cost. The first item costs $347.85. What is the retail price? You could calculate the mark-up and then add it to the cost as follows:

[C] 347.85 [×] .20 [=] 69.57 [+] 347.85 [=] 417.42   (answer)

Notice that the $347.85 was entered into the calculator twice (two chances to make a mistake). Instead, you could have obtained the same result by adding 20 percent to cost, which is 100 percent; thus the retail price would be 120 percent of cost. Using this method, you get the answer by the following computation:

[C] 347.85 [×] 1.2 [=] 417.42   (answer)

Try it. You will discover that it is faster and easier. And if you think of the general principle involved, you will see many applications for this technique. If you get a 10 percent discount on an item with a list price of $543.77, what is the price you pay?

[C] 543.77 [×] .9 [=] 489.39   (answer)

Example 2: Sequential Calculations

You wish to calculate a company's earnings after taxes. Its sales equal $75,950; cost of goods sold represents 75 percent of sales; interest expense is $1,000; and the tax rate is 40 percent. Using the usual method, the keystrokes would be:

[C] 75950 [×] .75 [=] 56962.50   (write down this number)
[C] 75950 [−] 56962.50 [=] 18987.50 [−] 1000 [=] 17987.50 [×] .4 [=] 7195
                                                   (write down this number)
[C] 17987.50 [−] 7195 [=] 10792.50   (answer)

Using the method described above, the same answer could have been determined by:

[C] 75950 [×] .25 [−] 1000 [×] .6 [=] 10792.50   (answer)

This method does *not* give you any of the intermediate answers, although they could, in part, be obtained by pushing the [=] key after each operation.

Suppose you wanted to find the cost of goods sold and the gross profit. The standard method would involve the following:

[C] 75950 [×] .75 [=] 56962.50   (write down number — the cost of goods sold)
[C] 75950 [−] 56962.50 [=] 18987.50   (gross profit)

The alternative method would be as follows:

[C] 75950 [×] .75 [=] 56962.50   (cost of goods sold)
[÷] .75 [×] .25 [=] 18987.50   (gross profit)

Notice that by remembering that all steps can be reversed mathematically by performing the opposite mathematical computation, you avoid the problem of having to enter long numbers more than once.

Example 3: Future Value of Cash Flow Streams

Suppose you need to find the future value of $100 one period from now, given a 10 percent interest rate — i.e., $100 \times (1 + .10)$ = future value. The keystrokes are:

[C] 100 [×] 1.1 [=] 110   (answer)

(Continued on back endpaper)

Principles of Managerial Finance

Principles of Managerial Finance

Fourth Edition

Lawrence J. Gitman
Wright State University

HARPER & ROW, PUBLISHERS, New York
Cambridge, Philadelphia, San Francisco, Washington,
London, Mexico City, São Paulo, Singapore, Sydney

Sponsoring Editor: John Greenman
Development Editor: Lauren S. Bahr
Project Editor: Susan Goldfarb
Text Design: T. R. Funderburk
Text Design Supervision: Mina Greenstein
Cover Design: Lawrence R. Didona
Text Art: Vantage Art, Inc.
Production: Jeanie Berke
Compositor: Progressive Typographers
Printer and Binder: R. R. Donnelley & Sons Company

Principles of Managerial Finance, Fourth Edition

Library of Congress Cataloging in Publication Data

Gitman, Lawrence J.
    Principles of managerial finance.

    Includes index.
    1. Corporations—Finance.   2. Business enterprises—
Finance.   I. Title.
HG4011.G5   1985   658.1'5   85-792

Regular edition ISBN: 0-06-042357-9
International edition ISBN: 0-06-350314-X

86 87 88 9 8 7 6 5 4 3

To my wife, Robin, our son, Zachary,
and our daughter, Jessica

Contents

Preface

Managerial finance is an interesting, exciting, and dynamic area of study, and its importance to the long-run success of today's business is unquestioned. But in recent years the environment created by the interaction of government, financial institutions, business firms, and individuals — both domestically and internationally — has been in a state of flux. The body of financial literature has continued to grow; existing theories and concepts have been challenged and refined; and new decision-making tools and techniques have been developed. At the same time, new and modified financial institutions have evolved in response to a changing regulatory environment; interest rates have declined from record levels and remain quite volatile; inflation has moderated but continues to challenge all participants in the economy; there have been continuing and significant revisions in the federal tax structure; and the personal microcomputer has become widely accepted and available to business people and students of managerial finance. These changes, coupled with my continuing commitment to convey up-to-date knowledge about the discipline, have prompted this significantly revised fourth edition of *Principles of Managerial Finance.*

The text is designed primarily for the introductory course at the undergraduate level. It may also be used with good results in the core MBA finance course, in management development programs, and in executive study programs. It is intended to make factual material as easily digestible as possible, so that the professor may concentrate on highlighting the theories, concepts, tools, and techniques that will help the student make reasonable real-world financial decisions. Examples that simplify concepts and catch the reader's interest are liberally provided throughout the text. In addition, to make it readable, the book has been written and revised with the student constantly in mind. The payoff of readability accrues not only to the student but also to the professor, who will find the job of teaching greatly simplified and considerably more rewarding.

Changes in the Fourth Edition

A variety of sources contributed toward the revision plan for the new edition. Mailed questionnaires, personal interviews, written reviews, feedback from adopters, colleagues, and students, and observations from my own use of the text provided valuable information. On-line financial managers scrutinized the plan to ensure that the real-world activities described truly reflect managerial finance as it is practiced today.

MAJOR CHANGES

Topic Sequence. Our research reconfirmed that the teachability of *Principles of Managerial Finance* is the primary reason for the book's widespread acceptance. The research also supported my sense that a shift is occuring in the structure of the managerial finance course. Today, most professors prefer to immediately follow the coverage of basic financial concepts (the time value of money, risk and return, and valuation) with such long-term financial decision topics as capital budgeting, cost of capital, leverage and capital structure, and dividend policy. The benefits of such a sequence seem to be threefold: (1) the long-term topics encompass applications of basic financial concepts just studied and should logically come right after them rather than later; (2) this sequence is consistent with the widely accepted "strategic approach" that begins with long-term policies and ends with short-term operational activities; and (3) given the limited time available in many courses, many professors prefer to fully develop the long-term *conceptual framework* first in order to assure that it receives adequate coverage, and then cover — often quickly — operational and descriptive material as time permits in the latter part of the course.

In order to provide early coverage of long-term financial concepts, this fourth edition's organizational structure is as follows:

Part I   The Financial Environment
Part II   Techniques of Financial Analysis and Planning
Part III   Basic Financial Concepts
Part IV   Long-Term Investment Decisions: Capital Budgeting
Part V   Cost of Capital, Leverage, Capital Structure, and Dividends
Part VI   The Management of Working Capital
Part VII   Sources of Long-Term Financing
Part VIII   Expansion and Failure

Two changes were made to arrive at this sequence. First, the discussion of techniques of financial analysis and planning (Part II), now precedes the discussion of basic financial concepts (Part III). This shift encourages students to gain a sound footing in financial analysis and planning before exploring major financial management concepts. Early coverage of these topics also provides a logical transition from the study of accounting to the study of finance. The second structural change was to place the coverage of long-term investment decisions, cost of capital, leverage, capital structure, and dividends *after* the presentation of basic financial concepts for the three reasons cited above. The restructuring allows financial analysis and planning and capital budgeting — two of the most likely areas of entry-level managerial finance employment — to be covered early in the course.

Despite the change in sequence, the text's strong coverage of working capital management has been preserved. Continuing periods of volatile and relatively high interest rates make this topic especially important. Consequently, *the text continues to place equal emphasis on short-term and long-term financial management.*

Tax Law Revisions. This edition fully describes the major tax revisions resulting from the *Economic Recovery Tax Act of 1981,* the *Tax Equity and Fiscal Responsibility Act of 1982,* and the *Tax Reform Act of 1984.* These acts have had, and will continue to have, major influence on financial decision making, especially as it relates to depreciation. The impact of these acts is dealt with frequently, both in text discussions and in end-of-chapter and ancillary materials. Information on the federal tax structure (in Chapter 2) has been completely revised to reflect these changes; the accelerated cost recovery system (ACRS) of asset depreciation, as well as changes in tax rates and credits, are clearly explained there. Chapter 9 illustrates the use of the ACRS normal recovery periods and depreciation percentages in determining investment cash flows. Chapter 10 has been revised to include a continuing example that illustrates the application of various capital budgeting techniques to investment decisions in a fashion consistent with the new legislation.

New Pedagogical Devices. In addition to the pedagogical features in earlier editions, a number of new devices have been integrated into the fourth edition of *Principles of Managerial Finance* to further strengthen its pedagogical effectiveness.

> *Learning Objectives:* Each chapter begins with six learning objectives that guide the student's understanding of the material presented.
>
> *Boxed Essays:* Each chapter contains two or more boxed essays describing real-world events or actual company situations that demonstrate text concepts.
>
> *Summary in List Format:* Each chapter summary is now presented as a bulleted list of major points that can be quickly reviewed.
>
> *Key Terms:* At the end of each chapter a list of key terms defined within the chapter (as well as in the glossary) is presented.
>
> *Expanded and Integrative Problems:* All end-of-chapter problems have been carefully reviewed and revised, with many new problems included. A number of new and longer integrative problems have been added.
>
> *Computer Disk Keyed To Text:* The use of *The Gitman Disk* — a user-friendly menu-driven personal computer disk containing 11 problem-solving routines (described in detail later) — is flagged in pertinent text discussions and before end-of-chapter problems that can be solved using the disk. These passages are identified by this symbol: ◼

OTHER STRUCTURAL AND CONTENT CHANGES

A number of other less sweeping changes have also been made:

1. Discussions of the changing role of financial intermediaries and interest rates, risk premiums, and required returns were added to Chapter 3 in order to establish early the concept of the fundamental tradeoff between risk and return.

2. An expanded review of basic financial statements begins Chapter 4 (on the analysis of financial statements). In addition, the concept of leverage is described, and the DuPont system of analysis is clearly explained.

3. The discussion of pro forma statements in Chapter 5 (on financial planning) has been clarified to include the use of both percent-of-sales and judgmental approaches for estimating external funds required.

4. The loan amortization process is now demonstrated by an example as part of the discussion of time value of money in Chapter 6.

5. There is now a separate chapter on risk and return—Chapter 7—that includes new discussions of the concepts of return, risk preferences, and normal probability distributions and an expanded discussion of correlation, diversification, risk, and return.

6. Valuation is now discussed in a separate chapter (Chapter 8). This chapter includes new material on the basic valuation concept and model, bond value behavior and yield to maturity, and common stock variable growth models.

7. Chapter 9 (on capital budgeting and cash flow principles) offers an expanded discussion of the capital budgeting process that includes a discussion of terminal cash flow and the effect, if any, of changes in net working capital.

8. Chapter 10, on capital budgeting techniques, includes new illustrated discussions of *NPV* and *IRR,* as well as a comprehensive problem that demonstrates the entire capital budgeting process for two mutually exclusive projects.

9. A new chapter on capital budgeting refinements and risk—Chapter 11—has been added. It includes comparisons of projects with unequal lives, using both the least common life and the annualized net present value approaches, and covers capital rationing, inflation in capital budgeting, and approaches for dealing with project risk, with particular emphasis given to the conceptual and practical aspects of certainty equivalents and risk-adjusted discount rates.

10. Chapter 13, on leverage and capital structure, begins with discussion of basic leverage concepts—breakeven analysis, operating leverage, financial leverage, and total leverage. This is followed by a discussion of capital structure that uses the debt ratio as a basis for evaluating both the theoretical and operational aspects of optimal capital structure decisions.

11. Discussion of dividend reinvestment plans has been added to the coverage of dividend policy in Chapter 14.

12. Chapter 16, on cash and marketable securities management, has been significantly revised to reflect the state of the art in cash management and explore the currently most popular marketable security investments.

13. An introductory illustrated discussion of credit scoring is now included in Chapter 17 (on accounts receivable and inventory management).

14. A single chapter, Chapter 18, is now devoted to sources of short-term financing. It covers all sources—spontaneous, unsecured (including

commercial paper), and secured — and includes a table summarizing the key features of each source at the end of the chapter.

15. In addition to coverage of long-term debt, Chapter 19 now includes material on investment banking. New discussions of deep discount and variable-rate bonds have been added, and a table summarizing the characteristics of popular types of bonds is included.

16. Chapter 21, on leasing, has been streamlined to better reflect current legal and accounting requirements for leases. Also, a brief discussion of leveraged leases is now included.

17. A discussion of the basic features of options — their markets, the logic of trading them, and their role in managerial finance — is now included in Chapter 22 (on convertibles, warrants, and options).

18. Chapter 23, on consolidations, mergers, and holding companies, includes a new multinational finance section concerned with international combinations.

19. In Chapter 24, on failure, reorganization, and liquidation, the discussion of priority of claims has been revised to better demonstrate the priorities for distributing funds in liquidation.

Pedagogical Features

ORGANIZATION

The text's organization conceptually links the firm's actions and its value as determined in the securities markets. Housed within this broad framework is a simple balance sheet structure that serves as a basis for analyzing many of the decisions confronting the financial manager. Each major decision area is presented in terms of both risk and return factors and their potential impact on the owner's wealth, as reflected by share value.

In organizing each chapter, I adhered to a managerial decision-making perspective. That is, I have not merely described a concept such as present value or operating leverage, but have also related it to the financial manager's overall goal of wealth maximization. Once a particular concept has been developed, its application is illustrated. Thus, the student is not left with just an abstract definition, but truly senses the decision-making considerations and consequences of each financial action. New terms are defined when first used, and the definitions are sometimes repeated in subsequent discussions to help the reader master the vocabulary of finance. Also, the list of key terms at the end of each chapter and the comprehensive glossary with chapter references at the back of the text make terms and definitions accessible in another way.

The fourth edition of *Principles of Managerial Finance* contains twenty-four chapters. It is designed to be read in sequence, but almost any chapter can be taken out of sequence and studied as a self-contained unit. Since each professor has particular topic preferences, the topic coverage in the book has deliberately been made both extensive and flexible. The manageable size of the book makes it suitable for courses of various lengths, from one quarter to two full semesters, and each professor will be able to adapt the text to fit his or her own teaching schedule.

EXAMPLES

Many well-marked examples occur throughout the text to demonstrate potentially troublesome concepts. The examples are detailed, and quite often the reason for using a particular approach is given along with the demonstration. Reviewers of this edition and users of earlier editions of this book have remarked that the content, quality, placement, and method of presenting the examples contribute greatly to teaching this material well and to learning it well.

QUESTIONS AND PROBLEMS

I am a strong believer in the use of many problems during all phases of the first finance course, at whatever level it is taught. Therefore, a comprehensive set of questions and problems at the end of each chapter serves as a review by which students may test their understanding of the material presented within the chapters. More than one problem is provided for each concept, to assure students multiple self-testing opportunities and to give professors a wide choice of assignable material. New integrative problems tying together related topics are included in this edition. A short caption at the beginning of each problem identifies the concept that the problem has been designed to test. Answers to selected end-of-chapter problems appear in Appendix B; these answers help students evaluate their progress in preparing detailed problem solutions.

MULTINATIONAL FINANCE

Another important feature of this fourth edition is its coverage of multinational finance. Rather than including a separate chapter on that topic, I continue to integrate it into relevant managerial finance discussions. *Eleven chapters include a section discussing the multinational dimensions of the chapter topic.* To aid the reader, these sections (and related end-of-chapter materials) are highlighted with a multinational globe symbol like the one shown above.

SUPPORT ITEMS

A complete set of financial tables for percentage rates between 1 and 50 percent is included in Appendix A. Also included for students' convenience is a removable laminated present-value table card that can be used in working problems. Another student aid is found on the endpapers inside the front and back cover, which illustrate procedures for performing routine financial calculations using a simple calculator. With a little practice, students following these procedures should improve their speed and accuracy in doing financial calculations described in the text.

Supplementary Materials

A number of additional materials are available to aid and enrich the learning and teaching processes.

STUDY GUIDE

The student review manual, *Study Guide to Accompany Principles of Managerial Finance,* Fourth Edition, coauthored with J. Markham Collins of the University of Tulsa, has been completely revised. Each chapter of the study guide contains a chapter summary, a chapter outline, a programmed self-test, and problems and detailed solutions. Where appropriate, discussions and problems are keyed to *The Gitman Disk.* In addition, material from the *Study Guide* will be available on *Study-Aid,* an interactive microcomputer program for use on the Apple II, II+, IIe, and IIc and on the IBM-PC.

CASEBOOK

A completely new casebook, *Casebook in Managerial Finance,* has been designed to accompany this text. Prepared by Bernard J. Winger of the University of Dayton, it includes analytical exercises and provides forms related to the cases in a study guide format. This new pedagogical approach to cases strengthens students' understanding of and facility with the case method. A separate instructor's manual accompanies this casebook.

INSTRUCTOR'S MANUAL

The comprehensive instructor's manual enables the professor to use the text easily and effectively in the classroom. Prepared by Cherie Mazer of Wright State University and me, it includes chapter outlines and detailed answers and solutions to all text questions and problems. Great care has been taken to ensure the accuracy of all answers and solutions.

QUIZ/EXAM FILE

Also prepared by Cherie Mazer and me, this supplement includes a quiz for each chapter and a prototype midterm and final examination, all with answers.

TEST BANK (BOTH IN PRINTED AND COMPUTER SOFTWARE DISK FORM)

A test bank containing 1200 multiple-choice questions and 200 problems with worked-out solutions has been developed by Douglas A. Hibbert of Fayetteville Technical Institute and Walter J. Reinhart of Loyola College in Maryland and is available in a separate test-bank manual and on MICROTEST, which is a microcomputer test-generation system that produces customized tests and carries a comprehensive set of descriptors for each multiple-choice question, including chapter number, item number, item type, level of difficulty, cognitive type, and page number in the text on which the correct answer is found. In addition, the available exam problems are also available on MICROTEST. MICROTEST is compatible with the Apple IIe and II+ and the IBM-PC.

ACETATE TRANSPARENCIES

A pack of 100 transparency acetates of key exhibits and problem solutions is available to adoptors.

THE GITMAN DISK

A new and unique computerized supplement for use with the Apple II and the IBM-PC, *The Gitman Disk* has been specifically developed by Frederick Rexroad to accompany this text. All routines are written in BASIC and can be transferred easily to other computers with little or no modification. *The Gitman Disk* includes 11 short programs, presented in a user-friendly menu-driven format, for use in solving financial problems. Applicability of the disk throughout the text and study guide is always keyed by a printed disk symbol like that shown above. Each routine on the disk includes page references to the text discussion of the technique being applied. *The Gitman Disk* is available free to adoptors. A detailed description of the disk and its use is given in Appendix C.

Acknowledgments

Many people have made significant contributions to this edition as well as to earlier editions. Without their classroom experience, guidance, and advice, this book would not have been written or revised. Receiving continual feedback from students, colleagues, and practitioners helps me create a truly teachable textbook. If you or your students are moved to write to me about any matters pertaining to this text package, please do. I welcome constructive criticism and suggestions for the book's further improvement.

Harper & Row obtained the experienced advice of a large group of excellent reviewers. I appreciate their many suggestions and criticisms, which have had a strong influence on various aspects of this volume. My special thanks go to the following people, who reviewed all or part of the manuscripts for earlier editions:

Ronald F. Anderson	Phil Harrington	Linda J. Martin
David A. Arbeit	George T. Harris	Vincent A. Mercurio
Richard E. Ball	Roger G. Hehman	Joseph Messina
Kenneth J. Boudreaux	Harvey Heinowitz	Gene P. Morris
Ron Baswell	Glenn Henderson	Edward A. Moses
Omer Carey	James Hoban	William T. Murphy
Patrick A. Casabona	Keith Howe	Don B. Panton
Thomas Cook	Kenneth M. Huggins	Ronda S. Paul
Joel J. Dauten	Dale W. Janowsky	Gerald W. Perritt
Lee E. Davis	Timothy E. Johnson	Stanley Piascik
Richard F. DeMong	Terrance E. Kingston	Gerald A. Poque
Peter A. DeVito	Harry R. Kuniansky	William B. Riley, Jr.
David R. Durst	William R. Lane	Ron Rizzuto
F. Barney English	Michael A. Lenarcic	William L. Sartoris
Ross A. Flaherty	A. Joseph Lerro	Carl J. Schwendiman
George W. Gallinger	Timothy Hoyt McCaughey	Carl Schweser
Gerald D. Gay	James C. Ma	Richard A. Shick
Philip W. Glasgo	William H. Marsh	A. M. Sibley
David A. Gordon	John F. Marshall	Stacy Sirmans

Gerald Smolen   Robert D. Tollen   John C. Woods
Gary Tallman   Kenneth J. Venuto   Charles W. Young
Harry Tamule   Grant J. Wells   Joe W. Zeman
Richard Teweles   Tony R. Wingler   J. Kenton Zumwalt

The following people provided useful input to the fourth edition:

Gary A. Anderson (University of Miami — Florida)
Russell L. Block (San Diego State University)
Calvin M. Boardman (The University of Utah)
Robert J. Bondi (Western Connecticut State University)
Roger G. Clarke (Brigham Young University)
Donnie L. Daniel (The University of Southern Mississippi)
Vincent R. Driscoll (Quinnipac College)
Anthony J. Giovino (State University of New York — Farmingdale)
I. Charles Granicz (State University of New York — Plattsburg)
Melvin W. Harju (Louisiana State University — Shreveport)
Nalina Jeypalan (Fresno State University)
Randy Myers (Rowan Technical Institute)
Jerome S. Osteryoung (Florida State University)
Kathleen F. Oppenheimer (Western Connecticut State University)
John Park (Frostburg State College)
Surendra S. Singhvi (ARMCO, Inc.)
Ira Smolowitz (Siena College)
Lester B. Strickler (Oregon State University)
James A. Verbrugge (University of Georgia)
Jonathan B. Welch (Northeastern University)
Howard A. Williams (Barrington College)

The three final draft in-depth reviewers deserve special attention for their outstanding and extremely useful input.

Donald A. Nast (Florida State University)
Dennis T. Officer (Arizona State University)
Gary Sanger (Ohio State University)

I am especially indebted to Mehdi Salehizadeh of San Diego State University for the outstanding job he did in preparing and revising the multinational finance discussions found throughout the book. Special thanks are due to Pieter A. Vandenberg, also of San Diego State University, for his reviews, as well as for preparing and revising the material on the front and back endpapers. I also extend thanks to Cherie Mazer for her help in preparing both the instructor's manual and the quiz/exam file. The work of Douglas A. Hibbert and Walter J. Reinhart in preparing the computer-based test bank is greatly appreciated. Thanks are also due to Fred Rexroad for developing *The Gitman Disk.* Thanks to my colleagues, tax experts Russel H. Hereth and John C. Talbott, and to Peter W. Bacon, Nicolas Gressis, Charles E. Maxwell, and Richard E. Williams for their continuing assistance and support. Special mention is due Cathie Dinnen Scott for her outstanding efforts in typing the manuscript, running numerous errands, and generally keeping things in order.

I am very appreciative of the useful feedback of J. Markham Collins and for his work in coauthoring the study guide. Special thanks also go to Bernard J. Winger for his reviews and for authoring the companion casebook. Thanks are also due to Lawrence Kryzanowski at Concordia University and to Devinder K. Gandhi at the University of Ottawa, who coauthored the Canadian edition of the text; to Michael D. Joehnk, Arizona State University, and George E. Pinches, University of Kansas, coauthors of our recently published graduate-level managerial finance text.

The staff of Harper & Row — particularly John Greenman, Lauren S. Bahr, Susan Goldfarb, and Jim Brennan — deserve special thanks for their professional expertise, creativity, enthusiasm, and continuing commitment to the text. An extra word of thanks to Lauren S. Bahr for tolerating and accommodating my obsession for perfection.

Finally, my wife, Robin, and our children, Zachary and Jessica, have played most important parts in patiently providing the support and understanding I needed during the writing of this book. To them I will be forever grateful.

LAWRENCE J. GITMAN

Part I

The Financial Environment

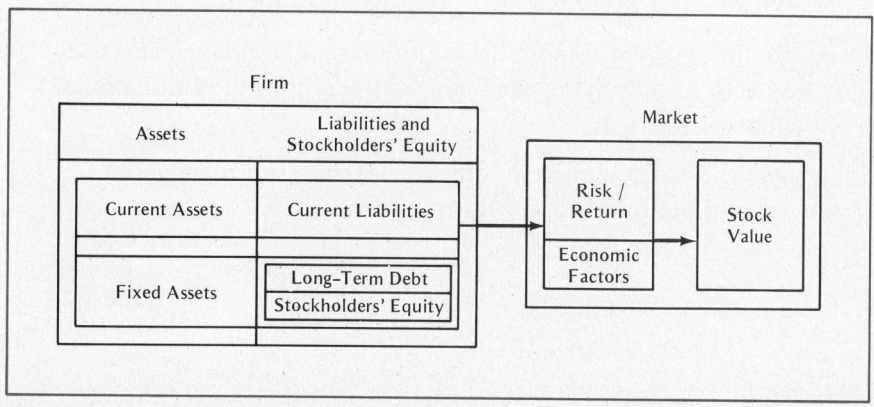

Chapter 1

The Role of Finance and the Financial Manager

After studying this chapter, you should be able to:

1. Differentiate finance from the closely related disciplines of economics and accounting.

2. Describe the location of the finance function within the broad organizational structure of the firm.

3. Discuss the primary functions of the financial manager within the firm.

4. Identify the wealth maximization goal of the financial manager and explain why it is preferred over profit maximization.

5. Recognize the growing importance of multinational finance and the major factors influencing the financial operations of multinational companies.

6. Understand the basic approach to the key concepts of managerial finance and the rationale for that approach.

A prerequisite to understanding financial theories, concepts, tools, and techniques is to answer two basic questions: What is finance? What are the functions and goal of the financial manager? Answering these questions will set the stage for an understanding of the important decision areas for the financial manager and the methods he or she uses to resolve problems. In addition, a brief overview of the multinational dimensions of finance and of its presentation in this text should lay the groundwork for the study of the financial manager's role in the modern business firm.

Finance, Economics, and Accounting

Financial management can be viewed as a form of applied economics that draws heavily on economic theory. Financial management also draws certain data from accounting, another area of applied economics. In this section, we discuss the relationship and key differences between finance and economics and also between finance and accounting.

FINANCE AND ECONOMICS

The importance of economics to the development of the financial environment and financial theory can best be described in terms of the two broad divisions of economics — macroeconomics and microeconomics. *Macroeconomics* is concerned with the overall institutional and international environment in which the firm must operate, while *microeconomics* concerns itself with the optimal operating strategies for firms or individuals. Each of these areas, as they relate to managerial finance, is discussed briefly below.

Macroeconomics. Macroeconomics is concerned with the institutional structure of the banking system, financial intermediaries, the federal treasury, and the economic policies available to the federal government for coping with and controlling the level of activity within the economy. Macroeconomic theory and policy know no geographic limits; rather, they are concerned with the establishment of an international framework in which funds flow freely between institutions and countries, economic activity is stabilized, and unemployment is controlled.

Since the business firm must operate in the macroeconomic environment, the financial manager must be aware of this institutional framework. The financial manager must also be alert to the consequences of varying levels of economic activity and changes in economic policy on his or her own environment. The financial manager must recognize the consequences of more restrictive fiscal or monetary policies on the firm's fund-raising and revenue-generating abilities. The financial manager must also be aware of the various financial institutions and their mode of operation to be able to evaluate potential investment or financing outlets.

Microeconomics. The theories of microeconomics provide for the efficient operation of a business firm. They are concerned with defining actions that will permit the firm to achieve success. The concepts involved in supply-and-demand relationships and profit-maximizing strategies are drawn from microeconomic theory. Issues related to the mix of productive factors, "optimal" sales levels, and product pricing strategies are all affected by microeconomic theories. Measurement of utility preferences, risk, and the determination of value are rooted in microeconomic theory. The rationale for depreciating assets is also derived from this area of economics. The primary principle that applies in managerial finance is *marginal analysis:* financial decisions should be made and actions taken only when marginal revenues exceed marginal costs. When this condition does exist, a given decision or action should result in an increase in profits. The importance of marginal analysis in making financial decisions will become apparent in subsequent chapters.

In summary, a knowledge of economics is necessary to understand both the financial environment and the decision theories that underlie contemporary managerial finance. Macroeconomics provides the financial manager with insight into the policies of government and private institutions by which economic activity is controlled. Operating within the "economic ballpark" created by these institutions, the financial manager draws on microeconomic theories of the operation of the firm and profit maximization to develop a winning game plan. The manager competes not only against other players in a particular industry but also against prevailing economic conditions.

FINANCE AND ACCOUNTING

Many people view the finance and accounting functions within a business as virtually the same. Although there is a close relationship between these functions, just as there is a close relationship between finance and economics, the accounting function is best viewed as a necessary input to the finance function — that is, as a subfunction of finance. This view is in line with the traditional organization of the activities of a firm into three basic areas — manufacturing, finance, and marketing. The accounting function is typically viewed as within the control of the financial vice-president. However, there are two key differences in viewpoint between finance and accounting — one related to the treatment of funds and the other to / decision making.

Treatment of funds. The accountant, whose primary function is to develop and provide \ data for measuring the performance of the firm, assessing its financial position, and paying taxes, differs from the financial manager in the way he or she views the firm's funds. The accountant, using certain standardized and generally accepted principles, prepares financial statements based on the premise that revenues should be recognized at the point of sale and expenses when they are incurred. This method is commonly referred to as the *accrual system.* Revenues resulting from the sale of merchandise on credit, for which the actual cash payment has not yet been received, appear on the firm's financial statements as *accounts receivable,* a temporary asset. Expenses are treated in a similar fashion — that is, certain liabilities are established to represent goods or services that have been received but have yet to be paid for. These items are usually listed on the balance sheet as *accounts payable,* or *accruals.*

The financial manager is more concerned with maintaining a firm's solvency by providing the *cash flows* necessary to satisfy its obligations and acquiring and financing the current and fixed assets needed to achieve the firm's goals. Instead of recognizing revenues at the point of sale and expenses when incurred, the financial manager recognizes revenues and expenses only with respect to inflows or outflows of cash.

A simple analogy may help to clarify the basic difference in viewpoint between the accountant and the financial manager. If we look on the human body as a business firm in which each pulsation of the heart represents a new sale, the accountant is concerned with each of these pulsations, entering these sales as revenues. The financial manager is concerned with whether the resulting flow of blood through the arteries reaches the right cells and keeps the various organs of the body functioning. It is possible for a body to have a strong heart but cease to function because of the development of blockages or clots in the circulatory system. Similarly, a firm may be profitable but still fail because it has an insufficient inflow of cash to meet its obligations as they come due.

EXAMPLE Thomas Corporation in the calendar year just ended made one sale in the amount of $100,000 of merchandise purchased during the year at a total cost of $80,000. Although the company paid in full for the merchandise during the year, it has yet to collect at year end from the customer to whom the sale was made. The accrual-based accounting view and the cash flow–oriented financial view of the firm's performance during the year are given by the income and cash flow statements, respectively.

Accounting view	Financial view
Thomas Corporation Income Statement for the Year Ended 12/31	Thomas Corporation Cash Flow Statement for the Year Ended 12/31

Accounting view		Financial view	
Sales revenue	$100,000	Cash inflow	$ 0
Less: Expenses	80,000	Less: Cash outflow	80,000
Net profit	$ 20,000	Net cash flow	($80,000)

It can be seen that whereas in an accounting sense the firm is quite profitable, it is a financial failure. Without adequate cash inflows to meet its obligations, the firm will not survive, regardless of its level of profits. ■

The lesson of the example is that accounting data do not fully describe the circumstances of the firm. The financial manager must look beyond financial statements to obtain insight into developing or existing problems. The Thomas Corporation's lack of cash flow resulted from the uncollected account receivable. The financial manager, by concentrating on cash flow, should be able to avoid insolvency and achieve the firm's financial goals.

Decision making. The duties of the financial manager differ from those of the accountant in that the accountant devotes the majority of his or her attention to the collection and presentation of financial data. The financial manager evaluates the accountant's statements, develops additional data, and makes decisions based on subsequent analyses. The accountant's role is to provide consistently developed and easily interpreted data on the firm's past, present, and future operations. The financial manager uses these data, either in raw form or after making certain adjustments and analyses, as an important input to the decision-making process. Of course, this does not mean that accountants never make decisions and financial managers never gather data; rather, the primary focuses of accounting and finance are different.

An Overview of the Finance Function

Since most business decisions are measured in financial terms, it is not surprising that the financial manager plays a key role in the operation of the firm. But people in all areas — accounting, manufacturing, marketing, personnel, operations research, and so forth — need a basic understanding of the finance function. In the recent past, the trend has been for more and more top executives to come from the finance area.[1] In response to this trend, enrollment in finance programs, both undergraduate and graduate, has increased.

To gain the needed understanding of the finance function, we must look closely at its role within the firm, the key functions of the financial manager, and his or her overall goal.

THE ROLE OF FINANCE IN THE BUSINESS FIRM

The size and importance of the finance function depends on the size of the firm. In small firms, the finance function is generally performed by the accounting depart-

---

[1] Five relatively recent articles lend support to the belief that finance remains the most common route to the top. See C. Patrick Fleenor, David L. Kurtz, and Louis E. Boone, "The Changing Profile of Business Leadership," *Business Horizons*, July-August 1983, pp. 43–46; John A. Pollock, John R. Bartol, Bruce C. Sherony, and George R. Carnahan, "Executives' Perceptions and Future MBA Programs," *Collegiate News and Views*, Spring 1983, pp. 23–25; George A. Weimer, "Finance Favored as Key to Executive Boardroom," *Iron Age*, April 16, 1979, pp. 36–38; Bernie J. Grablowsky and Dexter R. Rowell, "The Market for Finance Majors: The Myths and Realities Reconsidered," *Journal of Financial Education*, Fall 1980, pp. 33–41; and "Who Gets the Most Pay?" *Forbes*, June 7, 1982, pp. 74–78ff.

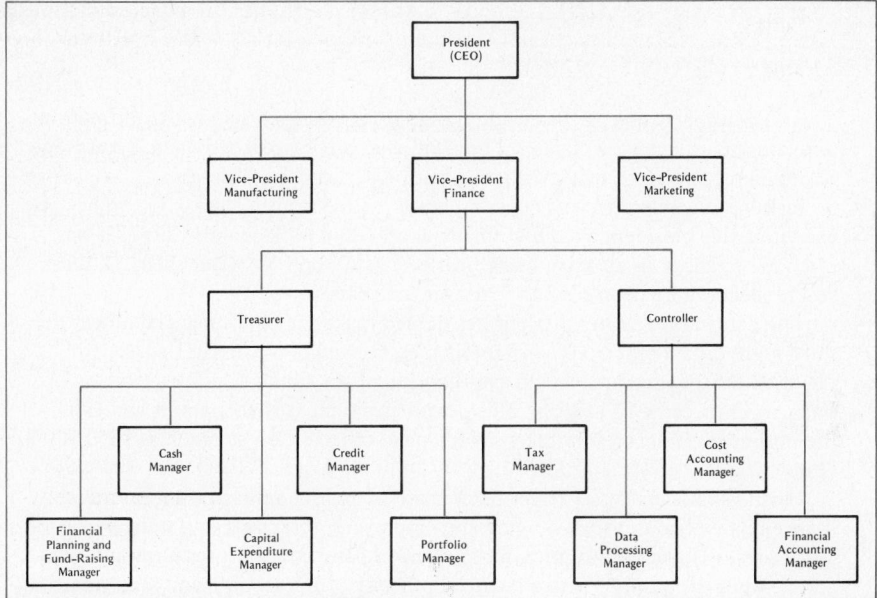

Figure 1.1 The finance activity within the firm

ment. As a firm grows, the importance of the finance function typically results in the evolution of a separate department, an autonomous organizational unit linked directly to the company president or chief executive officer (CEO) through a vice-president of finance. Figure 1.1 depicts a general organizational chart highlighting the structure of the finance activity within the firm. Reporting to the vice-president of finance are the treasurer and controller. The *treasurer* is commonly responsible for handling financial activities such as financial planning and fund raising, managing cash, making capital expenditure plans and decisions, managing credit activities, and managing the investment portfolio. The *controller* typically handles the accounting activities related to taxes, data processing, and cost and financial accounting. The emphasis here will be on the activities of the treasurer or financial manager.

THE FUNCTIONS OF THE FINANCIAL MANAGER

The financial manager's functions within the firm can be evaluated in terms of the firm's basic financial statements. His or her primary functions are (1) financial analysis and planning, (2) managing the firm's asset structure, and (3) managing the firm's financial structure.

All three functions are clearly reflected in the firm's balance sheet, which shows the current financial position of the firm. The financial manager evaluates the balance sheet data in order to assess the firm's overall financial position. In making this evaluation, he or she must monitor the firm's operations. In managing the firm's asset structure, the financial manager is, in effect, determining the construction of the left side of its balance sheet. In managing its financial structure, he or she is constructing the right side of the firm's balance sheet.

FINANCIAL OFFICERS IN HIGH DEMAND

The premium on expertise has made it harder for companies and accounting firms to retain their financial whizzes. "The good ones are approached daily," says Roger K. Williams, a recruiter with Williams, Roth & Krueger in Chicago.

Jack M. Greenberg left his job as a partner with Arthur Young & Co. to become executive vice president and chief financial officer of McDonald's Corp. "It was rare that a partner in an accounting firm ever left," says Mr. Greenberg. "I think you're seeing more people doing that over the years."

The demand for financial talent has helped make the chief financial officer the third highest-paid officer at many companies, recruiters say. A 1981 survey by Heidrick & Struggles Inc., a Chicago recruiting firm, found that the average financial chief earned $146,284, plus perquisites such as stock options and extra life insurance. Other headhunters say financial officers earn as much as $350,000 a year.

Financial officers get a greater percentage of their compensation from performance-related bonuses than do most top employees, according to a study by Hewitt Associates, a Chicago consulting firm. The company says short-term rewards can add between 40% and 50% to a financial officer's compensation, and long-term rewards can add another 35% to 40%.

"There is more risk — and more leverage — in the total compensation than would be the case for the top human resources man or the top legal person," says Hewitt's William R. James, chief compensation consultant. "There are more things that can be drawn upon to determine whether that guy has done a good or a bad job."

At troubled companies, the finance role can also be the route to the chief executive post. James C. Cotting, chief financial officer at International Harvester Co., is considered a possible candidate for a top job at the ailing maker of trucks and farm equipment. It took less than a year for Chief Financial Officer Joe B. Freeman to attain the chairmanship of AM International Inc., a Chicago office-equipment company that is in reorganization proceedings in bankruptcy court.

The vogue for financial experts may wane with economic recovery, however. "In periods of prosperity and easy money and strong economic growth, issues other than finance come to the fore," says RCA's [chief financial officer] Mr. [Richard W.] Miller. "A chief financial officer in that environment might have a diminished role."

SOURCE: Heywood Klein, "Financial Officers Often in Demand As Companies Seek Cost-Cutters," *The Wall Street Journal,* November 22, 1982, p. 1.

Financial analysis and planning. This function is concerned with the transformation of financial data into a form that can be used to monitor the firm's financial position, to evaluate the need for increased productive capacity, and to determine what additional financing is required.

Managing the firm's asset structure. The financial manager determines both the mix and the type of assets found on the firm's balance sheet. The *mix* refers to the number of dollars of current and fixed assets. Once the mix is determined, the financial manager must determine and attempt to maintain certain "optimal" levels of each *type* of current asset. He or she must also decide which are the best fixed assets to acquire and know when existing fixed assets need to be modified or replaced.

Managing the firm's financial structure. This function is concerned with the right-hand side of the firm's balance sheet. Two major decisions must be made about the firm's financial structure. First, the most appropriate mix of short-term and long-term financing must be determined. This is an important decision, since it affects the firm's profitability and overall liquidity. A second and equally important concern is which individual short-term or long-term sources of financing are best at a given point in time. Many of these decisions are dictated by necessity, but some require an in-depth analysis of the available alternatives, their costs, and their long-run implications.

THE GOAL OF THE FINANCIAL MANAGER

The goal of the financial manager should be to achieve the objectives of the firm's owners. In the case of corporations, the owners of a firm are normally distinct from the managers. The managers' function is not to fulfill their own objectives (which may include increasing their wages, becoming famous, or maintaining their positions). It is, rather, to maximize the owners' (stockholders') satisfaction. Presumably, if the managers are successful in this endeavor, they will also achieve their personal objectives.

Some people believe that the owner's objective is always the maximization of profits; others believe it is the *maximization of wealth.* Wealth maximization is the preferred approach for five basic reasons: It considers (1) the owner's realizable return, (2) a long-run viewpoint, (3) the timing of returns, (4) risk, and (5) the distribution of returns.

Owner's realizable return. The owner of a share of stock can expect to receive a return in the form of periodic cash dividend payments, through increases in the stock price, or both. The market price of a share of stock reflects a perceived value of expected future dividends as well as actual current dividends; a shareholder's (owner's) wealth in the firm at any point in time is measured by the market price of his or her shares.[2] If a stockholder in a firm wishes to liquidate his or her ownership, he or she has to sell the stock at or near the prevailing market price. Because it is the market price of the stock, and not the profits, that reflects an owner's wealth in a firm at any time, the financial manager's goal should be to maximize the market price of the stock, and thus the stockholders' wealth.

EXAMPLE   Four years ago, Harold Jenks purchased one share of Alpha Company and one share of Beta Company stock, each at a price of $100. Both companies are in the same line of business. Although their profits have differed over the four-year period, each of the firms has paid an annual dividend of $1 per share. Alpha has earned an annual profit of $2 per share, while Beta's annual profit has been $3 per share. The difference in earnings is attributed to the fact that Alpha has spent a great deal of money to develop an innovative new product, thereby lowering its profits. Alpha stock is currently selling for $130 per share;

---

[2] This viewpoint is the generally accepted one with respect to the value of stock. The basic constructs and techniques for valuing common stock are presented in Chapter 8. At this point, however, the reader should accept this statement as fact.

Beta stock sells for $110 per share. This situation reflects the fact that although the profits of Beta Company are greater, Alpha Company has a higher stock price. The higher price of Alpha shares can be attributed to the expectation that the successful sale of the new product will provide increased future profits, which will more than compensate for the lower profits experienced during the development period. Harold's wealth in Alpha Company is greater than his wealth in Beta Company in spite of the fact that Beta Company's profits are larger. ■

This example should make it quite clear that profit maximization and wealth maximization are not the same. Because the owners' financial position in a firm is reflected by the price at which they can sell their stock, the financial manager must attempt to maximize the owners' wealth as reflected by the share price.

Long-run viewpoint. Profit maximization is a short-run approach; wealth maximization considers the long run. From the preceding example, it should be clear that the higher stock price of Alpha Company has resulted from the fact that its short-term actions related to new-product development, although lowering short-run profits, are expected to result in higher future returns. A firm wishing to maximize profits could purchase low-grade machinery and use low-grade raw materials while making a strong sales effort to market its products at a price that yields a high profit per unit. This short-run strategy could result in high profits for the current year, but in subsequent years sales might decline significantly due to the low quality and the high maintenance costs associated with low-grade machinery. The impact of falling sales and rising costs, if unchecked, could result in the eventual bankruptcy of the firm. The potential consequences of short-run profit maximization are likely to be reflected in the current stock price, which will probably be lower than it would have been if the firm had pursued a longer-run strategy.[3]

Timing of returns. The profit maximization approach fails to reflect differences in the timing of returns, whereas wealth maximization tends to consider such differences. Use of the profit maximization goal places greater value on an investment that provides the highest total returns, while the wealth maximization approach explicitly considers the timing of returns and their impact on the stock price.

EXAMPLE The Cowell Company is attempting to choose between two machines. Both will provide returns over a period of five years and are assumed to cost $3.00 per share. The expected profits per share directly attributable to each of these machines are shown below.

Year	Machine A	Machine B
1	$ 0	$1.75
2	0	1.75
3	0	1.75
4	0	1.75
5	10.00	1.75
Total	$10.00	$8.75

---

[3] This expectation is based on the assumption that investors in the marketplace have perfect knowledge of the firm's actions. This assumption underlies the basic theory of value, which is presented in Chapter 8.

Although it appears, based solely on the profit maximization objective, that machine A would be preferred, it is quite possible that once the differences in timing of benefits are considered, the impact of machine B on the owner's wealth would be greater. If we assume that the owners of the firm can earn 10 percent on their investments in the machines elsewhere, certain financial analysis techniques will show that the impact of these investments on the stock price would be a $3.21 per share increase with A and a $3.63 per share increase with B.[4] In other words, the use of the wealth maximization objective considers differences in the timing of returns. ■

The example illustrates the superiority of wealth maximization over profit maximization. Wealth maximization recognizes that business people, all other things being equal, prefer to receive returns *sooner* as opposed to *later*. This preference is reflected by share price, not by earnings.

Risk. Profit maximization does not consider risk; wealth maximization gives explicit consideration to differences in risk. A basic premise of financial management is that a trade-off exists between risk and return: stockholders expect to receive higher returns from investments of higher risk, and vice versa.[5] Financial managers must therefore consider risk when evaluating potential investments.

EXAMPLE Drury Manufacturing is considering expanding its production into either of two new products, C or D. Product C is considered to be a relatively safe investment, while product D is considered a risky fad item. After considering all costs, the two products are expected to provide the profits per share over their five-year lives as shown:

Year	Product C	Product D
1	$ 2.00	$ 2.20
2	2.00	2.20
3	2.00	2.20
4	2.00	2.20
5	2.00	2.20
Total	$10.00	$11.00

If we ignore any risk differences and use a profit maximization approach, it would appear that product D is preferred. However, if product D is highly risky while product C represents a safe investment, the conclusion may not be so straightforward. The firm may only need to earn 10 percent on product C, but as compensation for the greater risk of product D it must earn 15 percent. Again by applying certain financial analysis techniques that reflect differences in the timing of the returns, it is found that product C is likely to increase the share price by $7.58, while product D is likely to result in a $7.37 increase in share price. It should be clear that the wealth maximization approach reflects differences in the risks associated with the receipt of earnings. ■

---

[4] The financial analysis techniques alluded to here are fully developed in Chapter 6. At this point, it is best merely to recognize that quantitative techniques for considering differences in timing are available.

[5] The trade-off between risk and return is introduced in Chapter 7 and is discussed in several other chapters. It is a concept that underlies nearly all aspects of financial theory and practice.

VICE-PRESIDENT OF FINANCE: A JOB DESCRIPTION

Basic function

Plan, direct, and execute the long-term financings required to fund corporate capital requirements at the lowest cost.

Primary responsibilities and duties

Plan and execute the financings required to fund corporate capital requirements while maintaining a balanced capital structure.

Direct, support, and review the actions of the department in obtaining long-term financing and maintaining positive relations with lenders and rating agencies.

Provide a capital budgeting and financial projection system.

Integrate projections of capital requirements with the status of credit markets and the company's capital structure.

Coordinate the activities of underwriters, lawyers, and accountants in order to complete financings in a timely manner.

Maintain contact with all company lenders and keep them informed of the company's goals and progress.

Provide financial support for various contractual arrangements.

Monitor pension fund assets and various special projects.

Types of decisions

Select underwriters, lenders, and counsel to structure financings.

Decide on the type of financing that is most appropriate to meet capital requirements and financial structure targets at the lowest cost.

Determine the timing of the issue of new financings.

Decisions are reviewed by the Senior Vice-President–Finance.

Organizational relationships

The incumbent directly supervises the AVP-Finance, Manager of Pension Investments, and Manager of Financial Analysis.

Work progress is discussed with the supervisor approximately once a year.

Because stockholders require higher returns for greater risks, the impact of risk upon their returns must be considered by the financial manager. The wealth maximization approach considers risk; profit maximization ignores it. Wealth maximization is therefore the preferred approach.

Distribution of returns. The profit maximization goal fails to consider that stockholders may wish to receive a portion of the firm's returns in the form of periodic dividends. In the absence of any preference for dividends, the firm could maximize profits from period to period by reinvesting all earnings to acquire new assets that will boost future profits. The wealth maximization strategy takes into consideration the fact that many owners place a value on the receipt of the *regular* dividend, regardless of its size. This *clientele effect* is used to explain the influence of dividend policy on the market value of shares. Making sure that stockholders

Work relationships

Frequently work with:

Bankers who are lenders and provide trustee services.
Long-term lenders (insurance companies).
Investment bankers.
Investment advisors who manage pension fund.
Industry groups.
Legal counsel.

Education and Experience

MBA in finance or two or three years of progressively responsible experience in financial/investment analysis.
Five to six years (including at least three years of management) experience in investment banking, financial consulting, or a comparable job.

Representative skills and knowledge

Should:

Be resourceful.
Be a good communicator.
Have analytical/problem solving/creative abilities.
Have high degree of verbal, quantitative, and interpersonal skills.
Understand business principles and practices.
Have complete understanding of financial management.
Be a quick, clear thinker.

Other

This is a complex job with very high responsibility and visibility both inside and outside of the company. Feedback on success and failure is quick. Stamina is required for the long hours and travel.

SOURCE: *Careers in Finance* (Tampa, Fla.: Financial Management Association, 1983), p. 10.

receive the return they expect is believed to have a positive effect on stock prices.[6] Since each stockholder's wealth at any time is equal to the market value of all his or her assets less the value of his or her liabilities, an increase in the market price of the firm's shares should increase the stockholder's wealth. A firm interested in maximizing owners' wealth may therefore pay dividends on a regular basis. A firm that wishes to maximize profits may opt to pay no dividends. But stockholders would certainly prefer an increase in wealth to the generation of an increasing flow of profits without concern for the market value of their holdings.

Because the stock price explicitly reflects the owners' realizable return, considers the firm's long-run prospects, reflects differences in the timing of returns, con-

[6] One school of thought does suggest that the payment of cash dividends has no effect on the value of a firm's stock. A discussion of this argument is included in Chapter 14, which is concerned specifically with dividend policy.

siders risk, and recognizes the importance of the distribution of returns, maximization of wealth as reflected in share price is viewed as the proper goal of financial management. Profit maximization can be part of a wealth maximization strategy. Quite often, the two objectives can be pursued simultaneously. But maximization of profits should never be permitted to overshadow the broader objective of wealth maximization.

 MULTINATIONAL FINANCE

An Overview

Since the 1960s, as world markets have become significantly more interdependent, international finance has become an increasingly important element in the management of many companies. More and more American firms (as well as companies based elsewhere in the world, especially in Western Europe and in Japan) have international assets and operations in foreign markets. The term *multinational company* (*MNC*) is used to refer to firms that have assets and operations in markets other than their respective home countries and draw part of total revenues and profits from such markets.

The principles of managerial finance presented in this text are applicable to the management of MNCs as well. However, certain factors unique to the international setting tend to complicate the financial management of multinational companies. A comparison between a domestic U.S. firm (firm A) and a U.S.-based MNC (firm B) will illustrate the major factors influencing the MNC's operations. Because the basic principles of finance apply to both, only certain chapters of the text have been extended to incorporate the international factors. These chapters will be identified as we compare firms A and B. Table 1.1 provides a summary of the factors (and thus the differences between firm A and firm B).

FOREIGN OWNERSHIP

Firm A has all its assets and capital owned by domestic people and organizations, under the usual forms, such as proprietorship, partnership, or corporation. Firm B, on the other hand, may have a portion of its total equity owned by foreign investors (both private and governmental). In fact, to operate in many of the world's countries, especially in developing nations, it is often essential for a firm to have a majority of its foreign (equity) investments owned by foreign partners. This type of constraint can influence both management decision making and the repatriation of capital, along with the remittance of profits for firm B. These aspects of multinational finance will be discussed in Chapter 2.

Furthermore, different tax liabilities distinguish the operations of the two firms. Firm A is liable only for domestic taxes. Firm B must pay both U.S. and foreign taxes. Some foreign governments maintain consistent, long-term tax treaties with the U.S. government, permitting companies such as firm B to take advantage of certain tax credits. Other nations, however, have internal tax schedules as well as external tax relationships that are subject to frequent fluctuation and changes. The international taxation of MNCs has become an important factor that must be taken into account, and Chapter 2 contains an analysis of this factor.

Table 1.1   The International Factors and Their Influence on MNCs' Operations

Factor	Firm A (Domestic)	Firm B (MNC)
Foreign ownership	All assets owned by domestic entities	Portions of equity of foreign investments owned by foreign partners thus affecting foreign decision making and profits
Foreign exchange risks	All operations in one currency	Fluctuations in foreign exchange markets can affect foreign revenues and profits as well as the overall value of the firm
Multinational accounting	All consolidation of financial statements based on one currency	The existence of different currencies and of specific translation rules influence the consolidation of financial statements into one currency
Multinational capital markets	All debt and equity structures based on the domestic capital market	Opportunities and challenges arise from the existence of different capital markets where debt and equity can be issued

Finally, unlike the domestic economic and political environment in the United States within which firm A operates, firm B's international assets and operations, particularly in some of the less-developed countries, are often subject to *"political risk."* In other words, assets in foreign countries can be subjected to confiscation, expropriation, or nationalization by local governments, without adequate — or any — compensation. This issue has in recent years become one of the most important factors affecting MNCs' global operations; a detailed review is provided in Chapter 7. In addition, international combinations of firms are discussed in Chapter 23.

FOREIGN EXCHANGE RISKS

Firm A conducts all its business in one currency, the U.S. dollar. It does not face any risks stemming from fluctuations in the foreign exchange markets. Moreover, its debt and equity structures are based entirely on the domestic capital markets and one currency. Firm B, on the other hand, has access to, and can potentially be influenced by, the international capital markets. A review of the foreign capital markets, including the opportunities and challenges they provide for MNCs, is given in Chapter 3.

The existence of different currencies can affect multinational companies' profits as well as their valuation by their respective owners. How MNCs can take advantage of foreign capital markets to combat foreign exchange risks is analyzed in Chapters 7 and 16, and the influence of foreign exchange on international cash flows and the evaluation of foreign investments are examined in Chapter 10.

MULTINATIONAL ACCOUNTING

Three issues separate the accounting procedures of firm A and firm B. First is the issue of the consolidation of the balance sheet and income statement. Firm A will undoubtedly present a consolidated view of its financial statements, but the application of this same rule by the U.S. government to an MNC (firm B) entails added complexities, since the consolidated statements have to be in U.S. dollars. In addition, the Financial Accounting Standards Board requires U.S.-based MNCs to follow certain procedures in translating the various accounts to be included in financial statements. This makes these firms subject to international currency fluctuations in reporting revenues, expenses, and profits. These points are covered in Chapter 4.

Second, firm A differs from firm B in its approach to the use of a required rate of return in evaluating investments. Firm A can apply its domestic rate, but firm B must often decide between the application of its global (average) rate and a local one that may be most appropriate for the local market. This complex issue is examined in Chapter 10, where attention is also focused on the third issue, the difference between domestic cash flows and those coming from foreign operations.

MULTINATIONAL CAPITAL MARKETS

Firm B, unlike firm A, has opportunities and challenges in the international capital markets. The firm can use these markets to raise funds as well as to invest excess cash. In addition to the material presented in Chapter 3, a more in-depth discussion, with an example of an MNC's activities in foreign capital markets, is presented in Chapter 18. Chapters 19 and 20, respectively, focus on specific aspects related to issuing long-term debt in international markets and to the use of common stocks in foreign direct investments. ●●

An Overview of the Text

The text is divided into eight parts, each devoted to some aspect of the financial manager's functions:

Part One: The Financial Environment
Part Two: Techniques of Financial Analysis and Planning
Part Three: Basic Financial Concepts
Part Four: Long-Term Investment Decisions: Capital Budgeting
Part Five: Cost of Capital, Leverage, Capital Structure, and Dividends
Part Six: The Management of Working Capital
Part Seven: Sources of Long-Term Financing
Part Eight: Expansion and Failure

This organization links the firm's activities to its value, as determined in the securities markets. Housed within this broad framework is a simple balance sheet structure that provides a basis for dissecting and investigating the various decisions that confront the financial manager. Each major decision area is presented in terms of both risk and return factors and their potential impact on the owner's wealth, as reflected by share value. Certain chapters include a final section on the multinational dimensions of the chapter topics. These sections are clearly marked with a globe symbol: .

Keyed to various parts of the text is *The Gitman Disk,* a menu-driven computer disk compatible with most personal computers that can be used as an aid in performing many of the routine financial calculations and procedures presented. Appendix C describes this decision aid, which for convenience is keyed to text discussions and end-of-chapter problems that can be solved with it. These sections are clearly marked with a disk symbol: .

A brief description of Parts One through Eight is given below. These descriptions are summarized by Figure 1.2, which relates each part of the text to the valuation framework.

PART ONE: THE FINANCIAL ENVIRONMENT

Part One sets the stage for subsequent discussion of the managerial finance function. This chapter relates finance to economics and accounting, describes the role and goal of finance and the financial manager, and provides a multinational finance overview. Chapters 2 and 3 describe the legal, operating, and tax environments of the firm and the structure and functions of financial intermediaries, markets, and interest rates.

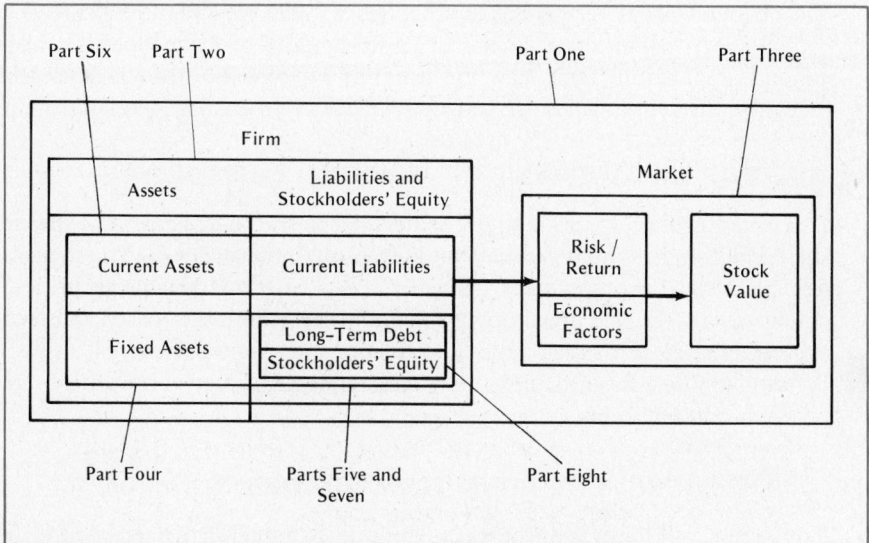

Figure 1.2   An overview of the major parts of the text

PART TWO: TECHNIQUES OF FINANCIAL ANALYSIS AND PLANNING

Part Two describes the basic tools of financial analysis and planning. Specific attention is given in Chapters 4 and 5 to the statement of changes in financial position, ratio analysis, cash budgeting, and pro forma statements. The preparation, interpretation, and importance of the key tools of financial analysis and planning are stressed.

PART THREE: BASIC FINANCIAL CONCEPTS

Part Three presents the basic financial concepts underlying contemporary financial management principles and practices. The time value of money, the concepts of risk and return, and the valuation process are discussed in Chapters 6, 7, and 8.

PART FOUR: LONG-TERM INVESTMENT DECISIONS: CAPITAL BUDGETING

Part Four is concerned with long-term investment decisions and capital budgeting. The primary focus of Chapter 9 is on capital budgeting and cash flow principles. In Chapter 10, capital-budgeting techniques under conditions of certainty are discussed. Chapter 11 discusses capital budgeting refinements and risk. A knowledge of each of these areas is necessary for a thorough understanding of the management and selection of fixed-asset investments.

PART FIVE: COST OF CAPITAL, LEVERAGE, CAPITAL STRUCTURE, AND DIVIDENDS

Part Five is devoted to three important topics — the cost of capital, leverage and capital structure, and dividend policy. These closely related topics are directly linked to the firm's value. The cost of capital, discussed in Chapter 12, is an important input in the capital-budgeting process; leverage and capital structure and dividend policy, presented in Chapters 13 and 14, affect the firm's cost of capital as well as its share value. An understanding of these topics shows how various suppliers of funds view the firm and enables the financial manager to recognize the key variables that must be considered in obtaining long-term funds.

PART SIX: THE MANAGEMENT OF WORKING CAPITAL

Part Six, Chapters 15 through 18, is devoted to the management of the firm's current accounts, which is called working capital management. The focus is on management of the firm's key current assets — cash, marketable securities, accounts receivable, and inventory — and liabilities — both unsecured and secured sources of short-term financing. The relationships between current assets and current liabilities are discussed, along with strategies aimed at the efficient management of these items.

PART SEVEN: SOURCES OF LONG-TERM FINANCING

Part Seven describes major sources of long-term financing. Chapters 19 through 22 discuss the cost, availability, inherent characteristics, and pros and cons of each of the following: long-term debt and investment banking, preferred and common stock, leasing, and convertibles, warrants, and options.

PART EIGHT: EXPANSION AND FAILURE

Part Eight discusses two topics related to decisions about the firm's future: external expansion through consolidations, mergers, and holding companies in Chapter 23, and the alternatives available to the failed business firm in Chapter 24.

CHAPTER SUMMARY

● Managerial finance is a form of applied economics. Macroeconomics provides an understanding of the institutional structure in which the flow of money and credit takes place. Microeconomics provides various profit maximization guidelines based on the theory of the firm.

● The accountant is primarily a source of data on the firm's past, present, and possible future financial position.

● The key differences between finance and accounting relate to the treatment of funds and decision making. The financial manager is concerned with cash flows, whereas the accountant focuses primarily on accruals. The financial manager also devotes attention to the analysis of data and decision making. The accountant's primary responsibility is the gathering and presentation of data.

● Since most business decisions must somehow be measured in financial terms, the financial manager performs a vital function within the firm. The degree of emphasis given to the finance function depends largely on the size of the firm. In large firms, it may be handled by a separate department headed by the vice-president of finance to whom both the treasurer and controller report; in small firms, the finance function is generally performed by the accounting department.

● The three functions of the financial manager are (1) financial analysis and planning, (2) managing the firm's asset structure, and (3) managing the firm's financial structure.

● The financial manager must perform these functions in light of the firm's overall goal of maximizing owners' wealth, which is a more important strategy than profit maximization. He or she is expected to consider realizable return, take a long-run view of the firm, consider the timing of returns, evaluate the risk-return trade-offs of managerial decisions, decide how returns are to be distributed, and take actions that will generally increase the market price of the firm's shares.

● Although many of the principles of managerial finance are applicable to international operations, multinational companies do face additional, unique factors in their foreign activities.

● The text is divided into eight major parts. Its organization uses a simple balance sheet structure to link the firm's activities to its value as determined in the securities marketplace.

KEY TERMS

accrual system
cash flows
clientele effect
controller
macroeconomics
marginal analysis

maximization of wealth
microeconomics
multinational company (MNC)
political risk
treasurer

QUESTIONS

1-1   Describe the general relationship between finance and economics and explain how the financial manager draws on the principles of macroeconomics and microeconomics.

1-2   How does the financial manager depend on the accountant? How does the output of accounting act as an input for finance?

1-3   What are the major differences between accounting and finance with respect to
a   The recognition of income and expenses?
b   Decision making?

1-4   How does the finance function evolve within the business firm? What kind of decisions does the financial manager make in the mature firm?

1-5   What are the three functions of the financial manager with respect to the firm's financial statements?

1-6   What is the goal of the financial manager? Discuss how one measures achievement of this goal.

1-7   The goal of managerial finance may conflict with profit maximization for any of five reasons. Briefly discuss these five reasons, showing how they support the goal of managerial finance.

1-8   Is it true that "if a firm is profitable, its survival is guaranteed"? Explain.

1-9   Briefly describe two of the major international factors that can influence the operations of MNCs.

1-10 What is *political risk,* and how does it affect multinational companies?

1-11 Indicate the main difference between the consolidation of financial statements for domestic firms and for MNCs.

Chapter 2

The Legal, Operating, and Tax Environments of the Firm

After studying this chapter, you should be able to:

1. Discuss the basic forms of business organization and their advantages and disadvantages.

2. Recognize the importance of and interrelationship among depreciation, cash flows, and interest and dividends.

3. Describe the basic features of personal taxes, including types of income and tax rates, determination of taxable income, and tax payment dates.

4. Discuss the fundamentals of corporate taxation of ordinary income and capital gains.

5. Understand the treatment of corporate tax losses, tax loss carrybacks and carryforwards, investment tax credit, S corporations, and tax payment dates.

6. Identify and recognize basic differences in the legal forms and taxation of multinational companies as compared to purely domestic companies.

To understand many financial decisions fully, a person must have a good understanding of the legal forms of business organization and their operating and tax environments. The basic assumption of this text is that the firm is a corporation. Since the primary emphasis in this book is on the corporate form, it is important to understand how corporate income is measured and taxed. Such an understanding makes it easier to see why certain financial variables must be considered in making decisions about the asset or financial structure of the firm. A knowledge of income measurement and tax treatment is also of key importance in financial analysis and planning. Familiarity with the legal organization of firms and the ways of measuring and taxing business income will give the reader a clear picture of the corporation's financial environment, on which subsequent discussions of the various aspects of financial planning and decision making can be based.

The Basic Forms of Business Organization

The three basic forms of business organization are the *sole proprietorship,* the *partnership,* and the *corporation.* Table 2.1 indicates their relative importance. The sole proprietorship is the dominant form of organization, accounting for 76 percent of all business firms. Partnerships and corporations account for only 8 percent and 16 percent, respectively. However, the corporation is by far the dominant form with respect to receipts and net profits. Corporations account for 88 percent of all business receipts and 78 percent of net profits. In general, corporations operate on a much larger scale than sole proprietorships or partnerships. The average business receipts and average net profits for each of these forms of business organization are given in Table 2.2. The figures support the contention that corporations, though less numerous than sole proprietorships and partnerships, operate on a much larger scale and therefore earn larger profits in absolute dollars, but not necessarily on a percentage basis.

Table 2.1   A Comparison of the Number, Business Receipts, and Net Profits of the Basic Forms of Business Organization

Form of business organization	Number of firms	% of total	Business receipts		Net profits	
			Millions of dollars	% of total	Millions of dollars	% of total
Sole proprietorship	12,701,597	76.0%	$ 505,885	7.8%	$ 55,450	17.5%
Partnership	1,299,593	7.8	242,654	3.7	15,206	4.8
Corporation	2,710,538	16.2	5,731,616	88.5	246,599	77.7
All Forms	16,711,728	100.0%	$6,480,155	100.0%	$317,255	100.0%

SOURCE: Data for sole proprietorships from U.S. Department of the Treasury, Internal Revenue Service, *Statistics of Income, 1979–1980 Sole Proprietorship Returns* (Washington, D.C.: U.S. Government Printing Office, 1982), p. 142. Data for partnerships from U.S. Department of the Treasury, Internal Revenue Service, *Statistics of Income, 1979 Partnership Returns* (Washington D.C.: U.S. Government Printing Office, 1982), p. 10. Data for corporations from U.S. Department of the Treasury, Internal Revenue Service, *Statistics of Income, 1980 Corporation Income Tax Returns* (Washington, D.C.: U.S. Government Printing Office, 1983), p. 16.

SOLE PROPRIETORSHIPS

A *sole proprietorship* is a business owned by one person who operates it for his or her own profit. In essence, the sole proprietor is self-employed. The typical sole proprietorship is a small firm, such as a neighborhood grocery, auto-repair shop, or shoe-repair business. Typically the proprietor, along with a few employees, operates the proprietorship. He or she normally raises capital from personal resources or by borrowing and is responsible for all decisions. The majority of sole proprietorships are in the wholesale, retail, service, and construction industries.

Advantages and disadvantages. The commonly cited advantages of a sole proprietorship, aside from being one's own boss, are as follows:

> *Ownership of all profits.* The sole proprietorship allows the owner to receive the fruits of his or her efforts; however, he or she must also absorb losses.
> *Low organizational costs.* No formal legal documents are required to form a

Table 2.2   Average Business Receipts and Average Net Profits of the Basic Forms of Business Organization

Item	Form of business organization		
	Sole proprietorship	Partnership	Corporation
Average business receipts	$39,828	$186,715	$2,114,568
Average net profits	$ 4,366	$ 11,701	$ 90,978

NOTE: These figures were obtained by dividing the business receipts and net profits for each form of business organization from Table 2.1 by the number of firms in each category.

sole proprietorship; at the most, the sole proprietor may have to purchase a license from the city or state.

Tax savings. The income of the sole proprietorship is taxed as personal income of the sole proprietor; in other words, the business is viewed as the job of the individual proprietor.

A possible high credit standing. If the sole proprietor has any wealth at all, it is quite likely that the proprietorship will have a higher credit standing than a corporation of equal size, since the owners' wealth is not considered when a corporation's credit is analyzed.

Other advantages. Secrecy and ease of dissolution.

There are a number of disadvantages of a sole proprietorship. In many cases, these may outweigh the advantages of this form of organization.

Unlimited liability. The sole proprietor's total wealth, not merely the amount he or she originally invested, can be taken to satisfy creditors.

Limitations on size. The fund-raising power of the sole proprietorship is limited to the amount one person can raise; generally, this is not enough to permit larger-scale operations.

Other disadvantages. (1) Difficulties in management resulting from the need to be a jack-of-all-trades; (2) a lack of opportunity for employees, since long-run incentives for a good employee to stay cannot be provided; and (3) a lack of continuity when the proprietor dies.

PARTNERSHIPS

A *partnership* consists of two or more owners doing business together for a profit. Partnerships are typically larger than sole proprietorships, but they are not generally large businesses (see Table 2.2). Finance, insurance, and real estate firms are the most common types of partnerships; wholesale and retail firms generate the largest amount of business receipts; and service firms provide the greatest net profits. One final (1979) statistic of interest is that the 1,299,593 partnerships in existence account for 6,954,767 partners, or an average of 5.4 per firm. Since many partnerships consist of only two or three partners, the data indicate that there are a number of large partnerships consisting of a few hundred partners. Public accounting and stock brokerage firms often have large numbers of partners.

The partnership contract. Most partnerships are established by a written contract known as the *articles of partnership.* If properly executed, it can eliminate many possible future problems between partners. Aside from descriptive data, the articles of partnership generally include (1) provisions for salaries, (2) a description of how profits and losses are to be divided, and (3) the procedure to be followed if a partner withdraws from the business or the firm is dissolved.

Limited partnerships. The most common of the special types of partnerships is the limited partnership. In a *general* (or regular) *partnership, all* the partners have unlimited liability; that is, their personal assets can be claimed if the firm defaults on its obligations. In a *limited partnership,* one or more partners can be designated as having limited liability as long as at least *one* partner has unlimited liability. The *limited partner* is normally prohibited from being active in the managment of the firm. Limited partnerships are quite common in real estate and oil speculation; their advantage is that an individual can invest money and expect a return without assuming any liability beyond the amount of his or her investment. In addition, these partnerships are commonly formed to obtain tax shelter benefits for income.

Advantages and disadvantages. The partnership is similar to the sole proprietorship with respect to taxes and organizational costs. A partner's income is taxed in the same manner as a sole proprietor's, and except for the possible legal cost of having the articles of partnership drawn up, the costs of organization are quite similar to those of the sole proprietorship. However, a partnership does have the following advantages over a sole proprietorship.

A larger amount of capital. The financial resources of more than one individual normally provide higher amounts of capital than the sole proprietor can raise.

A better credit standing. The personal assets of all the partners are available to satisfy the claims of creditors.

Other advantages. A partnership is advantageous in the sense that more brainpower and management skills are available than in the sole proprietorship. Also, a partnership is more likely to retain good employees because it can give them the opportunity to become partners.

Partnerships have a number of basic disadvantages that must be weighed against their advantages.

Unlimited liability. Partners have unlimited liability and are subject to *joint and several liability,* which means that if an equal partnership with three partners, A, B, and C, fails, with net losses beyond the liquidated value of the firm totaling *x* dollars, and if neither A nor B has any personal resources other than his or her investment in the business, the entire loss will fall on C if he or she has the assets to cover it. Partner C will, however, have a legal claim on A and B for the portion of their respective liabilities that C has paid.

Limited life. Technically, when a partner withdraws or dies, the partnership is dissolved.

Other disadvantages. It is difficult for a partner to liquidate or transfer money invested in a partnership. Although it can grow to a larger size than a sole proprietorship, the partnership still has difficulty achieving large-scale operations.

CORPORATIONS

As Table 2.2 shows, the corporation is the dominant form of business organization with respect to receipts and net profits. Although only 16 percent of all businesses

---

TYPICAL COMPENSATION OF OUTSIDE DIRECTORS

If you were wondering what the typical compensation is for outside directors of major U.S. corporations, the answer comes from a recent survey by Hewitt Associates, consultants on compensation and benefits.

Hewitt surveyed the top 100 industrials on the *Fortune* list and found the average annual retainer at $17,600, although the range was from a low of $8,000 to a high of $46,500.

The directors typically are paid for attending board meetings and committee meetings, but few receive any other benefits.

The "most common" board meeting fee, Hewitt says, is $500; for an audit committee meeting, the typical average fee is $650.

More than half the top 100 companies offer their directors the option of deferring their fees.

SOURCE: "$17,600 for Directors," *Dayton Daily News,* January 29, 1984, p. 1-E. Reprinted by permission of Hewitt Associates.

---

are corporations, the corporation accounts for 88 percent of business receipts and 78 percent of net profits. Corporations employ millions of people and have many thousands of shareholders; their activities affect the lives of everyone. The term *corporation* was officially defined by Chief Justice John Marshall of the U.S. Supreme Court in 1819, in the case of *Dartmouth College* v. *Woodward,* as follows: "A corporation is an artificial being; invisible, intangible, and existing only in contemplation of the law." [1] Because a corporation is an artificial being, it is often referred to as a *legal entity.* It has the powers of a human being in that it can sue and be sued, make and be party to contracts, and acquire property in its own name. Although a large number of corporations are involved in wholesale and retail trade and in finance, insurance, and real estate, manufacturing corporations as a group account for the largest portion of corporate business receipts and net profits.

Corporate organization. The major parties in a corporation are the *stockholders,* the *board of directors,* and the *president.* Figure 2.1 depicts the relationship among these parties. The stockholders are the true owners of the firm. The board of directors has the ultimate authority in guiding corporate affairs and making general policy. The president or chief executive officer (CEO) is responsible for managing day-to-day operations and carrying out the policies established by the board. He or she is required to report periodically to the board of directors.

Stockholders. Since the stockholders are the true owners of the firm, they vote periodically to select the members of the board of directors and to amend the corporate charter. The stockholder has the following basic rights:

1. To receive dividends in proportion to his or her ownership
2. To hold or sell his or her stock certificates

[1] *The Trustees of Dartmouth College* v. *Woodward,* 4 Wheaton 636 (1819).

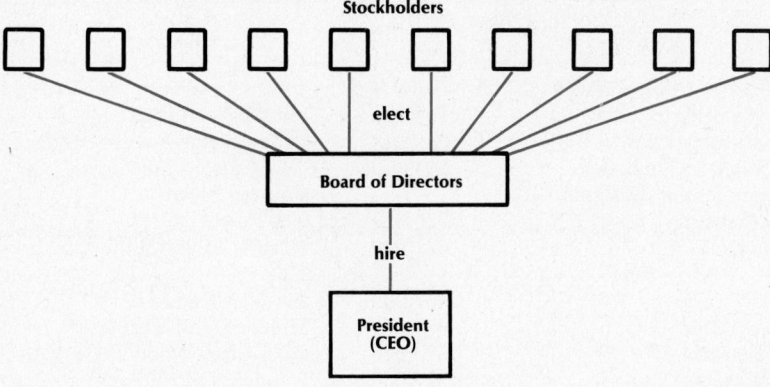

Figure 2.1   The general organization of a corporation

3. To share in liquidation
4. To purchase a pro rata portion of any new stock issues[2]
5. To inspect the firm's books and records

In small corporations, it is quite likely that the board of directors consists of the stockholders, who also manage the business. In a large corporation with thousands of shareholders, the firm's executives do not usually own a large number of shares. Table 2.3 presents a list of the 50 companies on the New York Stock Exchange with the largest number of shareholders. Large numbers of shareholders result in separation of ownership and management. In this situation, management is more likely to consider the total operating environment of the firm and attempt to maximize the owners' wealth by satisfying the needs not only of the owners but also of employees, customers, suppliers, the general public, and the government. This type of outlook is expected to provide share price maximization over the long run.

Advantages and disadvantages. Since corporations dominate our economy, the corporate form of organization must have certain advantages over the sole proprietorship and the partnership.

> *Limited liability.* The owners of a corporation have limited liability, which guarantees that they cannot lose more dollars than they invest.
> *Large size.* Because corporate shares are readily marketable and can be issued at low per-share prices, capital can be raised from many individuals through the sale of stock.
> *Transferability of ownership.* Corporate ownership is evidenced by stock certificates, which can easily be transferred to new owners. Organized

[2] This "preemptive" right is generally provided for in the corporate charter or by state law, although in some instances it may not be offered. It is discussed in greater detail in Chapter 20.

Table 2.3 NYSE Companies[a] with the Largest Number of
Common Stockholders of Record, Early 1983

Company	Stockholders	Company	Stockholders
American Telephone & Telegraph[b]	3,148,000	Northeast Utilities	230,000
General Motors	1,035,000	Ohio Edison	214,000
Exxon Corporation	865,000	Consolidated Edison	213,000
International Business Machines	726,000	Virginia Electric & Power	208,000
General Electric	481,000	Niagara Mohawk Power	207,000
GTE Corporation	467,000	Eastman Kodak	204,000
Sears, Roebuck	434,000	Middle South Utilities	201,000
Texaco Inc.	373,000	RCA Corporation	194,000
Southern Company	347,000	Standard Oil (Indiana)	192,000
American Electric Power	346,000	Union Electric	187,000
Ford Motor	328,000	Chrysler Corporation	187,000
Gulf Oil	296,000	Occidental Petroleum	182,000
Mobil Corporation	287,000	Long Island Lighting	181,000
Philadelphia Electric	283,000	Consumers Power	177,000
Commonwealth Edison	275,000	Pennsylvania Power & Light	169,000
British Petroleum	268,000	BankAmerica	165,000
Bell Canada	263,000	Westinghouse Electric	156,000
du Pont de Nemours	253,000	Southern California Edison	155,000
Pacific Gas & Electric	252,000	International Telephone & Telegraph	150,000
Detroit Edison	252,000	Matsushita Electric	145,000
Standard Oil of California	245,000	Dequesne Light	142,000
Tenneco Inc.	236,000	Dow Chemical	142,000
Atlantic Richfield	235,000	Union Carbide	137,000
United States Steel	232,000	Columbia Gas System	134,000
Public Service Electric & Gas	230,000	Pan American World Airways	130,000

[a] Foreign companies are not included in the survey.
[b] AT&T became eight separate companies on January 1, 1984.

SOURCE: *New York Stock Exchange 1983 Fact Book* (New York: New York Stock Exchange, 1983), p. 37.

stock exchanges facilitate the sale or purchase of stock and associated transfers of ownership.

Other advantages. Corporations also have a few other advantages: (1) They have a long life, since a corporation is not dissolved by the withdrawal or death of an owner; (2) professional managers can be hired to run the corporation, and if they do an unsatisfactory job, they can be replaced; (3) corporations can expand more easily than other types of organizations because of their ready access to capital markets and their generally large

INCORPORATING MAY NOT ALWAYS BE BEST

Recent changes in the tax laws . . . make this a good time to reconsider whether you should operate your business as a corporation. The Tax Equity and Fiscal Responsibility Act of 1982 (TEFRA) erased one of the primary benefits of incorporation. As of January 1 of this year [1984], owners of corporations can no longer put aside more money for retirement than sole proprietors or members of partnerships. . . .

"Now," concludes Robert L. Haddad, a tax partner in the Boston office of Price Waterhouse & Co., a national accounting firm, "the tax reasons for incorporating are not as material as they used to be."

Of course, incorporating still limits your personal liability if the business goes under or if the company is sued. That can be a real plus if your business is vulnerable to product-liability claims. In addition, there are some financial benefits that survived TEFRA. You can, for example, still deduct the costs of medical, life, and disability insurance for principals in the company, says Leah Belfort, tax manager in the New York office of the accounting firm of Fox & Co. . . .

Another disadvantage of operating your business as a corporation is that it is expensive. Take New York as an example. "In New York," says Belfort of Fox & Co., "there is a franchise tax for corporations. In New York City, there is an income tax on corporations. Add to that the bookkeeping and clerical costs, and you're out a lot of money."

With sole proprietorships and partnerships, the advantage is that income is recorded on your individual tax return. There is no corporate income tax form to file and no corporate tax to pay. "With a sole proprietorship especially," notes [Michael J.] Costello [a partner in the Boston office of the accounting firm of Laventhal & Horwath], "you can keep your overhead low. You don't need an accountant to do two forms, so you save yourself the extra accounting fees."

The disadvantages of operating as a sole proprietorship or partnership are that health, life, and disability insurance coverage for the principals in the business are not deductible. Also, the owners are personally liable for the debts of the business or if the company is sued for some other reason, such as product liability.

So which form of organization is best for you now? The answer partly depends on your business. "Every scenario is different," says Haddad, "so you really can't avoid pushing a pencil to make these decisions, because it's a little more intricate now. You don't have the overwhelming [pull] of the retirement plans."

Haddad's rule of thumb is to remain a corporation if you need protection from liabilities. "If you're a small retailer," he says, "you probably don't need to be incorporated. But if you're an insulation manufacturer with product liability [hanging over your head], it makes sense to incorporate."

And, Haddad adds, don't overlook the S-Corporation option. An S Corporation offers the same protection as a regular corporation, but income is not subject to the corporate tax. Rather, it flows through your personal tax return—just as it would if you operated your business as a sole proprietorship or partnership. You have to decide whether this is an advantage, given that you won't have the option of retaining some of the earnings in the corporation.

SOURCE: Donna Sammons Carpenter, "Alternatives to Incorporating," *INC.*, May 1984, p. 226.

size; (4) corporations receive a tax exemption on 85 percent of dividends they receive from other corporations; and (5) corporations are allowed to carry losses back and forward to achieve a more equitable tax treatment.

Corporations have certain disadvantages, most of which are closely related to their public nature.

Taxes. Because the income of a corporation is taxed and the same income is taxed again when it is distributed to the shareholder as dividends, the total tax burden is generally higher for corporations than for sole proprietorships and partnerships. In addition, franchise and income taxes are often levied on corporations by the states in which they operate.

Organizational expenses. The costs of incorporation and the issuance of shares often prove to be a drawback, especially for small businesses.

Government regulation. Since the corporation is a legal being, it is subject to regulation by various state and federal government departments. Often, a great deal of paperwork and information gathering is required to meet the requirements of regulatory agencies.

Other disadvantages. Other often-cited drawbacks of corporations are (1) a lack of personal interest in the firm by employees and (2) a lack of secrecy, since each stockholder must be provided with an annual report of the corporation's financial performance and financial position.

The Treatment of Corporate Income

Our emphasis here will be on the financial aspects of corporations. There are three basic reasons for this: (1) Corporations, due to their generally large size, provide a workshop in which to examine the greatest number of financial concepts. (2) Corporations are dominant in our economy. (3) Business school graduates will most likely end up working in and with corporations. Since corporate performance is measured by the net income shown on the firm's income statement, it is important to understand the basic concepts used in calculating that income. The key items to be examined are *depreciation, cash flows,* and *interest and dividends.*

DEPRECIATION

Corporations, as well as sole proprietorships and partnerships, are permitted to charge a portion of the cost of fixed assets to the annual revenues they generate. These costs show up as *depreciation.* For tax purposes, they are based on rules and guidelines established by the Internal Revenue Code, which underwent sweeping changes with passage of the *Economic Recovery Tax Act of 1981* and subsequent modification by the *Tax Equity and Fiscal Responsibility Act of 1982* and the *Tax Reform Act of 1984.* These rules state how certain assets can be depreciated and establish guidelines for the depreciable value and depreciable life of most fixed assets. Often a firm will use different methods for financial reporting purposes from those required for tax purposes. The student should not jump to the conclusion that the firm is trying to "cook the books" by keeping two different sets of records. The objectives of our tax laws are sometimes different from the objectives of financial reporting. For example, tax laws are used to accomplish certain economic goals such as providing incentives for firms to invest in certain types of capital goods. This, of course, is not usually the objective of financial reporting. Depreciation for tax purposes is determined using the *Accelerated Cost Recovery System (ACRS)* set down by the tax code, while for financial reporting purposes a variety of depreciation methods are available. However, before discussing the methods of depreciating an asset, we must first understand the relationship between depreciation and cash flows, the depreciable value of an asset, and the issue of the depreciable life of an asset.

Depreciation and cash flows. The financial manager is concerned with cash flows rather than net profits indicated by the income statement. To adjust the income statement to show cash flows from operations, all noncash charges must be added back. *Noncash charges* are expenses that are deducted on the income statement but do not involve an actual outlay of cash. Depreciation, amortization, and depletion allowances are examples. Since depreciation expenses are the most common noncash charges, we shall focus on their treatment; amortization and depletion charges are treated in a similar fashion.

The general rule for adjusting a firm's net profits after taxes to show cash flows from operations is to add back all noncash charges:

$$\text{Cash flow from operations} = \text{net profits after taxes} + \text{noncash charges} \qquad (2.1)$$

Applying Equation 2.1 to the income statement for the ABC Company in Table 2.4 yields a cash flow from operations of $18,000 because of the noncash nature of depreciation.

Net profit after taxes	$12,000
Plus: Depreciation	6,000
Cash flow from operations	$18,000

Table 2.4   ABC Company Income Statement

Sales		$100,000
Less: Returns and allowances		5,000
Net sales		$ 95,000
Less: Cost of goods sold		45,000
Gross profit		$ 50,000
Less: Expenses		
General and administrative expenses	$20,000	
Interest expense	4,000	
Depreciation	6,000	
Total		$ 30,000
Net profits before taxes		$ 20,000
Less: Federal taxes (40%)		8,000
Net profit after taxes		$ 12,000

But this value is only approximate, since not all sales are made for cash and not all expenses are paid when they are incurred.

Depreciation and other noncash charges shield the firm from taxes by lowering its taxable income. Many people do not accept depreciation as a source of funds; however, it is a source of funds in the sense that it is a "nonuse" of funds. Table 2.5 shows the ABC Company income statement prepared on a cash basis as an illustration of how depreciation shields income and acts as a nonuse of funds. Ignoring depreciation, except in determining the firm's tax liability, makes the resulting cash flow from operations equal to $18,000 — the same value obtained earlier. The adjustment of the firm's net profits after taxes by adding back noncash charges such as depreciation will be used on many occasions in this text to determine cash flows.

Depreciable value of an asset. Under ACRS the depreciable value (amount depreciated) of an asset is its *full cost* including outlays for installation. No adjustment is required for expected salvage value.

EXAMPLE   The ABC Company just acquired a new machine at a cost of $38,000, with installation costs of $2,000. Regardless of its expected salvage value, the depreciable value of the machine is $40,000 ($38,000 cost + $2,000 installation cost). ■

Depreciable life of an asset. The life over which an asset is depreciated can significantly affect the pattern of cash flows. The shorter the depreciable life, the quicker the cash flow created by the depreciation tax shield will be received. Given the financial manager's preference for faster receipt of cash flows, a shorter depreciable life is preferred to a longer one. Unfortunately, the firm must abide by certain Internal Revenue Service (IRS) regulations when setting depreciable life. These ACRS standards, which apply to both new and used assets, permit the taxpayer (1) to use the ACRS *normal recovery periods* or (2) to elect to take an *optional extended recovery period.* Table 2.6 briefly describes the four property classes (excluding real property — real estate) under ACRS for normal recovery period and shows the optional extended recovery periods associated with each class.

Table 2.5   ABC Company Income Statement
Calculated on a Cash Basis

Net sales		$95,000
Less: Cost of goods sold		45,000
Gross profit		$50,000
Less: Expenses		
General and administrative expenses	$20,000	
Interest expense	4,000	
Depreciation	0	
Total		$24,000
Cash flow before taxes		$26,000
Less: Taxes[a]		8,000
Cash flow from operations		$18,000

[a] Taxes are based on the inclusion of depreciation, as in Table 2.4.

Table 2.6   Property Classes and Normal and Optional Extended
Recovery Periods Under ACRS (Excluding Real Property)

Property class	Normal recovery period	Optional extended recovery periods
Autos, light-duty trucks, research and experiment equipment, and certain special tools	3 years	5 or 12 years
All other machinery and equipment	5 years	12 or 25 years
Certain public utility property, railroad tank cars, and residential manufactured homes	10 years	25 or 35 years
All other public utility property	15 years	35 or 45 years

Since for tax purposes the shorter normal recovery periods would be preferred, primary emphasis is given to them throughout the text.[3] As is customary, the four property classes (excluding real property) are referred to, in accordance with their normal recovery periods, as 3-year, 5-year, 10-year, and 15-year property.

Depreciation methods. For tax purposes, using the normal recovery periods, assets can be depreciated using the percentages shown in Table 2.7.[4] The firm can choose to depreciate the asset using straight-line depreciation over the normal or optional extended recovery periods.[5] Special tables of depreciation percentages for real property are available.[6] Although primary concern from a financial standpoint is given to tax depreciation, *for reporting purposes* a variety of other depreciation methods are available — straight-line, double-declining balance, and sum-of-the-years'-digits.[7] Since primary concern in managerial finance centers on cash flows, only tax depreciation methods will be utilized throughout this text. The applica-

[3] The optional extended recovery periods would be attractive only to firms anticipating negative predepreciation income in the near term. In such a case, deferring depreciation to later years when predepreciation income would be available would prove beneficial.

[4] The Economic Recovery Act of 1981, as modified by the Tax Reform Act of 1984, permits firms to elect to expense rather than to capitalize and depreciate up to a total of $5,000 per year in 1985, 1986, and 1987 for certain depreciable business assets. This amount is scheduled to increase to $7,500 per year in 1988 and 1989 and to $10,000 in 1990 and thereafter. Firms taking advantage of this feature must forgo certain other tax benefits that might be available if these assets were instead capitalized and depreciated.

[5] Firms electing to use straight-line depreciation over the normal or optional extended recovery periods must employ the *half-year convention*, which means that only one-half of the applicable straight-line depreciation can be taken in the first year. This convention therefore causes the final half year of depreciation to be taken in year $n + 1$ for an n-year normal recovery period. For example, using the straight-line method over a five-year normal recovery period would result in depreciation of 10 percent in the first year, 20 percent in years 2 through 5, and 10 percent in year 6.

[6] Rather than becoming involved in the intricacies of the tax laws, the decisions throughout this and subsequent chapters will tend to concentrate on the application of normal recovery periods and the percentages given in Table 2.7 to assets other than real property.

[7] For a review of these depreciation methods, as well as other aspects of financial reporting, see any recently published financial accounting text.

Table 2.7   Depreciation Percentage by Recovery Year Using Normal Recovery Periods Under ACRS (Excluding Real Property)

Recovery year	Percentage by recovery year			
	3-year	5-year	10-year	15-year public utility
1[a]	25	15	8	5
2	38	22	14	10
3	37	21	12	9
4		21	10	8
5		21	10	7
6			10	7
7 to 10			9	6
11 to 15				6

[a] The fact that the first-year depreciation percentage is lower than in subsequent years stems from the fact that the half-year convention is used. Under this convention, the first year is assumed to represent six months' use of the asset, regardless of when during the year the asset was actually acquired.

tion of the tax depreciation percentages given in Table 2.7 can be demonstrated by a simple example.

EXAMPLE   The ABC Company just acquired for an installed cost of $40,000 a machine having a normal recovery period of five years. Using the applicable depreciation percentages from Table 2.7, the depreciation in each year is calculated below.

Year	Cost (1)	Percentages (from Table 2.7) (2)	Depreciation [(1) × (2)] (3)
1	$40,000	15%	$ 6,000
2	$40,000	22	8,800
3	$40,000	21	8,400
4	$40,000	21	8,400
5	$40,000	21	8,400
Totals		100%	$40,000

It should be clear from column 3 that the total cost of the asset is written off over the five-year normal recovery period. ■

INTEREST AND DIVIDENDS

It is important to understand the difference in the treatment of interest and dividends. *Interest* is shown as an expense on the income statement and represents payments made by the firm to its creditors (lenders) for money borrowed. The repayment of a loan itself does not represent interest and is not shown on the income statement. The repayment must be from the firm's cash flows, but it does not affect income, since it merely represents the return of something that has been borrowed.

Table 2.8   The Format of a General
Income Statement

Sales
−Cost of goods sold
Gross profit
−Expenses other than interest
Operating profit
−Interest expense
Net profits before taxes
−Taxes
Net profits after taxes
−Preferred dividends
Earnings available for common stockholders
−Common stock dividends
To retained earnings

Dividends represent the distribution of earnings to the owners or stockholders of a corporation and are not tax-deductible. They must be paid from the firm's cash flows and are often deducted from net profits after taxes.[8] Both interest and dividends are payments for funds, but interest is a payment for funds *temporarily* lent to the firm, whereas dividends represent payment for *permanent* funds provided by the firm's owners. Moreover, dividend payments received by individuals must be claimed as personal income (except for a $100 exclusion on individual and $200 exclusion on joint returns) and are therefore subject to a second tax in the form of personal income tax. Dividends received by a corporation owning stock in other corporations are 85 percent tax-exempt.

A general income statement format is given in Table 2.8. This basic format will be used frequently throughout the text. One point to note is that before common stockholders can receive dividends, preferred stockholders' claims must be satisfied. Although both preferred and common stockholders are owners of the firm, preferred stockholders are given certain privileges, one of which is preference over common stockholders in the distribution of dividends.

Personal Taxes

The income of individuals is subject to a variety of federal taxes, the primary one being the federal income tax. This tax is levied on wages, salaries, dividends, interest, income from investments, and earnings from a sole proprietorship or partnership. Although the procedures for determining federal taxes owed on personal income can be quite complicated, it is important to understand the key aspects of personal taxation to be able to differentiate between the tax treatment given to individuals, which includes sole proprietorships and partnerships, and that given to corporations. This section presents a brief overview of personal

---

[8] A firm can pay cash dividends that exceed the current year's earnings, assuming that it has sufficient retained earnings to cover these dividends and the required amount of cash is available. A more in-depth discussion of this topic is included in Chapter 14.

taxation in three parts: types of income and tax rates, determining taxable income, and tax payments.

TYPES OF INCOME AND TAX RATES

The income of individuals can be classified as ordinary income or capital gain income. The method and rate of taxation depend on which of these types of income is earned.

Ordinary income. Income from all sources such as salaries, dividends, interest, income from investments, and earnings from a sole proprietorship or partnership are treated as ordinary income. After certain prescribed computations, these forms of income are taxed at *progressive rates,* which rise as the amount of taxable income rises. Although the applicable tax rates are dependent on an individual's filing status — single, married and filing jointly, married and filing separately, or unmarried head of household — Table 2.9, which is for single taxpayers, clearly illustrates the progressive nature of taxes on individual income.

EXAMPLE   The Smith sisters, June and Jane, wish to calculate their taxes for the current year. They are single individuals; June's taxable income is $11,000, and Jane's is $22,000. Their taxes are calculated as follows, using Table 2.9:

June: $1,203 + .18($11,000 − $10,800) = $1,203 + $36 = $1,239
Jane: $2,737 + .26($22,000 − $18,200) = $2,737 + $988 = $3,725

The *average tax rate* for June is 11.3 percent ($1,239 in taxes ÷ $11,000 taxable income), and Jane's average tax rate is 16.9 percent ($3,725 in taxes ÷ $22,000 taxable income). The progressive nature of the tax structure is also shown by the fact that although Jane's taxable income is twice that of June ($22,000 versus $11,000), her taxes are three times June's ($3,725 versus $1,239). ■

Ordinary individual income is often classified as either earned or unearned. Ordinary income that is earned includes salaries, wages, and income from proprietorships or partnerships directly attributable to the personal services provided by the proprietor or partner. Examples of earned proprietor or partnership income are fees received by an attorney, doctor, accountant, and so forth, for services provided to clients or patients. Unearned or passive income is income received in the form of dividends or interest or from nonincorporated business interests not fulfilling the requirements mentioned above. Prior to 1982, differing maximum tax rates applied to these two forms of individual income. The *Economic Recovery Tax Act of 1981* set the maximum tax rate on both forms of income at 50 percent. This maximum rate is clearly reflected in the tax column of Table 2.9.

Capital gains and losses. The other major form of income an individual may earn is capital gains. These gains result from the sale of capital assets at prices above the original purchase prices. A *capital asset* is property owned and used by the taxpayer for personal reasons, pleasure, or investment. The most common types are securities and real estate, including a home. A *capital gain* represents the amount by which

Table 2.9   1984 Tax Rates for Single Taxpayers[a]

Over	But not over	Tax	Of the amount over	Average tax rate on upper limit
$ 0	$ 2,300	$ 0 + 0%	$ 0	0%
2,300	3,400	0 + 11	2,300	3.6
3,400	4,400	121 + 12	3,400	5.5
4,400	6,500	241 + 14	4,400	8.2
6,500	8,500	535 + 15	6,500	9.8
8,500	10,800	835 + 16	8,500	11.1
10,800	12,900	1,203 + 18	10,800	12.3
12,900	15,000	1,581 + 20	12,900	13.3
15,000	18,200	2,001 + 23	15,000	15.0
18,200	23,500	2,737 + 26	18,200	17.5
23,500	28,800	4,115 + 30	23,500	19.8
28,800	34,100	5,705 + 34	28,800	22.0
34,100	41,500	7,507 + 38	34,100	24.9
41,500	55,300	10,319 + 42	41,500	29.1
55,300	81,800	16,115 + 48	55,300	35.3
81,800	—	28,835 + 50	81,800	—

[a]The taxes reflected in this table are those specified by the *Economic Recovery Tax Act of 1981* for the tax year 1984. Beginning January 1, 1985, the income tax brackets, zero-bracket amount (standard deduction), and personal exemptions are scheduled to be adjusted annually for inflation as reflected in the Consumer Price Index.

the proceeds from the sale of a capital asset exceeds its original purchase price. Capital gains can be classified as either short-term or long-term, depending on the length of time the asset was owned. As a result of the passage of the Tax Reform Act of 1984, *long-term capital gains* result on assets held for more than six months, while *short-term capital gains* are gains on assets held for six months or less. Short-term capital gains are taxed as ordinary income; long-term capital gains are taxed at only 40 percent of the ordinary tax rate, since only 40 percent of the gain is shown as taxable income.[9]

EXAMPLE   James McFail, who is in the 30 percent tax bracket, recently sold 100 shares of each of two stocks, A and B, for $10 and $14 per share, respectively. Stock A was originally purchased for $8 per share and held for 3 months, while stock B was purchased 15 months earlier for $12 per share. The total capital gain on stock A, therefore, amounted to $200 (100 shares × [$10 per share − $8 per share]), and the total capital gain on stock B also amounted to $200 (100 shares × [$14 per share − $12 per share]). Since stock A was held less than six months, the $200 gain on it will be taxed as ordinary income. Since James is in the 30 percent bracket, the tax on the *short-term* capital gain on stock A would amount to $60 (.30 × $200). The tax on the $200 *long-term* capital gain on stock B, which was held for longer than six months, would amount to $24 (.30 × .40 × $200). Although James's gain on each of the transactions was the same ($200), the taxes differ since the long-term gain on stock B is eligible for the more favorable treatment than the tax on the short-term capital gain. ■

[9] The maximum tax rate applicable to long-term gains is 20 percent (40 percent × 50 percent) of the total gain, which means that persons paying taxes on ordinary income at a rate of 50 percent will be taxed on long-term capital gains at a rate of only 20 percent.

Capital losses result when a capital asset is sold for less than its original purchase price. These losses may be either short-term or long-term, depending on whether the asset was held longer than six months. Before taxes are figured, all gains and losses must be netted out. Up to $3000 of *net* short-term losses can be applied against ordinary income, while one-half of *net* long-term losses up to an annual maximum of $3000 ($6000 of net long-term losses) can be applied against ordinary income. Losses that cannot be applied in the current year may be carried forward and used to offset future income subject to certain constraints.

DETERMINING TAXABLE INCOME

An individual's taxable income is determined by certain procedures outlined by the Internal Revenue Service (IRS) and computed with a variety of tax forms and schedules. The first step in this process involves the calculation of *gross income,* which is all income subject to federal taxes. Some types of income are *excluded* from gross income. One exclusion is the first $100 of dividends received. Married persons filing joint returns and jointly owning securities are eligible for a dividend exclusion of $100 each, or a total $200 exclusion. A number of deductions can then be made from gross income; these include a variety of trade and business expenses. The resulting balance after making these deductions is called *adjusted gross income.* From adjusted gross income a variety of nonbusiness expenses, or *itemized deductions,* can be taken.

Actually, the taxpayer may *itemize* these expenses, which include interest expenses, medical expenses, property taxes, and so forth, or take the *zero-bracket amount,* which is a type of blanket deduction. The zero-bracket amount is $2300 for unmarried individuals; $3400 for married taxpayers filing a joint return; and $1700 for married taxpayers filing a separate return. The choice depends, of course, on the level of eligible expenses. Filers who do not itemize can find *taxable income* by deducting any *personal exemptions,* which provide a $1000 deduction for the taxpayer and each of his or her dependents, from adjusted gross income. Taxpayers who itemize must subtract from adjusted gross income any excess itemized deductions in addition to personal exemptions in order to calculate taxable income. Using the tables and schedules provided by the IRS,[10] the taxpayer can find the tax associated with the given level of taxable income. From the tax amount the taxpayer can deduct any *tax credits,* such as the one allowed for child care, to find the *tax liability.*

EXAMPLE   Alice Majors, a single woman with no dependents, works as a tax accountant for a major public accounting firm. During 1984 she earned $38,000. In addition to her salary she received $500 in dividends on stock she owned and $400 interest from her money market account. During the year, she sold two stocks, resulting in a short-term capital gain of $500 and a long-term capital gain of $1,000. In 1984, Alice paid her own expenses of $400 to attend a special accounting seminar. Her itemized (nonbusiness) deductions totaled $9,300, while the applicable zero-bracket amount was $2,300. She claims one exemption

---

[10] Currently, persons with taxable incomes of less than $50,000 can use the tax tables, while those with taxable incomes in excess of $50,000 must calculate their tax liability from the tax rate schedules. Both tables and schedules have the zero-bracket amount built into them.

and is eligible for a $50 tax credit for political contributions. Alice has calculated her tax liability as follows:

Salary		$38,000
Dividends	$ 500	
Less: Exclusion	100	400
Interest earned		400
Capital gains		
Short-term	$ 500	
Long-term (taxable = .40 × $1,000)	400	900
Gross income		$39,700
Less: Alice's business expenses		400
Adjusted gross income		$39,300
Total itemized deductions	$9,300	
Less: Zero-bracket amount	2,300	
Less: Excess itemized deductions		7,000
Less: Personal exemption		1,000
Taxable income		$31,300
Tax (from Table 2.9)[a]		$ 6,555
Less: Credit for political contribution		50
Total tax liability		$ 6,505

[a] $5,705 + .34($31,300 − $28,800) = $5,705 + $850 = $6,555

Note that based on the data given, Alice's tax liability for 1984 is $6,505. ■

TAX PAYMENTS

The federal tax system is on a pay-as-you-go basis. This means that tax payments labeled "withholding taxes" are deducted from the wages and salaries of employees and are paid to the IRS by the employer. Persons who are self-employed, as well as employed persons with outside income from which taxes are not withheld, are required to make *estimated tax payments* on a quarterly basis to the IRS. Failure to make such payments results in a penalty. At the end of the year, once an individual's tax liability has been determined, the amount of taxes already paid through withholding and estimated payments is deducted from his or her tax liability to determine the amount of tax due (if the tax liability is greater than the amount paid in) or the size of the tax refund (if the paid-in taxes are greater than the tax liability). Individuals must file their tax returns by April 15 immediately following (or by the next business day if that date falls on a weekend or federal holiday) the tax year.

Corporate Taxes

To make sound financial decisions, a financial manager must understand the manner in which corporate income is taxed.[11] Corporations, like individuals, may

[11] This section deals only with corporations that are not part of a controlled group of corporations, since controlled groups of corporations have certain additional tax options. For a more detailed discussion of the material in this section of the chapter, see either *Federal Tax Course* (Englewood Cliffs, N.J.: Prentice-Hall) or *Federal Tax Course* (New York: Commerce Clearing House), both published annually.

earn either of two types of income, each subject to a different tax rate. Corporations can experience three types of tax losses — operating, depreciable assets, and capital losses — which may be carried back or forward and applied to other years. The manager also needs to be familiar with the investment tax credit, S corporations, and tax payment dates. This section of the chapter is divided into seven parts: ordinary income, capital gains, tax losses, tax loss carrybacks and carryforwards, investment tax credit, S corporations, and tax payment dates.

ORDINARY INCOME

The ordinary, or operating, income of a corporation is currently taxed at the following rates:

15 percent on first $25,000
18 percent on next $25,000
30 percent on next $25,000
40 percent on next $25,000
46 percent on the amount over $100,000

Corporations with taxable income in excess of $1 million must, in addition, increase the tax calculated using the above rate schedule by the lesser of $20,250 or 5 percent of taxable income in excess of $1 million.

EXAMPLE   Jessie Manufacturing, Inc., has before-tax earnings of $1,200,000. The tax on these earnings can be found by taking:

$$
\begin{aligned}
.15 \times \$25,000 &= \$\ \ 3,750\\
.18 \times \ \ 25,000 &= \ \ \ \ 4,500\\
.30 \times \ \ 25,000 &= \ \ \ \ 7,500\\
.40 \times \ \ 25,000 &= \ \ 10,000\\
.46 \times (1,200,000 - 100,000) &= \underline{506,000}
\end{aligned}
$$

Total $531,750

Plus: lesser of
$$
\left[
\begin{array}{c}
\$20,250\\
\text{or}\\
.05(\$1,200,000 - \$1,000,000)\\
= .05(\$200,000) = \$10,000
\end{array}
\right] = \underline{10,000}
$$

Total Taxes Due $\underline{\$541,750}$

The firm's total taxes on its before-tax earnings are therefore $541,750. If the firm had earned only $20,000 before taxes, its total tax liability would have been .15 × $20,000, or $3,000. ■

Average tax rates. The *average tax rate* paid on the firm's ordinary income can be found by dividing its taxes by its taxable income. Average tax rates range from 15 to 46 percent. The average tax rate reaches 46 percent when taxable income equals or exceeds $1,405,000 [($20,250 ÷ .05) + $1,000,000 = $1,405,000]. The average

Table 2.10   Pretax Income, Tax Liabilities, and Average Tax Rates

Pretax income (1)	Tax liability (2)	Average tax rate [(2) ÷ (1)] (3)
$ 25,000	$ 3,750	15.00%
50,000	8,250	16.50
100,000	25,750	25.75
250,000	94,750	37.90
500,000	209,750	41.95
1,000,000	439,750	43.98
1,250,000	567,250	45.38
1,405,000	646,300	46.00
2,500,000	1,150,000	46.00

tax rate paid by Jessie Manufacturing, Inc., in the example was 45.1 percent ($541,750 ÷ $1,200,000). Table 2.10 presents the firm's tax liability and average tax rate for various levels of pretax income. Figure 2.2 presents the average tax rates associated with various levels of taxable income. Again, it can be seen that the rate approaches and finally reaches 46 percent.

Marginal tax rates. The *marginal tax rate* represents the rate at which additional income is taxed. Due to the nature of the corporate tax structure, the marginal tax rate on income up to $25,000 is 15 percent; from $25,000 to $50,000 it is 18 percent; from

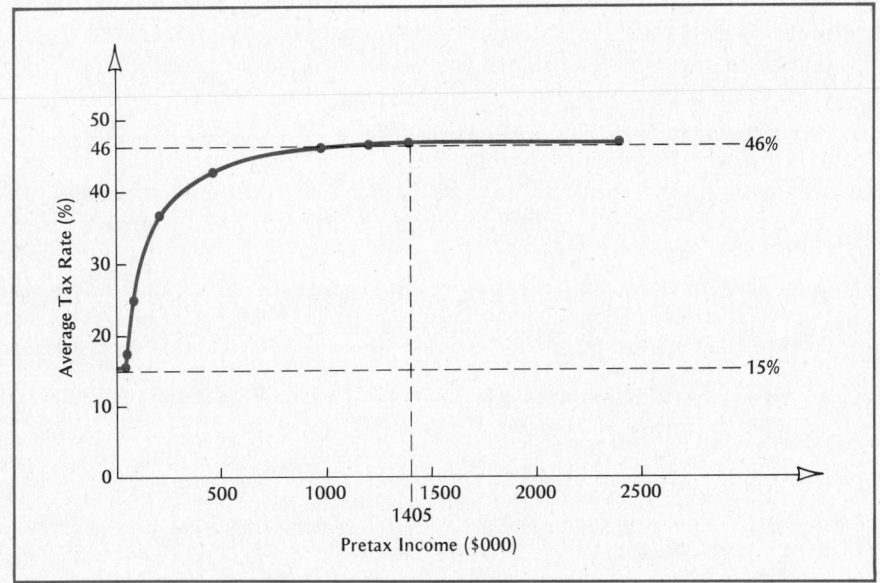

Figure 2.2   Average tax rates versus pretax income

$50,000 to $75,000 it is 30 percent; from $75,000 to $100,000 it is 40 percent; for income between $100,000 and $1,000,000 it is 46 percent; for income between $1,000,000 and $1,405,000 it is in excess of 46 percent due to the scheduled adjustment; and for income in excess of $1,405,000 it is 46 percent.[12]

EXAMPLE If Jessie Manufacturing's earnings go up to $1,300,000, the marginal tax rate on the additional $100,000 of income will become 51 percent. It will therefore have to pay additional taxes of $51,000 [(.46 × $100,000) + (.05 × $100,000)]. Total taxes on the $1,300,000, then, will be $592,750 ($541,750 + $51,000). To check this figure, we would take, using the ordinary tax rates, 15 percent of $25,000 plus 18 percent of $25,000 plus 30 percent of $25,000 plus 40 percent of $25,000 plus 46 percent of $1,200,000 (that is, $1,300,000 − $100,000) plus the lesser of (1) .05 × ($1,300,000 − $1,000,000) = $15,000 or (2) $20,250. This results in a total tax liability of $592,750 ($577,750 + $15,000) — the same value obtained by applying the marginal tax rate to the added income and adjusting the known tax liability. ■

CAPITAL GAINS

Corporations, like individuals and unincorporated businesses, are given special tax treatment with respect to certain capital gains. As in the case of individuals, if a firm sells certain capital assets for more than their initial purchase price, the difference between the sale price and the purchase price is called a capital gain.[13] Again, a short-term capital gain occurs when a capital asset held for six months or less is sold for more than its original purchase price; a long-term capital gain occurs when certain capital assets have been held for more than six months. For corporations as well as individuals, only long-term capital gains receive special tax treatment. The federal tax code provides for a rate of 28 percent or the ordinary rate, whichever is lower, on capital gains recognized as long-term. Taxation of long-term gains at the ordinary rate is advisable only when a firm's operating income is below $50,000, because the marginal tax rate for earnings over $50,000 is equal to or greater than 30 percent. When a firm sells an asset for more than its book value but less than its initial purchase price, the gain, which represents *recaptured depreciation,* is taxed as ordinary income. The 28 percent rate applies only to certain gains *above the initial purchase price* on assets held for longer than six months (long-term capital gains).[14] If a gain above the purchase price is realized on an asset held for six months or less, the total gain is taxed as ordinary income.

EXAMPLE The Commodore Company has operating earnings of $100,000 and has just sold for $40,000 a machine initially purchased two years ago for $36,000. The machine was being depreciated over a five-year normal recovery period according to the ACRS percentages

[12] To simplify the explanation of certain key concepts in the text, a 40 percent tax rate is assumed to be applicable to ordinary corporate income. This rate is not far out of line with the marginal tax rate of 46 percent and makes the calculations in the various examples easier to follow.

[13] The tax code specifically defines the types of assets eligible for this treatment. See William H. Hoffman, ed., *West's Federal Taxation: Corporations, Partnerships, Estates and Trusts* (St. Paul: West Publishing Company), published annually, for an excellent discussion of capital assets and capital gains.

[14] To simplify the computations presented in later chapters of the text, unless otherwise specified, a 30 percent tax rate is assumed to be applicable to long-term corporate capital gains.

(see Table 2.7). Because it was purchased two years ago, its current book value is $22,680, that is, $36,000 − [(.15 + .22) × $36,000]. The firm realized a total gain over book value of $17,320 ($40,000 − $22,680); $13,320 of this represents recaptured depreciation and is therefore recognized as ordinary income. The remainder of the gain, $4,000 ($40,000 − $36,000), may be subject to capital gain treatment and taxed at the 28 percent rate. Assuming this is the only depreciable asset sold during the year and there are no other capital gains or losses, the firm's total tax liability from its operating earnings and the sale of the machine is calculated as follows:

Taxable income
    Operations $100,000
    Total gain over book value   17,320
        Total $117,320
Less: Portion of gain recognized as long-term
    capital gain   4,000
        Ordinary income $113,320

Taxes
    Ordinary income:
    .15($25,000) + .18($25,000) + .30($25,000) +
        .40($25,000) + .46($113,320 − $100,000) =
        $3,750 + $4,500 + $7,500 + $10,000 +
        $6,127 = $31,877
    Capital gain (long-term):
    .28($4,000) =   1,120
        Total tax liability $32,997 ∎

If a firm sells certain assets for less than their original purchase price but more than book value, the gain above book value is taxed as ordinary income, as shown in the following example:

EXAMPLE If the Commodore Company sells the machine described in the preceding example for $30,000, only ordinary income will result. The firm would recapture depreciation of $7,320 ($30,000 − $22,680, the book value). It would therefore have a total taxable income of $107,320 ($100,000 + $7,320), on which the tax liability would be $29,117 [.15($25,000) + .18($25,000) + .30($25,000) + .40($25,000) + .46($107,320 − $100,000)].

If the company sells the machine for its exact book value of $22,680, no gain of any type will result, and the firm's only taxable income would be its $100,000 of operating income. Its taxes would then be $25,750[.15($25,000) + .18($25,000) + .30($25,000) + .40($25,000)]. ∎

TAX LOSSES

Three different tax loss situations may confront the firm.[15] It may have operating losses, losses on depreciable assets, or capital losses on capital assets.

Operating loss. An *operating loss* occurs when a firm has negative before-tax profits. It is permitted to apply this loss to past or future income, or both.

[15] For an in-depth discussion of operating and capital losses, see *Federal Tax Course* (Englewood Cliffs, N.J.: Prentice-Hall), published annually.

THE IRS VERSUS ACCOUNTANTS

When a company talks about taxes with its outside accountants, there's normally a candid exchange of information and opinions—a private conversation that's not for the eyes or ears of the Internal Revenue Service. But this frankness could be jeopardized by a little-publicized but landmark case now before the U.S. Supreme Court, which pits the IRS against the Big Eight accounting firm of Arthur Young & Co.

The IRS wants to get its hands on the "work papers" that Arthur Young auditors compiled several years ago when they tallied up the potential tax liabilities of Amerada Hess. The purpose of the work papers was to make sure the firm's financial statement set aside adequate reserves for possible taxes owed; the actual tax return was not involved. Nevertheless, the IRS argues that it has the legal right to demand all "relevant" information on taxpayers—and that the auditors' work papers are clearly relevant.

If the IRS wins its appeal of a lower court decision that denied the taxmen access to these papers, it will have a "chilling effect" on the relationship between accountants and their corporate clients, maintains Carl Liggio, who represented Arthur Young before the high court.

And that's just the beginning, add other experts, who predict the following consequences if the IRS wins:

● Companies will use lawyers instead of accountants for tax work in order to take advantage of the privacy of attorney-client privilege.

● Investors could be seriously misled by corporate financial statements if fear of the IRS zips executive lips when they talk to accountants. "Clearly, companies will take steps to shield themselves by not divulging everything," says the chief financial officer of a major multinational corporation.

● To avoid these adverse effects, accountants may simply throw away their work papers after filing a tax return—or put nothing in writing.

The IRS rejects Arthur Young's claim that it is "unfair" to give tax examiners access to work papers of independent accountants. "Under the revenue laws, taxpayers are required to collect and reveal a great deal of information that may ultimately be to their disadvantage," the government contends. "A corporate taxpayer is not free to play its cards close to its vest in the hope of going undetected or to turn the tax system into a sophisticated game of hide-and-seek."

Tax attorney Stuart Smith of Shea and Gould, who helped prepare the government's case, puts it this way: "These work papers will be helpful in identifying problems and ought not to be privileged. There are public considerations involved."

This kind of talk has an "appealing piety," admits Louis Craco, a spokesman for the American Institute of Certified Public Accountants. But he and others who support Arthur Young's position agree that the IRS has another "hidden agenda" in this case—saving time and money.

"The IRS has a lot to gain, because when it questions a company's taxes it must go through a long process of interviewing executives and poring through piles of paperwork," notes Kenneth Dirks, a partner in the accounting firm Main Hurdman. "But the IRS could cut the time significantly if it could just grab the accountant's work papers."

SOURCE: "The IRS vs. Accountants." *Dun's Business Month,* March 1984, pp. 42–45.

Loss on depreciable assets. If a firm sells a depreciable asset used in business or trade for less than its book value, a loss equal to the difference between the book value and the sale price may result. A loss on depreciable assets may be deducted from operating income for tax purposes.

EXAMPLE   If the Commodore Company sells the machine (a depreciable asset) described in the preceding examples for $18,000, it will experience a loss equal to the difference between the book value of $22,680 and the sale price of $18,000, or $4,680. This loss may be used to offset current, past, or future operating income. Since the company has operating earnings of $100,000, subtraction of the $4,680 loss from this figure would give it a taxable income of $95,320 and a tax liability of $23,878 [.15($25,000) + .18($25,000) + .30($25,000) + .40($95,320 − $75,000)]. ∎

Capital loss on capital assets. A firm experiences a capital loss when it sells a capital asset—a nondepreciable asset not used in business or trade—for less than its purchase price. A good example of a capital loss of this type would be the sale of marketable securities costing $1 million for $900,000. The firm would thus experience a $100,000 capital loss. A capital loss on capital assets can be used only to offset current, past, or future capital gains.

TAX LOSS CARRYBACKS AND CARRYFORWARDS

All three types of tax losses can be carried back 3 years; operating losses (includes losses on depreciable assets) can be carried forward for 15 years, and capital losses for 5 years.[16] The tax laws permit the carrying back and forward of losses to provide a more equitable tax treatment for corporations experiencing volatile patterns of income. This feature is especially attractive for firms in cyclic businesses such as durable goods manufacturing and construction since it effectively allows them to average out their taxes over the good and bad years. The law requires that the firm first net all losses against current gains, if any, and then carry losses back, applying them to the earliest year allowable and progressively moving forward until the loss has been fully recovered or the carryforward period has passed. Both operating losses and losses on the sale of depreciable assets used in business or trade may be applied against operating income, but capital losses on capital assets may be applied only against capital gains. Carrying tax losses back and forward means using the losses to offset past or future income and recomputing the firm's taxes based on the reduced income. The firm will then receive a tax refund (on a carryback) or have reduced future tax liabilities (on carryforwards).

EXAMPLE   The Regal Music Company's before-tax earnings and associated tax liabilities for the years 1981 through 1988 are presented in Table 2.11. Column 1 shows these amounts before any carrybacks or carryforwards have been made. In 1984 the firm had an operating loss of $500,000 as a result of a severe raw-material shortage. Column 2 indicates how this operating loss was carried back and then forward. By carrying the loss back three years and

---

[16] A corporation can elect to give up the three-year carryback for operating losses if such an election is made by the due date of filing the return for the year of the loss. See *Federal Tax Course* (Englewood Cliffs, N.J.; Prentice-Hall), published annually, for an in-depth discussion of tax loss carrybacks and carryforwards.

Table 2.11   Tax Loss Carryback and Carryforward Adjustments

Year	Item	Before carryback/carryforward (1)	After carryback/carryforward (2)
1981	Earnings	$ 115,000	$ 0
	Taxes	32,650	0
1982	Earnings	175,000	0
	Taxes	60,250	0
1983	Earnings	85,000	0
	Taxes	19,750	0
1984	Earnings	(500,000)	0
	Taxes	0	0
1985	Earnings	55,000	0
	Taxes	9,750	0
1986	Earnings	80,000	10,000
	Taxes	17,750	1,500
1987	Earnings	100,000	100,000
	Taxes	25,750	25,750
1988	Earnings	110,000	110,000
	Taxes	30,350	30,350

then forward, the firm was able to reduce its before-tax earnings by $115,000 in 1981, $175,000 in 1982, $85,000 in 1983, $55,000 in 1985, and $70,000 in 1986. The total tax savings was $138,650 ($32,650 in 1981, $60,250 in 1982, $19,750 in 1983, $9,750 in 1985, and $16,250 in 1986).

As soon as the company recognized the $500,000 loss in 1984, it was able to file for a tax refund of $112,650 ($32,650 + $60,250 + $19,750) for the years 1981–1983. It then carried the portion of the loss not used to offset past income forward to be applied against positive earnings for the next two years, 1985–1986. If the firm did not have sufficient earnings in the 15-year period 1985–1999 to permit it to write off the 1984 operating loss, it would have had no further tax recourse for recovering it, since such losses can be carried forward only 15 years, and the tax benefit would be lost forever. If the loss had been a capital loss instead of an operating loss, the carryback and carryforward procedure would have been similar, but the loss could have been applied only against the appropriate type of income and could have been carried forward only 5 instead of 15 years. ■

INVESTMENT TAX CREDIT (ITC)

At certain points in time, the Internal Revenue Service, in response to legislative action, has instituted an *investment tax credit (ITC)* permitting firms to receive a credit against federal income taxes for the purchase of certain depreciable property placed in service within the year. This feature of the tax law is intended to act as a stimulant to business investment and thereby help to foster expansion and growth in the economy. All qualifying[17] new property purchased during the year plus a

---

[17] Property that qualifies includes, with certain exceptions, only depreciable or amortizable property with lives of at least three years.

Table 2.12   Investment Tax Credit Options (ITC)

Normal recovery period grouping	Option 1		Option 2	
	ITC	Depreciable base (percent of cost)	ITC	Depreciable base (percent of cost)
3 years	6%	97%	4%	100%
5, 10, and 15 years	10%	95%	8%	100%

maximum of $125,000[18] in used property is eligible for this special treatment. The investment tax credit is applied to the total installed cost of an eligible asset. For instance, the credit would be applied to a $110,000 basis for an asset costing $100,000 and requiring an additional $10,000 in installation costs. The size of the ITC varies, depending on the assets' normal recovery period as well as which of the two available options is selected. The options available to assets with three-year normal recovery periods differ from those available to assets with longer (5-, 10-, or 15-year) normal recovery periods. Table 2.12 summarizes the two options available for each of the two normal recovery period groupings. The election depends on the firm's analysis of the financial and administrative factors related to each alternative.[19]

EXAMPLE   Dan Miller Clinics, Inc., acquired a new x-ray machine having a normal recovery period of five years for an installed cost of $160,000. The options available to the firm relative to the eligible investment tax credit would be:

Option 1: Take an investment tax credit of $16,000 (.10 × $160,000) and depreciate $152,000 (.95 × $160,000) over the five-year normal recovery period using ACRS depreciation percentages.

Option 2: Take an investment tax credit of $12,800 (.08 × $160,000) and depreciate $160,000 (1.00 × $160,000) over the five-year normal recovery period using ACRS depreciation percentages.

The firm will choose the option it deems most attractive from a financial and administrative viewpoint. ■

An investment tax credit cannot exceed a firm's tax liability in a given year. The maximum credit limit currently is $25,000 plus 85 percent of the tax liability in excess of $25,000. When the investment tax credit cannot be fully applied in a

---

[18] The Economic Recovery Tax Act of 1981 as modified by the Tax Reform Act of 1984 includes a scheduled increase to a limit of $150,000 in eligible used property, which is to take effect for taxable years beginning after 1987.

[19] For the sake of computational convenience, the use of option 2 — the lower ITC percentage and a depreciable base equal to 100 percent of cost — will be used throughout this text. Three-year assets will receive a 4 percent ITC, and longer-lived assets will receive an 8 percent ITC; the depreciable base in each instance will therefore equal 100 percent of cost.

given year because of this maximum-credit limitation, a 3-year carryback and a 15-year carryforward are permitted. These carrybacks and carryforwards are similar to those for operating, depreciable asset, and capital losses.

EXAMPLE   The Precision Milling Company's tax liability from operations for 1984 was $80,000. During 1984 the firm purchased two depreciable assets. One was a new machine (A) having a five-year normal recovery period and costing $900,000; the other was a used machine (B) having a three-year normal recovery period and costing $200,000. The total investment tax credit available can be calculated with respect to each machine, A and B.

$$\begin{array}{ll} \text{Machine A:} & 8\% \times \$900,000 = \$72,000 \\ \text{Machine B:} & 4\% \times \$125,000 = \underline{5,000} \\ \text{Total credit} & \underline{\$77,000} \end{array}$$

The $5,000 value for machine B is found by multiplying the $125,000 maximum for used property by the 4 percent rate applicable to eligible property having a normal recovery period of three years.

The maximum credit that can be applied to the current year's tax liability is $71,750 [$25,000 + .85($80,000 − $25,000)]. Since the firm is eligible for a credit of $77,000, the remaining credit of $5,250 ($77,000 − $71,750) can be carried back 3 years and then forward for as many as 15 years. ■

S CORPORATIONS

Subchapter S of the Internal Revenue Code permits corporations with 35 or fewer stockholders, all of whom are individuals, estates, and certain trusts — not other corporations — to be taxed like partnerships. That is, income is normally taxed as direct income of the shareholders, regardless of whether it is actually distributed to them. The *S corporation* is a tax-reporting entity rather than a tax-paying entity. The key advantage of this form of organization is that the shareholders receive all the organizational benefit of a corporation while escaping the double taxation normally associated with the distribution of corporate earnings to a firm's owners. S corporations do not receive certain types of tax advantages accorded other corporations, however. Many complexities and pitfalls can affect an S corporation and its shareholders, so taxpayers who wish to use this form should do so only after receiving competent advice.

TAX PAYMENT DATES

Corporations that expect to have an annual tax liability of $40 or more are required to make estimated tax payments. These estimated payments are commonly made in four installments, each covering 25 percent of the estimated liability. Estimated tax payments for the calendar year are made on April 15, June 15, September 15, and December 15. Any additional tax payments or refunds resulting from an under- or overpayment of estimated taxes must be settled by March 15 of the following year. Certain penalties may be levied on corporations that significantly underestimate tax liability.

MULTINATIONAL FINANCE

Foreign Ownership

In the present international legal environment, a multinational company must content itself with putting together a series of corporations created by the laws of different nation-states. The legal and economic complexities arising from this approach are significantly different from those a domestic firm would face.

LEGAL FORMS OF BUSINESS

In most other countries, operating a foreign business as a subsidiary or affiliate can take two forms, both similar to the U.S. corporation. In German-speaking countries, the two forms are the *Aktiengesellschaft* (A.G.) or the *Gesellschaft mit beschränkter Haftung* (GmbH); in many others the similar forms are a *Société Anonyme* (S.A.) or a *Société à Responsibilité Limitée* (S.A.R.L.). The A.G. or the S.A. is the most common form, but the GmbH or the S.A.R.L. enjoys much greater freedom and requires fewer formalities for formation and operation.

The establishment of a legal business organization in a form such as the S.A. can involve most of the provisions that govern a U.S.-based corporation, including the limited liability granted stockholders/owners. However, to operate in many foreign countries, especially in most of the less-developed nations, it is often essential to enter into joint-venture business agreements with private investors or with government-based agencies of the host. The governments of many Latin American countries, such as Brazil, Colombia, Mexico, and Venezuela, as well as the authorities in some of the nations of Southeast Asia, especially Malaysia, Indonesia, the Philippines, and Thailand, have in recent years instituted new laws and regulations governing MNCs. The result has been a reduction of ownership by MNCs of business ventures in their respective countries. The basic rule introduced by most of these countries requires that the majority ownership of such projects (i.e., at least 51 percent of the total equity) be by domestically based investors.

The existence of joint-venture laws and restrictions has certain implications for the operation of foreign-based subsidiaries. First of all, majority foreign ownership may result in a fair degree of foreign management and control. This can influence day-to-day operations in a manner that is detrimental to the managerial policies and procedures normally pursued by MNCs. Next, foreign ownership may result in disagreements among the partners as to the exact distribution of profits and the portion to be allocated for reinvestment. In many of the less-developed countries, for example, lack of domestic capital, along with frequent problems in the balance of payments position, has led to laws specifying minimum levels of reinvestment. Moreover, operating in foreign countries, especially on a joint-venture basis, can entail problems regarding the actual remission of profits. In the past, the governments of Argentina, Brazil, the People's Republic of China, and Thailand, among others, have imposed ceilings not only on the repatriation of capital by MNCs but also on profit remittances by these firms back to the parent companies. The shortage of foreign exchange is usually cited as the motivating factor by these governments.

Finally, from a "positive" point of view, it can be argued that to operate in many of the less-developed countries it would be beneficial for MNCs to enter into joint-venture agreements, given the potential risks stemming from political instability in the host countries. This issue will be addressed in detail in Chapter 7.

Multinational companies, unlike domestic firms, have financial obligations — as well as opportunities — in foreign countries. One of the basic responsibilities relates to international taxation, a topic we examine next. The international financial opportunities MNCs face will be discussed in Chapter 3.

INTERNATIONAL TAXES

International taxation is quite complex because national governments follow a variety of tax policies. In general, from the point of view of a U.S.-based MNC, several factors must be taken into account.

First, the *level* of foreign taxes needs to be examined. Certain countries are known for their "low" tax levels, including the Bahamas, Switzerland, Liechtenstein, Luxembourg, Panama, and Bermuda. These nations, unlike some of the major industrialized countries, typically have no withholding taxes on intra-MNC dividends. Next, there is a question as to the definition of *taxable income.* While some governments may regard profits to be taxable as received on a cash basis, others may treat the same profits as taxable as earned on an accrual basis. Differences can also exist on treatments of noncash charges, such as depreciation, amortization, and depletion.

Finally, the existence of tax agreements between the United States and other governments can influence the total tax bill of the parent MNC. For a U.S.-based MNC, the following elements and provisions must be noted. The U.S. government claims jurisdiction over *all* income of U.S. corporations, wherever earned. (Special rules apply to foreign corporations conducting business in the United States.) One of the major provisions is the possibility of taking foreign income taxes as a direct credit against U.S. tax liabilities. For the tax credit to be applicable, the MNC must have at least 10 percent of the equity of the foreign corporation. There can also be a pyramid effect, whereby the MNC parent can credit foreign income taxes paid by a subsidiary (2) owned by the foreign corporation (subsidiary 1) and the taxes paid by another subsidiary (3) owned by subsidiary 2. Each company must own at least 10 percent of the stock of the next lower firm, with the parent owning at least 5 percent (either directly or indirectly) of the stock of a subsidiary that paid taxes for it to be creditable. The overall technique is based on the "grossing up" procedure: The U.S. income is increased by the amount of foreign income (before the foreign taxes), and the U.S. tax calculation is then based on that higher level. The following example illustrates the procedure.

EXAMPLE   A U.S.-based MNC has three subsidiaries abroad as follows: subsidiary 1 (S1) is 40 percent owned by the MNC, with a taxable income of $20 million and local taxes of $10 million. The second subsidiary (S2) is 20 percent owned by S1 and has a taxable income of $48 million with local taxes of $16 million. The third subsidiary (S3) is 60 percent owned by S2 and has a taxable income of $15 million and local taxes of $9 million. In each case, the taxable income is the share belonging to the MNC. Assume a U.S. tax rate of 40 percent.

To calculate all the tax credits applicable to the MNC, the first part of the procedure is to establish the degree of ownership of each subsidiary by the MNC:

S1: 40 percent directly owned by the MNC
S2: (20 percent) $\times$ (40 percent) = 8 percent owned by the MNC
S3: (60 percent) $\times$ (20 percent) $\times$ (40 percent) = 4.8 percent owned by the MNC

Based on the regulations stated above, both S1 and S2 can be included in the calculation of tax credits, whereas S3, although more than 10 percent owned by S2, is still less than 5 percent owned by the parent MNC and is therefore not eligible. In terms of actual tax credits, if we assume that there are no withholding taxes in each of the local countries, the maximum credit against U.S. taxes would be 40 percent of the added income, or 40 percent of $68 million ($20 million from S1 and $48 million from S2), which is $27.2 million. Thus, the local taxes paid in foreign countries by S1 and S2 — amounting to $26 million — can be applicable as a credit in the United States for the MNC. ■

Additional provisions apply to tax deferrals by MNCs on foreign income; to operations set up in American possessions, such as the U.S. Virgin Islands, Guam, and American Samoa; to capital gains from the sale of stock in a foreign corporation; and to withholding taxes. A final point to note is that both the federal government and individual state governments in the United States have in recent years introduced new measures (mainly restrictions) that tend, overall, to treat the foreign operations and incomes of U.S.-based MNCs like the domestic activities of these firms or as part of a "unitary business" for tax purposes. State governments in the United States are using the courts as well as the U.S. Congress to clear the way to applying a special tax formula and thus taxing a share of the *total* income U.S.-based MNCs earn throughout the world. MNCs may face overlapping taxation of income by states and by foreign governments, since federal tax treaties with other countries do not apply to state taxation of MNCs.●●

CHAPTER SUMMARY

● The basic forms of business organization are the sole proprietorship, the partnership, and the corporation.

● Although there are more sole proprietorships than any other form of business organization, the corporation is dominant in terms of receipts and net profits. Since owners or stockholders have limited liability, corporations can raise large sums of money to grow and diversify.

● Corporations, like other forms of business, are permitted to allocate the past cost of certain assets to offset future income. The most common of these noncash expenditures are depreciation, amortization, and depletion.

● Depreciation is the most common type of noncash expenditure. The depreciable value of an asset and its depreciable life are determined using the Accelerated Cost Recovery System (ACRS) standards set out in the Economic Recovery Tax Act of 1981 and subsequently modified by the Tax Equity and Fiscal Responsibility Act of 1982 and the Tax Reform Act of 1984.

● The ACRS standards group assets (excluding real property) into four property classes based on length of recovery period — 3, 5, 10, or 15 years — with a schedule of yearly depreciation percentages for each period.

● Interest is a tax-deductible payment to lenders for money lent. It does not include return of the principal amount borrowed, which receives no special tax treatment and must be made from the firm's after-tax cash flow. Dividends are payments made by the firm to owners or stockholders and are not tax-deductible expenditures.

● The income of individuals, which includes proprietorships and partnerships, is subject to federal income taxes. Such income can be classified as ordinary income or capital gains, and each form is subject to a different tax treatment.

● On ordinary income, individuals are taxed on a progressive basis. The maximum tax rate on both earned and unearned income is 50 percent.

● On capital gains, which result when a capital asset is sold for more than its original purchase price, tax treatment depends on whether the gain is long-term or short-term. Long-term gains are taxed at only 40 percent of the ordinary tax rate up to a maximum rate of 20 percent. Short-term gains are taxed as ordinary income. The tax treatment of capital losses depends on whether they are short- or long-term.

● The taxable income and tax liability of individuals are found by following guidelines and using special forms provided by the IRS. By comparing the tax liability amount to total taxes paid through withholding and estimated tax payments during the tax year, the amount owed or the refund due is determined.

● The rates for and methods of taxing corporate income differ from the treatment of personal income and are quite complicated. The average tax rate paid by a firm can be found by dividing the taxes it pays by its taxable income. Average rates range from 15 to 46 percent. For our purposes, a 40 percent marginal tax rate can be assumed.

● If a firm sells certain capital assets for more than their initial purchase price, the amount by which the sale price exceeds the purchase price is considered a capital gain. If the asset has been held for six months or less, it is a short-term capital gain. If held for longer than six months, it is a long-term capital gain. Short-term capital gains are taxed at the firm's ordinary tax rate, while gains recognized as long-term can be taxed as ordinary income or at a flat 28 percent rate. In this book, a 30 percent rate is assumed.

● Firms often experience losses that can be used to offset past or future income. Operating losses and losses on depreciable assets used in business or trade can be applied against ordinary income. Capital losses on capital assets can be applied only against current, past, or future capital gains. Operating and depreciable asset losses may be carried back and forward, as may capital losses. In all cases, losses that cannot be fully applied in the carryforward period are lost forever.

● To stimulate economic activity, the federal government has instituted an investment tax credit entitling purchasers of new or used depreciable property to special tax deductions. The credit is based on the total installed cost of the asset, and the amount depends on the asset's normal recovery period as well as which of two optional treatments is elected. For our purposes, the smaller credit and full depreciable base can be assumed.

● The government also permits certain small businesses to file as S corporations, which are taxed as partnerships but have most of the rights of corporations.

● Setting up operations in foreign countries can entail special problems because of, among other things, the legal form of business organization chosen, the degree of ownership allowed by the host country, possible restrictions and regulations on capital repatriation and profit remittance, and international taxation.

KEY TERMS

Accelerated Cost Recovery System (ACRS)
adjusted gross income
articles of partnership

average tax rate
board of directors
capital asset

capital gain (long-term/short-term)
capital loss (personal)
capital loss on capital assets (corporate)
corporation
depreciation
dividends
Economic Recovery Tax Act of 1981
estimated tax payments
excess itemized deductions
exemptions (personal)
general partner
general partnership
gross income
interest
investment tax credit (ITC)
itemized deductions
joint and several liability
legal entity
limited partner
limited partnership
loss on depreciable assets

marginal tax rate
noncash charges
normal recovery period
operating loss
optional extended recovery period
partnership
president
progressive tax rates
recaptured depreciation
S corporation
sole proprietorship
stockholders
taxable income
tax credits
Tax Equity and Fiscal Responsibility Act
of 1982
tax liability
tax loss carryback/carryforward
Tax Reform Act of 1984
unlimited liability
zero-bracket amount

QUESTIONS

2-1 What are the three basic forms of business organization? Which form is most common? Which form is dominant in terms of business receipts and net profits?

2-2 What types of liability are related to the various forms of business organization? How does the expression *joint and several liability* relate to the business organization?

2-3 Why is the corporation often referrred to as a legal entity? Who is responsible for chartering a corporation?

2-4 How do the various legal and organizational aspects of corporations facilitate their growth into large businesses?

2-5 In what sense does depreciation act as a cash inflow? How can a firm's after-tax profits be adjusted to show cash flow from operations?

2-6 Briefly describe the Accelerated Cost Recovery System (ACRS) property classes, the normal recovery periods, and the optional extended recovery periods. Explain how the depreciation percentages are determined using the normal ACRS recovery periods.

2-7 How are interest and dividends different? How are they alike? What are the tax implications (if any) of each of these types of payments?

2-8 **a** For an individual, what is the difference between *earned income* and *unearned* or *passive income?*
       b What differences exist between short-term and long-term capital gains or losses? How are they treated for tax purposes by an individual?

2-9 In view of the progressive structure of personal income taxes, explain the difference between the average and marginal income tax rates for individuals. Does the same phenomenon exist for corporations? Explain.

2-10 Can a firm pay both an ordinary tax and a capital gains tax on the sale of an asset at a price
       a Greater than its purchase price?

       b Equal to its purchase price?

       c Equal to its book value?

2-11 What is the rationale for the investment tax credit? What election can the firm make relative to calculation of the credit? What are its tax implications?

2-12 Briefly discuss the major differences between the ownership of domestic business organizations and of foreign operations by multinational companies.

2-13 Why do some governments impose restrictions on profit remittances by MNCs? Be specific.

2-14 What is the "grossing up" procedure used in calculating the total U.S. tax liability of a U.S.-based MNC?

PROBLEMS

2-1 **(Liability Comparisons)** Marilyn Smith has personal assets with liquidation value of $125,000 and has invested $25,000 in the Research Marketing Company. The Research Marketing Company has recently become bankrupt and has $60,000 in unpaid debts. Explain the nature of payments (if any) by Ms. Smith in each of the following situations:

    a The Research Marketing Company is a sole proprietorship owned by Ms. Smith.

    b The Research Marketing Company is a 50-50 partnership of Ms. Smith and Arnold Jones. Mr. Jones has personal assets that can be readily liquidated for $15,000.

    c The Research Marketing Company is a corporation.

2-2 **(Cash Flow)** A firm had earnings after taxes of $50,000 in 1985. Depreciation charges were $28,000, and a $2,000 charge for amortization on a bond discount was incurred. What was the actual cash flow from operations?

2-3 **(Depreciation)** On January 1, 1984, Antex Corporation acquired two new assets. Asset A was a light-duty truck costing $17,000 and having a three-year normal recovery period. Asset B was a drill press having an installed cost of $45,000 and a five-year normal recovery period. Using the ACRS depreciation percentages given in Table 2.7, prepare a depreciation schedule for each of these assets.

2-4 **(Depreciation and Cash Flows)** A firm expects to have earnings before depreciation and taxes of $160,000 in each of the next five years. It is considering the purchase of a fixed asset costing $140,000, requiring $10,000 in installation costs, and having a normal recovery period of five years.

    a Calculate the annual depreciation for the asset purchase using the ACRS depreciation percentages given in Table 2.7.

    b Calculate the annual cash flows for each of the five years. Assume a 40 percent ordinary tax rate.

    c Compare and discuss your findings in **a** and **b**.

2-5 **(Depreciation and Cash Flow)** A firm in the third year of depreciating its only asset, originally costing $180,000 and being depreciated under ACRS over its normal five-year recovery period, has gathered the following data relative to the given year's operations.

Accruals	$ 15,000
Current assets	120,000
Interest expense	15,000
Total sales	400,000
Inventory	70,000
Total costs before depreciation, interest, and taxes	290,000
Tax rate on ordinary income	35%

    a Use the relevant data above to determine the *cash flow from operations* for the current year.

    b Explain the impact that depreciation, as well as any other noncash charges, has on a firm's cash flows.

2-6   **(Interest versus Dividends)**   The Randy Company expects earnings before interest and taxes to be $40,000 this period. Assuming an ordinary tax rate of 40 percent, compute the after-tax net profits and earnings available for common stockholders the firm will have if

    a The firm pays $10,000 in interest.

    b The firm pays $10,000 in preferred stock dividends.

2-7   **(Progressive Tax Rates)**   Juan Sandoval had a taxable income of $20,000, and his sister Maria had a taxable income of $12,000.

    a Compute the tax liability for each of these single persons using Table 2.9.

    b Compute the average tax rate for each person.

    c What taxation principle is illustrated by your findings in **b**?

2-8   **(Ordinary and Capital Gain Income for an Individual)**   During 1984 Rebecca Collins earned a salary of $23,500 and received $350 in interest on her passbook savings account. In addition, Rebecca sold two stocks—400 shares of X and 200 shares of Y. Stock X was purchased two years earlier for $15 per share and was sold for $17.50 per share. Stock Y, purchased five months earlier for $22 per share, was sold for $29 per share.

    a Calculate the amount of capital gain realized by Rebecca on each of her stock transactions and classify each as short-term or long-term.

    b Calculate Rebecca's gross income for 1984.

    c Rework **b** assuming that stock Y had been purchased ten months earlier.

    d Compare and contrast the gross income calculated in **b** and **c**.

2-9   **(Personal Tax Liability)**   José Chavez, a single person, during 1984 earned $18,500 from his job as salesman for Paxon Industries. During the year his employer withheld $2,500 for federal income tax purposes. In addition, José received interest of $500 on a money fund account and a dividend of $400 on stocks he owned. At the end of 1984 José sold two stocks, A and B. Stock A was sold for $800; it had been purchased four months earlier for $700. Stock B, which was sold for $1,500, had been purchased three years earlier for $700. José claimed only one exemption for tax purposes. José's total itemized deductions—including interest and tax outlays for his condominium—totaled $5,500 in 1984. In addition, José incurred $350 in unreimbursed business expenditures on an out-of-town business trip. José's only tax credit was $25 for a political contribution he made during the year.

    a Recognizing that José as a single person is eligible for a $100 dividend exclusion, a $2,300 zero-bracket amount, and a $1,000 exemption, calculate José's 1984 taxable income.

    b Using the tax schedule given in Table 2.9, calculate José's taxes.

    c In light of José's tax credit, how large is his tax liability?

    d Will José have to pay additional taxes or receive a refund? How large will this payment or refund be?

2-10   **(Average Corporate Tax Rates)**   Using the corporate tax rates given in the text:

    a Calculate the tax liability, after-tax earnings, and average tax rates for the following levels of corporate earnings before taxes: $10,000; $100,000; $500,000; $1 million; $5 million.

    b Plot the average tax rates (measured on the *y*-axis) against the pretax income levels (measured on the *x*-axis). What generalization can be made concerning the relationship between these variables?

2-11   **(Tax on Sale of Assets)**   Waters Manufacturing purchased a new machine three years ago for $80,000. It is being depreciated under ACRS over its normal five-year recovery period using the percentages given in Table 2.7. Assume a 40 percent ordinary tax rate and 30 percent tax rate on long-term capital gains.

a What is the book value of the machine?

b Calculate the firm's tax liability if it sells the machine for the following: $100,000; $56,000; $33,600; $25,000.

2-12 **(Total Tax Liability with Sale of Asset)**   The Lionel Corporation just sold a two-year-old machine that originally cost $500,000 and was being depreciated using the normal ACRS five-year recovery period and the applicable percentages given in Table 2.7. Assume that the firm has a 40 percent tax rate on ordinary income and 30 percent on long-term capital gains. The firm has before-tax operating earnings of $195,000.

a Calculate the total tax liability from ordinary and capital gains income assuming the firm sells the machine for $550,000.

b Recalculate the total tax liability assuming a sale for $450,000.

c Calculate the firm's total tax liability if the machine is sold for $250,000.

2-13 **(Total Tax Liability with Sale of Assets)**   A firm having ordinary operating income in the current year of $230,000, at year-end sold two assets, A and B, having the characteristics described below:

Characteristic	Asset A	Asset B
Original purchase price	$60,000	$20,000
Purchase date	2 years ago	3 years ago
Sale price	$45,000	$30,000
Depreciation (ACRS)	5-year normal recovery period	5-year normal recovery period

If ordinary income is taxed at 40 percent and long-term capital gains at 30 percent, calculate the total tax liability for the current year.

2-14 **(Integrative — Depreciation, Cash Flow, and Total Tax Liability)**   Adkins Running Store, Inc., during the year ended December 31, 1984, made the following asset transactions:

1. In January 1984, it sold its shoe-resoling machine, which originally cost $14,500, for $16,000. The machine was purchased two years earlier and was being depreciated under ACRS over its five-year normal recovery period.

2. The firm's only remaining depreciable asset was the delivery truck, which was being depreciated from its original $12,000 cost under ACRS over its three-year normal recovery period. The truck was in the second year of its depreciable life.

In addition, the firm has gathered the following data relative to the current year's (i.e., 1984) operations:

Current assets	$ 53,000
Inventory	$ 40,000
Total sales	$360,000
Accruals	$ 4,000
Interest expense	$ 22,000
Stockholders' equity	$ 63,000
Total cost before depreciation, interest, and taxes	$220,000

Ordinary tax rate   40%
Long-term capital gains tax rate   30%

a   Use the relevant data to determine the firm's *cash flow from operations* during 1984. (*Note:* Ignore any extraordinary gains or losses such as transaction 1 described above.)

b   Discuss the impact that depreciation and any other noncash charges have on a firm's cash flows.

c   Calculate the tax liability (or refund) associated with the sale of the resoling machine described in 1 above.

d   Based on your findings in **a** and **c**, what are the firm's *total cash flow* and *total tax liability* for the year ended December 31, 1984?

2-15   **(Carryback and Carryforward)**   The Ordway Shipbuilding Company had operating earnings, ordinary taxes, long-term capital gains, and capital gains taxes for the period 1981 through 1991 as indicated below.

Year	Operating earnings	Ordinary taxes	Long-term capital gains	Capital gains taxes
1981	$600,000	$240,000	$ 0	$ 0
1982	450,000	180,000	60,000	18,000
1983	200,000	80,000	20,000	6,000
1984				
1985	300,000	120,000	0	0
1986	400,000	160,000	0	0
1987	300,000	120,000	40,000	12,000
1988	500,000	200,000	90,000	27,000
1989	600,000	240,000	0	0
1990	300,000	120,000	0	0
1991	450,000	180,000	20,000	6,000

For each of the following cases, (1) calculate the adjusted incomes and taxes for each year and (2) indicate the amount of ordinary and capital gain tax relief, if any. The firm pays taxes of 40 percent on ordinary income and 30 percent on long-term capital gains. Explain your answers.

a   In 1984 Ordway had an operating loss of $1 million and no long-term capital gains.

b   In 1984 Ordway had operating income of $200,000 and long-term capital gains of $50,000.

c   In 1984 Ordway had an operating loss of $2 million and a capital loss on capital assets of $100,000.

d   In 1984 Ordway had operating income of $300,000 and a capital loss on capital assets of $250,000.

2-16   **(Investment Tax Credit Election)**   Zantus Corporation during 1984 acquired two new assets, R and S, briefly described below.

Asset	Cost	Installation cost	Normal recovery period
R	$125,000	$10,000	5 years
S	15,000	0	3 years

a Calculate the investment tax credit for each asset using both of the options available to the firm.

b Calculate the depreciable base for each asset under each of the available investment tax credit options.

c Discuss the alternative treatments for each asset in light of the investment tax credit and associated depreciable bases found in **a** and **b**.

2-17 **(Investment Tax Credit)**   In 1984 the Comet Manufacturing Company had a tax liability of $100,000. Assuming the firm has elected the option providing for the smaller investment tax credit and a 100 percent depreciable base, for each of the following assets calculate (1) the total investment tax credit for which the firm was eligible and (2) the amount of the credit applicable in 1984.

Asset	Installed cost	Normal recovery period	Status of asset when purchased
A	$ 600,000	3 years	new
B	70,000	15 years	used
C	1,500,000	5 years	new
D	90,000	3 years	new
E	200,000	10 years	used

2-18 **(Organizational Form and Taxes)**   The Palmer Products Company earns $80,000 before owner's salary and taxes. Mr. Palmer is considering changing his business organization from a sole proprietorship to a corporation. His sole criterion is whether such a move would decrease the level of his tax liability. Currently, he pays himself $45,000 in personal service income from the proprietorship. He has personal deductions of $15,000. If he operated as a corporation, he would receive a $35,000 salary and $10,000 in dividends. Using Table 2.9 and actual corporate tax rates, which business organization should he select?

2-19 **(MNC Tax Credits)**   A U.S.-based MNC has three subsidiaries as follows. Subsidiary 1, S1, is 50 percent owned by the MNC and has a taxable income of $200 million and local taxes of $85 million. Subsidiary 2, S2, is 20 percent owned by S1, with a taxable income of $120 million and local taxes of $38 million. The third subsidiary, S3, is 9 percent owned by the parent MNC and has taxable income of $80 million and local taxes of $53 million. Assume that there are no withholding taxes in any of the countries and that the U.S. tax rate is 40 percent. Also assume that the taxable incomes in each case are the shares belonging to the MNC. Calculate the total tax credits the MNC can have.

Chapter 3

Financial Intermediaries, Markets, and Interest Rates

After studying this chapter, you should be able to:

1. Discuss the role, importance, and interactions of financial intermediaries and markets in the U.S. economy.

2. Describe the key participants in financial transactions and the basic activities of major financial intermediaries.

3. Understand the money market—its operation, participants, and instruments.

4. Describe the role of capital markets, the functions and characteristics of securities exchanges, special stock transactions, and investment companies, and the role of the investment banker.

5. Discuss interest rate fundamentals—including the real and nominal rate of interest, the term structure of interest rates, risk premiums, and the basic trade-off between risk and return.

6. Identify the key characteristics and behaviors of international markets, particularly the Euromarket.

A corporation does not operate in a financial vacuum; it operates in close contact with the various financial intermediaries and markets. This close relationship allows the firm to obtain needed financing and also to invest idle funds in various financial instruments. Large corporations find it necessary to frequent the financial marketplace; small corporations may visit these markets relatively infrequently. Regardless of the size of the firm, the various financial media act as clearing mechanisms, matching the suppliers and demanders of funds and giving a structure to the fund-raising and investing process.

The emergence of strong financial intermediaries and markets is in large part responsible for the existence of large-scale business firms. Without some mechanism through which idle funds could be attracted by firms needing funds for investment in assets, companies such as American Telephone and Telegraph and General Motors would have been unable to reach their current size. These financial media not only make funds available but also allocate funds through the risk-return mechanism. Firms that have uncertain future prospects must compensate suppliers of funds by providing higher returns; firms with more predictable futures, such as public utilities, do not have to offer such high returns.

Financial Intermediaries and Markets: An Overview

Available funds can be transmitted to firms that require funds in three external ways. One is through a *financial intermediary,* an institution that accepts savings and transfers them to those needing funds. Another is through *financial markets,* organized forums where the suppliers and demanders of various types of funds can make transactions. A third is through private placement. Because of the unstructured nature of private placements, in this section we focus primarily on financial intermediaries and financial markets. However, private placement of funds is not unusual—especially in the case of debt instruments and preferred stock.

FINANCIAL INTERMEDIARIES

Financial intermediaries, or *financial institutions,* channel the savings of various parties into loans or investments.[1] The process by which savings are accumulated by financial institutions and then lent or invested is generally referred to as *intermediation.*[2] Many financial institutions directly or indirectly pay savers interest on deposited funds; others provide services for which they charge depositors. (For example, commercial banks levy service charges on checking accounts, thereby indirectly charging depositors in these accounts.) Some financial intermediaries accept savings and lend this money to their customers, others accept savings and then invest the funds in earning assets such as real estate or stocks and bonds, and still others both lend and invest money. In most instances, a financial intermediary must operate within certain legal constraints.

Key participants in financial transactions. The key suppliers and demanders of funds are individuals, businesses, and governments.

Individuals. The savings of individual consumers placed in certain financial institutions provide these institutions with a large portion of the funds they lend or invest. Individual savings may be kept in a checking or savings account in a commercial bank or in similar types of accounts in a mutual savings bank, a savings and loan association, or a credit union. They may be used to purchase life insurance, to contribute to pension funds, or to purchase mutual fund shares or make other types of deposits. Individuals not only act as suppliers of funds to intermediaries; they also obtain funds in the form of loans. Individuals may borrow money from commercial banks, mutual savings banks, savings and loan associations, credit unions, life insurance companies, and other institutions. Individuals can be viewed as both suppliers of funds to and demanders of funds from financial intermediaries. The important point is that individuals as a group are *net suppliers:* They save more money than they borrow.

Businesses. Business firms also place some of their funds with financial intermediaries, primarily in checking accounts with various commercial banks. Firms, like individuals, also obtain funds from various financial institutions. They borrow primarily from commercial banks, life insurance companies, pension funds, and mutual funds. Business firms as a group are *net demanders* of funds: They borrow more money than they save.

Governments. The federal government maintains deposits of temporarily idle funds, certain tax payments, and social security payments in commercial banks. It

---

[1] In this chapter the terms *loans* and *investments* are used interchangeably to mean the placement of funds in some type of earning instrument.

[2] During past inflationary periods as a result of the high interest rates available from media other than financial institutions, the process of *disintermediation* has taken place. Depositors withdrew their funds from financial institutions and invested them in the higher-yielding marketable securities. Today, with the *Depository Institutions Deregulation and Monetary Control Act of 1980* in effect, financial institutions are able to compete directly with other financial media, thereby drastically reducing disintermediation.

does not borrow funds directly from financial institutions but does obtain needed financing through the financial markets. State and local governments behave similarly by maintaining bank deposits and raising needed financing in the financial markets. When one considers the savings and borrowings of various levels of government in the financial marketplace, the government, like business firms, is typically *a net demander* of money: It borrows more than it saves.

Key financial intermediaries. The key financial intermediaries in the U.S. economy are commercial banks, mutual savings banks, savings and loan associations, credit unions, life insurance companies, pension funds, and mutual funds. These institutions attract funds from individuals, business, and government, combine them, and perform certain services to make attractive loans available to individuals and businesses. They may also make some of these funds available to fulfill various government demands for funds.

Commercial banks. The *commercial bank* is an important financial intermediary. It accepts both demand (checking) and time (savings) deposits and also offers *negotiable order of withdrawal (NOW) accounts,* which are interest-earning savings accounts against which checks can be written.[3] In addition, commercial banks currently offer *money market accounts* and *super NOW accounts,* which, subject to certain restrictions, pay interest at rates competitive with other short-term investment vehicles. The bank loans out its funds directly to borrowers or through the financial markets. The primary type of loan made by a commercial bank is a short-term unsecured business loan (see Chapter 18 for a full discussion). Commercial banks also make some installment and mortgage loans and provide lease financing to individuals and businesses.

Mutual savings banks. Mutual savings banks are similar to commercial banks except that they may not hold demand (checking) deposits.[4] They get their funds from savings, NOW, and money market account deposits, and they make these funds available to business firms. They generally lend or invest funds through financial markets rather than through negotiated loans, although they do make some residential real estate loans to individuals. Mutual savings banks are located primarily in New York, New Jersey, and the New England states.

Savings and loan associations. Savings and loan associations are similar to mutual savings banks in that they hold savings deposits, NOW accounts, and money market accounts, which they lend primarily to individuals for real estate mortgage loans. Some savings and loan funds are channeled into investments in the financial

---

[3] Prior to mid-November 1975, business firms (except certain charitable organizations) were legally prohibited from maintaining savings deposits in commercial banks. A change in the law at that time now permits businesses to maintain savings deposits of up to $150,000 at a commercial bank. This change in the law was made to provide small businesses with a mechanism whereby some return could be conveniently earned on temporarily idle funds; large businesses were not significantly affected by this change.

[4] Commercial banks are the *only* financial institutions legally permitted to hold checking accounts (demand deposits), although most depository institutions currently offer NOW and money market accounts, which are basically interest-earning checking accounts.

markets. Savings and loan associations also raise some of their capital through the sale of securities in the financial markets. Since savings and loan associations are dominant in the mortgage-lending area, federal agencies often become involved in lending money to them to finance certain types of real estate mortgages. Business firms do not generally become involved with savings and loan associations.

Credit unions. A *credit union* is a financial intermediary that deals primarily in transfers of funds between consumers. Membership in a credit union is generally based on some common bond such as working for the same employer or attending the same church. Credit unions accept members' savings deposits, NOW account deposits, and money market accounts and then lend the majority of these funds to other members, who typically use the money to purchase automobiles or appliances or make home improvements. If the demand for loans is not great enough to absorb all available funds, the credit union may channel some of its funds into short-term investments through the financial markets. When a credit union needs additional funds, it generally borrows them directly from a commercial bank.

Life insurance companies. Insurance companies, specifically *life insurance companies,* are the largest financial intermediary handling individual savings. Although a person generally purchases life insurance to provide for his or her beneficiaries after death, most life insurance (whole life and endowment policies) has a savings function. A portion of each premium payment goes to cover the death benefit; the remainder is invested to cover death losses in later years. In other words, life insurance companies receive large amounts of premium payments that must be invested to accumulate funds to cover future claims. They transfer the savings of individuals into loans and investments. Some life insurance money is lent directly to individuals, business, and government; another portion is channeled through the financial markets to those who demand funds.

Pension funds. Pension funds are set up so that employees of various corporations or government units can receive income after retirement. There are numerous types of pension plan arrangements. Quite often employers contribute to a pension fund, matching in some way the contributions of their employees; occasionally employer contributions are based on a profit-sharing arrangement. Pension fund dollars are loaned or invested in numerous areas. Some of the money is transferred directly to various borrowers, but the majority of it is lent or invested via the financial markets. The largest pension fund is the federal Old Age, Survivors, Disability, and Health Insurance System, or Social Security Plan, to which nearly all of us belong. Most Social Security funds are lent to other agencies of the federal government.

Mutual funds. A *mutual fund* is a type of financial intermediary that pools funds of savers and makes them available to business and government demanders. Mutual funds obtain funds through sale of shares and use the proceeds to acquire stocks and bonds issued by various business and governmental units. Their goal is to reduce risk by creating a diversified portfolio of securities that will achieve a specified investment objective such as liquidity with a high return, high growth, or tax-exempt income. There are hundreds of funds, with a variety of investment objectives. Many mutual funds are *no-load funds,* which do not charge any transaction fee; others, known as *load funds,* charge purchase fees ranging as high as 8.5 percent.

A currently popular type of mutual fund is the *money market fund,* which, by investing in short-term debt instruments of business and government, is able to provide competitive returns with high liquidity. Because many of these funds offer check-writing privileges, they are highly competitive with NOW, money market, and super NOW accounts offered by commercial banks, mutual savings banks, savings and loan associations, and credit unions. The very competitive returns offered by money market funds result from their use of professional management and certain cost savings resulting from their large-scale operations. Most money market funds are no-load funds.

Of the key intermediaries, commercial banks, life insurance companies, and pension funds are the major suppliers of loans and investments to business firms. Most of the dollars provided are not channeled directly to business firms but pass through the financial markets. Without these institutions, the funds available for business financing would be significantly reduced.

Changing role of financial intermediaries. Passage of the *Depository Institutions Deregulation and Monetary Control Act of 1980 (DIDMCA)* signaled the beginning of the "financial services revolution" that continues to change the nature of financial institutions. By eliminating interest-rate ceilings on most accounts and permitting certain institutions to offer new types of accounts and services such as NOWs, money market accounts, and discount brokerage, the DIDMCA intensified competition between these institutions and blurred traditional distinctions. What is evolving is the *financial supermarket,* at which a customer can obtain a full array of financial services such as checking, deposits, brokerage, insurance, and estate planning. This trend is expected to continue; soon institutions such as commercial banks, mutual savings banks, savings and loan associations, and credit unions will be virtually identical in terms of product and service offerings.

Testimony to the emergence of the financial supermarket is Sears, Roebuck and Company's "Sears Financial Network." In addition to its credit and insurance (Allstate) operations, Sears now owns a national real estate brokerage firm (Coldwell Banker), a major stock brokerage firm (Dean Witter), and a West Coast savings and loan (Allstate Savings and Loan). It offers all these financial services in a growing number of "Financial Networks" housed within its retail stores. Other large firms such as Kroger, American Express, and Prudential Insurance are also expanding their financial service offerings — often through acquisitions.

FINANCIAL MARKETS

Financial markets provide a forum in which suppliers and demanders of short-term and long-term loans and investments can transact business directly. Whereas the loans and investments of intermediaries are made without the direct knowledge of the fund suppliers (savers), suppliers in the financial marketplace know

CITIBANK: THE FIRST U.S. NATIONAL BANK?

Citibank unveiled a new strategy in its efforts to become a national consumer bank.

The big New York bank has begun marketing a "Citibank financial account" combining a credit card, savings, checking, a credit line and other features in three metropolitan areas, Atlanta, Tampa and Minneapolis-St. Paul.

It is the latest step by Citibank and its Citicorp parent to solicit consumer deposits and provide a full range of banking services around the U.S., skirting federal laws that generally prohibit interstate banking. In January, Citicorp acquired large, failing savings and loan associations in Illinois and Florida.

With the latest move, Citibank is gambling that it can successfully deliver full banking services cheaply to large numbers of consumers without a branch system, using cheaper mail, telephone and cash-dispensing machines in supermarkets and other locations. Banks generally aren't allowed to set up deposit-taking branches outside their home state. . . .

National banking

"National banking is here," said Ira S. Rimerman, a senior vice president and chairman of Citicorp's credit-card subsidiary. Although nothing in the Citibank account is particularly new to banking, he said, "We are the first bank to put this all together and offer it on a nationwide basis."

For the past two years, Citibank has been taking deposits by mail through its Visa and Mastercard holders attracting "hundreds of millions of dollars," according to Mr. Rimerman. The new account is a big expansion of the nationwide deposit-taking effort. . . .

Starting in the 1970s, Citicorp distributed millions of credit cards around the country, and lost hundreds of millions of dollars along the way. However, Citicorp now is the nation's biggest bank-card issuer with five million Visa and MasterCard accounts, 80% of them outside New York State.

Better prepared

Robert Albertson, an analyst at Smith Barney, Harris Upham & Co., said, "Citicorp is better prepared than anyone to take consumer banking nationwide in deposit taking. They have better processing capability and they have already made the acquaintance of the consumer nationwide" through credit cards, mortgage loans and other products. He added, "They can't be your bank like a bank with a branch in Tampa, but they can come pretty close."

Citicorp has long been looking to sell a range of consumer services through its bank cards. Mr. Rimerman said the bank's new financial account, which is linked to a Mastercard, is "a bank in a card."

To get cash to its existing credit-card customers, Citicorp has been linking up with automated teller machines or ATMs, in supermarket chains in Florida and California. It has an agreement to share 70 cash-dispensing machines in Publix supermarkets in Tampa, one of the three initial marketing areas for the new Citibank account. Now Citicorp is ready to "expand ATM availability around the country," including signing sharing agreements with other retailers and banks, Mr. Rimerman said.

SOURCE: Daniel Hertzberg, "Citibank Unveils New Marketing Strategy in Bid to Become National Consumer Bank," *The Wall Street Journal,* March 29, 1984, p. 13.

exactly where their funds are being lent or invested. The two key financial markets are the *money market* and the *capital market*. Transactions in short-term debt instruments, or marketable securities, take place in the money market. Long-term securities (bonds and stocks) are traded in the capital market.

All securities, whether they belong in the money or capital markets, are initially issued in the *primary market*. This is the only market in which the corporate or government issuer is directly involved in the transaction and receives direct benefit from the issue — that is, the company actually receives the proceeds from the sale of securities. Once the securities begin to trade between individual, business, government, or financial institution savers and investors, they become part of the *secondary market*. The primary market is where "new" securities are sold; the secondary market can be viewed as a "used" or "preowned" securities market.

THE RELATIONSHIP BETWEEN INTERMEDIARIES AND MARKETS

Financial intermediaries and financial markets are not independent of each other; on the contrary, it is quite common to find financial intermediaries actively participating in both the money market and the capital market, as both suppliers and demanders of funds. Figure 3.1 depicts the general flow of funds through and between financial intermediaries and financial markets; private placement transactions are also shown. The individuals, businesses, and governments that supply and demand funds may be domestic or foreign. In some instances there may be legal constraints on the operations of certain institutions in the financial marketplace. Because of the key importance of the money and capital markets to the business firm, the next two sections of this chapter will be devoted to these topics.

The Money Market

The *money market* is created by an intangible relationship between suppliers and demanders of *short-term funds*. It is not an actual organization housed in some central location, such as a stock market, although the majority of money market transactions culminate in New York City. Except for certain types of bank-to-bank transactions, money market transactions are made in marketable securities, which are short-term debt instruments such as Treasury bills, commercial paper, and negotiable certificates of deposit issued by government, business, and financial institutions, respectively. The money market exists because certain individuals, businesses, governments, and financial intermediaries have temporarily idle funds that they wish to place in some type of liquid asset or short-term interest-earning instrument. At the same time, other individuals, businesses, governments, and financial intermediaries find themselves in situations where they need seasonal or temporary financing. The money market brings together these suppliers and demanders of short-term funds.

THE OPERATION OF THE MONEY MARKET

Since the money market is intangible, how are suppliers and demanders of short-term funds brought together? Typically, they are matched through the facilities of

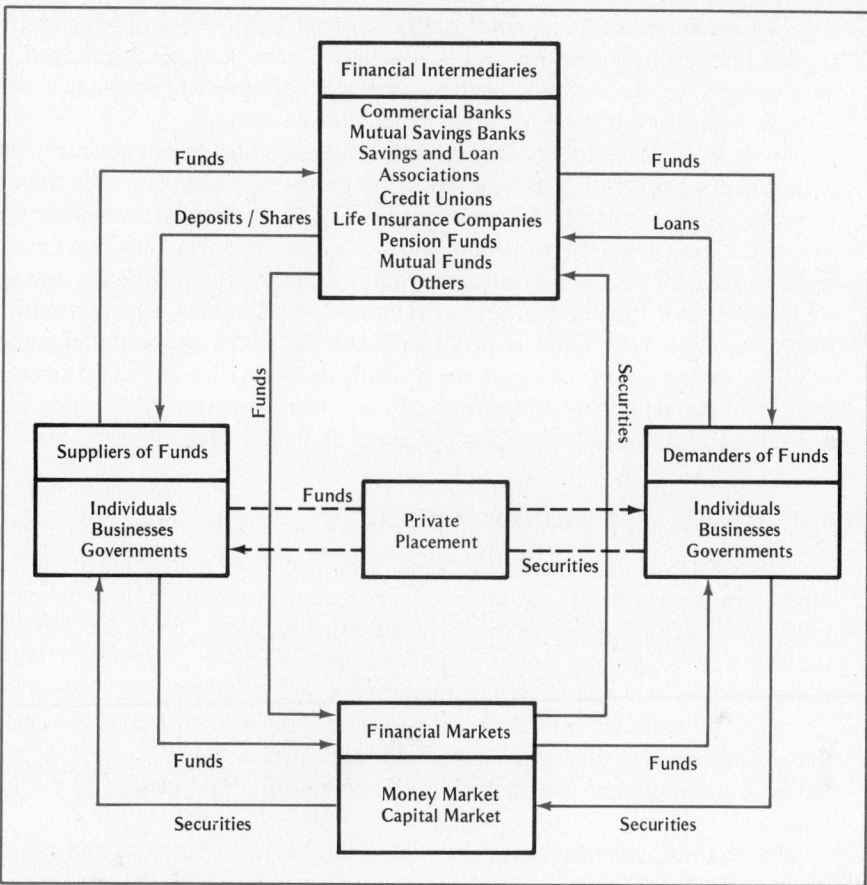

Figure 3.1   Flow of funds for financial intermediaries and markets

large New York banks, through government securities dealers, or through the Federal Reserve banks. The Federal Reserve banks become involved only in loans from one commercial bank to another; these loans are commonly referred to as transactions in *federal funds*. A number of stock brokerage firms purchase various money market instruments for resale to customers. If a brokerage firm does not have an instrument demanded by a customer, it will attempt to acquire it. In addition, financial intermediaries such as banks and mutual funds purchase money market instruments for their portfolios to provide attractive returns on their customers' deposits and share purchases.

Most money market transactions are negotiated by telephone. A firm wishing to purchase a certain marketable security may call its bank, which will then attempt to buy the securities by contacting a New York bank or another bank known to "make a market" or deal in the given security. The bank or the firm may also go directly to a *government security dealer,* a type of intermediary that purchases for resale various government securities and other money market instruments, to negotiate a transaction. Regardless of whether a business or government is issuing a money market instrument (demanding short-term funds) or purchasing a money market instrument (supplying short-term funds), one party must go directly to another party or use a middleperson, such as a commercial bank, government security dealer, or brokerage firm, to make a transaction.

The key to successful transactions in the money market is knowing *who* is willing to buy or sell a given instrument at a certain time. Firms that make frequent transactions in the money market become aware of the dealers in the market; firms that make less frequent transactions generally have to pay a bank, government security dealer, or brokerage firm to facilitate a transaction. Individuals wishing to purchase money market instruments (marketable securities) generally must go through a dealer firm. Purchasers of marketable securities must sell these securities to get their money back before the securities mature. The secondary (or resale) market for marketable securities is no different from the primary (or initial issue) market with respect to the basic transactions that are made.

PARTICIPANTS IN THE MONEY MARKET

As Figure 3.1 indicates, the key participants in the money market are individuals, businesses, governments, and financial intermediaries. Individuals participate as purchasers and as sellers of money market instruments. Their purchases are somewhat limited due to the large denominations — typically $100,000 or more — of money market instruments traded. Certain banks and stock brokerage firms will "break down" marketable securities and make them available in smaller denominations. Individuals sell marketable securities in the money market not as issuers but to liquidate the securities prior to maturity. Individuals do not issue marketable securities.

Business firms, governments, and financial institutions both buy and sell marketable securities. They may be the primary issuers, or they may sell securities they have purchased and wish to liquidate prior to maturity. They therefore may act as primary or secondary sellers of these securities. Of course, each of these parties can issue only certain money market instruments; a business firm, for example, cannot issue a Treasury bill. Some financial institutions purchase marketable securities specifically for resale, while others purchase these securities as short-term investments. Businesses and governments purchase marketable securities solely to earn a return on temporarily idle funds.

MONEY MARKET INSTRUMENTS

The key money market instruments include Treasury bills, federal agency issues, negotiable certificates of deposit, commercial paper, banker's acceptances, money market mutual funds, Eurodollars, and repurchase agreements. (These marketable securities are described in Chapter 16.) One characteristic common to all these instruments is liquidity. The annual rate of return, or yield, on these securities reflects directly the "tightness" or "looseness" of money. Figure 3.2 shows the prevailing rates of return for a variety of money market instruments on January 6, 1984, when the *prime rate of interest* — the base rate charged the best business borrowers — was 11 percent. A brief description of each instrument follows its

Prime rate: 11%. The base rate on corporate loans at large U.S. money center commercial banks.

Treasury bills: Results of the Tuesday, January 3, 1984, auction of short-term U.S. government bills, sold at a discount from face value in units of $10,000 to $1 million: 9.04% 13 weeks; 9.19% 26 weeks.

Agency issue (Federal Home Loan Mortgage Corp. — Freddie Mac): Posted yields on 30-year mortgage commitments for delivery within 30 days. 13%, standard conventional fixed-rate mortgages; 12.3%, three-year adjustable-rate mortgages.

Certificates of deposit (CDs): $9\frac{3}{8}$% one month; 9.40% two months; 9.45% three months; $9\frac{5}{8}$% six months; $9\frac{3}{4}$% one year. Typical rates paid by major banks on new issues of negotiable CDs, usually on amounts of $1 million and more. The minimum unit is $100,000.

Commercial paper: High-grade unsecured notes sold through dealers by major corporations in multiples of $1000: 9.35% 30 days; 9.35% 60 days; 9.35% 90 days.

Commercial paper placed directly by General Motors Acceptance Corp.: 9.20% 30 to 179 days; 9.05% 180 to 270 days.

Bankers' acceptances: 9.30% 30 days; 9.30% 60 days; 9.25% 90 days; 9.30% 120 days; 9.30% 150 days; 9.25% 180 days. Negotiable, bank-backed business credit instruments typically financing an import order.

Money market fund (Merrill Lynch Ready Assets Trust): 8.77%. Annualized average rate of return after expenses for the past 30 days; not a forecast of future returns.

London Late Eurodollars: $9\frac{3}{4}$% to $9\frac{5}{8}$% one month; $9\frac{7}{8}$% to $9\frac{3}{4}$% two months; $9\frac{15}{16}$% to $9\frac{13}{16}$% three months; 10% to $9\frac{7}{8}$% four months; $10\frac{1}{16}$% to $9\frac{15}{16}$% five months; $10\frac{1}{8}$% to 10% six months.

SOURCE: *The Wall Street Journal*, January 9, 1984, p. 22.

Figure 3.2 Rates (January 6, 1984) and brief descriptions of popular money market instruments

current annual interest rate. Differences in return between various instruments result from the different degrees of risk associated with the issuers. Although the list of securities is not all-inclusive, it does contain the key money market instruments available to the corporate purchaser. The only instrument backed solely by a nonfinancial corporate business is commercial paper.

The Capital Markets

Capital markets are created by a number of institutions and arrangements that allow the suppliers and demanders of *long-term funds* to make transactions. Included among these are transactions in the debt and equity issues of businesses and the debt issues of local, state, and federal governments. Capital markets are of key importance to the long-run growth and prosperity of business and government organizations since they provide the funds needed to acquire fixed assets and implement programs aimed at ensuring the organizations' continued existence. The backbone of the capital markets is the various securities exchanges, which provide a marketplace for debt and equity transactions.

THE FUNCTIONS OF SECURITIES EXCHANGES

Capital markets are necessary for the stock of capital goods in the economy to grow. They permit the segments of the economy that need capital to acquire plant and equipment to obtain funds from the savers in the economy. Just as financial intermediaries collect savings from numerous parties and lend them to acceptable borrowers, the capital markets permit the conversion of savings into investment, through loans or through the sale of ownership interests. They permit individuals, businesses, governments, and financial institutions to channel their savings into long-term loans or purchases of equity in businesses, government, and financial institutions. In addition, they provide a forum in which these loans and investments can be liquidated.

The key factor differentiating money and capital markets is that the capital markets provide permanent or long-term funds for the firm, while the money market provides short-term debt financing. Although both markets are important to the longevity of business and government, the capital markets provide the mechanism whereby large sums of money can be raised to increase the productive capability of the economy. The securities exchanges that make up the capital markets actually perform a number of important functions, such as creating a continuous market, allocating scarce capital, determining and publicizing security prices, and aiding in new financing.

Creating a continuous market. The key function of securities exchanges is to create a continuous market for securities at a price that is not very different from the price at which they were previously sold. The continuity of securities markets provides the *liquidity* necessary to attract investors' funds. Without exchanges, investors might have to hold debt securities to maturity and equity securities indefinitely. It is doubtful that many people would be willing to invest under such conditions. A continuous market also reduces the volatility of security prices, further enhancing their liquidity.

Allocating scarce capital. The securities exchanges help allocate scarce funds to the best uses. That is, by disclosing the price behavior of various securities and requiring the disclosure of certain corporate financial data, they allow prospective and existing investors to assess the securities' risk and return and to move their funds into the most promising investments. An *efficient market* is one that allocates funds to the most productive uses. The idea behind an efficient market is that the market price of securities always fully reflects available information and therefore is equal to the securities' value. This is especially true for securities that are actively traded on major exchanges, since the vigorous competition among profit-seeking investors tends to hold prices close to their correct level. Greater attention is given to this concept and its ramifications in Chapter 7.

Determining and publicizing security prices. Securities exchanges both determine and publicize security prices. The price of an individual security is determined by what is bought and sold, or the demand and supply for the security. Figure 3.3 depicts the interaction of the forces of demand (represented by line D_0) and supply (represented by line S) for a given security that is currently selling at an equilibrium price P_0. At that price, Q_0 shares of the stock are traded.

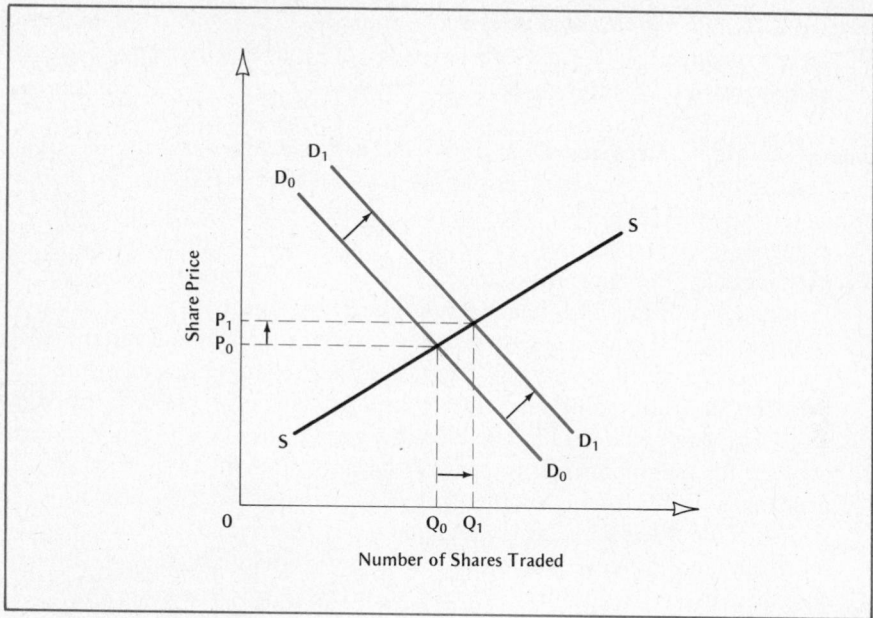

Figure 3.3   Supply and demand for a security

A capital market brings together buyers and sellers from all geographic areas while affording them some anonymity. This helps to ensure an efficient market in which the price reflects the true value of the security. Changing evaluations of a firm, of course, cause changes in the demand and supply for its securities and ultimately result in a new price for the securities. For example, if a favorable discovery by the firm shown in Figure 3.3 is announced and investors in the marketplace increase their valuations of the firm's shares resulting in a shift in demand from D_0 to D_1, Q_1 shares will be traded, and a new, higher equilibrium price of P_1 will result. The competitive market created by the major securities exchanges provides a forum in which share price is continuously adjusted to changing demand and supply. Since the prices are readily available to interested parties, they can use this information to make better purchase and sale decisions.

Aiding in new financing. Securities exchanges also provide firms with a method of obtaining new financing. Since the markets are continuous, thereby ensuring investor liquidity, new capital can be raised through new security issues. Of course, not all firms have access to those markets to raise new capital, but the presence of securities exchanges does give certain firms direct access to the savings of individuals, other firms, and financial institutions. Without these exchanges, new capital could be obtained only through direct negotiations with holders of large amounts of money. This obviously would be quite tedious.

CHARACTERISTICS OF SECURITIES EXCHANGES

Securities exchanges are the key institutions in capital markets. Many people refer to these exchanges as "stock markets," but this label is somewhat misleading.

Stocks, bonds, options, and a variety of other investment vehicles are traded on these exchanges. There are two key types of securities exchange — organized exchanges and the over-the-counter exchange.

Organized securities exchanges. *Organized securities exchanges* are tangible organizations on whose premises securities are traded. They are *secondary markets* in which "used" or already outstanding securities transactions are made. Organized exchanges account for over 72 percent of *total* share volume traded. The key exchanges are the New York Stock Exchange (NYSE) and the American Stock Exchange (AMEX), both headquartered in New York City and accounting for approximately 81 and 7 percent, respectively, of the total annual volume of shares traded on organized exchanges. Each of these exchanges has its own building, membership, and trading rules. Other regional exchanges, such as the Midwest Stock Exchange, the Pacific Stock Exchange, and the Boston Stock Exchange, account for only about 12 percent of the annual share volume on organized exchanges. In all, there are 14 regional exchanges that deal primarily in the trading of securities with local or regional appeal. Since most of the exchanges are modeled after the New York Stock Exchange, a brief discussion of its membership, its policies with respect to listing securities, trading activity, and reporting market activity is in order.

Membership. Membership in the New York Stock Exchange is expensive. To become a member, an individual or firm must own a seat on the exchange. (The word *seat* is used only figuratively, since members trade securities standing up.) There are a total of 1366 seats on the NYSE. Seats on the exchange have sold for as much as $515,000 (in 1968 and 1969) and as little as $4,000 (in 1876 and 1878), although most recently they have gone for about $350,000. Most seats are owned by brokerage firms, and many brokerage firms own more than one seat. The largest brokerage firm, Merrill Lynch Pierce Fenner & Smith, owns over 20 seats. Firms such as Merrill Lynch designate officers to occupy a seat. Only designated seat holders are permitted to make transactions on the floor of the exchange. The membership of the exchange is often divided into broad classes based on the members' activities. Membership on the American and other stock exchanges is obtained in a similar manner, but the cost of a seat is generally less, and the other requirements are not as strict.

Listing policies. To become listed on an organized stock exchange, a firm must file an application for listing. Some firms are listed on more than one exchange. The New York Stock Exchange has the most stringent listing requirements. Currently over 1500 firms, accounting for over 2200 stocks, and over 1030 issuers, accounting for over 3200 bonds, are listed on the NYSE. To be eligible for listing on the NYSE, a firm must have at least 2000 stockholders owning 100 shares (a *round lot*) or more. It must have a minimum of 1 million shares of stock outstanding that is publicly held; it must have a demonstrated earning power of $2.5 million before taxes at the time of the listing and $2 million before taxes for each of the preceding two years; it must have a total of $16 million in market value of publicly traded shares; and, finally, it must pay a listing fee. Once a firm's stock has been accepted

Receyp wase
of
Depreciation

for listing, it must meet certain requirements of the Securities and Exchange Commission (SEC), which regulates certain aspects of listed securities. If listed firms do not continue to meet requirements, they may be *delisted* from the exchange. The listing requirements of other exchanges are more lenient than those of the NYSE.

Trading activity. Trading is carried out on the floor of an exchange. The floor of the NYSE is an area about the size of a football field. On the floor are 18 trading posts, and around the perimeter are telephones and telegraphs, which are used primarily to transmit buy and sell orders from brokers' offices to the exchange floor and back again once an order has been executed. Certain stocks are traded at each of the 18 trading posts. At the NYSE, there is an annex where bonds and less active stocks are traded. All trades are made on the floor of the exchange by the occupants of seats. Only these people can make transactions on the floor. Trades are made primarily in round lots (lots of 100 shares), not odd lots (lots of less than 100 shares). Specialists, members who specialize in one or more stocks, make odd-lot transactions. The general procedure for placing and executing an order can be described by a simple example.

EXAMPLE   Sally Jones, who has an account with Merrill Lynch Pierce Fenner & Smith, wishes to purchase 200 shares of the Cities Service Company at the prevailing market price. Sally calls her account executive,[5] Abe Cohen of Merrill Lynch, and places her order. Abe immediately has the order transmitted to the New York headquarters of Merrill Lynch, which immediately forwards the order to the Merrill Lynch clerk on the floor of the exchange. The clerk dispatches the order to one of the firm's seat holders, who goes to the appropriate trading post, executes the order at the best possible price, and returns to the clerk, who then wires the execution price and confirmation of the transaction back to the brokerage office. Abe is given the relevant information and passes it along to Sally. Abe then has certain paperwork to do. ∎

Only minutes are required for an order, once placed, to be executed, thanks to sophisticated telecommunication devices. A sale of securities would have been handled in a similar manner.

All transactions on the floor of the exchange are made through an *auction process.* The goal is to fill all *buy orders* at the lowest price and to fill all *sell orders* at the highest price, thereby giving both purchasers and sellers the best possible deal. The actual auction process is quite complicated.

Reporting market activity. Information on the trading of listed securities on organized exchanges is reported in various media. Most big city newspapers report daily activity on major exchanges, although the key source of stock price information on listed securities is *The Wall Street Journal.* Figure 3.4 presents an example of some NYSE listings from *The Wall Street Journal.* Reporting these data daily enhances investor confidence in the continuity of the securities markets.

---

[5] The title "account executive" or "financial counselor" is often used to refer to an individual who traditionally has been called a "stockbroker." These titles are believed to add respectability to the position and change the image of the stockbroker from that of a salesperson to that of a personal financial manager who provides diversified financial services to his or her clients.

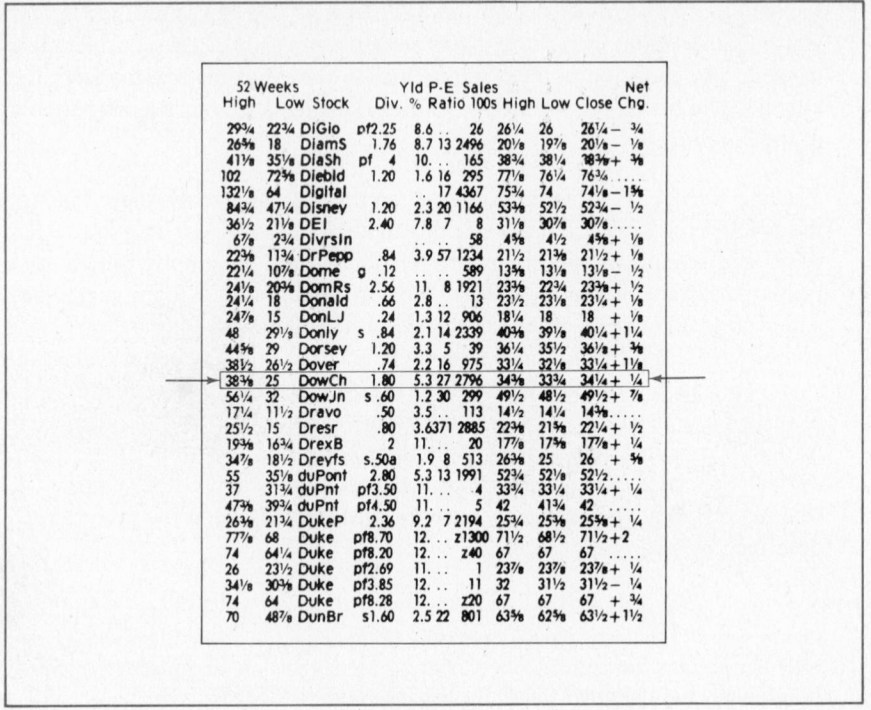

SOURCE: *The Wall Street Journal,* January 9, 1984, p. 38.

Figure 3.4   New York Stock Exchange stock price quotations

To see exactly what stock price information is reported, suppose we take a closer look at the data on Dow Chemical Company (Dow Ch) stock in Figure 3.4. The first two columns, labeled "High" and "Low," contain the highest ($38\frac{3}{8}$) and lowest ($25) price at which the stock sold during the latest 52-week period. The figure immediately following the company name is the cash dividend expected to be paid in 1984 ($1.80), based on the latest quarterly or semiannual declaration. The "Yld%" figure, which immediately follows the dividend, represents the dividend yield, which has been calculated by dividing the expected dividend ($1.80) by the stock's current or closing price ($34\frac{1}{4}$) and rounding the answer to the nearest tenth of a percent (5.3 percent).

The next entry is the price/earnings (P/E) ratio (27), the current market price divided by the previous year's per-share earnings. The P/E ratio is believed to reflect investor expectations concerning the firm's future activities. The daily volume follows the P/E ratio; 279,600 shares of Dow Chemical were traded on Friday, January 6, 1984.[6] The "High," "Low," and "Close" columns contain the highest, lowest, and last (closing) price, respectively, at which the stock sold on January 6. The prices of stocks are quoted and traded in eighths of a dollar.[7] The

[6] There is a one-day lag in reporting, which means that on Monday, January 9, 1984, *The Wall Street Journal* reported the Friday, January 6, 1984, transactions.

[7] Although the smallest divisor of security prices is one-eighth, the fractions are rounded off whenever possible. In other words, two-eighths, four-eighths, and six-eighths are expressed as one-fourth, one-half, and three-fourths.

final column shows the net change between the current day's closing price and the closing price on the preceding day. Dow Chemical closed at $34\frac{1}{4}$, up $\frac{1}{4}$, on January 6, 1984, which means that it must have closed at 34 ($\frac{1}{4}$ point lower) on January 5. Not all price quotations are as easy to read as this example, since quite often a number of footnotes are included in the listing.

The over-the-counter exchange. The over-the-counter exchange is not a specific institution; rather, it is a way of trading securities other than on an organized securities exchange. It accounts for nearly 28 percent of all share volume traded. The *over-the-counter (OTC) exchange* is the result of an intangible relationship among the purchasers and the sellers of securities. Active traders in this market are linked by a telecommunications network. The prices at which securities are traded over the counter are determined by competitive bids and negotiation. The actual process depends on the general activity of a security. A numeric majority of stocks are traded over the counter, as are most government and corporate bonds.

In addition to creating a secondary market for securities, the OTC market is a *primary market* in which new public issues — including those listed on organized exchanges — are sold. If they are listed, subsequent transactions will be made on the appropriate organized exchange; otherwise, they will continue to trade in the OTC. Some traders, known as *dealers,* make markets in certain securities by offering to buy or sell them at stated prices. Over 90 percent of all corporate bonds are traded in this market, and many of these bonds are also listed on the New York Stock Exchange. The *bid* and *ask* prices quoted on the OTC market represent, respectively, the highest price offered by the dealer to purchase a given security and the lowest price at which the dealer will sell the security. From the investor's perspective, stock can be sold at the (lower) bid price and can be bought at the (higher) ask price. The dealer, of course, profits from the spread between the two.

The OTC market today is linked through the National Association of Securities Dealers Automated Quotation System (NASDAQ), an automated system that provides up-to-date bid and ask prices on thousands of securities. NASDAQ provides a great deal of continuity in the OTC market because it allows buyers and sellers to locate each other to consummate a transaction. To trade in securities not quoted in NASDAQ, purchasers and sellers must find each other through references or through known dealers in the securities.

SPECIAL STOCK TRANSACTIONS

Two special types of stock market transactions that contribute to the markets' efficiency are margin purchases and short selling.[8] These transactions help stimulate market activity and add continuity to the securities markets.

Margin purchases. Purchases of securities made by borrowing a portion of the price are known as *margin purchases.* The Federal Reserve Board sets *margin requirements* that specify the proportion of the dollar price of a security purchase the buyer must provide; the purchaser is permitted to borrow the balance. By raising or lowering

---

[8] Numerous other types of orders and trades can be made on the security exchanges. For information on them, refer to any basic investments text, such as Lawrence J. Gitman and Michael D. Joehnk, *Fundamentals of Investing,* 2d ed. (New York: Harper & Row, 1984), chap. 2.

margin requirements, the Fed can depress or stimulate activity in the securities markets. Margin purchases must be approved by a broker. The brokerage firm then lends the purchaser the needed funds and retains the securities as collateral. Some brokerage firms have "in-house" margin requirements that are more restrictive than those of the Fed. Margin requirements most recently have been around 50 percent. Margin purchasers, of course, must pay interest at a specified rate on the amount they borrow.

EXAMPLE   Stan Washington wishes to purchase on margin 400 shares of Dow Chemical at $34.25 per share. If the margin requirement is 50 percent, Stan will have to pay 50 percent of the total purchase price of $13,700 ($34.25 × 400 shares), or $6,850. The remaining $6,850 of the purchase price will be lent to Stan by his brokerage firm. Stan will have to pay interest to his broker on the $6,850 he borrows, along with the appropriate brokerage fee. ■

Short selling. Most people, when they think of securities purchases, think of "buying low and selling high." These types of *long* transactions are most common, but there are some individuals who engage in *short selling,* which can be thought of as "selling high and buying low." Long transactions are made in anticipation of price increases, whereas *short transactions are made in anticipation of price decreases.* When an individual sells a security short, the broker borrows the security from someone else and then sells it on the short seller's behalf. These borrowed shares must be replaced by the short seller in the future. If the short seller can repurchase the shares at a lower price in the future and return them to their owner, the profit will be the difference between the proceeds of the initial sale and the repurchase price. If the short seller ends up repurchasing the shares at a higher price than he or she sold them for, the result is a loss. Numerous rules and regulations govern short sales.

EXAMPLE   Stan Washington wishes to sell short 200 shares of Dow Chemical at $34.25 per share. His broker borrows the shares and sells them, receiving proceeds of $6,850 ($34.25 × 200 shares). If the price of the stock drops as Stan expects it to and he repurchases the stock at $29.00 per share, Stan will make a profit, since the cost of replacing the stock, $5,800 ($29.00 × 200 shares), is less than his initial proceeds of $6,850. Stan's profit will be $1,050 ($6,850 − $5,800). If the stock prices rise above $34.25 per share and Stan repurchases it at, say $38.00 per share, he will sustain a loss of $750 [($38.00 × 200 shares) − ($34.25 × 200 shares)]. When Stan, or anyone, sells short, he is betting on a price decline; if he is wrong, the short seller suffers a loss. Stan, of course, will have to pay brokerage fees on his short sale transaction. ■

INVESTMENT COMPANIES

An *investment company* is a peculiar kind of financial organization that can be considered either a financial intermediary or a business firm. Investment companies pool funds of investors and invest them in a portfolio of securities. They are financial intermediaries in the sense that they channel individual savings into investments, but they are similar to business firms in that they sell both debt and equity, the proceeds from which they invest in certain earning assets — in this case, bonds and stocks of other companies. There are many types of investment companies, each specializing in certain types of securities. The *mutual fund*—defined earlier—is a common form of investment company.[9]

The attractiveness of investment companies lies in their ability to provide the small investor with the benefits of diversification, professional portfolio management, and skilled timing of purchases and sales. By purchasing a broad group of securities, the investment company attempts to maximize the return for a given level of risk. An individual owning one share in an investment company would probably be unable to obtain so diversified an investment in any other way, since it would require a large amount of money to assemble a portfolio similar to that of the investment company. An investment company allows the investor to buy a small portion of a diversified portfolio of securities for a modest outlay.

THE ROLE OF THE INVESTMENT BANKER

To raise money in the capital markets, firms can make either private placements or public offerings. *Private placement* involves the direct sale of a new security issue, typically debt or preferred stock, to an investor or group of investors such as an insurance company or pension fund. Most firms raise money through *public offerings* of securities. To make such offerings most firms use the services of an investment banker. The *investment banker* can be hired by the firm to find buyers for new security issues, whether they are to be privately placed or sold through a public offering.

The name *investment banker* is somewhat misleading, because an investment banker is neither an investor nor a banker; he or she neither makes long-term investments nor guards the savings of others. Instead, acting as a broker between the issuer and the buyer of new security issues, the investment banker purchases securities from corporations and governments and markets them to the public. This activity effectively creates a primary market for securities that will, in the case of public offerings, be traded in the secondary markets. Investment bankers, in addition to bearing the risk of selling a security issue, advise clients. Salomon Brothers Corporation and Merrill Lynch Capital Markets are two of the largest investment banking firms. Many investment banking firms operate in other financial areas as well; for example, Merrill Lynch is also the nation's largest retail stock brokerage firm. Detailed discussion of the activities, organization, and cost of investment banking is included in Chapter 19.

Interest Rates, Risk Premiums, and Required Returns

Financial intermediaries and markets were shown to provide a conduit through which funds flow between savers (suppliers) and investors (demanders). The level of funds flow between suppliers and demanders can significantly affect economic growth. It results from the interaction of a variety of economic factors, such as the money supply, trade balances, and economic policies, that are part of the cost of

---

[9] A *mutual fund,* also called an *open-end investment company,* sells its shares to the public and redeems these shares at a value representing their claim on the firm's total portfolio. Mutual funds are attractive in that they are open-ended. New shares can be sold so that the size of the fund increases.

A CAREER IN THE SECURITIES INDUSTRY

The stock market: is there any place in the U.S. business community where capitalism is seen in a purer form, where the credo of "buy low, sell high" is the cause of millions of hours of work to find how one's clients' assets should be managed? This extraordinarily intense study of dollars has been a magnet for generations of career-minded students.

Today, the normally hectic affairs of the investment community are reaching levels of frenzy that would have been unthinkable in years past. As with insurance, banking, and other financial services, the magic wand of deregulation has passed through Wall Street, leaving discount brokerage houses, futures indexes, and other new businesses in its wake. New players are entering the picture: through a series of mergers and expansions, new financial "supercompanies" such as Prudential-Bache, Shearson/American Express, and Citicorp have appeared, offering customers total financial planning and management.

The new market has generated a strong demand for stock market account executives, analysts, investment managers, and other personnel. "Last year we had significant expansion in staff, and this year we expect to exceed that," says Johanne Reid, vice-president and corporate employment manager for Merrill Lynch & Co.

Chet Piskorowski, senior vice-president and director of corporate resources for Prudential-Bache, says, "The Street is dynamic. Opportunities are unlimited. Several years ago our company had perhaps 30 core products (of investment instruments). Now we have something like 80, and I don't see the growth slowing down over the next few years."

Probably the best known entry-level job in the stock market is the account executive (broker), who searches for customers to buy stock issues, or to have their assets managed by the account executive's firm. At last count, there were about 63,000 such workers, according to the U.S. Dept. of Labor.

A sizable number of fresh college graduates are hired for such positions but many investment firms express an interest in more experienced, more mature individuals. "Younger people can't stand the repeated rejections from prospective clients. You have to be a strong, self-confident person to succeed in brokerage sales, and that's something that usually comes with maturity," said a Bache executive recently in *The New York Times.*

Piskorowski says, "We'll be hiring and training about 800 people for this job in the coming year. But we generally do not hire people right out of school; we prefer those with some work experience, especially in sales."

Indeed, the turnover rate is extremely high for account executives—some 95% within the first two years. The rewards, however, can be substantial—like other

money—the interest rate or required return. The level of this rate acts as a regulating device that controls the flow of funds between suppliers and demanders. In general, the lower the rate, the greater the funds flow and therefore the greater the economic growth, and vice versa. Interest rates and required returns are key variables influencing the actions of the financial manager.

INTEREST RATE FUNDAMENTALS

The interest rate or required return represents the cost of money. It is the rent or level of compensation a demander of funds must pay a supplier. When money is

salespeople, account execs start with a salary of $12,000 to $16,000, which is supplanted by commissions after the first year or so. Salaries of experienced brokers average over $40,000, and can more than double that figure.

There are many options for new grads entering the investment community. Among these are institutional investment, in which a broker manages a fund such as the pension of a company. Commercial underwriting involves developing the correct financial package for a new firm going into the market for the first time, or an existing firm going back to the market for more funds.

A large number of students, especially MBAs, are hired for securities analyst positions. For many of these analysts, the emphasis is on knowing everything there is to know about a particular industry—railroads, chemicals, computers, or whatever. The analyst then puts together reports that help his or her client, or the brokers of the firm, to decide how to invest in the industry. Because of their specialized knowledge, some of the stars in this field command salaries of more than $100,000 at an early age. The danger, however, is when one repeatedly makes the wrong assessment of companies; job security is then difficult to maintain.

A large number of so-called "back-office" jobs also exist at investment firms. They employ the people who manage the recordkeeping, sales reports, and financial analysis for the frontline brokers. According to an industry source, the enormous growth of new investment instruments has raised the number of back-office personnel from one to about 1.75 for every broker. For this reason, new computer technology to manage the paperwork has been a priority at investment firms, which are probably the most aggressive recruiters of data processing personnel of any industry.

Prudential-Bache's Piskorowski says, "We will be hiring many people for operations (what is traditionally known as back-office work). Operations has taken a higher profile in recent years. It is now becoming an increasingly important function of our business. We are specifically looking for BS grads. They will be put in a one-year training program. In some cases, our hiring isn't limited by job needs, but by office space."

Regardless of the initial job, securities firms have well-developed training programs for their new hires. Some of the bigger firms have a new class starting almost every month, to keep a steady supply of workers. According to Merrill Lynch's Reid, it matters very little whether one majored in business administration or modern literature in school; the training program provides the necessary financial background. "We seek to hire people with broad-based liberal arts backgrounds, because it's most important to be able to relate to people of all walks of life."

SOURCE: Nicholas Basta, "Securities Industry," *Business Week's Guide to Careers,* February/March 1984, p. 75.

lent by a supplier to a demander, the cost of borrowing the funds is the *interest rate;* when funds are invested by a supplier to obtain an ownership or "equity" interest in the demander's business, the cost is commonly called the *required return,* which reflects the level of expected return. In either instance the supplier is compensated for forgoing current consumption and accepting the risks associated with the transfer of funds to the demander. Ignoring risk factors, the nominal or actual interest rate (cost of funds) results from the real rate of interest adjusted for inflationary expectations and *liquidity preferences*—general preferences for shorter-term securities.

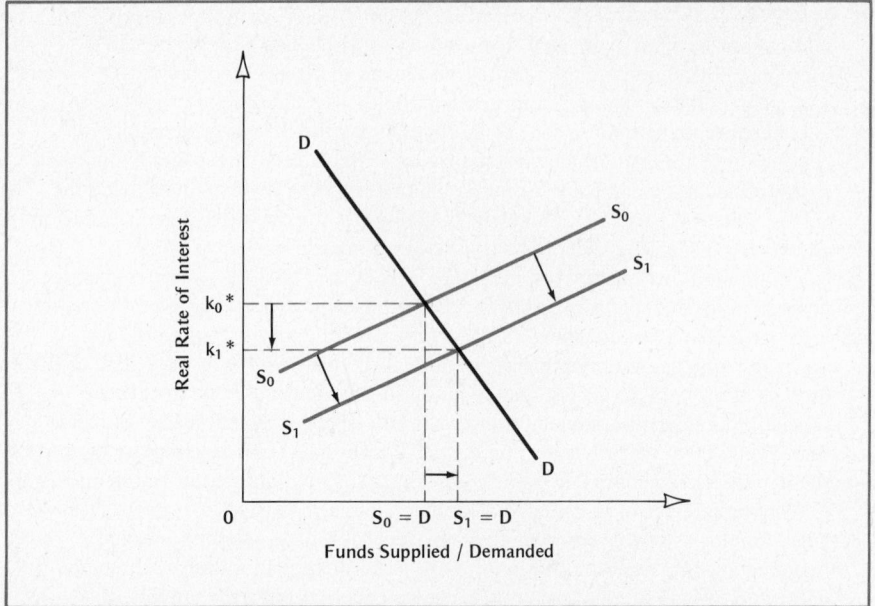

Figure 3.5 Supply of savings and demand for funds

The real rate of interest. In a perfect world in which there is no inflation, funds suppliers and demanders are indifferent to the term of loans or investments (they have no liquidity preference, and all outcomes are certain),[10] there would be one cost of money — the real rate of interest. The *real rate of interest* would be that which creates an equilibrium between the supply of savings and the demand for investment funds. The real rate of interest in the United States is assumed to be stable and equal to around 2 percent.[11] This supply-demand relationship is shown by the supply function (labeled S_0) and the demand function (labeled D) in Figure 3.5. It can be seen that an equilibrium between the supply of funds and the demand for funds ($S_0 = D$) occurs at a rate of interest k_0^*, the real rate of interest.

Clearly, the real rate of interest changes with changing economic conditions, tastes, and preferences. A favorable international trade balance could result in an increased supply of funds, causing the supply function in Figure 3.5 to shift to, say S_1. This could result in a lower real rate of interest, k_1^*, at equilibrium ($S_1 = D$). A

[10] These assumptions are made for expository convenience in order to describe the most basic interest rate, the real rate of interest. Subsequent discussions relax these assumptions in order to develop the broader concept of the interest rate and required return.

[11] The assumed 2 percent value for the real rate of interest is drawn from the findings of Roger G. Ibbotson and Rex A. Sinquefield, "Stocks, Bonds, Bills and Inflation: Update," *Financial Analysts Journal,* July-August 1979, adjusted for more recent observations. They found that over the period 1926–1978, U.S. Treasury bills provided an average annual real rate of return of about 0 percent, while during the period 1952–1978, the real rate of return was about .5 percent. Because prior to 1951 T-bill rates were intentionally pegged artificially low, the post-1951 real rate of return of .5 percent is believed to be more accurate. In view of the post-1973 economy, many economists believe the real rate to be around 2 percent.

change in tax laws or other factors could affect the demand for funds, causing the real rate of interest to rise or fall to a new equilibrium level.

Nominal or actual rate of interest (return). The *nominal rate of interest* is the actual rate of interest charged by the supplier and being paid by the demander. It differs from the real rate of interest, k^*, as a result of two factors: (1) inflationary expectations (IE) and (2) issuer and issue characteristics (IC). Using this notation, the nominal rate of interest for security l, k_l, is given in Equation 3.1:

$$k_l = \underbrace{k^* + IE}_{\substack{\text{risk-free} \\ \text{rate, } R_F}} + \underbrace{IC_l}_{\substack{\text{risk} \\ \text{premium}}} \qquad (3.1)$$

As noted with brackets, the nominal rate, k_l, actually can be viewed as having two basic components: (1) a risk-free rate of interest, R_F, plus (2) a risk premium, IC_l:

$$k_l = R_F + IC_l \qquad (3.2)$$

To simplify the discussion, we will assume that the risk premium, IC_l, is equal to zero and concern ourselves only with the *risk-free rate of interest,* which is defined as the required return on a risk-free asset.[12] Three-month *U.S. Treasury bills (T-bills),* which are short-term IOUs issued by the U.S. Treasury, are commonly considered the risk-free asset. We can therefore rewrite Equation 3.1[13] as

$$R_F = k^* + IE \qquad (3.3)$$

The risk-free rate embodies the real rate of interest plus the inflationary expectation.

The premium for *inflationary expectations* represents the average rate of *inflation* (price-level change) expected over the life of the loan or investment. It is *not* the rate of inflation experienced over the immediate past; rather, it reflects the forecasted rate. Take the risk-free asset: During the week ended January 6, 1984, three-month Treasury bills earned an 8.99 percent rate of return. Assuming an approximate 2 percent real rate of interest, fund suppliers were forecasting a 7 percent (annual) rate of inflation ($\approx 8.99\% - 2.00\%$) over the following three months. This expectation is in striking contrast to the 9.60 percent ($11.60\% - 2.00\%$) expected (annual) rate of inflation reflected by the 11.60 percent three-month T-bill rate two years earlier in the week ended January 8, 1982. The inflationary expectation premium changes over time in response to many factors, including recent inflation rates, government policies, and international events.

---

[12] In a later part of this discussion, the risk premium and its effect on the nominal rate of interest are discussed and illustrated.

[13] This equation is commonly called the *Fisher equation,* named for the renowned economist Irving Fisher, who first presented this approximate relationship between nominal interest and the rate of inflation. See Irving Fisher, *The Theory of Interest* (New York: Macmillan, 1930.)

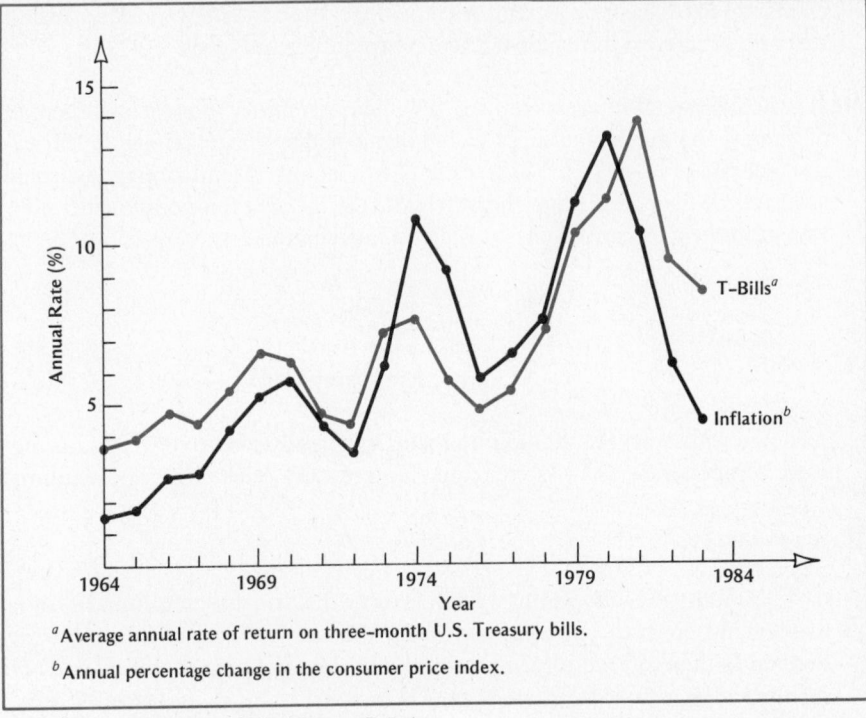

SOURCE: Data from selected *Federal Reserve Bulletins*.

Figure 3.6   Relationship between annual rate of inflation and three-month U.S.
Treasury bill yields

Figure 3.6 illustrates the movement of the rate of inflation and the risk-free rate of interest during the 20-year period 1964–1983. During this period, the two rates tended to move in a similar fashion. Between the Arab oil embargo of 1973 and early 1980, inflation and interest rates were quite high, peaking at over 13 percent in 1980–1981. Since 1981 these rates have declined to levels comparable to those existing prior to the oil embargo. The data clearly illustrate the significant impact of inflation on the nominal rate of interest for the risk-free asset.

TERM STRUCTURE OF INTEREST RATES

Thus far we have concerned ourselves solely with the risk-free asset, represented by a three-month Treasury bill. In fact, all Treasury securities are *riskless* in terms of the chance that the Treasury will default on the issue by failing to make scheduled interest and principal payments. Since it is believed to be easier to forecast inflation over shorter periods of time, the shorter-term three-month Treasury bill is considered the risk-free asset. Of course, differing inflation expectations associated with different maturities will cause nominal interest rates to vary, depending on the maturity of the security. Adding a maturity subscript, t, to it, Equation 3.3 can be rewritten as

$$R_{F_t} = k^* + IE_t \tag{3.4}$$

In other words, for U.S. Treasury securities, the nominal, or risk-free rate, for a given maturity varies with the inflation expectation over the term of the security.

EXAMPLE The nominal interest rate, R_{F_t}, for four maturities of U.S. Treasury securities on October 21, 1983, is given in column 1 of the table below. Assuming the real rate of interest is 2 percent, as noted in column 2, the inflation expectation for each maturity is found in

Maturity, t	Nominal interest rate, R_{F_t} (1)	Real interest rate, k^* (2)	Inflation expectation, IE_t [(1) − (2)] (3)
3 months	8.63%	2.00%	6.63%
1 year	9.69	2.00	7.69
5 years	11.36	2.00	9.36
30 years	11.51	2.00	9.51

column 3 by solving Equation 3.4 for IE_t. It can be seen that while a 6.63 percent rate of inflation is expected over the three-month period beginning October 21, 1983, a 7.69 percent average rate of inflation is expected over the one-year period, and so on. An analysis of the inflation expectations in column 3 for October 21, 1983, suggests that at that time, a general expectation of increasing inflation existed. ■

For any class of similar-risk securities, the *term structure of interest rates* relates the interest rate or rate of return to the time to maturity. For convenience we will continue to use Treasury securities as a class, but other classes could include securities that have similar overall quality or risk ratings such as Aaa utility bonds, Ba corporate bonds, and so on, as determined by independent agencies like Moody's and Standard & Poor's. The riskless nature of Treasury securities also provides a laboratory in which to develop the term structure. At any point in time the relationship between the rate of return or *yield*—the annual rate of interest one would earn on a security if purchased on the given day and held to maturity— and the time to maturity can be represented by the *yield curve.* This function is a graphic depiction of the term structure of interest rates. Figure 3.7 depicts two yield curves for U.S. Treasury securities—one at May 22, 1981, and the other at October 21, 1983.

The yield curve reflects (1) the general supply-demand conditions for money embodied in the real rate of interest, (2) the general preference of fund suppliers toward more liquid short-term securities, and (3) the general expectations of investors as to future interest rates. Interest rate expectations embody inflation expectations and reflect the fact that while short-term rates capture current behavior, long-term rates capture the level of expected future short-term interest rates. In Figure 3.7, it can be seen that on May 22, 1981, the yield curve was *downward-sloping,* reflecting lower expected future rates of interest. On October 21, 1983, the yield curve was *upward-sloping,* reflecting the prevailing expectation of higher future rates. Occasionally the yield curve is *flat,* indicating a stable expectation. The downward-sloping yield curve of May 1981 reflects an expectation of lower inflation and interest rates in the future. In Figure 3.6 it can be seen that at that time, the inflation rate was over 10 percent and the general expectation was for an economic recovery with reduced inflation. In October 1983, the upward-slop-

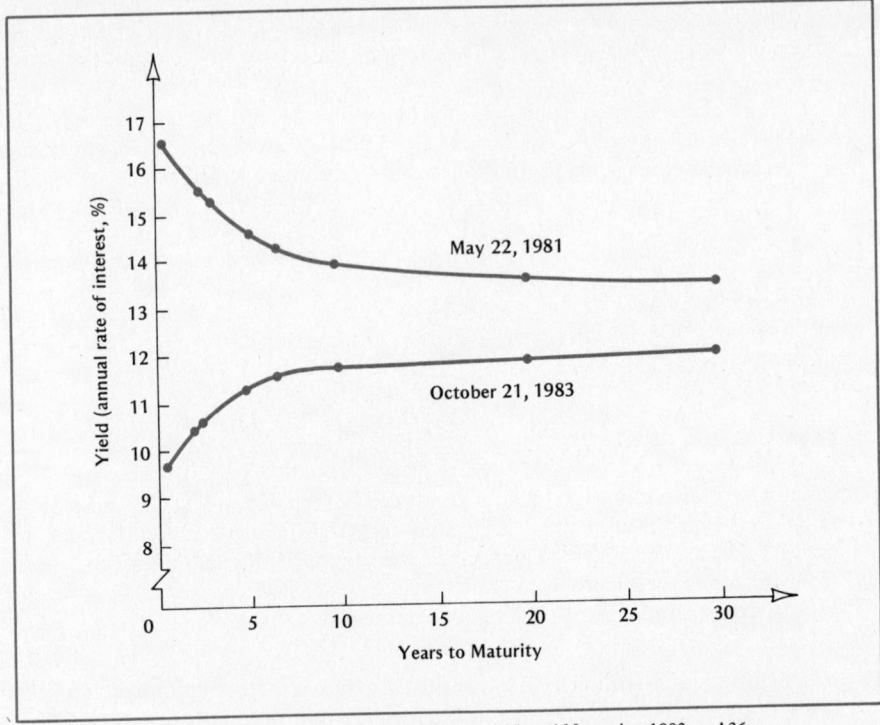

SOURCE: Data from *Federal Reserve Bulletin,* June 1981, p. A25, and November 1983, p. A26.

Figure 3.7   Yield curves for U.S. Treasury securities, May 22, 1981, and October 21, 1983

ing yield curve reflected a slightly increasing rate of inflation from the less than 5 percent rate at that time (see Figure 3.6). With the stock market hitting new highs, the looming record budget deficit, and the presidential elections, the rate of inflation and interest rates were expected to rise.

The financial manager needs to consider the yield curve when making a variety of decisions, since it provides information on current as well as future expectations for interest rates. While useful in the short-term investment process, the yield curve is of greatest importance in making financing decisions.

RISK PREMIUMS: ISSUER AND ISSUE CHARACTERISTICS

So far we have considered only risk-free U.S. Treasury securities. At this point we reintroduce the risk premium and assess it in view of risky non-Treasury issues. Recall that in Equation 3.1, restated here:

$$k_l = \underbrace{k^* + IE}_{\substack{\text{risk-free}\\ \text{rate, } R_F}} + \underbrace{IC_l}_{\substack{\text{risk}\\ \text{premium}}}$$

the nominal rate of interest for security 1, k_l, is equal to the risk-free rate, which consists of the real rate of interest (k^*) plus the inflation expectation premium (IE)

plus the risk premium. The *risk premium* varies with specific issuer and issue characteristics; it causes similar-maturity securities[14] to have differing nominal rates of interest.

EXAMPLE   On October 21, 1983, the nominal rates on a number of classes of long-term securities are as noted below.[15]

Security	Nominal interest (%)
U.S. Treasury bonds	11.16
Corporate bonds (by rating)	
Aaa	12.21
Aa	12.46
A	12.93
Baa	13.42
Utility bonds	12.33

Since the Treasury bond would represent the risk-free long-term security, we can calculate the risk premium associated with the other securities listed by subtracting the risk-free rate, 11.16 percent, from each yield.

Security	Risk premium (%)
Corporate bonds (by rating)	
Aaa	$12.21 - 11.16 = 1.05$
Aa	$12.46 - 11.16 = 1.30$
A	$12.93 - 11.16 = 1.77$
Baa	$13.42 - 11.16 = 2.26$
Utility bonds	$12.33 - 11.16 = 1.17$

These risk premiums reflect differing issuer and issue risks; it can be seen that the lower-rated corporate issues—A and Baa—have higher risk premiums than the higher-rated corporates—Aaa and Aa—while the utility issue has a risk premium comparable to the Aaa and Aa corporates. ■

The risk premium, IC_1, can be viewed as consisting of a number of issuer- and issue-related components including default, maturity, marketability, contractual provisions, and tax treatment.

Default. All securities other than those issued by the U.S. Treasury are subject to *default risk*—the possibility that the issuer will not pay the contractual interest or principal as scheduled. The greater the uncertainty as to the borrower's ability to meet these payments, the greater the risk premium. Bond ratings tend to reflect default risk: The higher the rating, the lower the default risk, and therefore the lower the interest rate, and vice versa.

---

[14] To provide for the same risk-free rate of interest, $k^* + IE$, it is necessary to assume equal maturities. By doing this, the inflationary expectations, IE, and therefore R_F, will be held constant, and the issuer and issue characteristics become the key factor differentiating the nominal rates of interest on various securities.

[15] These yields were obtained from the *Federal Reserve Bulletin,* November 1983, p. A26.

Maturity. Another component of the risk premium is *maturity risk* — the fact that a given change in interest rates will cause the value of the security to change by a greater amount the longer its maturity, and vice versa. This risk is often called *interest rate risk*. If interest rates on otherwise similar-risk securities suddenly rise due to a change in the money supply, the prices of long-term bonds will decline by more than the prices of short-term bonds, and vice versa. The longer the time to maturity for a bond, the more significant is the effect of a movement in interest rates on the price of the security.[16] Note that all securities with maturities beyond a few months are subject to this risk, regardless of other issuer and issue characteristics. This is why we used the *three-month* U.S. Treasury bill to represent the risk-free asset.

Marketability. Securities often differ as to their *marketability* — the ease with which they can be converted into cash without experiencing a loss in value. Generally, securities actively traded on major exchanges and over the counter are marketable. Less actively traded securities that have a "thin market" have low marketability. Since a potential loss in value will result from the need to quickly sell a security with low marketability, it would have a high *marketability risk*. This would raise its risk premium and therefore the nominal interest rate. The lower the marketability of a security, the greater its risk premium, and vice versa.

Contractual provisions. Another factor resulting in potential risk effects is the *contractual provisions* that are often included in a debt agreement or a stock issue. Examples would include working capital clauses or call features in a bond or voting rights in a stock. Certain of these features reduce the risk of a security, while others may increase risk. For example, ignoring all other risks, a *freely callable bond* (one that can be retired any time at the issuer's option) would be more risky than a bond that does not have a call feature. The issuer of the freely callable bond will have to offer a higher return to compensate the bondholder for this risk.

Tax treatment. Tax laws can affect a security's return. While tax treatment *does not* actually affect risk, it can be viewed as a component of the risk premium. Earnings on certain securities issued by agencies of state and local government are exempt from federal, and sometimes state and local, taxes.[17] Because of this benefit, their nominal interest rates tend to be reduced by an amount sufficient to allow their return to be equivalent to the after-tax return on a fully taxable issue with similar risk. For tax-exempt securities, we can adjust the nominal return by reducing the risk premium by an amount necessary to equate its return with that of a fully taxable issue of equivalent risk.

To summarize, it should be clear that the risk premium, IC_l, reflects the combined impact of default risk, interest rate risk, liquidity risk, contractual provisions, and tax treatment. In general, securities issued by firms with a high risk of default and

---

[16] A detailed discussion of the effects of interest rates on the price or value of bonds and other fixed-income securities is presented in Chapter 8.

[17] While all state and local issues are tax-exempt for federal income tax purposes, generally only those issued by the state or locality in which the taxpayer resides are exempt from state and local taxes, respectively. Securities that are exempt from federal, state, and local taxes are often called "triple tax-exempts."

long maturities that are traded in thin markets, have unfavorable contractual provisions, and are not tax-exempt tend to have the highest risk premiums and therefore the highest nominal returns, and vice versa.

RISK AND RETURN

The fact that a positive relationship exists between risk and the nominal or actual return should be evident. After assessing the risk embodied in a given security, investors tend to purchase those that are expected to provide a return commensurate with the perceived risk. The actual return earned on the security will affect their subsequent actions — whether they sell, hold, or buy additional securities. In addition, most investors look to certain types of securities to provide a certain range of risk-return behaviors.

Actual and expected return. The *actual return* on an investment, like interest rates and other financial costs, is measured as a percentage return on the initial price or amount invested. Equation 3.5 presents the basic expression for calculating the return on an investment.

$$\text{Return} = \frac{\text{ending value} - \text{initial value} + \text{cash distributions}}{\text{initial value}} \qquad (3.5)$$

Basically the equation expresses the sum of the change in value and any cash distributions as a percentage of the initial value. This method of calculating investment return is commonly applied over annual periods or expressed as an annual rate of return.[18]

EXAMPLE   Jane Ennick purchased 20 shares of Noranda, Inc., common stock for $37.00 per share one year ago. During the year she received cash dividends on the stock of $3.00 per share. The stock is currently selling for $41.50 per share. Ignoring any brokerage fees, we can find the rate of return earned by Jane if she sells the stock today. We first need to calculate the initial and ending value as well as the amount of cash distributions.

$$
\begin{aligned}
\text{Initial value} \quad &= \$37.00 \times 20 \text{ shares} = \$740 \\
\text{Ending value} \quad &= \$41.50 \times 20 \text{ shares} = \$830 \\
\text{Cash distribution} &= \$\ 3.00 \times 20 \text{ shares} = \$\ 60
\end{aligned}
$$

Substituting these values into Equation 3.5 yields:

$$\text{Return} = \frac{\$830 - \$740 + \$60}{\$740} = \frac{\$150}{\$740} = \underline{\underline{20.3\%}}$$

Over the one-year holding period, Jane therefore earned a 20.3 percent rate of return. ∎

The return calculated using Equation 3.5 is typically an actual rather than an expected return. When estimating *expected return,* the decision maker must

---

[18] The measurement of return over longer periods of time using internal rate of return and yield techniques is presented in subsequent chapters. For now this single "holding period return" measure is assumed.

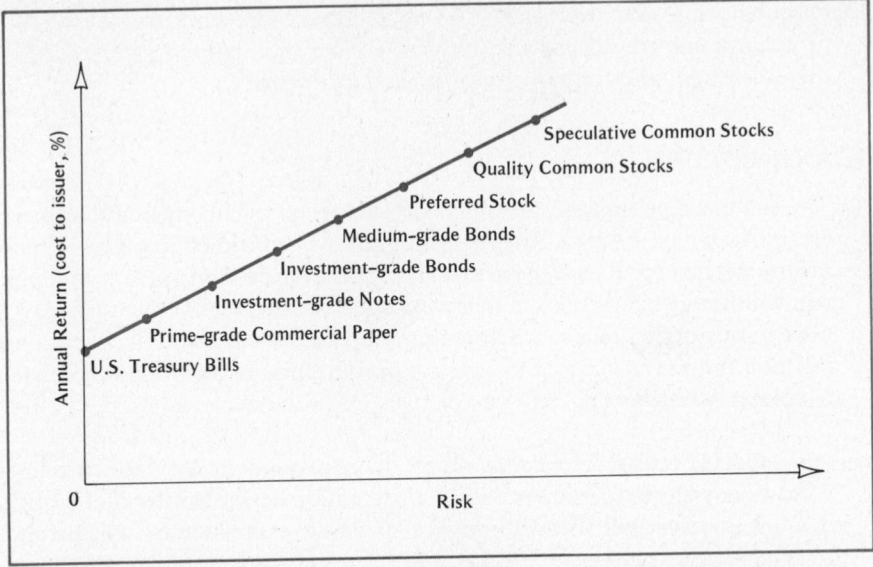

Figure 3.8   Risk-return profile for popular securities

forecast the ending value and cash distribution, thus introducing an element of risk or uncertainty as to the actual outcome. In general, the higher the uncertainty of the actual outcomes, the greater the risk, and vice versa. In spite of this uncertainty, Equation 3.5 represents the basic framework used to calculate both actual and expected returns. The use of this basic return measure is assumed throughout this text.

The basic trade-off. Earlier discussions have emphasized the existence of a *risk-return trade-off* such that investors must be compensated for accepting greater risk with the expectation of greater expected returns.[19] The theory holds that a close relationship exists between the return expected from a given class of securities and its exposure to risk. Figure 3.8 illustrates the typical relationship between risk and return for several popular securities. Clearly, higher returns (costs to the issuer) are expected with greater risk. Financial managers must attempt to keep financing costs down, but they must also consider the risks associated with each financing alternative. Their decision will ultimately rest on an analysis of the combined effect of risk and return on share price.

MULTINATIONAL FINANCE

International Financial Markets

During the last two decades the *Euromarket*—which provides for borrowing and lending of currencies outside their country of origin—has grown quite rapidly. Its

---

[19] The risk-return trade-off is discussed in detail in Chapter 7, where certain refinements are introduced to explain why investors are actually rewarded with higher returns for taking only certain types of "nondiversifiable" or inescapable risks.

overall size is now estimated to be over $1.5 trillion. The Euromarket provides multinational companies with an "external" opportunity to borrow or lend funds with the additional feature of less government regulation.

GROWTH OF THE EUROMARKET

Several reasons can be offered as to why the Euromarket has grown to such a magnitude. First, beginning in the early 1960s, the Russians wanted to maintain their dollar earnings outside the legal jurisdiction of the United States, mainly due to the cold war. Second, the consistently large U.S. balance of payments deficits helped "scatter" dollars around the world. Third, the existence of specific regulations and controls on dollar deposits in the United States, including interest rate ceilings imposed by the government, helped send such deposits to places outside the United States.

These and other factors have combined and contributed to the creation of an "external" capital market whose size cannot be accurately determined, mainly because of lack of controls and regulations. Several sources that periodically estimate its size are the Bank for International Settlements (BIS), Morgan Guar-

Table 3.1   External Assets of Banks in Individual Reporting Countries

Country	Amounts outstanding at year-end ($ billion)		
	1979	1981	1982
United States	136.4	256.3	361.4
of which: IBFs[a]	—	63.4	143.6
Foreign branches of U.S. banks[b]	127.6	172.0	172.0
Reporting European countries	776.0	998.4	1,023.6
of which: United Kingdom	285.5	432.1	457.8
France	123.6	143.4	148.1
Luxembourg	80.8	88.4	90.5
Germany	69.3	73.2	69.7
Switzerland	59.1	63.1	61.5
Netherlands	55.9	65.6	62.8
Belgium	43.0	61.5	60.3
Italy	29.6	36.3	34.5
Others[c]	29.2	34.8	38.4
Japan	45.4	84.6	90.9
Canada	25.6	38.2	38.8
Total	1,111.0	1,549.5	1,686.7
Memorandum item: non-reporting banks in off-shore centers[d]	135.0	239.0	256.0

[a] IBF represents an International Banking Facility.
[b] In the Bahamas, the Cayman Islands, Panama, Hong Kong, and Singapore.
[c] Austria, Denmark, Ireland, and Sweden.
[d] Estimates — at current exchange rates — for nonreporting banks in the five major offshore centers and for all banks located in Bahrain, Lebanon, and the Netherlands Antilles.

SOURCE: Bank for International Settlements.

anty Trust, the World Bank, and the Organization for Economic Cooperation and Development (OECD). The latest available estimate by BIS puts the overall size of the market at over $1.02 trillion *net* international lending. Table 3.1 shows the total size as well as the various portions of the total held in different countries. Figure 3.9 provides a summary of Euromarket jargon.

One aspect of the Euromarket is the so-called offshore centers. Certain cities around the world — including London, Singapore, Bahrain, Nassau, Hong Kong, and Luxembourg — have achieved prominence and are considered major (offshore) centers of Euromarket business. The availability of communication and transportation facilities, along with the importance of language, costs, time zones, taxes, and local banking regulations, are among the main reasons for the importance of these centers.

MAJOR PARTICIPANTS

The Euromarket is dominated by the dollar, and the big American banks have been among the most important participants in this market. In recent years, however, major banks from Europe, Japan, and Canada have increased their participation. In 1977 – 1980, for instance, U.S. bank lending to foreign countries

---

BIS: The Bank for International Settlements — a Swiss club for rich countries' central bankers whose annual report and periodic statistics are essential reading for all Euromarket watchers.

Eurobond: A long-term Euromarket loan, for which banks act like a marriage bureau. They bring together high-class borrowers (multinational companies, banks themselves) and lenders (insurance companies, other banks, and, so the myth goes, Belgian dentists).

Eurodollar: A greenback placed in a bank outside America.

LDCs: Less-developed countries — a polite way of describing poor countries, in comparison to (1) OECD — the club of 24 free-world industrial economies, (2) OPEC — the oil producers, and (3) CMEs — the centrally managed economies of the communist bloc.

Lead manager: The boss bank that organizes all the others in a syndicated loan (see below).

Libor: The London interbank offered rate, the interest rate paid by blue-blooded banks in London for borrowing dollars from other banks in London.

Offshore center: A place with lots of foreign banks — and a beach (Nassau, Singapore).

Recycling: Banks do nothing else. But the term is usually applied to the process whereby money used to pay for oil is lent through the banks to someone else to pay for more oil.

Spread (margin): The difference between what banks pay for deposits and what they charge to borrowers.

Syndicated loan: Several banks ganging together to raise huge sums ($1 billion or more) for a single borrower.

SOURCE: Adapted from *The Economist*, November 29, 1980, p. S-23.

Figure 3.9   Euromarket jargon

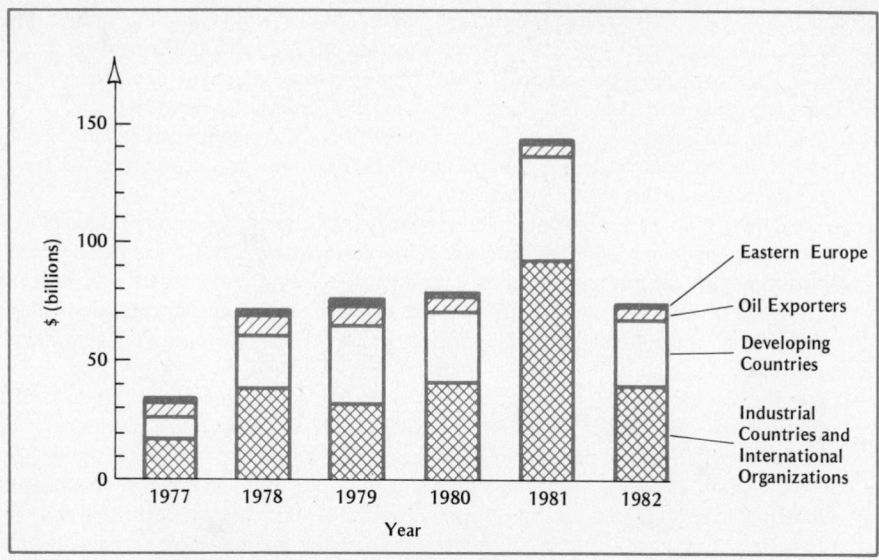

Figure 3.10   Where the oil money goes: international bank borrowing by country group (publicized long- and medium-term loans)

grew at an annual rate of 13.4 percent; non-U.S. bank lending abroad grew at a rate of 32.7 percent.

Following the 1973–1974 oil price increases by the Organization of Petroleum Exporting Countries (OPEC), massive amounts of dollars have been placed in short-term Euromarket bank deposits. The banks, in turn, have been lending to various groups of borrowers, led in recent years by the less-developed countries. Figure 3.10 shows the *redistribution* of "oil money" in terms of groups of countries borrowing from international banks. (These figures can be contrasted with a total borrowing for the year 1974 of less than $30 billion. It should also be noted that a large amount of borrowing is done through international bond issues; see Chapter 19.) Although developing countries have become a major borrowing group in recent years, the industrialized nations continue to borrow actively in international markets. Included in the latter group's borrowings are the funds obtained by multinational companies.

Multinational firms use the Euromarket to raise additional funds as well as to invest excess cash. Both Eurocurrency and Eurobond markets are used by MNCs. We will focus on MNCs' Euromarket activities in subsequent chapters, particularly Chapters 18 through 20. ●●

CHAPTER SUMMARY

● Financial intermediaries, or institutions, channel the savings of various individuals, businesses, and governments into the hands of demanders of these funds.

● The key financial intermediaries include commercial banks, mutual savings banks, savings and loan associations, credit unions, life insurance companies, pension funds, and mutual funds.

● The role of the intermediary is changing as a result of passage of the Depository

Institutions Deregulation and Monetary Control Act of 1980, which permits financial institutions to compete and has ushered in the era of the financial supermarket.

● The financial markets provide a forum in which suppliers and demanders of short-term and long-term loans and investments can transact business directly.

● The two components of the financial markets are the money market and the capital market. In both markets, securities are initially issued in the primary market; once issued, they are traded in the secondary market.

● The money market is the market in which short-term securities are traded. The key instruments of the money market include all the so-called marketable securities, which are short-term debt instruments such as Treasury bills, commercial paper, and negotiable certificates of deposit issued by government, business, and financial institutions. Participants in the money market include individuals, businesses, governments, and financial institutions.

● The capital market, where long-term debt and equity capital are raised, is of key importance to new capital formation. It is made up of the organized securities exchanges and the over-the-counter exchange. These exchanges create a continuous market, allocate scarce capital, determine and publicize security prices, and aid firms in obtaining new financing. The organized exchanges provide secondary markets for securities. The over-the-counter exchange is a telecommunications network linking active participants in this market. In addition to creating a secondary market for securities, the over-the-counter exchange is a primary market in which new public issues are sold.

● Securities can be traded in the capital markets not only by normal purchase and sale transactions but also by margin purchases and short selling.

● Investment companies enable individuals to purchase ownership in a portfolio of securities.

● Investment bankers can be hired to aid firms in finding buyers for new security issues; they also advise clients and bear the risk of selling a security issue.

● The flow of funds between suppliers and demanders is regulated by the interest rate or required return, which acts as compensation to the funds supplier for forgoing current consumption and accepting risk.

● In a perfect, inflation-free, certain world in which suppliers and demanders have no liquidity preferences, the real rate of interest creates equilibrium between the supply of savings and the demand for investment funds. The risk-free rate of interest can be defined as the sum of the real rate of interest and the inflationary expectation. This rate is the nominal or actual rate of interest (return) for a risk-free investment.

● The difference in nominal rates results from differing average rates of inflation expected over various maturities of the security. For any class of equal-risk securities, the term structure of interest rates reflects the relationship between the yield on the security and its maturity. Yield curves can be downward-sloping, flat, or upward-sloping, depending on inflation and interest rate expectations.

● The nominal yield on any security can be defined as the sum of the risk-free rate and a risk premium. The risk premium embodies a variety of factors, including default risk, maturity risk, marketability risk, contractual provisions, and tax treatment.

● Since investors must be compensated for taking risk, they expect higher returns for greater risk. Each type of security offers a range of potential risk-return trade-offs.

● The existence and expansion of dollars held outside the United States have contributed in recent years to the development of a major international financial market, the Euromarket. The large international banks participate in this market. Borrowers range from the industrialized nations to the less-developed countries; some oil-exporting countries are among the major lenders.

KEY TERMS

actual return
capital markets
commercial bank
contractual provisions
credit union
dealers
default risk
Depository Institutions Deregulation and
    Monetary Control Act of 1980
    (DIDMCA)
efficient market
expected return
Euromarket
federal funds
financial institutions
financial intermediary
financial markets
financial supermarket
freely callable bond
government security dealer
inflation
inflationary expectations
interest rate
interest rate risk
intermediation
investment banker
investment company
life insurance companies
liquidity preference
load fund
margin purchases
margin requirements

marketability
marketability risk
maturity risk
money market
money market account
money market fund
mutual fund
mutual savings bank
negotiable order of withdrawal (NOW)
    account
no-load fund
nominal rate of interest
organized securities exchanges
over-the-counter (OTC) exchange
pension funds
primary market
prime rate of interest
private placement
public offering
real rate of interest
required return
risk-free rate of interest (R_F)
risk premium
risk-return trade-off
savings and loan association
secondary market
short selling
super NOW account
term structure of interest rates
U.S. Treasury bill (T-bill)
yield
yield curve

QUESTIONS

3-1   What are *financial intermediaries* and *financial markets?* What is the fund-raising alternative to these media?

3-2   Who are the key participants in the financial intermediation process? Indicate who are net savers and who are net borrowers.

3-3   Briefly describe the key characteristics of the following financial intermediaries:
  a   commercial banks
  b   savings and loan associations
  c   life insurance companies
  d   mutual funds

3-4   Describe the changing role of financial intermediaries and explain how "financial supermarkets" fit into the evolving institutional environment.

3-5   What relationship exists between financial intermediaries and financial markets? Why does it exist?

3-6 What is the *money market?* Where is it housed? How does it differ from the capital market?

3-7 What is the *capital market?* What role do securities exchanges play in this market? What are *primary* and *secondary* markets?

3-8 How does the over-the-counter market operate? How does it differ from the organized exchanges? How is it linked? What are *bid* and *ask* prices?

3-9 What are *margin purchases* and *short-sale transactions?* Who controls margin requirements? When is an individual likely to make a short sale?

3-10 What is an *investment banker?* What role does he or she play in private placements and public offerings?

3-11 What is the *real rate of interest?* Differentiate it from the nominal rate of interest for the risk-free asset, a three-month U.S. Treasury bill.

3-12 What is the *term structure of interest rates* and how does it relate to the yield curve? For a given class of equal-risk securities, what expectation causes the yield curve to be downward-sloping, flat, or upward-sloping?

3-13 List and briefly describe the potential component risks embodied in the risk premium used to determine the nominal rate of interest on a risky security.

3-14 How are actual and expected returns measured and what is the difference between them? What is meant by the *risk-return trade-off?*

3-15 Discuss the major reasons for the emergence of the Euromarket.

3-16 What is an *offshore center?* What is *Libor* (see Figure 3.9)?

3-17 Name the major participants in the Euromarket.

PROBLEMS

3-1 **(Stock Quotations)** Given the following quotations for Mobil Corporation and NCR, from *The Wall Street Journal* on Tuesday, June 13, answer questions **a** through **j** for Mobil and NCR, respectively.

$70\frac{1}{2}$	$58\frac{1}{8}$	Mobil	4.20	6.4	7	254	$65\frac{3}{4}$	$64\frac{7}{8}$	$65\frac{5}{8}$	$+\frac{1}{4}$
$58\frac{5}{8}$	$34\frac{1}{2}$	NCR	1	1.7	10	600	$58\frac{3}{4}$	$57\frac{1}{4}$	$57\frac{1}{2}$	$-\frac{1}{4}$

a On what day did the trading activity occur?

b At what price did the stock sell at the end of the day on Friday, June 9?

c What are the highest and lowest prices at which the stock sold on the day quoted?

d How much is the firm's price-earnings ratio? What does it indicate?

e What is the firm's percentage dividend yield? What does it signify?

f What was the last price (or closing price) at which the stock was traded on the day quoted?

g How large a dividend is expected in the current year?

h What are the highest and lowest prices at which the stock has traded in the past 52 weeks?

i How many shares of the stock were traded on the day quoted?

j How much, if any, of a change in the stock price took place between the day quoted and the preceding trading day?

3-2 **(Margin Requirements)** For each of the following cases, indicate how much money Paula Lipski would have to put up to make the given transaction with the stated margin requirements.

Case	Number of shares	Price per share ($)	Margin requirement (%)
A	100	$22\frac{7}{8}$	55
B	80	$39\frac{1}{2}$	40
C	900	88	60
D	100	$26\frac{3}{4}$	35
E	250	$16\frac{7}{8}$	65
F	400	59	20

3-3   **(Margin and Interest)**   Wilma Marcotti is considering purchasing stock on margin. She has the following information. Use it to answer the questions below.

Stock	Number of shares	Price per share ($)	Margin requirement (%)	Interest on margin (%)	Holding period of stock (months)
A	100	25	20	12	3
B	50	$28\frac{1}{2}$	40	14	6
C	200	$37\frac{1}{4}$	60	18	1
D	450	$16\frac{7}{8}$	55	10	4

a   How much money will she have to put up in each case?

b   For each case, what amount of interest would she owe if she sells at the end of the given holding period?

3-4   **(Margin and Returns)**   On February 4, 1985, Winston Ross purchased 400 shares of CBA at $23\frac{1}{2}$ and 300 shares of DZC at $44\frac{7}{8}$. The margin requirement at the time was 40 percent, and the interest rate on margin purchases was 13 percent.

a   If Winston used the maximum amount of margin available, how much of his own money would he need for the purchase?

b   If he sold the stocks on June 4, 1985, how much interest would he pay on the transaction?

c   If the total brokerage fees for the purchase and sale were $62.50 and he sold CBA for $25 and DZC for $49\frac{3}{8}$, considering all costs, how much did Winston net from his purchases?

d   What was his rate of return on the funds he invested?

e   What would his net return have been if he had *not* bought on margin?

f   What would the return on his *invested funds* have been if he had *not* bought on margin?

3-5   **(Margin, Return, and Risk)**   Consider each of the following cases:

	Case			
	A	B	C	D
Number of shares purchased	300	150	150	80
Price per share ($)	31	$62\frac{1}{2}$	$62\frac{1}{2}$	254
Brokerage fees (total $)	60	100	100	90
Margin requirement (%)	65	55	55	45
Margin interest rate (%)	14	12	12	14
Holding period (months)	6	9	9	12
Sale price per share ($)	$37\frac{1}{4}$	55	70	302

    a Calculate the amount of money the purchaser must put up in each case assuming he or she uses the full amount of margin available.

    b Calculate the margin interest charged for the specified holding period.

    c Calculate the net profit (the proceeds after brokerage and margin costs) in each case.

    d Determine the return on the funds invested by the purchaser in each case.

    e Calculate the net profit in each case assuming margin is *not* used.

    f Determine the return on the funds invested by the purchaser assuming margin is *not* used.

    g What conclusions can you draw with respect to the risk-return trade-off provided by the use of margin? Explain this in light of cases B and C.

3-6 **(Margin Requirements and Purchase Ability)** Chung Li is considering the purchase of the common stock of Mountain Pass Food Processing, Inc. She has $8000 to invest, and the stock is currently selling at $50 per share.

    a How many shares can she purchase if the margin requirement is 100 percent? 50 percent? 10 percent?

    b From **a**, what conclusions can be drawn with respect to the effects of changes in the margin requirements on the ability to purchase securities?

3-7 **(Short Sale)** For each of the following cases, indicate the short profit or loss made (prior to brokerage fees) and the net profit after all costs.

Case	Number of shares	Price at which shares sold short ($)	Price at which shares repurchased ($)	Broker's commission ($)
A	100	50	55	25
B	700	80	70	280
C	300	$23\frac{7}{8}$	$32\frac{1}{4}$	120
D	1000	$32\frac{1}{2}$	$32\frac{1}{4}$	180

3-8 **(Short versus Long Position)** Ray Glaser, who is a real gambler, cannot decide whether to take a long or a short position in a given security. The stock is currently selling for $48 per share.

    a How much would Ray lose or gain if he bought 200 shares of the stock and later sold it for $54 per share?

    b How much would he have lost or gained had he taken a short position if the stock was repurchased at $54 per share?

    c Answer **a** and **b** above, assuming that the stock was sold or repurchased at $38 per share.

    d If Ray does some research into future stock price movements, what expectation will cause him to take a long position and what expectation will justify selling short? Explain.

3-9 **(Short versus Long Position)** Given the following stocks and expected prices now and six months from now, indicate whether you would take a long or short position in each stock and how much per share would be earned in each case if the expected prices matched the actual prices six months from now.

Stock	Current price per share ($)	Expected price per share ($) 6 months from now
A	44	50
B	37	$32\frac{1}{2}$
C	$14\frac{1}{4}$	$18\frac{1}{2}$
D	$19\frac{1}{8}$	22
E	47	47

3-10 **(Real Rate of Interest)**   To estimate the real rate of interest, the economics division of Lobonx Banks — a major bank holding company — has gathered the data summarized in the table below. Because there is a high likelihood that new tax legislation will be passed in the near future, current data as well as data reflecting the likely impact of passage of the legislation on the demand for funds are also included in the table. (*Note:* The proposed legislation will not have any impact on the supply schedule of funds.)

Amount of funds supplied/demanded ($ billion)	Currently		With passage of tax legislation
	Interest rate required by funds suppliers (%)	Interest rate required by funds demanders (%)	Interest rate required by funds demanders (%)
1	7	16	24
5	9	14	21
10	11	11	19
20	14	9	17
50	16	7	16
100	19	5	12

a   Draw the supply curve and the demand curve for funds using the current data. (*Note:* Unlike Figure 3.5, these functions will not appear as straight lines.)

b   Using your graph, label and note the real rate of interest using current data.

c   Add to the graph drawn in **a** the new demand curve expected in the event the proposed tax legislation becomes effective.

d   What is the new real rate of interest? Compare and analyze this finding in light of your analysis in **b**.

3-11 **(Nominal Interest Rates and Yield Curves)**   A recent study of inflationary expectations has disclosed that the consensus among economic forecasters yields the following average annual rates of inflation expected over the periods noted.

Period	Average Annual Rate of Inflation (%)
3 months	5
1 year	6
5 years	8
10 years	8.5
20 years	9

a If the real rate of interest is currently 2.5 percent, find the nominal interest rate on each of the following U.S. Treasury issues: 20-year bond, 3-month bill, 1-year note, 5-year bond.

b If the real rate of interest suddenly drops to 2 percent without any change in inflationary expectations, what effect, if any, would this have on your answers in a? Explain.

c Using your finding in a, draw a yield curve for U.S. Treasury securities. Describe the general shape and expectations reflected by the curve.

3-12 **(Nominal and Real Rates and Yield Curves)** A firm wishing to evaluate interest rate behavior has gathered nominal rate of interest and inflationary expectation data on five U.S. Treasury securities, each having a different maturity and each measured at a different point in time during the year just ended. This data is summarized in the table below.

U.S. Treasury security	Point in time	Maturity	Nominal rate of interest (%)	Inflationary expectation (%)
A	Jan. 7	1 year	12.6	9.5
B	Mar. 12	10 years	11.2	8.2
C	May 30	6 months	13.0	10.0
D	Aug. 15	20 years	11.0	8.1
E	Dec. 30	5 years	11.4	8.3

a Using the data above, find the real rate of interest at each point in time.

b Describe the behavior of the real rate of interest over the year. What forces might be responsible for such behavior?

c Draw the yield curve associated with this data, assuming that the nominal rates were measured at the same point in time.

d Describe the resulting yield curve in c and explain the general expectations embodied in it.

3-13 **(Term Structure of Interest Rates)** The following yield data for a number of highest-quality corporate bonds existed at each of the three points in time noted.

Time to Maturity (years)	Yield (%)		
	5 years ago	2 years ago	Today
1	9.1	14.6	9.3
3	9.2	12.8	9.8
5	9.3	12.2	10.9
10	9.5	10.9	12.6
15	9.4	10.7	12.7
20	9.3	10.5	12.9
30	9.4	10.5	13.5

a Draw the yield curve at each of the three points in time given, on the same set of axes.

b Label each curve in a as to its general shape (upward-sloping, flat, downward-sloping).

c Describe the general inflationary and interest rate expectation existing at each of the three points in time.

3-14 **(Risk-free Rate and Risk Premiums)** The real rate of interest is currently 3 percent, and the inflationary expectations and risk premiums for a number of securities are given below.

Security	Inflationary expectation (%)	Risk premium (%)
A	6	3
B	9	2
C	8	2
D	5	4
E	11	1

a Find the risk-free rate of interest, R_F, applicable to each security.

b Although not noted, what factor must be the cause of the differing risk-free rates found in **a**?

c Find the nominal rate of interest for each security.

3-15 **(Risk Premiums)** Alice Stamas is attempting to find the nominal rate of interest for each of two securities—A and B—issued by different firms at the same point in time. She has gathered the following data:

Characteristic	Security A	Security B
Time to maturity	3 years	15 years
Inflationary expectation	9.0%	7.0%
Risk premium for		
Default risk	1.0%	2.0%
Interest rate risk	0.5%	1.5%
Liquidity risk	1.0%	1.0%
Other risk	0.5%	1.5%

a If the real rate of interest is currently 2 percent, find the risk-free rate of interest applicable to each security.

b Find the total risk premium attributable to each security's issuer and issue risk.

c Calculate the nominal rate of interest for each security. Compare and discuss your findings.

3-16 **(Actual Rate of Return)** Alex Williams wishes to estimate his returns during the past year on a number of securities he owns. Using the data summarized in the table below, find the actual rate of return Alex would have earned during the year had he purchased the securities at the beginning price and sold them at the ending price without incurring any brokerage fees or taxes.

Security	Cash dividends or interest paid ($)	Market price Beginning ($)	Market price Ending ($)
A	2.00	30.00	34.00
B	0.00	25.00	27.00
C	2.50	17.50	16.00
D	1.00	86.00	89.50
E	3.00	63.50	54.00

3-17   (**Actual or Expected Return**)   The following data describe the actual return inputs as well as the expected returns on five securities for the year just ended.

Security	Cash dividends or interest paid ($)	Market price Beginning ($)	Market price Ending ($)	Expected return (%)
A	4.50	22.50	21.00	15
B	2.00	17.00	19.00	20
C	0.00	64.00	67.50	8
D	1.50	25.00	26.50	12
E	3.20	30.00	26.00	10

a   Calculate the actual return on each security for the year just ended.

b   Evaluate each security's actual return in view of the expected return.

c   If you held each of the securities, what action, if any, would you take in view of your findings in **b**? (*Note:* Ignore brokerage fees and taxes.)

d   What is likely to happen to the market prices of each of the securities, based on your comparison of actual and expected performance during the year? Explain.

Part II

Techniques of Financial Analysis and Planning

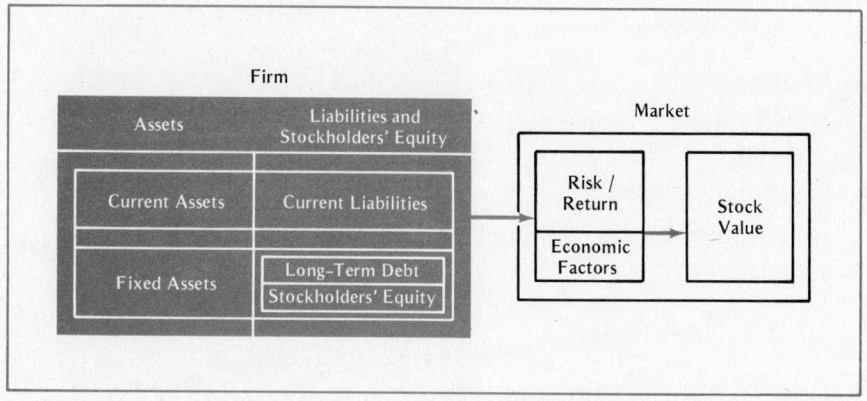

Chapter 4

The Analysis of Financial Statements

After studying this chapter, you should be able to:

1. Describe the structure, content, and information embodied in each of the four basic financial statements.

2. Understand the parties interested in performing financial ratio analysis and the type of ratio comparisons commonly made.

3. Calculate and interpret the popular financial ratios from the four basic groups—liquidity, activity, debt, and profitability.

4. Prepare and interpret an analysis of a firm's financial performance using the DuPont system.

5. Perform a complete ratio analysis of a firm's financial performance and condition and interpret and make recommendations based on your findings.

6. Discuss some of the major features that distinguish domestically oriented financial statements from internationally based reports.

The analysis of financial statements typically begins with an initial review of the four basic statements, followed by the calculation of ratios to evaluate the past, present, and future performance of the firm. The four basic financial statements are the income statement, the balance sheet, the statement of retained earnings, and the statement of changes in financial position. Each of these statements presents important information about the firm's recent performance or current financial position.

Ratio analysis is routinely used by shareholders, creditors, and the financial manager to assess a firm's financial condition. Ratios provide a *relative* measure of a company's performance and condition. The basic inputs to ratio analysis are the firm's income statement and balance sheet for the periods to be examined. The data provided by these statements can be used to calculate various ratios that permit an evaluation of certain aspects of financial performance and condition. Because ratios are routinely used by present and prospective stockholders to assess risk and return, the information they contain can significantly affect share price.[1]

Basic Financial Statements

Publicly held corporations must provide their stockholders with an annual *stockholders' report*. This report typically begins with a letter from the chairman of the board or the president describing the major events of greatest impact during the year. The letter will also likely point out plans for the coming year and the expected impact of these plans on the firm's financial condition. Following the

---

[1] The concepts and relationships of risk, return, and value are discussed in detail in Chapters 7 and 8. At this point, suffice it to say that the levels of risk and return perceived by investors in the marketplace are the determinants of the firm's value (share price), which the financial manager should attempt to maximize by making the "best" decisions.

statement of retained earnings, the statement of changes in financial position, and ratio analysis.

STATEMENT OF RETAINED EARNINGS

The *statement of retained earnings* reconciles the net income earned during the year, and any cash dividends paid, with the change in retained earnings between the start and end of the given year. Table 4.3 presents this statement for Dayton Oil for the year ended December 31, 1984. A review of the statement shows that the company began the year with $1,012,000 in retained earnings, had net profits after tax of $231,000, from which it paid $108,000 in dividends, resulting in year-end 1984 retained earnings of $1,135,000. This was a net increase of $123,000, as reflected in the final income statement entry in Table 4.1.

STATEMENT OF CHANGES IN FINANCIAL POSITION

The *statement of changes in financial position* provides a summary of the "funds flow" over the period of concern — typically the year just ended. The statement, which is sometimes called a source and use statement, provides insight into operations and financing. Interpretation of this statement requires a thorough understanding of basic financial principles. Before describing the statement, we need to discuss the definition of funds, cash flow through the firm, and the classification of sources and uses.

Definition of funds: Cash or working capital? The funds flow summarized in the statement of changes in financial position can be defined as cash or as *net working capital,* which is the amount of current assets minus the amount of current liabilities. Both forms of funds are necessary for the firm to function effectively. Cash is needed to pay bills currently due, and net working capital — especially in a seasonal business — is needed to provide a cushion for the payment of bills due in the near future. The use of net working capital as the pivotal element of the statement is based on the belief that current assets as well as cash can be used to pay current liabilities; the use of cash — the most basic form of funds — is based on a strict belief that only cash pays bills. While the accounting profession has been pushing

Table 4.3   Dayton Oil Company Statement of Retained Earnings ($000)

		For the year ended December 31, 1984
Retained earnings balance (January 1, 1984)		$1012
Plus: Net profit after taxes (for 1984)		231
Less: Cash dividends (paid during 1984)		
Preferred stock	($10)	
Common stock	(98)	(108)
Retained earnings balance (December 31, 1984)		$1135

for the required inclusion of a cash-based statement of changes in financial position in the stockholders' report, current corporate practice reflects a preference for the net-working-capital-based form of this statement. The cash-based statement is believed to be more informative because of its greater detail, so it is emphasized here.

Cash flow through the firm. Figure 4.1 is a diagram of the overall flow of cash through the firm. It shows (1) operating flows and (2) financial and legal flows. The *operating flows* relate to the firm's production cycle. Utilizing raw materials, labor, and fixed assets and incurring sales expenses and operating and administrative expenses such as salaries and rent, the firm produces and sells its finished goods. As Figure 4.1 shows, not all purchases are made for cash; many are made on credit through the establishment of an account payable or accrual. Similarly, not all sales are made for cash; many are made on credit, producing accounts receivable. The *financial and legal flows* depicted in Figure 4.1 include the payment and receipt of interest, the payment and refund of taxes, the incurrence and repayment of debt, the effect of distributions of equity through the payment of dividends and stock repurchases, and the cash inflow from the sale of stock.

These flows differ from operating flows in that they are not directly related to the production and sale of the firm's products. No division between operating

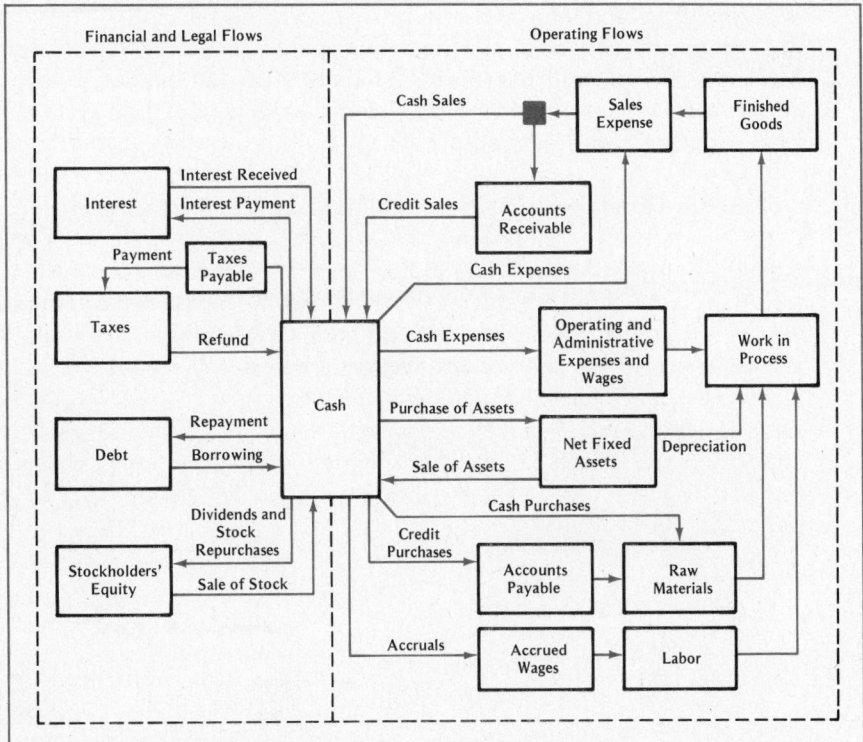

Figure 4.1   Cash flow through the firm

flows and financial and legal flows is made in the statement of changes in financial position, but the reader should recognize the difference between them.

Classifying sources and uses of cash. The cash-based statement of changes in financial position summarizes the sources and uses of cash during the period. An understanding of the scheme used to classify sources and uses of cash aids in interpreting the statement. Table 4.4 summarizes the basic sources and uses of cash. For example, if the firm's accounts payable increased by $1000 during a given year, this change would be a *source of cash*; if the firm's inventory increased by $2500 during the year, it would be a *use of cash*, since additional cash would have been tied up in inventory.

A few points should be clarified with respect to the classification scheme in Table 4.4.

1. A decrease in the cash *balance* is a source of cash *flow* because cash flow must have been released to provide a use of cash such as an increase in inventory. Similarly, an increase in the cash *balance* is a use of cash *flow* since the cash must have been drawn from some source of cash flow. Consider a firm confronted with two alternatives, using cash to purchase inventory or putting the cash in the bank. Both actions will consume cash, but the purchase of inventory will convert it into another type of asset, whereas placement in the bank will not. Both actions, however, will increase the firm's assets and therefore must be considered uses of cash.
2. In Chapter 2, Equation 2.1 and the discussion of it explained why depreciation and other noncash charges must be considered cash inflows, or sources of cash. Adding noncash charges back to the firm's net profits after taxes gives cash flow from operations:

   Cash flow from operations = net profits after taxes + noncash charges

   Note that it is possible for a firm to have a net loss but still have a positive cash flow from operations if depreciation during the period is greater than the net loss. In the statement of changes in financial position, net profits after taxes, net losses, and noncash charges are treated as separate items to increase the statement's information content.
3. Because depreciation is treated as a separate source of funds, only *gross* rather then *net* changes in fixed assets appear on the statement of changes

Table 4.4   The Sources and Uses of Cash

Sources	Uses
	Increase in Cash
Decrease in any asset	Increase in any asset
Increase in any liability	Decrease in any liability
Net profits after taxes	Net loss
Depreciation and other noncash charges	Cash dividends paid
Sale of stock	Repurchase or retirement of stock

Table 4.5   Dayton Oil Company Statement of Changes in Financial Position on a Cash Basis for the Year Ended December 31, 1984 ($000)

Sources of cash		Uses of cash	
Net profits after taxes	$231	Dividends ($10 + $98)	$108
Depreciation	239	Increase: Gross fixed assets	347
Decrease: Inventories	11	Increase: Cash	75
Increase: Accounts payable	112	Increase: Marketable securities	17
Increase: Accruals	45	Increase: Accounts receivable	138
Increase: Long-term debts	56	Decrease: Notes payable	20
Increase: Common stock	1	Total uses	$705
Increase: Paid-in capital	10		
Total sources	$705		

in financial position. Such treatment is necessary to avoid potential double counting of the effect of depreciation on cash flow.[6]

4. Direct entries of changes in retained earnings are *not* classified as sources or uses of cash; instead, entries for items that affect retained earnings appear as net profits or losses after taxes and cash dividends.

Interpreting the statement. The statement of changes in financial position prepared on a cash basis for Dayton Oil for the year ended December 31, 1984, is given in Table 4.5. It was prepared using Dayton Oil's 1984 income statement and its 1983 and 1984 balance sheets. The sources and uses of funds were determined from them; then certain accounting adjustments were made.

The statement of changes in financial position allows the financial manager to analyze the firm's past and possibly its future cash flow. The analyst will give special attention to major problems or symptoms of developing problems. Analysis of Dayton Oil Company's statement of changes in financial position does not seem to indicate the existence of any problems.[7]

The sources of funds seem to be distributed in a manner consistent with prudent financial management; the same is true of the firm's uses of funds. The statement seems to indicate that the firm is strong. Most of its funds have been generated through operations and increased accounts payable. These sources are consistent with efficient financial management. The major uses of funds have been an increase in fixed assets, the payment of dividends, and an increase in accounts receivable. These items, when viewed in light of the sources, tend to reflect moderate growth.

The financial manager may prepare a statement of changes in financial position

---

[6] For a detailed discussion of this refinement and of procedures for preparation of the statement of changes in financial position, see any leading accounting principles text, such as William W. Pyle and Kermit D. Larsen, *Fundamental Accounting Principles,* 10th ed. (Homewood, Ill.: Irwin, 1984), chap. 8, or a leading intermediate accounting text, such as Kieso and Weygandt, op. cit.

[7] Because thorough interpretation of the statement of changes in financial position presumes a reasonable understanding of basic financial principles, the interpretation presented here is by design superficial. Upon completion of this text, the reader should be able to interpret these statements more completely.

based on projected financial statements to determine whether a proposed financial plan is feasible in the sense that the appropriate mix and level of financing needed to support it will be available.

The Use of Financial Ratios

Before discussing the methods of calculating and interpreting financial ratios, we need to describe the various parties interested in financial ratio analysis and the types of comparisons commonly made using financial ratios.

INTERESTED PARTIES

Ratio analysis of a firm's financial statements is of interest to present and prospective shareholders, creditors, and the firm's own management. The present and prospective shareholder is interested in the current and future level of risk (liquidity, activity, and debt) and return (profitability). As will be explained in Chapters 7 and 8, these two dimensions directly affect share price.

The firm's creditors are primarily interested in the short-term liquidity of the firm and the ability of the firm to service its debts over the long run. Present creditors want to assure themselves that the firm is liquid and that it will be able to make scheduled interest and principal payments. Prospective creditors are concerned with determining whether the firm can support the additional debt that would result if they extended credit to the firm. A secondary interest of the present or prospective creditor is the firm's profitability; the creditor wants assurance that the firm is healthy and will continue to be successful.

Management, like the stockholders, must be concerned with all aspects of the firm's financial situation. Since it is aware of the aspects of the business evaluated by owners and creditors, it attempts to operate in a manner that will result in ratios that will be considered favorable by both parties. If the firm is successful, its share price should remain at an acceptable level and its creditworthiness should be unimpaired. In other words, the firm's ability to raise money through the sale of stock or the issuance of debt (bonds) should be maintained at a reasonably high level. A collateral objective of management is to use ratios to monitor the firm's performance from period to period. Any unexpected changes are examined to isolate developing problems.

TYPES OF COMPARISONS

Ratio analysis does not merely involve the application of a formula to financial data in order to calculate a given ratio. More important is the interpretation of the ratio value. To answer such questions as, Is it too high or too low? Is it good or bad?, a meaningful standard or basis for comparison is needed. Two types of ratio comparisons can be made: cross-sectional or time-series.

Cross-sectional analysis. *Cross-sectional analysis* involves the comparison of different firms' financial ratios at the same point in time. The typical business firm is interested in how well it performed in relation to its competitors. If the competitors are also corporations, their reported financial statements should be available for analysis. Often the firm's performance will be compared to that of the industry leader. The firm may uncover major operating differences, which, if changed, will increase efficiency. Another popular type of comparison is to industry averages. These figures can be found in the *Almanac of Business and Industrial Financial Ratios, Dun & Bradstreet's Key Business Ratios, Dun's Business Month, FTC Quarterly Reports, Robert Morris Associates Statement Studies,* and other sources such as industry association publications.[8] A sample of one available source of industry averages is given in Table 4.6 (pages 114 and 115).

The comparison to the standard is made to isolate any *deviations from the norm.* Many people mistakenly believe that in the case of ratios for which higher values are preferred, as long as the firm being analyzed has a value in excess of the industry average, it can be viewed favorably. This "bigger is better" viewpoint can be misleading. Quite often a ratio value that has a large but positive deviation from the norm can be indicative of problems that may, upon more careful analysis, be more severe than had the ratio been below the industry average.[9] It is therefore important to look for *large deviations to either side* of the industry standard; excessive deviation above *or* below the norm could mean a major problem.

The analyst must also recognize that ratio comparisons resulting in large deviations from the norm reflect only the symptom; further analysis of the firm's financial statements coupled with discussions with key managers is typically required to isolate the cause of such symptoms and develop prescriptive actions for correcting them. Of course, such an investigation may find that the large deviation to the desired side of the norm is acceptable and in fact reflects outstanding operating efficiencies and managerial actions. The fundamental issue is that *ratio analysis merely directs the analyst to potential areas of concern; it does not provide conclusive evidence as to the existence of a problem or an outstanding effort on the part of management.*

EXAMPLE In early 1985 the chief financial analyst at Duff Manufacturing gathered data on the firm's financial performance during 1984, the year just ended. The analyst calculated a variety of ratios and obtained industry averages for use in making comparisons. One ratio she was especially interested in was the inventory turnover, which reflects the speed with which the firm moves its inventory from raw materials through production into finished goods and to the customer as a completed sale. Generally, higher values of this ratio are preferred, since they are indicative of a quicker turnover of inventory. Duff Manufacturing's calculated inventory turnover for 1984 and the industry average inventory turnover were:

	Inventory turnover, 1984
Duff Manufacturing	14.8
Industry Average	9.7

---

[8] Cross-sectional comparisons of firms operating in several lines of business are difficult to perform. The use of weighted-average industry average ratios based on the firm's product line mix or, if data are available, analysis of the firm on a product-line-by-product-line basis, can be performed to analyze a multiproduct firm.

[9] Similarly, in the case of ratios for which "smaller is better," one must be as concerned with calculated values that deviate significantly *below* the norm, or industry average, as with values that fall above it. Significant deviations, regardless of the side of the norm, require further investigation by the analyst.

Table 4.6   Industry Average Ratios for Selected Lines of Business[a]

Line of business (number of concerns reporting)	Quick ratio (X)	Current ratio (X)	Current liabilities to net worth (%)	Current liabilities to inventory (%)	Total liabilities to net worth (%)	Fixed assets to net worth (%)	Collection period (days)	Net sales to inventory (X)	Total assets to net sales (%)	Net sales to net working capital (X)	Accounts payable to net sales (%)	Return on net sales (%)	Return on total assets (%)	Return on net worth (%)
Agriculture, construction, mining														
Agricultural production — Crops (133)	2.2	3.8	7.1	52.8	20.8	61.3	9.8	15.9	71.5	2.7	1.7	12.9	7.4	15.2
	0.6	2.0	18.7	111.0	57.9	96.7	25.1	6.4	189.6	4.6	3.3	4.4	4.7	7.1
	0.2	0.7	52.2	257.8	113.3	137.3	66.0	2.7	428.7	9.8	5.5	0.5	0.8	1.0
Crude petroleum and natural gas extraction (124)	1.9	4.5	7.3	280.7	13.0	15.4	25.9	34.8	84.9	1.2	5.0	30.0	9.3	28.5
	0.9	1.6	26.6	609.7	44.1	67.6	66.0	17.2	251.3	4.7	14.9	15.7	6.4	13.1
	0.6	1.0	116.1	999.9	271.0	157.8	170.8	11.6	409.6	12.8	42.4	4.9	1.6	3.8
General contractors — Houses (119)	2.6	4.3	8.8	75.0	27.2	28.2	5.8	99.2	42.2	2.9	1.3	13.1	17.9	25.5
	1.1	2.1	33.2	169.5	82.8	70.0	18.9	17.0	76.7	5.3	3.4	5.1	8.9	14.4
	0.3	1.3	86.5	587.9	132.9	104.8	48.9	4.5	152.8	11.8	6.7	2.1	4.6	7.8
Communication, transportation, utilities														
Electric services (112)	1.2	2.6	13.7	180.6	137.3	163.3	23.7	35.3	167.9	5.4	5.8	10.9	4.6	12.6
	0.8	1.7	23.0	268.7	211.3	234.9	32.4	20.1	207.1	8.3	7.0	6.3	3.2	10.4
	0.4	1.0	33.2	438.1	384.1	334.0	39.4	10.9	258.3	13.8	8.8	3.0	1.7	5.0
Radio broadcasting (168)	5.3	7.4	6.3	64.0	9.9	30.5	44.1	173.8	63.4	2.9	1.2	12.2	10.7	23.1
	2.2	3.1	17.3	400.8	35.1	57.4	56.9	85.9	81.0	4.6	2.2	6.9	6.8	8.4
	0.9	1.3	50.3	999.9	129.5	131.6	71.1	12.0	139.3	6.7	4.7	(0.5)	(1.6)	(2.4)
Manufacturing														
Aircraft parts including engines (170)	1.5	3.0	29.7	74.9	43.3	29.2	31.0	15.2	42.1	3.8	2.4	10.8	15.8	29.7
	1.1	2.2	56.1	119.2	87.8	48.6	43.8	7.4	54.3	5.7	4.9	6.2	10.6	19.0
	0.7	1.5	105.2	200.2	153.0	87.6	56.5	4.7	68.9	10.2	7.8	3.3	4.9	11.0
Metalworking machinery and equipment (102)	2.3	4.8	14.6	68.8	18.5	35.6	34.6	18.4	47.3	3.5	1.9	9.5	13.7	29.1
	1.3	2.3	38.9	140.0	54.6	61.3	48.2	8.3	67.0	4.7	3.8	5.7	8.8	18.8
	0.8	1.5	77.0	227.1	116.1	92.8	60.2	5.3	82.4	9.3	6.9	2.9	2.4	7.1

Line of business														

Retailing

Petroleum refining (99)	1.5	2.3	41.0	113.0	52.1	24.4	21.9	23.8	26.2	5.2	3.5	4.9	9.9	23.4
	1.0	**1.7**	**65.9**	**176.4**	**123.5**	**51.4**	**34.6**	**14.8**	**41.8**	**9.6**	**6.7**	**2.9**	**4.9**	**13.0**
	0.6	1.3	117.4	322.5	215.6	127.9	52.5	9.8	59.6	20.4	10.9	0.8	2.2	6.6
Department stores (108)	2.2	5.7	13.0	27.7	16.0	6.4	5.9	6.1	36.9	3.3	4.1	2.0	5.0	9.5
	1.3	**3.0**	**44.1**	**58.8**	**65.8**	**24.6**	**29.2**	**4.8**	**50.5**	**4.7**	**6.4**	**0.8**	**2.2**	**4.7**
	0.6	2.0	76.8	88.6	149.6	50.8	66.4	3.8	71.6	7.1	9.1	0.1	0.1	0.2
Grocery stores (100)	1.4	4.4	12.8	36.9	25.3	21.1	1.0	24.1	14.1	9.8	1.5	3.7	9.8	22.0
	0.8	**2.7**	**32.3**	**73.4**	**54.8**	**44.5**	**3.6**	**18.7**	**18.7**	**15.8**	**2.3**	**1.7**	**6.2**	**12.9**
	0.4	1.5	65.4	122.7	107.7	97.2	10.2	11.5	27.8	32.0	3.5	0.9	4.3	5.7
Motor vehicle dealers (new and used) (106)	0.3	1.7	129.8	81.2	138.3	11.1	2.5	8.2	19.2	10.7	0.5	2.7	7.5	27.4
	0.2	**1.3**	**217.9**	**94.6**	**227.6**	**21.3**	**4.7**	**6.2**	**24.9**	**18.3**	**0.9**	**1.5**	**4.3**	**13.7**
	0.1	1.2	352.2	104.0	366.1	42.7	9.1	4.9	30.6	31.5	1.5	0.6	1.8	5.0

Services

Computer and data processing services (116)	2.2	3.1	31.0	165.2	45.2	23.1	30.6	84.2	32.2	3.2	2.5	13.1	18.3	33.4
	1.2	**1.8**	**65.1**	**358.2**	**89.5**	**46.1**	**42.3**	**37.5**	**57.2**	**7.3**	**5.1**	**7.5**	**10.1**	**17.0**
	0.8	1.3	112.7	921.3	160.9	91.9	59.8	17.1	82.1	16.5	8.2	2.5	2.1	4.8
Hotels, motels, and tourist courts (100)	1.5	2.5	9.6	441.4	56.2	103.7	4.7	111.3	103.7	4.2	2.2	16.0	10.0	25.0
	0.6	**1.0**	**29.5**	**999.9**	**151.5**	**160.5**	**10.0**	**65.5**	**192.6**	**7.2**	**3.4**	**9.2**	**6.3**	**13.4**
	0.2	0.4	60.9	999.9	508.2	348.5	15.3	38.2	321.8	39.2	4.8	3.4	2.2	3.3

Wholesaling

Clothing and furnishings (117)	2.2	4.8	19.7	60.4	26.5	5.3	20.8	14.7	24.1	3.4	4.4	7.4	13.3	24.8
	1.1	**2.1**	**73.9**	**99.5**	**88.8**	**14.4**	**35.4**	**7.8**	**40.4**	**7.1**	**7.2**	**3.6**	**7.0**	**16.4**
	0.7	1.6	131.7	179.2	145.5	47.3	60.5	5.1	59.0	11.4	11.1	1.6	5.1	8.4
Petroleum and petroleum products (100)	2.0	3.5	19.6	93.3	31.0	28.4	13.5	59.8	13.6	9.4	2.0	4.0	11.8	23.3
	1.3	**1.8**	**57.8**	**185.4**	**78.7**	**45.9**	**21.9**	**32.0**	**18.5**	**18.2**	**3.3**	**1.5**	**5.8**	**13.8**
	0.9	1.4	109.9	311.3	144.2	79.6	36.8	18.2	31.9	28.4	5.2	0.7	2.6	5.8

[a] Three values are given for each ratio for each line of business. The center value in bold type is the *median*, and the values immediately above and below it are the *upper and lower quartiles*, respectively.

SOURCE: Adapted from "The Ratios," *Dun's Business Month*, February 1983, pp. 107–117.

The analyst's initial reaction to these data was that the firm had managed its inventory significantly better than the average firm in the industry. The turnover was in fact nearly 53 percent faster than the industry average. But upon reflection, the analyst felt there could be a problem, since a very high inventory turnover could result from maintaining very low levels of inventory. The consequence of low inventory could be excessive stockouts (lost sales due to insufficient inventory). The analyst's review of other ratios and discussions with persons in the manufacturing and marketing departments did in fact uncover such a problem: The firm's inventories during the year were extremely low, and numerous production delays and lost sales hindered its ability to meet demand. What had initially appeared to reflect extremely efficient inventory management was actually the symptom of a major problem. ■

Time-series analysis. *Time-series analysis* is done when a financial analyst evaluates performance over time. Comparison of current to past performance utilizing ratio analysis allows the firm to determine whether it is progressing as planned. Developing trends can be seen by using multiyear comparisons; knowledge of these trends should assist the firm in planning future operations. As in cross-sectional analysis, any significant year-to-year changes can be evaluated to assess whether they are symptomatic of a major problem. The theory behind time-series analysis is that the firm must be evaluated in relation to past performance, developing trends must be isolated, and appropriate action must be taken to direct the firm toward immediate and long-run goals. Time-series analysis is often helpful in checking the reasonableness of a firm's projected (pro forma) financial statements. A comparison of current and past ratios to those resulting from an analysis of projected statements may reveal discrepancies or overoptimism.

Combined analysis. The most informative approach to ratio analysis is one that combines cross-sectional and time-series analyses. A combined view permits assessment of the trend in the behavior of the ratio in relation to the trend for the industry. Figure 4.2 depicts this type of approach using Dayton Oil Company's average collection period in the years 1981–1984. Generally, lower values of this ratio, which reflects the average amount of time it takes the firm to collect bills, are preferred. A look at the figure quickly discloses that (1) Dayton Oil's effectiveness in collecting its receivables is poor in comparison to the industry and (2) there is a trend toward longer collection periods. Clearly Dayton Oil needs to shorten the collection period.

SOME WORDS OF CAUTION

Before discussing specific ratios, some cautions are in order. First, a single ratio does not generally provide sufficient information to judge the overall performance of the firm; only when a group of ratios is used can reasonable judgments be made. If an analyst is concerned only with specific aspects of a firm's financial position, one or two ratios may be sufficient. Second, an analyst should be sure that the dates of the financial statements being compared are the same. If not, the effects of seasonality may cause erroneous conclusions and decisions. Third, it is best to use audited financial statements for ratio analysis; if the statements have not been audited, there may be no reason to believe that the data contained in them reflect

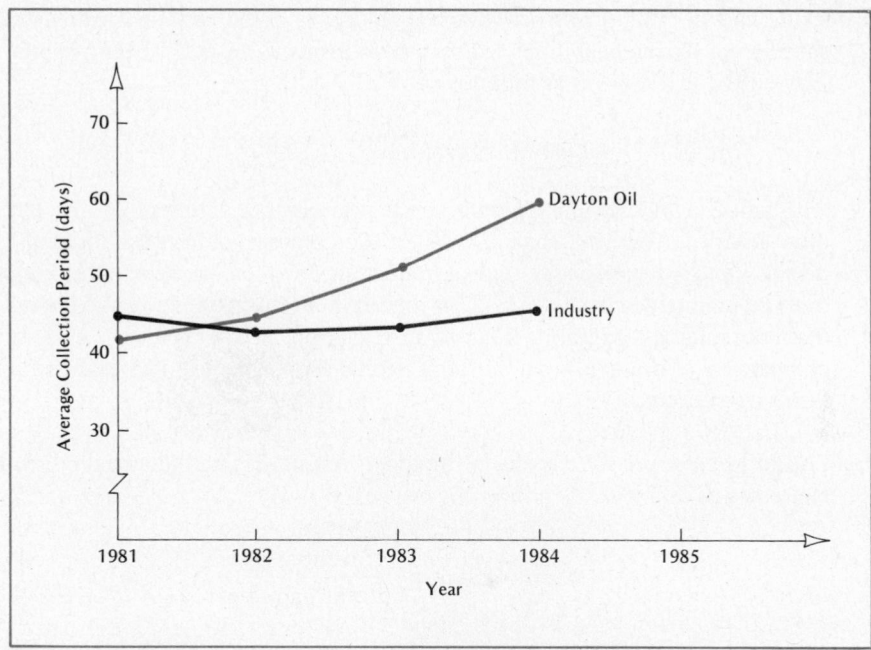

Figure 4.2   Combined cross-sectional and time-series view of Dayton Oil Company's average collection period, 1981–1984

the firm's true financial condition. The resulting ratios may be meaningless. Finally, it is important to make sure that the data being compared have been developed in the same way. The use of differing accounting treatments—especially relative to depreciation and inventory—can distort the results of ratio analysis, regardless of whether cross-sectional or time-series analysis is used.

Basic Financial Ratios

Financial ratios can be divided into four basic groups: liquidity ratios, activity ratios, debt ratios, and profitability ratios. As a rule, the necessary inputs to a good financial analysis include, at minimum, the income statement and the balance sheet. The important near-term elements are liquidity, activity, and profitability, since they provide the information critical to the short-run operation of the firm. And if the firm cannot survive in the short run, we need not be concerned with its longer-term prospects. Debt ratios are useful primarily when the analyst is sure the firm will successfully weather the short run.

MEASURES OF LIQUIDITY

The *liquidity* of a business firm is measured by its ability to satisfy its short-term obligations *as they come due.* Liquidity refers to the solvency of the firm's *overall* financial position. The three basic measures of liquidity are (1) net working capital, (2) the current ratio, and (3) the quick (acid-test) ratio.

Net working capital. The firm's net working capital, as noted earlier, is calculated by subtracting current liabilities from current assets. The net working capital for Dayton Oil in 1984 was as follows:

$$\text{Net working capital} = \$1,223,000 - \$620,000 = \$603,000$$

This figure is *not* useful for comparing the performance of different firms, but it is quite useful for internal control.[10] Often the contract under which a long-term debt is incurred specifically states a minimum level of net working capital that must be maintained by the firm. This requirement is intended to force the firm to maintain sufficient operating liquidity and helps protect the creditor. A time-series comparison of the firm's net working capital is often helpful in evaluating the firm's operations.

Current ratio. The *current ratio* is one of the most commonly cited financial ratios. It is expressed as follows:

$$\text{Current ratio} = \frac{\text{current assets}}{\text{current liabilities}}$$

The current ratio for Dayton Oil in 1984 is

$$\frac{\$1,223,000}{\$620,000} = 1.97$$

A current ratio of 2.0 is occasionally cited as acceptable, but an acceptable value depends on the industry in which a firm operates. For example, a current ratio of 1.0 would be considered acceptable for a utility but might be unacceptable for a manufacturing firm. Acceptability depends on the predictability of the firm's cash flows. The more predictable the cash flows, the lower the acceptable current ratio. The current ratio of 1.97 for Dayton Oil should be quite acceptable.

If the firm's current ratio is divided into 1.0 and the resulting quotient subtracted from 1.0, the difference multiplied by 100 represents the percentage by which the firm's current assets can shrink without making it impossible for the firm to cover its current liabilities. For example, a current ratio of 2.0 means that the firm can still cover its current liabilities even if its current assets shrink by 50 percent ([1.0 − (1.0 ÷ 2.0)] × 100).

A final point worthy of note is that whenever a firm's current ratio is 1.0, its net working capital is zero. If a firm has a current ratio of less than 1.0, it will have a negative net working capital. Net working capital is useful only in comparing the liquidity of the same firm over time and should not be used for comparing that of different firms; current ratio should be used instead.

---

[10] To make cross-sectional as well as better time-series comparisons, *net working capital as a percent of sales* can be calculated. For Dayton Oil in 1984 this ratio would be 19.6 percent ($603,000 ÷ $3,074,000). In general, the larger this value, the greater the firm's liquidity, and vice versa. Because of the relative nature of this measure, it is frequently used to make liquidity comparisons.

Quick (acid-test) ratio. The *quick (acid-test) ratio* is similar to the current ratio except for the fact that it excludes inventory from current assets. The basic assumption of the quick ratio is that inventory is generally the least liquid current asset and should therefore be excluded. The quick ratio is calculated as follows:[11]

$$\text{Quick ratio} = \frac{\text{current assets} - \text{inventory}}{\text{current liabilities}}$$

The quick ratio for Dayton Oil in 1984 is

$$\frac{\$1,223,000 - \$289,000}{\$620,000} = \frac{\$934,000}{\$620,000} = 1.51$$

A quick ratio of 1.0 or greater is occasionally recommended. Again, what is considered an acceptable value depends largely on the industry. This ratio provides a better measure of overall liquidity only when a firm's inventory cannot easily be converted into cash. If inventory is liquid, the current ratio is a preferred measure of overall liquidity.

MEASURES OF ACTIVITY

Activity ratios are used to measure the speed with which various accounts are converted into sales or cash. Measures of overall liquidity are generally inadequate because differences in the composition of a firm's current assets and liabilities can significantly affect the firm's "true" liquidity. For example, consider the current portion of the balance sheets for firms X and Y given in the following table:

Firm X

Cash	$ 0	Accounts payable	$ 0
Marketable securities	0	Notes payable	10,000
Accounts receivable	0	Accruals	0
Inventory	20,000		
Total current assets	$20,000	Total current liabilities	$10,000

Firm Y

Cash	$ 5,000	Accounts payable	$ 5,000
Marketable securities	5,000	Notes payable	3,000
Accounts receivable	5,000	Accruals	2,000
Inventory	5,000		
Total current assets	$20,000	Total current liabilities	$10,000

Although both firms appear to be equally liquid since their current ratios are both 2.0 ($20,000 ÷ $10,000), a closer look at the differences in the composition of

[11] Sometimes the quick ratio is defined as (cash + marketable securities + accounts receivable) ÷ current liabilities. If a firm were to show items other than cash, marketable securities, accounts receivable, and inventory as current assets, its quick ratio might vary, depending on the method of calculation.

A PICTORIAL ANALYSIS OF WESTINGHOUSE, 1978–1982

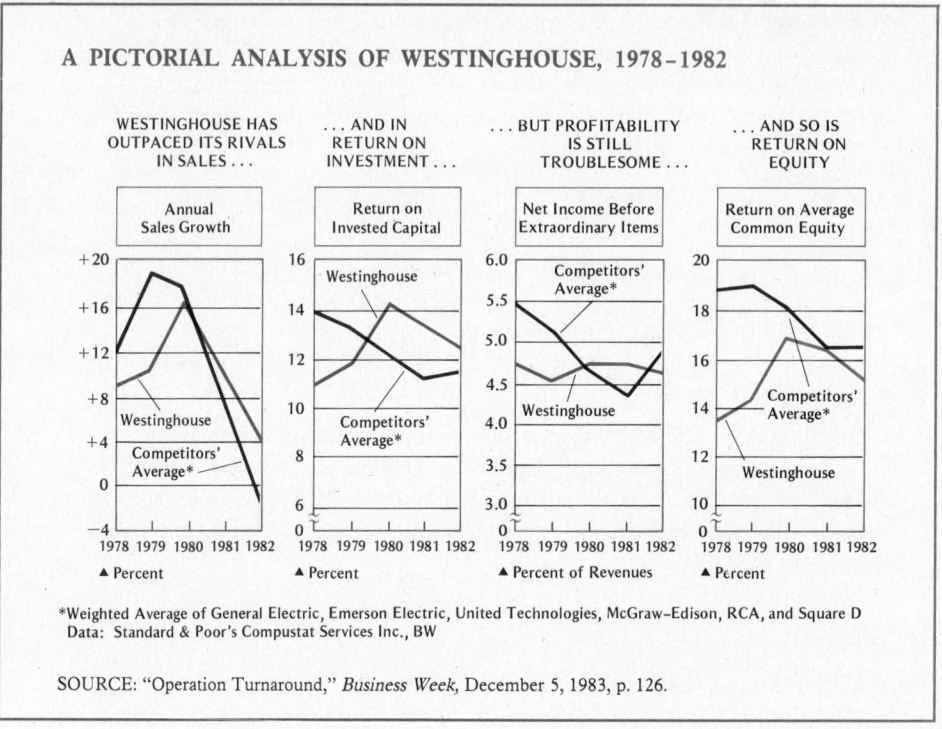

WESTINGHOUSE HAS OUTPACED ITS RIVALS IN SALES . . .

. . . AND IN RETURN ON INVESTMENT . . .

. . . BUT PROFITABILITY IS STILL TROUBLESOME . . .

. . . AND SO IS RETURN ON EQUITY

*Weighted Average of General Electric, Emerson Electric, United Technologies, McGraw–Edison, RCA, and Square D
Data: Standard & Poor's Compustat Services Inc., BW

SOURCE: "Operation Turnaround," *Business Week*, December 5, 1983, p. 126.

current assets and liabilities suggests that firm Y is more liquid than firm X. This results for two reasons: (1) Firm Y has more liquid assets in the form of cash and marketable securities than firm X, which has only a single and relatively illiquid asset in the form of inventory, and (2) firm Y's current liabilities are in general more flexible than the single current liability — notes payable — of firm X.

It is therefore important to look beyond measures of overall liquidity to assess the activity (or liquidity) of specific current accounts. A number of ratios are available for measuring the activity of the most important current accounts, which include inventory, accounts receivable, and accounts payable. The activity of fixed and total assets can also be assessed. The most common activity measures are discussed in the following pages. A basic simplifying assumption used in many of the calculations is that there are 360 days in the year and 30 days in each month.[12]

Inventory turnover. The activity, or liquidity, of a firm's inventory is commonly measured by its turnover. This is calculated as follows:

$$\text{Inventory turnover} = \frac{\text{cost of goods sold}}{\text{inventory}}$$

[12] Unless otherwise specified, a 360-day year consisting of twelve 30-day months is assumed throughout this text. This assumption allows some simplification of the calculations used to illustrate key concepts.

Applying this relationship to Dayton Oil in 1984 yields

$$\text{Inventory turnover} = \frac{\$2,088,000}{\$289,000} = 7.2$$

The resulting turnover is meaningful only when compared with that of other firms in the same industry or to the firm's past inventory turnover. An inventory turnover of 30.0 would not be unusual for a grocery store, whereas a common inventory turnover for an aircraft manufacturer would be 1.0. Differences in turnover rates result from the differing operating characteristics of various industries.

Many people believe that the higher the firm's inventory turnover, the more efficiently it has managed its inventory. This is true up to a point; beyond that point, as was illustrated earlier, a high turnover may signal problems. For example, one way to increase inventory turnover is to carry very small inventories. However, such a strategy could result in a large number of stockouts, which could damage future sales. For each industry, there is a range of inventory turnover that may be considered good. Values below this range may signal illiquid or inactive inventories; values above this range may indicate insufficient inventories and high stockouts.

Inventory turnover can easily be converted into an *average age of inventory* by dividing it into 360 — the number of days in a year. For Dayton Oil, the average age of inventory would be 50.0 days (360 ÷ 7.2). This value can also be viewed as the average number of days' sales in inventory.

Average collection period. The *average collection period,* or *average age of accounts receivable,* is useful in evaluating credit and collection policies.[13] It is found by dividing the average daily sales[14] into the accounts receivable balance:

$$\text{Average collection period} = \frac{\text{accounts receivable}}{\text{average sales per day}} = \frac{\text{accounts receivable}}{\dfrac{\text{annual sales}}{360}}$$

The average collection period for Dayton Oil in 1984 is

$$\frac{\$503,000}{\dfrac{\$3,074,000}{360}} = \frac{\$503,000}{\$8,539} = 58.9 \text{ days}$$

On the average it takes the firm 58.9 days to collect an account receivable.

The average collection period is meaningful only in relation to the firm's credit terms. If, for instance, Dayton Oil extends 30-day credit terms to customers, an average collection period of 58.9 days would indicate a poorly managed credit or collection department, or both. If it extended 60-day credit terms, the 58.9-day average collection period would be acceptable.

[13] A discussion of the evaluation and establishment of credit policies is presented in Chapter 17.

[14] The formula as presented assumes, for simplicity, that all sales are made on a credit basis. If such is not the case, average *credit* sales per day should be substituted for average sales per day.

Average payment period. The *average payment period,* or *average age of accounts payable,* is calculated in the same manner as the average collection period:

$$\text{Average payment period} = \frac{\text{accounts payable}}{\text{average purchases per day}} = \frac{\text{accounts payable}}{\dfrac{\text{annual purchases}}{360}}$$

The difficulty in calculating this ratio stems from the need to find annual purchases[15]—a value not available in published financial statements. Ordinarily, purchases are estimated as a given percentage of cost of goods sold. If we assume that Dayton Oil's purchases equaled 70 percent of its cost of goods sold in 1984, its average payment period is

$$\frac{\$382,000}{\dfrac{.70(\$2,088,000)}{360}} = \frac{\$382,000}{\$4,060} = 94.1 \text{ days}$$

This figure is meaningful only in relation to the average credit terms extended to the firm. If Dayton Oil's suppliers, on the average, have extended 30-day credit terms, an analyst would give it a low credit rating. If the firm has been generally extended 90-day credit terms, its credit would certainly be acceptable. Prospective lenders and suppliers of trade credit are especially interested in the average payment period, since it provides them with a sense of the bill-paying patterns of the firm.

Aging accounts. *Aging* is a technique for evaluating the composition of accounts receivable or accounts payable. It provides the analyst with information concerning the proportion of each type of account that has been outstanding for a specified period of time. By highlighting irregularities, it allows the analyst to pinpoint the cause of problems. Aging requires that the firm's accounts receivable and accounts payable be broken down into groups based on time of origin; this breakdown is typically made on a month-by-month basis, going back three or four months. Let us look at an example.

EXAMPLE   Assume that Dayton Oil extends 30-day credit terms to its customers. From its December 31, 1984, balance sheet, given in Table 4.2, it can be seen that the firm has $503,000 of accounts receivable on its books. An evaluation of the $503,000 of accounts receivable results in the following breakdown:

Days	Current	0–30	31–60	61–90	Over 90	
Month	December	November	October	September	August	Total
Accounts receivable	$151,000	$101,000	$166,000	$65,000	$20,000	$503,000
Percentage of total	30	20	33	13	4	100

[15] Technically, annual *credit* purchases—rather than annual purchases—should be used in calculating this ratio. For simplicity, this refinement is ignored here.

Since it is assumed that Dayton Oil gives its customers 30 days after the end of the month in which the sale is made to pay off their accounts, any December receivables still on the firm's books are considered current. November receivables are between zero and 30 days overdue, while October receivables still unpaid are 31 to 60 days overdue, and so on.

The table shows that 30 percent of the firm's receivables are current, 20 percent are one month late, 33 percent are two months late, 13 percent are three months late, and 4 percent are more than three months late.[16] While payment seems generally slow, a noticeable irregularity in these data is the high percentage represented by October receivables. This indicates that some problem may have occurred in October. Investigation may find that the problem can be attributed to the hiring of a new credit manager or the acceptance of a new account that has made a large credit purchase it has not yet paid for. When accounts are aged and such a discrepancy is found, the analyst should determine its cause. ■

The approach illustrated in this example can be applied in aging accounts payable, which would probably be of most interest to current and prospective creditors. Any discrepancies in the pattern of outstanding payables should be investigated. The benefit of aging lies in its ability to point up specific periods of apparent slowness in the collection or payment of accounts.

Fixed asset turnover. The *fixed asset turnover* is used to measure the efficiency with which the firm has been using its *fixed,* or earning, assets to generate sales. It is calculated by dividing the firm's sales by its net fixed assets:

$$\text{Fixed asset turnover} = \frac{\text{sales}}{\text{net fixed assets}}$$

The fixed asset turnover for Dayton Oil in 1984 is

$$\frac{\$3,074,000}{\$2,374,000} = 1.29$$

The company turns over its net fixed assets 1.29 times a year. Generally, higher fixed asset turnovers are preferred. Of course, the calculated value is meaningful only when viewed in light of the firm's past performance or an industry average.

One caution with respect to use of this ratio and the total asset turnover described in the following section stems from the fact that the calculations embody

---

[16] The average collection period can be estimated using the given data. By weighting the average age — not days overdue — by the percentage of accounts with the given age and summing the weighted values, the average collection period can be approximated. For example, the current (December) accounts would on average have an age of 15 days, the November accounts outstanding would have an average age of 45 days, and so on. Applying the given percentages to Dayton Oil, the average collection period is calculated as follows:

$$= .30(15 \text{ days}) + .20(45 \text{ days}) + .33(75 \text{ days}) + .13(105 \text{ days}) + .04(135 \text{ days})$$
$$= 4.50 + 9.00 + 24.75 + 13.65 + 5.40 = \underline{57.3 \text{ days}}$$

This approximation does not exactly agree with the 58.9-day average collection period calculated using the ratio presented earlier. This approximation can be applied in a similar fashion to an aging schedule of accounts payable.

the historical costs of fixed assets. Comparing these turnovers to those of firms that have significantly newer or older fixed assets can therefore sometimes be misleading. Because of inflation and the historically based net book values of assets, firms with newer assets will tend to have lower turnovers than those with older assets having lower book values.[17] The differences in these turnovers could result from more costly assets rather than differing operating efficiencies. Caution when using these ratios for cross-sectional comparisons is therefore recommended.

Total asset turnover. The *total asset turnover* indicates the efficiency with which the firm is able to use all its assets to generate sales dollars. Generally, the higher a firm's total asset turnover, the more efficiently its assets have been used. The total asset turnover is probably of greatest interest to management, since it indicates whether the firm's operations have been financially efficient. Other parties, such as creditors and prospective and present owners, will also be interested in this measure. The firm's total asset turnover is calculated as follows:

$$\text{Total asset turnover} = \frac{\text{sales}}{\text{total assets}}$$

The value of Dayton Oil's total asset turnover in 1984 is

$$\frac{\$3,074,000}{\$3,597,000} = 0.85 \qquad > 1$$

The company therefore turns its assets over .85 times a year. This value is meaningful only in light of the firm's past performance or an industry average.

 ## MEASURES OF DEBT

The debt position of the firm indicates the amount of other people's money that is being used in attempting to generate profits. Typically, the financial analyst is most concerned with long-term debts, since these commit the firm to pay interest over the long run and eventually repay the funds borrowed. Since the claims of creditors must be satisfied prior to the distribution of earnings to shareholders,[18] present and prospective shareholders pay close attention to degree of indebtedness and ability to repay debts. Lenders are also concerned about the firm's degree of indebtedness and ability to service debts, since the more indebted the firm, the higher the probability that the firm will be unable to satisfy the claims of all its

---

[17] This problem would not exist if firms were required to use current-cost accounting. Financial Accounting Standards Board (FASB) Statement No. 33, *Financial Reporting and Changing Prices*, issued in late 1979, prescribes procedures for inflation accounting. The standard currently requires only large publicly held corporations to include such reporting as *supplementary information* in their stockholders' reports. For a good discussion of FASB Statement No. 33, see A. N. Mosich and E. John Larsen, *"Intermediate Accounting,"* 5th ed. (New York: McGraw-Hill, 1982), pp. 1052–1070.

[18] The law requires that creditors' claims be satisfied prior to those of the firm's owners. This makes sense, since the creditor is providing a service to the owners and should not be expected to bear the risks of ownership.

creditors. Management obviously must be concerned with indebtedness in recognition of the attention paid to it by other parties and in the interest of keeping the firm solvent.

In general, the more debt a firm uses, the greater its *financial leverage,* which is a term used to describe the magnification of risk and return introduced through the use of fixed-cost financing such as debt and preferred stock. The more debt or financial leverage a firm uses, the greater will be its risk and return.

EXAMPLE   Joe Mendoza and Aaron Parsons are in the process of incorporating a new business venture they have formed. After a great deal of analysis, they have determined that an initial investment of $50,000 — $20,000 in current assets and $30,000 in fixed assets — is necessary. These funds can be obtained in either of two ways. The first is the no-debt plan, under which they would together invest the full $50,000 without borrowing. The other alternative, the debt plan, involves making a combined investment of $25,000 and borrowing the balance of $25,000 at 12 percent annual interest. Regardless of which alternative they choose, Joe and Aaron expect sales to average $30,000, costs and operating expenses to average $18,000, and earnings to be taxed at a 40 percent rate. The balance sheets and income statements associated with the no-debt and debt plans are summarized in Table 4.7.

The no-debt plan results in after-tax profits of $7,200, which represent a 14.4 percent rate of return on Joe and Aaron's $50,000 investment; the debt plan results in $5,400 of after-tax profits, which represent a 21.6 percent rate of return on their combined investment of $25,000. It therefore appears that the debt plan provides Joe and Aaron with a higher rate of return, but the risk of this plan is also greater, since the annual $3,000 of interest must be met prior to earnings' being available to them. ■

From the example, it should be clear that *with increased debt comes higher potential return as well as greater risk;* therefore, the greater the financial leverage,

Table 4.7   Financial Statements Associated with Joe and Aaron's Alternatives

Balance sheets	No-debt plan		Debt plan
Current assets	$20,000		$20,000
Fixed assets	30,000		30,000
Total Assets	$50,000		$50,000
Debt (12% interest)	$ 0		$25,000
(1) Equity	50,000		25,000
Total liabilities and equity	$50,000		$50,000
Income statements			
Sales	$30,000		$30,000
Less: Costs and operating expenses	18,000		18,000
Operating Profits	$12,000		$12,000
Less: Interest expense	0	.12($25,000) =	3,000
Net profit before taxes	$12,000		$ 9,000
Less: Taxes (rate = 40%)	4,800		3,600
(2) Net profit after taxes	$ 7,200		$ 5,400
Return on equity [(2) ÷ (1)]	$\dfrac{\$7{,}200}{\$50{,}000} = 14.4\%$		$\dfrac{\$5{,}400}{\$25{,}000} = 21.6\%$

the greater the potential return and risk, and vice versa. A detailed discussion of the impact of debt on the firm's risk, return, and value is included in Chapter 13. Here emphasis is given to the use of ratios to assess a firm's debt position externally.

Measures of the degree of indebtedness. The *degree of indebtedness* is typically measured using only balance sheet data. Two of the most commonly used measures are the debt ratio and the debt-equity ratio.

Debt ratio. The *debt ratio* measures the proportion of total assets provided by the firm's creditors. The higher this ratio, the greater the amount of other people's money being used in an attempt to generate profits. The ratio is calculated as follows:

$$\text{Debt ratio} = \frac{\text{total liabilities}}{\text{total assets}}$$

The debt ratio for Dayton Oil in 1984 is

$$\frac{\$1,643,000}{\$3,597,000} = .457 = 45.7\%$$

This indicates that the company has financed 45.7 percent of its assets with debt. The higher this ratio, the more financial leverage a firm has.

The following ratio differs from the debt ratio in that it focuses on long-term debts. Short-term debts, or current liabilities, are excluded, since most of them are spontaneous (that is, they are the natural result of doing business) and do not commit the firm to the payment of fixed charges over a long period of time.

Debt-equity ratio. The *debt-equity ratio* indicates the relationship between the *long-term* funds provided by creditors and those provided by the firm's owners. It is commonly used to measure the degree of financial leverage of the firm and is defined as follows:

$$\text{Debt-equity ratio} = \frac{\text{long-term debt}}{\text{stockholders' equity}}$$

The debt-equity ratio for Dayton Oil in 1984 is

$$\frac{\$1,023,000}{\$1,954,000} = .524 = 52.4\%$$

The firm's long-term debts therefore are only 52.4 percent as large as stockholders' equity. This figure is meaningful only in light of the firm's line of business. Firms with large amounts of fixed assets, stable cash flows, or both typically have high debt-equity ratios, while less capital-intensive firms, firms with volatile cash flows, or both tend to have lower debt-equity ratios. An industry average is a good figure to use when comparing a debt-equity ratio.

Measures of the ability to service debts. The ability to *service* debts refers to how readily a firm can meet the fixed contractual payments typically required on a scheduled basis over the life of a debt.[19] With debts come scheduled fixed-payment obligations for interest and principal (or sinking-fund) payments. Lease payments as well as preferred stock dividend payments also represent scheduled payment obligations. The firm's ability to meet certain fixed charges is measured using *coverage ratios.* The lower the firm's coverage ratios, the more risky the firm is considered to be. "Riskiness" here refers to the firm's ability to meet fixed obligations. If a firm is unable to meet these obligations, it will be in default, and its creditors may seek immediate repayment. In most instances, this would force a firm into bankruptcy. Two ratios of coverage — times interest earned ratio and the fixed-payment coverage ratio — are discussed below.[20] Actually, only the first of these ratios is concerned solely with debt; the second one considers other fixed-payment obligations in addition to debt service.

Times interest earned ratio. The *times interest earned ratio* is often called the firm's *total interest coverage ratio.* It measures ability to pay contractual interest payments. The higher the value of this ratio, the better able the firm is to fulfill its interest obligations. Times interest earned is calculated as follows:

$$\text{Times interest earned} = \frac{\text{earnings before interest and taxes}}{\text{interest}}$$

Applying this ratio to Dayton Oil yields the following 1984 value:

$$\text{Times interest earned} = \frac{\$418,000}{\$93,000} = 4.5$$

The value of earnings before interest and taxes is the same as the figure for operating profits shown in the income statements given in Table 4.1. The times interest earned ratio for Dayton Oil seems acceptable; as a rule, a value of at least 3.0 — and preferably closer to 5.0 — is suggested. If the firm's earnings before interest and taxes were to shrink by 78 percent [(4.5 − 1.0) ÷ 4.5], the firm would still be able to pay the $93,000 in interest it owes. Thus it has a good margin of safety. Creditors would probably consider extending a loan to Dayton Oil, since it appears to be able to cover its interest charges.

---

[19] The term *service* is used throughout this text to refer to the payment of interest and repayment of principal associated with a firm's debt obligations. When a firm services its debts, it pays, or fulfills, these obligations.

[20] Coverage ratios use data based on the application of accrual concepts (discussed in Chapter 1) to measure what in a strict sense should be measured with cash flows. This occurs since debts are serviced using cash flows, not the accounting values shown on the firm's financial statements. But because it is difficult to determine cash flows available for debt service from the firm's financial statements, the calculation of coverage ratios as presented here is quite common due to the ready availability of financial statement data.

Fixed-payment coverage ratio. The *fixed-payment coverage ratio* includes all fixed-payment obligations. Principal payments on debt, scheduled lease payments, and preferred stock dividends[21] are commonly included in this ratio. Since financial (long-term) lease payments are written off in a fashion similar to owned assets under current accounting standards, they do not require itemization; the principal payments and preferred stock dividends that must be paid from after-tax cash flows must be adjusted for taxes. The formula for the fixed-payment coverage ratio is as follows:[22]

$$\text{Fixed-payment coverage ratio} = \frac{\text{earnings before interest and taxes}}{\text{interest} + [(\text{principal payments} + \text{preferred stock dividends}) \times [1/(1 - t)]]}$$

where t is the corporate tax rate applicable to the firm's income. The term $1/(1 - t)$ is included to adjust the after-tax principal and preferred stock dividend payments back to a before-tax equivalent consistent with the before-tax value in the numerator. Applying the formula to Dayton Oil's 1984 data yields

$$\text{Fixed-payment coverage ratio}$$
$$= \frac{\$418,000}{\$93,000 + [(\$71,000 + \$10,000)[1/(1 - .29)]]}$$
$$= \frac{\$418,000}{\$207,000} = 2.0$$

The firm appears able to meet its fixed-payment obligations safely.

Like interest coverage, the fixed-payment coverage ratio measures risk. The lower the ratio, the more risky the firm is from the lenders' viewpoint. This risk results from the fact that if the firm were unable to meet scheduled fixed payments, it could be driven into bankruptcy. An examination of this ratio allows creditors to determine whether the firm is capable of handling additional debt.

The fixed-payment coverage ratio is of interest not only to creditors but also to present and prospective preferred and common stockholders. It measures the ability of the firm to cover all fixed financial payments. The higher it is, the safer the interests of creditors and preferred stockholders in the firm; also, the higher the firm's fixed-payment coverage ratio, the higher the levels of profit that can be expected by common stockholders.

[21] Although preferred stock dividends, which are stated at the time of issue, can be "passed" (not paid) at the option of the firm's directors, it is generally believed that the payment of such dividends is necessary. This text therefore treats the preferred stock dividend as if it were a contractual obligation not only to pay a fixed amount but also to make payments as scheduled.

[22] In the event a firm has operating (short-term) leases on its books, the fixed-payment coverage ratio would be

$$\frac{\text{earnings before oper. lease paymnts., int., and taxes}}{\text{oper. lease paymnts.} + \text{int.} + [(\text{prin. paymnts.} + \text{pref. stock div.}) \times [1/(1 - t)]]}$$

To simplify the text discussion, the presence of any operating leases is ignored.

MEASURES OF PROFITABILITY

There are many measures of profitability. Each relates the returns of the firm to its sales, assets, or equity. As a group, these measures allow the analyst to evaluate the firm's earnings with respect to a given level of sales, a certain level of assets, or the owners' investment. Without profits, a firm could not attract outside capital; moreover, present owners and creditors would become concerned about the company's future and attempt to recover their funds. Owners, creditors, and management pay close attention to boosting profits due to the great importance placed on earnings in the marketplace.

Common-size income statements. A popular approach for evaluating profitability in relation to sales is the *common-size income statement.*[23] By expressing each item on the income statement as a percentage of sales, the relationship between sales and specific revenues and expenses can be evaluated. Common-size income statements are especially useful in comparing performance for one year with that for another year. Common-size income statements for 1983 and 1984 for Dayton Oil are presented in Table 4.8. An evaluation of these statements reveals that the firm's cost of goods sold increased from 66.7 percent of sales in 1983 to 67.9 percent in 1984, resulting in a decrease in the gross profit margin from 33.3 to 32.1 percent. However, thanks to a decrease in operating expenses from 21.5 percent in 1983 to 18.5 percent in 1984, the firm's net profit margin rose from 5.8 percent of sales in 1983 to 7.5 percent in 1984. The decrease in expenses in 1984 more than compensated for the increase in the cost of goods sold. A decrease in the firm's 1984 interest expense (3.0 percent of sales as opposed to 3.5 percent in 1983) added to the increase in 1984 profits.

Table 4.8 Dayton Oil Company Common-Size Income Statements

	For the years ended December 31	
	1984	1983
Sales	100.0%	100.0%
Less: Cost of goods sold	67.9	66.7
(a) Gross profit margin	32.1%	33.3%
Less: Operating expenses		
Selling expense	3.3%	4.2%
General and administrative expenses	7.4	8.6
Depreciation expense	7.8	8.7
Total operating expense	18.5%	21.5%
(b) Operating profit margin	13.6%	11.8%
Less: Interest expense	3.0	3.5
Net profits before taxes	10.6%	8.3%
Less: Taxes	3.1	2.5
(c) Net profit margin	7.5%	5.8%

[23] This statement is sometimes called a "percent income statement." The same treatment is often applied to the firm's balance sheet to make it easier to evaluate changes in the asset and financial structures of the firm.

Three commonly cited ratios of profitability can be read directly from the common-size income statement: (a) the gross profit margin, (b) the operating profit margin, and (c) the net profit margin.

Gross profit margin. The *gross profit margin* indicates the percentage of each sales dollar remaining after the firm has paid for its goods. The higher the gross profit margin the better, and the lower the relative cost of merchandise sold. Of course, the opposite case is also true, as the Dayton Oil example shows. The gross profit margin is calculated as follows:

$$\text{Gross profit margin} = \frac{\text{sales} - \text{cost of goods sold}}{\text{sales}} = \frac{\text{gross profit}}{\text{sales}}$$

The value for Dayton Oil's gross profit margin for 1984 is

$$\frac{\$3,074,000 - \$2,088,00}{\$3,074,000} = \frac{\$986,000}{\$3,074,000} = 32.1\%$$

This value is shown on line (a) of the common-size income statement in Table 4.8.

Operating profit margin. The *operating profit margin* represents what are often called the *pure profits* earned on each sales dollar. Operating profits are pure in the sense that they ignore any financial or government charges (interest or taxes) and measure only the profits earned on operations. A high operating profit margin is preferred. The operating profit margin is calculated as follows:

$$\text{Operating profit margin} = \frac{\text{operating profit}}{\text{sales}}$$

The value for Dayton Oil's operating profit margin for 1984 is

$$\frac{\$418,000}{\$3,074,000} = 13.6\%$$

This value is shown on line (b) of the common-size income statement in Table 4.8.

Net profit margin. The *net profit margin* measures the percentage of each sales dollar remaining after all expenses, including taxes, have been deducted. The higher the firm's net profit margin, the better. The net profit margin is a commonly cited measure of the corporation's success with respect to earnings on sales. "Good" net profit margins differ considerably across industries. A net profit margin of 1 percent or less would not be unusual for a grocery store, while a net profit margin of 10 percent would be low for a jewelry store. The net profit margin is calculated as follows:

$$\text{Net profit margin} = \frac{\text{net profits after taxes}}{\text{sales}}$$

The value of Dayton Oil's net profit margin for 1984 is

$$\frac{\$231,000}{\$3,074,000} = 7.5\%$$

This value is shown on line (c) of the common-size income statement in Table 4.8.

Return on investment (*ROI*). The *return on investment (ROI),* which is often called the firm's *return on total assets,* measures the overall effectiveness of management in generating profits with its available assets. The higher the firm's return on investment, the better. The return on investment is calculated as follows:

$$\text{Return on investment} = \frac{\text{net profits after taxes}}{\text{total assets}}$$

The value of the Dayton Oil's return on investment in 1984 is

$$\frac{\$231,000}{\$3,597,000} = 6.4\%$$

This value appears to be quite acceptable, but only when it is compared to industry averages can conclusions be drawn. This value could have been derived using the DuPont system of analysis, which is described in a subsequent section.

Return on equity (*ROE*). The *return on equity (ROE)* measures the return earned on the owners' (both preferred and common stockholders') investment.[24] Generally, the higher this return, the better off the owners. Return on equity is calculated as follows:

$$\text{Return on equity} = \frac{\text{net profits after taxes}}{\text{stockholders' equity}}$$

The value of this ratio for Dayton Oil in 1984 is

$$\frac{\$231,000}{\$1,954,000} = 11.8\%$$

This value, which seems to be quite good, could also have been derived using the DuPont system of analysis.

Earnings per share (*eps*). The firm's *earnings per share (eps)* are generally of interest to present or prospective shareholders and management. The earnings per share

---

[24] This ratio includes preferred dividends in the profit figure and preferred stock in the equity value, but because the amount of preferred stock and its impact on a firm are generally quite small, or nonexistent, this formula is a reasonably good approximation of the true owners' — that is, the common stockholders' — return.

represent the number of dollars earned on behalf of each outstanding share of common stock. They are closely watched by the investing public and are considered an important indicator of corporate success. Earnings per share are calculated as follows:

$$\text{Earnings per share} = \frac{\text{earnings available for common stockholders}}{\text{number of shares of common stock outstanding}}$$

The value of Dayton Oil's earnings per share in 1984 is

$$\frac{\$221,000}{76,262} = \$2.90$$

This figure represents the dollar amount *earned* on behalf of each share outstanding. It does not represent the amount of earnings actually distributed to shareholders.

Price/earnings (P/E) ratio. Though not a true measure of profitability, the *price/earnings (P/E) ratio* is commonly used to assess the owners' appraisal of the value of the firm's earnings.[25] The P/E ratio represents the amount investors are willing to pay for each dollar of the firm's earnings. The level of the price/earnings ratio indicates the degree of confidence (or certainty) that investors have in the firm's future performance. The higher the P/E ratio, the greater investor confidence in the firm's future. The P/E ratio is calculated as follows:

$$\text{Price/earnings (P/E) ratio} = \frac{\text{market price per share of common stock}}{\text{earnings per share}}$$

If Dayton Oil's common stock at the end of 1984 was selling at $32\frac{1}{4}$, the P/E ratio at year-end 1984 is

$$\frac{\$32.25}{\$2.90} = 11.1$$

This figure indicates that investors were paying $11.10 for each $1.00 of earnings. Like most ratios, this multiple is more meaningful when compared to an industry average P/E ratio.

DuPont system of analysis. The *DuPont system of analysis* has for many years been used by financial managers as a structure for dissecting the firm's financial statements to assess its financial condition. The DuPont system merges the income statement and balance sheet into either of two summary measures of profitability, return on investment *(ROI)* and return on equity *(ROE)*. Figure 4.3 depicts the basic DuPont system with Dayton Oil's 1984 monetary and ratio values. The upper portion

[25] The use of the price/earnings ratio to estimate the value of the firm is included as part of the discussion of popular approaches to valuation in Chapter 8.

A GLIMPSE INTO PRIVATE FIRMS' FINANCES

Big company chiefs don't have a monopoly on million-dollar salaries. A number of small-business owners take $1 million or more out of their companies annually. Of about 500 private companies analyzed by business-acquisition specialists at Geneva Corp., more than 20 paid their owners seven-figure compensation.

Rather pedestrian kinds of businesses pay some impressive salaries, says Richard Rodnick, chairman of Geneva. The highest-paid owner that Geneva knows of gets $1.8 million a year, excluding retirement benefits, from a company that imprints messages on advertising specialties. Another million-a-year owner operates a metal-cutting business.

Geneva, based in Santa Ana, Calif., is privy to sensitive financial information because it can snoop through the books of private companies in its role as business broker and company-valuation specialist. It recently completed a computer analysis of financial information on 500 clients with revenues of $500,000 to $50 million a year.

Geneva analyzed the companies by age, geography and line of business. Owners of service businesses that were more than 16 years old and in the Eastern part of the country had the highest salaries in the group. The lowest paid were owners of wholesale or distribution companies 11 to 15 years old and in the Southwest.

Private companies tend to minimize profits to avoid income taxes. "It is almost impossible to buy a private company without recasting because the owner is understating profits," says Mr. Rodnick.

When Geneva recalculates a privately owned company's income statement and balance sheet, he says, "we treat it as if it were a profit center for a large corporation rather than the source of support for an owner's life style." The idea is to depict the company's earning power more accurately.

Financial statements are recast as if the company were operated by professional managers as a subsidiary of a big concern. Expenses for such things as the owner's salary and perks — expensive cars, homes and frequent first-class travel — are added back to profits and the expense of professional managers is deducted. Inventories usually have to be increased because they are often understated to minimize earnings.

Recasting more than doubled the average earnings of the nearly 500 companies Geneva analyzed. "The book figures," Mr. Rodnick says, "were about 43% of what we feel are their real profits."

Grouping the companies by age disclosed that those from one to five years old had higher average revenues — $3.7 million — than those between six and 10 years old — $3.3 million. "This might be due to burnout," Mr. Rodnick says, speculating that after five years of all-out effort to build a company, an owner slacks off, and that that accounts for the sales decline.

SOURCE: Sanford L. Jacobs, "Study Provides Rare Glimpse into Private Firms' Finances," *The Wall Street Journal*, June 11, 1984, p. 1.

of the chart summarizes the income statement – oriented ratios; the lower portion summarizes balance sheet – oriented ratios.

The DuPont system first brings together the *net profit margin,* which measures the firm's profitability on sales, with its *total asset turnover,* which indicates how efficiently the firm has used its assets to generate sales. The product of these two

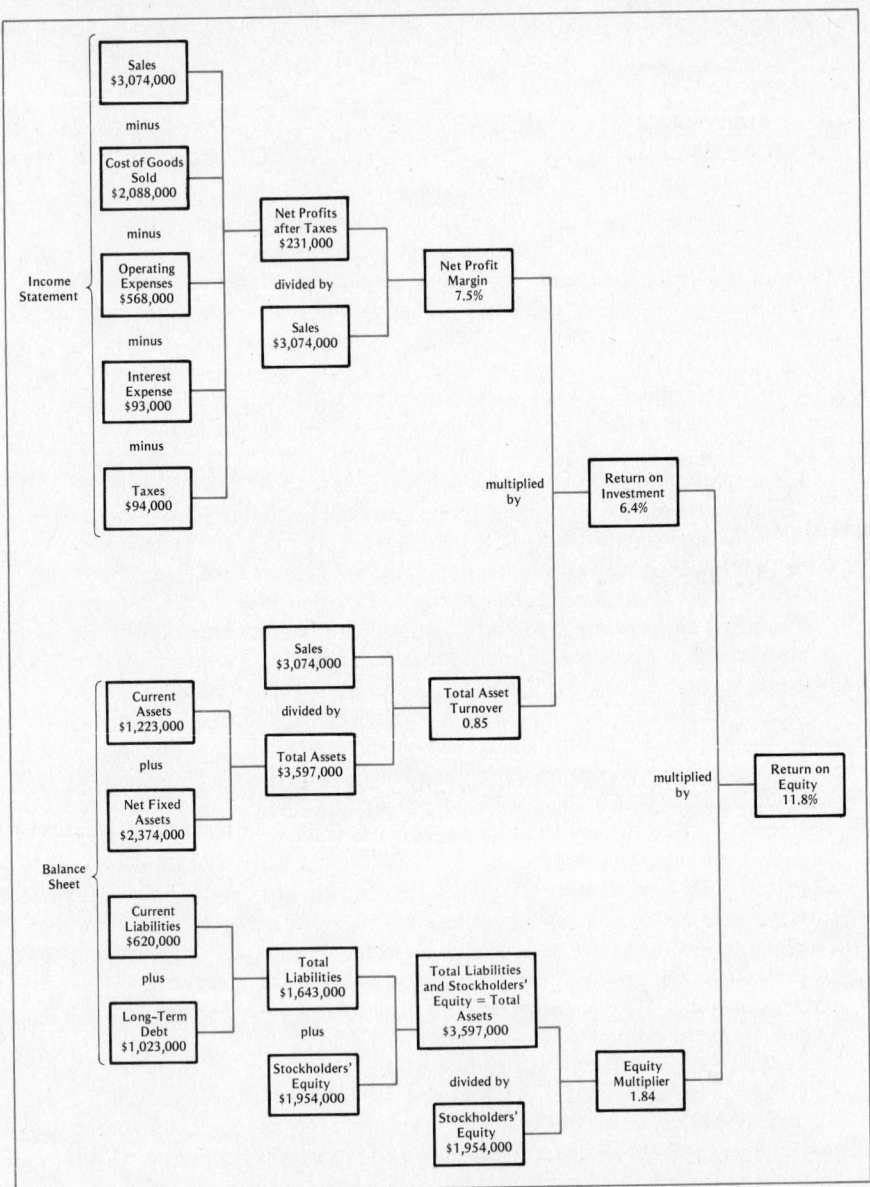

Figure 4.3   The DuPont system of analysis with application to Dayton Oil (1984)

ratios results in the *return on investment (ROI):*

$$ROI = \text{net profit margin} \times \text{total asset turnover}$$

Substituting the appropriate formulas into the equation and simplifying results in the formula given earlier,

$$ROI = \frac{\text{net profits after taxes}}{\text{sales}} \times \frac{\text{sales}}{\text{total assets}} = \frac{\text{net profits after taxes}}{\text{total assets}}$$

If the 1984 values of the net profit margin and total asset turnover of the Dayton Oil Company, calculated earlier, are substituted into the *DuPont formula,* the result is

$$ROI = 7.5\% \times 0.85 = 6.4\%$$

This result is what is expected. The DuPont formula allows the firm to break down its return into a profit-on-sales and an efficiency-of-asset-use component. Typically, a firm with a low net profit margin has a high total asset turnover, which results in a reasonably good return on investment. Often, the opposite situation exists. The relationship between the two components of the DuPont formula will depend largely on the industry in which the firm operates.

The second step in this system ties together the *return on investment (ROI)* and the degree of financial leverage as measured using the *equity multiplier,* which is the ratio of total assets to stockholders' equity,[26] to find the return earned on behalf of the firm's owners — the *return on equity (ROE):*

$$ROE = ROI \times \text{equity multiplier}$$

Substituting the appropriate formulas into the equation and simplifying results in the formula given earlier,

$$ROE = \frac{\text{net profits after taxes}}{\text{total assets}} \times \frac{\text{total assets}}{\text{stockholders' equity}} = \frac{\text{net profits after taxes}}{\text{stockholders' equity}}$$

Use of the equity multiplier to convert the *ROI* to the *ROE* reflects the impact of leverage (use of debt) on owners' return. Substituting the values for the *ROI* of 6.4% calculated earlier and the equity multiplier of 1.84 ($3,597,000 total assets ÷ $1,954,000 stockholders' equity) into the *modified DuPont formula* yields

$$ROE = 6.4\% \times 1.84 = 11.8\%$$

The 11.8 percent *ROE* calculated using the modified DuPont formula is the same as that calculated directly. The real strength of this approach is that it allows the firm to break its return on equity into a profit-on-sales component (net profit margin), an efficiency-of-asset-use component (total asset turnover), and a use-of-leverage component (equity multiplier). The total return to the owners can therefore be analyzed in light of these important dimensions.

---

[26] The equity multiplier is equivalent to $\dfrac{1}{1 - \text{debt ratio}}$ and represents 1 divided by the percentage of total financing raised with equity. For computational convenience, the equity multiplier is utilized here rather than the seemingly more descriptive debt ratio.

Table 4.9   Summary of Dayton Oil Company Ratios (1982–1984, including 1984 industry averages)

Ratio	Formula	Year 1982[a]	Year 1983[b]	Year 1984[b]	Industry average 1984[c]	Evaluation[d] Cross-sectional 1984	Evaluation[d] Time-series 1982–1984	Evaluation[d] Overall
Liquidity								
Net working capital	current assets − current liabilities	$583,000	$521,000	$603,000	$427,000	good	good	good
Current ratio	$\dfrac{\text{current assets}}{\text{current liabilities}}$	2.04	2.08	1.97	2.05	OK	OK	OK
Quick (acid-test) ratio	$\dfrac{\text{current assets} - \text{inventory}}{\text{current liabilities}}$	1.32	1.46	1.51	1.43	OK	good	good
Activity								
Inventory turnover	$\dfrac{\text{cost of goods sold}}{\text{inventory}}$	5.1	5.7	7.2	6.6	good	good	good
Average collection period	$\dfrac{\text{accounts receivable}}{\text{average sales per day}}$	46.9 days	51.2 days	58.9 days	44.3 days	poor	poor	poor
Average payment period	$\dfrac{\text{accounts payable}}{\text{average purchases per day}}$	75.8 days	81.2 days	94.1 days	66.5 days	poor	poor	poor
Fixed asset turnover	$\dfrac{\text{sales}}{\text{net fixed assets}}$	1.50	1.13	1.29	1.35	OK	OK	OK
Total asset turnover	$\dfrac{\text{sales}}{\text{total assets}}$	0.94	0.79	0.85	0.75	OK	OK	OK

Debt

Degree of indebtedness								
Debt ratio	$\dfrac{\text{total liabilities}}{\text{total assets}}$	36.8%	44.3%	45.7%	40.0%	OK	OK	OK
Debt-equity ratio	$\dfrac{\text{long-term debt}}{\text{stockholders' equity}}$	44.2%	53.1%	52.4%	50.0%	OK	OK	OK
Ability to service debts								
Times interest earned ratio	$\dfrac{\text{earnings before interest and taxes}}{\text{interest}}$	5.6	3.3	4.5	4.3	good	OK	OK
Fixed-payment coverage ratio	$\dfrac{\text{earnings before interest and taxes}}{\text{int.} + [(\text{prin.} + \text{pref. div}) \times [1/(1 - t)]]}$	2.7	1.5	2.0	1.5	good	OK	good

Profitability

Gross profit margin	$\dfrac{\text{gross profit}}{\text{sales}}$	31.4%	33.3%	32.1%	30.0%	OK	OK	OK
Operating profit margin	$\dfrac{\text{operating profit}}{\text{sales}}$	14.6%	11.8%	13.6%	11.0%	good	OK	good
Net profit margin	$\dfrac{\text{net profits after taxes}}{\text{sales}}$	8.8%	5.8%	7.5%	6.4%	good	OK	good
Return on investment (ROI)	$\dfrac{\text{net profits after taxes}}{\text{total assets}}$	8.3%	4.5%	6.4%	4.8%	good	OK	good
Return on equity (ROE)	$\dfrac{\text{net profits after taxes}}{\text{stockholders' equity}}$	13.1%	8.1%	11.8%	8.0%	good	OK	good
Earnings per share (eps)	$\dfrac{\text{earnings available for common stockholders}}{\text{number of shares of common stock outstanding}}$	$3.26	$1.81	$2.90	$2.26	good	OK	good
Price/earnings (P/E) ratio	$\dfrac{\text{market price per share of common stock}}{\text{earnings per share}}$	10.5	10.0	11.1	12.5	OK	OK	OK

a Calculated from data not included in the chapter.
b Calculated using the financial statements presented in Tables 4.1 and 4.2.
c Obtained from sources not included in this chapter.
d Represent subjective assessments based on data provided.

A Complete Ratio Analysis of Dayton Oil Company

As indicated earlier in the chapter, a single ratio is not adequate for assessing all aspects of the firm's financial condition. The 1984 ratio values calculated in the preceding section and the ratio values calculated for 1982 and 1983 for Dayton Oil, along with the industry average ratios for 1984, are summarized in Table 4.9 (pages 136 and 137). The table shows the formula used to calculate each ratio. Using these data, we can discuss the four key aspects of Dayton's performance — (1) liquidity, (2) activity, (3) debt, and (4) profitability — on a cross-sectional and a time-series basis.[27]

LIQUIDITY

The overall liquidity of the firm seems to exhibit a reasonably stable trend and has been maintained at a level that is reasonably consistent with the industry average in 1984. The firm's liquidity seems to be good.

ACTIVITY

Dayton Oil's inventory appears to be in good shape. Its inventory management seems to have improved, and in 1984 it performed at a level above that of the industry. The firm may be experiencing some problems with accounts receivable. The average collection period seems to have crept up to a level above that of the industry. The firm appears to be slow in paying its bills; Dayton is paying nearly 30 days slower than the average firm in the industry. Payment procedures should be examined to make sure that the company's credit standing is not adversely affected. While overall liquidity appears to be good, some attention should be given to the management of accounts receivable and payable. The fixed asset turnover and total asset turnover reflect sizable declines in the efficiency of fixed and total asset utilization between 1982 and 1983. Although in 1984 the total asset turnover rose to a level considerably above the industry average, it appears that the pre-1983 level of efficiency has not yet been achieved.

DEBT

The firm's indebtedness seems to have increased over the 1982–1984 period and is currently at a level slightly above the industry average. Although the increase in the ratios of the degree of indebtedness could be cause for alarm, a look at the coverage ratios indicates that the firm's ability to meet interest and fixed-payment obligations improved from 1983 to 1984 to a level that outperforms the industry. The firm's increased indebtedness in 1983 apparently caused a deterioration in its ability to service debt adequately. Dayton has evidently improved its income in 1984 so that it is able to meet its interest and fixed-payment obligations in a fashion consistent with the average firm in the industry. In summary, it appears that

---

[27] Since a complete ratio analysis is being performed, the use of the DuPont system of analysis is unnecessary, as it would tend to duplicate rather than add to the information provided.

although 1983 was an off year, the firm's debt position, both in terms of degree of indebtedness and ability to service debts, is acceptable in 1984.

PROFITABILITY

Dayton's profitability relative to sales in 1984 was better than that of the average company in the industry, although it does not match the firm's 1982 performance. While the *gross* profit margin in 1983 and 1984 was better than in 1982, it appears that higher levels of operating and interest expenses in these years have caused the 1984 *net* profit margin to fall below that of 1982. Dayton's 1984 net profit margin is certainly quite favorable when viewed in light of the industry average. The firm's return on investment, return on equity, and earnings per share seem to have behaved in a fashion similar to its net profit margin over the 1982–1984 period. The firm appears to have experienced a sizable drop in sales between 1982 and 1983 or a rapid expansion in assets during that period. The firm's shares appear to be selling at a multiple of earnings below that of the industry, although some improvement occurred between 1983 and 1984. The firm's above-average returns — *ROI, ROE,* and *eps* — may be attributable to its above-average risk as reflected by its below-industry-average P/E ratio. The owners' return, as evidenced by the exceptionally high 1984 level of return on equity, seems to suggest that the firm is performing quite well. The rebound in the firm's earnings per share reflects an improvement in the firm's profitability in 1984, although the 1984 *eps* are still below those of 1982.

In summary, it appears that the firm is growing and has recently gone through an expansion in assets, this expansion being financed primarily through the use of debt. The 1983–1984 period seems to reflect a period of adjustment and recovery from the rapid growth in assets. The firm's sales, profits, and other performance factors seem to be growing with the increase in the size of the operation. In short, the firm appears to have done quite well in 1984.

MULTINATIONAL FINANCE

International Consolidation

Several features distinguish domestically oriented financial statements and internationally based reports. Among these we have the issues of consolidation, translation of individual accounts within the financial statements, and overall reporting of international profits.

CONSOLIDATION

At the present time the rules in the United States require the consolidation of financial statements of subsidiaries according to the percentage of ownership by the parent of the subsidiary. Table 4.10 illustrates this rule.

As indicated, the regulations range from requiring a one-line income-item reporting of dividends, to a pro rata inclusion of profits and losses, to a full

Table 4.10   United States Rules for Consolidation of Financial Statements

Percentage of beneficial ownership by parent in subsidiary	Consolidation for financial reporting purposes
0–19%	Dividends as received
20–49%	Pro rata inclusions of profits and losses
50–100%	Full consolidation[a]

[a] Consolidation may be avoided in the case of some majority-owned foreign operations if the parent can convince its auditors that it does not have control of the subsidiary or there are substantial restrictions on the repatriation of cash.

SOURCE: Rita M. Rodriquez and E. Eugene Carter, *International Financial Management,* 3d ed. (Englewood Cliffs, N.J.: Prentice-Hall, 1984), p. 492.

disclosure in the balance sheet and income statement. (When ownership is less than 50 percent, since the balance sheet and thus the subsidiary's financing do not get reported, it is possible for the parent MNC to have off–balance sheet financing.)

TRANSLATION OF INDIVIDUAL ACCOUNTS

Unlike domestic items in financial statements, international items require translation back into U.S. dollars. Since December 1982 all financial statements of American MNCs have to conform to Statement No. 52 issued by the Financial Accounting Standards Board (FASB). The basic rules of FASB No. 52 are given in Figure 4.4.

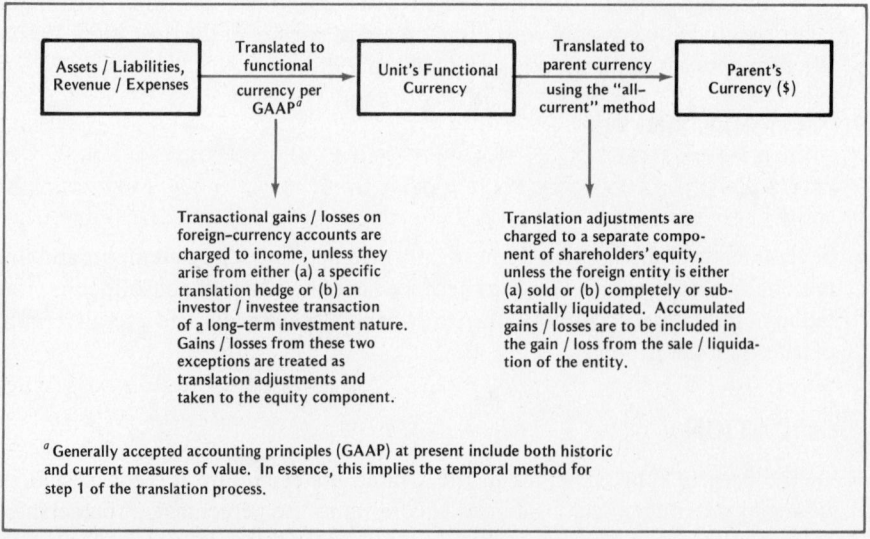

SOURCE: John B. Giannotti, "FAS 52 Gives Treasurers the Scope FAS 8 Denied Them," *Euromoney,* April 1982, pp. 141–151.

Figure 4.4   Details of FASB No. 52

Under FASB No. 52, the *current-rate method* is implemented in a two-step process. First, each entity's balance sheet and income statement are *measured* in terms of their functional currency by using "generally accepted accounting principles." In other words, various foreign-currency elements are translated by subsidiaries into the *functional currency* (the currency of the economic environment in which an entity primarily generates and expends cash) in which their accounts are maintained before financial statements are submitted to the parent for consolidation.

Through the second step, as shown in Figure 4.4, by using the all-current-rate method (which requires the translation of all balance sheet items at the closing rate and all income statement items at average rates), the functional currency-denominated financial statements are translated into the parent's currency.

Each of these steps can result in certain gains or losses. The first step can lead to transaction (cash) gains or losses, which, whether realized or not, are charged directly to net income. The completion of the second step can result in translation (accounting) adjustments, which are excluded from current income. Instead, they are disclosed and charged to a separate component of stockholders' equity.

INTERNATIONAL PROFITS

Prior to January 1976, the practice for most multinational companies was to utilize a special account called the *reserve account* to show "smooth" international profits. Excess international profits due to favorable exchange fluctuations were deposited in this account. Withdrawals were made during periods of high losses arising because of unfavorable exchange movements. The overall result was to display a smooth pattern in an MNC's international profits.

Between 1976 and 1982, however, FASB No. 8 was in existence. It required that both transaction gains or losses and translation adjustments be included in net income, with the separate disclosure of only the aggregate foreign exchange gain or loss. This requirement caused highly visible swings in the reported net earnings of U.S. multinationals. Under the current system, FASB No. 52, only certain transactional gains or losses are reflected in the income statement. Overall, assuming a positive income flow for a subsidiary, the income statement risk will be positive and be similarly enhanced or reduced by an appreciation or depreciation of the functional currency. ●●

CHAPTER SUMMARY

● The stockholders' reports of publicly traded corporations include, in addition to various kinds of subjective and factual information, four key financial statements—(1) the income statement, (2) the balance sheet, (3) the statement of retained earnings, and (4) the statement of changes in financial position—covering at least the two most recent years of operations.

● The income statement summarizes operating results during the specified period. The balance sheet presents a summary of the firm's financial position at a given point in time. The statement of retained earnings reconciles income earned during the year and any cash dividends paid with the change in retained earnings between the start and the end of the given year. The statement of changes in financial position provides a summary of funds flow over the period of interest — typically one year.

● Financial ratios allow interested parties to make an evaluation of certain aspects of a firm's performance. Interested parties typically include present and prospective stockholders and lenders, as well as the firm's management.

● Ratio analysis can be performed on a cross-sectional or a time-series basis. Cross-sectional analysis typically involves comparison of calculated ratios to those of an industry leader or to an industry average measured at the same point in time. Time-series analysis measures a firm's performance over time to isolate trends.

● A single ratio does not generally provide sufficient information to judge the overall performance of the firm; a group of ratios is often required. Ratios should be consistently applied to similar time periods to permit the most accurate comparisons. The use of audited financial statements is strongly recommended. Attention should also be given to consistency of accounting treatment.

● The most common ratios can be divided into four groups: measures of liquidity, measures of activity, measures of debt, and measures of profitability.

● The liquidity or ability of the firm to pay its bills as they come due can be measured by its net working capital, its current ratio, or its quick ratio.

● Activity ratios are used to measure the speed with which various accounts are converted into sales or cash. The activity of inventory can be measured by its turnover, that of accounts receivable by the average collection period, and that of accounts payable by the average payment period. Aging procedures can be applied to accounts receivable or accounts payable to gain further insight into their activity. Fixed asset turnover and total asset turnover can be used to measure the efficiency with which the firm has used its fixed and total assets to generate sales dollars.

● Debt ratios measure both degree of indebtedness and ability to service debts. They can be used to measure the firm's financial leverage to assess the risk-return trade-off resulting from its debt financing.

● Commonly used measures of indebtedness include the debt ratio and the debt-equity ratio. Measures of the ability to service debts and other contractual obligations such as interest, principal (or sinking-fund) payments, and preferred stock dividends are provided by coverage ratios such as times interest earned and fixed-payment coverage.

● Measures of profitability can be made in various ways. A common-size income statement, which shows all items as a percentage of sales, can be used to determine gross profit margin, operating profit margin, and net profit margin. Other measures of profitability include return on investment, return on equity, earnings per share, and the price/earnings ratio.

● The DuPont system of analysis provides a structure for dissecting the firm's financial statements to assess its financial position. It allows the firm to break the return on equity into a profit-on-sales component, an efficiency-of-asset-use component, and a use-of-leverage component.

 ● Certain regulations that apply to international operations tend to complicate the preparation of foreign-based financial statements. Included are rulings that pertain to the consolidation of subsidiaries, translation of accounts, and the overall reporting of international profits.

KEY TERMS

aging	balance sheet
average age of inventory	common-size income statement
average collection period	coverage ratios
average payment period	cross-sectional analysis

current-rate method

current ratio

debt-equity ratio

debt ratio

degree of indebtedness

DuPont formula

DuPont system of analysis

earnings per share *(eps)*

equity multiplier

FASB No. 52

financial and legal flows

financial leverage

fixed asset turnover

fixed-payment coverage ratio

functional currency

gross profit margin

income statement

inventory turnover

liquidity

long-term

modified DuPont formula

net profit margin

net working capital

operating flows

operating profit margin

price/earnings (P/E) ratio

quick (acid-test) ratio

ratio analysis

reserve account

return on equity *(ROE)*

return on investment *(ROI)*

service (of debts)

short-term

sources of cash

statement of changes in financial position

statement of retained earnings

stockholders' reports

time-series analysis

times interest earned ratio

total asset turnover

uses of cash

QUESTIONS

4-1 Briefly describe the basic contents, including the key financial statements, included in the stockholders' reports of publicly held corporations.

4-2 What basic information is contained in each of the following financial statements? Briefly describe each of them.
  a Income statement
  b Balance sheet
  c Statement of retained earnings

4-3 Describe the statement of changes in financial position and explain what are the basic sources of cash and uses of cash.

4-4 How is the statement of changes in financial position interpreted and used by the financial manager and other interested parties?

4-5 With regard to financial ratio analyses of a firm how do the viewpoints held by the firm's present and prospective shareholders, creditors, and management differ? How can these viewpoints be related to the firm's fund-raising ability?

4-6 How can ratio analysis be used for *cross-sectional* and *time-series* comparisons? Which type of comparison would be most common for internal analysis? Why?

4-7 When performing cross-sectional ratio analysis, to what types of deviations from the norm should the analyst devote primary attention? Explain why?

4-8 Financial ratio analysis is often divided into four areas: measures of liquidity, measures of activity, measures of debt, and measures of profitability. What is the purpose of these measures? Which is of greatest relative concern to present and prospective creditors?

4-9 How can a firm's having a high gross profit margin and a low net profit margin be explained? To what must this situation be attributable?

4-10 What is the significance of the firm's return on investment *(ROI)*? Why is the *ROI* considered a key measure of profitability?

4-11 What is the *price/earnings (P/E) ratio?* How do market participants often use it to assess the firm's risk? Is the P/E ratio actually a true measure of profitability?

4-12 Three areas of analysis or concern are combined in the *DuPont system of analysis*. What are these concerns and how are they combined to explain the firm's return on equity *(ROE)*? Can this formula yield useful information through cross-sectional or time-series analysis?

4-13 State the rules for consolidation of foreign subsidiaries.

4-14 Under FASB Standard No. 52, what are the balance sheet translation rules?

4-15 In terms of the reporting of international profits, are U.S. MNCs better off with the guidelines established under FASB No. 52 or those established under FASB No. 8? Explain.

PROBLEMS

4-1 **(Classifying Sources and Uses)**   Classify the following items as sources or uses of funds, or as neither.

Item	Change ($)	Item	Change ($)
Cash	+100	Accounts receivable	−700
Accounts payable	−1000	Net profits	+600
Notes payable	+500	Depreciation	+100
Long-term debt	−2000	Repurchase of stock	+600
Inventory	+200	Cash dividends	+800
Fixed assets	+400	Sale of stock	+1000

4-2 **(Reviewing Basic Financial Statements)**   The four basic financial statements for the year ended December 31, 1984, for Gold Equipment Company follow. Without calculating ratios:

a Briefly discuss the income statement, balance sheet, and statement of retained earnings for the year ended December 31, 1984.

b Discuss the information presented in the statement of changes in financial position and assess the firm's 1984 funds flow.

INCOME STATEMENT
GOLD EQUIPMENT COMPANY
FOR THE YEAR ENDED DECEMBER 31, 1984

Sales (all on credit)		$600,000
Less: Cost of goods sold		460,000
Gross profit		$140,000
Less: Operating expenses		
General and administrative expense	$30,000	
Depreciation	30,000	
Total		60,000
Operating profit		$ 80,000
Less: Interest		10,000
Net profit before taxes		$ 70,000
Less: Taxes		27,100
Net profit after taxes		$ 42,900
Less: Cash dividends		20,000
To retained earnings		$ 22,900

BALANCE SHEET
GOLD EQUIPMENT COMPANY
DECEMBER 31, 1984

Assets

Cash	$ 15,000
Marketable securities	7,200
Accounts receivable	33,000
Inventory	82,000
Prepaid rent	1,100
Total current assets	$138,300
Net plant and equipment	$270,000
Total assets	$408,300

Liabilities and stockholders' equity

Accounts payable	$ 57,000
Notes payable	13,000
Accruals	5,000
Total current liabilities	$ 75,000
Long-term debt	$150,000
Stockholders' equity	
Common stock equity (20,000 shares outstanding)	$110,200
Retained earnings	73,100
Total stockholders' equity	$183,300
Total liabilities and stockholders' equity	$408,300

STATEMENT OF RETAINED EARNINGS
GOLD EQUIPMENT COMPANY
FOR THE YEAR ENDED DECEMBER 31, 1984

Retained earnings balance (January 1, 1984)	$50,200
Plus: Net profit after taxes (for 1984)	42,900
Less: Cash dividends (for 1984)	(20,000)
Retained earnings balance (December 31, 1984)	$73,100

STATEMENT OF CHANGES IN FINANCIAL POSITION
GOLD EQUIPMENT COMPANY
FOR THE YEAR ENDED DECEMBER 31, 1984

Sources of cash		Uses of cash	
Net profit after taxes	$42,900	Dividends	$20,000
Depreciation	30,000	Increase: Gross fixed assets	15,000
Decrease: Cash	1,000	Increase: Inventory	32,000
Decrease: Marketable securities	800	Decrease: Notes payable	3,000
Decrease: Accounts receivable	7,000	Decrease: Accruals	1,000
Decrease: Prepaid rent	1,100	Decrease: Long-term debt	10,000
Increase: Accounts payable	8,000	Repurchase/retirement of stock	9,800
Total sources	$90,800	Total uses	$90,800

4-3 **(Liquidity Management)** The Houston Corporation's total current assets, net working capital, and inventory for each of the past four years is given below.

Item	1981	1982	1983	1984
Total current assets	$16,950	$21,900	$22,500	$27,000
Net working capital	7,950	9,300	9,900	9,600
Inventory	6,000	6,900	6,900	7,200

a   Calculate the firm's current and quick ratios for each year. Compare the resulting time series of each measure of liquidity (i.e., net working capital, the current ratio, and the quick ratio).
b   Comment on the firm's liquidity over the 1981–1984 period.
c   If you were told that the Houston Corporation's inventory turnover for each year in the 1981–1984 period and the industry averages were as follows, would this support or conflict with your evaluation in **b**? Why?

Inventory turnover	1981	1982	1983	1984
Houston Corporation	6.3	6.8	7.0	6.4
Industry average	10.6	11.2	10.8	11.0

4-4 **(Inventory Management)** The Davis Company has sales of $4 million and a gross profit margin of 40 percent. Its *end-of-quarter inventories* are as follows:

Quarter	Inventory
1	$ 400,000
2	800,000
3	1,200,000
4	200,000

a   Find the average quarterly inventory and use it to calculate the firm's inventory turnover and the average age of inventory
b   Assuming the company is in an industry with an average inventory turnover of 2.0, how would you evaluate the activity of Davis's inventory?

4-5 **(Accounts Receivable Management)** An evaluation of the books of Gordon's Supply Company shows the following end-of-year accounts receivable balance, which is believed to consist of amounts originating in the months indicated. The company had annual sales of $3 million of which *80 percent were on a credit basis.* The firm extends 30-day credit terms.

Month of origin	Amounts receivable
July	$ 3,875
August	2,000
September	34,025
October	15,100
November	52,000
December	193,000
Year-end accounts receivable	$300,000

a Use the year-end total to evaluate the firm's collection system. (*Note:* Only credit sales are relevant in this evaluation.)

b Age the accounts receivable to obtain additional information. What other observations can you make about the receivables collection policy?

c If the firm's peak season is from July to December, how would this affect the validity of your conclusion above? Explain.

4-6 **(Debt-Servicing Ability)** The Center City Bank is evaluating the Graham Corporation, which has requested a $4,000,000 loan, to assess its financial leverage and the financial risk involved.

INCOME STATEMENT
GRAHAM CORPORATION
FOR THE YEAR ENDED DECEMBER 31, 1984

Net sales (all on credit)		$30,000,000
Less: Cost of goods sold		21,000,000
Gross profits		$ 9,000,000
Less: Operating expenses		
Selling expense	$3,000,000	
General and administrative expenses	2,000,000	
Depreciation expense	1,000,000	
Total operating expense		6,000,000
Earnings before interest and taxes		$ 3,000,000
Less: Interest		1,000,000
Earnings before taxes		$ 2,000,000
Less: Taxes (rate = 40%)		800,000
Earnings after taxes		$ 1,200,000

BALANCE SHEET
GRAHAM CORPORATION
DECEMBER 31, 1984

Assets

Current assets	
Cash	$ 1,000,000
Marketable securities	3,000,000
Accounts receivable	12,000,000
Inventories	7,500,000
Total current assets	$23,500,000
Fixed assets	
Land and buildings	$11,000,000
Machinery and equipment	20,500,000
Furniture and fixtures	8,000,000
Total fixed assets	$39,500,000
Less: Accumulated depreciation	13,000,000
Net fixed assets	$26,500,000
Total assets	$50,000,000

(*continued*)

BALANCE SHEET *(Continued)*
GRAHAM CORPORATION
DECEMBER 31, 1984

Liabilities and stockholders' equity

Current liabilities	
Accrued liabilities	$ 500,000
Notes payable	8,000,000
Accounts payable	8,000,000
Total current liabilities	$16,500,000
Long-term debts[a]	$20,000,000
Stockholders' equity	
Preferred stock[b]	$ 2,500,000
Common stock (1 million shares at $5 par)	5,000,000
Paid-in capital in excess of par value	4,000,000
Retained earnings	2,000,000
Total stockholders' equity	$13,500,000
Total liabilities and stockholders' equity	$50,000,000

[a] Required annual principal payments are $800,000.
[b] 25,000 shares of $4.00 cumulative preferred stock outstanding.

Industry Averages

Debt ratio	0.51
Debt-equity ratio	1.07
Times interest earned ratio	7.30
Fixed-payment coverage ratio	1.85

a Based on the debt ratios for Graham, along with the industry averages and Graham's recent financial statements (presented below), evaluate and recommend appropriate action on the Graham request.
b A common-size income statement for the Graham Corporation's 1983 operations is presented below. Develop and compare it to the 1984 year-end common-size income statement. Which areas require further analysis or investigation?

COMMON-SIZE INCOME STATEMENT
GRAHAM CORPORATION
FOR THE YEAR ENDED DECEMBER 31, 1983

Net sales ($35,000,000)		100.0%
Less: Cost of goods sold		65.9
Gross profits		34.1%
Less: Operating expenses		
Selling expense	12.7%	
General and administrative expenses	6.9	
Depreciation expense	3.6	
Total operating expense		23.2%
Earnings before interest and taxes		10.9%
Less: Interest		1.5
Earnings before taxes		9.4%
Less: Taxes (rate = 40%)		3.8
Earnings after taxes		5.6%

4-7　(**DuPont System of Analysis**)　Use the following ratio information for Raimer Industries and the industry averages for Raimer's line of business to

　　a　Construct the DuPont system for both Raimer and the industry.
　　b　Evaluate Raimer (and the industry) over the three-year period.
　　c　Determine which areas of Raimer Industries require further analysis.

Raimer	1982	1983	1984
Equity multiplier	1.75	1.75	1.85
Net profit margin	.059	.058	.049
Total asset turnover	2.11	2.18	2.34

Industry averages			
Equity multiplier	1.67	1.69	1.64
Net profit margin	.054	.047	.041
Total asset turnover	2.05	2.13	2.15

4-8　(**Ratio Interpretation**)　Without referring to the text, indicate for each of the following ratios the formula for its calculation and the kinds of problems, if any, the firm is likely to be having if these ratios are too high relative to the industry average. What if they are too low relative to the industry? Create a table similar to that shown below and fill in the empty blocks.

Ratio	Too high	Too low
Current ratio =		
Inventory turnover =		
Times interest earned =	✕	
Gross profit margin =		
Return on investment =	✕	

4-9　(**Cross-Sectional Ratio Analysis**)　Use the financial statements for Gold Equipment Company for the year ended December 31, 1984, given in Problem 4-2 along with the following 1984 industry average ratios to

　　a　Prepare and interpret a ratio analysis of the firm's 1984 operations.
　　b　Summarize your findings and make recommendations.

Ratio	Industry average, 1984
Net working capital	$125,000
Current ratio	2.35
Quick ratio	.87
Inventory turnover	4.55
Average collection period	35.3 days
Fixed asset turnover	1.97

(*continued*)

(*Continued*) Ratio	Industry average, 1984
Total asset turnover	1.09
Debt ratio	.300
Debt-equity ratio	.615
Times interest earned ratio	12.3
Gross profit margin	.202
Operating profit margin	.135
Net profit margin	.091
Return on investment (*ROI*)	.099
Return on equity (*ROE*)	.167
Earnings per share (*eps*)	$3.10

4-10   **(Financial Statement Analysis)**   The financial statements of the Robin Manufacturing Company for the year ended December 31, 1984, are given below.

ROBIN MANUFACTURING COMPANY
BALANCE SHEET
DECEMBER 31, 1984

Cash	$ 500
Marketable securities	1,000
Accounts receivable	25,000
Inventories	45,500
Total current assets	$ 72,000
Land	$ 26,000
Buildings and equipment	90,000
Less: Accumulated depreciation	38,000
Net fixed assets	$ 78,000
Total Assets	$150,000
Accounts payable	$ 22,000
Notes payable	47,000
Total current liabilities	$ 69,000
Long-term debt	$ 22,950
Common stock	31,500
Retained earnings	26,550
Total liabilities and stockholders' equity	$150,000

ROBIN MANUFACTURING COMPANY
INCOME STATEMENT
FOR THE YEAR ENDED DECEMBER 31, 1984

Sales (all on credit)	$160,000
Cost of goods sold	106,000
Gross profit	$ 54,000
Operating expense:	
Selling expense	$ 16,000
General and administrative expenses	11,000
Depreciation	10,000
Total operating expense	$ 37,000
Operating profit	$ 17,000
Less: Interest	6,100
Net profit before taxes	$ 10,900
Less: Taxes	4,360
Net profit after taxes	$ 6,540

a   Use the preceding financial statements to complete the table below. Assume that the industry averages given in the table are applicable for both 1983 and 1984.

Robin Manufacturing Company Ratio Analysis

Ratio	Industry average	Actual 1983	Actual 1984
Current ratio	1.80	1.84	_____
Quick ratio	.70	.78	_____
Average collection period[a]	37 days	36 days	_____
Inventory turnover[a]	2.50	2.59	_____
Debt-equity ratio	50%	51%	_____
Times interest earned ratio	3.8	4.0	_____
Gross profit margin	38%	40%	_____
Net profit margin	3.5%	3.6%	_____
Return on investment	4.0%	4.0%	_____
Return on equity	9.5%	8.0%	_____

[a] Based on a 360-day year and on end-of-year figures.

b   Analyze Robin Manufacturing Company's financial condition as it relates to (1) liquidity, (2) activity, (3) debt, and (4) profitability. Summarize the company's overall financial condition.

4-11   **(Integrative — Complete Ratio Analysis)**   Given the following financial statements, historical ratios, and industry averages, calculate the Baker Company's financial ratios for the most recent year. Analyze its overall financial situation from both a cross-sectional and a time-series viewpoint. Break your analysis into an evaluation of the firm's liquidity, activity, debt, and profitability.

INCOME STATEMENT
BAKER COMPANY
FOR THE YEAR ENDED DECEMBER 31, 1984

Net sales (all on credit)		$10,000,000
Less: Cost of goods sold		7,500,000
Gross profit		$ 2,500,000
Less: Operating expenses		
Selling expense	$300,000	
General and administrative expenses	700,000	
Depreciation expense	200,000	1,200,000
Operating profits		$ 1,300,000
Less: Interest expense[a]		200,000
Profits before taxes		$ 1,100,000
Less: Taxes (40%)		440,000
Profits after taxes		$ 660,000
Less: Preferred stock dividends		50,000
Earnings available for common stockholders		$ 610,000
Less: Common stock dividends		200,000
To retained earnings		$ 410,000

[a] Interest expense includes the interest component of the annual financial lease payment as specified by the Financial Accounting Standards Board (FASB).

BALANCE SHEET
BAKER COMPANY
DECEMBER 31, 1984

Assets

Current assets		
Cash		$ 200,000
Marketable securities		50,000
Accounts receivable		800,000
Inventories		950,000
Total current assets		$ 2,000,000
Gross fixed assets (includes financial leases)[a]	$12,000,000	
Less: Accumulated depreciation	3,000,000	
Net fixed assets		$ 9,000,000
Other assets		1,000,000
Total assets		$12,000,000

Liabilities and stockholders' equity

Current liabilities	
Accrued liabilities	$ 100,000
Notes payable	200,000
Accounts payable[b]	900,000
Total current liabilities	$ 1,200,000
Long-term debts (includes financial leases)[c]	$ 3,000,000
Stockholders' equity	
Preferred stock (25,000 shares, $2 dividend)	$ 1,000,000
Common stock (200,000 shares at $3 par)[d]	600,000
Paid-in capital in excess of par value	5,200,000
Retained earnings	1,000,000
Total stockholders' equity	$ 7,800,000
Total liabilities and stockholders' equity	$12,000,000

[a] The firm has an eight-year financial lease requiring annual beginning-of-year payments. Five years of the lease have yet to run.
[b] Annual credit purchases of $6,200,000 were made during the year.
[c] The annual principal payment on the long-term debt is $100,000.
[d] On December 31, 1984, the firm's common stock closed at $27½.

HISTORICAL AND INDUSTRY-AVERAGE RATIOS
BAKER COMPANY

Ratio	1982	1983	Industry average 1984
Net working capital	$760,000	$720,000	$1,600,000
Current ratio	1.40	1.55	1.85
Quick ratio	1.00	.92	1.05
Inventory turnover	9.52	9.21	8.60
Average collection period	45.0 days	36.4 days	35.0 days
Average payment period	58.5 days	60.8 days	45.8 days
Fixed asset turnover	1.08	1.05	1.07
Total asset turnover	0.74	0.80	0.74
Debt ratio	0.20	0.20	0.30
Debt-equity ratio	0.25	0.27	0.39
Times interest earned ratio	8.2	7.3	8.0
Fixed-payment coverage ratio	4.8	4.5	4.5
Gross profit margin	0.30	0.27	0.25
Operating profit margin	0.12	0.12	0.10
Net profit margin	0.067	0.067	0.058
Return on investment (ROI)	0.049	0.054	0.043
Return on equity (ROE)	0.066	0.073	0.072
Earnings per share (eps)	$1.75	$2.20	$1.50
Price/earnings (P/E) ratio	12.0	10.5	11.2

Chapter 5

Financial Planning

After studying this chapter, you should be able to:

1. Understand the financial planning process and the role played by long-run and short-run financial plans.

2. Describe the short-run financial planning process and the key inputs to the cash budget and pro forma income statement and balance sheet.

3. Discuss the cash planning process, the role of sales forecasts, and the basic procedure for preparation of a cash budget.

4. Interpret a cash budget and recognize the problems introduced by uncertainty and cash flows within the month.

5. Develop, prepare, and interpret a pro forma income statement using the percent-of-sales method.

6. Apply the percent-of-sales method and judgmental approach to preparing a pro forma balance sheet and understand the assumptions and drawbacks of these simplified approaches.

Financial planning is an important part of the financial manager's job. Financial plans and budgets provide road maps for achieving the firm's objectives. In addition, they provide a structure for coordinating the activities of the firm and act as a control mechanism by establishing a standard against which actual outcomes can be evaluated.

Two important aspects of the process are *cash planning* and *profit planning*. Cash planning, which is commonly performed by preparation of the cash budget, is critical since cash is the lifeblood of the firm. Without adequate cash — regardless of the level of profits — the firm could fail. Profit planning is usually done with pro forma financial statements, which show anticipated levels of profits, assets, liabilities, and equity. Cash budgets and pro forma statements are not only useful for internal financial planning, but are routinely required by present and prospective lenders.

The Financial Planning Process

The *financial planning process* begins with the preparation of long-run financial plans that dictate the general parameters reflected in the short-run plans and budgets. Generally speaking, the short-run plans and budgets are operational guides for achieving the firm's long-run objectives. While the major emphasis in this chapter is on short-run financial plans and budgets, a few comments on the long-run plans are appropriate here.

LONG-RUN FINANCIAL PLANS

Long-run financial plans generally reflect the anticipated impact on the firm's finances from the implementation of planned actions by the firm. Such plans tend to cover periods ranging from two to ten years; the use of five-year plans, which are continuously revised as new information becomes available, is quite common. Generally, firms subject to high degrees of operating uncertainty, relatively short production cycles, or both tend to use shorter planning horizons. Long-run financial plans tend to focus on the implementation of proposed capital expenditures, research and development activities, marketing and product development actions, and major sources of financing. Also included would be termination of existing projects, product lines, or lines of business; repayment or retirement of outstanding debts; and any planned acquisitions. Such plans tend to be supported by a series of annual budgets and profit plans.

SHORT-RUN FINANCIAL PLANS

Short-run financial plans reflect the outcomes expected to result from near-term actions. These plans most often cover a one- to two-year period. Key inputs include the sales forecast and various forms of operating and financial data; key outputs include a number of operating budgets, the cash budget, and pro forma financial statements. The short-run financial planning process, from the initial sales forecast through the development of the cash budget and pro forma income statement and balance sheet, is presented in the flow diagram in Figure 5.1.

From the sales forecast is developed a production plan that takes into account the amount of lead time necessary to convert an item from a raw material into a finished good. The types and quantities of raw materials required during the forecast period can be estimated from the production plan. Based on these estimates, a schedule of when and how much of each raw material to purchase can be developed. Estimates of the amount of direct labor required, in either worker-hours or dollars, can be made. The firm's factory overhead outlays can also be estimated. Finally, operating expenses, specifically sales and administrative expenses, can be estimated based on the level of operations necessary to support forecast sales.

Once this series of plans has been prepared, the firm's pro forma income statement can be developed. The cash budget, based on monthly or quarterly breakdowns of cash receipts and disbursements, can also be created. With the pro forma income statement, the cash budget, the long-term financing plan, the capital expenditure plan, and the current-period balance sheet as basic inputs, the pro forma balance sheet can be developed. The pro forma income statement is needed to find the projected change in retained earnings, depreciation, inventory, and taxes. Data on the cash balance, marketable securities, level of accounts receivable, level of accounts payable, and level of notes payable can be obtained from the cash budget. The long-term financing plan provides information on changes in long-term debts and stockholders' equity attributed to financing decisions. The capital expenditure plan provides information with respect to expected changes in fixed assets.

The preceding-period balance sheet is needed in order to have initial values against which to measure changes in various balance sheet accounts such as fixed assets, common stock, and retained earnings. The beginning values for cash, marketable securities, accounts receivable, inventory, and liabilities are also derived from the most recent period's balance sheet. It is often quite helpful to compare the pro forma balance sheet with the current balance sheet to check the reasonableness of the forecast statement.

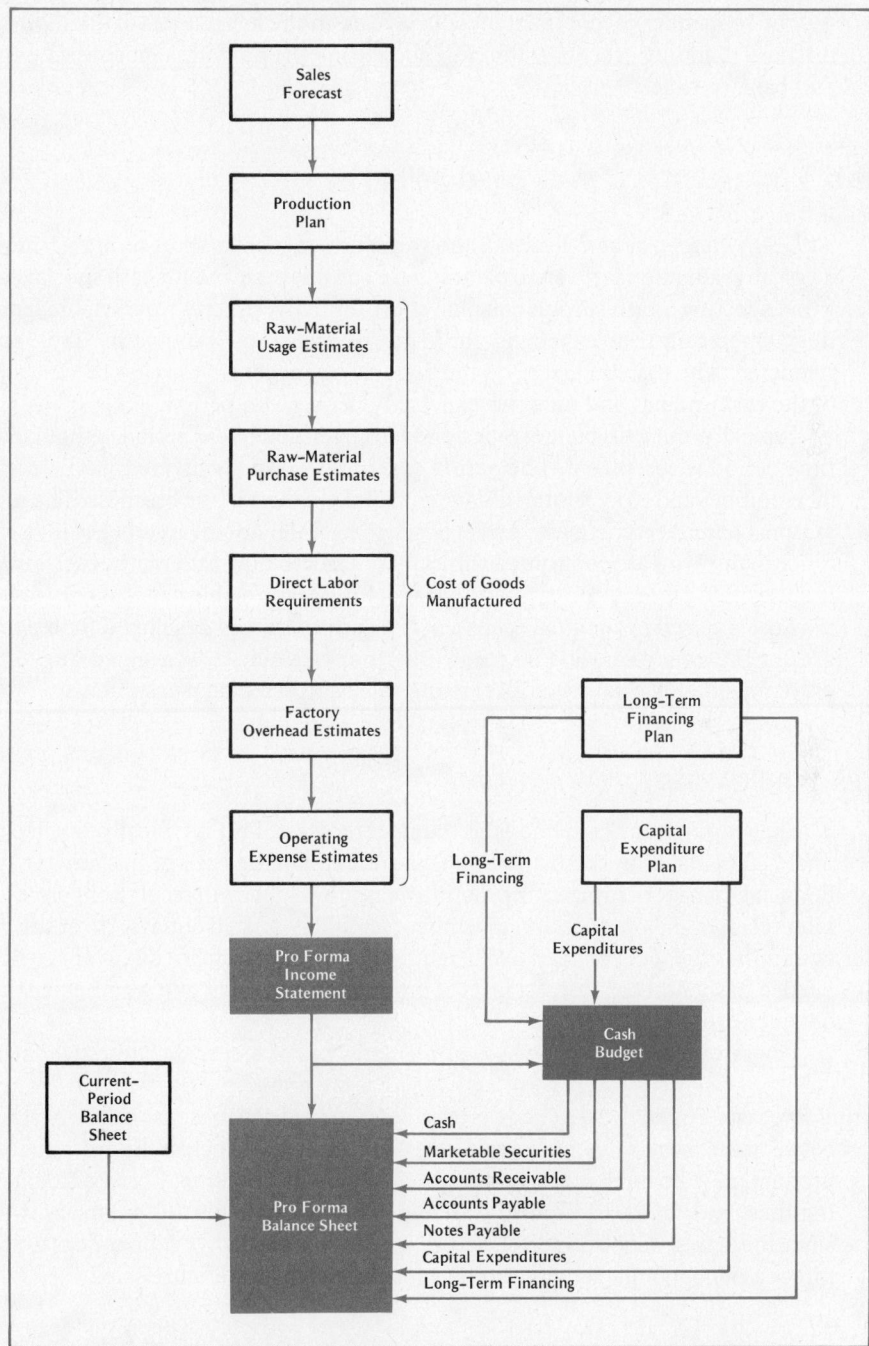

Figure 5.1   The short-run financial planning process

The remainder of this chapter concentrates on the key outputs of the short-run financial planning process — the cash budget and the pro forma income statement and balance sheet.

 ## Cash Planning: Cash Budgets

The *cash budget,* or *cash forecast,* allows the firm to plan its short-term cash needs. Typically, attention is given to planning for surplus cash and for cash shortages. A firm expecting a cash surplus can plan short-term investments (marketable securities), whereas a firm expecting shortages in cash must arrange for short-term financing. The cash budget gives the financial manager a clear view of the timing of the cash inflows and outflows expected over a given period.

Typically, the cash budget is designed to cover a one-year period, although any time period is acceptable. The period covered is normally divided into intervals. The number and type of intervals depend on the nature of the business. The more seasonal and uncertain a firm's cash flows, the greater are the number of intervals. Since many firms are confronted with a seasonal cash flow pattern, the cash budget is quite often presented on a monthly basis. Firms with stable patterns of cash flow may use quarterly or annual intervals. If a cash budget is developed for a period greater than one year, less frequent time intervals may be warranted due to the difficulty and uncertainty of forecasting sales and associated cash items.

SALES FORECAST

The key input to any cash budget is the *sales forecast.* This is typically given to the financial manager by the marketing department. On the basis of this forecast, the financial manager estimates the monthly cash flows that will result from projected sales receipts and production-, inventory-, and sales-related outlays. He or she also determines the level of fixed assets required; how much financing, if any, will be needed to support the forecast level of production and sales; and whether it can be obtained.

The sales forecast may be based on an analysis of external or internal data.[1]

External forecasts. An *external forecast* is based on the relationships that can be observed between the firm's sales and certain economic indicators such as the gross national product, new housing starts, and disposable personal income. Forecasts containing these indicators are readily available. The rationale for this approach is that since the firm's sales are often closely related to some aspect of economic activity, a forecast of economic activity should provide insight into future sales.

---

[1] A discussion of the calculation of the various forecasting techniques, such as regression, moving averages, and exponential smoothing, is not included in this text. The reader is referred to a basic statistics, econometrics, or management science text for a description of the technical side of forecasting. See, for example, Thomas H. Wonnacott and Ronald J. Wonnacott, *Introductory Statistics for Business and Economics,* 3rd edition (New York: John Wiley and Sons, Inc., 1984), Ch. 24 or Richard B. Chase and Nicholas J. Aquilano, *Production and Operations Management,* 3rd edition (Homewood, IL: Richard D. Irwin, 1981), Ch. 6.

Internal forecasts. *Internal forecasts* are based on a buildup of sales forecasts through the firm's sales channels. Typically, the salespeople in the field are asked to estimate the number of units of each type of product they expect to sell in the coming year. These forecasts are collected by the district sales manager, who may adjust the figures using his or her own knowledge of specific markets or the salesperson's forecasting ability. Finally, adjustments may be made for additional internal factors, such as production capabilities.

Firms generally use both external and internal forecast data in making the final forecast. The internal data provide insight into sales expectations, while the external data provide a way of adjusting these expectations by taking into account general economic factors. The nature of the product often affects the mix and types of forecasting methods used.

FORMAT OF THE CASH BUDGET

The general format of the cash budget is presented in Table 5.1. We will discuss each of its components individually.

Cash receipts. *Cash receipts* include the total of all items from which cash inflows result in any given month. The most common components of cash receipts are cash sales, collections of accounts receivable, and other cash receipts.

EXAMPLE   The ABC Company is developing a cash budget for October, November, and December. Sales in August and September were $100,000 and $200,000, respectively. Sales of $400,000, $300,000, and $200,000 have been forecast for October, November, and December, respectively. Historically, 20 percent of the firm's sales have been for cash, 50 percent have generated accounts receivable collected after one month, and the remaining 30 percent have generated accounts receivable collected after two months. Bad-debt expenses have been negligible.[2] In December, the firm will receive a $30,000 dividend from stock in a subsidiary. The schedule of expected cash receipts for the company is given in Table 5.2. It contains the following items.

Table 5.1   The General Format of the Cash Budget

	Jan.	Feb.	. . .	Nov.	Dec.
Cash receipts					
Less: Cash disbursements	____	____	. . .	____	____
Net cash flow					
Add: Beginning cash	____ ↗	____ ↗	. . . ↗	____ ↗	____
Ending cash					
Less: Minimum cash balance	____	____	. . .	____	____
Required total financing			. . .		
Excess cash balance			. . .		

[2] Normally it would be expected that the collection percentages would total slightly less than 100 percent to reflect the fact that some of the accounts receivable would be uncollectible. In this example the sum of the collection percentages is 100 percent (20% + 50% + 30%), which reflects the fact that all sales are assumed to be collected since bad debts are said to be negligible.

Table 5.2   A Schedule of Projected Cash Receipts
            for the ABC Company ($000)

	Aug.	Sept.	Oct.	Nov.	Dec.
Forecast sales	$100	$200	$400	$300	$200
Cash sales (.20)	$ 20	$ 40	$ 80	$ 60	$ 40
Collections of A/R:					
Lagged one month (.50)		50	100	200	150
Lagged two months (.30)			30	60	120
Other cash receipts					30
Total cash receipts			$210	$320	$340

Forecast sales   This initial entry is *merely informational.* It has been provided as an aid in calculating other sales-related items.

Cash sales   The cash sales shown for each month represent 20 percent of the sales forecast for that month.

Collections of A/R   These entries represent the collection of accounts receivable resulting from sales in earlier months.

Lagged one month   These figures represent sales made in the preceding month that generated accounts receivable collected in the current month. Since 50 percent of the current month's sales are collected one month later, the collections of accounts receivable with a one-month lag shown for September, October, November, and December represent 50 percent of the sales in August, September, October, and November, respectively.

Lagged two months   These figures represent sales made two months earlier that generated accounts receivable collected in the current month. Since 30 percent of sales are collected two months later, the collections with a two-month lag shown for October, November, and December represent 30 percent of the sales in August, September, and October, respectively.

Other cash receipts   These are cash receipts expected to result from sources other than sales. Items such as dividends received, interest received, proceeds from the sale of equipment, stock and bond sale proceeds, and lease receipts may show up here. For the ABC Company, the only other cash receipt is the $30,000 dividend due in December.

Total cash receipts   This figure represents the total of all the cash receipt items listed for each month in the cash receipt schedule. In the case of the ABC Company, we are concerned only with October, November, and December; the total cash receipts for these months are shown in Table 5.2. ■

Cash disbursements. Cash disbursements include all outlays of cash in the periods covered. The most common cash disbursements are these:

Cash purchases
Payments of accounts payable
Payments of cash dividends
Rent expense
Wages and salaries
Tax payments
Capital additions
Interest payments

Repayment of loans and sinking-fund payments
Repurchases or retirements of stock

It is important to recognize that *depreciation and other noncash charges are NOT included in the cash budget* because they merely represent a scheduled write-off of an earlier cash outflow. The impact of depreciation, as noted in Chapter 2, is reflected in the level of cash outflow represented by the tax payments.

EXAMPLE   The ABC Company has gathered the following data needed for the preparation of a cash disbursements schedule for the months of October, November, and December.

Purchases   The firm's purchases represent 70 percent of sales; 10 percent of this amount is paid in cash, 70 percent is paid in the month immediately following the month of purchase, and the remaining 20 percent is paid two months following the month of purchase.[3]

Cash dividends   Cash dividends of $20,000 will be paid in October.

Rent expense   Rent of $5,000 will be paid each month.

Wages and salaries   The firm's wages and salaries can be calculated by adding 10 percent of its monthly sales to the $8,000 fixed-cost figure.

Tax payments   Taxes of $25,000 must be paid in December.

Capital additions   A new machine costing $130,000 will be purchased and paid for in November.

Interest payments   An interest payment of $10,000 is due in December.

Sinking-fund payments   A $20,000 sinking-fund payment is also due in December.

Repurchases or retirements of stock   No repurchase or retirement of stock is expected to occur during the October–December period.

The firm's cash disbursement schedule, based on the data above, is presented in Table 5.3. Some items in Table 5.3 are explained in greater detail below.

Purchases   This entry is *merely informational.* The figures represent 70 percent of the

Table 5.3   A Schedule of Projected Cash Disbursements for the ABC Company ($000)

	Aug.	Sept.	Oct.	Nov.	Dec.
Purchases (.70 × sales)	$70	$140	$280	$210	$140
Cash purchases (.10)	$ 7	$ 14	$ 28	$ 21	$ 14
Payments of A/P:					
Lagged one month (.70)		49	98	196	147
Lagged two months (.20)			14	28	56
Cash dividends			20		
Rent expense			5	5	5
Wages and salaries			48	38	28
Tax payments					25
Capital additions				130	
Interest payments					10
Sinking-fund payments					20
Total cash disbursements			$213	$418	$305

[3] Unlike the collection percentages for sales, the total of the payment percentages should equal 100 percent since it is expected that the firm will pay off all of its accounts payable. In line with this expectation, the ABC Company's percentages total 100 percent (10% + 70% + 20%).

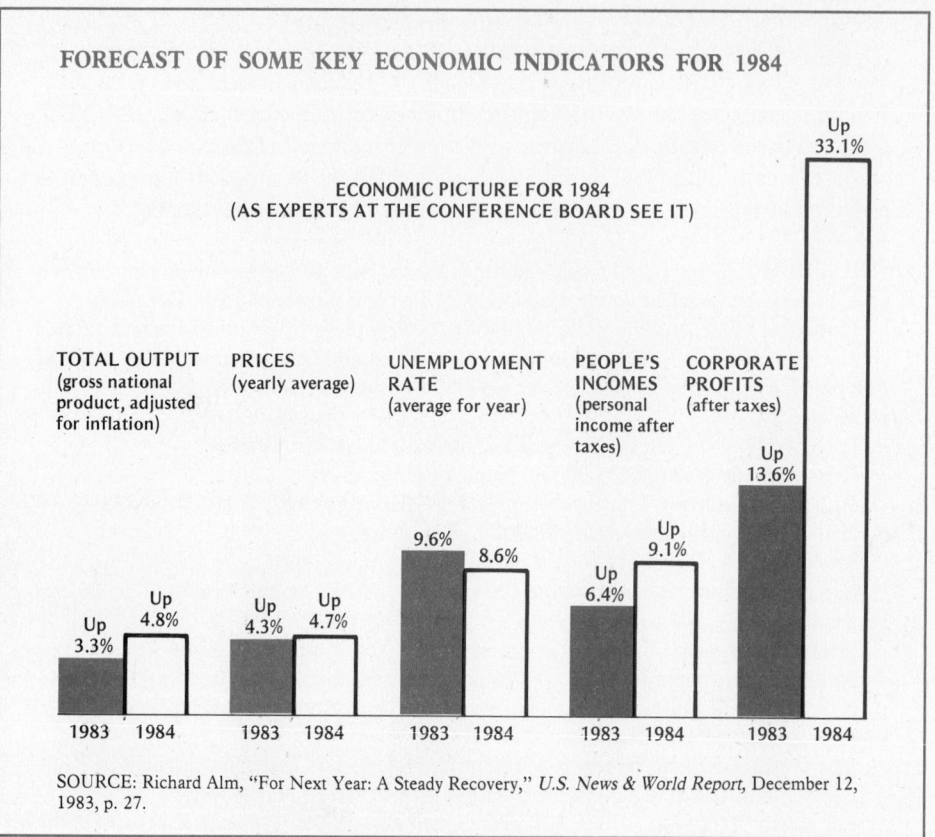

FORECAST OF SOME KEY ECONOMIC INDICATORS FOR 1984

ECONOMIC PICTURE FOR 1984
(AS EXPERTS AT THE CONFERENCE BOARD SEE IT)

| TOTAL OUTPUT (gross national product, adjusted for inflation) | PRICES (yearly average) | UNEMPLOYMENT RATE (average for year) | PEOPLE'S INCOMES (personal income after taxes) | CORPORATE PROFITS (after taxes) |

Up 33.1%

Up 13.6%

Up 3.3% — Up 4.8%
Up 4.3% — Up 4.7%
9.6% — 8.6%
Up 6.4% — Up 9.1%

1983 1984   1983 1984   1983 1984   1983 1984   1983 1984

SOURCE: Richard Alm, "For Next Year: A Steady Recovery," *U.S. News & World Report,* December 12, 1983, p. 27.

forecast sales for each month. They have been included to facilitate the calculation of the cash purchases and related payments.

Cash purchases   The cash purchases for each month represent 10 percent of the month's purchases.

Payments of A/P   These entries represent the payment of accounts payable resulting from purchases in earlier months.

Lagged one month   These figures represent purchases made in the preceding month that are paid for in the current month. Since 70 percent of the firm's purchases are paid for one month later, the payments lagged one month shown for September, October, November, and December represent 70 percent of the August, September, October, and November purchases, respectively.

Lagged two months   These figures represent purchases made two months earlier that are paid for in the current month. Since 20 percent of the firm's purchases are paid for two months later, the payments lagged two months for October, November, and December represent 20 percent of the August, September, and October purchases, respectively.

Wages and salaries   These values were obtained by adding $8000 to 10 percent of the *sales* in each month. The $8000 represents the salary component; the rest represents wages.

The remaining items on the cash disbursements schedule are self-explanatory. ■

Net cash flow, ending cash, financing, and excess cash. A firm's *net cash flow* is found by subtracting the cash disbursements from cash receipts in each month. By adding beginning cash to the firm's net cash flow, the *ending cash* for each month can be found. Finally, subtracting the minimum cash balance from ending cash yields the *required total financing* or the *excess cash balance.* If the ending cash is less than the minimum cash balance, *financing* is required; if the ending cash is greater than the minimum cash balance, *excess cash* exists.

EXAMPLE Table 5.4 presents the ABC Company's cash budget, based on the cash receipt and cash disbursement data already developed for the firm. ABC's end-of-September cash balance was $50,000, and the company wishes to maintain a minimum cash balance of $25,000.

For the ABC Company to maintain its required $25,000 ending cash balance, it will need to have borrowed $76,000 in November and $41,000 in December. In the month of October the firm will have an excess cash balance of $22,000, which can be placed in some interest-earning form. The required total financing figures in the cash budget refer to *how much will have to be owed at the end of the month;* they do *not* show the additional borrowing required during the month.

To clarify the meaning of these financing figures, Table 5.5 presents a different approach to evaluating the firm's required total financing.

Table 5.4 A Cash Budget for the ABC Company ($000)

	Oct.	Nov.	Dec.
Total cash receipts[a]	$210	$320	$340
Less: Total cash disbursements[b]	213	418	305
Net cash flow	$ (3)	$ (98)	$ 35
Add: Beginning cash	50	47	(51)
Ending cash	$ 47	$ (51)	$ (16)
Less: Minimum cash balance	25	25	25
Required total financing[c]	—	$ 76	$ 41
Excess cash balance[d]	$ 22	—	—

[a] From Table 5.2.
[b] From Table 5.3.
[c] Values are placed in this line when the ending cash is less than the minimum cash balance since in this instance financing is required.
[d] Values are placed in this line when the ending cash is greater than the minimum cash balance since in this instance an excess cash balance exists.

Table 5.5 Another View of the ABC Company's Financing Requirements ($000)

	Oct.	Nov.	Dec.
Net cash flow[a]	$ (3)	$(98)	$ 35
Add: Beginning cash	50	47	25
Less: Minimum cash balance	25	25	25
Less: Excess cash balance	22	0	0
Additional financing (repayment)	$ 0	$ 76	$(35)
Required total financing	$ 0	$ 76	$ 41

[a] From Table 5.4

INTERPRETING THE CASH BUDGET

The cash budget provides the firm with figures indicating the expected ending cash balance, which can be analyzed to determine whether a cash shortage or surplus is expected to result in each of the months covered by the forecast. The ABC Company can expect a surplus of $22,000 in October, a deficit of $76,000 in November, and a deficit of $41,000 in December. Each of these figures is based on the internally imposed requirement of a $25,000 minimum cash balance and represents the total balance at the end of the month.

The excess cash balance in October can be invested in marketable securities. The deficits in November and December will have to be financed by borrowing — typically, short-term borrowing (notes payable). Since it may be necessary for the firm to borrow up to $76,000 for the three-month period evaluated, the financial manager should be sure that a line of credit is opened or some other arrangement made to assure the availability of these funds. The manager will usually request or arrange to borrow more than the maximum financing indicated in the cash budget because of the uncertainty of the ending cash values, which are based on the sales forecast and other forecast values.

COPING WITH UNCERTAINTY IN THE CASH BUDGET

Aside from care in preparation of sales forecasts and other estimates included in the cash budget, there are two ways of coping with the uncertainty of the cash budget.[4] One is by preparing several cash budgets, one based on a pessimistic forecast, one based on the most likely forecast, and a third based on an optimistic forecast. An evaluation of these ending cash flows allows the financial manager to determine the amount of financing necessary to cover the most adverse situation. The use of a number of cash budgets, each based on differing assumptions, should also give the financial manager a sense of the riskiness of alternatives so that he or she makes more intelligent short-term financial decisions. The sensitivity analysis approach is commonly used to analyze cash flows under a variety of possible circumstances.

EXAMPLE   Table 5.6 presents the summary results of ABC Company's cash budget prepared for each month of concern for a pessimistic, most likely, and optimistic estimate of cash receipts and cash disbursements. The most likely estimate is based on the expected outcomes presented earlier in Tables 5.2 through 5.5; the pessimistic and optimistic outcomes are based on the worst and best possible outcomes, respectively. During the month of October, the ABC Company will need a maximum of $15,000 of financing, while at best it will have a $62,000 excess cash balance available for short-term investment. During November, its financing requirement will be between $0 and $185,000. It could experience an excess cash balance of $5,000 during November. The December projections reflect maximum borrowing of $190,000 with a possible excess cash balance of $107,000. By considering the extreme values reflected in the pessimistic and optimistic outcomes, the ABC Company should be better able to plan cash requirements. For the three-month period, the peak borrowing requirement under the worst circumstances would be $190,000, which

---

[4] The term *uncertainty* is used here to refer to the variability of the cash flow outcomes that may actually occur. A thorough discussion of risk and uncertainty is presented in Chapter 7.

Table 5.6   A Sensitivity Analysis of ABC Company's Cash Budget ($000)

	October			November			December		
	Pessi-mistic	Most likely	Opti-mistic	Pessi-mistic	Most likely	Opti-mistic	Pessi-mistic	Most likely	Opti-mistic
Total cash receipts	$160	$210	$285	$ 210	$320	$410	$ 275	$340	$422
Less: Total cash disbursements	200	213	248	380	418	467	280	305	320
Net cash flow	$ (40)	$ (3)	$ 37	$(170)	$ (98)	$ (57)	$ (5)	$ 35	$102
Add: Beginning cash	50	50	50	10	47	87	(160)	(51)	30
Ending cash	$ 10	$ 47	$ 87	$(160)	$ (51)	$ 30	$(165)	$ (16)	$132
Less: Minimum cash balance	25	25	25	25	25	25	25	25	25
Required total financing	$ 15	—	—	$185	$ 76	—	$ 190	$ 41	—
Excess cash balance	—	$ 22	$ 62	—	—	$ 5	—	—	$107

happens to be considerably greater than the most likely estimate for this period of $76,000. ■

A second and much more sophisticated way of coping with uncertainty in the cash budget is by *computer simulation*.[5] By simulating the occurrence of sales and other uncertain events, a probability distribution of the firm's ending cash flows for each month can be developed. The financial decision maker can then use the probability distribution to determine the amount of financing necessary to provide a desired degree of protection against a cash shortage.

CASH FLOW WITHIN THE MONTH

Since the cash flows presented in the cash budget are shown only on a total monthly basis, the information it provides is not necessarily adequate for assuring solvency. A firm must look more closely at its pattern of daily cash receipts and cash disbursements to make sure adequate cash is available for meeting bills as they come due. The following example illustrates the importance of monitoring daily cash flows in order to understand another source of variance.

EXAMPLE   The ABC Company found its actual pattern of cash receipt and cash disbursement during the month of October to be as shown in Table 5.7. It can be seen that, although the firm begins the month with $50,000 of cash and ends the month with $47,000 in cash, its cash balance is negative at various times within the month. Table 5.7 reflects negative cash balances during the periods October 2 through 11 and October 17 through 22. It can be seen that the largest deficit, of $72,000, occurs on October 4.

Although based on the cash budget presented in Table 5.4 it appears that the ABC Company will not require any financing during the month of October, since a $22,000 excess cash balance is expected, a look at the firm's daily cash flows during October makes it

[5] A more detailed discussion of the use of simulation is included as part of the discussion of capital budgeting under risk in Chapter 11.

Table 5.7   Daily Cash Flows During October for
the ABC Company ($000)

Date	Amount received	Amount disbursed	Cash balance[a]
10/1	Beginning balance		$50
10/2		$100	−50
10/4		22	−72
10/5	$65	15	−22
10/11	74		52
10/12	10	12	50
10/16		40	10
10/17	3	21	−8
10/22	35		27
10/26	20	1	46
10/29	3		49
10/31		2	47
Total	$210	$213	

[a] These figures represent ending cash balances without any financing.

quite clear that it will need additional financing in order to make payments as they come due. At the maximum, $72,000 is required to meet daily cash flow requirements. ■

The example makes it quite clear that while a firm's cash flows as reflected by the cash budget may be synchronized so that at month end receipts exceed disbursements, this still does not ensure that the firm can meet daily cash requirements. Since a firm's cash flows are generally quite variable when viewed on a daily basis, effective cash planning requires a look beyond the cash budget. Although the ABC Company's cash budget (Table 5.4) suggests it does not need to borrow during October, due to the nonsynchronized daily cash flows, the firm needs a maximum of $72,000 in additional funds. The financial manager must therefore plan and monitor cash flow more frequently than on a monthly basis. The greater the variability of cash flows from day to day, the greater is the attention required.

 ## Profit Planning: Pro Forma Statements

The profit-planning process centers on the preparation of *pro forma statements,* which are projected financial statements — income statements and balance sheets. Preparation of these statements requires a careful blending of a number of procedures to account for the revenues, costs, and expenses resulting from the firm's anticipated level of operations. The basic steps in this process were shown in the flow diagram presented in Figure 5.1. These detailed procedures are typically performed by an accountant. The financial manager concentrates on the use of simple approximations to estimate the pro forma statements. A variety of simplified approaches exist for preparing pro forma statements; the most popular are

WHAT IS CASH FLOW?: THE CHARTER COMPANY CONTROVERSY

Charter Co.'s financial position appears to be worse than the company admits.

The oil refining and insurance concern had a negative cash flow of at least $10 million — and possibly as much as $70 million — in the first nine months of this year [1983], according to several securities analysts and accounting experts who have studied figures Charter reported to the Securities and Exchange Commission on Nov. 4.

Charter insists that its cash flow is positive. The issue is important because financial analysts frequently use cash flow — the balance between cash coming in and cash going out — to determine a company's financial health. Charter Co.'s insurance subsidiaries have been hurt by publicity from the Chapter 11 bankruptcy filing of Baldwin-United Corp. and by Merrill Lynch & Co.'s decision to stop selling its annuities, but earnings from the insurance units aren't included in Charter's cash-flow figures. That means any cash-flow problems are from Charter's oil operations, and that Charter's troubles reach far beyond the insurance operations.

Cash flow "is a vital measure that would give you a clue as to whether this company is going to continue to function," says Samuel R. Sapienza, chairman of the accounting department at the University of Pennsylvania's Wharton School.

A "Nebulous Term"

James R. Whitley III, Charter's senior vice president for finance, says, "Physical cash received from continuing operations is positive." He says cash from operations was $14.6 million through Sept. 30, a figure in the SEC filing called "funds provided by operations." And he contends that cash flow is a "nebulous term."

But he concedes that the $14.6 million figure includes several nonrecurring items that accounting experts and securities analysts say don't reflect the profitability of continuing operations. And people who believe that Charter has a negative cash flow "have a preponderance of merit on their side," says George Sorter, an accounting professor at New York University's Graduate School of Business Administration. "Under any sort of calculations I made, they came out with a negative cash flow."

SOURCE: David B. Hilder, "Studies See Negative Cash Flow at Charter, Showing Troubles Beyond Insurance Lines," *The Wall Street Journal,* November 23, 1983, p. 29.

based on the belief that the financial relationships reflected in the firm's historical financial statements will not change in the coming period. The most common of these approaches is presented in the following material.

BACKGROUND INFORMATION

The inputs required for preparing pro forma statements using the simplified approaches are financial statements for the preceding year and a sales forecast for the coming year. A variety of assumptions must also be made when using simplified approaches. The company we will use to illustrate the simplified approaches to pro forma preparation is the DuBois Manufacturing Company, which manu-

Table 5.8 An Income Statement for the DuBois Manufacturing
Company for the Year Ended December 31, 1984

Sales		
Model X (1000 units at $20/unit)	$20,000	
Model Y (3000 units at $27/unit)	81,000	
Total sales		$101,000
Less: Cost of goods sold		
Labor	$28,500	
Material A	8,000	
Material B	5,500	
Overhead	38,000	
Total cost of goods sold		80,000
Gross profits		$ 21,000
Less: Operating expenses		10,000
Operating profits		$ 11,000
Less: Interest expense		1,000
Net profits before taxes		$ 10,000
Less: Taxes (.15 × $10,000)		1,500
Net profits after taxes		$ 8,500
Less: Common stock dividends		4,000
To retained earnings		$ 4,500

factures and sells one basic product, widgets. It has two basic models — model X
and model Y. Although each model is produced by the same process, each requires
different amounts of raw material and labor.

Past year's financial statements. The firm's income statement for the 1984 operations is
given in Table 5.8. It indicates that the firm paid $4000 in cash dividends in the
year just completed. The firm's balance sheet for the past year of operation, 1984,
is given in Table 5.9.

Sales forecast. As for the cash budget, the key input for the development of pro forma
statements is the sales forecast. The sales forecast by model for the coming year,

Table 5.9 A Balance Sheet for the DuBois Manufacturing
Company (December 31, 1984)

Assets		Liabilities and equities	
Cash	$ 6,000	Accounts payable	$ 7,000
Marketable securities	4,016	Taxes payable	375
Accounts receivable	13,000	Notes payable	8,260
Inventories	15,984	Other current liabilities	3,365
Total current assets	$39,000	Total current liabilities	$19,000
Net fixed assets	51,000	Long-term debts	$18,000
Total assets	$90,000	Stockholders' equity	
		Common stock	$30,000
		Retained earnings	$23,000
		Total liabilities and	
		stockholders' equity	$90,000

Table 5.10   1985 Sales Forecast for
              the DuBois Manufac-
              turing Company

Unit sales	
Model X	1,500
Model Y	2,800
Dollar sales	
Model X ($25/unit)	$ 37,500
Model Y ($35/unit)	98,000
Total	$135,500

1985, for the DuBois Company is given in Table 5.10. This forecast is based on
external and internal data. The unit sale prices given reflect an increase from $20
to $25 for model X and from $27 to $35 for model Y. These increases are required
to cover the firm's anticipated increases in labor, overhead, and operating expenses.

PRO FORMA INCOME STATEMENT

A simple way to develop a pro forma income statement is to use the *percent-of-
sales method,* which forecasts sales and uses values for the cost of goods sold,
operating expenses, and interest expense that are expressed as a percentage of
projected sales. The percentages used are likely to be the percentage of sales these
items equaled in the immediately preceding year. For the DuBois Manufacturing
Company, these percentages are as follows:

$$\frac{\text{Cost of goods sold}}{\text{Sales}} = \frac{\$80,000}{\$101,000} = 79.2\%$$

$$\frac{\text{Operating expenses}}{\text{Sales}} = \frac{\$10,000}{\$101,000} = 9.9\%$$

$$\frac{\text{Interest expense}}{\text{Sales}} = \frac{\$1,000}{\$101,000} = 1.0\%$$

The dollar values used are taken from the 1984 income statement (Table 5.8).
    Applying these percentages to the firm's forecast level of sales of $135,500,
developed in Table 5.10, and assuming that the firm will pay $4,000 in cash
dividends in 1985, results in the pro forma income statement in Table 5.11. The
expected contribution to retained earnings is $7,402, which represents a consider-
able improvement over the $4,500 in the preceding year.

Considering types of costs and expenses. The technique used to prepare the pro forma
income statement in Table 5.11 assumes that all the firm's costs are variable. This
occurs since the use of the historical (actual 1984) ratios of cost of goods sold,

Table 5.11   A Pro Forma Income Statement,
             Using the Percent-of-Sales
             Method, for the DuBois
             Manufacturing Company for the
             Year Ended December 31, 1985

Sales	$135,500
Less: Cost of goods sold (79.2%)	107,316
Gross profits	$ 28,184
Less: Operating expenses (9.9%)	13,415
Operating profits	$ 14,769
Less: Interest expense (1.0%)	1,355
Net profits before taxes	$ 13,414
Less: Taxes (.15 × $13,414)	2,012
Net profits after taxes	$ 11,402
Less: Common stock dividends	4,000
To retained earnings	$ 7,402

operating expenses, and interest expense to sales assumes that for a given percentage increase in sales, the same percentage increase in each of these cost and expense components will result. For example, as Dubois's sales increased by 34.2 percent (from $101,000 in 1984 to $135,500 projected for 1985), its cost of goods sold also increased by 34.2 percent (from $80,000 in 1984 to $107,316 projected for 1985).

Because of this fixed-percentage assumption, the firm's net profits before taxes also increased by 34.2 percent (from $10,000 in 1984 to $13,414 projected for 1985). This approach assumes all costs are variable; the firm has no fixed costs. The broader implication is that since the firm has no fixed costs, it will not receive the benefits often resulting from them.[6] Therefore, the use of past cost and expense ratios generally tends to understate profits, since the firm is likely to have certain fixed operating and financial costs. For high-fixed-cost firms, this approach will underestimate profits by more than would be true in the case of firms that have lower fixed costs. The best way to adjust for the presence of fixed costs when using the simplified approach for pro forma income statement preparation is to break the firm's historical costs into fixed and variable components and make the forecast using this relationship.[7]

[6] Detailed discussion and illustration of the potential returns as well as risks from the use of fixed (operating and financial) costs to create "leverage" are included in Chapter 13. The key point to recognize here is that fixed costs can magnify returns in the event the firm's revenue is increasing.

[7] The application of *regression analysis* — a statistically based technique for measuring the relationship between variables — to past cost data as it relates to past sales could be used to develop equations that recognize the fixed and variable nature of each cost. Such equations could be employed in preparing the pro forma income statement given the sales forecast. The use of the regression approach in pro forma income statement preparation is widespread, and many computer software packages for use in pro forma preparation rely on this technique. Expanded discussions of the application of this technique can be found in most second-level managerial finance texts.

EXAMPLE The XYZ Company's last and pro forma income statements, which are broken into fixed- and variable-cost components, are given below.

XYZ COMPANY INCOME STATEMENTS

	Last year	Pro forma
Sales	$100,000	$120,000
Less: Cost of goods sold		
Fixed cost	20,000	20,000
Variable cost (.40 × sales)	40,000	48,000
Gross profits	$ 40,000	$ 52,000
Less: Operating expense		
Fixed expense	5,000	5,000
Variable expense (.15 × sales)	15,000	18,000
Operating profits	$ 20,000	$ 29,000
Less: Interest expense (all fixed)	8,000	8,000
Net profits before taxes	$ 12,000	$ 21,000
Less: Taxes (.40 × net profits before taxes)	4,800	8,400
Net profits after taxes	$ 7,200	$ 12,600

By breaking its costs and expenses into fixed and variable components, the XYZ Company's pro forma profit is expected to provide a more accurate projection. Had the firm treated all costs as variable, its pro forma net profits before taxes would equal 12 percent of sales, just as was the case in the last year ($12,000 profits before taxes ÷ $100,000 sales). The net profits before taxes would therefore have been $14,400 (12% × $120,000 projected sales) instead of the $21,000 of net profits before taxes found using the firm's fixed-cost–variable-cost breakdown. ■

The example should make it clear that when using a simplified approach to pro forma income statement preparation, it is advisable to consider first breaking down costs and expenses into fixed and variable components. Due to a lack of available data, the pro forma income statement prepared for DuBois Manufacturing Company in Table 5.11 is based on the assumption that all costs are variable — which is likely *not* to be the case. Therefore, its projected profits may be understated.

 ## PRO FORMA BALANCE SHEET

One of two simplified procedures is commonly used to prepare a pro forma balance sheet: (1) the percent-of-sales method and (2) the judgmental approach.

Percent-of-sales-method. Like the pro forma income statement preparation process, the percent-of-sales method can be used to develop a firm's pro forma balance sheet. Justification for this approach is based on the fact that as a firm's sales increase, so does its need for additional assets and certain liabilities. For example, accounts receivable balances are usually directly related to sales — higher sales leads to higher accounts receivable, and vice versa. Table 5.12 recasts the 1984 balance sheet for DuBois Manufacturing Company (presented earlier as Table 5.9) on a

Table 5.12   A Percent-of-Sales Balance Sheet for the DuBois
Manufacturing Company (December 31, 1984)

Assets		Liabilities and equities	
Cash	5.9%	Accounts payable	6.9%
Marketable securities	4.0	Taxes payable	0.4
Accounts receivable	12.9	Notes payable	8.2
Inventories	15.8	Other current liabilities	3.3
Total current assets	38.6%	Total current liabilities	18.8%
Net fixed assets	50.5	Long-term debts	17.8%
Total assets	89.1%	Stockholders' equity	
		Common stock	29.7%
		Retained earnings	22.8%
		Total liabilities and stockholders' equity	89.1%

NOTE: The values in this table were calculated by dividing the dollar values of each account balance on the firm's balance sheet shown in Table 5.9 by $101,000—the actual sales during 1984 shown on the income statement in Table 5.8.

percentage-of-sales basis. Each asset, liability, and equity account balance is now shown as a percentage of 1984 sales, which were $101,000. The accounts receivable percentage of 12.9 was calculated by dividing the $13,000 accounts receivable balance by the $101,000 value of sales ($13,000 ÷ $101,000 = 12.9%).

Assuming that the historical percentages in Table 5.12 do not change and using the forecast sales of $135,500 for 1985, the firm's assets and current liabilities at year-end 1985 can be estimated as shown in Table 5.13. These asset and current liability values were found by multiplying the forecast sales of $135,500 by the historical percentages from Table 5.12. Inventories were found by taking 15.8 percent (from Table 5.12) of the $135,000 sales forecast (.158 × $135,500 = $21,409). The values for long-term debt and common stock were left unchanged from 1984 since changes in the levels of long-term financing are not spontaneous but rather require managerial action. The value for retained earnings is determined by adding the retained earnings of $7,402 from the pro forma income statement (Table 5.11) to the 1984 year-end retained earnings of $23,000 found on the historical balance sheet (Table 5.9).

The final entry is a balancing, or plug, figure called the *external funds required;* it represents the amount of additional funds needed to allow the firm to meet its financing needs in the coming year. Using the percent-of-sales method, it appears that the DuBois Manufacturing Company will need $16,855 in additional external financing during 1985. When this approach is used, a negative external funds requirement could result; it would indicate that the firm's spontaneous and retained earnings financing is in excess of its needs and therefore that funds will be available for repaying debt, repurchasing stock, or increasing the dividend to stockholders. Occasionally an analyst will use the percent-of-sales method for pro forma preparation to estimate financing needs in the coming year, but for our purposes this approach provides a rough approximation of the pro forma balance sheet. Most financial managers prepare a more detailed statement using the judg-

Table 5.13   A Pro Forma Balance Sheet, Using the Percent-of Sales Method, for DuBois Manufacturing Company (December 31, 1985)

Assets		Liabilities and equities	
Cash	$ 7,995	Accounts payable	$ 9,350
Marketable securities	5,420	Taxes payable	542
Accounts receivable	17,480	Notes payable	11,111
Inventories	21,409	Other current liabilities	4,472
Total current assets	$ 52,304	Total current liabilities	$ 25,475
Net fixed assets	68,428	Long-term debts[a]	$ 18,000
Total assets	$120,732	Stockholders' equity	
		Common stock[a]	$ 30,000
		Retained earnings[b]	$ 30,402
		Total	$103,877
		External funds required[c]	$ 16,855
		Total liabilities and stockholders' equity	$120,732

NOTE: All values were calculated by multiplying the historical percentage of sales from Table 5.12 by the forecast sales of $135,500, except as noted.

[a] These values were assumed unchanged from the preceding year and are drawn from Table 5.9.

[b] Calculated by adding the pro forma retained earning contribution of $7,402 from the pro forma income statement, Table 5.11, to the retained earnings of $23,000 from the 1984 balance sheet in Table 5.9 ($7,402 + $23,000 = $30,402).

[c] This adjustment reflects the level of external funds required to bring the liability and equity total up to $120,732 — the level of total assets. It was found by subtracting the total of current liabilities, long-term debt, common stock, and retained earnings of $103,877 from total assets ($120,732 − $103,877 = $16,855).

mental approach, which relies on more specific and detailed assumptions and estimates than the percent-of-sales approach.

Judgmental approach. Under the *judgmental approach* for developing the pro forma balance sheet, the values of certain balance sheet accounts are estimated while others are calculated. When this approach is used, the firm's external financing is used as a balancing, or plug, figure. To apply the judgmental approach to DuBois Manufacturing Company's balance sheet, a number of assumptions must be made:

1. A minimum cash balance of $6000 is desired.
2. Marketable securities are initially assumed to remain unchanged from their current level of $4016.
3. Accounts receivable will average one and one-half month's sales (i.e., a collection period of 1.50 × 30 days = 45 days). Since DuBois's annual sales are projected to be $135,500, the accounts receivable should average $16,938 ($\frac{1}{8}$ × $135,500) in any given month. (One-eighth represents one and one-half months expressed as a fraction of a year.)
4. The ending inventory should remain at a level of about $16,000, of which 25 percent (approximately $4,000) should be raw materials, while the remaining 75 percent (approximately $12,000) should consist of finished goods.

Table 5.14   A Pro Forma Balance Sheet, Using the Judgmental Approach, for the DuBois Manufacturing Company (December 31, 1985)

Assets			Liabilities and equities	
Cash		$ 6,000	Accounts payable	$ 8,130
Marketable securities		4,016	Taxes payable	503
Accounts receivable		16,938	Notes payable	8,260
Inventories			Other current liabilities	3,365
Raw materials	$ 4,000		Total current liabilities	$ 20,258
Finished goods	12,000		Long-term debts	$ 18,000
Total inventory		16,000	Stockholders' equity	
Total current assets		$ 42,954	Common stock	$ 30,000
Net fixed assets		63,000	Retained earnings	$ 30,402
Total assets		$105,954	Total	$ 98,660
			External funds required[a]	$ 7,294
			Total liabilities and stockholders' equity	$105,954

[a] The amount of external funds needed to force the firm's balance sheet to balance. Due to the nature of the judgmental approach to preparing the pro forma balance sheet, the balance sheet is not expected to balance without some type of adjustment.

quality of the estimated values and the degree of confidence he or she can have in them.

USING PRO FORMA STATEMENTS

In addition to estimating the amount, if any, of external financing required to support a given level of sales, pro forma statements provide a basis for analyzing in advance the level of profitability and overall financial performance of the firm in the coming year. Using pro forma statements, the financial manager, as well as lenders, can analyze the firm's sources and uses of funds as well as various aspects of performance, such as liquidity, activity, debt, and profitability. Sources and uses can be evaluated by preparing a pro forma statement of changes in financial position; various ratios can be calculated from the pro forma income statement and balance sheet to evaluate performance.

After analyzing the pro forma statements, the financial manager can take steps to adjust the coming year's operations to achieve short-run financial goals. For example, if profits on the pro forma income statement are too low, a variety of pricing or cost-cutting actions, or both, could be initiated; if the projected level of accounts receivable shown is too high, changes in credit policy may avoid this outcome. Pro forma statements are therefore of key importance in solidifying the firm's financial plans for the coming year.

CHAPTER SUMMARY

● The two key aspects of the financial planning process are cash planning and profit planning.

● Long-run financial plans, which reflect the anticipated impact on finances from implementation of planned actions by the firm, act as a guide for preparing short-run financial plans. They tend to cover periods ranging from two to ten years and are updated periodically.

● Key inputs to short-run plans are the sales forecast and various forms of operating and financial data; key outputs include operating budgets, the cash budget, and pro forma financial statements.

● The cash planning process centers on the preparation of the cash budget, which is often called the cash forecast. The cash budget relies heavily on the sales forecast as an input. Typically, the cash budget is prepared for a one-year period divided into monthly intervals.

● The basic format of the cash budget is such that cash receipts and disbursements for each period can easily be netted against each other to get the net cash flow in each period. By adding beginning cash to the net cash flow, ending cash can be estimated. After subtracting the minimum cash balance from the ending cash, the required total financing or excess cash balance can be determined.

● To cope with the uncertainty in the cash budget, sensitivity analysis or computer simulation can be used. One common sensitivity analysis approach involves preparing separate cash budgets based on pessimistic, most likely, and optimistic estimates.

● The profit planning process centers on preparation of pro forma statements, which are projected income statements and balance sheets.

● A pro forma income statement can be developed using past percentage relationships between certain cost and expense items and the firm's sales and applying these percentages to forecasts.

● A pro forma balance sheet can be estimated using either the percent-of-sales method or the judgmental approach. In either case, an entry for external funds required acts as a balancing, or plug, figure.

● Pro forma statements are useful for internal control; lenders also use them to make credit decisions.

KEY TERMS

cash budget
cash receipts
computer simulation
ending cash
excess cash balance
external forecast
external funds required
financial planning process
internal forecast
judgmental approach

long-run financial plans
net cash flow
percent-of-sales method
pro forma balance sheet
pro forma income statement
pro forma statements
required total financing
sales forecast
short-run financial plans

QUESTIONS

5-1   Describe the *financial planning process*. What are its two key components?

5-2   What is the purpose of the *cash budget* from the point of view of the financial manager?

5-3   The key input to the cash budget is a sales forecast. What is the difference between *external* and *internal* forecast data?

5-4   How can the bottom lines of the cash budget be used to determine the firm's short-term borrowing and investment requirements?

5-5   Normally, uncertainty is present in the cash budget. What is the cause of this uncertainty? What two techniques can be used to cope with this uncertainty?

5-6   Even with a monthly cash budget, the firm may not be assured of solvency. What actions or analysis beyond preparation of the cash budget should the financial manager undertake to assure that cash is available when needed?

5-7   What are *pro forma financial statements?* How do the pro forma income statement and pro forma balance sheet differ?

5-8   Which of the pro forma statements must be developed first? Why? What necessary inputs to the pro forma statement preparation process are provided by the cash budget?

5-9   Briefly describe the pro forma income statement preparation process using the percent-of-sales method. What are the strengths and weaknesses of this simplified approach?

5-10 Describe the two methods—percent-of-sales and judgmental—for simplified preparation of the pro forma balance sheet. Which approach is better?

5-11 What is the significance of the balancing, or plug, figure *external funds required,* used with the simplified approaches for preparing the pro forma balance sheet?

5-12 How may the financial analyst wish to evaluate pro forma statements? What is his or her objective in evaluating these statements?

PROBLEMS

5-1 **(Cash Receipts)** A firm has actual sales of $65,000 in April and $60,000 in May. It expects sales of $70,000 in June and $100,000 in July and in August. Assuming that sales are the only source of cash inflows and that half of these are for cash and the remainder are collected evenly over the following two months, what are the firm's expected cash receipts for June, July, and August?

5-2 **(Cash Budget — Basic)** Mary Schwartz, a financial analyst for MIS, Inc., has prepared the following sales and cash disbursement estimates for the period February–June of the current year.

Month	Sales	Cash Disbursements
February	$500	$400
March	600	300
April	400	600
May	200	500
June	200	200

Ms. Schwartz notes that historically 30 percent of sales have been for *cash*. Of *credit sales,* 70 percent are collected one month after the sale, and the remaining 30 percent are collected two months after the sale. The firm wishes to maintain a minimum ending balance in its cash account of $25. Balances above this amount would be invested in short-term government securities, while any deficits would be financed through short-term bank borrowing. The beginning cash balance at April 1 is $115.
  a Prepare a cash budget for the months of April, May, and June.
  b How much financing, if any, at a maximum would MIS, Inc., need to meet its obligations during this three-month period?
  c If a pro forma balance sheet dated at the end of June were prepared from the information presented, give the size of each of the following: cash, notes payable, marketable securities, accounts receivable.

5-3 **(Cash Budget — Basic)** The American Tire Company had sales of $50,000 in March and $60,000 in April. Forecast sales for May, June, and July are $70,000, $80,000, and $100,000, respectively. The firm has a cash balance of $5,000 on May 1 and wishes to maintain a minimum cash balance of $5,000. Given the following data, prepare and interpret a cash budget for the months of May, June, and July.
  (1) Twenty percent of the firm's sales are for cash, 60 percent are collected in the next month, the remaining 20 percent are collected in the second month following sale.
  (2) The firm receives other income of $2000 per month.
  (3) The firm's actual or expected purchases, all made for cash, are $50,000, $70,000, and $80,000 for the months of May through July, respectively.
  (4) Rent is $3000 per month.
  (5) Wages and salaries are 10 percent of the previous month's sales.
  (6) Cash dividends of $3000 will be paid in June.
  (7) Payment of principal and interest of $4000 is due in June.
  (8) A cash purchase of equipment costing $6000 is scheduled in July.
  (9) Taxes of $6000 are due in June.

5-4 (Cash budget — Advanced) Archer Appliance Company's actual sales and purchases for September and October 1984, along with its forecast sales and purchases for the period November 1984 through April 1985, follow.

Year	Month	Sales	Purchases
1984	September	$210,000	$120,000
1984	October	250,000	150,000
1984	November	170,000	140,000
1984	December	160,000	100,000
1985	January	140,000	80,000
1985	February	180,000	110,000
1985	March	200,000	100,000
1985	April	250,000	90,000

The firm makes 20 percent of all sales for cash and collects on 40 percent of its sales in each of the two months following the sale. Other cash inflows are expected to be $12,000 in September, February, and April and $15,000 in January, February, and March. The firm pays cash for 10 percent of its purchases. It pays for 50 percent of its purchases in the following month and for 40 percent of its purchases two months later.

Salaries and wages amount to 20 percent of the preceding month's sales. Rent of $20,000 per month must be paid. Interest payments of $10,000 are due in January and April. A principal payment of $30,000 is also due in April. The firm expects to pay cash dividends of $20,000 in January and April. Taxes of $80,000 are due in April. The firm also intends to make a capital outlay of $25,000 in December.

a Assuming that the firm has a cash balance of $22,000 at the beginning of November, determine the end-of-month cash balances for each month, November through April.

b Assuming that the firm wishes to maintain a $15,000 minimum cash balance, determine the monthly total financing requirements or excess cash balances.

c If the firm were requesting a line of credit to cover needed financing for the period November to April, how large would this line have to be? Explain your answer.

5-5 (Cash Budget — Sensitivity Analysis) Patterson's Parts Store expects to sell $100,000 in parts during each of the next three months. It is committed to accept monthly purchases of $60,000 during this time. Wages and salaries are $10,000 per month plus 5 percent of sales. Patterson's expects to make a tax payment of $20,000 in the next month, a capital expenditure of $15,000 in the second month, and receive $8,000 in cash from the sale of an asset in the third month. All sales and purchases are for cash. Beginning cash and the minimum cash balance are assumed to be zero.

a Construct a cash budget for the next three months.

b Patterson's is unsure of the sales levels, but all other figures are certain. If the most pessimistic sales figure is $80,000 per month and the most optimistic is $120,000 per month, what are the monthly minimum and maximum ending cash balances the firm can expect for each of the one-month periods?

c Combine **a** and **b** into a sensitivity analysis for Patterson's Parts Store. Briefly discuss how these combined data allow the financial manager to plan for his or her financing needs.

5-6 (Cash Flow Concepts) The following represent financial transactions that the Turner Company will be undertaking in the next planning period. For each transaction check the statement or statements that will be affected immediately.

	Statement		
	---	---	---
Transaction	Cash budget	Pro forma income statement	Pro forma balance sheet
Cash sale			
Credit sale			
Accounts receivable are collected			
Asset with five-year life is bought			
Depreciation is taken			
Amortization of goodwill is taken			
Sale of common stock			
Retirement of outstanding bonds			
Fire insurance premium is paid for the next three years			

5-7 **(Pro Forma Income Statement)**   The marketing department of Kaufman Manufacturing estimates that its sales in 1985 will be $1.5 million. Interest expense is expected to remain unchanged at $35,000, and the firm plans to pay $70,000 in cash dividends during 1985. Kaufman Manufacturing's income statement for the year ended December 31, 1984 is given below, followed by a breakdown of the firm's cost of goods sold and operating expenses into its fixed- and variable-cost components.

a   Use the *percent-of-sales method* to prepare a pro forma income statement for the year ended December 31, 1985 for Kaufman Manufacturing.

b   Use the *fixed- and variable-cost data* to develop a pro forma income statement for the year ended December 31, 1985 for Kaufman Manufacturing.

c   Compare and contrast the statements developed in **a** and **b**. Which statement will likely provide the better estimates of 1985 income? Explain why.

INCOME STATEMENT
KAUFMAN MANUFACTURING COMPANY
FOR THE YEAR ENDED DECEMBER 31, 1984

Sales	$1,400,000
Less: Cost of goods sold	910,000
Gross profits	$ 490,000
Less: Operating expenses	120,000
Operating profits	$ 370,000
Less: Interest expense	35,000
Net profits before taxes	$ 335,000
Less: Taxes (40%)	134,000
Net profits after taxes	$ 201,000
Less: Cash dividends	66,000
To retained earnings	$ 135,000

FIXED- AND VARIABLE-COST BREAKDOWN
KAUFMAN MANUFACTURING COMPANY
FOR THE YEAR ENDED DECEMBER 31, 1984

Cost of goods sold		
Fixed cost	$210,000	
Variable cost	700,000	
Total cost	$910,000	
Operating expenses		
Fixed expenses	$ 36,000	
Variable expenses	84,000	
Total expenses	$120,000	

5-8 (Pro Forma Balance Sheet)   Tucker Tool has 1984 sales of $10 million. It wishes to analyze expected performance and financing needs for 1986—two years ahead. Given the following information, answer questions **a** and **b**.

(1) The percent of sales for items that vary directly with sales are as follows:
Cash, 4 percent
Receivables, 12 percent
Inventory, 18 percent
Net fixed assets, 40 percent
Accounts payable, 14 percent
Accruals, 4 percent
Net profit margin, 3 percent

(2) Marketable securities and other current liabilities are expected to remain unchanged.

(3) No sale or retirement of long-term debt is expected.

(4) No sale or repurchase of common stock is expected.

(5) The dividend payout of 50 percent of net profits is expected to continue.

(6) Sales are expected to be $11 million in 1985 and $12 million in 1986.

(7) The December 31, 1984, balance sheet appears below.

a Prepare a pro forma balance sheet dated December 31, 1986.

b Discuss the financing changes suggested by the statement prepared in **a**.

TUCKER TOOL
BALANCE SHEET
DECEMBER 31, 1984
($000)

Assets		Liabilities and equities	
Cash	$ 400	Accounts payable	$1400
Marketable securities	200	Accruals	400
Accounts receivable	1200	Other current liabilities	80
Inventories	1800	Total current liabilities	$1880
Total current assets	$3600	Long-term debt	$2000
Net fixed assets	$4000	Common equity	$3720
Total assets	$7600	Total liabilities and stockholders' equity	$7600

5-9 (Integrative—Pro Forma Statements)   The O'Connor Daughters Corporation wishes to prepare financial plans. Using the financial statements below and the other information provided,

a   Prepare a pro forma income statement.
b   Prepare pro forma balance sheets using (1) the percent-of-sales method and (2) the judgmental approach.
c   Analyze these statements and discuss the resulting external funds required.

INCOME STATEMENT
O'CONNOR DAUGHTERS CORPORATION
FOR THE YEAR ENDED DECEMBER 31, 1984

Sales	$800,000
Less: Cost of goods sold	600,000
Gross profits	$200,000
Less: Operating expenses	100,000
Net profits before taxes	$100,000
Less: Taxes (40%)	40,000
Net profits after taxes	$ 60,000
Less: Cash dividends	20,000
To retained earnings	$ 40,000

BALANCE SHEET
O'CONNOR DAUGHTERS CORPORATION
DECEMBER 31, 1984

Assets		Liabilities and equities	
Cash	$ 32,000	Accounts payable	$100,000
Marketable securities	18,000	Taxes payable	20,000
Accounts receivable	150,000	Other current liabilities	5,000
Inventories	100,000	Total current	
Total current		liabilities	$125,000
assets	$300,000	Long-term debt	$200,000
Net fixed assets	$350,000	Common stock	$150,000
Total assets	$650,000	Retained earnings	$175,000
		Total liabilities	
		and stock-	
		holders' equity	$650,000

The following financial data are also available:
(1) The firm has estimated that its sales for 1985 will be $900,000.
(2) The firm expects to pay $35,000 in cash dividends in 1985.
(3) The firm wishes to maintain a minimum cash balance of $30,000.
(4) Accounts receivable represent approximately 18 percent of annual sales.
(5) The firm's ending inventory will change directly with changes in sales in 1985.
(6) A new machine costing $42,000 will be purchased in 1985. Total depreciation for 1985 will be $17,000.
(7) Accounts payable will change directly in response to changes in sales in 1985.
(8) Taxes payable will equal one-fourth of the tax liability on the pro forma income statement.
(9) Marketable securities, other current liabilities, long-term debt, and common stock will remain unchanged.

Part III

Basic Financial Concepts

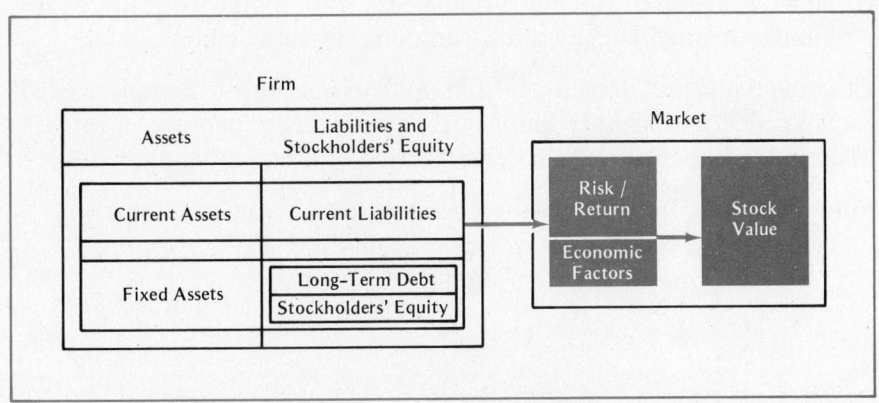

Chapter 6

The Time Value of Money

After studying this chapter, you should be able to:

1. Understand the concept of future value, with both annual and intrayear compounding.

2. Determine the future value of a single cash flow or an annuity mathematically or by using future-value tables.

3. Discuss the concept of present value and explain its relationship to the concept of future value.

4. Calculate the present value of a single cash flow, a mixed stream, or an annuity mathematically or by using present-value tables.

5. Describe the procedures involved in (a) determining the deposit needed to accumulate a future sum and (b) amortizing a loan into equal annual payments over a specified period of time.

6. Find interest or growth rates associated with cash flow streams and calculate the present value of a perpetuity.

Since we view the firm as a going concern, its value and the decisions of the financial manager must both be assessed in light of the future as well as the present. Taking such a long-run view means taking into account the time value of money.

The key concepts making up the time value of money are future value and present value. Future-value calculations are needed to evaluate future amounts resulting from current investment in an interest-earning medium. Present-value calculations are inversely related to future value. They are used to assess the value of the firm, as well as the future benefits expected to result from certain actions. Both future value and present value are needed to calculate the payments required to accumulate a predetermined future sum, to amortize loans by calculating loan payment schedules, and to determine interest or growth rates of money streams. In addition, a thorough understanding of the time value of money is helpful in finding internal rates of return and yields to maturity, concepts that will be discussed in subsequent chapters.

 ## Future Value

The concept of future value, often called "compound value," involves the application of compound interest to a present amount to result in some future amount. It is commonly used in savings institutions; for example, such institutions often advertise compound interest at a rate of x percent or x percent interest compounded semiannually, quarterly, monthly, weekly, or daily. The principles of future value are quite simple, regardless of the period of time involved. In this

Note: Many of the computations introduced in this chapter and applied throughout the text can be streamlined using a calculator or personal computer. Procedures for making routine financial calculations using a simple calculator having only the four standard math functions are described and illustrated on the endpapers inside the front and back covers of this text. The reader is strongly urged to learn these procedures once the basic underlying financial concepts are understood. With a little practice, both the speed and accuracy of financial computations using a calculator can be enhanced with application of the procedures presented.

section we will discuss three aspects of compounding: annual compounding, intrayear compounding, and finding the future value of an annuity.

ANNUAL COMPOUNDING

Annual compounding is the most common type. Interest is *compounded* when the amount earned on an initial deposit (the *initial principal*) becomes part of the principal at the end of the first compounding period. The term *principal* refers to the amount of money on which *interest* is paid.

The calculation of future value. The actual method by which future value is determined with annual compounding can be illustrated by a simple example.

EXAMPLE   If Steve Saver placed $100 in a savings account paying 8 percent interest compounded annually, at the end of one year he will have $108 in the account. This $108 represents the initial principal of $100 plus 8 percent ($8) in interest. The future value at the end of the first year is calculated using Equation 6.1:

$$\text{Future value at end of year 1} = \$100(1 + .08) = \$108 \tag{6.1}$$

If Steve were to leave this money in the account for another year, he would be paid interest at the rate of 8 percent on the new principal of $108. At the end of this second year, there would be $116.64 in the account. This $116.64 would represent the principal at the beginning of year 2 ($108) plus 8 percent of the $108 ($8.64) in interest. The future value at the end of the second year is calculated using Equation 6.2:

$$\text{Future value at end of year 2} = \$108(1 + .08) = \$116.64 \tag{6.2} \blacksquare$$

Substituting the right side of Equation 6.1 for the $108 figure in Equation 6.2 gives us Equation 6.3:

$$\text{Future value at end of year 2} = \$100(1 + .08)(1 + .08) \tag{6.3}$$
$$= \$100(1.08)^2$$
$$= \$116.64$$

The basic relationship in Equation 6.3 can be generalized to find the future value after any number of periods. Let

F_n = the future value or amount at the end of period n
P = the initial principal
k = the annual rate of interest paid on the account
n = the number of periods — typically years — the money is left in the account

Using this notation, a general equation for the future value at the end of period n can be formulated:

$$F_n = P(1 + k)^n \tag{6.4}$$

The usefulness of Equation 6.4 for finding the future value, F_n, in an account paying k percent interest compounded annually for n periods if P dollars were deposited initially can be illustrated by a simple example.

EXAMPLE   James Frugal has placed $800 in a savings account paying 6 percent interest compounded annually. He wishes to determine how much money will be in the account at the end of five years. Substituting $P = \$800$, $k = .06$, and $n = 5$ into Equation 6.4 gives him the amount at the end of year 5.

$$F_5 = \$800(1 + .06)^5 = \$800(1.338) = \$1070.40$$

James will have $1070.40 in the account at the end of year 5. This analysis can be depicted diagramatically on a time line as shown in Figure 6.1. ■

Future-value interest tables. Solving the preceding equation is quite time-consuming, since one must raise 1.06 to the fifth power. To simplify the calculations, future-value interest tables have been compiled. A table of the amount generated by the payment of compound interest on an initial principal of $1 is given as Appendix Table A-1. The table provides values for $(1 + k)^n$ in Equation 6.4.[1] This portion of Equation 6.4 is called the *future-value interest factor*. The future-value interest factor for an initial principal of $1 compounded at k percent for n periods is referred to as $FVIF_{k,n}$:

$$\text{Future-value interest factor} = FVIF_{k,n} = (1 + k)^n \qquad (6.5)$$

By accessing the table with respect to the annual interest rate, k, and the appropriate periods,[2] n, the factor relevant to a particular problem can be found. A sample

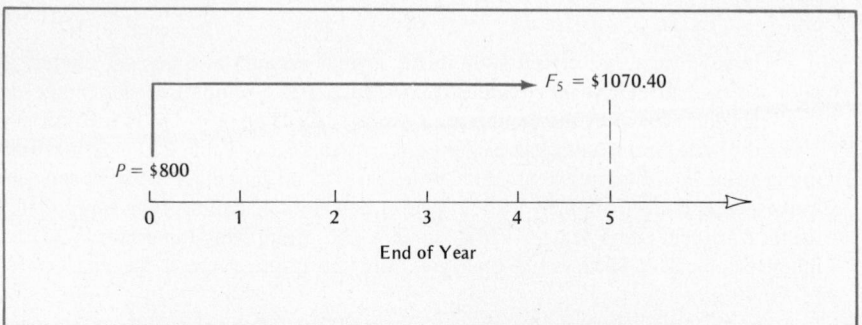

Figure 6.1   Time line for future value of a single amount ($800 initial deposit, earning 6 percent annual interest, at end of 5 years)

[1] This table is commonly referred to as a "compound interest table" or a "table of the future value of one dollar." As long as the reader understands the source of the table values, the various names attached to it should not create confusion, since one can always make a trial calculation of a value for one factor as a check.

[2] Although we commonly deal with years rather than periods, financial tables are frequently presented in terms of periods to provide maximum flexibility.

Table 6.1   The Future-Value Interest Factors for One Dollar, $FVIF_{k,n}$

Period	5.00 percent	6.00 percent	7.00 percent	8.00 percent	9.00 percent	10.00 percent
1	1.050	1.060	1.070	1.080	1.090	1.100
2	1.102	1.124	1.145	1.166	1.188	1.210
3	1.158	1.191	1.225	1.260	1.295	1.331
4	1.216	1.262	1.311	1.360	1.412	1.464
5	1.276	1.338	1.403	1.469	1.539	1.611
6	1.340	1.419	1.501	1.587	1.677	1.772
7	1.407	1.504	1.606	1.714	1.828	1.949
8	1.477	1.594	1.718	1.851	1.993	2.144
9	1.551	1.689	1.838	1.999	2.172	2.358
10	1.629	1.791	1.967	2.159	2.367	2.594

NOTE: All table values have been rounded to the nearest thousandth; the calculated values may differ slightly from the table values.

portion of Table A-1 is given in Table 6.1.[3] Because the factors in Table A-1 give the value for the expression $(1 + k)^n$ for various k and n combinations, by letting $FVIF_{k,n}$ represent the appropriate factor from Table A-1 we can rewrite Equation 6.4 as follows:

$$F_n = P \times (FVIF_{k,n}) \tag{6.6}$$

The expression indicates that to find the future value, F_n, at the end of period n of an initial deposit, we have merely to multiply the initial deposit, P, by the appropriate future-value interest factor from Table A-1. An example will illustrate the use of this table.

EXAMPLE   James Frugal has placed $800 in his savings account at 6 percent interest compounded annually. He wishes to find out how much would be in the account at the end of five years and does so by the cumbersome process of raising $(1 + .06)$ to the fifth power. Using the table for the future value of one dollar (Table 6.1 or Table A-1), he could find the future-value interest factor for an initial principal of $1 on deposit for five years at 6 percent interest compounded annually without performing any calculations. The appropriate factor for 6 percent and 5 years, $FVIF_{6\%,5\,\text{yrs}}$, is 1.338. Multiplying this factor by his actual initial principal of $800 would then give him the future value at the end of year 5, $1070.40. ■

Three important observations should be made about the table for the future value of one dollar. The first is that the factors in the table represent factors for

[3] Occasionally, in the absence of tables of future-value interest factors, the financial manager will want to estimate how long a given sum must earn at a given annual rate in order to double the amount. The *Rule of 72* is used to make this estimate; dividing the annual rate of interest into 72 results in the approximate period it will take to double one's money at the given rate. For example, to double one's money at a 10 percent annual rate of interest, it will take about 7.2 years ($72 \div 10 = 7.2$). Looking at Table 6.1, it can be seen that the future-value interest factor for 10 percent and 7 years is slightly below 2 (1.949); this approximation therefore appears to be reasonably accurate.

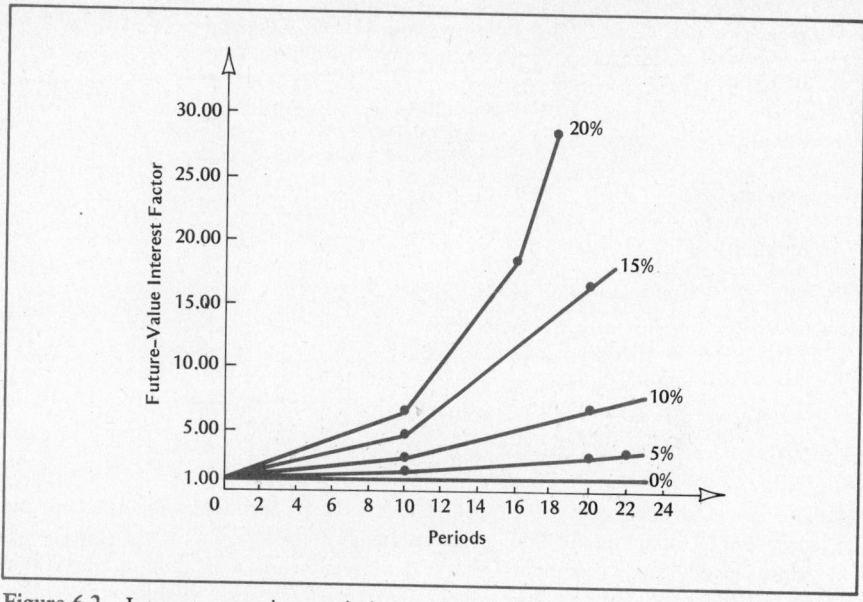

Figure 6.2   Interest rates, time periods, and future-value interest factors used to find the future value of one dollar

determining the future value of one dollar *at the end of the given period.* Second, *as the interest rate increases for any given period, the future-value interest factor also increases.* Thus the higher the interest rate, the greater is the future value. The third point is that *for a given interest rate, the future value of a dollar increases with the passage of time.* The relationship between various interest rates, the number of periods interest is earned, and future-value interest factors is illustrated in Figure 6.2. The fact that the higher the interest rate the higher the future-value interest factor is, and the longer the period of time the higher the future-value interest factor is, should be clear. Note that for an interest rate of 0 percent, the future-value interest factor always equals 1, and the future value therefore always equals the initial principal.

INTRAYEAR COMPOUNDING

Intrayear compounding of interest (interest is compounded more often than once a year) is used in various situations. Savings institutions compound interest semiannually, quarterly, monthly, weekly, daily, or even continuously. This section discusses semiannual and quarterly compounding and then presents a general equation for intrayear compounding. It also explains how to use future-value interest tables in these situations.

Semiannual compounding. *Semiannual compounding* of interest involves two compounding periods within the year. Instead of the stated interest rate being paid once a year, one-half of the stated interest rate is paid twice a year.

Table 6.2 The Future Value from Investing $100 at 8 Percent
Interest Compounded Semiannually over Two Years

Period	Beginning principal (1)	Future-value interest factor (2)	Future value at end of period [(1) × (2)] (3)
6 months	$100.00	1.04	$104.00
1 year	104.00	1.04	108.16
18 months	108.16	1.04	112.49
2 years	112.49	1.04	116.99

EXAMPLE Steve Saver has decided to invest $100 in a savings account paying 8 percent interest compounded semiannually. If he leaves his money in the account for two years, he will be paid 4 percent interest compounded over four periods—each six months long. Table 6.2 presents the calculations required to determine the amount Steve will have at the end of two years.

As the table shows, at the end of one year, when the 8 percent interest is compounded semiannually, Steve will have $108.16; at the end of two years, he will have $116.99. ■

Quarterly compounding. *Quarterly compounding* of interest involves four compounding periods within the year. One-fourth of the stated interest rate is paid four times a year.

EXAMPLE Steve Saver, after further investigation of his savings opportunities, has found an institution that will pay him 8 percent compounded quarterly. If he leaves his money in this

Table 6.3 The Future Value from Investing $100 at 8 Percent
Interest Compounded Quarterly over Two Years

Period	Beginning principal (1)	Future-value interest factor (2)	Future value at end of period [(1) × (2)] (3)
3 months	$100.00	1.02	$102.00
6 months	102.00	1.02	104.04
9 months	104.04	1.02	106.12
1 year	106.12	1.02	108.24
15 months	108.24	1.02	110.40
18 months	110.40	1.02	112.61
21 months	112.61	1.02	114.86
2 years	114.86	1.02	117.16

Table 6.4   The Future Value from Investing $100 at 8 Percent for Years 1 and 2 Given Various Compounding Periods

End of year	Compounding period		
	Annual	Semiannual	Quarterly
1	$108.00	$108.16	$108.24
2	116.64	116.99	117.16

account for two years, he will be paid 2 percent interest compounded over eight periods— each of which consists of one-fourth of a year. Table 6.3 presents the calculations required to determine the amount Steve will have at the end of two years. As the table shows, at the end of one year, when the 8 percent interest is compounded quarterly, Steve will have $108.24; at the end of two years, he will have $117.16.

Table 6.4 presents comparative values for Steve Saver's $100 at the end of years 1 and 2 given annual, semiannual, and quarterly compounding at the 8 percent rate. As the table shows, the *more frequently interest is compounded, the greater the amount of money accumulated.* This is true for any interest rate for any period of time. ■

A general equation for intrayear compounding. It should be clear from the preceding examples that, if m equals the number of times per year interest is compounded, Equation 6.4 (our formula for annual compounding) can be rewritten as

$$F_n = P\left(1 + \frac{k}{m}\right)^{m \times n} \tag{6.7}$$

If $m = 1$, Equation 6.7 reduces to Equation 6.4. Thus, if interest is compounded annually (once a year), Equation 6.7 will provide the same results as Equation 6.4. The general applicability of Equation 6.7 can be illustrated with a simple example.

EXAMPLE   In the preceding examples, the amount that Steve Saver would have at the end of two years if he deposited $100 at 8 percent interest compounded semiannually and quarterly was discussed. For semiannual compounding, m would equal 2 in Equation 6.7, while for quarterly compounding m would equal 4. Substituting the appropriate values for semiannual and quarterly compounding into Equation 6.7 would yield

1. *For semiannual compounding*

$$F_2 = \$100\left(1 + \frac{.08}{2}\right)^{2 \times 2} = \$100(1 + .04)^4 = \$116.99$$

2. *For quarterly compounding*

$$F_2 = \$100\left(1 + \frac{.08}{4}\right)^{4 \times 2} = \$100(1 + .02)^8 = \$117.16$$

If the interest were compounded monthly, weekly, or daily, m would equal 12, 52, or 365, respectively. In the case of *continuous compounding,* which implies compounding every microsecond, m would approach infinity and the use of calculus would be required to determine the future value. The results above agree with the values for F_2 in Tables 6.2 and 6.3. ■

Using a table for intrayear compounding. The table of future-value interest factors for one dollar, Table A-1, can be used to simplify the calculations required by Equation 6.7. Instead of indexing the table for k percent and n years, as we do when interest is compounded annually, we index it for $(k \div m)$ percent and $(m \times n)$ years. The usefulness of the table is usually somewhat limited, since only selected rates for a limited number of years can be found. The table can commonly be used to calculate the results of semiannual and quarterly compounding (i.e., when $m = 2$, 4), but when more frequent compounding is done, the aid of a financial calculator or computer may be necessary to solve Equation 6.7. The following example will clarify the use of the future-value interest factor table for intrayear compounding.

EXAMPLE In the earlier examples, Steve Saver wished to find the future value of $100 invested at 8 percent compounded both semiannually and quarterly for two years. The number of compounding periods, m, was 2 and 4, respectively, in these cases. The values by which the table for the future value of one dollar is accessed, along with the future-value interest factor in each case, are given below.

Compounding period	m	Percentage $(k \div m)$	Years $(m \times n)$	Future-value interest factor from Table A-1
Semiannual	2	$.08 \div 2 = .04$	$2 \times 2 = 4$	1.170
Quarterly	4	$.08 \div 4 = .02$	$4 \times 2 = 8$	1.172

The factor for 4 percent and four years is used for the semiannual compounding, while the factor for 2 percent and eight years is used for quarterly compounding. Multiplying each of the factors by the initial $100 deposit results in a value of $117.00 ($1.170 \times 100) for semiannual compounding and a value of $117.20 ($1.172 \times 100) for quarterly compounding. The corresponding values found by the long method are $116.99 and $117.16, respectively. The discrepancy can be attributed to the rounding of values in the table. ■

THE FUTURE VALUE OF AN ANNUITY

An *annuity* is a stream of equal annual cash flows. These cash flows can be received or deposited by an individual in some interest-earning form. The calculations required to find the future value of an annuity on which interest is paid at a specified rate compounded annually can be illustrated by a simple example.

EXAMPLE Mary Jones wishes to determine how much money she will have at the end of five years if she deposits $1000 annually in a savings account paying 7 percent annual interest. The deposits will be made at the end of each of the next five years. Table 6.5 presents the calculations required. This situation is depicted diagramatically on a time line in Figure 6.3. As the table and figure show, at the end of year 5 Mary will have $5751 in her account. Column 2 of the table indicates that since the deposits are made at the end of the year, the

Table 6.5   The Future Value of a $1000 Five-Year
Annuity Compounded at 7 Percent

End of year	Amount deposited (1)	Number of years compounded (2)	Future-value interest factors from Table A-1 (3)	Future value at end of year [(1) × (3)] (4)
1	$1000	4	1.311	$1311
2	1000	3	1.225	1225
3	1000	2	1.145	1145
4	1000	1	1.070	1070
5	1000	0	1.000	1000
	Future value of annuity at end of year 5			$5751

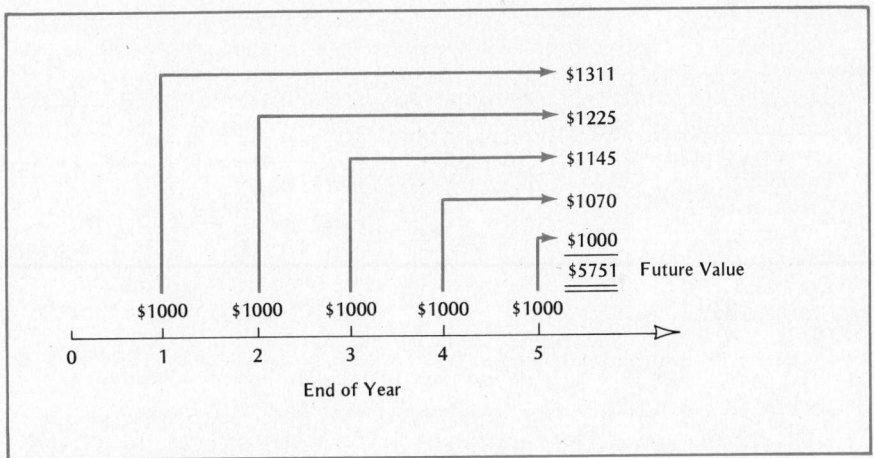

Figure 6.3   Time line for future value of an annuity ($1000 end-of-year deposit,
earning 7 percent, at end of 5 years)

first deposit will earn interest for four years, the second for three years, and so on. The
future-value interest factors in column 3 correspond to these interest-earning periods and
the 7 percent rate of interest. ■

Simplifying the calculations. The calculations required in the preceding example can be
simplified somewhat since each of the factors is actually multiplied by the same
dollar amount. Of course, this is true only in the case of an annuity. The actual
calculations required can be expressed as follows:

$$\text{Future value of annuity at end of year } 5 = \$1000(1.311) + \$1000(1.225) \qquad (6.8)$$
$$+ \$1000(1.145) + \$1000(1.070)$$
$$+ \$1000(1.000) = \$5751$$

Factoring out the $1000, Equation 6.8 can be rewritten as

MICROCOMPUTERS WIDELY USED IN FINANCE

A recent Dun and Bradstreet survey of firms with 500 or more employees has found that 63 percent now use microcomputers. The following table shows that large firms use microcomputers for financial analysis more than any other function, while small firms use them first for accounting and second for financial analysis.

How They Are Actually Used

In the larger companies, financial analysis is the major area in which microcomputers are used. Smaller firms find them most useful for accounting.

	Number of employees						
Function	1–19	20–99	100– 499	500– 999	1,000– 4,999	5,000– 24,999	Over 25,000
Accounting	80.7%	66.9%	55.9%	56.9%	51.3%	63.5%	64.3%
Financial analysis	59.6	61.3	66.1	67.7	69.8	80.0	80.0
Inventory control	34.2	36.3	38.6	27.7	21.2	31.3	37.1
Purchasing	20.2	18.5	11.8	16.9	6.9	15.7	14.3
Credit analysis of customers	29.8	29.0	25.2	12.3	9.0	21.7	15.7
Word processing	41.2	41.9	38.6	52.3	52.4	54.8	64.3
Database management	36.0	35.5	32.3	35.4	25.9	40.9	47.1
Other	8.8	5.6	10.2	10.8	12.7	5.2	1.4

SOURCE: Joseph W. Duncan, "Business Bets on Microcomputers," *Dun's Business Month,* August 1983, p. 45.

$$\text{Future value of annuity at end of year } 5 = \$1000(1.311 + 1.225 \quad (6.9)$$
$$+ 1.145 + 1.070$$
$$+ 1.000) = \$5751$$

Equation 6.9 indicates that to find the future value of the annuity, the annual amount must be multiplied by the sum of the appropriate future-value interest factors.

Using a future value of an annuity table. Appendix Table A-2 simplifies even further the calculations required to find the future value of an annuity. A portion of Table A-2 is given in Table 6.6. The *future-value interest factors for an annuity* included in this table are derived by summing the terms in parentheses in equations like Equation 6.9. In the case of Equation 6.9, this results in Equation 6.10.

$$\text{Future value of annuity at end of year } 5 = \$1000(5.751) = \$5751 \quad (6.10)$$

The values in the table are based on the assumption that deposits are made at the

Table 6.6   The Future-Value Interest Factors for a One-Dollar Annuity, $FVIFA_{k,n}$

Period	5.00 percent	6.00 percent	7.00 percent	8.00 percent	9.00 percent	10.00 percent
1	1.000	1.000	1.000	1.000	1.000	1.000
2	2.050	2.060	2.070	2.080	2.090	2.100
3	3.152	3.184	3.215	3.246	3.278	3.310
4	4.310	4.375	4.440	4.506	4.573	4.641
5	5.526	5.637	5.751	5.867	5.985	6.105
6	6.802	6.975	7.153	7.336	7.523	7.716
7	8.142	8.394	8.654	8.923	9.200	9.487
8	9.549	9.897	10.260	10.637	11.028	11.436
9	11.027	11.491	11.978	12.488	13.021	13.579
10	12.578	13.181	13.816	14.487	15.193	15.937

end of the period.[4] The formula for the future-value interest factor for an n-year annuity with end-of-year cash flows when interest is compounded annually at k percent, $FVIFA_{k,n}$, is[5]

$$FVIFA_{k,n} = \sum_{t=1}^{n} (1 + k)^{t-1} \qquad (6.11)$$

This formula merely states that the future-value interest factor for an n-year annuity is found by adding the sum of the first $n - 1$ future-value interest factors to 1.000 (i.e., $FVIFA_{k,n} = 1 + \sum_{t=1}^{n-1} FVIF_{k,t}$). This relationship can be easily verified by reviewing the terms in Equation 6.9. Letting S_n equal the future value of an n-year annuity, A equal the amount to be deposited annually at the end of each year, and $FVIFA_{k,n}$ represent the appropriate *future-value interest factor for an n-year annuity compounded at k percent,* the relationship among these variables can be expressed as follows:

$$S_n = A \times (FVIFA_{k,n}) \qquad (6.12)$$

Instead of using the equation presented earlier for the future value of an annuity, we can use Table A-2 and Equation 6.12. In Mary Jones's case, the interest factor for the future value of a one-dollar annuity at 7 percent for a five-year life can be obtained from Table A-2 and multiplied by the $1000 deposit.

[4] The discussions of annuities throughout this text concentrate on the more common form of annuity — the *ordinary annuity,* which is an annuity that occurs at the *end* of each period. An annuity that occurs at the *beginning* of each period is called an *annuity due.* The financial tables for annuities included in this book are prepared for use with ordinary annuities.

[5] The formula for the future-value interest factor for an *annuity due* is $\sum_{t=1}^{n} (1 + k)^t$, since in this case all deposits are made at the beginning of each year. The factor therefore merely represents the sum of the first n future-value interest factors, i.e., $\sum_{t=1}^{n} FVIF_{k,t}$.

Multiplying the table value of 5.751 by $1000 results in a future value for the annuity of $5751. The following example further illustrates the usefulness of Table A-2.

EXAMPLE   Randa Middleton wishes to determine the sum of money she will have in her savings account, which pays 6 percent annual interest, at the end of ten years if she deposits $600 at the end of each year for the next ten years. The appropriate interest factor for the future value at 6 percent for a ten-year annuity, $FVIFA_{6\%, 10\,yrs}$, is given in Table A-2 as 13.181. Multiplying this factor by the $600 deposit results in a future value of $7908.60. The simple calculations required to find the future value of an annuity using Table A-2 should be clear from this example. ■

Present Value

It is often useful to determine the "present value" of a future sum of money. The concept of present value, like the concept of future value, is based on the belief that the value of money is affected by when it is received. The axiom underlying this belief is that a dollar today is worth more than a dollar that will be received at some future date. In other words, the present value of a dollar that will be received in the future is less than the value of a dollar in hand today. The actual present value of a dollar depends largely on the earning opportunities of the recipient and the point in time the money is to be received. This section explores the present value of a single amount, a mixed stream, and an annuity.

THE PRESENT VALUE OF A SINGLE AMOUNT

The process of finding *present values,* or *discounting cash flows,* is actually the inverse of compounding. It is concerned with answering the question "If I can earn k percent on my money, what is the most I would be willing to pay for an opportunity to receive F_n dollars n periods from today?" Instead of finding the future value of present dollars invested at a given rate, discounting determines the present value of a future amount, assuming that the decision maker has an opportunity to earn a certain return, k, on the money. This return is often referred to as the *discount rate, required return, cost of capital,* or *opportunity cost.*[6] These terms will be used interchangeably in this text. The discounting process can be illustrated by a simple example.

EXAMPLE   Mr. Cotter has been given an opportunity to receive $300 one year from now. If he can earn 6 percent on his investments in the normal course of events, what is the most he should pay for this opportunity? To answer this question, we must determine how many dollars must be invested at 6 percent today to have $300 one year from now. Letting P equal this unknown amount, and using the same notation as in the compounding discussion, the situation can be expressed as follows:

$$P(1 + .06) = \$300 \tag{6.13}$$

[6] The theoretical underpinning of this "required return" is introduced in Chapter 7 and further refined in subsequent chapters.

Solving Equation 6.13 for P gives us Equation 6.14,

$$P = \frac{\$300}{1.06} \qquad (6.14)$$

$$= \$283.02$$

which results in a value of $283.02 for P. In other words, the "present value" of $300 received one year from today, given an opportunity cost of 6 percent, is $283.02. Mr. Cotter should be indifferent to whether he receives $283.02 today or $300.00 one year from now. If he can receive either by paying less than $283.02 today, he should, of course, do so. ∎

A mathematical expression for present value. The present value of a future amount can be found mathematically by solving Equation 6.4 for P. In other words, one merely wants to obtain the present value, P, of some future amount, F_n, to be received n periods from now, assuming an opportunity cost of k. Solving Equation 6.4 for P gives us Equation 6.15, which is the general equation for the present value of a future amount.

$$P = \frac{F_n}{(1 + k)^n} = F_n \left[\frac{1}{(1 + k)^n} \right] \qquad (6.15)$$

The similarity between this general equation for present value and the equation in the preceding example (Equation 6.14) should be clear. The use of this equation in finding the present value of a future amount can be illustrated by a simple example.

EXAMPLE   Jim McCarthy wishes to find the present value of $1700 that will be received eight years from now. Jim's opportunity cost is 8 percent. Substituting $F_8 = \$1700$, $n = 8$, and $k = .08$ into Equation 6.15 yields Equation 6.16.

$$P = \frac{\$1700}{(1 + .08)^8} \qquad (6.16)$$

To solve Equation 6.16, the term $(1 + .08)$ must be raised to the eighth power. The value

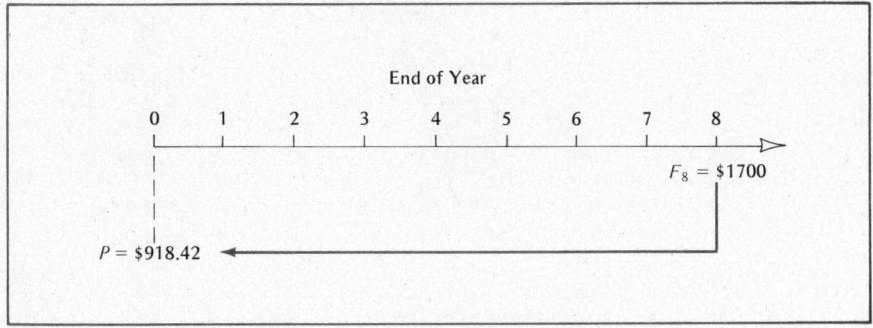

Figure 6.4   Time line for present value of a single amount ($1700 future amount, discounted at 8 percent, from end of 8 years)

resulting from this time-consuming calculation is 1.851. Dividing this value into $1700 yields a present value for the $1700 of $918.42. This analysis can be depicted diagramatically on a time line as shown in Figure 6.4. ■

Present-value interest tables. To simplify the present-value calculation, tables of present-value interest factors can be used. The table for the *present-value interest factor, $PVIF_{k,n}$*, gives values for the expression $1/(1 + k)^n$ where k is the discount rate and n is the number of periods — typically years — involved. Table A-3 in the Appendix presents present-value interest factors for various discount rates and periods. A portion of Table A-3 is presented in Table 6.7. Since the factors in Table A-3 give the value for the expression $1/(1 + k)^n$ for various k and n combinations, we can, by letting $PVIF_{k,n}$ represent the appropriate factor from Table A-3, rewrite Equation 6.15 as follows:

$$P = F_n \times (PVIF_{k,n}) \tag{6.17}$$

This expression indicates that to find the present value, P, of an amount to be received in a future period, n, we have merely to multiply the future amount, F_n, by the appropriate present-value interest factor from Table A-3. An example should help clarify the use of Equation 6.17.

EXAMPLE   Jim McCarthy wishes to find the present value of $1700 to be received eight years from now, assuming an 8 percent opportunity cost. Table A-3 gives us a present-value interest factor for 8 percent and eight years, $PVIF_{8\%, 8 \text{ yrs}}$, of .540. Multiplying this factor by the $1700 yields a present value of $918. This value is 42 cents less than the value obtained using the long method. This difference is attributable to the fact that the table values have been rounded to the nearest thousandth. ■

A few other points with respect to present-value tables are also important. First, *the present-value interest factor for a single amount is always less than 1;* only if the opportunity cost was 0 would this factor equal 1. Second, Table A-3 shows that *the higher the opportunity cost for a given year, the smaller is the present-value interest factor.* In other words, the greater an individual's opportunity cost, the less an amount to be received in a specified future year is worth today. Finally, obser-

Table 6.7   The Present-Value Interest Factors for One Dollar, $PVIF_{k,n}$

Period	5.00 percent	6.00 percent	7.00 percent	8.00 percent	9.00 percent	10.00 percent
1	.952	.943	.935	.926	.917	.909
2	.907	.890	.873	.857	.842	.826
3	.864	.840	.816	.794	.772	.751
4	.823	.792	.763	.735	.708	.683
5	.784	.747	.713	.681	.650	.621
6	.746	.705	.666	.630	.596	.564
7	.711	.665	.623	.583	.547	.513
8	.677	.627	.582	.540	.502	.467
9	.645	.592	.544	.500	.460	.424
10	.614	.558	.508	.463	.422	.386

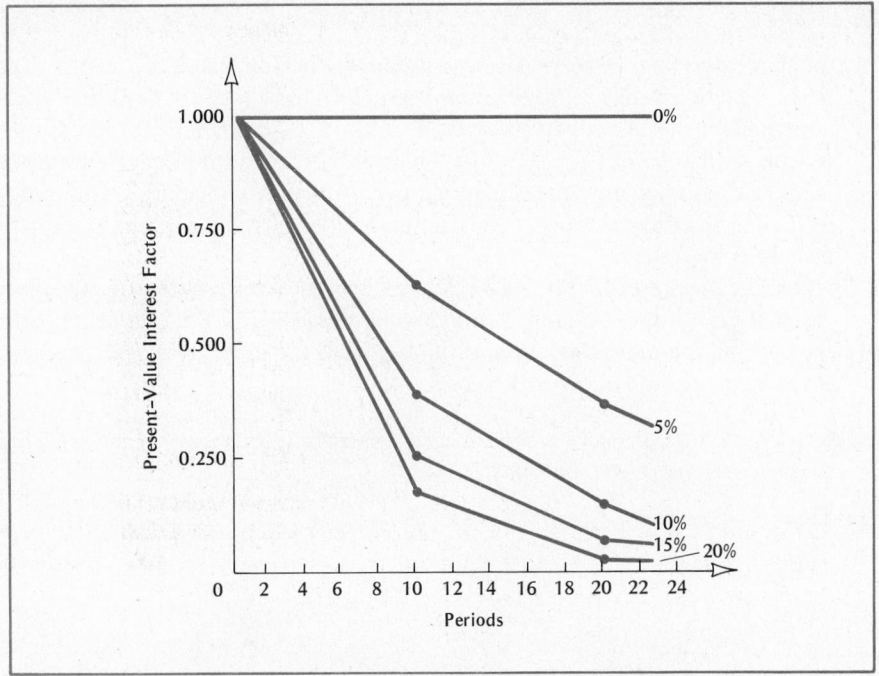

Figure 6.5 Discount rates, time periods, and present-value interest factors used to find the present value of one dollar

vation of the table values for a given discount rate indicates that *the further in the future a sum is to be received, the less it is worth presently.* The relationship among various discount rates, discount periods, and present-value interest factors is illustrated in Figure 6.5. Everything else being equal, the higher the discount rate, the lower is the present-value interest factor, and the longer the period of time, the lower is the present-value interest factor. The reader should also note that given a discount rate of 0 percent, the present-value interest factor always equals 1, and the future value of the funds therefore equals their present value.

Comparing present value and future value. A few important observations must be made with respect to present values. One is that the expression for the present-value interest factor for k percent and n periods, $1/(1 + k)^n$, is the inverse of the future-value interest factor for k percent and n periods, $(1 + k)^n$. This observation can be confirmed by dividing a present-value interest factor for k percent and n periods, $PVIF_{k,n}$, into 1 and comparing the resulting value to the future-value interest factor given in Table A-1 for k percent and n periods, $FVIF_{k,n}$. The two values should be equivalent. Because of the relationship between present-value interest factors and future-value interest factors, we can find the present-value interest factors given a table of future-value interest factors, and vice versa. The future-value interest factor from Table A-1 for 10 percent and five periods is 1.611. Dividing this value into 1 yields .621, which is the present-value interest factor given in Table A-3 for 10 percent and five periods.

THE PRESENT VALUE OF A MIXED STREAM

Quite often in finance there is a need to find the present value of a stream of cash flows to be received in various future years. Two basic types of cash-flow streams are possible: the mixed stream and the annuity. A *mixed stream* of cash flows reflects no particular pattern, while an *annuity* is a pattern of equal annual cash flows (the cash flows are the same each year). Since certain shortcuts are possible in finding the present value of an annuity, mixed streams and annuities will be discussed separately.

To find the present value of a mixed stream of cash flows, determine the present value of each future amount in the manner described in the preceding section, then add all the individual present values to find the present value of the stream. An example should clarify this process.

EXAMPLE　The CAM Company has been offered an opportunity to receive the following mixed stream of cash flows over the next five years:

Year	Cash flow
1	$400
2	800
3	500
4	400
5	300

If the firm must earn 9 percent, at minimum, on its investments, what is the most it should pay for this opportunity?

To solve this problem, the present value of each individual cash flow discounted at 9 percent for the appropriate number of years is determined. The sum of all these individual values is then calculated to get the present value of the total stream. The present-value interest factors required are obtained from Table A-3. Table 6.8 presents the calculations needed to find the present value of the cash flow stream, which turns out to be $1904.60. CAM should not pay more than $1904.60 for the opportunity to receive these cash flows, since paying $1904.60 would provide exactly a 9 percent return. This situation is depicted diagramatically on a time line in Figure 6.6.

Table 6.8　The Present Value of a Mixed Stream of Cash Flows

Year (n)	Cash flow (1)	$PVIF_{9\%,n}^a$ (2)	Present value [(1) × (2)] (3)
1	$400	.917	$366.80
2	800	.842	673.60
3	500	.772	386.00
4	400	.708	283.20
5	300	.650	195.00
	Present value of mixed stream		$1904.60

[a] Present-value interest factors at 9 percent are from Table A-3.

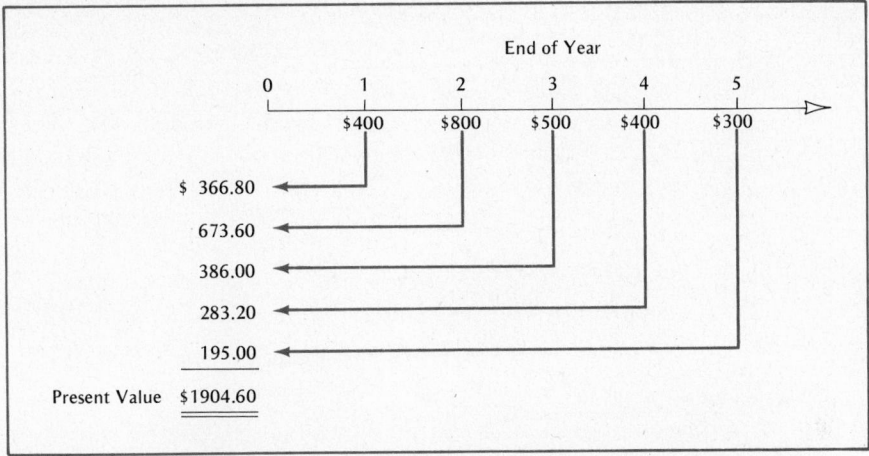

Figure 6.6 Time line for present value of a mixed stream (end-of-year cash flows, discounted at 9 percent, over corresponding number of years) ■

THE PRESENT VALUE OF AN ANNUITY

The present value of an annuity can be found in a manner similar to that used for a mixed stream, but a shortcut is possible.

EXAMPLE The Delco Company is attempting to determine the most it should pay to purchase a particular annuity. The firm requires a minimum return of 8 percent on all investments; the annuity consists of cash flows of $700 per year for five years. Table 6.9 shows the long way of

Table 6.9 The Long Method for Finding the Present Value of an Annuity

Year (n)	Cash flow (1)	$PVIF^a_{8\%,n}$ (2)	Present value [(1) × (2)] (3)
1	$700	.926	$648.20
2	700	.857	599.90
3	700	.794	555.80
4	700	.735	514.50
5	700	.681	476.70
Present value of annuity			$2795.10

[a] Present-value interest factors at 8 percent are from Table A-3.

finding the present value of the annuity, which is the same as the method used for mixed streams. This procedure yields a present value of $2795.10, which can be interpreted in the same manner as for the mixed cash flow stream in the preceding example. Similarly, this situation is depicted graphically on a time line in Figure 6.7.

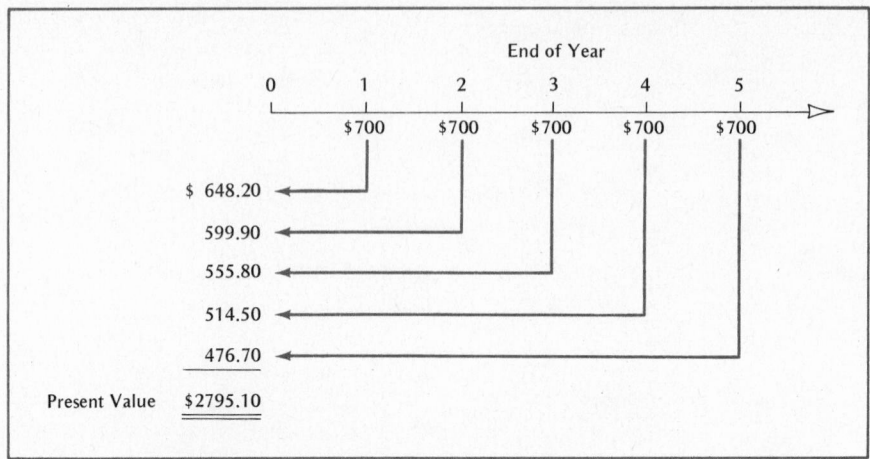

Figure 6.7   Time line for present value of an annuity ($700 end-of-year cash flows, discounted at 8 percent, over 5 years) ■

Simplifying the calculations. The calculations used in the preceding example can be simplified by recognizing that each of the five multiplications made to get the individual present values involved multiplying the annual amount ($700) by the appropriate present-value interest factor. This method of finding the present value of the annuity can also be written as an equation:

$$\text{Present value of annuity} = \$700(.926) + \$700(.857) \qquad (6.18)$$
$$+ \$700(.794) + \$700(.735)$$
$$+ \$700(.681) = \$2795.10$$

Simplifying Equation 6.18 by factoring out the $700 yields Equation 6.19.

$$\text{Present value of annuity} = \$700(.926 + .857 + .794 + .735 + .681) \qquad (6.19)$$
$$= \$2795.10$$

Thus the present value of an annuity can be found by multiplying the annual amount received by the sum of the present-value interest factors for each year of the annuity's life.

Using a present value of an annuity table. Appendix Table A-4 is a table of *present-value interest factors for an annuity* for specified rates and periods. It simplifies even further the calculations required to find the present value of any annuity. A portion of this table is presented in Table 6.10. The interest factors in the table are derived by summing the terms in the parentheses in equations like Equation 6.19. In the case of Equation 6.19, this results in Equation 6.20.

$$\text{Present value of annuity} = \$700(3.993) = \$2795.10 \qquad (6.20)$$

Table 6.10   The Present-Value Interest Factors for a One-Dollar Annuity, $PVIFA_{k,n}$

Period	5.00 percent	6.00 percent	7.00 percent	8.00 percent	9.00 percent	10.00 percent
1	.952	.943	.935	.926	.917	.909
2	1.859	1.833	1.808	1.783	1.759	1.736
3	2.723	2.673	2.624	2.577	2.531	2.487
4	3.546	3.465	3.387	3.312	3.240	3.170
5	4.329	4.212	4.100	3.993	3.890	3.791
6	5.076	4.917	4.767	4.623	4.486	4.355
7	5.786	5.582	5.389	5.206	5.033	4.868
8	6.463	6.210	5.971	5.747	5.535	5.335
9	7.108	6.802	6.515	6.247	5.995	5.759
10	7.722	7.360	7.024	6.710	6.418	6.145

The interest factors in Table A-4 actually represent the sum of the first n present-value interest factors in Table A-3 for a given discount rate. The formula for the present-value interest factor for an n-year annuity with end-of-year cash flows that are discounted at k percent, $PVIFA_{k,n}$, is

$$PVIFA_{k,n} = \sum_{t=1}^{n} \frac{1}{(1+k)^t} \qquad (6.21)$$

This formula merely states that the present-value interest factor for an n-year annuity is found by summing the first n present-value interest factors at the given rate (i.e., $PVIFA_{k,n} = \sum_{t=1}^{n} PVIF_{k,t}$). This relationship can be easily verified by reviewing the terms in Equation 6.19. Let P_n equal the present value of an n-period annuity, A equal the amount to be received annually at the end of each year, and $PVIFA_{k,n}$ represent the appropriate value for the *present-value interest factor for a one-dollar annuity discounted at* k *percent for* n *years*. The present value of the annuity can be found by the following equation:

$$P_n = A \times (PVIFA_{k,n}) \qquad (6.22)$$

The problem presented earlier involving the calculation of the present value of a five-year annuity of $700 assuming an 8 percent opportunity cost can be easily worked out with the aid of Table A-4 and Equation 6.22. The present-value interest factor for a one-dollar annuity in Table A-4 for 8 percent and five years, $PVIFA_{8\%,5 \text{ yrs}}$, is 3.993. Multiplying this factor by the $700 annuity provides a present value for the annuity of $2795.10. A simple example may help clarify the usefulness of Table A-4 in finding the present value of an annuity.

EXAMPLE   The Massachusetts Mining Company expects to receive $160,000 per year at the end of each of the next 20 years from a new mine. If the firm's opportunity cost of funds is 10 percent, how much is the present value of this annuity? The appropriate interest factor for the present value at 10 percent for a 20-year annuity, $PVIFA_{10\%,20 \text{ yrs}}$, is found in Table A-4 to be 8.514. Multiplying this factor by the $160,000 cash flow results in a present value of $1,362,240. ■

Applying Future-Value and Present-Value Techniques

Future-value and present-value techniques have a number of important applications. Four will be presented in this section: (1) the calculation of the deposits needed to accumulate a future sum, (2) the calculation of amortization on loans, (3) the determination of interest or growth rates, and (4) the calculation of the present value of perpetuities.

DEPOSITS TO ACCUMULATE A FUTURE SUM

Often an individual may wish to determine the annual deposit necessary to accumulate a certain amount of money so many years hence. Suppose a person wishes to purchase a house five years from now and recognizes that an initial down payment of $20,000 will be required at that time. She wishes to make equal annual end-of-year deposits in an account paying annual interest of 6 percent, so she must determine what size annuity will result in a sum equal to $20,000 at the end of year 5. The solution to this problem is closely related to the process of finding the future value of an annuity.

In an earlier section of this chapter, the future value of an n-year annuity, S_n, was found by multiplying the annual deposit, A, by the appropriate interest factor from Table A-2, $FVIFA_{k,n}$. The relationship of the three variables has been defined by Equation 6.12, which is rewritten here as Equation 6.23.

$$S_n = A \times (FVIFA_{k,n}) \tag{6.23}$$

We can find the annual deposit required to accumulate S_n dollars, given a specified interest rate, k, and a certain number of years, n, by solving Equation 6.23 for A. Isolating A on the left side of the equation gives us

$$A = \frac{S_n}{FVIFA_{k,n}} \tag{6.24}$$

Once this is done, we have only to substitute the known values of S_n and $FVIFA_{k,n}$ into the right side of the equation to find the annual deposit required.

EXAMPLE   In the problem just stated, a person wished to determine the equal annual end-of-year deposits required to accumulate $20,000 at the end of five years given an interest rate of 6 percent. Table A-2 indicates that the future-value interest factor for an annuity at 6 percent for five years, $FVIFA_{6\%,5 \text{ yrs}}$, is 5.637. Substituting $S_5 = \$20,000$ and $FVIFA_{6\%,5 \text{ yrs}} = 5.637$ into Equation 6.24 yields an annual required deposit, A, of $3,547.99 ($20,000 ÷ 5.637). If $3,547.99 is deposited at the end of each year for five years at 6 percent, at the end of the five years there will be $20,000 in the account. ■

TIME VALUE OF MONEY: A PERSONAL INVESTMENT PERSPECTIVE

On February 17, 1978, Larry—a corporate executive who "dabbles" in the market— bought 300 shares of Itek Corp., traded on the NYSE, at $26 per share. The total cost, including commissions, was $7,712. "I think I'll get a good bounce out of it," he said at the time. On Feb. 1, 1980, he sold the 300 shares at $30, which brought him $8,950. "It's topping out," he said, "It looks to me like it's gone as far as it's going to go. "The stock doesn't pay a dividend, so Larry's gain (if there were to be any) would have to come from capital appreciation. The stock's increase in price was the only source of potential profit.

How well did Larry do? In his own estimation, the answer is "very." What was his reason for that judgment? "Well," he said, "I spent about $7,700. And I got back $8,950. That's a $1,250 gain on a $7,700 investment. Not bad."

Is he right? Suppose he had invested the $7,700 in a one-year money market instrument that earned him 10% per annum, the interest to be paid in a lump sum at maturity. Ignoring tax considerations for a moment, suppose he then repeated the process. Investing the $7,700 + $770 = $8,470 at 10% would have brought him $847. At the second maturity date, Larry would have had $9,317.

He held his Itek stock for approximately two years. Even taking into consideration the more favorable tax treatment accorded capital gains than interest earned, he in fact did no better than he'd have done had his $7,700 remained in a money market fund. Actually, the picture was far worse than it seems, because during the period he owned it, the stock suffered a dramatic sinking spell, falling ten points from the price at which he bought it. At that point, he had a $3,000 loss on a $7,700 investment.

In essence he wasn't rewarded for the added risk he took in buying stocks instead of CDs or T-bills. Nor, of course, did he expect a guarantee that his profit would be greater merely because he was taking more of a chance. He simply hoped he'd do well, and in the end, he concluded that he definitely had.

Larry's view of stock market profits is entirely typical. What he omits from his calculations, the majority of investors . . . also overlook. Namely, the time value of money. A dollar you own today differs from the one you owned yesterday, and a dollar you receive tomorrow is not the same as one you receive today. There is a date attached to every investment you make, and the longer your money is invested, the more it has to earn just for you to break even.

That seemingly simple fact has a profound impact on the way seasoned investors calculate their stock market profits and make their investment decisions.

Gaining a sense of the time value of money is essential for two reasons: It will prevent you from thinking you've made a profit, when in fact you've barely broken even, and it will bring you into closer contact with the investment climate that now prevails. That doesn't mean you'll automatically make a killing in the market. . . . However, it will allow you to better understand the atmosphere of mild panic, which is an integral part of every period of high inflation, . . .

SOURCE: Srully Blotnick, "The Time Value of Money," *Forbes*, March 3, 1980, pp. 114–115.

LOAN AMORTIZATION

The expression *loan amortization* refers to the determination of the equal annual loan payments necessary to provide a lender with a specified interest return and repay the loan principal over a specified term. The loan amortization process involves finding the future payments (over the term of the loan) whose present value at the loan interest rate just equals the amount of initial principal borrowed. Lenders use loan amortization tables to find these payment amounts. In the case of home mortgages, these tables are used to find the equal monthly payments necessary to amortize or pay off the loan at a specified interest rate over a 20- to 30-year period.

The discussion here will deal only with the amortization of loans on which end-of-period payments are made, since the tables in this text are based on end-of-period amounts. Amortizing a loan actually involves creating an annuity out of a present amount. For example, an individual may borrow $6000 at 10 percent and agree to make equal annual end-of-year payments over four years. To determine the size of the payments, the four-year annuity discounted at 10 percent that has a present value of $6000 must be determined. This process is actually the inverse of finding the present value of an annuity.

Earlier in this chapter, the present value, P_n, of an n-period annuity of A dollars was found by multiplying the annual amount, A, by the present-value interest factor for an annuity from Table A-4, $PVIFA_{k,n}$. This relationship, which was originally expressed as Equation 6.22, is rewritten here as Equation 6.25:

$$P_n = A \times (PVIFA_{k,n}) \qquad (6.25)$$

To find the equal annual payment, A, required to pay off or amortize the loan, P_n, over a certain number of years at a specified interest rate, we need to solve Equation 6.25 for A. Isolating A on the left side of the equation gives us

$$A = \frac{P_n}{PVIFA_{k,n}} \qquad (6.26)$$

Once this is done, we have only to substitute the known values of P_n and $PVIFA_{k,n}$ into the right side of the equation to find the annual payment required.

EXAMPLE In the problem stated at the start of this section, a person wished to determine the equal annual end-of-year loan payments necessary to amortize fully a $6000, 10 percent loan over four years. Table A-4 indicates that the present-value interest factor for an annuity corresponding to 10 percent and four years, $PVIFA_{10\%,4\,yrs}$, is 3.170. Substituting $P_4 = \$6000$ and $PVIFA_{10\%,4\,yrs} = 3.170$ in Equation 6.26 and solving for A yields an annual loan payment of $1892.74 ($6000 ÷ 3.170). To repay the principal and interest on a $6000, 10 percent, four-year loan, equal annual end-of-year payments of $1892.74 are necessary.

The allocation of each loan payment to interest and principal in order to repay the loan fully can be seen in columns 3 and 4 of the *loan amortization schedule* given in Table 6.11. The portion of each payment representing interest (column 3) declines, and the portion going to principal repayment (column 4) increases over the repayment period. This is

Table 6.11   Loan Amortization Schedule ($6000 principal,
10 percent interest, 4-year repayment period)

End of year	Loan payment (1)	Beginning-of-year principal (2)	Payments		End-of-year principal [(2) − (4)] (5)
			Interest [.10 × (2)] (3)	Principal [(1) − (3)] (4)	
1	$1892.74	$6000.00	$600.00	$1292.74	$4707.26
2	1892.74	4707.26	470.73	1422.01	3285.25
3	1892.74	3285.25	328.53	1564.21	1721.04
4	1892.74	1721.04	172.10	1720.64	—[a]

[a] Due to rounding, a slight difference ($ .40) exists between the beginning-of-year-4 principal (in column 2) and the year-4 principal payment (in column 4).

typical of amortized loans because with level payments, as the principal is reduced, the interest component declines, leaving a larger portion of each subsequent payment to repay principal. ∎

DETERMINING INTEREST OR GROWTH RATES

It is often necessary to calculate the compound annual interest or growth rate associated with a stream of cash flows. In doing this, either future-value or present-value interest factors can be used. The approach using present-value interest tables is described in this section. The simplest situation is where one wishes to find the rate of interest or growth in a cash flow stream. This case can be illustrated by the following example.

EXAMPLE   Tom Richards wishes to find the rate of interest or growth of the following stream of cash flows.[7]

Year	Cash flow	
1984	$1520	4
1983	$1440	3
1982	$1370	2
1981	$1300	1
1980	$1250	

Interest has been earned (or growth experienced) for four years. To find the rate at which this has occurred, the amount received in the earliest year is divided by the amount received in the latest year. This gives the present-value interest factor for four years, $PVIF_{k,4\,\text{yrs}}$, which is 0.822 ($1250 ÷ $1520). The interest rate in Table A-3 associated with the factor closest to 0.822 for four years is the rate of interest or growth rate associated with the cash flows. Looking across year 4 of Table A-3 shows that the factor for 5 percent is 0.823—

[7] Since the calculations required for finding interest rates and growth rates, given certain cash flow or principal flow streams, are the same, this section refers to the calculations as those required to find interest *or* growth rates.

almost exactly the 0.822 quotient;[8] therefore, the rate of interest or growth rate associated with the cash flows given is 5 percent. ∎

Sometimes one wishes to determine the interest rate associated with an equal-payment loan. For instance, if a person were to borrow $2000 to be repaid in equal annual end-of-year amounts of $514.14 for the next five years, he or she might wish to determine the rate of interest being paid on the loan. Referring to Equation 6.25 shows that $P_5 = \$2000$ and $A = \$514.14$. Rearranging the equation and substituting these values results in a present-value interest factor for a five-year annuity, $PVIFA_{k,5\,\text{yrs}}$, of 3.890:

$$PVIFA_{k,5\,\text{yrs}} = \frac{P_5}{A} = \frac{\$2000}{\$514.14} = 3.890 \qquad (6.27)$$

The interest rate for five years associated with a factor of 3.890 in Table A-4 is 9 percent; therefore, the interest rate on the loan is 9 percent.

PERPETUITIES

A *perpetuity* is an annuity with an infinite life — in other words, an annuity that never stops providing its holder with A dollars at the end of each year. It is often necessary to find the present value of a perpetuity. The present value of an A-dollar perpetuity discounted at the rate k is defined by Equation 6.28.

Present value of an A-dollar perpetuity discounted at k percent   (6.28)

$$= A \times (PVIFA_{k,\infty}) = A \times \left(\frac{1}{k}\right)$$

---

[8] When making these and other types of interest or growth rate estimates using financial tables, *interpolation* can often be used to get a more exact answer. To illustrate, assume that for seven years of data, the quotient found by dividing the earliest by latest cash flow value is 0.575. Looking at the present-value interest table, Table A-3, for *six years* (the number of years of growth), the closest factors to 0.575 are 0.596 at 9 percent and 0.564 at 10 percent. Clearly, the growth rate is between 9 and 10 percent and is closer to the 10 percent value. To interpolate a more precise answer, the following steps are necessary:

1. Find the difference between the 9 and 10 percent present-value interest factors of 0.596 and 0.564. The difference is .032 (.596 − .564).
2. Find the *absolute* difference (i.e., ignore plus or minus sign) between the calculated quotient of .575 and the value of the present-value interest factor for the lower rate (9 percent), which is .596. This difference is .021 (.575 − .596).
3. Divide the value from step 2 by that found in step 1 to get the percent of total distance across the range attributable to the calculated value. The result is .6563 (.021 ÷ .032).
4. Multiply the percent found in step 3 by the interval width over which interpolation is being performed. In this case the interval width is 1 percent (10%–9%); multiplying we get .6563 percent (.6563 × 1%). Note that when interpolation is being performed over a wider interval, this step becomes more important.
5. Add the value found in step 4 to the interest rate associated with the lower end of the interval. The result is 9.6563 percent (9% + .6563%). The growth or interest rate is therefore 9.6563 percent.

Of course, an even more accurate result could easily be obtained using a financially oriented calculator. Using such a calculator, the rate for this preceding problem is found to be 9.6618 percent.

As noted in the equation, the appropriate factor, $PVIFA_{k,\infty}$, is found merely by dividing the discount rate, k (stated as a decimal), into 1. The validity of this method can be seen by looking at the factors in Table A-4 for 8 percent, 10 percent, and 20 percent. As the number of years approaches 50, the value of these factors approaches 12.500, 10.000, and 5.000, respectively. Dividing .08, .10, and .20 (for k) into 1 gives factors for finding the present value of perpetuities at these rates of 12.500, 10.000, and 5.000. An example may help clarify the application of Equation 6.28.

EXAMPLE   A person wishes to determine the present value of a $1000 perpetuity discounted at 10 percent. The appropriate present-value interest factor can be found by dividing 1 by .10. As prescribed by Equation 6.28, the resulting factor, 10, is then multiplied by the annual perpetuity cash inflow of $1000 to get the present value of the perpetuity, $10,000. In other words, the receipt of $1000 every year for an indefinite period is worth only $10,000 today if a person can earn 10 percent on investments. This is because, if the person had $10,000 and earned 10 percent interest on it each year, $1000 a year could be withdrawn indefinitely without affecting the initial $10,000, which would never be drawn down. ■

CHAPTER SUMMARY

● The key concepts related to the time value of money are future value and present value. The key time-value definitions and formulas are given in Table 6.12 (p. 212).

● Future value relies on compound interest to measure the value of future amounts. When interest is compounded, the initial principal or deposit in one period, along with the interest earned on it, becomes the beginning principal of the following period, and so on.

● Interest can be compounded annually, semiannually, quarterly, monthly, weekly, daily, or even continuously. The more frequently interest is compounded, the larger the future amount that will be accumulated.

● Present value represents the inverse of future value. In finding the present value of a future amount, we determine what amount of money today would be equivalent to the given future amount, considering the fact that we can earn a certain return on this money. As long as we can earn a return at a rate greater than 0 percent, the present value of a future cash flow is less than its future value.

● Occasionally it is necessary to find the present value of a stream of cash flows. Mixed streams consist of any cash flow pattern other than an annuity, which is a pattern of equal annual cash flows (the cash flows are the same each year).

● For mixed streams, the individual present values must be found and summed. In the case of an annuity, the present value can be found using the present-value interest factor for an annuity.

● By manipulating the equations for the future value and present value of single amounts and annuities in certain ways, the deposits needed to accumulate a future sum, loan amortization payments, and interest or growth rates can be calculated.

● The present value of a perpetuity, which is an annuity with an infinite life, can be calculated by multiplying the annual perpetuity cash flow by 1 divided by the appropriate discount rate.

KEY TERMS

annuity
compounding
continuous compounding
cost of capital
deposits to accumulate a future sum
discounting cash flows
discount rate
future-value interest factor ($FVIF_{k,n}$)
future-value interest factor for an annuity
  ($FVIFA_{k,n}$)
interest
intrayear compounding

loan amortization
loan amortization schedule
mixed stream
opportunity cost
perpetuity
present value
present-value interest factor ($PVIF_{k,n}$)
present-value interest factor for an annuity
  ($PVIFA_{k,n}$)
principal
quarterly compounding
required return
semiannual compounding

Table 6.12 Summary of Key Definitions and Formulas for Time Value of Money

---

Variable Definitions

F_n = future value or amount at the end of period n
P = initial principal
k = annual rate of interest
n = number of periods — typically years — over which money earns a return
m = number of times per year interest is compounded
t = period number index
S_n = future value of an n-year annuity
A = amount deposited or received annually at the end of each year
P_n = present value of an n-year annuity

Interest Factor Formulas

Future value of a single amount

$$FVIF_{k,n} = \left(1 + \frac{k}{m}\right)^{m \times n}$$

for annual compounding, $m = 1$

$$FVIF_{k,n} = (1 + k)^n \qquad \text{[Factors in Table A-1]}$$

Future value of an (ordinary) annuity

$$FVIFA_{k,n} = \sum_{t=1}^{n} (1 + k)^{t-1} \qquad \text{[Factors in Table A-2]}$$

Present value of a single amount

$$PVIF_{k,n} = \frac{1}{(1 + k)^n} \qquad \text{[Factors in Table A-3]}$$

Present value of an annuity

$$PVIFA_{k,n} = \sum_{t=1}^{n} \frac{1}{(1 + k)^t} \qquad \text{[Factors in Table A-4]}$$

Basic Equations

Future value (single amount): $F_n = P \times (FVIF_{k,n})$
Future value (annuity): $S_n = A \times (FVIFA_{k,n})$
Present value (single amount): $P = F_n \times (PVIF_{k,n})$
Present value (annuity): $P_n = A \times (PVIFA_{k,n})$

QUESTIONS

6-1 How is the *compounding process* related to the payment of interest on savings? What is the general equation for the future value, F_n, in period n if P dollars are deposited in an account paying k percent annual interest?

6-2 What effect would a *decrease* in the interest rate or an *increase* in the holding period of a deposit have on its future value? Why?

6-3 What effect does compounding interest more frequently than once per period have on the future value generated by a beginning principal? Why?

6-4 What is meant by the phrase "the present value of a future amount"? How are present-value and future-value calculations related?

6-5 What is the equation for the present value of a future amount, F_n, to be received in period n assuming that the firm requires a minimum return of k percent? How is this equation different from the equation for the future value of one dollar?

6-6 What effect do *increasing* (a) required return and (b) time periods have on the present value of a future amount? Why?

6-7 How can the present-value tables be used to find the present value of a mixed stream of cash flows? Why can the present value of an annuity be found by summing the individual present-value interest factors and multiplying the sum by the annual amount received?

6-8 How can the size of the equal annual end-of-year deposits necessary to accumulate a certain future value in a specified future period be determined? How might one of the financial tables discussed in this chapter aid in this calculation?

6-9 Describe the procedure used to amortize a loan into a series of equal annual payments. What is a *loan amortization schedule?*

6-10 Which financial table(s) would be used to find (a) the growth rate associated with a stream of cash flows and (b) the interest rate associated with an equal-payment loan? How would each of these be calculated?

6-11 What is a *perpetuity?* How might the factor for the present value of such a stream of cash flows be determined?

PROBLEMS

6-1 **(Future Value Calculation)** *Without tables,* use the basic formula for future value to calculate the future-value interest factor for the following rates, k, and number of periods, n. Compare the calculated value to the table value in Appendix Table A-1.

Case	Interest rate, k (%)	Number of periods, n
A	12	2
B	6	3
C	9	2
D	3	4

6-2 **(Future-Value Tables)** Use the future-value interest factors in Appendix Table A-1 in each of the following cases to estimate, to the nearest year, how long it would take an initial deposit assuming no withdrawals (a) to double and (b) to quadruple.

Case	Interest rate (%)
A	7
B	40
C	20
D	10

6-3 **(Future-Values)** For each of the following cases, calculate the future value of the cash flow that will be available at the end of the deposit period if the interest is compounded annually at the rate specified for the given period.

Case	Cash flow ($)	Interest rate (%)	Period (years)
A	200	5	20
B	4,500	8	7
C	10,000	9	10
D	25,000	10	12
E	37,000	11	5
F	40,000	12	9

6-4 **(Single-Payment Loan Repayment)** A person borrows $200 to be repaid in eight years with 14 percent annually compounded interest. The loan may be repaid at the end of any earlier year with no prepayment penalty.

a What amount would be due if the loan is repaid at the end of year 1?

b What is the repayment at the end of year 4?

c What amount is due at the end of the eighth year?

6-5 **(Changing Compounding Frequency)** Using annual, semiannual, and quarterly compounding periods, calculate the future amount if $5000 is deposited

a At 12 percent for five years.

b At 16 percent for six years.

c At 20 percent for ten years.

6-6 **(Compounding Frequency and Bank Choice)** Nancy Jackson has $10,000 that she can deposit in any of three savings accounts for a three-year period. Bank A pays interest on an annual basis, bank B pays interest twice each year, and bank C pays interest each quarter. If all banks have a stated annual interest rate of 8 percent but follow the different payment practices above,

a Which bank should Ms. Jackson deal with? Why?

b What amount would Ms. Jackson have at the end of the third year, leaving all interest paid on deposit, in each bank?

6-7 **(Future Value of an Annuity)** For each of the following cases, calculate the future value of the annuity at the end of the deposit period, assuming that the annuity cash flows occur at the end of each year.

Case	Amount of annuity ($)	Interest rate (%)	Deposit period (years)
A	2,500	8	10
B	500	12	6
C	30,000	20	5
D	11,500	9	8
E	6,000	14	30

6-8 **(Annuities and Compounding)** A person intends to deposit $300 per year in a credit union for the next ten years, and the credit union pays an annual rate of interest of 8 percent. Determine the future value the person will have (at end of ten years) given that end-of-period deposits are made and no interest is withdrawn if:

a $300 is deposited annually and the credit union pays interest annually.

b $150 is deposited semiannually and the credit union pays interest semiannually.

c $75 is deposited quarterly and the credit union pays interest quarterly.

6-9 **(Future Value of a Mixed Stream)** For each of the following mixed streams of cash flows, determine the future value at the end of the final year if deposits are made at the *beginning of each year* into an account paying annual interest of 12 percent, assuming no withdrawals are made during the period.

	Cash flow stream		
Year	A	B	C
1	$ 900	$30,000	$1,200
2	1,000	25,000	1,200
3	1,200	20,000	1,000
4		10,000	1,900
5		5,000	

6-10 **(Present-Value Calculation)** *Without tables,* use the basic formula for present value to calculate the present-value interest factor for the following rates, k, and number of periods, n. Compare the calculated value to the table value.

Case	Interest rate, k (%)	Number of periods, n
A	2	4
B	10	2
C	5	3
D	13	2

6-11 **(Present Values)** For each of the following cases, calculate the present value of the cash flow, discounting at the rate given and assuming that the cash flow will be received at the end of the period noted.

Case	Cash flow ($)	Discount rate (%)	Period (years)
A	7,000	12	4
B	28,000	8	20
C	10,000	14	12
D	150,000	11	6
E	45,000	20	8

6-12 **(Present Value)** Jay Martin has been offered a future payment of $500 three years from today. If his opportunity cost is 7 percent compounded annually, what value would he place on this opportunity?

6-13 **(Present Value)** An Ohio state savings bond can be converted to $100 at maturity six years from purchase. If the state bonds are to be competitive with U.S. Savings Bonds, which pay 8 percent annual interest (compounded annually), at what price will the state sell its bonds? Assume no cash payments on savings bonds prior to redemption.

6-14 **(Present Value — Mixed Streams)** Given the following mixed streams of cash flows:

Cash flow stream

Year	A	B
1	$ 50,000	$ 10,000
2	40,000	20,000
3	30,000	30,000
4	20,000	40,000
5	10,000	50,000
Totals	$150,000	$150,000

a Find the present value of each stream using a 15 percent discount rate.

b Compare the calculated present values and discuss them in light of the fact that the undiscounted total cash flows amount to $150,000 in each case.

 6-15 **(Present Value — Mixed Streams)** Find the present value of the following streams of cash flows. Assume that the firm's opportunity cost is 12 percent.

A		B		C	
Year	Amount	Year	Amount	Year	Amount
1	−$2,000	1	$10,000	1–5	$10,000/yr.
2	3,000	2–5	5,000/yr.	6–10	8,000/yr.
3	4,000	6	7,000		
4	6,000				
5	8,000				

6-16 **(Relationship between Future Value and Present Value)** Using *only* the following information:

Year (t)	Cash flow ($)	Future-value interest factor at 5 percent ($FVIF_{5\%,t}$)
1	800	1.050
2	900	1.102
3	1000	1.158
4	1500	1.216
5	2000	1.276

a Determine the *present value* of the mixed stream of cash flows using a 5 percent discount rate.

b How much would you be willing to pay for an opportunity to buy this stream, assuming that you can at best earn 5 percent on your investments.

c What effect, if any, would a 7 percent rather than 5 percent opportunity cost have on your analysis? (Explain verbally.)

 6-17 **(Present Value of an Annuity)** For each of the following cases, calculate the present value of the annuity, assuming that the annuity cash flows occur at the end of each year.

Case	Amount of annuity ($)	Interest rate (%)	Period (years)
A	12,000	7	3
B	55,000	12	15
C	700	20	9
D	140,000	5	7
E	22,500	10	5

6-18 **(Cash Flow Investment Decisions)**   Jerry Carney has an opportunity to invest in any of the following cash inflows at the prices given. What recommendation would you make, assuming that Mr. Carney can earn 10 percent on his investments?

cash In / Price
= .1667

Investment	Price ($)	Cash inflow ($)	Year of receipt
A	18,000	30,000	5
B	600	3,000	20
C	3,500	10,000	10
D	1,000	15,000	40

6-19 **(Investment Decision)**   You have a choice of accepting either of two 5-year cash flow streams or lump-sum payments. One cash flow stream is an annuity and the other is a mixed stream. You may accept alternative A or B—either as a cash flow stream or as a lump sum. Given the cash flow and lump-sum amounts associated with each, and assuming a 9 percent opportunity cost, which alternative (A or B) and in which form (cash flow stream or lump sum) would you prefer?

End of Year	Alternative A	Alternative B
Cash flow stream		
1	$700	$1100
2	700	900
3	700	700
4	700	500
5	700	300
Lump-sum amount		
At time zero	$2800	$2850

6-20 **(Accumulating a Future Sum)**   Mary Tewles wishes to accumulate $8000 by the end of five years by making equal annual end-of-year deposits over the next five years. If Mary can earn 9 percent on her investments, how much must she deposit at the end of each year to meet this goal?

6-21 **(Accumulating a Growing Future Sum)**   A retirement home at Marineworld Estates now costs $85,000. Inflation is expected to cause this price to increase at 6 percent per year over the 20 years before J. R. Rogers retires. How much will he need to save each year at an annual rate of 10 percent to have the cash to purchase his home upon retirement?

6-22 **(Loan Amortization)**   Determine the equal annual end-of-year payment required each year over the life of the following loans in order to repay them fully during the stated term of the loan.

Loan	Principal ($)	Interest rate (%)	Term of loan (years)
A	12,000	8	3
B	60,000	12	10
C	75,000	10	30
D	4,000	15	5

6-23 **(Loan Amortization Schedule)** Joe Smith borrowed $15,000 at a 14 percent annual rate of interest to be repaid over three years. The loan is amortized into three equal annual end-of-year payments.
  a Calculate the annual end-of-year loan payment.
  b Prepare a loan amortization schedule showing the interest and principal breakdown of each of the three loan payments.
  c Explain why the interest portion of each payment declines with the passage of time.

 **6-24** **(Growth Rates)** You are given the following series of cash flows:

		Cash flows	
Year	A	B	C
1	$500	$1500	$2500
2	560	1550	2600
3	640	1610	2650
4	720	1680	2650
5	800	1760	2800
6		1850	2850
7		1950	2900
8		2060	
9		2170	
10		2280	

  a Calculate the compound growth rate associated with each cash flow stream.
  b If year 1 values represent initial deposits in a savings account paying annual interest, what is the rate of interest earned on each account?
  c Compare and discuss the growth rates and interest rates found in a and b, respectively.

6-25 **(Rate of Return)** Julio Lopez has $1500 to invest. His investment counselor suggests an investment that pays no explicit interest but will return $2000 at the end of three years.
  a What annual rate of return will Mr. Lopez earn with this investment?
  b Mr. Lopez is considering another investment, of equal risk, which earns a return of 8 percent. Which investment should he take, and why?

6-26 **(Rate of Return — Annuity)** What is the rate of return on an investment of $10,606 if the company expects to receive $2,000 each year for the next ten years?

6-27 **(Loans Rates of Interest)** Bob Sherill has been shopping for a loan to finance the purchase of his new car. He has found three possibilities that seem attractive and wishes to select the one having the lowest interest rate. The information available with respect to each of the three $5000 loans follows.

Loan	Principal ($)	Annual payment ($)	Life (years)
A	5000	1352.81	5
B	5000	1543.21	4
C	5000	2010.45	3

a Determine the interest rate that would be associated with each of the loans.

b Which loan should Mr. Sherill take?

6-28 **(Perpetuities)** Given the following data, determine for each of the following perpetuities:

Perpetuity	Annual amount ($)	Discount rate (%)
A	20,000	8
B	100,000	10
C	3,000	6
D	60,000	5

a The appropriate present-value interest factor.

b The present value.

6-29 **(Annuity and Perpetuity)** You have decided to endow your favorite university with a scholarship in honor of your successful completion of managerial finance. It is expected that it will cost $6000 per year to attend the university into perpetuity. You expect to give the university the endowment in ten years and will accumulate it by making annual (end-of-period) deposits into an account. The rate of interest is expected to be 10 percent for all future time periods.

a How large must the endowment be?

b How much must you deposit at the end of each of the next ten years to accumulate the required amount?

6-30 **(Integrative — Future and Present Value)** A major corporation wishes to accumulate funds to provide a retirement annuity for a key executive. The executive by contract will retire at the end of exactly 12 years. Upon retirement the executive is entitled to receive an annual end-of-year payment of $42,000 for exactly 20 years. In the event the executive dies prior to the end of the 20-year period, the annual payments will pass to his heirs. During the 12-year "accumulation period," the corporation wishes to fund the annuity by making equal annual end-of-year deposits into an account earning 9 percent interest. Once the 20-year "distribution period" begins, the corporation plans to move the accumulated monies into an account earning a guaranteed 12 percent per year. At the end of the distribution period, the account balance will equal zero. How large must the equal annual end-of-year deposits into the account be over the 12-year accumulation period in order to allow the $42,000 annual end-of-year distributions to be made over the 20-year period? Note that the first deposit will occur at the end of year 1 and the first distribution payment at the end of year 13. (*Hint:* It may be helpful to draw a time line of cash flows before solving this problem.)

Chapter 7

Risk and Return

After studying this chapter, you should be able to:

1. Define *risk* and *return* as they relate to the decision-making activities of the financial manager.

2. Understand risk preferences and basic risk concepts, including risk and time, as they relate to a single asset.

3. Explain the concept of risk in a portfolio context as it relates to correlation and diversification.

4. Describe and differentiate between the two basic types of risk — diversifiable and nondiversifiable — that make up the total risk of a security or an asset.

5. Discuss beta and the capital asset pricing model (CAPM) and describe how it links the relevant risk and return of assets traded in efficient markets.

6. Understand the international dimensions of risk as they relate to the foreign exchange (economic) and political uncertainties faced by the multinational firm.

In Chapter 1 the goal of the firm and therefore of its financial manager was specified as owner wealth maximization. For the publicly traded corporation, the financial manager's primary mission is therefore to maximize the price of the firm's common stock.[1] To do this, the manager must learn to assess the two key determinants of share price: risk and return. Each financial decision presents certain risk and return characteristics, and all major financial decisions must be viewed in terms of expected risk, expected return, and their combined impact on share price. Because these "expected" values are often difficult to measure, the process requires considerable judgment as well as factual knowledge.

Risk Fundamentals

Risk can be viewed as it relates either to a single asset held in isolation or to a *portfolio* or collection of assets. Although portfolio risk is probably most important to the financial manager, the general concept of risk is most readily developed in terms of a single asset. Before considering risk in each of these forms, it is important to understand the fundamentals of risk, return, and risk preferences.

RISK DEFINED

In the most basic sense, *risk* can be defined as the chance of loss. Assets having greater chances of loss are viewed as more risky than those with lesser chances of loss. More formally, the term *risk* is used interchangeably with *uncertainty* to refer to the *variability of expected returns* associated with a given asset. For instance, a government bond that guarantees its holder $1000 interest after 30 days has no risk, since there is no variability associated with the return. An equivalent invest-

---

[1] Two important points should be recognized here: (1) While for convenience the publicly traded corporation is being discussed, the risk and return concepts presented apply equally well to all firms; and (2) Concern centers only on common stockholders' wealth, since they in fact represent the "residual owners" whose returns are in no way specified in advance.

ment in the common stock of a firm that may return over the same period anywhere from $0 to $2000 is very risky because of the high variability of returns. The more certain the return from an asset, the less variability and therefore the less risk.

The difference between risk and uncertainty as defined by the statistician is related to the decision maker's knowledge of the probabilities, or chances, of certain outcomes. *Risk* exists when the decision maker is able to estimate the probabilities associated with various outcomes. *Objective probability distributions* are normally based on historical data. For instance, if a person wishes to determine the probabilities associated with a given asset's returns, he or she can develop a distribution of probabilities based on historical return data on other assets of the same type. *Uncertainty* exists when the decision maker has no historical data and must make educated guesses in order to develop a *subjective probability distribution.* For example, if the proposed asset is new to the firm, the decision maker, through research and consultation with others, may be able subjectively to assign probabilities to various return outcomes. Throughout this section, we will use the terms *risk* and *uncertainty* interchangeably to refer to risky decision situations.

RETURN DEFINED

As noted in Chapter 3, the *return* on an investment is measured as the total gain or loss experienced on behalf of the owner over a given period of time. It is commonly stated as a percentage return on the beginning-of-period investment value. In the case of common stock, the rate of return earned over period t, k_t, is commonly defined as

$$k_t = \frac{P_t - P_{t-1} + D_t}{P_{t-1}} \tag{7.1}$$

where

k_t = actual, expected, or required rate of return[2] during period t
P_t = price (value) of stock at time t
P_{t-1} = price (value) of stock at time $t - 1$
D_t = cash dividends paid (cash flow) on the stock in the time period $t - 1$ to t

The return, k_t, reflects the combined effect of changes in value, $P_t - P_{t-1}$, and cash flow, D_t, realized over the period t.

Equation 7.1 is used to determine the expected rate of return on any asset, with the time period t being as short as one day or as long as ten years or more. However, in most cases t is equal to one year, and k therefore represents an annual rate of return. The beginning-of-period value, P_{t-1}, and the end-of-period value, P_t, are not necessarily *realized values.* They are commonly *unrealized,* which means that although the asset was *not* actually purchased at time $t - 1$ and sold at time t, the values P_{t-1} and P_t could have been realized had this happened.

---

[2] The terms *expected return* and *required return* are used interchangeably throughout this text since in an efficient market (discussed later) they would be expected to be equal. The actual return is an *ex post* value, while expected and required returns are *ex ante* values.

EXAMPLE   Zax Manufacturing wishes to determine the actual annual rate of return on two assets, C and D. Asset C was purchased exactly one year ago for $20,000 and currently has a market value of $21,500. During the year it generated $800 of cash flow. Asset D was purchased four years ago, and its value at the beginning and end of the year just completed declined from $12,000 to $11,800. During the year it provided $1,700 of cash flow.

Substituing into Equation 7.1, the annual rate of return, k, for each asset is calculated.

Asset C

$$k_C = \frac{\$21,500 - \$20,000 + \$800}{\$20,000} = \frac{\$2,300}{\$20,000} = \underline{\underline{11.5\%}}$$

Asset D

$$k_D = \frac{\$11,800 - \$12,000 + \$1,700}{\$12,000} = \frac{\$1,500}{\$12,000} = \underline{\underline{12.5\%}}$$

It can be seen that while the value of asset D declined during the year, its relatively high cash flow caused it to earn a higher rate of return than that earned by asset C during the same period. Clearly, it is the combined impact of changes in value and cash flow measured by the rate of return that is important. ■

RISK PREFERENCES

Because of differing managerial (firm) preferences, it is impossible to specify a generally acceptable level of risk.[3] The three possible behaviors — risk-averse, risk-indifferent, and risk-taking — are depicted graphically on a set of risk-return axes in Figure 7.1. It can be seen that as risk goes from B_1 to B_2, for the *risk-indifferent* manager, the return increases proportionally from k_1 to k_2, the increase in return corresponds directly to the increase in risk. In the case of the *risk-averse* manager, the required return increases more than proportionally; for the *risk taker,* it exhibits a less than proportional increase. *Most managers are risk-averse, since for a given increase in risk they require as compensation a greater than proportional increase in return.* Although in theory the risk preferences of managers could be measured, in practice managers tend to accept only those risks with which they feel comfortable. And they generally tend to be conservative rather than aggressive when accepting risk.

Basic Risk Concepts: A Single Asset

The concept of risk is most readily developed by first considering a single asset held in isolation. Such an approach creates a white laboratory in which the potential interactions of asset returns can be ignored. The relationship between risk and time is important in understanding the role of risk in financial decision making.

---

[3] The risk preferences of the managers in theory should be consistent with the risk preferences of the firm. While controversy exists as to whether managers in practice behave in a manner consistent with the firm's risk preferences, it is assumed here that such is the case. Therefore, the manager's risk preferences and those of the firm are assumed to be identical.

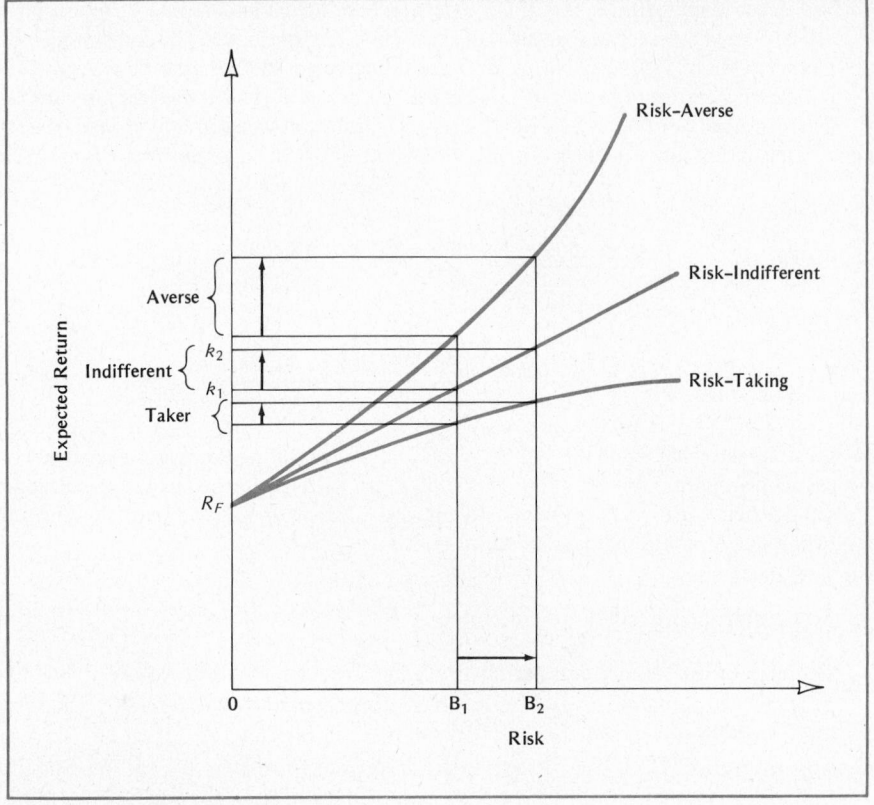

Figure 7.1   Risk preference functions

RISK OF A SINGLE ASSET

Although the risk of a single asset is measured in much the same way as the risk of a portfolio, it is important to differentiate between them, since certain benefits accrue to holders of portfolios. It is also useful to assess risk from both a behavioral and a quantitative point of view.

Sensitivity analysis. A simple behavioral view of risk can be obtained by using *sensitivity analysis,* the consideration of a number of possible outcomes when evaluating an asset investment. The basic procedure is to evaluate an asset using a number of possible return estimates to get a sense of the variability among outcomes. One common approach involves estimation of the pessimistic (worst), the most likely (expected), and the optimistic (best) return associated with a given asset. In this case the asset's risk will be reflected by the *range,* which can be found by subtracting the pessimistic outcome from the optimistic outcome. The greater the range for a given asset, the more variability or risk it is said to have.

EXAMPLE   Alfred Company is attempting to choose the best of two alternative asset investments, A and B, each requiring an initial investment of $10,000 and both having a *most likely*

Table 7.1 Assets A and B

	Asset A	Asset B
Initial investment	$10,000	$10,000
Annual rate of return		
Pessimistic	13%	7%
Most likely	15%	15%
Optimistic	17%	23%
Range	4%	16%

annual rate of return of 15 percent. Since the firm requires a 12 percent return on assets of this type, it would appear that either asset would be equally acceptable. Concentrating only on the level of expected return, though, fails to take risk into account. To evaluate the riskiness of these assets, management'has made *pessimistic* and *optimistic* estimates of the returns associated with each. The three estimates for each asset, along with their ranges, are given in Table 7.1. It can be seen that asset A appears to be less risky than asset B since its range of 4 percent (17 − 13 percent) is less than the range of 16 percent (23 − 7 percent) for asset B.

Table 7.1 illustrates that sensitivity analysis can produce some information about assets that appear equally desirable on the basis of the most likely estimates of their return. Comparing the range of annual return for asset A (4 percent) with that for asset B (16 percent), it should be clear that asset A is less risky. The financial decision maker's preference for asset A or B will depend on his or her attitude toward risk. A conservative decision maker will take asset A, thereby eliminating the possibility of a loss (earning 7 percent when the required return is 12 percent); a risk taker may take asset B due to the probability of receiving a very high return (23 percent). Although the use of sensitivity analysis and the range is rather crude, it does provide the decision maker with more than one estimate of return, which can be used to assess roughly the risk involved. ■

Probabilities and expected values. Probabilities are often used to assess more accurately the risk involved in an asset. The *probability* of an event's occurring may be viewed as the *percentage chance* of a given outcome. In other words, if it has been determined that an outcome has an 80 percent probability of occurrence, it is expected that the given outcome will occur eight out of ten times. If an outcome has a probability of 100 percent, it is certain to occur; outcomes having a probability of zero will never occur. By assigning probabilities to outcomes, the *expected value* of the return on an investment can be calculated.

The expected value of an asset is a weighted-average return, in which the weights used are the probabilities of the various outcomes. Although the expected value may never be realized, it is indicative of the likely return if the investment is repeated a large number of times. The most difficult aspect of determining expected values is estimating the probabilities associated with the various outcomes. Regardless of whether these probabilities are estimated objectively or subjectively, the expected value is calculated in the same manner. The calculation can be illustrated using the returns for assets A and B presented in Table 7.1.

EXAMPLE An evaluation of the Alfred Company's history of pessimistic, most likely, and optimistic estimates indicates that 25 out of 100 times, or 25 percent of the time, the pessimistic

LINDEN H. BLUE: A RISK TAKER IN THE AVIATION INDUSTRY

After 50 years of aging family management, Beech Aircraft Corp. has an outsider at the controls, and by any measure, he's charting a risky course.

Linden H. Blue, Beech's president, is gambling the company's future on a brand new airplane, the Starship. His goal is clear: to get the first of a new generation of business planes into the air before the competition gets one built.

He is taking that risk at a company that hasn't designed a new plane in two decades. He is spending $250 million to develop the Starship at a time when the general-aviation business is still recovering from its worst slump in 32 years. And he is staking Beech's success on a plane so radical in design that its appeal to business executives is in doubt.

For at least a year or two, the project will probably hurt the profits of Raytheon Co., Beech's parent company. But Mr. Blue says that he accepted his job with the understanding that "the time was right for Beech to make its technical thrust." And that "thrust" is the Starship. . . .

In keeping with Mr. Blue's style, there is nothing conservative about the design of the Starship. The plane has seven-foot-tall fins at the end of each main wing, an extra pair of wings under the cockpit, and no tail. Its turboprop engines are mounted backward to push the Starship at 400 miles an hour, instead of pulling it the way most propellers do. Its skin is made largely of graphite — the material used in expensive tennis rackets — rather than aluminum.

The 8- to 10-passenger Starship will fly almost as fast as a corporate jet and, at $2.75 million, will cost as much as some jets. But Beech says it will be 40% more fuel efficient than jets of comparable size.

Other companies have new planes in the works, but none are trying as many changes at once as Beech. Wolfgang Demisch, an analyst at First Boston Corp., suggests that the Starship is a "full generation ahead" of planes being produced by competitors.

But the Starship still faces problems. Although Beech has flown a scale-model, it hasn't yet built a full-sized plane or secured government approvals. Technical problems remain, such as devising a way to protect the plane's graphite skin from lightning without adding too much weight. . . .

SOURCE: David Wessel, "Beech's President Gambles Firm's Future on a Radically Designed Business Airplane," *The Wall Street Journal,* March 3, 1984, p. 29.

outcome occurred; 50 out of 100 times, or 50 percent of the time, the most likely outcome occurred; and 25 out of 100 times, or 25 percent of the time, the optimistic outcome occurred. Thus the probabilities of the pessimistic, most likely, and optimistic outcomes' occurring this time are 25 percent, 50 percent, and 25 percent, respectively. The sum of these probabilities must equal 100 percent; that is, they must be based on all the alternatives considered. Table 7.2 presents the calculations required to find the expected values of the returns from assets A and B.

A number of important points in Table 7.2 should be noted. First, the probabilities in each case sum to 1, which must be true when calculating expected values. Second, since the possible outcomes (pessimistic, most likely, and optimistic) considered for assets A and B are identical, the probabilities associated with them are the same in each case. Finally, the

Table 7.2   Expected Values of Returns for Assets A and B

Possible outcomes	Probability (1)	Returns (%) (2)	Weighted value (%) [(1) × (2)] (3)
Asset A			
Pessimistic	.25	13	3.25
Most likely	.50	15	7.50
Optimistic	.25	17	4.25
Total	1.00	Expected return	15.00
Asset B			
Pessimistic	.25	7	1.75
Most likely	.50	15	7.50
Optimistic	.25	23	5.75
Total	1.00	Expected return	15.00

expected return is equivalent to the most likely estimate in each case. This does not generally happen when expected returns are calculated.[4] ■

Probability distributions. Although the calculation of expected value does provide the decision maker with better inputs than the use of a single-point estimate or sensitivity analysis, it still does not give an exact picture of risk. If one were to compare the expected values of returns for assets A and B from Table 7.2, they would again be the same. Comparing the probability distribution associated with each asset does allow the decision maker to get a sense of the differing degrees of risk. A probability distribution can be graphed by plotting possible outcomes and associated probabilities on a set of outcome-probability axes.

The simplest type of probability distribution is the *bar chart,* or *discrete probability distribution,* which shows only a limited number of outcome-probability coordinates. The bar charts for assets A and B are shown in Figure 7.2. Although both assets have the same expected value of return, the range of return is much more dispersed for asset B than for asset A — 16 percent versus 4 percent.

A more descriptive probability distribution for an investment can be developed if the decision maker obtains the probabilities associated with every possible outcome. In the preceding example, we had only three possible return outcomes and associated probabilities; if we knew all the possible outcomes and associated probabilities, a *continuous probability distribution* could be developed. This type of distribution can be thought of as a bar chart for a very large number of outcomes. Figure 7.3 presents a graph of continuous probability distributions for assets A and B. (To draw these curves, a large number of outcomes would be required.)[5]

[4] As the reader may imagine, this example has been designed to highlight certain aspects of risk. For this reason the expected returns for the differing assets are equal.

[5] To develop a continuous probability distribution, one must have data on a large number of historical occurences. Then, by developing a frequency distribution indicating how many times each outcome has occurred over the given time horizon, one can convert these data into a probability distribution. Probability distributions for risky events can also be developed using *simulation*—a process discussed briefly in Chapter 11.

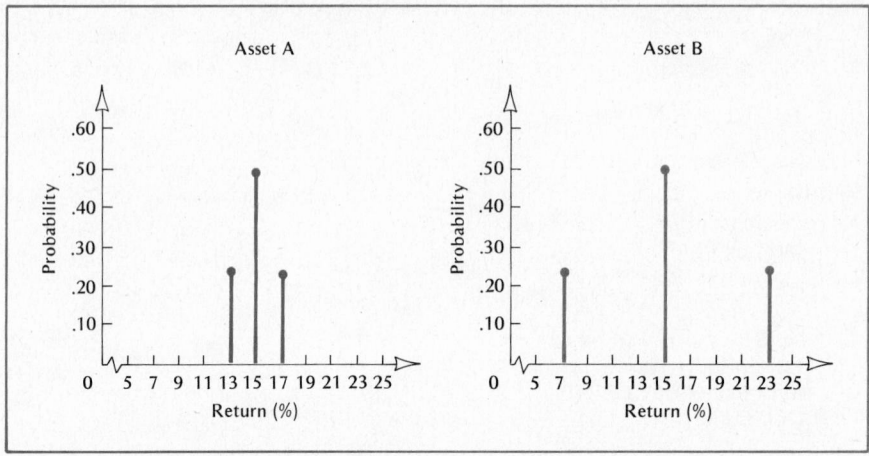

Figure 7.2   Bar charts for asset A's and asset B's returns

In the bar charts in Figure 7.2, assets A and B have the same probability (50 percent) of returns of 15 percent. In the continuous distribution these probabilities change because of the large number of additional outcomes considered. The area under each of the curves is equal to 1, which means that 100 percent of the outcomes, or all the possible outcomes, have been considered. Often distributions such as those in Figure 7.3 are converted into *cumulative probability distributions,* which allow the decision maker to determine easily the probability of obtaining at least a given value.[6] Note in Figure 7.3 that, although assets A and B have the same

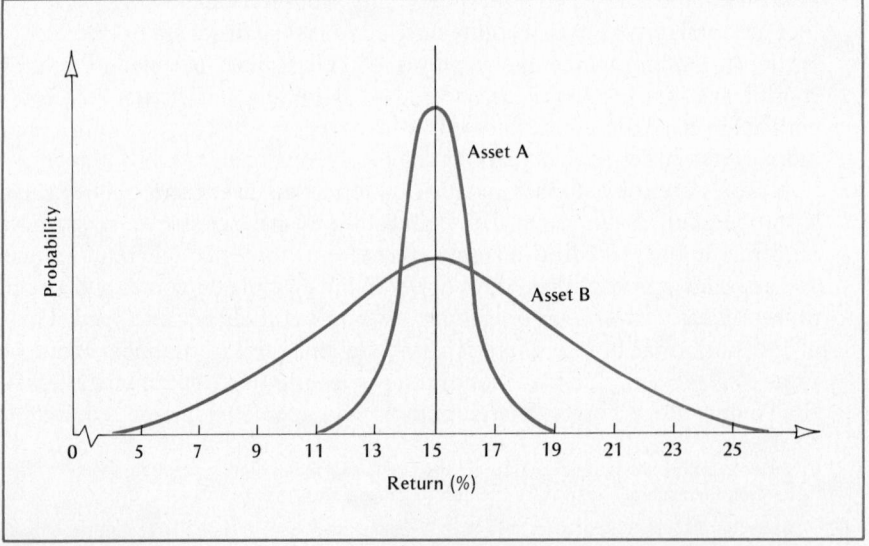

Figure 7.3   Continuous probability distributions for asset A's and asset B's returns

[6] A probability distribution can be converted into a *cumulative* distribution by determining the probability associated with obtaining at least each given value and plotting the cumulative probability of all occurrences less than or equal to the given value against the associated outcome.

expected return (15 percent), the distribution of returns for asset A is much tighter, or closer to the expected value, than that for asset B. The distribution for asset B would be said to have much greater *dispersion* than the distribution for asset A.

Standard deviation. The most common statistical measure of an asset's risk is the standard deviation from the mean or expected value of return.[7] The *standard deviation* of a distribution of asset returns represents the square root of the average squared deviations of the individual outcomes from the expected value. The first step in calculating the standard deviation of a distribution of returns is to find the *expected value of return, $\bar{k}$*, which is given by Equation 7.2.

$$\bar{k} = \sum_{i=1}^{n} k_i \times Pr_i \qquad (7.2)$$

where

k_i = the return for the ith outcome
Pr_i = the probability of occurence of ith return
n = the number of outcomes considered

The calculations of the expected value of returns, $\bar{k}$, for assets A and B were presented in Table 7.2. Column 1 gave the Pr_i's and column 2 gave the k_i's, n equaling 3 in each case. The expected value for each asset's returns was found to be 15 percent. The expression for the *standard deviation of the probability distribution of returns, σ_k*, is given by Equation 7.3.[8]

$$\sigma_k = \sqrt{\sum_{i=1}^{n} (k_i - \bar{k})^2 \times Pr_i} \qquad (7.3)$$

It can be seen from this equation that the standard deviation represents the square root of the sum of the product of each deviation from the expected value, $\bar{k}$, squared and the associated probability of occurrence.

EXAMPLE   Table 7.3 presents the calculation of the standard deviations for the returns for Alfred Company's assets A and B, based on the data presented earlier. The standard deviation of

---

[7] Although risk is typically viewed as determined by the variability, or dispersion, of outcomes around an expected value, many people believe it should be said to be present only when outcomes are below the expected value, since only returns below the expected value are considered bad. Nevertheless, the common approach is to view risk as determined by the variability on either side of the expected value, since the greater this variability, the less confident one can be of the outcomes associated with an asset investment.

[8] The formula commonly used to find the standard deviation of returns, σ_k, in a situation where *all* of the outcomes are known, and their related probabilities are assumed equal, is

$$\sigma_k = \sqrt{\frac{\sum_{i=1}^{n} (k_i - \bar{k})^2}{n}}$$

where n is the number of observations. Because when analyzing asset investments, returns and related probabilities are often available, the formula given in Equation 7.3 is emphasized in this chapter.

Table 7.3 The Calculation of the Standard Deviation of the Returns for Assets A and B

Asset A

i	k_i	$\bar{k}$	$k_i - \bar{k}$	$(k_i - \bar{k})^2$	Pr_i	$(k_i - \bar{k})^2 \times Pr_i$
1	13%	15%	−2%	4%	.25	1%
2	15	15	0	0	.50	0
3	17	15	2	4	.25	1

$$\sum_{i=1}^{3} (k_i - \bar{k})^2 \times Pr_i = 2\%$$

$$\sigma_{k_A} = \sqrt{\sum_{i=1}^{3} (k_i - \bar{k})^2 \times Pr_i} = \sqrt{2\%} = \underline{1.41\%}$$

Asset B

i	k_i	$\bar{k}$	$k_i - \bar{k}$	$(k_i - \bar{k})^2$	Pr_i	$(k_i - \bar{k})^2 \times Pr_i$
1	7%	15%	−8%	64%	.25	16%
2	15	15	0	0	.50	0
3	23	15	8	64	.25	16

$$\sum_{i=1}^{3} (k_i - \bar{k})^2 \times Pr_i = 32\%$$

$$\sigma_{k_B} = \sqrt{\sum_{i=1}^{3} (k_i - \bar{k})^2 \times Pr_i} = \sqrt{32\%} = \underline{5.66\%}$$

the returns for asset A is found to be 1.41 percent, and the standard deviation for Asset B is found to be 5.66 percent. The higher risk of asset B is clearly reflected in its higher standard deviation. ∎

A *normal probability distribution,* depicted in Figure 7.4, is one that always resembles a "bell-shaped" curve. It is symmetrical: From the peak of the graph, the curve's extensions are mirror images of each other. The symmetry of the curve means that half the curve's area lies to the left of the peak and half to the right. Therefore, half the probability is associated with the values to the left of the peak and half with values to the right. As noted on the figure, for normal probability distributions, 68 percent of the possible outcomes will lie between ±1 standard deviation from the expected value, 95 percent of all outcomes will lie between ±2 standard deviations from the expected value, and 99 percent of all outcomes will lie between ±3 standard deviations from the expected value.[9]

EXAMPLE If we assume that the probability distribution of returns for the Alfred Company is normal, 68 percent of the possible outcomes would be expected to have a return ranging

---

[9] Tables of values indicating the probabilities associated with various deviations from the expected value of a normal distribution can be found in any basic statistics text. These values can be used to establish confidence limits and make inferences about possible outcomes. Such applications are not discussed in this text but may be found in most basic statistics and upper-level managerial finance texts.

between 13.59 and 16.41 percent for asset A and 9.34 and 20.66 percent for asset B; 95 percent of the possible return outcomes would range between 12.18 and 17.82 percent for asset A and 3.68 and 26.32 percent for asset B; and 99 percent of the possible return outcomes would range between 10.77 and 19.23 percent for asset A and −1.98 and 31.98 percent for asset B. From these ranges, the greater risk of asset B is clearly reflected by its much wider range of possible returns at a given level of confidence (68 percent, 95 percent, etc.). ■

Our primary concern with standard deviation lies in its use in comparing asset risk. One must be careful in using the standard deviation to compare risk, since it is an *absolute measure of dispersion* and does not consider the dispersion of outcomes in relationship to an expected value. Since assets A and B have the same expected returns (15 percent), it would be safe to say that asset A is less risky than asset B because A has a smaller standard deviation than B (1.41 percent versus 5.66 percent).

Coefficient of variation. In comparing the risk of assets with differing expected returns, the use of the standard deviation can easily be improved upon by converting the standard deviation into a coefficient of variation. The *coefficient of variation, CV,* is calculated by dividing the standard deviation, σ_k, for an asset by its expected return, $\bar{k}$. Equation 7.4 presents the equation for the coefficient of variation.

$$CV = \frac{\sigma_k}{\bar{k}} \qquad (7.4)$$

The coefficients of variation for assets A and B are .094(1.41% ÷ 15%) and .377(5.66% ÷ 15%). The higher the coefficient of variation, the more risky the asset: Asset B is therefore more risky than asset A. Since both assets have the same

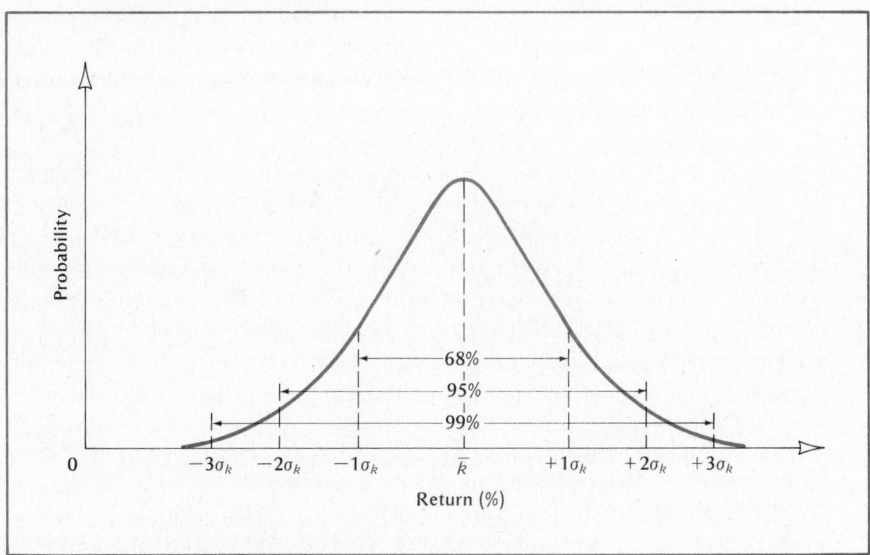

Figure 7.4   Normal probability distribution, with ranges

expected return, the coefficient of variation has not provided any more information than the standard deviation.

The real utility of the coefficient of variation is in comparing assets that have different expected returns. A simple example will illustrate this point.

EXAMPLE   A firm is attempting to select the least risky of two alternative assets — X and Y. The expected return, standard deviation, and coefficient of variation for each of these assets' returns is given below.

Statistics with respect to returns	Asset X	Asset Y
(1) Expected return	12%	20%
(2) Standard deviation	9%[a]	10%
(3) Coefficient of variation [(2) ÷ (1)]	.75	.50[a]

[a] Preferred asset using the given risk measure.

If the firm were to compare the assets solely on the basis of their standard deviations, it would prefer asset X, since asset X has a lower standard deviation than asset Y (9 percent versus 10 percent). Comparing the coefficients of variation of the assets shows that management would be making a serious error in accepting asset X in preference to asset Y since the relative dispersion, or risk, of the assets as reflected in the coefficient of variation is lower for asset Y than for asset X (.50 versus .75). This example should make clear that as a rule, the use of the coefficient of variation for comparing asset risk is better because it considers the relative size, or expected return, of assets.[10] ▪

RISK AND TIME

Risk can be viewed not only with respect to the current time period but also as an *increasing function of time.* Although the returns associated with a given asset may be expected to resemble an annuity and therefore have similar expected values for each time period, it is not unusual to find that they have differing degrees of risk. Even if the expected values are not believed to be equal in each year, the probability distributions of returns will become more dispersed with the passage of time due to the difficulty of accurately forecasting future outcomes. Generally, *the further into the future one forecasts, the more variable, and therefore the more risky, the forecasted values are.*

Figure 7.5 depicts increasing dispersion with the passage of time, assuming that the expected values of each year's returns are equal. A band representing ± 1 standard deviation, σ, from the expected return, $\bar{k}$, is indicated in the figure. It can be seen that the variability of the returns, and therefore the risk associated with the asset, increases with the passage of time. Generally, the longer-lived an asset investment, the greater is the risk due to increasing variability of returns resulting from increased forecasting errors for distant years.[11] Of course, if returns have been guaranteed, the standard deviation, and therefore the risk, is likely to be constant

[10] The only situation in which the standard deviation is sufficient is when the risks of two assets having the same expected value are being compared; in this case, risk rankings based on the standard deviation and coefficient of variation will agree.

[11] These forecasting errors are normal since, in most situations, uncontrollable factors, such as strikes, wars, and inflation, are difficult, if not impossible, to predict but can have a very real effect on future returns.

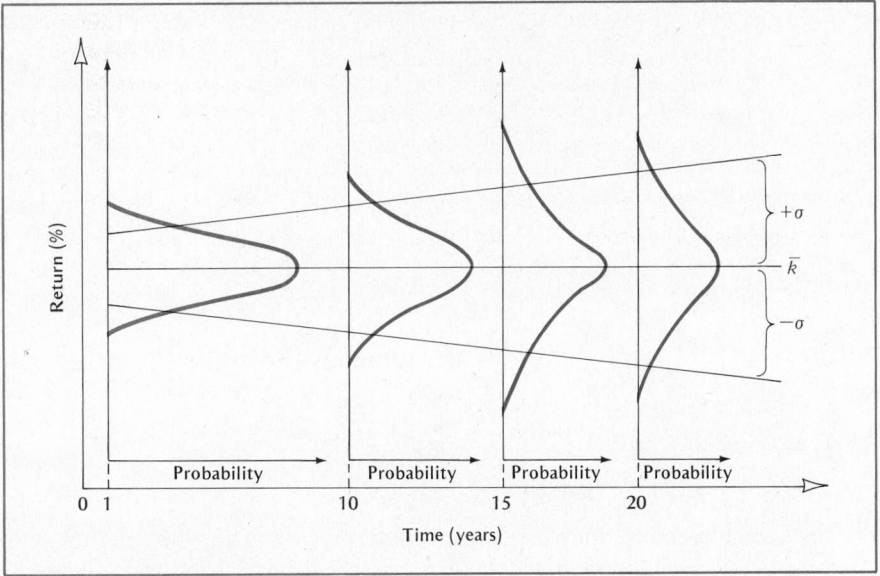

Figure 7.5   Risk as a function of time

over time. If the expected values of returns in each year differ, the coefficient of variation should be used to highlight the differences in risk.

Risk of a Portfolio

Thus far we have looked only at the evaluation of the risk of a single asset. But the risk of any single proposed asset investment cannot be viewed independently of other assets. Holders of assets should be viewed as having a *portfolio* selected in a fashion consistent with the wealth maximization goal.[12] New investments must be considered in light of existing assets and other proposed assets, and the assets selected must be those that best reduce risk while generating an acceptable return. Successful diversification may make the risk of a portfolio of assets less than the risk of the individual assets.

CORRELATION

In order to diversify risk to create an *efficient portfolio,* which is one that allows its owner to achieve the maximum return for a given level of risk or to minimize risk for a given level of return, the investor must understand the concept of correlation. *Correlation* is a statistical measure of the relationship, if any, between series of numbers representing anything from returns to test data. If two series move together, they are *positively correlated;* if the series are countercyclical, or move in

---

[12] In order to convey the portfolio risk concept efficiently, the portfolio of a firm, which would consist of its total assets, is not differentiated from the portfolio of an owner, which would likely contain a variety of different investment vehicles (i.e., assets). The differing characteristics of these two types of portfolios should become clear upon completion of Chapter 11.

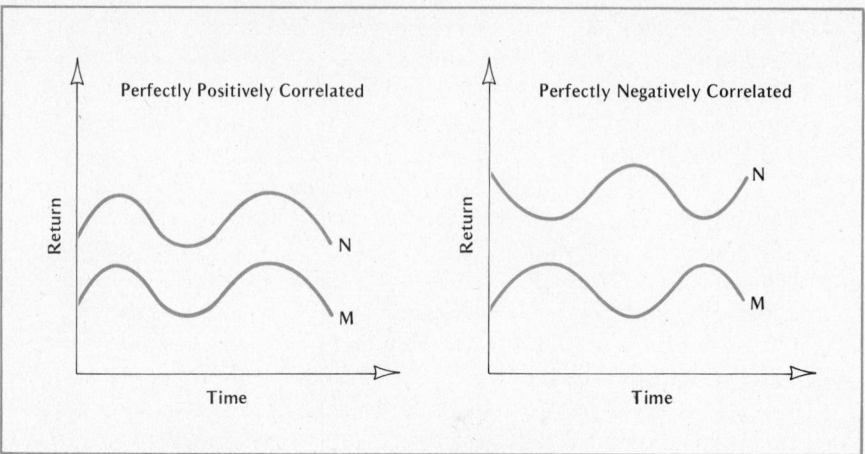

Figure 7.6   The correlation between series M and N

opposite directions, they are *negatively correlated.* The statistical measure of correlation, the *correlation coefficient,* has a range of +1 for *perfectly positively correlated* series and −1 for *perfectly negatively correlated* series. These two extremes are depicted for series M and N in Figure 7.6. The perfectly positively correlated series move exactly together, while the perfectly negatively correlated series more in exactly opposite directions. The existence of perfectly correlated — especially negatively corrrelated — assets is quite rare.

DIVERSIFICATION

To reduce overall risk, it is best to combine or add to the existing portfolio assets that have a negative (or low positive) correlation with existing assets. By combining negatively correlated assets, the overall variability of returns or risk, σ_k, can be reduced. The result of diversifying to reduce risk is illustrated in Figure 7.7. It

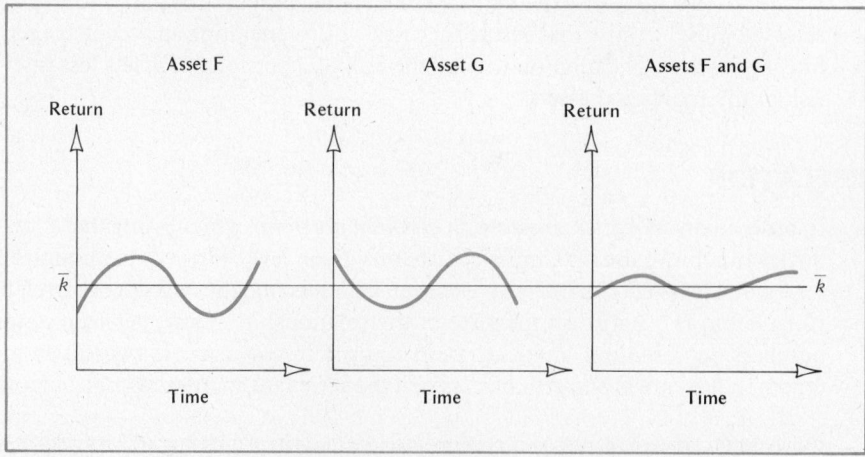

Figure 7.7   Combining negatively correlated assets to diversify risk

shows that a portfolio containing the negatively correlated assets F and G, both having the same expected return, $\bar{k}$, also has the return, $\bar{k}$, but less risk than either of the assets separately. Even if assets are not negatively correlated, the lower the positive correlation between them, the lower the resulting risk. Some assets are *uncorrelated;* that is, they are unrelated in the sense that there is very little, if any, interaction between their returns. Combining uncorrelated assets can reduce risk—not as effectively as combining negatively correlated assets, but more effectively than combining positively correlated assets. The correlation coefficient for uncorrelated assets is close to zero and acts as the midpoint between perfect positive and perfect negative correlation.

The creation of a portfolio by combining two assets having perfectly positively correlated returns cannot reduce the portfolio's overall risk below the risk of the least risky asset, whereas the creation of a portfolio by combining two assets that are perfectly negatively correlated *can* reduce the portfolio's total risk to a level below that of either of the component assets, which in certain situations may be zero. Combining assets with correlations that fall between perfect positive and perfect negative can therefore reduce the overall risk of a portfolio. An example of perfect positive correlation might be a meat packer's acquiring another meat packer; perfect negative correlation might result form the meat packer's acquiring a flour mill (as meat sales increase, flour sales decrease, and vice versa). Often a firm or individual must consider the correlation of a proposed asset with an existing portfolio of assets; this procedure is no different from that required when creating a portfolio of two new assets. Let us look at an example.

EXAMPLE   Table 7.4 presents the expected returns from three different assets—X, Y, and Z—over the next five years, along with their expected values and standard deviations. It can be seen that each of the assets has an expected return of 12 percent and a standard deviation of 2.83 percent. The assets therefore have equal return and equal risk, although their return patterns are not necessarily identical. A comparison of the return patterns of assets X and Y shows that they are perfectly negatively correlated, since they move in exactly opposite directions over time. Comparing assets X and Z, it should be clear that they are perfectly positively correlated, since they move in precisely the same direction (note that the returns for X and Z are identical).[13]

Portfolio XY   By combining equal portions of assets X and Y—the perfectly negatively correlated assets—portfolio XY (shown in Table 7.4) is created.[14] The risk in the portfolio created by this combination, as reflected in the standard deviation, is reduced to 0 percent, while the expected return value remains at 12 percent. Since both assets had the same expected return values, are combined in equal parts, and are perfectly negatively correlated, the combination results in the complete elimination of risk. Whenever assets are perfectly negatively correlated, an optimum combination (similar to the 50-50 mix in the case of assets X and Y) exists for which the resulting standard deviation will equal 0.

[13] It is *not* necessary for return streams to be identical in order for them to be perfectly positively correlated. Identical return streams are used in this example to permit the concepts to be illustrated in the simplest, most straightforward fashion. Any return streams that move (i.e., vary) exactly together—regardless of the relative magnitude of the returns—are perfectly positively correlated.

[14] Although the assets are not divisible in actuality, for illustrative purposes it has been assumed that each of the assets—X, Y, and Z—can be divided up and combined with other assets in order to create portfolios. This assumption is made only to permit the concepts, again, to be illustrated in the simplest, most straightforward fashion.

Table 7.4   Returns, Expected Values, and Standard Deviations
for Assets X, Y, and Z and Portfolios XY and XZ

	Assets			Portfolios	
Year	X	Y	Z	XY[a] (50%X + 50%Y)	XZ[b] (50%X + 50%Z)
1985	8%	16%	8%	12%	8%
1986	10	14	10	12	10
1987	12	12	12	12	12
1988	14	10	14	12	14
1989	16	8	16	12	16
Statistics:					
Expected value	12%	12%	12%	12%	12%
Standard deviation[c]	2.83%	2.83%	2.83%	0%	2.83%

[a] Portfolio XY, which consists of 50 percent of asset X and 50 percent of asset Y, illustrates *perfect negative correlation,* since these two return streams behave in completely opposite fashion over the five-year period.
[b] Portfolio XZ, which consists of 50 percent of asset X and 50 percent of asset Z, illustrates *perfect positive correlation,* since these two return streams behave identically over the five-year period.
[c] Since the probabilities associated with the returns are not given, the formula given earlier in Equation 7.3 could not be used to calculate the standard deviations, σ_k. Instead the general formula,

$$\sigma_k = \sqrt{\frac{\sum_{i=1}^{n} (k_i - \bar{k})^2}{n}}$$

where k_i = return i, $\bar{k}$ = expected value of the returns, and n = the number of observations, was used.

Portfolio XZ   By combining equal portions of assets X and Z—the perfectly positively correlated assets—portfolio XZ (shown in Table 7.4) is created. The risk in this portfolio, as reflected by its standard deviation, which remains at 2.83 percent, is unaffected by this combination, and the expected return remains at 12 percent. Whenever perfectly positively correlated assets such as X and Z are combined, the standard deviation of the resulting portfolio cannot be reduced below that of the least risky asset; the maximum portfolio standard deviation will be that of the riskiest asset. Since assets X and Z have the same standard deviation (2.83 percent), the minimum and maximum standard deviations are both 2.83 percent, which is the only value that could be taken on by a combination of these assets. This result can be attributed to the existence of the unlikely event that X and Z are identical assets. ■

CORRELATION, DIVERSIFICATION, RISK, AND RETURN

In general, the lower (less positive and more negative) the correlation between asset returns, the greater the potential diversification of risk (this should be clear from the behaviors illustrated in Table 7.4). For each pair of assets there is a combination that will result in the lowest risk (standard deviation) possible. The amount of potential risk reduction at this combination depends on the degree of correlation. This concept is a bit difficult to grasp since many potential combinations (assuming divisibility) could be made, given the expected return of each of

Table 7.5 Correlation, Return, and Risk for Various Two-Asset Portfolio Combinations

Correlation coefficient	Range of return	Range of risk
+1 (perfect positive)	Between returns of two assets held in isolation	Between risk of two assets held in isolation
0 (uncorrelated)	Between returns of two assets held in isolation	Between risk of most risky asset and less than risk of least risky asset, but greater than 0
−1 (perfect negative)	Between returns of two assets held in isolation	Between risk of most risky asset and 0

two assets, the standard deviation for each asset, and the correlation coefficient. Note that only one combination of the infinite number of possibilities will minimize risk.

Three possible correlations — perfect positive, uncorrelated, and perfect negative — can be used to illustrate the effect of correlation on the diversification of risk and return. Table 7.5 summarizes the impact of correlation on the range of return and risk for various two-asset portfolio combinations. It should be clear from the table that as we move from perfect positive correlation to uncorrelated assets to perfect negative correlation, the ability to reduce risk is improved. Note that in no case will creating portfolios of assets result in greater risk than that of the riskiest asset included in the portfolio. An example may clarify this concept further.

EXAMPLE A firm has carefully calculated the expected return, k, and risk, σ, for each of two assets — R and S — as summarized below:

Asset	Expected return, k	Risk (standard deviation), σ
R	6%	3%
S	8%	8%

From these data it can be seen that asset R is clearly a lower-risk, lower-return asset than asset S.

To evaluate possible combinations (assuming divisibility of the two assets), the firm considered three possible correlations — perfect positive, uncorrelated, and perfect negative. The results of the analysis are shown in frames A, B, and C and summarized in frame D of Figure 7.8 (p. 240). It can be seen that each endpoint represents a portfolio consisting of 100 percent of the given asset and 0 percent of the other asset. All points on the line joining the two endpoints (R and S) represent portfolios consisting of various combinations of assets R and S.

The ranges of return and risk exhibited are consistent with those noted in Table 7.5. In all cases the return will range between the 6 percent return of R and the 8 percent return of S. The risk, on the other hand, ranges between the individual risks of R and S (from 3 percent to 8 percent) in the case of perfect positive correlation (frame A), ranges from below 3 percent (the risk of R) but greater than 0 to 8 percent (the risk of S) in the uncorrelated case (frame B), and ranges between 0 percent and 8 percent (the risk of S) in the perfectly

TAKING RISK IS COMPANY POLICY AT QUAKER OATS

To inspire managers at Quaker Oats Co., Chairman William Smithburg tells them about his mistakes—the 1982 acquisition of a small video-games business that he has since closed or the French pet-accessory business he bought, then wrote off.

"I want you to take risks," he recently told 60 food-products marketers at a meeting. "There isn't one senior manager in this company who hasn't been associated with a product that failed, or some project that failed. That includes me. It's like learning to ski. If you're not falling down, you're not learning."

Mr. Smithburg has taken plenty of risks in reshaping Quaker, and he has had more successes than failures. In the past, the century-old food company had a patrician image and unaggressive manner. Since Mr. Smithburg became chief executive officer two years ago, Quaker has closed or sold weak businesses, improved marketing and introduced more products. And this summer [1983] he engineered Quaker's biggest acquisition ever, its purchase of Stokely-Van Camp Inc. That move has helped increase Quaker's stock price by about 20% since July [1983].

But Quaker has a way to go yet. Grocery products still account for 82% of its $2.6 billion in annual sales. And in many non-grocery areas Quaker's record has been dismal. Mr. Smithburg, a 45-year-old former advertising executive, is trying to change that. He became chairman Wednesday, succeeding Robert D. Stuart Jr., a member of one of Quaker's founding families.

"Quaker is a class company trying to figure out new ways to grow," says an executive at a competing company. Mr. Smithburg, he says, "is being tested as a leader."

negatively correlated case (frame C). Note that *only in the case of perfect negative correlation can the risk be reduced to 0.* It also can be seen in frame D, which includes all three cases plotted on the same set of axes, that as the correlation becomes less positive and more negative, the ability to reduce risk improves. Keep in mind that the amount of risk reduction achieved also depends on the proportions in which the assets are combined. While determination of the risk-minimizing combination is beyond the scope of this discussion, it is an important issue in developing portfolios of assets. ■

Risk and Return: The Capital Asset Pricing Model (CAPM)

Over the past 20 or so years,[15] a great deal of theory has been developed with respect to risk-return trade-offs. The most important aspect of risk is the overall risk of the firm as perceived by investors in the marketplace. This risk significantly affects investment opportunities—and even more important, the owners' wealth. The basic theory with respect to risk and return is commonly called the *capital*

[15] The key development of this theory is generally attributed to William F. Sharpe, "Capital Asset Prices: A Theory of Market Equilibrium Under Conditions of Risk," *Journal of Finance* 19 (September 1964), pp. 425–442, and John Lintner, "Security Prices, Risk, and Maximal Gains from Diversification," *Journal of Finance* 20 (December 1965), pp. 587–615. A number of authors have significantly advanced, refined, and tested this theory.

Grocery-Products Operations

Mr. Smithburg has already altered Quaker's grocery-products operations. He joined Quaker in 1966 as a frozen-waffle brand manager and rose rapidly, arguing for more aggressive marketing of Quaker's foods. As manager of the cereal division in the 1970s, he more than doubled sales of Life cereal by stressing flavor as well as nutrition. The best-known part of that change was a commercial featuring "Mikey," a tot whose older brother gives him a bowl of Life and discovers that "he likes it!"

Mr. Smithburg took risks. In the 1970s, when soaring commodity prices and federal price controls pinched Quaker's profit, Mr. Smithburg nonetheless maintained that spending on stagnated cereal brands should be increased. The company supported him, and the decision paid off when Quaker's cereal business started growing fast again.

He also played a role in improving profit on grocery products. Instead of milking mature food businesses for cash, as many food companies did, Mr. Smithburg tried to revitalize the businesses. For example, he promoted Quaker's instant oatmeal as a hot, ready-to-eat cereal instead of simply an instant version of oatmeal. That change, along with the introduction of new oatmeal flavors, led to big growth in Quaker's oldest product line.

Partly because of such moves, Quaker's return on U.S. grocery-product sales increased to 15% for the year ended June 30 [1983], compared with 11% for fiscal 1979. The company is spending much of that money on advertising and merchandising, which rose to 16% of sales last year from 10% five years earlier. "If you're in a mature business and you stand still, you will definitely lose," [he] says.

SOURCE: Sue Shellenbarger, "Quaker Oats Chairman to Continue to Make Changes in New Position," *The Wall Street Journal,* November 11, 1983, p. 25.

asset pricing model (CAPM). It was developed to explain the behavior of security prices and provide a mechanism whereby investors could assess the impact of a proposed security investment on their portfolio's overall risk and return.[16] In this section we will use CAPM to understand the basic risk-return trade-offs involved in all types of financial decisions.

ASSUMPTIONS OF THE MODEL

The capital asset pricing model relies on a number of assumptions that create a nearly perfect world. Although they appear to be unrealistic, empirical studies have confirmed their reasonableness and have provided support for the existence of the relationships described by CAPM. The basic assumptions are related to the efficiency of the markets and investor preferences.

Efficient markets. The marketplace in which investors make transactions in securities (or assets) is assumed to be highly efficient. This means that investors all have the same information with respect to securities. Investors are all assumed to view

[16] Although research on the application of the capital asset pricing model to "real assets" continues, the CAPM cannot be readily applied to these decisions because of their indivisibility, relatively large size, small number, and lack of an efficient market.

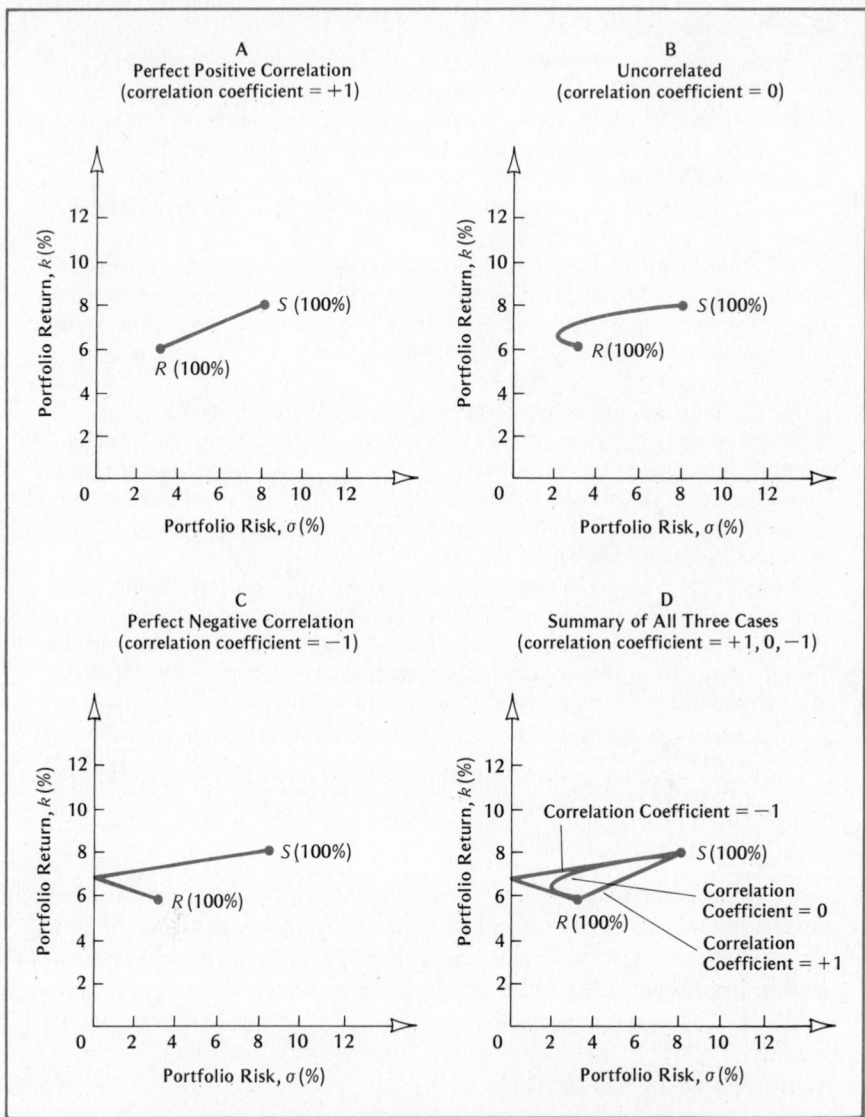

Figure 7.8   Portfolio risk (σ) and return (k) for combinations of assets R and S for various correlation coefficients

securities in light of a one-year common ownership (or holding) period. There are no restrictions on investment, no taxes, and no transaction costs. None of the investors is assumed to be large enough to affect the market price of the stock significantly.

Investor preferences. Investors are assumed to prefer to earn higher (versus lower) returns. At the same time, they are averse to risk, preferring lower (versus higher) risk. In general, they will prefer to invest in securities offering the highest return

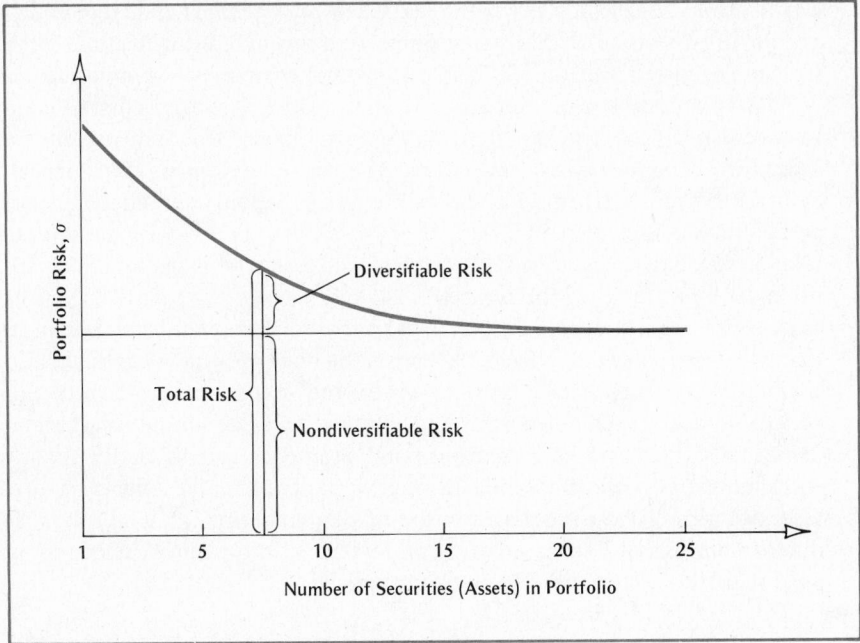

Figure 7.9   Portfolio risk and diversification

for a given level of risk or the lowest risk for a given level of return. They are assumed to measure return using the expected value and risk using the standard deviation.

TYPES OF RISK

To understand the basic types of risk, consider what happens when we begin with a single security (asset) in a portfolio and then expand the portfolio by randomly selecting additional securities from, say, the population of all actively traded securities. Using the standard deviation, σ, to measure the total portfolio risk, Figure 7.9 depicts the behavior of the total portfolio risk (y-axis) as additional securities are added (x-axis). When a single security is held in the portfolio, the total risk would equal the security's risk; as additional securities that are less than perfectly positively correlated are added, the total portfolio risk declines, due to the effects of diversification (as explained in the previous section), and tends to approach a limit. Research has shown that virtually all the benefits of diversification, in terms of risk reduction, can be gained by forming portfolios containing 10 to 20 randomly selected securities.[17] Figure 7.9 depicts this general behavior.

The *total risk* of a security can be viewed as consisting of two parts:

$$\text{Total security risk} = \text{nondiversifiable risk} + \text{diversifiable risk} \qquad (7.5)$$

[17] See, for example, W. H. Wagner and S. C. Lau, "The Effect of Diversification on Risk," *Financial Analysts Journal* 26 (November–December 1971), pp. 48–53, and Jack Evans and Stephen H. Archer, "Diversification and the Reduction of Dispersion: An Empirical Analysis," *Journal of Finance* 23 (December 1968), pp. 761–767.

Diversifiable risk, which is sometimes called *unsystematic risk,* represents the portion of an asset's risk that can be eliminated through diversification. It results from the occurrence of uncontrollable or random events, such as strikes, lawsuits, regulatory actions, loss of a key account, and so forth. The events that cause firms to have diversifiable risk vary from firm to firm; they are therefore unique to the given firm. *Nondiversifiable risk,* which is also called *systematic risk,* is attributed to forces that affect all firms. Factors such as war, inflation, international incidents, and political events account for nondiversifiable risk. This risk can be assessed in relation to the risk of a diversified portfolio of all assets, which is commonly called the *market portfolio* or "the market."

Because, as illustrated in Figure 7.9, any investor can create a portfolio of assets that will diversify away all diversifiable risk, the only *relevant risk* is the nondiversifiable risk. Any investor (or firm) must therefore be concerned solely with nondiversifiable risk, which reflects the contribution of an asset to the risk or standard deviation of the portfolio. This risk is not the same for each asset; different assets will affect the portfolio differently. In other words, the nondiversifiable risk of each asset depends on how it behaves in the market environment. The relevant risk differs from asset to asset, so its measurement is important in selecting assets possessing the desired risk-return characteristics.

THE MODEL: CAPM

The capital asset pricing model links the relevant risk and return for all assets. We will discuss it in four parts. The first part defines and describes the beta coefficient, which is an index of nondiversifiable risk. The second part presents an equation of the model, the third part graphically describes the relationship between risk and return, and the final part presents some general comments on CAPM.

Beta coefficient. To assess an asset's nondiversifiable risk, its *beta coefficient, b,* must be determined. The beta coefficient can be viewed as an *index* of the degree of responsiveness or comovement of asset return with market return. The beta coefficient for an asset can be found by examining the asset's historical returns relative to the returns for the market.[18] The market returns should be based on a broad index of *all* risky assets. Because such an index is not conveniently available, returns are typically measured by the average return on all (or a large sample of) assets. The Standard & Poor's 500 Stock Composite Index or some other stock index is

---

[18]The empirical measurement of beta is approached using regression analysis to find the regression coefficient (b_j) in the equation for the "characteristic line"

$$k_j = a_j + b_j k_m + e_j$$

where

k_j = the required (or expected) return on asset j
a_j = the intercept
b_j = the beta coefficient, which equals

$$\frac{Cov\,(k_j, k_m)}{\sigma_m^{\,2}}$$

Table 7.6 Betas for Selected Stocks
(March 9, 1984)

Stock	Beta
Apple Computer	1.75
Avon Products	1.00
Briggs & Stratton	.70
CBS Inc.	.95
Central Maine Power	.55
Delta Air Lines	1.05
Exxon Corporation	.90
General Motors	1.00
Gerber Scientific	1.70
International Business Machines	1.05
Merrill Lynch & Company	1.75
NCR Corporation	1.25
Paine Webber, Inc.	1.95
Reynolds & Reynolds	.95
Seagram Company	1.05
Standard Register	.75
Trans World Corporation	1.35
Union Electric	.65
U.S. Steel	1.05
Xerox Corporation	1.05

SOURCE: *Value Line Investment Survey* (New York: Arnold Bernhard and Company, March 9, 1984).

commonly used to measure market return. Betas for some selected stocks are given in Table 7.6. The beta for the market is equal to 1; all other betas are viewed in relation to this value. Asset betas may take on values that are either positive or negative; positive betas are much more common than negative betas. The majority of betas fall between .2 and 2. Table 7.7 gives some selected beta values and their associated interpretations.

The equation. Using beta as our index of nondiversifiable (relevant) risk, the capital asset pricing model is given in Equation 7.6.

$$k_j = R_F + b_j \times (k_m - R_F) \tag{7.6}$$

where

$Cov\ (k_j, k_m)$ = covariance of the return on asset j, k_j, and the market portfolio, k_m
σ_m^2 = variance of the return on the market portfolio
k_m = the required rate of return on the market portfolio of securities
e_j = random error term, which reflects the diversifiable or unsystematic risk of asset j

Because of the somewhat rigorous calculations involved in finding betas, the interested reader is referred to an advanced managerial finance or investments text for a more detailed discussion of this topic. Published security betas can be found in a variety of sources such as *Value Line*, as well as in the "Beta Books" now published by many of the leading stock brokerage firms such as Paine Webber, Inc., and Merrill Lynch, Pierce, Fenner & Smith, Inc.

Table 7.7   Selected Betas and Their Interpretations

Beta	Comment	Interpretation[a]
2.0 1.0 .5	Move in same direction as market	Twice as responsive, or risky, as the market Same response or risk as the market (i.e., average risk) Only half as responsive as the market
0		Unaffected by market movement
−.5 −1.0 −2.0	Move in opposite direction to market	Only half as responsive as the market Same response or risk as the market Twice as responsive as the market

[a] A stock that is twice as responsive as the market will experience a 2 percent change in its return for each 1 percent change in the return of the market portfolio, whereas the return of a stock that is half as responsive as the market will change by $\frac{1}{2}$ of 1 percent for each 1 percent change in the return of the market portfolio.

where

k_j = the required (or expected) return on asset j

R_F = the rate of return required on a risk-free asset, which is commonly measured by the yield on a U.S. government security such as a Treasury bill

b_j = the beta coefficient or index of nondiversifiable (relevant) risk for asset j

k_m = the required rate of return on the market portfolio of assets that can be viewed as the average rate of return on all assets

The required return on an asset, k_j, is an increasing function of beta, b_j, which reflects the relevant risk. In other words, the higher the risk, the higher the required return, and vice versa. The model can be broken into two parts: (1) the *risk-free rate, R_F;* and (2) the *risk premium,* $b_j \times (k_m - R_F)$. The $(k_m - R_F)$ portion of the risk premium could be called the *market risk premium* since it represents the premium the investor must receive for taking the average amount of risk associated with holding the market portfolio of assets. Let us look at an example.

EXAMPLE   Borst Corporation wishes to determine the required return on an asset — asset Z — that has a beta, b_z, of 1.5. The risk-free rate of return is found to be 7 percent, while the return on the market portfolio of assets is 11 percent. Substituting $b_z = 1.5$, $R_F = 7$ percent, and $k_m = 11$ percent into the capital asset pricing model given in Equation 7.6 yields a required return:

$$k_Z = 7\% + 1.5 \times (11\% - 7\%) = 7\% + 6\% = \underline{\underline{13\%}}$$

It can be seen that the market risk premium of 4 percent (11 percent − 7 percent), when adjusted for the assets index of risk (beta) of 1.5, results in a risk premium of 6 percent (1.5 × 4%), which when added to the 7 percent rate of return expected on a risk-free asset, results in a 13 percent required return. It should be clear that other things being equal, the higher the beta, the greater the required return, and vice versa. ■

The graph: the security market line (SML). When the capital asset pricing model (Equation 7.6) is depicted graphically, it is called the *security market line (SML).* It should be clear from Equation 7.6 that the SML will, in fact, be a straight line. It reflects for each level of nondiversifiable risk (beta) the required return in the marketplace. In the graph, risk as measured by beta, b, is plotted on the x-axis, and required returns, k, are plotted on the y-axis. Let us look at an illustration.

EXAMPLE   In the preceding example for the Borst Corporation, the risk-free rate, R_F, was 7 percent, and the required return on the market portfolio, k_m, was 11 percent. Since the betas associated with R_F and k_m, b_{R_F} and b_m, are by definition 0[19] and 1, respectively, the SML can be plotted using these two sets of coordinates. (i.e., $b_{R_F} = 0$, $R_F = 7\%$, and $b_m = 1$, $k_m = 11\%$). Figure 7.10 presents the security market line that results from plotting the coordinates given. As traditionally shown, the security market line in Figure 7.10 presents the required or expected return associated with all positive betas. The market risk premium of 4 percent (k_m of 11 percent minus R_F of 7 percent) has been highlighted. Using the beta for asset Z, b_Z, of 1.5, its corresponding required return, k_Z, is 13 percent. Also shown in the figure is asset Z's risk premium of 6 percent (k_Z of 13 % minus R_F of 7%). It should be clear that for assets with betas greater than 1, the risk premium is greater than that for the market; for assets with betas less than 1, the risk premium is less than that for the market.

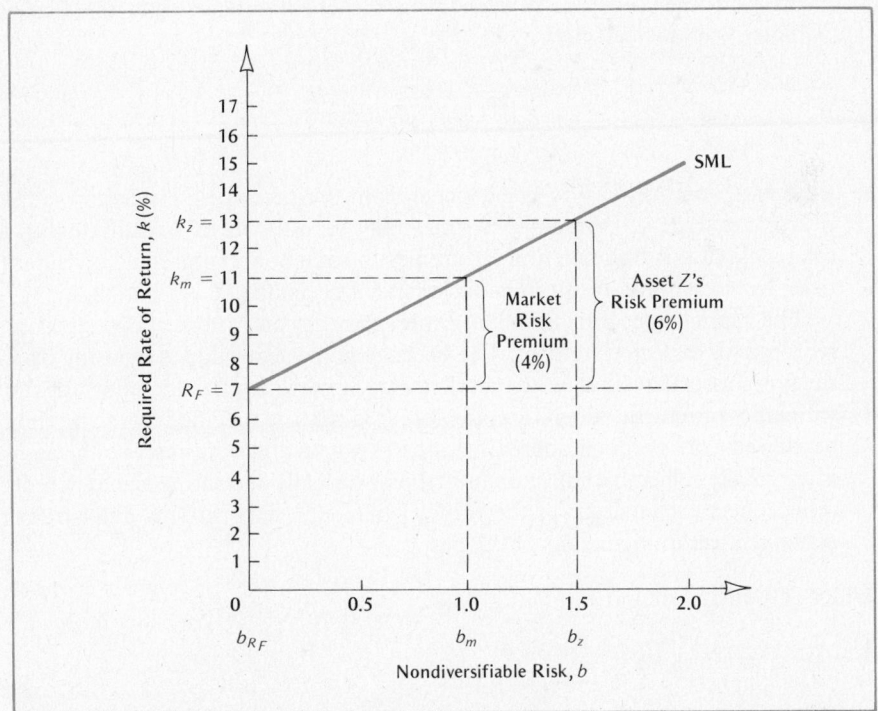

Figure 7.10   The security market line (SML) with Borst Corporation's asset Z data shown

[19] Since R_F is the rate of return on a risk-free asset, the beta associated with the risk-free asset, b_{R_F}, would equal 0. The 0 beta on the risk-free asset reflects not only its absence of risk but also that the asset's return is unaffected by movements in the market return.

DART PORTFOLIO VERSUS THE EXPERTS

It turns out that the old saw may be true. You can select a portfolio just by throwing darts at the stock tables and do at least as well in the market as the experts—if not better. Back in May (1981), Frank Lalli, the business and financial editor of the ailing New York *Daily News,* conceived a "battle of the brokers" to boost circulation. Four frequently quoted Wall Street professionals—Robert Stovall of Dean Witter Reynolds, Raymond DeVoe of Bruns Nordeman Rea, Michael Metz of Oppenheimer & Co. and William LeFevre of Purcell Graham & Co.— were each given an imaginary $30,000 to invest in the market for the ensuing two months. Pitted against this fearsome foursome were 10 *Daily News* business reporters armed with darts. By throwing one dart apiece at a stock table pinned on the wall, they selected 10 stocks in which they invested an imaginary $30,000. While the brokers were free to buy and sell the securities in their make-believe portfolio, the dart stocks were bought and held, so to speak.

When the contest was over at the end of June, the Dart Fund was up by $1,045.53, or 3.4%. The paper's fickle fingers of fate had outperformed all the experts save Stovall, whose portfolio had soared 26%. He got a plaque for his efforts. As for the losers? "They received a symbol of everlasting defeat," says Lalli. "Chicago Cubs baseball caps."

SOURCE: "The Dart Fund," *Money,* September 1981, p. 7.

Some comments on CAPM. The key concept from the preceding discussion is that a risk-return trade-off, which sometimes may be difficult to quantify, exists. An awareness of this trade-off and an attempt to somehow capture and consider the risk involved should result in better financial decisions.

The capital asset pricing model generally relies on historical data to estimate required (or expected) returns. The betas, which are developed by using data for the given asset as well as for the market, may or may not actually reflect the future variability of returns. Therefore, the required returns specified by the model can be viewed only as rough approximations. Analysts and other users of betas commonly make subjective adjustments to the historically determined betas in order to reflect their expectations of the future when such expectations differ from the actual risk-return behaviors of the past.

 **MULTINATIONAL FINANCE**

International Risks

The concepts of risk and return discussed earlier are applicable to international investments as well. However, additional factors must be taken into account, including both foreign exchange (economic) and political risks.

FOREIGN EXCHANGE RISKS

From the discussion in Chapter 3, we know that multinational companies operate in many different foreign markets, implying that portions of these firms' revenues and costs are based on foreign currencies. In order to understand the risks associated with such currencies, it is important to examine the relationship that exists among various currencies.

Since the mid-1970s, the major currencies of the world have had a *floating*—as opposed to *fixed*—relationship with respect to the U.S. dollar and to one another. The currencies regarded as major (or "hard") include the British pound (£), the Swiss franc (Sf), the Deutsche mark (DM), the French franc (Ff), the Japanese yen (¥), the Canadian dollar (C$), and, of course, the U.S. dollar (US$). The value of two currencies with respect to each other, or their *foreign exchange rate*, is expressed as follows:

$$US\$ \ 1.00 = Sf \ 2.24$$
$$Sf \ 1.00 = US\$ \ .45$$

The usual exchange quotation is given as Sf 2.24/US$, where the unit of account is the Swiss franc and the unit of currency being priced is one U.S. dollar.

For the major currencies, the existence of a floating relationship means that the value of any two currencies with respect to each other is allowed to fluctuate on a daily basis. On the other hand, most of the nonmajor currencies of the world try to maintain a *fixed* relationship with respect to one of the major currencies, a combination of major currencies, or some kind of international foreign exchange standard.

On any given day, the relationship between any two of the major currencies will contain two sets of figures, one reflecting the *spot* (that day's) *exchange rate*, and the other indicating the *forward* (a future day's) *exchange rate*. The foreign exchange rates given in Figure 7.11 can be used to illustrate these concepts.

For instance, the figure shows that on Monday, January 30, 1984, the spot rate for the Swiss franc was Sf 2.2425/US$, while the forward (future) rate was Sf 2.2305/US$ for 30-day delivery. In other words, on January 30, 1984, one could take a contract on forward Swiss francs for 30 days hence at an exchange rate of Sf 2.2305/US$. Forward *delivery* rates are also available for 90-day and 180-day contracts. For all such contracts, the agreements and signatures are completed on, say, January 30, 1984, whereas the actual exchange of dollars and Swiss francs between buyers and sellers will take place on the future date, say, 30 days later.

Figure 7.11 can also be used to illustrate the differences between floating and fixed currencies. All the major currencies previously mentioned have spot and forward rates with respect to the U.S. dollar. Moreover, a comparison of the exchange rates prevailing on January 30, 1984, *versus* those on Friday, January 27, 1984, indicates that the floating major currencies (or other currencies that also float in relation to the U.S. dollar, such as the Austrian schilling and the South African rand) have experienced changes in rates. Fixed currencies, such as the Chinese yuan and Saudi Arabian riyal, do not fluctuate on a daily basis with respect to the currency or currencies to which they are pegged (i.e., they have very limited movements with respect to either the U.S. dollar or other currencies).

A final point to note is the concept of changes in the value of a currency with respect to the U.S. dollar or another currency. For the floating currencies, changes in the value of foreign exchange rates are called *appreciation* or *depreciation*. For example, referring to Figure 7.11, it can be said that the value of the French franc

Foreign Exchange

Monday, January 30, 1984

The New York foreign exchange selling rates below apply to trading among banks in amounts of $1 million and more, as quoted at 3 p.m. Eastern time by Bankers Trust Co. Retail transactions provide fewer units of foreign currency per dollar.

Country	U.S. $ equiv. Monday	U.S. $ equiv. Friday	Currency per U.S. $ Monday	Currency per U.S. $ Friday
Argentina (Peso)	.03921	.04002	25.502	24.984
Australia (Dollar)	.9179	.9165	1.0894	1.0911
Austria (Schilling)	.05047	.05030	19.81	19.88
Belgium (Franc)				
Commercial rate	.01741	.01735	57.435	57.625
Financial rate	.01709	.01706	58.500	58.602
Brazil (Cruzeiro)	.0009722	.0009896	1028.50	1010.50
Britain (Pound)	1.4075	1.4058	.7104	.7113
30-Day Forward	1.4080	1.4064	.7102	.7110
90-Day Forward	1.4091	1.4074	.7096	.7105
180-Day Forward	1.4106	1.4089	.7089	.7097
Canada (Dollar)	.8009	.8015	1.2485	1.2477
30-Day Forward	.8008	.8014	1.2486	1.2478
90-Day Forward	.8008	.8014	1.2486	1.2478
180-Day Forward	.8009	.8016	1.2485	1.2475
Chile (Official rate)	.01135	.01138	88.04	87.83
China (Yuan)	.4834	.4834	2.0686	2.0686
Colombia (Peso)	.01108	.01118	90.19	89.42
Denmark (Krone)	.09815	.09793	10.1880	10.2110
Ecuador (Sucre)				
Official rate	.01791	.01803	55.81	55.45
Floating rate	.01129	.01109	88.55	90.15
Finland (Markka)	.1683	.1681	5.9400	5.9470
France (Franc)	.1162	.1161	8.6000	8.6125
30-Day Forward	.1160	.1158	8.6175	8.6275
90-Day Forward	.1153	.1151	8.6700	8.6825
180-Day Forward	.1141	.1139	8.7610	8.7755
Greece (Drachma)	.009685	.009689	103.25	103.20
Hong Kong (Dollar)	.1281	.1281	7.8010	7.8010
India (Rupee)	.0930	.0930	10.7526	10.75
Indonesia (Rupiah)	.001004	.001005	996.00	994.50
Ireland (Punt)	1.1000	1.0985	.9090	.9103
Israel (Shekel)	.008110	.008183	123.30	122.20
Italy (Lira)	.0005837	.0005827	1713.00	1716.00
Japan (Yen)	.004263	.004270	234.57	234.15
30-Day Forward	.004274	.004282	233.92	233.49
90-Day Forward	.004298	.004305	232.63	232.24
180-Day Forward	.004336	.004345	230.59	230.11
Lebanon (Pound)	.1706	.1734	5.86	5.765
Malaysia (Ringgit)	.4291	.4274	2.3300	2.3393
Mexico (Peso)				
Floating rate	.006060	.006060	165.00	165.00
Netherlands (Guilder)	.3162	.3153	3.1625	3.1710
New Zealand (Dollar)	.6505	.6508	1.5372	1.5365
Norway (Krone)	.1272	.1273	7.8575	7.8550
Pakistan (Rupee)	.07380	.07407	13.55	13.50
Peru (Sol)	.0004262	.0004302	2346.15	2324.50
Philippines (Peso)	.07142	.07137	14.00	14.01
Portugal (Escudo)	.007309	.007342	136.80	136.20
Saudi Arabia (Riyal)	.2849	.2849	3.5100	3.5100
Singapore (Dollar)	.4694	.4693	2.1303	2.1305
South Africa (Rand)	.7890	.7895	1.2674	1.2666
South Korea (Won)	.001250	.001254	799.60	797.00
Spain (Peseta)	.006307	.006291	158.55	158.95
Sweden (Krona)	.1222	.1225	8.1825	8.1575
Switzerland (Franc)	.4459	.4456	2.2425	2.2440
30-Day Forward	.4483	.4480	2.2305	2.2321
90-Day Forward	.4529	.4525	2.2078	2.2098
180-Day Forward	.4594	.4588	2.1765	2.1792
Taiwan (Dollar)	.02488	.02490	40.19	40.15
Thailand (Baht)	.04387	.04353	22.79	22.97
Uruguay (New Peso)				
Financial	.02144	.02179	46.63	45.88
Venezuela (Bolivar)				
Official rate	.1941	.1941	5.15	5.15
Floating rate	.07698	.07843	12.99	12.75
W. Germany (Mark)	.3556	.3549	2.8120	2.8170
30-Day Forward	.3567	.3561	2.8033	2.8082
90-Day Forward	.3590	.3583	2.7854	2.7905
180-Day Forward	.3620	.3614	2.7620	2.7668

SOURCE: *The Wall Street Journal,* January 31, 1984, p. 43.

Figure 7.11 Spot and future exchange rate quotations

has appreciated from Ff 8.6125 on Friday to Ff 8.6000 on Monday. In other words, it takes fewer francs to by one dollar. Meanwhile, during the same two days, the value of the Japanese yen has depreciated in relation to the dollar, since it takes more yen (234.57 versus 234.15 yen) to buy one dollar. For the fixed currencies, changes in values are called official revaluations or devaluations, but these terms have the same meanings as appreciation and depreciation, respectively. Multinational companies face foreign exchange risks under both floating and fixed arrangements. The case of the floating currencies can be used to illustrate these risks.

Using the U.S. dollar–Swiss franc relationship, we note that the forces of international supply and demand as well as internal and external economic and political elements help shape both the spot and the forward rates between these two currencies. Since our MNC cannot control much (or most) of these "outside" elements, the company faces potential changes in exchange rates in the forms of appreciation or depreciation that can in turn affect its revenues, costs, and profits to be measured in U.S. dollars. For currencies fixed in relation to each other, the risks come from the same set of elements indicated above. Again, these official changes, like the ones brought about by the market in the case of floating currencies, can affect the MNC's operations and its dollar-based financial position.

The risks stemming from changes in exchange rates can be illustrated by examining the balance sheet and income statement of MNC, Inc. We will focus on its subsidiary in Switzerland.

EXAMPLE   MNC, Inc., has a subsidiary in Switzerland that at the end of 1984 has the financial statements shown in Table 7.8. The figures for the balance sheet and income statement are given in the local currency, Swiss francs (Sf). Using the foreign exchange rate of Sf 2.10/US$ for December 31, 1984, the statements have been translated into U.S. dollars. For simplicity it is assumed that all the local figures are expected to remain the same during 1985. As a result, as of January 1, 1985, the subsidiary expects to show the same dollar figures on 12/31/85 as on 12/31/84. However, due to the change in the value of the Swiss franc relative to the dollar, from Sf 2.10/US$ to Sf 2.25/US$, it is clear that the translated dollar values of the items in the balance sheet, along with the dollar profit value on 12/31/85, are lower than those of the previous year, the changes being due only to fluctuations in foreign exchange. ■

There are additional complexities attached to each individual account in the financial statements. For instance, it is important whether a subsidiary's debt is all in the local currency, in U.S. dollars, or in several currencies. Moreover, it is important which curency (or currencies) the revenues and costs are denominated in. The risks exemplified so far relate to what is called the *accounting exposure.* In other words, foreign exchange fluctuations affect individual accounts in the financial statements. A different, and perhaps more important, risk element concerns *economic exposure.* Given that all future revenues and thus net profits can be subject to exchange rate changes, it is obvious that the present value of the net profits derived from foreign operations will have, as a part of its total diversifiable risk, an element reflecting appreciation (revaluation) or depreciation (devaluation) of various currencies with respect to the U.S. dollar.

What can MNC's management do about these risks? The actions will depend on the attitude of the management toward risk. This attitude, in turn, translates into how aggressively management wants to hedge the company's undesirable positions and exposures. The money markets, the forward (futures) markets, and the foreign currency options markets can be used — either individually or in conjunction with each other — to hedge foreign exchange exposures. Further details on certain hedging strategies will be provided in Chapters 16 and 18.

Another important component of the international diversifiable risk facing MNCs comes from political risks.

POLITICAL RISKS

The concept of *political risk* refers to the implementation by a host government of specific rules and regulations that can result in the discontinuity or seizure of the operations of a foreign company in that country. Political risk is usually manifested in the form of nationalization, expropriation, and confiscation. In general, the assets and operations of a foreign firm are taken over by the host government, usually without proper (or any) compensation.

Table 7.8   MNC, Inc.'s Swiss Subsidiary's Financial Statements

TRANSLATION OF BALANCE SHEET

| | 12/31/84 | | 12/31/85 | | | 12/31/84 | | 12/31/85 |
	Sf	US$	US$		Sf	US$	US$
Cash	8.00	3.81	3.55	Debt	48.00	22.86	21.33
Inventory	60.00	28.57	26.66	Paid-in Capital	40.00	19.04	17.77
Plant and Equipment (net)	32.00	15.23	14.22	Retained Earnings	12.00	5.71	5.33
Total	100.00	47.61	44.43	Total	100.00	47.61	44.43

TRANSLATION OF INCOME STATEMENT

| | 12/31/84 | | 12/31/85 |
	Sf	US$	US$
Sales	600.00	285.71	266.66
Cost of Goods Sold	550.00	261.90	244.44
Operating Profits	50.00	23.81	22.22

Note: This example is simplified to show how the balance sheet and income statement are subject to exchange fluctuations. For the applicable rules on the translation of foreign accounts, see the material at the end of Chapter 4.

Political risk has two basic paths: *macro* and *micro*. The former means that due to political change, a revolution, or the adoption of new policies by a host government, *all* foreign firms in the country will be subjected to political risk. An example of this is China in 1949 or Cuba in 1959–1960. In other words, no individual country or firm is treated differently; all assets and operations of foreign firms are taken over wholesale. Micro political risk, on the other hand, refers to the case in which an individual firm, a specific industry, or companies from a particular foreign country will be subjected to takeover. Examples include the nationalizations by a majority of the oil-exporting countries of the assets of the international oil companies in their territories.

Although political risk can take place in any country—even in the United States—the political instability of the Third World generally makes the positions of multinational companies most vulnerable there. At the same time, some of the countries in this group have the most promising markets for the goods and services being offered by MNCs. The main question, therefore, is how to engage in operation and foreign investment in such countries and yet avoid or minimize the potential political risk.

Table 7.9 shows some of the available short-term and long-term solutions MNCs may be able to adopt. The negative approaches are generally used by firms in extractive industries. The external approaches are also of limited use. The best policies MNCs can follow are the positive approaches, which involve both economic and political aspects.

In recent years MNCs have been relying on a variety of complex forecasting

Table 7.9   Coping with Political Risks

Positive approaches		Negative approaches
Prior negotiation of controls and operating contracts		License or patent restrictions under international agreements
Prior agreement for sale	Direct	Control of external raw materials
Joint venture with government or local private sector		Control of transportation to (external) markets
		Control of downstream processing
		Control of external markets
Use of locals in management		
Joint venture with local banks		
Equity participation by middle class	Indirect	
Local sourcing		
Local retail outlets		

External approaches to minimize loss
International insurance or investment guarantees
Thinly capitalized firms:
Local financing
External financing secured only by the local operation

SOURCE: Rita M. Rodriguez & E. Eugene Carter, *International Financial Management.* 3rd ed. (Englewood Cliffs, N.J.: Prentice-Hall, 1984), p. 512.

techniques whereby "international experts," using the available historical data, predict the chances for political instability in a host country and the potential effects on MNC operations. Events in Iran and Nicaragua, among others, however, point to the limited use of such techniques and tend to reinforce the usefulness of the positive approaches. ●●

CHAPTER SUMMARY

● *Risk* is commonly used interchangeably with *uncertainty* to refer to the variability of expected returns. Statistically, risk is present when the probability distribution of returns is known; uncertainty is present when the probability distributions are unknown.

● The return on an investment is measured as the total gain or loss experienced on behalf of its owner over a given period of time.

● Managers can exhibit risk-averse, risk-indifferent, or risk-taking behaviors; most are risk-averse since for a given increase in risk, they require as compensation a greater than proportional increase in return.

● The risk of a single asset is measured in much the same way as the risk of a portfolio, or collection, of assets, but it is often useful to differentiate between them, since certain benefits often accrue to holders of portfolios.

● Two approaches commonly used to get a sense of asset risk are sensitivity analysis and probabilities. Sensitivity analysis involves evaluating various estimates of asset returns, such as pessimistic, most likely, and optimistic. The range is often used to quantify risk by measuring the dispersion of these potential returns. A more sophisticated approach would be to assign probabilites to the various outcomes, either objectively or subjectively, to determine the expected value of the returns.

● Risk can be assessed visually by drawing either a bar chart or the entire probability distribution (if sufficient data are available) associated with an investment's returns.

● To obtain a more concrete measure of risk, statistical measures of variability can be used. Two statistics that provide a measure of an asset's risk are the standard deviation and the coefficient of variation.

● The timing of returns also affects an asset's risk. In general, the further into the future returns are to be received, the greater the variability of these returns.

● Portfolio risk is the relationship among differing asset returns. The correlation among assets in a portfolio, which is the degree to which their returns vary together, greatly affects the overall risk of the portfolio.

● A key consideration in financial decision making is the trade-off between risk and return. In a perfect world of efficient markets, the only relevant risk is nondiversifiable risk, which is inescapable since it is attributed to changes in the economy. Diversifiable risk, which is attributed to the firm itself and results from the occurrence of uncontrollable or random events, can be eliminated through diversification.

● The nondiversifiable risk can be measured by beta, an index that relates the responsiveness or comovement of an asset's return to that of the market.

● The capital asset pricing model (CAPM) uses beta to relate an asset's risk relative to the market to the asset's required return. Graphically, the capital asset pricing model is referred to as the security market line (SML), which depicts for each level of nondiversifiable risk (beta) the associated required return in the marketplace.

● Operating in international markets involves certain factors that can influence the risk and return characteristics of an MNC. Foreign exchange (economic) risk elements relate to the existence of different currencies and the potential impact they can have on the value of foreign operations. Political risks stem mainly from political instability in a number of countries and the associated implications for the assets and operations of MNCs.

KEY TERMS

accounting exposure	perfect negative correlation
bar chart	perfect positive correlation
beta coefficient	political risk (macro and micro)
capital asset pricing model (CAPM)	portfolio
coefficient of variation (*CV*)	positively correlated
continuous probability distribution	probability
correlation	range
correlation coefficient	realized values
cumulative probability distribution	relevant risk
discrete probability distribution	required return
dispersion	return
diversifiable risk	risk
diversification	risk-averse
economic exposure	risk-free rate, R_F
efficient portfolio	risk-indifferent
expected return	risk taker
expected value	risk premium
fixed currencies	security market line (SML)
floating currencies	sensitivity analysis
foreign exchange rate	spot exchange rate
foreign exchange risks	standard deviation
forward exchange rate	subjective probability distribution
market portfolio	systematic risk
market risk premium	total risk
negatively correlated	uncertainty
nondiversifiable risk	uncorrelated
normal probability distribution	unrealized values
objective probability distribution	unsystematic risk

QUESTIONS

7-1   Define *risk* as it relates to financial decision making. Why is it important for a decision maker to have some sense of the risk or uncertainty associated with an investment in an asset? Do any assets have perfectly certain returns?

7-2   Describe the basic calculation involved in finding the return on an investment. Differentiate between realized and unrealized returns.

7-3   Compare and contrast the following risk-preference behaviors and indicate which is most commonly exhibited by the financial manager.
   a   Risk-averse
   b   Risk-indifferent
   c   Risk-taking

7-4   How can *sensitivity analysis* be used to assess asset risk? What is one of the most common methods of sensitivity analysis? Define and describe the role of the *range* as an aid in sensitivity analysis.

7-5   How does a plot of the probability distribution of outcomes allow the decision maker to get a sense of asset risk? What is the difference between a bar chart and a continuous probability distribution?

7-6   What does the *standard deviation* of a distribution of asset returns indicate? What relationship exists between the size of the standard deviation and the degree of asset risk?

7-7   What is the *coefficient of variation?* How is it calculated? Why may the coefficient of variation be a better basis than the standard deviation for comparing the risk associated with different assets?

7-8   Why must assets be evaluated in a portfolio context? Why is the *correlation* between asset returns important?

7-9   How does diversification of risk in the asset selection process allow the investor to combine risky assets in such a fashion that the risk of the portfolio is less than the risk of the individual assets in it? What is an *efficient portfolio?*

7-10   What is the relationship of total risk, nondiversifiable risk, and diversifiable risk? Why would someone argue that nondiversifiable risk is the only relevant risk?

7-11   Using the beta coefficent as the measure of nondiversifiable risk, what is the equation for the *capital asset pricing model (CAPM)?* Explain the meaning of each variable. Assuming a risk-free rate of 8 percent and a market return of 12 percent, graph the risk-return trade-off as defined by the CAPM.

7-12   Define *spot* and *forward* exchange rates.

7-13   Discuss accounting and economic exchange rate exposures.

7-14   Discuss macro and micro political risk. Describe some techniques for dealing with political risk.

PROBLEMS

7-1   (**Rate of Return**)   Charles Marney, a financial analyst for Stornin Industries, wishes to estimate the rate of return for two similar-risk investments — X and Y. Marney's research indicates that the immediate past returns will act as reasonable estimates of future return. A year earlier, investment X had a market value of $20,000 and investment Y, $55,000. During the year, investment X generated cash flow of $1,500 and investment Y, $6,800. The current market values of investments X and Y are $21,000 and $55,000, respectively.

    a   Calculate the expected rate of return on investments X and Y using the most recent year's data.

    b   Assuming that the two investments are equally risky, which one would you prefer? Why?

7-2   (**Return Calculations**)   For each of the following investments, calculate the rate of return earned over the unspecified time period.

Investment	Beginning-of-period value ($)	End-of-period value ($)	Cash flow during period ($)
A	800	1,100	−100
B	120,000	118,000	15,000
C	45,000	48,000	7,000
D	600	500	80
E	12,500	12,400	1,500

7-3   (**Risk Preferences**)   Oren Wells, the financial manager for Winston Enterprises, wishes to evaluate three prospective investments — X, Y, and Z. Currently the firm earns 12 percent on its investments, which have a risk index of 6 percent. The three investments under consideration are profiled below in terms of expected return and expected risk.

Investment	Expected return (%)	Expected risk index (%)
X	14	8
Y	19	9
Z	20	10

a If Oren Wells were *risk-indifferent,* which investments would he select? Explain why.

b If Oren Wells were *risk-averse,* which investments would he select? Explain why.

c If Oren Wells were a *risk taker,* which investments would he select? Explain why.

d Given the traditional risk-preference behavior exhibited by financial managers, which investment would be preferred? Why?

7-4 **(Risk Analysis)** Bell Products is considering an investment in an expanded product line. Two possible types of expansion are being considered. After investigating the possible outcomes, the following estimates were made:

	Expansion A	Expansion B
Initial investment	$12,000	$12,000
Annual rate of return		
Pessimistic	16%	10%
Most likely	20	20
Optimistic	24	30

a Determine the range of the rates of return for each of the two projects.

b Which project is less risky? Why?

c If you were making the investment decision which one would you choose? Why? What does this imply about your feelings toward risk?

d Assume that expansion B's most likely outcome was 21 percent per year and all other facts remained the same. Does this change your answer to part **c**? Why?

7-5 **(Risk and Probability)** Micro-Pub, Inc., is considering the purchase of one of two microfilm cameras — R or S. Both should provide benefits over a ten-year period, and each requires an initial investment of $4000. Management has constructed the following table of estimates of probabilities and rates of return for pessimistic, most likely, and optimistic results:

	Camera R		Camera S	
	Amount	Probability	Amount	Probability
Initial investment	$4000	1.00	$4000	1.00
Annual rate of return				
Pessimistic	20%	.25	15%	.20
Most likely	25	.50	25	.55
Optimistic	30	.25	35	.25

a Determine the range for the rate of return for each of the two cameras.

b Determine the expected rate of return for each camera.

c Which camera is more risky? Why?

7-6 **(Bar Charts and Risk)** Wilbur's Sportswear is considering bringing out a line of

assumed degrees of correlation — perfect positive, uncorrelated, and perfect negative. The following expected return and risk values were calculated for each of the assets.

Asset	Expected return, $\bar{k}$ (%)	Risk (standard deviation), σ_k (%)
V	8	5
W	13	10

a If the returns of assets V and W are *perfectly positively correlated* (correlation coefficient $= +1$), describe the *range* of (1) expected return and (2) risk associated with all possible portfolio combinations.

b If the returns of assets V and W are *uncorrelated* (correlation coefficient $= 0$), describe the *approximate range* of (1) expected return and (2) risk associated with all possible portfolio combinations.

c If the returns of assets V and W are *perfectly negatively correlated* (correlation coefficient $= -1$), describe the *range* of (1) expected return and (2) risk associated with all possible portfolio combinations.

7-12 (Total, Nondiversifiable, and Diversifiable Risk) Martin Krone randomly selected securities from all those listed on the New York Stock Exchange to be included in a portfolio. He began with one security and added securities one by one until a total of 20 securities were held in the portfolio. After each security was added, Martin calculated the portfolio standard deviation, σ; the calculated values are given below:

Number of securities	Portfolio risk, σ (%)	Number of securities	Portfolio risk, σ (%)
1	14.50	11	7.00
2	13.30	12	6.80
3	12.20	13	6.70
4	11.20	14	6.65
5	10.30	15	6.60
6	9.50	16	6.56
7	8.80	17	6.52
8	8.20	18	6.50
9	7.70	19	6.48
10	7.30	20	6.47

a On a set of number of securities in portfolio (x-axis) – portfolio risk (y-axis) axes, plot the portfolio risk data given in the preceding table.

b Divide the total portfolio risk in the graph into its *nondiversifiable* and *diversifiable* risk components and label each of these on the graph.

c Describe which of the two risk components is the "relevant risk" and explain why it is relevant. How much of this risk exists in Martin Krone's portfolio?

7-13 (Interpreting Beta) A firm wishes to assess the impact of changes in the market return on one of its assets that has a beta of 1.20.

a If the market return increased by 15 percent, what impact would this have on the asset's return?

b If the market return decreased by 8 percent, what impact would this have on the asset's return?

    c If the market return did not change what impact, if any, would this have on the asset's return?

    d Would this asset be considered more or less risky than the market? Explain.

7-14 **(Betas)** Answer the questions below for each of the following assets.

Asset	Beta
A	0.50
B	1.60
C	−0.20
D	0.90

    a What impact would a *10 percent increase* in the market return have on each asset's return?

    b What impact would a *10 percent decrease* in the market return have on each asset's return?

    c If you were certain that the market return would *increase* in the near future, which asset would you prefer? Why?

    d If you were certain that the market return would *decrease* in the near future, which asset would you prefer? Why?

7-15 **(Betas and Risk Rankings)** Stock A has a beta of 0.80, Stock B has a beta of 1.40, and Stock C has a beta of −0.30.

    a Rank these stocks from the most risky to the least risky.

    b If the return on the market portfolio increases by 12 percent, what change in the return for each of the stocks would you expect?

    c If the return on the market portfolio declines by 5 percent, what change in the return for each of the stocks would you expect?

    d If you felt the stock market was just ready to experience a significant decline, which stock would you likely add to your portfolio? Why?

    e If you anticipated a major stock market rally, which stock would you add to your portfolio? Why?

7-16 **(Capital Asset Pricing Model — CAPM)** For each of the following cases, use the capital asset pricing model to find the required return.

Case	Risk-free rate, R_F (%)	Market return, k_m (%)	Beta, b
A	5	8	1.30
B	8	13	.90
C	9	12	−.20
D	10	15	1.00
E	6	10	.60

7-17 **(Manipulating CAPM)** Use the basic equation for the capital asset pricing model (CAPM) to work each of the following:

    a Find the *required return* for an asset with beta of 0.90 when the risk-free rate and market return are 8 percent and 12 percent, respectively.

    b Find the *risk-free rate* for a firm with a required return of 15 percent and a beta of 1.25 when the market return is 14 percent.

    c Find the *market return* for an asset with a required return of 16 percent and a beta of 1.10 when the risk-free rate is 9 percent.

    d Find the *beta* for an asset with a required return of 15 percent when the risk-free rate and market return are 10 percent and 12.5 percent, respectively.

7-18   **(Security Market Line — SML)**   Assume that the risk-free rate, R_F, is currently 9 percent and that the required return on the market portfolio, k_m, is currently 13 percent.

    a   Draw the security market line (SML) on a set of nondiversifiable risk (x-axis) – required return (y-axis) axes.

    b   Calculate and label on the axes in **a** the market risk premium.

    c   Given the data above, calculate the required return on asset A having a beta of 0.80 and asset B having a beta of 1.30.

    d   Draw in the beta and required returns calculated for assets A and B on the axes in **a**. Label the risk premium associated with each of these assets and discuss them.

7-19   **(Integrative — Risk, Return, and CAPM)**   The Jenkins Box Company must consider several investment projects, A through E, using the capital asset pricing model (CAPM) and its graphic representation, the security market line (SML). Using the table below,

Item	Rate of return (%)	Beta (b) value
Risk-free asset	9	0
Market portfolio	14	1.00
Project A	—	1.50
Project B	—	.75
Project C	—	2.00
Project D	—	0
Project E	—	− .50

    a   Calculate the rate of return and risk premium each project must produce given its level of nondiversifiable risk.

    b   Graph the security market line (required rate of return relative to nondiversifiable risk) for all projects listed in the table.

    c   Discuss the relative nondiversifiable risk of projects A through E.

Chapter 8

Valuation

After studying this chapter, you should be able to:

1. Describe the key inputs and fundamental concepts underlying the valuation process.

2. Identify the basic features of a corporate bond and use them to determine the value of the bond in view of current market conditions.

3. Understand the behavior of bond value, yield to maturity, semiannual interest, and perpetual bond and preferred stock valuations.

4. Recognize the popular approaches — book value, liquidation value, and price/earnings multiples — used to estimate stock values.

5. Perform basic common stock valuation using zero growth, constant growth, and variable growth assumptions as to future dividend behavior.

6. Discuss the relationship between decision making and common stock value and explain the impact of changes in expected return and risk on value.

*V*aluation is the process of determining the worth of an asset. Just like investors, financial managers must understand how to value stocks, bonds, and other assets to judge whether or not they are a "good buy."[1] Valuation couples the time value techniques presented in Chapter 6 with the risk and return factors developed in Chapter 7. Financial managers must understand how these forces interact to create value so that their decisions take into account any possible impact on the worth of the firm's bonds, stocks, and assets.

Valuation Fundamentals

The *valuation process* involves determining the worth of income- and cash-flow-generating assets. It is a relatively simple process that can be applied to expected streams of benefits from bonds, stocks, income properties, oil wells, and so on in order to determine their worth at a given point in time. To do this, the manager uses the time value of money techniques presented in Chapter 6 and the concepts of risk and return developed in Chapter 7.

KEY INPUTS

The key inputs to the valuation process include cash flows (returns), timing, and the discount rate (risk). Each is briefly described below.

Cash flows (returns). The value of any asset depends on the cash flow(s) it is expected to provide over the ownership period. Since cash is the common denominator used

---

[1] Theoretically, all assets traded *in active markets*, such as stocks on the New York Stock Exchange, are correctly priced at each point in time. This is based on the *efficient market hypothesis (EMH)*, which suggests that all market participants have full and complete information, pursue similar objectives, and therefore agree on a correct price at each point in time. In spite of this theory, many investors, and therefore financial managers as well, attempt to determine intrinsic as well as future values of assets using valuation techniques.

in finance to measure the costs of and benefits from financial transactions, the value of any asset — whether a *financial asset* such as a stock or bond or a *real asset* such as a machine or building — must derive from its cash flow. To have value, an asset does not have to provide an annual cash flow; it can provide intermittent cash flow or even a single cash flow over the period of analysis.

EXAMPLE   Millie Hobbs, the financial analyst for Jones Industries, wishes to estimate the value of three assets — common stock in Wortz United, an interest in an oil well, and an original painting by a well-known artist. Her cash flow estimates for each were:

> *Stock in Wortz United:* Expect to receive cash dividends of $300 per year indefinitely.
> *Oil well:* Expect to receive cash flow of $2,000 at the end of one year, $4,000 at the end of two years, and $10,000 at the end of four years, when the well is to be sold.
> *Original painting:* Expect to be able to sell the painting in five years for $85,000.

Having developed these cash flow estimates, Millie has taken the first step toward placing a value on each of these assets. ■

Timing. In addition to making cash flow estimates, the manager must specify the timing of the cash flows.[2] In general, the sooner a given cash flow is to be received, the greater its present value. It is customary to specify the timing along with the amounts of cash flow. For example, the cash flows of $2,000, $4,000, and $10,000 for the oil well in the example were scheduled to occur at the end of years 1, 2, and 4, respectively. In combination, the cash flow and its timing fully define the return expected from the asset.

Discount rate (risk). Risk, as noted in Chapter 7, is a relatively complex concept that can be used to describe the chance that an expected outcome will be realized. The level of risk associated with a given cash flow can significantly affect its value. In general, the greater the risk of (or the less certain) a given cash flow, the less value it will have for an assumed risk-averse investor. In terms of present value, greater risk can be incorporated into an analysis by using a higher discount rate or required return. Recall that in the capital asset pricing model (CAPM) in Chapter 7 (see Equation 7.6), the greater the risk as measured by beta (b), the higher the required (or expected) return (k). In the valuation process, the discount rate is used to incorporate risk into the analysis — the higher the risk, the greater the discount rate (required return), and vice versa.

EXAMPLE   Let's go back to Millie Hobbs's job of placing a value on Jones Industries' original painting, which is expected to provide a single cash flow through its sale in five years for an estimated $85,000, and consider two scenarios.

> *Scenario 1 — Certainty:* A major art gallery has contracted to buy the painting for $85,000 at the end of five years as part of their deferred purchase program. Because this is considered a certain situation, Millie views this as money in the bank and would use the prevailing risk-free rate of return, R_F, of 9 percent to calculate the value of the painting.

[2] Although cash flows can occur at any time during a year, for computational convenience as well as custom, they will be assumed to occur at the *end* of the year unless otherwise noted.

Scenario 2— High Risk: The value of original paintings by this artist has fluctuated widely over the past ten years, and although Millie expects to be able to get $85,000 for the painting, she realizes its sale price in five years could range between $30,000 and $140,000. Because of the high uncertainty surrounding the painting's value, Millie estimates that a 15 percent discount rate is appropriate. ■

These scenarios and Millie's associated estimates of the appropriate discount rate illustrate the role this rate plays in capturing risk when preparing to value an asset's estimated cash flows. The often subjective nature of such estimates is clear.[3]

THE BASIC VALUATION MODEL

Simply stated, the value of any asset is *the present value of all future cash flows it is expected to provide over the relevant time period.* The time period can be as short as one year or as long as infinity. The value of an asset is therefore determined by discounting the expected cash flows back to their present value, using a discount rate commensurate with the asset's exposure to risk. Utilizing the present-value techniques presented in Chapter 6, the value of any asset at time zero, V_0, can be expressed as

$$V_0 = \frac{CF_1}{(1 + k)^1} + \frac{CF_2}{(1 + k)^2} + \cdots + \frac{CF_n}{(1 + k)^n} \qquad (8.1)$$

where

$$V_0 = \text{value of the asset at time zero}$$
$$CF_t = \text{cash flow expected at the end of year } t$$
$$k = \text{appropriate discount rate}$$
$$n = \text{relevant time period}$$

Using present-value interest factor notation, $PVIF_{k,n}$, Equation 8.1 can be rewritten as

$$V_0 = CF_1(PVIF_{k,1}) + CF_2(PVIF_{k,2}) + \cdots + CF_n(PVIF_{k,n}) \qquad (8.2)$$

Given the expected cash flows, CF_t, over the relevant time period, n, the discount rate, k, appropriate to the risk of the expected cash flows can be used to determine the value of any asset.

EXAMPLE   Millie Hobbs, with the addition of appropriate discount rates, calculated the value of each asset as shown in Table 8.1 using Equation 8.2. The Wortz United stock has a value of $2,500, the oil well's value is estimated at $9,262, and the original painting has a value of $42,245. It should be clear that regardless of the nature of the expected cash flow

[3] Straightforward techniques for estimating discount rates do not exist. Actual practice tends to rely on subjective estimates based on the conceptual risk-return framework of the capital asset pricing model. Subsequent discussions describe some of these "practical" approaches.

Table 8.1   Valuation of Jones Industries' Assets by Millie Hobbs

Asset	Cash flow, CF		Appropriate discount rate (%)	Valuation
Wortz United stock[a]	$300/year indefinitely		12	$V_0 = \$300(PVIFA_{12\%,\infty})$ $= \dfrac{\$300}{.12} = \underline{\$2,500}$
Oil well[b]	Year (t)	CF_t	20	$V_0 = \$2,000(PVIF_{20\%,1})$ $+ \$4,000(PVIF_{20\%,2})$ $+ \$0(PVIF_{20\%,3})$ $+ \$10,000(PVIF_{20\%,4})$ $= \$2,000(.833)$ $+ \$4,000(.694)$ $+ \$0(.579)$ $+ 10,000(.482)$ $= \$1,666 + \$2,776$ $+ \$0 + \$4,820$ $= \underline{\$9,262}$
	1	$2,000		
	2	4,000		
	3	0		
	4	10,000		
Original painting[c]	$85,000 at end of year 5		15	$V_0 = \$85,000(PVIF_{15\%,5})$ $= \$85,000(.497)$ $= \underline{\$42,245}$

[a] This is a perpetuity (infinite-lived annuity), and therefore Equation 6.28 is applied.
[b] This is a mixed stream of cash flows and therefore requires finding the individual $PVIF$s noted.
[c] This is a lump-sum cash flow and therefore requires finding a single $PVIF$.

from an asset, the basic valuation equation can be applied to the estimated cash flows to determine value. In the case of perpetuities (like the Wortz United stock) and annuities, special present-value interest factors can be utilized to streamline the calculations. ∎

The next step involves customizing the basic equation for valuation of two key financial assets—bonds and stocks.

Bond Valuation

A quick examination of a firm's balance sheet clearly shows that corporations raise long-term funds from either of two sources—debt or equity. Attention here is devoted to corporate bonds because they are the dominant form of long-term financing used by corporations. Corporate *bonds,* which are described in detail in Chapter 19, are certificates evidencing that the corporation has borrowed a specified sum of money, which it has promised to repay in the future under clearly defined terms. Bonds are long-term debt instruments used to raise large sums of money from a diverse group of lenders. Before discussing the bond valuation process, it is helpful to understand some basics.

BOND FUNDAMENTALS

Corporate bonds typically have a *par*, or *face, value* of $1000 and pay interest—typically *semiannually* (every six months) at a specified *coupon rate,* which is fixed over the bond's *maturity.* Most *new issues* have *initial* maturities of 10 to 30 years; in the case of *outstanding (seasoned) bonds,* the *maturity date*—the specific year in which the bond matures—is always cited.[4] As noted in Chapter 3, new bonds are sold in the primary market; outstanding issues are traded in the secondary market, which includes the organized securities exchanges and the over-the-counter market. Whereas new issues are commonly sold at or near their par value, the *market price,* or value, of outstanding issues often varies from par.

EXAMPLE   The ABC Company has two bonds—a new issue and an outstanding issue. Each is described below.

> *New issue:* The firm just now (January 1, 1985) issued a 10 percent coupon, ten-year bond with a $1000 par value that pays interest semiannually. Investors who buy this bond receive the contractual right to (1) $100 annual interest (10 percent × $1000 par value) distributed as $50 ($\frac{1}{2}$ × $100) at the end of each six months for ten years and (2) the $1000 par value at the end of the tenth year. A holder of the bond could of course sell it at its market price some time prior to the stated maturity date.
>
> *Outstanding issue:* ABC Company also has outstanding a $1000 par, 12$\frac{1}{2}$ percent coupon bond that pays interest semiannually. The bond was initially issued with a 25-year maturity three years earlier, in January 1982; its maturity date is therefore 2007 (1982 + 25 years = 2007). Holders of these bonds receive the contractual right to (1) $125 annual interest (12.5 percent × $1000 par value) distributed as $62.50 ($\frac{1}{2}$ × $125) at the end of each six months for 22 years and (2) the $1000 par value at the end of the year 2007. Of course, the bond could be sold in the market prior to its maturity.

This example illustrates the key bond terminology: par value, coupon rate, maturity, new issue, outstanding bonds, and maturity date. ∎

Using data presented for ABC Company's new issue, we look now at basic bond valuation and related issues.

BASIC BOND VALUATION

At any point in time, the value of a bond is the present value of the contractual payments its issuer is obligated to make from the current time until it matures. The appropriate discount rate would be the required return, k_d, which depends on prevailing interest rates and risk. The basic valuation equation in Equation 8.1 is modified in Equation 8.3 to find the value, B_0, of a bond that pays *annual* interest of I dollars, has n years to maturity, has an M-dollar par value, and for which the required return is k_d.

---

[4] Bonds often have features that allow them to be retired by the issuer prior to maturity; these *call* and *conversion* features are presented in Chapters 19 and 22. For the purpose of the current discussion, these features are ignored.

$$B_0 = I\left[\sum_{t=1}^{n} \frac{1}{(1 + k_d)^t}\right] + M\left[\frac{1}{(1 + k_d)^n}\right] \qquad (8.3)$$

$$= I(PVIFA_{k_d,n}) + M(PVIF_{k_d,n}) \qquad (8.3a)$$

EXAMPLE   Using the ABC Company data for the January 1, 1985, new issue and *assuming that interest is paid annually* and that the required return is equal to the bond's coupon rate of interest, $I = \$100$, $k_d = 10$ percent, $M = \$1000$, and $n = 10$ years. Substituting these values in Equation 8.3a yields

$$B_0 = \$100(PVIFA_{10\%,10\,yrs}) + \$1000(PVIF_{10\%,10\,yrs})$$
$$= \$100(6.145) + \$1000(.386)$$
$$= \$614.50 + \$386.00 = \underline{\$1000.50}$$

The bond therefore has a value of approximately \$1000.[5] Note that the value calculated above is equal to par value; this will always be the case when the coupon rate of interest is equal to the required return. The computations involved in finding the bond value are depicted graphically on the time line in Figure 8.1. ∎

BOND VALUE BEHAVIOR

The value of a bond in the marketplace is rarely constant over its life. A variety of forces in the economy as well as the mere passage of time tend to affect value. Since these external forces are really in no way controlled by bond issuers or investors, it

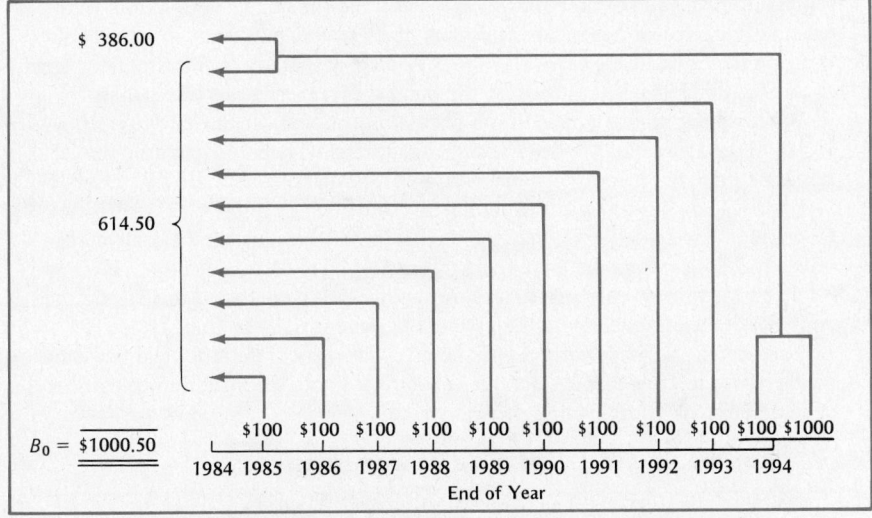

Figure 8.1   Graphic depiction of bond valuation (ABC Company's 10 percent coupon, 10-year maturity, \$1000 par, January 1, 1985 issue paying annual interest; required return = 10%)

[5] Note that a slight rounding error (\$.50) results here due to the use of the table factors rounded to the nearest thousandth.

HOW TO READ A BOND QUOTATION

New York Exchange Bonds
Tuesday, November 18, 1978

CORPORATION BONDS
Volume, $14,300,000

Bonds		Cur Yld	Vol	High	Low	Close	Net Chg.
ATT	2 3/4s80	3.0	5	91 3/8	91 3/8	91 3/8	−1/8
ATT	2 3/4s82	3.3	17	83 1/2	82 3/4	83 1/2	+3/4
ATT	3 1/4s84	4.3	22	76 1/8	76	76	−1/8
ATT	4 3/8s85	5.6	24	78 1/2	78 1/4	78 1/4	−1/2
ATT	2 5/8s86	3.8	5	68 1/8	68 1/8	68 1/8	−1/8
ATT	2 7/8s	4.3	11	66 1/2	66 1/2	66 1/2	−1/2
ATT	5 3/8s70	5.8	13	66 1/4	68 1/4	68 1/4	+1/2
ATT	8 3/400	8.9	155	98 3/4	98 1/2	98 5/8	−1/8
ATT	7s01	8.6	86	81 7/8	81 1/2	81 1/2	−1/4
ATT	6 1/2s79	6.7	24	96 3/4	96 3/8	96 3/4	−3/8
ATT	7 1/8s03	8.6	11	82 1/2	82 1/2	82 1/2	−1/8
ATT	8.80s05	9.0	173	96 1/8	98 1/8	98 1/4	−1/8
ATT	7 3/4s82	8.1	29	95 3/4	95 5/8	95 3/4	+1/8
ATT	8 5/8s07	6.9	28	96 1/2	96 1/2	96 1/4	−5/8
Amfac	5 1/494	cv	33	66 1/8	65 7/8	66 1/8	.....
Ampx	5 1/294	cv	61	60 3/4	60	60 1/4	+1/4
Anhr	9.20s05	9.1	5	100 7/8	100 7/8	100 7/8	+1/2
AppP	7 1/4s79	7.4	31	97 1/2	97 1/2	97 1/2	.....
Arco	8.70s81	8.9	20	98	97 1/2	97 1/2	−1/2
Arco	8s8s	8.3	147	96 3/8	95 1/4	96 3/8	+5/8
Arco	8 3/8s83	8.7	25	96 1/4	96 1/4	96 1/4	−5/8

Here is a typical example of the way bond market information might appear in your newspaper. We'll use an American Telephone bond to help decipher the information. First you see the **(1)** company name and the bond's description. In our example, we have an American Telephone bond paying a **(2)** coupon interest of 8¾% and maturing in the year **(3)** 2000. Next we see that **(4)** its actual current yield is not 8¾% but 8.9%. That's because the bond's **(5)** current price is less than $1,000. Skipping the volume column for a moment, you can see that **(6)** this bond's highest price for the day was 98¾. Traditionally, bond people drop the last zero on a price quotation. For our bond, "98" means $980 and the "¾" means ¾ of $10 or $7.50. So our bond sold at a price of $987.50 at its highest. **(7)** Its lowest price was 98½ or $985. **(8)** The "⅛" shows that on this day this bond closed at a price of $1.25 less than the previous day. Finally, **(9)** the volume column is simple. It tells you—with no code—exactly how many bonds were traded this day on the New York Stock Exchange. In the case of our American Telephone bond, 155. Looking down the page, you may see **(10)** "cv" instead of current yield for some bonds. This indicates that the bond is convertible into a specified number of shares of common stock of the issuing company.

SOURCE: *The Bond Book,* Merrill Lynch, Pierce, Fenner & Smith, Inc., 1981.

is useful to understand the impact that required return and time to maturity have on bond value.

Required return. Whenever the required return on a bond differs from the bond's coupon interest rate, the bond's value will differ from its par, or face, value. The required return on the bond is likely to differ from the coupon rate for either of two reasons:

1. *Shifts in the supply-demand relationship for money.* As noted in Chapter 3, these shifts will cause the basic cost of money—the interest rate—to rise or fall, depending on whether there is a reduction in supply relative to demand or an increase in supply relative to demand, respectively. Shifts in the supply-demand relationship result from various economic factors. Increases in the basic cost of money will cause the required return to rise, and vice versa.
2. *Changes in risk.* As noted in Chapter 7, these will affect the required return such that if the risk of the firm's bonds as perceived by market participants increases, the required return on them will rise, and vice versa.

Regardless of the exact cause, the important point is that when the required return is greater than the coupon rate of interest, the bond value, B_0, will be less than its par value, M. In this case the bond is said to sell at a *discount*, which will equal $M - B_0$. On the other hand, when the required rate of return falls below the coupon rate of interest, the bond value will be greater than par. In this situation the bond is said to sell at a *premium*, which will equal $B_0 - M$. An example will illustrate.

EXAMPLE In the preceding example it was shown that when the required return equaled the coupon rate of interest, the bond's value equaled its $1000 par value. If for the same bond the required return were to rise to 12 percent, its value would be

$$B_0 = \$100(PVIFA_{12\%,10\,yrs}) + \$1000(PVIF_{12\%,10\,yrs})$$
$$= \$100(5.650) + \$1000(.322) = \underline{\$887.00}$$

The bond would therefore sell at a *discount* of $113.00 ($1000 par value —$887.00 value). If, on the other hand, the required return fell to, say, 8 percent, the bond's value would be

$$B_0 = \$100(PVIFA_{8\%,10\,yrs}) + \$1000(PVIF_{8\%,10\,yrs})$$
$$= \$100(6.710) + \$1000(.463) = \underline{\$1134.00}$$

The bond would therefore sell at a *premium* of $134.00 ($1134.00 value —$1000 par value). Summarizing these results in Table 8.2, we can see that when the required return is above the coupon interest rate, the bond sells at a discount; the discount is necessary in order to cause the bond's return to equal the required return. When the required return is below the coupon rate, the bond sells at a premium; the premium is necessary in order to cause the bond's return to equal the required return. Figure 8.2 depicts graphically the relationship between the coupon rate and the required return for the ABC Company bond.

Table 8.2 Bond Values for Various Required Returns (10 percent Coupon Interest Rate, 10-Year Maturity, $1000 Par, Interest Paid Annually)

Required return, k_d (%)	Bond value, B_0	Status
12	$ 887.00	Discount
10	1000.00	Par value
8	1134.00	Premium

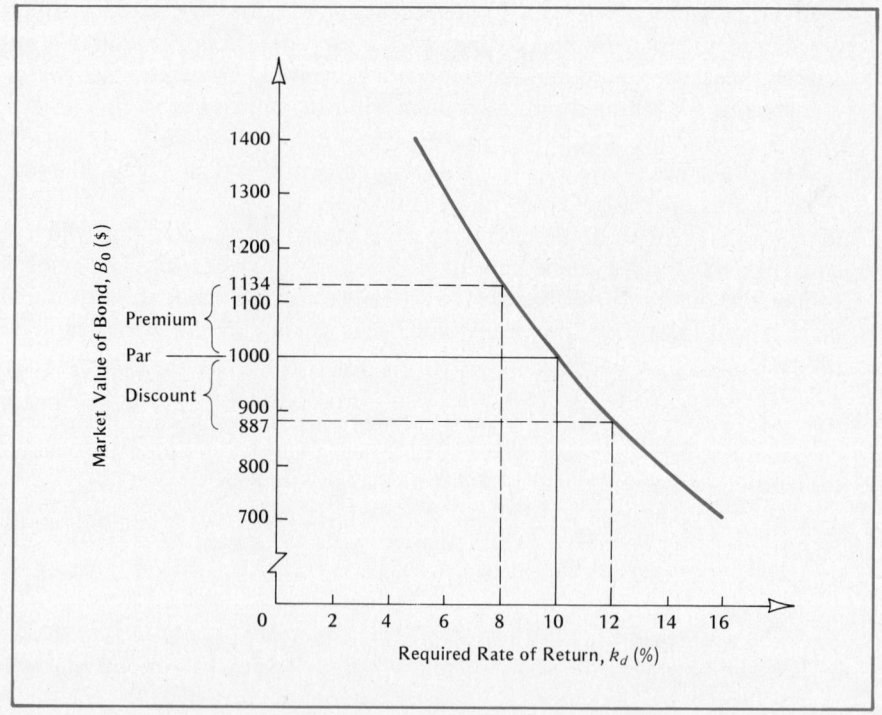

Figure 8.2 Bond value and required rate of return (ABC Company's 10 percent coupon, 10-year maturity, $1000 par, January 1, 1985 issue paying annual interest) ■

Time to maturity. Whenever the required return is different from the coupon rate, the amount of time to maturity affects bond value, even if the required return remains constant until maturity. Two important relationships exist among time to maturity, required return, and bond value. They are concerned with constant required returns and changing required returns.

1. Constant required returns. When the required return is different from the coupon rate and assumed *constant until maturity,* the value of the bond will approach its par value as the passage of time moves the bond's value closer to maturity. Of course, when the required return equals the coupon rate, the bond's value will remain at par until it matures.

EXAMPLE   Figure 8.3 depicts the behavior of the bond values calculated earlier and presented in Table 8.2 for ABC Company's 10 percent coupon bond paying annual interest and having ten years to maturity. Each of the three required returns—12 percent, 10 percent, and 8 percent—is assumed to remain constant over the ten years to the bond's maturity. It can be seen that the bond's value in each case approaches and ultimately equals the bond's $1000 par value at its maturity. At the 12 percent required return, the bond's discount declines with the passage of time as the bond's value increases from $887 to $1000. Since the 10 percent required return equals the bond's par value, value in this case remains unchanged at $1000 over its maturity. Finally, at the 8 percent required return, the bond's premium will decline as its value drops from $1134 to $1000 at maturity. With the required return assumed constant to maturity, the bond's value approaches its $1000 par or maturity value as the time to maturity declines. ■

2. Changing required returns. The shorter the amount of time until a bond's maturity, the less responsive is its market value to a given change in the required return. In other words, short maturities have less "interest rate risk" than do long maturities when all other features—coupon rate, par value, and interest payment frequency—are the same.

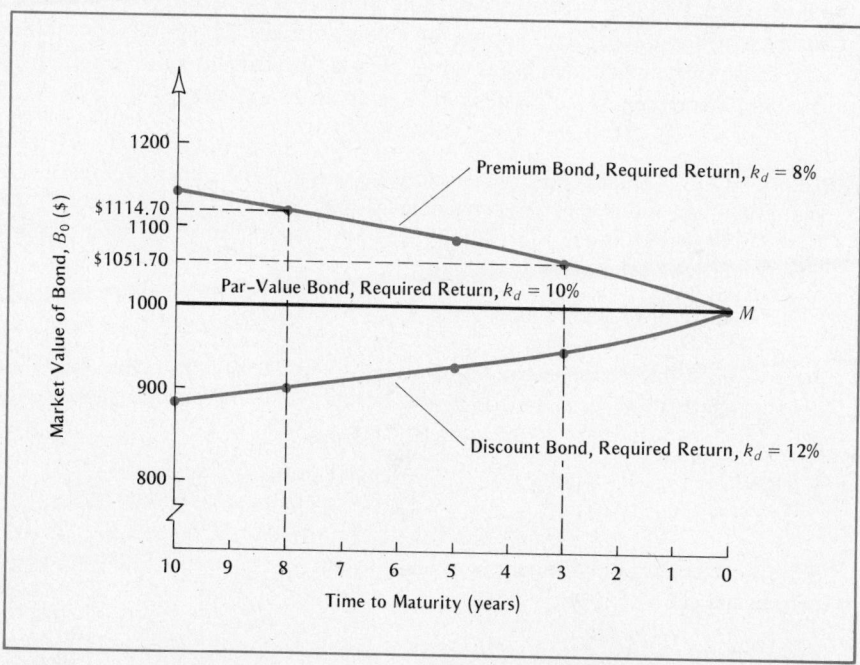

Figure 8.3   Relationship between time to maturity, required return, and bond value (ABC Company's 10 percent coupon, 10-year maturity, $1000 par issue paying annual interest)

EXAMPLE   The effect of changing required returns on bonds of differing maturity can be illustrated using ABC Company's bond and Figure 8.3. If, as noted by the dotted lines at eight years to maturity, the required return declines from 10 to 8 percent, the bond's value rises from $1000 to $1114.70 — an 11.47 percent increase. If the same change in required return had occurred with only three years to maturity, as noted by the dotted line, the bond's value would have risen to just $1051.70 — only a 5.17 percent increase. Similar types of responses can be seen in terms of the change in bond value associated with increases in required returns. The shorter the time to maturity, the smaller the impact on bond value caused by a given change in the required return. ■

YIELD TO MATURITY (YTM)

When investors evaluate and trade bonds they commonly consider *yield to maturity (YTM)*, which is the rate investors earn if they buy the bond at a specific price, B_0, and hold it until maturity. The yield to maturity on a bond with a current price equal to its par or maturity value (i.e., $B_0 = M$) will always equal the coupon rate. When the bond value differs from par, the yield to maturity will differ from the coupon rate. In such situations the yield to maturity can be calculated precisely or approximated by formula.

Calculation of YTM.   Assuming that interest is paid annually, the yield to maturity on a bond can be found by solving Equation 8.3 for k_d. In other words, the current value, B_0, the annual interest, I, the par value, M, and the years to maturity, n, are known, and the yield to maturity must be found. This is a difficult calculation to perform by hand. It involves finding the value of the bond at various rates until the rate causing the calculated bond value to equal the current value is found. This trial-and-error process is best described using an example.

EXAMPLE   The ABC Company bond, which currently sells for $1080, has a 10 percent coupon and $1000 par value, pays interest annually, and has ten years to maturity. Since $B_0 = \$1080$, $I = \$100$ $(.10 \times \$1000)$, $M = \$1000$, and $n = 10$ years, substituting into Equation 8.3a we get

$$\$1080 = \$100(PVIFA_{k_d,10\,yrs}) + \$1000(PVIF_{k_d,10\,yrs})$$

Since we know that a discount rate, k_d, of 10 percent would result in a value of $1000, the discount rate that would result in $1080 must be less than 10 percent. Trying 9 percent we get

$$\$100(PVIFA_{9\%,10\,yrs}) + \$1000(PVIF_{9\%,10\,yrs}) = \$100(6.418) + \$1000(.422)$$
$$= \$641.80 + \$422.00 = \$1063.80$$

Since the 9 percent rate is not quite low enough to bring the value up to $1080, we next try 8 percent and get

$$\$100(PVIFA_{8\%,10\,yrs}) + \$1000(PVIF_{8\%,10\,yrs}) = \$100(6.710) + \$1000(.463)$$
$$= \$671.00 + \$463.00 = \$1134.00$$

Since the resulting value of $1134 at the 8 percent rate is higher than $1080 and the $1063.80 value at the 9 percent rate is lower than $1080, the bond's yield to maturity must be between 8 and 9 percent. Since the $1063.80 is closest to $1080, to the nearest whole percent the YTM is 9 percent. Using interpolation, the more precise value of YTM is 8.77 percent.[6] For convenience, a YTM slightly below 9 percent is assumed. ■

A more practical alternative to the trial-and-error approach for finding the YTM is the approximate yield formula.

Approximate yield formula. The *approximate yield formula* is given in Equation 8.4.

$$\text{Approximate yield} = \frac{I + \dfrac{M - B_0}{n}}{\dfrac{M + B_0}{2}} \qquad (8.4)$$

Use of this formula can best be illustrated via an example.

EXAMPLE Substituting the ABC Company bond data from the preceding example into Equation 8.4 we get

$$\text{Approximate yield} = \frac{\$100 + \dfrac{\$1000 - \$1080}{10}}{\dfrac{\$1000 + \$1080}{2}}$$

$$= \frac{\$100 + (-\$8)}{\$1040} = \frac{\$92}{\$1040} = .0885 = \underline{\underline{8.85\%}}$$

The approximate YTM is therefore 8.85 percent, which does not differ greatly from the 8.77 percent YTM calculated earlier. ■

This approach is recommended because of the ease with which a reasonably accurate estimate of YTM can be made.

SEMIANNUAL INTEREST AND BOND VALUES

The procedure used to value bonds paying interest semiannually is quite similar to that illustrated in Chapter 6 for intrayear compounding — except that here we

---

[6] To interpolate in this case, the following steps are involved:

1. Find the difference between the bond values at 8 and 9 percent. The difference is $70.20 ($1134.00 − $1063.80).
2. Find the absolute difference between the desired value of $1080 and the value associated with the lower discount rate. The difference is $54 ($1134 − $1080).
3. Divide the value from step 2 by the value found in step 1 to get the percent of the distance across the discount rate range between 8 and 9 percent. The result is .77 ($54.00 ÷ $70.20).
4. Multiply the percent found in step 3 by the interval width of 1 percent (9 percent − 8 percent) over which interpolation is being performed. The result is .77 percent (.77 × 1 percent).
5. Add the value found in step 4 to the interest rate associated with the lower end of the interval. The result is 8.77 percent (8% + .77%). The yield to maturity is therefore 8.77 percent.

Of course, quicker and more accurate results can be obtained using a financially oriented calculator. Using such a calculator, the yield to maturity in this case is found to be 8.7662 percent.

need to find present instead of future value. It involves

1. Converting annual interest, I, to semiannual interest by dividing it by 2.
2. Converting the number of years to maturity, n, to the number of six-month periods to maturity by multiplying n by 2.
3. Converting the required return from an annual rate, k_d, to a semiannual rate by dividing it by 2.

Substituting the three changes noted above into Equation 8.3 yields

$$B_0 = \frac{I}{2} \left[\sum_{t=1}^{2n} \frac{1}{\left(1 + \frac{k_d}{2}\right)^t} \right] + M \left[\frac{1}{\left(1 + \frac{k_d}{2}\right)^{2n}} \right] \qquad (8.5)[7]$$

$$= \frac{I}{2} \left(PVIFA_{\frac{k_d}{2}, 2n} \right) + M \left(PVIF_{\frac{k_d}{2}, 2n} \right) \qquad (8.5a)$$

EXAMPLE   Assuming that the ABC Company bond pays interest semiannually and that the required return, k_d, is 12 percent, substituting into Equation 8.5a yields

$$B_0 = \frac{\$100}{2} \left(PVIFA_{\frac{12\%}{2}, 2 \times 10\, yrs} \right) + \$1000 \left(PVIF_{\frac{12\%}{2}, 2 \times 10\, yrs} \right)$$

$$= \$50(PVIFA_{6\%, 20\, periods}) + \$1000(PVIF_{6\%, 20\, periods})$$

$$= \$50(11.470) + \$1000(.312) = \underline{\$885.50}$$

Comparing this result to that found using annual compounding, shown in Table 8.2, it can be seen that the value is less when semiannual interest is used. This will always occur when the bond sells at a discount; for bonds selling at a premium, the opposite will occur (value with semiannual interest is greater than with annual interest). ■

PERPETUAL BONDS AND PREFERRED STOCK VALUATION

A *perpetual bond* is one that pays a stated amount of interest periodically (annually or semiannually) over an infinite time horizon; in other words, its par value, M, is never repaid. *Preferred stock,* while a form of equity, is like a perpetual bond in that it never matures.[8] It pays a fixed dividend amount stated on an annual basis and commonly paid in equal quarterly installments. Because it is a fixed-income security with preference over common stock in terms of both receipt of income and liquidation, *it is grouped with debt rather than equity for purposes of comparison.*

Since neither a perpetual bond nor a preferred stock ever matures, both can be viewed as perpetuities. Assuming for simplicity that each makes an *annual* pay-

---

[7] Although it may appear inappropriate to use the semiannual discounting procedure on the maturity value, M, this technique is necessary to find the correct bond value. One way to confirm the accuracy of this approach is to calculate the bond value in the case that the required return and coupon rate of interest are equal; for B_0 to equal M, as would be expected in such a case, the maturity value must be discounted on a semiannual basis.

[8] Technically, a firm may be able to retire preferred stock in a number of ways; a discussion of these and other features of preferred stocks is given in Chapters 20 and 22.

ment of interest or dividends, I, and that the required return is k_d, the value of either of these vehicles can be given by Equation 8.6.

$$B_0 = I\left(\frac{1}{k_d}\right) = \frac{I}{k_d}$$ (8.6)

Recall from Chapter 6 that in the case of a perpetuity, the present-value interest factor, $PVIFA_{k_d,\infty} = 1/k_d$, must be used. The application of this factor to find the value of the perpetuity can be noted in the first term to the right in Equation 8.6. An example will show how this is done.

EXAMPLE   The ABC Company has an issue of preferred stock outstanding that has a stated annual dividend of $5. The required return on the preferred stock has been estimated to be 13 percent. Substituting $I = \$5$ and $k_d = 13\%$ into Equation 8.6 yields a preferred stock value of $38.46 ($5 ÷ .13). In this example the preferred stock could just as readily have been a perpetual bond paying annual interest of $5 and having a required return of 13 percent. Equation 8.6 can be used to find the value of any perpetuity. ■

 ## Common Stock Valuation

Because common stockholders are the last to receive any return from their owner-ship interest, they are the true or residual owners of the firm. In exchange for purchasing common stock, these owners expect to be rewarded through the receipt of periodic cash dividends and an increasing — or at least nondeclining — share value. Prospective owners and security analysts are involved in the valuation process as well. They, like current owners, attempt to assess the firm's value. They choose to purchase the stock when they believe it to be *undervalued* (i.e., that its true value is greater than its market price) and to sell when they feel it is *overvalued* (i.e., that its market price is greater than its true value).[9]

POPULAR APPROACHES

Many popular approaches for measuring value exist, but only one is widely ac-cepted. The popular approaches to valuation include the use of book value, liquidation value, or some type of a price/earnings multiple.

Book value. *Book value per share* is simply the value of the firm's ownership per share in the event that all assets are liquidated for their exact book (accounting) value and that the proceeds remaining after paying all liabilities (including preferred stock) are divided among the common stockholders. This method lacks sophistication and can be criticized on the basis of its reliance on historical balance sheet data; it ignores the firm's expected earnings potential. Let us look at an example.

[9] A growing body of financial data tends to suggest that *widely held stocks that are actively traded* are always properly valued in the marketplace. In other words, the market price is always equal to the true share value. Such a conclusion tends to raise doubt about the recommendations of securities analysts. Because there remains much disagreement on the issue, further attention will not be given to it.

EXAMPLE   The Swanson Company currently (December 31, 1984) has total assets of $6 million, total liabilities including preferred stock of $4.5 million, and 100,000 shares of common stock outstanding. Its book value per share would therefore be

$$\frac{\$6,000,000 - \$4,500,000}{100,000 \text{ shares}} = \underline{\$15 \text{ per share}}$$

Since this value assumes that assets are liquidated for their book value, it may not represent the minimum share value. As a matter of fact, although most stocks sell above book value, it is not unusual to find stocks selling below book value. ■

Liquidation value. *Liquidation value per share* is the *actual* amount each common stockholder would expect to receive if the firm's assets are sold, creditors and preferred stockholders are paid, and any remaining money is divided among the common stockholders.[10] This measure is more realistic than book value, but it still fails to consider the earning power of the firm's assets. An example will illustrate.

EXAMPLE   The Swanson Company found upon investigation that it would obtain only $5.25 million if it liquidated its assets today. The firm's liquidation value per share would therefore be

$$\frac{\$5,250,000 - \$4,500,000}{100,000 \text{ shares}} = \underline{\$7.50 \text{ per share}}$$

Ignoring any expenses of liquidation, this would be the firm's minimum value. ■

Price/earning multiples. The average price/earnings (P/E) ratio in an industry can be used as a guide to a firm's value if it is assumed that investors value the earnings of a given firm in the same way (discount them at the required return) as they do the earnings of the average firm in the industry. The *price/earnings multiple approach to value* is a popular valuation technique whereby the expected per-share earnings of the firm are multiplied by the average P/E ratio for the industry, which gives an estimate of the value of the firm's shares. The average P/E for an industry can be obtained from a source such as *Standard & Poor's Industrial Ratios.*

This measure of value, like the preceding ones, lacks any deep theoretical roots. It is best looked on as a tool for forecasting a firm's future share price. The accuracy of the forecast depends on how "average" the company is. This technique is especially useful for valuing firms that are not publicly traded; the use of market price may be preferable in the case of a publicly traded firm. But in any case the price/earnings multiple approach is believed to be superior to the use of book or liquidation values, since it implicitly considers *expected* earnings. Before we discuss the most widely accepted approach, let us consider an example of price/earnings multiples.

EXAMPLE   The Swanson Company is expected to earn $2.60 per share next year (1985). This expectation is based on an analysis of the firm's historical earnings trend and certain

---

[10] In the event of liquidation, creditors' claims must be satisfied first, then those of the preferred stockholders. Anything left goes to common stockholders. A more detailed discussion of liquidation procedures is presented in Chapter 24.

industry factors expected to be operating in the coming year. The average price/earnings ratio for firms in the same industry is 7. Multiplying Swanson's expected earnings per share of $2.60 by this ratio gives us a value for the firm's shares of $18.20, assuming that investors will continue to measure the value of the firm at 7 times its earnings. The actual rate at which an investor is assumed to discount earnings is found by taking the inverse of the price/earnings ratio (i.e., 1/7 or .143). Dividing this into the firm's expected earnings of $2.60 would give us, once again, $18.20 for the value of the firm's shares.[11] It is easier to use the P/E ratio directly. ∎

BASIC COMMON STOCK VALUATION

Like bonds, the value of a share of stock is equal to the present value of all future benefits it is expected to provide. These benefits are viewed as a stream of dividends to be received over an infinite time horizon. This horizon is considered appropriate because the firm is viewed as a "going concern."[12] Simply stated, *the value of a share of stock is equal to the present value of all future dividends it is expected to provide over an infinite time horizon.* Although by selling stock at a price above that originally paid, a stockholder can earn capital gains in addition to dividends, from a strictly theoretical point of view what is really sold is the right to all future dividends. Therefore, from a valuation viewpoint, only dividends are relevant. Redefining terms, the basic valuation model given in Equation 8.1 can be specified for common stock as given in Equation 8.7.

$$P_0 = \frac{D_1}{(1 + k_s)^1} + \frac{D_2}{(1 + k_s)^2} + \cdots + \frac{D_\infty}{(1 + k_s)^\infty} \qquad (8.7)$$

where

$$P_0 = \text{the current value of common stock}$$
$$D_t(t = 1, \infty) = \text{the per-share dividend expected at the end of year } t$$
$$k_s = \text{the rate of return required on common stock}$$

The equation can be simplified somewhat by redefining each year's dividend, D_t, in terms of anticipated growth. Three cases are considered here — zero growth, constant growth, and variable growth.

Zero growth. The simplest approach to dividend valuation is one that assumes a constant, nongrowing dividend stream. In terms of the notation already introduced,

$$D_1 = D_2 = \cdots = D_\infty$$

---

[11] The price/earnings multiple approach to valuation, when viewed in this manner, does have a theoretical explanation. If we view 1 divided by the price/earnings ratio, or the earnings/price ratio, as the rate at which investors discount the firm's earnings, and if we assume that the projected earnings per share will be earned indefinitely, the price/earnings multiple approach can be looked on as a method of finding the present value of a perpetuity of projected earnings per share at a rate equal to the earnings/price ratio.

[12] The need to consider an infinite time horizon is not critical, since a sufficiently long period, say, 50 years, will result in about the same present value as an infinite period for moderate-sized required returns. For example, at 15 percent, a dollar to be received 50 years from now, $PVIF_{15\%, 50\,\text{yrs}}$, is worth only about $.001 today.

GREENWICH PHARMACEUTICALS: EXPECTATIONS CREATE VALUE

How do you run a business that has nothing to sell but spends an average of $650,000 a year? With a lot of anxiety and even more attention to raising capital.

Greenwich Pharmaceuticals Inc. has no sales and has had a number of crises in a hand-to-mouth existence. Yet, in the 14 years since it was formed, the company has obtained $6.5 million from investors willing to gamble that its patented compound, Therafectin, will become a commercially successful drug.

"People buy stock in the company in the hope that they have found the next new company that has found something of scientific value," says H. Lee Browne, the 36-year-old president of the Greenwich, Conn., concern and a major shareholder.

Managing a company in its development stage is much different from running one that has goods or services to sell. The pursuit of funds is constant. "I'm always knocking on doors," says Mr. Browne who, for the 10 years he has been with Greenwich Pharmaceuticals, has been explaining to the scientific and investment communities Therafectin's ability to regulate the body's immune system.

Mr. Browne, son of a former shipping industry executive and himself a successful real estate investor, believes the company has survived because of Therafectin's tantalizing possibilities.

Therafectin was developed by Paul Gordon, a pharmacologist and adjunct professor at Loyola University of Chicago's medical school. Mr. Gordon assigned his Therafectin patents to the corporation in 1969 for 3.7 million shares of stock. A group of private investors bought 73,000 shares at $33\frac{1}{3}$ cents a share.

This modest sum was to finance sufficient testing to demonstrate the drug's potential and attract additional investors to pay for further development. The first laboratory tests with biological materials were encouraging, but they weren't proof that the drug would work in humans. And before human testing could be done, tests in animals had to be performed.

Raising money was harder than the original investors had imagined. Ten years ago, the medical community had only a beginning interest in immune-system modulators, and the public was only slightly aware of immune-system research. Recently, publicity about Acquired Immune Deficiency Syndrome, or AIDS, has sparked intense interest in finding ways to control the immune system. So, in the last year both the medical and investment communities have looked more closely at Therafectin, Mr. Browne says. . . .

SOURCE: Sanford L. Jacobs, "Drug Concern with No Sales Survives on Investors' Hopes," *The Wall Street Journal*, January 30, 1984, p. 25.

Letting D_1 represent the amount of the annual dividend, Equation 8.7 under zero growth would reduce to

$$P_0 = D_1 \sum_{t=1}^{\infty} \frac{1}{(1 + k_s)^t} = D_1 \times (PVIFA_{k_s, \infty}) = \frac{D_1}{k_s} \qquad (8.8)$$

The equation shows that with zero growth, the value of a share of stock would equal the present value of a perpetuity of D_1 dollars discounted at a rate k_s. It should be clear that the form of this equation is identical to that of Equation 8.6, which is used to value perpetual bonds and preferred stock. Let us look at an example.

EXAMPLE The Vincent Company's dividend is expected to remain constant at $3 per share indefinitely. If the required return on its stock is 15 percent, the stock's value is $20 ($3 ÷ .15). ■

Constant growth. Probably the most widely cited dividend valuation model is one that assumes that dividends will grow at a constant rate, g, that is less than the required return, $k_s (g < k_s)$.[13] Letting D_0 represent the most recent dividend, Equation 8.7 can be rewritten as follows:

$$P_0 = \frac{D_0(1+g)^1}{(1+k_s)^1} + \frac{D_0(1+g)^2}{(1+k_s)^2} + \cdots + \frac{D_0(1+g)^\infty}{(1+k_s)^\infty} \tag{8.9}$$

If we simplify Equation 8.9, it can be rewritten as follows:[14]

$$P_0 = \frac{D_1}{k_s - g} \tag{8.10}$$

Although other dividend valuation models are available, the constant growth

---

[13] One of the assumptions of the constant growth model as presented is that earnings and dividends grow at the same rate. This assumption is true only in cases where a firm pays out a fixed percentage of its earnings each year (has a fixed payout ratio). In the case of a declining industry, a negative growth rate $(g < 0)$ might exist. In such a case the constant growth model, as well as the variable growth model presented in the next section, remains fully applicable to the valuation process.

[14] For the interested reader, the calculations necessary to derive Equation 8.10 from Equation 8.9 follow. The first step is to multiply each side of Equation 8.9 by $(1 + k_s)/(1 + g)$ and subtract Equation 8.9 from the resulting expression. This yields

$$\frac{P_0(1+k_s)}{1+g} - P_0 = D_0 - \frac{D_0(1+g)^\infty}{(1+k_s)^\infty} \tag{1}$$

Since k_s is assumed to be greater than g, the second term on the right side of Equation 1 should be zero. Thus,

$$P_0 \left(\frac{1+k_s}{1+g} - 1 \right) = D_0 \tag{2}$$

Equation 2 is simplified as follows:

$$P_0 \left(\frac{(1+k_s) - (1+g)}{1+g} \right) = D_0 \tag{3}$$

$$P_0(k_s - g) = D_0(1+g) \tag{4}$$

$$P_0 = \frac{D_1}{k_s - g} \tag{5}$$

Equation 5 equals Equation 8.10 above.

model in Equation 8.10 is the most commonly cited. It is sometimes called the *Gordon model.* An example will show how it works.

EXAMPLE   The Swanson Company has maintained a fixed dividend payout ratio from 1979 through 1984. The amount of these dividends is shown below.

Year	Dividend ($)
1984	1.40
1983	1.29
1982	1.20
1981	1.12
1980	1.05
1979	1.00

Using the table for the present-value interest factor, *PVIF* (Appendix Table A-3), in conjunction with the technique described for finding growth rates in Chapter 6, the annual growth rate of dividends, which is assumed to equal the expected constant rate of dividend growth, g, is found to equal 7 percent.[15] The company estimates that its dividend in 1985, D_1, will equal $1.50. The required return, k_s, was assumed to be 15 percent. Substituting these values into Equation 8.10, the value of the stock is

$$P_0 = \frac{\$1.50}{.15 - .07} = \frac{\$1.50}{.08} = \underline{\underline{\$18.75}}$$

Assuming that the assumptions of the model apply to this company and that the values of D_1, k_s, and g are accurately estimated, the Swanson Company's stock value is $18.75. ■

Variable growth. The zero and constant growth common stock models presented in Equations 8.8 and 8.10, respectively, do not allow for any shift in expected growth rates. Because future growth rates might shift up or down due to changing expectations, it is useful to consider *variable growth models* that allow for a change in the growth rate.[16] To determine the value of a share of stock given that a single shift in the growth rate occurs at the end of year N, the following four steps should be

[15] The technique involves solving the following equation for g:

$$D_{1984} = D_{1979}(1 + g)^5$$

$$\frac{D_{1979}}{D_{1984}} = \frac{1}{(1 + g)^5} = PVIF_{g,5}$$

Two basic steps can be followed. First, dividing the earliest dividend ($D_{1979} = \$1.00$) by the most recent dividend ($D_{1984} = \$1.40$), a factor for the present value of one dollar, *PVIF*, of .714 ($1.00 ÷ $1.40) results. Although six dividends are shown, they reflect only five years of growth. Looking across the table at the present-value interest factors, *PVIF*, for five years, the factor closest to .714 occurs at 7 percent (.713). Therefore, the growth rate of the dividends, rounded to the nearest whole percentage, is 7 percent.

[16] While more than one change in the growth rate can be incorporated in the model, to simplify the discussion only a single growth rate change is considered here. The number of variable growth valuation models is technically unlimited, but concern over all likely shifts in growth is unlikely to yield much more accuracy than a simpler model.

followed:

1. Find the value of the cash dividends at the end of *each year* during the initial growth period. This step may require adjusting the most recent dividend, D_0, using the growth rate expected during the initial period in order to calculate the dividend amount for each year.
2. Find the present value of the dividends expected during the initial growth period. Using the notation presented earlier, this value can be given as

$$\sum_{t=1}^{N} \frac{D_t}{(1 + k_s)^t}$$

3. Find the value of the stock at the end of the initial growth period, $P_N = \frac{D_{N+1}}{k_s - g}$, which is the present value of all dividends expected from year $N + 1$ to infinity—assuming a constant growth of dividends. It can be seen that this value is found by applying the constant growth model (presented as Equation 8.10 in the preceding section) to the dividends expected from year $N + 1$ to infinity. The present value of P_N would represent the value today of all dividends expected to be received from year $N + 1$ to infinity. This value can be represented by

$$\frac{1}{(1 + k_s)^N} \times \frac{D_{N+1}}{k_s - g} = PVIF_{k_s,N} \times P_N$$

4. Add the present-value components found in steps 2 and 3 to find the value of the stock, P_0, given in Equation 8.11.

$$P_0 = \underbrace{\sum_{t=1}^{N} \frac{D_t}{(1 + k_s)^t}}_{\substack{\text{Present value} \\ \text{of dividends} \\ \text{during initial} \\ \text{growth period}}} + \underbrace{\left(\frac{1}{(1 + k_s)^N} \times \frac{D_{N+1}}{k_s - g} \right)}_{\substack{\text{Present value of} \\ \text{price of stock at} \\ \text{end of initial} \\ \text{growth period}}} \qquad (8.11)$$

The application of these steps to a variable growth situation with only one growth rate change is illustrated in the following example.

EXAMPLE Clarn Industries' most recent (1984) annual dividend payment was $1.50 per share. The firm's financial manager expects that these dividends will increase at a 10 percent annual rate over the next three years (1985, 1986, and 1987) due to the introduction of a hot new product. At the end of the three years (end of 1987) the firm's mature product line is expected to result in a slowing of the dividend growth rate, g, to 5 percent per year forever. The firm's required return, k_s, is 15 percent. To estimate the current (end-of-1984) value of Clarn's common stock, $P_0 = P_{1984}$, the four-step procedure presented above must be applied to these data.

Table 8.3   Calculation of Present Value of Clarn Industries' Dividends (1985–1987)

t	End of year	$D_0 = D_{1984}$ (1)	$FVIF_{10\%,t}$ (2)	D_t [(1) × (2)] (3)	$PVIF_{15\%,t}$ (4)	Present value of dividends [(3) × (4)] (5)
1	1985	$1.50	1.100	$1.65	.870	$1.44
2	1986	1.50	1.210	1.82	.756	1.38
3	1987	1.50	1.331	2.00	.658	1.32

$$\text{Sum of present value of dividends} = \sum_{t=1}^{3} \frac{D_t}{(1+k_s)^t} = \underline{\underline{\$4.14}}$$

1. The value of the cash dividends in each of the next three years is calculated in columns 1, 2, and 3 of Table 8.3. The 1985, 1986, and 1987 dividends are $1.65, $1.82, and $2.00, respectively.
2. The present value of the three dividends expected during the 1985-to-1987 initial growth period is calculated in columns 3, 4, and 5 of Table 8.3. The sum of the present values of the three dividends is $4.14—the total of the column 5 values.
3. The value of the stock at the end of the initial growth period ($N = 1987$) can be found by first calculating $D_{N+1} = D_{1988}$:

$$D_{1988} = D_{1987}(1 + .05) = \$2.00(1.05) = \$2.10$$

Using $D_{1988} = \$2.10$, $k_s = .15$, and $g = .05$, the value of the stock at the end of 1987 can be calculated:

$$P_{1987} = \frac{D_{1988}}{k_s - g} = \frac{\$2.10}{.15 - .05} = \frac{\$2.10}{.10} = \$21.00$$

Finally, in this step, the share value of $21 at the end of 1987 must be converted into

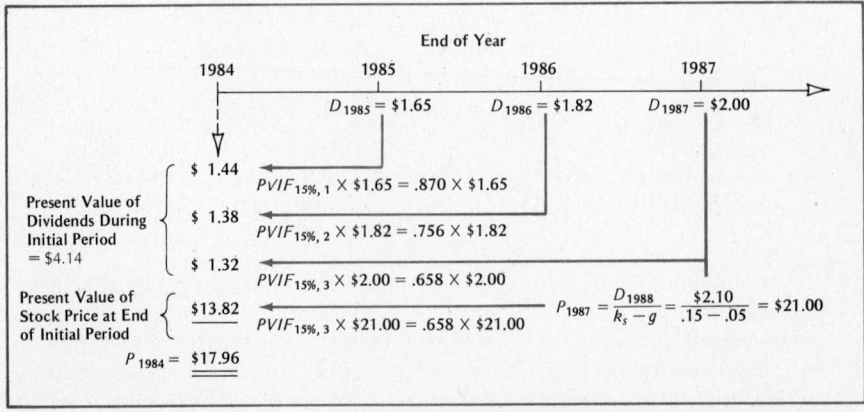

Figure 8.4   Finding Clarn Industries' current (end-of-1984) value with variable growth

a present (end-of-1984) value. Using the 15 percent required return we get

$$PVIF_{k_s,N} \times P_N = PVIF_{15\%,3} \times P_{1987} = .658 \times \$21.00 = \$13.82$$

4. Adding the present value of the initial dividend stream found in step 2 to the present value of the stock at the end of the initial growth period as specified in Equation 8.11, we get the current (end-of-1984) value of Clarn Industries' stock.

$$P_{1984} = \$4.14 + \$13.82 = \$17.96$$

The stock is currently worth \$17.96 per share; the calculation of this value is summarized diagramatically in Figure 8.4. ■

Decision Making and Common Stock Value

Valuation equations measure the stock value at a point in time based on expected return (D_1, g) and risk (k_s) data. The decisions of the financial manager, through their effect on these variables, can cause the value of the firm, P_0, to change. Figure 8.5 depicts the relationship among financial decisions, return, risk, and share value.

CHANGES IN EXPECTED RETURN

Assuming that economic conditions remain stable, any management action that would cause existing and prospective stockholders to raise their dividend expectations should increase the firm's value as long as the required return does not increase. In Equation 8.10[17] we can see that P_0 will increase for any increase in D_1 or g. Any action the financial manager can take that will increase the level of expected returns without changing the required return (risk) should be undertaken, since it will positively affect owners' wealth. An example will illustrate.

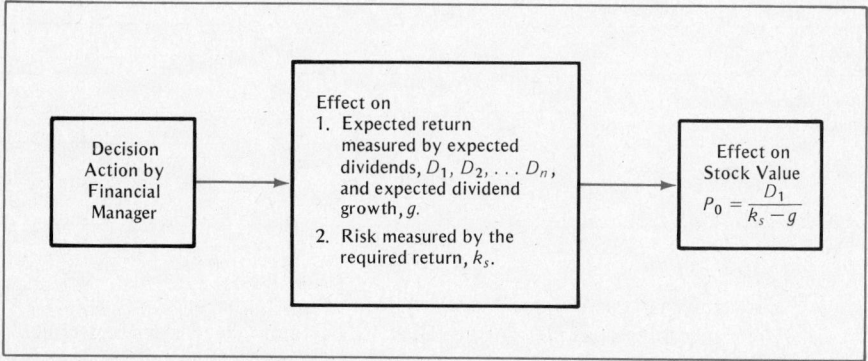

Figure 8.5   Financial decisions, return, risk, and share value

[17] To convey the interrelationship among financial decisions, return, risk, and share value, the constant growth dividend valuation model is used. Other models — zero growth or variable growth — could be used, but the simplicity of exposition using the constant growth model justifies its use here.

EVEN CHEAP STOCKS HAVE VALUE

There are more than 5,500 publicly traded shares, and over 1,200 of them now sell for $5 or less. The efficient market works well here, and the majority of these low-priced stocks deserve to be low-priced. Only about half of the group show earnings for the most recent fiscal year, and fewer than 200 earned any money at all during the most recent 12 months.

Is there gold to be found among all these tailings? To do some exploration, we asked our computer if any of these 200 companies that trade below $5 are sound enough to qualify as loaded laggards. These, to our way of thinking, are stocks with a potential value that may exceed current price.

Here are the criteria. We specified a debt-to-equity ratio of no more than 1.0. That eliminated companies with lots of borrowing on their balance sheets. Then, we culled further to find only those companies whose average annual four-year per-share earnings growth is positive. That eliminated moneylosers and declining businesses. Finally, to avoid paying premium prices, we specified that shares sell for no more than twice book value.

. . . the result [was] . . . 25 companies [—many of which] trade[d] well below book value. Some also [carried] unusually modest price/earnings ratios. This is a remarkable fact, given our tests for strong earnings growth and solid financial ratios. [The results for five of them are given below.]

These, of course, are low-priced stocks. But they carry value, too. Not, for all that, a crapshoot.

Stocks That Look Cheap, But May Hold Real Value

Company/business	Recent price	Latest 12 month EPS	Latest 12 month P/E	Current ratio	4-year earnings growth	Sales (millions)	Return on equity	Debt/ equity
Alaska Bancorporation/banking	$4\frac{1}{4}$	$1.16	3.7	1.05	29%	$15.6	18.3%	45%
Barco of California/apparel	$3\frac{3}{8}$	0.28	12.9	3.79	4	24.3	6.3	1
C&R Clothiers/retail	$1\frac{1}{2}$	0.12	12.5	1.63	86	36.4	3.1	24
Consumers Financial/insurance	$2\frac{1}{4}$	0.16	14.1	0.53	30	15.5	6.2	37
Dahlberg Electronics/health care products	$4\frac{7}{8}$	0.39	12.5	2.93	37	17.7	28.5	15

SOURCE: "Bargains Below $5," *Forbes*, May 21, 1984, p. 246.

EXAMPLE Imagine that the Swanson Company, which was found to have a share value of $18.75 in an earlier example, on the following day announced a major technological breakthrough that would revolutionize its industry. Current and prospective shareholders are not expected to adjust their required return of 15 percent, but they do expect that future dividends will be increased. Specifically, they feel that although the dividend next year, D_1, will remain at $1.50, the expected rate of growth will increase to 9 percent. Substituting $D_1 = \$1.50$, $k_s = .15$, and $g = .09$ into Equation 8.10, the resulting value is found to equal

$25 [i.e., $1.50 ÷ (.15 − .09)]. The increased value therefore resulted from the higher expected future dividends reflected in the increase in the growth rate, g. ∎

CHANGES IN RISK

Although k_s is defined as the required return, it is, as pointed out in Chapter 7, directly related to the nondiversifiable risk, which can be measured by beta. The capital asset pricing model (CAPM) given in Equation 7.6 is restated as Equation 8.12.

$$k_s = R_F + b \times (k_m - R_F) \qquad (8.12)$$

With the risk-free rate, R_F, and the required return on the market, k_m, held constant, the required return, k_s, depends directly on beta. In other words, any action of the financial manager that increases risk will increase required return. In Equation 8.10 it can be seen that with all else constant, an increase in the required return, k_s, will reduce share value, P_0, and vice versa. Any action of the financial manager that increases risk *contributes toward* a reduction in value, and vice versa. An example will illustrate.

EXAMPLE   Assume that the Swanson Company's 15 percent required return resulted from a risk-free rate, R_F, of 9 percent, a market return, k_m, of 13 percent, and a beta, b, of 1.50. Substituting into the capital asset pricing model, Equation 8.12, the 15 percent required return, k_s, results

$$k_s = 9\% + 1.50 \times (13\% - 9\%) = \underline{15\%}$$

Using this return, the value of the firm, P_0, was calculated to be $18.75 in the earlier example.

  Now imagine that the financial manager makes a decision that, without changing expected dividends, increases the firm's beta to 1.75. Assuming that R_F and k_m remain at 9 and 13 percent, respectively, the required return will increase to 16 percent [i.e., 9% + 1.75 × (13% − 9%)] to compensate stockholders for the increased risk. Substituting $D_1 = \$1.50$, $k_s = .16$, and $g = .07$ into the valuation equation, Equation 8.10, results in a share value of $16.67 [i.e., $1.50 ÷ (.16 − .07)]. As expected, the owners, by raising the required return (without any corresponding increase in expected return), cause the firm's share value to decline. Clearly the financial manager's action was not in the owners' best interest. ∎

COMBINED EFFECT

A financial decision rarely affects return and risk independently; most decisions affect both factors. In accordance with the risk-return trade-off, with increased return generally comes increased risk, and vice versa. Or, in terms of the measures presented, with an increase in beta one would expect an increase in D_1 or g, or both, assuming that k_m and R_F remain unchanged. Depending on the relative magnitude of the changes in these variables, the net effect on value can be assessed. Table 8.4 summarizes the effect on price expected from a change in each

Table 8.4 Effect of Increases in Key Valuation Variables on Price, P_0 (Assuming All Other Variables Remain Unchanged)

Increase in variable	Change in price, P_0 [increase (I) or decrease (D)]
R_F	D for $b < 1$; I for $b > 1$
k_m	D
b	D
k_s	D
D_1	I
g	I

Note: Decreases in each of the variables shown would have the opposite effect from that shown on P_0.

of the key variables discussed in this chapter. (The effect reported for each variable is based on the assumption that all other variables remain unchanged.) Note that general shifts in economic and market conditions, which have been ignored here, would in fact be introduced into the process through the risk-free rate, R_F, the market return, k_m, or both. An example shows why.

EXAMPLE If we assume that the two changes illustrated for the Swanson Company in the preceding examples occur simultaneously as a result of an action of the financial decision maker, key variable values would be $D_1 = \$1.50$, $k_s = .16$, and $g = .09$. Substituting into the valuation model, a price of $21.43 [i.e., $1.50 \div (.16 - .09)$] is obtained. The net result of the decision, which increased return (g from 7 to 9 percent) as well as risk (b from 1.50 to 1.75 and therefore k_s from 15 to 16 percent), is positive, since the share price increased from $18.75 to $21.43. Assuming that the key variables are accurately measured, the decision appears to be in the best interest of the firm's owners, since it increases their wealth. ■

The point to recognize from the foregoing examples is that risk and return are important dimensions of value. Most financial decisions affect both variables, and it is their combined effect on value that must be assessed by the financial manager.

CHAPTER SUMMARY

● The valuation process involves determining the worth of income- and cash-flow-generating assets.

● Key inputs to the valuation process include cash flows (returns), timing, and the discount rate (risk). The value of any asset is equal to the present value of all future cash flows it is expected to provide over the relevant time period.

● The value of a bond, which is a certificate evidencing that the corporation has borrowed a certain amount of money, is the present value of the periodic interest payments (annual or, more commonly, semiannual) plus the present value of the par, or maturity, value.

● The discount rate used to determine bond value is a required return that may differ from the coupon interest rate. The required return is affected by the supply-demand relationship for money and risk. If the required return is greater than the coupon rate, the bond will sell at a discount; if the required return is less than the coupon rate, the bond will sell at a premium.

● The amount of time to maturity affects bond values even if required return remains constant. When required return is constant, the value of a bond will approach its par value as the passage of time moves the bond closer to maturity. The shorter the amount of time until a bond's maturity, the *less* responsive its market value to a given change in the required return.

● When investors evaluate and trade bonds, they commonly consider yield to maturity (YTM), which can be calculated precisely or approximated by formula.

● The value of perpetual bonds and preferred stock is determined by applying the appropriate present-value interest factor for a perpetuity to the cash flow (interest or dividends, respectively).

● Popular approaches such as book value, liquidation value, and price-earnings multiples are often used to estimate stock value, but the best approach defines the share value as the present value of all future dividends expected to be received over an infinite time horizon.

● Three cases of dividend growth can be considered—zero growth, constant growth, and variable growth. The most widely cited model is the constant growth model.

● Because most financial decisions affect both return and risk, an assessment of their combined effect on value must be part of the financial decision-making process.

KEY TERMS

approximate yield formula	new issue
bond	outstanding (seasoned) bonds
book value per share	par value
constant growth model	perpetual bond
coupon rate	preferred stock
discount (bond)	premium (bond)
face value	price/earnings multiple approach to value
financial asset	real asset
Gordon model	semiannual interest
growth rate (dividends)	valuation
liquidation value per share	valuation process
market price	variable growth model
maturity	yield to maturity (YTM)
maturity date	zero growth model

QUESTIONS

8-1 Define *valuation* and explain why it is important for the financial manager to understand the valuation process.

8-2 Briefly describe the three key inputs—cash flows, timing, and the discount rate—to the valuation process. Does the valuation process apply to both financial and real assets?

8-3 Define and specify the general equation for the value of any asset, V_0, in terms of its expected cash flow, CF_t, in each year t, and the appropriate discount rate, k.

8-4 Define each of the following terms as they relate to corporate bonds.

a par, or face, value	**e** outstanding (seasoned) issue
b semiannual interest	**f** maturity date
c maturity	**g** market price
d new issue	

8-5 In terms of the coupon rate and the required return, what relationship between them will cause a bond to sell (a) at a discount? (b) at a premium? (c) at its par value? Explain.

8-6   If the required return on a bond differs from its coupon rate and is assumed constant until maturity, describe the behavior of the bond value as the passage of time moves the bond toward its maturity.

8-7   If you were a risk-averse investor, to protect against the potential impact of rising interest rates on bond value, would you prefer bonds with short or long periods until maturity? Explain why.

8-8   What is meant by the *yield to maturity (YTM)* on a bond? Briefly describe both the precise and the approximate approach for calculating YTM.

8-9   Describe the procedure used to estimate the value of perpetual bonds or preferred stock.

8-10   Explain each of the three popular approaches—(a) book value, (b) liquidation value, and (c) price/earnings multiples—for estimating common stock value. Which of these has the strongest theoretical roots?

8-11   Describe, compare, and contrast each of the following common stock valuation models.
   a   zero growth
   b   constant growth
   c   variable growth

8-12   Explain the linkages among financial decisions, return, risk, and share value. How do the capital asset pricing model (CAPM) and the Gordon model fit into this basic framework? Explain.

8-13   Assuming that all other variables remain unchanged, what impact would *each* of the following have on share price? Explain your answer.
   a   The risk-free rate of interest declines for a stock with a beta greater than 1.
   b   The stock's beta increases.
   c   The dividend expected next year decreases.
   d   The rate of growth in dividends is expected to increase.

PROBLEMS

8-1   (**Valuation Fundamentals**)   Imagine that you are trying to evaluate the economics of purchasing an automobile. Assume that you expect the car to provide annual after-tax cash benefits of $1200 and that you can sell the car for after-tax proceeds of $5000 at the end of the planned five-year ownership period. All funds for purchasing the car will be drawn from your savings, which are currently earning 9 percent after taxes.
   a   Is the car a financial or a real asset?
   b   Identify the cash flows, their timing, and the discount rate applicable to valuing the car.
   c   What is the maximum price you would be willing to pay to acquire the car? Explain why.

8-2   (**Valuation of Assets**)   Using the information provided, find the value of each of the following assets.

Asset	Cash flow End of year	Cash flow Amount ($)	Applicable discount rate (%)
A	1	5,000	18
	2	5,000	
	3	5,000	

(continued)

(*Continued*)

	Cash flow		
Asset	End of year	Amount ($)	Applicable discount rate (%)
B	1 through ∞	300	15
C	1	0	16
	2	0	
	3	0	
	4	0	
	5	35,000	
D	1 through 5	1,500	12
	6	8,500	
E	1	2,000	14
	2	3,000	
	3	5,000	
	4	7,000	
	5	4,000	
	6	1,000	

8-3 **(Asset Valuation and Risk)** Marla Ryland wishes to estimate the value of an asset expected to provide cash inflows of $3,000 per year at the end of years 1 through 4 and $15,000 at the end of year 5. Her research indicates that she must earn 10 percent on low-risk assets, 15 percent on average-risk assets, and 22 percent on high-risk assets.

    a What is the most Marla should pay for the asset if it is classified as (1) low risk? (2) average risk? or (3) high risk?

    b If Marla is unable to assess the risk of the asset and wants to be certain she makes a good deal, based on your findings in **a**, what is the most she should pay? Why?

    c All else being the same, what effect does increasing risk have on the value of an asset? Explain in light of your findings in **a**.

8-4 **(Bond Fundamentals)** For each of the following bonds, indicate its (1) par value, (2) coupon rate, (3) annual interest in dollars, and (4) initial maturity.

    Bond A: Issued 3 years ago and matures to $1000 in 17 more years. Pays annual interest of $120.

    Bond B: Issued with an initial maturity of 15 years and a $1000 par value six years ago. Pays $70 in interest each six months.

    Bond C: Has eight years to maturity and has paid $25 in interest each six months over the past 22 years. The coupon rate is 10 percent.

8-5 **(Basic Bond Valuation)** Redenour Supply has an issue of $1000-par-value bonds with a 12 percent coupon interest rate outstanding. The issue pays interest annually and has 16 years remaining to its maturity date.

    a If bonds of similar risk are currently selling to yield a 10 percent rate of return, how much will the Redenour Supply bond sell for today?

    b Describe the *two* possible reasons that similar-risk bonds are currently selling at a yield below the coupon rate on the Redenour Supply bond.

    c If the market rate of interest were at 12 percent instead of 10 percent, what would the current value of Redenour's bond be? Contrast this finding with **a** and discuss.

8-6 **(Bond Valuation — Annual Interest)** Calculate the value of each of the following bonds, all of which pay interest *annually*.

Bond	Par value ($)	Coupon interest rate (%)	Years to maturity	Required return (%)
A	1000	14	20	12
B	1000	8	16	8
C	100	10	8	13
D	500	16	13	18
E	1000	12	10	10

8-7 **(Bond Value and Changing Required Returns)** National Telephone has outstanding a bond issue that will mature to its $1000 par value in 12 years. The bond has a coupon rate of 11 percent and pays interest *annually*.

a Find the value of the bond if the required return is
  (1) 11 percent
  (2) 15 percent
  (3) 8 percent

b Plot your findings in **a** on a set of required return (*x*-axis) – market value (*y*-axis) axes.

c Use your findings in **a** and **b** to discuss the relationship between the coupon rate on a bond and the required return and the market value of the bond relative to its par value.

d What two reasons cause the required return to differ from the coupon rate?

8-8 **(Bond Value and Time — Constant Required Returns)** R. R. Booker has just issued a 15-year, 12-percent coupon, $1000-par bond that pays interest *annually*. The required return is currently 14 percent, and the company is certain it will remain at 14 percent until the bond matures in 15 years.

a Assuming that the required return does remain at 14 percent until maturity, find the value of the bond with: (1) 15 years, (2) 12 years, (3) 9 years, (4) 6 years, (5) 3 years, and (6) 1 year to maturity.

b Plot your findings on a set of time to maturity (*x*-axis) – market value of bonds (*y*-axis) axes.

c All else remaining the same, when the required return differs from the coupon rate and is assumed constant to maturity, what happens to the bond value as time moves toward maturity? Explain in light of the graph in **b**.

8-9 **(Bond Value and Time — Changing Required Returns)** Amy Baxter is considering investing in either of two outstanding bonds of SOW Industries. The bonds both have $1000 par values and 11 percent coupons and pay *annual* interest. Bond A has exactly 5 years to maturity, while the other, bond B, has 15 years remaining until it matures.

a Calculate the value of bond A if the required return is (1) 8 percent, (2) 11 percent, and (3) 14 percent.

b Calculate the value of bond B if the required return is (1) 8 percent, (2) 11 percent, and (3) 14 percent.

c From your findings in **a** and **b**, complete the following table and discuss the relationship between time to maturity and changing required returns.

Required return (%)	Value of bond A	Value of bond B
8	?	?
11	?	?
14	?	?

d If Amy wanted to minimize "interest rate risk," which bond would you recommend she purchase? Why?

8-10 **(Yield to Maturity — Precise and Approximate)** The Zen Company bond currently sells for $955, has a 12 percent coupon and $1000 par value, pays interest *annually,* and has 15 years to maturity.

a Calculate the yield to maturity on this bond using the more precise trial-and-error present-value-based approach.

b Use the approximation formula to estimate the yield to maturity on this bond.

c Compare the yields calculated in **a** and **b** and discuss the relative utility of the approximation formula. Which approach would you recommend?

d Explain the relationship that exists between the coupon rate and yield to maturity and the par value and market value of a bond.

8-11 **(Yield to Maturity)** Each of the following bonds pays interest *annually.*

Bond	Par value ($)	Coupon interest rate (%)	Years to maturity	Current value ($)
A	1000	9	8	820
B	1000	12	16	1000
C	500	12	12	560
D	1000	15	10	1120
E	1000	5	3	900

a Use the approximation formula to find the yield to maturity for each bond.

b Calculate the yield to maturity for each bond using the more precise trial-and-error present-value-based approach.

c Compare and contrast your findings in **a** and **b** for each bond. Comment on the accuracy of your estimates from **a**.

d What relationship exists between the coupon rate and yield to maturity and the par value and market value of the bond? Explain.

8-12 **(Bond Valuation — Semiannual Interest)** Find the value of a bond maturing in 6 years, with a $1000 par value and a coupon rate of 10 percent (5 percent paid semiannually) if the required return on similar-risk bonds is 14 percent annual interest (7 percent paid semiannually).

8-13 **(Bond Valuation — Semiannual Interest)** Calculate the value of each of the following bonds, all of which pay interest *semiannually.*

Bond	Par value ($)	Coupon interest rate (%)	Years to maturity	Required return (%)
A	1,000	10	12	8
B	1,000	12	20	12
C	500	12	5	14
D	1,000	14	10	10
E	100	6	4	14

8-14 **(Bond Valuation — Quarterly Interest)** Calculate the value of a $5000-par-value bond paying quarterly interest at an annual rate of 10 percent and having 10 years until maturity if the required return on similar-risk bonds is currently a 12 percent annual rate paid *quarterly.*

8-15 **(Preferred Stock Valuation)** Scott Stamping wishes to estimate the value of its outstanding preferred stock. The preferred issue has an $80 par value and pays an annual dividend of 8 percent (of par). Similar-risk preferred stocks are currently yielding a 9.3 percent annual rate of return.

a   What is the market value of the outstanding preferred stock?

b   If an investor purchases the preferred stock at the value calculated in **a**, how much would she gain or lose per share if she sells the stock when the required return on similar-risk preferreds has risen to 10.5 percent? Explain.

8-16   **(Perpetual Valuation and Beta)**   You have observed two different financial instruments currently actively traded in the financial markets. One is a bond issued in perpetuity that promises to pay 10 percent of its $100 par value once every year. The second is a preferred stock that promises a $10 annual dividend. The beta of the bond is .80, and the beta for the preferred stock is .90. Assuming that the risk-free rate is 8 percent and the return on the market portfolio is 12 percent,

a   Compute the value of the bond.

b   Compute the value of the preferred stock.

c   Assume that the preferred stock's beta is equal to .80. What is its value?

8-17   **(Book and Liquidation Value)**   The balance sheet for the Imperial Mill Company follows:

BALANCE SHEET
IMPERIAL MILL COMPANY
ENDING DECEMBER 31

Assets		Liabilities and stockholders' equity	
Cash	$ 40,000	Accounts payable	$100,000
Marketable securities	60,000	Notes payable	30,000
Accounts receivable	120,000	Accrued wages	30,000
Inventory	160,000	Total current liabilities	$160,000
Total current assets	$380,000	Long-term debt	$180,000
Fixed assets	$400,000	Preferred stock	$ 80,000
Total assets	$780,000	Common stock (5000 shares)	360,000
		Total liabilities and stock-holders' equity	$780,000

The following additional information with respect to the firm is available:

(1) Preferred stock can be liquidated for its book value.

(2) Accounts receivable and inventory can be liquidated at 90 percent of book value.

(3) The firm has 5000 shares of common stock outstanding.

(4) All interest and dividends are currently paid up.

(5) Fixed assets can be liquidated at 70 percent of book value.

(6) Cash and marketable securities can be liquidated at book value.

Given this information, answer the following:

a   What is Imperial Mill's book value per share?

b   What is their liquidation value per share?

c   Compare, contrast, and discuss the values found in **a** and **b**.

8-18   **(Valuation with Price/Earnings Multiples)**   For each of the following firms, use the data given to estimate their common stock value employing price/earnings multiples.

Firm	Forecast eps ($)	Price/earnings multiple
A	3.00	6.2
B	4.50	10.0
C	1.80	12.6
D	2.40	8.9
E	5.10	15.0

8-19 **(Common Stock Valuation — Zero Growth)** Stable Enterprises is a mature firm in the machine tool component industry. The firm's most recent common stock dividend was $2.40 per share. Due to its maturity as well as stable sales and earnings, the firm's management feels that their dividends will remain at the current level for the foreseeable future.

    a If the required return is 12 percent, what is the value of Stable Enterprises' common stock?

    b If the firm's risk as perceived by market participants suddenly increases, causing the required return to rise to 20 percent, what will be the common stock value?

    c Based on your findings in **a** and **b**, what impact does risk have on value? Explain.

8-20 **(Common Stock Value — Constant Growth)** Use the constant growth valuation model (Gordon model) to find the value of each of the following firms.

Firm	Dividend expected next year ($)	Dividend growth rate (%)	Required return (%)
A	1.20	8	13
B	4.00	5	15
C	.65	10	14
D	6.00	8	9
E	2.25	8	20

8-21 **(Common Stock Value — Constant Growth)** The Baxter Boiler Company has paid the following dividends over the past six years:

Year	Dividend per share ($)
1984	2.87
1983	2.76
1982	2.60
1981	2.46
1980	2.37
1979	2.25

The firm's dividend per share next year is expected to be $3.02.

    a If you can earn 13 percent on similar-risk investments, what is the most you would pay per share for this firm?

    b If you can earn only 10 percent on similar-risk investments, what is the most you would be willing to pay per share?

    c Compare and contrast your findings in **a** and **b** and discuss the impact of changing risk on share value.

8-22 **(Common Stock Value — Variable Growth)** Wallin Manufacturing is considering a cash purchase of the stock of Ellis Tool. During the year just completed, Ellis earned $4.25 per share and paid cash dividends of $2.55 per share. Ellis's earnings and dividends are expected to grow at 25 percent per year for the next three years, after which they are expected to grow at 10 percent per year to infinity. What is the maximum price per share Wallin should pay for Ellis if it has a required rate of return of 15 percent on investments with risk characteristics similar to those of Ellis?

8-23 **(Common Stock Value — Variable Growth)** Stone Industries' most recent annual dividend was $1.80 per share ($D_0 = \$1.80$), and the firm's required rate of return is 10 percent. Find the market value of Stone's shares when:

    a Dividends are expected to grow at 8 percent for three years followed by a 5 percent constant growth rate from year 4 to infinity.

    b Dividends are expected to grow at 8 percent for each of three years followed by zero growth in years 4 to infinity.

      c Dividends are expected to grow at 8 percent for three years followed by a 10 percent constant growth rate in years 4 to infinity.

 8-24 **(Common Stock Value — All Growth Models)** You are evaluating the potential purchase of a small business currently generating $42,500 of after-tax cash flow $(D_0 = \$42,500)$. Based on a review of similar-risk investment opportunities, you must earn an 18 percent rate of return on the proposed purchase. Since you are relatively uncertain as to future cash flows, you have decided to estimate the firm's value using several possible cash flow growth rate assumptions.

      a What is the firm's value if dividends are expected to grow at 0 percent to infinity?

      b What is the firm's value if dividends are expected to grow at a constant annual rate of 7 percent to infinity?

      c What is the firm's value if dividends are expected to grow at an annual rate of 12 percent for the first two years followed by a constant annual rate of 7 percent from year 3 to infinity?

8-25 **(Management Action and Stock Value)** Landis Enterprises' most recent dividend was $3 per share, its expected annual rate of dividend growth is 5 percent, and the required return is now 15 percent. A variety of proposals are currently being considered by management in order to redirect the firm's activities. For each of the proposed actions below, determine the resulting impact on share price and indicate the best alternative.

      a Do nothing, which will leave the key financial variables unchanged.

      b Invest in a new machine that will increase the dividend growth rate to 6 percent and lower the required return to 14 percent.

      c Eliminate an unprofitable product line, which will increase the dividend growth rate to 7 percent and raise the required return to 17 percent.

      d Merge with another firm, which will reduce the growth rate to 4 percent and raise the required return to 16 percent.

      e Acquire a subsidiary operation from another manufacturer. The acquisition should increase the dividend growth rate to 8 percent and increase the required return to 17 percent.

8-26 **(Integrative — Valuation and CAPM Formulas)** Given the following information for the stock of JCT Co., calculate its beta.

Current price per share of common	$50.00
Expected dividend per share next year	$ 3.00
Constant annual dividend growth rate	9%
Risk-free rate	7%
Expected return on market portfolio	10%

8-27 **(Integrative — Risk and Valuation)** SK Enterprises has a beta of 1.20, the risk-free rate of interest is currently 10 percent, and the required return on the market portfolio is 14 percent. The company, which plans to pay a dividend of $2.60 per share in the coming year, anticipates that its future dividends will increase at an annual rate consistent with that experienced over the 1978-to-1984 period, when the following dividends were paid:

Year	Dividend per share ($)	Year	Dividend per share ($)
1984	2.45	1980	1.82
1983	2.28	1979	1.80
1982	2.10	1978	1.73
1981	1.95		

a Use the capital asset pricing model (CAPM) to determine the required return on SK Enterprises' stock.

b Using the constant growth dividend valuation model and your finding in **a**, estimate the value of SK Enterprises' stock.

c Explain what effect, if any, a decrease in beta would have on the value of SK's stock.

8-28 **(Integrative — Valuation and CAPM)** Jackson Steel Company wishes to determine the value of Acme Foundry, a firm that it is considering acquiring for cash. Jackson wishes to use the capital asset pricing model (CAPM) to determine the applicable discount rate to use as an input to the constant growth valuation model. Because Acme's stock is not publicly traded, Jackson, after studying the betas of similar firms to Acme that are publicly traded, believes that an appropriate beta for Acme's stock would be 1.25. The risk-free rate is currently 9 percent, and the market return is 13 percent. Acme's historical dividend per share for each of the past six years is given below:

Year	Dividend per share ($)
1984	3.44
1983	3.28
1982	3.15
1981	2.90
1980	2.75
1979	2.75

a Given that Acme is expected to pay a dividend of $3.68 per share next year, determine the maximum cash price Jackson should pay for each share of Acme.

b Discuss the use of the CAPM for estimating the value of common stock and describe the effect on the resulting value of Acme of:

(1) An increase in the risk-free rate to 10 percent.

(2) A decrease in the beta to 1.

(3) An increase in the market return to 14 percent.

(4) All the above changes occurring simultaneously.

Part IV

Long-Term Investment Decisions: Capital Budgeting

great deal of attention must be given to the initial outlay and subsequent cash flows associated with long-term or fixed-asset investments. As time passes, fixed assets may become obsolete or require an overhaul; at these points too, financial decisions may be required. This section of the chapter discusses capital expenditures and briefly describes the steps in the capital budgeting process.

CAPITAL EXPENDITURE SITUATIONS

A *capital expenditure* is an outlay made by the firm that is expected to produce *benefits over a period of time greater than one year; current expenditures* result in benefits received *within* the year. Fixed-asset outlays are capital expenditures, but not all capital expenditures result in the receipt of a fixed asset. A $60,000 outlay for a new machine with a usable life of 15 years is a capital expenditure; so is an outlay for advertising that produces benefits over a long period. However, outlays for advertising are not normally capitalized as an asset on the firm's balance sheet.[1]

Capital expenditures can be made for many reasons. But although the motives differ, the evaluation techniques are the same. The basic motives for capital expenditures are to expand, replace, or renew fixed assets or to obtain some other less tangible benefit over a long period.

Expansion. Probably the most common motive for a capital expenditure is to expand the level of operations — typically through acquisition of fixed assets. A growing firm often finds it necessary to acquire new fixed assets rapidly. As a firm's growth slows and it reaches maturity, most of its capital expenditures will be for the replacement or renewal of obsolete or worn-out assets. It is important to remember that fixed assets include both plant and equipment. In other words, the purchase of additional physical facilities, such as an additional plant, is a capital expenditure.

The classic example of an expansion decision involves a firm that is operating at full capacity and is unable to fulfill the demand for its products. It must evaluate capital expenditure proposals to determine how best to increase its productive capacity. The proposals include the acquisition of an existing facility, an addition to the firm's current facility, or construction of a totally new facility. Techniques for making such a decision are presented in Chapter 10.

Replacement. The replacement decision is quite common in more mature firms. This type of capital expenditure does not always result from the outright failure of a piece of equipment or the inability of an existing plant to function efficiently. The need to replace existing assets must be periodically examined by the firm's financial manager. A machine does not break down and say, "Please replace me!" But each time a machine requires a major repair, the outlay for the repair must be evaluated in terms of the outlay to replace the machine and the benefits of replacement.

It should not take a breakdown to stir the financial manager to consider the

---

[1] Some firms do, in effect, capitalize advertising outlays if there is reason to believe the benefit of the outlay will be received at some future date. The capitalized advertising may appear as a deferred charge such as "deferred advertising expense," which is then amortized over the future. Expenses of this type are often deferred for reporting purposes in order to increase reported earnings, while for tax purposes the entire amount will be expensed in order to reduce the tax liability.

replacement of fixed assets. As machines become less able to hold required tolerances or become inefficient compared to new machines, the benefits of replacement should be evaluated. Due to electronic advances, numeric- and computer-controlled machines have made many existing machines obsolete. New materials also contribute to the obsolescence of machinery. If replacing an existing machine would permit the firm to produce the same product at a lower cost, the firm must analyze the costs and benefits of this change. An outlay for a new machine may be quite justifiable in light of the total cost savings that result. Only by keeping abreast of new developments and questioning outlays for repairs can the firm manage its fixed assets properly.

Renewal. The renewal of fixed assets is often an alternative to replacement. Firms wishing to improve efficiency may find that both replacing and renewing existing machinery are suitable solutions. Renewal may involve rebuilding, overhauling, or retrofitting an existing machine or facility. Perhaps an existing drill press could be renewed by replacing its motor and adding a numeric control system. Perhaps a physical facility could be renewed by rewiring, adding air conditioning, and so on.

Renewal decisions must be viewed in light of the relevant costs and benefits. The cost of renewing a machine or physical facility may well be justified by the benefits. However, the financial manager must be careful in analyzing renewal suggestions to be certain that other alternatives have been considered. He or she may find that the cost of renewing assets is actually greater than the cost of replacing them. And in some cases, although the cost of renewal may be less, replacement may be preferable because it results in the receipt of benefits over a longer period of time. Suppose a firm has the following two alternatives: (1) to renew a machine at a cost of $10,000 and generate savings of $5,000 per year for five years or (2) to replace the machine at a cost of $15,000 and generate savings of $5,000 a year for ten years. These decisions are difficult to make and must be approached with caution.

Other purposes. Some capital expenditures do not result in the acquisition or transformation of tangible fixed assets that are shown on the firm's balance sheet; rather, they involve a long-term commitment of funds by the firm in expectation of a future return. These expenditures include outlays for advertising, research and development, management consulting, and new products. Advertising outlays are expected to provide benefits in the form of increased future sales. Research and development outlays are expected to provide future benefits in the form of new product ideas. Management consulting outlays are expected to provide returns in the form of increased profits from increased efficiency of operation. New products are expected to contribute to a product mix that maximizes overall returns. Many capital expenditure proposals — especially those such as the installation of pollution-control devices mandated by the government — are hard to evaluate because it is difficult to measure the intangible returns they may generate.

STEPS IN THE PROCESS

The *capital budgeting process* can be viewed as consisting of five distinct but interrelated steps. It begins with proposal generation. This is followed by review and analysis, decision making, implementation, and follow-up. Each step in the process is important; major time and effort, however, are devoted to review and analysis and decision making. These are the steps given major attention in this and the following two chapters.

Proposal generation. Proposals for capital expenditures are made by people at all levels within a business organization. To stimulate a flow of proposals that could result in potential cost savings, many firms offer cash rewards to employees whose proposals are ultimately funded. Large firms typically provide forms that must be completed by the originator of the proposal. These forms require not only a description of the expenditure being proposed but also data on dollar amounts of the costs and benefits expected to result. Capital expenditure proposals typically travel from the originator to a reviewer at a higher level in the organization. For relatively minor expenditures, the review might be made at the next organizational level; major expenditure proposals will travel to a higher-level reviewer or review committee. Clearly, proposals that require large outlays will be much more carefully scrutinized than less costly expenditures.

Review and analysis. Capital expenditure proposals — especially those requiring major outlays — are formally reviewed (1) to assess their appropriateness in light of the firm's overall objectives and plans and (2) more important, to evaluate the economic validity of the proposal. The economic evaluation begins with an assessment of the costs and benefits. To develop and verify these estimates, technical consultants may be hired to review aspects of the proposed expenditure. The proposed costs and benefits are next converted into a series of relevant cash flows to which various capital budgeting techniques are applied to measure the investment merit of the proposed outlay. In addition, various aspects of the risk associated with the proposal are either incorporated into the economic analysis or somehow rated and recorded along with the economic measures.

Often the reviewer or review committee will screen the proposals before performing an economic analysis. The actual procedures used by the reviewers are described in detail later in this chapter as well as in Chapters 10 and 11. Once the economic analysis is completed, a summary report, often with a recommendation, is submitted to the decision maker or to a capital appropriations committee for action.

Decision making. The size of proposed capital expenditures can vary significantly. Some expenditures, such as the purchase of a hammer that will provide benefits for three years, are by definition capital expenditures, even if the cost is only $15.[2] The

---

[2] Even though purchases of items such as hammers are known to provide benefits over a period greater than a year, they are treated as expenditures in the year of purchase. There is a certain dollar limit beyond which outlays are capitalized and depreciated rather than expensed. This dollar limit depends largely on what the Internal Revenue Service will permit. (The *Economic Recovery Tax Act of 1981* as modified by the *Tax Reform Act of 1984* permits firms to expense rather than capitalize and depreciate up to a total of $5,000 per year in 1985, 1986, and 1987 for certain depreciable business assets. This amount is scheduled to increase to $7,500 per year in 1988 and 1989 and to $10,000 in 1990 and thereafter.) In accounting, the issue of whether to expense or capitalize an outlay is resolved using the *principle of materiality*, which suggests that any outlays deemed material (i.e., large) relative to the

THE MANAGER OF CAPITAL BUDGETING: A JOB DESCRIPTION

Basic function
Responsible for budgeting and administering the company's capital asset expenditure program.

Primary responsibilities and duties
Compile and control the company's capital asset expenditures and construction program.
Analyze requests for capital appropriations.
Project future cash flow needs and analyze the resulting financing requirements.
Determine the amount and timing of future debt and equity needs.
Project and analyze financial statements.
Develop and maintain the computer system relating to capital asset analysis.
Prepare and present monthly reports on the capital expenditures program and cash flow projections.
Distribute information to and work with other corporate departments.
Supervise the identification of industrial revenue bond projects.
Supervise and review the calculation of various loan covenants and financial restrictions.
Obtain lease financing and assist in the issuance of industrial revenue bonds.
Negotiate terms of leases with lessors.

Types of decisions
Decide what methods will be used to control capital expenditures.
Develop the computer system necessary to provide relevant management information.
Negotiate the terms of lease financing.
Determine investment and use of industrial revenue bond proceeds.
Influence asset-user and financing departments to comply with capital budget constraints.

Consequences of error
This position is very complex in that it concerns the entire company's operations rather than just one area; error may result in decisions to purchase assets with too low a return on investment resulting in an economic loss to the firm. . . .

Education and experience
MBA
3 years experience in accounting or management accounting.
3–4 years experience in financial analysis and reporting with emphasis on capital expenditure decisions and cash flow analysis.

SOURCE: *Careers in Finance* (Tampa, Fla.: Financial Management Association, 1983), p. 5.

---

firm's scale of operations should be capitalized; others should be expensed in the current period. Of course, the firm, by expensing instead of capitalizing outlays, avoids the clerical work required to set up and maintain a depreciation schedule for the item and at the same time receives the maximum tax relief.

purchase of a new machine costing $60,000 is also a capital expenditure because the machine is expected to provide long-run returns. The actual dollar outlay and the importance of a capital item therefore determine the organizational level at which the expenditure decision is made.

Dollar outlay. Firms delegate capital expenditure authority on the basis of certain dollar limits. Typically, the board of directors reserves the right to make final decisions on capital expenditures requiring outlays beyond a certain dollar amount, while the authority for making smaller expenditures is delegated to other organizational levels. An example of a scheme for delegating capital expenditure decision authority is presented in Table 9.1. As the dollar value of expenditures decreases, the decision-making authority moves to lower levels within the organization. Of course, the detail and formality of the economic analysis on which the decision is based tends to increase in rigor with the dollar value of the proposal.

The top management committee mentioned in Table 9.1 generally consists of high-level officers and members of the board of directors. This special committee, sometimes called an executive committee, an advisory committee, an operations committee, or a planning committee, often has the final authority for approving proposals concerning plant expansion, subsidiary acquisitions, and any other actions that would require a major financial commitment by the firm. The actual dollar limit on outlays that can be authorized at various organizational levels depends directly on the size of the operation. In a small firm, expenditures over a few hundred dollars may have to be approved by the company president, whereas in larger firms a procedure similar to that shown in Table 9.1 may be used.

Importance. Firms operating under critical time constraints with respect to production often find it necessary to provide for exceptions to a dollar-outlay scheme. The plant manager is often given the power to make decisions necessary to keep the production line moving, even though they entail outlays larger than those he or she would normally be allowed to authorize. These exceptions must be allowed because of the high cost of interrupting production. Certain decisions must be made immediately, and, in cases where many dollars would be lost should a shutdown occur, the authority to make these decisions must be given to those directly involved. It is wise to put some dollar limit on these critically important expenditures, but it can be set somewhat above the normal limit at that organizational level.

Large and important expenditures must be evaluated from a cost-benefit stand-

Table 9.1   A Scheme for Delegating Capital Expenditure Decision Authority

Size of expenditure	Decision-making authority
Over $100,000	Board of directors or specified top management committee
$50,000–$100,000	President and/or chair of board of directors
$20,000–$50,000	Vice-president in charge of division
$5,000–$20,000	Plant manager
Under $5,000	Persons designated by plant manager

point. If a critical machine breaks and the cost of repair is high, it is advisable for the decision maker to evaluate the possibility of replacing the machine. These decisions must be made in light of the lost dollars that would result from a shutdown, the cost of repair versus the cost of replacement or renewal, and the duration and dollar amount of the benefits that would result from replacement.

Implementation. Once a proposal has been approved and funding has been available,[3] the implementation phase begins. For minor outlays, implementation is relatively routine; the expenditure is made and payment is rendered. For major expenditures, greater control is typically required to make certain that what has been proposed and approved is actually acquired at the budgeted costs. Often the expenditures for a single proposal may occur in phases, with each outlay requiring the signed approval of specified company officers.

Because the economic analysis used to justify a proposal is based on certain cost assumptions, the control of actual cost in the implementation phase is important to the success of the project. When actual costs begin to deviate from those budgeted, a review and possible termination of a partially funded project may be appropriate. This situation has recently been faced by many utilities in the construction of nuclear power plants. Some have continued to complete their plants, while others have stopped construction of partially completed facilities. The decision depends on the circumstances and on the judgment of the firm's managers.

Follow-up. Equally important as controlling the cost incurred during the implementation phase is the monitoring of results during the operating phase of a project. Feedback and comparison of actual outcomes in terms of costs and benefits with those expected and those of previous projects are vital. When actual outcomes are below those projected, action may be required to improve the benefits or possibly to terminate the project. Some adjustment can be made in the early years of a project, but a *postimplementation audit* is generally recommended after a few years in order to evaluate formally the project's performance and take any appropriate action. In addition, through the follow-up process, new ideas and forecasting techniques for improving the capital expenditure analysis and decision steps are often discovered. Follow-up is often ignored in practice, but it is an important activity that can contribute favorably to the firm's overall returns, risk, and value.

Capital Budgeting Terminology

Before beginning to develop the theory, concepts, tools, and techniques related to the review and analysis and decision-making steps in the capital budgeting process, it is useful to understand some of the basic terminology of these areas. In addition, we present a number of key assumptions used to simplify the discussion in the balance of this chapter as well as in Chapters 10 and 11.

---

[3] Capital expenditures are often approved as part of the annual budgeting process, although funding will not be made available until the budget is implemented — often as long as six months after approval.

TYPES OF PROJECTS

The firm may be confronted with a number of different types of projects. Depending on the types of projects being considered, different decision-making approaches may be required. The two most common project types are (1) independent and (2) mutually exclusive projects.

Independent projects. *Independent projects* do not compete with one another; the acceptance of one *does not eliminate* the others from further consideration. If a firm has unlimited funds to invest, all the independent projects that meet its minimum investment criteria can be implemented.

Mutually exclusive projects. *Mutually exclusive projects* are projects that have the same function. The acceptance of one of a group of mutually exclusive projects *eliminates* all other projects in the group from further consideration. For example, if a firm is confronted with three ways to achieve its goal of increasing productive capacity, the three alternatives would be considered mutually exclusive. If each of these alternatives meets the firm's minimum acceptance criteria, some technique will have to be used to determine the "best" one. Acceptance of this "best" alternative will eliminate the need for either of the other two.

THE AVAILABILITY OF FUNDS

The availability of funds for capital expenditures affects the firm's decision environment.

Unlimited funds. If a firm has *unlimited funds* for investment, making capital budgeting decisions is quite simple. All independent projects that provide returns greater than some predetermined level can be accepted. Most firms are not in such a situation; typically, only a certain number of dollars are allocated for making capital expenditures. Normally the amount is specified in the firm's annual budget.

Capital rationing. Most firms operate under *capital rationing*. They have only a fixed number of dollars available for capital expenditures, and numerous projects compete for these limited dollars. The firm must therefore ration its funds by allocating them to projects that will maximize share value. Quite often, firms confronted with serious capital rationing are able to raise additional money to ease the budget constraint. The discussions that follow assume unlimited funds; procedures for dealing with capital rationing are presented in Chapter 11.

APPROACHES TO DECISION MAKING

Two basic approaches to capital budgeting decisions are available. These approaches are somewhat dependent on whether or not the firm is confronted with capital rationing, and they are affected by the type of project involved. The two are the accept-reject approach and the ranking approach.

The accept-reject approach. The *accept-reject approach* involves evaluating capital expenditure proposals to determine whether they are acceptable. This is a simple approach because it requires merely applying predetermined criteria to a proposal and comparing the resulting return to the firm's minimum acceptable return. This approach can be used if the firm has unlimited funds available. An accept-reject decision is also a preliminary step in evaluating mutually exclusive projects or in a situation in which capital must be rationed. If a mutually exclusive project does not meet the basic acceptance criterion, it should be eliminated from consideration. If the firm is evaluating projects with a view to capital rationing, only acceptable projects should be considered.

The ranking approach. A second approach involves *ranking* projects on the basis of some predetermined criterion such as the rate of return. The project with the highest return is ranked first, the project with the lowest acceptable return, last. Only acceptable projects should be ranked. Ranking is useful in selecting the "best" of a group of mutually exclusive projects and in evaluating projects with a view to capital rationing.

When the firm is confronted with a number of projects, some of which are mutually exclusive and some of which are independent, the proper approach is to determine the best of each group of mutually exclusive alternatives and therefore reduce the mixed group of projects to a group of independent projects. The best of the acceptable independent projects can then be selected. All acceptable projects can be implemented if the firm has unlimited funds. If capital rationing is necessary, the mix of projects that maximizes the firm's overall value should be accepted. Various decision-making techniques applicable in these situations are presented in Chapters 10 and 11. The following example illustrates the evaluation process.

EXAMPLE   A firm with unlimited funds must evaluate eight projects—A through H. Projects A, B, and C are mutually exclusive; projects G and H are also mutually exclusive; and projects D, E, and F are independent of the other projects. The projects are listed along with their returns:

Project	Status	Return (%)
A		16
B	Mutually exclusive	19
C		11
D	Independent	15
E	Independent	13
F	Independent	21
G	Mutually exclusive	20
H		17

To evaluate these projects, the best of the mutually exclusive groups must first be determined. On the basis of the given return figures, project B would be selected from mutually exclusive projects A, B, and C since it has the highest return of this group, and project G would be preferred to project H since it has the higher return. After the selection of the best of the two groups of mutually exclusive projects, the five remaining independent projects can be ranked on the basis of their returns:

Rank	Project	Return (%)
1	F	21
2	G	20
3	B	19
4	D	15
5	E	13

Given that the firm has unlimited funds, and assuming that all projects are acceptable, the ranking would not be especially useful. If the firm were operating in an environment of capital rationing, however, the rankings would be useful in choosing which projects to accept. ■

TYPES OF CASH FLOW PATTERNS

Cash flow patterns associated with capital investment projects can be classified as conventional or nonconventional. Another classification is as an annuity or a mixed stream.

Conventional cash flows. The *conventional cash flow pattern* consists of an initial outflow followed by a series of inflows. This pattern is associated with many types of capital expenditures. For example, a firm may spend $10,000 today and as a result expect to receive cash inflows of $2,000 at the end of each year for the next seven years and $8,000 at the end of the eighth year. This conventional pattern is diagramed in Figure 9.1. All conventional cash flow patterns can be diagramed in this way.

Nonconventional cash flows. A *nonconventional cash flow pattern* is any pattern in which an initial outlay is not followed by a series of inflows. Alternating inflows and outflows and an inflow followed by outflows are examples of such patterns. A common type of nonconventional pattern results from the purchase of an asset that generates cash inflows for a period of years, is overhauled, and again generates a stream of cash inflows for a number of years. For example, the purchase of a

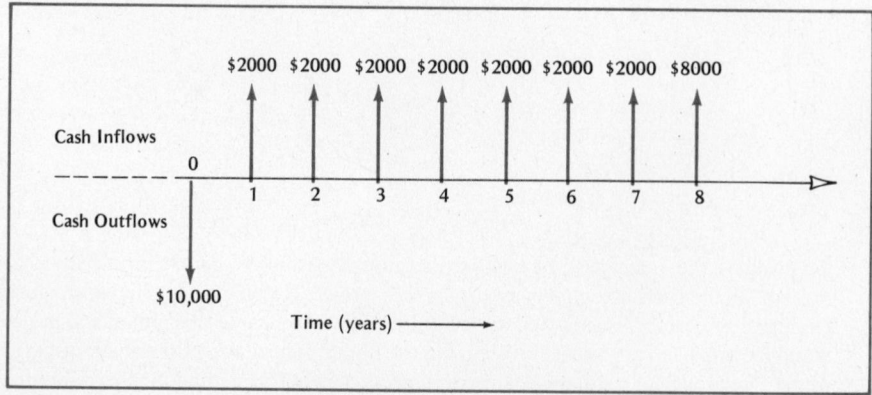

Figure 9.1 A conventional cash flow pattern

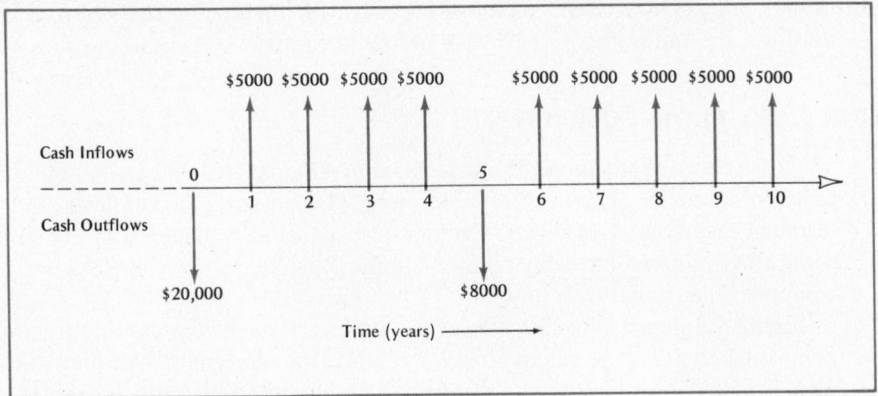

Figure 9.2   A nonconventional cash flow pattern

machine may require an initial cash outflow of $20,000 and generate cash inflows of $5,000 each year for four years. In the fifth year after the purchase, an outlay of $8,000 may be required to overhaul the machine, after which it generates inflows of $5,000 each year for five years. This nonconventional pattern is illustrated in Figure 9.2.

Difficulties often arise in evaluating projects involving a nonconventional pattern of cash flows. The discussions in the remainder of this chapter and in the following chapters will be limited to the evaluation of conventional patterns.

Annuity or mixed stream. As pointed out in Chapter 6, an *annuity* is a series of equal annual cash flows. A stream of cash flows that is not an annuity is referred to as a *mixed stream* of cash flows. Ignoring the eighth-year cash inflow, the cash inflows of $2000 per year (for seven years) in Figure 9.1 are inflows from an annuity, while the unequal pattern of inflows in Figure 9.4 on page 326 represents a mixed stream. As pointed out in Chapter 6, the techniques required to evaluate cash flows are much simpler to use when the pattern of flows is an annuity.

Developing Relevant Cash Flows[4]

To evaluate capital expenditure alternatives or "projects," the *after-tax cash outflows* and *inflows* associated with each project must be determined. As noted in Chapter 2, cash flows, rather than accounting figures, are used because it is these flows that directly affect the firm's ability to pay bills or purchase assets. Accounting figures and cash flows are not necessarily the same due to the presence of certain noncash expenditures on the firm's income statement. When a proposed purchase is intended to replace an existing asset, the *incremental* cash outflows and inflows that will result from the investment must be measured. The remainder

---

[4] The term *relevant* is used throughout this and the following two chapters to refer to cash flows that must be considered in analyzing various capital budgeting decision alternatives. The term is used to mean the *incremental after-tax cash flows* associated with a capital expenditure alternative.

of this chapter is devoted to the procedures for measuring the *relevant* cash outflows and inflows associated with proposed capital expenditures.

MAJOR CASH FLOW COMPONENTS

The cash flows of any project having the *conventional pattern* can include three basic components: (1) an initial investment, (2) operating cash inflows, and (3) terminal cash flow. All projects, whether for expansion, replacement, renewal, or some other purpose, have the first two components. Some, however, lack the final component, terminal cash flow.

Figure 9.3 depicts the cash flows for a project. Each of the cash flow components is labeled. The *initial investment,* which is the relevant cash outflow at time zero, is $50,000 for the proposed project. The *operating cash inflows,* which are the incremental after-tax cash inflows resulting from use of the project during its life, gradually increase from $4,000 in the first year to $10,000 in the tenth and final year of the project. The *terminal cash flow,* which is the after-tax nonoperating cash flow occurring in the final year of the project, generally attributable to liquidation of the project, is $25,000 received at the end of the project's ten-year life. Note that the terminal cash flow does *not* include the $10,000 operating cash inflow for year 10.

INITIAL INVESTMENT

The term *initial investment* as used here refers to the relevant cash outflow to be considered in evaluating a prospective capital expenditure. It is calculated by

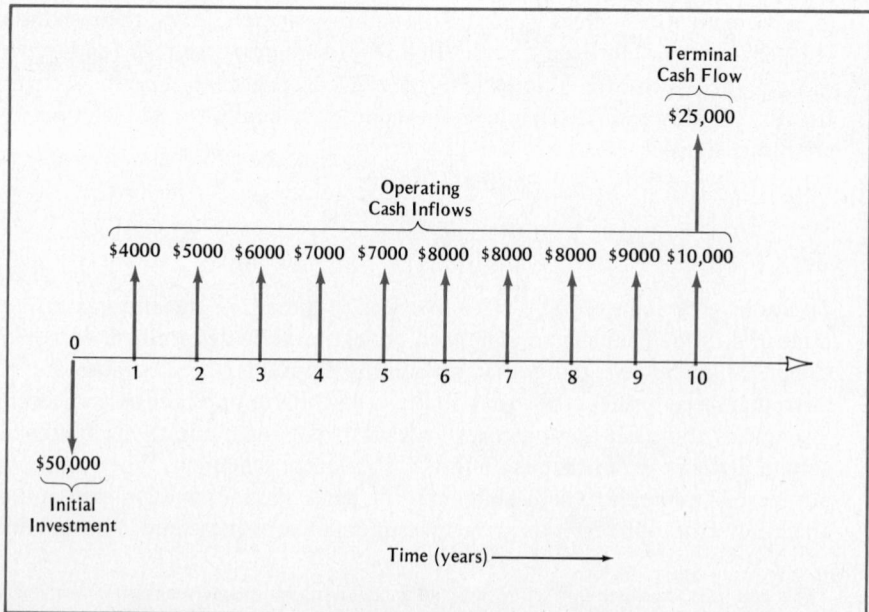

Figure 9.3 Major cash flow components

Table 9.2 The Basic Format for Determining Initial Investment

Cost of new asset
+ Installation costs
− Proceeds from sale of old assets
± Taxes on sale of old assets
− Investment tax credit on new asset
± Change in net working capital
Initial investment

netting out all outflows and inflows occurring at time zero (the time the expenditure is made) to get the initial outlay at time zero. Since our discussion of capital budgeting is concerned only with investments exhibiting conventional cash flows, a net outflow or initial investment must occur at time zero.

The basic variables that must be considered in determining the initial investment associated with a capital expenditure are the cost of the new asset, the installation costs (if any), the proceeds (if any) from the sale of old assets, the taxes (if any) resulting from the sale of old assets, the investment tax credit on the new asset (if applicable), and the change (if any) in net working capital. The basic format for determining initial investment is given in Table 9.2.

The cost of a new asset. The *cost* of a new asset is the outlay it requires. Typically we are concerned with the acquisition of a fixed asset for which a definite purchase price is paid. If the firm is not replacing an existing asset and there are no installation costs, the purchase price of the asset adjusted for the investment tax credit and any change in net working capital is equal to the initial investment. Each capital expenditure decision should be checked to make sure installation costs have not been overlooked.

Installation costs. The cost of installing a new asset once it has been acquired is considered part of the capital expenditure, since the Internal Revenue Service requires the inclusion of this cost in calculating depreciable value, which is written off over a period of years. *Installation costs* are defined as any added costs necessary to get an asset into operation.[5] The IRS frowns on firms expensing these costs since they actually should be capitalized.

Proceeds from the sale of old assets. If a new asset is intended to replace existing assets that are being sold, the proceeds from the sale are considered a cash inflow. If costs are incurred in the process of removing the old assets, the proceeds from the sale of the old assets are reduced by these *removal costs*. Some firms expense removal

---

[5] The IRS requires the firm to charge to the cost of the new asset all material installation costs. Even if a firm uses its in-house maintenance department to install the asset, if the cost of this installation is greater than a few hundred dollars, the installation cost should be added to the cost of the asset and depreciated over its recovery period. If the installation cost is not greater than a few hundred dollars, it should be expensed in the current period.

costs, but the IRS requires that they be deducted from the proceeds received on the sale of the asset. The proceeds from the sale of a replaced asset are often referred to as the *liquidation value* of the asset. These proceeds help to reduce the cost of the new asset, thereby reducing the firm's initial investment.

Taxes. Taxes must be considered in calculating the initial investment whenever a new asset replaces an old asset that has been sold.[6] The proceeds from the sale of the replaced asset are normally subject to some type of tax. The amount and how the proceeds are taxed depends on the relationship between the proceeds, the initial purchase price, and the book value of the asset being replaced. There are four possibilities: (1) The asset is sold for more than its initial purchase price; (2) the asset is sold for more than its book value but less than its initial purchase price; (3) the asset is sold for its book value; and (4) the asset is sold for less than its book value. An example will illustrate.

EXAMPLE   Let us assume that a firm purchased an asset two years ago for $100,000. The asset was being depreciated under the *Accelerated Cost Recovery System, ACRS* (see Chapter 2), over its five-year normal recovery period; its current book value is therefore $63,000.[7] What will happen if the firm now decides to sell the asset and replace it? Since the old asset has been held for longer than six months, certain gains (if there are any) from the sale will be subject to capital gains taxes (see Chapter 2). If the asset had not been held for longer than six months, all gains would be taxed at the firm's ordinary tax rate. The firm's ordinary rate is assumed to be 40 percent, and the tax rate on long-term capital gains is assumed to be 30 percent.[8] Let us consider each of the situations.

 The sale of the asset for more than its initial purchase price   If the firm sells the old asset for $110,000, it realizes a long-term capital gain of $10,000 (the amount by which the sale price exceeds the initial purchase price of $100,000). The firm also experiences ordinary income in the form of recaptured depreciation of $37,000 ($100,000 – $63,000), taxable at the ordinary rate.[9] The taxes on the total gain of $47,000 are calculated as follows:

Capital gain (long-term): $10,000 × .30 = $ 3,000
Ordinary gain: $37,000 × .40   = 14,800
   Total taxes   = $17,800

These taxes should be used in calculating the initial investment in the new asset being purchased, using the format in Table 9.2. In effect, they raise the amount of the firm's initial investment in the new asset by reducing the proceeds from the sale of the old.

[6] A detailed discussion of the tax treatment of ordinary income and losses and capital gains income and losses was presented in Chapter 2.

[7] Under ACRS, as shown in Table 2.7 on page 34, for a five-year recovery period, 15 percent would be depreciated in the first year and 22 percent in the second year. The book value of the $100,000 asset at the end of the second year was therefore determined as follows: $100,000 − [(.15 + .22) × $100,000] = $63,000.

[8] To emphasize the tax effects on various aspects of the initial investment and subsequent cash flows, a 40 percent ordinary income tax rate and a 30 percent long-term capital gains tax rate are used throughout this and following chapters. A discussion of actual corporate tax rates was included in Chapter 2.

[9] While the measurement of the amount of recaptured depreciation for movable business property is as described earlier and illustrated here, the treatment of real property such as buildings may be handled differently. For convenience, this difference is not addressed here.

The sale of the asset for more than its book value but less than its initial purchase price
If the firm sells the old asset for $80,000, which is less than its original purchase price but more than its book value, there is no capital gain. However, the firm still experiences a gain in the form of recaptured depreciation of $17,000 ($80,000 − $63,000), which is taxed as part of ordinary income. Since the firm is assumed to be in the 40 percent tax bracket, the taxes on the $17,000 gain are $6,800. This $6,800 in taxes should be used in calculating the initial investment in the new asset.

The sale of the asset for its book value   If the asset is sold for $63,000, which is its book value, the firm breaks even. Since no tax results from selling an asset for book value, there is no effect on the initial investment in the new asset.

The sale of the asset for less than its book value   If the firm sells the asset for $40,000, an amount less than its book value, it experiences a loss of $23,000 ($63,000 − $40,000). If it was a depreciable asset used in business or trade, the loss may be used to offset ordinary operating income. If the asset was a *capital asset*—a nondepreciable asset not used in business or trade—the capital loss can be used only to offset capital gains. Both types of losses can be applied currently or carried back three years. Depreciable asset losses can be carried forward 15 years and capital losses can be carried forward only five years, if necessary.[10] In this case, there are two possibilities:

1. If the asset is depreciable and used in business or trade and there are operating earnings the loss can be used to offset, the firm will save $9,200 in taxes ($23,000 × .40).
2. If the asset was *not* depreciable or was *not* used in business or trade but there are capital gains, the capital loss of $23,000 can be used to offset, the firm will save $6,900 in taxes ($23,000 × .30).

In either case, if current operating earnings or capital gains are not sufficient to offset the loss, the firm can carry portions of it back or forward. Losses treated in this way may affect the initial investment in the new asset. The impact of a carryback provides a refund that will effectively reduce the firm's initial investment, while carryforwards of tax losses will affect only the subsequent years' cash flows. ■

Investment tax credit. Because the capital budgeting process typically involves the acquisition of assets having long lives, the investment tax credit, described in detail in Chapter 2, is often applicable. This tax credit, which is based on the installed cost of the asset or project, varies with the recovery period. As shown in Table 2.12, two optional treatments of the credit are available. For our purpose, the more computationally straightforward Option 2, which is summarized in Table 9.3, is used throughout this text.[11] The calculation of the investment tax credit can be illustrated by a simple example.

[10] Refer to Chapter 2 for a more detailed discussion of tax loss carrybacks and carryforwards.

[11] Option 1 is computationally more rigorous since it involves an adjustment in the depreciable base of the asset. For assets with 3-year normal recovery periods the credit is 6 percent, but only 97 percent of the asset cost is used as a depreciable base, whereas for 5-, 10-, and 15-year normal recovery periods, a 10 percent credit and a depreciable base of 95 percent of cost are used.

Table 9.3   The Investment Tax Credit—Option 2[a]

Normal recovery period	Investment tax credit[b]
3 years	4%
5 years	8%
10 years	8%
15 years	8%

[a] Note that under this option, 100 percent of the full installed cost of the asset is its depreciable base.
[b] These are the percentages of the cost of the asset or project that can be taken as a *tax credit* in the year it is acquired.

EXAMPLE   Bemis Enterprises just acquired two assets, A and B, each having installed costs of $120,000. Asset A has a normal recovery period of 3 years, while asset B's normal recovery period is 10 years. Using the appropriate percentages from Table 9.3, the following investment tax credits result.

Asset	Investment tax credit
A	.04 × $120,000 = $ 4,800
B	.08 × 120,000 = 9,600
	Total A and B = $14,400

As a result of acquiring the two assets, the firm can use the total tax credit of $14,400 to reduce its tax liability by that amount. ∎

The presence of the investment tax credit lowers the initial investment required by reducing the tax liability. But under the option applied throughout this text, the *use of this credit in no way affects the depreciable value of an asset.* In the foregoing example, the installed cost of assets A and B for depreciation purposes remains $120,000 after calculation and use of the investment tax credit. In addition, the tax laws contain a variety of other rules and regulations on eligibility for the credit, application of the credit, and recapture of unearned investment tax credits.[12] Due to their relative complexity, these refinements are ignored in subsequent applications of the investment tax credit.

Change in net working capital. *Net working capital,* as noted in Chapter 4, is the amount by which a firm's current assets exceed its current liabilities. This topic is treated in depth in Part VI, especially in Chapter 15, but at this point it is important to note that changes in net working capital often accompany capital expenditure decisions, regardless of their motive. If a firm acquires new machinery to expand its

[12] Like depreciation, a firm that takes but does not fully earn an investment tax credit must recapture a specified portion of it upon sale of the asset. For example, under the liberalized provisions of the *Economic Recovery Tax Act of 1981* as modified by the *Tax Equity and Fiscal Responsibility Act of 1982,* a firm that takes a $10,000 credit as a result of acquiring an asset having a 10-year life must increase its tax liability by 80 percent of the $10,000—$8,000—if the asset is sold between years 1 and 2. This refinement is ignored for convenience in subsequent applications.

level of operations, accompanying such expansion will be increased levels of cash, accounts receivable, inventory, accounts payable, and accruals. As long as the expanded operations continue, the increased investment in current assets (cash, accounts receivable, and inventory) and increased current liability financing (accounts payable and accruals) would be expected to continue. The difference between the change in current assets and the change in current liabilities would be the *change in net working capital.* Generally, current assets increase by more than current liabilities, resulting in an increased investment in net working capital, which would be treated as an initial outflow associated with the project.[13] If the change in net working capital were negative, it would be shown as an initial inflow associated with the project. The change in net working capital — regardless of whether an increase or a decrease — *is not taxable* because it merely involves a net build-up or reduction of current accounts.

EXAMPLE Quirin Enterprises is contemplating expanding its operations to meet the growing demand for its products. In addition to Quirin's acquiring a variety of new capital equipment, financial analysts expect that the changes in current accounts summarized in Table 9.4 will occur and be maintained over the life of the expansion. Current assets are expected to increase by $22,000, and current liabilities are expected to increase by $9,000, resulting in a $13,000 increase in net working capital. In this case the increase would represent an increased working capital investment and be treated as a cash outflow in calculating the initial investment. ■

Calculating the initial investment. It should be clear that a variety of tax and other considerations enter into the initial investment calculation. The following example illustrates how the basic variables described in the preceding discussion are used to calculate the initial investment according to the format in Table 9.2.[14]

Table 9.4 Calculation of Change in Net Working Capital for Quirin Enterprises

Current account	Change in balance	
Cash	+ $ 4,000	
Accounts receivable	+ 10,000	
Inventory	+ 8,000	
(1) Current assets		+ $22,000
Accounts payable	+ $ 7,000	
Accruals	+ 2,000	
(2) Current liabilities		+ 9,000
Change in net working capital [(1) − (2)]		+ $13,000

[13] When net working capital changes apply to the calculation of the initial investment associated with a proposed capital expenditure, they are for convenience assumed to be spontaneous and thereby occurring at time zero. In practice, frequently the change in net working capital will occur over a period of months as the capital expenditure is implemented.

[14] Throughout the discussion of capital budgeting in this section, all assets evaluated as candidates for replacement are assumed to be depreciable assets that are directly used in the business, so any losses on the sale of these assets can be applied against ordinary operating income. These assets are also assumed to have been held for a period of time consistent with any investment tax credit initially taken — that is, there is no recaptured investment tax credit. The decisions are also structured so as to ensure that the life remaining on the old asset is just equal to the life of the new asset; this assumption permits the avoidance of the problem of unequal lives, which is discussed in greater detail in Chapter 11.

GM's $50 MILLION EXPENDITURE AT TARRYTOWN

General Motors Corp. said it plans to spend about $50 million in a "limited modernization" of its Tarrytown, N.Y., assembly plant. But the auto maker indicated that it might permanently close the aging plant within a few years.

GM said that in mid-September [1984] it would temporarily close the Tarrytown plant to upgrade and convert it to assembly of GM's popular, mid-size A-body cars from the compact X-body models it currently produces. When the modernization is complete at the end of November [1984], Tarrytown will join three other GM plants in making the A-bodies, which include such models as the Oldsmobile Cutlass Ciera and the Chevrolet Celebrity. Sales of those models have jumped substantially during the past year.

A GM spokesman, however, noted that the conversion to A-car production doesn't assure the plant's survival. "Instead, the product change provides us with interim production while other avenues are explored for the plant's long-term future," he said.

The conversion of Tarrytown would leave GM making the X-body cars only at its Willow Run, Mich., plant. Sales of the X-cars, which include such models as the Chevrolet Citation and the Buick Skylark, have leveled off recently. There has been much publicity concerning the cars' alleged braking problems, and many GM customers are turning to A-cars or subcompact J-body cars instead. The J-cars include such models as the Chevrolet Cavalier and Pontiac 2000.

GM said it would temporarily idle about 1,600 hourly workers during the conversion and retain the remaining 500 to 600 hourly workers, including many skilled tradesmen, to do some of the modernization work.

Built in 1915, Tarrytown is GM's oldest assembly plant. GM says it must find a way to get costs there in line with those at its other assembly plants to justify the substantial costs of renovating the facility. A $100 million to $200 million investment will be required in Tarrytown's paint system by 1987 to comply with new federal requirements for plant hydrocarbon emissions.

If the company doesn't significantly cut costs at Tarrytown, a spokesman said, "and we go into another slump and we need to cut capacity, Tarrytown would be one of the plants at the top of the list to be shut down."

Specifically, the spokesman said, the plant's problems include the highest utility costs of any GM assembly plant in the U.S., high taxes and shipping difficulties. GM officials have been meeting with local, state and federal officials, seeking tax abatements and, among other transportation improvements, the enlargement of tunnels around the city so that GM could ship cars out by rail. GM also is trying to get the United Auto Workers local at the plant to make cost-saving concessions in work rules.

SOURCE: "GM Plans to Spend $50 Million on Unit at Tarrytown, N.Y.," *The Wall Street Journal,* May 22, 1984, p. 7.

EXAMPLE   The Ajax Company is trying to determine the initial investment required to replace an old machine with a new, much more sophisticated model. The proposed machine's purchase price is $380,000 and an additional $20,000 will be required to install it. It will be depreciated under ACRS over its normal five-year recovery period. The installed cost of the proposed machine is eligible for an investment tax credit of $32,000, which equals 8 percent of its $400,000 cost ($380,000 purchase price plus $20,000 installation). The old machine was purchased three years ago at a cost of $240,000 and was being depreciated under ACRS over its normal five-year recovery period. The firm has found a buyer willing to pay $280,000 for the old machine and to remove it at his own expense. The firm expects that a $35,000 increase in current assets and an $18,000 increase in current liabilities will accompany the replacement; these changes will result in a $17,000 ($35,000 − $18,000) *increase* in net working capital. The firm is in the 40 percent ordinary tax bracket, and long-term capital gains are taxed at a rate of 30 percent.

The only component of the initial investment required by the proposed purchase that is difficult to obtain is taxes. Since the firm is planning to sell the old machine for $40,000 more than its purchase price, it will realize a long-term capital gain of $40,000. The book value of the old machine can be found using the depreciation percentages from Table 2.7 (page 34) of 15 percent, 22 percent, and 21 percent for years 1 through 3, respectively;[15] the resulting book value is $100,800 ($240,000 − [(.15 + .22 + .21) × $240,000]). An ordinary gain of $139,200 ($240,000 − $100,800) in recaptured depreciation is also realized on the sale. The total taxes on the gain are $67,680 [($40,000 × .30) + ($139,200 × .40)]. Substituting these taxes, along with the purchase price and installation cost of the new machine, the proceeds from the sale of the old machine, the investment tax credit on the new machine, and the change in net working capital, into the format in Table 9.2 results in an initial investment of $172,680. This represents the net cash outflow required at time zero:

Cost of new machine	$380,000	} Depreciable
+ Installation costs	20,000	} outlay
− Proceeds from sale of old machine	280,000	
+ Taxes on sale of old machine	67,680	
− Investment tax credit on new machine	32,000	
+ Change in net working capital	17,000	
Initial investment	$172,680	

In the example, the net proceeds from the sale of the old machine ($212,320) could have been found by subtracting the taxes from the sale price ($280,000 − $67,680). This is, in essence, the net amount that has been deducted from the sum of the purchase price, installation costs, and change in net working capital, less the investment tax credit on the new machine. Regardless of which approach is used, the resulting value for the initial investment is the same.

OPERATING CASH INFLOWS

The benefits expected from a capital expenditure are measured by its *operating cash inflows,* which are *incremental after-tax cash inflows.* In this section we develop clear definitions of the terms *after-tax, cash inflows,* and *incremental.* In addition, we present an alternative approach for determining relevant operating cash inflows.

Interpreting the term *after-tax.* Benefits expected to result from proposed capital expenditures must be measured on an after-tax basis, since the firm will not have the use of

---

[15] The depreciation percentages for assets having five-year normal recovery periods presented in Table 2.7 on page 34 and discussed in Chapter 2 were 15, 22, 21, 21, and 21 percent for years 1 through 5, respectively.

any benefits until it has satisfied the government's tax claims. These claims depend on the firm's taxable income, so the deduction of taxes *prior to* making comparisons between proposals is necessary for consistency. Consistency is required in evaluating capital expenditure alternatives, since the intention is to compare like benefits.

Interpreting the term *cash inflows*. All benefits expected from a proposed project must be measured on a cash flow basis. Cash inflows represent dollars that can be spent, not merely "accounting profits," which are not necessarily available for paying the firm's bills. A simple technique for converting after-tax net profits into operating cash inflows was illustrated in Chapter 2. The basic calculation requires adding any noncash charges deducted as expenses on the firm's income statement back to net profits after taxes. Probably the most common noncash charge found on income statements is depreciation. It is the only noncash charge that will be considered in this section. The following example shows how after-tax operating cash inflows can be calculated for a present and a proposed project.

EXAMPLE The Ajax Company's estimates of its revenues, expenses (excluding depreciation), and earnings before depreciation and taxes, with and without the proposed capital expenditure described in the preceding example, are given in Table 9.5.[16] The amount to be depreciated with the proposed machine is calculated by summing the purchase price of $380,000 and the installation costs of $20,000. Since the machine is to be depreciated under ACRS over a five-year normal recovery period, 15, 22, 21, 21, and 21 percent would be recovered in years 1 through 5, respectively (see Chapter 2 and Table 2.7 on page 34 for more detail). The resulting depreciation on this machine for each of the five years, as well as the remaining two years of depreciation on the old machine, are calculated in Table 9.6.[17]

The operating cash inflows in each year can be calculated as follows, using the projected earnings before depreciation and taxes.[18]

Projected earnings before depreciation and taxes
− Depreciation

Projected earnings before taxes
− Taxes

Projected earnings after taxes
+ Depreciation

Projected operating cash inflows

Treating the projected earnings before depreciation and taxes in Table 9.5 in this way results in the projected operating cash inflows. Using the data for year 4 for the proposed

---

[16] Note that both the proposed and present machines are assumed to have five-year usable lives.

[17] It is important to recognize that while both machines will provide five years of use, the proposed new machine will be depreciated over the five-year period, while the present machine — as noted in the preceding example — has been depreciated over three years and therefore has only its final two years of depreciation write-offs (i.e., 21 percent *each* year under ACRS) remaining.

[18] Sometimes it is not necessary to relate the effects of a proposed expenditure directly to after-tax profits. In these cases, the incremental after-tax operating cash inflows can be estimated directly by netting additional after-tax cash inflows and outflows for each period and adding the tax rate times the amount of additional depreciation expected to the net cash flows. This approach is discussed in greater detail and illustrated later in this chapter.

Table 9.5   Ajax Company's Revenues,
             Expenses (Excluding Depreciation), and Earnings
             Before Depreciation and Taxes

Year	Projected revenues (1)	Projected expenses (excl. depr.) (2)	Projected earnings before depreciation and taxes [(1) − (2)] (3)
With proposed machine			
1	$2,520,000	$2,300,000	$220,000
2	2,520,000	2,300,000	220,000
3	2,520,000	2,300,000	220,000
4	2,520,000	2,300,000	220,000
5	2,520,000	2,300,000	220,000
With present machine			
1	$2,200,000	$1,990,000	$210,000
2	2,300,000	2,110,000	190,000
3	2,400,000	2,230,000	170,000
4	2,400,000	2,250,000	150,000
5	2,250,000	2,120,000	130,000

and present machines and assuming a 40 percent tax rate, Table 9.7 demonstrates the procedure used to calculate the operating cash inflows in that year. The results from this and similar calculations of operating cash inflows for each of the five years for both projects are summarized in Table 9.8.

Table 9.6   Depreciation Expense for Proposed and Present Machines for
             the Ajax Company

Year	Cost (1)	Applicable ACRS cost recovery percentages (from Table 2.7) (2)	Depreciation [(1) × (2)] (3)
With proposed machine			
1	$400,000	15%	$60,000
2	400,000	22	88,000
3	400,000	21	84,000
4	400,000	21	84,000
5	400,000	21	84,000
Totals		100%	$400,000
With present machine			
1	$240,000	21% (year 4 of recovery period)	$ 50,400
2	240,000	21 (year 5 of recovery period)	50,400
3	} Since the present machine is at the end of the third year of its		0
4	} cost recovery period at the time the analysis is performed, it		0
5	} has only the final two years of cost recovery (years 4 and 5) yet applicable.		0
		Total	$100,800[a]

[a] The total of $100,800 represents the book value of the present machine at the end of the third year, which was calculated in the preceding example.

Table 9.7   Calculation of Operating Cash Inflows in Year 4 for Ajax
            Company's Proposed and Present Machines

| | Year 4 | |
Item	With proposed machine	With present machine
Projected earnings before depreciation and taxes[a]	$220,000	$150,000
− Depreciation[b]	84,000	0
Projected earnings before taxes	$136,000	$150,000
− Taxes (40%)	54,400	60,000
Projected earnings after taxes	$ 81,600	$ 90,000
+ Depreciation	84,000	0
Projected operating cash inflow	$165,600	$ 90,000

[a] From column 3 of Table 9.5.
[b] From column 3 of Table 9.6.

Table 9.8   Projected Operating Cash Inflows for
            the Ajax Company

| | Projected operating cash inflows | |
Year	With proposed machine (1)	With present machine (2)
1	$156,000	$146,160
2	167,200	134,160
3	165,600	102,000
4	165,600	90,000
5	165,600	78,000

Interpreting the term *incremental*. The final step in estimating the operating cash inflows to be used in evaluating a proposed project is to calculate the *incremental* or *relevant* cash inflows. Incremental operating cash inflows are needed, since our concern is *only* with how much more or less operating cash will flow into the firm as a result of the proposed project.

EXAMPLE   The figures given for each year in column 2 of Table 9.8 represent the amount of operating cash inflows the Ajax Company will receive without the proposed expenditure. If the proposed machine replaces the present machine, the firm's operating cash inflows for each year will be those shown in column 1 of Table 9.8. Just as earlier we were concerned only with the firm's incremental investment, so here we are concerned only with its incremental, or relevant, operating cash inflows.

Subtracting the operating cash inflows with the present machine from the operating cash inflows with the proposed machine in each year results in the incremental operating cash inflows for each year given in Table 9.9. These are the relevant inflows to be consid-

Table 9.9   Relevant or Incremental
            Operating Cash Inflows for
            the Ajax Company

Year	Relevant operating cash inflow
1	$ 9,840
2	33,040
3	63,600
4	75,600
5	87,600

ered in evaluating the benefits of making a capital expenditure for the proposed machine. ■

An alternative approach for determining relevant operating cash inflows. The operating cash inflows calculated in the preceding section can be determined more directly by finding the changes in revenues, changes in expenses (excluding depreciation), and changes in depreciation; adjusting these changes for taxes to determine the cash flows resulting from them; and adding the cash flows together to get the relevant operating cash inflow for each year. The factors for converting changes in revenues, expenses (excluding depreciation), and depreciation to (after-tax) cash flow changes are given in Table 9.10.

By multiplying the change in each of the items listed by the respective factors given in Table 9.10, the cash flow change caused by these items will result. By summing the individual changes for each year, one can determine the relevant operating cash inflow for the year.

The tax-adjustment factors for revenues and expenses are quite straightforward, but the depreciation adjustment may be a little less clear. The reader may feel that cash flows should be increased by the full amount of depreciation since, to find cash flow from operations, the amount of depreciation is added back to the after-tax profits. The following example should clarify why the depreciation tax-adjustment factor is defined as the tax rate times the change in depreciation.

EXAMPLE   A firm is contemplating whether or not to purchase an asset that is *not* expected to affect the firm's earnings in any way other than by increasing depreciation from its current level of zero to $10,000. The firm expects its earnings before depreciation and taxes to remain at $100,000 as a result of the proposed purchase. The firm, which is in the 40

Table 9.10   Factors for Converting Changes in Revenues,
             Expenses (Excluding Depreciation), and
             Depreciation into Changes in Cash Flow

Change in	Tax-adjustment factor
Revenues	(1 − tax rate)
Expenses (excluding depreciation)	−(1 − tax rate)
Depreciation	tax rate

percent tax bracket, has determined the operating cash flows resulting in each case as shown below:

	With purchase	Without purchase
Earnings before depreciation and taxes	$100,000	$100,000
Less: Depreciation	10,000	0
Earnings before taxes	$ 90,000	$100,000
Less: Taxes (.40)	36,000	40,000
Earnings after taxes	$ 54,000	$ 60,000
Plus: Depreciation	10,000	0
Operating cash flow	$ 64,000	$ 60,000
Difference in operating cash flow attributable to depreciation (.40 × $10,000)	$4000	

It should be clear from these data that the presence of depreciation causes the firm's operating cash flows with depreciation ($64,000) to exceed the operating cash flows resulting without the depreciation deduction ($60,000) by an amount ($4,000) equal to the product of the tax rate (.40) and the difference in depreciation ($10,000). Actually, the depreciation deduction increases cash flows by acting as a "tax shield" that reduces the firm's taxes by $4,000 (from $40,000 to $36,000). In other words, a change in depreciation will change a firm's operating cash flow by an amount equal to the tax rate times the amount of the change. ■

Table 9.11 Determination of Annual Changes in Revenues, Expenses (Excluding Depreciation), and Depreciation for the Ajax Company

Year	Revenues Proposed (1)	Present (2)	Change [(1) − (2)] (3)	Expenses (excl. depr.) Proposed (4)	Present (5)	Change [(4) − (5)] (6)
1	$2,520,000	$2,200,000	$320,000	$2,300,000	$1,990,000	$310,000
2	2,520,000	2,300,000	220,000	2,300,000	2,110,000	190,000
3	2,520,000	2,400,000	120,000	2,300,000	2,230,000	70,000
4	2,520,000	2,400,000	120,000	2,300,000	2,250,000	50,000
5	2,520,000	2,250,000	270,000	2,300,000	2,120,000	180,000

Year	Depreciation Proposed (7)	Present (8)	Change [(7) − (8)] (9)
1	$60,000	$50,400	$ 9,600
2	88,000	50,400	37,600
3	84,000	0	84,000
4	84,000	0	84,000
5	84,000	0	84,000

Note: The data in columns 1, 2, 4, and 5 are from Table 9.5, and the data in columns 7 and 8 are from Table 9.6.

Using the data presented earlier for the Ajax Company, the application of the alternative approach for determining relevant operating cash inflows using the factors given in Table 9.10 for converting changes in revenues, expenses (excluding depreciation), and depreciation into changes in cash flow is illustrated in the following example.

EXAMPLE   Using the Ajax Company data given in Table 9.5, the changes in revenues and expenses (excluding depreciation) are calculated in Table 9.11. Also calculated are the changes in depreciation found using the data from Table 9.6. Using the change data developed for revenues, expenses (excluding depreciation), and depreciation, the relevant operating cash inflows are determined in Table 9.12 by applying the tax adjustment factors presented earlier in Table 9.10. A comparison of the relevant operating cash inflows calculated in Table 9.12 with the operating cash inflows calculated earlier using the income statement approach and presented in Table 9.9 confirms the accuracy of the alternative approach. ■

TERMINAL CASH FLOW

The cash flow resulting from termination and liquidation of a project at the end of its economic life is its *terminal cash flow.* It represents the after-tax cash flows

Table 9.12   Determination of the Relevant Operating Cash Inflows for the Ajax Company Using the Alternative Approach

Year	Item	Amount (1)	Factor (2)	Cash inflow [(1) × (2)] (3)
1	Change in revenues	$320,000	(1 − .4)	$192,000
	Change in expenses	310,000	−(1 − .4)	− 186,000
	Change in depreciation	9,600	.4	3,840
	Relevant operating cash inflow			$ 9,840
2	Change in revenues	$220,000	(1 − .4)	$132,000
	Change in expenses	190,000	−(1 − .4)	− 114,000
	Change in depreciation	37,600	.4	15,040
	Relevant operating cash inflow			$ 33,040
3	Change in revenues	$120,000	(1 − .4)	$ 72,000
	Change in expenses	70,000	−(1 − .4)	− 42,000
	Change in depreciation	84,000	.4	33,600
	Relevant operating cash inflow			$ 63,600
4	Change in revenues	$120,000	(1 − .4)	$ 72,000
	Change in expenses	50,000	−(1 − .4)	− 30,000
	Change in depreciation	84,000	.4	33,600
	Relevant operating cash inflow			$ 75,600
5	Change in revenues	$270,000	(1 − .4)	$162,000
	Change in expenses	180,000	−(1 − .4)	− 108,000
	Change in depreciation	84,000	.4	33,600
	Relevant operating cash inflow			$ 87,600

Table 9.13 The Basic Format for
Determining Terminal
Cash Flow

Proceeds from sale of proposed asset
− Proceeds from sale of present asset
∓ Taxes on sale of proposed asset
± Taxes on sale of present asset
± Change in net working capital
Terminal cash flow

exclusive of operating cash inflows occurring in the final year of the project. When applicable, it is important to recognize these flows because they could significantly affect the capital expenditure decision. Consideration of these flows also provides closure to the analysis, allowing the firm to return to its initial position in terms of the expenditures being considered. Terminal cash flow, which is most often positive, can be calculated for replacement projects using the basic format presented in Table 9.13.

Proceeds from sale of assets. The proceeds from sale of the proposed and present asset represent the amount *net of any removal costs* expected upon termination of the project. For replacement projects, proceeds from both the proposed asset and the present asset must be considered as noted. For expansion, renewal, and other types of capital expenditures, the proceeds from the present asset would be zero. Of course, it is not unusual for the values of assets to be zero at termination of the project.

Taxes on sale of assets. Like the tax calculation on sale of old assets demonstrated earlier as part of finding the initial investment, taxes must be considered on the terminal sale of both the proposed and the present asset for replacement projects, and on only the proposed asset in other cases. The tax calculations apply whenever an asset is sold for a value different from its book value. If the net proceeds from the sale are expected to exceed book value, a tax payment shown as an *outflow* for the proposed asset and an *inflow* for the present asset would occur. A tax rebate shown as a cash *inflow* for the proposed asset and an *outflow* for the present asset would result when the net proceeds from the sale are below book value.[19] Of course, for assets sold to net exactly their book value, no taxes would be due.

Change in net working capital. The change in net working capital reflects the reversion to its original status of any net working capital investment reflected as part of the initial investment. Most often this will show up as a cash inflow attributed to the reduction in net working capital; with termination of the project, the need for the increased net working capital investment is assumed to end.[20] Since the net

---

[19] It is important to recognize that while the sign is negative for tax outflows on the proposed asset, it is positive for tax outflows on the present asset, and vice versa. This treatment is necessary to accomplish the proper netting of the *after-tax* sale proceeds of the proposed asset and the present asset measured at project termination.

[20] As noted earlier, the change in net working capital is for convenience assumed to occur spontaneously — in this case, upon termination of the project. In actuality, it may take a number of months for net working capital to be worked down to zero.

working capital investment is in no way consumed, the amount recovered at termination will equal the amount shown in the calculation of the initial investment. Tax considerations are not involved because the change in net working capital results from an internal reduction or build-up of current accounts. Of course, occasionally net working capital will not be changed by the proposed investment and therefore will not enter into the analysis.

It should be clear that the terminal value calculation, when applicable, involves the same procedures as those used to find the initial investment. The following example demonstrates how the terminal cash flow is calculated for a replacement decision.

EXAMPLE   Continuing with the Ajax Company presented in the earlier examples, assume that the firm expects to be able to liquidate the proposed machine at the end of its five-year life to net $50,000 after paying removal costs. The present machine can be liquidated at the end of the five years to net $0 because it will then be completely obsolete. The firm expects to recover its $17,000 net working capital investment upon termination of the project. As noted earlier, Ajax is in the 40 percent ordinary tax bracket, and long-term capital gains are taxed at a rate of 30 percent.

From the analysis of the operating cash inflows presented earlier, it can be seen that both the proposed and present machines will be fully depreciated and therefore have a book value of zero at the end of the five years. Since the sale price of $50,000 for the proposed machine is below its initial installed cost of $400,000 but greater than its book value of $0, taxes will have to be paid only on the recaptured depreciation of $50,000 ($50,000 sale proceeds − $0 book value). Applying the ordinary tax rate of 40 percent to the $50,000 results in a tax of $20,000 (.40 × $50,000) on the sale of the proposed machine. Since the present machine would net $0 at termination and its book value would be $0, no tax would be due on sale of the present machine. Substituting the tax values along with the proceeds values for each machine and the net working capital recovery into the format in Table 9.13 results in the terminal cash inflow value of $47,000 derived below. This represents the after-tax cash flow, exclusive of operating cash inflows, occurring upon termination of the project at the end of year 5.

Proceeds from sale of proposed machine	$50,000
− Proceeds from sale of present machine	0
− Taxes on sale of proposed machine	20,000
+ Taxes on sale of present machine	0
+ Change in net working capital	17,000
Terminal cash flow	$47,000

RELEVANT CASH FLOWS

The three cash flow components — initial investment, operating cash inflows, and terminal cash flow — together represent a project's *relevant cash flows.* These relevant cash flows can be viewed as the incremental, after-tax cash flows attributable to the proposed investment; they represent, in a cash flow sense, how much better or worse off the firm will be if it chooses to implement the proposal.

EXAMPLE   The relevant cash flows for the Ajax Company's proposed replacement expenditure can now be presented. They are shown graphically in Figure 9.4. As the figure shows, they follow a conventional pattern (an initial outlay followed by a series of inflows). Techniques

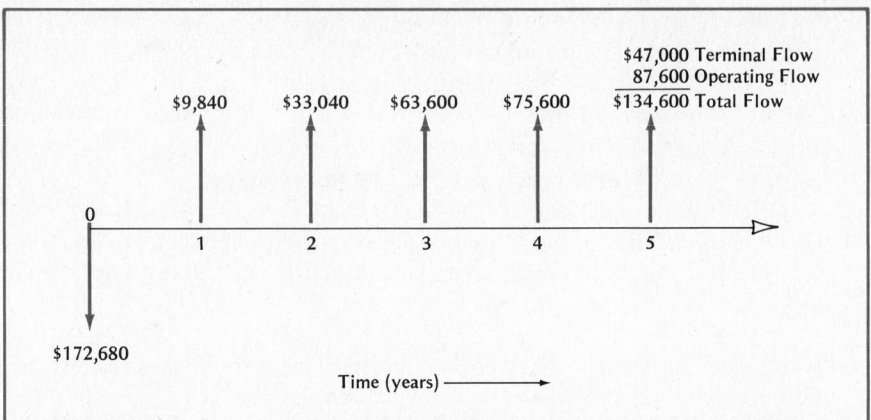

$9,840 $33,040 $63,600 $75,600 $47,000 Terminal Flow
                                        87,600 Operating Flow
                                       $134,600 Total Flow

0
  1   2   3   4   5

$172,680

Time (years) ⟶

Figure 9.4   The Ajax Company's relevant cash flows with the proposed machine

for analyzing this type of pattern to determine whether to undertake a proposed capital investment are discussed in Chapters 10 and 11. ■

CHAPTER SUMMARY

• Capital budgeting is the process used to evaluate and select long-term investments consistent with the goal of owner wealth maximization.

• Capital expenditures are long-term investments that generate benefits over a period greater than one year. They are made to expand, replace, or renew fixed assets or to obtain some other less tangible benefit over a long period.

• Regardless of the motive for capital expenditures, the basic format for analyzing proposals is the same.

• The capital budgeting process contains five distinct but interrelated steps: proposal generation, review and analysis, decision making, implementation, and follow-up.

• Capital expenditure proposals may be independent or mutually exclusive. Proposals are mutually exclusive if the acceptance of one eliminates the others from consideration. Independent proposals are not eliminated from consideration due to the acceptance of a given project.

• Most firms have only limited funds for capital investments and must ration them among carefully selected projects. To make investment decisions when proposals are mutually exclusive or capital must be rationed, projects must be ranked; otherwise accept-reject decisions must be made.

• Conventional cash flow patterns consist of an initial outflow followed by a series of inflows; any other pattern is nonconventional. These patterns can be either annuities or mixed streams.

• The relevant cash flows necessary for making capital budgeting decisions are the initial investment, the incremental after-tax operating cash inflows, and the terminal cash flow associated with a given proposal.

• The initial investment is the initial outlay required, taking into account purchase and installation costs, proceeds from sale of replaced assets, taxes (including the investment tax credit), and any change in net working capital.

• Incremental after-tax operating cash inflows are the additional cash flows received as a result of implementing a proposal.

● There are two basic approaches for determining the relevant operating cash inflows. One uses the income statement format to estimate the relevant operating cash inflows; the other is an alternative approach that directly adjusts changes in revenues, expenses (excluding depreciation), and depreciation for tax effects to determine the relevant operating cash inflows.

● The terminal cash flow results from liquidation of a project at the end of its economic life. It represents the after-tax cash flows, exclusive of operating cash inflows, occurring in the final year of the project. They are generally positive and found by subtracting taxes on sale of assets from the proceeds from asset sale and adjusting for any changes in net working capital.

KEY TERMS

accept-reject approach	installation costs
capital asset	labor-intensive firm
capital budgeting	liquidation value
capital budgeting process	mutually exclusive projects
capital expenditure	net working capital
capital-intensive firm	nonconventional cash flow pattern
capital rationing	operating cash inflows
change in net working capital	postimplementation audit
conventional cash flow pattern	ranking approach
current expenditure	relevant cash flows
earning assets	removal costs
incremental after-tax cash inflows	terminal cash flow
independent projects	unlimited funds
initial investment	

QUESTIONS

9-1 What does the fact that a firm is described as "capital-intensive" reveal about its production process and level of fixed assets? Why are fixed assets often referred to as *earning assets?*

9-2 What is *capital budgeting?* How do capital expenditures relate to the capital budgeting process? Are all capital expenditures fixed assets? Explain.

9-3 What are the basic motives described in the chapter for making capital expenditures? Discuss, compare, and contrast them.

9-4 Briefly describe each of the steps — proposal generation, review and analysis, decision making, implementation, and follow-up — involved in the capital budgeting process.

9-5 Define and differentiate between each of the following sets of capital budgeting terms.
  a Independent versus mutually exclusive projects
  b Unlimited funds versus capital rationing
  c Accept-reject versus ranking approach
  d Conventional versus nonconventional cash flows
  e Annuity versus mixed stream cash flows

9-6 Why is it important to evaluate capital budgeting projects on the basis of *incremental after-tax cash flows?* Why not use accounting data instead of cash flows?

9-7 Describe each of the following components of the initial investment and explain how the initial investment is calculated using them.

    a Cost of new asset
    b Installation costs
    c Proceeds from sale of old assets
    d Taxes on sale of old assets
    e Investment tax credit on new asset
    f Change in net working capital

9-8   Why are *installation costs* included in the cost of a new asset? What is the IRS's rationale for forcing a firm to include installation costs as part of the purchase price and forcing the firm to deduct any *removal costs* from the proceeds from the sale of an old asset?

9-9   What four tax situations may result from sale of an asset that is being replaced? Describe the tax treatment in each situation.

9-10 Using the framework for calculating initial investment given in this chapter, explain how a firm would calculate the value of depreciation needed to find operating cash inflows. How is the depreciation of an asset determined under the *Accelerated Cost Recovery System (ACRS)*?

9-11 Given the earnings before depreciation and taxes associated with a present asset and a proposed replacement for it, how would the projected operating cash inflows associated with the decision be calculated?

9-12 Two methods of calculating operating cash inflows are presented in this chapter. Explain how the alternative approach can yield the same result as the more detailed income statement approach. Why does the *alternative approach* use a different tax-adjustment factor for depreciation?

9-13 What is the *terminal cash flow*? Explain how the value of this cash flow is calculated for replacement projects.

9-14 Diagram and describe the three elements representing the *relevant cash flows* for a conventional capital budgeting project.

PROBLEMS

9-1   **(Classification of Expenditures)** Given the following list of outlays, indicate whether each would normally be considered a capital or a current expenditure. Explain your answers.
    a An initial lease payment of $5,000 for electronic point-of-sale cash register systems.
    b An outlay of $20,000 to purchase patent rights from the inventor.
    c An outlay of $80,000 for a large research and development program.
    d An $80,000 investment in a portfolio of marketable securities.
    e A $300 outlay for an office machine.
    f An outlay of $2,000 for a new machine tool.
    g An outlay of $240,000 for a new building.
    h An outlay of $1,000 for a marketing research report.

9-2   **(Basic Terminology)** A firm is considering the following three separate situations.
    Situation A: Build either a small office building or a convenience store on a parcel of land located in a high-traffic area. Adequate funding is available, and both projects are known to be acceptable. The office building will require an initial investment of $620,000 and is expected to provide operating cash inflows of $40,000 per year for 20 years; the convenience store is expected to cost $500,000 and provide a growing stream of operating cash inflows over its 20-year life. The initial operating cash inflow is $20,000 and will increase by 5 percent each year.

Situation B: Replace a machine with a new one requiring a $60,000 initial investment and providing operating cash inflows of $10,000 per year for the first five years. At the end of year 5, a machine overhaul costing $20,000 is required, and after it is completed, expected operating cash inflows are $10,000 in year 6, $7,000 in year 7, $4,000 in year 8, and $1,000 in year 9, at the end of which the machine will be scrapped.

Situation C: Invest in any or all of the four machines whose relevant cash flows are given in the following table. The firm has $500,000 budgeted to fund these machines, all of which are known to be acceptable. Initial investment for each machine is $250,000.

<table>
<tr><td></td><td colspan="4" align="center">Operating cash inflows</td></tr>
<tr><td>Year</td><td>Machine 1</td><td>Machine 2</td><td>Machine 3</td><td>Machine 4</td></tr>
<tr><td>1</td><td>$ 50,000</td><td>$70,000</td><td>$65,000</td><td>$90,000</td></tr>
<tr><td>2</td><td>70,000</td><td>70,000</td><td>65,000</td><td>80,000</td></tr>
<tr><td>3</td><td>90,000</td><td>70,000</td><td>80,000</td><td>70,000</td></tr>
<tr><td>4</td><td>−30,000</td><td>70,000</td><td>80,000</td><td>60,000</td></tr>
<tr><td>5</td><td>100,000</td><td>70,000</td><td>−20,000</td><td>50,000</td></tr>
</table>

For each situation or project, indicate
a   Whether the *situation* is independent or mutually exclusive.
b   Whether the availability of funds is limited or if capital rationing exists.
c   Whether accept-reject or ranking decisions are required.
d   Whether each *project's* cash flows are conventional or nonconventional.
e   Whether each *project's* cash flow pattern is an annuity or mixed stream.

9-3   **(Tax Calculations)**   For each of the following cases, describe the various taxable components of the funds received through sale of the asset and determine the total taxes resulting from the transaction. Assume a 40 percent ordinary tax rate and a 30 percent long-term capital gains tax. The asset was purchased for $80,000 two years ago and is being depreciated under ACRS over its five-year normal recovery period. (See Table 2.7 on page 34 for the applicable depreciation percentages.)
a   The asset is sold for $85,000.
b   The asset is sold for $65,000.
c   The asset is sold for $50,400.
d   The asset is sold for $35,000.

9-4   **(Investment Tax Credit Calculation)**   Ford Manufacturing is contemplating acquisition of two new assets. Asset A has a three-year normal recovery period, costs $73,000, and has no installation cost. Asset B has a five-year normal recovery, costs $400,000, and requires $30,000 in installation costs.
a   Using Option 2 summarized in Table 9.3, calculate the investment tax credit for each asset.
b   Describe the impact these credits will have on the size of the initial investment associated with each project.
c   Under the procedure used in **a**, how much depreciable value will result from each of these assets?

9-5   **(Change in Net Working Capital Calculation)**   Nicor Corporation is considering the purchase of a new machine to replace one they feel is obsolete. The firm has total current assets of $920,000 and total current liabilities of $640,000. As a result of the proposed replacement, the following *changes* are anticipated in the levels of the current asset and current liability accounts noted.

Account	Change
Accruals	+$ 40,000
Marketable securities	0
Inventory	− 10,000
Accounts payable	+ 90,000
Notes payable	0
Accounts receivable	+ 150,000
Cash	+ 15,000

    a Using the information given, calculate the change, if any, in net working capital expected to result from the proposed replacement action.

    b Explain why a change in these current accounts would be relevant to the analysis of the proposed capital expenditure.

    c Would the change in net working capital enter into any of the other cash flow components comprising the relevant cash flows? Explain.

9-6 **(Relevant Cash Flow Pattern Fundamentals)** For each of the following projects, determine the cash flows for each year, classify the cash flow pattern, and diagram the pattern. The investment tax credit (ITC) is applicable; use the schedule given in Table 9.3 to calculate the ITC.

    a A project costing $120,000 that generates annual operating cash inflows of $25,000 for the next 18 years. In each of the 18 years, maintenance of the project will require a $5,000 cash outflow.

    b A new machine costing $85,000. Sale of the old machine will yield $30,000 after taxes. Operating cash inflows generated by the replacement will amount to $20,000 in each year of a six-year period. At the end of six years, the terminal cash flow will be $15,000.

    c An asset costing $2 million that will yield annual operating cash inflows of $300,000 for each of the next ten years. Operating cash outlays will be $20,000 for each year except year 6, when an overhaul requiring an additional cash outlay of $500,000 will be required. The asset has a terminal cash flow of $250,000 at the end of year 10.

 9-7 **(Initial Investment — Basic Calculation)** Matthew T. Boone, Inc., is considering the purchase of a new grading machine to replace the existing one. The existing machine was purchased three years ago at an installed cost of $20,000; it was being depreciated under ACRS over its five-year normal recovery period. (See Table 2.7 on page 34 for the applicable depreciation percentages.) The existing machine is expected to have a usable life of at least five more years. The new machine would cost $35,000 and require $5,000 in installation costs; it would be depreciated over its five-year normal recovery period under ACRS. Although no investment tax credit was taken on the existing machine, an 8 percent credit would be taken on the new one, if acquired. The existing machine can currently be sold for $25,000 without incurring any removal costs. A $20,000 increase in net working capital is expected to accompany acquisition of the new grading machine. The firm pays 40 percent taxes on ordinary income and 30 percent on long-term capital gains. Calculate the *initial investment* associated with the proposed purchase of a new grading machine.

 9-8 **(Initial Investment at Various Sale Prices)** American Castings Corporation is considering replacement of one machine with another. The old machine was purchased three years ago for an installed cost of $10,000. The firm is depreciating the machine under ACRS over its five-year normal recovery period. (See Table 2.7 on page 34 for the applicable depreciation percentages.) The new machine costs $24,000 and requires $2,000 in installation costs. Although no investment tax credit was taken on the old machine, an 8 percent credit will be taken on the new one. As a result of purchasing the new machine, current assets are expected to increase by $30,000 and current liabilities by $20,000. Assume the firm has a 40 percent marginal tax rate on ordinary income and a 30 percent tax rate on long-term capital gains. In each of the following cases, calculate the initial investment of the replacement.

a   American Castings Corporation (ACC) sells the old machine for $11,000.

b   ACC sells the old machine for $7,000.

c   ACC sells the old machine for $4,200.

d   ACC sells the old machine for $3,000.

e   ACC must pay $2,000 to have the old machine removed and can only dispose of it by giving it away.

9-9   (**Depreciation and Operating Cash Inflows**)   A firm is evaluating the acquisition of an asset costing $64,000 and requiring $4,000 in installation costs. If the firm depreciates the asset under ACRS over its five-year normal recovery period (see Table 2.7 on page 34 for the applicable depreciation percentages),

a   Determine the annual depreciation charge.

b   If the firm has a 40 percent tax rate on ordinary income, what effect does this depreciation have on the firm's operating cash inflows? Explain your answer.

9-10   (**Incremental Operating Cash Inflows — Income Statement Approach**)   A firm is considering renewing its equipment to meet increased demand for its product. The cost of equipment modifications will be $1.9 million plus $100,000 in installation costs. The firm will depreciate the equipment modifications using ACRS over its five-year normal recovery period. (See Table 2.7 on page 34 for the applicable depreciation percentages.) Sales from the renewal should amount to $900,000 per year, and operating expenses and other costs (excluding depreciation) will amount to 40 percent of sales. The firm has an ordinary tax rate of 40 percent. (*Note:* Ignore any investment tax credit.)

a   What incremental earnings before depreciation and taxes will result from the renewal?

b   What incremental earnings after taxes will result from the renewal?

c   What incremental operating cash inflows will result from the renewal?

9-11   (**Incremental Operating Cash Inflows — Alternative Tax-Adjustment Approach**)   Tex-Tube Corporation is considering replacement of a machine. The replacement will reduce operating expenses by $8,000 per year for each of the five years the new machine is expected to last. Although the old machine has zero book value, it can be used for five more years. The depreciable value of the new machine is $48,000; the firm uses ACRS depreciation over the machine's five-year normal recovery period (see Table 2.7 on page 34 for the applicable depreciation percentages) to depreciate it and is subject to a 40 percent tax rate on ordinary income. Use the alternative tax-adjustment approach (see factors in Table 9.10) to estimate the incremental operating cash inflows generated by the replacement.

9-12   (**Incremental Operating Cash Inflows**)   The Dennis Tool Company has been considering replacement of a fully depreciated lathe that will last five more years. The replacement is expected to have a five-year life and depreciation charges of $1500 in year 1, $2200 in year 2, and $2100 in years 3, 4, and 5. The firm estimates the following *earnings before depreciation and taxes* with and without the proposed replacement. The firm has a 40 percent tax rate on ordinary income.

Year	With replacement	Without replacement
1	$10,000	$10,000
2	11,000	10,000
3	12,000	10,000
4	13,000	10,000
5	14,000	10,000

a   Calculate the after-tax operating cash inflows associated with each machine.

b   Calculate the incremental operating cash inflows resulting from the acquisition of the new machine.

c   Diagram the relevant operating cash inflows associated with the replacement decision.

9-13 (**Terminal Cash Flows — Various Lives and Sale Prices**)   Looner Industries is currently analyzing the purchase of a new machine costing $160,000, requiring $15,000 in installation costs, and having a five-year normal recovery period. Resulting from purchase of this machine is an increase in net working capital of $30,000 to support the expanded level of operations. The firm plans to depreciate the asset using ACRS and expects to sell the machine to net $10,000 before taxes at the end of its usable life.

a   Calculate the terminal cash flow for a usable life of (1) three years, (2) five years, and (3) seven years.

b   Discuss the effect of usable life on terminal cash flows using your findings in **a**.

c   Assuming a five-year usable life, calculate the terminal cash flow if the machine were sold to net (1) $0 or (2) $170,000 (before taxes) at the end of the five years.

d   Discuss the effect of sale price on terminal cash flows using your findings in **c**.

9-14 (**Terminal Cash Flow — Replacement Decision**)   J and S Enterprises is considering replacing a fully depreciated machine having a remaining useful life of ten years with a newer more sophisticated machine. The new machine will cost $200,000 and require $30,000 in installation costs. It will be depreciated using ACRS over its five-year normal recovery period. A $25,000 increase in net working capital will be required to support the new machine. The firm plans to evaluate the potential replacement over a four-year period. They estimate that the old machine could be sold at the end of four years to net $15,000 before taxes; the new machine at the end of four years will be worth $75,000 before taxes. Calculate the terminal cash flow relevant to the proposed purchase of the new machine. The firm is subject to a 40 percent ordinary tax rate and pays 30 percent taxes on long-term capital gains.

9-15 (**Relevant Cash Flows — No Terminal Value**)   The R. E. Williams Company is considering replacing an existing piece of machinery with a more sophisticated machine. The old machine was purchased three years ago at a cost of $50,000, and this amount was being depreciated using ACRS over a five-year normal recovery period. The machine has five years of economic life remaining. The new machine being considered will cost $76,000 and requires $4,000 in installation costs. The new machine would be depreciated using ACRS over a five-year normal recovery period. An 8 percent investment tax credit can be taken on the installed cost of the new machine; no investment tax credit was taken on the old machine. The old machine can currently be sold for $55,000 without incurring any removal costs. The firm pays 40 percent taxes on ordinary income and 30 percent on long-term capital gains. The earnings before depreciation and taxes associated with the new and the old machine for the next five years are given below. (Table 2.7 on page 34 contains the applicable ACRS depreciation percentages.)

| | Earnings before depreciation and taxes | |
Year	New machine	Old machine
1	$30,000	$14,000
2	30,000	16,000
3	30,000	20,000
4	30,000	18,000
5	30,000	14,000

a Calculate the initial investment associated with replacement of the old machine with the new one.

b Use the income statement approach to determine the relevant operating cash inflows associated with the proposed replacement.

c Use the alternative approach to determine the relevant operating cash inflows associated with the proposed replacement.

d Compare and discuss your computations in **b** and **c**. Which approach is most readily understood? Which is easiest to use?

e Diagram the relevant cash flows associated with the proposed replacement decision.

 9-16 (**Integrative — Determining Relevant Cash Flows**) A machine currently in use was originally purchased two years ago for $40,000. The machine is being depreciated under ACRS using its five-year normal recovery period; it has three more years of usable life remaining. The current machine can be sold today to net $42,000. A new machine, having a three-year normal recovery period, can be purchased at a price of $140,000. It will require $10,000 to install. The firm is eligible to take a 4 percent investment tax credit on the installed cost of the new machine; the investment tax credit was not taken on the current machine. If the new machine is acquired, net working capital is expected to increase by $20,000. With the new machine, *earnings before depreciation and taxes* are expected to increase from $70,000 to $120,000 in the first year and from $70,000 to $130,000 in each of the next two years. At the end of three years, the market value of the old machine would equal zero, but the new machine could be sold to net $35,000 before taxes. Ordinary corporate income is taxed at an annual rate of 40 percent, and long-term capital gains are subject to a 30 percent tax. (Table 2.7 on page 34 contains the applicable ACRS depreciation percentages.)

a Determine the initial investment associated with the proposed replacement decision.

b Calculate the relevant operating cash inflows for years 1 to 3 associated with the proposed replacement decision.

c Calculate the terminal cash flow associated with the proposed replacement decision.

d Diagram the relevant cash flows found in **a, b,** and **c** associated with the proposed replacement decision.

 9-17 (**Integrative — Determining Relevant Cash Flows**) The Salazar Company is contemplating the purchase of a new high-speed widget grinder to replace the existing grinder. The existing grinder was purchased two years ago at an installed cost of $60,000; it was being depreciated under ACRS over its five-year normal recovery period. The existing grinder is expected to have a usable life of at least five more years. The new grinder would cost $105,000 and require $5,000 in installation costs; it would be depreciated over its five-year normal recovery period using ACRS.

$$\text{Project B: } \frac{\$45,000}{2} = \$22,500$$

Project A requires an average investment of $21,000; project B requires an average investment of $22,500.

Ratio of the two. Dividing the average profits after taxes by the average investment results in the average rate of return for each project.

$$\text{Project A: } \frac{\$5,600}{\$21,000} = 26.67\%$$

$$\text{Project B: } \frac{\$5,000}{\$22,500} = 22.22\%$$

The results indicate that project A is preferable to project B because project A has a higher average rate of return. The actual percentages can be interpreted as the annual accounting rate of return expected on the average investment.

Methods of calculation. A number of alternate methods of calculating the average rate of return are available. One approach involves using average annual *cash inflows* instead of average annual accounting profits as the numerator. This approach has an appeal, since using returns measured as cash flows is in line with the financial rather than the accounting viewpoint. Another variation is to use the initial investment instead of the average investment as the denominator of the ratio. This cuts the calculated values in half. Thus the average rates of return for projects A and B would be 13.33 percent and 11.11 percent, respectively. It is up to the decision maker to determine which method provides the most useful information. To make decisions based on an average rate of return, the decision maker must compare the average rate of return to a predetermined cutoff rate or minimum acceptable average rate of return.

Pros and cons of the average rate of return. The most favorable aspect of using the average rate of return to evaluate projects is its ease of calculation. The only input required is projected profits, a figure that should be easily obtainable. There are three major weaknesses of this approach, however. The key conceptual weakness is the inability to specify the appropriate average rate of return in light of the wealth maximization goal. The second weakness stems from the use of accounting data. This weakness can be overcome by using average cash inflows in the numerator in Equation 10.1, as suggested in the preceding section. The third major weakness is that this method ignores the time factor in the value of money. Firms generally prefer to receive cash inflows today rather than in the future. The indifference to the time factor can be illustrated using Table 10.2.

Each project for which data are given in Table 10.2 has an average rate of return of 40 percent. Although the average rates of return are the same for all three projects, the financial manager would not be indifferent to them; he or she would

Table 10.2 Calculation of the Average Rate of Return for Three Alternative Capital Expenditure Projects

	Project X	Project Y	Project Z
(1) Initial investment *(II)*	$20,000	$20,000	$20,000
(2) Average investment [(1) ÷ 2]	$10,000	$10,000	$10,000
Year *(t)*	Profits after taxes (PAT_t)		
1	$ 2,000	$ 4,000	$ 6,000
2	3,000	4,000	5,000
3	4,000	4,000	4,000
4	5,000	4,000	3,000
5	6,000	4,000	2,000
(3) Average profits after taxes	$ 4,000	$ 4,000	$ 4,000
(4) Average rate of return [(3) ÷ (2)]	40%	40%	40%

prefer project Z to project Y and project Y to project X because project Z has the most favorable profit flow pattern, project Y has the next most favorable pattern, and project X has the least attractive pattern.

PAYBACK PERIOD

Payback periods are commonly used to evaluate proposed investments. The *payback period* is the number of years required to recover the initial investment. It is calculated by figuring *exactly* how long it takes to recover the initial investment from *cash inflows.*[3] For instance, in the case of project A, $42,000 must be recovered. After one year, $14,000 will be recovered; after two years, a total of $28,000 will be recovered ($14,000 in year 1 plus $14,000 in year 2). At the end of the third year, exactly $42,000 will be recovered ($28,000 total from years 1 and 2 plus the $14,000 recovered in year 3). The payback period for project A is therefore exactly three years. In the case of any *annuity,* such as project A, the payback period can be found by dividing the initial investment by the annual cash inflow ($42,000 ÷ $14,000 = 3 years).

Since project B generates a *mixed stream* of cash inflows, the calculation of the payback period is not quite as clear-cut. In year 1, the firm will recover $28,000 of its $45,000 initial investment. At the end of year 2, $40,000 ($28,000 from year 1 plus $12,000 from year 2) will be recovered. At the end of year 3, $50,000 ($40,000 from years 1 and 2 plus the $10,000 from year 3) will be recovered. Since the amount received by the end of year 3 is more than the initial investment of $45,000, the payback period is somewhere between two and three years. Only $5000 ($45,000 − $40,000) must be recovered during year 3. Actually, $10,000 is recovered, but only 50 percent of this cash inflow ($5000 ÷ $10,000) is needed to

---

[3] An alternative and less exact approach for calculating the payback period is available. The so-called *average payback period* is found by dividing the initial investment by the average cash inflows. Since this approach only approximates the actual payback period, it does not warrant attention.

complete the payback of the initial $45,000.[4] The payback period for project B is therefore 2.50 years (2 years plus 50 percent of year 3).

Project B would be preferred to project A since the former has a shorter payback period (2.50 years versus 3.00 years). Often companies establish a maximum payback period so that projects with longer paybacks are rejected; other projects will be accepted or further evaluated using a more sophisticated capital budgeting technique. In other words, the payback period is commonly used as an initial screening device for projects.

Pros and cons of payback periods. The payback period is a better measure than the average rate of return because it considers cash flows rather than accounting profits. The payback period is also a superior measure (compared to the average rate of return) in that it gives *some* implicit consideration to the timing of cash flows and therefore the time value of money. A final reason many firms use the payback period as a decision criterion or as a supplement to sophisticated decision criteria is that it is a measure of risk. The payback period reflects the liquidity of a project and thereby the risk of recovering the initial investment.[5] The more liquid an investment, the less risky it is assumed to be, and vice versa. Companies making international investments in countries with high inflation rates, unstable governments, or other problems use the payback period as a primary decision criterion because of their inability to forecast or measure such risks.

There are three primary disadvantages of using the payback period. The major disadvantage is that, like the average rate of return, this method is not able to specify the appropriate payback period in light of the wealth maximization goal. A second weakness is that this approach fails to take *fully* into account the time factor in the value of money; by measuring how quickly the firm recovers its initial investment, it only implicitly considers the timing of cash flows.[6] A third weakness is the failure to recognize cash flows that occur after the payback period. This weakness can be illustrated using the two investment opportunities given in Table 10.3. The payback period for project X is two years; for project Y, it is three years. Strict adherence to the payback approach suggests that project X is preferable to project Y. However, if we look beyond the payback period, we see that project X returns only an additional $1200 ($1000 in year 3, $100 in year 4, and $100 in year 5), while project Y returns an additional $7000 ($4000 in year 4 and $3000 in year 5). Based on this information, it appears that project Y is preferable. The payback

---

[4] This method of finding fractional payback periods implicitly assumes that the cash inflows from the project are received at a constant rate throughout a year. Although this may not be the case, this method is believed to provide the best estimate of payback periods.

[5] The liquidity of a capital project is determined by the speed with which the firm recovers the initial investment. The more liquid a project (the quicker the payback), the less risk, and vice versa. The longer one must wait to recover an investment, the greater the possibility of a calamity. The relationship between liquidity and risk is discussed in greater detail in Chapter 15.

[6] To consider differences in timing *explicitly* when using the payback method, the *present-value payback period* is sometimes used. It is found by first finding the present value of the cash inflows at the appropriate discount rate and then calculating the payback period using the present value of the cash inflows.

7. Calculate the *NPV* using the new discount rate. Repeat step 6. Stop as soon as two *consecutive* discount rates that cause the *NPV* to be positive and negative, respectively, have been found.[13] Whichever of these two rates causes the *NPV* to be closest to zero is the *IRR* to the nearest 1 percent.

In a number of the steps, the use of subjective estimates was suggested. A subjective feel for the amount of adjustment needed in the estimated *IRR* cannot be taught, but in working a number of these mixed-stream problems, one tends to develop such a feel. Another point that should be clarified is that step 4 can actually be skipped. The only advantage of step 4 is that it should provide a more accurate first estimate of the project's *IRR*.

EXAMPLE   The application of the seven-step procedure for finding the internal rate of return of a mixed stream of cash inflows can be illustrated using the Bosco Company's project B. The cash flows associated with the project were presented in Table 10.1.

1. Summing the cash inflows for years 1 through 5 results in total cash inflows of $70,000, which, when divided by the number of years in the project's life, results in an average annual cash inflow or "fake annuity" of $14,000 [($28,000 + $12,000 + $10,000 + $10,000 + $10,000) ÷ 5].
2. Dividing the initial outlay of $45,000 by the average annual cash inflow of $14,000 (calculated in step 1) results in a "fake payback period" (or present value of an annuity factor, *PVIFA*) of 3.214 years.
3. In Table A-4, the factor closest to 3.214 for five years is 3.199, the factor for a discount rate of 17 percent. The starting estimate of the *IRR* is therefore 17 percent.
4. Since the actual early-year cash inflows are greater than the average cash inflows of $14,000, a *subjective* increase of 2 percent is made in the discount rate. This makes the estimated *IRR* 19 percent.
5. Using the present-value interest factors *(PVIF)* for 19 percent and the correct year from Table A-3, the net present value of the mixed stream is calculated as follows:

Year *(t)*	Cash inflows *(CF_t)* (1)	$PVIF_{19\%,t}$ (2)	Present value at 19% [(1) × (2)] (3)
1	$28,000	.840	$23,520
2	12,000	.706	8,472
3	10,000	.593	5,930
4	10,000	.499	4,990
5	10,000	.419	4,190
		PV of cash inflows	$47,102
		— Initial investment *(II)*	45,000
		Net present value	$ 2,102

6 and 7. Since the net present value of $2102 calculated in step 5 is greater than zero,

---

[13] A shortcut method is to find a discount rate that results in a positive *NPV* and another that results in a negative *NPV*. Using only these two values, one can interpolate between the two discount rates to find the *IRR*. This approach, which may be nearly as accurate as that described above, can guarantee an answer after only two *NPV* calculations. Of course, because interpolation involves a straight-line approximation to an exponential function, the wider the interpolation interval, the less accurate the estimate.

EXAMPLE To prepare net present value profiles for Bosco Company's two projects, A and B, the first step is to develop a number of discount-rate—net-present-value coordinates. Three coordinates can easily be obtained for each project; they are at discount rates of 0 percent, 10 percent (the cost of capital, k), and the *IRR*. The net present value at a 0 percent discount rate is found by merely adding all the cash inflows and subtracting the initial investment. Using the data in Table 10.1, for project A we get ($14,000 + $14,000 + $14,000 + $14,000 + $14,000) − $42,000 = $28,000, and for project B we get ($28,000 + $12,000 + $10,000 + $10,000 + $10,000) − $45,000 = $25,000. The net present values for projects A and B at the 10 percent cost of capital were found to be $11,074 and $10,914, respectively, in Table 10.4. Since the *IRR*, as we have seen, is the discount rate for which net present value equals zero, the *IRR*s of 20 percent for project A and 22 percent for project B result in $0 *NPV*s. The three sets of coordinates for each of the projects are summarized in Table 10.5.

Plotting the data in Table 10.5 on a set of discount rate-*NPV* axes results in the net present value profiles for projects A and B plotted in Figure 10.1. An analysis of Figure 10.1 indicates that for any discount rate less than approximately 10.7 percent, the *NPV* for

Table 10.5 Discount Rate-*NPV* Coordinates for Projects A and B

Discount rate	Net present value	
	Project A	Project B
0%	$28,000	$25,000
10%	11,074	10,914
20%	0	—
22%	—	0

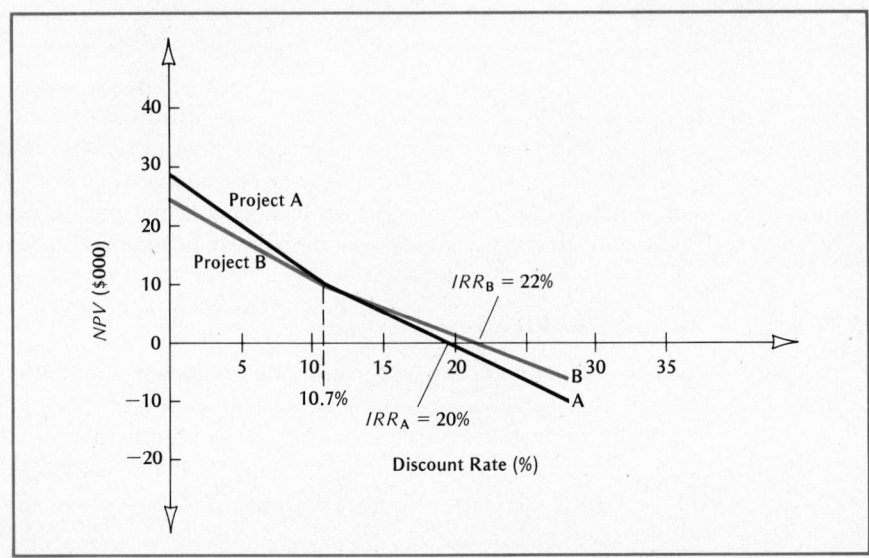

Figure 10.1 Net present value profiles for projects A and B

project A is greater than the *NPV* for project B. Beyond this point, the *NPV* for B is greater than that for A. Since the net present value profiles for projects A and B cross at a positive *NPV,* the *IRR*s for the projects cause conflicting rankings whenever they are compared to *NPV*s calculated at discount rates below 10.7 percent. ■

CONFLICTING RANKINGS

The possibility of *conflicting rankings* of projects by *NPV* and *IRR* should be clear. Ranking is an important consideration when projects are mutually exclusive or when capital rationing is necessary. When projects are mutually exclusive, ranking enables the firm to determine the best project from a financial viewpoint. When capital rationing is necessary, ranking projects may not determine the group of projects to accept, but it will provide a logical starting point.

Conflicts in project rankings using *NPV* and *IRR* result from *differences in the magnitude and timing of cash flows.* Although these two factors can be used to explain conflicting rankings, the underlying cause results from the implicit assumption concerning the reinvestment of *intermediate cash inflows* — cash inflows received prior to termination of the project. *NPV* assumes that intermediate cash inflows are reinvested at the cost of capital, k; *IRR* assumes that intermediate cash inflows can be invested at a rate equal to the project's *IRR*.[15]

In general, projects with similar-sized investments[16] and lower early-year cash inflows (lower cash inflows in the early years) tend to be preferred at lower discount rates, whereas projects having higher early-year cash inflows (higher cash inflows in the early years) tend to be preferred at higher discount rates. These behaviors can be explained by the fact that at high discount rates, later-year cash inflows tend to be severely penalized in present value terms. Of course, annuities (projects with level cash inflows) cannot be characterized in this fashion; they can best be evaluated in comparison to other cash inflow streams. Table 10.6 summarizes the preferences associated with extreme discount rates and dissimilar cash inflow patterns.

Table 10.6   Preferences Associated with Extreme Discount Rates and Dissimilar Cash Inflow Patterns

	Cash inflow pattern	
Discount rate	Lower early-year cash inflows	Higher early-year cash inflows
Low	Preferred	Not preferred
High	Not preferred	Preferred

[15] The *reinvestment rate assumption* is briefly discussed in the next section. Here, attention is given to classifying cash inflow patterns and describing how they can cause conflicting rankings.

[16] Because differences in the relative sizes of initial investments can also affect conflicts in rankings, the initial investments are assumed to be similar. This permits isolation of the effect of differences in magnitude and timing of cash inflows on project rankings.

EXAMPLE In an earlier example, the Bosco Company's projects A and B were found to have conflicting rankings at the firm's 10 percent cost of capital. This finding is depicted in Figure 10.1. If we review each project's cash inflow pattern as presented in Table 10.1, we can see that although the projects require similar initial investments, they have dissimilar cash inflow patterns — project A has level cash inflows and project B has higher early-year inflows. Table 10.6 indicates that project B would be preferred over project A at high discount rates. Figure 10.1 shows that this is in fact the case. At a discount rate in excess of 10.7 percent, project B's NPV rises above that of project A. Clearly the magnitude and timing of the cash inflows does affect their rankings. ∎

Although the classification of cash inflow patterns in Table 10.6 is useful in explaining conflicting rankings, differences in the magnitude and timing of cash inflows do not guarantee conflicts in ranking. In general, the greater the difference between the magnitude and timing of cash inflows, the greater the likelihood of conflicting rankings. Conflicts based on NPV and IRR can be reconciled computationally by creating and analyzing an incremental project reflecting the difference in cash flows between the two mutually exclusive projects. Because a detailed description of this procedure is beyond the scope of an introductory text, suffice it to say that IRR techniques can be used to generate consistently the same project rankings as would be obtained using NPV.

WHICH APPROACH IS BETTER?

The better approach for evaluating capital expenditures is difficult to determine because their theoretical and practical strengths are not well aligned. It is therefore wise to view both NPV and IRR techniques in light of each of the following dimensions.

Theoretical basis. On a purely theoretical basis, NPV is best. Its theoretical superiority is attributed to a number of factors. Most important is the fact that the use of NPV implicitly assumes that any intermediate cash inflows generated by an investment are reinvested at the firm's cost of capital. The use of IRR assumes reinvestment at the often unrealistic rate specified by the IRR. The concept of reinvestment of intermediate cash inflows is best illustrated with an example.

EXAMPLE Assume that you have $6000 you wish to invest in either of the two equal-risk investments described below.
    Savings account: You can place the $6000 in a savings account paying 12 percent interest compounded annually. At the end of three years, you would have $8430 ($6000 × $FVIF_{12\%,3}$ = $6000 × 1.405 = $8430).
    Loan to a friend: You can lend the $6000 to a friend at 12 percent annual interest to be repaid in three equal annual installments of $2498 ($6000 ÷ $PVIFA_{12\%,3}$ = $6000 ÷ 2.402 = $2498).
    If we calculate the internal rate of return on each of these investments it would be 12 percent.
Savings account

$$\frac{\$6000}{\$8430} = .711 = PVIF_{IRR,3}$$

$$IRR = 12\%$$

Table 10.7 Reinvestment of Loan Payments at 12 Percent

End of year	Loan payment received (1)	Number of periods earning (t) (2)	$FVIF_{12\%,t}$ (3)	Value at end of year 3 [(1) × (3)] (4)
1	$2498	2	1.254	$3132
2	2498	1	1.120	2798
3	2498	0	1.000	2498
	$7494	Total value at end of year 3		$8428

Loan

$$\frac{\$6000}{\$2498} = 2.402 = PVIFA_{IRR,3}$$

$$IRR = 12\%$$

Further examination reveals that although with the savings account alternative the 12 percent return is earned on the full $6000, the loan does not guarantee this return. Analyzing the loan in Table 10.7, we can see in column 1 that the total recovery over the three years is $7494—the sum of the three payment inflows. Only if these inflows can be reinvested at 12 percent would this alternative provide a 12 percent return on the full $6000. This can be seen in columns 2, 3, and 4 of the table, which illustrate the effect of reinvesting the intermediate cash inflows at the end of years 1 and 2 at the 12 percent rate. If this can be done, the value at the end of three years would be $8428 (column 3 total). This value is equivalent (with rounding) to the $8430 value resulting from the savings account.

The key point is that only by reinvesting the intermediate cash inflows at the 12 percent internal rate of return would the loan alternative generate the same future value as the savings alternative. In spite of the fact that both alternatives require an intial $6000 investment and have a 12 percent *IRR*, they are equivalent only if we are able to assume the ability to reinvest intermediate cash inflows at 12 percent. Thus an ability to reinvest intermediate cash inflows at the *IRR* is implied by the *IRR* technique. ■

The *IRR* technique assumes an ability to reinvest intermediate cash inflows at the *IRR*. Although not demonstrated, the use of *NPV* implies reinvestment of intermediate cash inflows at the cost of capital. Since the cost of capital tends to be a reasonable estimate of the rate at which the firm could actually reinvest intermediate cash inflows, whereas the *IRR* is often quite high, the use of *NPV* with its more conservative and realistic reinvestment rate is in theory preferred.

A second theoretical problem with the *IRR* is that it is not unusual for nonconventional patterns of cash flows to have *multiple rates of return*—more than one *IRR*. The multiple *IRR* problem results from certain mathematical properties of the calculations involved. Due to the technical nature of this problem, suffice it to say a project may have more than one *IRR*. When this occurs, difficult problems of interpretation result. A related criticism of *IRR* arises because certain projects may have mathematical properties such that an *IRR* does not even exist. Again, this technical problem may cause theoretical difficulties that will not occur with the *NPV* approach.

Practical basis. Because the *NPV* approach does not suffer from any of the deficiencies just described with respect to *IRR*, it is the theoretically preferred approach. In spite of this fact, evidence suggests[17] that financial managers of large corporations prefer to use *IRR*. This preference for *IRR* is attributable to the general disposition of business people toward *rates* of return rather than pure *dollar* returns. Because interest rates, profitability measures, and so on are most often cited as annual rates of return, the use of *IRR* makes sense to corporate decision makers. They tend to find *NPV* harder to use because, as was pointed out in the discussion of *PI* ratios, the *NPV* does not really measure the benefits relative to the amount invested. The *IRR*, by providing the decision maker with data on the returns relative to the initial investment, provides much more information from which to make an investment decision.

Summary view. Although *NPV* is theoretically preferable, the *IRR* is more popular due to the fact that financial decision makers can more readily relate it to available decision data. To answer the question of which technique is better, the reply must be *theoretically the NPV, but on a practical basis the IRR.* Because a variety of methods and techniques are available for avoiding the pitfalls of the *IRR,* its widespread use should not be viewed as reflecting a lack of sophistication on the part of financial decision makers. On a purely academic or theoretical basis, the *NPV* is the superior technique.

A Comprehensive Problem

The two major steps in the analytical phase of the capital budgeting process are (1) the development of relevant cash flows and (2) the application of appropriate decision techniques. This part of the chapter illustrates these two steps, using the example of a potential replacement decision. First the decision is described; then the relevant cash flows are developed and the major decision techniques applied to them to evaluate the desirability of the proposed action. Finally, the results of the analysis are evaluated and the recommended decision given.

THE DECISION PROBLEM   Thoro Publishing Company is considering the replacement of one of its printing presses with either of two new and more sophisticated ones, press A or press B. The characteristics of the old press and the proposed presses are summarized as follows:
   Old press: Originally purchased three years ago at an installed cost of $400,000, it is being depreciated using ACRS over its five-year normal recovery period. The investment tax credit was not originally taken on it. The old press has a remaining economic life of five years. It can be sold today to net $420,000 before taxes; if it is retained, it can be sold to net $150,000 before taxes at the end of five years.
   Press A: This highly automated press can be purchased for $830,000 and will require $40,000 in installation costs. It will be depreciated using ACRS over its five-year normal recovery period. At the end of the five years, the machine could be sold to net $400,000

[17] For example, see Lawrence J. Gitman and John R. Forrester, Jr., "A Survey of Capital Budgeting Techniques Used by Major U.S. Firms," *Financial Management,* 6 (Fall 1977), pp. 66–71, for a discussion of evidence with respect to capital budgeting decision-making practices in major U.S. firms.

Table 10.8 Earnings Before Depreciation and Taxes—Thoro Publishing Company

Year	Old press	Press A	Press B
1	$120,000	$250,000	$210,000
2	120,000	270,000	210,000
3	120,000	300,000	210,000
4	120,000	330,000	210,000
5	120,000	370,000	210,000

before taxes. If this machine is acquired, it is anticipated that the following current account changes would result:

Cash	+$ 35,000
Accounts receivable	+$180,000
Inventory	−$ 20,000
Accounts payable	+$ 35,000

Press B: This press is not as sophisticated as press A. It costs $640,000 and requires $20,000 in installation costs. It will be depreciated using ACRS over its five-year normal recovery period. At the end of five years, it can be sold to net $330,000 before taxes. If this press is acquired, a $40,000 increase in net working capital will be needed to support it.

The firm estimates that its *earnings before depreciation and taxes* with the old press and with press A or press B for each of the five years would be as shown in Table 10.8. The firm pays taxes of 40 percent on ordinary income and 30 percent on long-term capital gains. An 8 percent investment tax credit is applicable to the installed cost of assets. The firm's cost of capital, k, applicable to the proposed replacement is 14 percent.

DEVELOPING RELEVANT CASH FLOWS

The first step in analyzing the replacement decision is to convert the proposal into the relevant cash flows. Each of the three cash flow components—initial investment, operating cash inflows, and terminal cash flow—are developed separately and then summarized.

Initial investment. The initial investment associated with replacement of the old press with either press A or press B is calculated in Table 10.9 using the format presented in Table 9.2. In either case, the sale proceeds from the old press would be $420,000, and taxes of $98,800 would have to be paid on the transaction. The investment tax credit is 8 percent of the installed cost of each new press, and the change in net working capital reflects the net amount that will have to be invested to support the new presses. The more expensive press, press A, requires a significantly larger increase in net working capital than press B ($160,000 for A and $40,000 for B). The initial investment for press A is $639,200, whereas the less automated press, B, requires an initial investment of only $326,000. Of course, these values are meaningful only when viewed in light of the operating cash inflows resulting from the investment.

Table 10.9   Calculation of Initial Investment for
Thoro Publishing Company

Item	Press A	Press B
Cost of new press	$830,000	$640,000
+ Installation costs	40,000	20,000
− Proceeds from sale of old press	420,000	420,000
+ Taxes on sale of old press[a]	98,800	98,800
− Investment tax credit on new press[b]	69,600	52,800
+ Change in net working capital	160,000[c]	40,000
Initial investment *(II)*	$639,200	$326,000

[a]				
Sale price	$420,000	Purchase price		$400,000
− Purchase price	400,000	− Book value*		168,000
Long-term capital gain	$ 20,000	Recaptured depreciation		$232,000
× Capital gain tax rate	× .30	× Ordinary tax rate		× .40
Capital gains tax	$ 6,000	Ordinary taxes		$ 92,800

Total taxes on sale $98,800

* Book value = $400,000 − (.15 + .22 + .21)($400,000)
= $400,000 − (.58)($400,000)
= $400,000 − $232,000 = $168,000
[b] Press A: .08($830,000 + $40,000) = .08($870,000) = $69,600
Press B: .08($640,000 + $20,000) = .08($660,000) = $52,800
[c] Change in current assets − change in current liabilities
= ($35,000 + $180,000 − $20,000) − $35,000
= $195,000 − $35,000 = $160,000

Operating cash inflows. The first step in estimating operating cash inflows is to find the operating cash inflows over the next five years for the old press. These flows are calculated in Table 10.10 using the income statement approach. It can be seen from the table note that since the old press has been owned and depreciated for three years, only the final two years of ACRS depreciation remain in the five-year normal recovery period. Column 5 of the table gives the operating cash inflows for each of the five years; in this case, $105,600 is expected in years 1 and 2, followed by $72,000 in each of the last three years. These cash inflows would be received if the firm retains the old press and does nothing; they are therefore the basis against which the inflows from replacement presses A and B can be evaluated.

The relevant or incremental operating cash inflows for press A are developed in Table 10.11 using the income statement approach presented in Chapter 9. Column 5 shows the operating cash inflows for press A, and Column 7 shows the relevant or incremental operating cash inflows, which were obtained by deducting the operating inflows of the old press from those for press A. Press B's relevant or incremental operating cash inflows are developed in Table 10.12 using the alternative approach presented in Chapter 9. Since only earnings before depreciation and taxes *(EBDT)* were provided, they require the same tax adjustment as do revenues (i.e., 1 − tax rate); the process of converting *EBDT* to changes in cash inflows is illustrated for press B in columns 1 through 4. The changes in depreciation and conversion of them into cash inflow changes are shown in columns 5 and 6. The *relevant, or incremental,* cash inflows for press B are given in column 7.

FACTORY AUTOMATION AND PRODUCTIVITY

Technology's impact on industrial America is more extensive than is popularly recognized. "Factory automation is making incredibly rapid strides," observes Steven Walleck, a director of McKinsey & Company, a management-consultant firm in Cleveland. But Walleck also notes that the economic payoff among companies varies widely. "Some companies get up to 50 percent improvement in productivity," he says. "Others don't get any."

The auto industry, though a late starter, is a good illustration of one that is moving briskly to modernize its manufacturing process. "The auto industry has become a high-tech industry," says Philip Caldwell, chairman of Ford Motor Company in Dearborn, Mich.

Car makers have spent two thirds of a planned 80-billion-dollar investment to streamline products, plants and equipment. "Six years ago, we didn't have a single computer," says Nick Scheele, a Ford executive. "Today, they're all over the place, and more are coming."

Result: An industry being reborn, Caldwell predicts that a year from now more than half of the industry's 255 domestic auto plants will be rebuilt, re-equipped or retooled, with impressive productivity gains.

At Ford's 30-year-old assembly plant in Wayne, Mich., for example, the introduction of robotics and other automation has improved productivity, or output per hour of work, by 25 percent over the past four years. The remodeled factory now has 23 robots at work, with more on the way.

The paint shop is a rainbow of automation. Jets spray any combination of 25 different colors on a steady succession of auto chassis moved by conveyor. Only one human is needed to press the proper color button in a control booth, and several others stand by to apply finishing touches. In time, it is said, the color coordinator in the control booth may be automated out of his job by a bar code on each chassis similar to that which records the prices of goods at supermarket checkout counters.

"We're looking for a 7 percent productivity improvement each year," says Dave Porter, plant manager. "There's nothing in this plant, with a few exceptions, that we couldn't automate if we wanted to spend the money. But automation must be cost-effective."

SOURCE: Monroe W. Karmin, "High Tech: Blessing or Curse?" *U.S. News and World Report,* January 16, 1984, pp. 38–39.

The relevant or incremental operating cash inflows for both presses A and B represent the amount by which their operating cash inflows exceed the operating cash inflows of the old press.

Terminal cash flow. The terminal cash flows for the two presses are developed in Table 10.13 using the format developed in Table 9.13. The procedure involves determining the difference in after-tax proceeds from each new press and the old press and then adjusting for the amount of net working capital that will be recovered. The terminal cash flow from press A is $310,000, and a terminal cash flow of $148,000 is expected from press B.

Table 10.10   Operating Cash Inflows for Old Press

Year (t)	Earnings before depreciation and taxes (EBDT_t) (1)	Depreciation[a] (2)	Earnings before taxes [(1) − (2)] (3)	Earnings after taxes [(1 − .40)(3)] (4)	Operating cash inflows [(2) + (4)] (5)
1	$120,000	$84,000	$ 36,000	$21,600	$105,600
2	120,000	84,000	36,000	21,600	105,600
3	120,000	0	120,000	72,000	72,000
4	120,000	0	120,000	72,000	72,000
5	120,000	0	120,000	72,000	72,000

[a] Year	Depreciable value (1)	Recovery percentage (2)	Depreciation [(1) × (2)] (3)
1	$400,000	.21	$ 84,000
2	400,000	.21	84,000
3	400,000	0	0
4	400,000	0	0
5	400,000	0	0
			$168,000

Relevant cash flows. The relevant cash flows for the two presses are summarized in Table 10.14 and diagramed in Figure 10.2. It can be seen that the two replacement alternatives have conventional cash flow patterns. Also note that the initial investment as well as the cash inflows for press A — the highly automated press — are significantly greater than those for press B.

EVALUATING RELEVANT CASH FLOWS

To decide which, if either, of the new presses should be acquired to replace the existing press, the capital budgeting techniques developed earlier in the chapter can be applied to the relevant cash flows shown in Table 10.14. Here we will apply each of four techniques — payback period, net present value *(NPV)*, profitability index *(PI)*, and internal rate of return *(IRR)*. In addition, a comparison of the *NPV* and *IRR* for the two presses will be made using net present value profiles.

Payback period. The payback period for presses A and B is calculated in tabular form in Table 10.15. The payback period for press A is 4.06 years; for press B, 3.71 years. Although these payback periods are reasonably close, press B would be better according to this measure because shorter payback periods are preferred.

Net present value. Table 10.16 illustrates the   calculation of the net present value for presses A and B using the firm's 14 percent cost of capital. The *NPV* for press A is $64,517.32; for press B, $59,242.96. Since both have *NPV*s greater than zero, both are acceptable; press A is preferred over press B, since A has the higher *NPV*.

Table 10.11 Relevant or Incremental Operating Cash Inflows for Press A

Year (t)	Earnings before depreciation and taxes ($EBDT_t$) (1)	Depreciation[a] (2)	Earnings before taxes [(1) − (2)] (3)	Earnings after taxes [(1 − .40)(3)] (4)	Operating cash inflows [(2) + (4)] (5)	Old press operating cash inflows [col. 5, Table 10.10] (6)	Relevant (incremental) operating cash inflows (CF_t) [(5) − (6)] (7)
1	$250,000	$130,500	$119,500	$ 71,700	$202,200	$105,600	$ 96,000
2	270,000	191,400	78,600	47,160	238,560	105,600	132,960
3	300,000	182,700	117,300	70,380	253,080	72,000	181,080
4	330,000	182,700	147,300	88,380	271,080	72,000	199,080
5	370,000	182,700	187,300	112,380	295,080	72,000	223,080

[a]

Year	Depreciable value (1)	Recovery percentage (2)	Depreciation [(1) × (2)] (3)
1	$870,000	.15	$130,500
2	870,000	.22	191,400
3	870,000	.21	182,700
4	870,000	.21	182,700
5	870,000	.21	182,700
			$870,000

Table 10.12 Relevant or Incremental Operating Cash Inflows for Press B Using the Alternative Approach

Year (t)	Earnings before depreciation and taxes (EBDT_t) Press B (1)	Old press (2)	Change in EBDT [(1) − (2)] (3)	Change in cash inflow from change in EBDT [(1 − .40)(3)] (4)	Change in depreciation[a] (5)	Change in cash flow from depreciation change [.4(5)] (6)	Relevant (incremental) operating cash inflows (CF_t) [(4) + (6)] (7)
1	$210,000	$120,000	$90,000	$54,000	$ 15,000	$ 6,000	$ 60,000
2	210,000	120,000	90,000	54,000	61,200	24,480	78,480
3	210,000	120,000	90,000	54,000	138,600	55,440	109,440
4	210,000	120,000	90,000	54,000	138,600	55,440	109,440
5	210,000	120,000	90,000	54,000	138,600	55,440	109,440

[a]

Press B

Year	Depreciable value (1)	Recovery percentage (2)	Depreciation [(1) × (2)] (3)
1	$660,000	.15	$ 99,000
2	660,000	.22	145,200
3	660,000	.21	138,600
4	660,000	.21	138,600
5	660,000	.21	138,600
			$660,000

Old Press

Year	Depreciable value (4)	Recovery percentage (5)	Depreciation [(4) × (5)] (6)	Change in depreciation [(3) − (6)] (7)
1	$400,000	.21	$ 84,000	$ 15,000
2	400,000	.21	84,000	61,200
3	400,000	0	0	138,600
4	400,000	0	0	138,600
5	400,000	0	0	138,600
			$168,000	

Table 10.13 Calculation of Terminal Cash Flows for
Thoro Publishing Company

	Press A	Press B
Proceeds from sale of new press	$400,000	$330,000
− Proceeds from sale of old press	150,000	150,000
− Taxes on sale of new press[a]	160,000	132,000
+ Taxes on sale of old press[b]	60,000	60,000
+ Change in net working capital[c]	160,000	40,000
Terminal cash flow	$310,000	$148,000

[a]

	Press A	Press B
Sale price	$400,000	$330,000
− Book value*	0	0
Recaptured depreciation	$400,000	$330,000
× Ordinary tax rate	× .40	× .40
Tax on sale	$160,000	$132,000

* Equals zero for both assets because they are fully depreciated.

[b]

Sale price	$150,000
− Book value	0
Recaptured depreciation	$150,000
× Ordinary tax rate	× .40
Tax on sale	$ 60,000**

** This amount is shown as a positive value because tax outflows on sale
of old assets are to be shown this way, and vice versa, when calculating
terminal value.

[c] These values represent the recovery of the net working capital
investments shown as part of the initial investment calculated in Table
10.9.

Table 10.14 Relevant Cash Flows for Thoro Publishing Company's Replacement
Decision

	Press A		Press B
Initial investment *(II)*	$639,200		$326,000
Year *(t)*	Cash inflows *(CF_t)*		
1	$ 96,600		$ 60,000
2	132,960		78,480
3	181,080		109,440
4	199,080		109,440
5 Operating inflow $223,080		$109,440	
Terminal flow 310,000		148,000	
	533,080		257,440

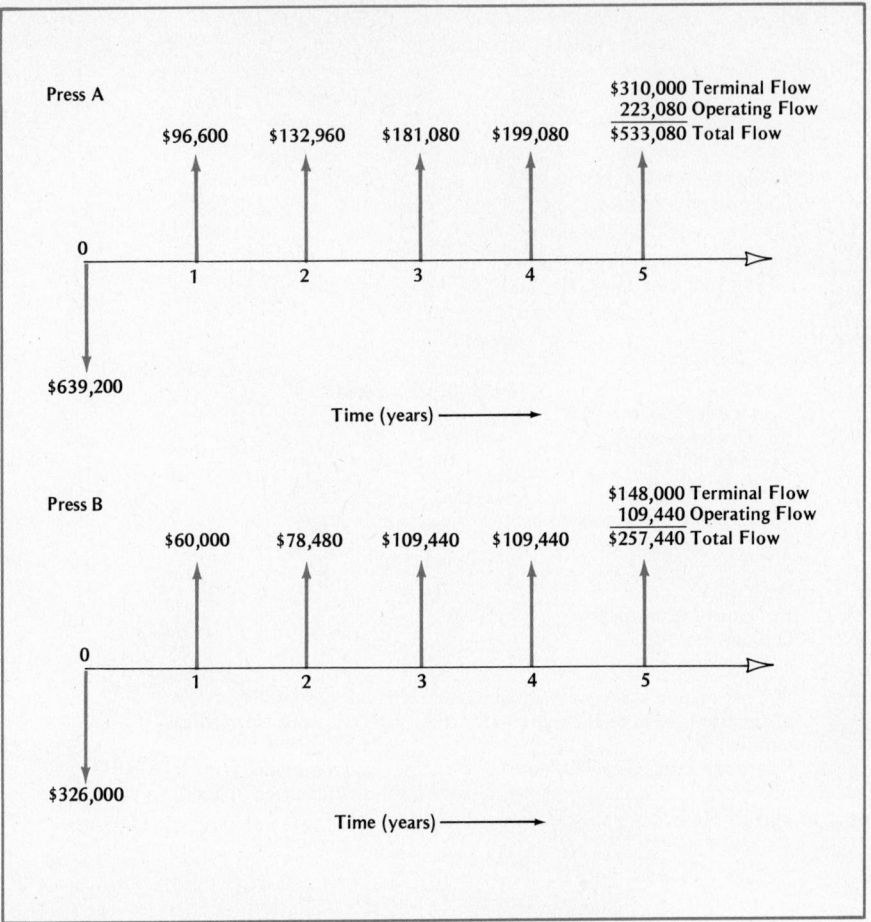

Figure 10.2 Relevant cash flows for Thoro Publishing Company

Table 10.15 Calculation of Payback Period for Presses A and B

Press A

Year (t)	Cash inflow (CF$_t$)	Cumulative cash inflow	
1	$ 96,600	$ 96,600	
2	132,960	229,560	Initial
3	181,080	410,640	investment
4	199,080	609,720	$639,200
5	533,080	1,142,800	

$$\text{Payback period} = 4 \text{ years} + \frac{\$639,200 - \$609,720}{\$533,080} = 4 + \frac{\$29,480}{\$533,080}$$

$$= \underline{4.06 \text{ years}}$$

Table 10.15   *(Continued)*

Press B

Year *(t)*	Cash inflow *(CF_t)*	Cumulative cash inflow	
1	$ 60,000	$ 60,000	Initial
2	78,480	138,480	investment
3	109,440	247,920	$326,000
4	109,440	357,360	
5	257,440	614,800	

$$\text{Payback period} = 3 \text{ years} + \frac{\$326,000 - \$247,920}{\$109,440} = 3 + \frac{\$ 78,080}{\$109,440}$$

$$= \underline{3.71 \text{ years}}$$

Table 10.16   Calculation of Net Present Value for Presses A and B

Press A

Year *(t)*	Cash inflow *(CF_t)* (1)	$PVIF_{14\%,t}$ (2)	Present value of cash inflows [(1) × (2)] (3)
1	$ 96,600	.877	$ 84,718.20
2	132,960	.769	102,246.24
3	181,080	.675	122,229.00
4	199,080	.592	117,855.36
5	533,080	.519	276,668.52
	Present value of inflows		$703,717.32
	− Initial investment *(II)*		639,200.00
	Net present value		$ 64,517.32

Press B

Year *(t)*	Cash inflow *(CF_t)* (1)	$PVIF_{14\%,t}$ (2)	Present value of cash inflow [(1) × (2)] (3)
1	$ 60,000	.877	$ 52,620.00
2	78,480	.769	60,351.12
3	109,440	.675	73,872.00
4	109,440	.592	64,788.48
5	257,440	.519	133,611.36
	Present value of inflows		$385,242.96
	− Initial investment *(II)*		326,000.00
	Net present value		$ 59,242.96

Profitability index. Using the present value of inflows for presses A and B in column 3 for each press in Table 10.16, we can calculate the profitability index *(PI)* for each of the presses by dividing the present value of inflows by the initial investment.

$$\text{Press A: } \frac{\$703,717.32}{\$639,200.00} = \underline{\underline{1.10}}$$

$$\text{Press B: } \frac{\$385,242.96}{\$326,000.00} = \underline{\underline{1.18}}$$

Since both presses have *PI*s greater than 1, both are acceptable. Press B's profitability index of 1.18 is higher than press A's *PI* of 1.10, so press B would be preferred using this measure.

Internal rate of return. The internal rate of return for each of the presses is calculated in Table 10.17. The *IRR* for press A is 17 percent; for press B, 20 percent. (Although the more precise values estimated using interpolation are shown in the table, the rounded values are used in subsequent discussion.) Using *IRR,* both presses are acceptable, since their *IRR*s are greater than the firm's cost of capital, $k = 14$ percent. Press B would be preferred, since its *IRR* is 3 percent higher.

Comparing *NPV* and *IRR*. The net present values and internal rates of return for the two presses can be evaluated using net present value profiles. The basic data used to draw the profiles are summarized in Table 10.18. Figure 10.3 shows the resulting profiles. It can be seen that at a cost of capital below approximately 14.5 percent,[18] press A is preferred over press B, while at costs greater than 14.5 percent, press B is preferred. Since the firm's cost of capital is 14 percent, conflicting rankings exist. Press A has a higher value and is therefore preferred over press B using *NPV,* whereas press B's *IRR* of 20 percent causes it to be preferred over press A, whose *IRR* is 17 percent using this measure.

[18] The point of intersection of the two profiles can be determined mathematically as the *IRR* on the incremental project found by subtracting the initial investment and annual cash inflows for the smaller project from the corresponding cash flows for the larger one. The calculations are as follows:

Year *(t)*	Press A (1)	Press B (2)	Incremental project [(1) − (2)] (3)	$PVIF_{14\%,t}$ (4)	PV at 14% [(3) × (4)] (5)	$PVIF_{15\%,t}$ (6)	PV at 15% [(3) × (6)] (7)
0	($639,200)	($326,000)	($313,200)	—	—	—	—
1	96,600	60,000	36,600	.877	$ 32,098.20	.870	$ 31,842.00
2	132,960	78,480	54,480	.769	41,895.12	.756	41,186.88
3	181,080	109,440	71,640	.675	48,357.00	.658	47,139.12
4	199,080	109,400	89,640	.592	53,066.88	.572	51,274.08
5	533,080	257,440	275,640	.519	143,057.16	.497	136,993.08
			PV of inflows		$318,474.36		$308,435.16
			−Initial investment *(II)*		313,200.00		313,200.00
			Net present value		$5,274.36		− $4,764.84

$$IRR = 14\% + \frac{\$\ 5,274.36}{\$10,039.20} = \underline{\underline{14.53\%}}$$

Table 10.17 Calculation of Internal Rate of Return for Presses A and B

Press A

Year(t)	Cash inflow (CF_t)	
1	$ 96,600	Fake annuity $= \dfrac{\$639,200}{\$228,560} = 2.797$
2	132,960	
3	181,080	$PVIFA_{x\%,5} = 2.797$
4	199,080	$x\% = 23\%$
5	533,080	
	$1,142,800 ÷ 5 = \$228,560	Try 17%

Year (t)	Cash inflows (CF_t) (1)	$PVIF_{17\%,t}$ (2)	Present value at 17% [(1) × (2)] (3)	$PVIF_{18\%,t}$ (4)	Present value at 18% [(1) × (4)] (5)
1	$ 96,600	.855	$ 82,593.00	.847	$ 81,820.20
2	132,960	.731	97,193.76	.718	95,465.28
3	181,080	.624	112,993.92	.609	110,277.72
4	199,080	.534	106,308.72	.516	102,725.28
5	533,080	.456	243,084.48	.437	232,955.96
	PV of inflows		$642,173.88		$623,244.44
	− Initial investment *(II)*		639,200.00		639,200.00
	Net present value		$ 2,973.88		−$ 15,955.56

IRR closest to 17%.

Interpolating: $17\% + \dfrac{\$ 2,973.88}{\$18,929.44} (1\%) = \underline{\underline{17.16\%}}$

Press B

Year (t)	Cash inflow (CF_t)	
1	$ 60,000	Fake annuity $= \dfrac{\$326,000}{\$122,960} = 2.651$
2	78,480	
3	109,440	$PVIFA_{x\%,5} = 2.651$
4	109,440	$x\% = 26\%$
5	257,440	
	$614,800 ÷ 5 = \$122,960	Try 19%

Year (t)	Cash inflows (CF_t) (1)	$PVIF_{19\%,t}$ (2)	Present value at 19% [(1) × (2)] (3)	$PVIF_{20\%,t}$ (4)	Present value at 20% [(1) × (4)] (5)
1	$ 60,000	.840	$ 50,400.00	.833	$ 49,980.00
2	78,480	.706	55,406.88	.694	54,465.12
3	109,440	.593	64,897.92	.579	63,365.76
4	109,440	.499	54,610.56	.482	52,750.08
5	257,440	.419	107,867.36	.402	103,490.88
	PV of inflows		$333,182.72		$324,051.84
	− Initial investment *(II)*		326,000.00		326,000.00
	Net present value		$ 7,182.72		−$ 1,948.16

IRR closest to 20%.

Interpolating: $19\% + \dfrac{\$7,182.72}{\$9,130.88} (1\%) = \underline{\underline{19.79\%}}$

Table 10.18   Basic Data Used to Draw Net
Present Value Profiles for Thoro
Publishing Company

| Discount rate | Net present value | |
	Press A	Press B
0%	$503,600.00[a]	$288,800.00[b]
14%	64,517.32	59,242.96
17%	0	—
20%	—	0

[a] $1,142,800 − $639,200 = $503,600
[b] $614,800 − $326,000 = $288,800

SELECTING THE BEST PRESS

The values for both presses for all four of the measures applied to the project's cash flows are summarized in Table 10.19. Included are notations indicating the preferred press using the given decision technique. Both presses are acceptable since they have positive *NPVs*, *PI*s greater than 1 and *IRR*s greater than the firm's 14

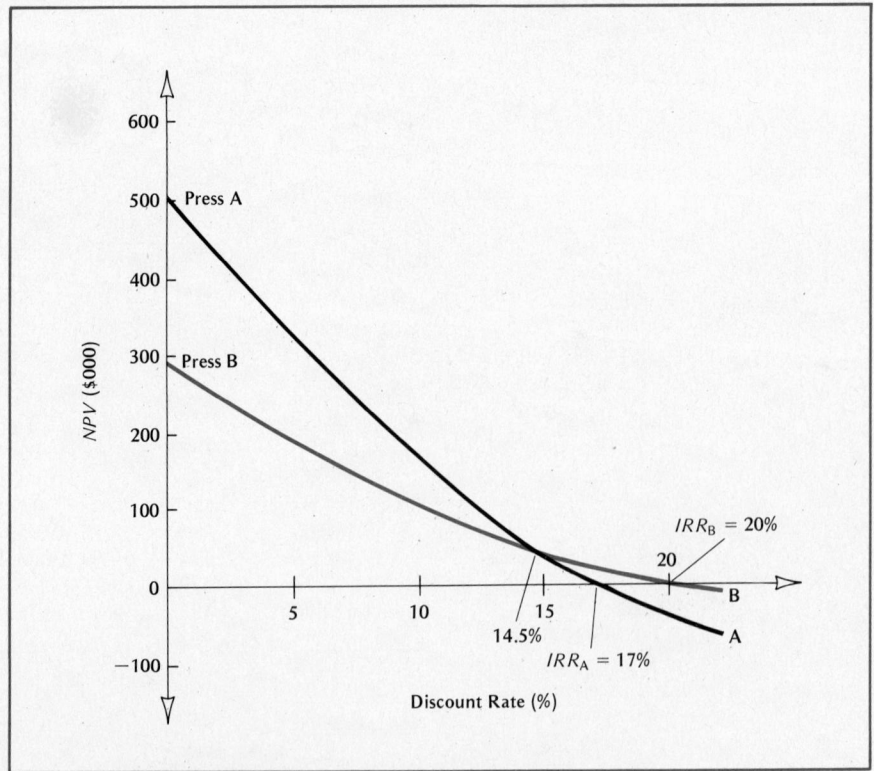

Figure 10.3   Net present value profiles for presses A and B

Table 10.19 Summary of Analysis with References for Presses A and B

Decision technique	Alternative		Preferred press using given decision technique
	Press A	Press B	
Payback period	4.06 years	3.71 years	B
Net present value *(NPV)*	$64,517.32	$59,242.96	A
Profitability index *(PI)*	1.10	1.18	B
Internal rate of return *(IRR)*	17%	20%	B

percent cost of capital. Rankings of the two presses using the four decision techniques show that press B is preferred by three of the techniques — payback, *PI*, and *IRR* — while press A is preferred by only *NPV*.

So which press is recommended? It depends on the firm's situation. If the firm has *unlimited funds* available for investment, press A would be recommended since it would add the most value (highest *NPV*). This technique is, in addition, the theoretically preferred one. If the firm is operating under *capital rationing* due to limited funds, press B *might* be preferable since it utilizes the funds more efficiently — it provides a better return per dollar invested.[19] Assuming that the firm has adequate funds available for either press A or press B, it is recommended that press A be acquired to replace the old press. Such an action is consistent with achievement of the firm's goal of owners' wealth maximization.

CHAPTER SUMMARY

● Unsophisticated capital budgeting techniques use the average rate of return or the payback period to evaluate the attractiveness of capital projects.

● The average rate of return is calculated by dividing the average profits after taxes by the average investment. The drawbacks of using the average rate of return are that it is not consistent with wealth maximization, it relies on accounting data, and it does not reflect the time value of money.

● The payback period is calculated by determining the amount of time it will take the firm to recover its initial investment. The payback method implicitly considers cash flow patterns, though it is inconsistent with the wealth maximization goal, fails to consider directly the time value of money, and ignores profits.

● Sophisticated techniques for capital budgeting consider the time factor in the value of money.

● The net present value *(NPV)* approach measures the difference between the present value of inflows and the initial investment, or present value of outflows, to determine the desirability of a project.

● The profitability index *(PI)* is similar to net present value, but it measures the ratio of the present value of inflows to the initial investment, indicating the present value return per dollar invested.

● The internal rate of return *(IRR)*, the discount rate that equates the net present value of a project with zero, is also used as a basis for capital budget decision making.

[19] The selection of projects under capital rationing is a difficult process; the best projects can only be determined when viewed in light of other projects competing for the firm's limited funds. Capital rationing is discussed in some detail in Chapter 11.

- Each of the sophisticated capital budgeting techniques uses the cost of capital in its decision criterion and provides the same accept-reject decisions for a given project, but there are often conflicts between the rankings of projects using these various techniques.
- Net present value profiles, which are graphs plotting the *NPV*s for a project against discount rates, are useful in comparing projects, especially when conflicting rankings exist between *NPV* and *IRR*.
- On a purely theoretical basis, *NPV* is preferred over *IRR* because the internal rate of return implicitly assumes reinvestment of intermediate cash inflows at the *IRR*. Also, the *IRR* for nonconventional cash flow patterns can result in more than one value, and in some cases the *IRR* may not even exist.
- *NPV* does not suffer from the deficiencies of the *IRR*, but the *IRR* is more commonly used by major firms because it is consistent with the general preference of financial decision makers for rates of return.

KEY TERMS

accounting rate of return	internal rate of return *(IRR)*
average investment	multiple rates of return
average profits after taxes	net present value *(NPV)*
average rate of return	net present value profile
benefit-cost ratio	opportunity cost
conflicting rankings	payback period
cost of capital *(k)*	profitability index *(PI)*
discount rate	yield criterion
intermediate cash inflows	

QUESTIONS

10-1   What adjustment is required to convert a stream of cash inflows into an after-tax profit figure? What is the rationale for this adjustment?

10-2   What weaknesses are associated with use of the *average rate of return* for measuring an investment's worth? How can a tie in the rankings be resolved using this technique?

10-3   What is the *payback period?* How is it calculated? What more efficient method can be used to find the payback for an annuity?

10-4   What weaknesses are commonly associated with the use of the *payback period* to measure an investment's worth? What factors are usually used to justify the use of the payback period? In what situations is it justifiable?

10-5   What is the one thing the so-called sophisticated capital budgeting techniques have in common that the unsophisticated techniques do not? What are the names commonly used to describe the rate at which cash flows are discounted in order to find present values?

10-6   What is the formula for finding the *net present value (NPV)* of a project with conventional cash flows? What is the acceptance criterion for *NPV?*

10-7   How is the *profitability index (PI)* calculated? What is its acceptance criterion? Is this measure consistent with the use of *NPV?* Explain.

10-8   What is the *internal rate of return (IRR)* on an investment? How is it determined? What is its acceptance criterion?

10-9   Do the net present value *(NPV)*, profitability index *(PI)*, and internal rate of return *(IRR)* always agree with respect to accept-reject decisions? Ranking decisions? Explain.

10-10 What is a *net present value profile?* How can it be used to compare projects when conflicting rankings exist?

10-11 What causes conflicts in the ranking of projects using net present value *(NPV)* and internal rate of return *(IRR)?* When comparing projects using *IRR,* what kind of cash inflow pattern tends to be preferred at low discount rates? Explain.

10-12 Explain what is meant by the "reinvestment rate assumption" and why, on a purely theoretical basis, the presence of this implied assumption tends to favor the use of net present value *(NPV)* rather than internal rate of return *(IRR).*

10-13 In practice, which of the two major capital budgeting techniques—net present value *(NPV)* or internal rate of return *(IRR)*—is preferred? Explain the rationale for this preference in light of the fact that it is inconsistent with theory.

10-14 When a conflict exists in the choice of the "best" project using net present value *(NPV)* and internal rate of return *(IRR),* what, if any, impact might the availability of funds—unlimited funds versus rationing—have on the selection? Explain.

PROBLEMS

10-1 (**Average Rate of Return**)   A firm is considering the acquisition of an asset that requires an initial investment of $10,000 and will provide after-tax profits of $1,000 per year for five years.
  a Calculate the average rate of return using the most common formula.
  b Calculate the average rate of return using the *initial* investment instead of the average investment in the denominator.
  c Calculate the average rate of return using the after-tax cash inflow instead of the after-tax profit in the numerator and using the average investment in the denominator. Assume that the firm depreciates the $10,000 initial investment at a constant (straight-line) rate over its five-year life.

10-2 (**Payback Period**)   The Lee Corporation is considering a capital expenditure that requires an initial investment of $42,000 and returns after-tax cash inflows of $7,000 per year for ten years. The company has established a maximum payback standard of eight years.
  a Determine the payback period for this project.
  b Should the company accept the project? Why or why not?

10-3 (**Average Rate of Return, Cash Inflows, and Payback**)   Walter's Sporting Equipment Company is evaluating a new machine. The initial investment of $20,000 will be written off over its normal recovery period of five years using the ACRS depreciation percentages (see Table 2.7 on page 34). The machine will generate earnings after taxes of $3,000 per year for each of the five years it will operate. The firm's ordinary income is taxed at a 40 percent rate.
  a Determine the average rate of return for the machine, using the most common formula.
  b Determine the after-tax cash inflows associated with the machine for each of the five years.
  c Determine the payback period for the machine.

10-4 (**Payback Comparisons**)   Houston Tool uses a five-year maximum payback standard. The firm is considering the purchase of a new machine and must choose between two alternative ones. The first machine requires an initial investment of $14,000 and generates annual after-tax cash inflows of $3,000 for each of the next seven years. The second machine requires an initial investment of $21,000 and provides an annual cash inflow after taxes of $4,000 for 20 years.
  a Determine the payback period for each machine.

b Comment on the acceptability of the machines assuming they are independent projects.

c Which machine should the firm accept? Why?

d Do the machines in this problem illustrate any of the criticisms of using payback? Discuss.

10-5 **(*NPV* for Varying Required Returns)** Bonnie's Beauty Aids is evaluating a new fragrance-mixing machine. The asset requires an initial investment of $24,000 and will generate after-tax cash inflows of $5,000 per year for eight years. For each of the required rates of return listed, (1) calculate the net present value, (2) indicate whether to accept or reject the machine, and (3) explain your decision.

a The cost of capital is 10 percent.

b The cost of capital is 12 percent.

c The cost of capital is 14 percent.

10-6 **(Net Present Value — Independent Projects)** Using a 14 percent cost of capital, calculate the net present value for each of the following independent projects and indicate whether or not each is acceptable.

	Project A	Project B	Project C	Project D	Project E
Initial investment *(II)*	$26,000	$500,000	$170,000	$950,000	$80,000
Year *(t)*			Cash inflows *(CF$_t$)*		
1	$ 4,000	$100,000	$ 20,000	$230,000	$ 0
2	4,000	120,000	19,000	230,000	0
3	4,000	140,000	18,000	230,000	0
4	4,000	160,000	17,000	230,000	20,000
5	4,000	180,000	16,000	230,000	30,000
6	4,000	200,000	15,000	230,000	0
7	4,000		14,000	230,000	50,000
8	4,000		13,000	230,000	60,000
9	4,000		12,000		70,000
10	4,000		11,000		

10-7 **(Average Rate of Return, Payback, and *NPV*)** Forrest Products has three projects under consideration. The cash flows for each of them are given below. The firm has a 16 percent cost of capital.

	Project A	Project B	Project C
Initial investment *(II)*	$40,000	$40,000	$40,000
Year *(t)*		Cash inflows *(CF$_t$)*	
1	$13,000	$ 7,000	$19,000
2	13,000	10,000	16,000
3	13,000	13,000	13,000
4	13,000	16,000	10,000
5	13,000	19,000	7,000

a Using the cash inflows, calculate the average rate of return for each project. Which project is preferred using this method?

b Calculate each project's payback period. Which project is preferred using this method?

c Calculate each project's net present value *(NPV)*. Which project is preferred using this method?

d Comment on your findings in **a**, **b**, and **c** and recommend the best project. Explain your recommendation.

10-8 (*NPV and PI*) Calculate the net present value *(NPV)* and profitability index *(PI)* for the following 20-year projects. Comment on the acceptability of each. Assume that the firm has an opportunity cost of 14 percent.

a Initial investment is $10,000; cash inflows are $2,000 per year.

b Initial investment is $25,000; cash inflows are $3,000 per year.

c Initial investment is $30,000; cash inflows are $5,000 per year.

10-9 (*NPV and PI*) A firm can purchase a fixed asset for a $13,000 initial investment. If the asset generates an annual after-tax cash inflow of $4,000 for four years:

a Determine the maximum required rate of return the firm can have and still accept the asset (closest whole-percentage rate).

b Determine the net present value of the asset assuming that the firm has a 10 percent cost of capital.

c Determine the profitability index assuming that the firm has a 10 percent cost of capital.

10-10 (*NPV and PI—Mutually Exclusive Projects*) Rollex Enterprises is considering the replacement of one of its old drill presses. Three alternative replacement presses are under consideration. The relevant cash flows associated with each are given. The firm's cost of capital is 15 percent.

	Press A	Press B	Press C
Initial investment *(II)*	$85,000	$60,000	$130,000
Year *(t)*	Cash inflows *(CF_t)*		
1	$18,000	$12,000	$ 50,000
2	18,000	14,000	30,000
3	18,000	16,000	20,000
4	18,000	18,000	20,000
5	18,000	20,000	20,000
6	18,000	25,000	30,000
7	18,000	—	40,000
8	18,000	—	50,000

a Calculate the net present value *(NPV)* of each press.

b Calculate the profitability index *(PI)* for each press.

c Using both *NPV* and *PI*, evaluate the acceptability of each press. Do the two techniques agree with respect to each press?

d Rank the presses from best to worst using each technique, *NPV* and *PI*. Do the rankings agree? Explain your findings.

10-11 (**Internal Rate of Return**) For each of the following projects, calculate the internal rate of return *(IRR)* and indicate for each project the maximum cost of capital the firm could have and find the *IRR* acceptable.

	Project A	Project B	Project C	Project D
Initial investment *(II)*	$90,000	$490,000	$20,000	$240,000
Year *(t)*		Cash inflows *(CF$_t$)*		
1	$20,000	$150,000	$ 7,500	$120,000
2	25,000	150,000	7,500	100,000
3	30,000	150,000	7,500	80,000
4	35,000	150,000	7,500	60,000
5	40,000	—	7,500	—

10-12 **(IRR—Mutually Exclusive Projects)** Tonus Corporation is attempting to choose the best of two mutually exclusive projects available for expanding the firm's warehouse capacity. The relevant cash flows for the projects are given. The firm's cost of capital is 15 percent.

	Project X	Project Y
Initial investment *(II)*	$500,000	$325,000
Year *(t)*	Cash inflows *(CF$_t$)*	
1	$100,000	$140,000
2	120,000	120,000
3	150,000	95,000
4	190,000	70,000
5	250,000	50,000

a Calculate the *IRR* to the nearest whole percent for each of the projects.
b Assess the acceptability of each project based on the *IRR*s found in **a**.
c Which project is preferred, based on the *IRR*s found in **a**?

10-13 **(IRR, Investment Life, and Cash Inflows)** Cincinnati Machine Tool (CMT) accepts projects earning more than the firm's 15 percent cost of capital. CMT is currently considering a ten-year project that provides annual cash inflows of $10,000 and requires an initial investment of $61,450. (*Note:* All amounts are after taxes.)
a Determine the *IRR* of this project. Is it acceptable?
b Assuming that the cash inflows continue to be $10,000 per year, how many *additional years* would the flows have to continue to make the project acceptable (have an *IRR* of 15 percent)?
c With the given life, initial investment, and cost of capital, what is the minimum annual cash inflow the firm should accept?

10-14 **(NPV, PI, and IRR)** Metropolitan Manufacturing Enterprises has prepared the following estimates for a long-term project it is considering. The initial investment will be $18,250, and the project is expected to yield after-tax cash inflows of $4,000 per year for seven years. The firm has a 10 percent required rate of return.
a Determine the net present value *(NPV)* of the project.
b Determine the profitability index *(PI)* for the project.
c Determine the internal rate of return *(IRR)* for the project.
d Would you recommend that Metropolitan accept or reject the project? Explain your answer.

10-15 **(ARR, Payback, NPV, PI, and IRR)** Don Reagan Enterprises is attempting to evaluate the feasibility of investing $95,000 in a piece of equipment having a five-year life. The firm has estimated the *profits after taxes* and *cash inflows* associated with the proposal as follows:

Year *(t)*	Profits after taxes *(PAT_t)*	Cash inflows *(CF_t)*
1	$ 5,000	$20,000
2	3,000	25,000
3	9,000	30,000
4	14,000	35,000
5	19,000	40,000

The firm has a 12 percent cost of capital.

a Calculate the average rate of return *(ARR)* for the proposed investment.

b Calculate the payback period for the proposed investment.

c Calculate the net present value *(NPV)* for the proposed investment.

d Calculate the profitability index *(PI)* for the proposed investment.

e Calculate the internal rate of return *(IRR)*, rounded to the nearest whole percent, for the proposed investment.

f Evaluate the acceptability of the proposed investment using *NPV, PI,* and *IRR.* What recommendation would you make relative to implementation of the project? Why?

10-16 (***NPV, IRR,* and *NPV* Profiles**)   Candor Enterprises is considering two mutually exclusive projects. The firm, which has a 12 percent cost of capital, has estimated its cash flows as follows:

	Project A	Project B
Initial investment *(II)*	$130,000	$85,000
Year *(t)*	Cash inflows *(CF_t)*	
1	$ 25,000	$40,000
2	35,000	35,000
3	45,000	30,000
4	50,000	10,000
5	55,000	5,000

a Calculate the *NPV* of each project and assess its acceptability.

b Calculate the *IRR* for each project and assess its acceptability.

c Draw the *NPV* profile for each project on the same set of axes.

d Evaluate and discuss the rankings of the two projects based on your findings in **a, b,** and **c.**

e Explain your findings in **d** in light of the pattern of cash inflow associated with each project.

10-17 (**All Techniques — Mutually Exclusive Investment Decision**)   The Comfort Chair Company is attempting to select the best of three mutually exclusive projects for increasing its aluminum extrusion capacity. The initial investment and after-tax cash inflows associated with each project are given in the table. Assume for each project that the initial investment equals total depreciable cost, that the project will be written off over its five-year normal recovery period using the ACRS depreciation percentages (see Table 2.7 on page 34), and that the firm is subject to a 40 percent tax rate on ordinary income.

Cash flow	Project A	Project B	Project C
Initial investment *(II)*	$60,000	$100,000	$110,000
Cash inflow *(CF)*, years 1–5	$20,000	$ 31,500	$ 32,500

a Calculate the average rate of return for each project using the most common formula.

b Calculate the payback period for each project.

c Calculate the net present value of each project assuming that the firm has a cost of capital equal to 13 percent.

d Calculate the internal rate of return for each project.

e Assuming that the cost of capital is 13 percent, which project would you recommend? Why?

10-18 **(All Techniques with *NPV* Profile — Mutually Exclusive Projects)** The following two proposals of equal risk have been made for the purchase of new equipment. The cash flows for each are given.

	Project A	Project B
Initial investment *(II)*	$80,000	$50,000
Year *(t)*	Cash inflows *(CF_t)*	
1	$15,000	$15,000
2	20,000	15,000
3	25,000	15,000
4	30,000	15,000
5	35,000	15,000

The firm's cost of capital is 13 percent.

a Use the firm's cash inflows to calculate the average rate of return *(ARR)* for each project.

b Calculate each project's payback period.

c Calculate the net present value *(NPV)* for each project.

d Calculate the profitability index *(PI)* for each project.

e Calculate the internal rate of return *(IRR)* for each project.

f Draw a net present value profile for each project on the same set of axes and discuss any conflict in ranking that may exist between *NPV* and *IRR*.

g Summarize the preferences dictated by each measure and indicate which project you would recommend if the firm has (1) unlimited funds and (2) capital rationing.

10-19 **(Integrative — Simple Investment Decision)** Yellow Springs Cash Register is considering opening a new plant in Pryor, Oklahoma. The total installed cost of the plant would be $2.2 million. This outlay would be partially offset by the sale of an existing facility in Tacoma, Washington. The Tacoma site has zero book value, cost $1 million in 1958, and can be sold currently for $250,000 before taxes. As a result of the new plant, sales are expected to increase by $800,000, but product costs (excluding depreciation) will represent 50 percent of sales. The plant will be written off over its 15-year normal recovery period using the ACRS depreciation percentages (see Table 2.7 on page 34). The firm is subject to a 40 percent tax rate on ordinary income and a 30 percent tax rate on long-term capital gains. Yellow Springs Cash Register's cost of capital is 11 percent. The flat 8 percent investment tax credit *(ITC)* is applicable. Net working capital is expected to remain unchanged, and terminal cash flows are assumed to equal zero.

a Determine the initial investment required by the new plant.

b Determine the operating cash inflows attributable to the new plant.

c Determine the payback period.

d Determine the net present value and the internal rate of return related to the proposed new plant.

e Make a recommendation to accept or reject the new plant and justify your answer.

10-20 **(Integrative — Investment Decision)** Kannon Textile is considering the replacement of an existing machine. The machine costs $1.2 million and requires installation costs of $150,000. The existing machine can be sold currently for $185,000 before taxes. It is two years old, cost $800,000 new, has a $504,000 book value, and has a remaining useful life of five years. It was being depreciated over a five-year normal recovery period using the ACRS depreciation percentages (see Table 2.7 on page 34) and therefore has the final three years of depreciation remaining. The investment tax credit was not taken on this machine when it was acquired. If held until the end of five years, the machine's market value would be zero. Over its five-year life, the new machine should reduce operating costs by $350,000 per year. The new machine will be depreciated over its five-year normal recovery period using the ACRS depreciation percentages (see Table 2.7 on page 34). The firm can take an 8 percent investment tax credit on the installed cost of the new machine. The machine can be sold for $200,000 net of removal costs at the end of five years. An increased investment in net working capital of $25,000 will be needed to support operations if the new machine is acquired. Assume the firm has adequate operating income against which to deduct any loss experienced on the sale of the existing machine. The firm has a 14 percent cost of capital, a 40 percent tax rate on ordinary income, and a 30 percent tax rate on long-term capital gains.

a Develop the relevant cash flows needed to analyze the proposed replacement.

b Determine the net present value of the proposal.

c Determine the internal rate of return on the proposal.

d Make a recommendation to accept or reject the replacement proposal and justify your answer.

e What is the highest cost of capital the firm could have and still accept the proposal? Explain.

10-21 **(Integrative — Complete Investment Decision)** Goolay Towing is contemplating replacement of one of its heavy-duty tow trucks with a newer, more fuel-efficient truck capable of towing a broader range of vehicles than the old truck. Two replacement tow trucks are being considered, A and B. The key characteristics of the old truck and the proposed trucks are summarized as follows:

Old truck: This truck was originally purchased four years ago at a delivered cost of $62,000 and is being depreciated using ACRS over its five-year normal recovery period. The investment tax credit was not originally taken on it. The old truck has a remaining economic life of five years. It can be sold today to net $68,000 before taxes; if retained, it can be sold to net $20,000 at the end of five years.

Truck A: This truck is not as automated as the other one being considered. Its delivered cost is $105,000. It would be depreciated using ACRS over its five-year normal recovery period. At the end of five years, it can be sold to net $35,000 before taxes. If it is acquired, a $5,000 increase in net working capital would be needed to support it.

Truck B: This highly automated truck can be purchased for a delivered cost of

$135,000. It would be depreciated using ACRS over its five-year normal recovery period. At the end of five years, the truck can be sold to net $40,000 before taxes. If the truck is acquired, it would result in a $40,000 increase in current assets and a $30,000 increase in current liabilities.

The firm estimates its *earnings before depreciation and taxes* with the old truck, with truck A, or truck B for each of the next five years as follows:

Year	Old truck	Truck A	Truck B
1	$30,000	$52,000	$55,000
2	30,000	52,000	58,000
3	30,000	52,000	63,000
4	30,000	52,000	70,000
5	30,000	52,000	75,000

The firm pays taxes of 40 percent on ordinary income and 30 percent on long-term capital gains. An 8 percent investment tax credit is applicable to the cost of assets. The firm's cost of capital applicable to the proposed replacement is 18 percent.

a   Find each of the following cash flow components associated with *each* of the two proposed replacement trucks: (1) initial investment, (2) operating cash inflows, (3) terminal cash flows.

b   Find and diagram the relevant cash flow stream associated with each of the alternatives using your findings in **a**.

c   Apply each of the following decision techniques to the relevant cash flow streams developed in **b**: (1) payback period, (2) net present value *(NPV)*, (3) profitability index *(PI)*, (4) internal rate of return *(IRR)*.

d   Draw net present value profiles for the two replacement trucks on the same set of axes and discuss conflicting rankings, if any, resulting from use of *NPV* and *IRR* decision techniques.

e   Recommend which, if either, of the trucks the firm should acquire if the firm has (1) unlimited funds and (2) capital rationing.

Chapter 11

Capital Budgeting Refinements and Risk

After studying this chapter, you should be able to:

1. Describe the procedures used to compare and select the best project from a group of mutually exclusive projects having unequal lives.

2. Discuss popular techniques for choosing projects under capital rationing and consider the effect of inflation in capital budgeting.

3. Recognize the relationship between risk and cash inflows and the basic approaches — sensitivity analysis, statistical, decision trees, and simulation — for dealing with project risk.

4. Understand the two basic risk-adjustment techniques — certainty equivalents (*CE*s) and risk-adjusted discount rates (*RADR*s).

5. Explain portfolio effects related to risk and the practical issues surrounding use of certainty equivalents versus risk-adjusted discount rates.

6. Identify the key factors unique to developing cash flows and making capital budgeting decisions in an international setting.

T hroughout the discussions of capital budgeting in Chapters 9 and 10, it was assumed that all projects had equal lives, the firm had unlimited funds, there was no inflation, and all projects' cash flows had the same level of risk as the firm. Since in fact very few decisions are made under these conditions, understanding the techniques for dealing with unequal lives, capital rationing, inflation, and risk is important. After presenting the basic refinements of unequal lives, capital rationing, and inflation, in this chapter we concentrate on the key considerations for dealing with risk. Primary emphasis is given to application of the basic risk concepts presented in Chapter 7 in order to adjust for project risk when making capital budgeting decisions.

Capital Budgeting Refinements

A number of refinements must often be made in the analysis of capital budgeting projects in order to accommodate special circumstances. These adjustments permit the relaxation of certain simplifying assumptions presented earlier. Three of the areas where special forms of analysis are frequently needed are (1) when comparing mutually exclusive projects having unequal lives, (2) when a binding budget constraint causes capital rationing, and (3) when future inflation rates are expected to be high.

COMPARING PROJECTS WITH UNEQUAL LIVES

The financial manager must often select the best of a group of unequal-lived projects. If the projects are independent, the length of the project lives is not critical. But when unequal-lived projects are mutually exclusive, the impact of differing lives must be considered because the projects do not provide service over comparable time periods. The following example illustrates the situation.

EXAMPLE The WS Company is in the process of evaluating two projects, X and Y. The relevant cash flows for each project are given in the table. The applicable cost of capital for use in evaluating these equally risky projects is 15 percent.

	Project X	Project Y
Initial investment *(II)*	$60,000	$75,000
Year *(t)*	Cash inflows *(CF_t)*	
1	$28,000	$35,000
2	33,000	30,000
3	38,000	25,000
4	—	20,000
5	—	15,000
6	—	10,000

Using the technique presented in Chapter 10, the net present value (*NPV*) of each project at the 15 percent cost of capital is found to be

$$NPV_X = [\$28,000(.870) + \$33,000(.756) + \$38,000(.658)] - \$60,000$$
$$= (\$24,360 + \$24,948 + \$25,004) - \$60,000$$
$$= \$74,312 - \$60,000 = \underline{\$14,312}$$

$$NPV_Y = [\$35,000(.870) + \$30,000(.756) + \$25,000(.658) + \$20,000(.572)$$
$$+ \$15,000(.497) + \$10,000(.432)] - \$75,000$$
$$= (\$30,450 + \$22,680 + \$16,450 + \$11,440 + \$7,455 + \$4,320) - \$75,000$$
$$= \$92,795 - \$75,000 = \underline{\$17,795}$$

The *NPV* for project X is $14,312, for project Y, $17,795. Ignoring the differences in project lives, it can be seen that both projects are acceptable (*NPV*s greater than zero) and that project Y is preferred over project X. In other words, if the projects are independent and, due to limited funds, only one could be accepted, project Y, with the larger *NPV*, would be preferred. On the other hand, if the projects are mutually exclusive, their differing lives must be considered; project X provides three years of service, and project Y provides six years of service. ∎

The analysis in this example is incomplete if the projects are mutually exclusive (our assumption throughout the remaining discussions). To compare these un-equal-lived mutually exclusive projects correctly, the differing lives must be considered in the analysis; an incorrect decision could result from use of *NPV* to select the better project. There are two common approaches for dealing with unequal lives: (1) the least common life approach and (2) the annualized net present value approach.

Least common life approach. To equalize and make comparable unequal-lived projects, the *least common life* can be determined. It is the shortest period of time over which projects can be repeated so as to cause them to terminate in the same year. For example, in the case of WS Company's three- and six-year-lived projects, the least common life would be six years. Repeating the three-year-lived project (X) once would cause it to terminate after six years—the life of project Y. The *least common life approach* involves the following four steps:

1. Find the least common life for the projects being compared.
2. Determine the relevant cash flow stream resulting from repeating each project the necessary number of times to reach the least common life.[1]
3. Using the cost of capital, find the net present value (*NPV*) of each project over the least common life using the cash flows developed in step 2.
4. Choose the project having the highest *NPV* based on step 3; it is the best one.

EXAMPLE   Returning to the WS Company, the four-step least common life procedure can be applied using the data presented earlier.

1. The least common life is six years, which means that project X will have to be repeated once and project Y does not have to be repeated.
2. Since only project X needs to be repeated in order to reach the six-year least common life, its relevant cash flows are found as shown here:

				End of year			
Project X	0	1	2	3	4	5	6
First purchase	−$60,000	$28,000	$33,000	$38,000			
Second purchase				− 60,000	$28,000	$33,000	$38,000
Relevant *CF*	−$60,000	$28,000	$33,000	−$22,000	$28,000	$33,000	$38,000

Note that the second purchase takes place at the beginning of year 4, which is equivalent to the end of year 3 as shown in the table.

3. Using the firm's 15 percent cost of capital, the net present value of the relevant cash flows for project X developed in the preceding step can be calculated:

$$
\begin{aligned}
NPV_X &= [\$28{,}000(.870) + \$33{,}000(.756) - \$22{,}000(.658) \\
&\quad + \$28{,}000(.572) + \$33{,}000(.497) + \$38{,}000(.432)] - \$60{,}000 \\
&= (\$24{,}360 + \$24{,}948 - \$14{,}476 + \$16{,}016 + \$16{,}401 \\
&\quad + \$16{,}416) - \$60{,}000 \\
&= \$83{,}665 - \$60{,}000 = \underline{\$23{,}665}
\end{aligned}
$$

Since project Y does not need to be repeated, its net present value is the same as that calculated in the earlier example.

$$
NPV_Y = \underline{\$17{,}795}
$$

4. Comparing the *NPV*s found in step 3, it can be seen that project X is preferred over project Y ($NPV_X = \$23{,}665 > NPV_Y = \$17{,}795$). In other words, once the lives are equalized, *project X is preferred*. Recall from the earlier example that when the differences in lives were ignored, project Y was preferred since its $17,795 *NPV* was

---

[1] Often, to reach the least common life, the projects being compared must each be repeated a number of times. For example, in comparing a three-year and a four-year project, the least common life is 12 years. The three-year-lived project would therefore have to be repeated four times and the four-year-lived project three times in this case.

greater than the single-cycle *NPV* of $14,312 for project X. Since these projects are mutually exclusive, the lives must be equalized, making project X preferred. ■

Annualized net present value (*ANPV*) approach. A second and much more efficient approach to selecting the best of unequal-lived mutually exclusive projects is the *annualized net present value (ANPV)*. The *ANPV* method, like the least common life approach, implicitly assumes that each project can be replaced up to the least common life for the same initial investment that will provide the same expected cash inflows. While this assumption may seem unreasonable, it does not detract from the usefulness of these techniques.[2]

The annualized net present value method converts the net present value of unequal-lived projects into an equivalent (in *NPV* terms) annual amount that can be used to select the best project. This net-present-value-based approach can be applied to unequal-lived mutually exclusive projects using the following steps.

1. Calculate the net present value of each project *j*, NPV_j, over its life, n_j, using the appropriate cost of capital, *k*.
2. Divide the net present value of each project having a positive *NPV* by the present-value interest factor for an annuity at the given cost of capital and the project's life to get the annualized net present value for each project *j*, $ANPV_j$.

$$ANPV_j = \frac{NPV_j}{PVIFA_{k,n_j}}$$
(11.1)

3. The project having the highest *ANPV* would be the best, followed by the project with the next highest *ANPV*, and so on. Application of these steps can be illustrated using data from the earlier example.

EXAMPLE   Using the WS Company data presented earlier for projects X and Y, the application of the three-step *ANPV* approach can be illustrated as follows:

1. The net present values of projects X and Y discounted at 15 percent — calculated earlier for a single purchase of each asset — are

$$NPV_X = \$14,312$$
$$NPV_Y = \$17,795$$

As noted earlier, based on these *NPV*s, which ignore the differing lives, project Y is preferred over project X.

2. Applying Equation 11.1 to the *NPV*s, the annualized net present value for each project can be calculated.

$$ANPV_X = \frac{\$14,312}{PVIFA_{15\%,3\,yrs}} = \frac{\$14,312}{2.283} = \underline{\$6,269}$$

$$ANPV_Y = \frac{\$17,795}{PVIFA_{15\%,6\,yrs}} = \frac{\$17,795}{3.784} = \underline{\$4,703}$$

[2] A brief discussion of the effect of inflation and changing technology on the initial investment and expected cash inflows from replacements when performing unequal-life project comparisons is included in the next section of this chapter.

3. Reviewing the *ANPV*s calculated in step 2, it can be seen that project X would be preferred over project Y. Comparing this conclusion to that obtained using the least common life approach, it should be clear that the *ANPV* ranking is the same as that obtained using the *NPV* for the least common lives (the rankings obtained using these alternative approaches will *always* agree). Given that projects X and Y are mutually exclusive, project X would be the recommended project because it provides the highest annualized net present value. ■

Inflation and changing technology. Both the least common life approach and the annualized net present value (*ANPV*) approach for selecting unequal-lived mutually exclusive projects assume *no inflation* and *no changes in technology.* These assumptions allow the projects to be repeated at the same cost with the same cash inflows when the least common life approach is used. Although not as obvious, the assumed absence of inflation and changes in technology is implicit in the annualized net present value approach. These assumptions do streamline the computations, especially when using the more efficient *ANPV* approach, but in periods of rapid inflation and changing technology they may not result in selection of the best project.

When inflation or changes in technology are expected to be significant, the procedures illustrated earlier can be modified to describe the situation more accurately. One technique involves using the least common life approach. The anticipated changes in initial investment and cash inflows for each replacement cycle over the least common life can be enumerated in the cash flows prior to finding the *NPV*s for the least common life. In the earlier example of the WS Company, if inflation and technology changes were anticipated, the cash flows for the second cycle of the three-year-lived project, X, would be estimated according to these changes prior to determining the relevant cash flows for the six-year least common life. The project with the higher *NPV* for the least common life would be preferred.

A second approach is to use the life of the shortest-lived project as the period of comparison. Projects with longer lives would be assumed to be liquidated at an estimated market value, which is treated as a cash inflow, at the end of the common life. For example if we wished to compare three-, five-, and six-year-lived projects, a three-year common life would be used, and the five- and six-year-lived projects would be treated as if they were liquidated at an estimated market value at the end of the third year. The project with the highest *NPV* for the three-year common life would be preferred. With this technique it would not be necessary actually to forecast the impact of inflation and changing technology on the cash flows.

CAPITAL RATIONING

Firms commonly find more acceptable projects than they have the money to undertake. The objective of *capital rationing* is to select the group of projects that will benefit the firm most. This is generally done by selecting the group that provides the *highest overall net present value* and does not require more dollars than are budgeted. Many capital rationing approaches are available. Whichever is used, remember that all projects considered must be independent; if there are any mutually exclusive projects, the best of these should be chosen and placed in the group of independent projects.[3] Only two basic approaches to project selection under capital rationing are discussed here, although sophisticated approaches are available.

Internal rate of return approach. The *internal rate of return approach* involves plotting *IRR*s, or yields, against total dollars on the basis of decreasing *IRR*s.[4] By drawing the cutoff-rate line and then imposing a budget constraint, the group of acceptable projects can be determined. The problem with this technique is that it does not guarantee maximum dollar return to the firm; it merely provides a satisfactory solution to capital rationing problems.

EXAMPLE   The Zink Fuel Company is confronted with six projects competing for the firm's fixed budget of $250,000. The *IRR* and initial investment for each project are as follows:

Project	Initial investment	*IRR*
A	$ 80,000	12%
B	70,000	20
C	100,000	16
D	40,000	8
E	60,000	15
F	110,000	11

The firm has a cost of capital of 10 percent. Figure 11.1 presents a graph of the six projects ranked in descending order based on *IRR*s. According to the graph, only projects B, C, and E should be accepted. Together they will absorb $230,000 of the $250,000 budget. Project D is not even worthy of consideration, since its *IRR* is less than the firm's 10 percent cost of capital, or cutoff rate. The drawback of this approach is that there is no guarantee that acceptance of projects B, C, and E will maximize total dollar returns and therefore owners' wealth. ■

Net present value approach. The *net present value approach* is based on the use of present values to determine the group of projects that will maximize owners' wealth. It can be approached by ranking projects on the basis of *IRR*s or *PI*s and then evaluating the present value of the benefits from each project to determine the combination with the highest overall present value. This is the same as maximizing net present value, since whether the entire budget is used or not it is viewed as the total initial investment for which maximum present value of benefits must be obtained. *The portion of the firm's budget that is not used does not increase the firm's value.* At best, the unused money can be invested in marketable

---

[3] When more sophisticated mathematical programing and statistical techniques are applied to capital rationing problems, the mutually exclusive projects are grouped in various ways and the mutually exclusive project that is best in light of the total portfolio of projects is chosen. Due to the basic level of this text, this approach is not described.

[4] The schedule of investment opportunities plotted on a set of investment-return axes beginning with the largest *IRR* and continuing in order of decreasing *IRR*s is often called the firm's *investment opportunities schedule (IOS)*. This schedule is developed in greater detail in Chapter 12 as part of the discussion of the cost of capital.

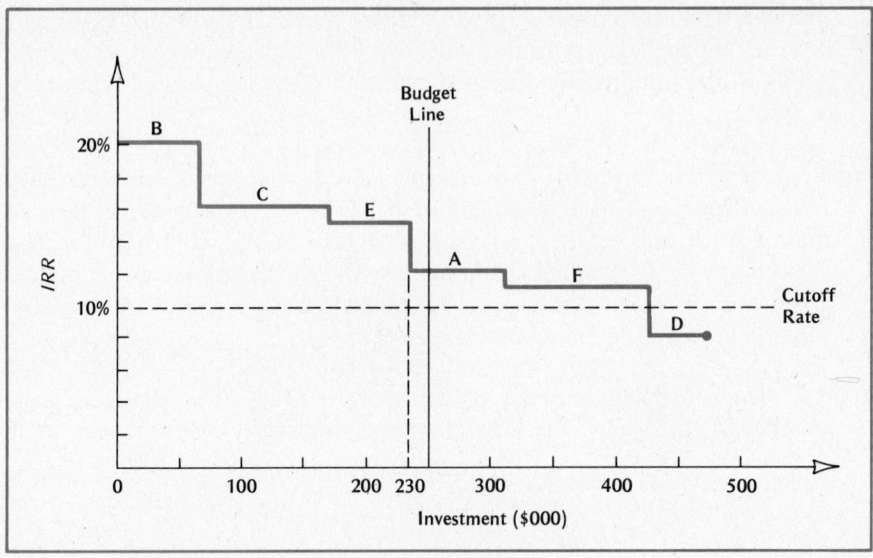

Figure 11.1   *IRRs* for the Zink Fuel Company projects

securities or returned to the owners in the form of cash dividends. In either case, the wealth of the owners is not likely to be enhanced.

EXAMPLE   The group of projects described in the preceding example is ranked in Table 11.1 on the basis of *IRRs*. The present value of the cash inflows associated with the projects is also included in the table. Projects B, C, and E, which together require $230,000, yield a return of $336,000. However, if projects B, C, and A were implemented, the total budget of $250,000 would be used and the present value of the cash inflows would be $357,000. This is greater than the return expected from selecting the projects with the highest *IRRs*. Implementing B, C, and A is preferable, since they maximize the present value of the firm's overall return for the given budget. *Our objective is to use the budget to generate the highest present value of inflows or net present value.*[5] Assuming that any unused portion of

Table 11.1   Rankings for the Zink Fuel Company Projects

Project	Initial investment	IRR	PV of inflows at 10%	
B	$ 70,000	20%	$112,000	
C	100,000	16	145,000	
E	60,000	15	79,000	
A	80,000	12	100,000	
F	110,000	11	126,500	Cutoff point
D	40,000	8	36,000	

[5] It may be conceptually difficult for the reader to understand why any unused portion of the budget does not increase the firm's value. One must view the situation as one in which the firm has a fixed amount of money available for which the firm is paying an annual cost equal to the cost of capital. Any unused portion of this money can, at best, be invested in marketable securities or paid out as cash dividends. Both alternatives will likely have negative *NPVs* and, therefore, will reduce the firm's value.

the budget does not gain or lose money, the total *NPV* for projects B, C, and E would be $106,000 ($336,000 − $230,000),[6] while for projects B, C, and A, the total *NPV* would be $107,000 ($357,000 − $250,000). In light of this comparison, it is clear that of the available acceptable projects, the optimal selection would be B, C, and A, since they generate the highest *NPV* from the available budget. Selecting projects B, C, and A will therefore maximize *NPV*. The technique described using either *IRR*s or *PI*s for the initial ranking is probably the best trial-and-error method for selecting projects when capital rationing is necessary. ■

CONSIDERING INFLATION IN CAPITAL BUDGETING

Inflation—a rise in price levels—can significantly affect the cash inflows from capital expenditures.[7] The cost of capital or required return, as noted in Chapter 3, contains an inflationary expectation component. When the rate of inflation is expected to be modest, managerial concern is low and inflation adjustments are not required, but when high rates are anticipated, greater attention is needed. The high rates of inflation experienced in recent years have caused financial managers to give explicit consideration to expected inflation when estimating project cash inflows.

The process of adjusting cash inflows for anticipated inflation is relatively simple. Any forecast cash outflows and inflows measured in today's dollars must be adjusted by the anticipated rate of inflation in order to estimate the expected cash flow in each year. Although this process is somewhat speculative, it is appropriate because management wants the best estimate of cash flows associated with a capital expenditure. Clearly no one can predict the future precisely, but good estimates are better than ignoring economic realities. An example will help to illustrate the importance as well as the process of adjusting expected cash inflows for inflation.

EXAMPLE Venture Industries is considering investing in a project requiring an initial investment of $64,400 and expected to provide relevant cash inflows over its five-year life as derived in Table 11.2. Using the firm's 14 percent cost of capital and the cash inflows from column 5 of Table 11.2, the net present value of the project is calculated as follows:

$$NPV = [\$13,200(.877) + \$16,960(.769) + \$18,480(.675) + \$20,280(.592)$$
$$+ \$22,080(.519)] - \$64,400$$
$$= (\$11,576.40 + \$13,042.24 + \$12,474.00 + \$12,005.76 + \$11,459.52)$$
$$- \$64,400.00$$
$$= \$60,557.92 - \$64,400.00 = \underline{-\$3,842.08}$$

Since the *NPV* of −$3,842.08 is less than zero, the project should be rejected.

Assume that before rejecting the project, the financial manager reviews the estimated

---

[6] Because it is likely that the *NPV* would be negative on the $20,000 excess ($250,000 available less $230,000 used) with projects B, C, and E (since they are paying more for the money than they earn on it), the *NPV* from this selection will be less than the $106,000 calculated.

[7] Note that similar concern and procedures could be applied in situations where *deflation*—a decline in price levels—is anticipated. Because it continues to dominate our economy, our attention here is devoted only to inflation.

Table 11.2   Derivation of Venture Industries' Relevant Cash Inflows

Year (t)	Earnings before depreciation and taxes ($EBDT_t$) (1)	Depreciation[a] (2)	Earnings before taxes [(1) − (2)] (3)	Earnings after taxes[b] [(1 − .40)(3)] (4)	Relevant cash inflows [(2) + (4)] (5)
1	$15,000	$10,500	$ 4,500	$2,700	$13,200
2	18,000	15,400	2,600	1,560	16,960
3	21,000	14,700	6,300	3,780	18,480
4	24,000	14,700	9,300	5,580	20,280
5[c]	27,000	14,700	12,300	7,380	22,080

[a] ACRS depreciation over the five-year normal recovery period was applied to the $70,000 depreciable value. Note the depreciable value of $70,000 is larger than the initial investment of $64,400: such a difference is not unusual.
[b] The firm's marginal tax rate on ordinary income is 40 percent.
[c] The terminal cash flow is zero, and therefore no adjustment to the year 5 operating cash inflow is required.

earnings before depreciation and taxes, finding that the analyst failed to adjust these figures for the annual 6 percent rate of inflation expected over the coming five years. To correct this error, the analyst applies a 6 percent compound growth rate to the estimates to make them more accurate. Table 11.3 shows the derivation of the relevant cash inflows incorporating the 6 percent rate of anticipated inflation. The inflation-adjusted earnings before depreciation and taxes ($EBDT$) is shown in column 3; these values were derived by adjusting $EBDT$ using the appropriate $FVIF$ factors at a 6 percent rate. After adjusting for depreciation and taxes, the inflation-adjusted relevant cash inflows are shown in column 7. As expected, these values are larger than those derived in Table 11.2.

Applying the 14 percent cost of capital to the inflation-adjusted relevant cash inflows from Table 11.3 results in the net present value:

$$
\begin{aligned}
NPV_{inflation\text{-}adjusted} &= [\$13,740(.877) + \$18,299(.769) + \$20,887(.675) \\
&\quad + \$24,053(.592) + \$27,556(.519)] - \$64,400 \\
&= (\$12,049.98 + \$14,071.93 + \$14,098.73 + \$14,239.38 \\
&\quad + \$14,301.56) - \$64,400.00 \\
&= \$68,761.58 - \$64,400.00 = \underline{\$4,361.58}
\end{aligned}
$$

The project's NPV of $4,361.58 now makes it acceptable. Clearly, attention must be given to the impact of potential inflation or deflation on future cash flows in the capital budgeting process, or the result may be poor decisions. ■

Approaches for Dealing with Risk

Up to this point, the discussion of capital budgeting techniques has been based on the assumption that all projects' cash flows have the same level of risk as the firm. Project cash inflows were equally risky. In actuality, there are very few capital budgeting projects for which cash inflows have the same risk as the firm. Using the basic risk concepts presented in Chapter 7, here we present some approaches for

Table 11.3   Derivation of Venture Industries' Relevant Cash Inflows Adjusted for Annual 6% Inflation

Year (t)	Earnings before depreciation and taxes $(EBDT_t)^a$ (1)	Inflation adjustment factor $FVIF_{6\%,t}$ (2)	Inflation-adjusted $EBDT$ $[(1) \times (2)]$ (3)	Depreciation[b] (4)	Inflation-adjusted earnings before taxes $[(3) - (4)]$ (5)	Inflation-adjusted earnings after taxes[c] $[(1 - .40)(5)]$ (6)	Inflation-adjusted relevant cash inflows $[(4) + (6)]$ (7)
1	$15,000	1.060	$15,900	$10,500	$ 5,400	$3,240	$13,740
2	18,000	1.124	20,232	15,400	4,832	2,899	18,299
3	23,000	1.191	25,011	14,700	10,311	6,187	20,887
4	24,000	1.262	30,288	14,700	15,588	9,353	24,053
5[d]	27,000	1.338	36,126	14,700	21,426	12,856	27,556

[a] Values from column 1 of Table 11.2.
[b] ACRS depreciation over the five-year normal recovery period was applied to the $70,000 depreciable value. Note the depreciable value of $70,000 is larger than the initial investment of $64,400; such a difference is not unusual.
[c] These values were rounded to the nearest whole dollar. The firm's marginal tax rate on ordinary income is 40 percent.
[d] The terminal cash flow is zero, and therefore no adjustment to the year 5 operating cash inflow is required.

dealing with risk in capital budgeting: risk and cash inflows, sensitivity analysis, statistical approaches, decision trees, and simulation.

RISK AND CASH INFLOWS

In the discussion of risk and return in Chapter 7, risk is defined as a chance of loss or, more formally, the variability of expected returns associated with a given asset. In the context of capital budgeting, *risk* refers to the chance that a project would prove unacceptable (i.e., $NPV < 0$, $PI < 1$, or $IRR < k$) or, more formally, the variability of expected cash flows. Projects with a small chance of being acceptable and a broad range of expected cash flows are more risky than projects having a high chance of acceptance and a narrow range of expected cash flows. In conventional capital budgeting projects,[8] risk stems almost entirely from cash inflows, since the initial investment is generally known with relative certainty. These inflows, of course, derive from a number of risky variables related to revenues, expenditures, and taxes. Examples would include the level of sales, costs of raw materials, labor rates, utility costs, and tax rates. We will concentrate on the risk in the cash inflows, but remember that this risk actually results from the interaction of these underlying variables. Therefore, to assess the risk of a proposed capital expenditure, the analyst needs to evaluate the probability that the cash inflows will be large enough to provide for project acceptance. This concept is best demonstrated by a simple example.

EXAMPLE Goodwear Tire Company is considering investing in either of two mutually exclusive projects, A and B, each requiring a $10,000 initial investment (*II*) and expected to provide equal annual cash inflows (*CF*) over their 15-year lives. For either project to be acceptable using the net present value (*NPV*) technique, its *NPV* must be greater than zero. Letting *CF* equal the annual cash inflow and *II* equal the initial investment, the following condition must be met for projects with annuity cash inflows, such as A and B, to be acceptable.

$$NPV = CF(PVIFA_{k,n}) - II \geq \$0 \qquad (11.2)$$

Substituting $k = 10\%$, $n = 15$ years, and $II = \$10,000$, the *breakeven cash inflow*—the level of cash inflow necessary for Goodwear's projects to be acceptable—can be found.

$$CF(PVIFA_{10\%,15\,yrs}) - \$10,000 \geq \$0$$
$$CF(7.606) \geq \$10,000$$

$$CF \geq \frac{\$10,000}{7.606} = \underline{\$1,315}$$

In other words, for the projects to be acceptable, they must have annual cash inflows of at least $1,315.

---

[8] Throughout the discussion of risk we will continue to assume that all projects have conventional cash flow patterns—an outflow followed by a series of inflows. This assumption is made for pedagogical convenience in order to provide a straightforward presentation of this important concept.

QUALIFICATIONS FOR CHIEF FINANCIAL OFFICERS (CFOs)

A quick survey of the literature concerning the qualifications employers look for in their financial officers suggests that firms expect a lot more from their chief financial officers (CFOs) than they did in the past. For example, they're looking for broader management experience, they're looking for more international "savvy," and they're emphasizing the "control" side over the "treasury" side.

Those judgments appeared in recent articles in the major business newspapers and periodicals, and they coincide with the observations of those at my firm.

I sat down with some of my colleagues and we agreed on some additional qualifications that prospective employers are looking for these days.

For example, everyone is aware that inflation has had a serious impact on the replacement value of plants and equipment. This is reflected in a demand for financial executives who can analyze replacement costs and determine the kind of return they can make on investments in new plants and equipment.

We've also noted that companies expect their financial people to concentrate on the management of corporate assets — real estate, offices, factories — as never before. They want financial executives who are extremely sophisticated in their ways of looking at fixed assets.

But after going through this informal and rather unscientific process, I decided to dig deeper. I dug into our files and pulled out the "spec" sheets for recruiting assignments about 12 years ago — in 1972 and 1973 — and compared them with our records for last year and this year. I think the results are very revealing.

For example, 12 years ago, not a single one of our clients explicitly insisted on international experience and knowhow. Currently, by way of contrast, at least half are citing international competence as a basic requirement.

As for the "control" function, the results are even more striking. Again, there was not any mention of this a decade ago, whereas now it's stressed more often than not. Obviously, companies are more concerned with cost containment and balance sheet management.

To quote a typical requirement: "Candidates must be proven managers with more experience in control than in treasury, and with a thoroughly operational orientation."

There are several other interesting and significant findings. One of them is that very few lists of qualifications demanded by our clients were specific, a decade ago, as to years of experience — and when they were, they usually cited 5, 10, or 15 years.

Employers now tend to be not only more specific but more demanding; they're more likely to insist on 15, 20, or even more years experience. But it's not just *years* that they're looking for — it's assurance that the people they're considering are executives who have gained experience through full business cycles — who have manned the rudder through fair days and foul.

Incidentally, on average, the compensation they're offering is usually at least triple the levels of 10 years ago, and it's not all because of inflation. Companies seem to be more aware of the value of good financial management, and they're willing to pay for it.

SOURCE: Ferdinand Nadherny, "The State-of-the-Art CFO," *Financial Executive*, April 1984, pp. 12–13.

Given this breakeven level of cash inflows, the risk of each project could be assessed by determining—using various statistical techniques beyond the scope of this text[9]—the probability that the firm's cash inflows will equal or exceed this breakeven level. Assume that such a statistical analysis results in the following:

Probability of $CF_A > \$1315$ 100%
Probability of $CF_B > \$1315$ 65%

Since project A is certain (100 percent probability) to have a positive net present value, while there is only a 65 percent chance that project B will have a positive NPV, project A is less risky than project B. Of course, the potential level of returns associated with each project must be evaluated in view of the firm's risk preference prior to selecting the preferred project. ■

The example clearly identified risk as it relates to the chance that a project is acceptable, but it didn't address the issue of cash flow variability. Even though project B had a greater chance of loss than project A, it might result in higher potential NPVs. Recall from Chapters 7 and 8 that it is the combination of risk and return that determines value. Similarly, the worth of a capital expenditure and its impact on the firm's value must be viewed in light of both risk and return. The analyst must therefore consider the variability of cash inflows and NPVs to assess project risk and return fully.

SENSITIVITY ANALYSIS

One of the simplest approaches for dealing with project risk to capture the variability of cash inflows and NPVs is sensitivity analysis. *Sensitivity analysis,* as noted in Chapter 7, involves using a number of possible inputs (cash inflows) to assess their impact on the firm's return (NPV). This technique is often useful in getting a feel for the variability of returns. In capital budgeting, one of the most common sensitivity approaches is to estimate the NPVs associated with pessimistic (worst), most likely (expected), and optimistic (best) cash inflow estimates. By subtracting the pessimistic-outcome NPV from the optimistic-outcome NPV, the range, which is the basic measure of variability, can be determined.

EXAMPLE   Returning to Goodwear Tire, assume that to gain greater insight into the riskiness of projects A and B, the financial manager made pessimistic, most likely, and optimistic estimates of the cash inflows for each project. The cash inflow estimates and resulting NPVs in each case are summarized in Table 11.4. Comparing the ranges of cash inflows—$1,000 ($2,500 − $1,500) for project A and $4,000 ($4,000 − $0) for project B—and, more important, the range of NPVs—$7,606 for project A and $30,424 for project B—makes it clear that project A is less risky than project B. Depending on the decision maker's attitude toward risk, he or she may choose either project. If risk-averse, the decision maker will take project A, thereby eliminating the possibility of loss; if a risk taker, the decision maker may take project B in light of the possibility of receiving a return with a high net present value.

[9] Normal distributions are commonly used to develop the concept of the probability of success—that is, of a project's having a positive NPV. The reader interested in learning more about this technique should see an M.B.A. or second-level managerial finance text such as Lawrence J. Gitman, Michael D. Joehnk, and George E. Pinches, *Managerial Finance* (New York: Harper & Row, 1985), Chapter 14.

Table 11.4   Sensitivity Analysis of Goodwear's
Projects A and B

	Project A	Project B
Initial investment	$10,000	$10,000
	Annual cash inflows	
Outcome		
Pessimistic	$1,500	$ 0
Most likely	2,000	2,000
Optimistic	2,500	4,000
Range	$1,000	$4,000
	Net present values[a]	
Outcome		
Pessimistic	$1,409	−$10,000
Most likely	5,212	5,212
Optimistic	9,015	20,424
Range	$7,606	$30,424

[a] These values were calculated using the corresponding cash inflows. A 10 percent cost of capital and a 15-year life for the annual cash inflows were used.

Although sensitivity analysis and the use of the range are still rather crude, they do provide the decision maker with more than one estimate of the project's outcome, and they can be used to make a rough assessment of the risk involved. ■

STATISTICAL APPROACHES

The use of the standard deviation and coefficient of variation to measure the risk of a single asset held in isolation[10] was presented in Chapter 7. These measures can be applied to a probability distribution of cash inflows or net present values to measure project risk statistically. As noted in Chapter 7, probability distributions can be *discrete* (having only a limited number of outcome-probability values) or *continuous* (having a large number of outcome-probability values). In practice, the financial manager may be faced with either type. The following example illustrates the application of these statistics to discrete *NPV* distributions.

EXAMPLE   The Goodwear Tire Company prepared a discrete probability distribution of *NPV*s for projects A and B by estimating the probability of the pessimistic, most likely, and optimistic outcomes. The *NPV* outcomes and associated probabilities for each of the projects is shown in Table 11.5. These values are also presented as a bar chart in Figure 11.2. Reviews of both the table and the figure clearly depict the greater variability of outcomes associated with project B.

To find the standard deviation of each project, the first step is to calculate the *expected*

[10] Our concern at this point is with the risk of a single project rather than the risk of a project held as part of a portfolio of projects. Portfolio effects as they relate to capital budgeting decisions are discussed later in this chapter.

Table 11.5   Discrete Probability Distributions of *NPV*s
for Goodwear's Projects A and B

i	Outcome$_i$	NPV_i^a	Probability, Pr_i^b
Project A			
1	Pessimistic	$ 1,409	.25
2	Most likely	5,212	.50
3	Optimistic	9,015	.25
Project B			
1	Pessimistic	−$10,000	.25
2	Most likely	5,212	.50
3	Optimistic	20,424	.25

[a] From Table 11.4.
[b] Values estimated subjectively, based on past experience.

net present value of each project. *The expected NPV, $\overline{NPV}$, can be calculated using*
Equation 7.2 from Chapter 7, rewritten as

$$\overline{NPV} = \sum_{i=1}^{n} NPV_i \times Pr_i \qquad (11.3)$$

where

$$NPV_i = \text{the } NPV \text{ for the } i\text{th outcome}$$
$$Pr_i = \text{the probability of occurrence of the } i\text{th } NPV$$
$$n = \text{the number of outcomes considered}$$

Substituting the data from Table 11.5, the expected *NPV* can be calculated for each project:

$$\overline{NPV}_A = \$1,409(.25) + \$5,212(.50) + \$9,015(.25)$$
$$= \$352.25 + \$2,606.00 + \$2,253.75 = \underline{\$5,212}$$

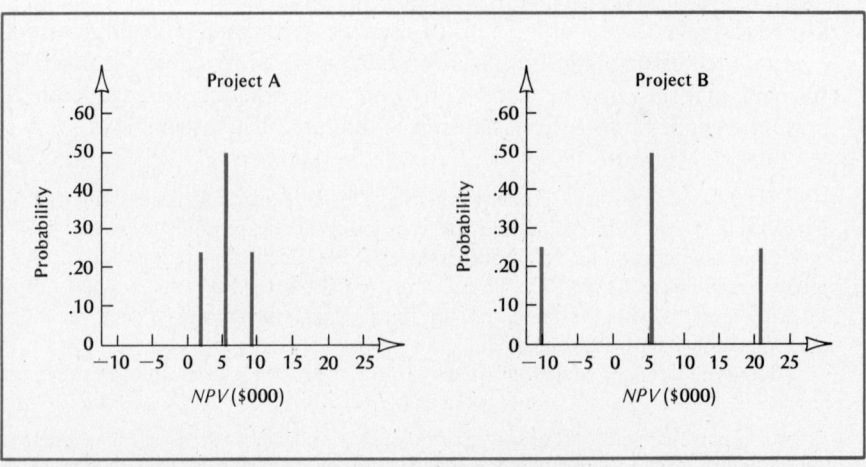

Figure 11.2   Bar charts for Goodwear Tire Company's projects A and B

Table 11.6 Calculation of the Standard Deviation of
NPV for Goodwear's Projects A and B

i	NPV_i	$\overline{NPV}$	$NPV_i - \overline{NPV}$	$(NPV_i - \overline{NPV})^2$	Pr_i	$(NPV_i - \overline{NPV})^2 \times Pr_i$
Project A						
1	$1,409	$5,212	−$ 3,803	$14,462,809	.25	$3,615,702
2	5,212	5,212	0	0	.50	0
3	9,015	5,212	3,803	14,462,809	.25	3,615,702

$$\sum_{i=1}^{3} (NPV_i - \overline{NPV})^2 \times Pr_i = \$7,231,404$$

$$\sigma_{NPV_A} = \sqrt{\sum_{i=1}^{3} (NPV_i - \overline{NPV})^2 \times Pr_i} = \sqrt{\$7,231,404} = \underline{\$\ 2,689}$$

i	NPV_i	$\overline{NPV}$	$NPV_i - \overline{NPV}$	$(NPV_i - \overline{NPV})^2$	Pr_i	$(NPV_i - \overline{NPV})^2 \times Pr_i$
Project B						
1	−$10,000	$5,212	$15,212	$231,400,000	.25	$ 57,850,000
2	5,212	5,212	0	0	.50	0
3	20,424	5,212	15,212	231,400,000	.25	57,850,000

$$\sum_{i=1}^{3} (NPV_i - \overline{NPV})^2 \times Pr_i = \$115,700,000$$

$$\sigma_{NPV_B} = \sqrt{\sum_{i=1}^{3} (NPV_i - \overline{NPV})^2 \times Pr_i} = \sqrt{\$115,700,000} = \underline{\$10,756}$$

$$\overline{NPV}_B = -\$10,000(.25) + \$5,212(.50) + \$20,424(.25)$$
$$= -\$2,500 + \$2,606 + \$5,106 = \underline{\$5,212}$$

Note that both projects have expected NPVs of $5,212 which also equals their most likely estimates.[11]

Once the expected NPV, $\overline{NPV}$, has been calculated, the *standard deviation of NPV*, σ_{NPV}, can be found using Equation 7.3 from Chapter 7, rewritten as

$$\sigma_{NPV} = \sqrt{\sum_{i=1}^{n} (NPV_i - \overline{NPV})^2 \times Pr_i} \qquad (11.4)$$

The calculation of the standard deviation of NPV for projects A and B using Equation 11.4 is given in Table 11.6. It can be seen that, as anticipated, project B's standard deviation of $10,756 is much higher than project A's standard deviation of $2,689. Based on this statistic, project B is clearly more risky than project A.

The *coefficient of variation, CV,* is another statistic commonly used to compare risk; as demonstrated in Chapter 7, it is especially useful for comparing the risk of projects of differing size. Since projects A and B have the same expected NPV, the coefficient of variation does not really improve the comparison. Applying Equation 7.4 from Chapter 7 to the NPV data, the coefficient of variation of NPV, CV_{NPV}, is defined as

$$CV_{NPV} = \frac{\sigma_{NPV}}{\overline{NPV}} \qquad (11.5)$$

---

[11] Because this example is designed to highlight certain aspects of risk, the expected NPVs for the two projects are equal.

Substituting σ_{NPV} and $\overline{NPV}$ for projects A and B into Equation 11.5 yields

$$CV_{NPV_A} = \frac{\sigma_{NPV_A}}{\overline{NPV_A}} = \frac{\$2,689}{\$5,212} = \underline{.516}$$

$$CV_{NPV_B} = \frac{\sigma_{NPV_B}}{\overline{NPV_B}} = \frac{\$10,756}{\$5,212} = \underline{2.064}$$

Clearly, project B, with a coefficient of variation of NPV of 2.064, is more risky than project A, which has a CV of .516. As expected, the coefficient of variation indicates that project B is more risky than project A. ■

DECISION TREES

An expected-value-based approach commonly used when making capital budgeting decisions is the *decision tree*. Decision trees are diagrams that permit the various decision alternatives and payoffs as well as their probabilities of occurrence to be mapped out in a clear fashion. They get their name from their resemblance to trees with a number of branches (see Figure 11.3). Decision trees can be viewed as a form of sensitivity analysis in which probabilities are attached to the outcomes (pessimistic, most likely, optimistic) considered.

Although decision trees provide a mechanism that allows the decision maker to

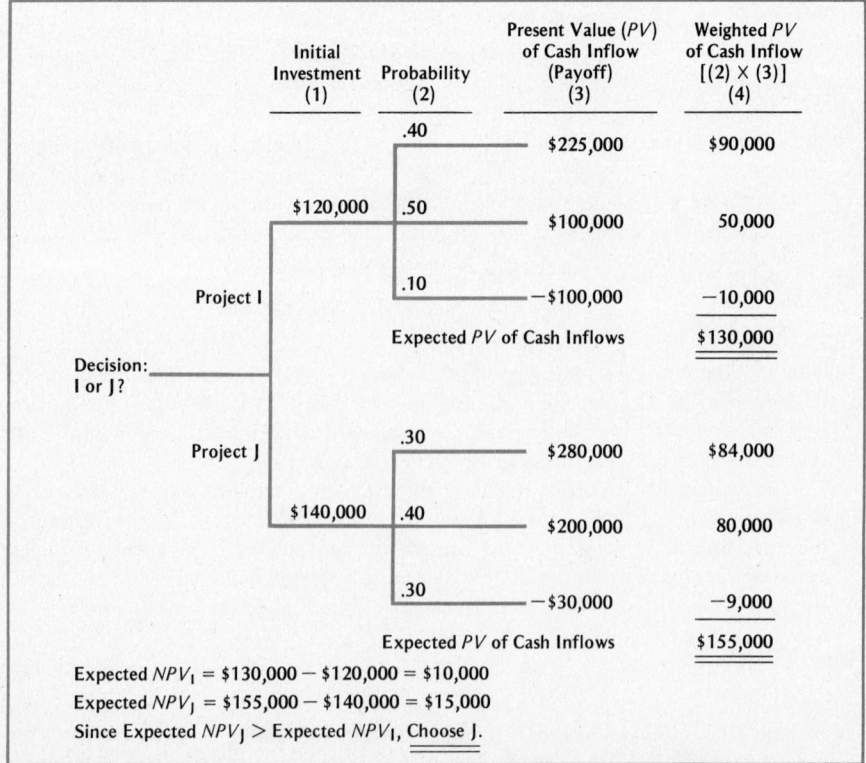

Figure 11.3   Decision tree for Elroy, Inc.'s choice between projects I and J

analyze choices more clearly and select courses of action, they are not especially sophisticated methods for dealing with risk.[12] They rely on estimates (normally subjective) of the probabilities associated with the outcomes (or payoffs) of competing courses of action. The payoffs associated with each course of action are weighted by the associated probability, the weighted payoffs for each course of action are summed, and the expected value of each course of action is then determined. The alternative providing the highest expected value would then be selected.

EXAMPLE   Elroy, Inc., wishes to choose between two equally risky projects, I and J. To make this decision, Elroy's management has gathered the necessary data, which are depicted in the decision tree in Figure 11.3. Project I requires an initial investment of $120,000; the calculation in column 4, based on the present values of cash inflow in column 3 and associated probabilities in column 2, gives an expected present value of cash inflows of $130,000. Project I's expected net present value, which is calculated below the decision tree, is therefore $10,000. Since the $15,000 expected net present value of project J, which is determined in a similar fashion, is greater than that for project I, project J would be preferred. ■

SIMULATION

Simulation is a sophisticated and statistically based approach for dealing with risk. Applying it to capital budgeting requires the generation of cash flows using predetermined probability distributions and random numbers. By tying the various cash flow components together in a mathematical model and repeating the process numerous times, a probability distribution of project returns can be developed. Figure 11.4 presents a flowchart of the simulation of the net present value of a project. The process of generating random numbers and using the probability distributions for cash inflows and outflows allows values for each of these variables to be determined. Substituting these values into the mathematical model results in a net present value. By repeating this process maybe a thousand times, a probability distribution of net present values is created. The key to simulating the distribution of returns is to identify accurately the probability distributions for the input variables and to formulate a mathematical model that truly reflects the existing relationships.

By simulating the various cash flows associated with a project and then calculating the *NPV* or *IRR* on the basis of these simulated cash flows, a probability distribution of each project's returns based on the *NPV* or the *IRR* criterion can be developed. Although only gross cash inflows and outflows are simulated in Figure 11.4, more sophisticated simulations in which each inflow and outflow component is simulated are quite common.[13] From the distribution of returns, regardless

---

[12] Decision trees are most useful when a series of sequential decisions must be made. In such cases, conditional probabilities must be determined, and in general the analysis is much more sophisticated than that described here. Even in the case of sequential decisions, the technique does not really capture risk; it instead relies on the use of expected values.

[13] Cash inflow components are such things as the number of units sold, the sale price per unit, and collection pattern of receivables. Cash outflow components include such items as maintenance costs, payments for raw materials, and wages. Sophisticated simulation models for capital budgeting consider the probability distribution of these and other cash flow components.

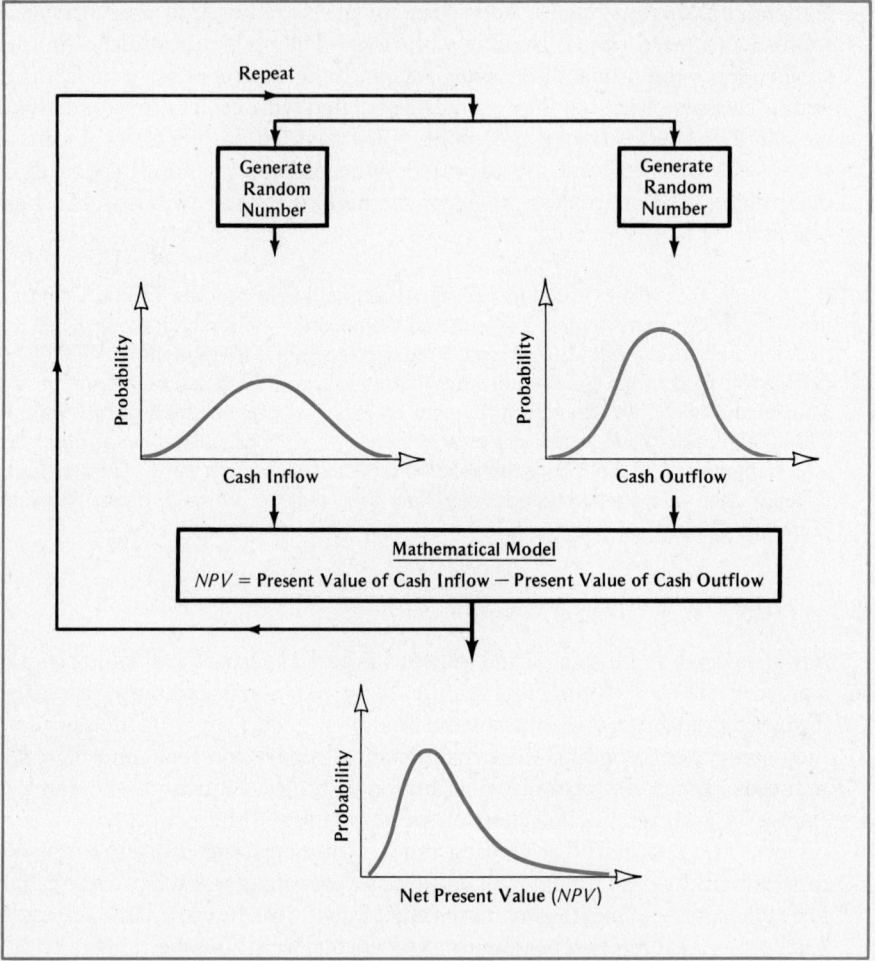

Figure 11.4   Flowchart of a net present value simulation

of how they are measured, the decision maker can determine not only the expected value of the return but also the probability of achieving or surpassing a given return. The use of computers has made this approach quite feasible. The output of simulation provides an excellent basis for decision making, since the decision maker can view a continuum of risk-return trade-offs instead of a single-point estimate.

Risk-Adjustment Techniques

The approaches for dealing with risk presented so far allow the financial manager to get a feel for project risk. Unfortunately, they do not really provide a straightforward basis for evaluating risky projects. We illustrate the two major risk-adjustment techniques using the net present value (*NPV*) decision method.[14] The *NPV* decision rule of accepting only those projects with *NPVs* ≥ 0 will continue to hold. The basic equation for *NPV* presented in Chapter 10 as Equation 10.2 is restated here as Equation 11.6.

$$NPV = \sum_{t=1}^{n} \frac{CF_t}{(1 + k)^t} - II \tag{11.6}$$

where

$$CF_t = \text{relevant cash inflow in year } t$$
$$k = \text{cost of capital or discount rate}$$
$$II = \text{initial investment}$$

Close examination of the equation should make it clear that since the initial investment (*II*), which occurs at time zero, is known with certainty, only the first term of the equation,

$$\sum_{t=1}^{n} \frac{CF_t}{(1 + k)^t}$$

embodies risk.

Two opportunities to adjust for risk in this term exist: (1) The cash flows, CF_t, can be adjusted, or (2) the discount rate, k, can be adjusted. Here we describe and compare two techniques — the cash flow adjustment process, known as certainty equivalents, and the discount rate adjustment process, known as risk-adjusted discount rates. In addition, we consider (1) the portfolio effects of project analysis, since it is important to consider the potential interrelationship of returns between proposed projects and the firm's existing portfolio of assets, and (2) the practical aspects of certainty equivalents and risk-adjusted discount rates.

CERTAINTY EQUIVALENTS (*CEs*)

One of the most direct and theoretically preferred approaches for risk adjustment is the use of *certainty equivalents (CEs),* which are factors that reflect the percent of a given cash inflow the financial decision maker would accept in exchange for the expected cash inflow. Equation 11.7 presents the basic expression for *NPV* when certainty equivalents are used for risk adjustment.

$$NPV = \sum_{t=1}^{n} \frac{\alpha_t CF_t}{(1 + R_F)^t} - II \tag{11.7}$$

where

---

[14] The *IRR* could just as well have been used, but since *NPV* is theoretically preferred, as noted in Chapter 10, it is used instead.

α_t = the certainty equivalent factor in year t ($0 \le \alpha_t \le 1$).

CF_t = relevant cash inflow in year t

R_F = the risk-free rate of return

In the equation, the *certainty equivalent factor*, α_t, for each year t is used to adjust the cash inflow to a certain amount, which is then discounted at the risk-free rate, R_F.[15]

The certainty equivalent in effect adjusts a risky cash inflow to a certain amount; it would equal 1 for a certain cash inflow and zero for the most risky cash inflow. The risk-free rate, R_F, is used to discount the certain cash inflows, $\alpha_t CF_t$, since, if a risk-adjusted rate were used, the risk would in effect be counted twice. Although the process of converting risky cash inflows to certain cash inflows is somewhat subjective, the technique is theoretically sound. The fact that the decision maker introduces his or her own risk preferences into the analysis is viewed as a positive aspect of the use of certainty equivalents.[16]

EXAMPLE   The Bosco Company wishes to consider risk in the analysis of two projects, A and B. The basic data for these projects were initially presented in Table 10.1 in Chapter 10, and the analysis of the projects using net present value and assuming the projects had equivalent risk was presented in Table 10.4. Ignoring risk differences and using net present value, it was shown earlier that at the firm's 10 percent cost of capital, project A was preferred over project B since its *NPV* of $11,074 was greater than B's *NPV* of $10,914. Assume that on further analysis the firm found that project A was actually more risky than project B. To consider the differing risk, the firm estimated the certainty equivalents for each project's cash inflows for each year. Columns 2 and 7 of Table 11.7 show the estimated values for projects A and B, respectively. Multiplying the risky cash inflows (given in columns 1 and 6) by the corresponding certainty equivalents (*CE*s) (columns 2 and 7, respectively) gives the certain cash inflows for projects A and B shown in columns 3 and 8, respectively.

Upon investigation, Bosco's management estimated the prevailing risk-free rate of return, R_F, to be 6 percent. Using the 6 percent risk-free rate to discount the certain cash inflows for each of the projects results in the net present values of $4,541 for project A and $10,141 for project B, as calculated in Table 11.7. Note that as a result of the risk adjustment, project B is now preferred. The usefulness of the certainty equivalent approach for risk adjustment should be quite clear; the only difficulty lies in the need to make subjective estimates of the certainty equivalents. ■

RISK-ADJUSTED DISCOUNT RATES (*RADRs*)

Another direct approach for risk adjustment involves the use of *risk-adjusted discount rates* (*RADRs*). Instead of adjusting the cash inflows for risk, as was done using the certainty equivalent approach, this approach adjusts the discount rate.[17]

[15] Alternately, the internal rate of return could be calculated for the risk-adjusted cash inflows and then compared to the risk-free rate in order to make the accept-reject decision.

[16] In theory, the risk preferences of the decision maker would derive from his or her utility function reflecting acceptable risk-return trade-offs. Unfortunately, as we point out later, it is quite difficult to operationalize the use of certainty equivalents.

[17] The risk-adjusted discount rate approach can be applied when using the internal rate of return as well as net present value. If the *IRR* is used, the risk-adjusted discount rate becomes the cutoff rate that must be equaled or exceeded by the *IRR* for the project to be accepted. When using *NPV*, the projected cash inflows are merely discounted at the risk-adjusted discount rate.

ONE PROFESSOR'S ATTEMPT TO DEFINE RISK

In the business world, we casually discuss this poor word as if just the mere verbalization of the concept relieves us of the responsibility to do anything about it. Or, conversely, we may do too much. How does such power emanate from such a wee word? In business academe, it's even worse: We think we know what we're talking about, but we couldn't recognize a good hard-core risk if it sat in one of our classrooms. I wouldn't presume to define for you, dear reader, what the word means; you've got your own perceptions, and that's all that really matters. Or is it? It's those damn perceptions that create the problems with risk.

Observe all the permutations and combinations of risk that we encounter: RISKless, RISKfree, RISK/return, RISK aversion, RISKy, margin of RISK, market RISK, business RISK . . . you fill in the blanks. Something as omnipotent as risk deserves respect and by God, it gets it. What else can cause such conservatism in business? Think of another word that separates business academe from the "hard" sciences as does risk (usually through the ubiquitous error term!). And doesn't risk befuddle economists and other central planners? It can't be all bad. What other concept restrains individuals from rash action and simultaneously gives rise to eminent authorities such as Murphy and Parkinson? Got the idea?

Huge sums are spent in reducing, measuring, compensating for, averting, and insuring against risk, usually without much success. The risk is always there. And, of course, the next question becomes, "Whose risk is it?" The task of handling risk has created a legion of business parasites, i.e., lawyers, accountants, regulators, consultants, insurance persons, and a host of staff functions. What an incredible overhead burden to protect one's ASSets against RISK. Are we really getting our money's worth for such a huge cost? I think not. And still risk remains, in spite of the sums we spend at the altar . . . .

Being true to my academic bent, I asked several colleagues to define what risk meant to them. The following random sample of five (with a confidence level of zero) led to these responses:

Finance type: variation about an expected return.
Accountant: errors and irregularities.
Management: making decisions in the face of unknown conditions.
Quantitative type: decision-making in which at least one decision variable is random.
Economist: uncertainty about the outcome.
Lawyer: not a legal concept (I loved this one).

Some consistency appears from these samples, but not enough for me to feel comfortable with real, live businessmen. Is this what we're really teaching? No wonder businessmen hold us in such low esteem—we're too parochial.

Now after all of this, you expect me to define what risk really is? No way . . . I'm a risk averter. But we might form a committee to . . .

SOURCE: Daniel L. Schneid, "Risk: Four-Letter Word," *Financial Executive,* January 1984, pp. 16–17.

Table 11.7   Analysis of the Bosco Company's Projects
A and B Using Certainty Equivalents

			Project A		
Year (t)	Cash inflows (CF_t) (1)	Certainty equivalent factors $(\alpha_t)^a$ (2)	Certain cash inflows $[(1) \times (2)]$ (3)	$PVIF_{6\%}$ (4)	Present value $[(3) \times (4)]$ (5)
1	$14,000	.90	$12,600	.943	$11,882
2	14,000	.90	12,600	.890	11,214
3	14,000	.80	11,200	.840	9,408
4	14,000	.70	9,800	.792	7,762
5	14,000	.60	8,400	.747	6,275
			PV of inflows		$46,541
			− Initial investment (II)		42,000
			Net present value (NPV)		$ 4,541

			Project B		
Year (t)	Cash inflows (CF_t) (6)	Certainty equivalent factors $(\alpha_t)^a$ (7)	Certain cash inflows $[(6) \times (7)]$ (8)	$PVIF_{6\%}$ (9)	Present value $[(8) \times (9)]$ (10)
1	$28,000	1.00	$28,000	.943	$26,404
2	12,000	.90	10,800	.890	9,612
3	10,000	.90	9,000	.840	7,560
4	10,000	.80	8,000	.792	6,336
5	10,000	.70	7,000	.747	5,229
			PV of inflows		$55,141
			− Initial investment (II)		45,000
			Net present value (NPV)		$10,141

Note: The basic cash flows for these projects were presented in Chapter 10, Table 10.1, and the analysis of the projects using *NPV* and assuming equal risk was presented in Table 10.4.
[a] These values were estimated by management; they reflect the risk managers perceive in the cash inflows.

Equation 11.8 presents the basic expression for *NPV* when risk-adjusted discount rates are used.

$$NPV = \sum_{t=1}^{n} \frac{CF_t}{(1 + RADR)^t} - II \qquad (11.8)$$

The risk-adjusted discount rate, *RADR*, reflects the return that must be earned on the given project to compensate the firm's owners adequately, thereby resulting in the maintenance or improvement of share price. The higher the risk of a project, the higher the *RADR* and therefore the lower the net present value for a given set of cash inflows. Because the logic underlying the use of *RADR*s is closely linked to the capital asset pricing model developed in Chapter 7, we evaluate some of its basic constructs before demonstrating the development and use of *RADR*s.

RADR and CAPM. In Chapter 7, the *capital asset pricing model (CAPM)* was used to link the *relevant* risk and return for all assets. Particular emphasis in that discussion was placed on assets traded in *efficient markets*— perfectly competitive markets in which full and complete information is available to market participants, none of whom is large enough to affect market price significantly and all of whom view securities and measure risk and return in the same fashion. In the development of the CAPM, the *total risk* of an asset was defined as

$$\text{Total risk} = \text{nondiversifiable risk} + \text{diversifiable risk} \qquad (11.9)$$

For assets traded in an efficient market, the *diversifiable risk,* which results from uncontrollable or random events, can be eliminated through diversification. The relevant risk is therefore the *nondiversifiable risk;* it is the risk for which owners of these assets are rewarded. Nondiversifiable risk for securities is commonly measured using *beta,* which is an index of the degree of responsiveness or comovement of asset return with the market return.

Using beta, b_j, to measure the relevant risk of any asset j, the CAPM is

$$k_j = R_F + b_j \times (k_m - R_F) \qquad (11.10)$$

where

$$k_j = \text{the required (or expected) return on asset } j$$
$$R_F = \text{the risk-free rate of return}$$
$$b_j = \text{the beta coefficient for asset } j$$
$$k_m = \text{the required rate of return on the market portfolio}$$

In Chapter 7 we demonstrated that the required return on any security, j, could be determined by substituting values of R_F, b_j, and k_m into the CAPM — Equation 11.10. Any security expected to earn in excess of its required return would be acceptable, and those expected to earn an inferior return would be rejected.

If we assume for a moment that real corporate assets such as computers, machine tools, and special-purpose machinery are traded in efficient markets, the CAPM could be redefined as noted in Equation 11.11.

$$k_{\text{project} j} = R_F + b_{\text{project} j} \times (k_m - R_F) \qquad (11.11)$$

The security market line (SML), which is a graphic depiction of the CAPM, is shown for Equation 11.11 in Figure 11.5. As noted, any project j having an *IRR* falling above the SML would be acceptable since its *IRR* would exceed the required return, $k_{\text{project} j}$, while any project j with an *IRR* below $k_{\text{project} j}$ would be

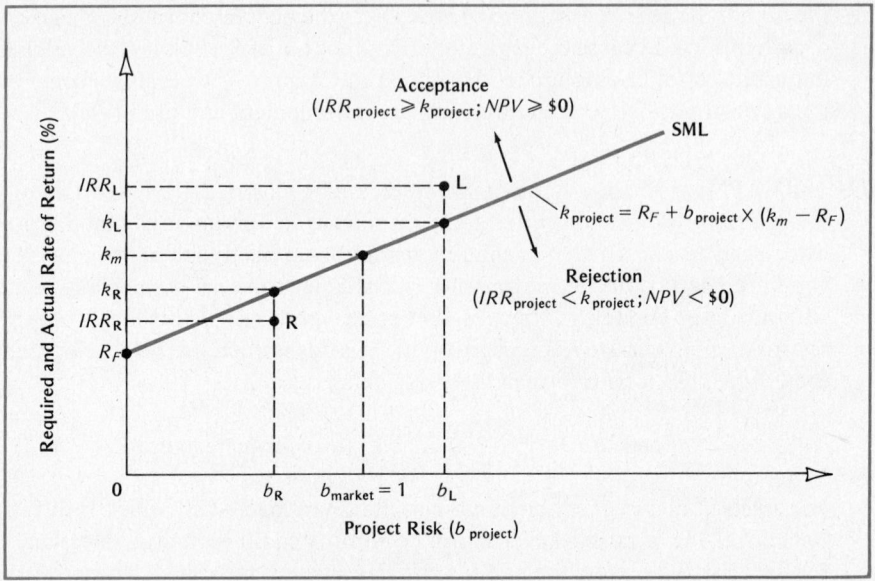

Figure 11.5   CAPM and SML in capital budgeting decision making

rejected. In terms of *NPV,* any project falling above the SML would have a positive *NPV* and any project falling below the SML a negative *NPV.*[18]

EXAMPLE   Two projects, L and R, are shown in Figure 11.5. Project L has a beta, b_L, and generates an internal rate of return, IRR_L. The required return for a project with risk b_L is k_L. Since project L generates a return greater than that required ($IRR_L > k_L$), project L would be acceptable. Project L would have a positive *NPV* when its cash inflows are discounted at its required return, k_L. Project R, on the other hand, generates an *IRR* below that required for its risk, b_R ($IRR_R < k_R$). This project would have a negative *NPV* when its cash inflows are discounted at its required return, k_R. Project R should be rejected. ∎

While the logic of the CAPM is quite appealing when adjusting the discount rate or required return for the risk of capital budgeting projects, the theory does not really apply in the case of real corporate assets. Rarely are real corporate assets traded in efficient markets. The market in which these assets are traded is *not* efficient; market participants do not possess full and accurate knowledge concerning the prices of such assets. Unlike securities traded in widely publicized competitive markets created by stock exchanges, it is unlikely that all buyers looking for a specific make and model of a machine tool will be able to bid for all such tools and thereby cause their prices to be the same. In addition, it would be difficult to estimate the market return, k_m, for a portfolio of all such assets.

[18] As explained in Chapter 10, whenever the *IRR* is above the cost of capital or required return ($IRR > k$), the *NPV* is positive, and whenever the *IRR* is below the cost of capital or required return ($IRR < k$), the *NPV* is negative. Since by definition the *IRR* is the discount rate that causes *NPV* to equal zero and the *IRR* and *NPV* always agree on accept-reject decisions, the relationship noted in Figure 11.5 logically follows.

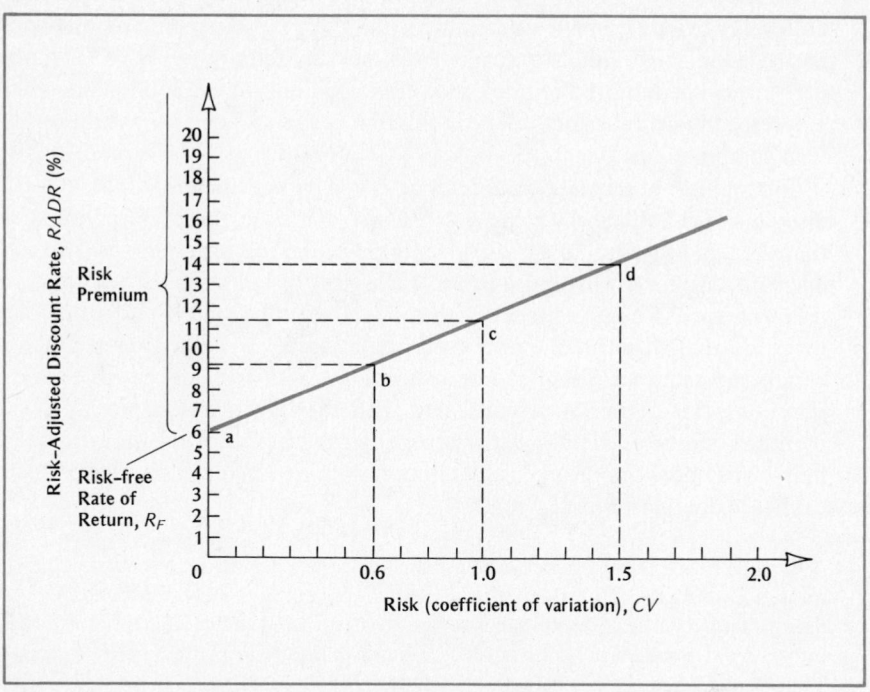

Figure 11.6 A hypothetical market indifference curve

Applying *RADRs*. Because the CAPM does not apply to real corporate assets, attention is commonly devoted to assessing the total risk of a project as measured by its standard deviation, σ, or coefficient of variation, *CV*. Relating these measures to the required level of return would then result in a risk-adjusted rate of return (*RADR*), which can be used in Equation 11.8 to find the *NPV*. To adjust the discount rate, it is necessary to develop a function that expresses the return for each level of project risk required in order to at least maintain the firm's value. One method of relating real-asset risk and return is to measure an asset's contribution to the portfolio owned by the firm and then relate for various degrees of risk the return required by prospective and existing shareholders as adequate compensation for the risks taken.

Using the coefficient of variation[19] as a measure of project risk, the firm can develop some type of *market indifference curve*, or *risk-return function*. An example of such a function is given in Figure 11.6, which relates the risk-adjusted discount rate, *RADR,* to the project risk as measured by the coefficient of variation, *CV*. In a fashion similar to CAPM, the relationship is assumed to be linear. The market indifference curve in Figure 11.6 indicates that project cash inflows associated with a riskless event ($CV = 0$) should be discounted at a 6 percent rate. This rate therefore represents the risk-free rate of return, R_F (point *a* in the figure). For

---

[19] The coefficient of variation is used here since it provides a relative basis for comparing risk. Although it is a project-specific measure that embodies both diversifiable and nondiversifiable risk, it is assumed to represent a reasonable measure of the relative risk of real-asset projects.

all levels of risk greater than certainty ($CV > 0$), the associated required rate of return is indicated. Points b, c, and d indicate that rates of return of 9, 11, and 14 percent will be required on projects with coefficients of variation of 0.6, 1.0, and 1.5, respectively. Investors will be indifferent as to a choice of any of these risk-return combinations.

Figure 11.6 is a *market indifference curve*, which means that investors will discount cash inflows with the given levels of risk at the corresponding rates; therefore, in order not to damage its market value, the firm must use the correct discount rate for evaluating a project. If a firm discounts a risky project's cash inflows at too low a rate and accepts the project, the firm's market price may drop as investors recognize that the firm itself has become more risky.[20] The amount by which the required discount rate exceeds the risk-free rate is called the *risk premium;* this definition is consistent with that given in Chapter 7. The risk premium increases directly with increasing project risk. A simple example may help clarify how the risk-adjusted discount rate, *RADR,* can be used to evaluate capital budgeting projects.

EXAMPLE The Bosco Company wishes to use the risk-adjusted discount rate approach to determine, according to *NPV,* whether to implement project A or project B. In addition to the data presented earlier, Bosco's management has estimated the coefficient of variation for project A as 1.5 and for project B as 1.0. According to Figure 11.6, the *RADR* for project A is 14 percent; for project B, it is 11 percent. Due to the more risky nature of project A, its risk premium is 8 percent (14 percent − 6 percent); for project B the risk premium is 5 percent (11 percent − 6 percent). The net present value of each project using its *RADR* is calculated in Table 11.8. The results clearly show that project B is preferable to project A, since

Table 11.8 Analysis of the Bosco Company's Projects A and B
Using Risk-Adjusted Discount Rates

Project A		Project B			
			Cash inflows (CF_t) (1)	$PVIF_{11\%,t}$ (2)	Present value [(1) × (2)] (3)
		Year (t)			
Annual inflow (CF)	$14,000	1	$28,000	.901	$25,228
× $PVIFA_{14\%,5 \text{ yrs}}$	3.433	2	12,000	.812	9,744
PV of inflows	$48,062	3	10,000	.731	7,310
− Initial investment (II)	42,000	4	10,000	.659	6,590
Net present value (NPV)	$ 6,062	5	10,000	.593	5,930
		PV of inflows			$54,802
		− Initial investment (II)			45,000
		Net present value (NPV)			$ 9,802

Note: Using Figure 11.6 and the coefficients of variation of 1.5 and 1.0 for projects A and B, respectively, a discount rate of 14 percent is used for project A and 11 percent for project B.

[20] It is also true that if the firm discounts a project's cash inflows at too high a rate, resulting in the rejection of an acceptable project, the firm's market price may drop because investors believe it is being overly conservative and sell their stock, putting downward pressure on the firm's market value.

its risk-adjusted net present value of $9802 is greater than the $6062 risk-adjusted *NPV* for project A. This is the same conclusion that resulted using certainty equivalents in the preceding example. As noted in Chapter 10 (see Table 10.4), when the discount rates are not adjusted for risk, project A would be preferred to project B. The usefulness of risk-adjusted discount rates should now be clear; the real difficulty of this approach lies in estimating the market indifference curve. ■

PORTFOLIO EFFECTS

As noted in Chapter 7, since investors are not rewarded for taking diversifiable risk, they should hold a diversified portfolio of securities. Since a business firm can be viewed as a portfolio of assets, is it similarly important that the firm maintain a diversified portfolio of assets?

By holding a diversified portfolio, the firm could reduce the variability of its cash flows. By combining two projects with negatively correlated cash inflows, the combined cash inflow variability — and therefore the risk — could be reduced. But are firms rewarded for diversifying risk in this fashion? If they are, the value of the firm could be enhanced through diversification into other lines of business. Surprisingly, the value of the stock of firms whose shares are traded publicly in an efficient marketplace is generally *not* affected by diversification. In other words, diversification is not normally rewarded and therefore is generally not necessary.

The lack of reward for diversification results from the fact that investors themselves can diversify by holding securities in a variety of firms; they do not need to have the firm do it for them. And investors can diversify more readily due to the ease of making transactions and at a lower cost due to the greater availability of information and trading mechanisms. Of course, if as a result of acquiring a new line of business the firm's cash flows tend to respond more to changing economic conditions (i.e., greater nondiversifiable risk), greater returns would be expected. If, for the additional risk, the firm earned a return in excess of that required (*IRR* > *k*), the value of the firm could be enhanced. Also, other benefits such as increased cash, greater borrowing capacity, guaranteed availability of raw materials, and so forth could result from, and therefore justify, diversification in spite of any immediate cash flow impact.

But in the absence of any reward for diversification, firms should generally evaluate the risks and rewards of projects independently using *total* risk and return rather than in terms of their impact on the total portfolio of assets. As long as investors can conveniently substitute personal diversification for corporate diversification, corporate diversification will not be rewarded.

CE VERSUS *RADR* IN PRACTICE

Certainty equivalents (*CEs*) are the theoretically preferred approach for project risk adjustment. Their theoretical superiority stems from the fact that *CEs* derive from utility theory and constitute a vehicle that accurately converts risky cash flows to certain cash flows. Risk-adjusted discount rates (*RADRs*), on the other hand, have a major theoretical problem: They implicitly assume that risk is an increasing function of time. This results from the basic mathematics of compounding and discounting. Rather than demonstrate this implicit assumption, suffice it to say that *CEs are theoretically superior to RADRs.*

Because of the complexity of developing *CEs, RADRs are most often used in practice.* Their popularity stems from two major facts: (1) They are consistent with the general disposition of financial decision makers toward rates of return,[21] and (2) they are easily estimated and applied to risky decision situations. The first reason is clearly a matter of personal preference, but the second one is based on the computational convenience involved in the use of *RADRs.* In practice, risk is often subjectively categorized rather than related to a continuum of *RADRs* associated with each level of risk, as illustrated by the market indifference curve in Figure 11.6. Firms often establish a number of *risk classes,* with an *RADR* assigned to each. Each project is then subjectively placed in the appropriate risk class, and the corresponding *RADR* is used to evaluate it. An example will help to illustrate this approach.

EXAMPLE Assume that the management of Bosco Company decided to use a more subjective but practical *RADR* approach to analyze projects. Each project would be placed in one of four risk classes according to its perceived risk. The classes ranged from Class I for the lowest-risk projects to Class IV for the highest-risk projects. Associated with each class was an *RADR* appropriate to the level of risk of projects in the class. A brief description of each class, along with the associated *RADRs,* is given in Table 11.9. It shows that lower-risk projects tend to involve routine replacement or renewal activities, whereas higher-risk projects involve expansion into new activities or replacement.

The financial manager of Bosco has assigned project A to Class III and project B to Class II. The cash flows for project A would therefore be evaluated using a 14 percent *RADR,* and project B's would be evaluated using a 10 percent *RADR.*[22] The net present value of project

Table 11.9 Bosco Company's Risk Classes and *RADRs*

Risk class	Description	Risk-adjusted discount rate, *RADR*
I	*Below-average risk:* Projects with low risk typically involve routine replacement without modernization of existing activities.	8%
II	*Average risk:* Projects similar to those currently implemented. Typically involve renewal or replacement of existing activities.	10%
III	*Above-average risk:* Projects with higher than normal, but not excessive, risk. Typically involves expansion of existing or similar activities.	14%
IV	*Highest risk:* Projects with very high risk. Typically involve expansion into new or unfamiliar activities.	20%

[21] Recall from Chapter 10 that while *NPV* was the theoretically preferred evaluation technique, *IRR* was more popular in actual business practice due to the general preference of business people toward rates of return rather than pure dollar returns. The preference for *RADRs* over *CEs* is therefore consistent with the preference for *IRR* over *NPV.*

[22] Note that the 10 percent *RADR* for project B using the risk classes in Table 11.9 differs from the 11 percent *RADR* found earlier for project B using the market indifference curve. This difference is attributable to the less precise nature of the use of risk classes.

A at 14 percent was calculated in Table 11.8 to be $6,062, and the *NPV* for project B at a 10 percent *RADR* was found to be $10,914 in Table 10.4 in Chapter 10. Clearly, with *RADR*s based on the use of risk classes, project B is preferred over project A. As noted earlier, this result is contrary to the findings in Table 10.4, where no attention was given to the differing risk of projects A and B. ∎

MULTINATIONAL FINANCE

International Capital Budgeting

The concepts and techniques outlined in Chapters 9 through 11 are also applicable to international operations, although certain additional factors unique to the international setting need to be discussed.

Elements relating to a parent company's investment in a subsidiary and the concept of taxes must be considered. For example, in the case of manufacturing investments, questions may arise as to the value of the equipment a parent may contribute to the subsidiary. Is the value based on the market conditions in the parent country or the local host economy? In general, the market value in the host country is the relevant "price." The existence of different taxes — as pointed out in Chapter 2 — can complicate measurement of the cash flows to be received by the parent because different definitions of taxable income can arise.

Furthermore, there are complications when it comes to the actual cash flows. From a parent's viewpoint, the cash flows are those repatriated from the subsidiary. In some countries, however, cash flows may be totally or partially blocked. Obviously, depending on the life of the project in the host country, the returns and net present values associated with such projects can significantly vary from the subsidiary's and the parent's point of view. For instance, for a project of only five years' duration, if all yearly cash flows are to be blocked by the host government, the subsidiary will show a "normal" return and *NPV*, while the parent may show no returns. On the other hand, for a project of longer life, even if cash flows are blocked for the first few years, the remaining years' cash flows can contribute toward the parent's returns and *NPV*. Depending on the exact regulations of host countries, the returns and *NPV*s associated with cash flows can reflect good performance on the part of subsidiaries and yet mean *no* returns for the parent.

Finally, there is the issue of risks attached to international cash flows. The three basic types of risk categories are (1) business and financial risks, (2) inflation and currency risks, and (3) political risks. The first category relates to the kind of industry the subsidiary is in as well as its financial structure (more details on financial risks will be presented in Chapters 19 and 20). We have already discussed the risks attached to having investments in different currencies and how profits, along with balance sheet items, are subject to exchange fluctuations (see Chapters 4 and 7). As for political risks, some of the potential impacts and how MNCs can combat them were presented in Chapter 7.

The important point to note here is that the presence of such risks will influence the discount rate (or the cost of capital) to be used in evaluating international cash flows. The basic rule, though, is that the *local* cost of equity capital (applicable to the local business and financial environments within which a subsidiary operates) is the starting discount rate to which risks stemming from currency and political factors can be added and from which benefits reflecting the parent's lower capital costs may be subtracted. ●●

CHAPTER SUMMARY

● A number of refinements in the capital budgeting process are often needed to accommodate special circumstances. Two approaches are commonly used to compare mutually exclusive projects having unequal lives. The least common life and annualized net present value approaches give the same best-project result, and both are based on the sometimes questionable assumptions of no inflation and no changes in technology.

● The least common life approach assumes that the projects can be repeated with the same cash flows enough times as necessary to cause them to terminate in the same year. The project with the highest *NPV* over the least common life is preferred.

● The annualized net present value (*ANPV*) approach is more efficient in that it merely converts the *NPV* for each project over its ownership period to an annual amount that can be used to select the best project.

● Common techniques for solving capital rationing problems include the internal rate of return approach and the net present value approach. Of the two, net present value best achieves the objective of using the budget to maximize the overall net present value resulting from the selection of a group of acceptable projects.

● Inflation can significantly affect the cash inflows from capital expenditures. Generally, when high rates of inflation are anticipated, some adjustment in the expected cash inflows is made. For conventional projects these adjustments are made to inflows using *FVIF* factors at the expected rate for the given number of periods. Once the inflation-adjusted relevant cash inflows are estimated, the *NPV* can be calculated.

● Risk in capital budgeting is concerned with the chance that a project will prove unacceptable, which is affected by the variability of cash inflows.

● Cash inflow variability stems from any of a number of revenue, expense, and tax variables. Finding the breakeven cash inflow and assessing the probability that it will be realized is one approach used to assess the chance of success.

● Sensitivity analysis is one of the simplest approaches for capturing the variability of cash inflows or *NPV*s.

● Statistical techniques for measuring project risk include the standard deviation and the coefficient of variation.

● Decision trees are an expected-value-based approach often used to evaluate capital budgeting decisions, especially when sequential decisions must be made.

● Simulation, which provides a probability distribution of project returns, usually requires a computer and allows the decision maker to get a feel for the risk involved in a proposed investment.

● The two major risk-adjustment techniques involve straightforward adjustment in the basic *NPV* calculation. Certainty equivalents (*CEs*) are used to adjust the risky cash inflows to certain amounts, which are discounted at a risk-free rate in order to find the *NPV*. The risk-adjusted discount rate (*RADR*) technique involves adjustment of the discount rate rather than the cash inflows. Risk-adjusted discount rates are the discount rates required in the marketplace to compensate for project risk.

● The *RADR* technique is closely linked to the CAPM, but because real corporate assets, unlike securities, are generally not traded in an efficient market, the CAPM cannot be applied directly to capital budgeting. A market indifference curve linking project risk measured by a statistic such as the coefficient of variation can be used to determine the risk-adjusted discount rate.

● Although portfolio effects are relevant when evaluating securities investments, the ability of shareholders to diversify makes project diversification by the firm unnecessary. Attention in capital budgeting is therefore given to the total risk.

● Certainty equivalents are the theoretically superior risk-adjustment technique, but because decision makers prefer rates of return and the ease of calculation, risk-adjusted discount rates are more commonly used.

● International cash flows can be subject to a variety of factors, including local taxes in host countries, host-country regulations that block cash flow repatriation, the usual business and financial risks, risks stemming from different currency and political actions by host governments, and the application of a "local" cost of capital.

KEY TERMS

annualized net present value (*ANPV*) approach

beta

breakeven cash inflow

capital asset pricing model (CAPM)

capital rationing

certainty equivalent (*CE*)

coefficient of variation (*CV*)

decision tree

diversifiable risk

efficient markets

expected net present value

inflation

internal rate of return (*IRR*) approach (capital rationing)

least common life

least common life approach

market indifference curve

net present value (*NPV*) approach (capital rationing)

nondiversifiable risk

risk (in capital budgeting)

risk-adjusted discount rate (*RADR*)

risk class

risk premium

risk-return function

sensitivity analysis

simulation

standard deviation of *NPV*

total risk

QUESTIONS

11-1   Explain why a mere comparison of the *NPV*s of unequal-lived mutually exclusive projects is inappropriate. How does the *least common life approach* resolve this problem?

11-2   Describe the *annualized net present value (ANPV) approach* for comparing unequal-lived mutually exclusive projects.

11-3   Do the least common life and annualized net present value approaches give the same recommendation when applied to unequal-lived projects? What common assumptions underlie these approaches? Explain.

11-4   What is meant by *capital rationing?* Is it unusual for a firm to ration capital? Why or why not?

11-5   Compare and contrast the *internal rate of return approach* and *net present value approach* to capital rationing. Which is better? Why?

11-6   In what situation is it important that explicit attention be given to inflation in capital budgeting? How can project cash inflows be adjusted for inflation? Explain.

11-7   Define *risk* in terms of the cash inflows from a project. How can determination of the *breakeven cash inflow* be used to gauge project risk? Explain.

11-8   Briefly describe the *standard deviation* and the *coefficient of variation* and explain how these statistics can be used in dealing with the risk of capital budgeting projects.

11-9 Briefly describe how each of the following techniques can be used to get a feel for project risk.
  a Sensitivity analysis
  b Decision trees
  c Simulation

11-10 Explain the concept of *certainty equivalents (CEs)*. How are they used in the risk-adjustment process?

11-11 Describe the logic as well as the basic procedures involved in using *risk-adjusted discount rates (RADRs)*. How does this approach relate to the *capital asset pricing model* (CAPM)? Explain.

11-12 Explain why a firm whose stock is actively traded in the securities markets need not concern itself with diversification. In view of this, how should the risk of capital budgeting projects be measured?

11-13 Compare and contrast certainty equivalents (*CEs*) and risk-adjusted discount rates (*RADRs*) from both a theoretical and a practical point of view. In practice, how are risk classes often used to apply *RADRs*? Explain.

11-14 Indicate how *NPV* can differ whether measured from the parent's point of view or that of the foreign subsidiary when cash flows may be blocked by local authorities.

11-15 Outline the three categories of risks influencing international cash flows.

PROBLEMS

11-1 **(Unequal Lives — Least Common Life Approach)**   Ron Industries wishes to select the better of two equally risky, mutually exclusive projects, A and B. The firm has a 12 percent cost of capital and uses net present value to evaluate project acceptability. The initial investment and annual cash inflows for project A, which has a two-year life, and project B, which has a three-year life, are summarized as follows:

	Project A	Project B
Initial investment (*II*)	$25,000	$40,000
Year (*t*)	Cash inflows (*CF$_t$*)	
1	$12,000	$24,000
2	20,000	18,000
3	—	9,000

  a Ignoring the differing lives, find the *NPV* for each project. Which is preferred?
  b Determine the least common life and calculate the relevant cash flows over that period for each project.
  c Find the *NPV* over the least common life of each project. Which is preferred?
  d Compare, contrast, and discuss your findings in **a** and **c**.

11-2 **(Converting *NPVs* to *ANPVs*)**   For each of the following projects, convert the *NPV* into an annualized net present value (*ANPV*) using the specified discount rate and project life.

Project	*NPV*	Discount rate	Life
A	$ 200,000	11%	25 years
B	37,500	18	4

(*continued*)

(Continued)

Project	NPV	Discount rate	Life
C	$ 60,000	7%	10 years
D	1,000,000	15	14
E	7,000	13	2
F	477,000	14	12

11-3 **(Unequal Lives — *ANPV* Approach)**   SDSU Enterprises wishes to select the best of three possible machines, each expected to fulfill the need for additional aluminum extrusion capacity. The three machines — A, B, and C — are equally risky. The firm plans to use a 12 percent cost of capital to evaluate each of them. The initial investment and annual cash inflows over the life of each machine are as follows:

	Machine A	Machine B	Machine C
Initial investment (II)	$92,000	$65,000	$100,500
Year (t)		Cash inflows (CF_t)	
1	$12,000	$10,000	$ 30,000
2	12,000	20,000	30,000
3	12,000	30,000	30,000
4	12,000	40,000	30,000
5	12,000	—	30,000
6	12,000	—	—

a Calculate the *NPV* for each machine over its life. Rank the machines in descending order based on *NPV*.

b Use the *annualized net present value* approach to calculate the *ANPV* of each machine. Rank the machines in descending order based on the *ANPV*.

c Compare and contrast your findings in **a** and **b**. Which machine would you recommend that the firm acquire? Why?

11-4 **(Unequal Lives — Least Common Life and *ANPV* Approaches)**   Decker Manufacturing is considering purchase of one of three mutually exclusive projects for increasing production efficiency. The firm plans to use a 14 percent cost of capital to evaluate these equal-risk projects. The initial investment and annual cash inflows over the life of each project are summarized as follows:

	Project X	Project Y	Project Z
Initial investment (II)	$78,000	$52,000	$66,000
Year (t)		Cash inflows (CF_t)	
1	$17,000	$28,000	$15,000
2	25,000	38,000	15,000
3	33,000	—	15,000
4	41,000	—	15,000
5	—	—	15,000
6	—	—	15,000
7	—	—	15,000
8	—	—	15,000

a Calculate the *NPV* for each project over its life. Rank the projects in descending order based on *NPV*.

b Use the *least common life approach* to calculate the *NPV* of each project. Rank the projects in descending order based on these *NPVs*.

c Use the *annualized net present value (ANPV)* approach to evaluate and rank the projects in descending order based on *ANPV*.

d Compare and contrast your rankings in **b** and **c** with those in **a**. Which method for comparing unequal-lived projects do you prefer? Why?

e What assumptions are common to both the least common life and *ANPV* approaches? Explain.

11-5 **(Capital Rationing — *NPV* Approach)** A firm must select the optimal group of projects from those in the table, given its capital budget of $1 million.

Project	Initial investment	*NPV*
A	$300,000	$ 84,000
B	200,000	10,000
C	100,000	25,000
D	900,000	90,000
E	500,000	70,000
F	100,000	50,000
G	800,000	160,000

a Calculate the *profitability index (PI)* associated with each project.

b Select the optimal group of projects, keeping in mind that unused funds are costly.

11-6 **(Capital Rationing — *IRR* and *NPV* Approaches)** J. Hadley and Sons is attempting to select the best of a group of independent projects competing for the firm's fixed capital budget of $4.5 million. The firm recognizes that any unused portion of this budget will earn less than its 15 percent cost of capital, thereby resulting in present value of inflows less than the initial investment. The firm has summarized the key data to be used in selecting the best group of projects in the following table.

Project	Initial investment	*IRR*	Present value of inflows at 15%
A	$5,000,000	17%	$5,400,000
B	800,000	18	1,100,000
C	2,000,000	19	2,300,000
D	1,500,000	16	1,600,000
E	800,000	22	900,000
F	2,500,000	23	3,000,000
G	1,200,000	20	1,300,000

a Use the *internal rate of return (IRR) approach* to select the best group of projects.

b Use the *net present value (NPV) approach* to select the best group of projects.

c Compare, contrast, and discuss your findings in **a** and **b**.

d Which projects should the firm implement? Why?

11-7 **(Inflation in Capital Budgeting — Basic)** Ronpred, Inc., wishes to analyze a proposed project using *NPV*. The firm has a 16 percent cost of capital. The initial investment (*II*) is $115,000; relevant cash inflows for the project are summarized as follows:

Year (t)	Cash inflows (CF_t)
1	$40,000
2	35,000
3	30,000
4	25,000
5	20,000
6	15,000

a Find the *NPV* for the project using the data given. Is the project acceptable?

b If the firm expects the *cash inflows* to increase by 4 percent a year due to inflation, what would be the inflation-adjusted cash inflows?

c Using the inflation-adjusted cash inflows from **b**, find the *NPV*. Is the project acceptable?

d Compare, contrast, and discuss your findings in **a** and **c**.

11-8 **(Inflation in Capital Budgeting — Advanced)** Zwart Industries is in the process of developing and analyzing, using *NPV*, the relevant cash inflows associated with the purchase of a new machine requiring an initial investment of $42,500. The firm has a 13 percent cost of capital and pays 40 percent in taxes on ordinary income. The projected earnings before depreciation and taxes and depreciation for each year over the machine's five-year usable life are summarized in the following table.

Year (t)	Earnings before depreciation and taxes ($EBDT_t$)	Depreciation
1	$ 8,000	$6,000
2	10,000	8,800
3	12,000	8,400
4	14,000	8,400
5	16,000	8,400

a From the data given, determine the relevant cash inflows associated with the proposed machine purchase.

b Calculate the *NPV* using your findings in **a**. Is the project acceptable?

c Assuming that a 5 percent rate of inflation in *earnings before depreciation and taxes (EBDT)* is expected over the five years but is not reflected in the *EBDT* data presented, find the inflation-adjusted relevant cash inflows.

d Use the inflation-adjusted relevant cash inflows from **c** to find the *NPV*. Is the project acceptable?

e Compare and discuss the *NPV*s calculated in **b** and **d**.

11-9 **(Breakeven Cash Inflows and Risk)** Ray Enterprises is considering investment in either of two mutually exclusive projects, X and Y. Project X requires an initial investment of $30,000; project Y, $40,000. Each project's cash inflows are five-year annuities; project X's inflows are $10,000 per year; project Y's, $15,000. The firm has unlimited funds and, in the absence of risk differences, accepts the project with the highest *NPV*. The cost of capital is 15 percent.

a Find the *NPV* for each project. Are the projects acceptable?

b Find the *breakeven cash inflow* for each project.

c The firm has estimated the probabilities of achieving various ranges of cash inflow for the two projects as noted in the following table. What is the probability that each project will achieve the breakeven cash inflow found in **b**?

Range of cash inflows	Probability of achieving cash inflow in given range	
	Project X	Project Y
$0 to $5,000	0%	5%
$5,000 to $7,500	10	10
$7,500 to $10,000	60	15
$10,000 to $12,500	25	25
$12,500 to $15,000	5	20
$15,000 to $20,000	0	15
Above $20,000	0	10

d Which project is more risky? Which project has the potentially higher *NPV*? Discuss the risk-return trade-offs of the two projects.

e If the firm wished to minimize losses (i.e., $NPV < 0$), which project would you recommend? Which would you recommend if the goal was instead achieving the highest *NPV?*

11-10 (Basic Sensitivity Analysis) Klauer Pharmaceutical is in the process of evaluating two mutually exclusive additions to their processing capacity. The firm's financial analysts have developed pessimistic, most likely, and optimistic estimates of the annual inflows associated with each project. These estimates are given in the following table.

	Project A	Project B
Initial investment	$8,000	$8,000
Outcome	Annual cash inflows	
Pessimistic	$ 200	$ 900
Most likely	1000	1000
Optimistic	1800	1100

a Determine the range of annual cash inflows for each of the two projects.

b Assume that the firm's cost of capital is 10 percent and that both projects have 20-year lives. Construct a table similar to that above for the *NPV*s for each project. Include the *range* of *NPV*s for each project.

c Do **a** and **b** provide consistent views of the two projects? Explain.

d Which project would you recommend? Why?

11-11 (Bar Charts, Expected NPV, and Risk) Using the net present values (*NPV*s) and associated probabilities for projects X and Y summarized in the table below,

a Prepare bar charts for the two projects' *NPV*s.

b Calculate and compare the expected *NPV*s of the projects.

c Compare the riskiness of the two projects.

Project X		Project Y	
NPV ($)	Probability	NPV ($)	Probability
−15,000	.01	−20,000	.00
0	.03	−10,000	.02
15,000	.03	0	.04
25,000	.05	10,000	.06
30,000	.15	20,000	.08
35,000	.50	30,000	.15
40,000	.15	40,000	.35
45,000	.05	50,000	.20
55,000	.03	60,000	.05
70,000	.00	70,000	.03
		80,000	.01
		90,000	.01
		100,000	.00

11-12 **(Statistical Evaluation of NPV)**   A clothing manufacturer is considering a new line. The following table summarizes the net present values (NPVs) and associated probabilities for various outcomes for the two lines being considered.

Market outcome	Probability	Net present value	
		Line S	Line T
Very poor	.05	−$ 6,000	500
Poor	.15	2,000	4,500
Average	.60	8,500	8,000
Good	.15	15,000	12,500
Excellent	.05	23,000	16,500

a Calculate the expected NPV for each line.
b Calculate the range of NPVs for each line.
c Calculate the standard deviation of NPV, σ_{NPV}, for each line.
d Calculate the coefficient of variation of NPV, CV_{NPV}, for each line.
e Using the statistics developed in **a** through **d**, evaluate the risk and return of the lines. Which do you prefer? Why?

11-13 **(Sensitivity Analysis and Statistics)**   Publishing Horizons is considering the purchase of one of two new word processors, P and Q. Both are expected to provide benefits over a ten-year period, and each has a required investment of $3000. The firm uses a 10 percent cost of capital. Management has constructed the following table of estimates of probabilities and cash inflows for pessimistic, most likely, and optimistic results:

	Processor P		Processor Q	
	Amount	Probability	Amount	Probability
Initial investment	$3000	1.00	$3000	1.00
Outcome	Cash inflows			
Pessimistic	$ 500	.25	$ 400	.20
Most likely	750	.50	750	.55
Optimistic	1000	.25	1200	.25

a Construct a table similar to that above for *NPVs* associated with each outcome for both processors.

b Find the range of *NPVs* and subjectively compare the risk of each processor.

c Calculate the expected *NPV* for each processor.

d Calculate the standard deviation of *NPV*, σ_{NPV}, for each processor.

e Calculate the coefficient of variation of *NPV*, CV_{NPV}, for each processor.

f Based on the analysis in **b** through **e**, discuss the risk-return trade-offs associated with the processors. Which processor do you recommend? Why?

11-14 **(Decision Trees)** The Emory Board-Games Company can bring out one of two new games this season. The *Signs Away* game has a higher initial cost but also has a higher expected return. *Monopolistic Competition*, the alternative, has a slightly lower initial cost but also has a lower expected return. The present values and probabilities associated with each game are listed in the following table.

Game	Initial investment	PV of cash inflows	Probabilities
Signs Away	$140,000		1.00
		$320,000	.30
		220,000	.50
		− 80,000	.20
Monopolistic Competition	$120,000		1.00
		$260,000	.20
		200,000	.45
		− 50,000	.35

a Construct a decision tree to analyze the games.

b Which game would you recommend (following a decision-tree analysis)?

c Has your analysis captured the differences in project risk? Explain.

11-15 **(Simulation)** Creighton Castings has compiled the following information on a capital expenditure proposal:

(1) The projected cash *inflows* are normally distributed with a mean of $36,000 and a standard deviation of $9,000.

(2) The projected cash *outflows* are normally distributed with a mean of $30,000 and a standard deviation of $6,000.

(3) The firm has an 11 percent cost of capital.

(4) The probability distributions of cash inflows and cash outflows are not expected to change over the project's 10-year life.

a Describe how the preceding data could be used to develop a simulation model for finding the net present value of the project.

b Discuss the advantages of using a simulation to evaluate the proposed project.

11-16 **(Certainty Equivalents — Accept-Reject Decision)** Westchester Ball Valve has constructed a table, shown below, that gives expected cash inflows and certainty equivalents for these cash inflows. These measures are for a new machine that lasts five years and requires an initial investment of $95,000. The firm has a 15 percent cost of capital, and the risk-free rate of return is 10 percent.

Year (t)	Cash inflows (CF_t)	Certainty equivalent (α_t)
1	$35,000	1.0
2	35,000	.8
3	35,000	.6
4	35,000	.6
5	35,000	.2

a What is the net present value (unadjusted for risk)?
b What is the certainty equivalent net present value?
c Should the firm accept the project? Explain.
d Management has some doubts about the estimate of the certainty equivalent for year 5. There is some evidence that it may not be any lower than for year 4. What impact might this have on the decision you recommended in **c**? Explain.

11-17 **(Certainty Equivalents — Mutually Exclusive Decision)** SAM Ventures, Inc., is considering investment in either of two mutually exclusive projects, C and D. The firm has a 14 percent cost of capital, and the risk-free rate of return is currently 9 percent. The initial investment, expected cash inflows, and certainty equivalents associated with each of the projects are presented in the following table.

	Project C		Project D	
Initial investment (II)	$40,000		$56,000	
Year (t)	Cash inflows (CF_t)	Certainty equivalent (α_t)	Cash inflows (CF_t)	Certainty equivalent (α_t)
1	$20,000	.90	$20,000	.95
2	16,000	.80	25,000	.90
3	12,000	.60	15,000	.85
4	10,000	.50	20,000	.80
5	10,000	.40	10,000	.80

a Find the net present value (unadjusted for risk) for each project. Which is preferred using this measure?
b Find the certainty equivalent net present value for each project. Which is preferred using this risk-adjustment technique?
c Compare and discuss your findings in **a** and **b**. Which, if either, of the projects would you recommend that the firm accept? Explain.

11-18 **(Risk-Adjusted Discount Rates — Basic)** Lee Charles, Inc., is considering investment in one of three mutually exclusive projects, E, F, and G. The firm's cost of capital, k, is 15 percent, and the risk-free rate of return, R_F, is 10 percent. The firm has gathered the following basic cash flow and risk index data for each project.

	Project (j)		
	E	F	G
Initial investment (II)	$15,000	$11,000	$19,000
Year (t)	Cash inflows (CF_t)		
1	$ 6,000	$ 6,000	$ 4,000
2	6,000	4,000	6,000
3	6,000	5,000	8,000
4	6,000	2,000	12,000
Risk index (RI_j)	1.80	1.00	0.60

a Find the net present value (NPV) of each project using the firm's cost of capital. Which project is preferred in this situation?
b The firm uses the following equation to determine the risk-adjusted discount rate, $RADR_j$, for each project j.

$$RADR_j = R_F + RI_j(k - R_F)$$

where

$$R_F = \text{risk-free rate of return}$$
$$RI_j = \text{risk index for project } j$$
$$k = \text{cost of capital}$$

Substitute each project's risk index into this equation to determine its *RADR*.

c   Use the *RADR* for each project to determine its risk-adjusted *NPV*. Which project is preferred in this situation?

d   Compare and discuss your findings in **a** and **c**. Which project would you recommend that the firm accept?

11-19   **(Integrative — Risk-Adjusted Discount Rates with Statistics)**   Preston Tire has recently investigated market risk-return trade-offs and has assembled the following data:

Coefficient of variation	Market discount rate
0.0	11%
0.2	12
0.4	13
0.6	14
0.8	15
1.0	16
1.2	17
1.4	18
1.8	20
2.2	22

a   Construct a graph of the *market indifference curve*. Be sure to label the axes and indicate the area of risk premiums.

b   The firm is evaluating the two following projects. Both have four-year lives and require initial investments of $4000.

Project P		Project Q	
Annual cash inflow ($)	Probability	Annual cash inflow ($)	Probability
−2000	.25	−1000	.20
2000	.50	1600	.50
6000	.25	3000	.30

(1)   Determine the expected value, standard deviation, and coefficient of variation for each project's *cash inflows*.

(2)   Use the market indifference curve to determine the appropriate risk-adjusted discount rate for each project. (Adjust to the nearest whole percent.)

(3)   Find the risk-adjusted *NPV* for each project. Which project do you recommend? Why?

11-20   **(Integrative — Certainty Equivalents and Risk-Adjusted Discount Rates)**   After a careful evaluation of investment alternatives and opportunities, the Joely Company has determined that the following is the best estimate of the market indifference curve:

Risk index	Appropriate discount rate
0.0	7.0% (risk-free rate)
0.2	8.0
0.4	9.0
0.6	10.0
0.8	11.0
1.0	12.0
1.2	13.0
1.4	14.0
1.6	15.0
1.8	16.0
2.0	17.0

The firm is faced with two mutually exclusive projects, A and B. The following are the data the firm has been able to gather about the projects:

	Project A	Project B
Initial investment	$20,000	$30,000
Project life	5 years	5 years
Annual cash inflow	$ 7,000	$10,000
Risk index	0.2	1.4

	Certainty equivalents	
Year	Project A	Project B
0	1.00	1.00
1	0.95	0.90
2	0.90	0.80
3	0.90	0.70
4	0.85	0.70
Greater than 4	0.80	0.60

All the firm's cash inflows have already been adjusted for taxes.

a   Evaluate the projects using *certainty equivalents.*

b   Evaluate the projects using *risk-adjusted discount rates.*

c   Discuss your findings in a and b and explain why the two approaches are alternative techniques for considering risk in capital budgeting.

11-21   (**Risk Classes and *RADR***)   Porch Industries is attempting to select the best of three mutually exclusive projects, X, Y, and Z. Though all the projects have five-year lives, they possess differing degrees of risk. Project X is in Class V, the highest-risk class; project Y is in Class II, the below-average-risk class; and project Z is in Class III, the average-risk class. The basic cash flow data for each project and the risk classes and *RADR*s used by the firm are given in the tables on the next page.

	Project X	Project Y	Project Z
Initial investment (II)	$180,000	$235,000	$310,000

Year (t)	Cash inflows (CF_t)		
1	$ 80,000	$ 50,000	$ 90,000
2	70,000	60,000	90,000
3	60,000	70,000	90,000
4	60,000	80,000	90,000
5	60,000	90,000	90,000

Risk Classes and *RADR*s

Class	Description	Risk-adjusted discount rate (*RADR*)
I	Lowest risk	10%
II	Below-average risk	13
III	Average risk	15
IV	Above-average risk	19
V	Highest risk	22

a Find the risk-adjusted *NPV* for each project.

b Which, if any, project would you recommend the firm undertake?

Part V

Cost of Capital, Leverage, Capital Structure, and Dividends

CHAPTERS IN THIS PART

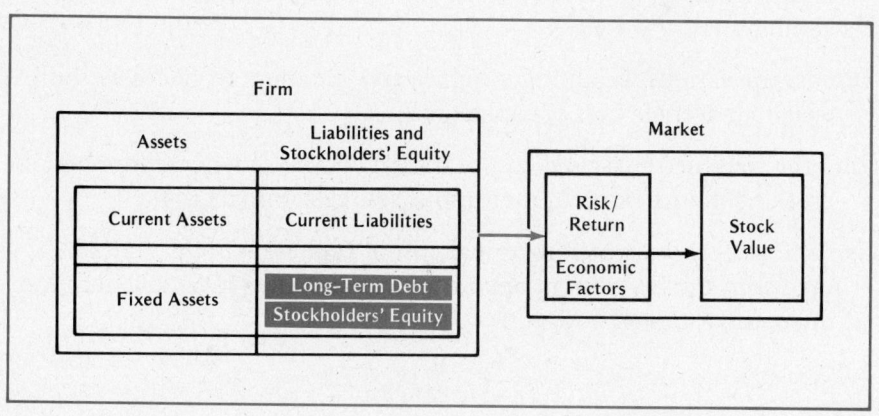

Chapter 12

The Cost of Capital

After studying this chapter, you should be able to:

1. Understand the underlying risk assumptions, the role of taxes, and the key factors affecting financing costs when finding the firm's cost of capital.

2. Describe the basic concept of cost of capital and the reasons that a weighted average is the appropriate cost measurement.

3. Calculate the cost of specific sources of long-term financing including long-term debt, bonds, preferred stock, common stock, and retained earnings.

4. Discuss the various weighting schemes and use them to calculate the weighted average cost of capital (*WACC*).

5. Find the weighted marginal cost of capital (*WMCC*) when a number of breaking points exists in the various sources of financing.

6. Explain how the weighted marginal cost of capital (*WMCC*) can be used with the investment opportunities schedule (*IOS*) to determine the optimal capital budget.

In earlier chapters we developed various techniques and concepts for evaluating investment alternatives. In discussions of the techniques of capital budgeting, the term *cost of capital* was often used. When net present values or profitability indexes are used to evaluate a project's cash flows, they are discounted at the firm's cost of capital. Although the cost of capital is not needed to calculate the internal rate of return of a project, it is needed to make accept-reject decisions. If a project's *IRR* is greater than or equal to the firm's cost of capital, the project is considered acceptable. Clearly, the cost of capital is an important financial concept. It acts as the major link between the firm's long-term decision-making activities and the wealth of the owners as determined by investors in the marketplace. This and the following two chapters provide theoretical as well as operational understanding of the linkage between capital budgeting, cost of capital, leverage and capital structure, dividends, and value. We begin with the cost of capital.

An Overview of the Cost of Capital

The *cost of capital* is the rate of return a firm must earn on its investments in projects having the same level of risk as the firm for the market value of the firm to remain unchanged.[1] It can also be thought of as the rate of return required by the market suppliers of capital in order to attract their funds to the firm. Holding risk constant, implementation of projects with a rate of return below the cost of capital will decrease the value of the firm.

[1] The value of the firm can be viewed as the present value of the firm's expected earnings. The cost of capital is the rate at which the firm's future earnings are discounted in the marketplace. It is dependent upon the level of nondiversifiable risk exhibited by the firm (see Chapters 7 and 8).

RISK

A basic assumption of traditional cost of capital analysis is that *the firm's business and financial risk are generally unaffected* by the acceptance and financing of projects.[2]

Business risk. *Business risk* is related to the response of the firm's earnings before interest and taxes (*EBIT*), or operating profits, to changes in sales. The projects accepted by a firm can greatly affect its business risk. If a firm accepts a project that is considerably more risky than average, suppliers of funds — debt or equity — will probably raise the cost of funds to compensate for the increased risk.[3] In analyzing the cost of capital, the projects accepted by the firm are assumed to possess the same level of risk as those already held. Therefore, the firm's *business risk is unchanged* (the projects accepted do not change the degree of responsiveness of *EBIT* to changes in sales).

Financial risk. *Financial risk* is related to the response of the firm's earnings per share (*eps*) to changes in earnings before interest and taxes (*EBIT*). It is affected by the mixture of long-term financing, or *capital structure,* of the firm. By increasing the proportion of fixed-cost financing — long-term debt, financial leases, and preferred stock — in its capital structure, the firm will increase its risk,[4] and thereby its financing costs. In analyzing the cost of capital, the proportional mix of long-term financing used is assumed to be the same as the existing capital structure. Therefore, the firm's *financial risk is unchanged* (the firm's financing decisions do not change the degree of responsiveness of *eps* to changes in *EBIT*).

TAXES

In the discussion of capital budgeting in earlier chapters, all cash flows were evaluated on an after-tax basis. To be consistent with this framework, the cost of capital, which is used to discount cash flows in determining net present values and profitability indexes and as the cutoff rate for internal rates of return, must also be measured on an after-tax basis. The only specific cost of capital component that actually requires any type of tax adjustment is the cost of debt.

[2] Although the acceptance of projects is independent of their financing, such a decision may or may not affect the business and financial risk of the firm. In fact, the use of the weighted marginal cost of capital — a topic discussed in the final section of this chapter — recognizes that by increasing the amount of financing, the firm's weighted average cost of capital is likely to increase. At this point in the analysis it is best to assume the complete independence of business and financial risk from the acceptance and financing of projects.

[3] There would obviously be a point at which the supplier would not make the funds available, regardless of the return the firm would be willing to provide. The firm would be too risky.

[4] Financial risk, or the likelihood that a firm will be able to meet its fixed financial charges, is often measured by a ratio of the degree of indebtedness, such as the debt ratio or a ratio of the ability to service debts such as times interest earned. (See Chapter 4 for a review of these ratios.) All these measures are rough indicators of ability to service debt.

OVERALL COST OF CAPITAL: SOME SURVEY DATA

In a relatively recent survey, firms in the *Fortune*'s 1000 were asked to indicate the approximate level of their cost of capital on October 15, 1980—a time when the yield on (risk-free) government bonds was about 12.4 percent. The table summarizes the responses to this question. The most frequent response indicated a cost of capital value of 15 to 17 percent, while nearly 65 percent of the 177 respondents had an overall cost of capital between 11 and 17 percent. Weighting the midpoint of each cost of capital range by the percentage of total responses in that range and summing the weighted values results in a mean value for the respondents of 14.3 percent.

Actual Cost of Capital (October 15, 1980)

Range of overall cost of capital	Percentage of 177 respondents
Less than 5%	1.7%
5% to 7%	0.6
7% to 9%	3.4
9% to 11%	10.1
11% to 13%	20.9 ⎤
13% to 15%	21.5 ⎬ —65%
15% to 17%	22.6 ⎦
17% to 19%	12.3
19% to 21%	4.0
21% to 23%	0.6
23% to 25%	0.6
Greater than 25%	1.7
Total	100.0%

SOURCE: Adapted from Lawrence J. Gitman and Vincent A. Mercurio, "Cost of Capital Techniques Used by Major U.S. Firms: Survey and Analysis of *Fortune*'s 1000," *Financial Management,* Winter 1982, p. 24.

and (2) flotation costs incurred when the debt is initially issued. To simplify the calculations in this section, *annual* interest payments on debt issues are assumed.[10]

Net proceeds. Most corporate long-term debts are incurred through the sale of bonds. The *net proceeds* from the sale of a bond are the funds received from the sale after all underwriting and brokerage fees have been paid. Sometimes the net proceeds from the sale of a bond are greater than the bond's *par,* or *face, value.* This is generally true when the *coupon rate* (stated interest rate) on the bond is greater than the interest rate associated with other, similar-risk debt instruments. The bond is sold for a *premium* (more than its par value) in order to equate the actual interest yield with the yields prevailing in the market. Bonds sold for less than par

[10] Interest on bonds is typically paid *semiannually.* The assumption of annual payments is made to simplify the required calculations while still conveying the key concepts. A discussion of how to treat bonds paying semiannual interest was included in the discussion of bond valuation in Chapter 8.

value, or at a *discount,* have coupon rates below the prevailing rates for similar-risk debt instruments. Selling bonds at a discount equates the effective yield (yield to maturity)[11] to the purchaser with yields of similar-risk debt instruments. *Flotation costs* — total costs of issuing and selling a security — reduce the net proceeds from the sale of a bond at a premium, at a discount, or at its par (face) value.

EXAMPLE   The Zero Company is contemplating selling $10 million worth of 20-year, 9 percent bonds, each with a par value of $1000. Since similar-risk debt instruments are yielding more than 9 percent, the firm must sell the bonds for $980 to compensate for the low coupon rate. The flotation costs paid the investment banker are 2 percent of the par value of the bond (2% × $1000), or $20.[12] The net proceeds to the firm from the sale of each bond are therefore $960 ($980 − $20). ■

Calculating the cost of debt. The before-tax cost of debt can be found by determining the internal rate of return on the bond cash flows. From the issuer's point of view, this value can be referred to as the *cost to maturity* of the cash flows associated with the debt.[13] The cost to maturity is calculated using the techniques presented in Chapter 10. It represents the annual before-tax percentage cost of the debt to the firm.

EXAMPLE   In the preceding example the net proceeds of a $1000, 9 percent, 20-year bond were found to be $960. Although the cash flows from the bond issue do not have a conventional pattern, the calculation of the annual cost is quite simple. Actually, the cash flow pattern is exactly the opposite of a conventional pattern in that it consists of an initial inflow (the net proceeds) followed by a series of annual outlays (the interest payments). In the final year, when the debt is retired, an outlay representing the repayment of the principal also occurs. The cash flows associated with the Zero Company's bond issue are as follows:

End of year(s)	Cash flow
0	$ 960
1 – 20	−$ 90
20	−$1000

The initial $960 inflow is followed by annual interest outflows of $90 (i.e., 9% of $1000) over the 20-year life of the bond. In year 20 an outflow of $1000, representing the repayment of the principal, occurs. The before-tax cost of the debt can be determined by finding the discount rate that equates the present value of the outflows with the initial inflow. Applying the trial-and-error internal rate of return techniques of Chapter 10 results in an approximate before-tax cost, or cost to maturity, of 9.47 percent.[14] ■

[11] The concept of *yield to maturity (YTM),* which is the actual rate of return investors would get if they purchase a bond at its current price and hold it to maturity, was fully developed and illustrated in the discussion of bond valuation in Chapter 8.

[12] As noted in Chapter 3, investment bankers are often hired by firms to find buyers for new security issues, regardless of whether they are privately placed or sold through a public offering. The flotation cost includes compensation to the investment banker for marketing the issue. Detailed discussion of the activities, organization, and cost of investment banking is included in Chapter 19.

[13] The internal rate of return on a bond investment, when *viewed by a purchaser* — not the issuer — is its *yield to maturity;* since our concern is from the viewpoint of the issuer, emphasis is placed on *cost to maturity.*

[14] In Chapter 6 (see footnote 8) an explanation was given of how to approximate interest or growth rates using *interpolation,* a simple technique for finding intermediate or fractional values when only integer

As was indicated earlier, the cost of debt must be stated on an after-tax basis, and since interest charges are tax deductible, a tax adjustment is required. The before-tax debt cost, k_d, can be converted to an after-tax debt cost, k_i, by the following equation:

$$k_i = k_d(1 - t) \qquad (12.2)$$

The t represents the firm's marginal tax rate.

EXAMPLE The before-tax debt cost for the Zero Company, which has a 40 percent marginal tax rate, is 9.47 percent. Applying Equation 12.2 results in an after-tax debt cost of 5.68 percent [i.e., 9.47% (1 − .40)]. Typically, the cost of debt is considerably less than the cost of any of the alternative forms of long-term financing. This is because the interest expense is tax deductible. ■

A shortcut for approximating the cost of debt. The cost of debt can be approximated using a shortcut approach that bypasses the need to find the internal rate of return (cost) for the cash flows associated with borrowing. This approach involves determining the average annual outflow, which consists of the annual interest plus the amortization of any premium or discount, and dividing this outflow by the average amount borrowed. If

I = the annual interest payment in dollars
N_d = the net proceeds from the sale of debt (bond)
n = the number of years to the bond's maturity

the approximate before-tax debt cost for a bond with a $1000 par value[15] can be found by the following equation:

---

data are available. To interpolate a more precise value for the internal rate of return, or cost to maturity, for the Zero Company's bond issue, the following steps are necessary:

1. Find the present value of the outflows at the two consecutive rates that straddle the initial inflow. In this case the present value of the outflows at 9 percent is $999.61; at 10 percent it is $915.26. The initial inflow is $960, which is between these values.
2. Find the difference between the present value of the two outflows, which in this case is $84.35 ($999.61 − $915.26).
3. Find the difference between the present value of the outflows at the lower rate ($999.61 at 9%) and the desired value, or initial inflow ($960), which in this case is $39.61 ($999.61 − $960.00).
4. Divide the result from step 3, which is $39.61, by the result from step 2, which is $84.35, to get the percent of total distance across the interval attributable to the calculated value. This results in a value, rounded to the nearest hundredth, of 0.47.
5. Multiply the percent found in step 4 by the interval width over which interpolation is being performed. In this case the interval width is 1 percent (10 percent − 9 percent); multiplying we get 0.47 percent (0.47 × 1 percent). Note that when interpolation is being performed over a wider interval, this step becomes more important.
6. Add the value from step 5 to the lower of the two rates developed in step 1, 9 percent. This results in an approximate cost to maturity of 9.47 percent (0.47 + 9.00).

[15] As demonstrated in Chapter 8 (Equation 8.4), this formula can be used to find yields to maturity by considering all cash flows from the point of view of an investor. For bonds with par values in an amount other than $1000, the par value can be substituted into Equation 12.3 for $1000 in order to apply the formula.

$$\text{Approximate before-tax debt cost} = \frac{I + \dfrac{\$1000 - N_d}{n}}{\dfrac{N_d + \$1000}{2}} \tag{12.3}$$

The first term in the numerator of Equation 12.3 represents the annual interest, the second term in the numerator represents the annual amortization of any premium or discount, and the denominator represents the average amount borrowed.

EXAMPLE   Substituting the appropriate values from the Zero Company example into Equation 12.3 results in an approximate before-tax debt cost of 9.39 percent.

$$\text{Approximate before-tax cost of debt} = \frac{\$90 + \dfrac{\$1000 - \$960}{20}}{\dfrac{\$960 + \$1000}{2}} = \frac{\$90 + \$2}{\$980}$$

$$= \frac{\$92}{\$980} = 9.39\%$$

Converting this value to an after-tax basis using Equation 12.2 results in an approximate after-tax debt cost of 5.63 percent [i.e., 9.39% (1 − .40)]. The accuracy of this approximation can be seen by comparing the approximate value of 5.63 percent to the actual after-tax debt cost of 5.68 percent calculated earlier. You may want to use this approximation in making rough calculations of the after-tax cost of debt. ■

THE COST OF PREFERRED STOCK

Preferred stock represents a special type of ownership interest in the firm. Preferred shareholders must receive their *stated* dividends prior to the distribution of any earnings to common shareholders. Since preferred stock is a form of ownership, the proceeds from the sale of preferred stock are expected to be held for an infinite period of time. A complete discussion of the various characteristics of preferred stock will be presented in Chapter 20. However, the one aspect of preferred stock that requires clarification at this point is dividends.

Preferred stock dividends. The amount of preferred stock dividends that must be paid each year before earnings can be distributed to common stockholders may be stated in dollars or as a percentage of the stock's par, or face, value.

Dollar amounts. Most preferred stock dividends are stated as "*x* dollars per year." When dividends are stated this way, the stock is often referred to as "*x* dollar preferred stock." A $4 preferred stock is expected to pay preferred shareholders $4 in dividends each year on each share of preferred stock owned.

Percentage amounts. Sometimes preferred stock dividends are stated as an annual percentage rate. This rate represents the percentage of the stock's par, or face, value that equals the annual dividend. For instance, an 8 percent preferred stock with a $50 par value would be expected to pay an annual dividend of $4 a share. Before calculating the cost of preferred stock, any dividends stated as percentages should be converted to annual dollar dividends.

Calculating the cost of preferred stock. The *cost of preferred stock, k_p,* is found by dividing the annual preferred stock dividend, D_p, by the net proceeds from the sale of the preferred stock, N_p. The net proceeds represent the amount of money to be received net of any flotation costs required to issue and sell the stock. For example, if a preferred stock is sold for $100 per share but $3 per share flotation costs are incurred, the net proceeds from the sale are $97. Equation 12.4 gives the cost of preferred stock, k_p, in terms of the annual dollar dividend, D_p, and the net proceeds from the sale of the stock, N_p:

$$k_p = \frac{D_p}{N_p} \qquad\qquad (12.4)$$

Since preferred stock dividends are paid out of the firm's *after-tax* cash flows, a tax adjustment is not required.

EXAMPLE   The Zero Company is contemplating issuance of a 9 percent preferred stock expected to sell for its $85 per share par value. The cost of issuing and selling the stock is expected to be $3 per share. The firm would like to determine the cost of the stock. The first step in finding this cost is to calculate the dollar amount of preferred dividends, since the dividend is stated as a percentage of the stock's $85 par value. The annual dollar dividend is $7.65 (9% of $85). The net proceeds from the proposed sale of stock can be found by subtracting the flotation costs from the sale price. This gives a value of $82 per share. Substituting the annual dividend, D_p, of $7.65 and the net proceeds, N_p, of $82 into Equation 12.4 gives the cost of preferred stock, 9.33 percent ($7.65 ÷ $82). ■

Comparing the 9.33 percent cost of preferred stock to the 5.68 percent cost of debt shows that the preferred stock is more expensive. This is true because (1) preferred stockholders accept more risk than debtholders who have a claim senior to that of preferred and (2) the cost of debt (interest) is tax deductible. If the dividends on the preferred stock of Zero Company had been stated in dollars, the calculations would have been simplified, since the dollar dividend could have been substituted directly into Equation 12.4.

THE COST OF COMMON STOCK

The *cost of common stock* is not as easy to calculate as the cost of debt or the cost of preferred stock. The difficulty arises from the definition of the cost, which is based on the premise that the value of a share of stock in a firm is determined by the present value of all future dividends expected to be paid on the stock. The rate at which these expected dividends are discounted to determine their present value represents the cost of common stock. The theory underlying this definition is rooted in the share-price valuation model, which was presented in Chapter 8.

The definition itself is based on a few key assumptions with respect to the behavior of individuals and their ability to forecast future values.

Share values. The basic assumption on which the cost of common stock is calculated is that the value of a share of stock is equal to the present value of all future dividends expected to be paid on the stock over an infinite period of time. Not all earnings are paid out as dividends, but it is expected that earnings that are retained and reinvested will boost future dividends. At infinity, a *liquidating,* or final, dividend is expected, which actually represents the distribution of the firm's assets. Since the firm is viewed as a going concern with an infinite life, the liquidating dividend does not have to be specified.

Growth rates. Another necessary assumption is that the rate of growth in dividends and earnings is *constant* over the infinite time horizon. This assumption implies a constant dividend payout (dividends per share that are a constant percentage of earnings per share) by the firm. The growth rate expected is assumed to be measurable, typically on the basis of the past growth in earnings demonstrated by the firm.

Risk classes. A final assumption concerns the riskiness of a firm as viewed by existing and prospective shareholders. Earlier in the chapter was presented a general expression for the relationship between risk and financing costs that showed that the cost of a specific type of funds is virtually the same for firms viewed by investors as having equivalent levels of business and financial risk. In the case of common stock, it is assumed that the expected earnings of firms perceived by investors as being equally risky (having the same degree of business and financial risk) will be discounted at the same rate. This same assumption underlies the capital asset pricing model (CAPM), developed in Chapter 7.

Common stockholders, just like bondholders and preferred stockholders, expect larger returns for higher levels of risk. In the case of bonds, if the firm becomes more risky, the returns to bondholders are increased by virtue of the fact that the bond sells at a discount in the marketplace. This is similar to what happens to preferred stock. In the case of common stock, increased risk must result in increased returns to the owners *or* the market price of their shares will fall. Of course, implicit in the assumption that the earnings of firms of equivalent risk are discounted at the same rate is the assumption that existing and prospective investors can accurately measure the riskiness of the firm and thereby agree on the rate at which to discount the firm's earnings.

Finding the cost of common stock equity. The *cost of common stock equity* can be generally stated as the rate at which investors discount the expected dividends of the firm in order to determine the market price of an ownership interest in the firm. The rate of discount is a function of the risk-free cost of funds adjusted for the business and financial risk associated with the firm. Two techniques for measuring the cost of common stock equity capital are available. One is the constant growth valuation method; the other relies on the capital asset pricing model (CAPM).

The constant growth valuation model. The *constant growth valuation model,* often called the *Gordon model,* is based on the widely accepted premise that the value of a share of stock is the present value of all anticipated dividends it will provide over an infinite time horizon. The key expression derived in Chapter 8 and presented as Equation 8.10 is restated in Equation 12.5:

$$P_0 = \frac{D_1}{k_s - g}$$ (12.5)

where

P_0 = the current value of common stock
D_1 = the per-share dividend expected at the end of year 1
k_s = the rate of return required on common stock
g = the constant annual rate of growth in dividends and earnings

Solving Equation 12.5 for k_s results in the following expression for the *cost of common stock equity:*

$$k_s = \frac{D_1}{P_0} + g$$ (12.6)

Equation 12.6 indicates that the cost of common stock equity can be found by dividing the dividend expected at the end of year 1 by the current price of the stock and adding the expected growth rate. The first term, D_1/P_0, represents the expected *dividend yield* on the stock. Since common stock dividends are paid from after-tax income, no tax adjustment is required.

EXAMPLE   The Zero Company wishes to determine its cost of common stock equity capital, k_s. The prevailing market price, P_0, of its common stock is $50 per share. The firm expects to pay a dividend, D_1, of $4 at the end of the coming year, 1985. The dividends paid on the outstanding common stock over the past six years (1979–1984) are as follows:

Year	Dividend
1984	$3.80
1983	3.62
1982	3.47
1981	3.33
1980	3.12
1979	2.97

The firm has maintained a fixed dividend payout ratio from 1979 to 1984. Using the table for the present-value interest factors, *PVIF* (Table A-3), in conjunction with the technique described for finding growth rates in Chapter 6, the annual growth rate of dividends, g, can be calculated.[16] It turns out to be approximately 5 percent. Substituting $D_1 = \$4$, $P_0 = \$50$, and $g = 5$ percent into Equation 12.6 results in the cost of common stock equity:

[16] The technique involves two basic steps. Dividing the earliest dividend ($2.97) by the latest dividend ($3.80) results in a factor for the present value of $1 of .782 ($2.97 ÷ $3.80). Although six dividends are shown, they reflect only five years of growth. Looking across the table for the present-value interest factors, *PVIF* (Table A-3), for five years, the factor closest to .782 occurs at 5 percent (.784). Therefore, the growth rate of the dividends rounded to the nearest whole percentage is 5 percent.

$$k_s = \frac{\$4}{\$50} + .05 = .08 + .05 = .13 = \underline{13\%}$$

The 13 percent cost of common stock equity capital represents the return required by *existing* shareholders on their investment in order to leave the market price of the firm's outstanding shares unchanged. ■

Using CAPM. The capital asset pricing model which was developed and discussed in Chapter 7 describes the relationship between the required return or cost of common stock equity capital, k_s, and the nondiversifiable or relevant risks of the firm as reflected by *beta, b* — its index of nondiversifiable risk. The basic CAPM is given in Equation 12.7.[17]

$$k_s = R_F + b \times (k_m - R_F) \tag{12.7}$$

where

R_F = the rate of return required on a risk-free asset, which is commonly measured by the yield on a U.S. government security such as a Treasury bill
k_m = the required rate of return on the market portfolio of assets that can be viewed as the average rate of return on all assets

The use of CAPM to measure the cost of common stock equity capital relies on the securities market to reflect the returns required from a firm having a specified level of nondiversifiable or relevant risk. This risk is measured by the firm's security beta, *b*.

EXAMPLE   The Zero Company, which calculated its cost of common stock equity capital, k_s, using the constant growth valuation model in the preceding example, also wishes to calculate this cost using the capital asset pricing model. From information provided by the firm's investment advisers and its own analyses, it is found that the risk-free rate, R_F, equals 7 percent; the firm's beta, *b*, equals 1.50; and the return on the market, k_m, equals 11 percent. Substituting these values into the CAPM (Equation 12.7), it has estimated the cost of common stock equity capital, k_s, as follows:

$$k_s = 7\% + 1.50 \times (11\% - 7\%) = 7\% + 6\% = \underline{13\%}$$

The 13 percent cost of common stock equity capital represents the required return of investors in Zero Company common stock. This return, which is the same as that found using the constant growth valuation model in the preceding example,[18] represents the

---

[17] For a more complete development and discussion of CAPM, see the discussion of risk and return in Chapter 7. Comparison of Equation 12.7 and Equation 7.6 reveals a few minor differences in notation. These were made to simplify the current discussion of cost of capital; they do not alter the model in any way.

[18] The agreement between the cost of common stock equity capital, k_s, of 13 percent calculated using CAPM and the 13 percent cost found earlier using the constant growth valuation model has been intentionally arranged to avoid any problems that may arise from differing values. In actual situations, the cost of common stock equity capital calculated using these alternative approaches will not necessarily agree, owing to differences in the models.

return that must be earned by investors to compensate them for the nondiversifiable or relevant risk involved. The 13 percent cost of common stock equity capital can be viewed as consisting of a 7 percent risk-free rate plus a 6 percent risk premium, which reflects the fact that Zero Company's return is 1.50 times more responsive than the market portfolio to the factors affecting nondiversifiable or relevant risk. ∎

Use of the CAPM to measure the cost of common stock equity capital is becoming more popular. CAPM differs from the constant growth valuation model in that it directly considers the firm's risk as reflected by beta in order to determine the *required* return or cost of common stock equity capital. The constant growth model does not look at risk; it uses the market price, P_0, as a reflection of the *expected* risk-return preference of investors in the marketplace. Although both techniques are theoretically sound, the use of the constant growth valuation model is often preferred because the data required are more readily available. Obtaining the data required to apply the CAPM is currently a bit more time consuming.

Another difference lies in the fact that when the constant growth valuation model is used to find the cost of common stock equity capital, it can easily be adjusted for underpricing and flotation costs to find the cost of new common stock; the CAPM does not provide such an adjustment mechanism. The difficulty in adjusting the cost of common stock equity capital calculated using CAPM for these costs stems from the fact that the model does not include the market price, P_0, a variable that is needed to make such an adjustment.

Until the problems in application and definition associated with the use of CAPM to measure the costs of common stock equity capital and new common stock are dealt with, the apparent preference for use of the valuation-based model is expected to continue. Throughout the remainder of this text, the traditional constant growth valuation model will be used for measuring both the cost of common stock equity capital and the cost of new common stock. Discussion of the use of this model to determine the cost of new common stock follows.

The cost of new issues of common stock. Since our purpose in finding the firm's overall cost of capital is to determine the after-tax cost of *new* funds required for financing projects, attention must be given to the cost of *new* issues of common stock. Assuming that new funds are raised in the same proportions as the current capital structure, the only additional data required for finding the *cost of new issues of common stock* are the amount of underpricing and flotation costs associated with them. It is quite likely that, to sell a new issue, the sale price will have to be below the current market price, reducing the proceeds below the current market price, P_0. The stock must be *underpriced* by an amount that will result in a "fair price" in light of the dilution of ownership that will take place. Another factor that will reduce these proceeds is flotation costs paid for issuing and selling the new issue.

The cost of new issues can be calculated by determining the net proceeds after underpricing and flotation costs, using the constant growth valuation model expression for the cost of existing common stock, k_s, as a starting point. If we let N_n represent the net proceeds from the sale of new common stock after allowing for underpricing and flotation costs, the cost of the new issue, k_n, can be expressed as follows:[19]

$$k_n = \frac{D_1}{N_n} + g \qquad (12.8)$$

Since the net proceeds from sale of new common stock, N_n, will be less than the current market price, P_0, the cost of new issues, k_n, will always be greater than the cost of existing issues, k_s. The cost of new common stock is normally greater than any other long-term financing cost. Since common stock dividends are paid from after-tax cash flows, no tax adjustment is required.

EXAMPLE   In the example using the constant growth valuation model, an expected dividend, D_1, of \$4, a current market price, P_0, of \$50, and an expected growth rate of dividends, g, of 5 percent were used to calculate Zero Company's cost of common stock equity capital, k_s, which was found to be 13 percent. To determine its cost of new common stock, k_n, the Zero Company, with the aid of its advisers, has estimated that on average, new shares can be sold for \$49. The \$1 per share underpricing is necessary due to the competitive nature of the market. A second cost associated with a new issue is an underwriting fee of \$.80 per share that would have to be paid to cover the costs of issuing and selling the new issue. The total underpricing and flotation costs per share are therefore expected to be \$1.80 (\$1.00 per share underpricing plus \$.80 per share flotation).

Subtracting the \$1.80 per share underpricing and flotation cost from the current \$50 share price, P_0, results in expected net proceeds, N_n, of \$48.20 per share (\$50.00 − \$1.80). Substituting $D_1 = \$4$, $N_n = \$48.20$, and $g = 5$ percent into Equation 12.8 results in a cost of new common stock, k_n, as follows:

$$k_n = \frac{\$4.00}{\$48.20} + .0500 = .0830 + .0500 = .1330 = \underline{\underline{13.30\%}}$$

Zero Company's relevant cost of new common stock, k_n, is therefore 13.30 percent. This is the value to be used in the subsequent calculation of the firm's overall cost of capital. ∎

THE COST OF RETAINED EARNINGS

The *cost of retained earnings* is closely related to the cost of common stock. If earnings were not retained, they would be paid out to the common stockholders as dividends. Retained earnings are often looked on as a *fully subscribed issue of additional common stock,* since they increase the stockholders' equity in the same way as a new issue of common stock. The cost of retained earnings must therefore be viewed as the opportunity cost of the forgone dividends to the *existing* common stockholders.

---

[19] An alternative, but computationally less straightforward, form of this equation is

$$k_n = \frac{D_1}{P_0(1 - f)} + g \qquad (12.8a)$$

where f represents the *percentage* reduction in current market price expected as a result of underpricing and flotation costs. Simply stated, N_n in Equation 12.8 is equivalent to $P_0(1 - f)$ in Equation 12.8a. For convenience, Equation 12.8 is used to define the cost of new common stock, k_n.

If the firm is unable to earn as much on its retained earnings as other firms with a comparable level of risk, it is assumed that shareholders will prefer to receive these earnings in the form of dividends so they can invest in the other firms. When the company retains earnings, it assumes that the shareholders cannot for a comparable risk earn more on the money elsewhere than the firm can earn through reinvestment.

If retained earnings are viewed as a fully subscribed issue of additional common stock, the firm's cost of retained earnings, k_r, can be assumed to be equal to the cost of common stock equity as given by Equations 12.6 and 12.7.[20] That is,

$$k_r = k_s \tag{12.9}$$

It is not necessary to adjust the cost of retained earnings for either underpricing or flotation costs. By retaining earnings, the firm bypasses these costs and still raises the equity capital.

EXAMPLE   The cost of retained earnings for the Zero Company was actually calculated in the preceding examples, since it is equal to the cost of common stock equity when underpricing and flotation costs are ignored. Thus k_r equals 13 percent. The cost of retained earnings is always lower than the cost of a new issue of common stock, which in this case is 13.30 percent. This is because of the absence of underpricing and flotation costs in financing projects with retained earnings. ■

Measuring the Overall or Weighted Average Cost of Capital (*WACC*)

Now that methods for calculating the cost of specific sources of financing have been reviewed, we can present techniques for determining the overall cost of capital to be used to evaluate prospective investments. As noted earlier, the *weighted average cost of capital (WACC)* is found by weighting the cost of each specific type of capital by its proportion in the firm's capital structure. Let us look at the common weighting schemes and the procedures and considerations involved.

WEIGHTING SCHEMES

Weights can be calculated as book value or market value and as historic or target.

Book value versus market value. *Book value weights* are based on the use of accounting values to assess the proportion of each type of capital in the firm's structure. *Market value weights* measure the proportion of each type of financing at its market value.

---

[20] Technically, if a stockholder received dividends and wished to invest them in additional shares of the firm's stock, he or she would have first to pay taxes on the dividends and then pay brokerage fees prior to acquiring additional shares. If pt were the average stockholder's personal tax rate and bf the average brokerage fees stated as a percentage, the cost of retained earnings, k_r, could be specified as $k_r = k_s(1 - pt)(1 - bf)$. Due to the difficulty in estimating pt and bf, only the simpler definition of k_r given in Equation 12.9 is used here.

Market value weights are theoretically more appealing, since the market values of securities closely approximate the actual dollars to be received from their sale. Moreover, since the costs of the various types of capital are calculated using prevailing market prices, it seems only reasonable to use market value weights. However, it is more difficult to calculate the market values of a firm's sources of equity financing than to use book values. The weighted average cost of capital based on market value weights is typically greater than the weighted average cost based on book value, since it is not unusual for preferred and common stocks to have market values above their book values. Since these sources of long-term funds have higher specific costs than debt, the overall cost of capital normally increases when market instead of book value weights are used. *Market value weights are clearly preferred over book value weights* and will be used in the discussions that follow.

Historic versus target. *Historic weights* can be book or market weights based on actual data. For example, past as well as current book proportions would constitute a form of historic weighting. Likewise, past or current market proportions would represent a historic weighting scheme. Such a weighting scheme would therefore be based on actual — rather than desired — proportions. *Target weights,* which can also be based on book or market values, reflect the desired capital structure proportions. Firms using target weights establish these proportions on the basis of the "optimal" capital structure they wish to achieve. Firms that believe their existing capital structure is optimal will use historic weights, since in such a case these in fact reflect the target capital structure.

Unless a firm's existing capital structure differs significantly from the optimal, the weighted average cost of capital using historic market value weights is not expected to differ greatly from the weighted average calculated using target market value proportions. When one considers the somewhat approximate nature of these calculations, the choice of weights may not be critical. *From a strictly theoretical point of view, the preferred weighting scheme is target market value proportions,* and these will be used throughout this chapter.

CALCULATING THE WEIGHTED AVERAGE COST OF CAPITAL (*WACC*)

Once the cost of the specific sources of financing and the appropriate weighting scheme have been determined, the weighted average cost of capital (*WACC*) can be calculated. This calculation is performed by multiplying the specific cost of each form of financing by its proportion in the firm's capital structure and summing the weighted values. As an equation, the weighted average cost of capital, k_a, can be specified as follows:

$$k_a = w_i k_i + w_p k_p + w_s k_{r \text{ or } n} \tag{12.10}$$

where

w_i = proportion of long-term debt in capital structure
w_p = proportion of preferred stock in capital structure
w_s = proportion of common stock equity in capital structure
$w_i + w_p + w_s = 1$

Two important points should be noted in Equation 12.10:

1. *The sum of weights must equal 1.* Simply stated, all capital structure components must be accounted for.
2. The firm's common stock equity weight, w_s, is multiplied by either the cost of retained earnings, k_r, or the cost of new common stock, k_n. The specific cost used in the common stock equity term will depend on whether the firm's common stock equity financing would be obtained using retained earnings, k_r, or new common stock, k_n. This distinction should become clearer in the discussion of the weighted marginal cost of capital (*WMCC*) in the next section.

EXAMPLE   Earlier in the chapter, the costs of the various types of capital for the Zero Company were found to be as follows:

Cost of debt, k_i = 5.68 percent
Cost of preferred stock, k_p = 9.33 percent
Cost of new common stock, k_n = 13.30 percent
Cost of retained earnings, k_r = 13.00 percent

The company has determined what it believes to be the optimal capital structure it is trying to achieve. Zero Company uses this target capital structure, which is based on market values, to calculate the weighted average cost of capital. The target market value proportions are as follows:

Source of capital	Target market value proportions
Long-term debt	40%
Preferred stock	10
Common stock equity	50
Total	100%

Table 12.1   Calculation of the Weighted Average Cost of Capital for the Zero Company

Source of capital	Target proportion (1)	Cost (2)	Weighted cost [(1) × (2)] (3)
Long-term debt	40%	5.68%	2.272%
Preferred stock	10	9.33	.933
Common stock equity	50	13.00	6.500
Totals	100%		9.705%

Weighted average cost of capital = 9.705%

COST OF CAPITAL WEIGHTING SCHEMES

In Gitman and Mercurio's 1981 study of *Fortune's* 1000 firms, the 177 responses summarized in the table below relative to the general approach to cost of capital and method used to weight capital components if a weighted average cost of capital was used were obtained. It can be seen that the majority of respondents used some type of weighted average when determining their cost of capital. Somewhat surprising is the fact that rather than using a weighted average cost of capital, nearly 17 percent of the respondents used the cost of the specific source of funds employed as a cutoff rate for making financial decisions. Such an approach clearly runs counter to theory and suggests that a number of respondents were acting very differently from what theory suggests.

General Approach and Weighting Schemes

Approach or weighting scheme	Percentage of 177 respondents
Use the cost of specific source of financing planned for funding the alternative	16.9%
Use a weighted average cost of capital based on *book value* weights	16.4
Use a weighted average cost of capital based on target *capital structure* weights	41.8
Use a weighted average cost of capital based on current *market value* weights	28.8
Use a weighted average cost of capital based on some other weighting scheme	0.6
Total	104.5%[a]

[a] Note that the total is greater than 100 percent because a number of respondents gave multiple responses.

Of the firms using a weighted average, the majority appear to use target capital structure weights. Second most popular are market value weights, followed by book value and other weighting schemes. The dominance of target and market value weights seems to be consistent with the literature. Although theoretically unsound, the use of book value weights by about 16 percent of respondents may reflect the fact that they chose this weighting scheme either for convenience or because they feel their book value proportions are identical to target proportions. In general, it should be clear that about 80 percent of the respondents using a weighting scheme use the theoretically preferred target or market value weights.

SOURCE: Adapted from Lawrence J. Gitman and Vincent A. Mercurio, "Cost of Capital Techniques Used by Major U.S. Firms: Survey and Analysis of *Fortune's* 1000," *Financial Management,* Winter 1982, pp. 22–23.

Because the firm expects to have a sizable amount ($300,000) of retained earnings available, it plans to use its cost of retained earnings, k_r, as the common stock equity cost component. Using this value along with the other data presented, Zero Company's weighted average cost of capital is calculated in Table 12.1. The resulting weighted average cost of capital for Zero Company is 9.705 percent. In view of this cost of capital, the firm should accept all projects (that do not change the firm's risk) whose net present value discounted at 9.705 percent is greater than or equal to zero, whose profitability index calculated using the 9.705 percent discount rate is greater than or equal to 1, or whose internal rate of return is greater than or equal to 9.705 percent. ■

Weighted Marginal Cost of Capital (*WMCC*)

The weighted average cost of capital may vary at any time depending on the volume of financing the firm plans to raise. As the volume of financing increases, the costs of the various types of financing will increase, raising the firm's weighted average cost of capital. A schedule or graph relating the firm's weighted average cost of capital to the level of new financing is called the *weighted marginal cost of capital (WMCC).*[21] These increasing costs are attributable to the fact that suppliers of capital will require greater returns in the form of interest, dividends, or growth to compensate for the increased risk introduced as larger volumes of *new* financing are incurred. A second factor relates to the use of common stock equity financing. The portion of new financing provided by common stock equity will be taken from available retained earnings until exhaused and then obtained through new common stock financing. Since retained earnings are a less expensive form of common stock equity financing than the sale of new common stock, it should be clear that once retained earnings have been exhausted, the weighted average cost of capital will rise with the addition of more expensive new common stock. Because firms will first use all retained-earnings financing available prior to selling new common stock, it is best to view the firm as having three types of capital: (1) long-term debt, (2) preferred stock, and (3) common stock equity, which includes both retained-earnings and new common stock financing.

CALCULATING THE WEIGHTED MARGINAL COST
OF CAPITAL (*WMCC*)

To calculate its weighted marginal cost of capital, the firm must first determine the cost of each source of financing at various levels of total new financing. To do this, the firm must take the following steps:

1. The cost of each source of financing for various levels of use of that type of financing must be determined through an analysis of current market conditions.
2. Using the historic or target capital structure proportions of debt, preferred stock, and common stock equity, the levels of *total new financing* at which

---

[21] Some authors refer to this function as the *marginal cost of capital (MCC),* but for descriptive clarity the term *weighted marginal cost of capital (WMCC)* is used.

the cost of the new components change must be determined. The levels at which the component costs increase are called *breaking points*. They can be calculated using the relationship given in Equation 12.11:

$$BP_j = \frac{TF_j}{w_j} \qquad (12.11)$$

where

BP_j = breaking point for financing source j
TF_j = total new financing from source j at the breaking point
w_j = capital structure proportion (historic or target) for financing source j

EXAMPLE   A firm expects to have available $200,000 of retained earnings for investment in the coming year. The cost of these earnings has been calculated as 12 percent. Once the retained earnings have been exhausted, common stock equity financing will have to be obtained through the sale of new common stock; the cost of new common stock is 13 percent. The target capital structure contains 40 percent common stock equity, which consists of retained earnings and common stock. To find the breaking point, or level of total new financing, at which the cost of common equity will rise, the firm applies Equation 12.11 as follows:

$$BP_{\text{common equity}} = \frac{\$200,000}{.40} = \underline{\underline{\$500,000}}$$

This result indicates that at levels of *total* new financing up to $500,000, the firm's cost of common stock equity would be 12 percent; at a level of total new financing greater than $500,000, the cost of equity would increase to 13 percent, since retained earnings would be exhausted and the more expensive new common stock would have to be utilized. As a check to this conclusion, it should be clear that to maintain 40 percent equity at a total new financing level of $500,000, $200,000 (.40 × $500,000) of common equity is needed. Since only $200,000 of retained earnings will be available, more expensive new common stock financing will be required to obtain more than $500,000 in total new financing and maintain the required target capital structure. Therefore, the $500,000 level of total new financing is a breaking point for common stock equity. ■

3. Once the breaking points have been determined, the weighted average cost of capital over the range of total financing between breaking points must be calculated. First, the weighted average cost of capital for a level of total new financing between zero and the first breaking point is found. Next, the weighted average cost of capital for a level of total new financing between the first and second breaking points is found, and so on. By definition, for each of the ranges of total new financing between breaking points, certain component capital costs will increase, causing the weighted average cost of capital to increase to a higher level than over the preceding range.

4. Once the weighted average cost of capital for each range of total new financing has been determined, a schedule of these results is prepared. The

schedule shows the related weighted average cost of capital for each range of total new financing. This relationship is called the *weighted marginal cost of capital* because it shows the weighted average cost of capital for each level of total new financing.

The use of these steps to find a firm's weighted marginal cost of capital can best be demonstrated by using a simple example.

EXAMPLE The Zero Company wishes to determine its weighted marginal cost of capital. In making the required calculations, the firm wishes to use the target capital structure proportions given earlier in column 1 of Table 12.1 and restated in column 1 of Table 12.2. Using these data, the steps just presented can be followed to find Zero Company's weighted marginal cost of capital.

1. After consulting a variety of sources, the Zero Company finds the cost of each of its three capital sources over various ranges of the respective sources of new financing. Columns 2 and 3 of Table 12.2 present this information for each of the three sources. The specific costs given in column 3 are calculated using the applicable techniques presented earlier in this chapter.
2. Using the target capital structure proportions given in column 1 of Table 12.2 and the financing ranges given in column 2, the breaking points for each source of capital are calculated in column 3 of Table 12.3. The resulting ranges of total new financing are given in column 4 of Table 12.3.
3. An examination of columns 3 and 4 of Table 12.3 indicates that the firm's weighted

Table 12.2 Data for Use in Calculating the Weighted Marginal Cost of Capital (*WMCC*) for the Zero Company

Source of capital	Target proportion (1)	Range of new financing[a] (2)	Cost (3)
Long-term debt	40%	$0 to $400,000 $400,000 to $800,000 $800,000 and above	5.68% 6.50% 7.10%
Preferred stock	10%	$0 to $100,000 $100,000 and above	9.33% 10.60%
Common stock equity	50%	$0 to $300,000 $300,000 to $750,000 $750,000 and above	13.00%[b] 13.30%[c] 15.50%

[a] These ranges are for the corresponding sources of capital. They do *not* represent levels of total new financing.
[b] The firm expects it will have $300,000 available from earnings after paying cash dividends. This amount of common equity will therefore have a cost of 13.00 percent, which is the cost of retained earnings calculated earlier.
[c] The 13.30 percent cost assigned to this range of new financing is the cost of new common stock calculated earlier in the chapter. This cost applies because once the $300,000 of expected retained earnings is exhausted, new common stock must be sold to obtain additional common stock equity.

Table 12.3 Determination of Breaking Points for Zero Company's Capital Sources

Source of capital	Cost (1)	Range of new financing (2)	Breaking point (3)	Range of total new financing (4)
Long-term debt	5.68%	$0 to $400,000	$\dfrac{\$400,000}{.40} = \$1,000,000$	$0 to $1,000,000
	6.50%	$400,000 to $800,000	$\dfrac{\$800,000}{.40} = \$2,000,000$	$1,000,000 to $2,000,000
	7.10%	$800,000 and above	—	$2,000,000 and above
Preferred stock	9.33%	$0 to $100,000	$\dfrac{\$100,000}{.10} = \$1,000,000$	$0 to $1,000,000
	10.60%	$100,000 and above	—	$1,000,000 and above
Common stock equity	13.00%	$0 to $300,000	$\dfrac{\$300,000}{.50} = \$600,000$	$0 to $600,000
	13.30%	$300,000 to $750,000	$\dfrac{\$750,000}{.50} = \$1,500,000$	$600,000 to $1,500,000
	15.50%	$750,000 and above	—	$1,500,000 and above

Key:
Column 1: These costs are strictly notational; they were initially given in column 3 of Table 12.2.
Column 2: Ranges of new financing from column 2 of Table 12.2.
Column 3: Breaking points calculated by dividing the upper limit of the new financing ranges by the appropriate target capital structure proportion from column 1 of Table 12.2. The breaking point is calculated using Equation 12.11.
Column 4: Using the breaking point calculated in column 3, the range of *total* new financing corresponding to each financing range given in column 2 is determined.

average cost of capital will change at levels of total new financing of $600,000, $1 million, $1.5 million, and $2 million. These breaking points are listed in increasing order. In Table 12.4, the weighted average cost of capital over the ranges of total new financing between increasing breaking points is calculated. Note that some component costs change as the new financing increases from one breaking point to the next. The effect of these increases in component costs is to raise the firm's weighted average cost of capital as the range of total new financing increases.

4. A schedule of the weighted average cost of capital associated with each range of total new financing is given in Table 12.5. This schedule represents the weighted marginal cost of capital (*WMCC*). The increasing nature of this relationship should be quite evident from the data presented. Figure 12.1 presents the *WMCC* graphically. Graph *a* shows a plot of the actual data; graph *b* presents a smoothed function that more realistically depicts the firm's *WMCC*. Again, it is quite clear that the *WMCC* is an increasing function of the amount of total new financing raised.

Table 12.4   Weighted Average Cost of Capital for Ranges of Total
New Financing for the Zero Company

Range of total new financing	Source of capital (1)	Target proportion (2)	Cost[a] (3)	Weighted cost [(2) × (3)] (4)
$0 to $600,000	Debt	.40	5.68%	2.272%
	Preferred	.10	9.33	.933
	Common	.50	13.00	6.500
		Weighted average cost of capital		9.705%
$600,000 to $1,000,000	Debt	.40	5.68%	2.272%
	Preferred	.10	9.33	.933
	Common	.50	13.30	6.650
		Weighted average cost of capital		9.855%
$1,000,000 to $1,500,000	Debt	.40	6.50%	2.600%
	Preferred	.10	10.60	1.060
	Common	.50	13.30	6.650
		Weighted average cost of capital		10.310%
$1,500,000 to $2,000,000	Debt	.40	6.50%	2.600%
	Preferred	.10	10.60	1.060
	Common	.50	15.50	7.750
		Weighted average cost of capital		11.410%
$2,000,000 and above	Debt	.40	7.10%	2.840%
	Preferred	.10	10.60	1.060
	Common	.50	15.50	7.750
		Weighted average cost of capital		11.650%

[a] The costs given for each range of total new financing were obtained from a comparison of columns 1 and 4 of Table 12.3.

Table 12.5   Weighted Marginal Cost of
Capital for the Zero Company

Range of total new financing	Weighted average cost of capital
$0 to $600,000	9.705%
$600,000 to $1,000,000	9.855
$1,000,000 to $1,500,000	10.310
$1,500,000 to $2,000,000	11.410
$2,000,000 and above	11.650

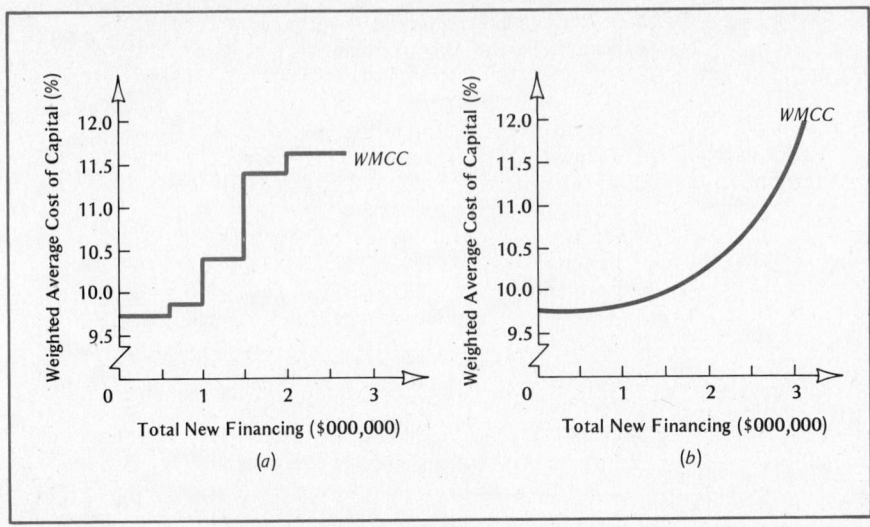

Figure 12.1   Weighted marginal cost of capital functions for the Zero Company   ■

USE OF THE *WMCC* FOR DECISION MAKING

The *WMCC* should be used in conjunction with the firm's *investment opportunities schedule (IOS)*, which is a ranking of investment possibilities from best to worst, to choose investments to be implemented. As long as a project's internal rate of return[22] is greater than the weighted marginal cost of new financing, the project should be accepted. As a firm increases the amount of money available for investment in capital projects, the return (*IRR*) on the projects will decrease, since generally the first project accepted will have the highest return, the next project selected the second highest, and so on. In other words, the return on investments will decrease as the firm accepts additional projects. At the same time, as more projects are accepted, the weighted marginal cost of capital will increase because greater amounts of new financing will be required. The firm would therefore *accept projects up to the point where the marginal return on its investment just equals its weighted marginal cost of capital.* Beyond that point its investment return will be less than its capital cost.[23] An example should clarify this relationship.

EXAMPLE   The Zero Company's current investment opportunities schedule (*IOS*) lists the best (highest internal rate of return) to the worst (lowest internal rate of return) investment possibilities in column 1 of Table 12.6. In column 2 of the table, the initial investment required by the project is shown, and in column 3, the cumulative total invested funds required to finance all projects better than and including the corresponding investment opportunity are given. Plotting the project *IRR*s against the cumulative investment (col-

[22] Although other sophisticated measures of project acceptability could be used to make these decisions, the internal rate of return is used here because of the ease of comparison it offers.

[23] So as not to confuse the discussion presented here, the fact that the use of the *IRR* for selecting projects may not provide optimum decisions is ignored. The problems associated with the *IRR* and its use in capital rationing were discussed in greater detail in Chapters 10 and 11, respectively.

Table 12.6   Investment Opportunities Schedule
              (*IOS*) for the Zero Company

Investment opportunity	Internal rate of return (*IRR*) (1)	Initial investment (2)	Cumulative investment[a] (3)
A	16%	$ 200,000	$ 200,000
B	15	400,000	600,000
C	14	1,000,000	1,600,000
D	13	100,000	1,700,000
E	12	300,000	2,000,000
F	11	500,000	2,500,000
G	10	200,000	2,700,000
H	9	400,000	3,100,000
I	8	100,000	3,200,000
J	7	300,000	3,500,000

[a] The cumulative investment represents the total amount invested in projects with higher *IRR*s plus the investment required for the given investment opportunity.

umn 1 against column 3 in Table 12.6 on a set of total new financing or investment–weighted average cost of capital and *IRR* axes), the firm's investment opportunities schedule (*IOS*) results. A graph of the *IOS* for Zero Company is given in Figure 12.2. The firm's *WMCC* is also shown in Figure 12.2. Using these two functions in combination, the firm's optimal capital budget ("X" in Figure 12.2) is determined. By raising $2 million of new financing and investing these funds in projects A, B, C, D, and E, the wealth of the firm's owners should be maximized, since the 12 percent return on the last dollar invested (in

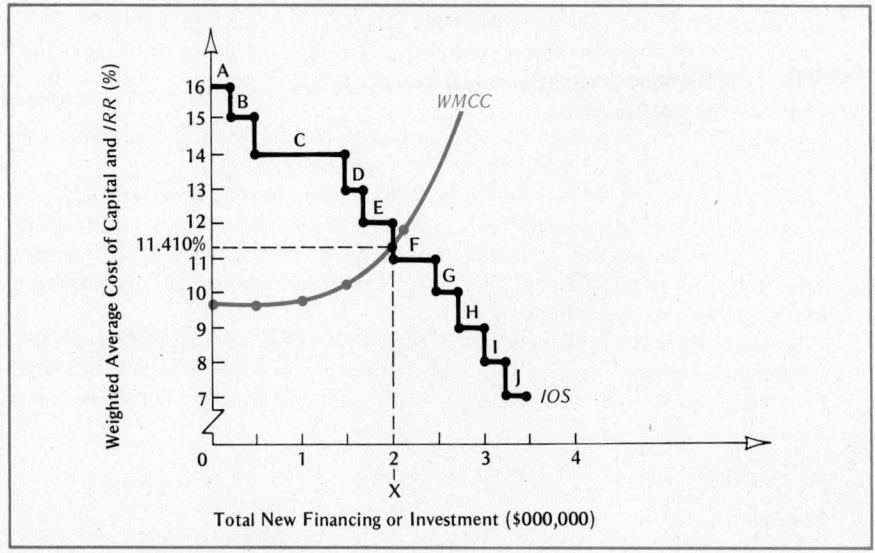

Figure 12.2   Using the *IOS* and *WMCC* to select projects

project E) exceeds its 11.410 percent weighted average cost. Investment in project F is not feasible because its 11 percent return is less than the 11.650 percent cost of funds available for investment. The importance of the *IOS* and *WMCC* for investment decision making should now be quite clear. ■

CHAPTER SUMMARY

● The cost of capital is the rate of return required by the market suppliers of capital to allow the firm's market price to remain unchanged.

● The basic factors underlying the cost of capital for a firm are the degree of risk associated with the firm, the taxes it must pay, and the supply of and demand for various types of financing.

● In evaluating the cost of capital, we have assumed that (1) firms are acquiring assets that do not change their business risk and (2) these acquisitions are financed in such a way as to leave financial risk unchanged.

● Since investment opportunities are evaluated after taxes, a firm must measure its cost of capital on this basis to be consistent.

● The cost of capital is used to discount project cash flows in finding net present values or in calculating profitability indexes and as the cutoff rate when evaluating internal rates of return.

● Since business and financial risk are assumed to be fixed, the key factor differentiating the cost of various types of financing is the supply of and demand for each type of funds.

● Because of the interrelatedness of the sources of long-term financing, a firm must utilize a combined or weighted average cost of capital rather than the cost of a specific source to evaluate its investment opportunities.

● The specific costs of the basic types of capital (long-term debt, preferred stock, common stock, and retained earnings) can be calculated individually. Only the cost of debt must be adjusted for taxes, since the costs of the other forms are paid from after-tax cash flows.

● The cost of debt is the cost to maturity of the cash flows associated with the debt adjusted for taxes.

● The cost of preferred stock is the stated annual dividend expressed as a percentage of the net proceeds from the sale of preferred shares.

● The calculation of the cost of common stock equity is rooted in the theory of the value of the firm. It can be calculated using the constant growth valuation model or the capital asset pricing model (CAPM).

● The cost of new common stock incorporates an adjustment in the cost of common stock equity to reflect underpricing, flotation costs, or both.

● The cost of retained earnings is equal to the cost of common stock equity.

● A firm's weighted average cost of capital (*WACC*) can be determined by combining the costs of specific types of capital after weighting each cost using historical book or market value weights or target book or market value weights. The theoretically preferred approach uses target weights based on market values.

● A firm's weighted marginal cost of capital (*WMCC*) function can be developed by finding the weighted average cost of capital for various levels of total new financing. The function relates the weighted average cost of capital to each level of total new financing.

KEY TERMS

book value weights
breaking point

business risk
capital structure

constant growth valuation model
cost of capital
cost of common stock
cost of common stock equity
cost of long-term debt
cost of new issues of common stock
cost of preferred stock
cost of retained earnings
cost to maturity
dividend yield
financial risk
flotation costs

historic weights
investment opportunities schedule (*IOS*)
market value weights
net proceeds
overall cost of capital
specific cost (of financing)
target capital structure
target weights
underpriced (stock)
weighted average cost
weighted average cost of capital (*WACC*)
weighted marginal cost of capital (*WMCC*)

QUESTIONS

12-1 How is the cost of capital used in the capital budgeting process? Specifically, how is it connected with the net present value, profitability index, and internal rate of return techniques for determining project acceptability?

12-2 Why, in using the cost of capital for evaluating investment alternatives, was it assumed that the acceptance of proposed projects would not affect the *business risk* of the firm?

12-3 What is *financial risk?* Why is it necessary to assume that the firm's capital structure remains unchanged when evaluating the firm's cost of capital? Why is this assumption awkward?

12-4 Why is the cost of capital most appropriately measured on an after-tax basis? What effect, if any, does this have on specific cost components?

12-5 You have just been told, "Since we are going to finance this project with debt, its required rate of return should only exceed the cost of debt." Do you agree or disagree? Explain.

12-6 What is meant by the *net proceeds* from the sale of a bond? In what circumstances is a bond expected to sell at a discount or a premium?

12-7 What sort of general approximation is used to find the before-tax cost of debt? What do the numerator and denominator of this expression represent?

12-8 How would you calculate the cost of preferred stock? Why do we concern ourselves with the net proceeds from the sale of the stock instead of the sale price?

12-9 What assumptions underlie the use of the constant growth valuation model (Gordon model) to measure the cost of common stock equity, k_s? What does each component of the equation represent?

12-10 If retained earnings are viewed as a fully subscribed issue of additional common stock, why is the cost of financing a project with retained earnings technically less than the cost of using a new issue of common stock?

12-11 Describe the logic underlying the use of *target capital structure weights* and compare and contrast this approach to the use of historic weights.

12-12 Outline the basic steps involved in calculating the *weighted marginal cost of capital (WMCC)*. Be sure to discuss the significance and computations involved in determining the breaking points.

12-13 What does the weighted marginal cost of capital function represent? Why does this function increase, and how can it be used in conjunction with the *investment opportunities schedule (IOS)* to select acceptable investments?

PROBLEMS

12-1 **(Cost of Debt — Risk Premiums)** The Three N Company's cost of long-term debt last year was 10 percent. This rate was attributable to a 7 percent risk-free cost of long-term debt, a 2 percent business risk premium, and a 1 percent financial risk premium. The firm currently wishes to obtain a long-term loan.

    a If the firm's business and financial risk are unchanged from the previous period and the risk-free cost of long-term debt is now 8 percent, at what rate would you expect the firm to obtain a long-term loan?

    b If, as a result of borrowing, the firm's financial risk will increase enough to raise the financial risk premium to 3 percent, how much would you expect the firm's borrowing cost to be?

    c One of the firm's competitors has a 1 percent business risk premium and a 2 percent financial risk premium. What is that firm's cost of long-term debt likely to be?

12-2 **(Concept of Cost of Capital)** Fee Manufacturing is in the process of analyzing its capital budgeting/cost of capital decision-making procedures. The two projects evaluated by the firm during the past month were projects 263 and 264. The basic variables surrounding each project analysis using the *IRR* decision technique and the resulting decision actions are summarized in the following table.

Basic variables	Project 263	Project 264
Cost	$64,000	$58,000
Life	15 years	15 years
IRR	8%	15%
Least-cost financing		
Source	Debt	Equity
Cost (after-tax)	7%	16%
Decision		
Action	Accept	Reject
Reason	8% *IRR* > 7% cost	15% *IRR* < 16% cost

    a Evaluate the firm's decision-making procedures and explain why the acceptance of project 263 and rejection of project 264 may not be in the owners' best interest.

    b If the firm maintains a capital structure containing 40 percent debt and 60 percent equity, find its weighted average cost using the data in the table.

    c Had the firm used the weighted average cost calculated in **b**, what actions would have been taken relative to projects 263 and 264?

    d Compare and contrast the firm's actions with your findings in **c**. Which decision method seems most appropriate? Explain why.

 12-3 **(Cost of Debt Using Both Methods)** Currently Krick and Company can sell 15-year, $1000 par-value bonds paying annual interest with a 12 percent coupon. As a result of current interest rates, the bonds can be sold for $1010 each; flotation costs of $30 per bond will be incurred in this process. The firm is in the 40 percent marginal tax bracket.

    a Find the net proceeds from sale of the bond, N_d.

    b Show the cash flows from the firm's point of view over the maturity of the bond.

    c Use the *IRR approach* with interpolation (see footnote 14) to estimate the before-tax and after-tax cost of debt.

    d Use the *shortcut approximation* to estimate the before-tax and after-tax cost of debt.

e Compare and contrast the cost of debt calculated in **c** and **d**. Which approach do you prefer? Why?

12-4 **(Cost of Debt Using the Shortcut Approximation)** For each of the following $1000 bonds, assuming annual interest payment and a 40 percent marginal tax rate, calculate the *after-tax* cost to maturity using the *shortcut approximation* presented in the chapter.

Bond	Life	Underwriting fee	Discount (−) or premium (+)	Coupon rate
A	20 years	$25	$−20	9%
B	16	40	$+10	10
C	15	30	$−15	12
D	25	15	Par	9
E	22	20	$−60	11

12-5 **(Cost of Preferred Stock)** The Flat-Free Tire Company has just issued preferred stock. The stock has a 12 percent annual dividend and a $100 par value and was sold at $97.50 per share. In addition, flotation costs of $2.50 per share must be paid.
a Calculate the cost of the preferred stock.
b If the firm had sold the preferred stock with a 10 percent annual dividend and a $90.00 net price, what would its cost have been?

12-6 **(Cost of Preferred Stock)** Determine the cost for each of the following preferred stocks.

Preferred stock	Par value	Sale price	Flotation cost	Annual dividend
A	$100	$101	$9.00	11%
B	$ 40	38	$3.50	8%
C	$ 35	37	$4.00	$5.00
D	$ 30	26	5%	$3.00
E	$ 20	20	$2.50	9%

12-7 **(Cost of Common Stock Equity)** Tasty Meat Packing wishes to measure its cost of common stock equity. The firm's stock is currently selling for $57.50. The firm expects to pay a $3.40 dividend at the end of the year. The dividends for the past five years were as follows:

Year	Dividend
1984	$3.10
1983	2.92
1982	2.60
1981	2.30
1980	2.12

After underpricing and flotation costs, the firm expects to net $52 per share on a new issue.
a Determine the growth rate of dividends.
b Determine the net proceeds, N_n, the firm acutally receives.
c Using the constant growth valuation model, determine the cost of new common stock equity.

d Using the constant growth valuation model, determine the cost of retained earnings.

12-8 **(New Common Stock versus Retained Earnings)**   For the following firms, calculate the cost of new common stock and the cost of retained earnings using the constant growth valuation model.

Firm	Current market price per share	Dividend growth rate	Projected dividend per share next year	Underpricing per share	Flotation cost per share
A	$50.00	8%	$2.25	$2.00	$1.00
B	20.00	4	1.00	0.50	1.50
C	42.50	6	2.00	1.00	2.00
D	19.00	2	2.10	1.30	1.70

12-9 **(Cost of Equity — CAPM)**   Tucker and Tucker (T&T) common stock has a measure of responsiveness to the overall market of 1.2 ($b = 1.2$). If the risk-free rate is 6 percent and the required return on the market portfolio is 11 percent,
  a Determine the risk premium on T&T common stock.
  b Determine the required rate of return T&T common stock should provide.
  c Determine T&T's after-tax cost of common equity using the CAPM.

12-10 **(WACC — Book Weights)**   Ohio Tire has on its books the following amounts and specific (after-tax) costs for each source of capital:

Source of capital	Book value	Specific cost
Long-term debt	$700,000	5.25%
Preferred stock	50,000	12.00
Common stock equity	650,000	16.00

  a Calculate the firm's weighted average cost of capital using book weights.
  b Explain how the firm can use this cost in the capital-budgeting decision-making process.

12-11 **(WACC — Book Weights and Market Weights)**   The Cool Air Company has compiled the following information:

Source of capital	Book value	Market value	After-tax cost
Long-term debt	$4,000,000	$3,840,000	6.00%
Preferred stock	40,000	60,000	13.00
Common stock equity	1,060,000	3,000,000	17.00
Totals	$5,100,000	$6,900,000	

  a Calculate the weighted average cost of capital using book value weights.
  b Calculate the weighted average cost of capital using market value weights.
  c Compare the answers obtained in **a** and **b**. Explain the differences.

12-12 **(WACC and Target Weights)**   After careful analysis, the McCall Company has determined that its optimal capital structure is composed of the following sources and target market value proportions:

Present-Value Interest Factors for One Dollar Discounted at k Percent for n Periods: $PVIF_{k,n} = \dfrac{1}{(1+k)^n}$

Period	1%	2%	3%	4%	5%	6%	7%	8%	9%	10%	11%	12%	13%	14%	15%	16%	17%
1	.990	.980	.971	.962	.952	.943	.935	.926	.917	.909	.901	.893	.885	.877	.870	.862	.855
2	.980	.961	.943	.925	.907	.890	.873	.857	.842	.826	.812	.797	.783	.769	.756	.743	.731
3	.971	.942	.915	.889	.864	.840	.816	.794	.772	.751	.731	.712	.693	.675	.658	.641	.624
4	.961	.924	.888	.855	.823	.792	.763	.735	.708	.683	.659	.636	.613	.592	.572	.552	.534
5	.951	.906	.863	.822	.784	.747	.713	.681	.650	.621	.593	.567	.543	.519	.497	.476	.456
6	.942	.888	.837	.790	.746	.705	.666	.630	.596	.564	.535	.507	.480	.456	.432	.410	.390
7	.933	.871	.813	.760	.711	.665	.623	.583	.547	.513	.482	.452	.425	.400	.376	.354	.333
8	.923	.853	.789	.731	.677	.627	.582	.540	.502	.467	.434	.404	.376	.351	.327	.305	.285
9	.914	.837	.766	.703	.645	.592	.544	.500	.460	.424	.391	.361	.333	.308	.284	.263	.243
10	.905	.820	.744	.676	.614	.558	.508	.463	.422	.386	.352	.322	.295	.270	.247	.227	.208
11	.896	.804	.722	.650	.585	.527	.475	.429	.388	.350	.317	.287	.261	.237	.215	.195	.178
12	.887	.789	.701	.625	.557	.497	.444	.397	.356	.319	.286	.257	.231	.208	.187	.168	.152
13	.879	.773	.681	.601	.530	.469	.415	.368	.326	.290	.258	.229	.204	.182	.163	.145	.130
14	.870	.758	.661	.577	.505	.442	.388	.340	.299	.263	.232	.205	.181	.160	.141	.125	.111
15	.861	.743	.642	.555	.481	.417	.362	.315	.275	.239	.209	.183	.160	.140	.123	.108	.095
16	.853	.728	.623	.534	.458	.394	.339	.292	.252	.218	.188	.163	.141	.123	.107	.093	.081
17	.844	.714	.605	.513	.436	.371	.317	.270	.231	.198	.170	.146	.125	.108	.093	.080	.069
18	.836	.700	.587	.494	.416	.350	.296	.250	.212	.180	.153	.130	.111	.095	.081	.069	.059
19	.828	.686	.570	.475	.396	.331	.277	.232	.194	.164	.138	.116	.098	.083	.070	.060	.051
20	.820	.673	.554	.456	.377	.312	.258	.215	.178	.149	.124	.104	.087	.073	.061	.051	.043
21	.811	.660	.538	.439	.359	.294	.242	.199	.164	.135	.112	.093	.077	.064	.053	.044	.037
22	.803	.647	.522	.422	.342	.278	.226	.184	.150	.123	.101	.083	.068	.056	.046	.038	.032
23	.795	.634	.507	.406	.326	.262	.211	.170	.138	.112	.091	.074	.060	.049	.040	.033	.027
24	.788	.622	.492	.390	.310	.247	.197	.158	.126	.102	.082	.066	.053	.043	.035	.028	.023
25	.780	.610	.478	.375	.295	.233	.184	.146	.116	.092	.074	.059	.047	.038	.030	.024	.020
30	.742	.552	.412	.308	.231	.174	.131	.099	.075	.057	.044	.033	.026	.020	.015	.012	.009
35	.706	.500	.355	.253	.181	.130	.094	.068	.049	.036	.026	.019	.014	.010	.008	.006	.004
40	.672	.453	.307	.208	.142	.097	.067	.046	.032	.022	.015	.011	.008	.005	.004	.003	.002
45	.639	.410	.264	.171	.111	.073	.048	.031	.021	.014	.009	.006	.004	.003	.002	.001	.001
50	.608	.372	.228	.141	.087	.054	.034	.021	.013	.009	.005	.003	.002	.001	.001	.001	*

Period	18%	19%	20%	21%	22%	23%	24%	25%	26%	27%	28%	29%	30%	35%	40%	45%	50%
1	.847	.840	.833	.826	.820	.813	.806	.800	.794	.787	.781	.775	.769	.741	.714	.690	.667
2	.718	.706	.694	.683	.672	.661	.650	.640	.630	.620	.610	.601	.592	.549	.510	.476	.444
3	.609	.593	.579	.564	.551	.537	.524	.512	.500	.488	.477	.466	.455	.406	.364	.328	.296
4	.516	.499	.482	.467	.451	.437	.423	.410	.397	.384	.373	.361	.350	.301	.260	.226	.198
5	.437	.419	.402	.386	.370	.355	.341	.328	.315	.303	.291	.280	.269	.223	.186	.156	.132
6	.370	.352	.335	.319	.303	.289	.275	.262	.250	.238	.227	.217	.207	.165	.133	.108	.088
7	.314	.296	.279	.263	.249	.235	.222	.210	.198	.188	.178	.168	.159	.122	.095	.074	.059
8	.266	.249	.233	.218	.204	.191	.179	.168	.157	.148	.139	.130	.123	.091	.068	.051	.039
9	.225	.209	.194	.180	.167	.155	.144	.134	.125	.116	.108	.101	.094	.067	.048	.035	.026
10	.191	.176	.162	.149	.137	.126	.116	.107	.099	.092	.085	.078	.073	.050	.035	.024	.017
11	.162	.148	.135	.123	.112	.103	.094	.086	.079	.072	.066	.061	.056	.037	.025	.017	.012
12	.137	.124	.112	.102	.092	.083	.076	.069	.062	.057	.052	.047	.043	.027	.018	.012	.008
13	.116	.104	.093	.084	.075	.068	.061	.055	.050	.045	.040	.037	.033	.020	.013	.008	.005
14	.099	.088	.078	.069	.062	.055	.049	.044	.039	.035	.032	.028	.025	.015	.009	.006	.003
15	.084	.074	.065	.057	.051	.045	.040	.035	.031	.028	.025	.022	.020	.011	.006	.004	.002
16	.071	.062	.054	.047	.042	.036	.032	.028	.025	.022	.019	.017	.015	.008	.005	.003	.002
17	.060	.052	.045	.039	.034	.030	.026	.023	.020	.017	.015	.013	.012	.006	.003	.002	.001
18	.051	.044	.038	.032	.028	.024	.021	.018	.016	.014	.012	.010	.009	.005	.002	.001	.001
19	.043	.037	.031	.027	.023	.020	.017	.014	.012	.011	.009	.008	.007	.003	.002	.001	*
20	.037	.031	.026	.022	.019	.016	.014	.012	.010	.008	.007	.006	.005	.002	.001	.001	*
21	.031	.026	.022	.018	.015	.013	.011	.009	.008	.007	.006	.005	.004	.002	.001	*	*
22	.026	.022	.018	.015	.013	.011	.009	.007	.006	.005	.004	.004	.003	.001	.001	*	*
23	.022	.018	.015	.012	.010	.009	.007	.006	.005	.004	.003	.003	.002	.001	*	*	*
24	.019	.015	.013	.010	.008	.007	.006	.005	.004	.003	.003	.002	.002	.001	*	*	*
25	.016	.013	.010	.009	.007	.006	.005	.004	.003	.003	.002	.002	.001	.001	*	*	*
30	.007	.005	.004	.003	.003	.002	.002	.001	.001	.001	.001	*	*	*	*	*	*
35	.003	.002	.002	.001	.001	.001	.001	*	*	*	*	*	*	*	*	*	*
40	.001	.001	.001	*	*	*	*	*	*	*	*	*	*	*	*	*	*
45	.001	*	*	*	*	*	*	*	*	*	*	*	*	*	*	*	*
50	*	*	*	*	*	*	*	*	*	*	*	*	*	*	*	*	*

*PVIF is zero to three decimal places.

Present-Value Interest Factors for a One-Dollar Annuity Discounted at k Percent for n Periods: $PVIFA_{k,n} = \sum_{t=1}^{n} \dfrac{1}{(1+k)^t}$

Period	1%	2%	3%	4%	5%	6%	7%	8%	9%	10%	11%	12%	13%	14%	15%	16%	17%
1	.990	.980	.971	.962	.952	.943	.935	.926	.917	.909	.901	.893	.885	.877	.870	.862	.855
2	1.970	1.942	1.913	1.886	1.859	1.833	1.808	1.783	1.759	1.736	1.713	1.690	1.668	1.647	1.626	1.605	1.585
3	2.941	2.884	2.829	2.775	2.723	2.673	2.624	2.577	2.531	2.487	2.444	2.402	2.361	2.322	2.283	2.246	2.210
4	3.902	3.808	3.717	3.630	3.546	3.465	3.387	3.312	3.240	3.170	3.102	3.037	2.974	2.914	2.855	2.798	2.743
5	4.853	4.713	4.580	4.452	4.329	4.212	4.100	3.993	3.890	3.791	3.696	3.605	3.517	3.433	3.352	3.274	3.199
6	5.795	5.601	5.417	5.242	5.076	4.917	4.767	4.623	4.486	4.355	4.231	4.111	3.998	3.889	3.784	3.685	3.589
7	6.728	6.472	6.230	6.002	5.786	5.582	5.389	5.206	5.033	4.868	4.712	4.564	4.423	4.288	4.160	4.039	3.922
8	7.652	7.326	7.020	6.733	6.463	6.210	5.971	5.747	5.535	5.335	5.146	4.968	4.799	4.639	4.487	4.344	4.207
9	8.566	8.162	7.786	7.435	7.108	6.802	6.515	6.247	5.995	5.759	5.537	5.328	5.132	4.946	4.772	4.607	4.451
10	9.471	8.983	8.530	8.111	7.722	7.360	7.024	6.710	6.418	6.145	5.889	5.650	5.426	5.216	5.019	4.833	4.659
11	10.368	9.787	9.253	8.760	8.306	7.887	7.499	7.139	6.805	6.495	6.207	5.938	5.687	5.453	5.234	5.029	4.836
12	11.255	10.575	9.954	9.385	8.863	8.384	7.943	7.536	7.161	6.814	6.492	6.194	5.918	5.660	5.421	5.197	4.988
13	12.134	11.348	10.635	9.986	9.394	8.853	8.358	7.904	7.487	7.103	6.750	6.424	6.122	5.842	5.583	5.342	5.118
14	13.004	12.106	11.296	10.563	9.899	9.295	8.745	8.244	7.786	7.367	6.982	6.628	6.302	6.002	5.724	5.468	5.229
15	13.865	12.849	11.938	11.118	10.380	9.712	9.108	8.560	8.061	7.606	7.191	6.811	6.462	6.142	5.847	5.575	5.324
16	14.718	13.578	12.561	11.652	10.838	10.106	9.447	8.851	8.313	7.824	7.379	6.974	6.604	6.265	5.954	5.668	5.405
17	15.562	14.292	13.166	12.166	11.274	10.477	9.763	9.122	8.544	8.022	7.549	7.120	6.729	6.373	6.047	5.749	5.475
18	16.398	14.992	13.754	12.659	11.690	10.828	10.059	9.372	8.756	8.201	7.702	7.250	6.840	6.467	6.128	5.818	5.534
19	17.226	15.679	14.324	13.134	12.085	11.158	10.336	9.604	8.950	8.365	7.839	7.366	6.938	6.550	6.198	5.877	5.584
20	18.046	16.352	14.878	13.590	12.462	11.470	10.594	9.818	9.129	8.514	7.963	7.469	7.025	6.623	6.259	5.929	5.628
21	18.857	17.011	15.415	14.029	12.821	11.764	10.836	10.017	9.292	8.649	8.075	7.562	7.102	6.687	6.312	5.973	5.665
22	19.661	17.658	15.937	14.451	13.163	12.042	11.061	10.201	9.442	8.772	8.176	7.645	7.170	6.743	6.359	6.011	5.696
23	20.456	18.292	16.444	14.857	13.489	12.303	11.272	10.371	9.580	8.883	8.266	7.718	7.230	6.792	6.399	6.044	5.723
24	21.244	18.914	16.936	15.247	13.799	12.550	11.469	10.529	9.707	8.985	8.348	7.784	7.283	6.835	6.434	6.073	5.746
25	22.023	19.524	17.413	15.622	14.094	12.783	11.654	10.675	9.823	9.077	8.422	7.843	7.330	6.873	6.464	6.097	5.766
30	25.808	22.396	19.601	17.292	15.373	13.765	12.409	11.258	10.274	9.427	8.694	8.055	7.496	7.003	6.566	6.177	5.829
35	29.409	24.999	21.487	18.665	16.374	14.498	12.948	11.655	10.567	9.644	8.855	8.176	7.586	7.070	6.617	6.215	5.858
40	32.835	27.356	23.115	19.793	17.159	15.046	13.332	11.925	10.757	9.779	8.951	8.244	7.634	7.105	6.642	6.233	5.871
45	36.095	29.490	24.519	20.720	17.774	15.456	13.606	12.108	10.881	9.863	9.008	8.283	7.661	7.123	6.654	6.242	5.877
50	39.196	31.424	25.730	21.482	18.256	15.762	13.801	12.233	10.962	9.915	9.042	8.304	7.675	7.133	6.661	6.246	5.880

Period	18%	19%	20%	21%	22%	23%	24%	25%	26%	27%	28%	29%	30%	35%	40%	45%	50%
1	.847	.840	.833	.826	.820	.813	.806	.800	.794	.787	.781	.775	.769	.741	.714	.690	.667
2	1.566	1.547	1.528	1.509	1.492	1.474	1.457	1.440	1.424	1.407	1.392	1.376	1.361	1.289	1.224	1.165	1.111
3	2.174	2.140	2.106	2.074	2.042	2.011	1.981	1.952	1.923	1.896	1.868	1.842	1.816	1.696	1.589	1.493	1.407
4	2.690	2.639	2.589	2.540	2.494	2.448	2.404	2.362	2.320	2.280	2.241	2.203	2.166	1.997	1.849	1.720	1.605
5	3.127	3.058	2.991	2.926	2.864	2.803	2.745	2.689	2.635	2.583	2.532	2.483	2.436	2.220	2.035	1.876	1.737
6	3.498	3.410	3.326	3.245	3.167	3.092	3.020	2.951	2.885	2.821	2.759	2.700	2.643	2.385	2.168	1.983	1.824
7	3.812	3.706	3.605	3.508	3.416	3.327	3.242	3.161	3.083	3.009	2.937	2.868	2.802	2.508	2.263	2.057	1.883
8	4.078	3.954	3.837	3.726	3.619	3.518	3.421	3.329	3.241	3.156	3.076	2.999	2.925	2.598	2.331	2.109	1.922
9	4.303	4.163	4.031	3.905	3.786	3.673	3.566	3.463	3.366	3.273	3.184	3.100	3.019	2.665	2.379	2.144	1.948
10	4.494	4.339	4.192	4.054	3.923	3.799	3.682	3.570	3.465	3.364	3.269	3.178	3.092	2.715	2.414	2.168	1.965
11	4.656	4.486	4.327	4.177	4.035	3.902	3.776	3.656	3.544	3.437	3.335	3.239	3.147	2.752	2.438	2.185	1.977
12	4.793	4.611	4.439	4.278	4.127	3.985	3.851	3.725	3.606	3.493	3.387	3.286	3.190	2.779	2.456	2.196	1.985
13	4.910	4.715	4.533	4.362	4.203	4.053	3.912	3.780	3.656	3.538	3.427	3.322	3.223	2.799	2.469	2.204	1.990
14	5.008	4.802	4.611	4.432	4.265	4.108	3.962	3.824	3.695	3.573	3.459	3.351	3.249	2.814	2.478	2.210	1.993
15	5.092	4.876	4.675	4.489	4.315	4.153	4.001	3.859	3.726	3.601	3.483	3.373	3.268	2.825	2.484	2.214	1.995
16	5.162	4.938	4.730	4.536	4.357	4.189	4.033	3.887	3.751	3.623	3.503	3.390	3.283	2.834	2.489	2.216	1.997
17	5.222	4.990	4.775	4.576	4.391	4.219	4.059	3.910	3.771	3.640	3.518	3.403	3.295	2.840	2.492	2.218	1.998
18	5.273	5.033	4.812	4.608	4.419	4.243	4.080	3.928	3.786	3.654	3.529	3.413	3.304	2.844	2.494	2.219	1.999
19	5.316	5.070	4.843	4.635	4.442	4.263	4.097	3.942	3.799	3.664	3.539	3.421	3.311	2.848	2.496	2.220	1.999
20	5.353	5.101	4.870	4.657	4.460	4.279	4.110	3.954	3.808	3.673	3.546	3.427	3.316	2.850	2.497	2.221	1.999
21	5.384	5.127	4.891	4.675	4.476	4.292	4.121	3.963	3.816	3.679	3.551	3.432	3.320	2.852	2.498	2.221	2.000
22	5.410	5.149	4.909	4.690	4.488	4.302	4.130	3.970	3.822	3.684	3.556	3.436	3.323	2.853	2.498	2.222	2.000
23	5.432	5.167	4.925	4.703	4.499	4.311	4.137	3.976	3.827	3.689	3.559	3.438	3.325	2.854	2.499	2.222	2.000
24	5.451	5.182	4.937	4.713	4.507	4.318	4.143	3.981	3.831	3.692	3.562	3.441	3.327	2.855	2.499	2.222	2.000
25	5.467	5.195	4.948	4.721	4.514	4.323	4.147	3.985	3.834	3.694	3.564	3.442	3.329	2.856	2.499	2.222	2.000
30	5.517	5.235	4.979	4.746	4.534	4.339	4.160	3.995	3.842	3.701	3.569	3.447	3.332	2.857	2.500	2.222	2.000
35	5.539	5.251	4.992	4.756	4.541	4.345	4.164	3.998	3.845	3.703	3.571	3.448	3.333	2.857	2.500	2.222	2.000
40	5.548	5.258	4.997	4.760	4.544	4.347	4.166	3.999	3.846	3.703	3.571	3.448	3.333	2.857	2.500	2.222	2.000
45	5.552	5.261	4.999	4.761	4.545	4.347	4.166	4.000	3.846	3.704	3.571	3.448	3.333	2.857	2.500	2.222	2.000
50	5.554	5.262	4.999	4.762	4.545	4.348	4.167	4.000	3.846	3.704	3.571	3.448	3.333	2.857	2.500	2.222	2.000

Source of capital	Target market value proportions
Long-term debt	30%
Preferred stock	15
Common stock equity	55
Total	100%

The cost of debt is estimated to be 7.2 percent, the cost of preferred stock is estimated to be 13.5 percent, the cost of new common stock is estimated to be 16.5 percent, and the cost of retained earnings is estimated to be 16 percent. All these are after-tax rates. Currently, the company's debt represents 25 percent, the preferred stock represents 10 percent, and the common stock equity represents 65 percent of the capital structure based on market values of the three components. The company expects to have a significant amount of retained earnings available and does not expect to sell any additional common stock.

a Calculate the weighted average cost of capital based on market weights.

b Calculate the weighted average cost of capital based on target weights.

 12-13 **(Calculation of Specific Costs, *WACC,* and *WMCC*)**   Cloak, Inc., is interested in measuring its overall cost of capital. Current investigation has gathered the following data. The firm is in the 40% tax bracket.

Debt. The firm can raise an unlimited amount of debt by selling $1000, 8 percent, 20-year bonds on which annual interest payments will be made. To sell the issue, an average discount of $30 per bond would have to be given. The firm also must pay flotation costs of $30 per bond.

Preferred stock. The firm can sell 8 percent preferred stock at its $95-per-share par value. The cost of issuing and selling the preferred stock is expected to be $5 per share. An unlimited amount of preferred stock can be sold under these terms.

Common stock. The firm's common stock is currently selling for $100 per share. The firm expects to pay cash dividends of $7 per share next year. The firm's dividends have been growing at an annual rate of 6 percent, and this is expected to continue into the future. The stock will have to be underpriced by $3 per share, and flotation costs are expected to amount to $5 per share. The firm can sell an unlimited amount of new common stock under these terms.

Retained earnings. When measuring this cost, the firm does not concern itself with the tax bracket or brokerage fees of owners. It expects to have available $100,000 of retained earnings in the coming year; once these retained earnings are exhausted, the firm will use new common stock as the form of common stock equity financing.

a Calculate the specific cost of each source of financing. (Round answers to the nearest .10 percent).

b The firm's target capital structure proportions used in calculating its weighted average cost of capital are given. (Round answer to the nearest .01 percent in this part).

Source of capital	Target capital structure proportion
Long-term debt	30%
Preferred stock	20
Common stock equity	50
Total	100%

(1) Calculate the single breaking point associated with the firm's financial situation. (*Hint:* This point results from exhaustion of the firm's retained earnings.)

(2) Calculate the weighted average cost of capital associated with total financing below the breaking point calculated in (1).

(3) Calculate the weighted average cost of capital associated with total financing above the breaking point calculated in (1).

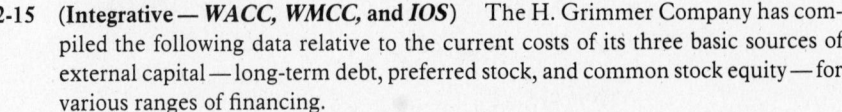

12-14 (**Integrative — *WACC* and *WMCC***)   Keystone Pump has charged Martin Drywater, its financial manager, with measuring the cost of each specific type of capital as well as the weighted average cost of capital. The weighted average cost is to be measured using the firm's target capital structure weights. The firm wishes to finance projects using 40 percent long-term debt, 10 percent preferred stock, and 50 percent common stock equity (retained earnings, new common stock, or both). The firm's marginal tax rate is 40 percent on ordinary income.

Debt. The firm can sell a ten-year, $1000-par-value bond having a 10 percent annual coupon for $980. A flotation cost of 3 percent of the face value would be required in addition to the discount of $20 per bond.

Preferred stock. 8 percent preferred stock having a par value of $100 can be sold for $65. An additional fee of $2 per share must be paid to the underwriters.

Common stock. The firm's common stock is currently selling for $50 per share. The dividend expected to be paid at the end of the coming year (1985) is $4. Its dividend payments, which have been approximately 60 percent of earnings per share in each of the past five years, were as follows:

Year	Dividend
1984	$3.75
1983	3.50
1982	3.30
1981	3.15
1980	2.85

It is expected that to sell, new common stock must be underpriced $3 per share and the firm must also pay $2 per share in flotation costs. Dividend payments are expected to continue at 60 percent of earnings.

a Calculate the specific cost of each source of financing. (Assume that $k_r = k_s$.)

b If earnings available to common shareholders are expected to be $7 million, what is the breaking point associated with the exhaustion of retained earnings?

c Determine the weighted average cost of capital between zero and the breaking point given in **b**.

d Determine the weighted average cost of capital just beyond the breaking point calculated in **b**.

12-15 (**Integrative — *WACC, WMCC,* and *IOS***)   The H. Grimmer Company has compiled the following data relative to the current costs of its three basic sources of external capital — long-term debt, preferred stock, and common stock equity — for various ranges of financing.

Source of capital	Range of new financing	After-tax cost
Long-term debt	$0 to $200,000 $200,000 to $300,000 $300,000 and above	6% 7 9
Preferred stock	$0 to $100,000 $100,000 and above	17% 19
Common stock equity	$0 to $220,000 $220,000 to $320,000 $320,000 and above	22% 24 26

The firm's current earnings, of which 40 percent will be retained, amount to $200,000. The cost of these retained earnings to the firm has been estimated to be 20 percent. The company's target capital structure proportions used in calculating its weighted average cost of capital are as follows:

Source of capital	Target capital structure
Long-term debt	40%
Preferred stock	20
Common stock equity	40
Total	100%

a Determine the breaking points and ranges of *total* new financing associated with each source of capital. (*Hint:* Be sure to recognize that any available retained earnings would be exhausted prior to using new common stock equity.)

b Using the data developed in **a**, determine the levels of *total* new financing at which the firm's weighted average cost of capital will change.

c Calculate the weighted average cost of capital for each range of total new financing found in **b**.

d Using the results of **c** along with the following information on the available investment opportunities, draw the firm's weighted marginal cost of capital (*WMCC*) function and investment opportunities schedule (*IOS*) on the same set of total new financing or investment (*x*-axis)–weighted average cost of capital and *IRR* (*y*-axis) axes.

Investment opportunity	Initial investment	Internal rate of return (*IRR*)
A	$200,000	19%
B	300,000	15
C	100,000	22
D	600,000	14
E	200,000	23
F	100,000	13
G	300,000	21
H	100,000	17
I	400,000	16

e Which, if any, of the available investments would you recommend the firm accept? Explain your answer.

12-16 **(Integrative — Specific Costs, *WACC, WMCC,* and *IOS*)** Humble Manufacturing is interested in measuring its overall cost of capital. Current investigation has gathered the following data. The firm is in the 40 percent marginal tax bracket.

Debt. The firm can raise an unlimited amount of debt by selling $1000, 10 percent, ten-year bonds on which annual interest payments will be made. To sell the issue, an average discount of $30 per bond would have to be given. The firm must also pay flotation costs of $20 per bond.

Preferred stock. The firm can sell 11 percent preferred stock at its $100-per-share par value. The cost of issuing and selling the preferred stock is expected to be $4 per share. An unlimited amount of preferred stock can be sold under these terms.

Common stock. The firm's common stock is currently selling for $80 per share. The firm expects to pay cash dividends of $6 per share next year. The firm's dividends have been growing at an annual rate of 6 percent, and this is expected to continue in the future. The stock will have to be underpriced by $4 per share, and flotation costs are expected to amount to $4 per share. The firm can sell an unlimited amount of new common stock under these terms.

Retained earnings. When measuring this cost, the firm does not concern itself with the tax bracket or brokerage fees of owners. It expects to have available $225,000 of retained earnings in the coming year; once these retained earnings are exhausted, the firm will use new common stock as the form of common stock equity financing.

a Calculate the specific cost of each source of financing. (Round to the nearest .10.)

b The firm's target capital structure proportions used in calculating its weighted average cost of capital are given. (Round to the nearest .01 in this part.)

Source of capital	Target capital structure proportion
Long-term debt	40%
Preferred stock	15
Common stock equity	45
Total	100%

(1) Calculate the single breaking point associated with the firm's financial situation. (*Hint:* This point results from the exhaustion of the firm's retained earnings.)

(2) Calculate the weighted average cost of capital associated with total financing below the breaking point calculated in (1).

(3) Calculate the weighted average cost of capital associated with total financing above the breaking point calculated in (1).

c Using the results of **b** along with the following information on the available investment opportunities, draw the firm's weighted marginal cost of capital (*WMCC*) function and investment opportunities schedule (*IOS*) on the same set of total new financing or investment (*x*-axis)–weighted average cost of capital and *IRR* (*y*-axis) axes.

Investment opportunity	Initial investment	Internal rate of return (*IRR*)
A	$100,000	11.2%
B	500,000	9.7
C	150,000	12.9
D	200,000	16.5
E	450,000	11.8
F	600,000	10.1
G	300,000	10.5

d Which, if any, of the available investments would you recommend the firm accept? Explain your answer.

Chapter 13

Leverage and Capital Structure

After studying this chapter, you should be able to:

1. Understand the fundamentals of breakeven analysis and operating leverage—including its measurement—and the interrelationship between them.

2. Discuss financial leverage and total leverage—including their measurement—and the interrelationship among operating, financial, and total leverage.

3. Define capital structure, pointing out the basic types of capital, external assessment of capital structure, and the basic theory of capital structure.

4. Explain business risk and financial risk and how, with business risk assumed constant, the effect of various capital structures on financial risk can be evaluated.

5. Apply the *EBIT-eps* approach to evaluate alternative capital structures and explain the basic shortcoming of this analytical technique for choosing the best capital structure.

6. Demonstrate the linkage of capital structure, risk, and value and describe other important factors to be considered when evaluating capital structures.

462

Leverage and capital structure are closely related concepts linked to cost of capital (Chapter 12) and therefore capital budgeting decisions (Chapters 9 through 11). *Leverage* is the use of fixed-cost assets or sources of funds to magnify returns to owners. Changes in leverage result in changes in level of return and associated risk. *Risk* in this context refers to the degree of uncertainty associated with the firm's ability to cover its fixed-payment obligations. Generally, increases in leverage result in increases in return and risk; decreases in leverage result in decreased return and risk. The amount of leverage in the firm's *capital structure* — the mix of long-term debt and equity utilized by the firm — can significantly affect its value by affecting return and risk. Poor capital structure decisions can result in a high cost of capital, making more investments unacceptable. Good decisions can lower the cost of capital, resulting in more acceptable investments that will add to owners' wealth.

Leverage

The two basic types of leverage and their total effect can best be defined with reference to the firm's income statement. Table 13.1 presents a general income statement format. The portions of the statement related to the firm's operating leverage, that of its financial leverage, and that of its total leverage are clearly labeled. *Operating leverage* is concerned with the relationship between the firm's sales revenue and its earnings before interest and taxes.[1] *Financial leverage* is concerned with the relationship between the firm's earnings before interest and taxes and the earnings available for common stockholders. *Total leverage* is concerned with the relationship between the firm's sales revenue and the earnings available for common stockholders.

---

[1] The firm's earnings before interest and taxes are often referred to as "operating profits." Earnings before interest and taxes are used as the pivotal point in defining operating and financial leverage because they divide the firm's income statement into operating and financial portions.

Table 13.1   A General Income Statement Format

Operating leverage {	Sales revenue Less: Cost of goods sold Gross profits Less: Operating expenses Earnings before interest and taxes *(EBIT)* Less: Interest Earnings before taxes
Financial leverage {	Less: Taxes Earnings after taxes Less: Preferred stock dividends Earnings available for common stockholders

Total leverage

BREAKEVEN ANALYSIS

Before developing the concept of operating leverage, it is important to understand various aspects of breakeven analysis. *Breakeven analysis,* which is sometimes called *cost-volume-profit analysis,* is important to the firm because it allows the firm (1) to determine the level of operations it must maintain to cover all operating costs and (2) to evaluate the profitability associated with various levels of sales. To understand breakeven analysis, it is necessary to analyze further the firm's operating costs. An examination of the upper portion of Table 13.1 reveals that to calculate the firm's earnings before interest and taxes, the cost of goods sold and operating expenses must be subtracted from sales revenue.

The firm's cost of goods sold and its operating expenses contain fixed and variable operating-cost components. *Fixed operating costs* are a function of time, not sales, and are typically contractual. They require the payment of a certain number of dollars each accounting period. Rent is a fixed operating cost. *Variable operating costs* vary directly with sales. They are a function of volume, not time. Production and delivery costs are variable operating costs. In some cases, *semivariable operating costs*—partly fixed and partly variable operating costs[2]—result. One example of semivariable operating costs might be sales commissions. These commissions may be fixed over a certain range of volume and increase to higher levels for higher volumes. The firm's cost of goods sold and its operating expenses can be grouped into fixed and variable operating costs.[3] The top portion of Table 13.1 can then be recast as shown in the left-hand side of Table 13.2. Using this framework, the firm's operating breakeven point can be determined either algebraically or graphically, and the impact of changing costs on the operating breakeven point can be demonstrated.

The algebraic approach. Using the following variable names, the operating portion of the firm's income statement can be represented as shown in the right-hand portion of Table 13.2:

[2] Semivariable costs are sometimes called *semifixed* costs. Regardless of how these costs are labeled, they have the characteristics described here.

[3] Semivariable costs are ignored here and in the discussions that follow because they can be broken down into fixed and variable components.

Table 13.2 Operating Leverage, Costs, and Breakeven Analysis

	Item	Algebraic representation
Operating leverage	Sales revenue	$p \times X$
	Less: Fixed operating costs	$- \quad F$
	Less: Variable operating costs	$-(v \times X)$
	Earnings before interest and taxes	$EBIT$

$X =$ sales volume in units
$p =$ sale price per unit
$F =$ fixed *operating* cost per period
$v =$ variable *operating* cost per unit

Rewriting the algebraic calculations in Table 13.2 as a formula for earnings before interest and taxes yields Equation 13.1:

$$EBIT = (p \times X) - F - (v \times X) \tag{13.1}$$

Simplifying Equation 13.1 yields

$$EBIT = X(p - v) - F \tag{13.2}$$

The firm's *operating breakeven point* is defined as the level of sales at which all fixed and variable *operating* costs are covered — that is, the level at which *EBIT* equals zero.[4] Setting *EBIT* equal to zero and solving Equation 13.2 for the firm's sales volume, X, yields

$$X = \frac{F}{p - v} \tag{13.3}$$

This equation is used to find the firm's breakeven volume, X. Let us look at an example.

EXAMPLE   Assume that a firm has fixed operating costs of $2500, the sale price per unit of its product is $10, and its variable operating cost per unit is $5. Applying Equation 13.3 to these data yields

$$X = \frac{\$2500}{\$10 - \$5} = \frac{\$2500}{\$5} = 500 \text{ units}$$

At sales of 500 units, or $5000 ($10 × 500 units), the firm's *EBIT* should just equal zero. ∎

---

[4] You should recognize that the operating breakeven point defined in this chapter refers to the point at which *all operating costs are covered,* or where *EBIT* just equals zero. Quite often the breakeven point is calculated so that it represents the point at which all operating *and* financial costs are covered. Our concern in this chapter is not with this overall breakeven point, although its calculation is quite similar.

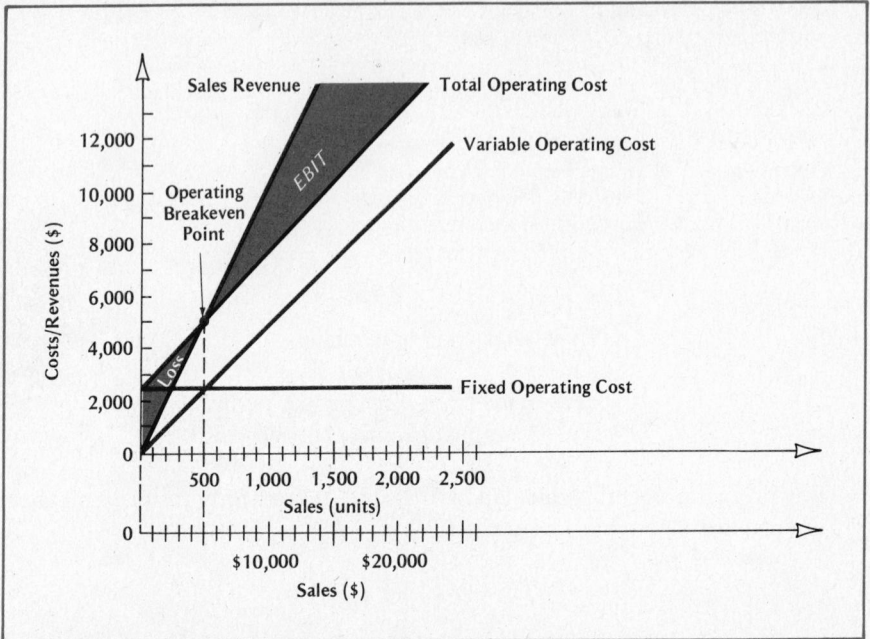

Figure 13.1   Graphic operating breakeven analysis

In the example, the firm will have positive *EBIT* for sales greater than 500 units and negative *EBIT,* or a loss, for sales less than 500 units. The reader can confirm this by substituting values above and below 500 units, along with the other values given, into Equation 13.1.

The graphic approach. The firm's operating breakeven point can also be calculated graphically. Figure 13.1 presents breakeven analysis of the data in the example. It has two base-line axes, one represents sales in units, the other, sales in dollars. Breakeven charts can be presented using either of these axes, but the use of units is the simpler approach.[5]

[5] The *operating breakeven point in dollars, D*, can be found by using the formula

$$D = \frac{F}{1 - \dfrac{TV}{S}}$$

where

S = total sales revenue in dollars
TV = total variable operating costs paid to achieve S dollars of sales
F = fixed operating costs paid during the period in which S dollars of sales are achieved.

The term $1 - \dfrac{TV}{S}$ is the *contribution margin,* which reflects the per-dollar contribution toward meeting fixed operating costs and profits provided by each sales dollar.

The operating breakeven point can also be found on a cash basis. Assuming that the firm has noncash charges (such as depreciation), N, included in its fixed operating costs,

Table 13.3   Sensitivity of Operating Breakeven Point
to Increases in Key Breakeven Variables

Increase in variable	Effect on operating breakeven point
Fixed operating cost (F)	Increase
Sale price per unit (p)	Decrease
Variable operating cost per unit (v)	Increase

Note: Decreases in each of the variables shown would have the opposite effect from that indicated on the breakeven point.

In Figure 13.1, the firm's breakeven point is the point at which total operating cost equals its sales revenue. A firm's *total operating cost* is defined as the sum of its fixed and variable operating costs. Using the notation introduced earlier, we can define the equation for the total operating cost as follows:

$$\text{Total operating cost} = F + (v \times X) \qquad (13.4)$$

Also depicted in Figure 13.1 are the firm's fixed and variable operating costs. The general cost characteristics defined earlier are shown by the lines representing each of these costs.

Figure 13.1 shows that a loss occurs when the firm's sales are below the operating breakeven point. For sales of less than 500 units ($5000), total operating costs exceed sales revenue. For sales levels greater than the operating breakeven point, *EBIT* is greater than zero. The absolute amount of the loss increases as the level of sales decreases from the operating breakeven point; the absolute amount of *EBIT* increases as the level of sales increases beyond the operating breakeven point.

Changing costs and the operating breakeven point. A firm's operating breakeven point is sensitive to a number of variables: fixed operating costs (F), the sale price per unit (p), and the variable operating cost per unit (v). The effects of increases or decreases in each of these variables can be readily assessed by referring to Equation 13.3. The sensitivity of the breakeven sales (X) to an *increase* in each of these variables is summarized in Table 13.3. As might be expected, Table 13.3 indicates that an increase in cost (F or v) tends to increase the breakeven point, while an increase in revenue (p) will decrease the breakeven point.

EXAMPLE   Assume that the firm wishes to evaluate the impact of (1) increasing fixed operating costs to $3000, (2) increasing the sale price per unit to $12.50, (3) increasing the variable operating cost per unit to $7.50, and (4) simultaneously implementing all three of these changes. Substituting the appropriate data into Equation 13.3 yields the following:

$$\text{Cash operating breakeven point} = \frac{F - N}{p - v}$$

This equation determines the number of units the firm must sell to have breakeven operating *cash flow*.

$$(1) \quad \text{Operating breakeven point} = \frac{\$3000}{\$10 - \$5} = 600 \text{ units}$$

$$(2) \quad \text{Operating breakeven point} = \frac{\$2500}{\$12.50 - \$5} = 333\tfrac{1}{3} \text{ units}$$

$$(3) \quad \text{Operating breakeven point} = \frac{\$2500}{\$10 - \$7.50} = 1000 \text{ units}$$

$$(4) \quad \text{Operating breakeven point} = \frac{\$3000}{\$12.50 - \$7.50} = 600 \text{ units}$$

Comparing the resulting operating breakeven points to the initial value of 500 units, we can see that, as noted in Table 13.3, the cost increases (1 and 3) increase the breakeven point (600 units and 1000 units, respectively), while the revenue increase (2) decreases the breakeven point to $333\tfrac{1}{3}$ units. In this case the combined effect (4) results in an increased breakeven point of 600 units. ∎

Weaknesses of breakeven analysis. Although breakeven analysis is widely used by business, it has a number of inherent weaknesses. First, it assumes that the firm faces linear total revenue and total operating cost functions. Generally, neither the firm's sale price per unit nor variable cost per unit is independent of sales volume. The sale price per unit generally decreases with volume while the cost per unit generally increases with volume thereby resulting in *curved,* rather than straight, revenue and cost functions. Recognition of these curved functions complicates the analysis and may result in solutions significantly different from those obtained using linear revenue and cost functions. A second weakness of breakeven analysis is the difficulty of classifying semivariable costs, which are fixed over certain ranges of volume, but vary between them. Another weakness occurs in the application of breakeven analysis to multiproduct firms. Due to the difficulty of allocating costs to products, special more sophisticated multiproduct breakeven models must be used to determine breakeven points for each product line. Finally, the short-term — typically one year — time horizon of breakeven analysis often limits its use. A large outlay in the current period could raise the breakeven point, although the benefits may occur over a period of years. Expenses for advertising and research and development are examples of such outlays. Clearly one must consider these potential weaknesses when applying breakeven analysis.

OPERATING LEVERAGE

Operating leverage results from the existence of fixed *operating* costs in the firm's income stream. Using the framework presented in Table 13.2, *operating leverage* can be defined as the ability to use fixed operating costs to magnify the effects of changes in sales on earnings before interest and taxes.

EXAMPLE   Using the data presented earlier (sale price, $p = \$10$ per unit; variable operating costs, $v = \$5$ per unit; fixed operating costs, $F = \$2500$), Figure 13.2 presents the operating breakeven chart for these data, which was originally shown in Figure 13.1. It can be seen from the additional notations on the chart that as the firm's sales increase from 1000 to 1500 units (X_1 to X_2), its *EBIT* increase from \$2500 to \$5000 ($EBIT_1$ to $EBIT_2$). In other

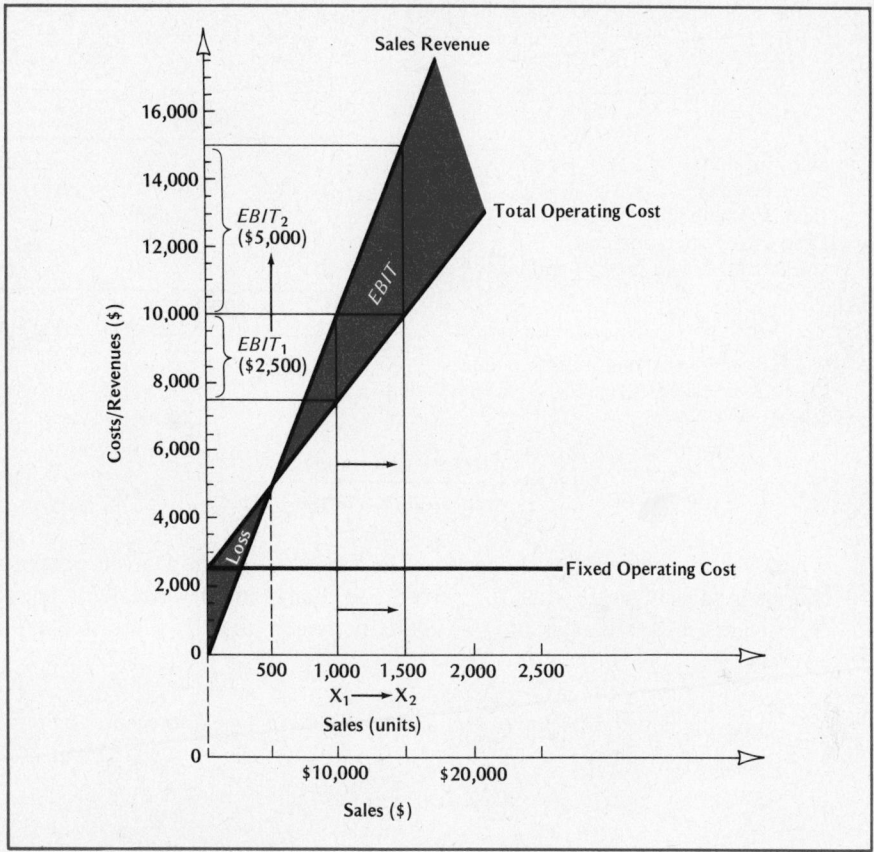

Figure 13.2   Breakeven analysis and operating leverage

words, a 50 percent increase in sales (1000 to 1500 units) results in a 100 percent increase in *EBIT*. Table 13.4 includes the data relating to Figure 13.2 as well as relevant data associated with a 500-unit sales level. Using the 1000-unit sales level as a reference point, two cases can be illustrated.

Case 1   A 50 percent *increase* in sales (from 1000 to 1500 units) results in a 100 percent *increase* in earnings before interest and taxes (from $2500 to $5000).

Case 2   A 50 percent *decrease* in sales (from 1000 to 500 units) results in a 100 percent *decrease* in earnings before interest and taxes (from $2500 to zero). ■

Operating leverage works in both directions. When a firm has fixed operating costs, operating leverage is present. An increase in sales results in a more than proportional increase in earnings before interest and taxes; a decrease in sales results in a more than proportional decrease in earnings before interest and taxes.

Measuring the degree of operating leverage (DOL). The *degree of operating leverage (DOL)* can be measured using the following equation.[6]

[6] The degree of operating leverage is also a function of the base level of sales used as point of reference. The closer the base sales level used is to the operating breakeven level, the more operating leverage there is. A comparison of the operating leverage ratios of two firms is valid only when the base level of sales used for each firm is the same.

Table 13.4   *EBIT* for Various Sales Levels

		Case 2		Case 1
		−50%		+50%
Sales (in units)		500	1,000	1,500
Sales revenue[a]		$5,000	$10,000	$15,000
Less: Variable operating costs[b]		2,500	5,000	7,500
Less: Fixed operating costs		2,500	2,500	2,500
Earnings before interest and taxes *(EBIT)*		$ 0	$ 2,500	$ 5,000
			−100%	+100%

[a] Sales revenue = $10/unit × sales in units.
[b] Variable operating costs = $5/unit × sales in units.

$$DOL = \frac{\text{percentage change in } EBIT}{\text{percentage change in sales}} \qquad (13.5)$$

Whenever the percentage change in *EBIT* resulting from a given percentage change in sales is greater than the percentage change in sales, operating leverage exists. This means that as long as *DOL* is greater than 1, there is operating leverage.

EXAMPLE   Applying Equation 13.5 to cases 1 and 2 in Table 13.4 yields the following results:[7]

$$\text{Case 1: } \frac{+100\%}{+50\%} = 2.0$$

$$\text{Case 2: } \frac{-100\%}{-50\%} = 2.0$$

Since the resulting quotient is greater than 1, operating leverage exists. For a given base level of sales, the higher the value resulting from applying Equation 13.5, the greater the degree of operating leverage. ■

A more direct formula for calculating the degree of operating leverage at a base sales level, *X*, is shown in Equation 13.6, using the notation given earlier:[8]

$$DOL \text{ at base sales level } X = \frac{X(p - v)}{X(p - v) - F} \qquad (13.6)$$

EXAMPLE   Substituting $X = 1000$, $p = \$10$, $v = \$5$, and $F = \$2500$ into Equation 13.6 yields the following result:

[7] Because the concept of leverage is *linear,* positive and negative changes of equal magnitude will always result in equal degrees of leverage when the same base sales level is used as a point of reference. This relationship holds for all types of leverage discussed in this chapter.

[8] Technically, the formula for *DOL* given in Equation 13.6 should include absolute-value signs because it is possible to get a negative *DOL* when the *EBIT* for the base sales level is negative. Since we assume that the *EBIT* for the base level of sales is positive, the absolute value signs are not included.

$$DOL \text{ at 1000 units} = \frac{1000(\$10 - \$5)}{1000(\$10 - \$5) - \$2500} = \frac{\$5000}{\$2500} = 2.0$$

It should be clear that the use of the formula given in Equation 13.6 provides a more direct method for calculating the degree of operating leverage than the approach illustrated using Table 13.4 and Equation 13.5.[9] ■

Fixed costs and operating leverage. Changes in fixed operating costs affect operating leverage significantly. This effect can be best illustrated by continuing with our example.

EXAMPLE   Assume that the firm discussed earlier is able to exchange a portion of its variable operating costs for fixed operating costs. This exchange results in a reduction in the variable operating cost per unit from \$5 to \$4.50 and an increase in the fixed operating costs from \$2500 to \$3000. Table 13.5 presents an analysis similar to that given in Table 13.4 using these new costs. Although the *EBIT* of \$2500 at the 1000-unit sales level is the same as before the shift in operating cost structure, it should be clear from Table 13.5 that by shifting to greater fixed operating costs, the firm has increased its operating leverage.

With the substitution of the appropriate values into Equation 13.6, the degree of operating leverage at the 1000-unit base level of sales becomes

$$DOL \text{ at 1000 units} = \frac{1000(\$10 - \$4.50)}{1000(\$10 - \$4.50) - \$3000} = \frac{\$5500}{\$2500} = 2.2$$

Comparing this value to the *DOL* of 2.0 before the shift to more fixed costs should make it clear that the higher the firm's fixed operating costs relative to variable operating costs, the greater the degree of operating leverage.

Table 13.5   Operating Leverage and Increased Fixed Costs

	Case 2		Case 1
	−50%		+50%
Sales (in units)	500	1,000	1,500
Sales revenue[a]	\$5,000	\$10,000	\$15,000
Less: Variable operating costs[b]	2,250	4,500	6,750
Less: Fixed operating costs	3,000	3,000	3,000
Earnings before interest and taxes *(EBIT)*	−\$250	\$ 2,500	\$ 5,250
	−110%		+110%

[a] Sales revenue was calculated as indicated in Table 13.4.   ■
[b] Variable operating costs = \$4.50/unit × sales in units.

[9] When total sales in dollars—instead of unit sales—are available, the following equation in which S = dollar level of base sales and TV = total variable operating costs in dollars can be used.

$$DOL \text{ at base dollar sales } S = \frac{S - TV}{S - TV - F}$$

This formula is especially useful for finding the *DOL* for multiproduct firms. It should be clear that since in the case of a single product firm $S = p \times X$ and $TV = v \times X$, substitution of these values into Equation 13.6 would result in the equation given here.

Because leverage works both ways, the shift toward more fixed costs tends to increase the magnitude of potential losses. This increased risk is quite clear when one compares, in the foregoing examples, the operating breakeven points before and after the shift. Before the shift, the firm's operating breakeven point is found to be 500 units [$2500 ÷ ($10 − $5)], whereas after the shift the operating breakeven point becomes 545 units [$3000 ÷ ($10 − $4.50)]. The increased breakeven point reflects the fact that the firm must achieve a higher level of sales to meet increased fixed operating costs.

FINANCIAL LEVERAGE

Financial leverage results from the presence of fixed *financial* charges in the firm's income stream.[10] These fixed charges do not vary with the firm's earnings before interest and taxes; they must be paid regardless of the amount of *EBIT* available to pay them. An examination of the lower portion of Table 13.1 indicates that the two fixed financial charges normally found on the firm's income statement are (1) interest on debt and (2) preferred stock dividends. Financial leverage is concerned with the effects of changes in earnings before interest and taxes on the earnings available for the common stockholders. Throughout the following analysis, it is assumed that all preferred stock dividends are paid. This assumption is required in order to measure the amount of money actually available to be distributed to common shareholders.[11]

Financial leverage is defined as the firm's ability to use fixed financial charges to magnify the effects of changes in earnings before interest and taxes on the firm's earnings per share *(eps)*. Earnings per share are commonly considered instead of earnings available for common stock because *eps* represent the number of dollars earned on behalf of each outstanding share of common stock; as noted in Chapter 4, the calculation of *earnings per share* is done by dividing the earnings available for common stockholders by the number of shares of common stock outstanding. Taxes, as well as the financial costs of interest and preferred stock dividends, are deducted from the firm's income stream. However, these taxes do not represent a fixed cost, since they change with changes in the level of earnings before taxes *(EBT)*. As a variable cost, they have no direct effect on the firm's financial leverage.

EXAMPLE   A firm expects earnings before interest and taxes of $10,000 in the current year. It has a $20,000 bond with a 10 percent coupon and an issue of 600 shares of $4 (dividend per share) preferred stock outstanding; it also has 1000 shares of common stock outstanding. The annual interest on the bond issue is $2,000 (.10 × $20,000). The annual dividends on the preferred stock are $2,400 ($4.00/share × 600 shares). Table 13.6 presents the levels of earnings per share resulting from levels of earnings before interest and taxes of $6,000, $10,000, and $14,000 assuming the firm is in the 40 percent tax bracket. Two situations are illustrated in the table.

[10] The expression *trading on the equity* is often used interchangeably with *financial leverage*.

[11] Preferred stock dividends may be *passed* (unpaid) during a period, but only if no dividends are paid to the common shareholders either. Preferred stock is generally such that unpaid dividends accrue and must be satisfied prior to any distribution of earnings to common stockholders. A discussion of the characteristics of preferred stock is included in Chapter 20.

Table 13.6　The *eps* for Various *EBIT* Levels

	Case 2		Case 1
	−40%		+40%
EBIT	$6,000	$10,000	$14,000
Less: Interest *(I)*	2,000	2,000	2,000
Earnings before taxes *(EBT)*	$4,000	$ 8,000	$12,000
Less: Taxes *(T)(t* = .40)	1,600	3,200	4,800
Earnings after taxes *(EAT)*	$2,400	$ 4,800	$ 7,200
Less: Preferred stock dividends *(PD)*	2,400	2,400	2,400
Earnings available for common *(EAC)*	$　0	$ 2,400	$ 4,800
Earnings per share *(eps)*	$\dfrac{\$0}{1000} = \$0$	$\dfrac{\$2400}{1000} = \$2.40$	$\dfrac{\$4800}{1000} = \$4.80$
	−100%		+100%

Case 1　A 40 percent *increase* in *EBIT* (from $10,000 to $14,000) results in a 100 percent *increase* in earnings per share (from $2.40 to $4.80).

Case 2　A 40 percent *decrease* in *EBIT* (from $10,000 to $6,000) results in a 100 percent *decrease* in earnings per share (from $2.40 to $0). ■

The effect of financial leverage is such that an increase in the firm's *EBIT* results in a greater than proportional increase in the firm's earnings per share, while a decrease in the firm's *EBIT* results in a more than proportional decrease in *eps*.

Measuring the degree of financial leverage *(DFL).* The *degree of financial leverage (DFL)* can be measured in a fashion similar to that used to measure the degree of operating leverage. The following equation presents one approach for measuring *DFL*.[12]

$$DFL = \frac{\text{percentage change in } eps}{\text{percentage change in } EBIT} \tag{13.7}$$

Whenever the percentage change in *eps* resulting from a given percentage change in *EBIT* is greater than the percentage change in *EBIT*, financial leverage exists. This means that whenever *DFL* is greater than 1, there is financial leverage.

EXAMPLE　Applying Equation 13.7 to cases 1 and 2 in Table 13.6 yields

$$\text{Case 1: } \frac{+100\%}{+40\%} = 2.5$$

$$\text{Case 2: } \frac{-100\%}{-40\%} = 2.5$$

[12] This statement is true only when the base level of *EBIT* used to calculate and compare such quotients is the same. In other words, the base level of *EBIT* must be held constant to compare the financial leverage associated with different levels of fixed financial costs.

THE EFFECTS OF SLOWING GROWTH IN FIXED COSTS AND INCREASING SALES ON THE BIG THREE AUTOMAKERS

This series of graphs depicts the expected outcomes in terms of earnings, cash flow, and capital investment for the Big Three automakers if they can slow growth in fixed costs and increase sales. The impact of total leverage on returns is clearly reflected by these graphs.

IF THEY CAN SLOW THE GROWTH OF THEIR FIXED COSTS . . .

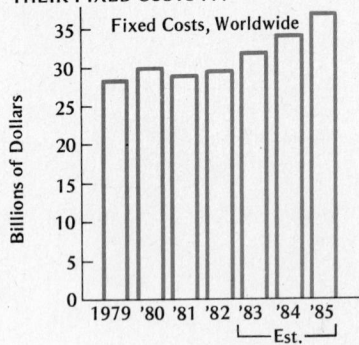

. . . AND ACHIEVE A HIGHER VOLUME OF AUTO SALES . . .

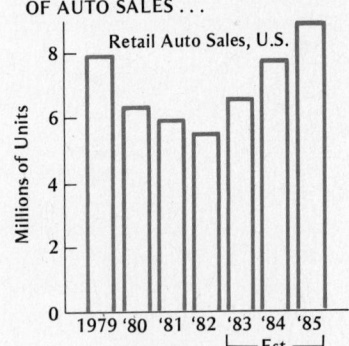

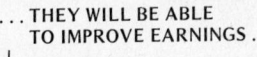

. . . THEY WILL BE ABLE TO IMPROVE EARNINGS . . .

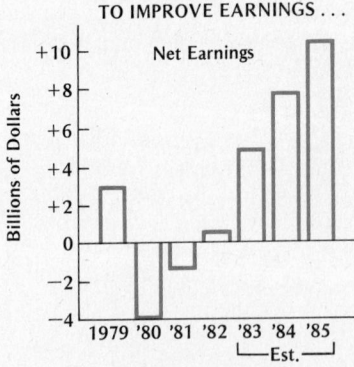

. . . GENERATE STRONGER CASH FLOW . . .

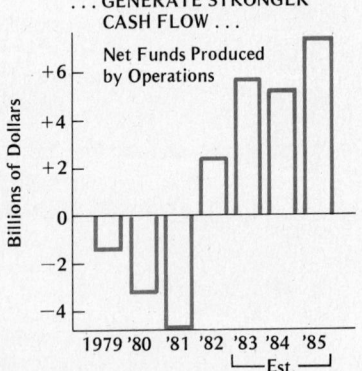

. . . AND BOOST PRODUCTIVITY THROUGH HEAVY CAPITAL INVESTMENT

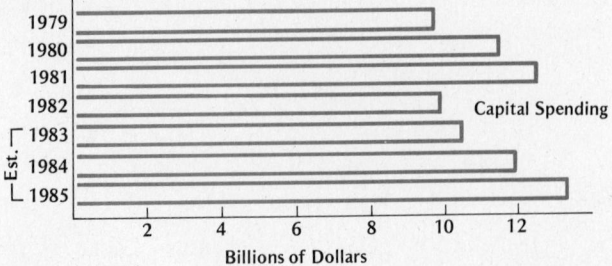

SOURCE: Sanford C. Bernstein & Co.

In both cases, the quotient is greater than 1, and financial leverage exists. The higher this quotient, the greater the degree of financial leverage. ∎

A more direct formula for calculating the degree of financial leverage at a base level of *EBIT* is given by Equation 13.8, using the notation from Table 13.6.[13]

$$\text{DFL at base level } EBIT = \frac{EBIT}{EBIT - I - \left(PD \times \frac{1}{1-t}\right)} \tag{13.8}$$

EXAMPLE   Substituting $EBIT = \$10{,}000$, $I = \$2{,}000$, $PD = \$2{,}400$, and the tax rate ($t = .40$) into Equation 13.8 yields the following result:

$$\text{DFL at } \$10{,}000 \; EBIT = \frac{\$10{,}000}{\$10{,}000 - \$2{,}000 - \left(\$2{,}400 \times \frac{1}{1-.40}\right)} = \frac{\$10{,}000}{\$4{,}000} = 2.5$$

It should be apparent that the formula given in Equation 13.8 provides a more direct method for calculating the degree of financial leverage than the approach illustrated using Table 13.6 and Equation 13.7. ∎

Because financial leverage, like operating leverage, works in both directions, magnifying the effects of increases and decreases in the firm's *EBIT,* higher levels of risk are again attached to higher degrees of leverage. High fixed financial costs thus increase the firm's financial leverage *and* its financial risk.

TOTAL LEVERAGE: THE COMBINED EFFECT

The combined effect of operating and financial leverage on the firm's risk can be assessed using a framework similar to that used to develop the individual concepts of leverage. This combined effect, or *total leverage,* can be defined as the firm's ability to use fixed costs, both operating and financial, to magnify the effect of changes in sales on the firm's earnings per share. Total leverage can therefore be viewed as the total impact of the fixed costs in the firm's operating and financial structure.

EXAMPLE   A firm expects sales of 20,000 units at $5 per unit in the coming year and must meet the following: variable operating costs at $2 per unit, fixed operating costs of $10,000, interest of $20,000, and preferred stock dividends of $12,000. The firm is in the 40 percent tax bracket and has 5,000 shares of common stock outstanding. Table 13.7 presents the levels of earnings per share *(eps)* associated with the expected sales of 20,000 units and with sales of 30,000 units.

The table illustrates that as a result of a 50 percent increase in sales (20,000 to 30,000 units), the firm would experience a 300 percent increase in earnings per share ($1.20 to $4.80). Although not shown in the table, a 50 percent decrease in sales would, conversely,

[13] Using the formula for *DFL* in Equation 13.8, it is possible to get a negative value for the *DFL* if the *eps* for the base level of *EBIT* is negative. Rather than show absolute value signs in the equation, it is instead assumed that the base-level *eps* is positive.

Table 13.7   The Total Leverage Effect

Sales (in units)	20,000	30,000	
Sales revenue[a]	$100,000	$150,000	
Less: Variable operating costs[b]	40,000	60,000	
Less: Fixed operating costs	10,000	10,000	
Earnings before interest and taxes (EBIT)	$ 50,000	$ 80,000	$DOL = \dfrac{+60\%}{+50\%} = 1.2$
Less: Interest	20,000	20,000	
Earnings before taxes	$30,000	$60,000	
Less: Taxes (40%)	12,000	24,000	
Earnings after taxes	$18,000	$36,000	
Less: Preferred stock dividends	12,000	12,000	
Earnings available for common	$ 6,000	$24,000	$DFL = \dfrac{+300\%}{+60\%} = 5.0$
Earnings per share (eps)	$\dfrac{\$6,000}{5,000} = \$1.20$	$\dfrac{\$24,000}{5,000} = \$4.80$	$DTL = \dfrac{+300\%}{+50\%} = 6.0$

Sales (in units): +50%

EBIT: +60%

Earnings available for common / eps: +300%

[a] Sales revenue = $5/unit × sales in units.
[b] Variable operating costs = $2/unit × sales in units.

result in a 300 percent decrease in earnings per share. The linear nature of the leverage relationship accounts for the fact that sales changes of equal magnitude in opposite directions result in earnings per share changes of equal magnitude in the corresponding direction. At this point, it should be clear that whenever a firm has fixed costs—operating or financial—in its structure, total leverage will exist. ■

Measuring the degree of total leverage (DTL). The *degree of total leverage (DTL)* can be measured in a fashion similar to that used to measure operating and financial leverage. The following equation presents one approach for measuring *DTL*.[14]

$$DTL = \frac{\text{percentage change in } eps}{\text{percentage change in sales}} \qquad (13.9)$$

Whenever the percentage change in *eps* resulting from a given percentage change in sales is greater than the percentage change in sales, total leverage exists. This means that as long as the *DTL* is greater than 1, there is total leverage.

EXAMPLE   Applying Equation 13.9 to the data in Table 13.7 yields

$$DTL = \frac{+300\%}{+50\%} = 6.0$$

Since this quotient is greater than 1, total leverage exists. The higher this quotient, the greater the degree of total leverage. ■

A more direct formula for calculating the degree of total leverage at a given base level of sales, X, is given by Equation 13.10,[15] which uses the same notation presented earlier:

$$DTL \text{ at base sales level } X = \frac{X(p - v)}{X(p - v) - F - I - \left(PD \times \dfrac{1}{1 - t}\right)} \qquad (13.10)$$

EXAMPLE   Substituting $X = 20{,}000$, $p = \$5$, $v = \$2$, $F = \$10{,}000$, $I = \$20{,}000$, $PD = \$12{,}000$, and the tax rate ($t = .40$) into Equation 13.10 yields the following result:

DTL at 20,000 units

$$= \frac{20{,}000(\$5 - \$2)}{20{,}000(\$5 - \$2) - \$10{,}000 - \$20{,}000 - \left(\$12{,}000 \times \dfrac{1}{1 - .40}\right)}$$

$$= \frac{\$60{,}000}{\$10{,}000} = 6.0$$

[14] This statement is true only when the base level of sales used to calculate and compare such quotients is the same. In other words, the base level of sales must be held constant in order to compare the total leverage associated with different levels of fixed costs.

[15] Using the formula for *DTL* in Equation 13.10, it is possible to get a negative value for the *DTL* if *eps* for the base level of sales is negative. For our purposes, rather than show absolute value signs in the equation, we instead assume that the base-level *eps* is positive.

Clearly, the formula given in Equation 13.10 provides a more direct method for calculating the degree of total leverage than the approach illustrated using Table 13.7 and Equation 13.9. ■

Since total leverage, like operating and financial leverage, works in both directions, magnifying the effects of both increases and decreases in the firm's sales, higher levels of risk are attached to higher degrees of total leverage. High fixed costs thus increase total leverage *and* total risk.

The relationship of operating, financial, and total leverage. Total leverage reflects the combined impact of operating and financial leverage on the firm. High operating and financial leverage will cause total leverage to be high. The opposite will also be true. The relationship between operating and financial leverage is multiplicative rather than additive. The relationship between the degree of total leverage *(DTL)* and the degrees of operating *(DOL)* and financial *(DFL)* leverage is given by Equation 13.11.

$$DTL = DOL \times DFL \tag{13.11}$$

EXAMPLE Substituting the values calculated for *DOL* and *DFL,* shown on the right-hand side of Table 13.7, into Equation 13.11 yields

$$DTL = 1.2 \times 5.0 = 6.0$$

The resulting degree of total leverage of 6.0 is the same value that was calculated directly in the preceding section. The fact that the combined effect of operating and financial leverage on the firm's total leverage is multiplicative rather than additive should be clear. ■

The Firm's Capital Structure

Capital structure is one of the most complex areas of financial decision making because of the interrelationships among capital structure and various other financial decision variables. Therefore, an ability to assess the firm's capital structure and to understand its relationship to risk, return, and value is a necessary skill. This section ties together concepts presented in Chapters 4, 7, 8, and 12 and the discussion of leverage in this chapter.

TYPES OF CAPITAL

The two basic types of capital are debt capital and equity capital. Although both represent sources of funds to the firm, they have certain characteristic differences. The term *capital* denotes the long-term funds of the firm. All the items on the right side of the firm's balance sheet, excluding current liabilities, are sources of capital. The simplified balance sheet shown here indicates the basic breakdown of the firm's long-term financing into its debt and equity components.

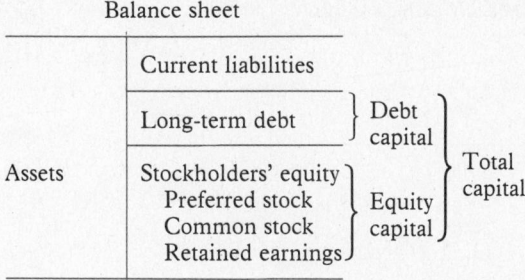

Debt capital includes any type of long-term funds obtained by borrowing.[16] The various types and characteristics of long-term debt are discussed in detail in Chapter 19. In Chapter 12 the cost of debt was found to be considerably less than the cost of other forms of financing. The "cheapness" of debt capital is attributable to the fact that as creditors, holders of such debt have the least risk of any long-term contributors of capital: First, they have a higher priority of claim against any earnings or assets available for payment; second, they have a legal pressure against the company to make payment far stronger than that of preferred or common stock; third, the treatment of interest payments as tax-deductible expenses lowers the cost substantially.

Equity capital consists of the long-term funds provided by the firm's owners. Unlike borrowed funds that must be repaid at a specified future date, equity capital is expected to remain in the firm for an indefinite period of time. The three basic sources of equity capital are preferred stock, common stock, and retained earnings. Most corporate financial managers think of preferred stock not as equity but as a substitute for debt that does not have a fixed maturity date. As far as common stockholders are concerned, preferred stock is a senior claim to their right to receive income from earnings through cash dividends. As we saw in Chapter 12, the cost of each of these sources of equity capital differs. Common stock is typically the most expensive, followed by retained earnings and preferred stock, respectively. The characteristics of retained earnings are discussed as part of the dividend presentation in Chapter 14; preferred and common stock are further discussed in Chapter 20.

Our concern here is not with the specific types of equity capital but with the gross relationship between debt and equity capital. Key differences between these two forms of capital relative to voice in management, claims on income and assets, maturity, and tax treatment are summarized in Table 13.8. It should be clear that because of its secondary position relative to debt, suppliers of equity capital take greater risk and therefore must be compensated with higher expected returns.

EXTERNAL ASSESSMENT OF CAPITAL STRUCTURE

Certain ratio measures of debt were presented in Chapter 4. These ratios indicate, directly and indirectly, the degree of financial leverage possessed by the firm. The

---

[16] Included as part of debt capital would be any *financial leases,* which are long-term contracts requiring the firm to make scheduled payments for the use of an asset. (This topic is discussed in detail in Chapter 21.)

Table 13.8   Key Differences Between Debt and Equity Capital

Characteristic	Type of capital	
	Debt	Equity
Voice in management[a]	No	Yes
Claims on income and assets	Senior to equity	Subordinate to debt
Maturity	Stated	None
Tax treatment	Interest deduction	No deduction

[a] In default, debtholders and preferred stockholders *may* receive a voice in management; otherwise, only common stockholders have voting rights.

direct measures concerned with the degree of indebtedness included the *debt ratio* and the *debt-equity ratio;* the higher these ratios, the greater the firm's financial leverage. The measures of the ability to service debts, which included *times interest earned* and the *fixed-payment coverage ratio,* provide indirect information on leverage. The smaller these ratios, the less able the firm is to meet its obligations as they come due. Generally speaking, low debt-service ratios are associated with high degrees of financial leverage.

An acceptable degree of financial leverage for one industry or line of business could be highly risky in another because of differing operating characteristics between industries or lines of business. Table 13.9 presents three ratios — debt, debt-equity, and times interest earned — for selected industries and lines of business. Significant industry differences can be seen in these data. For example, the debt ratio for electronic computing equipment manufacturers is 52.1 percent, while for auto retailers it is 71.8 percent. Of course, differences in debt positions are likely to exist *within* an industry or line of business as well. The amount of financial leverage within a given firm is largely the result of the decision maker's attitude toward risk. The more risk a firm is willing to take, the greater will be its financial leverage. In theory, the firm's financial leverage should be the result of creating a capital structure that minimizes its weighted average cost of capital, thereby maximizing owners' wealth.

BASIC THEORY OF CAPITAL STRUCTURE

The theory of capital structure is closely related to the firm's cost of capital. Many debates over whether an "optimal" capital structure exists are found in the financial literature. The debate began in the late 1950s, and there is as yet no resolution of the conflict. Theorists who assert the existence of an optimal capital structure are said to take a *traditional approach,* while those who believe such a structure does not exist are called supporters of the *M and M approach,* named for its initial proponents, Franco Modigliani and Merton H. Miller.

To provide some insight into what is meant by an optimal capital structure, we

Table 13.9   Debt Ratios for Selected Industries and Lines of Business (Fiscal Years Ended 6/30/82 Through 3/31/83

Industry or line of business	Debt ratio (%)	Debt-equity ratio (%)	Times interest earned ratio
Manufacturing industries			
Books: Publishing and printing	67.5%	64.6%	3.2
Dairy products	63.5	50.7	2.3
Electronic computing equipment	52.1	36.1	3.1
Fertilizers	62.7	47.2	1.6
Iron and steel foundries	53.0	48.1	1.2
Jewelry, precious metals	61.4	33.4	1.9
Motor vehicles	60.1	40.9	1.6
Wines, distilled liquors, liqueurs	58.6	36.2	1.6
Women's dresses	50.9	21.4	4.4
Wholesaling industries			
Furniture	62.8	33.9	2.4
General groceries	65.6	48.5	2.1
Hardware and paints	59.2	31.9	1.8
Men's and boys' clothing	58.0	20.7	2.0
Petroleum products	68.3	52.1	1.9
Retailing industries			
Autos—new and used	71.8	42.6	1.6
Department stores	53.7	44.9	2.0
Radio, television, record players	68.3	49.5	2.4
Restaurants	70.7	116.0	2.2
Shoes	60.9	36.6	2.2
Service industries			
Accounting, auditing, bookkeeping	48.8	39.5	5.8
Advertising agencies	73.6	43.6	3.3
Auto-repair shops	62.4	55.6	2.5
Insurance agents and brokers	80.1	74.4	2.0
Physicians	61.2	65.5	3.2
Travel agencies	65.6	34.0	3.0

Note: These ratios were derived from data appearing in the "All Sizes" column from the source cited.

SOURCE: *Annual Statement Studies, 1983* (fiscal years ended 6/30/82 through 3/31/83) (Philadelphia: Robert Morris Associates, 1983). Copyright © 1983 by Robert Morris Associates.

INTERPRETATION OF STATEMENT STUDIES FIGURES
Robert Morris Associates recommends that Statement Studies data be regarded only as general guidelines and not as absolute industry norms. There are several reasons why the data may not be fully representative of a given industry:
(1) The financial statements used in the *Statement Studies* are not selected by any random or statistically reliable method. RMA member banks voluntarily submit the raw data they have available each year, with these being the only constraints: (a) The fiscal year-ends of the companies reported may not be from April 1 through June 29, and (b) their total assets must be less than $100 million.
(2) Many companies have varied product lines; however, the *Statement Studies* categorize them by their primary product Standard Industrial Classification (SIC) number only.
(3) Some of our industry samples are rather small in relation to the total number of firms in a given industry. A relatively small sample can increase the chances that some of our composites do not fully represent an industry.
(4) There is the chance that an extreme statement can be present in a sample, causing a disproportionate influence on the industry composite. This is particularly true in a relatively small sample.
(5) Companies within the same industry may differ in their method of operations which in turn can directly influence their financial statements. Since they are included in our sample, too, these statements can significantly affect our composite calculations.
(6) Other considerations that can result in variations among different companies engaged in the same general line of business are different labor markets; geographical location; different accounting methods; quality of products handled; sources and methods of financing; and terms of sale.
For these reasons, RMA does not recommend the Statement Studies figures be considered as absolute norms for a given industry. Rather the figures should be used only as general guidelines and in addition to the other methods of financial analysis. RMA makes no claim as to the representativeness of the figures printed in this book.

will examine the traditional approach.[17] The material presented here is based on a number of simplifying assumptions;[18] more sophisticated theories have eliminated the need for many of the restrictive assumptions on which the traditional model is based. In the traditional approach to capital structure, the value of the firm is maximized when the cost of capital is minimized. Using a simple zero growth valuation model (see Equation 8.8 in Chapter 8), the value of the firm, V, can be defined by Equation 13.12, where $EBIT$ equals earnings before interest and taxes and k_a is the weighted average cost of capital.

$$V = \frac{EBIT}{k_a} \tag{13.12}$$

Clearly, if we assume that $EBIT$ is constant, the value of the firm is maximized by minimizing the weighted average cost of capital, k_a.

Cost functions. It can be seen from Figure 13.3 that three cost functions—the cost of debt, k_i; the cost of equity, k_s; and the overall cost of capital, k_a—are plotted as a function of financial leverage measured by the debt ratio (debt-to-total assets). The *cost of debt, k_i,* remains constant as financial leverage increases, until a point is reached at which lenders feel the firm is becoming financially risky. At this point, the cost of debt will increase. The *cost of equity, k_s,* also increases with increasing financial leverage, but much more rapidly than the cost of debt. The faster increase in the cost of equity occurs because market participants recognize that the earnings of the firm must be discounted at a higher rate as leverage increases in order to compensate for the higher degree of financial risk. The *overall cost of capital, k_a,* results from a weighted average of the firm's debt and equity capital.[19] At a debt ratio of zero, the firm is 100 percent equity-financed. As debt is substituted for equity and the debt ratio increases, the overall cost of capital declines because the debt cost is less than the equity cost ($k_i < k_s$). As the debt ratio continues to increase, the increased debt cost eventually causes the overall cost of capital to rise (point M in Figure 13.3). This behavior results in a U-shaped or saucer-shaped overall cost of capital function, k_a.

Optimal capital structure. Since the maximization of value, V, is achieved when the overall cost of capital, k_a is at a minimum, the *optimal capital structure is therefore that at which the overall cost of capital, k_a, is minimized.* The point labeled M in

---

[17] You may wonder why attention is given only to the traditional approach and not to the Modigliani and Miller approach. The chief reason is that the M and M model is algebraically somewhat rigorous, and it is more important at this level to become familiar with the key concepts that affect managerial decisions than to delve deeply into the theory of finance. Business people tend to believe the traditional as opposed to the M and M approach.

[18] The key assumptions are that financing is done using only bonds and stocks, all earnings are paid out as dividends, there are no income taxes, earnings before interest and taxes *(EBIT)* is known and constant, business risk is constant, and changes in leverage are achieved through substitution of bonds for stock or stock for bonds.

[19] The overall cost of capital and the weighted average cost of capital are one and the same. The term *overall cost of capital* is used here because it is more common in the theoretical literature.

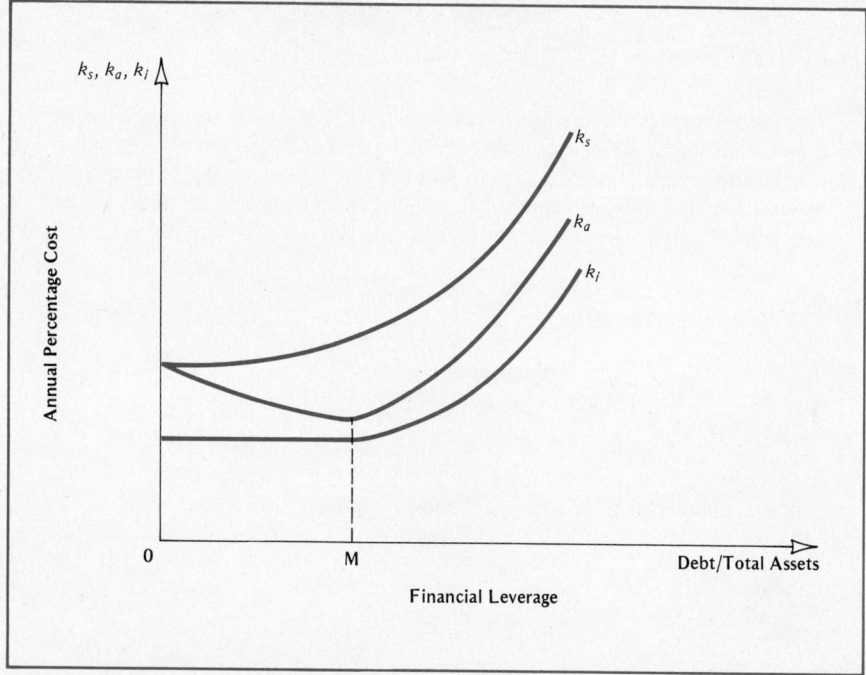

Figure 13.3   The traditional theory of capital structure

Figure 13.3 represents the point of optimal financial leverage and hence capital structure for the firm, since it results in a minimum overall cost of capital, k_a.[20]

The basic relationship of the cost of debt, k_i, the cost of equity, k_s, and the resulting overall cost of capital, k_a, should now be clear. The lower the firm's overall or weighted average cost of capital, the higher the expected returns to owners. Given a fixed capital budget, the less the firm's money costs, the greater the difference between the return on a project and the cost of money, and the greater the profits from the project. Reinvesting these increased profits will increase the firm's expected future earnings and therefore its value.

RISK AND CAPITAL STRUCTURE

A firm's capital structure must be developed with an eye toward risk because it is a direct link to value. Risk comes into play in two ways: (1) The capital structure must be consistent with the business risk, and (2) the capital structure results in a certain level of financial risk. In other words, the prevailing business risk tends to act as an input into the capital structure decision process, the output of which is a certain level of financial risk.

---

[20] In the Modigliani and Miller approach, the firm's overall cost of capital, when plotted on a graph similar to Figure 13.3, is represented by a horizontal line parallel to the x-axis. In other words, *the M and M approach suggests that there is no optimal capital structure* since the method by which the firm finances itself has no effect on its overall cost of capital. These conclusions are logically sound, given M and M's assumptions, but their assumptions are highly unrealistic.

INDUSTRY LEVERAGE: LEAST TO MOST

The following table summarizes the industries with extreme leverage positions drawn from recent three-year financial data for 890 of the nation's largest nonfinancial and industrial corporations in 36 key industries (fiscal years ending between October 1982 and September 1983). The wide divergence in the use of debt and associated coverage is apparent in this table.

How Industry Balance Sheets Stack Up:
The Three-Year Average

Capital position[a] (Debt as percent of total invested capital)			
The least leveraged		The most leveraged	
Office equipment	22.2%	Food & lodging	48.3%
Leisure time	22.3	Utilities	50.1
Drugs	22.6	Services	54.0
Instruments	23.3	Airlines	64.0
Personal care	24.0	Real estate	65.0

Coverage ability[b] (Fixed-charge coverage ratio)			
The best		The worst	
Drugs	8.8%	Tire & rubber	2.1%
Office equipment	8.2	Building materials	1.9
Natural resources	8.0	Real estate	1.6
Trucking	7.8	Airlines	Negative
Personal care	7.8	Automotive	Negative

[a] All-industry average 38.4%
[b] All-industry average 3.8

DATA: Standard & Poor's Compustat Services Inc.

Business risk. In Chapter 12, *business risk* was conveniently defined as the relationship between the firm's sales and its earnings before interest and taxes *(EBIT)*. In general, the greater the firm's operating leverage—the use of fixed operating cost—the higher its business risk. Although operating leverage is an important factor affecting *business risk,* two other factors also affect it—revenue stability and cost stability. *Revenue stability* refers to the relative variability of the firm's sales revenues. This behavior depends on both the stability of demand and the price of the firm's products. Firms with reasonably stable levels of demand and products with stable prices have stable revenues that result in low levels of business risk. Firms with highly volatile product demand and price have unstable revenues that result in high levels of business risk. *Cost stability* is concerned with the relative predictability of input prices such as labor and materials. The more predictable and stable these input prices are, the lower is the business risk, and vice versa.

In general, firms with low operating leverage, stable revenues, and stable costs have low business risk, while firms with high operating leverage, volatile revenues, and volatile costs have high business risk. Of course, the level of operating leverage employed by the firm quite often depends on its revenue and cost stability. Firms with stable revenues and costs can accept greater operating leverage (that is, fixed operating costs) than those with volatile patterns of revenues and costs. Business risk varies among firms, regardless of line of business, and is not affected by capital structure decisions. The level of business risk must be taken as given. The higher a firm's business risk, the more cautious the firm must be in establishing its capital structure. Firms with high business risk therefore tend toward less highly levered capital structures, and vice versa.

As in Chapter 12, we will hold business risk constant throughout the discussions that follow. Since business risk is an input to the capital structure decision process, once it has been specified, we can devote our attention to the financial risk expected to result from alternative capital structures. Let us look at an example.

EXAMPLE   The JSG Company, in preparing to make a capital structure decision, has obtained estimates of sales and the associated levels of *EBIT*. The firm's forecasting group feels there is a 25 percent chance sales will total $400,000, a 50 percent chance sales will total $600,000, and a 25 percent chance sales will total $800,000. Variable operating costs equal 50 percent of sales and fixed operating costs total $200,000. These data are summarized and the resulting earnings before interest and taxes *(EBIT)* calculated in Table 13.10.

It can be seen that there is a 25 percent chance *EBIT* will be zero, a 50 percent chance it will be $100,000, and a 25 percent chance it will equal $200,000. The financial manager must accept as given these levels of *EBIT* and associated probabilities when developing the firm's capital structure.[21] These *EBIT* data effectively reflect a certain level of business risk that captures the firm's sales variability, cost variability, and operating leverage. ∎

Financial risk. The firm's capital structure directly affects its *financial risk,* which was described earlier in this chapter as the risk resulting from the use of financial leverage. Financial leverage is concerned with the relationship between earnings before interest and taxes *(EBIT)* and earnings per share *(eps)*. The more fixed-cost financing — debt (including financial leases) and preferred stock — a firm has in

Table 13.10   Sales and Associated *EBIT* Calculations for JSG Company ($000)

Probability of sales	0.25	0.50	0.25
Sales	$400	$600	$800
— Variable operating costs (50% of sales)	200	300	400
— Fixed operating costs	200	200	200
Earnings before interest and taxes *(EBIT)*	$ 0	$100	$200

[21] As noted earlier in this chapter, by changing the firm's operating cost structure, the financial manager can affect its business risk. To isolate the capital structure decision, the firm's operating cost structure, and therefore its operating leverage, is assumed to be given and constant.

its capital structure, the greater its financial risk. Since the level of this risk and the associated level of return *(eps)* are key inputs to the valuation process, the financial manager must estimate the potential impact of alternative capital structures on these factors and ultimately on value in order to select the best capital structure. Fund suppliers will, of course, raise the cost of funds as the firm's financial leverage increases.

EXAMPLE   For simplicity, let us assume that the JSG Company is considering seven alternative capital structures. If we measure these structures using the debt ratio,[22] they are associated with ratios of 0, 10, 20, 30, 40, 50, and 60 percent. If (1) the firm has no current liabilities, (2) its capital structure currently contains all equity as shown, and (3) the total amount of capital remains constant[23] at $500,000, the mix of debt and equity associated with the debt ratios just stated would be as noted in Table 13.11. Also shown in the table is the number of shares of common stock remaining outstanding under each alternative.

Current capital structure

Long-term debt	$ 0
Common stock equity (25,000 shares at $20)	500,000
Total capital	$500,000

Associated with each of the debt levels in column 3 of Table 13.11 would be an interest rate that is expected to increase with increases in financial leverage, as reflected in the debt ratio. The level of debt, the associated interest rate (assumed to apply to *all* debt), and the dollar amount of annual interest associated with each of the alternative capital structures is summarized in Table 13.12. Since both the level of debt and the interest rate increase with increasing financial leverage (debt ratios), the annual interest increases as well.

Table 13.11   Capital Structures Associated with Alternative Debt Ratios

	Capital structure ($000)			Shares of common stock
Debt ratio (%) (1)	Total assets[a] (2)	Debt [(1) × (2)] (3)	Equity [(2) − (3)] (4)	outstanding (000) [(4) ÷ $20][b] (5)
0%	$500	$ 0	$500	25.00
10	500	50	450	22.50
20	500	100	400	20.00
30	500	150	350	17.50
40	500	200	300	15.00
50	500	250	250	12.50
60	500	300	200	10.00

[a] Because the firm, for convenience, is assumed to have no current liabilities, its total assets equal its total capital of $500,000.
[b] The $20 value represents the book value per share of common stock equity noted earlier.

[22] The debt ratio, rather than the debt-equity ratio, is used throughout this chapter to measure financial leverage for computational convenience. In theory, the debt-equity ratio may be a better measure of financial leverage because it considers only the firm's *long-term* debt financing.

[23] This assumption is needed to permit the assessment of alternative capital structures without having to consider the returns associated with the investment of additional funds raised. Concern here need be given only to the *mix* of capital rather than its investment.

Table 13.12 Level of Debt, Interest Rate, and Dollar
Amount of Interest Associated with JSG
Company's Alternative Capital Structures

Capital structure debt ratio (%)	Debt ($000) (1)	Interest rate on *all* debt (%) (2)	Interest ($000) [(1) ×(2)] (3)
0%	$ 0	0.0%	$ 0.00
10	50	9.0	4.50
20	100	9.5	9.50
30	150	10.0	15.00
40	200	11.0	22.00
50	250	13.5	33.75
60	300	16.5	49.50

Using the levels of earnings before interest and taxes *(EBIT)* and associated probabilities developed in Table 13.10, the number of shares of common stock found in column 5 of Table 13.11, and the interest values calculated in column 3 of Table 13.12, and assuming a 40 percent ordinary tax rate, calculation of the earnings per share *(eps)* for debt ratios of 0, 30, and 60 percent is illustrated in Table 13.13. Also shown are the resulting expected *eps,* the standard deviation of *eps,* and the coefficient of variation of *eps* associated with each debt ratio.

Table 13.13 Calculation of *eps* for Selected Debt Ratios ($000)

Debt ratio = 0%

Probability	0.25	0.50	0.25
EBIT (Table 13.10)	$ 0.00	$100.00	$200.00
− Interest (Table 13.12)	0.00	0.00	0.00
Earnings before taxes	$ 0.00	$100.00	$200.00
− Taxes (.40)	0.00	40.00	80.00
Earnings after taxes	$ 0.00	$ 60.00	$120.00
eps (25.0 shares, Table 13.11)	$ 0.00	$ 2.40	$ 4.80
Expected eps[a]		$2.40	
Standard deviation of eps[a]		$1.70	
Coefficient of variation of eps[a]		0.71	

Debt ratio = 30%

Probability	0.25	0.50	0.25
EBIT (Table 13.10)	$ 0.00	$100.00	$200.00
− Interest (Table 13.12)	15.00	15.00	15.00
Earnings before taxes	($15.00)	$ 85.00	$185.00
− Taxes (.40)	(6.00)[b]	34.00	74.00
Earnings after taxes	($ 9.00)	$ 51.00	$111.00
eps (17.50 shares, Table 13.11)	($ 0.51)	$ 2.91	$ 6.34
Expected eps[a]		$2.91	
Standard deviation of eps[a]		$2.42	
Coefficient of variation of eps[a]		0.83	

(continued)

Table 13.13   *(Continued)*

	Debt ratio = 60%		
Probability	0.25	0.50	0.25
EBIT (Table 13.10)	$ 0.00	$100.00	$200.00
−Interest (Table 13.12)	49.50	49.50	49.50
Earnings before taxes	($49.50)	$ 50.50	$150.50
−Taxes (.40)	(19.80)[b]	20.20	60.20
Earnings after taxes	($29.70)	$ 30.30	$ 90.30
eps (10.00 shares, Table 13.11)	($ 2.97)	$ 3.03	$ 9.03
Expected eps[a]		$3.03	
Standard deviation of eps[a]		$4.24	
Coefficient of variation of eps[a]		1.40	

[a] The procedures used to calculate the expected value, standard deviation, and coefficient of variation were presented as equations 7.2, 7.3, and 7.4, respectively, in Chapter 7.
[b] It is assumed that the firm receives the tax benefit from its loss in the current period as a result of carrying back the loss against profits in earlier periods. (See Chapter 2 for a discussion of tax loss carrybacks and carryforwards.)

The resulting statistics from the calculations in Table 13.13, along with the same statistics for the other debt ratios (10, 20, 40, and 50 percent — calculations not shown), are summarized for the seven alternative capital structures in Table 13.14. Because the coefficient of variation measures the risk relative to the expected *eps*, it is the preferred risk measure for use in comparing capital structures. It should be clear that as the firm's financial leverage increases, so does its coefficient of variation of *eps*. As expected, an increasing level of risk is associated with increased levels of financial leverage.

The relative risk of two of the capital structures evaluated in Table 13.13 (debt ratio = 0% and 60%) can be illustrated by showing the probability distribution of *eps*

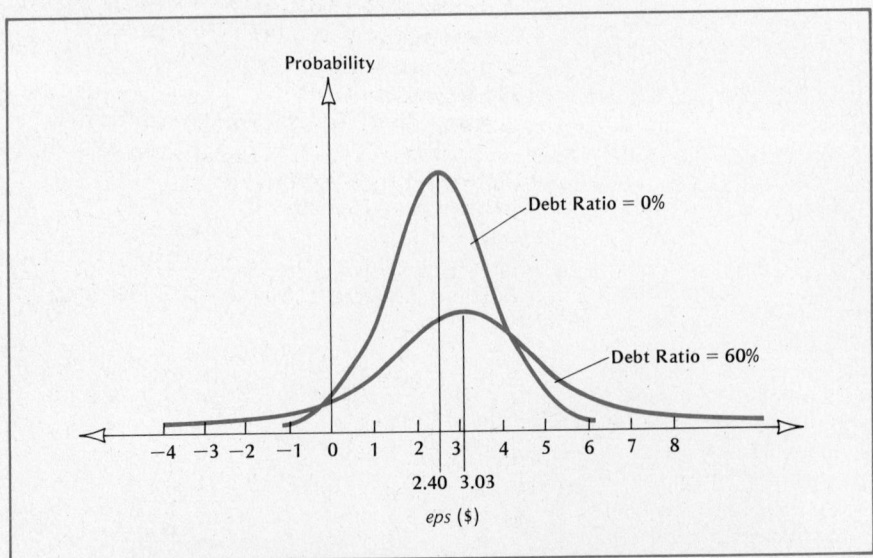

Figure 13.4   Probability distribution of *eps* for debt ratios of 0 and 60 percent

Table 13.14 Expected *eps*, Standard Deviation, and Coefficient of
Variation for Alternative Capital Structures

Capital structure debt ratio (%)	Expected *eps* ($) (1)	Standard deviation of *eps* ($) (2)	Coefficient of variation of *eps* [(2) ÷ (1)] (3)
0%	$2.40	$1.70	0.71
10	2.55	1.88	0.74
20	2.72	2.13	0.78
30	2.91	2.42	0.83
40	3.12	2.83	0.91
50	3.18	3.39	1.07
60	3.03	4.24	1.40

associated with each of them. Figure 13.4 shows these two distributions. It can be seen that while the expected level of *eps* increases with increasing financial leverage, so does risk, as reflected in the relative dispersion of each of the distributions. Clearly, the uncertainty of the expected *eps* as well as the chance of experiencing negative *eps* is greater when higher degrees of leverage are employed.

The nature of the risk-return trade-off associated with the seven capital structures under consideration can clearly be observed by plotting the *eps* and coefficient of variation relative to the debt ratio. Plotting the data obtained from Table 13.14 results in Figure 13.5. An analysis of the figure shows that as debt is substituted for equity (as the debt ratio increases), the level of earnings per share rises and then begins to fall (graph *a*). Based on the graph, it can be seen that the peak earnings per share occur at a debt ratio of 50 percent. The decline

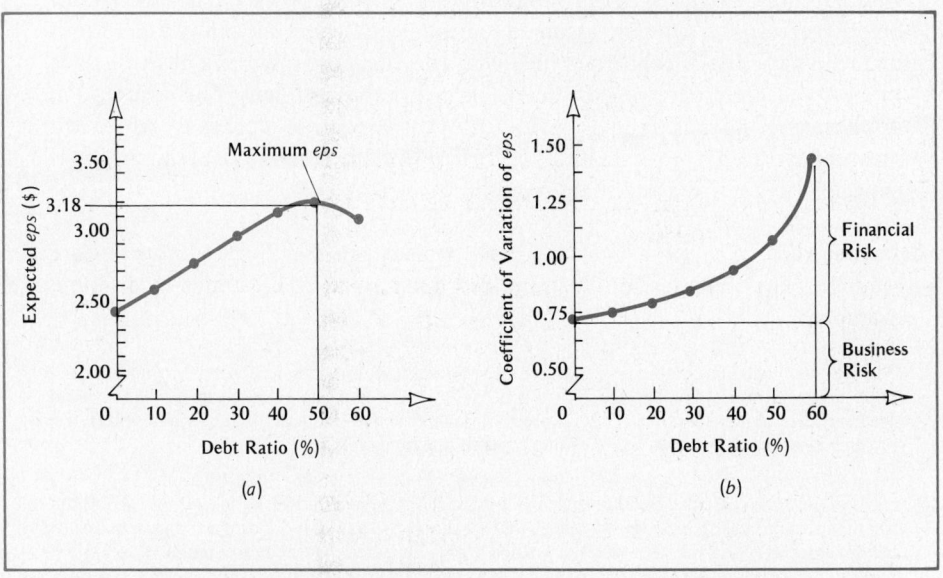

Figure 13.5 Expected *eps* and coefficient of variation of *eps* for alternative capital structures for the JSG Company

in earnings per share beyond that ratio results from the fact that the significant increases in interest are not fully compensated for by the reduction in the number of shares of common stock outstanding. If we look at the risk behavior as measured by the coefficient of variation, we can see that risk increases with increasing leverage (graph *b*). As noted, a portion of the risk can be attributed to business risk, while that portion changing in response to increasing financial leverage would be attributed to financial risk. Clearly, a risk-return trade-off exists relative to the use of financial leverage. How to combine these risk-return factors into a valuation framework will be addressed later in the chapter. The key point to recognize here is that as a firm introduces more leverage into its capital structure, it will experience increases in both the expected level of return and the associated risk. ■

The *EBIT-eps* Approach to Capital Structure

The *EBIT-eps approach* to capital structure involves selecting the capital structure that maximizes earnings per share *(eps)* over the expected range of earnings before interest and taxes *(EBIT)*. Here the main emphasis is on the effects of various capital structures on owners' returns. Since one of the key variables affecting the market value of the firm's shares is its earnings, earnings per share *(eps)* can be used to measure the effect of various capital structures on shareholders' investment.[24]

PRESENTING A FINANCING PLAN GRAPHICALLY

In analyzing the effects of a firm's capital structure on the returns to the firm's owners, we need to be concerned only with the relationship between earnings before interest and taxes *(EBIT)* and earnings per share *(eps)*. Expected earnings before interest and taxes are assumed to be constant, since an analysis of a firm's financial structure is concerned only with the effects of financing costs, such as interest and preferred stock dividends, on owners' investment. This assumption implies a constant business risk. As indicated earlier, earnings per share is used as a measure of the effects of operations on owners' wealth, since a close relationship is expected between *eps* and share prices.[25]

The data required. To graph a financing plan, at least two *EBIT-eps* coordinates are required. The approach for obtaining coordinates can be illustrated by a simple example.

[24] In the event that investors did not require risk premiums (additional returns) as the firm increases the proportion of debt in its capital structure, a strategy involving maximizing earnings per share would also maximize owners' wealth. Since risk premiums increase with increases in financial leverage, the maximization of *eps* does *not* assure owners' wealth maximization.

[25] The relationship expected to exist between earnings per share and owners' wealth is not one of cause and effect. As was indicated in Chapter 1, the maximization of profits does not necessarily assure the firm that owners' wealth is also being maximized. Profit maximization is a short-run approach; wealth maximization is a long-run approach. Nevertheless, it is expected that the movement of earnings per share will have some effect on owners' wealth since *eps* data constitute one of the few pieces of information investors receive, and they often bid the firm's share prices up or down in response to the level of these earnings.

Table 13.15 *EBIT-eps* Coordinates for JSG Company Selected Capital Structures (from Table 13.13)

Capital structure debt ratio (%)	EBIT	
	$100,000	$200,000
	Earnings per share *(eps)*	
0%	$2.40	$4.80
30	2.91	6.34
60	3.03	9.03

EXAMPLE The JSG Company data developed earlier can be used to illustrate the *EBIT-eps* approach. The *EBIT-eps* coordinates can be found by assuming two *EBIT* values and calculating the *eps* associated with them.[26] Such calculations for three capital structures— debt ratios of 0, 30, and 60 percent—for the JSG Company were presented in Table 13.13. Using the *EBIT* values of $100,000 and $200,000, the associated *eps* values calculated there are summarized in Table 13.15. ■

Plotting the data. The data summarized for the JSG Company in Table 13.15 can now be plotted on a set of *EBIT-eps* axes, as shown in Figure 13.6. Since our concern is only with positive levels of *eps,* the graphs have not been extended below the x-axis. The figure shows the level of *eps* expected for each level of *EBIT.* For levels of *EBIT* below the x-axis intercept—known as the *financial breakeven point*—a loss (negative *eps*) would result.

COMPARING ALTERNATIVE CAPITAL STRUCTURES

The graph presented in Figure 13.6 is most useful as a mechanism for comparing various capital structures, as in the following simple example.

EXAMPLE The JSG Company's capital structure alternatives were plotted on the *EBIT-eps* axes in Figure 13.6. An analysis of this figure discloses that over certain ranges of *EBIT,* each capital structure reflects superiority over the others in terms of maximizing *eps.* The zero-leverage capital structure (debt ratio = 0 percent) would be superior to either of the other capital structures for levels of *EBIT* between $0 and $50,000; between $50,000 and $95,500 of *EBIT,* the capital structure associated with a debt ratio of 30 percent would be

---

[26] A convenient method for finding one *EBIT-eps* coordinate is to calculate the *financial breakeven point,* the level of *EBIT* for which the firm's *eps* just equals zero. It is the level of *EBIT* needed to satisfy all fixed charges—interest *(I)* and preferred stock dividends *(PD).* The equation for the financial breakeven point is

$$\text{Financial breakeven point} = I + \frac{PD}{1 - t}$$

where t is the tax rate. It can be seen that when $PD = 0$, the financial breakeven point is equal to I, the annual interest payment.

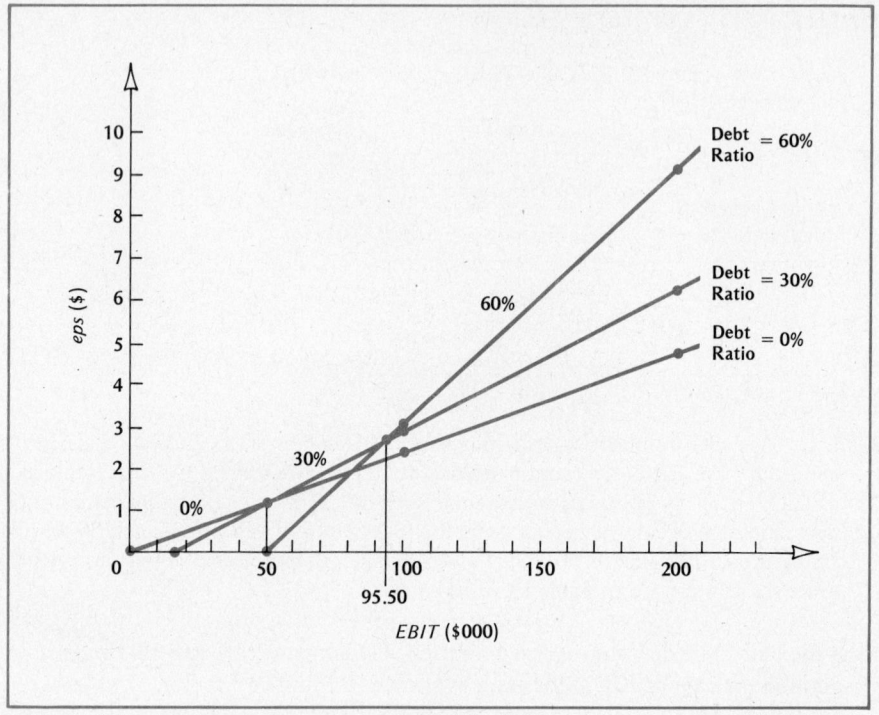

Figure 13.6 A graphic comparison of selected capital structures for JSG Company

preferred; while at a level of *EBIT* in excess of $95,500, the capital structure associated with a debt ratio of 60 percent would provide the highest earnings per share.[27] ■

[27] Algebraic techniques for finding the points of indifference between various capital structures are available. These techniques involve expressing each capital structure as an equation stated in terms of earnings per share, setting the equations for two capital structures equal to each other, and solving for the level of *EBIT* that causes the equations to be equal. Using the notation from footnote 26 and letting *n* equal the number of shares of common stock outstanding, the general equation for the earnings per share from a financing plan is

$$eps = \frac{(1 - t)(EBIT - I) - PD}{n}$$

Comparing the 0 percent and 30 percent capital structures, we get

$$\frac{(1 - .40)(EBIT - \$0) - \$0}{25.00} = \frac{(1 - .40)(EBIT - \$15.00) - \$0}{17.50}$$

$$\frac{.60\ EBIT}{25.00} = \frac{.60\ EBIT - \$9.00}{17.50}$$

$$10.50\ EBIT = 15.00\ EBIT - \$225.00$$

$$\$225.00 = 4.50\ EBIT$$

$$EBIT = \$50$$

The calculated value of the indifference point between the 0 percent and 30 percent capital structure is therefore $50,000, as can be seen in Figure 13.6.

INTERPRETING *EBIT-eps* ANALYSIS

When interpreting *EBIT-eps* analysis, it is important to assess accurately the risks involved with each of the capital structure alternatives. It is also important to recognize certain weaknesses associated with this approach.

Graphically, the risk of each capital structure can be viewed in light of the financial breakeven point *(EBIT*-axis intercept) and the degree of financial leverage reflected in the slope of the capital structure line. The higher the financial breakeven point and the steeper the slope of the capital structure line, the greater the financial risk.[28] Further assessment of risk can be performed using ratios. With increased financial leverage, as measured using the debt ratio, one would expect a corresponding decline in the firm's ability to service its debt, as measured using the times interest earned ratio.

EXAMPLE Reviewing the three capital structures plotted for the JSG Company in Figure 13.6, we can see that as the debt ratio increases, so does the financial risk of each alternative. Both the financial breakeven point and the slope of the capital structure lines increase with increasing debt ratios. If we refer to Table 13.13 and use the $100,000 *EBIT* value, the times interest earned ratio *(EBIT* ÷ interest) for the zero-leverage capital structure is infinity ($100,000 ÷ 0), for the 30 percent debt case it is 6.67 ($100,000 ÷ $15,000), and for the 60 percent debt case it is 2.02 ($100,000 ÷ $49,500). Since lower times interest earned ratios reflect higher risk, these ratios support the earlier conclusion that the risk of the capital structures increases with increasing financial leverage. The capital structure for a debt ratio of 60 percent is more risky than that for a debt ratio of 30 percent, which is more risky than the capital structure for a debt ratio of 0 percent. ■

The most important point to recognize when using *EBIT-eps* analysis is that this technique tends to concentrate on maximization of earnings rather than maximization of owners' wealth. Although there may be a positive relationship between these two objectives, the use of an *eps*-maximizing approach does not capture risk. To select the best capital structure, both return *(eps)* and risk (via the required return, k_s) must be integrated into a valuation framework in a fashion consistent with the capital structure theory presented earlier.

Choosing the Optimal Capital Structure

Creating a wealth maximization framework for use in making capital structure decisions is not easy. While the two key factors — return and risk — can be used to make capital structure decisions, integration of them into a market value context should provide improved results. This section describes the procedures for linking the return and risk associated with alternative capital structures to market value in order to select the best capital structure.

LINKAGE

To determine the firm's value under alternative capital structures, the risk associated with each structure must be linked to the required rate of return in the

---

[28] The degree of financial leverage *(DFL)* is reflected in the slope of the *EBIT-eps* function. The steeper the slope, the greater the degree of financial leverage since the change in *eps* (y-axis) resulting from a given change in *EBIT* (x-axis) will increase with increasing slope, and vice versa.

market. Given that the share price is the result of interactions among market participants, the firm must determine the level of return that must be earned in order to compensate investors and owners for the risk being incurred. Such a framework is consistent with the overall valuation framework developed in Chapter 8 and applied to capital budgeting decisions in Chapters 10 and 11.

The required return associated with a given level of financial risk can be estimated in a number of ways. Theoretically, the preferred approach would center on first estimating the beta associated with each alternative capital structure and using the CAPM framework presented in Chapter 7 (see Equation 7.6) to calculate the required return, k_s. Another approach would involve linking the financial risk associated with each capital structure alternative directly to the required return. Such an approach, which is similar to the market indifference curve presented in Chapter 11 (see Figure 11.6), would require estimation of the required return associated with each level of financial risk as measured by a statistic such as the coefficient of variation of *eps*. Regardless of the approach used, one would expect that the required return would be greater the greater the financial risk involved. An example will illustrate.

EXAMPLE   The JSG Company, using the coefficients of variation of *eps* associated with each of the seven alternative capital structures (see column 3 of Table 13.14) as a risk measure, estimated the associated required returns, k_s, to be as shown in Table 13.16. As expected, it can be seen that the estimated required return, k_s, increases with increasing risk, as measured by the coefficient of variation of *eps*. ∎

ESTIMATING VALUE

The value of the firm associated with alternative capital structures can be estimated using one of the standard valuation models. If, for simplicity, we assume that all earnings are paid out as dividends, a zero growth valuation model such as that developed in Chapter 8 can be used.[29] The model, originally stated in Equation 8.8, is restated here with *eps* substituted for dividends, since in each year the dividends would equal *eps*.

$$P_0 = \frac{eps}{k_s} \tag{13.13}$$

By substituting the estimated level of *eps* and the associated required return, k_s, into Equation 13.13, the value of the firm, P_0, can be estimated.

EXAMPLE   Returning again to the JSG Company, we can now estimate the value of its stock under each of the alternative capital structures. Substituting the expected *eps* (from column 1 of Table 13.14) and the required returns, k_s (from column 2 of Table 13.16), into Equation 13.13 for each of the seven alternative capital structures results in the share values given in

[29] While other valuation models such as the constant growth model, also presented in Chapter 8 (see Equation 8.10), can be applied, only the zero growth model is used here. The simplicity of this model provides for the most straightforward application of the valuation concept to the capital structure decision and is therefore preferred for explanatory convenience.

Table 13.16   Required Returns for JSG Company's
Alternative Capital Structures

Capital structure debt ratio (%)	Coefficient of variation of *eps* (from column 3 of Table 13.14) (1)	Estimated required return, k_s (%) (2)
0%	0.71	11.5%
10	0.74	11.7
20	0.78	12.1
30	0.83	12.5
40	0.91	14.0
50	1.07	16.5
60	1.40	19.0

Table 13.17   Calculation of Share Value Estimates Associated with
Alternative Capital Structures for the JSG Company

Capital structure debt ratio (%)	Expected *eps* ($) (from column 1 of Table 13.14) (1)	Estimated required rate of return, k_s (from column 2 of Table 13.16) (2)	Estimated share value ($) [(1) ÷ (2)] (3)
0%	$2.40	.115	$20.87
10	2.55	.117	21.79
20	2.72	.121	22.48
30	2.91	.125	23.28
40	3.12	.140	22.29
50	3.18	.165	19.27
60	3.03	.190	15.95

column 3 of Table 13.17. Plotting the resulting share values against the associated debt ratios as shown in Figure 13.7 clearly illustrates that the maximum share value occurs at the capital structure associated with a debt ratio of 30 percent; at that debt ratio, the share value is expected to equal $23.28. ■

MAXIMIZE VALUE VERSUS MAXIMIZE *eps*

Throughout this text, for a variety of reasons, the goal of the financial manager has been specified as maximizing owners' wealth, not profit. Although there is some relationship between the level of expected profit and value, there is no reason to believe that profit-maximizing strategies necessarily result in wealth maximization. It is therefore the wealth of the owner as reflected in the estimated share value that should act as the criterion for selecting the best capital structure. A final look at the JSG Company will help to highlight the point.

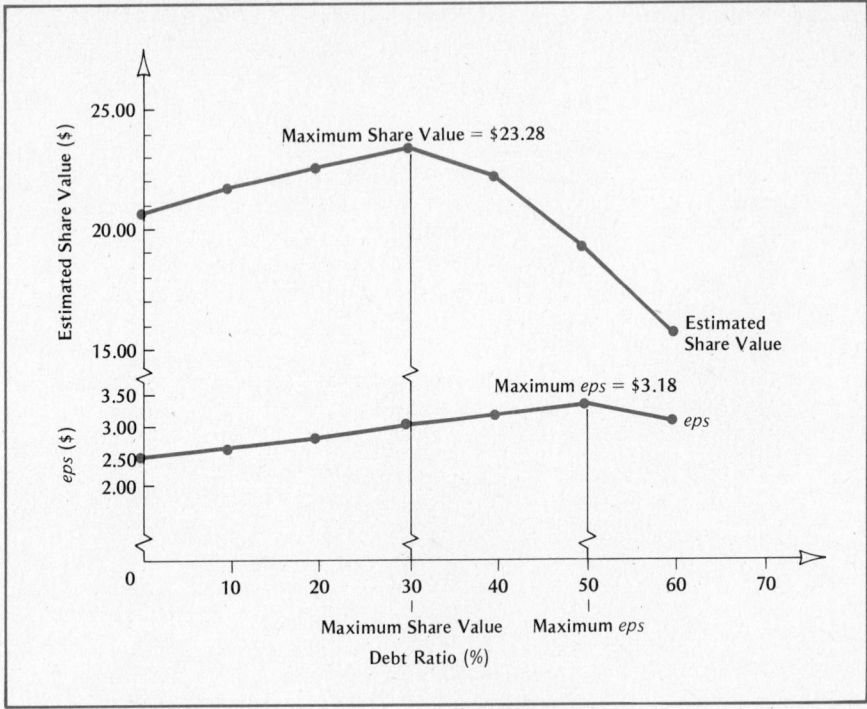

Figure 13.7 Estimated share value and *eps* for alternative capital structures for JSG Company

EXAMPLE Further analysis of Figure 13.7 clearly shows that while the firm's profits *(eps)* are maximized at a debt ratio of 50 percent, share price is maximized at a 30 percent debt ratio. In this case, the preferred capital structure would be the 30 percent debt ratio. The failure of the *eps*-maximization approach to provide a similar conclusion stems from its lack of consideration of risk. Based solely on the quantitative analysis presented, JSG Company should employ the capital structure resulting in a 30 percent debt ratio. ■

SOME OTHER IMPORTANT CONSIDERATIONS

Any quantitative analysis of capital structure must be tempered with other important considerations. A nearly endless list of additional factors relative to capital structure decisions could be created; some of the more important of these factors are briefly discussed here.

Cash flow. The key concern of the firm when considering a new capital structure must center on its ability to generate the necessary cash flows to meet obligations. Cash forecasts reflecting an ability to service debts (and preferred stock) must support any capital structure shift. The fact that it is cash flow — not accrued earnings — that is used to meet obligations must be reflected in the decision process. Although the additional debt or preferred stock will place an increased burden on cash flow, the sale of stock can effectively improve the firm's cash flow.

THE DISTINCTION BETWEEN DEBT AND EQUITY FOR CLOSELY HELD CORPORATIONS

Should you finance your corporation through debt or equity, or a combination of both? On the surface, it may seem that a clear-cut case can be made in favor of debt financing, but that isn't always true. The Internal Revenue Service takes a dim view of closely held corporations whose debts represent a large part of their working capital. It is the IRS's contention that debt provided by shareholders may be, in reality, equity, and thus the corporation shouldn't be allowed to deduct the interest paid on these debts. Beyond that, says the IRS, the corporation should have to pay additional taxes on that interest.

Although numerous cases and court decisions have revolved around this issue, there are no clearly defined guidelines a closely held corporation can follow to determine what the "proper" amount of debt or equity is or what the debt-to-equity ratio should be. In 1980, the IRS issued rules on debt-and-equity financing, which were to become effective on January 1, 1982. The proposed regulations brought public outcry, particularly from representatives of small start-up companies who faced the prospect of having their debt suddenly converted to equity. As a result, the IRS scrapped the regulations and came up with a new set of rules originally scheduled to take effect on July 1, 1983, but now postponed for further revision. Reaction to the latest proposals has been mixed because, although there are improvements, there are still many drawbacks for closely held corporations.

The proposals deal only with transactions between corporations and their shareholders. They don't affect transactions between corporations and independent lenders. The rules will probably require that loans made to a corporation be classified as debt or equity immediately after the loans are made.

Such classification may be complicated, however. For example, a written loan — such as a bond, note, or debenture — may be treated differently than an unwritten loan. Any loan repaid within 120 days after the end of the taxable year in which the loan was made won't be subject to the proposed rules if an arm's-length interest rate (the going rate) is charged. But they also prohibit artificial repayments by stating that a loan won't be considered repaid if another loan is made during the prohibited period — a period beginning on the day the loan is repaid and extending for the number of days the first loan was outstanding.

SOURCE: Allan I. Weiss, "Is It Debt, or Is It Equity?" *Inc.*, April 1983, p. 118.

Revenue stability. As noted earlier, the behavior of the firm's revenue function can significantly affect its capital structure. Firms having stable and predictable revenues can more safely undertake highly levered capital structures than firms with volatile patterns of sales revenue. Firms with increasing revenues (growing sales) tend to be in the best position to benefit from added debt because they can reap the positive benefits of leverage, which tends to magnify the effect of these increases. Firms that are experiencing volatile or declining patterns of revenue can be severely damaged by the use of leverage; they tend toward less highly levered capital structures.

Control. Since voting control of the firm lies in the hands of its common stockholders, the sale of additional shares of stock can affect who controls the firm. A management concerned about control may prefer to issue debt rather than common stock to raise funds. Of course, if market conditions are favorable, a firm that wanted to sell equity could issue *nonvoting shares* or make a *preemptive offering,* allowing each shareholder to maintain proportionate ownership. These features are discussed further in Chapter 20. Generally, only in closely held firms or firms threatened by takeover does control become a major concern in the capital structure decision process.

Contractual obligations. Sometimes, as a result of earlier capital structure decisions, a firm may be constrained with respect to the type or form of funds it subsequently raises. For example, a contract describing conditions of an earlier bond issue might prohibit the firm from selling additional debt except where the claims of holders of such debt are made subordinate to the existing debt. Contractual constraints on the sale of additional stock as well as the ability to distribute dividends on stock might also exist. Previous contractual obligations can therefore limit the firm's capital structure decisions.

Management preferences. Occasionally a firm will impose an internal constraint on the use of debt to limit the firm's risk exposure to a level deemed acceptable to its management. In other words, due to risk aversion, the firm's management constrains the firm's capital structure at a certain level, which may or may not be the true optimum.

External risk assessment. Because lenders as well as bond rating agencies carefully consider the firm's financial ratios and estimated cash flows when making loans or rating the firm's risk, the financial manager must assess the potential impact of capital structure decisions on these factors. The firm's ability to raise funds quickly and at favorable rates will clearly depend on the external risk assessments of lenders and bond raters. The financial manager must therefore consider the potential impact of capital structure decisions not only on share value but also on published financial statements from which lenders and raters tend to assess the firm's risk.

Timing. Timing is an important factor in capital structure decisions. At certain points in time, when the general level of interest rates is low, the use of debt financing might be more attractive; when interest rates are high, the sale of stock may become more appealing. Sometimes the sources of both debt and equity capital dry up and become unavailable under what would be viewed as reasonable terms. General economic conditions—especially those of the capital market—can thus significantly affect capital structure decisions.

CHAPTER SUMMARY

● Leverage is the use of fixed-cost assets or sources of funds to magnify returns to owners.

● Breakeven analysis is used to measure the level of sales necessary to cover total operating costs. The breakeven point may be calculated algebraically or determined graphically. It is sensitive to changes in fixed costs, the selling price of the firm's product, and variable costs.

● Operating leverage is closely related to operating breakeven analysis. It is defined as the ability of the firm to use fixed operating costs to magnify the effects of changes in sales on earnings before interest and taxes *(EBIT)*. The higher the firm's fixed operating costs are, the greater is its operating leverage.

● Financial leverage is defined as the ability of the firm to use fixed financial costs to magnify the effects of changes in earnings before interest and taxes *(EBIT)* on earnings per share *(eps)*. The higher the fixed financial costs are — typically interest and preferred stock dividends — the greater is the financial leverage.

● The total leverage of the firm is defined as its ability to use fixed costs — both operating and financial — to magnify the effects of changes in sales on earnings per share. Total leverage reflects the combined effect of operating and financial leverages.

● A firm's capital structure is determined by the mix of long-term debt and equity it uses in financing its operations.

● The basic differences between debt and equity capital are related to voice in management, the claims on income and assets of the providers of each type of capital, the length of time funds are available to the firm, and tax treatment.

● External assessments of capital structure tend to rely on the use of ratios such as the debt ratio, the debt-equity ratio, times interest earned, and the fixed-payment coverage ratio.

● The traditional approach to capital structure suggests that the optimal capital structure for a firm is that for which the overall cost of capital is minimized, thereby maximizing share value.

● Both the cost of debt and the cost of equity are increasing functions of leverage. The cost of debt typically increases only beyond a certain level of leverage.

● A firm's capital structure must be consistent with its business risk and results in a certain level of financial risk.

● In general, the higher the business risk, the less highly levered is the firm's capital structure, and vice versa. The firm's capital structure directly affects its financial risk, which results from financial leverage — the use of fixed-cost financing such as debt (including financial leases) and preferred stock.

● The *EBIT-eps* approach can be used to evaluate various capital structures in light of the degree of financial risk they entail and the returns they provide the firm's owners. Using the *EBIT-eps* approach, the preferred capital structure would be the one expected to provide maximum *eps* over the range of *EBIT* the firm expects to have. Graphically, this approach reflects risk in terms of the financial breakeven point and the slope of the capital structure line.

● The optimal capital structure can be selected from available alternatives by using a valuation model to link return and risk factors. The preferred capital structure would be the one that results in the highest estimated share value — not profits *(eps)*.

● In addition to quantitative findings, the capital structure decision must be tempered by other important considerations such as cash flow, revenue stability, control, contractual obligations, management preferences, external risk assessment, and timing.

KEY TERMS

breakeven analysis	capital structure
business risk	cost stability
capital	cost-volume-profit analysis

debt capital
degree of financial leverage *(DFL)*
degree of operating leverage *(DOL)*
degree of total leverage *(DTL)*
EBIT-eps approach (capital structure)
equity capital
financial breakeven point
financial leverage
financial risk
fixed operating costs
leverage

M and M approach (capital structure)
operating breakeven point
operating leverage
optimal capital structure
revenue stability
risk
semivariable operating costs
total leverage
total operating cost
traditional approach (capital structure)
variable operating costs

QUESTIONS

13-1   What is meant by the term *leverage?* What is a firm's *capital structure?*

13-2   What is the *operating breakeven point?* How do changes in fixed operating costs, the selling price per unit, and the variable operating cost per unit affect it?

13-3   What is meant by *financial leverage?* What items on the firm's income statement affect the degree of financial leverage present in a given firm?

13-4   What is the general relationship among operating leverage, financial leverage, and the total leverage of the firm? Do these types of leverage complement each other? Why or why not?

13-5   How do *debt* and *equity* capital differ?

13-6   Do all firms agree on the amount of financial leverage that is optimal? Explain.

13-7   Under the traditional approach to capital structure, what happens to the cost of debt and the cost of equity as the firm's financial leverage increases? Describe the resulting overall cost of capital.

13-8   Define *business risk* and discuss the three factors that affect it. What is the influence of business risk on a firm's capital structure?

13-9   Explain the *EBIT-eps approach* to capital structure. Include in your answer a graph indicating the financial breakeven point; label the axes.

13-10   Do *maximizing value* and *maximizing eps* lead to the same conclusion about the optimal level of financial leverage? If the conclusions are different, what is the cause?

13-11   How might a firm go about determining its optimal capital structure?

13-12   In addition to wealth considerations, what other factors might a firm consider when making capital structure decisions?

PROBLEMS

13-1   **(Breakeven Comparisons)**   Given the following price and cost data for each of the three firms I, J, and K, answer the questions.

Data	Firm I	Firm J	Firm K
Sale price per unit	$ 18.00	$ 21.00	$ 30.00
Variable operating cost per unit	$ 6.75	$ 13.50	$ 12.00
Fixed operating cost	$45,000.00	$30,000.00	$90,000.00

    a What is the operating breakeven point in units for each firm?

    b How would you rank these firms in terms of their risk?

13-2 **(Breakeven—Sensitivity)** The Alaska Press publishes the *Annual Alaska Almanac.* Last year, the book sold for $10 with variable operating costs per book of $8 and fixed operating costs of $40,000. How many books must Alaska Press sell this year to achieve the breakeven point for the operating costs, given the following different circumstances?

    a All figures remain the same as for last year.

    b Fixed operating costs increase to $44,000; all other figures remain the same as for last year.

    c The selling price increases to $10.50; all costs remain the same as for last year.

    d Variable operating costs per book increase to $8.50; all other figures remain the same.

    e What conclusions about the operating breakeven point can be drawn from your answers?

13-3 **(*EBIT* Sensitivity)** The Bush Company sells its finished product for $9 per unit. Its fixed operating costs are $20,000 and the variable operating cost per unit is $5.

    a Calculate the firm's earnings before interest and taxes *(EBIT)* for sales of 10,000 units.

    b Calculate the firm's *EBIT* for sales of 8,000 and 12,000 units, respectively.

    c Calculate the percentage change in sales (from the 10,000-unit base level) and associated percentage changes in *EBIT* for the shifts in sales indicated in **b**.

13-4 **(Degree of Operating Leverage)** The Island Paper Company has fixed operating costs of $380,000, variable operating costs per unit of $16, and a selling price of $63.50 per unit.

    a Calculate the operating breakeven point in units.

    b Calculate the firm's *EBIT* at 9,000, 10,000, and 11,000 units, respectively.

    c Using *10,000 units as a base,* what are the percentage changes in units sold and *EBIT* as sales move from the base to the other sales levels used in **b**?

    d Use the percentages computed in **c** to determine the degree of operating leverage *(DOL).*

    e Use the degree of operating leverage formula to determine the *DOL* at 10,000 units.

13-5 **(Breakeven—Graphic)** Advance Design, Inc., has fixed operating costs of $72,000, variable operating costs of $6.75 per unit, and a selling price of $9.75 per unit.

    a Calculate the operating breakeven point in units.

    b Compute the degree of operating leverage *(DOL)* for the following base unit sales levels: 25,000, 30,000, 40,000. Use the formula given in the chapter.

    c Graph the *DOL* figures you computed in **b** (on the *y*-axis) against base sales levels (on the *x*-axis).

    d Compute the degree of operating leverage at 24,000 units; add this point to your graph.

    e What principle is illustrated by your graph and figures?

13-6 **(*eps* Calculations)** The Power Tool Corporation has $60,000 of 16 percent bonds outstanding, 1,500 shares of preferred stock paying an annual dividend of $5 per share, and 4,000 shares of common stock outstanding. Assuming the firm has a 40 percent tax rate, compute earnings per share *(eps)* for the following levels of *EBIT*:

    a $24,600

    b $30,600

    c $35,000

13-7 **(Degree of Financial Leverage)** The Spring Water Company has *EBIT* of $67,500. Interest costs are $22,500, and the firm has 15,000 shares of common stock outstanding. Assume a 40 percent tax rate.

    a Use the degree of financial leverage *(DFL)* formula to calculate the *DFL* for the firm.

    b Using a set of *EBIT-eps* axes, plot the Spring Water financing plan.

    c Assuming that the firm also has 1,000 shares of preferred stock paying a $6.00 annual dividend per share, what is the *DFL*?

    d Plot the financing plan including the 1,000 shares of $6.00 preferred stock on the axes used in **b**.

    e Briefly discuss the graphs of the two financing plans.

13-8 **(Integrative — Multiple Leverage Measures)** Rose Oil Cosmetics produces skin-care products, selling 400,000 bottles a year. Each bottle produced has a variable operating cost of $.84 and sells for $1.00. Fixed operating costs are $28,000. The firm has current interest charges of $6,000, preferred dividends of $2,000, and a 40 percent tax rate.

    a Calculate (1) the operating breakeven point in units, (2) the financial breakeven point in dollars, and (3) the total (including both operating and financial costs) breakeven point in units.

    b Use the degree of operating leverage *(DOL)* formula to calculate *DOL*.

    c Use the degree of financial leverage *(DFL)* formula to calculate *DFL*.

    d Use the degree of total leverage *(DTL)* formula to calculate *DTL*. Compare this to the product of *DOL* and *DFL* calculated in **b** and **c**.

13-9 **(Integrative — Leverage and Risk)** Firm A has a *contribution margin* (see footnote 5) of $.30 per unit, fixed operating costs of $6,000, and sales of 100,000 units. Interest is $10,000 per year. Firm B has a *contribution margin* of $1.50 per unit, fixed operating costs of $62,500, and sales of 100,000 units. Interest is $17,500 per year. Assume that both firms are in the 40 percent tax bracket.

    a Compute the degree of operating, financial, and total leverage for firm A.

    b Compute the degree of operating, financial, and total leverage for firm B.

    c Compare the relative risks of the two firms.

    d Discuss the principles of leverage illustrated in your answers.

13-10 **(Integrative — Leverage)** CSD's most recent sales were $750,000, its variable operating costs represent 40 percent of sales, and its fixed operating costs are $250,000. Annual interest charges total $80,000, and the firm has 8,000 shares of $5 (annual dividend) preferred stock outstanding. It currently has 20,000 shares of common stock outstanding. Assume that the firm has a 40 percent tax rate.

    a At what level of sales would the firm break even on operations (i.e., *EBIT* = 0)?

    b Calculate the firm's earnings per share *(eps)* in tabular form at (1) the current level of sales and (2) at a $900,000 sales level.

    c Using the *$750,000 level of sales as a base,* calculate the firm's degree of operating leverage *(DOL)*.

    d Using the *EBIT associated with the $750,000 level of sales as a base,* calculate the firm's degree of financial leverage *(DFL)*.

    e Use the degree of total leverage *(DTL)* concept to determine the effect (in percentage terms) of a 50 percent increase in CSD's sales from the $750,000 base level on its earnings per share.

13-11 **(Various Capital Structures)** The Zachary Corporation currently has $1 million in total assets and is totally equity-financed. It is contemplating a change in capital structure. Compute the amount of debt and equity that would be outstanding if the firm were to shift to one of the following debt ratios (the amount of total assets would not change): 10, 20, 30, 40, 50, 60, and 90 percent. Is there a limit to the debt ratio's value?

13-12 (*eps* **and Debt Ratio**)   The JTV Corporation has made the following forecast of sales. Also given is the probability of each level of sales.

Probability	Sales forecast
.20	$200,000
.60	300,000
.20	400,000

The firm has fixed operating costs of $75,000 and variable operating costs of 70 percent of the sales level. The company pays $12,000 in interest per period. The tax rate is 40 percent.

a   Compute the earnings before interest and taxes *(EBIT)* for each level of sales.

b   Compute the expected earnings per share *(eps)*, standard deviation of the *eps*, and the coefficient of variation of *eps* for each level of forecast sales, assuming that there are 10,000 shares of common stock outstanding.

c   JTV has the opportunity to reduce leverage to zero and pay no interest. This will require that the number of shares outstanding be increased to 15,000. Repeat **b** under this assumption.

13-13 (*eps* **and Optimal Debt Ratio**)   Jessica Swimwear has estimated, at various debt ratios, the expected earnings per share and the standard deviation of the earnings per share as follows:

Debt ratio (%)	Earnings per share (*eps*)	Standard deviation of *eps*
0%	$2.30	$1.15
20	3.00	1.80
40	3.50	2.80
60	3.95	3.95
80	3.95	5.53

a   Estimate the optimal debt ratio based on the relationship between earnings per share and the debt ratio. You will probably find it helpful to graph the relationship.

b   Graph the relationship between the coefficient of variation and the debt ratio. Label the areas associated with business risk and financial risk.

13-14 (*EBIT* **and** *eps*)   Western Oil Corporation has a current capital structure consisting of $250,000 of 16 percent debt and 2,000 shares of common stock. The firm pays taxes at the rate of 40 percent on ordinary income.

a   Using *EBIT* values of $80,000 and $120,000, determine the associated earnings per share.

b   Calculate the financial breakeven point for this capital structure.

c   Graph the firm's current capital structure on a set of *EBIT-eps* axes.

13-15 (*EBIT-eps* **and Structure**)   Parker Petroleum is considering two capital structures. The key information follows. Assume a 40 percent tax rate on ordinary income.

Source of capital	Structure A	Structure B
Long-term debt	$100,000 at 16%	$200,000 at 17%
Common stock	4,000 shares	2,000 shares

a Calculate two *EBIT-eps* coordinates for each of the structures.
b Plot the two capital structures on a set of *EBIT-eps* axes.
c Indicate over what *EBIT* range, if any, each structure is preferred.
d Discuss the leverage and risk aspects of each structure.
e If the firm is fairly certain its *EBIT* will exceed $75,000, which structure would you recommend? Why?

13-16 (*EBIT-eps* **and Preferred Stock**) Wonder Diaper is considering two possible capital structures, A and B:

Source of capital	Structure A	Structure B
Long-term debt	$75,000 at 16%	$50,000 at 15%
Preferred stock	$10,000 at 18%	$15,000 at 18%
Common stock	8,000 shares at $20	10,000 shares at $20

a Calculate the financial breakeven point for each structure. Assume a 40 percent tax rate on ordinary income.
b Graph the two capital structures on the same set of *EBIT-eps* axes.
c Discuss the leverage and risk associated with each of the structures.
d Over what range of *EBIT* would each structure be preferred?
e Which structure would you recommend if the firm expects its *EBIT* to be $35,000? Explain.

13-17 (**Optimal Capital Structure**) The Hawaiian Macadamia Nut Company has collected the following data with respect to its capital structure, expected earnings per share, and required rates of return.

Capital structure debt ratio (%)	Expected earnings per share ($)	Required rate of return, k_s (%)
0%	$3.12	13%
10	3.90	15
20	4.80	16
30	5.44	17
40	5.51	19
50	5.00	20
60	4.40	22

a Compute the estimated share value using the simplified method described in this chapter (see Equation 13.13).
b Determine the optimal capital structure based on (1) maximization of expected earnings per share and (2) maximization of share value.
c Which capital structure do you recommend? Why?

13-18 (**Integrative — Optimal Capital Structure**) The Homes Corporation has made the following forecast of sales, with the associated probability of occurrence noted.

Sales	Probability
$200,000	.20
300,000	.60
400,000	.20

The company has fixed operating costs of $100,000 per year, and variable operating costs represent 40 percent of sales. The existing capital structure consists of

25,000 shares of common stock that have a $10 per share book value. No other capital items are outstanding. The marketplace has assigned the following discount rates to risky earnings per share.

Coefficient of variation of eps	Estimated required return, k_s (%)
.43	15%
.47	16
.51	17
.56	18
.60	22
.64	24

The company is contemplating *shifting its capital structure* by substituting debt in the capital structure for common stock. Three different debt ratios are under consideration, given here with the estimate of the required interest rate on *all* the debt.

Debt ratio (%)	Interest rate on all debt
20%	10%
40	12
60	14

The tax rate is 40 percent on ordinary income. The market value of the equity for a levered firm can be found using the simplified method (see Equation 13.13).

a   Calculate the expected earnings per share, the standard deviation of *eps*, and the coefficient of variation of *eps* for the three proposed capital structures.

b   Determine the optimal capital structure, assuming (1) maximization of earnings per share and (2) maximization of share value.

c   Construct a graph (similar to Figure 13.7) showing the relationships in **b**. (*Note:* You will probably have to sketch the lines, since you have only three data points.)

13-19   (**Integrative — Optimal Capital Structure**)   Triple D Corporation, which has fixed operating costs of $300,000 and variable operating costs equal to 40 percent of sales, has made the following three sales estimates, with their probabilities noted.

Sales	Probability
$ 600,000	.30
900,000	.40
1,200,000	.30

The firm wishes to analyze five possible capital structures—0, 15, 30, 45, and 60 percent debt ratios. The firm's total assets of $1 million are assumed constant. Its common stock is valued at $25 per share, and the firm is in the 40 percent tax bracket. The following additional data has been gathered for use in analyzing the five capital structures under consideration.

Capital structure debt ratio (%)	Cost of debt, k_i (%)	Required rate of return, k_s (%)
0%	0.0%	10.0%
15	8.0	10.5
30	10.0	11.6
45	13.0	14.0
60	17.0	20.0

a   Calculate the level of *EBIT* associated with each of the three levels of sales.

b   Calculate the amount of debt, the amount of equity, and the number of shares of common stock outstanding for each of the capital structures being considered.

c   Calculate the annual interest on the debt under each of the capital structures being considered. (*Note:* The cost of debt, k_i, is the interest rate applicable to *all* debt associated with the corresponding debt ratio.)

d   Calculate the *eps* associated with each of the three levels of *EBIT* calculated in **a** for each of the five capital structures being considered.

e   Calculate the (1) expected *eps*, (2) standard deviation of *eps*, and (3) coefficient of variation of *eps* for each of the capital structures, using your findings in **d**.

f   Plot the *eps* and coefficient of variation of *eps* against the capital structures (*x*-axis) on separate sets of axes and comment on the return and risk relative to capital structure.

g   Using the *EBIT-eps* data developed in **d**, plot the 0, 30, and 60 percent capital structures on the same set of *EBIT-eps* axes and discuss the ranges over which each is preferred. What is the major problem with the use of this approach?

h   Using the valuation model given in Equation 13.13 and your findings in **e**, estimate the share value for each of the capital structures being considered.

i   Compare and contrast your findings in **f** and **h**. Which structure is preferred if the goal is to maximize *eps*? Which structure is preferred if the goal is to maximize value? Which capital structure do you recommend? Explain.

Chapter 14

Dividend Policy

After studying this chapter, you should be able to:

1. Explain how retained earnings act as a source of financing and explain cash dividend payment procedures and dividend reinvestment plans.

2. Discuss the residual theory of dividends and the arguments concerning the irrelevance or relevance of dividends.

3. Understand the key factors affecting dividend policy.

4. Describe the common objectives of dividend policy and the basic types of dividend policies employed by firms.

5. Contrast the basic features, objectives, and procedures of stock dividends with stock splits.

6. Explain the basic accounting procedures, motives, and process for making stock repurchases.

The expected level of cash dividends is the key return variable from which owners and investors in the marketplace determine share value. The establishment of an effective dividend policy is therefore of major importance to the firm's overall objective. The development of such a policy is not easy. In each period, any earnings that remain after satisfying obligations to creditors, the government, and preferred stockholders can be retained, paid out as cash dividends, or divided between retained earnings and cash dividends. Retained earnings can be invested in assets that will help the firm expand or maintain its present rate of growth. On the other hand, the owners of the firm generally desire some current return on their equity investment—the payment of a cash dividend, which reduces the amount of earnings retained.

Procedural and Theoretical Considerations

To understand the mechanics and importance of the dividend decision, you must understand how retained earnings act as a source of long-term funds for the firm as well as understand the procedures for paying cash dividends and certain theoretical viewpoints on the importance of dividend payments. This section discusses retained earnings as a source of financing, cash dividend payment procedures, dividend reinvestment plans, and the residual theory of dividends.

RETAINED EARNINGS AS A SOURCE OF FINANCING

Retained earnings are viewed as a source of financing, since paying out earnings as cash dividends to common stockholders results in the reduction of the asset cash. To increase assets back to the level that would have prevailed had dividends not been paid, the firm must obtain additional debt or equity financing. By forgoing dividend payments and retaining earnings, the firm can avoid having to raise a given amount of funds or can eliminate certain existing sources of financing. In either case, *the retention of earnings is a source of funds.* A simple example will clarify this point.

EXAMPLE The Miller Flour Company's financial statements, presented in Table 14.1, have been constructed on the assumption that the company has paid out all its earnings as dividends. In addition, assume that the firm has already made its investment decisions and that asset values are at their optimal levels. Miller had $40,000 of earnings available after paying all claims other than those of common stockholders, and it decided to distribute the entire $40,000 as cash dividends to these owners, reinvesting none of these earnings in the firm. Had Miller gone to the other extreme and retained all $40,000 of its earnings available for common, the bottom portion of its income statement would be as follows:

Earnings available for common	$40,000
Less: Common stock dividends	0
To retained earnings	$40,000

Table 14.2 presents the firm's balance sheet when it retains the $40,000 in earnings. Comparing the balance sheet in Table 14.2 to that in Table 14.1 shows that Miller has available an added $40,000 of financing as a result of retaining (instead of paying out in common stock dividends) the $40,000 of earnings available to be paid out to common stockholders.[1]

Table 14.1 The Miller Flour Company's Financial Statements When All Earnings Are Paid Out as Dividends

Balance Sheet

Assets		Liabilities and stockholders' equity	
Cash	$ 20,000	Accounts payable	$ 30,000
Marketable securities	30,000	Notes payable	150,000
Accounts receivable	100,000	Accruals	20,000
Inventories	200,000	Total current liabilities	$ 200,000
Prepaid items	10,000	Long-term debt	$ 300,000
Total current assets	$ 360,000	Common stock at par	$ 100,000
Fixed assets (net)	640,000	Paid-in capital in excess of par	200,000
Total assets	$1,000,000	Preferred stock at 8%	100,000
		Retained earnings	100,000
		Total stockholders' equity	$ 500,000
		Total liabilities and stockholders' equity	$1,000,000

Income statement

Sales	$1,500,000
Less: Cost of goods sold	1,000,000
Gross profits	$ 500,000
Less: Expenses	420,000
Profits before taxes	$ 80,000
Less: Taxes (.40)	32,000
Profits after taxes	$ 48,000
Less: Preferred stock dividends	8,000
Earnings available for common	$ 40,000
Less: Common stock dividends	40,000
To retained earnings	$ 0

[1] Firms can pay out in cash dividends more than the current period's earnings. The two items that may act as constraints are the amount of cash available and the total amount of retained earnings. The maximum amount of cash dividends a firm can pay in a given period is discussed later in the chapter.

Table 14.2 The Miller Flour Company's Balance Sheet
When All Earnings Are Retained

Assets		Liabilities and stockholders' equity	
Cash	$ 60,000	Accounts payable	$ 30,000
Marketable securities	30,000	Notes payable	150,000
Accounts receivable	100,000	Accruals	20,000
Inventories	200,000	Total current liabilities	$ 200,000
Prepaid items	10,000	Long-term debt	$ 300,000
Total current assets	$ 400,000	Common stock at par	$ 100,000
Fixed assets (net)	640,000	Paid-in capital in excess of par	200,000
Total assets	$1,040,000	Preferred stock at 8%	100,000
		Retained earnings	140,000
		Total stockholders' equity	$ 540,000
		Total liabilities and stockholders' equity	$1,040,000

Regardless of how Miller disposes of the $40,000 in financing provided by the current period's operation, the firm, by retaining earnings, has raised $40,000 in long-term funds. Had it paid out these earnings as dividends, it would have to borrow or sell preferred or common stock to attain the asset and financial structure shown in the balance sheet in Table 14.2. Retained earnings are actually funds obtained from common stockholders. Since another way to obtain funds from this source is to sell new shares of common stock, retained earnings are often viewed as a fully subscribed issue of additional common stock. The implications of this fact for the firm's cost of capital were discussed in Chapter 12. ■

The example should make it clear that *the dividend decision is actually a financing decision,* since, assuming asset decisions are already made optimally, paying a dividend directly affects the firm's financing.

CASH DIVIDEND PAYMENT PROCEDURES

The payment of cash dividends to corporate stockholders is decided by the board of directors. The directors normally hold a quarterly or semiannual dividend meeting at which they evaluate the past period's financial performance to determine whether and in what amount dividends should be paid. The payment date of the cash dividend (if one is declared) must also be established.

Amount of dividends. Whether dividends should be paid and, if they are, how large they should be are important decisions that depend largely on the firm's dividend policy. Most firms pay some cash dividends each period. The amount is generally fixed, although significant increases or decreases in earnings may justify changing it. Most firms have a set policy with respect to the amount of the periodic dividend, but the firm's directors can change the amount at the dividend meeting.

Relevant dates. If the directors declare a dividend, they will also indicate the record and payment dates associated with the dividend. Typically, the directors issue a statement indicating their dividend decision, the record date, and the payment date. This statement is generally quoted in *The Wall Street Journal, Barron's,* and other financial news media.

Record date. All persons whose names appear as stockholders in the firm's stock ledger on the *date of record,* which is set by the directors, will receive a declared dividend.[2] These stockholders are often referred to as *holders of record.* Because of the time needed to make bookkeeping entries when a stock is traded, the stock will sell *ex dividend* for four business days prior to the date of record. The NYSE and other stock exchanges allow four business days for recording changes of ownership. When a stock sells ex dividend, purchasers do not receive the dividends. When a stock is selling prior to the ex dividend date, it is said to be selling with *dividends on* or *cum dividends.*

Payment date. The payment date is also set by the directors. It is generally set a few weeks after the record date. The *payment date* is the actual date on which the company will mail the dividend payment to the holders of record. An example will clarify the various dates and accounting entries.

EXAMPLE   At the quarterly dividend meeting of the Wiseley Company, held June 10, the directors declared an $.80 per share cash dividend for holders of record on Monday, July 1. The firm has 100,000 shares of common stock outstanding. The payment date for the dividend is August 1. Before the dividend was declared, the key accounts of the firm were as follows:

Cash	$200,000	Dividends payable	$ 0
		Retained earnings	1,000,000

When the dividend was announced by the directors, $80,000 ($.80 per share × 100,000 shares) of the retained earnings was transferred to the dividends payable account. The key accounts thus became

Cash	$200,000	Dividends payable	$ 80,000
		Retained earnings	920,000

The Wiseley Company's stock sold ex dividend for four business days prior to the date of record, which is June 25. Purchasers of Wiseley's stock on June 24 or earlier received the rights to the dividends; those purchasing the stock on or after June 25 did not.[3] When the August 1 payment date arrived, the firm mailed dividend checks to the holders of record as of July 1. This produced the following balances in the key accounts of the firm:

Cash	$120,000	Dividends payable	$ 0
		Retained earnings	920,000

The net effect of declaration and payment of the dividend was to reduce the firm's total assets (and stockholders' equity) by $80,000. ■

[2] The *stock ledger* is the official book in which the records of the current owners of the firm's outstanding shares are kept. All state corporation laws require firms to maintain a stock ledger. *Transfer agents,* which are generally major commercial banks, maintain the stock ledgers for large corporations. They are, of course, paid by the firms for their services.

[3] A simple way to determine the first day on which the stock sells ex dividend is to subtract four from the date of record; if a weekend intervenes, subtract two additional days. One business day prior to the first ex dividend day is the last day the stock will sell with dividends on. This, of course, will be five business days prior to the date of record. The relationship between the record date and ex dividend date is the same for stock dividends. In the case of rights offerings (discussed in Chapter 20), the ex rights date is similar to the ex dividend date.

DIVIDEND REINVESTMENT PLANS

A growing number of firms offer *dividend reinvestment plans,* an approach long used by mutual funds, which enable stockholders to acquire shares — even fractional shares — at little or no transaction cost. Sometimes discounts from the existing market price are offered, especially among utilities. These plans can be handled by the company in either of two ways. Both allow the stockholder to elect to have dividends reinvested in the firm's shares. In one situation, a third-party trustee buys the firm's shares in the open market on behalf of the shareholders who wish to reinvest their dividends. The second approach involves buying *newly issued* shares from the firm; this approach allows the firm to raise new capital while at the same time permitting owners to reinvest their dividends, often at a discount below the current market price.

Starting in 1982, shareholders in public utilities such as electric companies, telephone companies, and natural gas distributors gained a new tax break if they participated in the utilities' dividend reinvestment program. This is because up to $750 in reinvested dividends ($1500 for married taxpayers filing joint returns) may be excluded from current income taxes. Normally, cash dividends (or the value of the stocks received through a dividend reinvestment plan) are taxed as ordinary income, except for the $100 or $200 dividend exclusion. When the acquired utility shares are sold, a capital gains tax may have to be paid if the proceeds are in excess of the original purchase price. However, the much lower capital gains tax rate results in a smaller tax bite than would have been incurred if the utility dividends were taxed as ordinary income. The existence of dividend reinvestment plans — especially in the case of public utility stocks — may enhance the appeal of a firm's shares.

THE RESIDUAL THEORY OF DIVIDENDS

One school of thought — the *residual theory of dividends* — suggests that the dividend paid by a firm should be viewed as a residual — the amount left over after all acceptable investment opportunities have been undertaken. Using this approach, the firm would treat the dividend decision in three steps, as follows:

1. Determine its optimum level of capital expenditures, which would be the level generated by the point of intersection of the investment opportunities schedule *(IOS)* and weighted marginal cost of capital *(WMCC)* function (see Chapter 12).
2. Using the optimal capital structure proportions (see Chapter 13), it would estimate the total amount of equity financing needed to support the expenditures generated in step 1.
3. Because the cost of retained earnings, k_r, is less than the cost of new common stock, k_n (see Chapter 12), retained earnings would be used to meet the equity requirement determined in step 2. If retained earnings are inadequate to meet this need, new common stock would be sold. If the available retained earnings are in excess of this need, the surplus amount would be distributed as dividends.

As long as the firm's equity need is in excess of the amount of retained earnings, no cash dividend would be paid. If an excess of retained earnings exists, the residual amount would be distributed as a cash dividend. This view of dividends tends to suggest that the required return of investors in the marketplace, k_s, is not influenced by the firm's dividend policy — a premise that suggests that dividend policy is irrelevant. Let us look at an example.

EXAMPLE   Suntime Industries has available from the current period's operations $1.8 million that can be retained or paid out in dividends. The firm's optimal capital structure is at a debt ratio of 30 percent, which represents 30 percent debt and 70 percent equity. Figure 14.1 depicts the firm's weighted marginal cost of capital *(WMCC)* function along with three investment opportunities schedules, IOS_1, IOS_2, and IOS_3. For each *IOS,* the level of total new financing or investment determined by the point of intersection of the *WMCC* and the *IOS* has been noted. For IOS_1 it is $1.5 million, for IOS_2 it is $2.4 million, and for IOS_3 it is $3.2 million. While only one *IOS* will actually exist, it is useful to look at the dividend decisions generated by applying the residual theory in each of the three cases. Table 14.3 summarizes this analysis.

It can be seen from Table 14.3 that if IOS_1 exists, the firm would pay out $750,000 in dividends, since only $1,050,000 of the $1,800,000 of available earnings is needed. A 41.7 percent payout ratio results. For IOS_2, dividends of $120,000 (a payout ratio of 6.7 percent) results. Should IOS_3 exist, the firm would pay no dividends (a zero payout ratio), since its retained earnings of $1,800,000 are less than the $2,240,000 of earnings needed. In this case the firm would have to obtain additional new common stock financing to meet the new

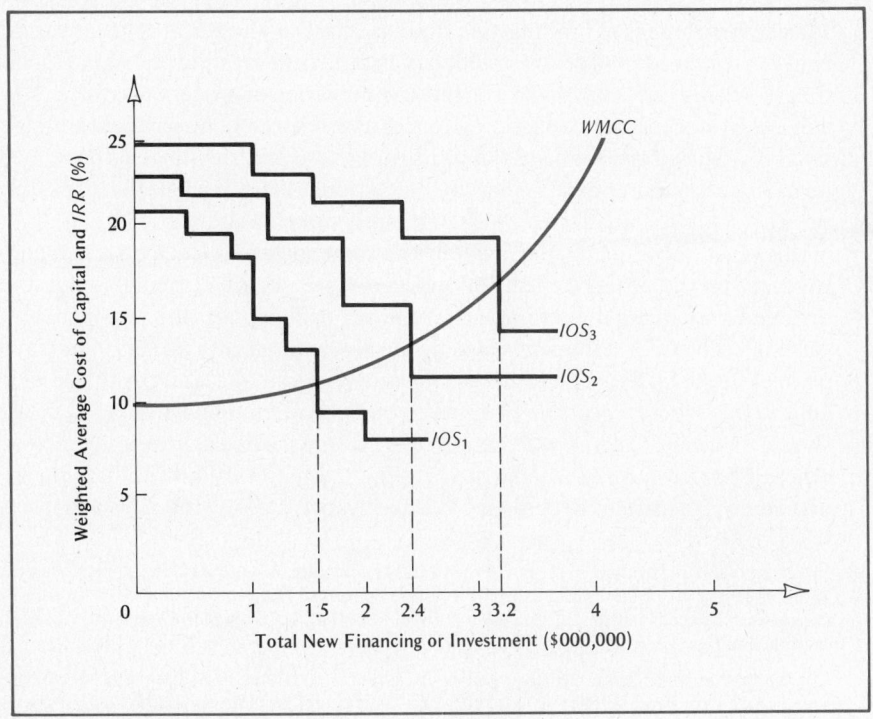

Figure 14.1   *WMCC* and *IOS*s for Suntime Industries

Table 14.3 Applying the Residual Theory of Dividends to Suntime Industries for Each of Three IOSs (shown in Figure 14.1)

Item	Investment opportunities schedules		
	IOS_1	IOS_2	IOS_3
(1) New financing or investment (Fig. 14.1)	$1,500,000	$2,400,000	$3,200,000
(2) Retained earnings available (given)	$1,800,000	$1,800,000	$1,800,000
(3) Equity needed [70% × (1)]	1,050,000	1,680,000	2,240,000
(4) Dividends [(2) − (3)]	$ 750,000	$ 120,000	$ 0[a]
(5) Dividend payout ratio [(4) ÷ (2)]	41.7%	6.7%	0%

[a] In this case additional new common stock in the amount of $440,000 ($2,240,000 needed − $1,800,000 available) would have to be sold; no dividends would be paid.

requirements generated by the intersection of the IOS_3 and *WMCC*. Depending on which *IOS* exists, the firm's dividend would in effect be the residual, if any, remaining after financing all acceptable investments. ■

The irrelevance of dividends. The residual theory of dividends tends to imply that dividends are irrelevant — that the value of the firm is independent of its dividend policy. The major advocates of this view are Franco Modigliani and Merton H. Miller (commonly referred to as M and M). They argue, for a variety of reasons and subject to a number of limiting assumptions, that the way a firm splits its earnings between dividends and reinvestment has no direct effect on value.[4] As part of their theory, Modigliani and Miller suggest the existence of a *clientele effect:* A firm will attract stockholders whose preferences with respect to the payment and stability of dividends correspond to the payment pattern and stability exhibited by the firm. Since the shareholders get what they expect, M and M argue that the value of the firm's stock is unaffected by changes in dividend policy.

However, recognizing that dividends do somehow affect stock prices, M and M suggest that the positive effects of dividend increases are attributable not to the dividend itself but to the *informational content* of dividends with respect to future earnings. The information provided by the dividends causes owners to bid up the price of the stock based on future expectations. M and M's arguments lead one to believe that when acceptable investment opportunities are not available, the firm should distribute the unneeded funds to the owners, who can invest the money in other firms that have acceptable investment alternatives. This residual theory of dividends is consistent with M and M's irrelevance theory.[5] It suggests that since,

[4] Because of the highly theoretical nature of M and M's work, detailed presentation and analysis are not appropriate as part of this initial exposure to these concepts. The interested reader is prompted to review an advanced managerial finance text. See, for example, Lawrence J. Gitman, Michael D. Joehnk, and George E. Pinches, *Managerial Finance* (New York: Harper & Row, 1985).

[5] In the case of small firms, the treatment of dividends as a residual remaining after all acceptable investments have been initiated is quite common. This occurs because small firms do not normally have ready access to capital markets. The use of retained earnings therefore acts as a key source of financing for growth, which is generally an important goal of a small firm.

DO DIVIDENDS REALLY MATTER?

Dividends may not be the stuff of suspense novels, but so far this year [1984] they have made headlines. A reinvigorated Chrysler reinstated its quarterly payout, American Telephone and Telegraph threatened to cut its dividend for the first time ever, two big utilities—Long Island Lighting and Public Service of New Hampshire—halted their common stock dividends, and just last week [May 1984], General Motors surprised Wall Street by raising its quarterly payout by 25 percent.

But whether dividends are actually good for shareholders is not altogether clear. While some old-line companies, such as General Electric, have paid dividends for years, rapid-growth, high-tech concerns, such as Apple Computer, often do not pay dividends at all. Nor is the meaning of dividend changes easy to decipher.

A dividend cut, for example, could be good news if a company is plowing back funds into promising ventures. Moreover, as the economy changes to high-technology oriented industry and as companies spend more on research and development, such a trend to leaner dividends could become more pronounced. Consequently, the American investing public may have to depend less on dividends for total returns.

In fact, there is a growing sentiment that the [role] of dividends should be played down and that cash payouts, because they are taxed more highly than long-term capital gains, are actually a very costly way to compensate shareholders.

"Why firms continue to pour out vast quantities of dividends in the face of these tax differentials is one of the great puzzles of our time," says Merton H. Miller, the Leon Carroll Marshall Professor of Finance at the University of Chicago.

In fact, for more than two decades, academicians, Wall Street professionals and corporate executives have struggled to understand the role of dividends in investing, and in particular to determine if companies might better serve shareholders by reinvesting profits.

Some, like Prof. Robert Litzenberger at Stanford University, have done studies suggesting that corporations might increase their stock prices by reducing dividends. Others, such as John F. Childs, a dividend expert at Kidder, Peabody & Company, argue that dividends are vital to cushion shareholders against losses and to signal managers' confidence—or lack of it—in their companies.

A third group, led by Professor Miller, argues that dividend policies usually do not matter—and sometimes can penalize shareholders. For the average investor, he says, bleeding out more cash in the form of dividends does not make shareholders any richer. And wealthy, high-tax-bracket individuals, he adds, are better off with a dollar of capital gains than with a dollar of dividends.

"Paying out funds as dividends may bring you applause for your generosity at the annual meeting from some of the odd-lot holders who have nothing better to do than eat a box lunch at your expense," Professor Miller says. "But it can be a considerable imposition on your upper-tax-bracket stockholders." . . .

It follows logically that when a company changes its dividend, it is sending a message to investors. A dividend increase signals that earnings are expected to rise, whereas a dividend cut means earnings are about to nosedive.

SOURCE: Eric N. Berg, "Rethinking the Meaning of Dividends," *The New York Times,* May 13, 1984, p. F-10.

given certain assumptions, dividends are irrelevant to the firm's value, the firm does not need to have a dividend policy.

The relevance of dividends. Another school of thought suggests that in the absence of M and M's limiting assumptions, their argument collapses. A key belief of those supporting dividend relevance is that because current dividend payments reduce investor uncertainty, investors will discount the firm's earnings at a lower rate, k_s, thereby placing a higher value on the firm's stock. If dividends are not paid, investor uncertainty will increase, raising the required rate of return, k_s, and lowering the stock's value.

The dividend relevance school's leading proponent, Myron J. Gordon, suggests that stockholders do have a preference for current dividends — that there is, in fact, a direct relationship between the dividend policy of a firm and its market value. Gordon argues that investors are generally risk averters and attach less risk to current as opposed to future dividends or capital gains. This "bird-in-the-hand" argument suggests that a firm's dividend policy is relevant since investors prefer some dividends now to reduce their uncertainty. When investors are less uncertain about their returns, they discount the firm's future earnings at a lower rate — therefore placing a higher value on the firm. The general behavior of business-people and investors seems to suggest that Gordon's arguments are more widely accepted in practice than are M and M's. Since our concern in this text is with the real-world behavior of business firms, the remainder of this chapter incorporates the general belief that dividends *are relevant* — that each firm must develop a dividend policy that fulfills the goals of owners and maximizes their wealth in the long run.

Factors Affecting Dividend Policy

Before discussing the objectives and types of dividend policies, we should consider the factors involved in formulating dividend policy. These include certain legal, contractual, and internal constraints; the firm's growth prospects; owner considerations; and market considerations.

LEGAL, CONTRACTUAL, AND INTERNAL CONSTRAINTS

The firm's dividend policy is often constrained by legal, contractual, and internal factors. The legal factors result from state and federal laws, the contractual constraints typically result from certain loan provisions, and the internal constraints are the result of the firm's liquid-asset position.

Legal constraints. Four basic legal constraints confront the corporation with respect to cash dividend payments: capital impairment, earnings, insolvency, and the accumulation of excess earnings.

Capital impairment. Most states prohibit corporations from paying out as cash dividends any portion of the firm's capital stock as measured by the par value of common stock. Other states define capital to include not only the par value of the common stock but also any paid-in capital in excess of par. Capital impairment restrictions are generally established to provide a sufficient equity base to protect creditors' claims. An example will clarify the different definitions of capital.

EXAMPLE   The Miller Flour Company balance sheet presented in Table 14.2 indicated that the firm has common stock with a par value of $100,000, paid-in capital in excess of par of $200,000, and retained earnings of $140,000. In states where the firm's capital is defined as the par value of its common stock, the firm could pay out $340,000 ($200,000 + $140,000) in cash dividends without impairing its capital. In states where the firm's capital includes all paid-in capital, the firm could pay out only $140,000 in cash dividends. ■

Earnings. The earnings requirement is similar to the capital impairment requirement in that it limits the amount of dividends to the sum of the firm's present and past earnings. In other words, the firm cannot pay more in cash dividends than the sum of its most recent and past retained earnings. This requirement has the same effect as the capital impairment rule. However, *the firm is not prohibited from paying more in dividends than its current earnings.*[6]

EXAMPLE   The Miller Flour Company's income statement, presented in Table 14.1, indicates that the firm currently has $40,000 in earnings available for common stock dividends. An analysis of the balance sheet in Table 14.1 indicates that the firm has past retained earnings of $100,000. Thus it could pay dividends of up to $140,000. ■

Insolvency. If a firm has overdue liabilities or is legally insolvent or bankrupt (if the fair market value of its assets is less than its liabilities), most states prohibit the payment of cash dividends. This restriction is intended to protect creditors by prohibiting the liquidation of a near-bankrupt firm through the payment of cash dividends to owners, which could seriously impair creditors' claims in bankruptcy.

The accumulation of excess earnings. The Internal Revenue Service prohibits firms from accumulating excess earnings. A firm's owners must pay income taxes on dividends when received, but the owners are not taxed on capital gains in market value until the stock is sold. A firm may retain a large portion of earnings in order to provide capital gain opportunities to the owners. If the IRS can determine that a firm has accumulated an excess of earnings to avoid ordinary income taxes, it may levy an *excess earnings accumulation tax* on any retained earnings above $250,000 — the amount currently exempt from this tax for all firms except personal corporations. A firm that has paid low or no cash dividends, has high retained earnings, and has a great deal of cash and marketable securities is a likely candidate for an IRS investigation. The federal government's dim view of a firm's retaining earnings so that owners can avoid income taxes is an incentive to pay dividends when attractive investment opportunities do not exist.

---

[6] A firm having an operating loss in the current period could still pay cash dividends as long as sufficient retained earnings were available and, of course, as long as it had the cash with which to make the payments.

Contractual constraints. Often the firm's ability to pay cash dividends is constrained by certain restrictive provisions in a term loan agreement, a bond indenture, a preferred stock agreement, or a lease contract. Generally, these contraints prohibit the payment of cash dividends until a certain level of earnings has been achieved or limit the amount of dividends paid to a certain amount or percentage of earnings. Constraints on dividend payments help to protect creditors, preferred stockholders, and lessors from losses due to insolvency on part of the firm. Contractual constraints on dividend payments are quite common, and their violation is generally grounds for a request for immediate repayment by the funds supplier affected.

Internal constraints. The firm's ability to pay cash dividends is generally constrained by the amount of excess cash available. Of course it is possible for a firm to borrow funds to pay dividends, but if borrowing were necessary, the minimum dividend would most likely be paid. Lenders are not especially interested in lending money for dividend payments, since they produce no tangible or operating benefits that will help the firm repay the loan. Although a firm may have high earnings, its ability to pay dividends may be constrained by a low level of liquid assets (cash and marketable securities).

EXAMPLE   The Miller Flour Company's financial statements, presented in Table 14.1, indicate that if the firm's capital is defined as all paid-in capital, the firm can pay $140,000 in dividends (since it has $100,000 in past retained earnings plus $40,000 in current earnings available for common stock). The firm has total liquid assets of $50,000 ($20,000 in cash plus marketable securities worth $30,000), but $35,000 of this is needed for operations. Therefore, the maximum dividend the firm can pay is $15,000. ■

GROWTH PROSPECTS

The firm must plan its needed financing in light of its growth prospects. The availability of outside financing and the exact timing of funds needs will greatly affect the need for retained earnings to finance growth. Two factors related to growth — financial requirements and the availability of funds — are discussed.

Financial requirements. The firm's financial requirements are directly related to the degree of asset expansion anticipated. If the firm is in a growth stage, it may need all the funds it can get to finance capital expenditures. A growing firm also requires funds to maintain and improve its assets. High-growth firms typically find themselves constantly in need of funds. Their financial requirements may be characterized as large and immediate. Firms exhibiting little or no growth may periodically need funds to replace or renew assets.

Availability of funds. A firm must evaluate its financial position from a profitability and a risk standpoint to develop insight into its ability to raise capital externally. It must determine not only its ability to raise funds but also the cost and speed with which financing can be obtained. Generally, a large, mature firm has greater access to new capital. For this reason, the funds available to a rapidly growing firm may not be sufficient to support the numerous acceptable projects. A growth firm is likely to have to depend heavily on internal financing through retained earnings to take advantage of profitable projects and is likely to pay out only a very small percentage of its earnings as dividends. However, not all growth firms are small, struggling enterprises; IBM is considered a growth firm with a low dividend payout.

A more stable firm that needs capital funds only for planned outlays is better advised to pay out a large proportion of its earnings, especially if it has ready sources of financing. The firm's owners, it is assumed, can earn a greater return on other investments. Only when the firm's external sources of funds are limited should it retain earnings for a planned future outlay.

OWNER CONSIDERATIONS

In establishing a dividend policy, the primary concern should be to maximize owners' wealth over the long run. Although it is impossible to establish a policy that will maximize each owner's wealth, the firm must establish a policy that has a favorable effect on the wealth of the majority of the owners. Three factors that must be considered are the tax status of the owners, the owners' investment opportunities, and the dilution of ownership.

Tax status of the firm's owners. The tax status of a firm's owners can have a significant effect on the firm's dividend policy. If a firm has a large percentage of wealthy stockholders who are in a high tax bracket, it may pay out a lower percentage of its earnings in order to provide its owners with income in the form of capital gains as opposed to dividends.[7] Since the capital gains tax rate is considerably less than the ordinary tax rate, these wealthy owners would find their tax liability reduced. Lower-income shareholders who need dividend income will prefer a higher payout of earnings.

It is quite difficult for the financial manager of a large, diversely held firm to know the tax status of the owners; he or she can base assessments only on feedback from directors and data obtained in the marketplace. If the directors believe a low dividend payout is preferable, any owners who disagree with this strategy can divest themselves of their holdings and purchase the stock of another firm.

Owner investment opportunities. A firm should not retain funds for investment in projects yielding lower returns than the owners could obtain from external investments of equal risk. The firm should evaluate the returns expected on its investment opportunities and, using present-value techniques, determine whether greater returns are obtainable from external investments such as government securities or other corporate stocks. If it appears that the owners have better opportunities externally, the firm should pay out a high percentage of its earnings. If the firm's investment opportunities are at least as good as similar-risk external investments, a low payout is justifiable. A firm should not retain funds in the form

---

[7] The consideration of the owners' tax status in making dividend policy decisions is illegal, although it is quite difficult for the IRS to police this law. Rather, the IRS will look for high retained earnings and high liquidity. Firms in this situation are penalized through an excess earnings accumulation tax. It is quite difficult, if not impossible, to determine the extent to which the tax status of a firm's owners affects dividend policy decisions.

of marketable securities in order to make some future outlay; rather, it should pay out these earnings now and raise the needed funds later when the outlay must be made.

Dilution of ownership. Since the most comparable alternative to the use of retained earnings as a source of equity financing is the sale of additional common stock, attention must be given to the dilution of ownership interests that may result from a high-payout policy. If a firm pays out a high percentage of earnings, new equity capital will have to be raised with common stock, which may result in the dilution of both control and earnings for the existing owners. By paying out a low percentage of its earnings, the firm can minimize the possibility of dilution.

It is most important that the stockholders recognize the firm's motives for retaining or paying out a large percentage of earnings. Although the ultimate dividend policy depends on numerous factors, the avoidance of shareholder discontent is important. If the shareholders become dissatisfied with the existing dividend policy, they may sell their shares, increasing the possibility that control of the firm will be seized by some outside group. The takeover of a firm is more likely when owners are dissatisfied with its dividend policy. It is the financial manager's responsibility to keep in touch with the owners' general attitude toward dividends.

MARKET CONSIDERATIONS

Since the wealth of the firm's owners is reflected in the market price of the firm's shares, an awareness of the market's probable response to certain types of policies is helpful in formulating a suitable dividend policy.

Fixed-dollar or increasing dividends. Stockholders are believed to value a fixed or increasing level of dividends as opposed to a fixed payout ratio. If the *payout ratio,* which is found by dividing the dividends per share by the earnings per share, is held constant, the shareholders may receive no dividends in lean periods and high dividends in fat ones. Since paying a fixed or increasing dividend eliminates uncertainty about the magnitude of dividends, the earnings of the firm are likely to be discounted at a lower rate and the value of the firm's stock is likely to remain at a reasonably high level.

Continuous dividend payments. The marketplace generally values not only a fixed or increasing dividend level but also a policy of continuous dividend payment. The continuous payment of cash dividends, regardless of their magnitude, reduces shareholder uncertainty and lowers the rate at which earnings are discounted. The net effect should be an increase in the market value of the firm's stock and therefore increased owners' wealth.

The informational content of dividends. A final market consideration is the informational content of dividends. Shareholders often view the firm's dividend payments as an indicator of future success. A stable, continuous dividend conveys to the owners that the firm is in good health and that there is no reason for concern. If the firm passes a dividend payment in a given period due to a loss or very low earnings, shareholders are quite likely to react unfavorably. The nonpayment of the dividend creates uncertainty about the future, and this uncertainty is likely to result in lower stock values. When current earnings are temporarily low, a firm should continue its dividend payment to avoid conveying negative information to owners and prospective investors. Owners and investors generally construe a dividend payment during a period of losses as an indication that the loss is temporary.

The marketplace views the firm's dividends as a source of information. The firm should attempt to develop a dividend policy that provides owners and prospective investors with positive and correct information, thus reducing uncertainty about the firm's future. By paying fixed or increasing dividends on a continuous basis, the firm gives its owners a feeling of confidence.

Objectives and Types of Dividend Policies

It is the responsibility of the financial manager and the board of directors to establish a dividend policy that best fulfills the firm's overall objectives. This section discusses the basic objectives of dividend policy and the most common types of policies.

OBJECTIVES OF DIVIDEND POLICY

The firm's dividend policy represents a plan of action to be followed whenever the dividend decision must be made. The policy must be formulated with two basic objectives in mind—maximizing the wealth of the firm's owners and providing for sufficient financing. These objectives are interrelated. They must be fulfilled in light of a number of constraints—legal, contractual, internal, growth, owner-related, and market-related—that limit the alternatives available to the decision maker when establishing dividend policy.

Wealth maximization. The firm's dividend policy must be designed not merely to maximize the share price in the coming year but to maximize wealth in the *long run,* since the firm is assumed to have an infinite life. Of course, theoretically we expect that shareholders and prospective investors will recognize the long-run effects of a dividend policy on their ownership and that this recognition will be reflected in the level of future returns they forecast. In actuality, owners are often not fully aware of the implications of certain dividend policies, and as a result their actions may cause the stock price to drop. It is the responsibility of the firm's management to make the owners aware of the objectives and implications of dividend policy so that the market reaction is favorable.

Providing for sufficient financing. Without sufficient financing to implement acceptable projects, the wealth maximization process cannot be carried out. The firm must forecast its future funds needs and, taking into account the external availability of funds and certain market considerations, determine both the amount of equity financing needed and the amount of retained earnings available *after* the minimum dividends have been paid. Most businesspeople and investors accept the view that dividend policy is relevant. In other words, *dividend payments generally are not viewed as a residual but rather as a required outlay,* after which any remaining funds can be reinvested in the firm. In investing retained earnings in profitable projects and paying out only "extra," or residual, retained earnings, the financial manager is attaching little importance to the cash dividend. Only in rare instances should the firm cut its dividend in order to obtain funds. The important point to remember here is that the amount of retained-earnings financing available must be forecast on an *after-dividend basis* because the market can be expected to react adversely to the unanticipated decline in or absence of cash dividends.

TYPES OF DIVIDEND POLICIES

Although an infinite number of possible dividend policies are available to the business firm, most have one of a number of basic features. Three of the more commonly used policies are a constant-payout-ratio dividend policy, a regular dividend policy, and a low-regular-and-extra dividend policy. A particular firm's cash dividend policy may incorporate elements of each.

Constant-payout-ratio dividend policy. One type of dividend policy occasionally adopted by firms is the use of a constant payout ratio.[8] With a *constant-payout-ratio dividend policy,* the firm simply establishes a certain percentage of earnings to be paid out each period. The problem with this policy is that if the firm's earnings drop or a loss occurs in a given period, the dividends will be low or even nonexistent. Since dividends are often considered a source of information about the firm's future, the firm's stock may be adversely affected by this type of action. An example will clarify the problems stemming from a constant-payout-ratio policy.

EXAMPLE　The Nader Motor Company has a policy of paying out 40 percent of earnings in cash dividends. In periods when a loss occurs, the firm's policy is to pay no cash dividends. Nader's earnings per share, dividends per share, and average price per share for the past six years were as follows:

Year	Earnings/share	Dividends/share	Average price/share
1979	$4.50	$1.80	$50.00
1980	2.00	0.80	46.00
1981	−1.50	0.00	38.00
1982	1.75	0.70	48.00
1983	3.00	1.20	52.00
1984	−0.50	0.00	42.00

Dividends increased in 1981–1982 and 1982–1983 and decreased in 1979–1980, 1980–1981, and 1983–1984. It can be seen that in years of decreased dividends, the firm's stock price dropped; when dividends increased, the price of the stock increased. Nader's sporadic

---

[8] The *payout ratio,* by definition, is the firm's cash dividend per share divided by its earnings per share. It indicates the percentage of each dollar earned that is distributed to the owners in the form of cash.

A HISTORIC LOOK AT DIVIDENDS AND CASH FLOW

As can be seen in the graph, corporations have been paying out a lower proportion of their cash flow (earnings after taxes plus depreciation) than they once did. Because of much improved cash flows, firms are expected to boost payments in 1984 and into 1985.

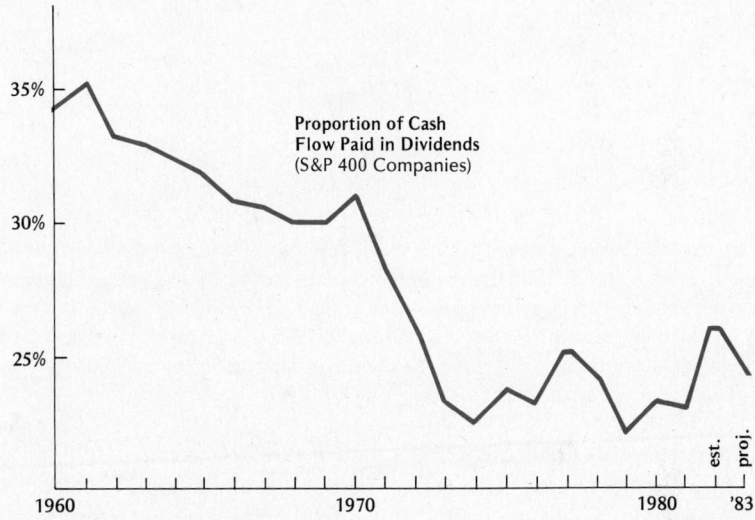

Proportion of Cash
Flow Paid in Dividends
(S&P 400 Companies)

SOURCE: Graph from Elizabeth S. Silverman, "Good Times Ahead for Dividends," *Fortune,* December 26, 1983, p. 167.

dividend payments appear to make its owners uncertain about the returns they can expect from their investment in the firm and therefore generally depress the stock's price. Although a constant-payout-ratio dividend policy is used by some firms, it is *not* recommended. ■

Regular dividend policy. Another type of dividend policy is based on the payment of a fixed-dollar dividend in each period. The *regular dividend policy* provides the owners with generally positive information indicating that the firm is okay, thereby minimizing their uncertainty. Often, firms using this policy will increase the regular dividend once a *proven* increase in earnings has occurred. Under this policy, dividends are almost never decreased. An example will clarify how a regular dividend policy works.

EXAMPLE   The Tulsa Oil Company's dividend policy is to pay annual dividends of $1.00 per share until per-share earnings have exceeded $4.00 for three consecutive years, at which time the annual dividend is raised to $1.50 per share and a new earnings plateau established. The firm does not anticipate decreasing its dividend unless its liquidity is in jeopardy. Tulsa's earnings per share, dividends per share, and average price per share for the past 12 years were as follows:

Year	Earnings/share	Dividends/share	Average price/share
1973	$3.00	$1.00	$35.00
1974	2.80	1.00	33.50
1975	0.50	1.00	33.00
1976	0.75	1.00	33.00
1977	3.00	1.00	36.00
1978	6.00	1.00	38.00
1979	2.00	1.00	38.50
1980	5.00	1.00	42.00
1981	4.20	1.00	43.00
1982	4.60	1.50	45.00
1983	3.90	1.50	46.50
1984	4.50	1.50	47.50

It can be seen that regardless of the level of earnings, Tulsa paid dividends of $1.00 per share through 1981. In 1982 the dividend was raised to $1.50 per share, since earnings of $4.00 per share had been achieved for three years. In 1982 the firm would also have had to establish a new earnings plateau for further dividend increases. Tulsa Oil Company's average price per share exhibited a stable, increasing behavior in spite of a somewhat volatile pattern of earnings. ■

Often, a regular dividend policy is built around a *target dividend-payout ratio.* The firm attempts to pay out a certain percentage of earnings, but rather than let dividends fluctuate, it pays a stated dollar dividend and adjusts it toward the target payout as proven increases in earnings occur. For instance, the Tulsa Oil Company appears to have a target payout ratio of around 35 percent. The payout was about 33 percent ($1.00 ÷ $3.00) when the dividend policy was set in 1973, and the dividend was raised to $1.50 (about a 35 percent payout ratio during 1982–1984) when per-share earnings exceeded $4.00. The use of a target payout ratio with a regular dividend policy is not unusual.

Low-regular-and-extra dividend policy. Some firms establish a *low-regular-and-extra dividend policy* — policy of a low regular dividend, supplemented by an additional dividend when earnings warrant it. If earnings are higher than normal in a given period, the firm may pay this additional dividend, which will be designated an *extra dividend.* By designating the amount by which the dividend exceeds the regular payment as an extra dividend, the firm avoids giving existing and prospective shareholders false hopes. The use of the "extra" designation is especially common among companies that experience cyclical shifts in earnings.

By establishing a low regular dividend that is paid each period, the firm gives investors the stable income necessary to build confidence in the firm, while the extra dividend permits them to share in the spoils if the firm experiences an especially good period. Firms using this policy must raise the level of the regular dividend once proven increases in earnings have been achieved. The extra dividend should not be a regular event, or it becomes meaningless. The use of a target payout ratio in establishing the regular dividend level is advisable.

Other Forms of Dividends

A number of other forms of dividends are available to the firm. One uncommon approach, which will not be discussed here, is the payment of dividends in merchandise produced by the firm. We will discuss two other methods of paying dividends — stock dividends and stock repurchases — as well as a closely related topic, stock splits. Stock dividends are easily recognizable as a dividend payment. Stock splits, although not strictly a form of dividend payment, have a similar effect on the firm. The repurchase of stock also has an effect similar to the payment of cash dividends, since it can be viewed as an alternative method of distributing funds to the firm's owners.

STOCK DIVIDENDS

Often, firms pay stock dividends as a replacement for or a supplement to cash dividends. Although stock dividends do not have a real value, stockholders may perceive them to represent something they did not have before and therefore have value. By definition, a *stock dividend* is a payment of stock to existing owners.

Accounting aspects. In an accounting sense, the payment of a stock dividend is a shifting of funds between capital accounts rather than a use of funds. When a firm declares a stock dividend, the general procedures with respect to announcement and distribution are the same as those described earlier for a cash dividend. The difference is that the owner receives additional stock, which in actuality represents something he or she already owns. It does not change the shareholder's proportional ownership or increase the assets of the firm. An example of the accounting entries associated with the payment of stock dividends is given in the following example.

EXAMPLE   The J and L Company's current stockholders' equity on its balance sheet is as follows:

Preferred Stock	$ 300,000
Common stock (100,000 shares at $4 par)	400,000
Paid-in capital in excess of par	600,000
Retained earnings	700,000
Total stockholders' equity	$2,000,000

If J and L declares a 10 percent stock dividend and the market price of its stock is $15 per share, $150,000 (10% × 100,000 shares × $15 per share) of retained earnings will be capitalized. The $150,000 will be distributed between common stock and paid-in capital in excess of par accounts based on the par value of the common stock. The resulting account balances are as follows:

Preferred Stock	$ 300,000
Common stock (110,000 shares at $4 par)	440,000
Paid-in capital in excess of par	710,000
Retained earnings	550,000
Total stockholders' equity	$2,000,000

Obviously, the stockholders' equity has not changed as a result of the payment of a 10 percent stock dividend. Since 10,000 (10 percent of 100,000) new shares have been issued and the prevailing market price is $15 per share, $150,000 ($15 per share × 10,000 shares) has been shifted from retained earnings to the common stock and paid-in capital accounts. A total of $40,000 ($4 par × 10,000 shares) has been added to common stock, and the remaining $110,000 [($15 − $4) × 10,000 shares] has been added to the paid-in capital in excess of par. The firm's stockholders' equity has not changed; funds have only been redistributed among stockholders' equity accounts. ■

Since certain legal constraints relating to capital impairment and earnings may limit cash dividend payments, it is important to recognize that since the payment of stock dividends reduces the firm's retained earnings, it reduces the aggregate amount of cash dividends that can be paid out. Because the availability of cash is typically more binding on the firm's ability to pay cash dividends, the reduction of retained earnings as the result of stock dividend payments generally does not affect the firm unfavorably.

The shareholder's viewpoint. The shareholder receiving a stock dividend receives nothing of value. After the dividend is paid, the per-share value of the shareholder's stock will decrease in proportion to the dividend in such a way that the market value of his or her total holdings in the firm will remain unchanged. The shareholder's proportion of ownership in the firm will also remain the same, and as long as the firm's earnings remain unchanged, so will his or her share of total earnings. An example will clarify this point.

EXAMPLE   Mr. X owned 10,000 shares of the J and L Company's stock. The company's most recent earnings were $220,000, and earnings are not expected to change in the near future. Before the stock dividend, Mr. X owned 10 percent (10,000 shares ÷ 100,000 shares) of the firm's stock, which was selling for $15 per share. Earnings per share were $2.20 ($220,000 ÷ 100,000 shares). Since Mr. X owns 10,000 shares, his earnings were $22,000 ($2.20 per share × 10,000 shares). After receiving the 10 percent stock dividend, Mr. X has 11,000 shares, which again is 10 percent (11,000 shares ÷ 110,000 shares) of the ownership. The market price of the stock can be expected to drop to $13.64 per share [$15 × (1.00 ÷ 1.10)], which means that the market value of Mr. X's holdings will be $150,000 (11,000 shares × $13.64 per share). This is the same as the initial value of his holdings (10,000 shares × $15 per share). The future earnings per share will drop to $2 ($220,000 ÷ 110,000 shares), since the same $220,000 in earnings must now be divided among 110,000 shares. Since Mr. X still owns 10 percent of the stock, his share of total earnings is still $22,000 ($2 per share × 11,000 shares). In summary, if the firm's earnings remain constant and total cash dividends do not increase, a stock dividend will result in a lower per-share market value for the firm's stock. ■

Sometimes when a firm that has been paying cash dividends issues a stock dividend, it will maintain the cash dividend per share, thereby increasing the total dividends paid out, since more shares are outstanding. This type of action actually represents an increase in dividends and may result in an increased market value for the firm's stock. The effect is somewhat dependent on the existing investment opportunities and the firm's funds needs. Another plus for the stock dividend is its informational content. Although it has no current value, the stock dividend may indicate to owners that if the firm retains and reinvests its earnings, its earnings will grow enough to more than offset the decreased per-share market value and earnings resulting from the payment of the stock dividend.

The company's viewpoint. Stock dividends are more costly to issue than cash dividends, but the advantages generally outweigh these costs. Firms find the stock dividend a means of giving owners something without having to use cash. Generally, when a firm is growing rapidly and needs internal financing to perpetuate this growth, a stock dividend is used. As long as the investors recognize that the firm is reinvesting its earnings in a manner that should tend to maximize future earnings, the market value of the firm should at least remain unchanged. If the stock dividend is paid so that cash can be retained to satisfy past-due bills, a decline in market value may result.

STOCK SPLITS

Although not a type of dividend, *stock splits* have an effect on a firm's share price similar to that of stock dividends. Stock splits are commonly used to lower the market price of a firm's stock. Quite often, a firm believes that its stock is priced too high and that lowering the market price will enhance trading activity. Stock splits are often made prior to new issues of a stock to enhance the marketability of the stock and stimulate market activity.

A stock split has no effect on the firm's financial structure. It commonly increases the number of shares outstanding and reduces the stock's per-share par value. In other words, when a stock is split, a specified number of new shares are exchanged for a given number of outstanding shares. In a 2-for-1 split, two new shares are exchanged for each old share; in a 3-for-2 split, three new shares are exchanged for each two old shares, and so on.

EXAMPLE The Krantz Company had 200,000 shares of $2 par-value common stock and no preferred stock outstanding. Since the stock is selling at a high market price, the firm has declared a 2-for-1 stock split. The total before- and after-split stockholders' equity is given below.

Before split	
Common stock (200,000 shares outstanding with a $2 par value)	$ 400,000
Paid-in capital in excess of par	4,000,000
Retained earnings	2,000,000
Total stockholders' equity	$6,400,000

After 2-for-1 split	
Common stock (400,000 shares outstanding with a $1 par value)	$ 400,000
Paid-in capital in excess of par	4,000,000
Retained earnings	2,000,000
Total stockholders' equity	$6,400,000

The insignificant effect of the stock split on the firm's books is obvious. ∎

Stock can be split in any way desired. Sometimes *reverse stock splits* are made: a certain number of outstanding shares are exchanged for one new share. For example, in a 1-for-2 split, one new share is exchanged for two old shares; in a 2-for-3 split, two new shares are exchanged for three old shares, and so on. Reverse stock splits are initiated when a stock is selling at too low a price to appear respectable.[9]

It is not unusual for a stock split to cause a slight increase in the market value of the stock. This is attributable to the informational content of stock splits and the fact that *total* dividends paid commonly increase slightly after a split.

The stock dividend, since it does tend to lower the price of a firm's shares, has an effect similar to that of a stock split. A lower per-share price may mean increased trading activity in the stock. However, the use of stock dividends to lower the market price of shares must be considered as only a collateral objective. The primary use of stock dividends, from the firm's viewpoint, is as a means of avoiding paying out cash while still giving owners a type of psychological or informational income; the primary objective of a stock split is to stimulate trading activity in the firm's shares.

STOCK REPURCHASES

In the recent past, firms have increased their repurchasing of shares of outstanding common stock in the marketplace. Such *stock repurchases* are made for a number of reasons: to obtain shares to be used in acquisitions, to have shares available for stock option plans, to achieve a gain in the book value of equity when shares are selling below their book value, or merely to retire outstanding shares. This section is concerned with the repurchase of shares for retirement, since this type of repurchase is similar to the payment of cash dividends.

Accounting entries. The accounting entries that result when common stock is repurchased are a reduction in cash and the establishment of an asset account called "treasury stock," which is typically shown as a deduction from stockholders' equity. The label *treasury stock* is used to indicate the presence of repurchased shares on the balance sheet. The repurchase of stock can be viewed as a cash dividend, since it involves the distribution of cash to the firm's owners, who are the sellers of the shares.

Motives for the retirement of shares. When common stock is repurchased for retirement, the underlying motive is to distribute excess cash to the owners. Retiring stock means that the owners receive cash for their shares. The general rationale for this action is that as long as earnings remain constant, the repurchase of shares reduces the number of outstanding shares, raising the earnings per share and therefore the market price per share. The retirement of common stock can be viewed as a type of

---

[9] If a firm's stock is selling at a low price — possibly less than a few dollars — many investors are hesitant to purchase it because they believe it is "cheap." These somewhat unsophisticated investors correlate cheapness and quality, and they feel that a low-priced stock is a low-quality investment. A reverse stock split raises the stock price and increases per-share earnings.

reverse dilution, since the earnings per share and the market price of stock are increased by reducing the number of shares outstanding. A simple example will clarify this point.

EXAMPLE   The Terrell Company has released the following financial data:

Earnings available for common stockholders	$1,000,000
Number of shares of common outstanding	400,000
Earnings per share ($1,000,000 ÷ 400,000)	$2.50
Market price per share	$50
Price/earnings ratio ($50 ÷ $2.50)	20

The firm is contemplating paying cash dividends of $2 per share, which will raise the price of the stock to $52 (since the market price is currently $50) while the stock is selling with dividends on. The total amount of dividends to be paid by the firm will be $800,000 (400,000 shares × $2 per share). However, instead of paying $800,000 in cash dividends, the firm could repurchase stock at $52 per share. With $800,000, it could repurchase approximately 15,385 shares ($800,000 ÷ $52 per share). As a result of this repurchase, 384,615 shares (400,000 shares − 15,385 shares) of common stock would remain outstanding. Earnings per share would rise to $2.60 ($1,000,000 ÷ 384,615), and if the stock still sold at 20 times earnings, its market price would rise to $52 per share. The market price per share would be the same, $52, regardless of whether the cash dividend was paid[10] or stock was repurchased.

The impact of the stock repurchase illustrated is attributable to two key assumptions: (1) The shares could be repurchased at $52 each, and (2) the price/earnings ratio remains at 20 in either case (cash dividend or repurchase). If the firm were to buy the shares for less than $52, the remaining shareholders would gain, while at more than $52, the remaining shareholders would lose. If the price/earnings ratio rose as a result of repurchase, the remaining shareholders would gain, and if it were to drop, they would lose. In other words, the assumptions made with respect to the repurchase price and the price/earnings ratio significantly affect the analysis of a proposed stock repurchase in lieu of paying cash dividends. ■

The advantages of stock repurchases are an increase in per-share earnings and certain tax benefits. The tax advantage stems from the fact that if the cash dividend is paid, the owners will have to pay ordinary income taxes on it, whereas the $2 increase in the market value of the stock due to the repurchase will be taxable at the more favorable long-term capital gains rate (assuming that the stock has been held for at least six months). The IRS allegedly watches firms that regularly repurchase stock and levies a penalty if it believes the repurchases have been made to shield the stockholders from taxes. Enforcement in this area appears to be relatively lax.

Although the use of repurchases to retire shares is commonly viewed as a dividend decision, some people view it as an investment or a financing decision. A stock repurchase is an investment decision in the sense that the firm has excess

---

[10] When the stock is selling with dividends on, its price would be $52; once the dividend is paid, the stock price would drop by the $2-per-share dividend to $50. Of course, the shareholders would have gained the $2 per share dividend, while in the case of the repurchase, the remaining shareholders would have experienced a $2-per-share increase in the market price (from $50 to $52 per share).

THE BENEFITS OF STOCK REPURCHASES

At the end of 1971, Teledyne had the equivalent of 88.8 million common shares outstanding, earned 61 cents a share and the stock was selling for $8. Then Teledyne began buying back its stock. By the end of this week [May 27, 1984], after its eighth such repurchase in the past 13 years, Teledyne will have only about 15 million shares outstanding, earnings of about $20 a share and a stock price of almost $200—a 2,300 percent appreciation from 1971.

Teledyne's case may be somewhat unique, but in our opinion its stock appreciation is not a market fluke. Rather, it is the result of astute financial management. If that assessment is correct, then the current recovery in corporate profits combined with the tax savings being derived from the 1981 Economic Recovery [Tax] Act should make many companies consider such unconventional methods as stock repurchases to build sagging shareholder value.

And indeed, some other companies are following suit. Eastman Kodak this month [May 1984] announced the first stock buyback in its history, and just last Tuesday [May 22, 1984], the Standard Oil Company (Indiana) announced the largest stock repurchase ever—a $1.7 billion offer for 10.3 percent of its shares. . . .

But the benefits of repurchase are more than just a communications tool. They are based on financial precepts that every business should follow and those are to minimize the tax impact for the shareholder and to seek the highest return on investment. The shareholder's return on a repurchase comes in the form of a capital gain which is taxed at a maximum capital gains rate of 20 percent, instead of at the marginal ordinary income rate, which can reach 50 percent on cash dividends. The company also saves the dividend on the repurchased shares.

The benefits of repurchase also go beyond the predictable rewards to the shareholders. Repurchases benefit the economy as a whole by liberating redundant capital to move to other uses in faster-growing industries, thereby creating greater employment and improved economic well-being for all.

SOURCE: Michael Sherman and Michael Seely, "The Wisdom of Stock Buy-Backs," *The New York Times,* May 27, 1984, p. F-3.

cash but no acceptable investment opportunities except to repurchase shares. This can be thought of as an investment in the company's own shares, which in the long run should help to maximize the remaining owners' wealth. The retirement of stock through repurchase may be considered a financing decision in the sense that it enables the firm to shift its debt ratio to a more highly levered position. When debt or preferred stock is used to raise funds for a repurchase of shares, it is more likely to be viewed as a financing decision.

The repurchase process. When a company intends to repurchase a block of outstanding shares, it should make shareholders aware of its intentions. Specifically, it should advise them of the purpose of the repurchase (acquisitions, stock options, gain in book value, retirement, and so forth) and the disposition (if any) planned for the repurchased shares (traded for shares of another firm, distribution to executives, held in the treasury, and so forth). Three basic methods of repurchase are commonly used. One is to purchase shares on the *open market.* This places upward pressure on the price of shares if the number of shares being repurchased is reasonably large in comparison with the total number outstanding. The second method is through tender offers.[11] A *tender offer* is a formal offer by the firm to purchase a given number of shares at a specified price. The price at which a tender offer is made is set above the current market price in order to attract sellers. If the number of shares desired cannot be repurchased through the tender offer, open-market purchases can be used to obtain the additional shares. Tender offers are preferred when large numbers of shares are repurchased since the company's intentions are clearly stated and each stockholder has an opportunity to sell his or her shares at the tendered price. The third method sometimes used to repurchase shares involves arranging to purchase on a *negotiated basis* a large block of shares from one or more major stockholders. Again, in this case the firm would have to state its intentions and make certain that the purchase price is fair and equitable in view of the interests and opportunities of the remaining shareholders.

CHAPTER SUMMARY

● Any earnings remaining after cash dividends have been paid become retained earnings, which represent reinvested funds. Because retained earnings are a source of long-term financing, the dividend decision is sometimes considered a financing decision. Retained earnings are therefore often viewed as a fully subscribed issue of additional common stock, since they represent new ownership capital.

● The cash dividend decision is normally a quarterly decision made by the corporate board of directors. The amount (if any) of dividends is set by the board, which establishes the record date and payment date.

● Many firms offer dividend reinvestment plans that allow stockholders to acquire shares, in lieu of cash dividends, at an attractive price. Special tax benefits are available on the dividend reinvestment plans of public utilities.

● The residual theory of dividends suggests that the firm determines the optimal capital structure and uses retained earnings to the extent that they are available to meet equity needs. Any unused retained earnings would be paid out as dividends. This theory suggests that dividends are irrelevant.

● Another school of thought argues that dividends are relevant and are an important factor in maximizing owners' wealth. Paying dividends reduces the owners' uncertainty concerning the future of the firm, causing them to discount its earnings at a lower rate. The effect of this lower discount rate is to raise the market value of the firm's stock.

● Certain factors must be considered in setting dividend policy. State laws prohibit paying out capital, which is defined either as the par value of the stock or all paid-in capital. Some laws limit dividends to an amount equal to current and past retained earnings only. Most states prohibit insolvent firms from paying cash dividends. Loan provisions, bond indentures, preferred stock agreements, and lease contracts often limit dividends. The amount of cash and marketable securities a firm has often acts as an internal constraint. Other factors that require consideration are growth prospects, owners' tax status, owners' other investment opportunities, dilution, and certain market considerations.

---

[11]Tender offers are discussed in greater detail in Chapter 23. The motive for these offers may be to acquire control of another firm rather than to tender the firm's own shares.

● The firm must establish a dividend policy that maximizes the wealth of its owners in the long run while allowing it sufficient financing to perpetuate itself.

● Commonly used dividend policies include a constant payout ratio, regular dividends, or low-regular-and-extra dividends. Most firms try to establish dividend policies that will not require them to decrease dividends.

● Occasionally, firms may pay stock dividends, which involves capitalizing retained earnings.

● Although not a type of dividend, stock splits, which are used to enhance trading activity in a firm's shares, are sometimes initiated. They tend to have effects similar to those of a stock dividend in that they most often increase the number of shares outstanding without providing any inflow of new capital.

● Another method similar to paying cash dividends is stock repurchases. Firms having excess cash can repurchase and retire stock in order to increase the earnings and market price per share.

● Some firms repurchase stock for acquisitions, for stock options, to achieve a gain in book value, or for retirement.

● Making stock repurchases in lieu of cash dividend payments may provide tax benefits to the firm's owners by providing them with long-term capital gains income instead of ordinary income, which would be taxed at a higher rate.

● Stock repurchases can be made directly in the open market, through tender offers, or on a negotiated basis from holders of large blocks of shares.

KEY TERMS

clientele effect	payment date (dividend)
constant-payout-ratio dividend policy	payout ratio
cum dividends	regular dividend policy
date of record	residual theory of dividends
dividends on	reverse stock split
dividend reinvestment plan	stock dividend
ex dividend	stock repurchase
excess earnings accumulation tax	stock split
extra dividend	target dividend-payout ratio
holders of record	tender offer
informational content (dividends)	treasury stock
low-regular-and-extra dividend policy	

QUESTIONS

14-1 How are retained earnings a source of funds to the business firm? If earnings were not retained, what might the financial consequences for the firm be?

14-2 How do the date of record and the holders of record relate to the payment of cash dividends? What do the terms *ex dividend* and *dividends on,* or *cum dividends,* mean? Who sets the dividend payment date?

14-3 What is a *dividend reinvestment plan*? Describe the two ways companies can handle such plans. What special benefit is available on public utility dividend reinvestment plans?

14-4 Describe the *residual theory of dividends.* Would following this approach lead to a stable dividend? Explain.

14-5 What are the two key positions with respect to the relevance of dividend policy? Explain.

14-6 What are some *contractual and internal constraints* on the firm's ability to pay dividends? Why do contractual constraints exist?

14-7   Why must the firm's dividend policy be based on its growth prospects?

14-8   What are the two broad objectives of dividend policies? Are these objectives mutually exclusive? Why or why not?

14-9   What are (1) a constant-payout-ratio dividend policy, (2) a regular dividend policy,
and (3) a low-regular-and-extra dividend policy? What are the ramifications of
these policies?

14-10   If it is more costly to issue stock than to pay cash dividends, why do firms issue *stock
dividends?* Are there any similarities between stock dividends and stock splits?
What are they?

14-11   What is a *stock split?* Compare a stock split with a stock dividend. What is a *reverse
stock split?*

14-12   What is the logic behind *repurchasing shares* of common stock to redistribute
excess cash to the firm's owners? How might this raise the per-share earnings and
market price of outstanding shares?

PROBLEMS

14-1   **(Dividend Payment Procedures)**   Wisconsin Widget, at the quarterly dividend
meeting, declared a cash dividend of $1.10 per share for holders of record on
Monday, July 10. The firm has 300,000 shares of common stock outstanding and
has set a payment date of July 31. Prior to the dividend declaration, the firm's key
accounts were as follows:

Cash	$500,000	Dividends payable	$ 0
		Retained earnings	2,500,000

    a   Show the entries after the meeting adjourned.
    b   When is the ex dividend date?
    c   After the July 31 payment date, what values would the key accounts have?
    d   What effect, if any, will the dividend have on the firm's total assets?

14-2   **(Residual Dividend Policy)**   As president of Jensen's of California, a large clothing chain, you have just received a letter from a major stockholder. The stockholder
asks about the company's dividend policy. In fact, the stockholder has asked you to
estimate the amount of the dividend you are likely to pay next year. You have not
yet collected all the information about the expected dividend payment, but you do
know the following:
    (1)   The company will follow a residual dividend policy.
    (2)   The total capital budget for next year is likely to be one of three amounts,
depending on the results of capital budgeting studies currently under way.
The capital expenditure amounts are $2 million, $3 million, and $4 million.
    (3)   The forecasted level of potential retained earnings next year is between $2
million and $2.5 million.
    (4)   The target or optimal capital structure is a debt ratio of 40 percent.
You have decided to respond by sending the stockholder the best information
available to you.
    a   Describe a residual dividend policy.
    b   There are three possible capital expenditure levels and two extremes for the
level of potential retained earnings, making a total of six possible combinations.
Compute the amount of the dividend (or the amount of new equity needed) and
the dividend payout ratio for each combination.

14-3   **(Dividend Constraints)**   The Big D Company's stockholders' equity account is as
follows:

Preferred stock	$ 500,000
Common stock (400,000 shares at $4 par value)	1,600,000
Paid-in capital in excess of par	1,000,000
Retained earnings	1,900,000
Total stockholders' equity	$5,000,000

The earnings available for common stockholders from this period's operations are $100,000, which have been included as part of the $1.9 million retained earnings.

a What is the maximum dividend per share the firm can pay? (Assume that capital includes *all* paid-in capital.)

b If the firm has $160,000 in cash, what is the largest per-share dividend it can pay without borrowing?

c Indicate the accounts and changes, if any, that will result if the firm pays the dividends indicated in **a** and **b**.

d Indicate the effects of an $80,000 cash dividend on stockholders' equity.

14-4 **(Dividend Constraints)**   A firm has $800,000 in paid-in capital, retained earnings of $40,000 (including the current year's earnings), and 25,000 shares of common stock outstanding. It earned $29,000 after taxes and preferred stock dividends in the most recent year.

a What is the most the firm can pay in cash dividends to each common shareholder? (Assume that capital includes *all* paid-in capital.)

b What effect would a cash dividend of $.80 per share have on the firm's balance sheet entries?

c If the firm cannot raise any new funds from external sources, what do you consider the key constraint with respect to the magnitude of the firm's dividend payments? Why?

14-5 **(Alternative Dividend Policies)**   A firm has had the indicated earnings per share over the past 10 years:

Year	Earnings per share
1984	$4.00
1983	3.80
1982	3.20
1981	2.80
1980	3.20
1979	2.40
1978	1.20
1977	1.80
1976	−0.50
1975	0.25

a If the firm's dividend policy was based on a constant payout ratio of 40 percent for all years with positive earnings and a zero payout otherwise, determine the annual dividend for each year.

b If the firm had a dividend payout of $1.00 per share, increasing by $.10 per share whenever the dividend payout fell below 50 percent for two consecutive years, what annual dividend did the firm pay each year?

c If the firm's policy was to pay $.50 per share each period except when earnings per share exceed $3.00, when an extra dividend equal to 80 percent of earnings beyond $3.00 would be paid, what annual dividend did the firm pay each year?

d Discuss the pros and cons of each dividend policy described in **a** through **c**.

14-6 **(Alternative Dividend Policies)** Given the following earnings per share over the period 1977–1984 determine the annual dividend per share under each of the policies set forth in **a** through **d**.

Year	Earnings per share
1984	$1.40
1983	1.56
1982	1.20
1981	−0.85
1980	1.05
1979	0.60
1978	1.00
1977	0.44

  a Pay out 50 percent of earnings in all years with positive earnings.

  b Pay $.50 per share and increase to $.60 per share whenever earnings per share rise above $.90 per share for two consecutive years.

  c Pay $.50 per share except when earnings exceed $1.00 per share, when there would be an extra dividend of 60 percent of earnings above $1.00 per share.

  d Combine policies in **b** and **c**. When the dividend is raised (in **b**), raise the excess dividend base (in **c**) from $1.00 to $1.10 per share.

  e Compare and contrast each of the dividend policies described in **a** through **d**.

14-7 **(Stock Dividend — Firm)** FMA has a stockholders' equity account, given here. The firm's common stock has a current market price of $30 per share.

Preferred stock	$100,000
Common stock (10,000 shares at $2 par)	20,000
Paid-in capital in excess of par	280,000
Retained earnings	100,000
Total stockholders' equity	$500,000

  a Show the effects on FMA of a 5 percent stock dividend.

  b Show the effects of (1) a 10 percent and (2) a 20 percent stock dividend.

  c In light of your answers to **a** and **b**, discuss the effects of stock dividends on stockholders' equity.

14-8 **(Cash versus Stock Dividend)** Hadley-Walsh Steel has a stockholders' equity account as given. The firm's common stock currently sells for $4 per share.

Preferred stock	$ 100,000
Common stock (400,000 shares at $1 par)	400,000
Paid-in capital in excess of par	200,000
Retained earnings	320,000
Total stockholders' equity	$1,020,000

  a Show the effects on the firm of a $.01, $.05, $.10, and $.20 per-share *cash* dividend.

  b Show the effects on the firm of a 1 percent, 5 percent, 10 percent, and 20 percent *stock* dividend.

  c Compare the effects in **a** and **b**. What are the significant differences in the two methods of paying dividends?

14-9 **(Stock Dividend — Investor)** Betty Clark currently holds 400 shares of Mountain Grown Coffee. The firm has 40,000 shares outstanding. The firm most recently had earnings available for common stockholders of $80,000, and its stock has been selling for $22 per share. The firm intends to retain its earnings and pay a 10 percent stock dividend. The retention of earnings is deemed necessary to finance a planned expansion. The firm expects the rate of return on the expansion to equal the rate of return the firm now earns on stockholders' equity.

a   How much does the firm currently earn per share?

b   What proportion of the firm does Betty Clark currently own?

c   What proportion of the firm will Ms. Clark own after the stock dividend? Explain your answer.

d   At what market price would you expect the stock to sell after the stock dividend?

e   Discuss what effect, if any, the payment of stock dividends will have on Ms. Clark's share of the ownership and earnings of Mountain Grown Coffee.

14-10   **(Stock Dividend — Investor)**   The Mission Company has outstanding 50,000 shares of common stock currently selling at $40 per share. The firm most recently had earnings available for common stockholders of $120,000, but it has decided to retain these funds and is considering a 5 percent or a 10 percent stock dividend in lieu of a cash dividend.

a   Determine the firm's current earnings per share.

b   If Jack Frost currently owns 500 shares of the firm's stock, determine his proportion of ownership currently and under each of the proposed dividend plans. Explain your findings.

c   Calculate and explain the market price per share under each of the stock dividend plans.

d   For each of the proposed stock dividends, calculate the earnings per share after payment of the stock dividend.

e   How much would the value of Jack Frost's holdings be under each of the plans? Explain.

f   As Mr. Frost, would you have any preference with respect to the proposed stock dividends? Why or why not?

14-11   **(Stock Split — Firm)**   The U.S. Oil Company's current stockholders' equity account is as follows:

Preferred stock (5% cumulative, $100 par)	$ 400,000
Common stock (600,000 shares at $3 par)	1,800,000
Paid-in capital in excess of par	200,000
Retained earnings	800,000
Total stockholders' equity	$3,200,000

a   Indicate the change, if any, expected if the firm declares a 2-for-1 stock split.

b   Indicate the change, if any, expected if the firm declares a 1-for-1½ *reverse* stock split.

c   Indicate the change, if any, expected if the firm declares a 3-for-1 stock split.

d   Indicate the change, if any, expected if the firm declares a 6-for-1 stock split.

e   Indicate the change, if any, expected if the firm declares a 1-for-4 *reverse* stock split.

14-12   **(Stock Split — Firm)**   The Big Company is considering a 3-for-2 stock split. It currently has the stockholders' equity position shown below. The current stock price is $120 per share. The most recent period's earnings available for common is included in retained earnings.

Preferred stock	$ 1,000,000
Common stock (100,000 shares at $3 par)	300,000
Paid-in capital in excess of par	1,700,000
Retained earnings	10,000,000
Total stockholders' equity	$13,000,000

   a   What effects on Big Company would result from the stock split?

   b   What change in stock price would you expect to result from the stock split?

   c   What is the maximum cash dividend *per share* the firm could pay before and after the stock split? (Assume that capital includes *all* paid-in capital.)

   d   Contrast your answers to **a** through **c** with the circumstances surrounding a 50 percent stock dividend.

   e   Explain the differences between stock splits and stock dividends.

14-13 **(Stock Repurchase)**   The following financial data on the Victor Stock Company are available:

Earnings available for common stockholders	$800,000
Number of shares of common outstanding	400,000
Earnings per share ($800,000 ÷ 400,000)	$2
Market price per share	$20
Price/earnings ratio ($20 ÷ $2)	10

The firm is currently contemplating paying cash dividends of $1 per share, which will raise the stock price to $21 per share while dividends are on.

   a   Approximately how many shares of stock can the firm repurchase at the $21-per-share price using the funds that would have gone to pay the cash dividend?

   b   Calculate earnings per share after the repurchase. Explain your calculations.

   c   If the stock still sells at 10 times earnings, how much will the market price be after the repurchase?

   d   Compare and contrast the pre- and post-repurchase earnings per share. Discuss the tax implications of this action.

   e   Compare and contrast the pre- and post-repurchase market price. Discuss your findings.

14-14 **(Stock Repurchase)** The Off Shore Steel Company has earnings available for common stockholders of $2 million and 500,000 shares of common stock outstanding at $60 per share. The firm is currently contemplating the payment of $2 per share in cash dividends.

   a   Calculate the firm's current earnings per share and price/earnings ratio.

   b   If the firm's stock is expected to sell at $62 per share with dividends on and the firm can repurchase shares at this price, how many shares can be purchased in lieu of making the proposed cash dividend payment?

   c   How much will the earnings per share be after the proposed repurchase? Why?

   d   If the stock will sell at the old price/earnings ratio, what will the market price be after repurchase?

   e   Compare and contrast the earnings per share and market price per share before and after the proposed repurchase.

   f   Describe and discuss the differences, if any, in balance sheet entries resulting from the payment of cash dividends and the proposed repurchase. Be specific.

   g   What recommendations and cautions might you offer Off Shore Steel with respect to the proposed stock repurchase? Why?

THE FIVE BEST-MANAGED COMPANIES IN 1983

"Each honest calling, each walk of life, has its own elite, its own aristocracy based on excellence of performance," educator James Bryant Conant once observed. The five elite companies chosen by *Dun's Business Month* as the best-managed of 1983 spring from many walks of business life — from soft drinks, paper products and financial services to retailing and health care. Three are renowned; two are something less than household names. Yet all five are foremost exponents of Conant's crucial criterion: excellent performance.

It may be argued that in 1983, a recovery year marked by easing interest rates, low inflation and an all-time-high stock market, many companies looked good. But for the Five Best-Managed Companies — American Express Co., Baxter Travenol Laboratories, Coca-Cola Co., James River Corp. and R.H. Macy & Co. — 1983 was another record year in a long history of growth, achieved in bad times and good. More than that, they shared a strategem common to all goal achievers: By making bold, risk-taking thrusts into new markets, they demonstrated both a singular vision of where they were headed and an aggressive resolve to get there. In short, they had the right corporate stuff.

1983 Winners: The Growth Record

Company	Revenues			Earnings per share				
	Est. 1983 (billions)	One-year increase	Five-year annual growth rate	Est. 1983	One-year increase	Five-year annual growth rate	Latest 12-month dividend	Recent yield
American Express	$9.6	18.5%	17.2%	$3.45	14.2%	17.0%	$1.85	5.4%
Baxter Travenol	1.9	13.7	14.6	1.45	19.0	18.4	0.26¾	0.5
Coca-Cola	7.1	14.5	12.5	4.25	7.6	9.5	2.68	5.1
James River	2.2[a]	29.4	55.5	2.90[a]	31.2	25.5	0.33⅓	1.1
R.H. Macy	3.5[b]	16.4	13.6	3.72[b]	35.8	22.5	0.80	1.4

[a] Estimate for year ending April 24, 1984.
[b] Actual for year ending July 30, 1983.

SOURCE: "The Five Best-Managed Companies," *Dun's Review*, December 1983, p. 37.

Combined effects. The combined effects of changes in current assets and in current liabilities can be measured by considering them simultaneously. In the preceding examples, the effects of a decrease in the ratio of current to total assets and the effects of an increase in the ratio of current liabilities to total assets were illustrated. Both changes, considered independently, were shown to increase the firm's profitability while increasing its risk. Logically, then, the combined effect of these actions should be to increase profits and risk and decrease net working capital.

EXAMPLE   Table 15.4 illustrates the effects of combining the changes in current assets and current liabilities presented in Tables 15.2 and 15.3. The values in Table 15.4 show that the combined effect of the two changes illustrated earlier is an increase in profits of $63 and a decrease in net working capital (liquidity) of $600.

Table 15.4   The Combined Effects of Changes in GHI's
Current Assets and Current Liabilities

Change	Change in profits	Change in net working capital
Decrease in ratio of current to total assets	+$39	−$300
Increase in ratio of current liabilities to total assets	+$24	−$300
Combined effect	+$63	−$600

The trade-off here is obvious; the firm has increased its profitability by increasing its risk. Table 15.4 shows that the firm's net working capital has been reduced by $600 (from its initial level of $1100 to $500). The firm's *initial net profit* can be thought of as the difference between the initial profits on total assets and the initial cost of financing. The initial profit on total assets was $699, and the initial cost of financing was $642. The initial net profit was therefore $57 ($699 − $642). After the changes in current assets and current liabilities, the firm's profits on total assets increase to $738 while the cost of financing decreases to $618. Net profits therefore increase to $120 ($738 − $618). The change in net profits is therefore $63 ($120 − $57). ∎

Determining the Financing Mix

One of the most important decisions that must be made with respect to current assets and liabilities is how current liabilities will be used to finance current assets. One of the critical factors is that only a limited amount of short-term financing (current liabilities) is available to any business firm. The amount of current liabilities available is limited by the dollar amount of purchases in the case of accounts payable, by the dollar amount of accrued liabilities in the case of accruals, and by the amount of seasonal borrowing considered acceptable by lenders in the case of notes payable. Lenders make short-term loans to allow a firm to finance seasonal buildups of accounts receivable or inventory; *they generally do not lend short-term money for long-term uses.*[10]

The firm's financing requirements can be broken into a permanent and a seasonal need. The *permanent need,* which consists of fixed assets plus the permanent portion of the firm's current assets, remains unchanged over the year, while the *seasonal need,* which is attributable to the existence of certain temporary current assets, varies over the year. The relationship between current and fixed assets and permanent and seasonal funds requirements can be illustrated graphically with the aid of a simple example.

EXAMPLE   The GHI Company's estimate of current, fixed, and total asset requirements on a monthly basis for the coming year is given in columns 1, 2, and 3 of Table 15.5. Note that

---

[10] The rationale for, techniques of, and parties to short-term business loans are discussed in detail in Chapter 18. The primary sources of short-term loans to businesses, commercial banks, make these loans only for seasonal or self-liquidating purposes such as temporary buildups of accounts receivable or inventory.

Table 15.5 Estimated Funds Requirements for the GHI Company

Month	Current assets (1)	Fixed assets (2)	Total assets[a] [(1) + (2)] (3)	Permanent requirement (4)	Seasonal requirement [(3) − (4)] (5)
January	$4,000	$13,000	$17,000	$13,800	$3,200
February	3,000	13,000	16,000	13,800	2,200
March	2,000	13,000	15,000	13,800	1,200
April	1,000	13,000	14,000	13,800	200
May	800	13,000	13,800	13,800	0
June	1,500	13,000	14,500	13,800	700
July	3,000	13,000	16,000	13,800	2,200
August	3,700	13,000	16,700	13,800	2,900
September	4,000	13,000	17,000	13,800	3,200
October	5,000	13,000	18,000	13,800	4,200
November	3,000	13,000	16,000	13,800	2,200
December	2,000	13,000	15,000	13,800	1,200

[a] This represents the firm's total funds requirement.

the relatively stable level of total assets over the year reflects, for convenience, an absence of growth by the firm. Columns 4 and 5 present a breakdown of the total requirement into its permanent and seasonal components. The permanent component (column 4) is the lowest level of total funds required during the period, while the seasonal portion is the difference between the total funds requirement (i.e., total assets) for each month and the permanent funds requirement.

By comparing the firm's fixed assets (column 2) to its permanent funds requirement (column 4), it can be seen that the permanent funds requirement exceeds the firm's level of fixed assets. This result occurs because a portion of the firm's current assets are permanent, since they are apparently always being replaced. The size of the permanent component of current assets is $800 for the GHI Company. This value represents the base level of current assets that remains on the firm's books throughout the entire year. This value can also be found by subtracting the level of fixed assets from the permanent funds requirement ($13,800 − $13,000 = $800). The relationships presented in Table 15.5 are depicted graphically in Figure 15.2. ■

There are a number of approaches to determining an appropriate financing mix. The three basic approaches — (1) the aggressive approach, (2) the conservative approach, and (3) a trade-off between the two — are discussed below.[11]

THE AGGRESSIVE APPROACH

The *aggressive approach* requires that the firm finance its short-term needs with short-term funds and its long-term needs with long-term funds. Seasonal variations in the firm's requirements are met from short-term sources, while permanent

[11] The discussions that follow do not explicitly address the various types of financing used and currently found on the firm's books. Rather, they are based on the assumption that the firm has a flexible financial structure that can be adjusted as required.

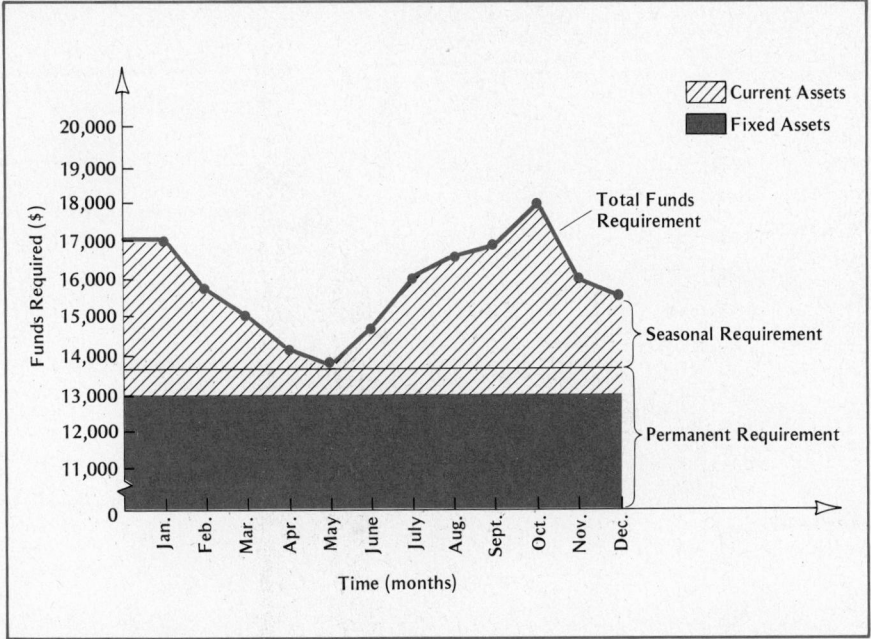

Figure 15.2   GHI Company's estimated funds requirements

financing needs are met from long-term sources. Short-term borrowing is geared to the actual need for funds. In other words, the aggressive approach involves a process of *matching* maturities of debt with the duration of each of the firm's financial needs. This approach can be illustrated graphically using the GHI Company data developed earlier.

EXAMPLE   The GHI Company's estimate of its total funds requirements (i.e., total assets) on a monthly basis for the coming year has been given in Table 15.5, column 3. Columns 4 and 5 divide this total funds requirement into permanent and seasonal components.

   The aggressive approach requires that the permanent portion of the firm's funds requirement be financed with long-term funds and that the seasonal portion be financed with short-term funds. The application of this financing plan to the firm's total funds requirement is illustrated graphically in Figure 15.3 (p. 554). ∎

Using the aggressive approach, the firm in this example would have net working capital in an amount equal to the portion of current assets financed using long-term funds. The GHI Company's net working capital would therefore amount to $800, which is the portion of its current assets financed using long-term funds ($13,800 permanent financing − $13,000 in fixed assets). This strategy would therefore be quite risky due to the low level of net working capital maintained.

Cost considerations. If the cost of short-term funds needed by GHI in the example is 3 percent and the cost of long-term funds is 11 percent, the cost of the financing plan can be estimated as follows:

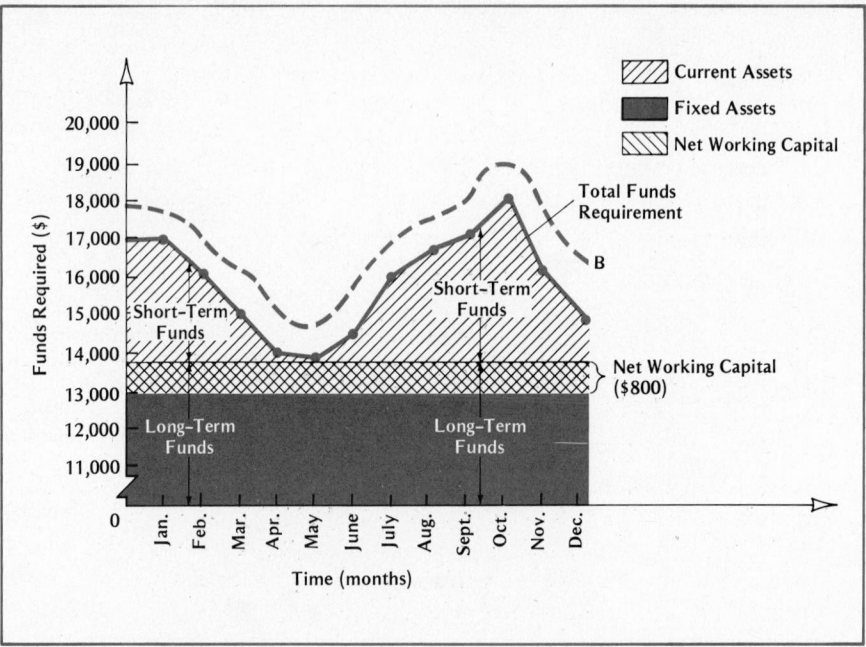

Figure 15.3   Applying the aggressive approach to the GHI Company's funds requirements

Cost of the short-term funds. The cost of the short-term funds can be estimated by calculating the average annual seasonal funds requirement and multiplying this amount by the annual cost of short-term funds of 3 percent. The average annual short-term funds requirement can be estimated by dividing the sum of the monthly seasonal funds requirements (column 5 in Table 15.5) by 12.[12] The sum of the seasonal funds requirements is $23,400, and the average short-term funds requirement is $1,950 ($23,400 ÷ 12). Thus the cost of short-term funds under this plan is $58.50 (3% × $1950).

Cost of the long-term funds. The cost of the long-term funds can be calculated by multiplying the average annual permanent funds requirement of $13,800 (from column 4 in Table 15.5) by the annual cost of long-term funds of 11 percent. The resulting cost of long-term funds under the aggressive plan is $1518 (11% × $13,800).

Total cost of the aggressive plan. The total cost of the aggressive plan can be found by adding the cost of the short-term funds ($58.50) and the cost of the long-term funds ($1518). The total cost of the plan is thus $1576.50. This figure will become more meaningful when compared to the cost of various other plans.

[12] In calculating the average funds requirement, we have merely converted the monthly funds requirements into an equivalent balance for the entire year. In other words, instead of calculating the cost for each month and summing the monthly amounts, we have multiplied the average balance by the annual interest rate to find the annual interest cost.

Risk considerations. The aggressive plan operates with minimum net working capital, since only the permanent portion of the firm's current assets is being financed with long-term funds. For the GHI Company, the level of net working capital is therefore equal to $800, which is the amount of permanent current assets ($13,800 permanent requirement − $13,000 in fixed assets).

The aggressive plan is risky not only from the standpoint of low net working capital but also because the firm is drawing as heavily as possible on its short-term sources of funds to meet seasonal fluctuations in its requirements. If its total requirement actually turns out to be, say, the level represented by the dashed line B in Figure 15.3, the firm may find it difficult to obtain a sufficient amount of short-term funds. Moreover, it may be impossible to obtain longer-term funds quickly enough to satisfy short-term needs. This aspect of risk associated with the aggressive approach results from the fact that a firm has only a limited amount of short-term borrowing capacity. If it draws too heavily on this capacity, unexpected needs for funds may become difficult to satisfy.

A final aspect of risk associated with the aggressive approach's maximum use of short-term financing is the fact that the high volatility of short-term interest rates could result in significantly higher borrowing costs as the short-term debt is refinanced; with long-term financing, a less volatile rate and less frequent refinancing needs result in greater certainty and less risk.

THE CONSERVATIVE APPROACH

The most *conservative approach* would be to finance all projected funds requirements with long-term funds and use short-term funds in the event of an emergency or an unexpected outflow of funds. It is hard to imagine how this approach could actually be implemented, since certain short-term financing tools are virtually unavoidable. It would be quite difficult for a firm to keep accounts payable and accruals low. It would also be unwise, since accounts payable and accruals rise naturally in the process of doing business.

In illustrating this approach, the spontaneous short-term financing provided by payables and accruals will be ignored. For GHI, the conservative approach would involve meeting all the forecast funds requirements, even the entire $18,000 needed in October, with long-term funds and reserving the use of short-term financing for contingencies.

EXAMPLE   Figure 15.4 (p. 556) shows graphically the application of the conservative approach to the estimated funds requirements for GHI given in Table 15.5. All the funds required over the one-year period, including the entire $18,000 forecast for October, are financed with long-term funds. The firm's net working capital, defined here as the portion of the firm's current assets financed by long-term funds, amounts to $5,000 ($18,000 − $13,000).[13] Any long-term financing in excess of the $13,000 in fixed asset requirements provides net working capital. ■

---

[13] The level of net working capital is constant throughout the year since the firm has $5000 in current assets that will be fully financed with long-term funds. Because the portion of the $5000 in excess of the scheduled level of current assets is assumed to be held as marketable securities, the firm's current asset balance will increase to this level.

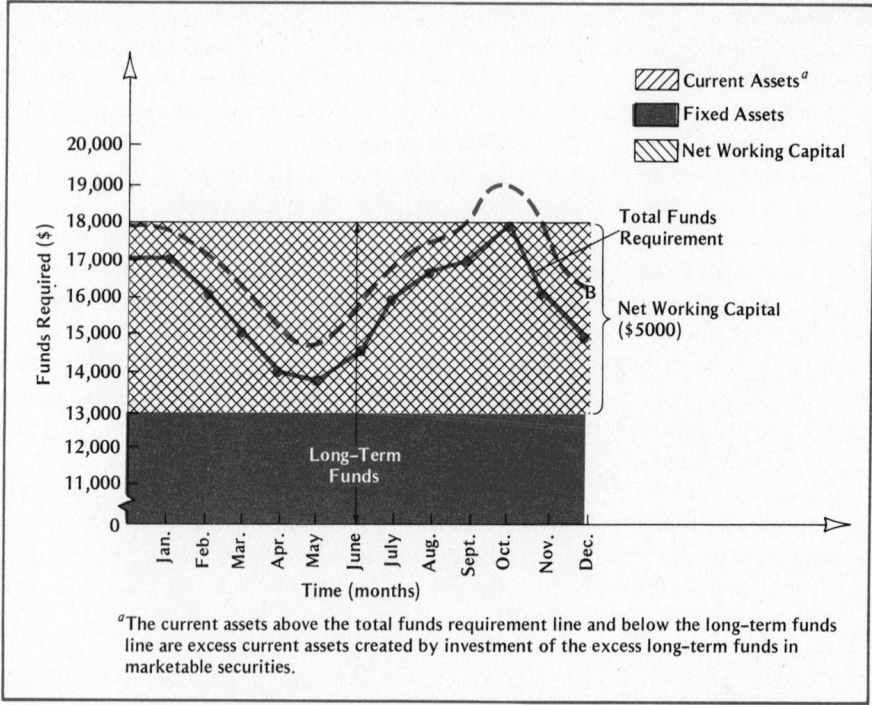

^aThe current assets above the total funds requirement line and below the long-term funds
line are excess current assets created by investment of the excess long-term funds in
marketable securities.

Figure 15.4   Applying the conservative approach to the GHI Company's funds
requirements

Cost considerations. The effects of the conservative approach on profitability can be
measured by determining the cost of this financing plan. In the example just given,
the cost of long-term funds was given as 11 percent per year. Since the average
long-term financing balance with the conservative financing plan is $18,000, the
total cost of this plan is $1,980 (11% × $18,000).[14] Comparing this figure to the
total cost of $1,576.50 using the aggressive approach indicates the more expensive
nature of the conservative approach. Why the conservative approach is so expensive can be seen by looking at Figure 15.4. The area above the total funds requirement line and below the long-term funds line represents the level of funds not
actually needed but on which the firm is paying interest — the amount of excess
funds available. In spite of the fact that the financial manager will invest these idle
funds in some type of marketable security so as partially to offset their cost, it is
highly unlikely that the manager can earn more on the funds than their interest
cost. So these temporarily unneeded funds are costly to the firm.

Risk considerations. The $5,000 of net working capital ($18,000 long-term financing
— $13,000 of fixed assets) associated with this plan should mean a very low level of

[14] For expository convenience, any potential earnings from investment of the excess funds in marketable securities is ignored. Clearly, the financial manager would be expected to invest surplus funds,
thereby reducing the total (net) cost of the conservative approach.

risk for the firm. The firm's risk should also be lowered by the fact that the plan does not require the firm to use any of its limited short-term borrowing capacity. In other words, if total required financing actually turns out to be the level represented by the dashed line B in Figure 15.4, sufficient short-term borrowing capacity should be available to cover the unexpected needs and avoid technical insolvency. In addition, the need to frequently refinance high levels of short-term financing, possibly at high rates, is avoided, thereby lowering further the risk of the conservative approach.

Comparison with the aggressive approach. Unlike the aggressive approach, the conservative approach requires the firm to pay interest on unneeded funds. The lower cost of the aggressive approach, therefore, makes it more profitable than the conservative approach, but the aggressive approach is much more risky. The contrast between these two approaches should clearly indicate the trade-off between profitability and risk. The aggressive approach provides high profits but also high risk, while the conservative approach provides low profits and low risk. A trade-off between these extremes should result in an acceptable financing strategy for most firms.

A TRADE-OFF BETWEEN THE TWO APPROACHES

Most firms use a financing plan somewhere between the high-profit, high-risk aggressive approach and the low-profit, low-risk conservative approach. The exact trade-off between profitability and risk depends largely on the decision maker's attitude toward risk. One of many possible trade-offs in GHI Company's case is described in this example.

EXAMPLE   After careful analysis, the GHI Company has decided on a financing plan based on an amount of permanent financing equal to the midpoint of the minimum and maximum monthly funds requirements for the period. An examination of Table 15.5 reveals that the minimum monthly funds requirement is $13,800 (in May) and the maximum monthly funds requirement is $18,000 (in October). The midpoint between these two values is $15,900 [($13,800 + $18,000) ÷ 2]. Thus the firm will use $15,900 in long-term funds each month and raise any additional funds required from short-term sources. The breakdown of long- and short-term funds under this plan is given in Table 15.6.

Column 3 in Table 15.6 shows the amount of short-term funds required each month. These values were found by subtracting $15,900 from total funds required each month, given in column 1. For the months March, April, May, June, and December, the level of total funds required is less than the level of long-term funds available; therefore, no short-term funds are needed.

Implementing this plan would result in a level of net working capital of $2,900 ($15,900 long-term funds −$13,000 of fixed assets). This should give the firm a risk position somewhere between the high-risk level of the aggressive approach (which provides $800 of net working capital) and the low-risk position of the conservative approach (which provides $5,000 of net working capital). ■

Figure 15.5 (p. 559) presents graphically the trade-off plan described in Table 15.6 along with the plan based on the aggressive approach and the conservative

Table 15.6   A Financing Plan Based on a Trade-off Between
             Profitability and Risk for the GHI Company

Month	Total assets[a] (1)	Long-term funds (2)	Short-term funds (3)
January	$17,000	$15,900	$1,100
February	16,000	15,900	100
March	15,000	15,900	0
April	14,000	15,900	0
May	13,800	15,900	0
June	14,500	15,900	0
July	16,000	15,900	100
August	16,700	15,900	800
September	17,000	15,900	1,100
October	18,000	15,900	2,100
November	16,000	15,900	100
December	15,000	15,900	0

[a] This represents the firm's total funds requirement from column 3 of Table 15.5.

approach. The area above the total funds requirement line and below the long-term financing line, line 3, represents the level of funds not actually needed but on which the firm is paying interest — the amount of excess funds available.

Cost considerations. The cost of the trade-off plan can be calculated by finding the average short- and long-term funds required and multiplying these amounts by the short- and long-term financing costs of 3 and 11 percent, respectively. The sum of these two cost components is the overall cost of the plan.

Cost of the short-term funds. The cost of the short-term funds can be estimated by calculating the average short-term funds requirement and multiplying this by 3 percent. The average annual short-term funds required can be calculated by dividing the sum of the monthly (seasonal) funds requirements (from column 3 of Table 15.6) by 12. The sum of the seasonal funds requirements is $5400. The average short-term funds requirement is thus $450 ($5400 ÷ 12), and the cost of short-term funds with this plan is $13.50 (3% × $450).

Cost of the long-term funds. The cost of the long-term funds can be calculated by multiplying the average long-term funds requirement of $15,900 (from column 2 of Table 15.6) by the annual cost of long-term funds of 11 percent. The cost of long-term funds with the trade-off is therefore $1,749.

Total cost of the trade-off plan. The total cost of the trade-off plan can be found by adding the cost of short-term funds ($13.50) and the cost of long-term funds ($1749). The total cost of the trade-off plan is therefore $1762.50.[15]

[15] For expository convenience, any potential earnings from investment of the excess funds in marketable securities is ignored. Clearly, the financial manager would be expected to invest surplus funds, thereby reducing the total (net) cost of the trade-off plan.

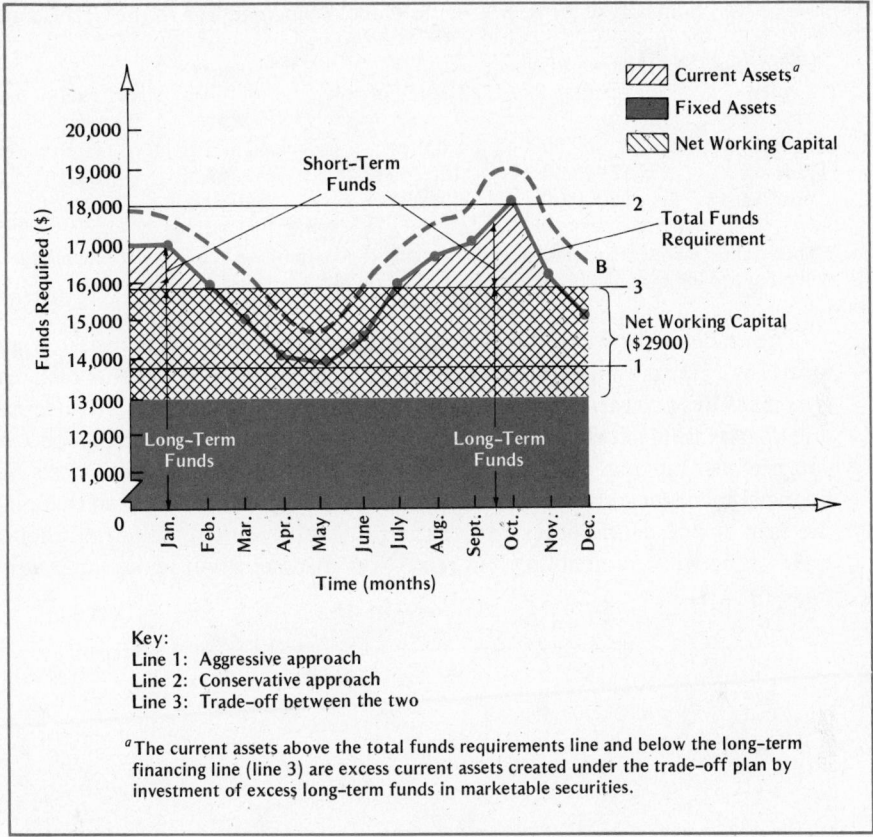

Figure 15.5 Three alternative financing plans for the GHI Company

Risk considerations. As Figure 15.5 shows, the trade-off plan is less risky than the aggressive approach but more risky than the conservative approach. With the trade-off plan, if the total funds requirement is actually at the level represented by the dashed line B in Figure 15.5, the likelihood that the firm will be able to obtain additional short-term financing is good, since a portion of its short-term financial requirements is actually being financed with long-term funds. The risk of having to refinance frequently at possibly higher interest rates falls between those of the aggressive and conservative approaches. With respect to cost, the trade-off plan also falls between the aggressive approach, which has the lowest cost, and the conservative approach, which has the highest cost.

A SUMMARY COMPARISON OF APPROACHES

Table 15.7 summarizes the results of the analysis of each of the plans. It indicates that the lower the firm's net working capital, the higher the risk present. The table also indicates that the higher the risk of insolvency, the higher the firm's profits are expected to be.

Table 15.7   Summary of the Results of the Three Financing Plans for the GHI Company

Financing plan	Net working capital[a]	Degree of risk	Total cost of funds	Level of profits
Aggressive	$ 800.00	Highest	$1576.50	Highest
Trade-off	$2900.00	Intermediate	$1762.50	Intermediate
Conservative	$5000.00	Lowest	$1980.00	Lowest

[a] These values represent the amount of net working capital provided by each financing plan as determined in the examples.

The trade-off between the risk and profitability can be demonstrated more clearly by a graph, as in Figure 15.6. In analyzing Figure 15.6, note that each of the axes measures two variables. As you move to the right on the x-axis, risk decreases due to increasing net working capital; unfortunately, profits decrease too, because you are also moving up the y-axis, encountering increasing funds costs. The financial manager must determine whether to select a financing plan that places the firm at one or the other end of the profitability-risk function, or choose a trade-off between profitability and risk. Most managers will make some type of trade-off.

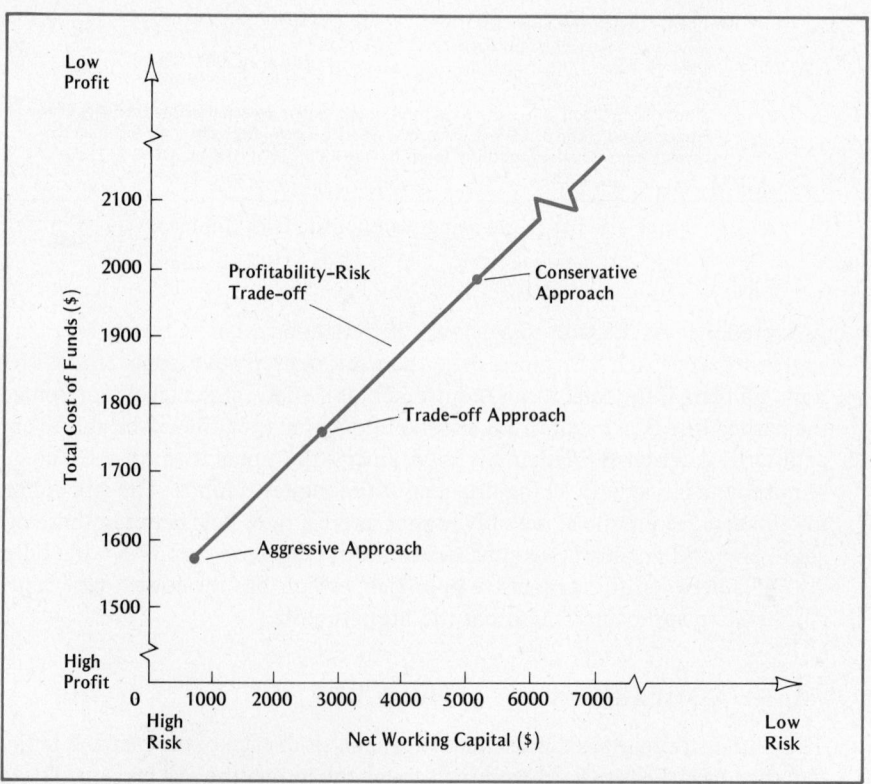

Figure 15.6   Graph of the profitability-risk trade-off for the GHI Company

ASSISTANT TREASURER—CASH CONTROL: A JOB DESCRIPTION

Basic function

Responsible for operations of the Treasury Department involving cash management operations with specific attention to the effective direction and control of corporate funds internally and through the company's various bank accounts.

Primary responsibilities and duties

Manage, in conjunction with lock box banks retained by company, the processing of over 120,000 customer payments daily.

Disbursement of all company funds, including payrolls, pensions, and vendor payments.

Direct the management staff to assure compliance with our stated objectives and planning in order to assure the effectiveness of the organization.

Sign checks and review and approve various documents such as wire transfer confirmations and investment letters.

Meet with banks and their representatives.

Perform various assignments for senior management.

Also responsible for the risk management/insurance function.

Types of decisions

Personnel: disciplinary action, hire, fire, promote, and transfer.

Anything of significant impact on the budget.

Kinds of insurance coverage to purchase.

Approve all changes in operating procedures in all areas of this department. . . .

Education and experience

Minimum B. A.

Formerly held positions as Director of auditing, General Manager—Administration, and Division Manager—Customer Service.

Representative skills and knowledge

Should:

Be familiar with cash control operations, including bank operations such as check processing and lock box, and Federal Reserve check-clearing operations.

Have knowledge of bank dispersing and other bank services.

Must:

Have a working knowledge of customer service activities such as billing, collections, and the business office's operations.

Possess the analytical skills to review financial statements and understand certain loss and reserve relationships.

Have the ability to communicate in all forms effectively.

Be creative and resourceful.

Be able to motivate personnel.

SOURCE: *Careers in Finance* (Tampa, Fla.: Financial Management Association, 1983), pp. 21–22.

CHAPTER SUMMARY

● Net working capital is defined as the difference between current assets and current liabilities. The appropriate level of net working capital depends on cash flow patterns. Firms maintain net working capital to provide a cushion between cash outflows and inflows.

● Net working capital is often used as a measure of the risk of technical insolvency by the firm. The more liquid a firm is, the less likely it will be unable to satisfy its current obligations as they come due.

● An alternative definition of net working capital is the portion of a firm's current assets financed with long-term funds.

● The higher a firm's ratio of current to total assets, the less profitable the firm, and the less risky it is. The converse is also true. The higher a firm's ratio of current liabilities to total assets, the more profitable and more risky the firm is. The converse of this statement is also true. These trade-offs between profitability and risk must be considered in evaluating the net working capital position.

● Since net working capital can be considered the portion of a firm's current assets financed by long-term funds, the mix between short-term and long-term financing is directly related to the profitability-risk trade-off and net working capital.

● By forecasting funds requirements, the financial manager can evaluate the consequences of various financing plans.

● Financing requirements can be broken down into seasonal and permanent needs. The permanent need is attributable to fixed assets and the permanent portion of current assets, while the seasonal need is attributable to the existence of certain temporary current assets.

● The aggressive approach for determining an appropriate financing mix is a high-profit, high-risk financing plan whereby seasonal needs are financed with short-term funds and permanent needs are financed with long-term funds. The maturity of debt is matched with the duration of each of the firm's financial needs.

● The conservative approach is a low-profit, low-risk financing plan: All funds requirements—both seasonal and permanent—are financed with long-term funds; short-term funds are saved for emergencies.

● Most firms use a trade-off plan whereby some seasonal needs are financed with long-term funds; this approach falls between the high-profit, high-risk aggressive approach and the low-profit, low-risk conservative approach.

KEY TERMS

aggressive approach (working capital)
conservative approach (working capital)
long-term funds
maturity structure of debt
net profit (working capital)
net working capital

permanent (funds) need
profitability (working capital)
risk (working capital)
seasonal (funds) need
technical insolvency
working capital management

QUESTIONS

15-1 Why is working capital management considered so important by stockholders, creditors, and the firm's financial manager? What is the definition of *net working capital?*

15-2 What relationship would you expect to exist between the predictability of a firm's cash flows and its required level of net working capital?

15-3   How are net working capital, liquidity, technical insolvency, and risk related?

15-4   Why is an increase in the ratio of current to total assets expected to decrease both profits and risk as measured by net working capital?

15-5   How can changes in the ratio of current liabilities to total assets affect profitability and risk?

15-6   How would you expect an increase in a firm's ratio of current assets to total assets and a decrease in its ratio of current liabilities to total assets to affect profit and risk? Why?

15-7   What is the basic premise of the *aggressive approach* for meeting a firm's funds requirements? What are the effects of this approach on the firm's profitability and risk?

15-8   What is the *conservative approach* to financing funds requirements? What kind of profitability-risk trade-off is involved?

15-9   If a firm has a constant funds requirement throughout the year, which, if any, of the three financing plans is preferable? Why?

15-10   As the difference between the cost of short-term and long-term financing becomes smaller, which financing plan — aggressive or conservative — becomes more attractive? Would the aggressive or the conservative approach be preferable if the costs were equal? Why?

PROBLEMS

15-1   **(Liquidity, Risk, and Return)**   Last year, the NRC Corporation had the following balance sheet:

Assets		Liabilities and equity	
Current assets	$ 6,000	Current liabilities	$ 2,000
Fixed assets	14,000	Long-term funds	18,000
Total	$20,000	Total	$20,000

The firm estimated it earned 10 percent on current assets, current liabilities cost 14 percent, fixed assets earned 25 percent, and long-term funds cost 16 percent.

For the coming year, calculate the expected profits on total assets, financing costs, net profit, and current ratio under the following different circumstances:

a   There are no changes.

b   The firm shifts $1000 from current assets to fixed assets and $500 from long-term funds to current liabilities.

c   Discuss the changes in risk and return illustrated by **a** and **b**.

15-2   **(Liquidity, Risk, and Return)**   The Badger Company had the following balance sheet at the end of 1984:

Assets		Liabilities and equity	
Current assets	$ 30,000	Current liabilities	$ 15,000
Fixed assets	90,000	Long-term funds	105,000
Total	$120,000	Total	$120,000

a   Calculate profits on total assets, financing costs, net profits, current ratio, and return on investment (*ROI*) if the firm (1) expects to earn 8 percent on current assets and 20 percent on fixed assets, current liabilities cost 12 percent, and long-term funds cost 16 percent; and (2) expects to earn 10 percent on current assets and 20 percent on fixed assets, pay 11 percent on current liabilities, and pay 15 percent on long-term funds.

b The firm wishes to decrease net working capital by $10,000. This could be accomplished by either decreasing current assets or increasing current liabilities. Under each circumstance—**a**(1) and **a**(2)—would this goal be most profitably accomplished by decreasing current assets or increasing current liabilities? Explain.

15-3 **(Average Borrowing Costs)**   What is the average loan balance and the annual loan cost, given an annual interest rate on loans of 15 percent, for a firm with total monthly borrowings as follows?

Month	Amount	Month	Amount
Jan.	$12,000	July	$6,000
Feb.	13,000	Aug.	5,000
Mar.	9,000	Sept.	6,000
Apr.	8,000	Oct.	5,000
May	9,000	Nov.	7,000
June	7,000	Dec.	9,000

15-4 **(Aggressive versus Conservative)**   International Tool has forecast its total funds requirements for the coming year as follows:

Month	Amount	Month	Amount
Jan.	$2,000,000	July	$12,000,000
Feb.	2,000,000	Aug.	14,000,000
Mar.	2,000,000	Sept.	9,000,000
Apr.	4,000,000	Oct.	5,000,000
May	6,000,000	Nov.	4,000,000
June	9,000,000	Dec.	3,000,000

a Calculate the total financing costs of the aggressive approach and the conservative approach if (1) the cost of short-term funds is 12 percent and the cost of long-term funds is 17 percent; and (2) the cost of short-term funds is 11 percent and the cost of long-term funds is 12 percent. (*Note:* Use the average loan balance when appropriate.)

b Discuss the profitability-risk trade-offs associated with the aggressive plan and the conservative plan.

c Which plan would more closely approximate your choice in **a**(1) and **a**(2)? Why?

15-5 **(Aggressive versus Conservative)**   Petro-Gas has forecast its seasonal financing needs for the next year as follows:

Month	Seasonal requirement	Month	Seasonal requirement
Jan.	$2,400,000	July	$ 800,000
Feb.	500,000	Aug.	400,000
Mar.	0	Sept.	0
Apr.	300,000	Oct.	300,000
May	1,200,000	Nov.	1,000,000
June	1,000,000	Dec.	1,800,000

Assuming that the firm's permanent funds requirement is $5 million, calculate the total financing costs under the aggressive plan and the conservative plan and recommend one of the plans under the following conditions:

a   Short-term funds cost 10 percent and long-term funds cost 16 percent.

b   Short-term funds cost 11 percent and long-term funds cost 14 percent.

c   Both short-term and long-term funds cost 12 percent.

15-6   (Testing Assumptions)   Stop-and-Shop has seasonal financing needs that vary from zero to $2 million. For each separate condition in **a** through **f**, would the condition tend to move the firm toward an aggressive financing plan or toward a conservative financing plan?

a   The difference between short-term and long-term financing costs has decreased.

b   The average seasonal financing need is $400,000.

c   The average seasonal financing need is $1.8 million.

d   The long-term financing cost is much higher than the short-term cost.

e   The firm has a high proportion of its assets in current assets.

f   Sales are very difficult to predict.

15-7   (Aggressive, Conservative, and Trade-off)   Mile High Enterprises expects to need the following amounts of funds next year:

Month	Amount	Month	Amount
Jan.	$10,000	July	$10,000
Feb.	10,000	Aug.	9,000
Mar.	11,000	Sept.	8,000
Apr.	12,000	Oct.	8,000
May	13,000	Nov.	9,000
June	11,000	Dec.	9,000

a   What is the average amount of funding needed during the year?

b   If short-term financing costs 8 percent and long-term financing costs 20 percent, what will be the total financing costs for the aggressive and conservative financing plans, respectively?

c   If the firm finances $10,000 with long-term financing, what will be the total financing cost?

15-8   (Aggressive versus Conservative: No Seasonality)   Snyder Supply has financing needs of $250,000 per month forecast for every month of the coming year. The cost of short-term financing is 12 percent and the cost of long-term financing is 14 percent.

a   What are the total costs of the aggressive and conservative financing plans?

b   Which plan is preferable? Why?

Chapter 16

Cash and Marketable Securities Management

After studying this chapter, you should be able to:

1. Discuss the three basic cash management strategies and demonstrate their impact on the firm's minimum operating cash using the cash cycle model.

2. Define *float*, including its three basic components, and explain the firm's major objective with respect to the levels of collection float and disbursement float.

3. Describe the basic cash management techniques, including popular collection procedures, disbursement procedures, and the role of strong banking relationships.

4. Understand marketable security fundamentals, including the basic motives for holding these securities, their key characteristics, and the optimum proportion to hold.

5. List and briefly describe the basic features of the popular marketable securities, including government issues and nongovernment issues.

6. Discuss the multinational aspects of cash management related to foreign exchange risk.

Cash and marketable securities are the firm's most liquid assets. They provide the ability to pay bills as they come due. Collaterally, these liquid assets provide a pool of funds to cover unexpected outlays, thereby reducing the risk of a "liquidity crisis." Since the other major current assets (accounts receivable and inventories) will eventually be converted into cash through collections and sales, cash is the common denominator to which all liquid assets can be reduced.

Marketable securities are short-term investment instruments used by the firm to obtain a return on temporarily idle funds. When a firm recognizes that too large an amount of cash has been accumulated, it will often put a portion into an interest-earning instrument. Although commercial banks often pay interest on demand deposits (checking accounts), business customers tend to be compensated for the balances they maintain by receiving reduced activity fees, lower interest rates on loans, or both. Because the "earnings rate" or rate of interest applied by banks is quite low, firms tend to move excess bank balances into other instruments. A number of highly liquid interest-earning instruments allow the firm to profit on its idle cash without sacrificing much liquidity.

The Efficient Management of Cash[1]

The basic strategies that should be employed by the business firm in managing cash are as follows:

1. Pay accounts payable as late as possible without damaging the firm's credit rating, but take advantage of any favorable cash discounts.[2]

---

[1] The conceptual model used in this part to demonstrate basic cash management strategies was developed by Lawrence J. Gitman in "Estimating Corporate Liquidity Requirements: A Simplified Approach," *The Financial Review,* 1974, pp. 79–88, and refined and operationalized by Lawrence J. Gitman and Kanwal S. Sachdeva in "A Framework for Estimating and Analyzing the Required Working Capital Investment," *Review of Business and Economic Research,* Spring 1982, pp. 35–44.

[2] A discussion of the variables to consider in determining whether to take cash discounts appears in Chapter 18. A cash discount is often an enticement to pay accounts payable early to reduce the purchase price of goods. Strategies for the use of accruals as a free source of short-term financing are also discussed in Chapter 18.

2. Turn over inventory as quickly as possible, avoiding stockouts that might result in shutting down the production line or in a loss of sales.

3. Collect accounts receivable as quickly as possible without losing future sales because of high-pressure collection techniques. Cash discounts, if they are economically justifiable, may be used to accomplish this objective.

The overall implications of these strategies for the firm can be demonstrated by looking at cash cycles and cash turnovers.

CASH CYCLES AND CASH TURNOVERS

The *cash cycle* of a firm is defined as the amount of time that elapses from the point when the firm makes an outlay to purchase raw materials to the point when cash is collected from the sale of the finished good produced using that raw material. *Cash turnover* refers to the number of times each year the firm's cash is actually turned over. The relationship between the cash cycle and cash turnover is similar to the relationship between the average age and turnover of inventory discussed in Chapter 4. The concept of cash cycles and cash turnovers can be better defined using a simple example.

EXAMPLE   The KLM Company currently purchases *all* its raw materials on a credit basis and sells all its merchandise on credit.[3] The credit terms extended the firm currently require payment within 30 days of a purchase, while the firm currently requires its customers to pay within 60 days of a sale. The firm's calculations of the average payment period and average collection period indicate that it is taking, on the average, 35 days to pay its accounts payable and 70 days to collect its accounts receivable. Further calculations reveal that, on the average, 85 days elapse between the point a raw material is purchased and the point the finished good is sold. In other words, the average age of the firm's inventory is 85 days.

Cash cycle   The firm's cash cycle can be shown by a simple graph, as in Figure 16.1. There are 120 days between the cash outflow to pay the account payable (on day 35) and the cash inflow from the collection of the account receivable (on day 155). During this period, the firm's money is tied up.

At time zero the firm purchases raw materials, which are initially placed in the raw materials inventory. Eventually the raw materials are used in the production process, becoming part of the work-in-process inventory. When the work in process is completed, the finished good is placed in the finished goods inventory until it is sold. The total amount of time that elapses, on the average, between the purchase of raw materials and the ultimate sale of finished goods is the average age of inventory, 85 days in Figure. 16.1.

When the firm initially purchased the raw materials (on day 0), an account payable was established. It remained on the firm's books until it was paid, 35 days later. It was at this point that a *cash outflow* occurred. After the sale of the finished good (on day 85), the firm established an account receivable. This account receivable remained on its books until it was collected 70 days later. It was therefore 70 days after the item was sold, on day 155 (70 days beyond the 85th day, which was the day of sale) that a *cash inflow* occurred.

A firm's cash cycle is calculated by finding the average number of days that elapse

---

[3] This assumption of *all* credit purchases and credit sales simplifies the cash management model. Although purchases and sales for cash could easily be incorporated into it, they have not been in order to convey the key cash management strategies with a minimum of algebraic complexity.

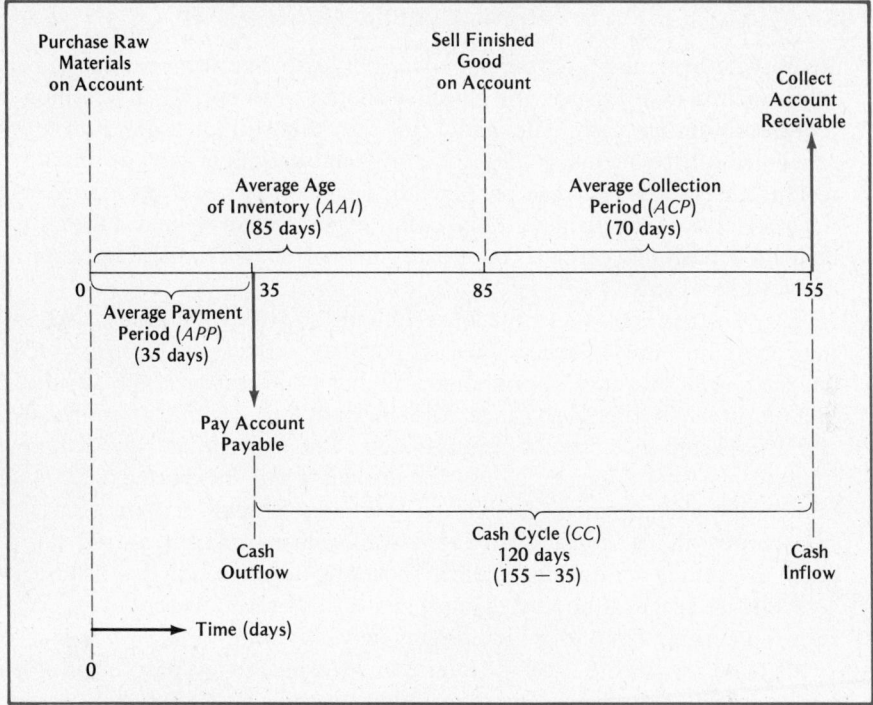

Figure 16.1   The KLM Company's cash cycle

between the cash outflows associated with paying accounts payable and the cash inflows associated with collecting accounts receivable. Stated as an equation, the cash cycle (CC) is

$$CC = AAI + ACP - APP \qquad (16.1)$$

where:

$$AAI = \text{average age of inventory}$$
$$ACP = \text{average collection period}$$
$$APP = \text{average payment period}$$

Substituting $AAI = 85$ days, $ACP = 70$ days, and $APP = 35$ days into Equation 16.1, KLM's cash cycle is found to be 120 days (85 days + 70 days − 35 days). This result can be seen in Figure 16.1.

   Cash turnover   A firm's cash turnover (CT) can be calculated by dividing the cash cycle into 360.

$$CT = \frac{360}{CC} \qquad (16.2)$$

The KLM Company's cash turnover is currently 3 (360 days ÷ 120 days). The higher a firm's cash turnover, the less cash the firm requires. Cash turnover, like inventory turnover, should be maximized. However, the firm does not want to run out of cash. ■

DETERMINING A FIRM'S MINIMUM OPERATING CASH[4]

Because the firm must forgo various opportunities to invest or repay debts in order to maintain a cash balance, the objective should be to operate in a fashion that requires minimum cash. The amount of cash that will allow the firm to meet scheduled bill payments as they come due and provide a margin of safety for making unscheduled payments or scheduled payments when expected inflows are not available must be planned. This "cash," of course, can be held in the form of a demand deposit (checking account balance) or in some type of interest-earning marketable security.

There are a variety of quantitative techniques and rules of thumb for determining "optimum" cash balances. The cash budget, discussed in Chapter 5, presents one method for planning cash requirements, but it does not deal explicitly with the question of the appropriate balance. The optimum level depends on both expected and unexpected receipts and disbursements. The appropriate balance is sometimes set at a level sufficient to meet both expected and unexpected requirements or to meet the requirements established by lenders, whichever is greater. In other cases, firms will plan to maintain a zero cash balance using a prearranged line of credit as a source of immediate cash for covering negative cash flows. The use of zero-balance accounts (discussed later) and lines of credit (described in Chapter 18) for managing cash flows is common today.

A simple approach is to set the minimum level of cash as a percentage of sales. For example, a firm that wishes to maintain a cash balance equal to 8 percent of annual sales, which are expected to be \$2 million, would maintain a balance of \$160,000 (.08 × \$2,000,000). More sophisticated approaches are based on techniques using calculus and statistics. For purposes of illustration, a simple yet appealing and practical technique is used to estimate the minimum liquidity level required. Using the framework already developed, the minimum level of operating cash needed by a firm can be estimated by dividing the firm's total annual outlays (TAO) by its cash turnover rate.[5] Letting TAO equal total annual outlays, the *minimum operating cash (MOC)* is

$$MOC = \frac{TAO}{CT} \qquad (16.3)$$

[4] The expression "minimum operating cash" as used throughout this part of the chapter can more correctly be viewed as the *net working capital investment required to support a specified level of operations.* Although minimum operating cash would be held in a variety of forms — cash, marketable securities, accounts receivable, or inventory — the expression is used here for pedagogical convenience. In other words, this model illustrates key concepts of cash management rather than its operational characteristics.

[5] The logic of this calculation rests on the existence of the following equation for a firm's cash turnover:

$$\text{Cash turnover} = \frac{\text{total annual outlays}}{\text{average cash balance}}$$

Solving this equation for the average cash balance produces the following equation:

$$\text{Average cash balance} = \frac{\text{total annual outlays}}{\text{cash turnover}}$$

This model assumes that the *average* amount of cash required by the firm in order to operate is the same as the *minimum* amount.

EXAMPLE   If the KLM Company spends approximately $12 million annually on operating outlays (*TAO*), its minimum operating cash (*MOC*) is $4 million ($12,000,000 ÷ 3). This means that if it begins the year with $4 million in cash, it should have sufficient cash to pay bills as they come due. It should not have to borrow additional funds in these circumstances. If the opportunity cost of holding cash is 10 percent, the cost of maintaining a $4 million cash balance will be $400,000 (.10 × $4,000,000) per year. ∎

Opportunity cost concept. The opportunity cost of 10 percent in the example is based on the fact that the firm, if it were free to use the $4 million, could invest it in an equally risky investment yielding a return of 10 percent per year or repay a debt costing 10 percent per year. Since there is a cost of maintaining idle cash balances, a firm should attempt to reduce the amount of operating cash it requires.

Analysis of the cash cycle model. This discussion of cash cycles, cash turnovers, and minimum operating cash is based on a number of limiting assumptions. First, is that the technique explicitly ignores profit — the fact that inflows will actually exceed outflows. The model assumes that inflows equal outflows and, therefore that no profit exists. Second, the model assumes that *all* outflows occur at the same time that the raw materials are paid for (payment of accounts payable). It should be clear that in actuality value will be added to the raw material at various stages throughout the production-sale process. This assumption tends to cause minimum operating cash to be overestimated. Third, it is assumed that the firm's purchases, production, and sales occur at a constant rate throughout the year. In situations where this assumption is not valid, minimum operating cash can be estimated by using the cash turnover rate for the most cash-dependent period of operation. Finally, the amount of uncertainty, or variability, in a firm's cash requirements will certainly affect the minimum level of operating cash maintained. Although for simplicity this uncertainty has been ignored here, the amount of cash held by a firm is a function of the uncertainty of its cash inflows and outflows as well as the financial manager's disposition toward risk. In general, the larger the cash balance (or line of credit) available, the lower the risk (of technical insolvency) and return (due to greater opportunity cost), and vice versa.

Although these limiting assumptions may subtract from the practical applicability of this technique, its usefulness for illustrating recommended cash management strategies warrants its application in the following examples.

CASH MANAGEMENT STRATEGIES

The effects of implementing each of the strategies mentioned earlier are described in the following paragraphs, using the KLM Company data. Note that while the costs of implementing each proposed strategy are ignored in the following discussion, in practice they would be estimated and compared with the calculated savings in order to make the cash management strategy decision.

Stretching accounts payable. One strategy available to KLM is to *stretch accounts payable* — that is, to pay its bills as late as possible without damaging its credit rating. Although this is a financially attractive strategy, it raises an important ethical issue since it may cause the firm to violate an agreement with a supplier.

Clearly, a supplier would not look kindly upon a customer who purposely post-poned paying for merchandise or equipment.[6]

EXAMPLE If KLM Company can stretch the payment period from the current average of 35 days to an average of 45 days, its cash cycle will be reduced to 110 days (CC = 85 days + 70 days − 45 days = 110 days). By stretching its accounts payable 10 additional days, the firm increases its cash turnover rate from 3 to 3.27 (CT = 360 days ÷ 110 days = 3.27). This increased cash turnover rate results in a decrease in the firm's minimum operating cash requirement from $4,000,000 to approximately $3,670,000 ($MOC$ = $12,000,000 ÷ 3.27 = $3,670,000). The reduction in required operating cash of approximately $330,000 ($4,000,000 − $3,670,000) represents an annual savings to the firm of $33,000 (.10 × $330,000), which is the opportunity cost of tying up that amount of funds. ■

The payoff from stretching accounts payable for KLM should be clear. How-ever, only if suppliers are dependent on the firm for a large portion of their business can a firm really capitalize on stretching. Many firms offer cash discounts as enticements to customers to pay accounts promptly. Had KLM's suppliers offered cash discounts for early payment, the firm might have found that the cheapest overall strategy would be to pay early and take the discount. Occasionally a sup-plier may let a customer stretch accounts, if the customer is a young, growing firm and the payoff from helping it grow will be increased business in the future. Stretching accounts payable is certainly a strategy to be considered by a firm that wants to reduce its cash requirements and therefore its operating costs.[7]

Efficient inventory-production management. Another way of minimizing required cash is to increase inventory turnover. This can be achieved in any of the following ways:

Increasing raw materials turnover. By using more efficient inventory control techniques, the firm may be able to increase raw materials turnover.

Decreasing the production cycle. With better production planning, scheduling, and control techniques, the firm can reduce the length of the production cycle. Reducing the production cycle will cause the firm's work-in-process inventory turnover to increase.

Increasing the finished-goods turnover. The firm can increase its finished-goods turnover through better forecasting of demand and better planning of production to coincide with these forecasts. More efficient control of the finished-goods inventory will contribute to a faster finished-goods inventory turnover.

---

[6] The resolution of this ethical issue is not further addressed in this text. Suffice it to say that although the use of various techniques to slow down payments is widespread due to its financial appeal, it may not be justifiable on purely ethical grounds.

[7] In periods of tight money such as 1974–1975 and 1978–1982, a firm's ability to stretch payables becomes limited, especially when the supplier can live without the customer's business. During periods of tight money, many suppliers levy or enforce interest charges on a daily basis for payments received after the end of a credit period.

Regardless of what aspects of the firm's overall inventory turnover are adjusted, the result will be a reduction in the amount of operating cash required. Let us see how these techniques work.

EXAMPLE   If KLM manages to reduce the average age of its inventory from the current level of 85 days to 70 days—a reduction of 15 days—the effects on its minimum operating cash will be as follows: There will be a reduction of 15 days in the cash cycle, from 120 days to 105 days (CC = 70 days + 70 days − 35 days = 105 days). The decreased average age of inventory for KLM increases the annual cash turnover rate from the initial level of 3 to 3.43 (CT = 360 days ÷ 105 days = 3.43). The increased cash turnover rate results in a decrease in the firm's minimum operating cash requirement from \$4 million to approximately \$3.5 million (MOC = \$12,000,000 ÷ 3.43 = \$3,500,000). The reduction in required operating cash of approximately \$500,000 (\$4,000,000 − \$3,500,000) represents an annual savings to the firm of \$50,000 (.10 × \$500,000). Since \$500,000 less must be tied up, the firm will be able to earn 10 percent on these funds. This savings clearly indicates the importance of efficiency in inventory and production management. ∎

Speeding the collection of accounts receivable. Another way of reducing the operating cash requirement is to speed up the collection of accounts receivable. Accounts receivable, just like inventory, tie up dollars that could be invested in additional assets. Accounts receivable are a necessary cost to the firm, since the extension of credit to customers normally allows the firm to achieve higher levels of sales than it could by operating on a strictly cash basis. The actual *credit terms* extended are normally dictated by the industry in which the firm operates.[8] Typically, they are related to the nature of the product sold—to the way it is transported and the way it is used.

In industries where virtually undifferentiated products are sold, credit terms may be a critical factor in sales. Normally in these industries, all firms match the best credit terms given in order to maintain their competitive position. In industries where relatively differentiated types of products are sold, there may be greater variance in credit terms.

The firm's collection period is affected not only by its credit terms but also by credit and collection policies. *Credit policies* are the firm's criteria for determining to whom credit should be extended; *collection policies* determine the effort put forth by the firm to collect accounts receivable promptly. Changes in credit terms, credit policies, and collection policies can all be used to decrease the average collection period while maintaining or increasing overall profits. Typically, the initiation of a cash discount for early payment, the use of more restrictive credit policies, or the initiation of more aggressive collection policies will decrease the average collection period. An example will help to clarify the effects of faster collections on the minimum operating cash requirement.

EXAMPLE   If the KLM Company, by changing its credit terms, is able to reduce the average collection period from the current level of 70 days to 50 days, this will reduce its cash cycle by 20 days (70 days − 50 days) to 100 days (CC = 120 days − 20 days = 100 days). The

---

[8] A discussion of various types of credit terms and their implications is presented in Chapter 17, which covers the management of accounts receivable. Credit terms state when payment is due and whether or not and under what conditions a cash discount is offered.

decrease in the collection period from 70 to 50 days raises the annual cash turnover rate from the initial level of 3 to 3.60 (CT = 360 days ÷ 100 days = 3.60). The increased cash turnover results in a decrease in the firm's minimum operating cash requirement from $4,000,000 to approximately $3,330,000 ($MOC$ = $12,000,000 ÷ 3.60 = $3,330,000). The reduction in required operating cash of approximately $670,000 ($4,000,000 − $3,330,000) represents an annual savings to the firm of approximately $67,000 (.10 × $670,000). By speeding the collection of accounts receivable by 20 days, the firm releases $670,000 in funds, which can be invested or used to repay debts. Again, the efficient management of accounts receivable thus provides the firm with definite financial rewards. ∎

COMBINING CASH MANAGEMENT STRATEGIES

We have illustrated the individual effects of implementing each of the suggested strategies on the firm's overall operating cash requirement. The stretching of accounts payable, the speeding of the inventory turnover, and the speeding of the collection of accounts receivable were all shown to have favorable effects on overall cash turnover. In actuality, firms would not attempt to implement just one of these strategies; they would attempt to use them all to reduce their operating cash requirement. Using a combination of these strategies would have the following effects on KLM.

EXAMPLE If KLM simultaneously increased the average payment period by 10 days, decreased the average age of inventory by 15 days, and sped the collection of accounts receivable by 20 days, its cash cycle would be reduced to 75 days, as shown here.

Initial cash cycle	120 days
Reduction due to:	
1. Increased payment period	
35 days to 45 days =	10 days
2. Decreased inventory age	
85 days to 70 days =	15 days
3. Decreased collection period	
70 days to 50 days =	20 days
Less: Total reduction in cash cycle	45 days
New cash cycle	75 days

KLM's annual cash turnover rate increases from 3 to 4.80 (CT = 360 days ÷ 75 days = 4.80). The increased cash turnover reduces the minimum operating cash requirement from $4 million to approximately $2.5 million ($MOC$ = $12,000,000 ÷ 4.80 = $2,500,000). The reduction in required operating cash of approximately $1.5 million ($4,000,000 − $2,500,000) represents an annual savings to the firm of $150,000 (.10 × $1,500,000). This savings represents a sizable decrease in the firm's opportunity costs, from an initial level of $400,000 (.10 × $4,000,000) to $250,000 (.10 × $2,500,000). ∎

Consciously implementing the basic accounts payable, inventory, and accounts receivable strategies outlined here should maximize profits with respect to the use of cash. However, when implementing these policies, care should be taken not to damage the firm's credit rating by overstretching accounts payable, to avoid having a large number of stockouts or a production stoppage due to carrying too small an inventory, and to avoid losing sales due to overly restrictive credit terms, credit policies, or collection policies.

Cash Management Techniques

Financial managers have at their disposal a variety of techniques, consistent with the basic cash management strategies, that can provide additional savings. These techniques are aimed at minimizing the firm's cash requirements by taking advantage of certain imperfections in the collection and payment system. Assuming that the firm has done all it can to stimulate customers to pay promptly and to select vendors offering the most attractive and flexible credit terms, certain techniques can further speed collections and slow disbursements. These procedures take advantage of the float existing in the collection and payment systems.

FLOAT

In the broadest sense, *float* refers to funds that have been dispatched by a payer (the firm or individual *making* payment) but are not in a form that can be spent by the payee (the firm or individual *receiving* payment). Float also exists when a payee has received funds in a spendable form but these funds have not been withdrawn from the account of the payer. Certain environmental as well as institutional imperfections create delays in the collection-payment system and are responsible for float. With electronic payments systems as well as deliberate action by the Federal Reserve system, it seems clear that in the not too distant future float will virtually disappear. Until that event happens, however, financial managers must continue to understand and take advantage of float.

Currently business firms and individuals can experience both collection and disbursement float as part of the process of making financial transactions. *Collection float* results from the delay between the time when a customer deducts a payment from the checking account ledger and the time when the vendor actually receives these funds in a spendable form. *Disbursement float* results from the lapse between the time when a firm deducts a payment from its checking account ledger and the time when funds are actually withdrawn from its account. Collection float is experienced by a payee and is a delay in receipt of funds; disbursement float is experienced by the payer and results in a delay in the actual withdrawal of funds.

Float has three basic components:

1. *Mail float.* The amount of time that elapses between the time when a payment is placed in the mail and the time when it is received by the payee.
2. *Processing float.* The amount of time that elapses between the receipt of a check by the payee and the actual deposit of it in the firm's account.
3. *Transit float.* The amount of time that elapses between the deposit of a check by the payee and the actual availability of the funds. This component

THE FUTURE OF FLOAT

From the moment the treasurer puts a check in the mail, an invoice is considered paid. The "mailbox rule," a custom since 1818, sets the postmark on the envelope as the date of payment. But that money won't actually leave the corporate bank account for days, perhaps even weeks. So the same money that has been used to pay the bill can be used again—invested, or left in a bank account to compensate for loans.

Taking advantage of this anomaly—"playing the float"—is fundamental to cash management today. Lengthening float time can contribute substantially to earnings: for each million dollars disbursed, extending float by one additional day can earn a company more than $100,000 per year. A large company that disbursed $5 million a day earned more than $1 million a year, by extending its float a few days. . . .

The current controversy

Since the early 1970's, companies have slowed down cash outflows by increasing float. They have learned to "criss-cross" payments, drawing checks on remote banks and mailing them from distant points. By writing checks on a western bank and mailing them from the South, the treasurer of one midwestern company stretched his float to more than fifteen days. "Man's ingenuity can be startling," lamented a Federal Reserve Bank officer in 1977, "and it applies to this field as well."

Federal Reserve banks had good cause to complain. Float extension techniques were exacerbating the problem of "Fed float"—funds the Fed makes available to banks before the checks they deposit have actually cleared. Fed float more than doubled in a decade, from a daily average of $3.2 billion in 1969 to $6.5 billion in 1979.

Concern about the cost of that float led to provisions of the Monetary Control Act of 1980, directing the Fed to eliminate float or to charge for it. The Fed responded by instituting charges for its check-clearing services, and by designing an electronic check collection plan. . . .

The emerging new system

An electronic payment system can save business from this deluge of paper. Using this system, the supplier's account is credited and the customer's account is debited simultaneously. The technology and the network for such a system exist. But why should a company go out of its way to speed up its payments? The typical treasurer's attitude has been, "I'll pay electronically when I'm paid that way!" . . .

Corporate treasurers are beginning to consider offering higher discounts, or longer payment terms, to customers who pay them electronically in immediately usable funds. These alternative credit terms would enable disbursing companies to make up for some of their lost float by sharing in the efficiencies of electronic payment. As more firms begin doing this, a new payment system will emerge.

In the long run, the new payment process may be part of an electronic system embracing all inter-company transactions. Electronic data interchange could largely replace the traditional paper flow of orders, invoices, and shipping data, as well as payments.

SOURCE: "The End of Float: Is Cash Management Sunk?" advertisement for Mellon Bank, Pittsburgh, Pa.

USING CONTROLLED DISBURSEMENT TO PROFIT FROM FLOAT

Many large companies find controlled disbursement pleasantly profitable. On float alone—by the companies' own calculations—National Distillers earns $3 million a year, American Brands $5 million, and Foremost-McKesson $5.5 million.

Prior to 1979, what is now called controlled disbursement was generally called remote disbursement, the term referring to the distance—the greater the better—between the location of the bank on which a check is drawn and the location of the recipient of that check. If a New York company, say, paid a New York supplier by a check drawn on a Montana bank, the payer picked up an extra two or three days' float—free use of the money—before the check was debited to his account. At 10% interest, one day's float of $1 million throughout the year is worth $100,000; two days' float, $200,000.

In 1979, however, the Federal Reserve Board issued a statement strongly disapproving of remote disbursement on the grounds that it denied consumers and small businesses "prompt access to funds," in addition to undermining the efforts of the Fed staff to "improve the speed and efficiency of the check-clearing system." In a twinkling the term "remote disbursement" disappeared from the sales pitches of banks, to be replaced by "controlled disbursement." . . .

Some corporate treasurers are candid about seeking float. When Herbert W. Eames Jr. became chief financial officer three years ago at J. Walter Thompson, the mammoth advertising agency headquartered in New York, he discovered that the company was getting minimal float, issuing checks drawn on a New York bank. Paying for advertising time, it disbursed checks to the networks by hand. Messengers from the networks and some vendors would appear at the cashier's office on the eighth floor of the Graybar Building so that the checks could be deposited as soon as possible.

Eames soon set matters right. He opened a remote disbursement account (he candidly uses the term) at the Waukesha branch of the First Wisconsin National Bank. Thompson calculates that it now gets an average of $1\frac{1}{2}$ days' additional float, even though some checks are still picked up by hand.

Whether it is called "remote" or "controlled," the phenomenon has grown enormously in the last few years. That is evident from a survey by Greenwich Research Associates, a financial consulting firm. Covering 1,217 large companies, including most of the *Fortune* 500, the survey showed that 59% maintained controlled disbursement accounts last year, up from 49% two years before. Also, 18% of the companies reported using remote disbursement, but the published data did not indicate how much overlap there was between the two groups.

A company wanting to make use of controlled disbursement has to find a bank that offers such accounts, but that's not much of a problem. They are now offered by over 130 banks around the country, including most of the leading banks in the East. As recently as 1978, perhaps three dozen banks offered controlled disbursement accounts.

SOURCE: Irwin Ross, "The Race Is to the Slow Payer," *Fortune,* April 18, 1983, pp. 75–76.

able securities portfolio—into the account, causing the account balance to remain at zero. The bank will charge a fee or require that balances be maintained in other accounts as compensation for this service. As long as the benefits of control as well as additional earnings are greater than the cost of such a system, its use is recommended.

THE ROLE OF STRONG BANKING RELATIONSHIPS

Establishing and maintaining strong bank relations is one of the most important elements in an effective cash management system. Banks have become keenly aware of the profitability of corporate accounts and in recent years have developed a number of innovative services and packages designed to attract various types of businesses. No longer are banks simply a place to establish demand deposit accounts and secure loans; instead, they have become the source of a wide variety of cash management services. For example, in addition to providing advice and assistance with government securities portfolios, banks are selling sophisticated information-processing packages to commercial clients; these packages deal with everything from basic accounting and budgeting to complex multinational disbursement and centralized cash control. All are designed to help financial managers maximize day-to-day cash availability and facilitate short-term investing.

Today most bank services are offered to corporations on a direct-fee basis, but some of the depository functions are still paid for with deposit balances rather than direct charges. Banks prefer the "compensating balance" approach, since it fosters deposit growth and provides a foundation for the future growth of bank earnings. Bank services available to cash managers should be used only if the benefits derived from their use are greater than their costs.

EXAMPLE A firm has been offered a cash management service that should eliminate "excess" cash on deposit and reduce certain administrative and clerical costs. Assume that the service, which costs $50,000 per year, involves the collection, movement, and reporting of corporate cash. The purported benefits are these: (1) The firm should be able to reduce the cash required to support operations by some $600,000 (as a result of tighter control over the cash flow), and (2) administrative and clerical costs should drop by about $1,000 per month (since the bank will be taking on administrative and clerical duties as part of the service). Using a 10 percent opportunity cost, the benefits and costs would be as follows:

Benefits (annual)	
Extra returns from reduced cash on hand (.10 × $600,000)	$60,000
Reduced administrative and clerical costs ($1,000 × 12)	12,000
Total benefits	$72,000
Less: Costs (annual)	
Bank service charges	50,000
Net benefits (annual)	$22,000

From a benefit-cost perspective, the proposal looks promising; the major risk, of course, is that the purported benefits will fall far short of the mark. Management, however, can at least get an idea of such risk. A simple calculation, for example, may be used to estimate the minimum reduction in cash or opportunity cost required to generate a sufficient level of total benefits. On the other hand, some positive risk reductions may result from adoption of the bank's program, such as less exposure to volatile interest rates, and these should obviously also be considered. ■

Marketable Securities Fundamentals

Marketable securities are short-term money market instruments that can easily be converted into cash.[13] Marketable securities are often referred to as part of the firm's liquid assets.

MOTIVES FOR HOLDING MARKETABLE SECURITIES

There are three motives for maintaining liquidity (cash *or* marketable securities) and therefore for holding marketable securities, which by definition represent a storehouse of liquidity. Each motive is based on the premise that a firm should attempt to earn a return on temporarily idle funds. The type of marketable security purchased will depend on the motive for the purchase. The basic motives are the *transactions motive,* the *safety motive,* and the *speculative motive.*

Transactions motive. Marketable securities that will be converted into cash to make some known future payment are said to be held for transactions purposes. Firms that must make certain payments in the near future may already have the cash with which to make these payments. To earn some return on these funds, they invest them in a marketable security that matures or can be easily liquidated on or just before the required payment date. For example, in the cases of quarterly tax payments and outlays for the acquisition of fixed assets, both the amount to be spent and the timing of the expenditure are normally known in advance. Since the exact timing of the payments is known, the firm can invest its cash in an interest-earning instrument until the payment date.

Safety motive. Marketable securities held for safety are used to service the firm's cash account. These securities must be very liquid, since they are bought with funds that will be needed, though exactly when is unknown. They protect the firm against the possibility of being unable to satisfy unexpected demands for cash.

Speculative motive. Marketable securities held because the firm currently has no other use for certain funds are said to be held for speculative reasons. Although such situations are not extremely common, some firms occasionally have excess cash. Until a firm finds a suitable use for this money, it invests it in more speculative types of marketable securities. In many cases, these dollars are placed in long-term instruments, which do not fall within the category of marketable securities. This motive is by far the *least common* one for holding marketable securities. Many firms would consider a company with such investments to be in an enviable position.

[13] As explained in Chapter 3, the *money market* results from an intangible relationship between the suppliers and demanders of short-term funds, that is, marketable securities.

CHARACTERISTICS OF MARKETABLE SECURITIES

The basic characteristics of marketable securities affect the degree of their marketability. To be truly marketable, a security must have two basic characteristics: (1) a ready market and (2) no likelihood of a loss in value (safety of principal).

A ready market. The market for a security should have both breadth and depth to minimize the amount of time required to convert it into cash. Common definitions of marketable securities suggest that they are securities that can be converted into cash in a short period of time, typically a few days.

Breadth of the market. The *breadth of a market* is determined by the number of participants. A broad market is one that has many participants. The term *breadth* is also used to refer to the geographic dispersion of a market. The more scattered the participants (assuming there are many), the more breadth the market is considered to have.

Depth of the market. The *depth of a market* is determined by its ability to absorb the purchase or sale of a large dollar amount of securities. Thus it is possible to have a broad market that has no depth. As many as 100,000 participants each willing to purchase one share is less desirable than 1,000 participants each willing to purchase 2,000 shares. Although both characteristics are desirable, it is much more important for a market to have depth than breadth for a security to be marketable.

No likelihood of a loss in value (safety of principal). The second key determinant of marketability is whether the market price received when liquidating a security deviates significantly from the amount invested. There should be little or no loss in the value of a marketable security over time. Consider a security recently purchased for $1000. If it can be sold quickly for $500, does that make it marketable? No. According to the definition of marketability, the security must not only be salable quickly but must also be salable for close to the $1000 initially invested.

This aspect of marketability is often overlooked. It is commonly referred to as the *safety of the principal.* The risk associated with a loss in the value of the principal invested in a marketable security is probably the most important aspect of the selection process. Only securities that can be easily converted into cash without experiencing any reduction in principal are candidates for short-term investment. It should be clear that the firm would be better off leaving the balances in cash if the alternative were to risk a significant reduction in principal.

THE OPTIMUM PROPORTION OF MARKETABLE SECURITIES IN THE FIRM'S ASSET MIX

A major decision confronting the business firm is exactly what mix of cash and marketable securities should be maintained.[14] This decision is difficult to make

---

[14] Numerous quantitative models for determining the optimum amounts of marketable securities to hold in certain circumstances have been developed. One of the most popular of these models is based on the inventory theory underlying the EOQ model, which is briefly described in Chapter 17. A discussion of these cash–marketable security models is beyond the scope of this text.

because it involves a trade-off between the opportunity to earn a return on idle funds during the holding period and the brokerage costs associated with the purchase and sale of marketable securities.

EXAMPLE Assume that a firm must pay $35 in brokerage costs to purchase and sell $4500 worth of marketable securities yielding an annual return of 8 percent that will be held for one month. Since the securities will be held for $\frac{1}{12}$ of a year, the firm will earn interest of .67 percent ($\frac{1}{12} \times 8\%$), or $30 (.0067 $\times$ $4500). Since this is less than the $35 cost of the transaction, the firm should *not* make the investment. This trade-off between interest returns and brokerage costs is a key factor in determining just what proportion of liquid assets should be held in the form of marketable securities. ■

The Popular Marketable Securities

The securities most commonly held as part of the firm's marketable securities portfolio are divided into two groups: (1) government issues and (2) nongovernment issues. Table 16.1 presents the January 6, 1984, yields for the marketable securities described in the following pages.

GOVERNMENT ISSUES

The short-term obligations issued by the federal government and available as marketable security investments are Treasury bills, Treasury notes, and federal agency issues.

Treasury bills. *Treasury bills* are obligations of the U.S. Treasury that are issued weekly on an auction basis. The most common maturities are 91 and 182 days, although

Table 16.1 Yields on Popular Marketable Securities for the Week Ending January 6, 1984

Security	Maturity period	Yield (%)
Bankers acceptances	3 months	9.31%
Certificates of deposit	3 months	9.57
Commercial paper	3 months	9.32
Eurodollar deposits	3 months	9.88
Federal agency issues[a]	3 months	9.17
Money market mutual funds[b]	approx. 30 days	9.10
Treasury bills	3 months	8.95
Treasury notes	1 year	10.02

[a] A Federal Home Loan Bank (FHLB) issue maturing in April 1984 is used here in the absence of any average yield data.
[b] A Boston Company Cash Fund with an average maturity of 30 days is used here in the absence of any average yield data.

SOURCE: All data except for that of federal agency issues and money market mutual funds were obtained from *Federal Reserve Bulletin*, February 1984 (Washington, D.C.: Board of Governors of the Federal Reserve System, 1984), p. A26. Data for federal agency issues and money market mutual funds were obtained from *The Wall Street Journal*, January 9, 1984, pp. 27, 37.

bills with one-year maturities are occasionally sold. Treasury bills are sold by competitive bidding. Because they are issued in bearer form, there is a strong *secondary (resale) market.* The bills are sold at a discount from their face value, the face value being received at maturity. The smallest denomination of Treasury bills currently available is $10,000. Since Treasury bills are issues of the United States government, they are considered virtually risk-free. For this reason, and because of the strong secondary market for them, Treasury bills are one of the most popular marketable securities. The yields on Treasury bills are generally lower than those on any other marketable securities due to their virtually risk-free nature.

Treasury notes. *Treasury notes* have initial maturities of between one and seven years, but due to the existence of a strong secondary market, they are quite attractive marketable security investments. They are generally issued in minimum denominations of $5000, carry a fixed-interest coupon rate, and pay interest semiannually. A firm that purchases a Treasury note that has less than one year left to maturity is in the same position as if it had purchased a marketable security with an initial maturity of less than one year. Due to their virtually risk-free nature, Treasury notes generally have a relatively low yield.

Federal agency issues. Certain agencies of the federal government issue their own debt. These *federal agency issues* are not part of the public debt, are not a legal obligation of the U.S. Treasury, and are not even guaranteed by the U.S. Treasury. Nevertheless, regardless of their lack of direct government backing, the issues of government agencies are readily accepted as low-risk securities, since most purchasers feel they are implicitly guaranteed by the federal government. Agency issues generally have minimum denominations of $5000 and are issued either with a stated coupon rate or at a discount. These agencies commonly issue short-term instruments:

1. Bank for Cooperatives (BC)
2. Federal Home Loan Banks (FHLB)
3. Federal Intermediate Credit Banks (FICB)
4. Federal Land Banks (FLB)
5. Federal National Mortgage Association (FNMA)

Most agency issues have short maturities and offer slightly higher yields than Treasury issues having similar maturities. Agency issues have a strong secondary market, which is most easily reached through government security dealers.

NONGOVERNMENT ISSUES

A number of additional marketable securities are issued by banks or businesses. These nongovernment issues typically have slightly higher yields than government issues due to the slightly higher risks associated with them. The main nongovernment marketable securities are negotiable certificates of deposit, commercial paper, banker's acceptances, Eurodollar deposits, money market mutual funds, and repurchase agreements.

GOVERNMENT CASH MANAGEMENT: A NEW ERA?

Each year the government spends or collects $1.7 trillion—almost $971 million every working hour, $16.2 million every minute. With this magnitude of cash flow, the manner in which the government handles its transactions can have a major financial effect on taxpayers.

This observation begins a discussion of federal cash management by President Reagan's commission on government waste, headed by Peter Grace. Some federal officeholders have knocked the Grace commission's report, issued in January [1984]. They say it overstates the money that might be saved through its 2,500 recommendations.

But many bureaucrats do not fault the report. At the Treasury Department, in fact, they're grateful to Grace's team for lending support to what Treasury insiders have been saying for years: Government cash management practices are outdated, and money to improve them would be well spent.

Under Secretary Donald Regan, the department has not been waiting for the Grace commission to tell it how to save. Indeed, in the two years since the commission started work, the Treasury has so improved its cash management that the report is now obsolescent.

Take a commission suggestion to award performance bonuses. The Grace commission found that federal cash managers had no strong incentive to speed the government's money intake or to regulate its outflow. (The Treasury issues some 640 million checks a year.) Coming and going, the cash was costing a lot in interest.

The report advanced a solution: a system of bonuses for the most efficient cash managers. Assistant Secretary Carole Dineen thought it would work. She had begun planning a bonus system months ago. "The problem will be finding the money," Dineen says. "We're talking about 10 awards a year that would range up to $10,000 apiece. It's not easy to find a loose $100,000, but I'm sure we'll do it.". . .

Dineen, herself a cash management whiz from Bankers Trust Co., says the Treasury has greatly improved its own operations even without bonuses. The Treasury and 104 other agencies have taken about 300 specific steps to improve cash management in the past few years, saving more than $600 million, she says, in fiscal 1983. Neither supercomputers nor accounting gimmickry were involved, she says. Rather, some fundamental private-sector procedures were adopted: the use of lockboxes, for example, employed for years by corporations to speed the processing and deposit of checks collected from geographically dispersed operations.

Another improvement involves concentration banking. One good example of an agency using this system is the Farmers Home Administration. Previously some $8 billion in FHA loan repayments flowed from some 2,200 county offices to a processing center in St. Louis, which would deposit them in the St. Louis Federal Reserve. "Between the mail float and the processing float, you had about eight days in there," Dineen says. With the help of the Treasury, the FHA created a system in which county offices deposit payments at local banks. From there they move electronically to one concentrator bank on a prearranged schedule. The money usually begins earning interest three days after the initial deposit at the county level, instead of eight.

SOURCE: Kevin McManus, "Performance Game," *Forbes,* March 26, 1984, p. 40.

Negotiable certificates of deposit (CDs). *Negotiable certificates of deposit (CDs)* are negotiable instruments evidencing the deposit of a certain number of dollars in a commercial bank. The amounts and maturities are normally tailored to the investor's needs. Average maturities of 30 days are quite common. A good secondary market for CDs exists. Normally, the smallest denomination for a negotiable CD is $100,000. The Federal Reserve system currently establishes maximum initial interest rates only on CDs with denominations of less than $2500. The yields on CDs are initially set on the basis of size, maturity, and prevailing money market conditions; they are typically above those on Treasury bills and slightly above the yield on commercial paper.

Commercial paper. *Commercial paper* is a short-term, unsecured promissory note issued by a corporation with a very high credit standing.[15] These notes are issued, generally in multiples of $100,000, by all types of firms and have initial maturities of anywhere from 3 to 270 days.[16] They can be sold directly by the issuer or through dealers. The yield on commercial paper typically is slightly below that available on negotiable CDs but above that paid on government issues with similar maturities.

Banker's acceptances. *Banker's acceptances* arise from a short-term credit arrangement used by businesses to finance transactions, especially those involving firms in foreign countries or firms with unknown credit capacities. The purchaser, to assure payment to the seller, requests its bank to issue a *letter of credit* on its behalf, authorizing the seller to draw a *time draft* — an order to pay a specified amount at a specified time — on the bank in payment for the goods. Once the goods are shipped, the seller presents a time draft along with proof of shipment to its bank. The seller's bank then forwards the draft with appropriate shipping documents to the buyer's bank for acceptance and receives payment for the transaction. The buyer's bank may either hold the acceptance to maturity or sell it at a discount in the money market.

As a result of its sale, the banker's acceptance becomes a marketable security that can be traded in the marketplace. The initial maturities of banker's acceptances are typically between 30 and 180 days, 90 days being most common. A banker's acceptance is a low-risk security because at least two, and sometimes three, parties may be liable for its payment at maturity. The yields on banker's acceptances are similar to those on commercial paper.

Eurodollar deposits. *Eurodollar deposits* are deposits denominated in U.S. dollars and deposited in banks located outside the United States. The nationality of the bank makes no difference; it might be a foreign bank or the foreign branch of an American bank. The deposit is always a time deposit or negotiable CDs in large denominations, typically in units of $1 million. London is the center of the Eurodollar market; other important centers are in Paris, Frankfurt, Zürich, Nassau

---

[15] An in-depth discussion of commercial paper, from the point of view of the issuer, is deferred until Chapter 18, which is devoted to the various sources of short-term financing available to business.

[16] The maximum maturity is 270 days because the Securities and Exchange Commission (SEC) requires formal registration of corporate issues having maturities greater than 270 days.

(Bahamas), Singapore, and Hong Kong. Deposits in Singapore and Hong Kong are called "Asia dollars" but are virtually identical to Eurodollars in yield, maturity, and other characteristics. The maturities of Eurodollar deposits range from overnight to several years, with most of the money held in the one-week to six-month maturity range. Because of the added foreign exchange risks, Eurodollar deposits tend to provide yields above nearly all other marketable securities, government or nongovernment. An active secondary market allows Eurodollar deposits to be used to meet both transactions and safety needs.

Money market mutual funds. *Money market mutual funds,* often called "money funds," are portfolios of marketable securities such as those described earlier. Shares or interests in these funds can be easily acquired — often without paying any brokerage commissions. A minimum initial investment of as low as $500, but generally $1000 or more, is required. Money funds provide instant liquidity in much the same fashion as a checking or savings account. In exchange for investing in these funds, investors earn returns that — especially during periods of high interest rates — are higher than those obtainable from most other marketable securities. Because of the high liquidity, competitive yields, and often low transactions costs, these funds have achieved significant growth in size and popularity in recent years.

Repurchase agreements. A *repurchase agreement* is not a specific security; it is an arrangement whereby a bank or security dealer sells specific marketable securities to a firm and agrees to repurchase the securities at a specific price at a specified point in time. In exchange for the tailor-made maturity date provided by this arrangement, the bank or security dealer provides the purchaser with a return slightly below that obtainable through outright purchase of similar marketable securities. The benefit to the purchaser is the guaranteed repurchase, the tailor-made maturity date ensures that the purchaser will have cash at a specified point in time. The actual securities involved may be government or nongovernment issues. Although the issues used in these agreements are generally short-term, money managers have been showing increased interest recently in using long-term bonds as a way to obtain increased returns without violating the intent of this mechanism. Repurchase agreements are ideal for marketable securities investments made to satisfy the transactions motive.

MULTINATIONAL FINANCE

International Cash Management

The concepts discussed so far in this chapter are equally applicable in an international setting. One basic difference is that a multinational company deals with many currencies in its international operations. Therefore, as pointed out in Chapter 7, the foreign exchange risk is a challenge for MNCs.

In its international cash management, an MNC can respond to foreign exchange risks by covering (hedging) its undesirable cash and marketable securities exposures or by certain adjustments in its operations. The first approach involves actions to be taken in the international financial markets in the form of borrowing or lending in different currencies and making transactions in the futures markets. More details on this approach will be given in Chapter 18 (also see Chapter 7). The second procedure is the one we will elaborate here.

In responding to exchange fluctuations, international cash flows can be given some protection through appropriate adjustments in assets and liabilities. Two routes are available to a multinational company. The first centers on the operating relationships that a subsidiary of an MNC maintains with *other* firms—"third parties." Depending on management's expectation of a local currency's position, adjustments in operations would involve the reduction of liabilities if the currency is appreciating or the reduction of financial assets if it is depreciating. For if a U.S.-based MNC with a subsidiary in Mexico expects the Mexican currency to appreciate in value relative to the U.S. dollar, local customers' accounts receivable would be increased and accounts payable would be reduced if at all possible. With the dollar being the currency in which the MNC parent will have to prepare consolidated financial statements, the net result of this action is to increase (or decrease) the Mexican subsidiary's resources in local currency when that currency is appreciating (or depreciating).

The second route focuses on the operating relationship a subsidiary has with its own parent (or with other subsidiaries within the same MNC). In dealing with exchange risks, a subsidiary can rely on "intra-MNC" accounts. Specifically, undesirable foreign exchange exposures can be corrected to the extent that the subsidiary can take the following steps:

1. In revaluation-prone countries, intra-MNC accounts receivable are collected as soon as possible, while payment of intra-MNC accounts payable is delayed as long as possible.
2. In devaluation-prone countries, intra-MNC accounts receivable are not collected for as long as possible, while intra-MNC accounts payable are paid as soon as possible.

Again using the example of a Mexican subsidiary, the net result of step 1 or step 2 would be the potential increase (or decrease) of that subsidiary's resources in the Mexican currency when that currency is appreciating (or depreciating) relative to the parent MNC's main currency, the U.S. dollar.

From a *global* point of view and as far as an MNC's consolidated intracompany accounts are concerned, manipulation of such accounts by one subsidiary can mean the opposite results for another subsidiary (or the parent firm). In other words, if an MNC's subsidiaries in, for instance, Brazil and Mexico are dealing with each other, the Brazilian subsidiary's manipulations of intra-MNC accounts — along the lines just discussed — in anticipation of an appreciation of that country's currency relative to that of Mexico's can mean exchange gains for the Brazilian subsidiary and losses for the Mexican one. The exact degree and direction of the actual manipulations, however, may depend on the tax status of each country, the MNC obviously wanting to have the exchange losses in the country with the higher tax rate. Finally, changes in intra-MNC accounts can be subject to restrictions and regulations put foward by the respective host countries of various subsidiaries.

Potential manipulations of both third party and intra-MNC accounts are among the approaches available to an MNC and its subsidiaries in facing foreign exhange risks. The existence of cash and marketable securities in different currencies, moreover, provides an MNC with challenges as well as opportunities in raising and investing funds in the international financial arena. Chapter 18 presents additional details on these challenges and opportunities. ●●

CHAPTER SUMMARY

● Cash and marketable securities make up the firm's liquid assets and give the firm the liquidity it needs to satisfy financial obligations as they come due.

● Cash is held in the form of a checking deposit at a commercial bank, which pays little or no interest.

● There are many forms of marketable securities, each with different characteristics, but all earning some kind of return.

● The efficient management of cash is based on three basic strategies: (1) paying accounts payable as late as possible, (2) managing the inventory-production cycle efficiently to maximize the inventory turnover rate, and (3) collecting accounts receivable quickly.

● Although the cash budget is useful for cash planning, decisions on the appropriate cash balance depend on the magnitude of both expected and unexpected cash receipts and cash disbursements as well as the financial manager's disposition toward risk.

● Financial managers can use a variety of techniques to capitalize on certain imperfections in the collection and payment system to take advantage of float in order to minimize the firm's cash requirements.

● Popular collection techniques include concentration banking, lockboxes, direct sends, preauthorized checks (PACs), depository transfer checks (DTCs), and wire transfers.

● Disbursement techniques include controlled disbursing, playing the float, overdraft systems, and zero-balance accounts.

● Establishment and maintenance of strong banking relationships is crucial to effective cash management.

● A firm holds marketable securities to earn a return on temporarily idle funds.

● Marketable securities are held for a number of reasons: the transactions motive, the safety motive, and the speculative motive.

● For a security to be considered marketable, it must have a ready market that has both breadth and depth. The risks associated with the safety of the principal must be quite low.

● The proportion of a firm's liquid assets made up of marketable securities depends on the trade-off between the return earned during the holding period and the brokerage costs associated with purchasing and selling securities.

● The most popular marketable securities are government and nongovernment issues.

● Government issues include Treasury bills, Treasury notes, and federal agency issues.

● The most common nongovernment issues are negotiable certificates of deposit, commercial paper, banker's acceptances, Eurodollar deposits, money market mutual funds, and repurchase agreements.

 ● An MNC has a variety of means available to it for managing its international cash position. The foreign exchange risks that complicate international cash management can be overcome through manipulations of accounts receivable and accounts payable from and to third parties and intra-MNC units.

KEY TERMS

banker's acceptance

breadth of a market

cash cycle (*CC*)

cash turnover (*CT*)

collection float

collection policy

commercial paper

concentration banking

controlled disbursing

credit policy

credit terms

depository transfer check (DTC)

depth of a market

direct send

disbursement float

Eurodollar deposit

federal agency issue

float

lockbox system

mail float

marketable securities

minimum operating cash (*MOC*)

money market mutual fund

negotiable certificate of deposit (CD)

overdraft system

payable-through draft

playing the float

preauthorized check (PAC)

processing float

repurchase agreement

safety motive

safety of principal

speculative motive

stretching accounts payable

time draft

transactions motive

transit float

Treasury bill

Treasury note

wire transfer

zero-balance account

QUESTIONS

16-1 What is the objective of the financial manager in cash management? What conditions must be satisfied in meeting this objective?

16-2 What are the *key strategies* with respect to accounts payable, inventory, and accounts receivable for the firm that wants to manage its cash efficiently?

16-3 What is a firm's "cash cycle"? How are the cash cycle and cash turnover of a firm related? What should a firm's objective with respect to cash cycle and cash turnover be?

16-4 If a firm reduces the average age of its inventories, what effect might this action have on the cash cycle? On the firm's total sales? Is there a trade-off between average inventory and sales? Give reasons for your answer.

16-5 Define *float* and describe its three basic components. Compare and contrast collection and payment float and cite the financial manager's goal with respect to each of these types of float.

16-6 Briefly describe the key features of each of the following collection techniques.

    a Concentration banking   **d** Preauthorized checks (PACs)

    b Lockboxes   **e** Depository transfer checks (DTCs)

    c Direct sends   **f** Wire transfers

16-7 Briefly describe the key features of each of the following disbursement techniques.

    a Controlled disbursing   **c** Overdraft systems

    b Playing the float   **d** Zero-balance accounts

16-8 Describe the role of strong banking relationships in the cash management process. How should available bank services be evaluated?

16-9 What are the possible motives for holding marketable securities? What two characteristics are essential for a security to be deemed "marketable"?

16-10 For each of the following government-based marketable securities, give a brief description emphasizing maturity, liquidity, risk, and return.

    a Treasury bill

    b Treasury note

    c Federal agency issue

16-11 Describe the basic features—including maturity, liquidity, risk, and return—of each of the following nongovernment marketable securities.

    a Negotiable certificate of deposit (CD)   **c** Banker's acceptance

    b Commercial paper   **d** Eurodollar deposit

16-12 Briefly describe the basic features of the following marketable securities and explain how they both involve other marketable securities.

    a Money market mutual funds

    b Repurchase agreements

 **16-13** Discuss the steps to be followed in adjusting a subsidiary's accounts relative to "third parties" when that subsidiary's local currency is expected to appreciate in value in relation to the currency of the parent company.

 **16-14** Outline the changes to be undertaken in intra-MNC accounts if a subsidiary's currency is expected to depreciate in value relative to the currency of the parent MNC.

PROBLEMS

16-1 **(Cash Cycle and Minimum Operating Cash)** Western Supply is concerned about managing cash in an efficient manner. On the average, accounts receivable are collected in 60 days, and inventories have an average age of 90 days. Accounts payable are paid approximately 30 days after they arise. The firm spends $30 million each year, at a constant rate. Assuming a 360-day year,

    a Calculate the firm's cash cycle.

    b Calculate the firm's cash turnover.

    c Calculate the minimum operating cash balance the firm must maintain to meet its obligations.

16-2 **(Cash Cycle and Minimum Operating Cash)** The Denver Company has an inventory turnover of 12, an average collection period of 45 days, and an average payment period of 40 days. The firm spends $1 million per year. Assuming a 360-day year,

    a Calculate the firm's cash cycle.

    b Calculate the firm's cash turnover.

    c Calculate the minimum operating cash balance the firm must maintain to meet its obligations.

16-3 **(Comparison of Cash Cycles)** A firm collects accounts receivable, on the average, after 75 days. Inventory has an average age of 105 days, and accounts payable are paid an average of 60 days after they arise. What changes will occur in the cash cycle and cash turnover with each of the following circumstances? Assume a 360-day year.

    a The average collection period changes to 60 days.

    b The average age of inventory changes to 90 days.

    c The average payment period changes to 105 days.

    d The circumstances in **a**, **b**, and **c** occur simultaneously.

16-4 **(Changes in Cash Cycles)** A firm is considering several plans that affect working capital accounts. Given the following five plans and their probable results, which one would you favor? Explain.

	Change		
Plan	Average age of inventory	Average collection period	Average payment period
A	+30 days	+20 days	+5 days
B	+20 days	−10 days	+15 days
C	−10 days	0 days	−5 days
D	−15 days	+15 days	+10 days
E	+5 days	−10 days	+15 days

16-5   **(Annual Savings and the Cash Cycle)**   The Watson Manufacturing Company pays accounts payable on the tenth day after purchase. The average collection period is 30 days, and the average age of inventory is 40 days. Annual cash outlays are approximately $18 million. The firm is considering a plan that would stretch its accounts payable by 20 days. If the firm can earn 12 percent on equal-risk investments, what annual savings can it realize by this plan? Assume no discount for early payment of trade credit and a 360-day year.

16-6   **(Changing Cash Cycle)**   Cooper Industries turns its inventory eight times each year, has an average payment period of 35 days, and has an average collection period of 60 days. The firm's total annual outlays are $3.5 million.
   a   Calculate the firm's minimum operating cash, assuming a 360-day year.
   b   Assuming that the firm can earn 14 percent on its short-term investments, how much would the firm earn annually if it could *favorably change* its current cash cycle by 20 days?

16-7   **(Multiple Changes in Cash Cycle)**   Fisher Corporation turns its inventory six times each year, has an average payment period of 30 days, and has an average collection period of 45 days. The firm's total annual outlays are $3 million.
   a   Calculate the firm's minimum operating cash, assuming a 360-day year.
   b   Find the firm's minimum operating cash in the event that it makes the following changes simultaneously.
     (1)   Extends average payment period by 10 days.
     (2)   Shortens the average age of inventory by five days.
     (3)   Speeds the collection of accounts receivable by an average of 10 days.
   c   If the firm can earn 13 percent on its short-term investments, how much, if anything, could it earn annually as a result of the changes in b?
   d   If the annual cost of achieving the savings in c is $35,000, what action would you recommend to the firm? Why?

16-8   **(Float)**   Levin Industries has daily cash receipts of $65,000. A recent analysis of its collections indicated that customers' payments were in the mail an average of $2\frac{1}{2}$ days. Once received the firm spends $1\frac{1}{2}$ days processing payments, and once deposited, it takes an average of three days for these receipts to clear the banking system.
   a   How much collection float (in days) does the firm currently have?
   b   If the firm's opportunity cost is 11 percent, would it be economically advisable for the firm to pay an annual fee of $16,500 in order to reduce collection float by three days? Explain why or why not.

16-9   **(Concentration Banking)**   Consumer Products Corporation sells to a national market and bills all credit customers from the New York City office. Using a continuous billing system, the firm has collections of $1.2 million per day. Under consideration is a concentration banking system that would require customers to mail payments to the nearest regional office to be deposited in local banks.

Consumer Products estimates that the collection period for accounts will be shortened an average of $2\frac{1}{2}$ days under this system. The firm also estimates that *annual* service charges and administrative costs of $300,000 will result from the proposed system. The firm can earn 14 percent on equal-risk investments.

a How much cash will be made available for other uses if the firm accepts the proposed concentration banking system?

b What savings will the firm realize on the $2\frac{1}{2}$-day reduction in the collection period?

c Would you recommend the change? Explain your answer.

16-10 **(Concentration Banking — Range of Outcomes)** The Frazee Toy Company markets its Crazee Frazee through widely dispersed distributors in the United States. It currently takes between six and nine days for cash-receipt checks to become available to the firm once they are mailed. Through use of a concentration banking system, the firm estimates that the collection float can be reduced to between two and four days. Daily cash receipts currently average $10,000. The firm's minimum opportunity cost is 5.5 percent — the rate paid on passbook savings accounts.

a Use the data given to determine the minimum and maximum annual savings from implementing the proposed system.

b If the annual cost of the concentration banking system is $7500, what recommendation would you make?

c What impact, if any, would the fact that the firm's opportunity cost is 12 percent have on your analysis? Explain.

16-11 **(Lockbox System)** A firm that has an opportunity cost of 9 percent is contemplating installation of a lockbox system at an annual cost of $90,000. The system is expected to reduce mailing time by $2\frac{1}{2}$ days and reduce check clearing time by $1\frac{1}{2}$ days. If the firm collects $300,000 per day, would you recommend the system? Explain.

16-12 **(Lockbox System)** Eastern Oil feels a lockbox system can shorten its accounts receivable collection period by three days. Credit sales are $3,240,000 per year, billed on a continuous basis. The firm has other equally risky investments with a return of 15 percent. The cost of the lockbox system is $9,000 per year.

a What amount of cash will be made available for other uses under the lockbox system?

b What net benefit (cost) will the firm receive if it adopts the lockbox system?

16-13 **(Direct Send — Single)** Catalan Industries of San Diego, California, just received a check in the amount of $800,000 from a customer in Bangor, Maine. If the firm processes the check in the normal manner, the funds will become available in six days. To speed up this process, the firm could send an employee to the bank in Bangor on which the check is drawn to present it for payment. Such action will cause the funds to become available after two days. If the cost of the direct send is $650 and the firm can earn 11 percent on these funds, what recommendation would you give them? Explain.

16-14 **(Direct Sends — Multiple)** Tom Morris Enterprises just received four sizable checks drawn on various distant banks throughout the United States. The following data on these checks has been assembled. The firm, which has a 12 percent opportunity cost, can lease a small business jet with pilot to fly the checks to the cities of the banks on which they are drawn and present them for immediate payment. This task can be accomplished in a single day — thereby reducing to one day the funds availability from each of the four checks. The total cost of leasing the jet with pilot and other incidental expenditures is $4500. Analyze the proposal and make a recommendation as to the proposed action.

Check	Amount	Number of days until funds are available
1	$ 600,000	7 days
2	2,000,000	5 days
3	1,300,000	4 days
4	400,000	6 days

16-15   **(Controlled Disbursing)**   A large Midwestern firm has annual cash disbursements of $360 million made continuously over the year. Although annual service and administrative costs would increase by $100,000, the firm is considering writing all disbursement checks on a small bank in Georgia. The firm estimates this will allow an additional $1\frac{1}{2}$ days of cash usage. If the firm earns a return on other equally risky investments of 12 percent, should it change to the distant bank? Why or why not?

16-16   **(Playing the Float)**   Cartgate Enterprises routinely funds its checking account to cover all checks when written. A thorough analysis of its checking account discloses that the firm could maintain an average account balance 25 percent below the current level and adequately cover all checks presented. The average account balance is currently $900,000. If the firm can earn 10 percent on short-term investments, what, if any, annual savings would result from maintaining the lower average account balance?

16-17   **(Checking Account Management)**   Walter's Window has a weekly payroll of $250,000. The payroll checks are issued on Friday afternoon each week. In examining the check-cashing behavior of its employees, it has found the following pattern:

Number of business days[a] since issue of check	Percentage of checks cleared
1	20
2	40
3	30
4	10

[a] Excludes Saturday and Sunday.

Given this information, what recommendation would you give the firm with respect to managing its payroll account? Explain.

16-18   **(Zero-Balance Account)**   Caminito Industries is considering establishment of a zero-balance account. The firm currently maintains an average balance of $420,000 in its disbursement account. As compensation to the bank for maintaining the zero-balance account, the firm will have to pay a monthly fee of $1,000 and maintain a $300,000 noninterest-earning deposit in the bank. The firm currently has no other deposits in the bank. Evaluate the proposed zero-balance account and make a recommendation to the firm assuming it has a 12 percent opportunity cost.

16-19   **(Marketable Securities — Economics of Purchase)**   To purchase and sell $25,000 in marketable securities, a firm must pay $800. If the marketable securities have a yield of 12 percent annually, recommend purchasing or not if
a   The securities are held for one month.
b   The securities are held for three months.
c   The securities are held for six moths.
d   The securities are held for one year.

16-20 **(Marketable Securities — Comparison and Selection)** Alice Piper is cash manager for Carousel Corporation. The cash budget indicates that excess cash of $20,000 will be available for the next 90 days. She is considering an investment of this sum in one of the instruments listed below. Ignoring taxes, calculate the expected rate of return for each and select the best investment. Explain your choice.

   a Common stock costing $40 per share and paying a $2 annual dividend ($.50 each quarter); the stock is expected to increase in price by 18 percent per year.

   b Preferred stock that pays a $6 annual dividend ($1.50 each quarter), currently selling for $50 a share. No increase in price is anticipated.

   c Municipal bonds issued by the city of Houston, Texas, maturing in 2005. Currently and in the near future, these are expected to sell at par. They have an 8 percent annual coupon (2 percent per quarter).

   d A 90-day certificate of deposit paying 12 percent annual interest (3 percent per quarter).

   e Ninety-day commercial paper selling at 97 percent of face value (commercial paper sells at a discount).

   f A money market mutual fund expected to yield 11.8 percent per year.

Chapter 17

Accounts Receivable and Inventory Management

After studying this chapter, you should be able to:

1. Discuss credit scoring and the fundamental aspects of credit standards, including the key variables to consider, procedures for determining their value, and their use in making credit decisions.

2. Describe the basic sources of credit information and their use in analyzing credit applicants.

3. Understand the key components of credit terms—cash discount, cash discount period, and credit period—and the effects of changes in them on profits.

4. Explain key features of collection policies, including the basic trade-offs, available collection techniques, and the role of the computer in accounts receivable management.

5. Understand the key characteristics of inventory, its role as an investment, and the relationship between inventory and accounts receivable.

6. Describe common inventory management techniques, including the ABC system, the basic economic order quantity (EOQ) model, and the reorder point.

600

Accounts receivable represent the extension of credit on open account by the firm to its customers. In order to keep current customers and attract new ones, most manufacturing concerns find it necessary to offer credit. Inventory is also a necessary current asset in that it permits the production-sale process to operate with a minimum of disturbances. A stock of raw materials and work in process is needed to ensure that required items are available when demanded. Finished goods inventories must be available to provide a buffer stock that will enable the firm to satisfy demands as they arise. Accounts receivable and inventory are closely related: When a credit sale is made, the appropriate amount of finished goods inventory is effectively converted into an account receivable.

Accounts receivable and inventory are the dominant current assets held by most firms. For the average manufacturer, they account for over 78 percent of *current assets.* Table 17.1 presents data on the level of accounts receivable and inventory held by a selected sample of manufacturing firms in late 1983. Together, accounts receivable and inventory account for nearly 33 percent of the *total assets* of manufacturing corporations. Although there are industry differences in the relative size of these accounts, it is clear that these two current assets are of key importance. The financial manager tends to have direct control over accounts receivable, and he or she must act as a "watchdog" and adviser in matters concerning inventory — an asset that tends to be under the direct control of the manufacturing department.

Credit Policies

A firm's *credit policy* provides guidelines for determining whether to extend credit to a customer and how much credit to extend. The firm must concern itself not only with the establishment of credit standards but also with the correct use of these standards in making decisions. Appropriate sources of credit information and methods of credit analysis must be developed. Each of these aspects of credit policy is important to the successful management of accounts receivable. Poor

Table 17.1   Accounts Receivable and Inventory as a Percentage of Total
Assets for Selected Industries (Third Quarter, 1983)

	Percentage of total assets		
Industry group	Accounts receivable	Inventory	Accounts receivable plus inventory
All manufacturers	15.5%	17.1%	32.6%
Chemicals and allied products	15.0	14.1	29.1
Food and kindred products	14.7	18.9	33.6
Electrical and electronic equipment	20.7	24.0	44.7
Paper and allied products	13.4	12.5	25.9
Petroleum and coal products	8.4	6.0	14.4
Primary metal industries	14.3	15.6	29.9
Rubber and miscellaneous plastic products	24.0	18.3	42.3
Textile mill products	26.5	26.4	52.9
Transportation equipment	13.6	28.8	42.4

SOURCE: U.S. Bureau of the Census, *Quarterly Financial Report for Manufacturing, Mining and Trade Corporations.* Third Quarter, 1983 (Washington, D.C.: U.S. Government Printing Office, 1983).

implementation of a good credit policy or successful implementation of a poor credit policy will not produce optimal results. A brief look at credit scoring will help place credit policy in proper perspective.

CREDIT SCORING

Consumer credit decisions, because they involve a large group of homogeneous applicants, each representing a small part of the firm's total business, can be handled using impersonal computer-based credit decision models. One popular approach is *credit scoring*— a procedure resulting in a score reflecting the applicant's overall credit strength, derived as a weighted average of the scores obtained on a variety of key financial and credit characteristics. Credit scoring is often used by large credit card operations such as oil companies and department stores. The technique can best be presented using an example.

EXAMPLE   Pete's Petroleum Company uses a credit scoring model to make its consumer credit decisions. Each credit applicant fills out and submits a credit application to the company. The application is then reviewed and scored by one of the company's credit analysts and entered into the computer; the rest of the process, including making the credit decision, generating a letter of acceptance or rejection to the applicant, and dispatching preparation and mailing of a credit card, is automated.

Table 17.2 demonstrates the calculation of Joe Customer's credit score. The firm's predetermined credit standards are summarized in Table 17.3. The cutoff scores shown were developed to accept the group of credit applicants that will result in a positive contribution to share value. In evaluating Joe Customer's credit score of 80.25 in light of the firm's credit standards, the decision would be to *extend standard credit terms* to him (80.25 > 75). ■

Table 17.2   Credit Scoring of Joe Customer by Pete's Petroleum Company

Financial and credit characteristics	Score (0 to 100) (1)	Predetermined weight (2)	Weighted score [(1) × (2)] (3)
Credit references	80	.15	12.00
Home ownership	100	.15	15.00
Income range	70	.25	17.50
Payment history	75	.25	18.75
Years at address	90	.10	9.00
Years on job	80	.10	8.00
	Total	1.00 Credit score	80.25

Key:
Column 1: Scores assigned by analyst and computer using company guidelines on the basis of data presented in credit application. Scores range from 0 (lowest) to 100 (highest).
Column 2: Weights based on the company's analysis of the relative importance of each financial and credit characteristic in predicting whether or not a customer will pay an account. These weights must sum to 1.00.

The attractiveness of credit scoring should be clear from the example. Unfortunately, most manufacturers sell to a diversified group of different-sized businesses. The statistical characteristics necessary for applying credit scoring to decisions regarding *mercantile credit*—business firms extending credit to other business firms—rarely exist. In the following discussion we concentrate on the basic concepts of mercantile credit decisions, which cannot easily be made in quantifiable terms.

CREDIT STANDARDS

The firm's *credit standards* define the minimum criteria for the extension of credit to a customer. Such things as credit ratings, credit references, average payment periods, and certain financial ratios provide a quantitative basis for establishing and enforcing credit standards. Our concern here is not with the individual components of credit standards but with the restrictiveness or nonrestrictiveness of a firm's overall policy. Knowing the key variables that must be considered when a firm is contemplating relaxing or tightening its credit standards will give a general feel for the kinds of decisions involved.

Table 17.3   Credit Standards for Pete's Petroleum Company

Credit score	Action
Greater than 75	Extend standard credit terms.
65 to 75	Extend limited credit; if account is properly maintained, it converts to standard credit terms after one year.
Less than 65	Reject application.

Key variables. The major variables that should be considered in evaluating proposed changes in credit standards are sales volume, the investment in accounts receivable, and bad debt expenses.[1]

Sales volume. Changing credit standards can be expected to change the volume of sales. As credit standards are relaxed, sales are expected to increase; a tightening of standards is expected to reduce sales. The effects of these changes on net profits will depend on their impact on revenues and costs.

Investment in accounts receivable. There is a cost associated with carrying accounts receivable. The higher the firm's average accounts receivable, the more expensive they are to carry, and vice versa. If the firm relaxes its credit standards, the average level of accounts receivable should rise. Thus a relaxation of credit standards can be expected to result in higher carrying costs.

The changes in the level of accounts receivable associated with changes in credit standards result from two factors — changes in sales and changes in collections.[2] Increased sales will result in higher average accounts receivable, and decreased sales will result in lower average account receivable. When credit terms are relaxed, credit is extended to less creditworthy customers, who will probably take longer to pay their bills. Since relaxing credit standards results in more slower paying customers, it raises the average level of accounts receivable. In short, changes in sales and changes in collections work together to produce higher carrying costs for accounts receivable when credit standards are relaxed and reduced carrying costs for accounts receivable when standards are tightened. These reactions also occur when changes are made in credit terms or collection procedures.

Bad debt expenses. Another variable that is expected to be affected by changes in credit standards is bad debt expenses. The probability (or risk) of acquiring a bad debt increases as credit standards are relaxed.

The basic changes and effects on profits expected to result from the *relaxation* of credit standards are tabulated as follows:

Variable	Direction of change	Effect on profits
Sales volume	Increase	Positive
Average collection period	Increase	Negative
Bad debt expenses	Increase	Negative

If credit standards were tightened, the opposite effects would be expected.

[1] A relaxation of credit standards would be expected to add to the *clerical costs* as a result of the need for a larger credit department, while a tightening of credit standards might save clerical costs. Because these costs are assumed to be included in the variable cost per unit, they are not explicitly isolated in the analyses presented in this chapter. These costs are most likely *semivariable*: As the credit department expands, certain points are reached at which new people must be employed, but between hirings the department cost remains fixed.

[2] Due to the forward-looking nature of accounts receivable analysis, certain items such as sales, collections, and bad debts resulting from changes in the management of accounts receivable must be estimated. The need to estimate these future values may introduce a great deal of uncertainty into the decision process. Some of the techniques discussed in Chapter 11, such as sensitivity analysis, statistics, and simulation, can be applied to these estimates to adjust them for uncertainty.

Determining values of key variables. The way in which the key variables involved in the credit standard decision are determined can be illustrated by a simple example.[3]

EXAMPLE   The XYZ Company is currently selling a product for $10 per unit. Sales (all on credit)[4] for the most recent year were 60,000 units. The variable cost per unit is $6, and the average cost per unit, given a sales volume of 60,000 units, is $8. The difference of $2 between the average cost per unit and the variable cost per unit represents the contribution of each of the 60,000 units toward the firm's fixed costs. Working backward, since each of the 60,000 units sold contributes $2 to fixed costs, the firm's total fixed costs must be $120,000.

The firm is currently contemplating a relaxation of credit standards that is expected to result in a 5 percent increase in unit sales to 63,000 units, an increase in the average collection period from its current level of 30 days to 45 days, and an increase in bad debt expenses from the current level of 1 percent of sales to 2 percent. The firm's required return on equal-risk investments is 15 percent.

To determine whether the XYZ Company should implement the proposed relaxation in credit standards, the effect on the firm's additional profit contribution from sales, the cost of the marginal investment in accounts receivable, and the cost of marginal bad debts must be calculated.

Additional profit contribution from sales   The additional profit contribution from sales expected to result from the relaxation of credit standards can be calculated easily. The firm's profit contribution from sales will increase by an amount equal to the product of the number of additional units sold and the profit contribution per unit. Because fixed costs are "sunk" and thereby unaffected by a change in the level of sales, the only cost relevant to a change in sales would be out-of-pocket or variable costs. Sales are expected to increase by 5 percent, or 3,000 units. The profit contribution per unit[5] will equal the difference between the sale price per unit ($10) and the variable cost per unit ($6). The profit contribution per unit would therefore be $4. The total additional profit contribution from sales will be $12,000 (3,000 units $\times$ $4 per unit).

Cost of the marginal investment in accounts receivable   The cost of the marginal investment in accounts receivable can be calculated by finding the difference between the cost of carrying receivables before and after the introduction of the relaxed credit standards. The average investment in accounts receivable can be calculated using the following formula.

$$\text{Average investment in accounts receivable} = \frac{\text{cost of annual sales}}{\text{turnover of accounts receivable}} \quad (17.1)$$

where:

---

[3] Because various credit policy decisions tend to commit the firm to long-run behaviors, a number of authors have suggested that credit policy decisions should be made using a present-value framework. See Yong H. Kim and Joseph C. Atkins, "Evaluating Investments in Accounts Receivable: A Maximizing Framework," *Journal of Finance* 33 (May 1978), pp. 402–412. Although their suggestions are valid, a more recent article by Kanwal S. Sachdeva and Lawrence J. Gitman, "Accounts Receivable Decions in a Capital Budgeting Framework," *Financial Management* 10 (Winter 1981), pp. 45–49, has shown that single-period decision rules similar to those applied throughout this chapter will provide correct accept-reject decisions without the computational rigor of the present-value approach.

[4] Although all sales have been assumed to be made on credit throughout this chapter, the analytical techniques presented could easily be adapted to situations in which only a portion of sales were made on credit. The simpler all-credit sale assumption is used to avoid confusing the key issues by complicating the analytical procedure.

[5] The *profit contributions per unit* or *contribution margin* represents the amount of each sales dollar available for meeting fixed costs and profits. In the example, the amount by which the sale price per unit exceeds the variable cost per unit is viewed as contributing directly toward profits (or reducing losses).

$$\text{Turnover of accounts receivable}^6 = \frac{360}{\text{average collection period}}$$

The cost of annual sales under the proposed and present plans can be found as noted below.
Cost of annual sales:

$$\text{Proposed plan: (\$8)(60,000 units)} + \text{(\$6)(3,000 units)}$$
$$\$480,000 + \$18,000 = \$498,000$$
$$\text{Present plan: (\$8)(60,000 units)} = \$480,000$$

The cost calculation for the present plan involves the straightforward use of the average cost per unit of $8. The cost under the proposed plan is found by adding to the total cost of producing 60,000 units the marginal cost of producing an additional 3,000 units ($6 per unit). In spite of the fact that by definition fixed costs do not change, the total — fixed plus variable — cost must be determined for both the proposed and present plans. *Fixed costs are included because the time pattern of their recovery is affected by the length of the average collection period.* The longer the average collection period is, the slower the firm will recover its fixed as well as variable costs and therefore the greater its average investment will be in accounts receivable, and vice versa.

The turnover of accounts receivable in each case is found by dividing the average collection period into 360 — the number of days in a year.
Turnover of accounts receivable:

$$\text{Proposed plan: } \frac{360}{45} = 8$$

$$\text{Present plan: } \frac{360}{30} = 12$$

It can be seen that with implementation of the proposed plan, the accounts receivable turnover would drop from 12 to 8.

Substituting the cost and turnover data just calculated into Equation 17.1 for each case, the following average investments in accounts receivable result:
Average investment in accounts receivable:

$$\text{Proposed plan: } \frac{\$498,000}{8} = \$62,250$$

$$\text{Present plan: } \frac{\$480,000}{12} = \$40,000$$

The marginal investment in accounts receivable as well as its cost is calculated as follows:
Cost of marginal investment in accounts receivable:

Average investment with proposed plan	$62,250
Average investment with present plan	40,000
Marginal investment in accounts receivable	$22,250
× required return on investment	.15
Cost of marginal investment in A/R	$ 3,338

---

[6] The turnover of accounts receivable can also be calculated by *dividing annual sales by accounts receivable.* For the purposes of this chapter, only the formula transforming the average collection period to a turnover of accounts receivable is emphasized.

ACCOUNTS RECEIVABLE: MOST IMPORTANT
WORKING CAPITAL ACTIVITY

A March 1983 survey yielding 238 responses from chief financial officers of the respondent firms in the *Fortune* 1000 listing provides some interesting insights into the related importance of various working capital activities. As can be seen in the table below, based on the weighted average responses, accounts receivable require slightly more time than cash management and short-term financial planning and budgeting. While "time spent" and "importance" may not necessarily coincide, these data tend to suggest that accounts receivable are a very important working capital activity.

Time Spent on Individual Working Capital Activities

	Percent of time spent on activity						Weighted average response[a]
Working capital activity	<10%	10%– 20%	20%– 30%	30%– 40%	40%– 50%	>50%	
	Response percentages[b]						
Accounts receivable	25.2	32.9	30.3	5.1	4.7	1.7	18.95
Cash management	23.3	39.2	24.1	7.3	4.3	1.7	18.84
Short-term financial planning and budgeting	22.3	34.3	31.8	9.9	1.3	.4	18.56
Inventory management	31.9	32.3	23.1	7.0	4.4	1.3	17.62
Banking relationships	42.4	38.6	16.5	1.3	1.3	.0	13.08
Accounts payable management	52.8	31.2	10.4	3.9	1.3	.4	12.17
Short-term investment management	54.0	31.9	9.4	3.0	.9	.9	11.97
Short-term borrowing	62.3	25.9	9.2	1.3	1.3	.0	10.34

[a] Weighted average response for each factor is calculated as the sum of the product of the response percentage and the midpoint of the time/percent range across all values. For example, the weighted average response for accounts receivable is calculated as follows: $[(.252 \times .05) + (.329 \times .15) + (.303 \times .25) + (.051 \times .35) + (.047 \times .45) + (.017 \times .75)] \times 100 = 18.95$.
[b] Percentages may not total 100% due to rounding.

SOURCE: Lawrence J. Gitman and Charles E. Maxwell, "Financial Activities of Major U.S. Firms: Survey and Analysis of *Fortune*'s 1000," unpublished manuscript, 1984, Exhibit 7.

It should be clear that the cost of investing an additional $22,250 in accounts receivable was found by multiplying it by 15 percent (the firm's required return on investment). The resulting value of $3,338 is considered a cost because it represents the maximum amount that could have been earned on the $22,250 had it been placed in the best equal-risk investment alternative available.

Cost of marginal bad debts   The cost of marginal bad debts is found by taking the difference between the level of bad debts before and after the relaxation of credit standards, as shown here.

Cost of marginal bad debts:

Proposed plan: (.02)($10/unit)(63,000 units) = $12,600
Present plan: (.01)($10/unit)(60,000 units) = 6,000
        Cost of marginal bad debts $ 6,600

The key factor to note is that *the unit cost of a bad debt equals its sale price per unit*—$10 in this case. The entire sale price is lost and must be deducted in the analysis to offset the fact that the additional profit contribution from sales has been calculated on the assumption that the full sales price will be received. ■

Making the credit standard decision. To decide whether the firm should relax its credit standards, the additional profit contribution from sales must be compared to the sum of the cost of the marginal investment in accounts receivable and the cost of marginal bad debts. If the additional profit contribution is greater than marginal costs, credit standards should be relaxed; otherwise, current standards should remain unchanged. Let us look at an example.

EXAMPLE The results and key calculations relative to the XYZ Company's decision to relax its credit standards are summarized in Table 17.4. It can be seen that since the additional profit contribution from the increased sales would be $12,000, which exceeds the sum of the cost of the marginal investment in accounts receivable and the cost of marginal bad debts, the firm *should* relax its credit standards as proposed. The net addition to total profits resulting from such an action will be $2,062 per year. ■

The technique described here for making a credit standard decision is commonly used for evaluating other types of changes in the management of accounts receivable as well. If the firm in the preceding example had been contemplating more restrictive credit standards, the cost would have been a reduction in the profit contribution from sales, and the return would have been reductions in the cost of the marginal investment in accounts receivable and in bad debts. Another application of this analytical technique is described later in the chapter.

CREDIT ANALYSIS

Once the firm has established its credit standards, it must develop procedures for *credit analysis*—evaluating credit applicants. Often the firm must not only determine the creditworthiness of a customer but also it must estimate the maximum amount of credit the customer is capable of supporting. Once this is done, the firm can establish a *line of credit,* the maximum amount the customer can owe the firm at any time. Lines of credit are established to eliminate the necessity of checking a major customer's credit each time a purchase is made.

Whether the firm's credit department is evaluating the creditworthiness of a customer desiring credit for a specific transaction or that of a regular customer in order to establish a line of credit, the basic procedures are the same. The only difference is in the depth of the analysis. A firm would be unwise to spend $50 to investigate the creditworthiness of a customer making a one-time $40 purchase, but $50 for a credit investigation may be a good investment in the case of a

Table 17.4 The Effects of a Relaxation of Credit
Standards on the XYZ Company

Additional profit contribution from sales [(3,000 units)($10 − $6)]		$12,000
Cost of marginal investment in A/R[a]		
Average investment with proposed plan:		

$$\frac{(\$8)(60,000) + (\$6)(3,000)}{8} = \frac{\$498,000}{8} \qquad \$62,250$$

Average investment with present plan:

$$\frac{(\$8)(60,000)}{12} = \frac{480,000}{12} \qquad \underline{40,000}$$

Marginal investment in A/R	$22,250	
Cost of marginal investment in A/R[(.15)($22,250)]		($ 3,338)
Cost of marginal bad debts		
Bad debts with proposed plan [(.02)($10)(63,000)]	$12,600	
Bad debts with present plan [(.01)($10)(60,000)]	6,000	
Cost of marginal bad debts		($ 6,600)
Net profit from implementation of proposed plan		$ 2,062

[a] The denominators 8 and 12 in the calculation of the average investment in accounts receivable for the proposed and present plans are the accounts receivable turnovers for each of these plans (360/45 = 8 and 360/30 = 12).

customer who is expected to make credit purchases of $60,000 annually. The two basic steps in the process are (1) obtaining credit information and (2) analyzing the information.

Obtaining credit information. When a firm is approached by a customer desiring credit terms, the credit department typically begins the evaluation process by requiring the applicant to fill out various forms requesting financial and credit information and references. Working from the application, the firm obtains additional information from other sources. If the firm has previously extended credit to the applicant, it will have its own information on the applicant's payment history. The major external sources of credit information are as follows:

Financial statements. By requiring the credit applicant to provide financial statements for the past few years, the firm can analyze the applicant's liquidity, activity, debt, and profitability positions. Although no specific information with respect to past payment patterns is shown, insight into the firm's financial position may indicate the nature of its overall financial management. The willingness of the applicant firm to provide these statements may be indicative of its financial position. Audited financial statements are a must for applicants desiring to make large credit purchases or to obtain lines of credit.

Dun & Bradstreet. Dun & Bradstreet, Inc., is the largest mercantile credit-reporting agency. It provides subscribers with a copy of a reference book containing

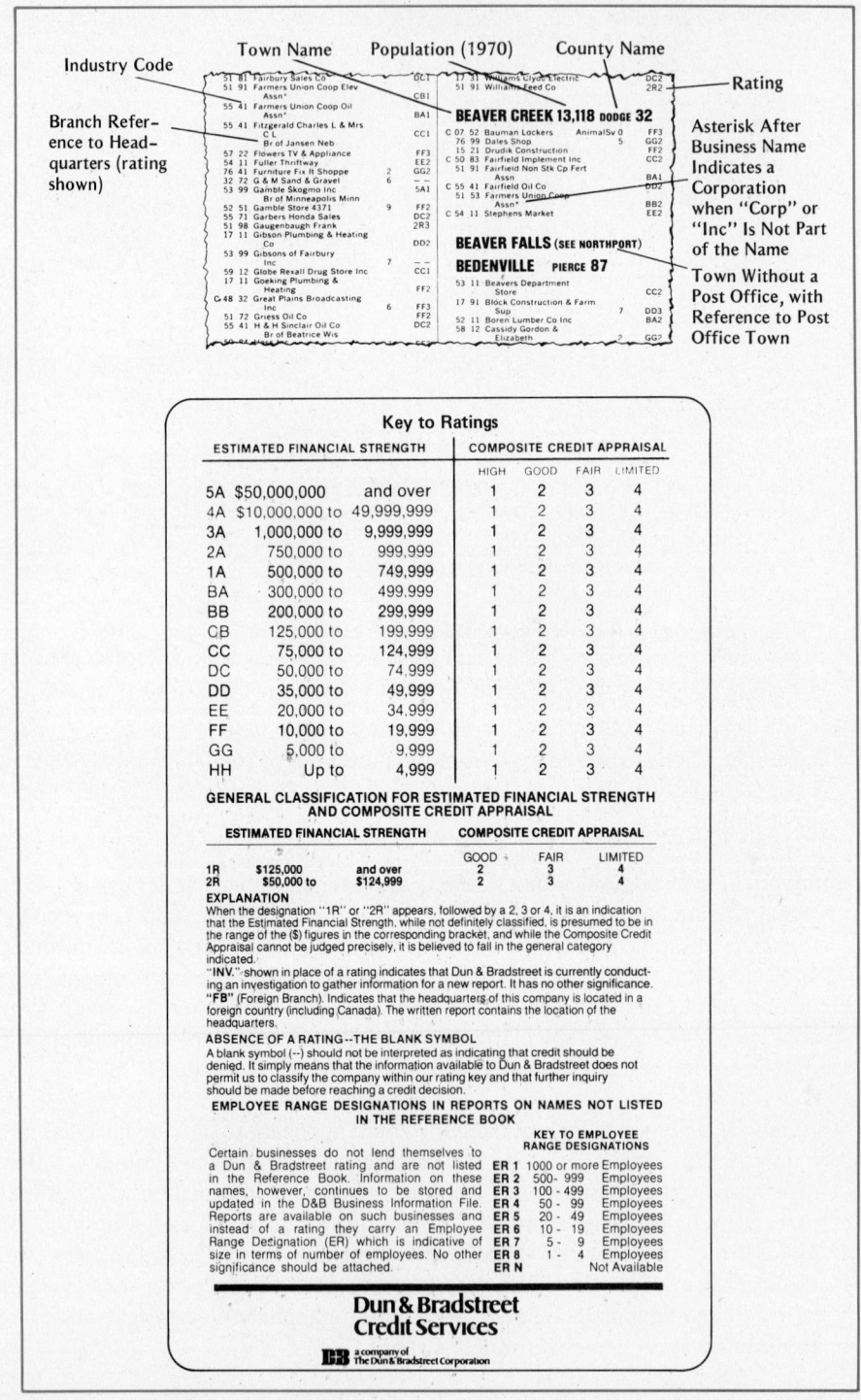

SOURCE: Dun & Bradstreet, Inc., New York, 1984.

Figure 17.1 Excerpts from the *Dun & Bradstreet Reference Book* and the *Key to Ratings*

credit ratings and keyed estimates of overall financial strength for approximately 3 million U.S. and Canadian firms. A sample book page along with a key to the ratings is given in Figure 17.1. For an additional charge, subscribers can obtain a Business Information Report on a specific company. This report provides summary information about the firm and its Dun & Bradstreet rating and information on the firm's payments, finances, banking, history, and operations. When applicable, the Business Information Report also includes information on special events in the business such as changes in the business, updates in the business's activities, and public filings such as suits, judgments, tax liens, and so forth. A sample report containing many of these elements is presented in Figure 17.2.

Credit interchange bureaus. Firms may obtain credit information through the National Credit Interchange System, a national network of local credit bureaus that exchange information on a reciprocal basis. By agreeing to provide information to the credit bureau on its present customers, a firm receives the right to make inquiries concerning prospective customers. The reports obtained through these

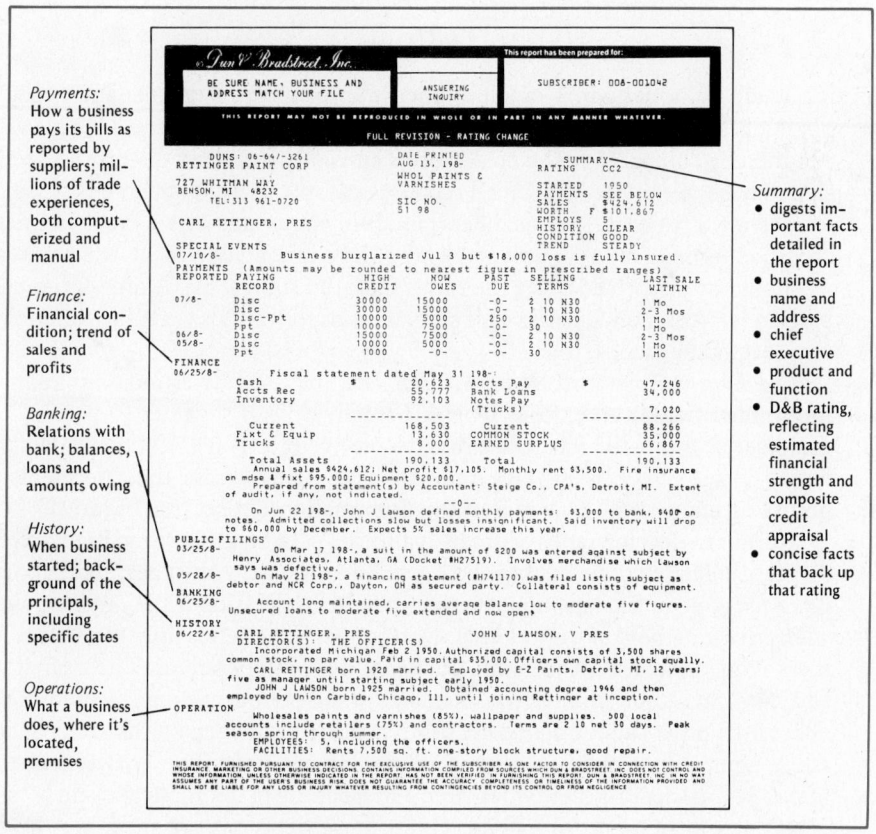

SOURCE: Dun & Bradstreet, Inc., New York, 1984.

Figure 17.2   A Dun & Bradstreet *Business Information Report*

exchanges are factual rather than analytical. A fee is usually levied for each inquiry.

Direct credit information exchanges. Another way of obtaining credit information may be through local, regional, or national credit associations. These associations may be organized as part of certain industry or trade organizations. Often, an industry association maintains certain credit information that is available to members. Another method is to contact other suppliers selling to the applicant and ask what its payment patterns are like. Often, cooperation with such requests for information can be obtained with an agreement to reciprocate.

Bank checking. It may be possible for the firm's bank to obtain credit information from the applicant's bank. However, the type of information obtained is most likely to be vague unless the applicant aids the firm in obtaining it. This is true because the credit applicant's bank cannot disclose specific information such as account balances, loan balances, and so forth, without the consent of the applicant. Typically, an estimate of the firm's cash balance is provided. For instance, it may be found that a firm maintains a "high five-figure" balance.

Analyzing credit information. A credit applicant's financial statements and accounts payable ledger can be used to calculate its "average payment period." This value can then be compared to the credit terms currently extended the firm. A second step may be to age the applicant's accounts payable so as to obtain better insight into payment patterns. For customers requesting large amounts of credit or lines of credit, a thorough ratio analysis of the firm's liquidity, activity, debt, and profitability should be performed using the firm's financial statements. A time-series comparison (discussed in Chapter 4) of similar ratios for various years should uncover any developing trends.

The *Dun & Bradstreet Reference Book* can be used for estimating the maximum line of credit to extend. Dun & Bradstreet itself suggests 10 percent of a customer's "estimated financial strength" (see Figure 17.1). Additional data providing insight into creditworthiness can be obtained from the "payments reported" section of the D & B Business Information Report (see Figure 17.2).

A firm can develop ratios or credit evaluation schemes tailored to its own credit standards. There are no established procedures; the firm must gear its analysis to its needs. One of the key inputs to the final credit decision is the credit analyst's *subjective judgment* of a firm's creditworthiness. Experience provides a "feel" for the nonquantifiable aspects of the quality of a firm's operations. The analyst will add his or her knowledge of the character of the applicant's management, references from other suppliers, and the firm's historic payment patterns to any quantitative figures developed to determine creditworthiness. The analyst will then make the final decision as to whether to extend credit to the applicant, and possibly what amount of credit to extend. Often these decisions are made not by one individual but by a credit review committee.

Credit Terms

A firm's *credit terms* specify the repayment terms required of all credit customers.[7] Typically, a type of shorthand is used. For example, credit terms may be stated as *2/10 net 30,* which means that the purchaser receives a 2 percent cash discount if the bill is paid within 10 days after the beginning of the credit period; if the customer does not take the cash discount, the full amount must be paid within 30 days after the beginning of the credit period. Credit terms cover three things: (1) the cash discount, if any (in this case 2 percent), (2) the cash discount period (in this case 10 days), and (3) the credit period (in this case 30 days). Changes in any aspect of the firm's credit terms may have an effect on its overall profitability. The positive and negative factors associated with such changes, and quantitative procedures for evaluating them, are presented in this section.

CASH DISCOUNTS

When a firm initiates or *increases* a cash discount, the following changes and effects on profits can be expected:

Variable	Direction of change	Effect on profits
Sales volume	Increase	Positive
Average collection period	Decrease	Positive
Bad debt expenses	Decrease	Positive
Profit per unit	Decrease	Negative

The sales volume should increase because, if a firm is willing to pay by day 10, the price per unit decreases. If demand is elastic, sales should increase as a result. The average collection period should decrease, reducing the cost of carrying accounts receivable. The reduction in receivables results from the fact that some customers who did not previously take the cash discount will now take it. The bad debt expense should fall since, as people on the average pay earlier, the probability of a bad debt should decrease.[8] Both the decrease in the average collection period and the decrease in the bad debt expense should result in increased profits. The negative aspect of an increased cash discount is a decreased profit per unit as more people take the discount and pay the reduced price. Decreasing or eliminating a cash discount would have opposite effects. The quantitative effects of changes in cash discounts can be evaluated by a method similar to that used to evaluate changes in credit standards.

[7] An in-depth discussion of credit terms as viewed by the recipient is presented in Chapter 18. The emphasis there is on the analysis of credit terms in order to evaluate trade credit as a source of short-term financing. In this chapter, our concern is with credit terms from the point of view of the offerer.

[8] This contention is based on the fact that the longer it takes a person to pay, the less likely it is that the person will pay. The more time that elapses, the more opportunities there are for a customer to become technically insolvent or bankrupt. Therefore, the probability of a bad debt is expected to increase directly with increases in the average collection period.

EXAMPLE   Assume that the XYZ Company is contemplating initiating a cash discount of 2 percent for payment prior to day 10 after a purchase. The firm's current average collection period is 30 days [turnover = (360/30) = 12], credit sales of 60,000 units are made, the variable cost per unit is $6, and the average cost per unit is currently $8. The firm expects that if the cash discount is initiated, 60 percent of its sales will be on discount, and sales will increase by 5 percent to 63,000 units. The average collection period is expected to drop to 15 days [turnover = (360/15) = 24]. Bad debt expenses are expected to drop from the current level of 1 percent of sales to .5 percent of sales. The analysis of this decision is presented in Table 17.5. It can be seen that the calculations are quite similar to those presented for the credit standard decision in Table 17.4[9] except for the final entry, "cost of cash discount." This cost of $7,560 reflects the fact that profits will be reduced as a result of a 2 percent cash discount being taken on 60 percent of the new level of sales. The XYZ Company can increase profit by $10,178 by initiating the proposed cash discount; such an action therefore seems advisable. This type of analysis can also be applied to decisions concerning the elimination or reduction of cash discounts.

Table 17.5   The Effects of Initiating a Cash Discount on the XYZ Company

Additional profit contribution from sales [(3,000 units)($10 − $6)]		$12,000
Cost of marginal investment in A/R		
Average investment with proposed plan:		
$\dfrac{(\$8)(60,000) + (\$6)(3,000)}{24} = \dfrac{\$498,000}{24}$	$20,750	
Average investment with present plan:		
$\dfrac{(\$8)(60,000)}{12} = \dfrac{\$480,000}{12}$	40,000	
Marginal investment in A/R	($19,250)	
Cost of marginal investment in A/R [(.15)($19,250)]		2,888 [a]
Cost of marginal bad debts		
Bad debts with proposed plan [(.005)($10)(63,000)]	$ 3,150	
Bad debts with present plan [(.01)($10)(60,000)]	6,000	
Cost of marginal bad debts		2,850[a]
Cost of cash discount[b][(.02)(.60)($10)(63,000)]		(7,560)
Net profit from implementation of proposed plan		$10,178

[a] This value is positive since it represents a savings rather than a cost.
[b] This calculation reflects the fact that a 2 percent cash discount will be taken on 60 percent of the new level of sales — 63,000 units at $10 each.   ∎

[9] The calculation of the average investment in accounts receivable presented for both the present and proposed plans is not entirely correct. Whenever a change in credit terms or some other aspect of accounts receivable is expected to change the payment pattern of existing customers, formal analysis should recognize that the firm's pattern of receipt of both cost *and* profit from these customers is being altered. Therefore, the average investment in receivables for existing customers whose payment patterns have been altered should be measured at the sale price, not cost. For an excellent discussion of this point, see Edward A. Dyl, "Another Look at the Investment in Accounts Receivable," *Financial Management* (Winter 1977), pp. 67–70. To convey the key concepts throughout the remainder of this chapter without confusing the reader, the average accounts receivable investment is calculated at cost regardless of whether or not existing customers' payment patterns are altered by the proposed action.

CASH DISCOUNT PERIOD

The net effect of changes in the cash discount period is quite difficult to analyze due to the nature of the forces involved. For example, if the cash discount period were *increased,* the following changes could be expected:

Variable	Direction of change	Effect on profits
Sales volume	Increase	Positive
Average collection period due to non-discount takers now paying earlier	Decrease	Positive
Average collection period due to discount takers still getting cash discount but paying later	Increase	Negative
Bad debt expenses	Decrease	Positive
Profit per unit	Decrease	Negative

The problems in determining the exact results of changes in the cash discount period are directly attributable to the two forces affecting the firm's average collection period. When the cash discount period is increased, there is a positive effect on profits because many people who did not take the cash discount in the past will now take it, decreasing the average collection period. However, there is also a negative effect because people who already were taking the cash discount will still be able to take it and pay later, increasing the average collection period. The net effect of these two forces on the average collection period is difficult to quantify.

If the firm were to shorten the cash discount period, the effects would be the opposite of those just described. Due to the many assumptions necessary to illustrate changes in the cash discount period analytically, no example of these effects is given. However, the basic calculations described earlier can be applied to this decision.

CREDIT PERIOD

Changes in the credit period also affect the firm's profitability. The following effects on profits can be expected from an *increase* in the credit period.

Variable	Direction of change	Effect on profits
Sales volume	Increase	Positive
Average collection period	Increase	Negative
Bad debt expenses	Increase	Negative

Increasing the credit period should increase sales, but both average collection period and bad debt expenses are likely to increase as well. Thus the net effect on profits of the sales increase is positive, while the increases in collection period and bad debt expenses will negatively affect profits. A decrease in the credit period is likely to have the opposite effect. The credit period decision is analyzed in the same way as the credit standard decision illustrated earlier in Table 17.4.

Collection Policies

The firm's *collection policies* are the procedures followed to collect accounts receivable when they are due. The effectiveness of these policies can be partly evaluated by looking at the level of bad debt expenses. This level depends not only on collection policies but also on the policies on which the extension of credit is based. If one assumes that the level of bad debts attributable to credit policies is relatively constant, increasing collection expenditures can be expected to reduce bad debts. This relationship is depicted in Figure 17.3. As the figure indicates, beyond point A, additional collection expenditures will not reduce bad debt losses enough to justify the outlay of funds. The firm must determine the level of collection expenditures that is "optimal" from a cost-benefit viewpoint.

BASIC TRADE-OFFS

The basic trade-offs expected to result from an *increase* in collection efforts are as follows:

Variable	Direction of change	Effect on profits
Sales volume	None or decrease	None or negative
Average collection period	Decrease	Positive
Bad debt expenses	Decrease	Positive
Collection expenditures	Increase	Negative

Increased collection expenditures should reduce the average collection period and bad debt expenses, increasing profits. The costs of this strategy may include lost sales in addition to increased collection expenditures if the level of collection

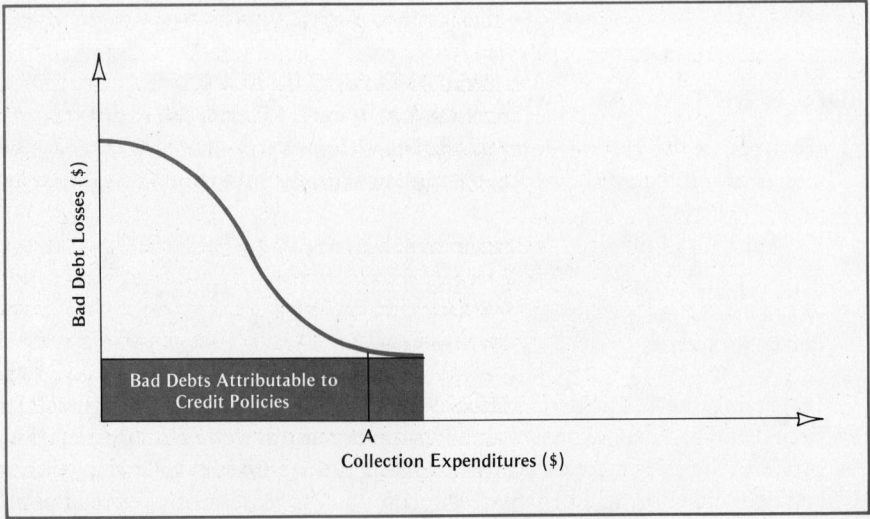

Figure 17.3 Collection expenditures and bad debt losses

effort is too intense. In other words, if the firm pushes its customers too hard to pay their accounts, they may be angered and take their business elsewhere. The firm should be careful not to be overly aggressive. If payments are not received on the due date, the firm should wait a reasonable period of time before initiating collection procedures.

The basic trade-offs just described can be evaluated quantitatively in a manner similar to that used to evaluate the trade-offs for credit standards and cash discounts. By calculating the sum of the marginal cost of increased collection efforts and the decreased profit contribution from sales (if any) and comparing this to the savings from decreased investment in accounts receivable and reduced bad debt expenses, various strategies for increasing the level of collection effort can be assessed. Proposed reductions in the level of effort can be evaluated in a similar manner.

TYPES OF COLLECTION TECHNIQUES

A number of collection techniques are employed. As an account becomes more and more overdue, the collection effort becomes more personal and more strict. The basic techniques are presented in the order typically followed in the collection process.

Letters. After an account receivable becomes overdue a certain number of days, the firm normally sends a polite letter reminding the customer about his or her obligation. If the account is not paid within a certain period of time after the letter has been sent, a second, more demanding letter is sent. This letter may be followed by yet another letter, if necessary. Collection letters are the first step in the collection process for overdue accounts.

Telephone calls. If letters prove unsuccessful, a telephone call may be made to the customer to personally request immediate payment. If the customer has a reasonable excuse, arrangements may be made to extend the payment period. A call from the company's attorney may be used if all other discussions seem to fail.

Personal visits. This technique is much more common at the consumer credit level, but it may be employed by industrial suppliers. Sending a local salesperson, or a collection person, to confront the customer can be a very effective collection procedure. Payment may be made on the spot.

Using collection agencies. A firm can turn uncollectible accounts over to a collection agency or an attorney for collection. The fees are typically quite high; the firm may receive less than 50 cents on the dollar for accounts collected in this way.

Legal action. This is the most stringent step in the collection process. It is an alternative to the use of a collection agency. Not only is direct legal action expensive, but it may force the debtor into bankruptcy, thereby reducing the possibility of future business without guaranteeing the ultimate receipt of the overdue amount.

COMPUTERIZATION OF ACCOUNTS RECEIVABLE MANAGEMENT

The use of computers in the billing and collection of accounts is widespread. A computer is used to bill credit customers at the appropriate time following a purchase. As payments are received, a record of them is keyed into the computer. A computer can be programmed to monitor accounts receivable after a customer has been billed. Periodic checks are automatically made at certain points in time after billing to see if the accounts have been paid. If payment has not been received at certain predetermined points, collection letters are sent. After a prescribed number of these letters have been sent without any receipt of payment, a special notice will be generated, probably as part of a report to the credit manager. At this point, the collection efforts become more directly personal. Actions such as telephone calls, personal visits, and use of a collection agency will then be taken. Legal action is also a possibility.

Currently computers are being used not only to monitor accounts but also as an aid in the credit decision process. Data on each customer's payment patterns are maintained and can be called forth to evaluate requests for renewed or additional credit. A computer can also be used to monitor the effectiveness of the collection department by generating data on the status of outstanding accounts. Although the computer cannot carry out the entire accounts receivable management function, it will continue to reduce the amount of paperwork required.

Inventory Management

As shown in Table 17.1, inventory, like accounts receivable, represents a significant investment on the part of most firms. In Chapter 16 the importance of turning over inventory quickly in order to minimize this investment was illustrated. This financial objective often conflicts with the objective of carrying sufficient inventories to satisfy production demands and minimize stockouts. The firm must determine the "optimal" level of inventories that reconciles these conflicting objectives. The financial manager does not directly control inventory and therefore tends to have only indirect input into the inventory management process. Let us look at some key aspects of inventory management, including basic characteristics, inventory as an investment, the relationship between inventory and accounts receivable, and inventory management techniques.

BASIC CHARACTERISTICS OF INVENTORY

Two aspects of inventory require some elaboration. One aspect is the types of inventory; the other concerns differing viewpoints as to the appropriate level of inventory held by certain functional areas of the firm.

Types of inventory. The basic types of inventory are raw materials, work-in-process, and finished goods inventories.

Raw materials. The *raw materials inventory* contains items purchased by the firm, usually basic materials such as screws, plastic, raw steel, or rivets. If a firm manufactures complex products with numerous parts, the raw materials inventory may consist of manufactured items that have been purchased from another firm or another division of the same corporation. For example, radios, tires, or transmissions might be purchased by a Ford Motor Company assembly plant from other Ford divisions or from outside vendors. All manufacturing firms have a raw materials inventory of some kind. The actual level of each raw material maintained depends on the lead time it takes to receive orders, the frequency of use, the dollar investment required, and the physical characteristics of the inventory.

Work in process. The *work-in-process inventory* consists of all items currently in the production process. These are normally partially finished goods at some intermediate stage of production. Pieces of metal on which some machining has been performed but which will have additional characteristics at the end of the production process are considered work in process. The level of work in process depends on the length and complexity of the production process. If 50 operations, each requiring approximately two days of production time, are required to convert a raw material into a finished good, an item will remain in the work-in-process inventory for a long period of time. Even if only a few operations are required, their complexity may make the production process long, resulting in a high work-in-process inventory.

Finished goods. The *finished goods inventory* consists of items that have been produced but not yet sold. Some manufacturing firms that produce to order carry very low finished goods inventories, since virtually all items are sold before they are produced. Our concern here is with the general manufacturing firm producing and selling a diversified group of products. Most merchandise is produced in anticipation of sales. The level of finished goods is largely dictated by projected sales demands, the production process, and the investment in finished goods required.

Functional viewpoints with respect to inventory levels. Conflicting viewpoints concerning appropriate inventory levels commonly exist within the business firm. The functional areas generally involved are finance, marketing, manufacturing, and purchasing. Each area views inventory levels in light of its own objectives.

Finance. The financial manager's basic responsibility is to make sure that the firm's cash flows are managed efficiently. The financial manager must monitor the levels of all assets in light of this overall objective, making sure that the firm does not tie up its funds in redundant or excess assets. Inventory, which typically involves a sizable investment by the firm, must be scrutinized closely. The financial manager's general disposition toward inventory levels is to keep them low. The financial manager must police the inventories, making sure that the firm's money is not being unwisely invested in excess inventory.

Marketing. The marketing manager is concerned with the level of finished goods inventories. He or she would like to have large inventories of each of the firm's finished products. This would ensure that all orders could be filled quickly and eliminate the need for backorders due to stockouts. Since the marketing department's effectiveness is usually evaluated, and the sales force is often compensated, on the basis of the dollar volume of sales generated, these people want to make sure that no sales are lost because a product cannot be delivered quickly to a customer. Carrying high inventories should reduce the probability of lost sales due to stockouts.

Manufacturing. The manufacturing manager's main concern is with the level of the raw materials and work-in-process inventories. His or her actions with respect to these inventories directly affect the level of finished goods inventories. The manufacturing manager's major responsibility is to make sure that the production plan is correctly implemented and that it results in the desired amount of finished goods. The manufacturing manager is evaluated not only on the basis of the efficient delivery of finished goods but also on keeping the production cost per unit low. In fulfilling his or her role, the manufacturing manager would keep high raw materials inventories in order to avoid production delays and cause high finished goods inventories by making large production runs in order to lower unit production costs.

Purchasing. The purchasing manager is concerned solely with the raw materials inventories; he or she is responsible for seeing that the raw materials required by production are available in the correct quantities at the desired times.[10] The purchasing manager is concerned not only with the size and timing of raw materials purchases but also with buying such materials at a favorable price. Since raw material costs are an important component of the estimated product cost, on the basis of which pricing decisions may be made, it is important for the purchasing manager to buy raw materials wisely. Without proper control, the purchasing manager may purchase larger quantities than are actually needed in order to receive quantity discounts or in anticipation of rising prices or a shortage of a certain material.

A CLOSER VIEW OF INVENTORY AS AN INVESTMENT

On numerous occasions in the foregoing discussion we have referred to inventory as an investment. Inventory is an investment in the sense that it requires the firm to tie up its money. The analyses earlier in this chapter illustrated how the average investment in accounts receivable could be calculated using the cost of annual sales and the turnover of accounts receivable. The average investment in inventory can be calculated in a similar manner, as the following example shows.

---

[10] Organizationally, the purchasing function is quite often under the control of the manufacturing or plant manager rather than being an autonomous function. This arrangement makes sense, since the purchasing activity exists primarily to service the manufacturing function.

EXAMPLE   A firm is contemplating making larger production runs in order to reduce the high setup costs associated with production of its only product. The total *annual* reduction in setup costs that can be obtained has been estimated to be $20,000. Currently the firm's inventories turn over six times a year; with the proposed larger production runs, the inventory turnover rate is expected to drop to four. The larger production runs are not expected to have any effect on sales revenues. The cost of goods sold is expected to remain at the current level of $1.2 million. The firm has a required return on equal-risk investments of 25 percent. Should the firm implement the proposed system?

The first step in determining whether to increase the size of the production runs is to calculate the average investment in inventory under both the proposed and present systems. The value of the firm's average inventory can be calculated, given the cost of goods sold and the inventory turnover, by the following formula:

$$\text{Average inventory} = \frac{\text{cost of goods sold}}{\text{inventory turnover}}$$

Since inventory is carried at cost on the firm's books, this formula can be used to calculate the average investment in inventory under both the proposed and present systems.[11]

Average investment in inventory:

$$\text{Proposed system: } \frac{\$1,200,000}{4} = \$300,000$$

$$\text{Present system: } \frac{\$1,200,000}{6} = \$200,000$$

The slower inventory turnover associated with the proposed system is due to the fact that in the process of running larger lots, the firm must maintain higher average raw materials, work-in-process, and finished goods inventories. The result of this slower turnover is a higher average investment in inventory than was previously required. It is the cost of the *marginal* investment in inventory that must be examined. The marginal investment is calculated by subtracting the present average investment ($200,000) from the average investment under the proposed system ($300,000). The marginal investment in inventory is therefore $100,000.

On this additional investment of $100,000 in inventory, the firm must earn 25 percent per year at a minimum, or $25,000. This can be viewed as the annual cost of carrying the higher inventories associated with the proposed system. Comparing the annual $25,000 cost of the system with the annual savings of $20,000 shows that the proposal should be *rejected,* since it results in a net annual loss of $5,000. ∎

The procedure presented in this example should not be construed as a universal tool to be applied to all inventory decisions. It has been presented to illustrate a way of thinking, especially in the sense of recognizing the relationship between the level of inventory and the number of dollars invested in it. In general, the higher a firm's average inventories, the larger the dollar investment required, and vice versa. In evaluating planned changes in inventory levels, the financial manager should consider them from a benefit-cost standpoint.

[11] Recall that in determining the firm's average investment in accounts receivable it is necessary to take into account the fact that receivables are based on the sale price — not the cost — of the firm's products. Since inventory is carried on the firm's books at cost, no special adjustment is required to estimate the average investment in inventory.

THE RELATIONSHIP BETWEEN
INVENTORY AND ACCOUNTS RECEIVABLE

The level and the management of inventory and accounts receivable are closely related. Generally in the case of manufacturing firms, when an item is sold, it moves from inventory to accounts receivable and ultimately to cash. Because of the close relationship between these current assets, the inventory management and accounts receivable management functions should not be viewed independently of each other. For example, the decision to extend credit to a customer can result in an increased level of sales, which can be supported only by higher levels of inventory and accounts receivable.[12] The credit terms extended will also affect the investment in inventory and receivables, since longer credit terms may allow a firm to move items from inventory to accounts receivable. Generally there is an advantage to such a strategy, since the cost of carrying an item in inventory is greater than the cost of carrying an account receivable. This is true because the cost of carrying inventory includes, in addition to the required return on the invested funds, the costs of storing, insuring, and otherwise maintaining the physical inventory. This relationship can be shown using a simple example.

EXAMPLE   The Erker Company estimates that the annual cost of carrying $1 of merchandise in inventory for a one-year period is 25 cents, while the annual cost of carrying $1 of receivables is 15 cents. The firm currently maintains average inventories of $300,000 and an average *investment* in accounts receivable of $200,000. The firm believes that by altering its credit terms, it can cause its customers to purchase in larger quantities on the average, thereby reducing its average inventories to $150,000 and increasing the average investment in accounts receivable to $350,000. The altered credit terms are not expected to generate new business but will result only in a shift in purchasing and payment patterns. The costs of the present and proposed inventory–accounts receivable systems are calculated in Table 17.6.

Table 17.6 shows that by shifting $150,000 of inventory to accounts receivable, the Erker Company is able to lower the cost of carrying inventory and accounts receivable from $105,000 to $90,000—a $15,000 ($105,000 − $90,000) addition to profits. This profit is achieved without changing the level of average inventory and accounts receivable investment from its $500,000 total. Rather, the profit is attributed to a shift in the mix of these

Table 17.6   Analysis of Inventory–Accounts Receivable Systems for the Erker Company

		Present		Proposed	
Variable	Cost/return (%) (1)	Average balance ($) (2)	Cost ($) [(1) × (2)] (3)	Average balance ($) (4)	Cost ($) [(1) × (4)] (5)
Average inventory	25	$300,000	$ 75,000	$150,000	$37,500
Average receivables	15	200,000	30,000	350,000	52,500
Total		$500,000	$105,000	$500,000	$90,000

[12] Accounts payable (a spontaneous liability) will also change in response to changes in sales. Discussion of this important source of short-term financing is included in Chapter 18.

WHY BUSINESS HOLDS LOWER INVENTORY TODAY

Fundamental changes in the economic environment explain why business wants to hold much lower inventories.

First, because of the high cost of rebuilding and holding inventories, the inventory cycle is critically sensitive to the level of interest rates. Moreover, the sensitivity of the up-and-down cycle of inventories to borrowing costs has increased over the last four years, as real interest rates have risen to all-time highs.

Corporate strategies toward holding inventories did not change immediately, in part because of the brevity of the 1980 recession and uncertainty as to whether the restrictive stance of monetary policy would be maintained. However, by the latter part of 1981, as interest rates remained high and business faced a huge volume of unsold goods, corporations shifted to a strategy of holding inventories at much lower levels. To a substantial degree, high interest rates explain the low level of inventories since 1982.

The impact of interest rates on inventory levels has also been heightened by business cash flow problems. During the late 1970's, the expansion of corporate debt meant that a larger share of current earnings was diverted into debt service, compelling business to increase its cash flow by reducing costs. Since inventories represent a variable cost that can be lowered, their current low inventory strategy is also due to still-fragile corporate balance sheets in many industries.

Greater volatility in the business cycle itself has led to increased efforts by business to reduce inventories. Over the past five years, total demand has shown unusual instability with two discrete recessionary episodes separated by a short-lived period of reflation. Under these circumstances, business has experienced extreme difficulty in forecasting the actual level of demand and in gauging the correct level of inventory relative to consumer purchases. Consequently, business has become more cautious in holding large inventories in order to minimize the risk of unanticipated surpluses due to increased business-cycle volatility.

Another fundamental factor causing the cutback in inventory levels is related to lower inflation. Normally, higher inflation is associated with inventory buildups, since profit margins can be raised by adding to inventories and selling them later when inflation has pushed their prices up. Now, however, expectations on inflation have been adjusted substantially downward. And that adjustment has lowered the rate at which companies build up their stocks, since there is little possibility of raising profit margins through inventory speculation.

SOURCE: Jerry J. Jasinowski, "Less Stockpiling, More Stability," *The New York Times,* June 17, 1984, p. F-3.

current assets so that a larger portion of them is held in the form of accounts receivable, which is less costly to hold than inventory. ∎

The inventory–accounts receivable relationship is affected by decisions made in all areas of the firm — finance, marketing, manufacturing, and purchasing. The financial manager should consider the interactions between inventory and accounts receivable when developing strategies and making decisions related to the production-sale process. This interaction is especially important when making credit decisions, since the required as well as actual levels of inventory will be directly affected.

INVENTORY MANAGEMENT TECHNIQUES

Techniques commonly used in managing inventory are (1) the ABC system, (2) the basic economic order quantity (EOQ) model, and (3) the reorder point. Although these techniques are not strictly financial, it is helpful for the financial manager to understand them.

The ABC system. A firm using the *ABC system* segregates its inventory into three groups—A, B, and C. The A items are those in which it has the largest dollar investment. In Figure 17.4, which depicts the typical distribution of inventory items, this group consists of the 20 percent of the inventory items that account for 90 percent of the firm's dollar investment. These are the most costly or slowest-turning items of inventory. The B group consists of the items accounting for the next largest investment. In Figure 17.4, the B group consists of the 30 percent of the items accounting for about 8 percent of the firm's dollar investment. The C group typically consists of a large number of items accounting for a small dollar investment. In Figure 17.4, the C group consists of approximately 50 percent of all the items of inventory but accounts for only about 2 percent of the firm's dollar investment. Such items as screws, nails, and washers would be in this group.

Dividing its inventory into A, B, and C items allows the firm to determine the level and types of inventory control procedures needed. Control of the A items should be most intensive due to the high dollar investments involved, while the B and C items would be subject to correspondingly less sophisticated control procedures.

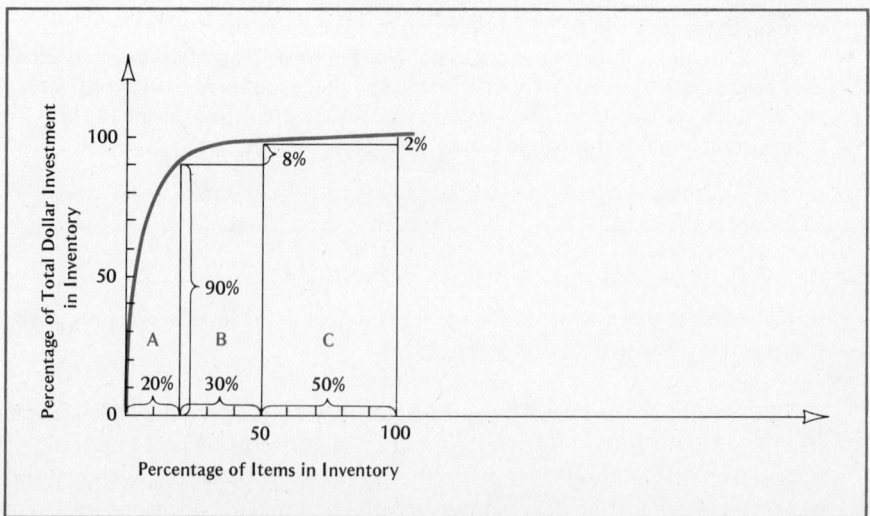

Figure 17.4 A typical distribution of inventory items

The basic economic order quantity (EOQ) model. One of the most commonly cited sophisticated tools for determining the optimal order quantity for an item of inventory is the *economic order quantity (EOQ) model.* This model could well be used to control the firm's A items. It takes into account various operating and financial costs and determines the order quantity that minimizes total inventory costs. The discussion of the economic order quantity model here will cover (1) the basic costs, (2) a graphic approach, and (3) a mathematical approach.

Basic costs. Excluding the actual cost of the merchandise, the costs associated with inventory can be divided into three broad groups — order costs, carrying costs, and total cost. Each has certain key components and characteristics.

Order costs. Order costs include the fixed clerical costs of placing and receiving an order — the cost of writing a purchase order, of processing the resulting paperwork, and of receiving an order and checking it against the invoice. Order costs are normally stated as dollars per order.

Carrying costs. Carrying costs are the variable costs per unit of holding an item in inventory for a specified time period. These costs are typically stated as dollars per unit per period. Carrying costs have a number of components, including storage costs, insurance costs, the cost of deterioration and obsolescence, and, most important, the opportunity cost of tying up funds in inventory. The *opportunity cost* is the *financial cost* component; it is the value of the returns that have been forgone (in equal-risk investments) in order to have the current investment in inventory. A commonly cited rule of thumb suggests that the cost of carrying an item in inventory for one year represents approximately 20 percent to 25 percent — and even as much as 30 percent — of the cost (value) of the item.

Total cost. The *total cost* of inventory is defined as the sum of the order and carrying costs. Total cost is important in the EOQ model, since the model's objective is to determine the order quantity that minimizes it.

A graphic approach. The stated objective of the EOQ approach is to find the order quantity that minimizes the firm's total inventory cost.[13] The economic order quantity can be found graphically by plotting order quantities on the x-axis and costs on the y-axis. Figure 17.5 shows the general behavior of these costs. The minimum total cost occurs at the point labeled EOQ. The EOQ occurs at the point where the order cost line and the carrying cost line intersect; since this is always true for this model when the costs are defined as strictly fixed and strictly variable,[14] the mathematical calculations required to determine the EOQ are quite simple.

[13] The EOQ methodology is also applied to situations in which the firm wishes to minimize a total cost with fixed and variable components. It is commonly used to determine optimal production quantities when there is a fixed setup cost and a variable operating cost. The EOQ methodology has also been used in the financial cash – marketable security decision process.

[14] In situations where one or more of the component costs has both fixed and variable elements, the EOQ will likely *not* occur at the point of intersection of the order cost and carrying cost lines. To simplify this presentation, only the situation where order cost is strictly fixed and carrying cost is strictly variable is considered.

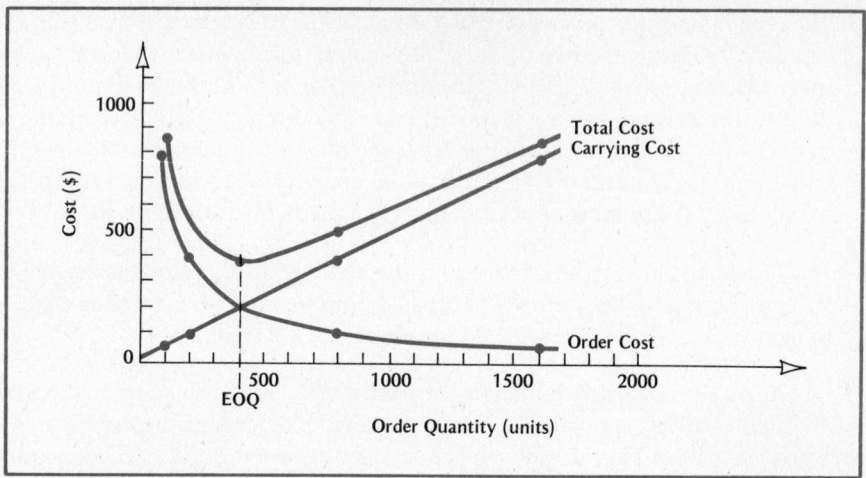

Figure 17.5   A graphic presentation of an EOQ

It is important to recognize the nature of the cost functions in Figure 17.5. The order cost function varies inversely with the order quantity. In other words, as order quantity increases, the order cost for the period decreases. This can be explained by the fact that, since the annual usage is fixed, if larger amounts are ordered, fewer orders and therefore lower order costs are incurred. Carrying costs are directly related to order quantities. The larger the order quantity, the larger the average inventory and therefore the higher the firm's carrying cost.

The total cost function exhibits a U shape, which means that a minimum value for the function exists. The total cost line represents the sum of the order costs and carrying costs for each order quantity. Within a range of plus or minus 20 percent of the EOQ, the total cost function is quite flat, indicating that total cost is relatively insensitive to small shifts away from the EOQ.

A mathematical approach. A formula can be developed for determining the firm's EOQ for a given inventory item. By letting

$$S = \text{usage in units per period}$$
$$O = \text{order cost per order}$$
$$C = \text{carrying cost per unit per period}$$
$$Q = \text{order quantity in units}$$

the firm's total cost equation can be developed. The first step in deriving the total cost equation is to develop an expression for the order cost function and the carrying cost function. The order cost can be expressed as the product of the cost per order and the number of orders. Since the number of orders equals the usage during the period divided by the order quantity (S/Q), the order cost can be expressed as follows:

$$\text{Order cost} = O \times S/Q \qquad\qquad (17.2)$$

The carrying cost is defined as the cost of carrying a unit per period multiplied by the firm's average inventory $(Q/2)$. The average inventory is defined as the order quantity divided by 2, since inventory is assumed to be depleted at a constant rate. Thus the carrying cost can be expressed as follows:

$$\text{Carrying cost} = C \times Q/2 \qquad (17.3)$$

Analyzing Equations 17.2 and 17.3 shows that as the order quantity, Q, increases, the order cost will decrease while the carrying cost increases proportionately.

The total cost equation is obtained by combining the order cost and carrying cost expressions in Equations 17.2 and 17.3, as follows:

$$\text{Total cost} = (O \times S/Q) + (C \times Q/2) \qquad (17.4)$$

Since the EOQ is defined as the order quantity that minimizes the total cost function, Equation 17.4 must be solved for the EOQ.[15] The following formula results:

$$\text{EOQ} = \sqrt{\frac{2SO}{C}} \qquad (17.5)$$

EXAMPLE Assume that a firm uses 1600 units of an item annually and that its order costs are $50 per order and carrying costs are $1 per unit per year. Substituting $S = 1,600$, $O = \$50$, and $C = \$1$ into Equation 17.5 yields an EOQ of 400 units:

$$\text{EOQ} = \sqrt{\frac{2 \times 1,600 \times \$50}{\$1}} = \sqrt{160,000} = \underline{\underline{400 \text{ units}}}$$

If the firm orders in quantities of 400 units, it will minimize its total inventory cost. ∎

Although even the simple EOQ model has weaknesses, it certainly provides decision makers with better grounds for a decision than subjective observations. While the financial manager is normally not directly associated with the use of the EOQ model, he or she must be aware of its utility. The financial manager must also

[15] The solution can be found by taking the first derivative of Equation 17.4 with respect to Q or by setting the order cost equal to the carrying cost and solving for Q, the EOQ, as demonstrated below.

(1) Multiply both sides by Q	$O \times \dfrac{S}{Q} = C \times \dfrac{Q}{2}$
(2) Multiply both sides by 2	$O \times S = C \times \dfrac{Q^2}{2}$
(3) Divide both sides by C	$2OS = C \times Q^2$
(4) Take the square root of both sides	$\dfrac{2OS}{C} = Q^2$
	$\sqrt{\dfrac{2SO}{C}} = Q = \text{EOQ}$

provide certain financial inputs, specifically with respect to inventory carrying costs, to permit the use of the EOQ model.

The reorder point. Once the firm has calculated its economic order quantity, it must determine when to place an order. In the EOQ model, it was assumed that orders are received instantaneously when the inventory level reaches zero. Actually, a reorder point is required that considers the lead time needed to place and receive orders.

Assuming again a constant usage rate for inventory, the *reorder point* can be determined by the following equation:

$$\text{Reorder point} = \text{lead time in days} \times \text{daily usage} \qquad (17.6)$$

For example, if a firm knows that it requires ten days to receive an order once the order is placed and it uses five units of inventory daily, the reorder point would be 50 units (10 days × 5 units per day). As soon as the firm's inventory level reaches 50 units, an order will be placed for an amount equal to the economic order quantity. This order would be received exactly when the inventory level reaches zero. This reorder-point formula is based on the assumptions of a fixed lead time and fixed daily usage. More sophisticated statistical reorder-point models, based on less restrictive assumptions, are available to handle the uncertainty of lead times and order flow.

CHAPTER SUMMARY

● The two dominant current assets—accounts receivable and inventory—represent sizable investments to the firm and therefore should be quickly turned into cash while maintaining an adequate level of service.

● The management of accounts receivable centers on credit policies, credit terms, and collection policies.

● Credit scoring is commonly used to make consumer credit decisions because they involve a large number of homogeneous credit applicants, each representing a small part of the firm's total business.

● Credit policies have two dimensions: credit standards and credit analysis. The basic trade-offs here are the profit contribution from sales, the cost of investment in accounts receivable, and the cost of bad debts.

● Credit analysis is devoted to the collection and evaluation of credit information on applicants in order to determine whether they can meet the firm's standards. The subjective judgment of the credit analyst is an important input to the credit decision.

● Credit terms have three components: the cash discount, the cash discount period, and the credit period. Changes in each of these variables affect the firm's sales, average collection period, bad debt expenses, and profit per unit.

● Collection policies determine the type and degree of effort exercised to collect overdue accounts. Quantitative procedures for evaluating collection policies are quite similar to those used to evaluate credit policies and terms.

● The basic collection techniques include letters, telephone calls, personal visits, the use of collection agencies, and legal action.

● The financial manager should attempt to make sure that not too many dollars are invested in all types of inventory—raw materials, work in process, and finished goods.

● The viewpoints held by marketing, manufacturing, and purchasing managers relative to the appropriate levels of various types of inventory tend to conflict with that of the financial manager.

● The financial manager, who views inventory as an investment that consumes dollars, must consider the interrelationship between inventory and accounts receivable when making production-sale decisions.

● Several techniques are used to manage inventory. The ABC system is aimed at determining which inventories require the most attention. One of the most common techniques for determining optimal order quantities is the economic order quantity (EOQ) model. The economic order quantity is the order quantity that minimizes the firm's total inventory cost. Once the optimal order quantity has been determined, the firm can set a reorder point, the level of inventory at which an order will be placed.

KEY TERMS

ABC system (inventory)
carrying cost (inventory)
collection policies
credit analysis
credit interchange bureaus
credit policy
credit scoring
credit standards
credit terms
Dun & Bradstreet, Inc.

economic order quantity (EOQ) model
finished goods inventory
line of credit
mercantile credit
order cost (inventory)
raw materials inventory
reorder point
total cost (inventory)
work-in-process inventory

QUESTIONS

17-1 What do the *accounts receivable* of a firm typically represent? What is meant by a firm's *credit policy*?

17-2 Describe *credit scoring* and explain why this technique is typically applied to consumer credit decisions rather than to mercantile credit decisions.

17-3 What key variables should be considered in evaluating possible changes in a firm's credit standards? What are the basic trade-offs in a tightening of credit standards?

17-4 What is *credit analysis*? Describe the two basic steps in the credit investigation process and summarize the basic sources of credit information.

17-5 Discuss what is meant by *credit terms*. Explain how they relate to the firm's accounts receivable and on what basis they are typically dictated.

17-6 What are the expected effects of a *decrease* in a firm's cash discount on sales volume, average collection period, bad debt expenses, and per-unit profits?

17-7 What are the expected effects of a *decrease* in the firm's credit period? What is likely to happen to sales volume, average collection period, and bad debt expenses?

17-8 What is meant by a firm's *collection policy*? Explain the basic trade-offs involved and describe the popular types of collection techniques.

17-9 What is the financial manager's role with respect to the management of inventory? What trade-off must the financial manager make with respect to turnover of inventory, inventory cost, and stockouts?

17-10 What are likely to be the viewpoints of each of the following managers with respect to the levels of the various types of inventory?
    a Finance   **c** Manufacturing
    b Marketing   **d** Purchasing

17-11 Explain the relationship between inventory and accounts receivable. What effects on inventory levels are likely to result from easing credit standards and lengthening credit terms? Distinguish between the immediate and longer-term effects.

17-12 What is meant by the *ABC system* of inventory control? On what key premise is this system based?

17-13 What is the *EOQ model*? What are its assumptions and objectives? To what group of inventory items is it most applicable? What costs does it consider? What financial cost is involved?

PROBLEMS

17-1 **(Credit Scoring)** Moses Department Store uses credit scoring to evaluate retail credit applications. The financial and credit characteristics considered and weights indicating their relative importance in the credit decision are as follows:

Financial and credit characteristics	Predetermined weight
Credit references	.25
Education	.15
Home ownership	.10
Income range	.10
Payment history	.30
Years on job	.10

The firm's credit standards are to accept all applicants with credit scores of 80 or more, to extend limited credit on a probationary basis to applicants with scores of greater than 70 and less than 80, and to reject all applicants with scores below 70.

The firm currently needs to process three applications recently received and scored by one of its credit analysts. The scores for each of the applicants on each of the financial and credit characteristics are summarized in the following table:

Financial and credit characteristics	Applicant		
	A	B	C
	Score (0 to 100)		
Credit references	60	90	80
Education	70	70	80
Home ownership	100	90	60
Income range	75	80	80
Payment history	60	85	70
Years on job	50	60	90

a Use the data presented to find the credit score for each of the applicants.

b Recommend the appropriate action for each of the three applicants.

17-2 **(Accounts Receivable and Costs)** Wilson Water Products currently has an average collection period of 45 days and annual credit sales of $1 million. Assume a 360-day year.

a What is the firm's average accounts receivable balance?

b If the average cost of each product is 60 percent of sales, what is the average investment in accounts receivable?

    c If the equal-risk opportunity cost of the investment in accounts receivable is 12 percent, what is the total opportunity cost of the investment in accounts receivable?

17-3 **(Changes in Credit Policy Without Bad Debts)** Eastinghome Appliance currently has credit sales of $600 million per year and an average collection period of 60 days. Assume that the price of Eastinghome's products is $100 per unit, the variable costs are $55 per unit, and the average costs are $85 per unit at the current level of sales. The firm is considering changing its credit policy. This will result in a 20 percent increase in sales and an equal 20 percent increase in the average collection period. No change in bad debts is expected. The firm's equal-risk opportunity cost on its investment in accounts receivable is 14 percent.

    a What are the firm's fixed costs with and without the policy change?

    b Calculate the additional profits from new sales the firm will realize it if changes its credit policy.

    c What marginal investment in accounts receivable will result?

    d Calculate the cost of the marginal investment in accounts receivable.

    e Should the firm change its credit policy? What other information would be helpful in your analysis?

17-4 **(Bad Debt Policy)** A firm is evaluating a credit policy change that would increase bad debts from 2 to 4 percent of sales. Sales are currently 50,000 units, the selling price is $20 per unit, variable cost per unit is $9, and average cost per unit is $11 at the current level of sales. As a result of the change in accounts receivable policy, sales are forecast to increase to 60,000 units.

    a What are bad debts in dollars for the present and proposed plans?

    b Calculate the cost of the marginal bad debts to the firm.

    c Ignoring the profitability from increased sales, if the policy saves $3,500 and causes no change in the average investment in accounts receivable, would you recommend the policy change? Explain.

    d Considering *all* changes in costs and benefits, would you recommend this policy change? Explain.

    e Compare and discuss your answers in **c** and **d**.

17-5 **(Changing Credit Standards — Bad Debt Losses)** Nelson-Hall Menswear feels its credit costs are too high. By raising its credit standards, bad debts will fall from 5 percent of sales to 2 percent. However, sales will fall from $100,000 to $90,000 per year. If the variable cost per unit is 50 percent of the sale price, fixed costs are $10,000, and the average investment in receivables does not change,

    a What cost will the firm face in a reduced contribution to profits from sales?

    b Should the firm raise its credit standards? Explain your answer.

17-6 **(Relaxation of Credit Standards)** Jones Industries is considering relaxing its credit standards in order to increase its currently sagging sales. As a result of the proposed relaxation, sales are expected to increase by 10 percent from 10,000 to 11,000 units during the coming year, the average collection period is expected to increase from 45 to 60 days, and bad debts are expected to increase from 1 percent to 3 percent of sales. The sale price per unit is $40, the variable cost per unit is $31, and the average cost per unit at the current 10,000 unit sales volume is $36. If the firm's required return on investment is 25 percent, evaluate the proposed relaxation and make a recommendation to the firm.

17-7 **(Initiating a Cash Discount)** Paul's Products currently makes all sales on credit and offers no cash discount. The firm is considering a 2 percent cash discount for payment within 15 days. The firm's current average collection period is 60 days, sales are 40,000 units, selling price is $45 per unit, variable cost per unit is $36, and average cost per unit is $40 at the current sales volume. The firm expects that the change in credit terms will result in an increase in sales to 42,000 units, that 70 percent of the sales will take the discount, and that the average collection period will fall to 30 days. If the firm's required rate of return on equal-risk investments is 25 percent, should the proposed discount be offered?

17-8 **(Credit Term Change — Shortening the Credit Period)** A firm is contemplating *shortening* its credit period from 40 to 30 days and believes that as a result of this change its average collection period will decline from 45 to 36 days. Bad debt expenses are expected to decrease from 1.5 percent to 1 percent of sales. The firm is currently selling 12,000 units but believes that as a result of the proposed change, sales will decline to 10,000 units. The sale price per unit is $56, its variable cost per unit is $45, and the average cost per unit at the 12,000-unit volume is $53. The firm has a required return on investment of 25 percent. Evaluate this decision and make a recommendation to the firm.

17-9 **(Credit Term Change — Lengthening the Credit Period)** The Henry Equipment Company is considering lengthening its credit period from 30 to 60 days. All customers will continue to pay on the net date. The firm currently bills $450,000 for sales, has $345,000 in variable costs, and has $45,000 in fixed costs. The change in credit terms is expected to increase sales to $510,000. Bad debt expense will increase from 1 percent to 1.5 percent of sales. The firm has a required rate of return on equal-risk investments of 20 percent.

a   What additional profit contribution from sales will be realized from the change?

b   What changes in the cost of financing the investment in accounts receivable and bad debts will the firm face?

c   Do you recommend this change in policy? Why?

17-10 **(Easing Collection Efforts)** The Rapp Rug Repair Company is attempting to evaluate whether it should ease collection efforts. The firm repairs 72,000 rugs per year at an average price of $32 each. Bad debt expenses are 1 percent of sales, and collection expenditures are $60,000. The average collection period is 40 days, the average cost per unit is $29 at the current sales level, and the variable cost per unit is $28. By easing the collection efforts, Rapp expects to save $40,000 per year in collection expense. Bad debts will increase to 2 percent of sales, and the average collection period will increase to 58 days. Sales will increase by 1,000 repairs per year. If the firm has a required rate of return on equal-risk investments of 24 percent, what recommendation would you give the firm? Use your analysis to justify your answer.

17-11 **(Inventory — The ABC System)** Ready Supply has 16 different items in its inventory. The average number of units held in inventory and the average unit cost are listed below for each item. The firm wishes to introduce an ABC system of inventory control. Suggest a breakdown of the items into classifications of A, B, and C. Justify your selection and point out items that could be considered borderline cases.

Item	Average number of units in inventory	Average cost per unit
1	1800	$ 0.54
2	1000	8.20
3	100	6.00
4	250	1.20
5	8	94.50
6	400	3.00

(continued)

(Continued)

Item	Average number of units in inventory	Average cost per unit
7	80	45.00
8	1600	1.45
9	600	0.95
10	3000	0.18
11	900	15.00
12	65	1.35
13	2200	4.75
14	1800	1.30
15	60	18.00
16	200	17.50

17-12 **(Inventory Investment)**   What is the firm's average investment in inventory in the following cases?

    a The firm has sales of $25 million and a gross profit margin of 40 percent, and the average age of inventory is 45 days.

    b The firm has an annual cost of goods sold of $200,000 and an inventory turnover ratio of 6.

    c The firm's sales are $2 million, its gross profit margin is 20 percent, and its average age of inventory is 30 days.

17-13 **(Changes in Inventory Turnover)**   Nieman Brothers has sales of $200,000, a gross profit margin of 20 percent, and an average age of inventory of 45 days.

    a What will be the change in the average investment in inventory if the firm's inventory turnover ratio changes to 7?

    b If the firm's required rate of return on investments of equal-risk is 18 percent, what additional profits (or losses) result from the change in **a**?

17-14 **(Inventory versus Accounts Receivable Costs)**   Franklin Tire estimates the annual cost of carrying a dollar of inventory is $.27, while the annual carrying cost of an equal investment in accounts receivable is $.17. The firm's current balance sheet reflects its average inventory of $400,000 and average investment in accounts receivable of $100,000. If the firm can convince its customers to purchase in large quantities, the average level of inventory can be reduced by $200,000 and the average investment in receivables increased by the same amount. Assuming no change in annual sales, what addition to profits will be generated from this shift? Explain your answer.

17-15 **(Graphic EOQ Analysis)**   Washington Textile uses 10,000 units of raw material per year on a continuous basis. The firm estimates the cost of carrying one unit in inventory at 25 cents per year. Placing and processing an order for additional inventory costs $200 per order.

    a What are annual order costs, carrying costs, and total costs of inventory if the firm orders in quantities of 1000, 2000, 3000, 4000, 5000, 6000, and 7000 units, respectively?

    b Graph order costs and carrying costs (*y*-axis) relative to quantity ordered (*x*-axis). Label the EOQ.

    c Based on your graph, in what quantity would you order? Is this consistent with the EOQ equation? Explain why or why not.

17-16 **(EOQ Analysis)**   Lyons Electronics purchases 100,000 units per month of one component. Monthly carrying costs of the item are 10 percent of the item's $2 cost. Fixed costs per order are $25.

    a Determine the EOQ, average level of inventory, number of orders, and total cost of inventory under the following conditions: (1) no changes, (2) the carrying cost is zero, (3) the order cost is zero.

b What do your answers illustrate about the EOQ model? Explain.

17-17 **(Reorder Point)** Columbus Gas and Electric (CG&E) is required to carry a minimum of 20 days' average coal usage, which is 100 tons of coal. It takes ten days between order and delivery. At what level of coal would CG&E reorder?

17-18 **(EOQ and Reorder Point)** The Williams Paint Company uses 60,000 gallons of pigment per year. The cost of carrying the pigment in inventory is $1 per gallon per year, and the cost of ordering pigment is $200 per order. The firm uses pigment at a constant rate throughout the year.

a Calculate the EOQ.

b Calculate the total cost of the plan suggested by the EOQ.

c Determine the total number of orders suggested by this plan. If the value is fractional, find the best ordering plan using complete orders.

d Assuming that it takes 20 days to receive an order once it has been placed, determine the reorder point in terms of gallons of pigment.

17-19 **(EOQ, Reorder Point, and Safety Stock)** A firm uses 800 units of a product per year on a continuous basis. The product has carrying costs of $2 per unit per year and fixed costs of $50 per order. It takes five days to receive a shipment after an order is placed, and the firm wishes to hold in inventory ten days' usage as a safety stock.

a Calculate the EOQ.

b Determine the average level of inventory.

c Determine the reorder point.

d Which of the following variables change in the event the firm does not hold the safety stock: (1) carrying costs, (2) order costs, (3) reorder point, (4) total inventory cost, (5) average level of inventory, (6) number of orders per year, (7) economic order quantity? Explain.

Chapter 18

Sources of Short-Term Financing

After studying this chapter, you should be able to:

1. Describe the role and basic features of the major sources of spontaneous short-term financing.

2. Calculate the cost of trade credit and use this cost to decide under various conditions whether to take or forgo cash discounts and stretch accounts payable.

3. Discuss the basic forms and key features of unsecured short-term bank loans, and define commercial paper and explain its role in short-term financing.

4. Compare the characteristics of secured and unsecured short-term loans, describe acceptable collateral, and note the key institutions extending these types of loans.

5. Describe the methods by which accounts receivable and inventory can be used as short-term loan collateral.

6. Explain the characteristics, challenges, and opportunities for short-term financing available to multinational companies with operations and subsidiaries in different markets.

Short-term financing, which consists of obligations that are expected to mature in one year or less, is required to support a large portion of the firm's current assets, such as cash, marketable securities, accounts receivable, and inventory. The discussions of cash budgeting and pro forma statements in Chapter 5 emphasized the importance of planning for short-term financial needs. In Chapters 15 through 17 primary attention was given to specific current assets, again emphasizing the importance of efficient financial management.

In this chapter we discuss the characteristics of both unsecured and secured short-term financing. *Secured short-term financing* has specific assets pledged as collateral, whereas *unsecured short-term financing* does not. These forms of financing show up on the balance sheet as accounts payable, accruals, and notes payable. Accounts payable and accruals are spontaneous sources of short-term funds since they arise from the normal operations of the firm; notes payable, though often unsecured, result from some type of negotiated borrowing by management. As a firm incurs greater and greater amounts of unsecured short-term financing, a threshold level is reached beyond which suppliers of short-term funds believe the firm is too risky to be extended additional unsecured credit. Other firms are unable to obtain any unsecured short-term loans, and secured financing is therefore their only resource.

A firm should always attempt to obtain all the unsecured short-term financing it can before seeking any secured short-term loans. Unsecured short-term borrowing is normally cheaper than a secured short-term loan. The firm should also use short-term financing, unsecured or secured, to finance seasonal needs for increased accounts receivable or inventories. The importance of this strategy to the firm's overall profitability and risk position was emphasized in the overview of working capital management in Chapter 15. Short-term funds allow the firm to match maturity with period of need. A summary table of the key features of the common sources of short-term financing is included as Table 18.6 in the chapter summary.

Spontaneous Sources of Short-Term Financing

The two major spontaneous sources of short-term financing are accounts payable and accruals. Each of these sources is unsecured and results from normal business operations. As the firm's sales increase, accounts payable increase in response to the increased purchases required to produce at higher levels. Also in reponse to increasing sales, the firm's accruals increase as wages and taxes rise as a result of greater labor requirements and the increased taxes on the increased earnings. There is normally no explicit cost attached to either of these current liabilities, although they do have certain implicit costs. The firm should take advantage of these often "interest-free" sources of short-term financing whenever possible.

ACCOUNTS PAYABLE

Accounts payable are generally created by the purchase of raw materials "on open account." Open-account purchases are the major source of unsecured short-term financing for business firms. They include all transactions in which merchandise is purchased but no formal note is signed evidencing the purchaser's liability to the seller. The purchaser, by accepting shipped merchandise, in effect agrees to pay the supplier the amount required in accordance with the supplier's terms of sale. Although the obligation of the purchaser to the supplier may not seem as legally binding as it would be if the supplier had required the purchaser to sign a note, there is no legal difference between the two arrangements. The credit terms extended in such transactions are normally stated on the supplier's invoice. These credit terms are of key importance to the purchaser and should be noted in planning all purchases.

In this chapter we deal only with the use of accounts payable for purchasing raw materials. Among the most important aspects of accounts payable are the types of credit terms offered by suppliers, the cost of trade credit, and the payoffs that may result from stretching accounts payable. The discussion of accounts payable here is presented from the viewpoint of the purchaser, not the supplier of trade credit. The account payable of a purchaser is an account receivable on the supplier's books.[1]

Credit terms. The firm's credit terms state the credit period, the size of the cash discount, the cash discount period, and the date the credit period begins. Each of these aspects of a firm's credit terms is concisely stated in such expressions as "2/10 net 30 EOM." The terms contain all the key information concerning the length of the credit period (30 days), the cash discount (2 percent), the cash discount period (10 days), and the time the credit period begins, the end of the month (EOM). Although credit terms typically differ among industries, there are a number of commonly used terms, each of which is discussed.

Credit period. The *credit period* is the number of days until payment in full is required. Regardless of whether a cash discount is offered, the credit period

---

[1] Chapter 17 highlighted the key strategies and considerations involved in extending credit to customers.

associated with a transaction must be indicated. Credit periods usually range from zero to 120 days, although in certain instances longer times are provided.[2] Often, suppliers require payment on delivery. The term *COD,* for "cash on delivery," is normally attached to these credit terms. In other instances, suppliers require payment before delivery. The term *CBD,* for "cash before delivery," is used to designate this type of arrangement, which is used on some contracted manufacturing jobs. COD and CBD terms *do not* represent an extension of credit by the supplier to the customer and are *not* evidenced by an account payable on the purchaser's books. They can be thought of as cash purchases.

Most credit terms include a net period typically referred to as "net 30 days," "net 60 days," and so on. The word *net* indicates that the face amount of the purchase must be paid within the number of days indicated from the beginning of the credit period. For example, the term "net 30 days" indicates that the firm must make *full payment* within 30 days of the beginning of the credit period. A firm that stretches its accounts payable will pay beyond the stated credit period. The extent to which terms may be stretched depends on the vendor's collection policy, the prevailing competitive conditions, and the relative importance of the customer to the vendor. Stretching is most effective when the vendor has a lax collection policy, there is a buyer's market, and the firm is a major customer of the vendor.

Suppliers in seasonal businesses, such as clothing and sporting goods firms, often use *seasonal datings.* This provides a considerably longer credit period than that normally extended, possibly as long as 180 days. The supplier ships finished goods to the purchaser in advance of the selling season but does not require payment until shortly after the actual demand for the seasonal items is expected. Both parties to the transaction stand to gain from seasonal dating. The seller saves physical inventory carrying costs related to storage, insurance, and deterioration and obsolesence. Many manufacturers of seasonal merchandise produce at a constant rate throughout the year, and if they could not pass these inventory carrying costs on to their customers, they would have to absorb them.[3] The purchaser gains through assurances of having merchandise available for the peak season and not having to pay for it until the season arrives. As long as the purchaser has adequate inventory facilities, the use of seasonal dating works to the benefit of both parties concerned.

Cash discounts. If a *cash discount* is offered as part of the firm's credit terms, it is normally between 1 and 5 percent. It is actually a percentage deduction from the purchase price if the purchaser pays within the cash discount period. A 2 percent cash discount indicates that the purchaser of $100 of merchandise need pay only $98 if payment is made within the discount period. Many purchasers will stretch

[2] The credit period is zero days when purchases are made for cash.

[3] As previously noted (Chapter 17), a commonly cited rule of thumb with respect to inventory carrying costs states that the cost of carrying an item in inventory for one year represents approximately 20 to 25 — and even as much as 30 — percent of the cost (or value) of the item. In spite of the fact that more than half of this cost is attributable to the cost of financing the inventory, which would *not* be eliminated if the goods are sold on credit, very real savings in physical inventory carrying costs should result for suppliers using seasonal datings.

their cash discounts by taking the discount even when paying after the cash discount period.

From the point of view of the supplier of credit, whose objective it is to collect accounts receivable quickly, a cash discount provides an incentive to pay early. The reduction in proceeds due to the discount is compensated for by the speeding up of collections. The purchaser, whose objective is to stretch accounts payable by paying as late as possible, must determine whether it is advantageous to take the cash discount. Techniques for analyzing the benefits of each alternative will be discussed in a later section.

Cash discount period. The *cash discount period* specifies the maximum number of days after the beginning of the credit period that the cash discount can be taken. Typically, the cash discount period is between 5 and 20 days. In certain industries, more than one cash discount is offered. The discount period is shortest for the largest discount offered and longest for the smallest discount offered. Often, large customers of smaller firms use their position as key customers as a form of leverage, enabling them to take cash discounts far beyond the end of the cash discount period. This strategy, although ethically questionable, is frequently encountered.

The current trend toward the elimination of cash discounts is the result of two factors. The first is the widespread use of computers for paying accounts payable. When the payments are computerized, most firms take the cash discount regardless of when payment is made. A firm may end up paying 20 days after the end of the discount period but still take the discount. The second reason for the trend is the difficulty of policing the discounts and collecting the amount due when a discount has been incorrectly taken. In addition, many firms now charge interest at a specified rate for each day beyond the credit period it takes a customer to pay. This late charge is intended to deter firms from stretching accounts payable.

Beginning of the credit period. The beginning of the credit period is stated as part of the supplier's credit terms. One of the most common designations for the beginning of the credit period is the *date of invoice.* Both the cash discount period and the net period are then measured from the invoice date. *End of month (EOM)* indicates that the credit period for all purchases made within a given month begins on the first day of the month immediately following. These terms simplify record keeping on the part of the firm extending credit. The date of the invoice is recognized as the date of sale.[4] *Middle of month (MOM)* indicates that the month is broken into two separate credit periods. The credit period for all sales made (invoices dated) between the first and fifteenth of the current month begins on the sixteenth of the month. The credit period for all sales made between the sixteenth and the last day of the month begins on the first day of the month immediately following. (Thirty-day months are assumed.) These credit terms speed up the firm's collections because payments for purchases made prior to the fifteenth of the month are collected earlier than when EOM terms are offered. MOM terms are

---

[4] Occasionally firms receive invoices prior to receiving the actual merchandise purchased. In these situations the beginning of the credit period is not tied to the invoice date, which could be 30 days prior to the receipt of goods.

not common. The following example may help to clarify the differences among the various types of credit period beginnings.

EXAMPLE   The Grimes Company made two purchases from a certain supplier offering credit terms of 2/10 net 30. One purchase was made on September 10 and the other on September 20. The payment dates for both purchases, based on credit periods that begin at various points, are given in Table 18.1. The payment dates if the firm takes the cash discount and if it pays the net amount are shown.

Table 18.1 illustrates that, from the point of view of the recipient of trade credit, a credit period beginning at the end of the month is preferable in all cases, since purchases made early in the month can be paid for at a later date than otherwise would have been the case. When the credit period begins on the date of the invoice, the credit recipient must pay earlier regardless of whether it takes the cash discount or pays the net amount. The difference between the EOM and MOM terms can be recognized by noting that, for the September 10 purchase, MOM terms require quicker payment than EOM terms. For the September 20 purchase, EOM and MOM terms result in the same payment dates. ∎

Receipt of goods (ROG) terms are commonly used when goods purchased may be received considerably later than the purchase date. This happens when merchandise is purchased from a geographically distant supplier and the shipping process takes a period of months. A large number of backorders, strikes, and other problems may also delay the receipt of goods. ROG terms indicate that the credit period does not begin until the purchaser has actually received the merchandise.

Credit terms are generally standardized within a given industry because credit terms are often viewed as a competitive device. In order to maintain their competitive position, firms within an industry offer the same terms. In many cases, stated credit terms are not the terms actually given to a customer; special arrangements or "deals" are made that provide certain customers with more favorable terms. This is often done to attract key accounts or to help a growing firm that is low on working capital. The prospective purchaser is wise to look closely at the credit terms of suppliers when making a purchase decision. In many instances, concessions may be available.

Cost of trade credit. Although no explicit cost is levied on the recipient of trade credit, the firm extending the credit does incur a cost in the sense that its money is tied up for the interim. Extending credit to customers requires the investment of money that could be used elsewhere, and this cost is indirectly passed on to the purchaser in

Table 18.1   Payment Dates for the Grimes Company Given Various Assumptions

| Beginning of credit period | September 10 purchase | | September 20 purchase | |
	Discount taken	Net amount paid	Discount taken	Net amount paid
Date of invoice	Sept. 20	Oct. 10	Sept. 30	Oct. 20
EOM	Oct. 10	Oct. 30	Oct. 10	Oct. 30
MOM	Sept. 25	Oct. 15	Oct. 10	Oct. 30

the cost of the merchandise. In the same way that a supplier extends trade credit to a customer, so too the supplier's supplier generally extends trade credit, thereby helping the supplier to absorb a portion of the cost. A detailed discussion of trade credit from the point of view of the issuer (accounts receivable) was presented in Chapter 17.

Taking or forgoing the cash discount. If a firm is extended credit terms that include a cash discount, it has two options. Its first option is to *take the cash discount.* If a firm intends to take a cash discount, it should pay on the last day of the discount period. In subsequent analyses, it will be assumed that this is what happens — firms that take cash discounts pay on the final day of the cash discount period. There is no implicit cost associated with taking a cash discount. The second option open to the firm is to *forgo the cash discount* and pay at the end of the credit period. Although there is no direct cost associated with forgoing a cash discount, there is an implicit cost. If the cash discount is forgone, the firm should pay on the final day of the credit period.

EXAMPLE The Russell Corporation purchased $1000 worth of merchandise on February 27 from a supplier extending terms of 2/10 net 30 EOM. If the corporation takes the cash discount, it will have to pay $980 [$1000 − .02($1000)] on March 10. If it forgoes the discount, it will have to pay the full $1000 on March 30. The factors involved in deciding whether or not the discount should be forgone are explained in the following paragraphs. ∎

Cost of forgoing a cash discount. There is an implicit *cost of forgoing a cash discount*[5] because to delay paying its bill for an additional number of days, the firm must forgo an opportunity to pay less for the items it has purchased. The cost of forgoing a cash discount can be illustrated by a simple example. The example assumes that if the firm takes a cash discount, payment will be made on the final day of the cash discount period, and if the cash discount is forgone, payment will be made on the final day of the credit period.

EXAMPLE The Russell Corporation has been extended credit terms of 2/10 net 30 EOM. If it takes the cash discount on its February 27 purchase, payment will be required on March 10. If the cash discount is forgone, payment can be made on March 30. To keep its money for an extra 20 days (from March 10 to March 30), the firm must forgo an opportunity to pay $980 for its $1000 purchase. In other words, it will cost the firm an extra $20 to delay payment for 20 days. Figure 18.1 shows the payment options open to the corporation.

To calculate the cost of forgoing the cash discount, the *true purchase price* must be viewed as the discounted cost of the merchandise. For the Russell Corporation, this discounted cost would be $980. To delay paying the $980 for an extra 20 days, the firm must pay $20 ($1000 − $980). The annual percentage cost of forgoing the cash discount can be calculated using Equation 18.1.[6]

---

[5] Note that this "cost" actually represents the *financing cost* and therefore does not consider earnings or savings opportunities expected to result from having funds available for an additional period of time. Since our concern here is solely with the financing cost, attention is not given to the employment of these funds. Clearly the firm would not forgo the discount unless it has opportunities to earn or save at a rate in excess of the cost of forgoing the discount.

[6] Equation 18.1 as well as the related discussions are based on the assumption that there is only one discount period. In the event that multiple discount periods are offered, calculation of the cost of forgoing the discount must be made for each alternative.

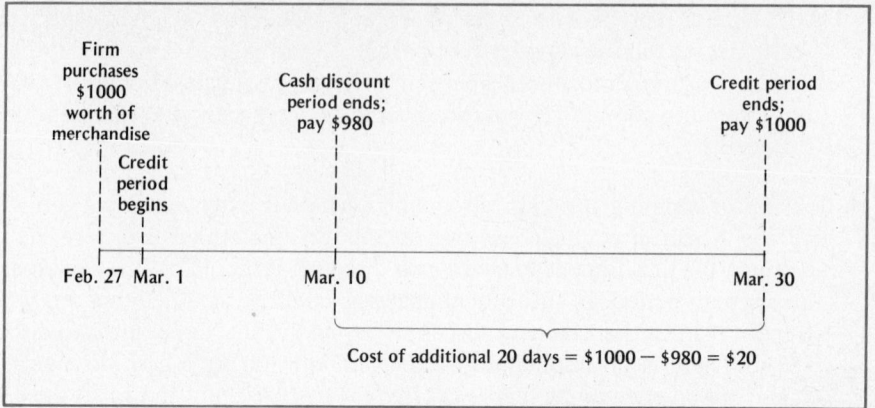

Figure 18.1 Payment options for the Russell Corporation

$$\text{Cost of forgoing cash discount} = \frac{CD}{1 - CD} \times \frac{360}{N} \tag{18.1}$$

where

$CD =$ the stated cash discount in decimal terms
$N =$ the number of days payment can be delayed by forgoing the cash discount

Substituting the values for CD (.02) and N (20 days) into Equation 18.1 and solving results in a cost of forgoing the cash discount of 36.73 percent [(.02 ÷ .98) × (360 ÷ 20)]. A 360-day year is assumed.

The same answer could have been obtained by substituting for the first term of Equation 18.1 the quotient obtained by dividing the dollar cash discount ($20) by the price of the merchandise if the cash discount is taken ($980). However, the use of Equation 18.1 is less complicated. A simple way to *approximate* the cost of a forgone discount is to use the stated cash discount percentage, CD, in place of the first term of Equation 18.1.

$$\text{Approximate cost of forgoing cash discount} = CD \times \frac{360}{N} \tag{18.2}$$

The smaller the cash discount, the closer the approximation of the cost of forgoing the discount is to the actual cost of forgoing the cash discount. Using this approximation, the cost of forgoing the cash discount for the Russell Corporation is found to be 36 percent [.02 × (360 ÷ 20)]. ■

Using the cost of forgoing a cash discount in decision making. The financial manager must determine whether it is advisable to take a cash discount. A number of other decisions with respect to cash discounts may confront the financial manager. Each can be illustrated by a simple example.

EXAMPLE   The Gup Company has four possible suppliers, each offering different credit terms. Except for the differences in credit terms, their products and services are identical. Table 18.2 presents the credit terms offered by each supplier, A, B, C, and D, and the cost of

Table 18.2 Cash Discounts and Associated
Costs for the Gup Company

Supplier	Credit terms	Approximate cost of forgoing cash discount
A	2/10 net 30 EOM	36.0%
B	1/10 net 55 EOM	8.0
C	3/20 net 70 EOM	21.6
D	4/10 net 60 EOM	28.8

forgoing the cash discounts. The approximation method of calculating the cost of forgoing a cash discount has been used to simplify the analysis. The cost of forgoing the cash discount from supplier A is 36 percent; from supplier B, 8 percent; from supplier C, 21.6 percent; and from supplier D, 28.8 percent. Let us now see how the information in Table 18.2 might be used in a number of decision situations.[7]

Case 1: A one-by-one analysis If the firm needs short-term funds, which are currently available from its commercial bank at 15 percent, and if each of the suppliers (A, B, C, and D) is viewed *separately,* which (if any) of the suppliers' cash discount will the firm forgo? To answer this question, each supplier's terms must be evaluated as they would be if it were the firm's sole supplier. A decision can then be made based on the consequences of the stated credit terms. In dealing with supplier A, the firm will take the cash discount since the cost of forgoing it is 36 percent. The firm will then borrow the funds it requires from its commercial bank at 15 percent interest. In dealing with supplier B, the firm will do better to forgo the cash discount since the cost of this action is less than the cost of borrowing money from the bank (8 percent as opposed to 15 percent). In dealing with either supplier C or supplier D, the firm should take the cash discount since in both cases the cost of forgoing the discount is greater than the 15 percent cost of borrowing from the bank.

Case 2: The firm must forgo a discount If the Gup Company knows that it must forgo cash discounts because it needs money and has no alternate sources of short-term financing, from which of its four alternative suppliers will the purchase be made? In this case, the main concern is *not* the cost of forgoing the cash discount but rather *which supplier can be paid latest.* Since the cash discount must be forgone, all suppliers will be paid the full amount for their merchandise. Thus the supplier that can be paid latest is preferable. In this case, supplier C will be selected because it can be paid on day 70, later than any of the other suppliers.

Case 3: The firm must take a discount If the Gup Company already has sufficient short-term financing, from which supplier should it make the purchase? In this situation, the firm *will* take the cash discount, so the cost of forgoing it is *not* relevant. The chief consideration is *who can be paid the least the latest.* Table 18.3 presents the firm's options with respect to the percentage of the purchase price that must be paid and the payment date if the cash discount is taken. The four alternatives can easily be reduced to two by comparing the terms of suppliers A, B, and D. Each of these suppliers requires payment on day 10, but supplier D is preferable because it requires payment of only 96 percent of the purchase price at that time. In other words, supplier D can be paid less than supplier A or supplier B at the same point in time.

[7] The analysis of the various decisions implicitly assumes that the firm will continuously make purchases from the given supplier since this permits the term of the loan provided to be aligned with the firm's actual financial need. In actuality, a 20-day loan obtained by forgoing a cash discount may not fulfill a firm's actual funds need.

Table 18.3   The Percentage of the Purchase Price
Paid and Payment Dates When the Cash
Discount Is Taken by the Gup Company

Supplier	Percentage of purchase price paid	Payment date
A	98%	Day 10
B	99	Day 10
C	97	Day 20
D	96	Day 10

The comparison of suppliers C and D is not quite so straightforward. Supplier C can be paid 97 percent on day 20, and supplier D can be paid 96 percent on day 10. To delay payment ten days, the firm must pay an additional 1 percent of the purchase price. To determine if supplier C is preferable to supplier D, the question of whether it is worth this much money (1 percent) to delay payment ten days must be answered. The cost of such an action is approximately 36 percent [.01 × (360 ÷ 10)]. Since the firm's cost of borrowing is 15 percent, it seems advisable for the firm to make its purchase from supplier D and avoid the 36 percent marginal borrowing cost. ∎

The examples show that the cost of forgoing a cash discount is relevant only when evaluating a single supplier's credit terms in light of certain bank borrowing costs. In comparing various suppliers' credit terms, the cost of forgoing the cash discount is not the most important factor in the decision process.

Effects of stretching accounts payable. If a firm anticipates stretching accounts payable, the cost of forgoing a cash discount is reduced. Stretching accounts payable is sometimes suggested as a reasonable strategy for a firm as long as it does not damage its credit rating. As noted in Chapter 16, although this strategy is financially attractive, it raises an important ethical issue: It may cause the firm to violate the agreement it entered into with its supplier when it purchased merchandise or equipment. Clearly, a supplier would not look kindly on a customer who purposely postponed paying for purchases. Let us look at an example of stretching payments.

EXAMPLE   The Russell Corporation was extended credit terms of 2/10 net 30 EOM. The cost of forgoing the cash discount, assuming payment on the last day of the credit period, was found to be approximately 36 percent [.02 × (360 ÷ 20)]. If the firm were able to stretch its account payable to 70 days without damaging its credit rating, the cost of forgoing the cash discount would be only 12 percent [.02 × (360 ÷ 60)]. Stretching accounts payable reduces the implicit cost of forgoing a cash discount. ∎

ACCRUALS

The second spontaneous source of short-term financing for a business is accruals. *Accruals* are liabilities for services received for which payment has yet to be made. The most common items accrued by a firm are wages and taxes. Since taxes are payments to the government, their accrual cannot be manipulated by the firm. It can, however, manipulate the accrual of wages to some extent.

Although there is no explicit or implicit cost associated with accruals, a firm can save money by accruing as many dollars of wages as possible. Employees provide services for which they are normally not paid until a specified period of time has elapsed. The pay period for hourly employees is often governed by union regulations or state or federal law. However, in other cases the frequency of payment is at the discretion of the company's manager. The following example shows how accruals can be used to increase the firm's financing.

EXAMPLE   The Smith Company currently pays its salaried employees every two weeks. The payroll for two weeks is normally about $3 million. If the opportunity cost is 10 percent on equal-risk investments, how much would the firm save by changing the pay period from two weeks to one month? If the firm paid monthly, the payroll at the end of each month would be approximately $6 million. Currently the average amount accrued for the salaried payroll is $1.5 million ($3 million ÷ 2), since the accrued payroll is expected to increase at a constant rate until payment is actually made. For the first half of the payroll period the accrued payroll will be below $1.5 million, and for the second half of the payroll period it will be greater than $1.5 million.

Under the new plan, the average amount accrued would be $3 million ($6 million ÷ 2), using the same logic as above. Implementing the proposed plan would therefore increase the average amount of accruals by $1.5 million ($3 million − $1.5 million). In effect, this increase in average accrued salaries increases the firm's free financing by $1.5 million. This amount of funds can now be used elsewhere at an opportunity cost of 10 percent. The annual savings from this change in the salary payment interval is $150,000 (.10 × $1,500,000). By increasing accruals, the firm can save this amount of funds. ∎

The use of accruals as an interest-free source of financing is consistent with the general philosophy of paying bills as late as possible as long as the firm does not damage its credit standing. In the case of accrued wages, the firm must be careful not to delay payment of wages too long. Since the government requires quarterly tax payments by corporations, tax accruals may be thought of as having an average value of one-half of the quarterly tax liability. Sometimes firms pay rent or lease expenses at the end of a lease period; if they do, these expenditures are accrued.

Unsecured Sources of Short-Term Loans

Businesses obtain unsecured short-term loans from two major sources — banks and commercial paper. Unlike the spontaneous sources of unsecured short-term financing, these sources are negotiated and result from the discretionary actions of the financial manager. Bank loans are more popular because they are available to firms of all sizes; commercial paper tends to be available only to large firms.

BANK LOANS

The major type of loan made by banks to businesses is the *short-term self-liquidating loan.* Loans are referred to as self-liquidating when the bank's motive for making them is to provide the firm with financing to meet seasonal needs — for example, to cover seasonal increases in accounts receivable or inventories. Self-liquidating loans are intended merely to carry the firm through seasonal peaks in financing needs attributed primarily to buildups of accounts receivable and inventory. It is expected that as receivables and inventories are converted into cash, the funds needed to retire these loans will automatically be generated. In other words, the use to which the borrowed money is put provides the mechanism through which the loan is repaid.

Unsecured short-term loans made by commercial banks represent the primary source of *negotiated* short-term funds to businesses; the primary source of unsecured short-term funds to business in general is trade credit (accounts payable). Banks lend unsecured short-term funds in three basic ways — through single-payment notes, lines of credit, and revolving credit agreements.

Single-payment notes. A *single-payment note* can be obtained from a commercial bank by a creditworthy business borrower. Typically, this type of loan is a "one-shot" deal made when a borrower needs additional funds for a short period but does not believe this need will continue. The resulting instrument is a *note,* which must be signed by the borrower. The note states the terms of the loan, which include the length of the loan (the maturity date) and the interest rate charged. This type of short-term note generally has a maturity of 30 days to 9 months or more. The interest charged on the note is generally tied in some fashion to the prime rate of interest.

The *prime rate of interest* is the lowest rate of interest charged on business loans to the best business borrowers by the nation's leading banks. The prime rate fluctuates with changing supply and demand relationships for short-term funds.[8] Banks typically determine the rate charged on loans to various borrowers by adding some type of premium to the prime rate to adjust it for the borrower's "riskiness." This riskiness is a composite of the perceived business and financial risk of the borrower. The premium may amount to 4 percent or more, although most unsecured short-term notes carry premiums of less than 2 percent. In general, commercial banks do not make short-term unsecured loans to businesses that are believed to be questionable risks.

These notes can have fixed or floating interest rates. On *fixed-rate notes,* the rate of interest is determined initially as a set increment above the prime rate and remains at that fixed rate until maturity. On *floating-rate notes,* the increment above the prime rate is initially established and the rate of interest is allowed to "float" at that increment above prime over the term of the note. Generally the increment above prime on a floating-rate note will be *lower* than on a fixed-rate note of equivalent risk because the lender bears less risk with a floating-rate note. The highly volatile nature of the prime rate in recent years, coupled with the widespread use of computers by banks to monitor and calculate loan interest, has been responsible for the current dominance of floating-rate notes and loans. Let us look at an example.

EXAMPLE   The ZAG Company recently borrowed $100,000 from each of two banks — bank A and bank B. The loans were incurred on the same day, when the prime rate of interest was

---

[8] From 1975 through the third quarter of 1978 the prime rate was generally below 9 percent. Since the end of 1978 the prime rate has remained above 10 percent. In late December 1980 the prime rate reached a record high, 21.5 percent; it had fallen to about 11 percent by January 1984.

12 percent; each loan involved a 90-day note. The interest rate was set at $1\frac{1}{2}$ percent above the prime rate on bank A's fixed-rate note; this means that over the 90-day period the rate of interest will remain at $13\frac{1}{2}$ percent (12 percent prime rate + $1\frac{1}{2}$ percent increment) regardless of fluctuations in the prime rate. The interest rate was set at 1 percent above the prime rate on bank B's floating-rate note; this means that the rate charged over the 90 days will vary directly with the prime rate. Initially the rate will be 13 percent (12 percent + 1 percent), but when the prime rate changes, so will the rate of interest on the note. For instance, if after 30 days the prime rate rises to 12.5 percent and after another 30 days drops to 12.25 percent, the firm would be paying 13 percent interest for the first 30 days, 13.5 percent for the next 30 days, and 13.25 percent for the last 30 days. It should be clear that depending upon fluctuations in the prime rate over the 90 days, the ZAG Company could pay more or less interest on the floating-rate loan from bank B than on the fixed-rate loan from bank A. ■

Lines of credit. A *line of credit* is an agreement between a commercial bank and a business that states the amount of unsecured short-term borrowing the bank will make available to the firm over a given period of time. A line of credit agreement is typically made for a period of one year and often places certain constraints on the borrower. A line of credit agreement is *not a guaranteed loan* but indicates that if the bank has sufficient funds available, it will allow the borrower to owe it up to a certain amount of money. The amount of a line of credit is *the maximum amount the firm can owe the bank* at any point in time. Technically, it is possible for a firm to *borrow* more than the amount of its line of credit, but at no time can the *loan balance* exceed the line of credit.

EXAMPLE   The Holcomb Company has a line of credit of $1 million with its bank. The borrowing against this line of credit during the first six months of the year, along with the firm's loan balance, is given in Table 18.4. The firm's borrowings of $1.2 million appear to exceed its $1 million line of credit because some funds were borrowed, repaid, and later re-borrowed during the six-month period. Note that Holcomb's loan balance never exceeded its $1 million line of credit.[9]

Table 18.4   The Holcomb Company's Borrowing
Against Its Line of Credit

Month	Transaction		Loan balance
	Borrow	Repay	
January	$ 200,000	0	$200,000
February	$ 600,000	0	$800,000
March	0	$ 200,000	$600,000
April	0	$ 100,000	$500,000
May	$ 400,000	0	$900,000
June	0	$ 900,000	0
Total	$1,200,000	$1,200,000	

■

[9] If the average loan were to exceed the maximum line of credit, it would indicate that at some point during the period the firm borrowed more than the amount permitted by the line of credit. If the firm owed exactly the maximum amount allowed over the entire period, its average borrowing would equal that amount.

IS THE PRIME RATE FIXED?

First Interstate Bank of Oregon illegally conspired with other banks to fix its prime lending rate at an artificially high level, a federal jury decided Tuesday [May 15, 1984].

Four plaintiffs whose cases were consolidated for trial were awarded a total of $500,000, an amount that would be tripled under federal antitrust law.

Keith Borman of the bank's legal department said the verdict would be appealed.

The plaintiffs alleged that the bank, Oregon's second-largest, agreed with other banks to move the prime rate in "lockstep" without regard to the cost of funds used to make loans, or other operating expenses. They alleged the practice was designed to fix the price of commercial loans for "middle market" borrowers at a high level, although large corporate borrowers could still get money from the banks at rates below the prime.

The bank said its prime rate was in line with 12,000 other banks in the country most of the time, and that it reflected market forces.

The prime rate traditionally was defined as that charged a bank's most credit-worthy commercial customers, but bankers now describe the prime lending rate as the base on which they figure short-term business loans. Consumer rates, while not tied directly to the prime, are influenced to the point that the prime is reflective of other market interest rates.

Both sides agreed during the two-week trial that First Interstate's prime rate was identical to that of most banks and generally was the same as the "national prime."

Henry Carey, an attorney for the plaintiffs, described the system as a "national electronic price fix."

"It's been a massive deception that only you can straighten out," he told the jury. "First here, and hopefully throughout the country."

When one bank announces a change in its prime it is generally followed within hours by most other major banks.

Bank officials testified they had instant access to the information when other banks changed their prime lending rates. Chairman P. W. Wilke said First Interstate Bank of Oregon used the "count-to-four" method: It monitored seven major West Coast banks, and changed its prime rate as soon as any four made a move.

SOURCE: "Prime Rate Movement Is Price Fix, Jury Rules," Dayton *Journal Herald,* May 16, 1984, p. 24.

To obtain a line of credit, a borrower must apply for it. The application may require the borrower to submit such documents as its cash budget, its pro forma income statement, its pro forma balance sheet, and its recent financial statements. If the bank finds the customer acceptable, the line of credit will be extended. The major attraction of a line of credit from the bank's point of view is that it eliminates the need to examine the creditworthiness of a customer each time it borrows money. A few characteristics of lines of credit require further explanation.

Interest rates. Like single-payment notes, the interest charge on a line of credit is normally stated as the *prime rate plus x percent.* If the prime rate changes, the interest rate charged on new as well as outstanding borrowing will automatically change.[10] The amount a borrower is charged in excess of the prime rate depends on its creditworthiness. The more creditworthy the borrower, the lower the interest increment above prime, and vice versa.

EXAMPLE   The Raine Company is negotiating a line of credit with the First National Bank. After evaluating the Raine Company's financial statements, the bank sets an interest rate for the line of credit that is 2 percent more than the prime rate. The prime rate is currently 11.5 percent, so the Raine Company will have to pay 13.5 percent for current borrowing. If the prime rate drops to 11 percent in the future, the interest charge on Raine's borrowing will drop to 13 percent. As the prime rate fluctuates, so will the interest rate on the Raine Company's line of credit. ■

Once the rate of interest charged a given customer has been established, the method of computing interest should be determined. Interest can be paid when a loan matures or in advance. If interest is paid when a loan matures, the *effective rate of interest* — the actual rate of interest paid — is equal to the stated interest rate. The effective rate of interest is found by dividing the dollar interest paid by the amount of loan proceeds available to the borrower. When interest is paid in advance, it is deducted from the loan so that the borrower actually receives less money than it requested. Paying interest in advance therefore raises the effective rate of interest above the stated rate. Let us look at an example.

EXAMPLE   The Bressler Company wants to borrow $10,000 at a stated rate of 12 percent interest for one year. If the interest on the loan is paid at maturity, the firm will pay $1,200 (.12 × $10,000) for the use of the $10,000 for the year. The effective rate of interest will therefore be

$$\frac{\$1,200}{\$10,000} = 12.0 \text{ percent}$$

If the money is borrowed at the same rate but interest is paid in advance, the firm will still pay $1,200 in interest, but it will receive only $8,800 ($10,000 − $1,200). The effective rate of interest in this case is

$$\frac{\$1,200}{\$8,800} = 13.6 \text{ percent}$$

Paying interest in advance thus makes the effective rate of interest greater than the stated rate. Loans on which interest is paid in advance are often called *discount loans.* Most commercial bank loans to business require the interest payment at maturity. ■

Operating change restrictions. In a line of credit agreement, a bank may retain the right to revoke the line if any major changes occur in the firm's financial condition or operations. The firm is typically required to submit for review periodically —

---

[10] As noted earlier, most banks not only adjust the interest rate charged on *new borrowing* but also make floating-rate loans that provide for automatic adjustment of the rate charged against *outstanding loans* for changes in the prime rate. In these situations, the borrower is not assured that the rate of interest at the time of borrowing will remain fixed over the maturity of the note; if the prime rate changes, so will the rate of interest charged over the remaining term of the note.

generally quarterly or semiannually — up-to-date and, preferably, audited financial statements. In addition, the bank typically needs to be informed of shifts in key managerial personnel or in the firm's operations prior to changes taking place because changes in personnel or operations may affect the future success and debt-servicing ability of the firm and could alter its status as a credit risk. If the bank does not agree with the proposed changes and the firm makes them anyway, the bank has the right to revoke the line of credit agreement.

Compensating balances. To ensure that the borrower will be a good customer, most short-term unsecured bank loans — single-payment notes, and lines of credit — require the borrower to maintain a *compensating balance* in a demand deposit account (checking account) equal to a certain percentage of the amount borrowed.[11] Compensating balances of 10 to 20 percent are normally required. A compensating balance not only forces the borrower to be a good customer of the bank but may also raise the interest cost to the borrower, thereby increasing the bank's earnings. An example will illustrate.

EXAMPLE   A company has borrowed $1 million under a line of credit agreement. It must pay a stated interest charge of 12 percent and maintain a compensating balance of 20 percent of the funds borrowed, or $200,000, in its checking account. Thus it actually receives the use of only $800,000. To use the $800,000 for a year, the firm pays $120,000 (.12 × $1,000,000). The effective rate of interest on the funds is therefore 15 percent ($120,000 ÷ $800,000), 3 percent more than the stated rate of 12 percent.

If the firm normally maintains a balance of $200,000 or more in its checking account, the effective interest cost will equal the stated interest rate of 12 percent because none of the $1 million borrowed is needed to satisfy the compensating balance requirement. If the firm normally maintains a $100,000 balance in its checking account, only an additional $100,000 will have to be tied up, leaving it with $900,000 ($1,000,000 − $100,000) of usable funds. The effective interest cost in this case would be 13.3 percent ($120,000 ÷ $900,000). A compensating balance raises the cost of borrowing *only* if it is larger than the firm's normal cash balance. ∎

Annual cleanups. To ensure that money lent under a line of credit agreement is actually being used to finance seasonal needs, many banks require an *annual cleanup.* This means that the borrower must have a loan balance of zero for a certain number of days during the year. Forcing the borrower to carry a zero loan balance for a certain period of time ensures that short-term loans do not turn into long-term loans. A look back at Table 18.4 shows that the Holcomb Company cleaned up its loans during the month of June.

All the characteristics of a line of credit agreement are negotiable to some extent. Today, banks bid competitively to attract large, well-known firms. A prospective borrower should attempt to negotiate a line of credit with the most favorable interest rate, for an optimal amount of funds, and with a minimum of restrictions. Lenders typically will accept fees instead of deposit balances, and vice versa, as

[11] Sometimes the compensating balance will be stated as a percentage of the amount of the line of credit rather than the amount borrowed. In other cases the compensating balance will be linked to both the amount borrowed and the amount of the line of credit.

compensation for loans and other services rendered to their commercial customers. The lender will attempt to get a good return with maximum safety. The negotiations should produce a line of credit suitable to both borrower and lender.

Revolving credit agreements. A *revolving credit agreement* is nothing more than a *guaranteed line of credit.* It is guaranteed in the sense that the commercial bank making the arrangement guarantees the borrower that a specified amount of funds will be made available regardless of the tightness of money. It is not uncommon for a revolving credit agreement to be for a period greater than one year; two- or three-year agreements may be made.[12] The requirements for a revolving credit agreement are similar to those for a line of credit. Of course, each of these agreements is negotiable; a standard arrangement does not actually exist.

Since the bank guarantees the availability of funds to the borrower, a *commitment fee* is normally charged on a revolving credit agreement. This fee often applies to the average unused balance of the credit agreement.[13] It is normally about .5 percent of the average unused portion of the funds. An example may clarify the nature of commitment fees.

EXAMPLE The Smith Company has a $2 million revolving credit agreement with its bank. Its average borrowing under the agreement for the past year was $1.5 million. The bank charges a commitment fee of .5 percent. Since the average unused portion of the committed funds was $500,000 ($2 million − $1.5 million), the commitment fee for the year was $2500 (.005 × $500,000). Of course, Smith also had to pay interest on the actual $1.5 million borrowed under the agreement. Although more expensive than a line of credit, a revolving credit agreement can be less risky from the borrower's viewpoint, since the availability of funds is guaranteed by the bank. ■

COMMERCIAL PAPER

Commercial paper consists of short-term, unsecured promissory notes issued by firms with a high credit standing. Generally, only quite large firms of unquestionable financial soundness are able to issue commercial paper. Most commercial paper has maturities ranging from 3 to 270 days. Although there is no set denomination, commercial paper is generally issued in multiples of $100,000 or more. A large portion of the commercial paper issued today is issued by finance companies; manufacturing firms account for a smaller portion of this type of financing.

As was indicated in Chapter 16, businesses often purchase commercial paper, which they hold as marketable securities, to provide a reserve of liquidity. Commercial banks, individuals, insurance companies, pension funds, and other types of financial institutions also purchase commercial paper. In each case, the motive

---

[12] Many authors classify the revolving credit agreement as a form of *intermediate-term financing*, defined as having a maturity of one to seven years. In this text, the intermediate-term financing classification is not used; only short-term and long-term classifications are made. Since many revolving credit agreements are for more than one year, they can be classified as a form of long-term financing; however, they are discussed here because of their similarity to line of credit agreements.

[13] Some banks not only require payment of the commitment fee but also require the borrower to maintain, in addition to the compensating balance against actual borrowings, a compensating balance of 10 percent or so against the unused portion of the commitment.

for purchasing the paper is the need to find an interest-earning medium in which to place temporarily idle funds.

Because most purchasers of commercial paper hold it to maturity, the secondary market for commercial paper is not well developed. To provide investors with the liquidity they desire, the issuing firm or selling dealer will often agree to repurchase the paper at a discount price prior to maturity. Commercial paper is generally considered a safe investment, since the issuers are the most creditworthy of the nation's corporations. In addition, most paper is backed by unused bank lines of credit that can be used to refund the paper at maturity in the event of adverse market conditions. However, issues of commercial paper have been known to go sour. Like corporate bonds (see Chapter 19) commercial paper is rated as to its quality by Moody's and Standard & Poor's, the two dominant independent rating firms.

Interest on commercial paper. The interest paid by the issuer of commercial paper is determined by the size of the discount and the length of time to maturity. Commercial paper is sold at a discount from its par, or face, value and the actual interest earned is determined by certain calculations. These can be illustrated by a simple example.

EXAMPLE   The Howell Corporation has just issued $1 million worth of commercial paper that has a 90-day maturity and sells for $970,000. At the end of 90 days the purchaser of this paper will receive $1 million for his or her $970,000 investment. The interest paid on the financing is therefore $30,000 on a principal of $970,000. This is equivalent to an annual interest rate for the Howell Corporation commercial paper of 12.4 percent [($30,000 ÷ $970,000) × (360 days ÷ 90 days)]. ■

An interesting characteristic of commercial paper is that it *normally* has a yield 1 to 2 percent below the prime bank lending rate. In other words, firms are able to raise funds through the sale of commercial paper more cheaply than by borrowing from a commercial bank. This is because many suppliers of short-term funds do not have the option of making low-risk business loans at the prime rate; they can invest only in marketable securities such as Treasury bills and commercial paper. Since commercial paper is an extremely safe marketable security with a higher yield than Treasury bills and most other marketable securities, it is an attractive investment. Many commercial banks purchase commercial paper that yields less than a prime-rate loan. This is generally because of certain limits on bank loans to one borrower[14] and the fact that the smaller commercial banks do not have many opportunities to lend to high-quality business borrowers. Compared to lower-yielding Treasury bills, commercial paper is quite attractive to these institutions.

Although the cost of borrowing through the sale of commercial paper is typically lower than the prime bank loan rate, one must keep in mind that interest on a bank loan is paid only on the outstanding balance. Since commercial paper, once

---

[14] Commercial banks are legally prohibited from lending an amount greater than 15 percent (plus an additional 10 percent for loans secured by readily marketable collateral) of their unimpaired capital and surplus to any one borrower. This restriction is intended to protect depositors by forcing the commercial bank to spread its risk across a number of borrowers.

issued, does not mature for a given period, the firm may pay interest on funds it does not actually need. A second point is that a firm must maintain a good working relationship with its bank. Even if it is slightly more expensive to borrow from a commercial bank, it may be advisable to do so in order to establish the necessary rapport with a banker. This strategy ensures that when money is tight, funds can be obtained promptly. The commercial bank should be the primary source of negotiated unsecured short-term money for the firm, and commercial paper should be a secondary source.

Sale of commercial paper. Commercial paper is *directly placed* with investors by the issuer or sold by *commercial paper dealers.* For performing the marketing function, the commercial paper dealer is paid a fee. Most commercial paper is placed directly with other corporations, life insurance companies, or pension funds. Dealers purchase the paper from the issuer and place it with banks and other large investors.

Secured Sources of Short-Term Loans

Once a firm has exhausted its unsecured sources of short-term financing, it may be able to obtain additional short-term financing on a secured basis. A *secured loan* is a loan for which the lender requires *collateral.*[15] The collateral commonly takes the form of an asset, such as accounts receivable or inventory. The lender obtains a security interest in the collateral through the execution of a contract (security agreement) between it and the borrower. The *security agreement* specifies the collateral held against the loan. In addition, the terms of the loan against which the security is held are attached to or form part of the security agreement. They specify the conditions required for the security interest to be removed, along with the interest rate on the loan, repayment dates, and other loan provisions. A copy of the security agreement is filed in a public office within the state — typically a county or state court. Filing provides subsequent lenders with information about which assets of a prospective borrower are free to be used as collateral. The filing requirement protects the lender by legally establishing his or her security interest.

CHARACTERISTICS OF SECURED SHORT-TERM LOANS

Although many people believe that holding collateral as security reduces the risk of the loan, lenders do not usually view loans in this way. Lenders recognize that by having an interest in collateral they can reduce losses if the borrower defaults, but *as far as changing the risk of default, the presence of collateral has no impact.* Lenders require collateral if they feel the firm is too risky and want to be able to recover some portion of the loan in the event of default. They do not want to have

---

[15] The terms *security* and *collateral* are used interchangeably to refer to the items used by a borrower to back up a loan. Loan security or collateral may be any assets against which a lender, as a result of making a loan, has a legal claim that is exercisable if the borrower defaults on some provision of the loan. If the borrower defaults, the lender can sell the security or collateral to satisfy his claim against the borrower. Some of the more technical aspects of loan defaults are presented in Chapter 24.

to administer and liquidate collateral; the lender would like to be repaid as scheduled. In general, they would prefer to make less risky loans at lower rates of interest than to be in a position in which they may have to liquidate collateral.

Due to the additional paperwork and higher degree of risk, secured short-term loans are generally not as favorable as unsecured short-term borrowing. Depending on the exact arrangement, the borrower may or may not retain control of the loan collateral. The following brief discussions of the nature of the collateral and terms of secured short-term loans and the types of institutions normally extending secured short-term loans to firms are presented in light of the constraints placed on the short-term secured borrower.

Collateral and terms. A number of factors must be highlighted with respect to the characteristics desirable in collateral and the basic terms of secured short-term loans. These factors include the life of the collateral, the activity of the collateral, the percentage advance, and the interest rate and fees charged.

Life of the collateral. Lenders of secured short-term funds prefer collateral that has a life closely related to the term of the loan. This requirement assures the lender that the security can be used to satisfy the loan in the event of a default. For short-term loans, the likely candidates as collateral are a firm's short-term or current assets. Current assets — accounts receivable, inventories, and marketable securities — are generally the most desirable collateral for short-term loans since they usually (automatically) turn into cash much sooner than do fixed assets. The use of fixed assets is better for long-term loans since they retain their value over a long period and, if necessary, can be converted into cash in the future in order to satisfy unpaid debts.

The strategy of securing short-term loans with current assets and long-term loans with fixed assets is similar to the aggressive approach presented in Chapter 15, which suggested financing seasonal needs (primarily current assets) with short-term funds and permanent needs (primarily fixed assets) with long-term funds. By the same token, *it is normally suggested that short-term loans be secured with current assets and long-term loans be secured with fixed assets.* By closely aligning the maturity (turnover) of the collateral with the loan maturity, the lender is assured of protection throughout the life of the loan and is somewhat assured that the funds can be readily recovered through liquidation of the collateral in the event of default.

Activity of the collateral. Another important consideration in evaluating possible collateral is its *activity*— the speed with which it can be converted into cash. Although current assets are the most common candidate as collateral for short-term loans, not all current assets are equally desirable. Desirability is determined largely by the borrower's line of business because the line of business of a firm largely determines the nature of its accounts receivable and inventories, which are the primary sources of short-term collateral. From the discussions of ratio analysis in Chapter 4, we know that even within a given industry, the activity of current assets often differs. The short-term lender of secured funds is more apt than not to find only liquid current assets acceptable as collateral. Accounts receivable or inventories having average ages of 180 days are questionable candidates as security for a 90-day note.

Percentage advance. Having isolated the acceptable collateral of a given firm, the lender must determine what amount he or she is willing to lend against the book value of this collateral. Typically, the lender determines the desirable *percentage advance* to make against certain collateral. This percentage advance is normally between 30 and 100 percent of the book value of collateral; it varies not only according to the type and activity of collateral but also according to the type of security interest being taken.

Interest rate and fees. The interest rate charged on secured short-term loans is typically *higher* than the rate on unsecured short-term loans. This stems from the fact that the primary suppliers of unsecured short-term loans are commercial banks that make loans only to the better business borrowers. If a customer is not a good enough credit risk to warrant an unsecured loan, commercial banks generally prefer to make unsecured loans to other acceptable borrowers. Commercial banks and other institutions do not normally look on secured loans as being less risky than unsecured loans and therefore require higher interest rates on them.

Negotiating and administering secured loans is more troublesome for the lender than negotiating and administering unsecured loans; therefore, the lender normally requires added compensation in the form of a service charge, a higher interest rate, or both. The higher cost of secured as opposed to unsecured borrowing can therefore be attributed to the greater risk of default and the increased administration costs.

Institutions extending secured short-term loans. The primary sources of secured short-term loans to business are commercial banks and commercial finance companies. Both institutions deal in short-term loans secured primarily by accounts receivable and inventory. Since you should be familiar with commercial banks, the primary emphasis in this section will be on the commercial finance company.

Commercial banks. Typically, only large commercial banks extend secured loans, due to their ability to achieve certain economies in administration. By making a number of loans of this type, the larger banks are able to justify the employment of specialists for analyzing, administering, and policing them. Also, small banks are more constrained with respect to the maximum loan they can extend to a single borrower.[16]

Commercial finance companies. A *commercial finance company* is a financial institution without a bank charter that makes loans secured with accounts receivable, inventories, or chattel mortgages on fixed assets. Commercial finance companies are also known to finance the installment purchase of commercial and industrial equipment by businesses. Commercial finance companies make only secured loans to businesses; some of the loans are short-term and others are

---

[16] See footnote 14.

long-term arrangements. The leading commercial finance companies include the Commercial Investors Trust (CIT) Corporation and Westinghouse Credit Corporation, Industrial Division. These firms offer the same types of short-term secured financing as commercial banks. The primary type of loan extended by the commercial finance company is the accounts receivable loan, although loans against inventory and other collateral are not uncommon.

Commercial finance companies do not make unsecured business loans, nor are they permitted to hold demand deposits. Borrowers in need of short-term financing rely primarily on commercial banks. Only when their unsecured and secured short-term borrowing power from the commercial bank is exhausted will they turn to the commercial finance company for additional secured borrowing. Because the finance company typically ends up with higher-risk borrowers, its interest charges on secured short-term loans are generally higher than those of commercial banks. Another reason for the slightly higher charges of commercial finance companies is the fact that a portion of their financing is often obtained through commercial bank borrowing at wholesale rates. Since commercial banks are limited with respect to the amount they can lend to a single customer, it is not unusual for a bank to refer certain borrowers to a finance company.

THE USE OF ACCOUNTS RECEIVABLE AS COLLATERAL

Two commonly used means of obtaining short-term financing with accounts receivable are pledging accounts receivable and factoring accounts receivable. Actually, only a pledge of accounts receivable creates a secured short-term loan; factoring really entails the *sale* of accounts receivable at a discount. Although factoring is not actually a form of secured short-term borrowing, it does involve the use of accounts receivable to obtain needed short-term funds.

Pledging accounts receivable. A *pledge* or an assignment of accounts receivable is often used to secure a short-term loan. Because accounts receivable are normally quite liquid, they are an attractive form of short-term collateral. Both commercial banks and commercial finance companies extend loans against pledges of accounts receivable.

Types of pledges. Accounts receivable are normally pledged on a *selective basis.* The prospective lender analyzes the past payment records of the firm's accounts to determine which accounts represent acceptable loan collateral. A lender will generally advance money only against accounts determined to be acceptable credit risks. A lender is likely to advance as much as 90 percent of the collateral's value against a pledge of selected accounts.

A second method of pledging accounts receivable is to take a lien[17] on *all* the firm's accounts receivable. This type of *floating lien* arrangement is normally used when a firm has many accounts that, on the average, have only a small dollar value. In this case, the cost of evaluating each account separately would not be warranted.

---

[17] *Lien* is a legal term for a claim on the property of another, such as a security interest against the payment of a legal debt. A lien must be filed by the lender against the collateral in a legal office such as a county or state court.

Instead, the lender places a lien on all the firm's accounts receivable. The lender in this situation keeps track of the total dollar amount of pledged accounts. Due to the difficulty of identifying each item of collateral and therefore of policing this arrangement, the percentage advanced against a floating lien on accounts receivable is normally less than 50 percent of the book value of the accounts. This situation is more risky from the lender's viewpoint, since the borrower has opportunities to misrepresent accounts.

The pledging process. When a firm approaches a prospective lender to request a loan against accounts receivable, the lender will first evaluate the firm's accounts receivable to determine their desirability as collateral. The lender will make a list of the acceptable accounts, along with the billing dates and amounts. If the borrowing firm requests a loan for a fixed amount, the lender will need to select only enough accounts to secure the funds requested. In some instances the borrower may want the maximum loan available. In this situation, the lender will evaluate all the accounts to select the maximum amount of acceptable collateral. Let us look at an example.

EXAMPLE   The Second National Bank is analyzing the Crowe Company's accounts receivable ledger to find acceptable collateral for a pledge of accounts receivable. Each of Crowe's accounts receivable, along with its age and average payment period, is given in Table 18.5. Since Crowe extends credit terms of 2/10 net 30 EOM, the bank eliminates from further consideration all accounts that are currently overdue (those whose age is greater than 30 days). This immediately eliminates the accounts of customers C, E, and I.

The second step in the bank's evaluation process is to analyze the historical payment patterns of the customers. After calculating the average payment period for each customer (given in the last column of Table 18.5), the Second National Bank decides to eliminate customer B, whose account, although not currently overdue, normally requires 60 days to collect. Having eliminated the accounts of customers B, C, E, and I, the bank is left with $45,000 of acceptable accounts from customers A, D, F, G, and H (who owe $10,000, $4,000, $6,000, $14,000, and $11,000, respectively). The Crowe Company therefore has $45,000 of acceptable accounts receivable collateral. Each account used as collateral will be marked in the Crowe Company's ledger, and a list of the billing dates and amounts will be kept by the Second National Bank.

Table 18.5   The Crowe Company's Accounts Receivable

Customer	Account receivable	Age[a]	Average payment period
A	$10,000	20 days	35 days
B	8,000	5	60
C	15,000	50	45
D	4,000	14	30
E	3,000	70	60
F	6,000	10	20
G	14,000	3	10
H	11,000	23	10
I	3,000	45	45

[a] Number of days since beginning of credit period.

After selecting the acceptable accounts, the lender will normally adjust the dollar value of these accounts for expected returns or allowances. If a customer whose account has been pledged returns merchandise or receives some type of allowance, such as a cash discount for early payment, the amount of the collateral is automatically reduced. For protection from such occurrences, the lender will normally reduce the value of the acceptable collateral by a fixed percentage.

EXAMPLE   The $45,000 of acceptable accounts receivable selected by the Second National Bank from the Crowe Company's books must be adjusted for returns and allowances. The bank decides, after evaluating the company's accounts, that a 5 percent adjustment is appropriate. After this adjustment, the Crowe Company has acceptable collateral of $42,750 [$45,000 × (1 − .05)]. ■

Once the lender has determined the acceptable accounts and made adjustments for returns and allowances, the percentage to be advanced against the collateral must be determined based on the lender's overall evaluation of the quality of the acceptable receivables and the expected cost of their liquidation. For selected accounts receivable, this will range between 50 and 90 percent.

EXAMPLE   After a reexamination of the Crowe Company's acceptable accounts receivable *and* general operations, the Second National Bank decides to advance 85 percent of the value of the adjusted acceptable collateral. This means that the bank will lend the company $36,337.50 ($42,750 × .85). ■

Pledges of accounts receivable are normally made on a *nonnotification* basis. This means that the customer whose account has been pledged is not notified of this action. Instead, the customer continues to remit payments to the firm. If a pledge of accounts receivable is made on a *notification* basis, the customer is notified to remit payments directly to the lender. Nonnotification arrangements are preferred by borrowers, since their customers may construe the fact that their accounts have been pledged to mean that the firm is in financial difficulty. The nonnotification arrangement is a type of *trust receipt loan,* since the borrower still collects the pledged account receivable and the lender *trusts* that the borrower will remit these payments as they are received. To police a trust arrangement, the lender will check frequently to see if the customers whose accounts have been pledged and are currently listed as uncollected have actually paid any of these accounts. As the lender receives payments of accounts, the loan principal is reduced by the amount collected.

Cost of pledges of accounts receivable. The stated cost of a pledge of accounts receivable is normally 2 to 5 percent above the prime rate. It may be even higher on pledges from commercial finance companies. In addition to the stated interest rate, a service charge of up to 3 percent may be levied. Although the interest payment is expected to compensate the lender for loaning the money, the service charge is needed to cover the administrative costs incurred by the lender. These administrative costs result from the need to inspect accounts, keep records of pledged accounts, make entries as collections of accounts are received, and police

BUSINESSES' HEAVY RELIANCE ON SHORT-TERM BORROWING

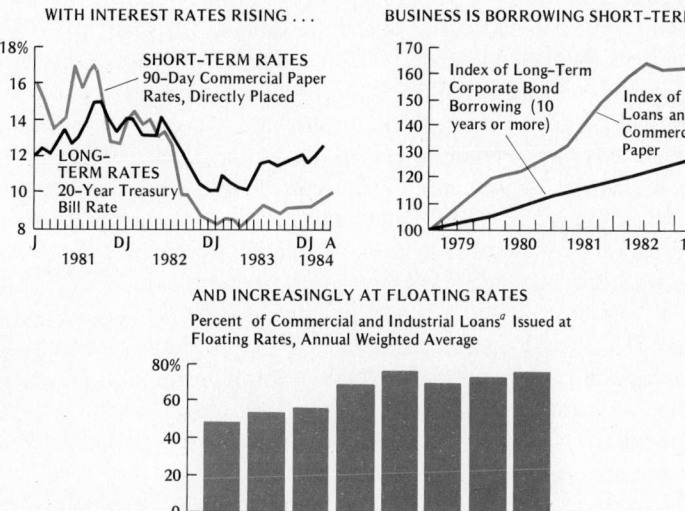

WITH INTEREST RATES RISING . . .

SHORT-TERM RATES
90–Day Commercial Paper
Rates, Directly Placed

**LONG–
TERM RATES**
20–Year Treasury
Bill Rate

J   DJ   DJ   DJ A
1981   1982   1983   1984

BUSINESS IS BORROWING SHORT–TERM . . .

Index of Long–Term
Corporate Bond
Borrowing (10
years or more)

Index of Bank
Loans and
Commercial
Paper

1979   1980   1981   1982   1983

AND INCREASINGLY AT FLOATING RATES
Percent of Commercial and Industrial Loans[a] Issued at
Floating Rates, Annual Weighted Average

1977 1978 1979 1980 1981 1982 1983 1984[b]

[a] For one year or longer
[b] Estimate based on first quarter, 1984 data

SOURCE: E. F. Hutton Economics and Federal Reserve

New debt has been rising at a 31 percent annual rate since the start of the year [1984], more than triple the usual growth at this stage of a recovery, according to Abraham Gulkowitz, an economist at the Bankers Trust Company.

Nearly half these new loans are short-term, extended for up to a year at interest rates usually under 11 percent. Moreover, even the so-called long-term debt of American business is taking on the coloration of short-term borrowing. According to the Federal Reserve, 75 percent of all new debt being extended these days—in maturities greater than one year—is issued at floating rates. That means a loan's interest rate can rise and fall *dozens* of times before the loan itself expires.

And it means that business has a new vulnerability and potentially, a new problem: If interest rates continue to move up, as they have in recent weeks, financing costs could soar. And that eventually could provoke a wave of bankruptcies among companies unable to repay maturing loans—either because they would be too shaky financially to obtain new financing or they could not afford the crushing cost of rising rates. At risk in this scenario is the financial health of many corporations that could find themselves in much the same predicament as homeowners who face higher installment payments because of variable rate mortgages.

"Right now, the rise in short-term debt is manageable," said Leo C. O'Neill, group vice president of Standard & Poor's, the bond-rating agency. "But if the economy hits the brakes, the risk is there.". . . A similar risk brought on the near collapse of the Chrysler Corporation and the International Harvester Company in 1981, and the bankruptcy of AM International in 1982. All three companies were burdened with huge amounts of short-term debt during a period of steeply rising rates.

SOURCE: Robert A. Bennett, "Risky Trend in Business Borrowing," *The New York Times,* May 27, 1984, p. F-1.

the lending arrangement. The stated cost of a pledge of accounts receivable is normally 1 to 3 percent higher than the cost of an unsecured bank loan.

The effective cost of accounts receivable pledges may not be much greater than the cost of unsecured financing. With unsecured financing, the borrower pays interest on the full amount borrowed for the term of the loan; when accounts receivable are pledged as collateral, the loan principal on which interest is calculated is reduced as accounts are collected. It is possible that with an unsecured note the borrower will be paying interest on funds not actually needed; under a pledge, interest is paid only on the amount needed (the declining loan balance). In comparing the advantages of unsecured and secured notes, this point is worthy of consideration. Although the stated interest rate is higher for a pledge of accounts receivable than for an unsecured loan, the principal is quite likely to be lower for the pledge, since the loan balance decreases as payment is received.

Pledges as a continuous source of financing. Quite often, pledging accounts receivable is used as a continuous source of financing by the firm. As accounts are collected, new accounts acceptable to the lender are substituted, allowing the firm to maintain a relatively constant loan balance with the lender. If the lender finds all the firm's accounts receivable acceptable and continuously takes them as collateral, it ends up financing all the firm's accounts receivable. The firm may find this arrangement quite beneficial from a cost standpoint.

Factoring accounts receivable. *Factoring* accounts receivable involves their outright sale to a factor or other financial institution.[18] Although the factor is the primary factoring institution, some commercial banks and commercial finance companies also factor accounts receivable. Factoring accounts receivable is not actually the same as obtaining a short-term loan, but it is similar to borrowing with accounts receivable as collateral. Factoring is commonplace in the textile and carpeting industries and is used extensively in lumber, sporting goods, chemicals, and toys. Although factoring is used only in selected industries, it accounts for approximately one-third of the total financing secured by accounts receivable (including factoring) and inventory in the United States today.

The factor. A *factor* is a financial institution that purchases accounts receivable from businesses. The factor generally accepts all the credit risks associated with the accounts receivable it purchases. Factoring initially began in the textile industry as a result of the long credit period required by purchasers of textiles.[19]

[18] The use of bank cards such as MasterCard and VISA by consumers has some similarity to factoring, since the vendor accepting the card is reimbursed at a discount for purchases made using the card. The difference between factoring and bank cards is that the bank cards are nothing more than a line of credit extended by the bank card company, which charges the vendors a fee for accepting the cards. In factoring, the factor does not analyze credit until after the sale has been made; in many cases (except where factoring is done on a continuous basis) the initial credit decision is the responsibility of the vendor, not the factor who purchases the account.

[19] Because of the seasonal nature of the sales of clothing and other textile items, textiles must be produced in large quantities well in advance of the selling season. Manufacturers use seasonal datings; they send merchandise to purchasers as soon as it is produced to avoid physical inventory carrying costs but do not require payment until after the selling season begins. They therefore end up with very high levels of receivables, which they factor to get working capital for use in supporting the production and inventory outlays required to meet the next season's demand.

at the warehouse designated by the lender, the *warehouse official* checks the merchandise in, listing each item received on a *warehouse receipt,* noting the quantity, serial or lot numbers, and estimated value. The receipt is forwarded to the lender, who advances a specified percentage of the collateral value to the borrower and files a lien on all the items listed on the receipt.[23]

Under the *field warehouse* arrangement, the lender hires a field warehousing company to set up a warehouse on the borrower's premises or lease part of the borrower's warehouse. A number of companies specialize in establishing field warehouses for a fee. Once they have isolated the inventory, the procedures followed by the field warehouse personnel are quite similar to those followed by the terminal warehouse personnel. A field warehouse may take the form of a fence around a stock of raw materials located outdoors, it may consist of a roped-off section of the borrower's warehouse, or it may actually be a warehouse constructed by the warehousing company on the borrower's premises, a portion of which may have been leased by the warehousing company.

Regardless of whether a terminal or field warehouse is established, the warehousing company places a guard over the inventory. Terminal warehouses always have a guard; under a field warehousing arrangement, a guard is stationed near the warehoused collateral. The guard or warehouse official is not permitted to release the collateral without authorization from the lender. In other words, the lender has complete control over the inventory used to collateralize the loan. Only upon written approval of the lender can any portion of the secured inventory be released.

The loan agreement. The actual lending agreement specifically states the requirements for the release of inventory. As in the case of other secured loans, the lender accepts only collateral believed to be readily marketable and advances only a portion—generally 75 to 90 percent—of the collateral's value. The types of collateral normally found most acceptable for warehouse receipt loans are canned foods, lumber, refined products, and basic metal stocks.

Cost of warehouse receipt loans. The specific costs of warehouse receipt loans are generally higher than those of any other secured lending arrangements due to the need to hire and pay a third party (the warehousing company) to guard and attend to the collateral. The basic interest charged on warehouse receipt loans is higher than that charged on unsecured loans. It generally ranges from 3 to 5 percent above the prime rate. In addition to the interest charge, the borrower must absorb the costs of warehousing by paying the warehouse fee, which is generally between 1 and 3 percent of the amount of the loan. These charges vary with the size of the loan and other factors. In some instances the firm's marginal warehousing costs are small because it has to warehouse the inventory anyway. The borrower is normally required to pay the insurance costs on warehoused merchandise.

[23] Although most warehouse receipts are nonnegotiable, some are *negotiable,* which means that they may be transferred by the lender to other parties. If the lender wants to remove a warehouse receipt loan from its books, it can sell a negotiable warehouse receipt to another party, who then replaces the original lender in the agreement. In some instances, the ability to transfer a warehouse receipt to another party may be desirable.

MULTINATIONAL FINANCE

International Short-Term Financing

In international operations the usual domestic sources of short-term financing, along with other sources, are available to MNCs. Included are accounts payable as well as accruals, bank and nonbank sources in each subsidiary's local environment, and the Euromarket discussed in Chapter 3. Our emphasis here is on the "foreign" sources.

For a subsidiary of a multinational company, its local economic market is a basic source of both short- and long-term financing. Moreover, the subsidiary's borrowing (and lending) status, relative to a local firm in that economy, can be superior, since it can rely on the potential backing and guarantee of its parent MNC. One drawback, however, is that most local markets (and local currencies) are regulated by local authorities. So a subsidiary may choose to turn to the Euromarket and take advantage of borrowing and lending in unregulated capital markets.

The Euromarket offers financing opportunities for both the short term (Euro-currency) and the long term (Eurobonds). (We will cover Eurobonds in Chapter 19.) In the case of short-term financing, the forces of supply and demand are among the main factors determining exchange rates in *Eurocurrency markets,* with each currency's nominal interest rate being influenced by economic policies pursued by the respective "home" governments. In other words, the interest rates offered in the Euromarket on, for example, the U.S. dollar are greatly affected by the prime rate inside the United States, and the dollar's exchange rates with other major currencies are influenced by the supply and demand forces acting in such markets (and in response to interest rates).

Unlike borrowing in the domestic markets, where only one currency and *nominal* interest rate is involved, financing activities in the Euromarket can involve several currencies and both nominal and *effective* interest rates. Effective rates are equal to nominal rates plus (minus) any forecast appreciation (depreciation) of a currency relative to the currency of the MNC parent, say, the U.S. dollar. An example will illustrate the issues involved.

EXAMPLE A multinational company, MNC, Inc., has subsidiaries in Switzerland (with local currency, Swiss franc, Sf) and Belgium (Belgian franc, Bf). Based on each subsidiary's forecast operations, the financial needs of each (in equivalent U.S. dollars) are as follows:

> Switzerland: $80 million excess cash to be invested (lent)
> Belgium: $60 million funds to be raised

Based on all the available information, the parent firm has provided each subsidiary with the following figures regarding exchange rates and interest rates (the figures for the effective rates shown are derived by adding the forecast percentage revaluation numbers to the nominal rates):

existence of the Euromarket, in particular, allows MNCs to take advantage of unregulated capital markets to invest (lend) and raise funds in a variety of currencies and to protect themselves against foreign exchange risk exposures.

KEY TERMS

accruals

annual cleanup

captive finance company

cash discount

cash discount period

collateral

commercial finance company

commercial paper

commercial paper dealer

commitment fee

compensating balance

cost of forgoing a cash discount

credit period

date of invoice

directly placed (commercial paper)

discount loans

effective rate of interest

end of month (EOM)

Eurocurrency markets

factor

factoring (accounts receivable)

field warehouse

fixed-rate notes

floating lien

floating-rate notes

floor planning

line of credit

middle of month (MOM)

nonnotification

nonrecourse (factoring)

notification

percentage advance

pledge (accounts receivable)

prime rate of interest

receipt of goods (ROG)

recourse (factoring)

revolving credit agreement

seasonal datings

secured loan

secured short-term financing

security agreement

single-payment note

terminal warehouse

trust receipt loan

unsecured short-term financing

warehouse receipt

warehouse receipt loan

QUESTIONS

18-1   What are the two key sources of spontaneous short-term financing for a firm? Why are these sources considered spontaneous, and how are they related to the firm's sales? Do they normally have an explicit cost?

18-2   Is there a cost associated with taking a cash discount? Is there any cost associated with forgoing a cash discount? How is the decision to take a cash discount affected by the firm's opportunity cost of short-term funds?

18-3   What are *accruals?* What items are most commonly accrued by the firm? How attractive are accruals as a source of financing to the firm?

18-4   What is the primary source of *negotiated* short-term loans to business? When are loans considered short-term self-liquidating loans?

18-5   What are the basic terms and characteristics of a single-payment note? How is the prime interest rate relevant to the cost of short-term bank borrowing? What is a *floating-rate note?*

18-6   What is a *line of credit?* Describe each of the following features commonly included in these agreements.

    a   Operating change restrictions

    b   Compensating balance

    c   Annual cleanup

18-7   What is meant by a *revolving credit agreement?* How does this arrangement differ from the line of credit agreement? What is a commitment fee?

18-8   How is commercial paper used to raise short-term funds? Who can issue commercial paper? Who buys commercial paper? How is it sold?

18-9   What are the key differences between unsecured and secured forms of short-term borrowing? In what circumstances do firms borrow short-term money on a secured basis?

18-10 Many people argue that secured loans have lower effective interest costs than unsecured loans; they argue that the collateral lowers risk. The text stresses that these two statements are not necessarily complementary. Explain why.

18-11 In general, what kind of interest rates and fees are levied on secured short-term loans? Why are these rates generally *higher* than the rates on unsecured short-term loans?

18-12 Compare, contrast, and describe the basic features of
   a Pledging accounts receivable
   b Factoring accounts receivable
   Be sure to mention the institutions offering each of them.

18-13 Describe the basic features and compare each of the following methods of using *inventory* as short-term loan collateral.
   a Floating lien
   b Trust receipt loan
   c Warehouse receipt loan

18-14 Explain why a subsidiary may choose to turn to the Euromarkets rather than the domestic market for borrowing and lending activities.

18-15 Point out the difference between the *nominal* and *effective* rates of interest in international operations.

PROBLEMS

18-1   **(Payment Dates)**   Determine when a firm must make payment for purchases made on November 25 under each of the following credit terms.
   a net 30   **d** COD
   b net 30 EOM   **e** CBD
   c net 45 MOM

18-2   **(Cost of Forgoing Cash Discounts)**   Determine the cost of forgoing cash discounts under each of the following terms of sale.
   a 2/10 net 30   **e** 1/10 net 60
   b 1/10 net 30   **f** 3/10 net 30
   c 2/10 net 45   **g** 4/10 net 180
   d 3/10 net 45

18-3   **(Cash Discount versus Loan)**   Ann Daniels works in the accounts payable department of Penrod Industries. She has attempted to convince her boss to take advantage of the 3/10 net 45 credit terms most suppliers offer, but her boss argues that the 3 percent discount is less costly than a short-term loan at 14 percent. Prove that either Ann or her boss is incorrect.

18-4   **(Credit Terms and Strategies)**   The credit terms for each of three suppliers are as follows:

Supplier	Credit terms
X	1/10 net 55 EOM
Y	2/10 net 30 EOM
Z	2/20 net 60 EOM

    a Determine the *approximate* cost of forgoing the cash discount from each supplier.

    b Assuming that the firm needs short-term financing, recommend whether or not it would be better to forgo the cash discount or borrow from the bank at 14 percent annual interest. Evaluate each supplier separately.

    c What impact, if any, would the fact that the firm could stretch its accounts payable (net period only) by 20 days from supplier Z have on your answer in **b** relative to this supplier?

18-5 **(Cash Discount Decisions)** Barrett Manufacturing has four possible suppliers, each offering different credit terms. Except for the differences in credit terms, their products and services are virtually identical. The credit terms offered by each supplier are as follows:

Supplier	Credit terms
Q	1/10 net 30 EOM
R	2/20 net 80 EOM
S	1/20 net 60 EOM
T	3/10 net 55 EOM

    a Calculate the *approximate* cost of forgoing the cash discount from each supplier.

    b If the firm needs short-term funds, which are currently available from its commercial bank at 16 percent, and if each of the suppliers is viewed *separately* (one-by-one analysis), which, if any, of the suppliers' cash discounts should the firm forgo? Explain why.

    c If the company knows that it must forgo cash discounts because it needs money and has no alternate sources of financing, from which of its four alternative suppliers should the purchase be made? Why?

    d If the company already has sufficient short-term financing, from which supplier should it make the purchase? Why?

    e Compare, contrast, and discuss your findings in **a**, **c**, and **d**.

18-6 **(Changing Payment Cycle)** Upon accepting the position of chief executive officer and chairman of American Cash Register, Robert Adamson changed the firm's weekly payday from Monday afternoon to the following Friday afternoon. The firm's weekly payroll was $10 million, and the cost of short-term funds was 13 percent. If the effect of this change was to delay check clearing by one week, what annual savings, if any, were realized?

18-7 **(Cost of Bank Loan)** Stick Enterprises has obtained a 90-day bank loan at an annual interest rate of 15 percent. If the loan is for $10,000, how much interest (in dollars) will the firm pay?

18-8 **(Effective Loan Costs)** A financial institution lends a firm $10,000 for one year at 10 percent on a discounted basis and requires compensating balances of 20 percent of the face value of the loan. Determine the effective annual interest rate associated with this loan.

18-9 **(Comparison of Loan Terms)** Wisconsin Can wishes to establish a prearranged borrowing agreement with its local commercial bank. The bank's terms for a line of credit are 3.30 percent over the prime rate, and the borrowing must be reduced to zero for a 30-day period. For an equivalent revolving credit agreement, the rate is 2.80 percent over prime with a commitment fee of .50 percent on the average unused balance. With both loans, the compensating balance is 20 percent of the amount borrowed. The prime rate is currently 8 percent. The revolving credit agreement is for $1 million. Wisconsin Can expects on average to borrow $500,000 during the year no matter which loan agreement it decides to use.

a   What is the effective interest cost of the line of credit?

b   What is the effective interest cost of the revolving credit agreement? (*Hint:* Compute the ratio of the dollars the firm will pay in interest and commitment fees to the dollars the firm will effectively have use of.)

c   Under what conditions does the revolving credit agreement have a lower or higher effective interest cost than the line of credit?

d   If the firm does expect to borrow an average of half the prearranged funds, which arrangement would you recommend for the borrower? Explain why.

18-10   (**Cost of Commercial Paper**)   Commercial paper is usually sold at a discount. GMAT has just sold an issue of 90-day commercial paper with a face vaue of $1 million. The firm has received $978,000.

a   What effective *annual* interest rate will the firm pay for financing with commercial paper?

b   If a brokerage fee of $9,612 was paid from the initial proceeds to an investment banker for selling the issue, what effective annual interest rate will the firm pay?

18-11   (**Accounts Receivable as Collateral**)   Kansas City Castings (KCC) is attempting to obtain the maximum loan possible using accounts receivable as collateral. The firm extends net 30-day credit. The amounts owed KCC by its 12 credit customers, the average age of each account, and the customers' average payment period are as follows:

Customer	Account receivable	Average age of account	Average payment period of customer
A	$37,000	40 days	30 days
B	42,000	25 days	50 days
C	15,000	40 days	60 days
D	8,000	30 days	35 days
E	50,000	31 days	40 days
F	12,000	28 days	30 days
G	24,000	30 days	70 days
H	46,000	29 days	40 days
I	3,000	30 days	65 days
J	22,000	25 days	35 days
K	62,000	35 days	40 days
L	80,000	60 days	70 days

a   If the bank will accept all accounts that can be collected in 45 days or less as long as the customer has a history of paying within 45 days, which accounts will be acceptable? What is the total dollar amount of accounts receivable collateral? (Accounts receivable that have an average age greater than the customer's average payment period are also excluded.)

b   In addition to the conditions in **a**, the bank recognizes that 5 percent of credit sales will be lost to returns and allowances. Also, the bank will lend only 80 percent of the acceptable collateral (after adjusting for returns and allowances). What level of funds would be made available through this lending source?

18-12   (**Accounts Receivable as Collateral**)   Pottsburg Plate and Glass wishes to borrow $80,000 from the Pottsburg National Bank using its accounts receivable to secure the loan. The bank's policy is to accept as collateral any accounts that are normally paid within 30 days of the end of the credit period so long as the average age of the account is not greater than the customer's average payment period. Pottsburg Plate's accounts receivable, their average ages, and the average payment period for each customer are given. The company extends terms of net 30 days.

Customer	Account receivable	Average age of account	Average payment period of customer
A	$20,000	10 days	40 days
B	6,000	40 days	35 days
C	22,000	62 days	50 days
D	11,000	68 days	65 days
E	2,000	14 days	30 days
F	12,000	38 days	50 days
G	27,000	55 days	60 days
H	19,000	20 days	35 days

a Calculate the dollar amount of acceptable accounts receivable collateral held by Pottsburg Plate and Glass.

b The bank reduces collateral by 10 percent for returns and allowances, what is the level of acceptable collateral under this condition?

c The bank will advance 75 percent against the firm's acceptable collateral (after adjusting for returns and allowances). What amount can Pottsburg Plate and Glass borrow against these accounts?

18-13 **(Factoring)** Dynamic Finance factors the accounts of the Russell Allen Company. All eight factored accounts are listed, with the amount factored, the date due, and the status as of May 30. Indicate the amounts Dynamic should have remitted to Russell Allen as of May 30 and the dates of those remittances. Assume that the factor's commission is 2 percent.

Account	Amount	Date due	Status on May 30
A	$200,000	May 30	Collected May 15
B	90,000	May 30	Uncollected
C	110,000	May 30	Uncollected
D	85,000	June 15	Collected May 30
E	120,000	May 30	Collected May 27
F	180,000	June 15	Collected May 30
G	90,000	May 15	Uncollected
H	30,000	June 30	Collected May 30

18-14 **(Cost of Factoring Advance — Single Amount)** Duff Duds wishes to receive an *advance* from its factor on an account of $100,000 due in 30 days. The factor holds a 10 percent factor's reserve, charges a 2 percent factoring commission, and charges 16 percent annual interest (paid in advance) on advances.

a Calculate the maximum dollar amount of interest to be paid.

b What amount will the firm actually receive?

c What is the effective interest cost on this transaction?

18-15 **(Cost of Factoring — Multiple Accounts)** The Rohio Oil Company factors all its accounts. The factor charges a 1 percent factoring commission, holds a 15 percent reserve, and charges 10 percent interest (paid in advance) on advances. Rohio wishes to receive an advance against the following accounts as of September 1:

Account	Amount	Date due
A	$ 60,000	September 30
B	100,000	September 30
C	120,000	September 30
D	75,000	September 30
E	40,000	September 30

a Calculate the actual amount the firm can borrow.

b Calculate the maximum dollar amount of interest that must be paid.

c What is the effective interest cost of this advance?

d What is the annual factoring cost (in percent)? Can this rate be compared to a straight loan of the same amount? Why or why not?

e Why might the actual interest and factoring costs be less than the amounts calculated in **b** and **d**?

18-16 (Pledging versus Factoring) American Manufacturing is considering obtaining funding through advances against receivables. Total credit sales are $12 million, terms are net 30 days, and payment is made on the average in 30 days. City State Bank will advance funds under a pledging arrangement for 15 percent annual interest. On the average, 80 percent of credit sales will be accepted as collateral. Friendly Finance offers factoring on a nonrecourse basis for a 2.5 percent factoring commission, charging 1 percent per month on advances and requiring a 20 percent factor's reserve. Under this plan, the firm would factor all accounts and close its credit and collection department, saving $300,000 per year.

a What is the effective interest rate and the average amount of funds made available under pledging and under factoring?

b What other effects must be considered in choosing either of these plans?

c Which plan do you recommend and why?

18-17 (Inventory Financing) Prescott Turbine Company faces a liquidity crisis — it needs a loan of $100,000 for 30 days. Having no source of additional unsecured borrowing, the firm must find a secured short-term lender. The firm's accounts receivable are quite low, but its inventory is considered liquid and reasonably good collateral. The book value of the inventory is $300,000, of which $120,000 is finished goods.

(1) Center City Bank will make a $100,000 trust receipt loan against the finished goods inventory. The annual interest rate on the loan is 12 percent on the outstanding loan balance plus a .25 percent administration fee levied against the $100,000 initial loan amount. Because it will be liquidated as inventory is sold, the average amount owed over the month is expected to be $75,000.

(2) First Local Bank is willing to lend $100,000 against a floating lien on the book value of inventory for the 30-day period at an annual interest rate of 13 percent.

(3) North Mall Bank and Trust will loan $100,000 against the finished goods inventory and charge 15 percent annual interest on the outstanding loan balance. A .5 percent warehousing fee will be levied against the average amount borrowed. Because the loan will be liquidated as inventory is sold, the average loan balance is expected to be $60,000.

a Calculate the cost of each of the proposed plans for obtaining an initial loan amount of $100,000.

b Which plan do you recommend? Why?

c If the firm had made a purchase of $100,000 for which it had been given terms

The importance of long-term debt to the firm's capital structure was emphasized in earlier discussions of the cost of capital, leverage, and capital structure. The presence of debt provides financial leverage, which tends to magnify the effects of increased operating profits on owners' returns. Since debt is normally the cheapest form of long-term financing, due to the tax-deductibility of interest, it is a desirable component of capital structure. The presence of long-term debt in the firm's capital structure generally lowers the cost of capital,[1] permitting the firm to select from a larger group of acceptable investment alternatives.

Long-term debt financing can be obtained in two ways. One is to borrow the money directly. *Term loans,* with varying requirements, are available from a number of major financial institutions. A second method of raising long-term debt funds is to sell marketable debt in the form of *bonds* and raise small parts of the total debt financing from various purchasers. The process of selling bonds, as well as stock, is generally accomplished using an *investment banker*—an institution that can assist in private placements and take a lead role in public offerings. Firms—especially multinationals—may have opportunities to obtain international long-term debt financing.

Characteristics of Long-Term Debt Financing

Long-term debt is defined as debt having a maturity of greater than one year.[2] The long-term debts of businesses typically have maturities of between 5 and 20 years.

[1] This is commonly the case due to the tax-deductibility of interest, which causes the cost of debt (discussed in Chapter 12) to be quite low. Of course, as was pointed out in Chapter 13, the introduction of *large* quantities of debt into the firm's capital structure can result in high levels of financial risk, which can cause the weighted average cost of capital to rise.

[2] Some texts classify debts with maturities of one to seven years as *intermediate-term debt.* This text uses a strict short-term–long-term classification. Debts with maturities of less than one year are considered short-term, and debts with maturities greater than one year are considered long-term. This type of classification is more in line with the firm's balance sheet classification of current liabilities and long-term debts.

When a long-term debt is within a year of its maturity, many accountants will move the debt balance from the long-term debt account to the current liabilities account because at that point the long-term debt has actually become a short-term obligation. Similar treatment is given to portions of long-term debts payable in the coming year. These entries are normally labeled "current portion of long-term debt."

STANDARD LOAN PROVISIONS

A number of *standard provisions* are included in long-term loan agreements. These provisions should not place a burden on the financially sound business. The borrower is required to maintain satisfactory accounting records, render financial statements, pay its taxes and other liabilities, and maintain all its facilities in good condition.

Maintenance of satisfactory accounting records. The borrower is required to maintain satisfactory accounting records in accordance with generally accepted accounting principles. This guarantees the lender that the financial data of the borrower are presented accurately and permits easy interpretation of operating results.

Rendering of financial statements. The borrower is required to supply, at certain dates, audited financial statements that provide the lender with a yardstick for enforcing certain restrictive covenants and enable it to monitor the firm's progress. Often, the lender requires copies of the firm's bank statements to evaluate its spending behavior.

Payment of taxes and other liabilities. The borrower is required to pay taxes and other liabilities when due. The lender is not only concerned with receiving its required payments; it must also make sure that the borrower does not default on any of its other obligations, since default on any payment could result in bankruptcy. If the borrower does not pay bills, the lender can force repayment of the loan.

Repair and maintenance requirements. The lender requires the borrower to maintain all its facilities in good working order. This ensures the lender that the borrower will not let assets deteriorate to the point where their market value is negligible. In a sense, it forces the borrower to act as a "going concern."

RESTRICTIVE LOAN PROVISIONS

Long-term lending agreements, whether resulting from a negotiated term loan or a bond issue, normally include certain *restrictive covenants,* contractual clauses placing certain financial and operating *constraints* on the borrower. Since the lender is committing funds for a long period, it seeks to protect itself. Restrictive covenants generally require the firm to maintain a specified financial condition and managerial structure. These covenants stay in force for the life of the loan agreement. Generally, they include working capital restrictions, constraint on sale of receivables, fixed-asset restrictions, constraints with respect to subsequent borrowing, prohibition on leases, combination restrictions, salary restrictions, management restrictions, constraints on security investment, constraints on the use of loan proceeds, and dividend restrictions.

Working capital restrictions. One of the most common restrictions placed on the long-term borrower by the lender requires the borrower to maintain a minimum level of net working capital at all times. The level is determined through negotiations between borrower and lender. If the net working capital of the firm falls below the predetermined level, this is construed as an indicator of a deteriorating financial position and entitles the lender to *call* the loan prior to the firm's downfall.[3] Although a firm whose net working capital falls below the predetermined level may not be on the road to bankruptcy, this provision gives the lender the opportunity to evaluate the borrower's financial position and decide whether to continue the lending arrangement.

In addition to a net working capital requirement, many loan agreements contain provisions specifying minimum levels of current assets, minimum current ratios, or both. These provisions are also aimed at forcing the firm to maintain its liquidity, since if the firm cannot survive in the short run, there will be no long run.

Constraint on sale of receivables. Borrowers are prohibited from selling accounts receivable to generate cash, since this could result in a long-run cash flow shortage — especially if the firm must use the proceeds to meet current obligations. Selling accounts receivable is viewed as a sacrifice of the firm's long-run liquidity to satisfy short-term obligations. From a long-term lender's viewpoint, this behavior is not desirable.

Fixed-asset restrictions. Long-term lenders commonly place constraints on the firm with respect to the liquidation, acquisition, and encumbrance of fixed assets.

Liquidation of fixed assets. Lenders often prohibit the liquidation of fixed assets. A firm that does not have sufficient liquidity to make required payments can sell fixed assets to get cash. However, this strategy may damage the firm's ability to repay a term loan. Some firms sell fixed assets because they are no longer useful; if this is the case, the lender may find the liquidation of assets acceptable. By including a restrictive covenant, the lender at least retains the right to pass judgment in such a situation. The lender may merely require the borrower to get its approval prior to liquidating any fixed assets. In some cases, the working capital provision specifically restricts the sale of fixed assets to obtain liquidity.

Acquisition of fixed assets. Lenders sometimes prohibit the borrower from making capital expenditures to acquire new fixed assets. They may specify a maximum

---

[3] When a loan is "called," the lender demands immediate repayment. Violation of any standard or restrictive loan provision generally gives the lender the right to call a loan. In other words, violation of the covenants means the borrower has failed to abide by the terms of the loan contract. The lender's recourse is to require the immediate return of its money along with any accrued interest. Sometimes the lender will merely request some type of concession, such as representation on the borrower's board of directors, as an alternative to calling the loan; of course, the acceptance of such a concession is controlled by the lender, not the borrower.

dollar capital expenditure per year. The purpose of this restriction is to require the firm to maintain liquidity by keeping its dollars in current assets. A lender normally permits a level of capital expenditures sufficient to allow for adequate maintenance and repair of assets. It may waive the capital expenditure restriction if a large capital expenditure is shown to be justifiable.

Encumbrance of fixed assets. Quite often lenders will prohibit the use of fixed assets as collateral for a loan. By forcing the borrower to leave fixed assets unencumbered, the lender protects itself in case of liquidation. If the assets were used as collateral for another loan and the firm failed, the proceeds from the sale of the encumbered assets would be unavailable to satisfy the term lender's claims.

Constraints on subsequent borrowing. Many lending agreements prohibit the borrower from incurring any additional long-term debt. Short-term borrowing, which is a necessity for a seasonal business, is not usually limited. The restriction on long-term borrowing may require only that additional borrowing be *subordinated* to the original loan. Subordination of subsequent debt means that the subordinated creditors agree to wait until all the claims of the existing or *senior debt* are satisfied prior to receiving any distribution of assets in the event of liquidation.[4] The lender may require only that all subsequent long-term loans be unsecured.

Prohibition on leases. Borrowers may be prohibited from entering into financial leases. Often a certain dollar limit is placed on the amount of lease liability acceptable to the lender. If the firm were permitted to make unlimited lease agreements, the effectiveness of restrictive provisions with respect to capital expenditures and debt would be minimal. The similarity between a lease and a long-term debt obligation will be discussed in Chapter 21. The lender's objective is to ensure that financial lease commitments, which also are a form of long-term financing, are kept under control.

Combination restrictions. Occasionally, the lender requires the borrower to agree not to merge, consolidate, or combine in any way with another firm. Such an action could completely change the firm's operating and financial structure, and the changed structure could make the firm more financially risky than it was when the loan was initially negotiated. The lender may also prohibit the firm from changing its line of business by internally diversifying into new areas. The lender may permit the borrower to make certain changes if it has the lender's approval.

Salary restrictions. To prevent liquidation through large salary payments, the lender may prohibit salary increases for specified employees. The clause may permit salary increases up to a certain annual percentage. Restrictions on salary increases are intended to prevent the firm from paying out dollars that could be used to increase liquidity and operating profits. Normally included in this provision is a statement

---

[4] Debts are quite often subordinated in such a way that the senior debt's recovery in liquidation is greater than that of the general creditors. An example of how the subordination feature works in liquidation is given later in this chapter.

prohibiting employee loans or advances, since the effect of either is similar to that of a large salary payment.

Management restrictions. The lender may require the borrower to maintain certain "key employees" without whom the future success of the firm is uncertain. The lender may also retain the privilege of calling the loan or taking part in the selection of a new executive if a key officer were to resign. To protect itself in the event of the death of a key executive, the lender may also require the firm to maintain a *key employee life insurance* policy on specified executives. The policies may be payable to the company or directly to the lender to retire the loan. These management-related provisions are needed only when the presence of certain individuals is considered critical to the success of the firm.

Constraints on security investment. Occasionally the lender includes a covenant limiting the borrower's security investment alternatives. For example, the firm may be limited to highly marketable securities such as Treasury bills and negotiable certificates of deposit. By limiting the borrower's alternatives, the lender protects itself and prohibits the firm from making investments in securities with limited marketability. This increases the probability that the borrower will survive a liquidity crisis.

Constraints on the use of loan proceeds. Occasionally a covenant specifically requiring the borrower to spend the borrowed funds on certain items is included in the loan agreement. This restriction assures the lender that the funds will not be diverted outside the company or to some less productive use than that for which the money was initially borrowed. It forces the borrower to act in a manner consistent with its proven financial need.

Dividend restrictions. A relatively common provision in long-term loan agreements limits the firm's cash dividend payout to a maximum of 50 to 70 percent of its net earnings. Occasionally the dividend restriction is stated as a maximum dollar amount per year. Many lenders also place restrictions on the *repurchase* of stock, which, as pointed out in Chapter 14, is merely an alternative method of distributing corporate earnings to stockholders.

These are the most common loan restrictions. In the process of negotiating the terms of long-term borrowing, borrower and lender must ultimately agree to acceptable restrictive covenants; if agreement is not reached, the loan will not be made. Often the lender is in control and insists on the restrictions it believes are necessary to protect itself. Of course, the financial manager has the right to negotiate on the severity of the restrictions. Thus, a good financial manager will know in advance the relative impact of each restriction on the firm and will try to hold the line on restrictions that may have a severe negative impact.

    The violation of any standard or restrictive provisions by the borrower gives the lender the right to demand immediate repayment of the loan principal and any accrued interest. The lender will not normally demand immediate repayment, but it will evaluate the situation to determine whether the violation is serious enough to jeopardize the loan. On the basis of this evaluation it may call the loan, waive the violation and continue the loan, or waive the violation but alter the terms of the initial agreement.

COST OF LONG-TERM FINANCING

The cost of long-term financing is generally higher than that of short-term financing due to the high degree of uncertainty associated with the future. The long-term financing agreement specifies the actual interest rate charged to the borrower, the timing of the payments, and the dollar amount of the payments. An important consideration for the borrower is the rate of interest, or the cost of borrowing the funds. The major factors affecting the cost of money for a given borrower are the loan maturity, the size of the loan, the business and financial risk of the borrower, and the basic cost of money.

Maturity of the loan. Generally, long-term loans have higher interest rates than short-term loans. The difference in rates is attributable to the fact that lenders cannot accurately predict the future behavior of interest rates. The longer the term of a loan, the less accuracy in predicting interest rate patterns to maturity and therefore the greater the uncertainty associated with the loan. To compensate for both the uncertainty of future interest rates and the fact that the longer the term of a loan the higher the probability that the borrower will default, the lender typically charges a higher interest rate on long-term loans.

If a lender expects future interest rates to be higher than current (short-term) interest rates, it will definitely charge more for long-term loans. In certain periods when short-term rates are quite high (third quarter of 1978 through third quarter of 1982, for example), lenders will make long-term loans at rates below the prevailing short-term rate. A firm needing funds is advised to use an alternate form of financing (short-term debt, preferred stock, or common stock) when long-term rates are high. There is obviously a trade-off between these alternative forms of financing and long-term debt. The borrower should attempt to quantify the differences and determine whether an alternate form of financing (if available) would be preferable. The commitment resulting from a long-term debt financing decision suggests the need for careful study by the borrower before a long-term loan agreement is signed.

Size of the loan. The size of the loan affects the interest cost of borrowing in an inverse manner. Loan administration costs per dollar borrowed are likely to decrease with increasing loan size, but the risk to the lender increases. The size of the loan sought by each borrower must be evaluated to determine the net administrative cost-risk trade-off. The size of the loan with respect to the lender's total funds also affects interest cost. If a lender lends 20 percent of its money to one borrower, it will charge a rate reflecting the riskiness of the loan. This risk will be high because of the lender's failure to diversify its loans.

AMERICAN MOTORS' UNUSUAL LOAN

Early in 1982, when the recession was bottoming out, American Motors badly needed more cash to pay for its ambitious car and Jeep product programs. So it turned to an unconventional source for a loan: its unionized work force.

For the United Auto Workers, A.M.C.'s request was a first. That same year, General Motors and Ford, troubled by their own financial problems, were asking their workers for more direct wage and benefit concessions. A.M.C., instead, proposed that each of its 14,000 hourly workers loan it $8,000 to $9,000 apiece from wages and benefits over a three-year period ending in 1985. A.M.C. said it would pay back the loan by 1988 at 10 percent interest. After running into some initial opposition among A.M.C.'s militant work force, the plan was ratified by the workers in May, 1982. Through this plan, the union not only saved jobs, but eventually helped fund the development of A.M.C.'s hatchback Encore as well as its new down-sized Jeeps.

Under the unique plan, A.M.C.'s hourly workers made the loan by agreeing to forgo their 3 percent annual raises in 1983 and 1984, six quarterly cost-of-living allowance adjustments, and 28 days' pay over a three-year period. Under the original agreement, all of these benefits will have been restored to workers by the start of 1985.

The plan, says A.M.C., has provided the company with $120 million. But next year [1985], A.M.C. is scheduled to begin paying back the loan — when the troubled automaker, once again, sorely needs the money to fund new product lines. The repayment agreement to employees is complex, giving the union the option of two different methods of calculating how much each worker is to be paid. Under the first, A.M.C. would be required to pay out up to 25 percent of its automotive profits.

If A.M.C. isn't sufficiently profitable to make payments under the first plan, a second calls for A.M.C. to pay each worker $100 for every one of the first 200,000 cars produced during the year, plus an additional $150 for each vehicle beyond the first 200,000. Workers would also receive 10 percent of A.M.C.'s automotive profits for the year. In either case, A.M.C. has from 1985 to 1988 to repay its entire debt to its workers, plus interest.

The uncertain nature of how the employees will be repaid makes it difficult for analysts to forecast A.M.C.'s 1985 earnings. While David Eisenberg, automotive analyst with Sanford C. Bernstein & Company, believes that A.M.C. could earn as much as $70 million next year, he remains uncertain how much will be eaten up by the U.A.W. deal — and how much will be left over for product development.

SOURCE: "American Motors Repays an Unusual Loan," *The New York Times,* January 29, 1984, p. F-13.

Business and financial risk of the borrower. As noted in Chapter 13, a firm's operating leverage, revenue stability, and cost stability result in a certain level of business risk. The higher the operating leverage and the less stable the firm's revenues and costs, the greater is its business risk. The higher the borrower's debt ratio, the greater its financial risk is considered to be. A low times-interest-earned ratio also reflects this financial risk. The lender's main concern is with the ability of the borrower to repay the loan. If the lender's assessment of the borrower's business and financial risk indicates that the borrower would be unable to service readily the debt, the loan will not be made. The overall assessment of the borrower's business and financial risk, along with information on past payment patterns, is used by the lender in setting the interest rate on any term loan. In the case of bonds, ratings by independent agencies reflect their risk and thereby affect the associated interest rate.[5] It should be clear that a careful credit analysis of a borrower by the lender or potential bondholder is necessary to assess the riskiness of the prospective borrower.

Basic cost of money. The cost of money is the basis for determining the actual interest rate charged a prospective borrower. It is defined as the interest rate on long-term debt issues that are virtually risk-free. Generally, the rate on government bonds with equivalent maturities is used as the basic cost of money. Each lender will add premiums related to such factors as the maturity date of the loan, the size of the loan, and the business and financial risk of the borrower. If the lender agrees that the prevailing rate of interest on equal-maturity government issues accurately reflects interest rate expectations, it may not need to make any adjustment for the maturity of the loan. Adjustments for the size of the loan and for business and financial risk are much more common. Generally, the basic cost of long-term money adjusted for certain specific factors determines the rate of interest charged.

Some lenders determine a prospective borrower's risk class[6] and find the rates charged on similar-maturity loans to firms believed to be in the same risk class. Instead of having to determine a risk premium, the lender can use the risk premium prevailing in the marketplace for similar loans. The key to the successful use of this approach is to be able to measure and classify the business and financial risk of a given firm accurately. Regardless of which approach is used for determining the interest rate on a long-term loan, it is important that both the borrower and the lender feel comfortable with the rate, since both commit themselves to it for a long period of time.

Term Loans

Long-term loans are made by financial institutions to business firms. These loans generally have maturities of 5 to 12 years; shorter maturities are available, but minimum five-year maturities are most common. These loans are often made to finance *permanent* working capital needs, to purchase machinery and equipment, or to liquidate other loans — to change their maturities or to lower the interest cost.

---

[5] A brief discussion of bond ratings is included in a later section of this chapter.

[6] A *risk class* reflects the firm's overall risk profile. One must envision a continuum of risk, break it into discrete classes, and place the firm in an appropriate class. Looking at other firms perceived to be in the same risk class will help the lender make certain decisions with respect to the appropriate rate of interest. For publicly traded firms, betas (see Chapter 7) are often used to classify firms into homogeneous risk classes.

CHARACTERISTICS OF TERM LOAN AGREEMENTS

The actual term loan agreement is a formal contract of a few to a few hundred pages. These agreements are normally prepared by the lender's attorneys. The following items are commonly specified in the loan agreement: the amount and maturity of the loan, payment dates, the interest rate, standard provisions, restrictive provisions, the collateral (if any), the purpose of the loan, the action to be taken in the event of default, and stock-purchase options. Of these, only payment dates, collateral requirements, and stock-purchase options require further discussion.

Payment dates. Term loan agreements generally require monthly, quarterly, semiannual, or annual payments. Generally, these equal payments fully amortize the principal and interest over the life of the loan. Occasionally a term loan agreement will require periodic payments over the life of the loan followed by a large lump-sum payment at maturity. This lump-sum, or *balloon payment,* represents the entire loan principal if the periodic payments represent only interest. If the lending agreement specifies a large balloon payment, the borrower is often required to make periodic payments into a *sinking fund,* which is a type of deposit or investment that at maturity is equal to the required balloon payment. The use of sinking funds is much more common in the case of bond financing. Term loan agreements commonly include prepayment penalties of 2 to 10 percent of the outstanding loan balance. This is because term lenders generally prefer to have their loans held to maturity.

Collateral requirements. Term lending arrangements may be unsecured or secured in a fashion similar to short-term loans. Whether collateral is required depends on the lender's evaluation of the borrower's financial condition. Common types of collateral include machinery and equipment, plant, pledges of accounts receivable, and pledges of securities. The lender can obtain a security interest in any of these assets by filing certain documents that become part of the term loan agreement in a public office. When fixed assets are used as collateral, the lender files a mortgage on them; in many instances the loan is actually made to finance the purchase of these fixed assets. If current assets such as accounts receivable and marketable securities are used as collateral, the lender requires continuous pledges of acceptable accounts and securities.

Stock-purchase options. A recent trend in term lending is for the lender to require the borrower to provide stock-purchase options in addition to the required interest payments. Stock-purchase options are *warrants* that allow the holder to purchase a stated amount of common stock in the firm at a specified price over a certain period of time. These options can be made available only by corporate borrowers. They are used to entice institutional lenders to make term loans. (Warrants are discussed in greater detail in Chapter 22.)

TERM LENDERS

The primary financial institutions making term loans to business are commercial banks, insurance companies, pension funds, regional development companies, the

Small Business Administration, small business investment companies, commercial finance companies, and equipment manufacturers. Although the characteristics and provisions of term lending agreements made by these institutions are quite similar, a number of basic differences exist.

Commercial banks. Large commercial banks make some term loans to business. These loans are generally for periods of no more than 12 years except in the case of real estate loans, which may have maturities of as long as 25 years. Since commercial banks are limited in the amount they can lend to a single borrower (no more than 15 percent of the bank's unimpaired capital and surplus), many commercial banks are unable to make loans requested by creditworthy borrowers. Often a commercial bank will syndicate a large loan by forming a credit group made up of a number of banks. Each bank provides a certain percentage of the total loan. Sometimes loans are syndicated not because of a constraint on lending but to spread, or diversify, the risk. Commercial banks generally require collateral for term loans.

The advantages of commercial bank term loans include the establishment of a working relationship with a banker, advice and counsel from experts in business loans, a source of credit information on customers, and the establishment of a possible source of information on mergers and acquisitions. The disadvantages include the need to divulge confidential information and the general control given the lender by the provisions of the loan agreement. Many of these advantages and disadvantages are present in term loans from other financial institutions as well.

Insurance companies. Insurance companies — especially life insurance firms such as The Prudential Insurance Company of America — make term loans with maturities of 10 to 20 years. Insurance company loans are generally for much larger amounts than commercial bank loans. Insurance companies make term loans to large firms, while commercial banks generally make term loans to smaller firms. Insurance companies make both unsecured and mortgage (secured) term loans. The mortgage loans are generally made for not more than two-thirds to three-fourths of the value of the collateral. The basic covenants and terms of insurance company loans are the same as for bank loans. The major advantages of insurance company loans over bank loans are the longer maturities and larger amounts of money available. The basic disadvantage is that the rate of interest charged is in many cases slightly higher than that charged on commercial bank loans.

Pension funds. Employee pension funds invest a small portion of their funds in term loans to business. These loans are generally mortgage loans to large firms. The provisions and costs of pension fund loans are similar to those of life insurance company loans. This similarity is largely attributable to the fact that many pension funds are managed by life insurance companies.

Regional development companies. Term loans to business are often made by *regional development companies,* which are associations, generally attached to local or regional governments, that attempt to promote business development in specific geographic areas. These associations attempt to make it possible for businesses with good prospects of success and companies desiring to expand to fulfill these objectives. Regional development companies obtain funds from various governmental bodies and from the federal government. By making long-term loans at competitive rates, they attract new and expanding businesses into an area. Their long-run objective is to increase the economic base and promote favorable economic conditions in the given geographic area.

Small Business Administration. The Small Business Administration (SBA), which is an agency of the federal government, makes loans to firms that fulfill certain eligibility requirements. The SBA often joins with a private lending institution in making these loans. It lends a portion of the principal or guarantees repayment of a portion of a privately made loan. The SBA makes "direct loans," rather than providing guarantees, only when a qualified borrower cannot obtain SBA-guaranteed financing from private lending institutions. The SBA will guarantee loans through banks for up to $500,000; direct loans are limited to $150,000 except under special circumstances, when they can be increased to $350,000. Generally, SBA loans are for less than $100,000. The rates on SBA loans are equal to or below commercial bank rates. The SBA makes some loans to regional development companies.

Small business investment companies. A *small business investment company (SBIC)* is an institution licensed by the government that makes both debt and equity investments in small firms. The small business investment company raises its capital by borrowing from the Small Business Administration or from other sources. The owners of an SBIC are primarily interested in placing their money in companies with high growth potential. An SBIC loan to a company normally provides the SBIC with an opportunity to receive an equity interest in the borrowing firm. The payoff is expected to result from capital gains on the SBIC's equity interest. Term loans made by SBICs have maturities of from 5 to 20 years and interest rates slightly higher than those for bank loans.

Commercial finance companies. Commercial finance companies (CFCs) make secured long-term loans to business firms. CFCs are generally involved in the financing of equipment purchases by manufacturing firms. Often the commercial finance company is a subsidiary of the manufacturer of the equipment. The term of CFC loans is generally less than ten years. The borrower is required to make a specified down payment followed by equal installment payments over the life of the loan. Title to the equipment may or may not initially pass to the borrower. The cost of term loans from CFCs is generally high in comparison with the cost of long-term loans from other sources.

Equipment manufacturers. The manufacturer or seller of equipment may finance long-term installment sales to businesses. The characteristics of manufacturers' loans to customers are similar to those of loans made by commercial finance companies. Many manufacturers have their own commercial financing subsidiaries.

Corporate Bonds

A *bond* is a certificate indicating that a corporation has *borrowed* a certain amount of money and promises to repay it in the future under clearly defined terms. The issuing corporation agrees to pay bondholders a stated amount of interest at specified time intervals (usually semiannually). Most bonds are issued with maturities of 10 to 30 years and with a par, or face, value of $1,000. However, maturities of less than ten years and par values of $100 to $10,000 are not uncommon. Bonds with a par value of less than $500 are referred to as *baby bonds.* The coupon interest rate on a bond represents the percentage of the bond's par value that will be paid out annually. Purchasers of bonds are creditors who expect to receive specified periodic interest and repayment of the principal amount (par value) at maturity.

LEGAL ASPECTS OF CORPORATE BONDS

Since a corporate bond issue may be for millions of dollars obtained by selling portions of the debt to numerous unrelated persons, certain legal arrangements are required to protect purchasers. Bondholders are protected legally primarily through the indenture and the trustee.

Bond indenture. A *bond indenture* is a legal document stating the conditions under which a bond has been issued. It specifies both the rights of the bondholders and the duties of the issuing corporation. The actions that may be taken by bondholders if the issuer violates any of the clauses in the indenture are also clearly specified. An indenture is normally a complex and lengthy legal document. In addition to specifying the interest and principal payments and dates, it contains various standard and restrictive provisions, sinking-fund requirements, and provisions with respect to a security interest (if the bond is secured).

Standard and restrictive provisions. The standard and restrictive provisions of a bond issue are virtually the same as those in a term loan agreement.

Sinking-fund requirements. One other restrictive provision that is normally included in a bond indenture is a sinking-fund requirement. The objective of this requirement is to provide for the systematic retirement of the outstanding bonds prior to maturity. Bondholders generally favor this activity, since it reduces the firm's debt and thereby its financial risk as the bond approaches maturity. To simplify the sinking fund retirement, a *call feature* is normally included in the indenture. This feature permits the issuer to repurchase outstanding bonds at a specified price. The firm may be required to make fixed or variable sinking-fund payments. *Fixed sinking-fund payments* represent prespecified annual dollar repurchases; *variable sinking-fund payments* require the firm to repurchase an amount of bonds equal to a certain percentage of earnings. Since the variable plan requires that few or no bonds be repurchased in a lean year, bondholders prefer fixed requirements. Even the fixed payment plans sometimes provide for a balloon payment to retire outstanding bonds at maturity. Most bond issues require fixed-dollar sinking-fund payments.

Under a sinking-fund requirement, the issuer can purchase the bonds in the marketplace or call them at the specified call price. The issuer will call bonds only when sufficient bonds cannot be purchased in the marketplace or when the market

tion of its claim.[8] Without the subordinated debentures, the senior debtholder would have received only 60 percent of this amount ($1.8 million instead of $3.0 million). ■

Income bonds. An *income bond* requires the payment of interest only when earnings are available from which to make the payment. These bonds are commonly issued during the reorganization of a failed or failing firm. The unpaid interest generally accumulates and must be paid prior to any distribution of funds to stockholders. Due to the weak claim of the income bondholder on the firm's assets, the stated rate of interest is generally quite high.

Mortgage bonds. A *mortgage bond* is a bond secured with a lien on real property or buildings. Normally the market value of the collateral is greater than the amount of the mortgage bond issue. Some mortgage bonds are secured by *blanket mortgages* such that all the assets of the firm act as collateral. A *first-mortgage bond* gives the holder the first claim on secured assets. A *second-mortage bond* gives the holder a secondary claim on assets already secured by the first mortgage. The first-mortgage bond is obviously the more secure, since the holder has the first claim on the pledged assets. Although first and second mortgages are most common, subsequent mortgages can be filed. The claims of first-mortgage bondholders must be satisfied prior to the payment of any subsequent mortgage claims. A number of features may be included in a mortgage bond indenture.

Open-end mortgages. An *open-end mortgage* permits the issuance of additional bonds under the same mortgage contract. This arrangement provides the issuer with some flexibility in financing. Creditors are usually protected under this arrangement by restrictions on the amount of additional borrowing.

Limited open-end mortgages. A *limited open-end mortgage* allows the firm to issue additional bonds up to a specified maximum, which is typically stated as a percentage of the original cost of the pledged property. This arrangement provides more protection to existing bondholders than the open-end mortgage.

Closed-end mortgages. A *closed-end mortgage* does not permit additional borrowing on a given mortgage. The only way additional funds can be raised is through a new or subsequent mortgage. Creditors are well protected under this arrangement.

After-acquired clauses. Many mortgages, especially open-end mortgages, contain an *after-acquired clause.* This clause provides that all property acquired after the first mortgage be added to the property already pledged as security under the first mortgage. The clause protects the claim of current mortgage holders by giving them a lien on any additional property acquired.

---

[8] A more detailed example of the place of senior and subordinated debtholders in the liquidation process is included in Chapter 24. The example illustrates the rights of holders of both debt and equity in the liquidation process.

SWAPPING FIXED AND FLOATING DEBT

The difficulty and expense of raising long-term, fixed-rate money has been driving many corporate borrowers into the arms of banks, which are themselves seeking new clients for so-called innovative financing techniques. Among the most popular of these fee-producing services is "interest-rate swaps."

When all works well, a corporation can get fixed-rate money at below-market interest rates by exchanging its floating-rate payment obligations with another borrower—usually a foreign financial company—that wants to switch its floating-rate payments from fixed-rate payments.

The corporation prefers fixed-rate debt because it then knows exactly what its interest costs will be, eliminating the risk that its financing costs might soar. A foreign bank or financial company might want a floating-rate obligation that would move in line with the interest rates it charges on its short-term loans.

Last January, for example, the Niagara Mohawk Power Corporation wanted to convert $50 million of a floating-rate loan it had from its banks into a seven-year, fixed-rate loan with an interest rate of less than 13 percent.

Interest on the floating-rate loan was set at one-half a percentage point above Libor—the London Interbank Offered Rate. It is at that rate that banks in the London market trade deposits among themselves.

The company could have fixed its interest payments by issuing seven-year bonds in the United States, which would have cost about $13\frac{1}{4}$ percent at the time. Niagara Mohawk decided that it could lower that cost through a swap deal.

As a result, it asked for bids on a swap arrangement, and Citicorp won the bid by offering a fixed rate for seven years at a total cost of $12\frac{3}{4}$ percent. Thus, Niagara Mohawk saved about $1.75 million in interest expenses.

Citicorp did not make the fixed-rate loan. It found a financial company in Asia that wanted floating-rate debt in place of fixed-rate that it held. Citicorp, in effect, arranged to have Niagara Mohawk pay the fixed-rate interest on behalf of the Asian financial company, and the Asian company agreed to pay the floating rate for Niagara Mohawk. Each side deals through Citicorp. No principal was exchanged, only interest payments.

According to Stephanie R. Warren, vice president of Citicorp, "everyone ended up happy"—if maybe a little confused.

SOURCE: "Swapping Fixed and Floating Debt," *The New York Times*, May 27, 1984, p. F-8.

Collateral trust bonds. If the security held by a trustee consists of stock and (or) bonds of other companies, the secured bonds issued against this collateral are called *collateral trust bonds*. Since the assets of *holding companies* generally consist of stocks and bonds of their subsidiaries, holding companies are the primary issuers of collateral trust bonds.[9] Many of these bonds provide for the substitution of fixed assets as collateral as long as a predefined collateral premium over the amount borrowed is maintained. The value of the collateral generally must be 25 to 35 percent greater than the value of the bonds it supports.

---

[9] A *holding company* is a corporation having a controlling interest in one or more other corporations. To maintain this controlling interest, ownership of between 10 and 20 percent of the outstanding shares of the firm's stock is generally required. A discussion of holding companies is included in Chapter 23.

Equipment trust certificates. *Equipment trust certificates* were originally used primarily by railroads to finance the purchase of equipment. Today they are commonly used by airlines, truck lines, and barge lines to finance their "rolling stock"—airplanes, trucks, or boats. To obtain the equipment, a down payment of 20 to 25 percent is made by the firm (borrower) to the trustee, which is normally a bank. The trustee sells certificates to raise the additional funds required to purchase the equipment from the manufacturer. The firm makes periodic lease payments to the trustee, which then pays dividends to the trust certificate holders. The trust certificates mature serially and are retired by the trustee, using the balance of the lease payments. The final lease payment is used to retire any remaining trust certificates. After the final payment, the trustee passes title of the equipment to the firm. The annual lease payment to the trustee is set to cover the cost of dividends, retiring certificates, and the expenses of the trust in each period of the trust agreement's life. Equipment trust certificates are essentially a form of leasing (see Chapter 21).

Deep discount (and zero coupon) bonds. *Deep discount bonds* are issued with very low coupons; to provide a competitive yield, they are therefore sold at a price far below par value. As noted in Chapter 8, the difference between the deeply discounted cost of the bond and its par value increases the yield. Generally, the coupons on these bonds are initially set at 50 to 60 percent of competitive yields, resulting in initial offering prices of around 50 percent of par. The most deeply discounted bonds are *zero coupon bonds,* which have a zero coupon rate, thereby causing an investor's yield to result solely from their gain in value. These bonds are generally callable only at their par value, thus assuring investors they will not be called. As a result, they are sold at initial yields of 1 percent or so below the prevailing rate on similar-risk bonds. In addition to the lower cost, deep discount bonds are appealing to issuers because they require very low periodic interest cash outflows, although some tax benefits—through writing off (amortizing) of the discount—are received annually. Of course, in addition to being unable to call the bond, the issuer must be prepared to retire the bonds at their par value, which will be significantly higher than the initial proceeds, at their maturity. Despite the fact that the IRS has taken some of the tax benefits away from investors in these bonds, they remain popular among various institutional investors in low tax brackets.

Variable-rate bonds. Typically the coupon rate of interest on a bond is fixed. *Variable-rate bonds* are bonds that have a floating coupon — one that is adjusted periodically in response to market conditions. Adjustments are typically tied to a specific money or capital market rate such as Treasury-bill or Treasury-note rates and are commonly limited to some maximum change each period as well as over the maturity of the bond. Variable-rate bonds, or "floaters," tend to be used when a great deal of uncertainty surrounds inflation and future interest rate movements. Because the bond's coupon rate will generally equal the market rate for similar-risk bonds, variable-rate bonds generally sell in the market at a price close to par.[10]

[10] The discussion of bond valuation procedures in Chapter 8 demonstrated that when the coupon rate is equal to the market rate for similar-risk bonds, market value is equal to par value. See Equation 8.3 and the surrounding discussion for clarification of this point.

BOND-REFUNDING OPTIONS

A firm that wishes to retire or refund a bond prior to maturity has two options. Both require some foresight on the part of the issuer.

Serial issues. The borrower can issue *serial bonds,* a certain proportion of which come due each year. When serial bonds are issued, a schedule showing the yields, interest rates, and prices associated with each maturity is given. An example would be a $30 million, 20-year bond issue for which $1.5 million of the bonds mature each year. The interest rate associated with the shorter maturities would, of course, differ from the rates associated with the longer maturities. Although serial bonds cannot necessarily be retired at the option of the issuer, they do permit the issuer to retire the debt over its life. Not only does this type of bond appeal to the firm, but it can also attract purchasers because such an issue offers a variety of yields and maturities from which the investor can select. This type of bond is issued primarily by governmental units.

Refunding bonds by exercising a call privilege. If interest rates drop after the issuance of a bond, the issuer may wish to refund the bond with new bonds at the lower interest rate. If a call feature has been included in the issue, the issuer can easily retire it. The desirability of such an action is not necessarily obvious but can be determined by a type of cost-benefit analysis using present-value techniques. The actual process used to make these decisions can be illustrated by a simple example. However, a few tax-related points should be clarified first.

Call premiums. The amount by which the call price exceeds the par value of the bond is the *call premium.* It is paid by the issuer to the bondholder to buy back outstanding bonds prior to maturity. The call premium is treated as a tax-deductible expense in the year of the call.

Bond discounts and premiums. When bonds are sold at a discount or at a premium, the firm is required to amortize the discount or premium over the life of the bond. The amortized discount is treated as a tax-deductible expenditure, while the amortized premium is treated as income. If a bond is retired prior to maturity, any unamortized portion of a discount or premium is deducted or treated as income at that time.

Flotation or issuance costs. Any costs incurred in the process of issuing a bond must be amortized over the life of the bond. The annual write-off is therefore a tax-deductible expenditure. If a bond is retired prior to maturity, any unamortized portion of this cost is deducted at that time.

EXAMPLE The Flaherty Company is contemplating calling $30 million of 30-year, $1000 bonds issued five years ago at a coupon rate of 14 percent. The bonds have a call price of $1140 and initially netted proceeds of $29.1 million due to a discount of $30 per bond. The initial flotation cost was $360,000. The company intends to sell $30 million of 12-percent, 25-year bonds to net proceeds for retiring the old bonds.[11] The firm intends to sell the new bonds at their par value of $1,000. The underwriting costs on the new issue are estimated to be $440,000. The firm is currently in the 40 percent tax bracket and estimates its after-tax cost of debt to be 8 percent.[12] It expects a four-month period of overlapping interest, during which interest must be paid on both the old and the new bonds.

The first step is to calculate the incremental initial outlay, or initial investment, involved in implementing the proposed refunding. Table 19.3 presents the calculations required, which indicate that the Flaherty Company must pay out $3,380,000 now in order to implement the refunding plan. The second step is to determine the annual cash flow savings that will result from the new bond. The annual cash flow savings each year are the same, since the old bond has 25 years remaining to maturity and the life of the new bond is 25 years. Table 19.4 shows how the annual cash flow savings are calculated by subtracting the annual cash outflows with the new bond from the annual cash outflows with the old bond. The new bond results in cash flow savings of $350,240 per year.

Table 19.3   Calculating the Incremental Initial
Outlay for the Flaherty Company

Initial cash outflows	
Cost of calling old bonds ($1,140 × 30,000)	$34,200,000
Cost of issuing new bonds	440,000
Interest on old bonds during overlap period	
(.14 × 4/12 × $30,000,000)	1,400,000
(1) Total cash outflows	$36,040,000

Initial cash inflows	
Proceeds from new bond	$30,000,000
Tax shields[a]	
Call premium (.40 × $140 × 30,000)	1,680,000
Unamortized discount on old bond	
($900,000 × 25/30 × .40)	300,000
Unamortized issue cost of old bond	
($360,000 × 25/30 × .40)	120,000
Overlapping interest	
(.14 × 4/12 × $30,000,000 × .40)	560,000
(2) Total cash inflows	$32,660,000
Incremental initial outlay [(1) − (2)]	$ 3,380,000

[a] These are treated as a cash inflow, although they actually represent a negative cash outflow.

[11] To simplify this analysis, the maturity of the new bonds has been set equal to the number of years to maturity remaining on the old bonds. A procedure using annualized net present value (ANPV) techniques as presented in Chapter 11 would be required in comparing bonds having unequal maturities remaining. Refer to an advanced text for a detailed description of the application of these techniques.

[12] Ignoring any flotation costs, the firm's after-tax cost of debt would be 7.2 percent [12 percent debt cost × (1 − .40 tax rate)]. To reflect the flotation costs associated with selling new debt, the use of an after-tax debt cost of 8 percent was believed to be the applicable discount rate. A more detailed discussion of techniques for calculating a firm's after-tax cost of debt can be found in Chapter 12.

Table 19.4 Calculating the Annual Cash Flow Savings
for the Flaherty Company

Old bond	Annual cash outflow
Annual interest (.14 × $30,000,000)	$4,200,000
Less: Tax savings[a]	
Interest (.14 × $30,000,000 × .40)	(1,680,000)
Amortization of discount [($900,000 ÷ 30) × .40]	(12,000)
Amortization of issuing cost [($360,000 ÷ 30) × .40]	(4,800)
(1) Annual cash outflows with old bond	$2,503,200

New bond	
Annual interest (.12 × $30,000,000)	$3,600,000
Less: Tax savings[a]	
Interest (.12 × $30,000,000 × .40)	(1,440,000)
Amortization of issuing cost [($440,000 ÷ 25) × .40]	(7,040)
(2) Annual cash outflows with new bond	$2,152,960
Annual cash flow savings from new bond [(1) − (2)]	$ 350,240

[a] Tax savings are treated as cash inflows because of the tax shield they provide.

The final step in the analysis is to compare the initial outlay of $3,380,000 required to retire the old bond and issue the new bond to the annual cash savings of $350,240 resulting from the new bond. Because of the difference in the timing of these cash flows, the present value of the 25-year annuity of $350,240 must be found using the after-tax cost of debt. The *after-tax cost of debt* is used because the decision involves very low risk.[13] The present value of the $350,240, 25-year annuity, discounted at 8 percent, is $3,738,812 (10.675 × $350,240). Subtracting the incremental initial outlay of $3,380,000 from the present value of the cash savings ($3,738,812) yields a net present value of $358,812. Since a positive net present value results, the proposed refunding plan is recommended. ■

The analytical approach illustrated for bond refunding can be applied to all refunding problems. Certain modifications may be required, but the basic process of finding the incremental initial outlay and annual cash flow savings and comparing the present value of the savings to the initial outlay to make the decision is always the same. Care is required in the treatment of interest, call premiums, bond discounts and premiums, flotation or issuance costs, and interest overlaps, since these items are tax-deductible.

[13] Because the refunding decision involves the choice between retaining an existing debt or substituting a new, lower-cost debt, it is viewed as a low-risk decision that will not significantly affect the firm's financial risk. While some controversy surrounds the appropriate discount rate, the low-risk nature of the decision warrants the use of a very low rate, such as the firm's after-tax cost of debt.

Investment Banking

Investment banking plays an important role in aiding firms to raise long-term financing — both debt and equity — in the capital markets. It is the investment banker's job to find buyers for new security issues. As noted briefly in Chapter 3, *investment bankers* are neither investors nor bankers; they neither make long-term investments nor guard the savings of others. Instead investment bankers act as intermediaries between the issuing firm and purchasers of new security issues; they purchase securities from corporate and government issuers and market them to the public. Salomon Brothers and Merrill Lynch Capital Markets are two of the largest investment banking firms. Many investment banking firms operate in other areas as well; for example, Merrill Lynch is also the nation's leading securities brokerage firm.

FUNCTIONS OF THE INVESTMENT BANKER

The investment banker's primary function is underwriting security issues. A secondary function is advising clients.

Underwriting. When *underwriting* a security issue, an investment banker guarantees the issuer that it will receive at least a specified minimum amount from the issue. The banker buys the securities at a lower price than he or she plans to sell them for, thereby making a profit. The investment banker therefore bears the risk of price changes and a market collapse between the time of purchase and the time of sale of securities. There is always the possibility that the banker will be "stuck" with a large amount of the securities. In some instances, he or she may be able to sell the securities only at a price lower than the initial purchase price.

EXAMPLE   The First Big Corporation has agreed to underwrite a new $50 million common stock issue for the Taco Oil Company. It has agreed to purchase the stock for $48 million. Since First Big must pay Taco $48 million for the stock, it must attempt to sell the stock for net proceeds of at least $48 million. Actually, it will attempt to sell the stock for at least $50 million, thereby obtaining a $2 million commission. If it is unable to raise $50 million, the investment banking firm will not realize the full $2 million commission and will possibly lose part of the $48 million spent for the stock initially. In some cases, a security issue can be sold in a few days; in other, less fortunate situations, months are required to negotiate a sale. The investment banker therefore bears the risk of unfavorable price changes before the issue is sold as well as the risk of being unable to sell the issue at all. ■

Many security issues are not underwritten but rather are *privately placed* or sold on a *best efforts* basis. These functions are also handled by investment bankers.

Private placement. Private placement occurs when an investment banker arranges for the direct purchase of a new security issue by an individual, several individuals, a firm, or a group of firms. The investment banker is then paid a commission for acting as an intermediary in the transaction.

Best efforts. In the case of some public offerings, the investment banker may not actually underwrite the issue; rather, the banker may use his or her resources to sell the securities on a *best efforts* basis. In this case, the banker does not take on the risk associated with underwriting, and compensation is based on the number of securities sold.

Advising. The investment banker performs an advisory function by analyzing the firm's financial needs and recommending appropriate means of financing. Since an investment banker has a feel for the pulse of the securities markets, he or she can provide useful advice on mergers, acquisitions, and refinancing decisions.

ORGANIZATION OF INVESTMENT BANKING ACTIVITY

The investment banker's functions of underwriting security issues and advising clients come into play as a result of a logical sequence of events. The process begins when a firm in need of additional financing selects an investment banking firm, which then confers with the issuer, syndicates the underwriting, forms a selling group, fulfills legal requirements for a sale, sets a price, distributes the issue, and stabilizes the price.

Selecting an investment banker. A firm that needs additional financing through the capital markets initiates the fund-raising process by selecting an investment banker to underwrite the new issue and provide advice. The investment banker may be selected through *competitive bidding* or chosen by the issuing firm. In the case of competitive bidding, the investment banker or group of bankers that bids the highest price for the issue receives it. If the investment banker is merely hired by the issuing firm, the security issue is called a *negotiated offering.*

Conferring with the issuer. Once selected, the investment banker aids the firm in determining how much capital should be raised and in what form, debt or equity. The banker analyzes the firm's financial position and proposed disposition of the funds to be raised to make sure that the firm is financially sound and that the proposed expenditures are justifiable. After an examination of certain legal aspects of the firm and its proposed offering, a tentative underwriting agreement is drawn up.

Syndicating the underwriting. Due to the size of many new security issues, it is often necessary for the investment banker to form an *underwriting syndicate,* which is a group of investment banking firms. The use of an underwriting syndicate lessens the risk of loss to any single firm. Each underwriter in the syndicate must sell its portion of the issue. This is likely to result in a wider distribution of the new securities.

Forming a selling group. Each of the underwriters in the syndicate forms a selling group to sell the securities once they have been purchased. These *selling groups* consist of other investment bankers and stock brokerage firms. Members of the selling

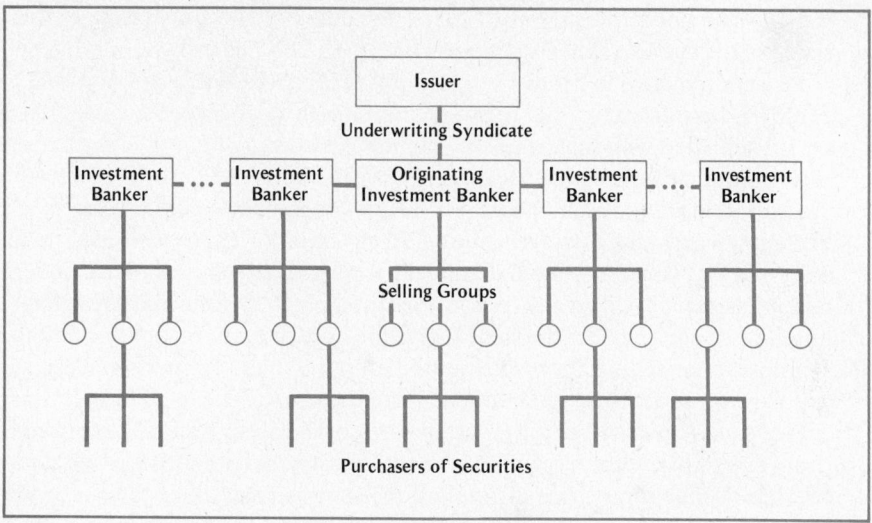

Figure 19.1　Distribution channels for a new security issue

group are paid a certain amount for each security sold.[14] Figure 19.1 depicts the distribution channels for a new issue.

Fulfilling legal requirements. Through the Securities and Exchange Commission, the federal government regulates the initial and subsequent trading of securities. Initial regulation tends to center on the registration of new issues; subsequent regulation is concerned with the securities exchanges and markets.

Registration requirements. Before a new security can be issued, the issuer must obtain the approval of the Securities and Exchange Commission (SEC). According to the Securities Act of 1933, which was passed to ensure the full disclosure of information with respect to new security issues and prevent a stock market collapse similar to the one that occurred in 1929–1932, the issuer is required to file a registration statement with the SEC. The firm cannot sell the security until the SEC approves the registration statement. This usually requires 20 days.

One portion of the registration statement is called the *prospectus.* This prospectus may be issued to potential buyers during the waiting period between filing the registration statement and its approval as long as a *red herring,* which is a statement indicating the tentative nature of the offer, is printed in red on the prospectus. Once the registration statement has been approved, the new security can be offered for sale if the prospectus is made available to all interested parties. If the registration statement is found to be fraudulent, the SEC will not only reject the issue but can also sue the directors and others responsible for the misrepresentation. Approval of the registration statement by the SEC does not mean that the

[14] The selling group is usually compensated in the same fashion as the underwriter. In other words, the selling group buys the securities at a discount from the sale price and profits from the *spread* between the price at which it purchases and the price at which it sells the security.

security is a good investment; it indicates only that the facts presented in the statement accurately reflect the firm's operating and financial position.

As an alternative to filing a lengthy registration statement and awaiting SEC approval, large firms (with at least $150 million in stock owned by investors who are not affiliated with management) can use a procedure known as *shelf registration*. This procedure, which became effective in March 1982, allows a firm to file a "master registration statement"—a single document summarizing planned financing—covering a two-year period. At any time during the two years, the firm, after filing a "short statement," can sell securities already approved under the master statement. Using this procedure, the approved securities are effectively warehoused and kept "on the shelf" until the need exists or market conditions are appropriate for selling the securities. The use of shelf registration is especially popular with large firms that frequently need access to the capital markets to raise debt or equity funds. To date the vast majority of shelf registrations have been debt issues rather than equity issues, and the equity issues have often been initial public offerings. While some firms using shelf registration can reduce their reliance on investment bankers, the investment banker continues to be the key link between the firm and the capital markets.

Trading requirements. Another important piece of legislation regulating the securities markets is the Securities Exchange Act of 1934, which is aimed at controlling the secondary trading of securities by providing for the regulation of securities exchanges, listed securities, and the general activities of the securities markets. The act provides for the disclosure of information on and accurate representation of securities traded. This piece of legislation and the Securities Act of 1933 are the key laws protecting participants in the capital markets. Many states also have laws aimed at regulating the sale of securities within their borders. These *blue sky laws* protect investors by preventing the sale of securities that provide "nothing but blue sky."

Pricing the issue. Underwriting syndicates generally wait until the end of the registration period to price securities so that they will have a feel for the current mood of the market. The pricing decision is important because it affects the ease with which the issue can be sold and also the issuer's proceeds. The investment banker's "feel" for the market should result in a price that achieves the optimum mix of marketability and financial return.

Distributing the issue. Prior to the actual offering of a new security for sale, the issue is publicized. This can be done only after the registration statement has been approved. Publicity is obtained through advertising and personal contacts through the brokerage firms handling the issue. When the security is formally placed on the market, orders are accepted from the selling groups and from outsiders. If the issue is sold out, it is considered *oversubscribed;* if all shares are not sold immediately, it is said to be *undersubscribed.*

Stabilizing the price. Once an issue has been offered for sale, the original underwriter attempts to stabilize its price so that the entire issue can be sold at the initial offering price. By placing orders to buy the security, the original investment

MORGAN STANLEY: FORMERLY THE NUMBER ONE UNDERWRITER

The ties between Exxon and Morgan Stanley, premier names in oil and investment banking, date back at least half a century. For decades, whenever Exxon turned to Wall Street to issue new stocks or bonds, Morgan Stanley was by its side, usually as the lead underwriter for the money-raising effort under way. Even today, the two companies occupy the same gleaming skyscraper in midtown Manhattan.

But when Exxon set its financing for 1983—a modest $77.7 million in tax-exempt bonds—it did not turn to its traditional investment banker. The oil giant opted, instead, for E. F. Hutton and its "lower floaters," a new kind of long-term bond with a floating interest rate. Explained W. Allen Harrison, Exxon's assistant treasurer: "Morgan Stanley does not have a product here."

Therein lies a key problem for Morgan Stanley & Company and the new, younger management team that took charge of the nation's pre-eminent investment bank last December. In a deregulated and hotly competitive financial world, where innovation and hard selling have begun to overtake tradition in importance, Morgan Stanley—the upright, venerable and still highly profitable Wall Street firm—is proving to be a dawdler. . . .

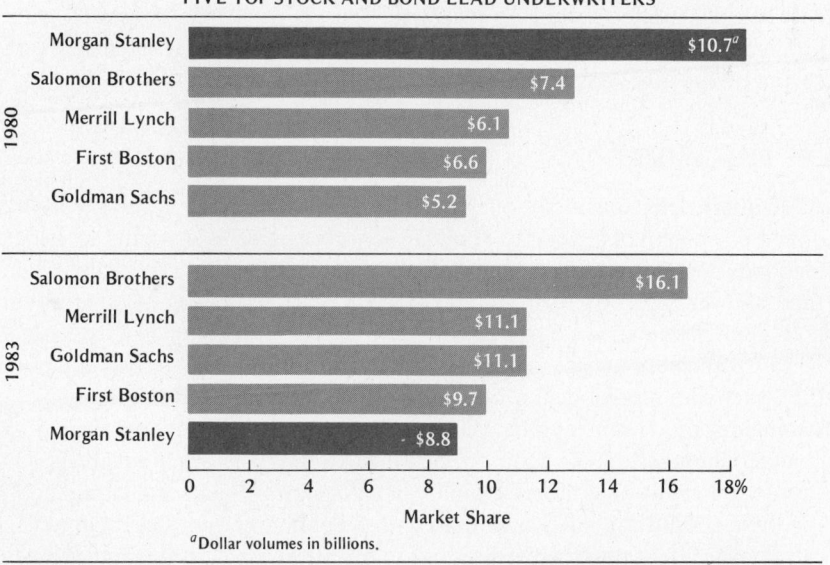

FIVE TOP STOCK AND BOND LEAD UNDERWRITERS

There are those on the street, however, who doubt that Morgan can ever again assume such heights. They cite deregulation, volatile financial markets, increasingly sharp corporate financial officers, the rise of the institutional investor and the advent of shelf registration. These fundamental changes, they say, have combined to make the investment banking game, even for a firm with Morgan's grand history, too difficult and fast-changing for any one company to remain supreme for long.

SOURCE: Michael Blumstein, "Morgan Stanley Fights for No. 1," *The New York Times,* April 1, 1984, pp. F-1, F-8.

banker can keep the demand for the issue and therefore the price at the desired level. This activity, sometimes referred to as *price pegging,* is legal as long as the intent is disclosed in the registration statement filed with the SEC. Price pegging is in the best interests of both the issuer and the underwriting syndicate in that it reduces the syndicate's risk, thereby lowering the issuance charges to the issuer.

COST OF INVESTMENT BANKING SERVICES

The investment banker is compensated by purchasing the security issue at a discount from the proposed sale price. The discount on an individual per-bond or per-share basis is referred to as the *spread.* The size of the spread depends on the cost of investigations, printing, and registration, the discount to the underwriting syndicate, and the discount given to the selling group. The cost of an issue is a function of two basic components — administrative cost and underwriting cost. Generally, the larger the issue, the lower the overall cost in percentage terms. It is also generally true that the overall flotation cost for common stock is highest, preferred stock and bonds following in that order. The overall flotation cost ranges from as little as .5 percent of the total proceeds on a large bond issue to as much as 20 percent on a small common stock issue. The type of security issued affects the cost because it affects the ease with which large blocks can be placed with one purchaser. A firm that is contemplating a security issue must therefore weigh the cost of public sale against the cost and feasibility of private placement.

PRIVATE PLACEMENT

As an alternative to a public offering, a firm can sometimes negotiate private (or direct) placement of a security issue. Ordinarily, private placements are used only for bonds or preferred stock. Common stock is sometimes directly placed when the firm believes that the existing shareholders might purchase the issue through an arrangement known as a *rights offering,* which is described in detail in Chapter 20. Private placement usually reduces issuance and administrative costs and provides the issuer with a great deal of flexibility, since the firm need not file registration statements and is not required to obtain the approval of the Securities and Exchange Commission. In addition, private placement is often advantageous because the borrower has more flexibility in tailoring covenants and later renegotiating them should the need arise than with a public offering. On the other hand, private placement poses a disadvantage to the buyer who at some future date may wish to sell the securities on the open market because prior to public sale registration and approval by the Securities and Exchange Commission is required. In the case of private placements, an investment banker is usually employed to assist in finding a buyer and provide pricing advice.

Direct placement of common stock is sometimes achieved through stock options or stock-purchase plans. *Stock options* are generally extended to management and permit it to purchase a certain number of shares of the firm's common stock at a specified price over a stated period of time. These options are intended to stimulate managerial actions that increase the long-run success of the firm. *Stock-purchase plans* are a fringe benefit offered to a firm's employees. They allow the employees to purchase the firm's stock at a discount or on a matching basis whereby the firm absorbs part of the cost. Both plans provide equity capital and at the same time increase employee motivation and interest in the company.

MULTINATIONAL FINANCE

International Long-Term Debt

Chapter 3 contained certain information on international loans. Here the focus is on international bonds used by MNCs in their global operations.

INTERNATIONAL BONDS

In general, an *international bond* initially sold outside the country of the borrower is often distributed in several countries. When a bond is sold primarily in the country of the currency of the issue, it is called a *foreign bond.* For example, an MNC based in West Germany might float a bond issue in the French capital market underwritten by a French syndicate and denominated in French francs. When an international bond is sold primarily in countries other than the country of the currency in which the issue is denominated, it is called a *Eurobond.* For example, an MNC based in the United States might float a Eurobond in several European capital markets, underwritten by an international syndicate and denominated in U.S. dollars.

Tables 19.5 and 19.6 show new issues of foreign bonds and Eurobonds outside the United States for the period 1978–1982. As can be seen, state enterprises and international organizations tend to dominate the foreign bond market, and the Swiss franc is the dominant currency. In the case of new issues of Eurobonds, companies outside the United States have shown consistent dominance during the

Table 19.5 Foreign Bond Issues Outside the United States (in millions of U.S. dollars)

	1978	1979	1980	1981	1982
Foreign bonds, total	$14,359	$17,749	$14,521	$13,817	$20,535
By category of borrower					
U.S. companies	245	217	307	592	1,969
Foreign companies	2,110	3,463	3,157	3,384	4,447
State enterprises	3,163	3,284	2,830	3,701	5,421
Governments	5,771	7,663	4,086	2,762	3,575
International organizations	3,070	3,122	4,141	3,378	5,123
By currency of denomination					
Deutsche mark	3,789	5,379	4,839	1,310	2,951
Swiss franc	5,698	9,777	7,617	8,285	11,597
Dutch guilder	385	75	259	481	919
Japanese yen	3,826	1,833	1,088	2,457	3,414
Other	671	685	718	1,284	1,654

SOURCE: Morgan Guaranty Trust Company, *World Financial Markets,* New York, various issues.

Table 19.6   New Eurobond Issues (in millions of U.S. dollars)

	1978	1979	1980	1981	1982
Eurobonds, total	$14,125	$18,726	$23,959	$31,616	$52,161
By category of borrower					
U.S. companies	1,122	2,872	4,100	6,176	13,126
Other companies	4,540	7,183	9,032	12,882	13,647
State enterprises	3,291	4,524	5,835	7,496	14,297
Governments	3,643	2,433	3,045	2,629	7,415
International organizations	1,529	1,714	1,947	2,431	3,676
By currency of denomination					
U.S. dollar	7,290	12,565	16,420	26,830	45,048
Deutsche mark	5,251	3,626	3,607	1,277	2,587
Dutch guilder	394	531	1,050	529	645
Canadian dollar	—	425	279	634	1,201
European unit of account	165	253	65	309	1,385
Other	1,025	1,326	2,538	2,037	1,295

SOURCE: Morgan Guaranty Trust Company, *World Financial Markets,* New York, various issues.

1978–1982 period, with the U.S. dollar the most desired currency. (Oil price increases, in dollars, can partially account for both sets of figures.)

INTERNATIONAL FINANCIAL INSTITUTIONS

For foreign bonds, the underwriting institutions are those that handle bond issues in the respective countries in which such bonds are issued. For Eurobonds, a number of financial institutions in the United States and Western Europe form international underwriting syndicates. The underwriting costs for Eurobonds are comparable to those for bond flotation in the United States' domestic market.

To raise funds through international bond issues, many MNCs establish their own financial subsidiaries. Many American-based MNCs, for example, have created subsidiaries in the United States and Western Europe, especially in Luxembourg. Such subsidiaries can be used to raise large amounts of funds in "one move," with the funds redistributed wherever MNCs need them. (Special tax rules applicable to such subsidiaries also make them desirable to MNCs.)

INTEREST RATES

In the case of foreign bonds, interest rates are usually directly correlated with the domestic rates prevailing in the respective countries. For Eurobonds, several interest rates may be influential. For instance, for a Eurodollar bond, the interest rate will reflect the U.S. long-term rate, the Eurodollar rate, and long-term rates in other countries. ●●

CHAPTER SUMMARY

● Certain standard and restrictive loan provisions are common to all long-term borrowing arrangements.

● The standard provisions are generally concerned with the maintenance of satisfactory accounting records, the rendering of financial statements, the payment of obligations, and the repair and maintenance of assets.

● Restrictive provisions are generally concerned with net working capital minimums, accounts receivable, fixed assets, subsequent borrowing, financial lease commitments, business combinations, executive salaries, management, security investments, the disposition of loan proceeds, and dividend payments.

● The intention of all loan provisions is to protect the lender by permitting it to break the loan agreement and demand immediate repayment when the borrower's financial position appears to be weakening.

● The cost of long-term loans is normally higher than the cost of short-term borrowing. The difference depends on loan maturity, loan size, the business and financial risks of the borrower, and the basic cost of money.

● Long-term loans generally require monthly, quarterly, semiannual, or annual installment payments. Some loans provide for balloon payments at maturity; others require that sinking-fund payments be made to retire the loan.

● Term loans may be unsecured or secured; secured term loans are normally collateralized with fixed assets. Some term lenders require stock-purchase options, which give them an opportunity to take an equity interest in the borrowing company.

● Loans can be obtained directly from a number of financial institutions. The primary term lenders are commercial banks and life insurance companies, but term loans are also available from pension funds, regional development companies, the Small Business Administration, small business investment companies, commercial finance companies, and equipment manufacturers.

● Bonds are certificates carrying a promise to pay interest and principal at specified future dates. The agreement under which the bond is issued is called an indenture, and the enforcement of the indenture is placed in the hands of a trustee. Bonds are typically issued in $1000 denominations and have 10- to 30-year maturities.

● Many bonds have a conversion feature, a call feature, or stock-purchase warrants attached.

● Bond ratings, which are issued by independent agencies such as Moody's and Standard & Poor's, are important indicators of the risk of a new or outstanding bond.

● Unsecured bonds are called debentures. Some debentures are subordinated to other types of debt. Income bonds are another type of unsecured bonds that pay interest only when earnings are available.

● Secured bonds include mortgage bonds, collateral trust bonds, and equipment trust certificates. The mortgage bond is the most common type of secured bond.

● Bonds, whether unsecured or secured, may be issued as deep discount (zero coupon) or variable-rate bonds.

● Bond refunding is an important consideration for a firm. When serial bonds are issued, refunding is on a planned basis since the bonds' maturities are originally set to provide for orderly retirement. The inclusion of a call feature allows the issuer to refund a bond prior to maturity. Refunding is done when there is a drop in interest rates great enough to provide savings if the old bond is called and new bonds are issued at the lower rate.

● Investment bankers play an important role in assisting firms to raise long-term debt and equity financing. They underwrite or sell total issues of securities, receiving compensation in the form of a spread between the price at which they purchase and sell a security issue. They also assist in private placements and can be hired to sell new issues on a best efforts basis. Investment bankers provide advice to issuers in addition to underwriting.

● Generally, the originating investment banker will syndicate large issues with other investment bankers.

● Legal requirements, monitored by the Securities and Exchange Commission, must be met for registration and trading of securities. Shelf registration has helped to streamline registration.

● An alternative to public offerings is private (or direct) placement of securities—especially bonds and preferred stocks. In private placements, an investment banker is usually employed to assist in finding a buyer and to provide pricing advice.

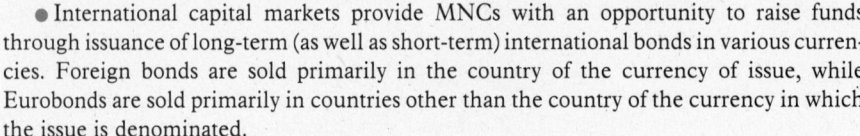 ● International capital markets provide MNCs with an opportunity to raise funds through issuance of long-term (as well as short-term) international bonds in various currencies. Foreign bonds are sold primarily in the country of the currency of issue, while Eurobonds are sold primarily in countries other than the country of the currency in which the issue is denominated.

KEY TERMS

after-acquired clause	open-end mortgage
baby bond	oversubscribed (security issue)
balloon payment	price pegging
best efforts	private placement
blanket mortgage	prospectus
blue sky laws	red herring
bond indenture	regional development company
bond	restrictive covenant (debt)
call feature	rights offering
call premium	second-mortgage bond
call price	selling group
closed-end mortgage	senior debt
collateral trust bond	serial bond
competitive bidding	shelf registration
conversion feature	sinking fund
debenture	small business investment company (SBIC)
deep discount bond	spread
equipment trust certificate	standard provisions (debt)
Eurobond	stock option
first-mortgage bond	stock-purchase plan
fixed sinking-fund payment	subordinated debenture
foreign bond	term loans
income bond	trustee
international bond	undersubscribed (security issue)
investment banker	underwriting
key employee life insurance	underwriting syndicate
limited open-end mortgage	variable-rate bond
long-term debt	variable sinking-fund payment
mortgage bond	warrants
negotiated offering	zero coupon bond

QUESTIONS

19-1 Why is long-term debt an important component of a firm's capital structure? What are the two key methods of raising long-term debt?

19-2 What motives does the lender have for including certain *restrictive provisions* in a loan agreement? How do these covenants differ from the so-called *standard provisions?*

19-3   What sort of negotiation process is required in settling on a set of restrictive loan covenants? What are the consequences of violation of a standard or restrictive provision?

19-4   What is the general relationship between the cost of short-term and long-term borrowing? Why are long-term rates generally higher than short-term rates? How may interest rate expectations affect financing decisions?

19-5   What types of interest and principal payment dates are generally associated with a term loan agreement? What are *balloon payments?* How do they differ from *sinking-fund payments?*

19-6   What role do commercial banks play in term lending to business? What are some of the "extras" that may result from borrowing through a commercial bank?

19-7   What role do insurance companies, pension funds, regional development companies, the Small Business Administration, small business investment companies, commercial finance companies, and equipment manufacturers play in lending long-term funds to business?

19-8   What sorts of maturities, denominations, interest payments, and types of purchasers are associated with a typical corporate bond?

19-9   What does it mean if a bond has a *conversion feature? A call feature? Warrants?* How are bonds rated and why?

19-10   Describe the basic characteristics of each of the following popular types of bonds.
  a Debentures   **d** Deep discount (zero coupon) bonds
  b Subordinated debentures   **e** Variable-rate bonds
  c Income bonds

19-11   Describe, compare, and contrast the basic features of the following secured bonds.
  a Mortgage bond
  b Collateral trust bond
  c Equipment trust certificate

19-12   What two options may be available to a firm that wants to retire an outstanding bond issue prior to maturity? Must these options be provided for in advance of issuance? Why might the issuer wish to retire a bond prior to maturity?

19-13   Describe the role and functions performed by the *investment banker.* Explain the sequence of events involved in the investment banking activity.

19-14   How is the investment banker compensated for his or her services? How are underwriting costs affected by the size and type of an issue? What, if any, role does an investment banker play in private placements?

 **19-15**   Describe and differentiate between *foreign bonds* and *Eurobonds.* Explain how each is sold and discuss the determinant(s) of their interest rates.

PROBLEMS

19-1   **(Priority of Claims)**   Thompson and Thompson have $25 million of debentures currently outstanding; $15 million are straight debentures, and the remaining $10 million are subordinated to the straight debentures. The firm has recently become bankrupt; the assets have been liquidated for $15 million, and there are $15 million of general creditor claims.
  a Determine how much of the $15 million will be distributed to each creditor.
  b Calculate the percentage of each debt recovered by each creditor.
  c Explain why debenture holders may permit the issuance of only subordinate debt when the firm raises new capital.

19-2   **(Priority of Claims)**   The Shoestring Company currently has $10 million of unsecured debt outstanding. The unsecured debt has the following components:

Debt	Amount	Subordinated?
General creditors' claims	$1,000,000	No
Debenture A	2,000,000	No
Debenture B	3,000,000	No
Debenture C	2,000,000	Yes, to debenture A
Debenture D	2,000,000	Yes, to debentures A and B
Total	$10,000,000	

The firm has just become bankrupt and has no secured debt outstanding. The liquidation of the firm has produced $5 million.

a Determine the amount each debtholder would have gotten if all the creditors had been general creditors.

b Given the actual nature of the firm's indebtedness, how much money, if any, will each creditor receive?

c Determine the percentage of claims recovered by each creditor.

d Discuss the advantage to debenture holders of subordinating subsequent indebtedness.

19-3 **(Bond Discounts or Premiums)** The initial proceeds per bond, the size of the issue, the initial maturity of the bond, and the years remaining to maturity are given for a number of bonds. In each case the firm is in the 40 percent tax bracket and the bond has a $1000 par value.

Bond	Proceeds per bond	Size of issue	Initial maturity of bond	Years remaining to maturity
A	$ 980	20,000 bonds	25 years	20
B	1,020	14,000 bonds	20 years	12
C	1,000	10,500 bonds	10 years	8
D	950	9,000 bonds	30 years	21
E	1,030	3,000 bonds	30 years	15

a Indicate whether each bond was sold at a discount, at a premium, or at its par value.

b Determine the total discount or premium for each issue.

c Determine the annual amount of discount or premium amortized for each bond.

d Calculate the unamortized discount or premium for each bond.

e Determine the after-tax cash flow associated with the retirement now of each of these bonds, using the values developed in **d**.

19-4 **(Cost of a Call)** For each of the callable bond issues in the table, calculate the after-tax cost of calling the issue. Each bond has a $1000 par value; the various issue sizes and call prices are summarized in the table. The firm is in the 40 percent tax bracket.

Bond	Size of issue	Call price
A	8,000 bonds	$1,080
B	10,000 bonds	1,060
C	6,000 bonds	1,010
D	3,000 bonds	1,050
E	9,000 bonds	1,040
F	13,000 bonds	1,090

19-5 **(Amortization of Issue Cost)** The initial issuance cost, the initial maturity, and the number of years remaining to maturity are given for a number of bonds. The firm is in the 40 percent tax bracket.

Bond	Initial issuance cost	Initial maturity of bond	Years remaining to maturity
A	$500,000	30 years	24
B	200,000	20 years	5
C	40,000	25 years	10
D	100,000	10 years	2
E	80,000	15 years	9

a Calculate the annual amortization of the issuance cost for each bond.
b Determine the after-tax cash inflow, if any, expected to result from the unamortized issuance cost if the bond were called today.

19-6 **(Interest Overlap Cost and Tax Shield)** For each of the bond issues in the table,
a Calculate the dollar amount of interest that must be paid during the interest overlap period.
b Calculate the tax shield resulting from the overlapped interest if the firm is in the 40 percent tax bracket.

Bond	Principal	Coupon rate	Interest overlap period
A	$ 2,000,000	12.0%	2 months
B	60,000,000	14.0	4 months
C	40,000,000	10.0	3 months
D	10,000,000	11.0	4 months
E	25,000,000	9.5	1 month

19-7 **(Refunding Decision — No Interest Overlap)** The Hunt Company is contemplating calling an outstanding $30 million bond issue and replacing it with a new $30 million bond issue. The firm wishes to do this to take advantage of the decline in interest rates that has occurred since the initial bond issuance. The old and new bonds are described below. The firm is in the 40 percent tax bracket.
Old bonds: The outstanding bonds have a $1000 par value and a 14 percent coupon rate. They were issued five years ago with a 25-year maturity. They were initially sold for their par value of $1000, and the firm incurred $250,000 in issuance costs. They are callable at $1140.
New bonds: The new bonds would have a $1000 par value and a 12 percent coupon. They would have a 20-year maturity and could be sold at their par value. The issuance cost of the new bonds would be $400,000. The firm does not expect to have any overlapping interest.
a Calculate the after-tax cash inflow expected from the unamortized portion of the old bonds' issuance cost.
b Calculate the annual after-tax cash inflow from the issuance cost of the new bonds, assuming the 20-year amortization.
c Calculate the after-tax cash outflow from the call premium required to retire the old bonds.
d Determine the incremental initial outlay required to issue the new bonds.
e Calculate the annual cash flow savings, if any, expected from the bond refunding and reissue.

f If the firm has a 7 percent after-tax cost of debt, would you recommend the proposed refunding and reissue? Why or why not?

19-8 **(Refunding Decision — With Interest Overlap)** Lawrence Furniture is considering calling an outstanding bond issue of $10 million and replacing it with a new $10 million issue. The firm wishes to do this to take advantage of the decline in interest rates that has occurred since the original issue. The two bond issues are discussed below; the firm is in the 40 percent tax bracket.

Old bonds: The outstanding bonds have a $1000 par value and a 17 percent coupon rate. They were issued five years ago with a 20-year maturity. They were initially sold at a $20 discount per bond and a $120,000 issuance cost was incurred. They are callable at $1170. *New bonds:* The new bonds would have a 15-year maturity, a par value of $1000, and a 14 percent coupon rate. It is expected that these bonds can be sold at par for a flotation cost of $200,000. The firm expects the two issues to overlap by two months.

a Calculate the incremental initial outlay required to issue the new bonds.

b Calculate the annual cash flow savings, if any, expected from the bond refunding and reissue.

c If the firm uses its after-tax cost of debt of 8 percent to evaluate low-risk decisions, would you recommend refunding? Explain your answer.

19-9 **(Refunding Decision — With Interest Overlap and Sensitivity Analysis)** The Korrect Kopy Company is considering the calling of an outstanding bond issue of $14 million and replacing it with a new $14 million issue. The details of both bond issues are outlined below. The firm has a 40 percent marginal tax rate.

Old bonds: Korrect's old issue has a coupon rate of 14 percent, was issued six years ago, and had a 30-year maturity. The bonds sold at a $15 discount from their $1000 par value, flotation costs were $120,000, and their call price is $1140.

New bonds: The new issue is expected to sell at par ($1000), have a 24-year maturity, and have a flotation cost of $360,000. The firm will have a one-month period of overlapping interest while it retires the old bond.

a What is the incremental initial outlay required to issue the new bonds?

b What are the annual cash flow savings, if any, from refunding and reissuing if
(1) The new bonds have a 12.5 percent coupon.
(2) The new bonds have a 13 percent coupon.

c Construct a table showing the net benefits of refunding under the two circumstances given in **b**, when
(1) The firm has an after-tax cost of debt of 6 percent.
(2) The firm has an after-tax cost of debt of 8 percent.

d Discuss the set(s) of circumstances when the reissue is favorable and when it is not.

e If the four circumstances were equally probable (each had .25 probability), would you recommend the refunding and reissue? Why or why not?

19-10 **(Underwriting Spread)** The Gray Company is interested in selling common stock to raise capital for plant expansion. The firm has consulted the First Omaha Company, a large underwriting firm, which believes the stock can be sold for $80 per share. The underwriter, on investigation, has found that its administrative costs will be 2 percent of the sale price and its selling costs will be 1.5 percent of the sale price. If the underwriter requires a profit of 1 percent of the sale price, how much will the *spread* have to be *in dollars* to cover the underwriter's costs and profit?

19-11 **(Bond Underwriting Analysis)** The Philip-Marrow Company wishes to sell $100 million of bonds whose net proceeds will be used in the acquisition of Unsoda Soft Drinks. The company has estimated that the net proceeds after paying the underwriter costs should provide an amount sufficient to make the acquisition. The underwriter, Morris Lunch & Co., believes the 100,000 bonds can be sold to the public at their $1000 par value. The underwriter estimates that its administrative costs will be $3.5 million. It also must sell the bonds at a .75 percent discount from their par value to members of the selling group. Morris Lunch's underwriting commission (in addition to recovery of its administrative costs) is 1 percent of the par value of the offering.

a Calculate the per-bond spread required by the underwriter to cover its costs.

b How much will Philip-Marrow net from the issue?

c How much will the selling group receive? How much will the underwriter receive?

d Assuming that this is a public offering, describe the nature of the underwriter's risk.

Chapter 20

Preferred and Common Stock

After studying this chapter, you should be able to:

1. Differentiate between debt and equity capital in terms of ownership rights, claims on income and assets, maturity, and tax treatment.

2. Understand the basic rights of preferred stockholders and the features normally included as part of a preferred stock issue.

3. Explain the key advantages and disadvantages of preferred stock financing.

4. Discuss the distinguishing characteristics of common stock, including important aspects of voting rights.

5. Describe stock rights and their role in common stock financing and cite the key advantages and disadvantages of common stock financing.

6. Understand the features that distinugish the use of international capital markets from the use of domestic markets to raise equity capital.

This chapter is devoted to the two sources of external equity capital for a business — preferred and common stock. Retained earnings, internally generated equity capital, were discussed with dividend policy in Chapter 14. The use of preferred stock, and especially common stock, to raise equity capital is necessary for a corporation's continued existence.

Chapters 12 and 13 discussed the firm's cost of capital, leverage, and capital structure. The cost of capital discussion indicated that preferred stock is generally a less expensive source of financing than common stock. The lower cost of preferred stock was attributed primarily to the fact that preferred dividends are fixed. The cost of common was found to depend primarily on the riskiness of the firm as perceived by investors and the historical pattern of dividend payments. The discussion of leverage and capital structure emphasized the need for an equity base large enough to allow the firm to raise sufficient low-cost debt to build an optimal capital structure.

The Nature of Equity Capital

Equity capital differs from debt capital in a number of key ways. Various differences between debt and equity capital were summarized in Chapter 13 (see Table 13.8). The four basic differences between debt and equity capital relate to the ownership of the firm, the claims on its income and assets, the maturity of the two types of capital, and the tax treatment of the two types of capital.

OWNERSHIP RIGHTS

Unlike creditors, holders of equity capital (preferred and common stockholders) are owners of the firm. The dollars invested by equity holders do not mature at some future date; they represent permanent capital that is expected to remain on the firm's books indefinitely. Holders of equity capital often receive voting rights that permit them to select the firm's directors and to vote on special issues.

Debtholders receive voting privileges only when the firm has defaulted or violated the terms of a loan agreement or bond indenture. As long as the firm meets all the requirements of loan agreements, only certain equity holders are given a voice in management.

CLAIMS ON INCOME AND ASSETS

Holders of equity capital receive claims on both income and assets that are secondary to the claims of creditors.

Claims on income. The claims of equity holders on income cannot be paid until the claims of all creditors have been satisfied. These claims include both interest and principal, regardless of whether the principal payment is in the form of a sinking-fund payment. Once these claims have been satisfied, the board of directors can decide whether to distribute any of the remaining funds to the owners. Certain owners may have preference over other owners with respect to the distribution of earnings. A firm's ability to make these payments may be constrained by its cash position or certain loan provisions. The firm may have sufficient earnings but no cash; it is the availability of cash that permits the firm to distribute earnings to owners.

Claims on assets. The claims of equity holders on the firm's assets are secondary to the claims of creditors. The stockholder's claims on assets are relevant primarily when the firm becomes bankrupt.[1] When this happens, assets are liquidated and the proceeds distributed first to employees and customers, then to the government, then to secured creditors, then to general creditors, and finally to equity holders. Since the liquidation value of the firm's assets is generally below their book value, equity holders rarely receive the book value of their equity in the event of liquidation. Because equity holders are the last to receive any distribution of assets during bankruptcy proceedings, they expect greater compensation in the form of dividends or rising market prices.

As noted in Chapter 12, the costs of the various forms of equity financing are generally higher than debt costs. This is partially explained by the fact that the firm must compensate suppliers of equity more than suppliers of debt capital because the suppliers of equity capital take a higher risk. This higher risk results from the secondary claims of equity on income and assets. Despite its being more costly, equity capital is necessary for the firm to grow and mature. All firms must initially be capitalized with some form of equity.

MATURITY

Unlike debt, equity capital is a permanent form of financing. It does not mature, and therefore repayment of the initial capital is not required. However, owners of equity capital are often able to liquidate their holdings through the various securities exchanges. Even equity in closely held corporations can be sold, although the process of finding a suitable buyer may be a bit more difficult than in the case of

---

[1] The procedures followed in bankruptcy proceedings are described in Chapter 24.

of debt is only 4.8 percent [8 percent $\times$ (1 — .40)].[5] On an after-tax basis, the firm must therefore pay its long-term creditors $1,440 (.048 $\times$ $30,000) and its preferred stockholders $3,000 (.10 $\times$ $30,000), leaving $7,560 ($12,000 — $1,440 — $3,000) available for the common stockholders. The return on the common stock equity is therefore 18.9 percent ($7,560 ÷ $40,000). The presence of the preferred stock increases the firm's leverage and magnifies the return to the common stockholders, since the 12 percent return on total capital is greater than the 10 percent cost of preferred stock financing.

If the Robin Company had earned the same amount but had $30,000 worth of bonds, no preferred stock, and $70,000 worth of common stock, the earnings available for common stockholders would have amounted to $10,560 ($12,000 — $1,440). The return on the common stock equity would thus have been only 15.1 percent ($10,560 ÷ $70,000). The decreased return to common stockholders is due to the decreased leverage resulting from the replacement of the $30,000 worth of preferred stock with an additional $30,000 worth of common stock. It should be clear from this example how preferred stock can be used to increase the firm's leverage, thereby magnifying the effects of increased earnings on common stockholders' returns. ■

Flexibility. Although preferred stock does provide added leverage in much the same way as a bond, it differs from a bond in that the issuer can pass a dividend or sinking-fund payment without suffering the consequences that result when an interest or sinking-fund payment is missed on a bond. Preferred stock allows the issuer to keep its levered position without running as great a risk of being forced out of business in a lean year as it might if it missed interest or sinking-fund payments on debt.

Use in mergers and acquisitions. Preferred stock has been used successfully to merge or acquire firms. Often, preferred stock is exchanged for the common stock of an acquired firm; the preferred dividend is set at a level equivalent to the historic dividend of the acquired firm. This lets the acquiring firm state at the time of the acquisition that only a fixed dividend will be paid. All other earnings can be reinvested to perpetuate the growth of the merged enterprise. This approach permits the owners of the acquired firm to be assured of a continuing stream of dividends equivalent to that which may have been provided prior to acquisition. Quite often, preferred stock used for mergers and acquisitions is convertible.

Disadvantages. The two major disadvantages of preferred stock are the seniority of the holders' claims and its cost.

Seniority of the holders' claims. Since holders of preferred stock are given preference over common stockholders with respect to the distribution of earnings and assets, the presence of preferred stock in a sense jeopardizes common shareholders' returns. If the firm's after-tax earnings are quite variable, its ability to pay at least token dividends to common stockholders may be seriously impaired.

[5] Recall from Chapter 12, which was concerned with the cost of capital, that since interest is tax-deductible, the after-tax cost of debt to the firm is calculated by multiplying the stated cost by 1 minus the tax rate. In this example, since the $12,000 represents earnings measured *before interest and after taxes,* in order to get earnings *after* interest and taxes, the interest cost times 1 minus the tax rate [interest $\times$ (1 — tax rate)] must be subtracted from the earnings before interest and after taxes.

Cost. The cost of preferred stock financing is generally higher than the cost of debt financing. This is because the payment of dividends to preferred stockholders is not guaranteed, whereas the payment of interest to bondholders is. Since preferred shareholders are willing to accept the added risk of purchasing preferred stock rather than long-term debt, they must be compensated with a higher return. Another factor causing the cost of preferred stock to be significantly greater than that of long-term debt is the fact that interest on debt is tax-deductible, while preferred dividends must be paid from after-tax earnings.[6]

In summary, the desirability of using preferred stock to raise funds depends not only on the firm's current capital structure and the state of the financial markets but also on the trade-offs among the cost, risk, and control of the alternate forms of long-term financing. The firm must weigh the long-run benefits and costs of preferred stock against the advantages and disadvantages of both long-term debt and common stock. Consideration must also be given to whether the stock will be cumulative or noncumulative, participating or nonparticipating, callable or non-callable, convertible or nonconvertible. In many instances, the preferred stock financing decision is a difficult one. Of the major external sources of long-term funds, preferred stock financing is the least commonly used.

Common Stock

The true owners of business firms are the common stockholders, who invest their money in the firm only because of their expectation of future returns. A common stockholder is sometimes referred to as a *residual owner,* since in essence he or she receives what is left after all other claims on the firm's income and assets have been satisfied. As a result of this generally uncertain position, the common stockholder expects to be compensated with adequate dividends and capital gains.

This section of the chapter discusses the characteristics of common stock, how stock rights can be used to raise additional capital, the non-rights sale of new common stock, the basic values of common stock, and some of the key advantages and disadvantages of common stock financing.

CHARACTERISTICS OF COMMON STOCK

An issue of common stock has a number of distinguishing characteristics. In this section we discuss par value; authorized, outstanding, and issued stock; voting rights; dividends; stock repurchases; and the distribution of earnings and assets.

Par value. Common stock may be sold with or without a par value. A *par value* is a relatively useless value arbitrarily placed on the stock in the corporate charter. It is generally quite low, since in many states the firm's owners can be held legally

---

[6] From time to time, discussion of making preferred stock dividends tax-deductible occurs in Congress and other legal forums. Tax reform recommendations made by President Ford to Congress during his term in office included such a proposal. Currently (July, 1984), no legislation relative to the tax-deductibility of preferred stock dividends is under congressional consideration.

liable for an amount equal to the difference between the par value and the price paid for the stock if the price paid for the stock is less than the par value. Setting the par value quite low, in the range of $1, reduces the possibility that the stock will sell for less than its par value. Firms often issue *no-par stock,* in which case they may assign it a value or place it on the books at the price at which it is sold.

A low par value may also be advantageous in states where certain corporate taxes are based on the par value of stock; if a stock has no par value, the tax may be based on an arbitrarily determined per-share figure. The accounting entries resulting from the sale of common stock can be illustrated by a simple example.

EXAMPLE   The Quixon Company has issued 1000 shares of $2 par-value common stock, receiving proceeds of $50 per share. This results in the following entries on the firm's books:

Common stock (1000 shares at $2 par)	$ 2,000
Paid-in capital in excess of par	48,000
Common stock equity	$50,000

Sometimes the entry labeled "paid-in capital in excess of par" may be labeled "capital surplus." Firms are usually prohibited by state law from distributing any paid-in capital as dividends.[7] ■

Authorized, outstanding, and issued stock. A corporate charter must state the number of shares of common stock the firm is *authorized* to issue. Not all authorized shares will necessarily be *outstanding.* Since it is often difficult to amend the charter to authorize the issuance of additional shares, firms generally attempt to authorize more shares than they plan to issue. A possible disadvantage of this approach is the fact that in some states corporates taxes are based on the number of shares authorized. It is possible for the corporation to have *issued* more shares of common stock than are currently outstanding if it has repurchased stock. Repurchased stock, as noted in Chapter 14, is called *treasury stock.* The amount of treasury stock is therefore found by subtracting the number of outstanding shares from the number of shares issued.

Voting rights. Generally, each share of common stock entitles the holder to one vote in the election of directors and in other special elections. Votes are generally assignable and must be cast at the annual shareholders' meeting. Occasionally, *nonvoting common stock* is issued when the firm's present owners wish to raise capital through the sale of common stock but do not want to give up any voting power. When this is done, the common stock will be classed. Class A common is typically designated as nonvoting, while class B common would have voting rights. Because class A shares are not given voting rights, they typically are given preference over class B shares in the distribution of earnings and assets. Treasury stock, which resides within the corporation, generally *does not* have voting rights. Three aspects of voting require special attention — proxies, majority voting, and cumulative voting.

[7] The various legal, contractual, and internal considerations with respect to the payment of cash dividends were discussed in Chapter 14. A firm can pay out more dollars in cash dividends than it earns in a given period if sufficient cash and retained earnings are available.

Proxies. Since most small stockholders cannot attend the annual meeting to vote, they may sign a *proxy* statement giving their votes to another party. The solicitation of proxies from shareholders is closely controlled by the Securities and Exchange Commission, since there is a possibility that proxies will be solicited on the basis of false or misleading information. The existing management generally receives the stockholders' proxies, since it is able to solicit them at company expense. Occasionally, when the ownership of the firm is widely disseminated, outsiders may attempt to gain control by waging a *proxy battle.* This requires soliciting a sufficient number of votes to unseat the existing management. To win a corporate election, votes from a majority of the shares voted—not outstanding—is required. Proxy battles generally occur when the existing management is performing poorly; however, the odds of a nonmanagement group winning a proxy battle are generally slim.

Majority voting. In the *majority voting system,* each stockholder is entitled to one vote for each share of stock owned. The stockholders vote for each position on the board of directors separately, and each stockholder is permitted to vote all of his or her shares for *each* director he or she favors. The directors receiving the majority of the votes are elected. It is impossible for minority interests to select a director, since each shareholder can vote his or her shares for as many of the candidates as he or she wishes. As long as management controls a majority of the votes, it can elect all the directors. An example will clarify this point.

EXAMPLE   The Baker Company is in the process of electing three directors. There are 1000 shares of stock outstanding, of which management controls 60 percent. The management-backed candidates are A, B, and C; the minority candidates are D, E, and F. By voting its 600 shares (60 percent of 1000) for *each* of its candidates, management can elect A, B, and C; the minority shareholders, with only 400 votes for each of their candidates, cannot elect any directors. Management's candidates will receive 600 votes each, and other candidates will receive 400 votes each. ■

Cumulative voting. Some states require and others permit the use of a *cumulative voting system* to elect corporate directors. This system gives a number of votes equal to the number of directors to be elected to each share of common stock. The votes can be given to *any* director(s) the shareholder desires. The advantage of this system is that it provides the minority shareholders with an opportunity to elect at least some directors.

EXAMPLE   The Able Company, like the Baker Company, is in the process of electing three directors. In this case, however, each share of common entitles the holder to three votes, which may be voted in any manner desired. Again, there are 1000 shares outstanding, and management controls 600. It therefore has a total of 1800 votes (3 × 600), while the minority shareholders have 1200 votes (3 × 400). In this situation, the majority shareholders can elect only two directors, and the minority shareholders can elect at least one director. The majority shareholders can split their votes evenly among the three candidates (give them 600 votes each); but if the minority shareholders give all their votes to one of their candidates, he or she will win. ■

A commonly cited formula for determining the number of shares necessary to elect a certain number of directors, *NE,* is given by Equation 20.1.

$$NE = \frac{O \times D}{T + 1} + 1 \qquad (20.1)$$

where

NE = number of shares needed to elect a certain number of directors
O = total number of shares of common stock outstanding
D = number of directors desired
T = total number of directors to be elected

EXAMPLE Substituting the values in the preceding example for O and T into Equation 20.1 and letting $D = 1, 2,$ and 3 yields values of NE equal to 251, 501, and 751. Since the minority stockholders control only 400 shares, they can elect only one director. ■

The advantage of cumulative voting from the point of view of minority shareholders should be clear from the example. However, even with cumulative voting, certain election procedures such as staggered terms for directors can be used to prevent minority representation on a board. Also, the majority shareholders may control a large enough number of shares or the total number of directors to be elected may be small enough to prevent minority representation.

Dividends. The payment of corporate dividends is at the discretion of the board of directors. Most corporations pay dividends quarterly. Dividends may be paid in cash, stock, or merchandise. Cash dividends are most common; merchandise dividends are least common. Stock splits, which have some similarity to stock dividends, are sometimes used to enhance the trading activity of a stock. The common stockholder is not promised a dividend, but he or she grows to expect certain payments from the historical dividend pattern of the firm. Before dividends are paid to common stockholders, the claims of all creditors, the government, and preferred stockholders must be satisfied. Because of the great importance of the dividend decision to the growth and valuation of the firm, Chapter 14 was devoted to a discussion of dividend policy.

Stock repurchases. Another characteristic of common stock, alluded to earlier in the discussion of authorized, outstanding, and issued stock, is the repurchase of stock. Firms occasionally repurchase stock to change their capital structure or to increase the returns to the owners. The effect of repurchasing common stock is similar to that of the payment of cash dividends to stockholders. The repurchase of stock has become quite popular among firms that are in a very liquid position with no attractive investment opportunities. Since stock repurchases are similar to cash dividend payments, they too were given coverage in Chapter 14.

Distribution of earnings and assets. As was mentioned in previous sections, holders of common stock have no guarantee of receiving any periodic distribution of earnings in the form of dividends, nor are they guaranteed anything in the event of liquidation. Common stockholders are likely to receive nothing as a result of bankruptcy proceedings. However, one thing they are assured of is that as long as they pay more than the par value for the stock, they cannot lose any more than they have invested in the firm. Moreover, the common stockholder can receive unlimited returns through the distribution of earnings and through appreciation in the value of holdings. Nothing is guaranteed, but the possible rewards for providing risk capital can be great.

STOCK RIGHTS

Stock rights, which provide certain purchase privileges to existing shareholders, are an important tool of common stock financing. Without them, shareholders run the risk of losing their proportionate control of the corporation.

Preemptive rights. Most issues of common stock provide shareholders with *preemptive rights,* which allow stockholders to maintain their proportionate ownership in the corporation when new issues are made. Most states require that shareholders be extended this privilege unless it is explicitly prohibited by the corporate charter. Preemptive rights permit existing shareholders to maintain their voting control and protect against the dilution of their ownership and earnings. *Dilution* of ownership usually results in the dilution of earnings, since each shareholder will have a claim on a smaller part of the firm's earnings. Of course, if earnings simultaneously increase, the long-run effect may be an overall increase in earnings per share. From the firm's viewpoint, the use of preemptive rights offerings to raise new equity capital may be cheaper than a public offering of stock. An example may help clarify the use of rights.

EXAMPLE The Maverick Company currently has 100,000 shares of common stock outstanding and is contemplati issuing an additional 10,000 shares through a rights offering. Each existing shareho' r will receive one right per share, and each right will entitle the shareholder to purchase one-tenth of a share of new common stock (10,000 ÷ 100,000), so 10 rights will be required to purchase one share of the stock. The holder of 1000 shares of existing common stock will receive 1000 rights, each permitting the purchase of one-tenth of a share of new common stock, for a total of 100 shares of new common stock. If the shareholder exercises his or her rights, he or she will end up with a total of 1100 shares of common stock, or 1 percent of the total number of shares outstanding (110,000). This is the same proportion the shareholder had prior to the rights offering. ■

Mechanics of rights offerings. When a company makes a rights offering, the board of directors must set a *date of record,* which is the last date on which the recipient of a right must be the legal owner indicated in the company's stock ledger. Due to the lag in bookkeeping procedures, stocks are usually sold *ex rights* (without rights) four business days prior to the date of record. Prior to this point, the stock is sold *cum rights* or *rights on,* which means that purchasers will receive the rights.

The issuing firm sends rights to holders of record, who are free to exercise them, sell them, or let them expire. Rights are transferable, and many are traded actively enough to be listed on the various stock exchanges. They are exercisable for a specified period of time, generally not more than a few months, at a price, which is called the *subscription price,* set somewhat below the prevailing market price. Since fractions of shares are not always issued, it is sometimes necessary to purchase additional rights or sell any extra rights. The value of a right depends largely on the number of rights needed to purchase a share of stock and the amount by which the right subscription price is below the current market price. If the rights have a very low value and an individual owns only a small number of shares, the rights may be permitted to expire.

Management decisions. A firm's management must make two basic decisions when preparing for a rights offering. The first is the price at which the right holders can purchase a new share of common stock. The subscription price must be set *below* the current market price, but how far below depends on management's evaluation of the sensitivity of the market demand to a price change, the degree of dilution in ownership and earnings expected, and the size of the offering. Management will consider the rights offering successful if approximately 90 percent of the rights are exercised.

Once management has determined the subcription price, it must determine the number of rights required to purchase a share of stock. Since the amount of funds to be raised is known in advance, the subscription price can be divided into this value to get the total number of shares that must be sold. Dividing the total number of shares outstanding by the total number of shares to be sold will give management the number of rights required to purchase a share of stock.

EXAMPLE   The Boone Company intends to raise $1 million through a rights offering. The firm currently has 160,000 shares outstanding, which have been most recently trading for $53 to $58 per share. The company has consulted an investment banking firm, which has recommended setting the subscription price for the rights at $50 per share. It believes that at this price the offering will be fully subscribed. The firm must therefore sell an additional 20,000 shares ($1,000,000 ÷ $50 per share). This means that 8 rights (160,000 ÷ 20,000) will be needed to purchase a new share at $50. Each right will entitle its holder to purchase one-eighth of a share of common stock. ∎

Value of a right. Theoretically, the value of a right should be the same if the stock is selling *with rights on (cum rights)* or *ex rights.* In either case, the market value of a right may differ from its theoretical value.

With rights on. Once a rights offering has been declared, shares will trade for only a few days with rights on. Equation 20.2 is used to find the value of a right when the stock is trading with rights on, R_o.

$$R_o = \frac{M_o - S}{N + 1} \qquad (20.2)$$

where

R_o = theoretical value of a right when stock is selling with rights on
M_o = market value of the stock with rights on

S = subscription price of the stock
N = number of rights needed to purchase one share of stock

EXAMPLE The Boone Company's stock is currently selling with rights on at a price of $54.50 per share, the subscription price is $50 per share, and 8 rights are required to purchase a new share of stock. According to Equation 20.2, the value of a right is $.50 [($54.50 − $50.00) ÷ (8 + 1)]. A right should therefore be worth $.50 in the marketplace. ■

Ex rights. When a share of stock is traded ex rights, meaning that the value of the right is no longer included in the stock's market price, the share price is expected to drop by the value of a right. Equation 20.3 is used to find the market value of the stock trading ex rights, M_e. The same notation is used as in Equation 20.2.

$$M_e = M_o - R_o \qquad (20.3)$$

The value of a right when the stock is trading ex rights, R_e, is given by Equation 20.4.

$$R_e = \frac{M_e - S}{N} \qquad (20.4)$$

The use of these equations can be illustrated by returning to the Boone Company example.

EXAMPLE According to Equation 20.3, the market price of the Boone Company stock selling ex rights is $54 ($54.50 − $.50). Substituting this value into Equation 20.4 gives the value of a right when the stock is selling ex rights, which is $.50 [($54.00 − $50.00) ÷ 8]. The theoretical value of the right when the stock is selling with rights on or ex rights is therefore the same. ■

Market behavior of rights. As indicated earlier, stock rights are negotiable instruments traded on stock exchanges. The market price of a right will generally differ from its theoretical value. The extent to which it will differ will depend on how the firm's stock price is expected to behave during the period when the right is exercisable. By buying rights instead of the stock itself, investors can achieve much higher returns on their money when stock prices rise.

Under- and oversubscribed offerings. Rights offerings may be made through an investment banker or directly by the issuing company. Most rights offerings are made through investment bankers, who underwrite and issue the rights. In most underwriting agreements, the investment banker agrees to a *standby arrangement,* which is a formal guarantee that any shares not subscribed or sold publicly will be purchased by the investment banker. This guarantee assures the firm that the entire issue will be sold; it will not be *undersubscribed.* The investment banker, of course, requires an additional fee for making this guarantee.

Most rights offerings include an *oversubscription privilege,* which provides for the distribution of shares for which the rights were not exercised to interested shareholders on a pro rata basis at the stated subscription price. This privilege is a method of restricting ownership to the same group, although ownership proportions may change slightly. Shares that cannot be sold through the oversubscription privilege may be offered to the public. If an investment banker is used, the disposition of unsubscribed shares may be left up to the banker.

NON-RIGHTS SALE OF NEW COMMON STOCK

Aside from the sale of new common stock through a rights offering, the firm may be able to place new shares of common stock directly through some type of stock option or stock-purchase plan. As pointed out in Chapter 19, *stock options* are generally extended to management and permit it to purchase a certain number of shares of their firm's common stock at a specified price over a certain period of time, while *stock-purchase plans* are fringe benefits occasionally offered to employees that allow them to purchase the firm's stock at a discount or on a matching basis, with the firm absorbing part of the cost.

New issues of common stock, of course, can also be sold publicly through an investment banker. This approach is commonly used in situations in which rights offerings are not required or are unsuccessful. The public offering of common stock through an investment banker is generally more expensive than any type of private placement, but the investment banker does provide a convenient mechanism for selling new common. A detailed discussion of the functions, organization, and operation of the investment banker in selling corporate securities was presented in Chapter 19.

BASIC VALUES OF COMMON STOCK

The value of a share of common stock may be measured in a number of ways. It has a book value, a liquidation value, a market value, and a theoretical value. The book value and the liquidation value do not reflect the value of the firm as a going concern, but rather view the firm as a conglomeration of assets and liabilities without any earning power. Book value measures the firm's common stock value as the per-share amount of common stock equity recorded on the firm's balance sheet. Liquidation value is based on the fact that the book value of the firm's assets is not generally equal to their market value. It is calculated by taking the market value of the firm's assets, subtracting its liabilities and the claims of preferred stockholders from this value, and dividing the result by the number of shares of common stock outstanding.

The most accepted way of determining the true (or theoretical) value of a share is to find the present value of all future per-share dividends expected over the firm's assumed infinite life. In an efficient market, the theoretical value would be expected to equal the market value. A discussion of efficient markets and common stock valuation was presented in Chapter 8.

PAYSOPs: A PIECE OF THE ACTION FOR EMPLOYEES

Employees at a growing number of companies are more than just wage earners. They're also stockholders.

One out of 3 owners of Dow Chemical is an employee; together, they hold 7 percent of the shares. Employees hold 20 percent of Sherwin Williams, 33 percent of People Express and 70 percent of Dan River. Before its breakup, 1 out of 7 shareholder accounts at AT&T was for an employee.

Cutting workers in for a piece of the action isn't new—employee stock plans have been around for years, based on the belief that workers who own part of their firm are more productive. But now a financial assist from Uncle Sam is causing more firms to look at the idea.

The latest spur to employee stock is a tax break under which the government picks up the tab. Each year, corporations can subtract dollar for dollar from their income tax an amount equal to 0.5 percent of payroll—rising to 0.75 percent in 1985—if that much in company stock is given to employees. . . .

Double benefit

A firm may even come out ahead if, rather than buying shares for employees, it issues new stock. That means no cash outlay for shares, but still a tax-cutting credit.

Called a PAYSOP, for payroll-based employee-stock-ownership plan, the arrangement was authorized by the 1981 tax-cut bill and took effect last year [1983]. It replaced a less popular incentive in which the credit for issuing stock to employees was equal to a percentage of spending for new equipment and facilities. For most firms, basing the credit on payroll means a larger rebate and thus meatier shifts of stock to workers.

As many as 3 out of 4 large companies will likely adopt PAYSOPs, estimates Corey Rosen, executive director of the National Center for Employee Ownership in Arlington, Va. . . .

Still, PAYSOPs have drawbacks. One is their limited punch. The benefit is too small to brighten employee attitudes, critics say. A worker earning $25,000 a year, for example, may get only $125 in stock this year. . . .

Broader plans?

Many backers of employee stockholding, nevertheless, are counting on PAYSOPs to whet appetites for more generous employee-stock-ownership programs, broadly known as ESOPs. Under these employer-sponsored setups, there is no direct tax credit, but companies get business-expense deductions for their outlays, and workers defer tax on the benefits while building a stake in the firm, typically as part of a retirement plan. In many cases, employees get stock equal to 10 percent or more of their pay each year.

SOURCE: "Employees Get Another Piece of the Company Action," *U.S. News and World Report,* February 27, 1984, pp. 70–71.

ADVANTAGES AND DISADVANTAGES OF COMMON STOCK

Common stock has a number of advantages and disadvantages. Some of the factors to be reckoned with in considering common stock financing are discussed in the following paragraphs.

Advantages. The basic advantages of common stock stem from the fact that it is a source of financing that places a minimum of constraints on the firm. Since dividends do not *have* to be paid on common stock and their nonpayment does not jeopardize the receipt of payment by other security holders, common stock financing is quite attractive. The fact that common stock has no maturity, thereby eliminating future repayment of obligations, also enhances the desirability of common stock financing. Another advantage of common stock over other forms of long-term financing is its ability to increase the firm's borrowing power. The more common stock the firm sells, the larger the firm's equity base and therefore the more easily and cheaply long-term debt financing can be obtained.

Disadvantages. The disadvantages of common stock financing include the potential *dilution* of voting power and earnings. Only when rights are offered and exercised by their recipients can this be avoided. Of course, the dilution of voting power and earnings resulting from new issues of common stock may go unnoticed by the small shareholder. Another disadvantage of common stock financing is its high cost. In Chapter 12 common stock equity was shown to be, normally, the most expensive form of long-term financing. This is because dividends are not tax-deductible and because common stock is a riskier security than either debt or preferred stock.

MULTINATIONAL FINANCE

International Equity Capital

International capital markets provide multinational companies with a setting in which equity funds can be raised. Several characteristics of such a setting distinguish it from a domestic one.

The basic aspects of foreign ownership of international operations were discussed in Chapter 2. Recent laws and regulations enacted by a number of host countries require MNCs to maintain less than 50 percent ownership in their subsidiaries in those countries. For a U.S.-based MNC, for example, establishing foreign subsidiaries in the form of joint ventures means that a certain portion of the firm's total international equity stock is held by foreign owners. Chapter 2 provided some of the advantages and disadvantages of joint ventures. A number of MNCs have the parent's equity stock distributed internationally and owned by stockholders of different nationalities. Capital markets in Western Europe and in Japan are the usual channels used by U.S.-based MNCs that desire international ownership of their equity. For MNCs based elsewhere, United States capital markets serve a similar function.

In establishing a foreign subsidiary, an MNC may wish to have as little equity and as much debt as possible, with the debt coming from local sources in the host country or the MNC itself. Each of these actions can be supported. The host country may allow more *local* debt for a subsidiary; this is a good protective measure in terms of lessening the potential impacts of political risk (see Chapter 7). In other words, since local sources are involved in the capital structure of a subsidiary, there may be fewer threats from local authorities in the event of changes in government or the enactment of new regulations on foreign businesses.

In support of the other action, having more MNC-based debt in a subsidiary's capital structure, it is true that many host governments are less restrictive — in terms of taxation and actual repatriation — toward intra-MNC interest payments than toward intra-MNC dividend remittances. The parent firm may therefore be in a better position if it has more MNC-based debt than equity in the capital structure of its subsidiaries.

A final point to note is that in international capital markets, as in domestic capital markets, different *classes* of equity — such as preferred and common — can be issued. ●●

CHAPTER SUMMARY

● Both preferred and common stock are instruments for raising long-term equity funds. Both securities represent forms of ownership and have claims on income and assets that are secondary to those of debt. These securities have no maturity and do not receive tax benefits like those given on interest payments to debtholders.

● Preferred stock is considered a security senior to common stock since the holders of preferred are given preference over common stockholders with respect to the distribution of earnings and assets.

● Preferred stock is similar to debt in that though some adjustable-rate (or floating-rate) issues exist, it generally has a fixed annual dividend. Since preferred stockholders' claims are given preference over the claims of common stockholders, these investors do not run the same risks as common stockholders, who are the firm's true owners. They therefore do not receive any voting privileges.

● Preferred stock issues may have certain restrictive covenants similar to those of bond issues. They may also have such features as cumulative dividends, participation in earnings, a call feature, a conversion feature, and retirement options.

● The basic advantages for the use of preferred stock financing include its ability to increase leverage, the flexibility of the obligation, and its use in mergers and acquisitions.

● Disadvantages include its preference over the common stockholders and its relatively high cost.

● Some firms issue various classes of common stock. Class A stock may have no voting rights but has preference over class B shares with respect to the receipt of distributions of earnings, assets, or both.

● Various voting systems are available for providing minority representation on the board of directors.

● Purchasers of common stock normally expect to receive some type of dividend; sometimes common stock is repurchased to meet a variety of objectives.

● Holders of common stock generally receive a preemptive right that gives them an opportunity to purchase any new common stock on a pro rata basis to maintain their proportion of votes and earnings.

● Stock rights are used to pass a purchase option to the owners. A certain number of rights are required to purchase shares at a reduced price, which causes the rights to have a value. Rights may be exercised, sold, purchased, or allowed to expire.

● Common stock may be privately placed with the purchaser by the issuer or sold through public offering by an investment banker. In addition to the use of rights offerings, private placement can be achieved through the use of stock options or stock-purchase plans.

● The worth of a share of common stock may be judged by its book value, liquidation value, market value, or theoretical value.

● The basic advantages of common stock stem from the fact that it is a source of financing that places a minimum of constraints on the firm with respect to periodic payments and retirement. Common stock also allows the firm to enhance its borrowing power.

● Disadvantages of common stock include the potential dilution of voting power and earnings and the high cost of this form of financing.

● Multinational companies can use international capital markets to raise equity. In establishing foreign subsidiaries, it may be more advantageous to issue debt (either local or MNC-based) than MNC-owned equity.

KEY TERMS

adjustable-rate (floating-rate) preferred
   stock
authorized stock
cum rights
cumulative preferred stock
cumulative voting system
dilution (of ownership)
ex rights
issued stock
majority voting system
noncumulative preferred stock
nonparticipating preferred stock
nonvoting common stock
no-par stock

outstanding stock
oversubscription privilege
participating preferred stock
par value (stock)
passed (dividends)
preemptive rights
proxy
proxy battle
rights on
standby arrangement
stock rights
subscription price
treasury stock

QUESTIONS

20-1 How do debt and equity capital differ? What are the key differences between them with respect to ownership, claims on income and assets, maturity, and tax treatment?

20-2 What is *preferred stock*? What claims do preferred stockholders have on earnings and assets? How are dividends on preferred stock typically stated? What is an *adjustable-rate* (or *floating-rate*) *preferred stock*?

20-3 What are *participating*, and *nonparticipating* preferred stock? How is the degree of participation specified? In what circumstance would you expect participating preferred to be issued?

20-4 What is a *call feature* in a preferred stock issue? When and at what price does the call usually take place? What benefit does the call offer the issuer of preferred stock?

20-5 What are the key advantages and disadvantages of using preferred stock financing as a source of new capital funds?

20-6 Why is the common stockholder considered the true owner of a firm? What risks do common stockholders take that other suppliers of long-term capital do not?

20-7   What are *proxies*? How are they used? What are *proxy battles,* and why are they initiated? Why is it difficult for minority shareholders to win such battles?

20-8   How do majority and cumulative voting systems differ? Which of these voting systems would be preferred by the small stockholder? Why?

20-9   What is a *date of record* for stock rights? What do the terms *ex rights* and *cum rights* or *rights on* mean? Are stock rights marketable?

20-10   What is a right *subscription price*? How is it determined? Given the subscription price, what must the firm know to determine the number of rights to offer?

20-11   What are the key advantages and disadvantages of using common stock financing as a source of new capital funds?

 20-12   What are the long-run advantages of having more *local* debt and less MNC-based equity in the capital structure of a foreign subsidiary?

PROBLEMS

20-1   **(Preferred Dividends)**   Sinderson, Schaefer, and Schloff has an outstanding issue of preferred stock with an $80 par value and an 11 percent annual dividend.

    a   What is the annual dollar dividend? If it is paid quarterly, how much will be paid each quarter?

    b   If the preferred stock is *noncumulative* and the board of directors has passed the preferred dividend for the last three years, how much must preferred stockholders be paid prior to paying dividends to common stockholders?

    c   If the preferred stock is *cumulative* and the board of directors has passed the preferred dividend for the last three years, how much must be paid to preferred stockholders prior to paying dividends to common stockholders?

20-2   **(Preferred Dividends)**   In each case in the table, how many dollars of preferred dividends per share must be paid to preferred stockholders prior to paying common dividends?

Case	Type	Par value	Dividend per share per period	Periods of dividends passed
A	Cumulative	$ 80	$5	2
B	Noncumulative	110	8%	3
C	Noncumulative	100	$11	1
D	Cumulative	60	8.5%	4
E	Cumulative	90	9%	0

20-3   **(Participating Preferred Stock)**   The Korrect Kan Company has outstanding an issue of 3000 shares of participating preferred stock that has a $100 par value and an 8 percent annual dividend. The preferred stockholders participate fully (on an equal per-share basis) with common shareholders in dividends of more than $9 per share for common stock. The firm has 5000 shares of common stock outstanding.

    a   If the firm pays preferred stockholders their dividends and then declares an additional $100,000 in dividends, how much will be the total dividend per share for preferred and common stock, respectively?

    b   If the firm pays preferred stockholders their dividends and then declares an additional $40,000 in dividends, what is the total dividend per share for each type of shareholder?

    c   If the firm's preferred stock is cumulative and the past two years' dividends have been passed, what dividends will be received by each type of shareholder if the firm declares a *total* dividend of $30,000?

d Rework **c** assuming that the total dividend payment is $20,000.

e Rework **a** and **b** assuming that the preferred stock is nonparticipating.

20-4 **(Leverage and Preferred Stock)** The Great Plains Corporation had earnings *before interest and after taxes* of $300,000 last year. The firm has a marginal tax rate of 40 percent and currently has the following capital structure:

Source of capital	Amount	Percentage of total capital
Long-term debt at 10%	$ 600,000	25%
Preferred stock at 11%	600,000	25
Common stock equity	1,200,000	50
Total capital	$2,400,000	100%

a Calculate the firm's *before-interest and after-tax* return on its total capital.

b Calculate the firm's after-tax return on common equity.

c If the firm had retired the $600,000 of preferred stock capital using the proceeds from the sale of $600,000 of additional common stock, what would its after-tax return on common equity have been?

d If the firm had shifted the preferred stock financing to debt (at the same 10 percent cost), what effect would this have had on the after-tax return on common equity?

e Use the answers in **b** through **d** to evaluate the effects of preferred stock on the firm's financial leverage.

20-5 **(Leverage and Preferred Stock)** Zesto-Presto currently has the following capital structure:

Source of capital	Amount	Percentage of total capital
Long-term debt at 12%	$100,000	20%
Preferred stock at 12%	50,000	10
Common stock equity	350,000	70
Total capital	$500,000	100%

The firm had earnings *before interest and after taxes* of $80,000 in the last year and has a 40 percent tax rate.

a What was the firm's after-tax return on common equity?

b What effect on the after-tax return on common equity would result from a $50,000 shift from long-term debt to preferred stock?

c What effect on the after-tax return on common equity would result from a $50,000 shift from common stock to preferred stock?

d What information concerning preferred stock leverage is illustrated by **b** and **c**?

20-6 **(Accounting for Common Stock)** What accounting entries on the firm's balance sheet would result from the following cases?

a A firm sells 10,000 shares of $1-par common stock at $13 per share.

b A firm sells 20,000 shares of $2-par common and receives $100,000.

c A firm sells 200,000 shares of no-par common stock for $8 million.

d A firm sells 14,000 shares of common stock for the par value of $5 per share.

20-7 **(Majority versus Cumulative Voting)** Max-an'-Maud's, a fast-food franchise, is electing five new directors to the board. The company has 1000 shares of common stock outstanding. The management, which controls 54 percent of the common shares outstanding, backs candidates A through E; the minority shareholders are backing candidates F through J.

  a If the firm uses a *majority voting system*, how many directors will each group elect?

  b If the firm uses a *cumulative voting system,* how many directors will each group elect?

  c Discuss the differences between these two approaches and the resulting election outcomes.

20-8 **(Majority versus Cumulative Voting)** Determine the number of directors that can be elected by the minority shareholders using (1) majority voting and (2) cumulative voting in each of the following cases.

Case	Number of shares outstanding	Percentage of shares held by minority	Number of directors to be elected
A	140,000	20%	3
B	100,000	40	7
C	175,000	30	4
D	880,000	40	5
E	1,000,000	18	9

20-9 **(Number of Rights)** Indicate (1) how many shares of stock one right is worth and (2) the number of shares a given stockholder, X, can purchase in each of the following cases:

Case	Number of shares outstanding	Number of new shares to be issued	Number of shares held by stockholder X
A	900,000	30,000	600
B	1,400,000	35,000	200
C	800,000	40,000	2,000
D	60,000	12,000	1,200
E	180,000	36,000	1,000

20-10 **(Theoretical Value of Rights)** Determine the theoretical value of the right when the stock is selling (1) with rights on and (2) ex rights in each of the following cases:

Case	Market value of stock with rights on	Subscription price of stock	Number of rights needed to purchase one share of stock
A	$20.00	$17.50	4
B	56.00	50.00	3
C	41.00	30.00	6
D	50.00	40.00	5
E	92.00	82.00	8

20-11 **(Value of a Right)**   Your brother-in-law is a stockholder in a corporation that just recently declared a rights offering. In need of cash, he has offered to sell you his rights for 30 cents each. The key data relative to the stock and associated rights is given as follows:

Current stock price	$37.25/share
Subscription price of rights	$36.00/share
Number of rights needed to purchase one share of common stock	4

   a   Determine the theoretical value of the rights with *rights on*.
   b   Determine the theoretical value of the rights when the stock is selling *ex rights*.
   c   Discuss your findings in **a** and **b**. Would you accept your brother-in-law's offer?

20-12 **(Sale of Common Equity — Rights)**   Utah Gas wishes to raise $1 million in common equity financing using a rights offering. The company has 500,000 shares of common stock outstanding that have recently traded for $25 to $28 per share. The firm believes that if the subscription price is set at $25, the shares will be fully subscribed.
   a   Determine the number of new shares the firm must sell to raise the desired amount of capital.
   b   How many shares will each right entitle a holder of one share to purchase?
   c   Rework **a** and **b** assuming that the subscription price is $10.
   d   What is the theoretical value of a right if the current market price is $27 and the subscription price is $25? Answer for both the *rights on* and *ex rights* situations.
   e   Rework **d** assuming that the subscription price is $10.
   f   Which subscription price ($25 or $10) will be more likely to assure complete subscription? Why?

20-13 **(Sale of Common Equity — Rights)**   The Flint Paper Corporation is interested in raising $600,000 of new equity capital through a rights offering. The firm currently has 300,000 shares of common stock outstanding. It expects to set the subscription price at $25 and anticipates that the stock will sell for $29 with rights on.
   a   Calculate the number of new shares the firm must sell to raise the desired amount of funds.
   b   How many rights will be needed to purchase one share of stock at the subscription price?
   c   Cogburn Jones holds 48,000 shares of Flint Paper common stock. If he exercises his rights, how many additional shares can he purchase?
   d   Determine the theoretical value of a right when the stock is selling (1) with rights on and (2) ex rights.
   e   Approximately how much could Jones get for his rights immediately after the stock goes ex rights?
   f   If the date of record for the Flint Paper Company was Monday, March 15, on what days would the stock sell (1) with rights on and (2) ex rights?

Chapter 21

Leasing

After studying this chapter, you should be able to:

1. Describe the basic types of leases and the arrangements commonly available as part of any lease.

2. Discuss the legal requirements for tax-deductibility of lease payments and the key items normally included in a lease contract.

3. Understand tax considerations, timing of payments, and the basic procedure used by the lessor to calculate the lease payment.

4. Explain the effects of leasing on the firm's future financing opportunities.

5. Analyze—using appropriate cash flow and present-value techniques—the decision whether to lease or to purchase a given asset.

6. Summarize the commonly cited advantages and disadvantages associated with leasing rather than borrowing to obtain the use of an asset.

*L*easing involves obtaining the use of specific fixed assets, such as land and equipment, without actually receiving title to them. The *lessee* receives the services of the assets *leased* to him or her (or "it" in the case of a firm) by the *lessor,* who owns the assets. In exchange for the use of the assets, the lessee pays the lessor a fixed periodic payment, which is normally made in advance of each lease period. The lease payment is treated as a tax-deductible expenditure by the lessee; lease receipts are treated as income by the lessor. The popularity of leasing has increased over the past 25 years as a result of the growing awareness of the financial power of leasing.

The use of leasing as a source of financing can best be understood by comparing the lease to the purchase of a specific asset. If a firm wishes to obtain the service of a specific asset, it has two alternatives: purchase or lease. To purchase the asset, the firm must pay out a lump sum or agree to some type of installment purchase plan that involves incurring a long-term liability. Both the asset purchased and the associated long-term debt will show up on the firm's balance sheet. Leasing the desired asset provides the firm with the asset's service without necessarily increasing any balance sheet accounts.[1] Leasing is a source of financing in that it enables the firm to obtain the use of a fixed asset in exchange for agreeing to make a series of scheduled lease payments.

Characteristics of Leases

Leasing arrangements can take a number of forms. Here we discuss the basic types of leases and leasing arrangements, with special emphasis on the effects of leasing on the corporation. The legal requirements of leases and the lease contract are also briefly described.

[1] Rulings by the Financial Accounting Standards Board (FASB) make it mandatory that certain types of lease commitments be shown as an asset and corresponding liability on the firm's balance sheet. This treatment and other aspects of lease commitment disclosure are discussed later in this chapter.

BASIC TYPES OF LEASES

The two basic types of leases available to a business are *operating* and *financial* leases, the latter of which are often called *capital leases* by accountants. An operating lease generally represents a short-term arrangement by which the service of certain assets is obtained by the firm. The primary difference between operating and financial leases is that a financial lease is a long-term arrangement that cannot be canceled at the option of the lessee.

Operating leases. An *operating lease* is normally a contractual arrangement whereby the lessee agrees to make periodic payments to the lessor for five or fewer years for an asset's services. Such leases are generally *cancelable* at the option of the lessee, who may be required to pay a predetermined penalty for cancellation. Assets leased under operating leases generally have a usable life *longer* than the term of the lease. Usually, they would become less efficient and technologically obsolete if they were leased for a longer period of years. Computer systems are prime examples of assets whose relative efficiency is expected to diminish with new technological developments; the operating lease is therefore a common arrangement for obtaining such systems, as well as for such items as automobiles.

If an operating lease is held to maturity, the lessee at that time returns the leased asset to the lessor, who may lease it again or sell the asset. Normally the asset has a positive market value at the termination of the lease. In some instances, the lease contract will give the lessee the opportunity to purchase the leased asset. Generally, the total payments made by the lessee to the lessor are *less* than the initial cost of the leased asset paid by the lessor. Since the operating lease is normally for a period of less than the asset's usable life, the lessor expects to be able to sell the asset (for an amount greater than its unrecovered cost)[2] when the lease matures.

Financial (or capital) leases. A *financial (or capital) lease* is a *longer-term* lease than an operating lease. Financial leases are *noncancelable* and therefore obligate the lessee to make payments for the use of an asset over a predefined period of time. Even if the lessee does not require the service of the leased asset, it is contractually obligated to make payments over the life of the lease contract. Financial leases are commonly used for leasing land, buildings, and large pieces of fixed equipment. The noncancelable feature of the financial lease makes it quite similar to certain types of long-term debt.[3] The lease payment becomes a fixed, tax-deductible expenditure that must be paid at predefined dates over a definite period. Failing to make the contractual payments may mean bankruptcy for the lessee.

Another distinguishing characteristic of the financial lease is that total payments over the lease period are *greater* than the cost of the leased asset to the lessor. The lease period is therefore generally closely aligned with the economic life of

---

[2] This implies that the original cost of the leased asset to the lessor, along with the financial charges incurred less the costs recovered through the lease payments received from the lessee, results in an end-of-lease investment by the lessor that is below the asset's market value at that time. The lessor therefore usually gains on the sale of the asset at termination of the lease.

[3] Some authors classify financial leases as *intermediate-term financing,* where the intermediate term is assumed to represent a period of one to seven years. In this text the intermediate classification is not used; any debt having a maturity of greater than one year is classified as *long-term.*

the asset. If the salvage value of the asset is expected to be negligible, the lessor must receive more than the asset's purchase price in order to earn its required return on the dollars it has invested in the asset. The emphasis in this chapter will be on financial leases, since this type of lease results in an inescapable financial commitment by the firm. Some financial leases give the lessee a purchase option at maturity.

LEASING ARRANGEMENTS

Certain options are available as part of any lease. One of these is concerned with the manner in which leased assets are acquired by the lessor. A second is related to the maintenance of the leased assets. A third concerns the renewability of the contract. A final option is related to the types of lessors available.

Acquisition of leased assets. Lessors use three primary techniques for obtaining assets to be leased. The method depends largely on the desires of the prospective lessee. The three techniques are direct leases, sale-leaseback arrangements, and leveraged leases.

Direct leases. A *direct lease* results when a lessor owns or acquires the assets that are leased to a given lessee. In other words, the lessee did not previously own the assets it is leasing. The lessor may be the actual manufacturer of the asset, or it may be a leasing firm or subsidiary that acquires the assets from the manufacturer and then leases them to the lessee. A lessee will normally specify the manufacturer, model number, and other relevant characteristics of the asset it wishes to lease.

Sale-leaseback arrangements. A second technique used by lessors to acquire leased assets is to purchase assets already owned by the lessee and lease them back. This type of arrangement is quite common. A *sale-leaseback arrangement* is normally initiated by a firm that needs funds for operations. By selling an existing asset to a lessor and then leasing it back, the lessee receives cash for the asset immediately while at the same time obligating itself to make fixed periodic payments for use of the leased asset. The sale-leaseback of an existing old asset provides the firm with a mechanism whereby its liquidity can be strengthened. Certain other advantages that may also accrue to the lessee under this arrangement will be discussed later. The periodic lease payments charged the lessee will be set by the lessor at a level that allows the lessor to recover its investment in the leased asset and obtain its required return on the dollars invested.

Leveraged leases. Leasing arrangements that include one or more third-party lenders are *leveraged leases*. Unlike direct and sale-leaseback arrangements, under a leveraged lease the lessor acts as an equity participant supplying only about 20 percent of the cost of the asset, and the lender supplies the balance. The loan is secured by a first mortgage on the asset and an assignment of legal control over the lease payments. A trustee is hired to enforce the agreement, hold title to the leased asset, and collect the lease payments. Receipts are distributed by the trustee first to the lender to satisfy scheduled debt service payments; any surpluses are given to the lessor. If lease payments are less than the debt service, the lessor will of course have to make up the difference. In recent years, leveraged leases have become especially popular in structuring leases of very expensive assets.

Maintenance provisions. A lease agreement normally specifies whether the lessee is responsible for maintenance of the leased assets. *Operating leases* normally include *maintenance clauses* requiring the lessor to maintain the assets. Maintenance normally includes not only repairs but also insurance and tax payments. The lessor, of course, will include in the lease payment sufficient compensation for the expected maintenance costs of the leased assets. Since operating leases are relatively short-term agreements, the lessor is generally able to estimate accurately the maintenance outlays expected for the duration of the lease.

Financial leases almost always require the lessee to pay maintenance costs. In other words, the lease payment under a financial lease is a payment for the use of the asset only. Since the term of a financial lease is normally closely aligned with the economic life of the leased asset (except in the case of land), the lessee's position is quite similar to that of an owner; the responsibility and cost of maintaining the asset is in its hands. Since a financial lease is a long-term agreement, it would be quite difficult for the lessor to estimate maintenance costs for the asset's life so that they could be fairly reflected in the lease payment.

Renewability. The lessee is usually given the option to renew a lease at its expiration. *Renewal options* are especially common in operating leases, since they have shorter lives and the chance that the leased assets will become obsolete is reduced. Lease payments are normally lower after renewal. The renewal option, of course, does not come into play until the term of the original lease has expired.

Types of lessors. The lessor can be one of a number of parties. In operating lease arrangements, the lessor is quite likely to be the manufacturer of the leased item. Manufacturers such as IBM and Xerox have their own leasing divisions, which are responsible for negotiating leases for their products. Independent leasing companies also exist. Companies such as Hertz and Avis provide operating leases. Financial leases are often offered by large financial institutions such as commercial banks and life insurance companies. Life insurance companies are especially active in real estate leasing. A large amount of life insurance investments is currently being placed in land and buildings leased to various business concerns. Commercial banks, though not a dominant force in leasing, have been increasing their activities in an attempt to provide a full range of financial services to business customers. Pension funds have also been moving into the general area of leasing, although to date their penetration has been negligible.

LEGAL REQUIREMENTS OF LEASES

To prevent firms from using leasing arrangements as a disguise for what is actually an installment loan, the Internal Revenue Service specifies certain conditions under which lease payments are tax-deductible. If a lease arrangement does not meet these basic requirements, the lease payments are not completely tax-deduct-

---

SALE-LEASEBACKS: A KEY TO ARKANSAS WAFFLES' GROWTH

As interest rates soared out of control, the ambitious growth plans of Arkansas Waffles Inc., a chain of family restaurants, might well have been shelved until better times arrived. The business, based in Jacksonville, Ark., had opened its first 24-hour restaurant in 1971, and the owners were eager to continue penetrating their market by constructing a network of similar units throughout their statewide franchising territory. But by 1981, rates on long-term mortgages for commercial properties were creeping to 17% and higher, far more than most businesses would even dream of paying.

"The cost of financing should never be out of line with the economics of the business you're in," says R. Bert Alexander, president of Arkansas Waffles.

Yet even in 1981, when commercial mortgage rates reached their high-water mark, Alexander and his partner, Charles Menser Jr., the company's secretary/treasurer, managed to open two new restaurants without a hitch, thanks to a creative financing technique that kept the rate they paid—and their own capital requirements for the business—to a minimum. Through a series of sale-leaseback transactions, the two entrepreneurs have built Arkansas Waffles into a chain of 14 restaurants with combined 1982 revenues of about $7 million.

While four of the company's properties are owned by Alexander and Menser, the remainder have been sold to private investors with whom Arkansas Waffles has negotiated 20-year leases at fixed rates several percentage points below the prevailing mortgage rates. When rates hit 18% in 1981, for instance, "we signed lease agreements for at least seven points less," Alexander says.

By definition, the use of sale-leasebacks limits the amount of equity the company will build in the land and restaurants. But this doesn't bother the principals, who see their primary business goal as running a chain of restaurants featuring "good food fast," with enough profits to support growth of at least three new restaurants a year. "Doing that," says Menser, "is worth more to us than accumulating real estate." . . .

"The sale-leaseback is a way of renting money," explains Menser. "We see the restaurants and the real estate as two separate businesses. We've left our credit lines open to finance equipment and other things." Without having to tie up capital— amounting to about $250,000 per restaurant—in land or buildings, Alexander adds, "we can concentrate on becoming a bigger operating company."

SOURCE: Bruce G. Posner, "Renting Money," *INC.*, April 1983, p. 121.

---

ible.[4] The requirements specified by the IRS prior to 1981 were quite restrictive, but the Economic Recovery Tax Act of 1981 liberalized them significantly. Because the 1981 act was too liberal, the Tax Equity and Fiscal Responsibility Act (TEFRA) of 1982 was passed to resolve its major shortcomings. To conform with

---

[4] The IRS's concern stems from the fact that the full lease payment is tax-deductible, while in the case of an installment loan only the interest component of the payment is tax-deductible. To obtain high current tax deductions, the firm would lease the asset over a specified period, at the end of which it could purchase the asset for a nominal amount. Such a scheme would permit the firm to maximize its tax deductions and still ultimately own the asset.

the IRS code under TEFRA, a leasing arrangement must meet the following major conditions[5]:

1. The lessor must own the property and anticipate earning a pretax profit from leasing it.
2. The lessor and lessee must agree that the transaction is a lease, the term of the lease must conform to IRS requirements, and the lessor must specify it as "designated lease property" on its income tax return.
3. The lease must be entered into within 90 days after the property is placed in service.
4. The lessee can be given the option to purchase the property, but the price must be equal to or greater than 10 percent of the original purchase price.

THE LEASE CONTRACT

The key items in the lease contract normally include the term of the lease, provisions for its cancellation, lease payment amounts and dates, renewal features, purchase options, maintenance and associated cost provisions, and other provisions specified in the lease negotiation process. Many provisions are optional. A lease can be cancelable or noncancelable, but if cancellation is permitted, the penalties must be clearly specified. The lease may be renewable. If it is, the renewal procedures and costs should be specified. The lease agreement may provide for the purchase of the leased assets during the contract period or at the termination of the lease. The costs and conditions of the purchase must be clearly specified. In the case of operating leases, it is likely that maintenance costs, taxes, and insurance will be paid by the lessor. In the case of a financial lease, these costs will generally be borne by the lessee. The bearer of these costs must be specified in the lease agreement.

The leased assets, the terms of the agreement, the lease payment, and the payment interval must be clearly specified in all lease agreements. The consequences of missing a payment or violating any other lease provisions must also be clearly stated in the contract. The consequences of violation of the agreement by the lessor must be specified. Once the lease contract has been drawn up and agreed to by lessee and lessor, the notarized signatures of these parties bind them to the terms of the contract.

Leasing as a Source of Financing

Leasing is considered a source of financing provided by the lessor to the lessee. The lessee receives the service of a certain fixed asset for a specified period of time.

---

[5] This is not an exhaustive listing of the conditions, but it reflects what are believed to be the most important and limiting requirements. In addition, certain transitional rules are scheduled to take effect through 1986. To avoid excessive detail and streamline this discussion, other conditions and refinements are not addressed here. For a more detailed discussion, see either *Federal Tax Course* (Englewood Cliffs, N.J.: Prentice-Hall) or *Federal Tax Course* (New York: Commerce Clearing House), both published annually.

In exchange for the use of this asset, the lessee commits itself to a fixed periodic payment. The only other way the lessee could obtain the services of the given asset would be to purchase it outright, and the outright purchase of the asset would require financing. The lessee might have sufficient funds to purchase the asset outright without borrowing, but the funds used would not be free, since there is an opportunity cost associated with the use of cash. It is the fixed-payment obligation for a set period that forces us to view the financial lease as a source of long-term financing. Although at this point the rationale for leasing may seem no different than that for borrowing when a cash purchase cannot be made, certain other considerations with respect to the lease-purchase decision do exist.

LEASE COSTS

The lease cost results from tax considerations, payment timing, and lease payment calculations.

Tax considerations. Lease payments are treated as tax-deductible expenditures on the firm's income statement. A lease payment can be deducted from the firm's before-tax income *in the period in which the service for which the payment is made is received.* The tax-deductibility of lease payments makes leasing quite competitive with the alternative of borrowing to purchase an asset. Many financial leases involve the leasing of land, which cannot be depreciated. The tax-deductibility of the total lease payment may make it more advantageous to lease rather than to buy land. The lease payment received by the lessor must be treated as taxable income.

Payment timing. A lessor normally requires *lease payments in advance.* In the case of yearly payments, the lessee will be required to make its lease payment at the beginning of the year, although the benefits from the leased asset will not yet have been received. In evaluating lease-purchase decisions, it is important to specify when lease payments are to be made. Since the tax laws permit the deduction of lease expenses only in the period in which the lease benefits have been received, making a lease payment in advance may cause the actual tax benefits of the payment to lag as much as one year behind the actual outlay. An example will illustrate.

EXAMPLE   The Kulsrud Corporation has recently entered into a leasing agreement with the First National Leasing Company. The agreement requires Kulsrud to make annual beginning-of-year payments of $39,535.89 for the next 12 years. In exchange, Kulsrud will receive the use of a 10,000-square-foot warehouse. Kulsrud is in the 40-percent tax bracket. The lease payment pattern required, the tax benefits, and the after-tax cash outflows for the Kulsrud Corporation over the life of the lease are given in Table 21.1. The lag in the tax benefits resulting from the advance payment can be clearly seen in the table. The effect of this lag must be considered in the lease evaluation process. ■

 Lease payment calculations. The lessor charges the lessee a payment that will provide the lessor with a certain required return. In determining these payments, the lessor takes into account its required return, the lease term, and the expected salvage value (if any) of the leased asset at the termination of the lease. The calculations

Table 21.1   Lease-Related Cash Flows for the Kulsrud Corporation

End of year(s)	Lease payments (1)	Tax benefits from lease payments[a] (2)	After-tax cash outflows [(1) − (2)] (3)
0	$39,535.89	$ 0	$39,535.89
1–11	39,535.89	15,814.36	23,721.53
12	0	15,814.36	(15,814.36)

[a] Tax benefits are calculated by multiplying the lease payment deductible in the year indicated by the tax rate of 40 percent.

required are based on the present-value concepts developed in Chapter 6. These calculations can be illustrated by a simple example.

EXAMPLE   The First National Leasing Company is attempting to determine the annual lease payment to be paid at the start of each year by the Kulsrud Corporation. Kulsrud is leasing a warehouse that was purchased by First National for $300,000 and is expected to have a salvage value of $100,000 at the end of the 12-year lease period. First National wishes to determine the annual lease payment it must charge Kulsrud at the start of each year in order to earn a 12 percent return on the leasing arrangement.[6]

1. Calculating the initial investment (net of salvage)   The first step in the analysis is to determine First National's initial investment (net of salvage) in the warehouse. Since the warehouse can be sold for its $100,000 book value at the end of year 12, subtracting the present value of the $100,000 discounted at the 12 percent required rate of return from the $300,000 outlay gives us the initial investment (net of salvage):

Current outlay to purchase warehouse	$300,000
Less: Present value of salvage	
$100,000 ($PVIF_{12\%, 12\,yrs.}$ = .257)	−25,700
Initial investment in warehouse (net of salvage)	$274,300

The initial investment (net of salvage) in the warehouse is $274,300.

2. Calculating the payments   The second step is to determine the 12 equal payments that will amortize the initial investment (net of salvage) while providing a 12 percent return to First National. Since the lease payment is made at the start of each of the 12 years, the 12 payments actually consist of an initial (beginning of year 1) payment followed by 11 end-of-year payments. The beginning of any year is considered equivalent to the end of the immediately preceding year. Equation 21.1 equates the initial investment (net of salvage) of $274,300 with the present value of the annual lease payment, x, discounted at the required return of 12 percent:

$$\$274,300 = 1.000x + 5.938x \qquad (21.1)$$

[6] The payment value calculated in this example actually represents the *after-tax cash inflow* the lessor must receive annually to provide its required return. In actuality, the lessor would adjust this cash flow for the benefit of depreciation and the investment tax credit, any administrative or maintenance expenses associated with the lease, and the tax effects of each of the aforementioned items as well as any other expenses borne by the lessor. Rather than confuse the issue at this time, it is assumed that the after-tax lessor cash inflow requirement represents the amount of the lease payment charged the lessee to provide the lessor with its required return.

Since present-value tables are based on year-end cash flows, the present-value factor for the end of year zero (the beginning of year 1) payment is 1.000. The remaining 11 payments can be viewed as an 11-year annuity, since they are made at the end of years 1 through 11. The present-value interest factor for an annuity, *PVIFA*, discounted at 12 percent with an 11-year life, is 5.938 (the coefficient of the second term on the right side of Equation 21.1).

Simplifying Equation 21.1 and solving for *x*, the annual lease payment, yields a lease payment, *x*, of $39,535.89. By requiring the lessee to make this payment at the beginning of each year for the next 12 years, and selling the warehouse for $100,000 at the end of this period, the First National Leasing Company will earn its required 12 percent return on the lease to the Kulsrud Corporation. The only "tricky" step in the calculation of the lease payments is due to the fact that payments are made at the beginning of each year. ■

EFFECTS OF LEASING ON FUTURE FINANCING

Since leasing can be considered a type of financing, its effects on the firm's future financing must be discussed. Because lease payments are tax-deductible, they are shown as an expense on the firm's income statement. Anyone analyzing the firm's income statement would probably recognize that an asset is being leased, although the actual details of the amount and term of the lease would be unclear. This section will discuss the lease disclosure requirements established by the Financial Accounting Standards Board (FASB) of the American Institute of Certified Public Accounts (AICPA) and the effect of leases on financial ratios.

Lease disclosure requirements. After many years of debate and controversy, the Financial Accounting Standards Board (FASB) in November 1976 in Standard No. 13, "Accounting for Leases," finally established requirements for the explicit disclosure of certain types of lease obligations on the firm's balance sheet. Standard No. 13 established criteria for classifying various types of leases and set reporting standards for each class. The standard defines a capital (financial) lease as one having *any* of the following elements:

1. The lease transfers ownership of the property to the lessee by the end of the lease term.
2. The lease contains an option to purchase the property at a "bargain" price.
3. The lease term is equal to 75 percent or more of the estimated economic life of the property.
4. At the beginning of the lease, the present value of the lease payments is equal to 90 percent or more of the fair market value of the leased property less any investment tax credit received by the lessor.

If a lease meets any of these criteria, it must be *capitalized* by finding the present value of the scheduled lease payments. The lessee must show the capitalized value on its balance sheet as an asset captioned "lease property under capital lease" and a corresponding obligation (liability) captioned "obligation under capital lease." If it does not meet any of these criteria, it is an operating lease and need not be capitalized, but its basic features must be disclosed in a footnote to the financial statements. The standard, of course, establishes detailed guidelines to be used in capitalizing leases to reflect them as an asset and corresponding liability on the balance sheet. In addition to requirements placed on the lessee, Standard No. 13 also provides explicit guidelines for the disclosure of leases by the lessor. Subsequent standards have further refined lease capitalization and disclosure procedures. Let us look at an example.

EXAMPLE The Graber Company is leasing an asset under a ten-year lease requiring annual beginning-of-year payments of $15,000. The lease can be capitalized merely by calculating the present value of the lease payments over the life of the lease. However, the rate at which the payments should be discounted is difficult to determine.[7] If 10 percent were used, the present value (capitalized value) of the lease would be $101,385 [$15,000 × (1.000 + 5.759)]. The method used is similar to that given in Equation 21.1, except that now the x's are known and their present value must be determined. The capitalized value of the lease would be shown as an asset and corresponding liability on the firm's balance sheet. This should result in an accurate reflection of the firm's true financial position. ■

Leases and financial ratios. Since the consequences of missing a financial lease payment are the same as those of missing an interest or principal payment on debt, a financial analyst must view the lease as a long-term financial commitment of the lessee. With FASB No. 13, the inclusion of financial (capital) leases as an asset and corresponding liability (i.e., long-term debt) provides for a balance sheet that more accurately reflects the firm's financial status and thereby permits various types of financial ratio analyses to be performed directly on the statement by any interested party.

The Lease-Purchase Decision

The lease-purchase, or lease-buy, decision is one that commonly confronts firms contemplating the acquisition of new fixed assets. The alternatives available are (1) to lease the assets, (2) to borrow to purchase the assets, or (3) to purchase the assets using available liquid cash. Alternatives 2 and 3, although they differ, can be analyzed in a similar fashion. Even if the firm has liquid resources with which to purchase the assets, the use of these dollars should be viewed as a form of borrowing. This is true since the opportunity cost of the funds is at least equal to the prevailing interest rate on borrowing, which the firm is assumed always to have available by having the ability to retire outstanding debt. Because the cash purchase and borrowing alternatives can be viewed as much the same, we need to compare only the leasing and borrowing alternatives here. Most firms do not generally have sufficient cash on hand to make cash purchases of fixed assets.

This section presents the analytical framework for comparing leasing and

---

[7] The rate at which a financial lease is capitalized should be closely related to the cost of financing associated with the outright purchase alternative. The Financial Accounting Standards Board in Standard No. 13 established certain guidelines with respect to the appropriate rate to use when capitalizing leases. Most commonly, the rate that at the inception of the lease the lessee would have incurred to borrow the funds necessary to buy the asset with a secured loan having terms similar to the repayment schedule of the lease would be used. This simply represents the before-tax cost of a secured debt.

purchasing alternatives. Basically, what is needed is an *after-tax, incremental, present-value comparison.* As in the earlier discussion of capital budgeting, all costs will be measured on an after-tax cash flow basis. To keep the analysis simple, the lease obligation or additional borrowing is assumed to be small relative to the total capital structure, thereby causing the firm's capital structure and risk to remain basically unchanged. The required analysis is presented in three sections. The first is devoted to converting lease payments to after-tax cash outflows. The second is concerned with determining the after-tax cash outflows associated with the borrowing alternative. The final section presents the techniques required for comparing the lease and purchase (borrowing) alternatives to make the lease-purchase decision.

LEASE PAYMENTS AND AFTER-TAX CASH OUTFLOWS

The after-tax cash outflows associated with leasing are relatively easy to calculate. If the lease payments are properly aligned with the resulting tax benefits, the after-tax cash outflows for each period of the lease's life can be found simply by determining the difference between the lease payment and the tax benefit in each period. An example will clarify the calculations.

EXAMPLE   The Moore Company is contemplating acquiring a new machine tool costing $24,000. Discussions with various financial institutions have shown that leasing or borrowing arrangements can be made to obtain the use of the machine. The leasing alternative would require the firm to sign a five-year financial lease requiring annual lease payments made in advance, although for tax purposes the payments could not be deducted until the services of the asset had actually been received. The annual payments would be set at a level that would give the lessor a 14 percent return on its investment. The machine is expected to have no salvage value at the end of its life. All maintenance, insurance, and other costs would be borne by the lessee.[8] The firm pays a 40 percent tax on its ordinary income.

   1. Finding the annual lease payment   Substituting the appropriate values for this problem into Equation 21.1 results in Equation 21.2.

$$\$24,000 = 1.000x + 2.914x \tag{21.2}$$

The coefficient 2.914 represents the present-value interest factor for an annuity, *PVIFA,* from Table A-4 discounted at 14 percent for four years. Simplifying the equation and solving for *x* yields an annual lease payment of approximately $6132.[9]

   2. Finding the cash outflows   Table 21.2 presents the after-tax cash outflows associated with each of the five years of the lease agreement.[10] Column 3 of the table presents the

---

[8] If maintenance, insurance, and other costs were to be borne by the lessor, the lessor, in calculating the required lease payments to earn a specified return, would have to include the present value of the after-tax cash outflows associated with these items as part of its initial investment. The present value of these cash outflows would be calculated using the lessor's required rate of return.

[9] As pointed out in footnote 6, the value referred to here as the lease payment would actually represent the lessor's cash inflow requirement, which is likely to differ from the lease payment amount. To simplify this discussion, the payment calculated is assumed to represent the actual lease payment.

[10] Although other cash outflows such as maintenance, insurance, and operating expenses may be relevant here, they would be the same under the lease and the purchase alternatives and, therefore, would cancel out in the final analysis.

Table 21.2 After-Tax Cash Outflows Associated with
Leasing for the Moore Company

End of year	Lease payments (1)	Tax benefits from lease payments[a] (2)	After-tax cash outflows [(1) − (2)] (3)
0	$6,132	$ 0	$6,132
1	6,132	2,453	3,679
2	6,132	2,453	3,679
3	6,132	2,453	3,679
4	6,132	2,453	3,679
5	0	2,453	(2,453)

[a] Tax benefits are calculated by multiplying the lease payment deductible in the year indicated by the tax rate of 40 percent.

relevant after-tax cash outflows associated with the lease. The cash inflow of $2453 shown for year 5 is due to the fact that no actual lease payment is made in year 5 and the tax savings from the year 4 lease payment are realized in that year. ∎

BORROWING AND AFTER-TAX CASH OUTFLOWS

The cash outflows associated with borrowing are more difficult to obtain due to the need to identify both the interest on the loan and the depreciation expense associated with borrowing to purchase the asset. The calculation of the cash outflows associated with borrowing has two steps. The first step is to determine the annual interest component; the second is to calculate the depreciation and total the cash outflows.

1. Calculating the interest Since the Internal Revenue Service allows the deduction of interest only — not the principal of a loan — from income for tax purposes, it is often necessary to split a loan payment into interest and principal components. The technique used to do this can be illustrated by continuing the Moore Company example.

EXAMPLE The purchase of the machine tool needed by the Moore Company could be financed by a 9 percent, 5-year loan requiring equal end-of-year installment payments of $6170.[11] These payments include both interest and principal. Table 21.3 presents the calculations required to split the loan payments into their interest and principal components. Columns 3 and 4 show the annual interest and principal paid in each of the five years. ∎

2. Finding the cash outflows The cash outflows[12] associated with borrowing to purchase the machine can be calculated once the loan payment has been broken

---

[11] The annual loan payment on the 9 percent, five-year loan of $24,000 is calculated using the loan amortization technique described in Chapter 6. Dividing the present-value interest factor for an annuity, *PVIFA*, from Table A-4 at 9 percent for five years (3.890) into the loan principal of $24,000 results in the annual loan payment of $6170. For a more detailed explanation of loan amortization, see Chapter 6.

[12] Although other cash outflows such as maintenance, insurance, and operating expenses may be relevant here, they would be the same under the lease and the purchase alternatives and, therefore, would cancel out in the final analysis.

Table 21.3 Determining the Interest and Principal Components
of the Moore Company Loan Payments

End of year	Loan payments (1)	Beginning-of-year principal (2)	Payments Interest [.09 × (2)] (3)	Payments Principal [(1) − (3)] (4)	End-of-year principal [(2) − (4)] (5)
1	$6,170	$24,000	$2,160	$4,010	$19,990
2	6,170	19,990	1,799	4,371	15,619
3	6,170	15,619	1,406	4,764	10,855
4	6,170	10,855	977	5,193	5,662
5	6,170	5,662	510	5,660	—[a]

[a] The values in this table have been rounded to the nearest dollar, which results in a slight difference ($2) between the beginning-of-year 5 principal (in column 2) and the year 5 principal payment (in column 4).

into the interest and principal components. Again, we can continue the Moore Company example.

EXAMPLE The only pertinent information we still need on the Moore Company is its depreciation schedule. The company intends to depreciate the $24,000 machine under ACRS over its five-year normal recovery period. Using the applicable depreciation percentages — 15 percent in year 1, 22 percent in year 2, and 21 percent in years 3 through 5 — given in Table 2.7 on page 34, the annual depreciation for each year given in column 2 of Table 21.4 results. Table 21.4 presents the calculations required to determine the cash outflows associated with borrowing to purchase the new machine. Column 6 of the table presents the after-tax cash outflows associated with the borrowing alternative. A few points should be clarified with respect to the calculations in Table 21.4. The major cash outflow is the total loan payment for each year given in column 1. This outflow is reduced by the tax savings from writing off the depreciation and interest associated with the new machine and its financing, respectively. The resulting cash outflows are the after-tax cash outflows associated with the borrowing alternative.

Table 21.4 After-Tax Cash Outflows Associated with
Borrowing for the Moore Company

End of year	Loan payments (1)	Depreciation (2)	Interest[a] (3)	Total deductions [(2) + (3)] (4)	Tax shields [.40 × (4)] (5)	After-tax cash outflows [(1) − (5)] (6)
1	$6,170	$3,600	$2,160	$5,760	$2,304	$3,866
2	6,170	5,280	1,799	7,079	2,832	3,338
3	6,170	5,040	1,406	6,446	2,578	3,592
4	6,170	5,040	977	6,017	2,407	3,763
5	6,170	5,040	510	5,550	2,220	3,950

[a] From Table 21.3, column 3.

COMPARING LEASE AND PURCHASE ALTERNATIVES

To compare lease and purchase alternatives, the present value of the stream of after-tax cash outflows associated with each must be calculated. This is because the cash outflows occur at different points in time. The discount rate used to evaluate the cash flows should be the *after-tax cost of debt,*[13] since the decision involves very low risk. The procedure for comparing the two alternatives can be illustrated using the Moore Company example.

EXAMPLE At the time the Moore Company must make the lease-purchase decision, its after-tax cost of debt is approximately 6 percent.[14] By comparing the present value of the after-tax cash outflows associated with each of the alternatives, the decision whether to lease or purchase the machine can be made. The alternative for which the present value of the cash outflows is the lowest will be the most acceptable, since it will be the cheapest alternative in terms of today's dollars. Table 21.5 presents the calculations required.

The sum of the present values of the cash outflows for leasing and borrowing (the totals of columns 3 and 6, respectively, in Table 21.5) indicates that borrowing is preferable. This is because the present value of the borrowing cost is less than the present value of the leasing

Table 21.5 A Comparison of the Cash Outflows Associated with Leasing and Borrowing for the Moore Company

	Leasing			Borrowing		
End of year	After-tax cash outflows[a] (1)	Present-value factors[b] (2)	Present value of outflows [(1) × (2)] (3)	After-tax cash outflows[c] (4)	Present-value factors[b] (5)	Present value of outflows [(4) × (5)] (6)
0	$6,132	1.000	$ 6,132	$ 0	1.000	$ 0
1	3,679	.943	3,469	3,866	.943	3,646
2	3,679	.890	3,274	3,338	.890	2,971
3	3,679	.840	3,090	3,592	.840	3,017
4	3,679	.792	2,914	3,763	.792	2,980
5	(2,453)	.747	(1,832)	3,950	.747	2,951
	PV of cash outflows		$17,047	PV of cash outflows		$15,565

[a] From column 3, Table 21.2.
[b] From Table A-3, *PVIF,* for 6 percent and the corresponding year.
[c] From column 6, Table 21.4.

[13] Although a great deal of controversy surrounds the appropriate discount rate, the after-tax cost of debt is used to evaluate the lease-purchase decision because the decision itself involves the choice between two financing alternatives having very low risk. If we were evaluating whether a given machine should be acquired, the appropriate risk-adjusted rate or cost of capital would be used, but in this type of analysis we are attempting only to determine the best *financing* technique — leasing or borrowing.

[14] Ignoring any flotation costs, the firm's after-tax cost of debt would be 5.4 percent [9% debt cost × (1 − .40 tax rate)]. To reflect both the flotation costs associated with selling new debt and the need to sell the debt at a discount, the use of an after-tax debt cost of 6 percent was believed to be the applicable discount rate. A more detailed discussion of techniques for calculating the after-tax cost of debt can be found in Chapter 12.

cost ($15,565 versus $17,047). The *incremental savings* achieved by borrowing rather than leasing would be $1,482 ($17,047 − $15,565). Thus borrowing and purchasing the machine will save the firm $1,482 in today's dollars. Had the present value of the cash outflows associated with leasing been less than the present value of the cash outflows associated with borrowing, leasing would have been preferable. ■

The techniques described here for comparing leasing and borrowing (purchase) alternatives may be applied in different ways. The approach illustrated using the Moore Company data is one of the most straightforward. Some of the factors to be considered in making lease-purchase decisions are inexpensive borrowing opportunities, high required lessor returns, and a low risk of obsolescence. All these would increase the attractiveness of borrowing. Subjective factors must also be included in the decision-making process. Like most financial decisions, the lease-purchase decision requires a certain degree of judgment or intuition.

Advantages and Disadvantages of Leasing

Leasing has a number of commonly cited nonquantifiable advantages and disadvantages that should be considered in making a decision between leasing and borrowing. Although not all these advantages and disadvantages hold in every case, it is not unusual for a number of them to be relevant to a given lease-purchase decision.

ADVANTAGES OF LEASING

The basic advantages commonly cited for leasing are the ability it gives the lessee, in effect, to depreciate land, its effects on financial ratios, its effect on the firm's liquidity, the ability it gives the firm to obtain 100 percent financing, the limited claims of lessors in the event of bankruptcy or reorganization, the fact that the firm may avoid assuming the risk of obsolescence, the lack of many restrictive covenants, and the flexibility provided. The following critical evaluation of these commonly cited advantages shows that some of them may not be advantageous to the lessee.

Effective depreciation of land. Leasing allows the lessee, in effect, to depreciate land, which is prohibited if the land were purchased. Since the lessee who leases land is permitted to deduct the total lease payment as an expense for tax purposes, the effect is the same as it would be if the firm purchased the land and then depreciated it. The greater the amount of land included in a lease agreement, the more advantageous this factor becomes from the point of view of the lessee. However, this advantage is somewhat tempered by the fact that land generally has a salvage value for its purchaser, which it does not for a lessee.

Effects on financial ratios. Since it results in the receipt of service from an asset possibly without increasing the assets or liabilities on the firm's balance sheet, leasing may result in misleading financial ratios. With the passage of FASB No. 13, this

THE FINANCIAL MANAGEMENT ASSOCIATION (FMA)

The Financial Management Association was established in 1970 in order to develop a continuing relationship between successful financial practitioners and leading academicians and to encourage the free exchange of ideas, techniques, and advances in the field of financial management and business finance. . . .

Financial management

The quarterly journal of the Association, *Financial Management,* is dedicated to the common interests of financial managers and academicians. Articles report on and refine the most advanced academic research and review developments made by practitioners in many financially oriented fields. The journal's scope includes major business concerns operating in a variety of areas, regulated industries, non-profit organizations, financial institutions, and a variety of other public and private sector concerns. . . .

Annual meetings

Participatory interaction is a central goal of the Association. The annual meeting draws from both practitioners and academicians to ensure that FMA actively meets its objective of bringing theory and practice together. Recent meetings in San Diego, Atlanta, Denver, New Orleans, Cincinnati, San Francisco, and Atlanta have involved up to 1,400 participants. Future meeting sites include: Toronto (1984), Denver (1985), New York (1986), Las Vegas (1987), and New Orleans (1988). . . .

Student chapters program

FMA sponsors student finance clubs throughout the U.S. and Canada in order to provide students of finance, banking, and investments an association which will encourage their professional development and increase the interaction between business executives, faculty, and students. FMA student chapters are a valuable link for students to a successful future as professionals in finance. . . .

National Honor Society

The purpose of the National Honor Society is to encourage and reward scholarship and accomplishment in business and nonbusiness finance and banking among undergraduate and graduate students, to provide an association for college students actively interested in these fields, and to encourage an interaction between business executives and students of finance and banking. The National Honor Society is the *only* national honorary [organization] for students of finance. . . . For information on membership contact:

> Financial Management Association
> College of Business Administration
> University of South Florida
> Tampa, FL 33620
> (813) 974-2084

SOURCE: *Careers in Finance* (Tampa, Fl.: Financial Management Association, 1983), pp. 51, 52.

advantage no longer applies to financial leases, although in the case of operating leases it remains a potential advantage. Of course, even in the case of operating leases, the American Institute of Certified Public Accountants requires disclosure of the lease in a footnote to the firm's statements. Today, most analysts are aware of the impact of leasing on the firm's financial statements and will make certain adjustments to these statements that will more accurately reflect the effect of any existing operating leases on the firm's financial position.

Increased liquidity. The use of sale-leaseback arrangements may permit the firm to increase its liquidity by converting an *existing* asset into cash, which can be used as working capital. A firm short of working capital or in a liquidity squeeze can sell an owned asset to a lessor and lease the asset back for a specified number of years. Of course, this action binds the firm to making fixed payments over a period of years. The benefits of the increase in current liquidity are therefore tempered somewhat by the added fixed financial payments incurred through the lease.

100 percent financing. Another advantage of leasing is that it provides 100 percent financing. Most loan agreements for the purchase of fixed assets require the borrower to pay a portion of the purchase price as a down payment. As a result, the borrower receives only 90 to 95 percent of the purchase price of the asset. In the case of a lease, the lessee is not required to make any type of down payment; the lessee must make only a series of periodic payments. In essence, a lease permits a firm to receive the use of an asset for a smaller initial out-of-pocket cost than borrowing. However, since large initial lease payments are often required in advance, it is possible to view the initial advance payment as a type of down payment.[15]

Limited claims in the event of bankruptcy or reorganization. When a firm becomes bankrupt or is reorganized, the maximum claim of lessors against the corporation is three years of lease payments.[16] If debt is used to purchase an asset, the creditors have a claim equal to the total amount of unpaid financing. In such a case, an owned asset may have a salvage value that can be used to defray the firm's obligations to its creditors.

Avoidance of the risk of obsolescence. In a lease arrangement, the firm may avoid assuming the risk of obsolescence if the lessor, in setting the lease payments, fails accurately to anticipate the obsolescence of assets. This is especially true in the case of operating leases, which generally have relatively short lives. However, most lessors are perceptive enough to require sufficient compensation in both the term and the amount of lease payments to protect themselves against obsolescence.

---

[15] Since lease payments are normally made in advance, there is no guarantee that leasing a given asset provides more financing than borrowing; in many instances it may provide less financing than borrowing.

[16] This limitation is specified in Chapter 7 of the Bankruptcy Reform Act of 1978. A description of the key aspects of the Bankruptcy Reform Act, along with a discussion of the various bankruptcy, reorganization, and liquidation procedures, is included in Chapter 24.

Lack of many restrictive covenants. A lessee avoids many restrictive covenants that are normally included as part of a long-term loan.[17] Requirements with respect to minimum net working capital, subsequent borrowing, changes in management, and so on are *not* normally found in a lease agreement; the only restrictive covenant occasionally included in the lease relates to subsequent lease commitments. The general lack of restrictive covenants allows the lessee much greater flexibility in its operations.

Flexibility. In the case of low-cost assets that are infrequently acquired, leasing — especially operating leases — may provide the firm with needed financing flexibility. The firm does not have to arrange other financing for these assets and can somewhat conveniently obtain them through a lease. The firm also retains its ability to raise funds in economically preferred quantities at the right time, again helping to lower its overall capital costs. Flexibility is also provided in the sense that with a short-term operating lease the firm can buy time to shop around for an owned asset that may be more advantageous from the standpoint of long-run owners' wealth maximization.

DISADVANTAGES OF LEASING

The commonly cited disadvantages of leasing include high interest costs, the lack of salvage value, the difficulty of making property improvements, and obsolescence considerations. Though not relevant in every case, they may bear importantly on the lease-purchase decision in certain instances.

High interest costs. As pointed out earlier, a lease does not have an explicit interest cost; rather, the lessor builds a return into the lease payment. In many leases the implicit return to the lessor is quite high, so the firm might be better off borrowing to purchase the asset. The lessee should estimate this return in the manner illustrated earlier, using Equation 21.1, to determine whether it is reasonable.

Lack of salvage value. At the end of the term of the lease agreement, the salvage value of an asset, if any, is realized by the lessor. If the firm had purchased the asset, it could have realized its salvage value. If an asset is expected to appreciate over the life of a lease agreement, it may be wiser to purchase it, although various other factors must be considered in making this decision. Appreciation in the value of an asset is especially likely when land or buildings, or both, are involved. If the lease contains a purchase option, this disadvantage may not apply.

Difficulty of property improvements. Under a lease, the lessee is generally prohibited from making improvements on the leased property without the approval of the lessor. If the property were owned, this difficulty would not arise. Related to this disadvantage is the fact that it is often hard to obtain financing for improvements

[17] An in-depth discussion of the various *restrictive covenants,* which are certain financial and operating constraints contractually placed on the firm, included in long-term loan agreements was presented in Chapter 19. It is possible that even under a lease certain contractual constraints may be placed on the firm as part of the lease agreement.

on leased property since it is difficult for the lender to obtain a security interest in the improvements. On the other hand, the lessor may agree in the initial lease contract to finance or make certain leasehold improvements specified by the lessee.

Obsolescence considerations. If a lessee leases (under financial lease) an asset that subsequently becomes obsolete, it still has to make lease payments over the remaining life of the lease. This is true even if it is unable to use the asset. This type of situation can weaken a firm's competitive position by raising (or failing to lower) production costs and therefore forcing the sale price of its products to be increased in order to earn a profit.

CHAPTER SUMMARY

● A lease is a contractual arrangement with a specified term, series of lease payments, payment dates, penalties, and other important features that allows the lessee to obtain the use of assets owned by the lessor without actually receiving title to them.

● The basic types of leases are operating and financial leases: operating leases are generally short-term and cancelable at the option of the lessee; financial leases tend to be long-term, noncancelable arrangements.

● Since the alternative to leasing is the outright purchase of assets, which normally requires borrowing, leasing can be viewed as a source of financing to the firm.

● A financial lease can be initiated in three ways—as a direct lease, a sale-leaseback arrangement, or a leveraged lease.

● Under a direct lease, the lessor owns or acquires specified assets and leases them to the firm.

● Under a sale-leaseback arrangement, the lessor purchases the assets from the lessee and then leases them back to the same firm.

● Under a leveraged lease, a third-party lender is used to finance the lessor's purchase of the leased assets.

● Most financial leases require the lessee to maintain, insure, and pay taxes on leased assets; operating leases, on the other hand, normally include maintenance clauses whereby the lessor absorbs these costs. Leases may be renewable, although most financial leases are not.

● The IRS provides guidelines specifying which lease payments are tax-deductible.

● Since lease payments are tax-deductible, the cost of leasing is reduced by the tax shield provided. Most lease payments are made in advance, although the tax deduction cannot be taken until the service provided by the lease has been received.

● The amount of the annual lease payment is determined by the lessor, which seeks to assure itself of a specified return over the term of the lease. In calculating payments, present values must be taken into account.

● The lessee firm is required by the Financial Accounting Standards Board of the American Institute of Certified Public Accountants to disclose the existence of leases on its financial statements. In the case of financial (or capital) leases, FASB Standard No. 13 requires and outlines detailed procedures for capitalization of the lease commitment as an asset and corresponding liability. In the case of operating leases, only a footnote to the firm's statements indicating the key features of the lease is required.

● A lease-purchase decision can be evaluated by calculating the after-tax cash outflows associated with the lease and purchase alternatives. The most desirable alternative is the one that has the lower present value of after-tax cash outflows.

● Commonly cited advantages of leasing include the effective depreciation of land, potential favorable ratio effects, increased liquidity, the ability to obtain 100 percent financing, limited claims of lessors in bankruptcy or reorganization, avoidance of obsolescence risk, lack of restrictive covenants, and flexibility.

● Disadvantages include high interest costs, lack of salvage value, difficulty of property improvements, and obsolescence considerations.

KEY TERMS

capitalized (lease payments)
direct lease
financial (or capital) lease
leasing
lessee
lessor

leveraged lease
maintenance clause
operating lease
renewal option
sale-leaseback arrangement

QUESTIONS

21-1 What is *leasing?* What roles are played by the lessor and the lessee? How are lease payments treated for tax purposes?

21-2 What is an *operating lease?* What are its key characteristics? What is true about the market value of a leased asset at the termination of an operating lease?

21-3 What is a *financial lease?* How is it different from an operating lease?

21-4 Describe, compare, and contrast the following three methods for acquiring leased assets.
  a Direct lease
  b Sale-leaseback arrangement
  c Leveraged lease

21-5 List and briefly describe the four major conditions required by the IRS for lease payments to be tax-deductible.

21-6 What are the major similarities and differences between lease and debt financing? In what circumstances may leasing be more attractive?

21-7 How are lease payments timed? What effect might advance payments have on the tax benefits of a lease arrangement and the after-tax cash outflows associated with the lease?

21-8 Why is leasing often viewed as a source of financing? Why, under the current disclosure requirements, might *operating leases* be referred to as a form of "off-balance-sheet financing"?

21-9 According to FASB No. 13, what types of leases must be *capitalized* and shown on the balance sheet? How does a financial manager capitalize a lease?

21-10 What cash flows are used in evaluating leasing and purchasing alternatives? How are they calculated?

21-11 Why are the cash outflows associated with both leasing and borrowing discounted at the *after-tax cost of debt* when evaluating a lease-purchase decision?

21-12 What are the commonly cited advantages and disadvantages of leasing as a source of financing? Which of these advantages and disadvantages are most important in a subjective lease-purchase evaluation?

PROBLEMS

21-1 **(Lease Cash Flows)** The Lima Company's lease on a warehouse requires annual lease payments of $40,000 to be made at the beginning of each year for the next 12 years. Determine the after-tax cash outflows each year, assuming that the firm is in the 40 percent tax bracket.

21-2   **(Lease Cash Flows)**   Given the following lease payments and terms, determine the yearly after-tax cash outflows for each firm, assuming that lease payments are made at the start of each year and that the firm is in the 40 percent tax bracket.

Firm	Annual lease payment	Term of lease
A	$100,000	4 years
B	80,000	14 years
C	150,000	8 years
D	60,000	25 years
E	20,000	10 years

21-3   **(Initial Lease Investment)**   The American Leasing Company is attempting to determine the initial investment (net of salvage value) it must make in a number of leases. The firm's required rate of return is 16 percent. Given the following costs, salvage values, and terms, determine the initial investment required under each of the leasing alternatives.

Leasing alternative	Cost of leased asset	Salvage value	Term of lease
A	$100,000	$ 25,000	14 years
B	150,000	30,000	18 years
C	400,000	40,000	8 years
D	440,000	100,000	16 years
E	38,000	3,000	7 years

21-4   **(Lease Payments — Net of Salvage)**   For each of the following initial investments (net of salvage), required returns, and lease terms, determine the annual beginning-of-period lease payments required to justify the lease.

Lease	Initial investment (net of salvage)	Required return	Term of lease
A	$400,000	10%	15 years
B	320,000	12	8 years
C	180,000	13	13 years
D	65,000	9	7 years
E	13,000	15	4 years
F	723,000	11	19 years

21-5   **(Lease Payments)**   Leasecorp is in the business of leasing slot machines. Each slot machine costs $25,000 and is leased for a five-year term, at the end of which it is sold to net $3,000. The company's required rate of return on such leases is 15 percent. Assuming that lease payments are made at the beginning of the period and ignoring taxes, calculate the lease payment that Leasecorp should charge its customers.

21-6   **(Cash Flow Patterns)**   The Confederated Financial Corporation is considering leasing a facility costing $280,000 to the Klink-Klenke Aviation Company. K-K wants a ten-year lease and is in the 40 percent tax bracket. Confederated has estimated a $40,000 salvage value at the end of ten years. Confederated wishes to earn 15 percent on each leasing deal. The lease payment will be made at the beginning of each year.

a Determine the required initial investment (net of salvage) if Confederated accepts the lease.

b Determine the annual lease payments K-K must make to Confederated to justify the arrangement.

c Determine the annual after-tax cash outflow for K-K resulting from the lease.

21-7 **(Sale-Leaseback — Lessor Selection)** The Big Warehouse Company is in need of cash and is considering a sale-leaseback arrangement involving one of its warehouse buildings. Three leasing companies have been approached, and as a result of industrial espionage, Big Warehouse has obtained certain information with respect to each of the prospective lessors — R, S, and T. Each lessor is expected to require beginning-of-year lease payments and a ten-year lease commitment. Each is willing to purchase the firm's warehouse for its current $120,000 book value. Big Warehouse is currently in the 40 percent tax bracket. The lessors' estimates of the salvage value for the building and their required returns are as follows:

Lessor	Expected salvage value of building	Required rate of return
R	$12,000	11%
S	30,000	12
T	20,000	13

a Calculate the initial investment (net of salvage) required of each lessor.

b Determine the annual lease payments that would be charged by the three lessors, respectively, if each receives its required rate of return.

c Determine the annual after-tax cash outflow for Big Warehouse under each of the leasing arrangements.

d Which of the lessors should Big Warehouse do business with? Why?

21-8 **(Financial Analysis and Leases)** The Rapid American Company is considering either leasing or purchasing a new machine costing $60,000. If the machine is purchased, it will be depreciated $3,000 each year over its 20-year life. A $60,000, 15 percent loan will be used to finance the purchase. The leasing arrangement would entail a 20-year lease requiring annual beginning-of-year payments of $8,200. The firm's most recent financial statements are given.

FINANCIAL STATEMENTS
RAPID AMERICAN COMPANY
YEAR ENDING DECEMBER 31

Income statement	
Sales	$200,000
Less: Cost of goods sold	140,000
Gross profits	$ 60,000
Less: Operating expenses excluding depreciation, lease, and interest expense	$ 10,000
Depreciation expense	10,000
Lease expense	0
Interest expense	15,000
Profits before taxes	$ 25,000
Less: Taxes (40%)	10,000
Profits after taxes	$ 15,000

(continued)

(Continued)

Balance sheet

Current assets	$ 30,000	Current liabilities	$ 20,000
Fixed assets (net)	120,000	Long-term debt	50,000
Total assets	$150,000	Total liabilities	$ 70,000
		Stockholders' equity	$ 80,000
		Total liabilities and stock-holders' equity	$150,000

---

a Recast the Rapid American Company's *income statement* on the assumption that as a result of acquiring the new machine, sales increased to $283,000, the cost of goods sold increased to $196,000, and operating expenses excluding depreciation, lease, and interest expense increased to $40,000.

(1) Show the income statement if borrowing is used to purchase the asset.

(2) Show the income statement if the asset is leased.

b Recast the Rapid American Company's *balance sheet* on the assumption that all items will remain unchanged other than those affected by the new machine. Use 15 percent as the capitalization rate.

(1) Show the balance sheet if the borrowing alternative is selected.

(2) Show the balance sheet if the leasing alternative is selected.

c Based on the income statements and balance sheets generated for the borrowing and leasing alternatives, calculate the following items in each case.

(1) The debt ratio. (*Hint:* In doing this you are forced to include the lease as debt or equity. Which seems most appropriate?)

(2) The total asset turnover.

(3) The return on investment.

(4) The cash flow per year for the firm.

d Discuss the effects of each of the alternatives (borrowing or leasing) on the firm's financial picture as indicated by the ratios calculated in **c**.

21-9 **(Capitalized Leases)** Rocky Smith, a credit analyst for Winger City Bank, has been charged with analyzing the financial statements of the Wayne Corporation. An abbreviated income statement and balance sheet for the company are presented at the top of page 768. *(continued)*

FINANCIAL STATEMENTS
WAYNE CORPORATION
YEAR ENDING DECEMBER 31

Income statement

Sales		$400,000
Less: Cost of goods sold		260,000
Gross profits		$140,000
Less: Expenses		
General and administrative	$80,000	
Depreciation	8,000	
Lease^a	20,000	
Interest	12,000	
Total expenses		120,000
Profits before taxes		$ 20,000
Less: Taxes (40%)		8,000
Profits after taxes		$ 12,000

Balance Sheet

Current assets	$120,000	Current liabilities	$ 60,000
Fixed assets (net)	360,000	Long-term debt	240,000
Total assets	$480,000	Total liabilities	$300,000
		Stockholders' equity	$180,000
		Total liabilities and stockholders' equity	$480,000

^{a} The firm has a lease obligation requiring annual beginning-of-year payments of $20,000 for the next 15 years.

a Calculate the firm's cash outflow resulting from the lease for each year, assuming that the firm pays taxes of 40 percent on ordinary income.

b Calculate the following items, using the data in the financial statements.
(1) The debt ratio.
(2) The total asset turnover.
(3) The return on investment.
(4) The cash flow per year for the firm.

c If the capitalization rate was 11 percent, what would the capitalized value of the lease be?

d Using the result of c, prepare a balance sheet for the firm showing the capitalized lease value.

e Using the new balance sheet, calculate the items indicated in b.

f Compare the items derived in b and e. Which do you believe are most indicative of the firm's true financial position? Explain.

21-10 **(Capitalized Lease Values)** Given the following lease payments, terms remaining until the leases expire, and capitalization rates, calculate the capitalized value of each lease, assuming that lease payments are made annually at the beginning of each year.

Lease	Lease payment	Remaining term	Capitalization rate
A	$ 40,000	12 years	10%
B	120,000	8 years	12
C	9,000	18 years	14
D	16,000	3 years	9
E	47,000	20 years	11

21-11 **(Loan Payments and Interest)** The Walker Company wishes to purchase an asset costing $117,000. The full amount needed to finance the asset can be borrowed at 14 percent interest. The terms of the loan require equal end-of-year payments for the next six years. Determine the total annual loan payment and break it into the amount of interest and the amount of principal paid for each year.

21-12 **(Loan Amortization Schedules)** For each of the following loan amounts, loan payments, and loan terms, calculate the interest rate and interest paid each year over the term of the loan, assuming that loan payments are made at the end of each year.

Loan	Amount	Payment	Term
A	$ 30,000	$13,358	3 years
B	80,000	27,456	4 years
C	40,000	10,018	5 years
D	150,000	60,313	3 years
E	100,000	24,325	6 years

21-13 **(Loan Payments and Interest)** For each of the following loan amounts, interest rates, and loan terms, calculate the annual loan payment and annual interest paid each year over the term of the loan, assuming that the payments are made at the end of each year.

Loan	Amount	Interest rate	Term
X_1	$14,000	10%	4 years
X_2	17,500	12	2 years
X_3	2,400	13	3 years
X_4	49,000	14	5 years
X_5	26,500	16	6 years

21-14 **(Lease versus Purchase)** The Haunted House Restaurant wishes to evaluate two plans, leasing and borrowing to purchase, for financing an oven.
Leasing: The restaurant could lease the oven under a five-year lease requiring annual beginning-of-year payments of $5,000. The lease payment is not deductible for tax purposes until the end of the year.
Purchase: The oven costs $20,000 and will have a five-year life. The asset will be depreciated under ACRS over its five-year normal recovery period. (See Table 2.7 on page 34 for the applicable depreciation percentages.) The total purchase price will be financed by a five-year, 15 percent loan requiring equal annual end-of-year payments. The firm is in the 40 percent tax bracket.
a For the leasing plan, calculate the following:
  (1) The after-tax cash outflows each year.
  (2) The present value of the cash outflows using a 9 percent *discount* rate.

    b For the purchase plan, calculate the following:
      (1) The annual end-of-year loan payment.
      (2) The annual interest expense deductible for tax purposes for each of the five years.
      (3) The after-tax cash outflows resulting from the purchase for each of the five years.
      (4) Using a 9 percent *discount* rate, the present value of the cash outflows.
    c Compare the present value of the cash-outflow streams from each plan and determine which would be preferable. Explain your answer.

21-15 **(Lease versus Purchase)** The Tony Corporation is attempting to determine whether to lease or purchase a new light-duty truck. The firm is in the 40 percent tax bracket, and its after-tax cost of debt is currently 8 percent. The terms of the lease and the purchase are as follows:

Lease: Annual advance lease payments of $25,200 are required over the three-year life of the lease. The lease payment is not deductible for tax purposes until the end of each year.

Purchase: The truck, costing $60,000, can be financed entirely with a 14 percent loan requiring annual end-of-year payments of $25,844 for three years. The firm in this case would depreciate the truck under ACRS over its normal three-year recovery period. (See Table 2.7 on page 34 for the applicable depreciation percentages.)

    a Calculate the after-tax cash outflows associated with each alternative.
    b Calculate the present value of each cash outflow stream.
    c Which alternative would you recommend and why?

21-16 **(Integrative — Lease versus Purchase)** The Tucson Tube Company needs to expand its facilities. To do so, the firm must acquire a machine costing $80,000. The machine can be leased or purchased. The firm is in the 40 percent tax bracket, and its after-tax cost of debt is 9 percent. The terms of the lease and purchase plans are as follows:

Lease: The leasing arrangement would require beginning-of-year payments that for tax purposes could not be deducted until the end of the year. The lease would be for five years, and the machine is expected to have a salvage value of $10,000 at the end of that period. The lessor intends to charge equal annual lease payments that would allow a return of 16 percent on the investment.

Purchase: If the firm purchases the machine, its cost of $80,000 would be financed with a five-year, 14 percent loan requiring equal end-of-year payments of $23,302. The machine would be depreciated under ACRS over its normal five-year recovery period. (See Table 2.7 on page 34 for the applicable depreciation percentages.)

    a Calculate the annual lease payment required to provide the lessor with a 16 percent rate of return.
    b Determine the after-tax cash outflows of Tucson Tube under each alternative.
    c Find the present value of the after-tax cash outflows using the after-tax cost of debt.
    d Which alternative, lease or purchase, would you recommend? Why?

Chapter 22

Convertibles, Warrants, and Options

After studying this chapter, you should be able to:

1. Describe the basic types of convertible securities and their general features.

2. Discuss the key motives and other considerations for financing with convertibles.

3. Demonstrate the procedures for determining the straight value, conversion or stock value, and market value of a convertible security.

4. Explain the basic characteristics of stock-purchase warrants and compare and contrast them with convertibles and rights.

5. Calculate the theoretical value of a warrant and use its market value to find the warrant premium.

6. Define options and discuss the basics of calls and puts, options markets, options trading, and the role of options in managerial finance.

Chapters 19 through 21 presented the various methods of raising long-term funds externally — term loans, bonds, preferred stock, common stock, and leasing. In this chapter we focus on two optional features of security issues — conversion features and stock-purchase warrants — and one other security — options.

Both conversion features and warrants allow the firm through actions of investors to shift its future capital structure. The *conversion feature,* which may be part of a bond or preferred stock, permits the firm's capital structure to be changed without increasing the total financing. *Stock-purchase warrants* may be attached to a long-term loan, a bond, or preferred stock. They permit the firm to raise added funds at some point in the future by selling common stock. The use of warrants shifts the firm's capital structure toward a less highly levered position, since new equity capital is obtained.

Both conversion features and warrants are commonly used today. Bonds that can be converted into common stock are the most common type of convertible security; warrants attached to corporate bond issues are the most common type of warrants. Both convertible securities and warrants may be listed and traded on organized securities exchanges and over the counter.

An *option* is a special type of security that provides its holder with the right to buy or sell a specified asset at a stated price on or before its expiration date. Options have grown in popularity in recent years, although they are not often used by corporate fund raisers.

Characteristics of Convertible Securities

A *conversion feature* is an option included as part of a bond or preferred stock issue that permits the holder of the bond or stock to convert the security into a different type of security. A conversion feature often adds to the marketability of an issue.

TYPES OF CONVERTIBLE SECURITIES

Corporate bonds or preferred stocks may be convertible. These securities are most commonly convertible into common stock, although in the case of bonds conversion into preferred stock occurs in rare instances.[1] The most common type of convertible security is the bond. Both convertible bonds and convertible preferred stock normally have a *call feature* accompanying the conversion feature. The call feature permits the issuer to retire or encourage conversion of outstanding convertibles.

Convertible bonds. A *convertible bond* is almost always a debenture or an unsecured bond with a call feature. It is most commonly convertible into a predefined number of shares of common stock. Because the conversion feature provides the purchaser of a convertible bond with the possibility of becoming a stockholder on favorable terms, convertible bonds are generally a less expensive form of financing than similar-risk nonconvertible or *straight bonds.* A conversion feature adds a degree of speculation to a bond issue, though the issue still maintains its value as a bond.

Convertible preferred stock. Occasionally a preferred stock will contain a conversion feature. Often this feature is included to enhance the marketability of the issue. *Convertible preferred stock* can normally be sold with a lower stated dividend than a similar-risk nonconvertible or *straight preferred stock.* This is because the convertible preferred holder is assured of the fixed dividend payment associated with a preferred stock and also may receive the appreciation resulting from increases in the market price of the common stock. Convertible preferred stocks are usually convertible over an unlimited time horizon; convertible bonds are normally convertible only for a specified period of years.

GENERAL FEATURES OF CONVERTIBLES

The general features of convertible securities include the conversion ratio, the conversion period, the conversion value, and the conversion premium.

Conversion ratio. The *conversion ratio* is the ratio in which the convertible security can be exchanged for common stock. The conversion ratio can be stated in two ways.

1. Sometimes the conversion ratio is stated by indicating that the security is convertible into *x* shares of common stock. In this situation the conversion ratio is *given,* and to find the *conversion price,* the par value (not the market value) of the convertible security must be divided by the conversion ratio.

EXAMPLE   International Widget Company has outstanding two convertible security issues—a bond with a $1000 par value convertible into 25 shares of common stock and preferred stock with a par value of $114 convertible into 3 shares of common stock. The conversion ratios

---

[1] It is quite uncommon for a bond to be convertible into preferred stock. The discussion throughout this chapter deals only with the near universal case of conversion into common stock.

for the bond and the preferred stock are 25 and 3, respectively. The conversion price for the bond is $40 ($1000 ÷ 25), and the conversion price for the preferred stock is $38 ($114 ÷ 3). ∎

2. Sometimes, instead of the conversion ratio, the conversion price is given. The conversion ratio can be obtained by dividing the par value of the convertible by the conversion price. Often the conversion price is not constant, changing in response to the length of time the issue has been outstanding or the proportion of the issue that has been converted. A convertible security could have a conversion price of $30 for the first ten years and $35 after ten years. Or the conversion price could be $30 for the first 30 percent of the securities converted and $35 for all subsequent conversions. These types of acceleration features are often included in a bond indenture or preferred stock covenants to give the issuer the power to encourage conversion.

EXAMPLE   The Ginsberg Company has outstanding a convertible 20-year bond with a par value of $1000. The bond is convertible at $50 per share into common stock for the next five years and at $55 for the remainder of its life. The conversion ratio for the first five years is 20 ($1000 ÷ $50), and for the remainder of the bond's life it is 18.18 ($1000 ÷ $55). ∎

When a conversion ratio indicates the issuance of *fractional shares,* the issuer may issue the fractional shares, permit the converter to purchase the balance of a fractional share in order to get a full share, or pay the converter the fractional share price upon conversion. The treatment of fractional shares on conversion must be specified in the initial bond indenture or preferred stock agreement.

The issuer of a convertible security normally establishes a conversion ratio or conversion price that makes the conversion price per share at the time of issuance of the security somewhere between 10 and 20 percent above the current market price of the firm's stock. The premium above the market price must be set at a level realistic enough so that at some point during the convertible's life conversion is expected to become feasible. In other words, the conversion price must be a price that the firm's common stock can realistically be expected to fetch in the market at some time prior to the maturity of the convertible. If prospective purchasers do not expect conversion ever to be feasible, they will purchase a straight security or another convertible issue. A predictable chance of conversion must be provided for to enhance the marketability of a convertible security.

Conversion period. Convertible securities are often convertible only within or after a certain period of time. Sometimes conversion is not permitted until two to five years have passed. In other instances conversion is permitted only for a limited number of years, say for five or ten years after issuance of the convertible. Other issues are convertible at any time during the life of the security. Convertible preferred stocks are generally convertible for an unlimited time. Time limitations on conversion are imposed by the issuer to suit the firm's forecast long-run financial needs.

Conversion value. The *conversion value* is the value of the security measured in terms of the market price of the security into which it may be converted. Since most convertible securities are convertible into common stock, the conversion value can generally be found simply by multiplying the conversion ratio by the current market price of the firm's common stock.

EXAMPLE The Krohn Electronics Company has outstanding a $1000 bond that is convertible into common stock at $62.50 a share. The conversion ratio is therefore 16 ($1000 ÷ $62.50). Since the current market price of the common stock is $65 per share, the conversion value is $1040 (16 × $65). Since the conversion value is above the bond value of $1000, conversion is a viable option for the owner of the convertible security. Of course, the security holder may anticipate a still greater conversion value and therefore maintain his or her present position if the issuer does not use its call privilege to encourage conversion. ■

Conversion premium. The *conversion premium* is the percentage difference between the conversion price and the market price of a security. As pointed out earlier, the conversion premium is normally set initially in the 10 to 20 percent range. The actual size of the premium depends largely on the nature of the company. If the company's stock is not expected to appreciate greatly over the coming years, a low premium will be used; if considerable appreciation is expected, the conversion premium may be in the 15 to 20 percent range. The conversion premium given to a convertible security can greatly affect the future success of the security.

EXAMPLE The Oliver Book Company, a high-growth book publisher, has just issued a $1000 convertible bond. The bond is convertible into 20 shares of the firm's common stock at a price of $50 per share. Since the firm's common stock is currently selling at $42 per share, the conversion premium is $8 per share ($50 − $42), or $160 ($8 per share × 20 shares). The conversion premium can be stated as a percentage by dividing the difference between the conversion price per share and the market price per share by the market price per share. For the Oliver Book Company, the conversion premium is approximately 19 percent ($8 ÷ $42), which would not be unusual for a high-growth company. ■

MOTIVES FOR CONVERTIBLE FINANCING

The motives or advantages for the use of convertible financing to raise long-term funds are generally consistent with the long-run view of the firm's capital structure discussed in Chapters 12 through 14. A basic theme is the importance of timing security issues so as best to capitalize on varying financial costs, which are dictated to some extent by activity in the capital markets. Convertibles may be used as a form of deferred common stock financing, as a sweetener for financing, and for raising temporarily cheap funds.

Deferred common stock financing. The use of convertible securities provides for future common stock financing. When a convertible security is issued, both issuer and purchaser expect the security to be converted into common stock at some point in the future. If the purchaser did not have this expectation, he or she would not accept the lower return normally associated with convertible issues. However, since the convertible security is sold with a conversion premium that sets the conversion price above the current market price of the firm's stock, conversion is initially not feasible.

The issuer of a convertible could sell common stock instead, but it could be marketed only at the current market price or below. By selling the convertible, the issuer in effect makes a deferred sale of common stock. As the market price of the firm's common stock rises to a higher level, conversion may occur voluntarily or be encouraged using the call feature. By deferring the issuance of new common stock until the market price of the stock has increased, the firm is able to decrease the dilution of both earnings and control. Of course, prior to conversion, financial leverage and hence risk will be greater with the convertibles than it would be if common stock were initially issued. The earnings benefit of using convertible securities as a form of deferred common stock financing can be illustrated by a simple example.

EXAMPLE   The Green Manufacturing Company needs $1 million of new long-term financing. The firm is considering the sale of common stock or a convertible bond. The current market price of the common stock is $20 per share. To sell the new issue, the stock would have to be underpriced by $1 and sold for $19 per share. This means that approximately 52,632 shares ($1,000,000 ÷ $19 per share) would have to be sold. The alternative would be to issue 30-year, 12 percent, $1000 par-value convertible bonds. The conversion price would be set at $25 per share, and the bond could be sold at par (for $1000). Thus 1000 bonds ($1,000,000 ÷ $1,000 per bond) would have to be sold. The firm currently has outstanding 200,000 shares of common stock. Most recently, the earnings available for common stock were $500,000 or $2.50 per share ($500,000 ÷ 200,000 shares).

If we assume that the earnings available for common stock will remain at the $500,000 level, the dilution benefit of using a convertible security to defer common stock financing can easily be illustrated. The earnings per share with both common stock financing and a convertible bond are given in the following table.

Financing alternative	Number of shares outstanding	Earnings per share
Common stock	252,632	$1.98
Convertible bond		
Before conversion	200,000	$2.50[a]
After conversion[b]	240,000	$2.08

[a] To simplify this example, the additional interest expense on the convertible bond has been ignored. If we assumed a 40 percent tax rate, the $500,000 should be reduced by the after-tax cost of debt of $72,000 [.12 × $1,000,000 × (1 − .40)], resulting in earnings available for common stock of $428,000 ($500,000 − $72,000). Dividing the $428,000 of available earnings by the 200,000 shares outstanding, the correct earnings per share value of $2.14 results.
[b] Assuming that all bonds are converted.

After conversion of the convertible bond, 40,000 additional shares of common stock are outstanding. ∎

A convertible security is a useful tool for deferring common stock financing to a time when the price of the stock is higher and the dilution of earnings is reduced. In the example, the use of the convertible bond has not only resulted in a smaller dilution of earnings per share ($2.08 per share versus $1.98 per share) but also in a

FEATURES OF SOME ACTIVELY TRADED CONVERTIBLES

The table summarizes the key features of some actively traded convertibles. Following the issuer's name is the coupon rate and maturity date for bonds and the annual dividend for preferreds. The Standard & Poor's (S&P) rating, amount outstanding, and conversion ratio are shown, respectively, in the three columns at the right. For example, the Mapco convertible bond has a 10 percent coupon, matures in 2005, is rated BBB — by S&P, is a $140 million issue, and has a conversion ratio of 21.86, which translates into a conversion price of $45.75 per share ($1000 ÷ 21.86).

Issue	S&P rating	Amount outstanding (millions)	Conversion ratio
Convertible bonds ($1000 par)			
Amfac 5¼ (1994)	BB+	$ 31.1	22.90
Bank of NY 6¼ (1994)	NR[a]	24.7	26.67
Computer Sciences 6 (1994)	B—	39.7	37.04
Eastern Air Lines 11¾ (2005)	CCC	35.0	76.92
Ford Motor Credit 4⅞ (1998)	A—	87.4	18.04
Georgia-Pacific 5¼ (1996)	BBB+	119.0	32.39
Gulf States Utilities 7¼ (1992)	BBB—	20.5	75.47
Mapco 10 (2005)	BBB—	140.0	21.86
Northwest Bancorp 6¾ (2003)	AA	50.0	33.33
U.S. Steel 5¾ (2001)	A—	353.0	15.94
Convertible preferreds[b]			
American Tel & Tel $4 pfd	AA	6.5	1.05
Atlantic Richfield $2.80 pfd	AA	3.1	2.40
Beatrice Foods $3.38 pfd	AA	5.0	1.86
Champion International $4.60 pfd	BBB	3.0	1.67
GAF Corp. $1.20 pfd	CCC	2.5	1.25
Gulf & Western $2.50 pfd	BB	2.0	2.50
Ingersoll-Rand $2.35 pfd	BBB+	2.8	.60
Libby-Owens-Ford $4.75 pfd	BBB	1.0	1.50
Pitney-Bowes $2.12 pfd	NR[a]	2.8	1.00
Weyerhaeuser $2.80 pfd	A+	4.0	1.21

[a] NR = nonrated issue; not rated by this particular rating agency.
[b] The amount outstanding for preferreds is measured in millions of shares.

SOURCE: Table data from Standard & Poor's *Bond Guide* and *Stock Guide,* November 1982.

smaller number of shares outstanding (240,000 versus 252,632), preserving the voting control of the owners. In actuality, the firm's earnings would be expected to increase as a result of the new financing, providing some per-share earnings increase in both cases. The per-share earnings increase would be larger with the convertible bond due to the smaller number of owners.

A sweetener for financing. The conversion feature often makes the bond or preferred stock issue more attractive to the purchaser. The holder of debt or preferred stock is given an opportunity to become a common stockholder and share in the potential growth of the firm. Since the purchaser of the convertible security is given the opportunity to share in the firm's future success, *convertibles can normally be sold with lower interest or dividend rates than nonconvertibles.* Therefore, from the firm's viewpoint, including a conversion feature as part of a bond or preferred stock issue reduces the effective interest or preferred dividend cost, whichever is applicable. The purchaser of the issue sacrifices a portion of his or her fixed return in order to have the opportunity to become a common stockholder in the future.

Raising temporarily cheap funds. The discussion of the cost of capital in Chapter 12 indicated that the cost of both debt and preferred stock financing is normally less than the cost of common stock. By using convertible securities, the firm can raise temporarily cheap funds. When a firm raises funds to finance a specific project that is expected to boost future earnings, the use of low-cost financing during the start-up period can minimize the financial pressures on the firm. Once the project is on line, the firm may wish to shift its capital structure to a less highly levered position. A conversion feature gives the issuer the opportunity through actions of convertible holders to shift its capital structure at a future point in time.

The general pattern for a growing firm is to sell convertible securities to finance expansion, thereby minimizing financial costs. Once expansion has been achieved and a higher level of revenues is being generated, the fixed payment obligations can be shifted to common stock equity, assuming that conversion is feasible.[2] With a larger equity base, the firm can obtain new low-cost debt funds for further expansion. Often a conversion feature may be the factor that makes the sale of debt or preferred stock feasible during a period of tight money. This too must be considered a possible advantage of convertible security financing.

OTHER CONSIDERATIONS

Two other considerations with respect to convertible security issues require discussion — forcing conversion and overhanging issues.

Forcing conversion. A firm issues a convertible security with the expectation that the price of its common stock will rise by enough to make conversion attractive. It hopes that once the market price of the common stock exceeds the conversion price, the purchaser will convert the security into the common stock. This expectation is only logical, since one of the motives for issuing a convertible security is to provide for a change in capital structure when the firm's stock price becomes higher.

When the price of the firm's common stock rises above the conversion price, the market price of the convertible security will normally rise to a level close to its

---

[2] The option to convert is actually placed in the hands of the holder of the security, not the issuing firm. The *call* feature can be used by the issuer to encourage conversion, although as we shall see later, sometimes the economics of the situation result in an "overhanging issue." If the stock price appreciates sufficiently above the conversion price, conversion should occur.

conversion value. When this happens, many convertible holders will not convert the security, for two major reasons. The first is that it already has the market price benefit obtainable from conversion and still receives fixed periodic interest or dividend payments that are probably larger than the dividends that would be paid after conversion. Of course, future increases in the stock price will continue to be reflected in corresponding increases in the market price of the convertibles. The second reason is generally a lack of confidence in the current market price of the common stock. If the stock price has not exhibited some stability or there is no reason to believe that it will stay above the conversion price, the convertible security holder may feel safer holding the convertible.[3] Once there is reason to believe that the common stock price will remain stable at a sufficiently high level, the holder may convert the security.

As indicated earlier, virtually all convertible securities have a call feature that enables the issuer to encourage or "force" conversion. The call price of the security is generally about 10 percent above its par value. Quite commonly the call price exceeds the security's par value by an amount equal to one year's stated interest on the security. Although the issuer must pay a premium for calling a security, the call privilege is generally not exercised until the conversion value of the security is 10 to 15 percent *above the call price.* This type of premium above the call price helps to assure the issuer that when the call is made, the holders of the convertible will convert it instead of accepting the call price. When the convertible holders believe the stock price to be quite volatile, the conversion value must be considerably above the call price for the call to be effective.

EXAMPLE The Felix Company currently has outstanding a 12 percent, $1000 convertible bond. The bond is convertible into 50 shares of common stock at a conversion price of $20 per share ($1000 ÷ 50 shares) and callable at $1120. Since the bond is convertible into 50 shares of common stock, calling it would be equivalent to paying each common stockholder $22.40 per share ($1120 ÷ 50 shares). If the firm issues the call when the stock is selling for $24 per share, a convertible security holder is likely to take the $1120 instead of converting the security even though he or she realizes only $22.40 per share instead of $24. This is because the holder recognizes that the stock price is likely to drop as soon as the conversion occurs. Also, if the holder wishes to sell the stock after conversion, he or she will have to pay brokerage fees and taxes on the transaction.

If the Felix Company waited until the market price exceeded the call price by 10 to 15 percent — if, say, the call was made when the market price of the stock reached $25 — most of the convertible holders would probably convert the security. The market price of $25 per share would be approximately 11.6 percent above the call price per share of $22.40 — high enough to cover any movements in the stock price or brokerage fees and taxes associated with conversion. At least 30 days' advance notice is normally given prior to a call. ■

When a call privilege is exercised, it is likely that a small percentage of the convertibles will be called and not converted. As indicated in an earlier discussion, the conversion price often increases at intervals to decrease the conversion ratio and make conversion more likely. Prior to a scheduled decrease in the conversion

---

[3] Of course, the holder of the convertible could convert the security and then sell the stock, but he or she would have to pay both brokerage fees and taxes on the sale. By converting and holding the stock or not converting at all, he or she delays or avoids these expenses.

ratio, conversion is likely. Since these changes are determined at the time of issuance, it is difficult to force conversion at a chosen point in time; the superiority of the call feature in this respect should be obvious. Increasing common stock dividends to raise the common stock price and thereby the conversion value is sometimes effective in forcing conversion.

Overhanging issues. There are instances when the market price of a security does not reach a level sufficient to stimulate the conversion of associated convertibles. In some cases the market price may not exceed the conversion price; in others the market price may rise to within a few percentage points of the call price per share. In either case, conversion is not a viable alternative for the holders of the security. A convertible security that cannot be forced into conversion is called an *overhanging issue.*

An overhanging issue can be quite detrimental to a firm. If the firm were to call the issue, not only would it have to pay the call premium, but additional financing would be required to raise the money for the call. If the firm raised these funds through the sale of equity, a great deal of dilution would result due to the low market price. The firm might actually have been better off selling equity initially instead of selling the convertible. Another source of financing would be the use of debt or preferred stock, but this would leave the firm's capital structure at least as levered or more highly levered than prior to the call.

Although convertible securities are an attractive type of deferred equity financing, the issuer must have confidence in its ability to use the funds to stimulate increases in the value of its common stock to make conversion feasible. The issuer must recognize the possibility that the convertible securities may not be converted and that new equity financing may not be forthcoming. Ways of handling an overhanging convertible should be planned in advance; if not, the firm may find itself unable to obtain future long-term financing on favorable terms.

Determining the Value of Convertibles

The key characteristic of convertible securities that greatly enhances their marketability is their ability to minimize the possibility of a loss while providing a possibility of capital gains. Closely related to this characteristic is the fixed pattern of interest or dividend income. This section discusses the three values of a convertible security — the straight bond or preferred stock value, the conversion or stock value, and the market value — along with a few special considerations.

STRAIGHT BOND OR PREFERRED STOCK VALUE

The *straight bond,* or *preferred stock, value* of a convertible security is the price at which it would sell in the market without the conversion feature. It is found by determining the value of a *nonconvertible* bond or preferred stock issued by a firm having the same business and financial risk. As indicated earlier, a convertible security's value will normally be greater than that of a straight bond or preferred stock. The straight bond or preferred stock value is typically the *floor,* or minimum, price at which a convertible bond or preferred stock will be traded.

Calculating the straight bond value. The straight value of a convertible bond can be found by discounting the bond interest payments and par value (at maturity) at the rate of interest that would have to be charged on a straight bond issue by the company. In other words, the bond value of a convertible bond is equal to the present value of its interest and principal payments discounted at the straight bond interest rate.

EXAMPLE   The Rich Company has just sold a $1000, 20-year convertible bond with a 12 percent coupon. The bond interest will be paid at the end of each year, and the principal will be repaid at maturity.[4] A straight bond could have been sold with a 14 percent coupon, but the addition of the conversion feature compensates for the lower rate on the convertible. The straight bond value of the convertible is calculated as follows:

Year(s)	Payments (1)	Present-value interest factor at 14 percent (2)	Present value [(1) × (2)] (3)
1–20	$ 120[a]	6.623[b]	$794.76
20	1000	.073[c]	73.00
		Straight bond value	$867.76

[a] $1000 at 12% = $120 interest per year.
[b] Present-value interest factor for an annuity, *PVIFA*, discounted at 14% for 20 years, from Table A-4.
[c] Present-value interest factor for $1, *PVIF*, discounted at 14% for year 20, from Table A-3.

This value, $867.76, is the minimum price at which the convertible bond is expected to sell. Generally, only in certain instances where the stock's market price is below the conversion price will the bond be expected to sell at this level. ■

Calculating the straight preferred stock value. The minimum price at which a convertible preferred stock is expected to sell can be found in a similar manner. Since the preferred stock is a form of ownership, its life is assumed to be infinite, and therefore the present-value interest factor used to find its value is not readily available. The straight preferred stock value of a convertible preferred stock is assumed to equal the present value of preferred dividends over an infinite life discounted at the yield on a straight preferred stock. The present-value interest factor for an infinite-lived annuity is given by Equation 22.1.[5]

$$PVIFA_{k,\infty} = \frac{1}{k} \qquad (22.1)$$

where

$PVIFA_{k,\infty}$ = present-value interest factor for an infinite-lived annuity discounted at rate k
k = the appropriate discount rate

[4] As indicated earlier, bond interest is typically paid semiannually, which means that calculating a bond value requires a process using semiannual discounting to find the present value. The techniques for finding a bond value for a bond paying semiannual interest were described in Chapter 8.

[5] The interest factor for the present value of an infinite-lived annuity, or *perpetuity,* as it is called, was discussed in Chapter 6.

An example will clarify the calculations required to find the straight value of convertible preferred stock.

EXAMPLE   The Rich Company has just issued a 13 percent convertible preferred stock with a $100 par value. If the firm had issued a nonconvertible preferred stock, the annual dividend would probably have been 15 percent. Dividends are paid annually at the end of each year. Multiplying the annual dividend of $13 (.13 × $100) by the factor for the present value of an infinite-lived annuity discounted at 15 percent, which is 6.67(1 ÷ .15), yields a value for the preferred stock of $86.71 ($13 × 6.67). In other words, the straight value of the preferred stock is $86.71. If the market price of common stock fell below the conversion price, the preferred stock would be expected to sell for no less than $86.71. ■

CONVERSION OR STOCK VALUE

The *conversion,* or *stock, value* of a convertible security was defined earlier as the value of the convertible measured in terms of the market price of the common stock into which the security can be converted. When the market price of the common stock exceeds the conversion price, the conversion, or stock, value is expected to exceed the straight bond or preferred stock value of the convertible. An example will clarify the point.

EXAMPLE   The Rich Company's convertible bond described earlier is convertible at $50 per share. This means that it can be converted into 20 shares, since it has a $1000 par value. The conversion value of the bond when the stock is selling at $30, $40, $50, $60, $70, and $80 per share is shown in the following table.

Market price of stock	Conversion value
$30	$ 600
40	800
50	1000
60	1200
70	1400
80	1600

Since the straight value of this bond is $867.76, it will (in a stable environment) never sell for less than this amount, regardless of how low its conversion value is. If the market price per share were $30, the bond would still sell for $867.76 — not $600 — because its value as a bond would dominate. ■

MARKET VALUE

The market value of a convertible is likely to be greater than its straight value or its conversion value. The amount by which the market value exceeds the straight or conversion value is often called the *market premium.* The market premium is larger the closer the straight value is to the conversion value. Even when the conversion value is below the straight value, a premium based on expected stock price movements exists. The same type of premium exists when the conversion value is above the straight value; this premium is also attributed to the convertible

AN AESTHETICALLY APPEALING DEBENTURE

A brawny man on a couch is flanked by a blonde in a flimsy nightgown and a brunette in a blue slip and black leather jacket.

Sound like the cover of a bad detective novel? Actually, it's a debenture.

Most debentures are bland, paper documents on which companies promise to repay investors. This one is a 4-by-5-foot oil painting in aqua, magenta and gold leaf.

It's a $10,000 debenture of Minsky Finances Inc., a newly formed company in the New York City borough of Queens that plans to buy and sell art. The painting is due in 1994 and yields 10% interest — well below the current rate [March 1984] of about 12.4% on 10-year U.S. Treasury notes.

Richard Minsky, a 37-year-old artist, hit on the idea of a series of oil-painted debentures as a way to raise $2 million over the next few years. "A lot of people would want to hang this type of financial instrument on their walls," he says. "It's museum quality."

Painted above the trio on the couch on the first debenture — which is still drying — is the name of the company in gold leaf. Below the couch are the words "Love Me Tender" in white. Bordering the canvas are 10 smaller scenes of couples swimming, dancing and wrestling.

To receive the $1,000 interest each year, the investor must clip one of the smaller scenes and send it to Mr. Minsky. Of course, this would create a series of holes. "The investor may find that the painting is more likely to appreciate in value if he doesn't redeem the coupons," Mr. Minsky says.

When the painting "matures" in 10 years, he says, Minsky Finances will buy it back for $10,000. Or the investor could try to sell to someone else for a higher price.

Next in the series will be a more abstract debenture with swirls of red, white and blue. Then Mr. Minsky plans to offer a convertible debenture, featuring a gold Cadillac Eldorado convertible and convertible into Minsky Finances common shares.

Mr. Minsky says interest payments will come from the sale of art owned by his fledgling company. So far the assets include one medieval, leather book cover, one Guatemalan marimba and 12 paintings.

How risky is this investment? An investor considering Mr. Minsky's first debenture isn't concerned. "It's secured by his talent," says Rose Slivka, a New York art critic, "and that's more stable than anything else."

SOURCE: Kathleen A. Hughes "New Company Issues a Debenture That's Secured by a Picture Frame," *The Wall Street Journal,* March 26, 1984, p. 27.

security purchaser's expectations. The general relationship of the straight value, conversion value, market value, and market premium for the Rich Company's convertible bond is shown in Figure 22.1.[6] The straight bond value acts as a floor for the security's value, and when the market price of the stock exceeds a certain value, the conversion value of the bond exceeds the straight bond value. Also, due to the expectations of investors about movements in the price of the firm's com-

---

[6] We have discussed the method of finding the straight value, conversion value, market value, and market premium associated with a convertible bond. The values of a convertible preferred stock would be found in a similar fashion. Bond examples are used throughout the chapter because convertible bonds are more common than convertible preferred stock.

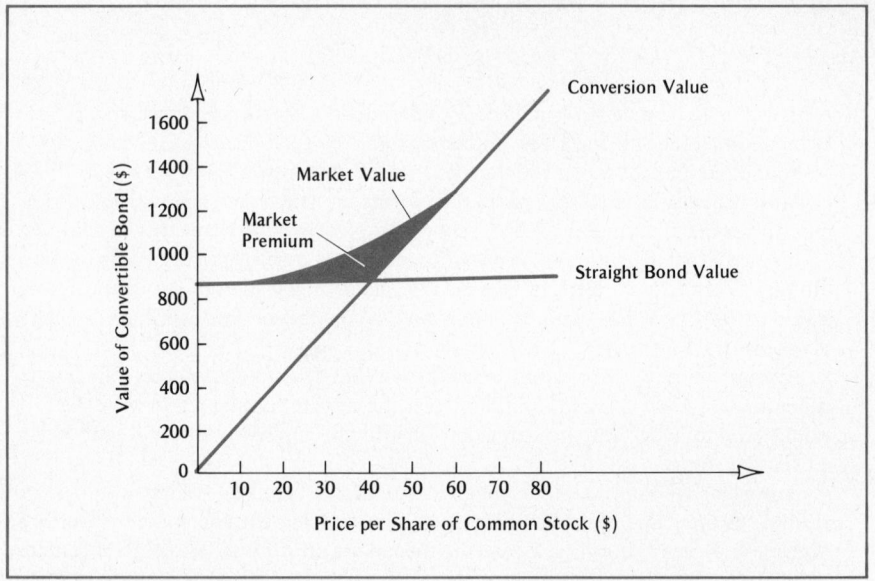

Figure 22.1 The values and market premium for the Rich Company's convertible bond

mon stock, the market value of the convertible often exceeds both the straight and conversion values of the security, resulting in a market premium on the security.

SPECIAL CONSIDERATIONS

The behavior of convertible security values — specifically the straight value of a convertible — is not precisely as described. The straight value of a bond or preferred stock is not necessarily fixed over a long period of time. It can be affected by a number of factors. If the firm runs into operating or financial difficulties, it is quite possible that the risk associated with its securities will increase. The rate at which the payments associated with its bonds or preferred stock are discounted will rise, lowering their straight value. Likewise, a decrease in business or financial risk could cause the discount rate to drop, thereby raising the straight value.

The second factor affecting straight values is interest rate movements in the capital markets. If money becomes tighter, interest rates will rise, causing the present value of the cash flows associated with a bond or a preferred stock to decline. If money loosens up and capital market rates decline, the straight value of a convertible bond or preferred stock can be expected to increase.

Regardless of which factor causes a change in the straight value of a convertible, the conversion value, although it may also change, will act as a floor for the convertible security's value. The market value of the stock into which a convertible may be converted is thus the absolute minimum value of the convertible. Only if a firm were to become bankrupt with no liquidable assets would the market value of its convertible securities approach zero. However, when the firm's risk increases or market interest rates rise, the alleged attraction of the floor price as a downside protection for purchasers of convertibles may deteriorate.

Stock-Purchase Warrants

Stock-purchase warrants are quite similar to stock rights, which were described in detail in Chapter 20. A *warrant* gives the holder an option to purchase a certain number of shares of common stock at a specified price. Warrants also bear some similarity to convertibles in that they provide for the injection of additional equity capital into the firm at some future date.

CHARACTERISTICS OF WARRANTS

Some of the basic characteristics of stock-purchase warrants discussed here are the use of warrants as sweeteners, exercise prices, the life of a warrant, warrant trading, a comparison of warrants and convertibles, and a comparison of warrants and rights.

Warrants as sweeteners. Warrants are often attached to debt or preferred stock issues as sweeteners. When a firm makes a large issue of debt or preferred stock, the attachment of stock-purchase warrants may add to the marketability of the issue while lowering the required interest or preferred dividend rate. As sweeteners, warrants are similar to conversion features. When money is tight, the attachment of warrants may be the key factor enabling the firm to raise needed funds. Also, when a firm is believed to be financially risky, warrants may enable it to obtain debt or preferred stock financing. Often, when a new firm is being capitalized, suppliers of debt or preferred stock will require warrants to permit them to share in whatever success the firm achieves. Since the initial capital is generally considered risk capital, its suppliers expect an opportunity to share in the rewards they hope will result from the use of the funds they supply. Warrants are often used to pay for the services acquired in mergers and to compensate investment bankers for underwriting services.

Exercise prices. The price at which holders of warrants can purchase the specified number of shares is normally referred to as the *exercise price* or the *option price.* This price is normally set 10 to 20 percent above the market price of the firm's stock at the time of issuance. Until the market price of the stock exceeds the exercise price, holders of warrants would not be advised to exercise them, since they could purchase the stock more cheaply in the marketplace. Occasionally the exercise price of a warrant is not fixed but changes at certain predefined points in time. An exercise price will rise to give holders of warrants an incentive to exercise them. The exercise price of a warrant is automatically adjusted for stock dividends and stock splits.

Life of a warrant. Warrants normally have a life of no more than ten years, although some warrants do have infinite lives. While warrants cannot be called like convertible securities, their finite life acts as an impetus for holders to exercise them if the exercise price is below the market price of the firm's stock.

Warrant trading. Warrants are usually *detachable,* which means that the recipient of a warrant may sell it without selling the security to which it is attached. Many detachable warrants are listed and actively traded on organized securities exchanges and on the over-the-counter exchange. The majority of actively traded warrants are listed on the American Stock Exchange. Warrants, as demonstrated in a later section, often provide investors with better opportunities for gain (with increased risk) than the underlying securities themselves.

Comparison of warrants and convertibles. The potential effects on the firm's capital structure of the exercise of warrants is best explained in light of the use of convertibles. One effect of the exercise of stock-purchase warrants is a dilution of earnings and control because a number of new shares of common stock are automatically issued. Of course, the conversion of a convertible security generally results in a greater dilution of earnings and control due to the considerably larger number of shares of common issued.

The exercise of a warrant shifts the firm's capital structure to a less highly levered position because new common stock equity capital is created without any change in debt or preferred stock capital. If a convertible issue were converted, the reduction in leverage would be even more pronounced, since the new common equity would be created through a corresponding reduction in debt or preferred stock. The exercise of warrants reduces the firm's leverage, but not to the degree that the conversion of a convertible security issue does.

The key difference between the result of exercising a warrant and converting convertibles is that the warrant provides an influx of new capital; with convertibles the new capital is raised when the securities are originally issued rather than when converted. When a warrant is exercised, new common stock is issued. The firm's total capital is increased through an increase in equity funds. The conversion of a convertible security does not change the firm's total capital; it merely shifts debt or preferred stock into common stock. The influx of new equity capital resulting from the exercise of a warrant does not occur until the firm has achieved a certain degree of success that is reflected in an increased price for its stock. At that time, new equity capital is created automatically, without a public offering. In this best case, the firm conveniently obtains needed funds.

Comparison of warrants and rights. The similarity between a warrant and a right should be clear. Both result in new equity capital, although the warrant provides for deferred equity financing. The right provides for the maintenance of pro rata ownership by existing owners, whereas the warrant has no such feature; rather, the warrant is generally used to make other forms of financing more attractive. The life of a right is typically less than a few months; a warrant is generally exercisable for a period of years. Rights are issued with a subscription price below the prevailing market price of the stock; warrants are generally issued at an exercise price 10 to 20 percent above the prevailing market price.

THE VALUE OF WARRANTS

Like a convertible security, a warrant has both a theoretical and a market value. The difference between these values, or the *warrant premium*, depends largely on investor expectations and the ability of the investors to get more leverage from the warrants than from the underlying stock.

Theoretical value of a warrant. The *theoretical value* of a stock-purchase warrant is the amount one would expect the warrant to sell for in the marketplace. Equation 22.2 gives the theoretical value of a warrant:

$$TVW = (P_o - E) \times N \tag{22.2}$$

where

TVW = theoretical value of a warrant
P_o = current market price of a share of common stock
E = exercise price of the warrant
N = number of shares of common stock obtainable with one warrant

The use of Equation 22.2 can be illustrated by a simple example.

EXAMPLE   The Classic Car Company has outstanding warrants that are exercisable at $40 per share and entitle holders to purchase three shares of common stock. The warrants were initially attached to a bond issue to sweeten the bond. The common stock of the firm is currently selling for $45 per share. Substituting $P_o = \$45$, $E = \$40$, and $N = 3$ into Equation 22.2 yields a theoretical warrant value of $15 [($45 − $40) × 3]. Therefore, Classic's warrants should sell for $15 in the marketplace. ∎

Market value of a warrant. The market value of a stock-purchase warrant is generally above the theoretical value of the warrant. Only when the theoretical value of the warrant is very high are the market and theoretical values close. The general relationship between the theoretical and market values of the Classic Car Company's warrants is presented graphically in Figure 22.2. The market value of the

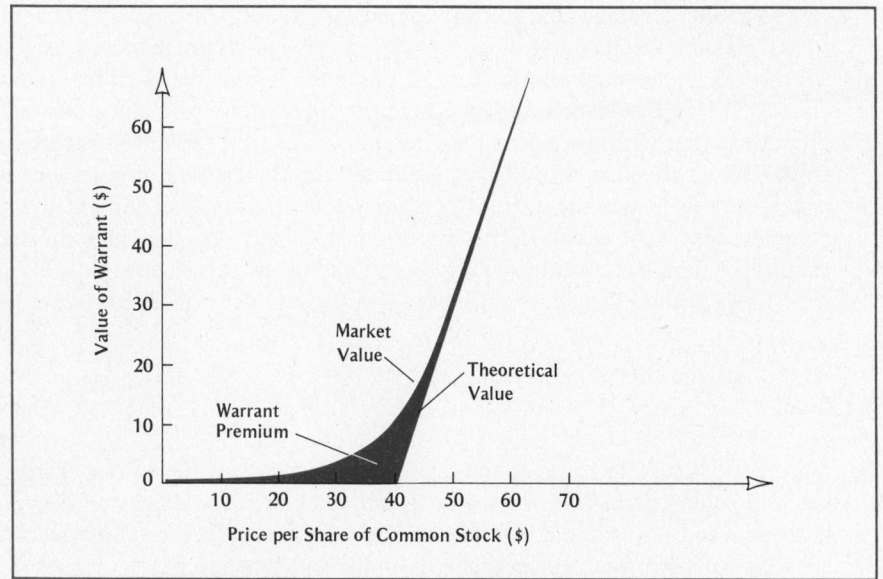

Figure 22.2   The values and warrant premium for the Classic Car Company's stock-purchase warrants

warrants generally exceeds the theoretical value by the greatest amount when the stock's market price is close to the warrant exercise price per share.

Warrant premium. The *warrant premium,* or amount by which the market value of the Classic Car Company's warrants exceeds the theoretical value of these warrants, is also shown in Figure 22.2. This premium results from a combination of investor expectations and the ability of the investor to obtain much larger potential returns by trading in warrants rather than stock. If an investor has a fixed amount of money to spend, the potential returns (and risk) from trading warrants are typically greater than those obtainable from trading the underlying stock. An example will clarify the effect of expectations of stock price movements on warrant market values.

EXAMPLE   John Investor has $2430 he is interested in investing in the Classic Car Company. Classic's stock is currently selling for $45 per share, and its warrants are selling for $18 per warrant. Each warrant entitles the holder to purchase three shares of Classic's common stock at $40 per share. Since Classic's stock is selling for $45 per share, the theoretical warrant value, calculated in the preceding example using Equation 22.2, is $15 [($45 − $40) × 3].

The warrant premium is believed to result from investor expectations and leverage opportunities. John Investor could spend his $2430 in either of two ways. Ignoring brokerage fees, he could purchase 54 shares of common stock at $45 per share or 135 warrants at $18 per warrant. If Mr. Investor purchases the stock, its price rises to $48, and if he then sells the stock, he will gain $162 ($3 per share × 54 shares). If instead of purchasing the stock he purchases the 135 warrants and the stock price increases by $3 per share, Mr. Investor will make approximately $1215. Since the price of a share of stock rises by $3, the price of each warrant can be expected to rise by $9, since each warrant can be used to purchase three shares of common stock. A gain of $9 per warrant on 135 warrants means a total gain of $1215 on the warrants. ∎

The greater leverage (and risk) associated with trading warrants should be clear from the example. Of course, leverage works both ways. If the market price fell by $3, the loss on the stock would be $162, while the loss on the warrants would be close to $1215. The leverage effect is not perfectly symmetrical, since the warrant premium varies with the price of the common stock, as depicted in Figure 22.2. Other factors affecting the warrant premium are the stability of common stock prices, the nearness to the warrant's maturity or expiration date, and the dividend policies of the firm. Stock rights, discussed in Chapter 20, also give their purchasers the same opportunity to achieve a more highly levered position, although their life is limited to a short period of time, generally less than a few months.

Options

During the past 10 to 15 years, the establishment of organized options exchanges has stimulated a great deal of research as well as investment activity on the part of individual and institutional investors. In the most general sense, an *option* can be viewed as an instrument that provides its holder with an opportunity to purchase or sell an asset at a specified price on or before its *expiration date.* Options can be purchased on a security or financial asset such as common stock or real property such as a parcel of land. Options can be acquired for a variety of reasons. Stock options are often given to executives as part of their compensation package, options on adjacent parcels of land often pass to buyers in commercial real estate transactions, and investors can acquire options on stocks through organized options exchanges.

Today the interest in options centers on options on common stock. The development of organized options exchanges has created markets in which to trade these options, which themselves are securities. These securities options are acquired by investors in order to capitalize on expected changes—increases or decreases—in the prices of common stock. Aside from attempting to profit from changes in the price of the underlying securities, options are sometimes used in "hedging" to protect existing investment positions against losses. The three basic forms of options are rights, warrants, and calls and puts. Rights were discussed in Chapter 20, and warrants were described in the preceding section.

CALLS AND PUTS

The two most common types of options are calls and puts. A *call option* is an option to purchase a specified number of shares (typically 100) of a stock on or before some future date for a specified price. Call options usually have initial lives of one to nine months, occasionally one year. The *striking price* is the price at which the holder of the option can buy the stock at any time prior to the option's expiration date; it is generally set at or near the prevailing market price of the stock at the time the option is issued. For example, if the stock of Altex Corporation is currently selling for $50 per share, a call option on the stock initiated today would likely have a striking price set at $50 per share. To purchase a call option, a specified price of normally a few hundred dollars must be paid.

A *put option* is an option to sell a given number of shares of stock on or before a specified future date for a stated striking price. Like the call option, the striking price of the put is close to the market price of the underlying stock at the time of issuance. The lives and costs of puts are also quite similar to those of calls. Other types of options, made up of some combination of calls and puts, do exist, but calls and puts are the most common types.

HOW THE OPTIONS MARKETS WORK

There are two ways of making options transactions. The first involves making a transaction through one of 20 or so call and put options dealers with the help of a stockbroker. The other, more popular mechanism is the organized options exchanges. The main exchanges are the *Chicago Board Options Exchange (CBOE)* and the *American Stock Exchange (AMEX)*. Although from their inception (April 1973 on the CBOE and January 1975 on AMEX) until June 1977 each dealt only in call options, both exchanges now provide organized marketplaces in which purchases and sales of both call and put options can be made in an orderly fashion. The options traded on the options exchanges are standardized and are considered registered securities. Each option is for 100 shares of the underlying stock. The

THE CHRYSLER WARRANTS: EXPECTATION . . . AND OUTCOME

Expectation

The Chrysler Loan Guarantee Board has decided to auction its holding of 14.4 million Chrysler Corp. warrants, each of which permits the owner to buy one Chrysler common share at $13. Chrysler's stock is currently [August, 1983] trading at about $28. Treasury Secretary Donald T. Regan, who heads the board, is to announce the bidding procedure soon. The board turned down an offer from Chrysler to repurchase the warrants for $17 each, or $250 million, after it had received a higher bid from Shearson/American Express Inc. Among others expected to bid are Prudential Bache Securities Inc. and Goldman, Sachs & Co. The board obtained the warrants in 1981, when Chrysler asked to draw down part of the $1.2 billion in loans the federal government guaranteed to help Chrysler survive. . . .

Outcome

Chrysler Corp. is free and clear of its Washington connection. The company was the winning bidder for the 14.4 million warrants to buy Chrysler stock that the Treasury Dept. has held since 1980 as part of the federal government's bailout program for the No. 3 auto maker. Offering $21.60 for each warrant, or a total of $311 million, Chrysler beat out three Wall Street syndicates. The company will retire the warrants, clearing the way for future equity offerings and increased earnings per share. Salomon Bros. Inc., Chrysler's investment banker, advanced the money for the purchase, and the company has six months to decide how to fund the deal. This summer, Chrysler paid off $1.2 billion in federally guaranteed loans seven years ahead of schedule.

SOURCE: "The U.S. Mines Its Chrysler Lode," *Business Week,* August 15, 1983, p. 38, and "Chrysler Wins Its Warrants," *Business Week,* September 26, 1983, p. 50.

---

price at which options transactions can be made is determined by the forces of supply and demand. Options on over 100 listed securities are available on both the CBOE and AMEX.

An investor can become an option buyer or an option writer. The *buyer* of options purchases and sells options that were initially written by the *writer.* In other words, a three-month call option for 100 shares of Altex Corporation with a striking price of $50, if exercised, would allow the buyer to purchase 100 shares of Altex for $50 per share. The writer of the option would be responsible for providing the 100 shares of Altex. Thus when an investor writes a call option, a contractual obligation is made to sell 100 shares of the stock to the buyer of the call at the striking price.[7] Writers of puts must be prepared to purchase from the buyer of the put 100 shares of the stock at the striking price. Although far less than half of all options are ever exercised, the option writer must be prepared to fulfill his or her contractual obligations to the option buyer. Most individual investors who trade options only buy and sell them; they normally do not write them.

---

[7] A writer of a call option does not necessarily have to own the stock against which the option is written. Call options written without holding the stock to back it up are called *naked options;* call options written against stock that is held by the writer are called *covered options.*

LOGIC OF OPTIONS TRADING

The most common motive for purchasing call options is the expectation that the market price of the underlying stock will rise by more than enough to cover the cost of the option and thereby allow the purchaser of the call to profit.

EXAMPLE   Assume that Walter Hart pays $250 for a three-month call option on Altex Corporation at a striking price of $50. This means that by paying $250 Walter is guaranteed that he can purchase 100 shares of Altex at $50 per share at any time during the next three months. Ignoring any brokerage fees, the stock price must climb $2.50 per share ($250 ÷ 100 shares) to $52.50 per share to cover the cost of the option. If the stock price were to rise to $60 per share during the period, Walter's net profit would be $750 [(100 shares × $60/ share) − (100 shares × $50/share) − $250]. Since this return would be earned on a $250 investment, it illustrates the high potential return on investment that options offer. Of course, had the stock price not risen above $50 per share, Walter would have lost the $250 since there would have been no reason to exercise the option. Had the stock price risen to between $50 and $52.50 per share, Walter probably would have exercised the option in order to reduce his loss to an amount less than $250. ■

Put options are purchased in the expectation that the share price of a given security will decline over the life of the option. Purchasers of puts commonly own the shares and wish to protect a gain they have realized since their initial purchase. By buying a put, they lock in the gain because it enables them to sell their shares at a known price during the life of the option. Investors gain from put options when the price of the underlying stock declines by more than the per-share cost of the option. The logic underlying the purchase of a put is exactly the opposite of that underlying the use of call options.

ROLE OF OPTIONS IN MANAGERIAL FINANCE

Although options are an extremely popular investment vehicle, they play *no* direct role in the fund-raising activities of the financial manager. Options are issued by investors, not businesses. *They are not a source of financing to the firm.* Corporate pension managers, whose job it is to invest and manage corporate pension funds, may use options as part of their investment activities to earn a return or to protect or lock in returns already earned on securities. The presence of options trading in the firm's stock could — by increasing trading activity — stabilize the firm's share price in the marketplace, but the financial manager has no direct control over this. Buyers of options do not have any say in the firm's management or any voting rights; only stockholders are given these privileges. Despite the popularity of options as an investment vehicle, the financial manager has very little need to deal with them, especially as part of fund-raising activities.

CHAPTER SUMMARY

● Two optional features of long-term debt or preferred stock are convertibles and warrants.

● Corporate bonds or preferred stocks may be convertible into common or preferred stock, although the conversion of bonds into preferred stock is relatively uncommon. Most convertibles have a call feature.

● A convertible's conversion ratio indicates the number of shares it can be converted into. A conversion privilege may have a limited life, or the conversion ratio may decrease at predefined points in time.

● The major motives for the use of convertibles are to obtain deferred common stock financing, to sweeten security issues, and to raise temporarily cheap funds.

● When the value of a stock rises to a level at which conversion becomes attractive, the firm may use the call feature to encourage or "force" conversion.

● Occasionally, conversion does not become attractive and the firm cannot force it. An overhanging issue may then place the firm in an undesirable financial position.

● The value of a convertible can be measured in a number of ways. Generally the minimum value at which a convertible will trade is the value of a straight (nonconvertible) security issued by a firm having the same business and financial risk. The conversion value of a convertible is its value measured in terms of the securities into which it may be converted. The market value of a convertible is generally above these values, especially when the straight security value and conversion value are quite close.

● The amount by which the market value exceeds the straight or conversion value is the market premium. The straight value of the convertible may fluctuate in response to changes in the firm's risk and interest rate movements in the capital markets.

● Stock-purchase warrants are generally attached to debt or preferred stock issues to sweeten them and lower their cost. Sometimes warrants are used in mergers or to compensate underwriters.

● A warrant provides the holder with the privilege of purchasing a certain number of shares of common stock at a specified price, called the exercise price.

● Warrants generally have limited lives, although infinite-lived warrants do exist. They are generally detachable, and many are traded on organized securities exchanges and on the over-the-counter exchange.

● Warrants are quite similar to convertibles, but exercising them has a less pronounced effect on the firm's leverage and brings in new funds. They are also similar to stock rights, except that their exercise generally results in a dilution of earnings and ownership control. The life of a warrant is also generally longer than that of a right.

● The exercise price of a warrant is initially set above the underlying stock's current market price, whereas the subscription price of a right is set below the prevailing market price of the stock.

● The market value of a warrant is usually greater than its theoretical value due to investor expectations and the ability of investors to obtain considerably more leverage (and risk) from trading warrants than from trading the underlying stock.

● The warrant premium, or amount by which the market value of a warrant exceeds its theoretical value, generally declines as the warrant approaches maturity or in response to internal firm factors.

● An option is an instrument that provides its holder with an opportunity to purchase or sell an asset at a specified price on or before its expiration date.

● Rights, warrants, and calls and puts are forms of options.

● Calls are options to purchase common stock, and puts are options to sell common stock.

● Investors can buy or write call and put options.

● Options play no direct role in the fund-raising activities of the financial manager, although they may be used by corporate pension managers in investment management activities.

KEY TERMS

buyer (of option)
call option
Chicago Board Options Exchange (CBOE)
conversion feature
conversion period
conversion premium
conversion price
conversion ratio
conversion (or stock) value
convertible bond
convertible preferred stock
exercise (or option) price
expiration date (of option)

fractional shares (of stock)
market premium
option
overhanging issue
put option
straight bond
straight preferred stock
striking price
theoretical value (of warrant)
warrant
warrant premium
writer (of option)

QUESTIONS

22-1 What are the key similarities and differences between *convertible securities* and *stock-purchase warrants?* What effect do these instruments have on the firm's capital structure?

22-2 What is a *conversion ratio?* How may it be stated? Is a conversion ratio always fixed over the conversion period?

22-3 What is the *conversion value* of a convertible security? How can the conversion value be calculated if you know the conversion ratio and the current market price of the firm's stock?

22-4 When the market price of the stock rises above the conversion price, why may a convertible security *not* be converted?

22-5 What is a *call feature?* Why do virtually all convertible securities have a call feature? At what level is the call price generally set, and how far above the call price must the conversion value be before the call is exercised?

22-6 What is meant by the *straight bond or preferred stock value* of a convertible security? How is this value calculated, and why is it often viewed as a floor for the convertible's value?

22-7 Graphically depict the general relationship among the straight value, conversion value, market value, and market premium associated with a convertible bond.

22-8 What are *stock-purchase warrants?* How do they differ from stock rights? How are warrants issued, and how are they similar to convertibles?

22-9 What are the similarities and key differences between the effects of convertibles and warrants on the firm's ownership, its earnings per share, its capital structure, and its ability to raise new capital?

22-10 What is the general relationship between the theoretical and market values of a warrant? In what circumstances are these values quite close?

22-11 What factors other than the price of the underlying common stock affect the *warrant premium?*

22-12 What is an *option?* Why have options grown in popularity during the past 10 to 15 years? Are rights and warrants options? Explain.

22-13 Define *calls* and *puts.* What role do the *buyer* and *writer* play in options transactions? What is the logic of buying a call and buying a put?

22-14   Describe what role, if any, options play in the fund-raising activities of the financial manager. Why is the role as described?

PROBLEMS

22-1   **(Conversion Price)**   Calculate the conversion price for each of the following convertible issues.
   a   A $1000-par-value bond convertible into 20 shares of common stock.
   b   Preferred stock with a $104 par value that is convertible into 13 shares of common stock.
   c   A $1000-par-value bond convertible into 50 shares of common stock.
   d   A $90-par-value preferred stock convertible into six shares of common stock.

22-2   **(Conversion Ratio)**   What is the conversion ratio for each of the following securities?
   a   A $115-par-value preferred stock convertible into common stock at $20 per share.
   b   A $1000-par-value bond convertible into common stock at $25 per share.
   c   An $80-par-value preferred stock convertible into common stock at $5 per share.
   d   A $600-par-value bond convertible into common stock at $30 per share.

22-3   **(Conversion Value)**   What is the conversion value for each of the following convertible securities?
   a   A $1000 bond convertible into 25 shares of common stock. The common stock is currently selling at $50 per share.
   b   A $1000 bond convertible into 12.5 shares of preferred stock. The preferred stock is currently selling for $42 per share.
   c   A $1000 bond convertible into 100 shares of common stock. The common stock is currently selling for $10.50 per share.
   d   A $60 preferred stock convertible into two shares of common stock. The common stock is currently selling for $30 per share.

22-4   **(Changing Conversion Price and Ratio)**   Market Manufacturing Company has two convertible issues outstanding. One is an $85-par-value convertible preferred stock that is convertible into common stock at $40 per share for the next year, after which it is convertible at $42.50 per share for the next three years. After four years, the conversion feature expires. The other convertible issue is a bond with a $1000 par value. It is convertible into 20 shares of common stock in the first year and 18 shares of common stock thereafter.
   a   Calculate the conversion ratio for the preferred issue in the first year and in the following three years.
   b   Calculate the conversion price for the convertible bond in the first year and thereafter.
   c   Explain the rationale for increases in the conversion price (decreases in the conversion ratio) with the passage of time.
   d   If the current market price of common stock is $35, which issue would you expect to be converted first? Explain your answer.

22-5   **(Conversion Premiums and Value)**   The Hoben Medical Supply Corporation has just issued a convertible bond with a par value of $1000. The bond may be converted into 12.5 shares of common stock. The stock is currently selling at $73 per share.

    a What is the per-share conversion premium associated with this issue?

    b Calculate the total conversion premium for the bond.

    c State the conversion premium as a percentage of the current share price.

    d If the market price increased to $80, $85, and $100 per share of common stock, what would be the conversion value of the bond in each case?

22-6 **(Conversion Value and Premiums)** Give the conversion value, conversion premium, and conversion premium in percentage terms (of the current market price) for the following convertibles.

Convertible	Par value	Conversion ratio	Current market price of stock
A	$1000	25	$42.25
B	800	16	50.00
C	1000	20	44.00
D	100	5	19.50

22-7 **(Convertibles and *eps*)** The Glen Watkins Company is considering two alternatives for raising a needed $1 million. The first involves a sale of common stock at $37 per share, underpriced by $3 relative to the current market price of $40. The second alternative would be to sell $1000-par-value convertible bonds. These carry a 13 percent interest coupon and can be sold at par value. The conversion ratio would be 22. The firm currently has 150,000 shares of common stock outstanding. The earnings available for common stockholders are expected to be $600,000 per year for each of the next several years.

    a Determine the number of shares of common stock outstanding and the earnings per share under the common stock financing alternative.

    b Determine the number of shares of common stock outstanding and the earnings per share associated with the bond prior to its conversion under the convertible bond financing alternative. (Ignore bond interest.)

    c Determine the number of shares outstanding and the earnings per share associated with the bond alternative once all bonds have been converted.

    d Discuss which of the two alternatives, stock or convertible bonds, is preferable in terms of maximizing earnings per share.

22-8 **(Convertibles and *eps*)** Atlanta Ice must decide whether to obtain a needed $2 million of financing by selling common stock at its currently depressed price or selling convertible bonds. The firm's common stock is currently selling for $32 per share; new shares can be sold for $30 per share, an underpricing of $2 per share. The firm currently has 100,000 shares of common stock outstanding. Convertible bonds can be sold for their $1000 par value and would be convertible at $34. The firm expects its earnings available for common stockholders to be $200,000 each year over the next several years.

    a Calculate the earnings per share of common stock resulting from

        (1) The sale of common stock.

        (2) The sale of the convertible bonds prior to conversion. (Ignore bond interest.)

        (3) The sale of convertible bonds after all bonds have been converted.

    b Which of the two financing alternatives would you recommend the company adopt? Why?

22-9 **(Straight Values)** Calculate the straight value for each of the following:

Case	Par or face value	Coupon or dividend rate (paid annually)	Coupon or dividend rate on equal-risk straight instruments	Years to maturity (bonds)
Bond A	$1000	10%	14%	20
Preferred stock R	80	11	13	—
Bond B	800	12	15	14
Preferred stock S	60	10	21	—
Bond C	1000	13	16	30
Preferred stock T	50	9	14	—
Bond D	1000	14	17	25

22-10   (**Determining Values — Convertible Bond**)   The Western Clock Company has an outstanding issue of convertible bonds with a $1000 par value. These bonds are convertible into 40 shares of common stock. They have a 12 percent coupon and a 20-year maturity. The interest rate on a straight bond of similar risk is currently 15 percent.

    a Calculate the conversion value of the bond when the market price of the common stock is $20, $25, $28, $35, and $50 per share.

    b Calculate the straight value of the bond.

    c For each of the stock prices given in **a**, at what price would you expect the bond to sell? Why?

    d What is the least you would expect the bond to sell for regardless of the common stock price behavior?

22-11   (**Determining Values — Convertible Preferred Stock**)   Mrs. Tom's Fish Company has an outstanding issue of convertible preferred with a $50 par value. These preferred stocks are convertible into four shares of common stock. They have a 13 percent dividend, whereas the dividend rate on straight preferred of similar risk is 16 percent.

    a Calculate the conversion value of the preferred stock when the market price is $9, $12, $13, $15, and $20 per share of common stock.

    b Calculate the straight value of this preferred stock.

    c For each of the common stock prices given in **a**, at what price would you expect the preferred stock to sell? Why?

    d Graph the conversion value and straight value of the preferred stock for each common stock price given. Plot the common stock prices on the x-axis and the preferred stock values on the y-axis. Use this graph to indicate the minimum market value of preferred stock associated with each common stock price.

22-12   (**Warrant Values**)   Elmer's Electronics has warrants that allow the purchase of three shares of its outstanding common stock at $50 per share. The common stock price per share and the market value of the warrant associated with that stock price are summarized as follows:

Common stock price per share	Market value of warrant
$42	$ 2
46	8
48	9
54	18
58	28
62	38
66	48

   a For each of the values given, calculate the theoretical warrant value.

   b Graph on a set of common stock price–warrant value axes the theoretical and market values of the warrant.

   c If the warrant value is $12 when the market price of common stock is $50, does this contradict or support the graph you have constructed? Explain why or why not.

   d Specify the area of warrant premium. Why does this premium exist?

   e If the expiration date of the warrants is quite close, would you expect your graph to look different? Explain.

22-13 **(Common Stock versus Warrants)** Gayle Graham is evaluating the Ever-On Battery Company's common stock and warrants in order to choose the best investment. The firm's stock is currently selling for $50 per share; its warrants to purchase three shares of common stock for $45 are selling for $20. Ignoring transactions costs, Ms. Graham has $8000 to invest. She is quite optimistic with respect to Ever-On because she has certain "inside information" about the firm's prospects with respect to a large government contract.

   a How many shares of stock and how many warrants can Ms. Graham purchase?

   b Suppose Ms. Graham purchased the stock, held it one year, then sold it for $60 per share. Ignoring brokerage fees and taxes, what return would she realize? What would be her rate of return on this investment?

   c Suppose Ms. Graham purchased warrants and held them for one year, and the market price of the stock increased to $60 per share. Ignoring brokerage fees and taxes, what return would she realize if the market value of warrants increased to $45 and she sold out?

   d What benefit, if any, would the warrants provide? Are there any differences in the risk of these two alternative investments? Explain.

22-14 **(Common Stock versus Warrants)** Mark Christian can invest $5000 in the common stock or the warrants of Kettering Engineering Center, Inc. The common stock is currently selling for $30 per share; its warrants, which provide for the purchase of two shares of common stock at $28 per share, are currently selling for $7. The stock is expected to rise to a market price of $32 within the next year, so the expected theoretical value of a warrant over the next year is $8. The expiration date of the warrant is one year from the present.

   a If Mr. Christian purchases the stock, holds it for one year, and then sells it for $32, what is his rate of return? (Ignore brokerage fees and taxes.)

   b If Mr. Christian purchases the warrant and converts to common stock in one year, what rate of return would he earn if the market price of common shares is actually $32? (Ignore brokerage fees and taxes.)

   c Repeat **a** and **b** assuming that the market price of the stock in one year is (1) $30 and (2) $28.

   d Discuss the two alternatives and the trade-offs associated with them.

22-15 **(Options Profits and Losses)** For each of the following *100-share options,* use the underlying stock price at expiration and other information to determine the amount of profit or loss an investor would have had, ignoring brokerage fees.

(continued)

Option	Type of option	Cost of option	Striking price per share	Underlying stock price per share at expiration
A	Call	$200	$50	$55
B	Call	350	42	45
C	Put	500	60	50
D	Put	300	35	40
E	Call	450	28	26

22-16 **(Call Option)** Jane Butler is considering buying 100 shares of Iris, Inc., at $62 per share. Because she has read that the firm will likely soon receive certain large orders from abroad, she expects the price of Iris, Inc., to increase to $70 per share. As an alternative, Jane is considering purchase of a call option for 100 shares of Iris, Inc., at a striking price of $60. The 90-day option will cost $600. Ignore any brokerage fees or dividends.

  a What would Jane's profit be on the stock transactions if its price does rise to $70 and she sells?

  b How much would Jane earn on the option transaction if the underlying stock price rises to $70?

  c How high must the stock price rise in order for Jane to break even on the option transaction?

  d Compare, contrast, and discuss the relative profit and risk from the stock and the option transactions.

22-17 **(Put Option)** Charles Vogel, the pension fund manager for Jayson Industries, is considering purchase of a put option in anticipation of a price decline in the stock of Stick, Inc. The option to sell 100 shares of Stick, Inc., at any time during the next 90 days at a striking price of $45 can be purchased for $380. The stock of Stick, Inc., is currently selling for $46 per share.

  a Ignoring brokerage fees, what profit or loss would Charles make if he buys the option and the lowest price of Stick, Inc. stock during the 90 days is $46, $44, $40, $35, respectively?

  b What effect would the fact that the price of Stick, Inc.'s stock slowly rose from its initial $46 level to $55 at the end of 90 days have on Charles's purchase?

  c In light of your findings, discuss the potential risks and returns from using put options to attempt to profit from an anticipated decline in share price.

Part VIII

Expansion and Failure

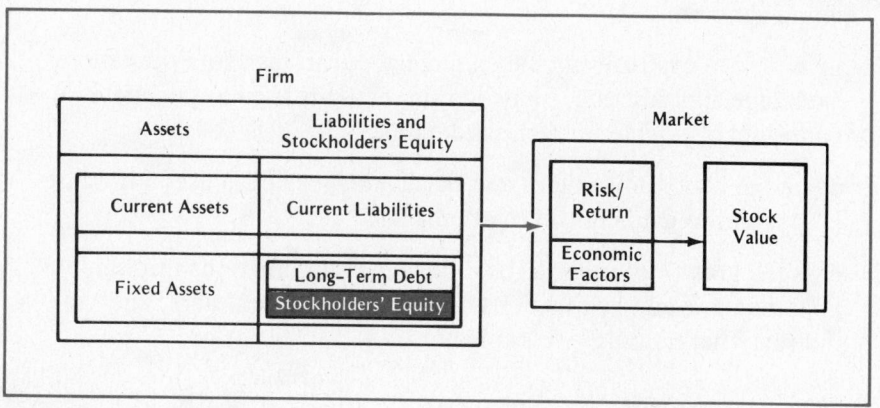

Chapter 23

Consolidations, Mergers, and Holding Companies

After studying this chapter, you should be able to:

1. Describe the basic characteristics, similarities, and differences among the major types of business combinations.

2. Understand the common motives for business combinations and the relevant variables the financial manager considers when evaluating the impact of combinations on owners' wealth.

3. Demonstrate the procedures used to evaluate cash purchases of companies acquired either as a conglomeration of assets or as a going concern.

4. Explain how to evaluate stock-exchange acquisitions using the ratio of exchange and describe the two basic methods used to negotiate control of a suitable merger candidate.

5. Evaluate the major advantages and disadvantages of the use of holding companies to gain control of other firms.

6. Discuss the growth of international business combinations through joint ventures and acquisitions, foreign direct investment, and international holding companies.

A major boom in business combinations began in the early 1980s. In 1983 over 2500 business combinations, accounting for $73.1 billion in value, were completed or pending. This nine-year record seemed likely to be broken in 1984. Some of the better-known mergers of this period include American Express, Shearson Loeb Rhoades, and Lehman Brothers to create Shearson Lehman/ American Express, the purchase of Conoco by DuPont, and the purchase of Getty Oil by Texaco. These mergers demonstrate that often, for any of a number of possible motives, firms find combination an attractive means for external expansion. Typically, these firms wish to increase their productive capacity, their earnings, or the market price of their stock rapidly or to take advantage of certain liquidity benefits. The most common forms of business combination are consolidations, mergers, and holding companies. Consolidations and mergers are similar to each other; the holding company arrangement is quite distinct. These business combinations differ not only with respect to the procedures involved but also with respect to their objectives.

The Fundamentals of Business Combinations

TYPES OF BUSINESS COMBINATIONS

The key forms of business combinations are *consolidations, mergers,* and *holding companies.* These arrangements have certain basic similarities and differences.

Consolidations. A *consolidation* involves the combination of two or more companies to form a completely new corporation. The new corporation normally absorbs the assets and liabilities of the companies from which it is formed. The old corporations cease to exist. Consolidations normally occur when the firms to be combined are of similar size. They are carried out by issuing to shareholders in the old firms a certain number (or fraction) of shares of stock in the new firm in exchange for each share of the old firm. The number of new shares issued for each old share may differ depending on differences in the size of the firms to be consolidated.

Mergers. A *merger* is quite similar to a consolidation except that, when one or more firms are merged, the resulting firm maintains the identity of one of the firms. Mergers are generally confined to combinations of two firms that are unequal in size; the identity of the larger of the two firms is normally maintained. Usually, the assets and liabilities of the smaller firm are consolidated into those of the larger firm. The merger may be used by a larger firm to obtain the assets or the common stock of a smaller company. The larger firm pays for its acquisition with cash or with preferred or common stock.

There are two key differences between consolidations and mergers. One is that consolidations result in the creation of a new corporation, while in mergers one of the merged companies remains in existence. The second key difference is that in consolidations common stock is exchanged for common stock, while mergers may involve the exchange of cash or stock for the assets or common stock of the second party to the merger. Because of the great similarity between consolidations and mergers, the remainder of this chapter will not differentiate between these forms of combination. *The term* merger *will be used to refer to both.*

Holding companies. A *holding company* is a corporation that has a controlling interest in one or more other corporations. Having a controlling interest in large, widely held companies generally requires the ownership of between 10 and 20 percent of the outstanding stock. A holding company must own enough shares to have *voting* control of the firms it holds. The companies controlled by a holding company are normally referred to as *subsidiaries.* A holding company obtains control of a subsidiary by purchasing (generally for cash) a sufficient number of shares of its stock.

A holding company consists of a group of subsidiary firms, each operating as a separate corporate entity, whereas a consolidated or merged firm is a single corporation. The holding company arrangement permits a firm greater asset control per dollar than a consolidation or merger. This is because the holding company does not acquire the entire firm, whereas in consolidations and mergers entire firms are acquired.

MOTIVES FOR COMBINATIONS

Firms combine through mergers or holding company arrangements to fulfill certain objectives. The most common motives for combination include growth or diversification, synergistic effects, fund raising, increased managerial skills, tax considerations, and increased ownership liquidity.

Growth or diversification. Companies that desire rapid growth in *size* or *market share* or diversification in *the range of their products* may find that some form of combination will fulfill this objective. Instead of going through the time-consuming process of internal growth or diversification, the firm may achieve the same objective in a short period of time by acquiring or combining with an existing firm. If a firm that wants to expand operations in existing or possibly new product areas can find a suitable partner, it may avoid many of the risks inherent in achieving the same objective through internal growth. The risks associated with the design, manufacture, and sale of new products or more products are eliminated if the firm can acquire a going concern. Moreover, when a firm expands or extends its product line by acquiring another firm, it also removes a potential competitor.[1]

Mergers and holding companies may be used to achieve horizontal or vertical growth, or conglomerate diversification. Each of these situations is briefly described in the following paragraphs.

Horizontal growth. Horizontal growth occurs when firms in the same line of business are combined. For example, the merger of two machine tool manufacturers is a form of horizontal growth. This type of growth allows the firm to expand its operations in an existing product line and at the same time eliminate a competitor. Certain economies result from this type of growth due to the elimination of staff and support functions to avoid duplication. For example, two vice-presidents of finance or two purchasing agents may no longer be required. Economies are also expected to result through the purchase of merchandise in larger quantities and the elimination of duplicate sales channels. Often, a horizontal combination of firms increases sales by increasing the diversity of styles and sizes of the finished products. Horizontal growth is commonly referred to as *horizontal integration.*

Vertical growth. Vertical growth occurs when a firm acquires suppliers of its raw materials or purchasers of its finished products. In other words, vertical growth involves expansion either backward toward the firm's suppliers or forward toward the ultimate consumer. The economic benefits of vertical growth, which is commonly referred to as *vertical integration,* stem from greater control over the acquisition of raw materials or the distribution of finished goods. A firm that is *totally integrated* controls the entire production process from the extraction of raw materials to the sale of finished goods. An example of vertical growth would be the merger of a machine tool manufacturer with a supplier of castings.

Conglomerate diversification. Conglomerate diversification involves the combination of firms in unrelated businesses. This type of combination was quite popular in the late 1960s when, for example, Jimmy Ling built the LTV empire, which subsequently faced financial difficulties. This conglomerate consisted of firms as diverse as sporting goods companies and manufacturers of aircraft components. At this writing (mid-1984) widespread activity in conglomerate diversification is continuing. Since a conglomerate consists of firms in unrelated businesses, no real operating economies are expected from this type of growth. The key benefit of conglomerates lies in their ability to *diversify risk* by combining firms in a manner that provides a minimum risk and a maximum return. Conglomerate diversification should be most attractive to firms that have seasonal or cyclic patterns of

---

[1] You may recognize that certain legal constraints on growth — especially where the elimination of competition is expected — exist. The various antitrust laws, which are closely enforced by the Federal Trade Commission (FTC) and the Justice Department, prohibit business combinations that eliminate competition, especially when the resulting enterprise would be a monopoly.

THE TEN LARGEST MERGERS

The table shows the buyer and the company bought, the cost to the buyer, and the year the transaction was made for the ten largest mergers involving U.S. companies.

	Buyer/Bought	Cost	Date
1.	Socal/Gulf*	$13.4 bil.	1984
2.	Texaco/Getty	$10.1 bil.	1984
3.	Du Pont/Conoco	$ 7.4 bil.	1981
4.	U.S. Steel/Marathon Oil	$ 6.5 bil.	1981
5.	Mobil/Superior Oil*	$ 5.7 bil.	1984
6.	Royal Dutch Shell/Shell Oil*	$ 5.2 bil.	1984
7.	Santa Fe/Southern Pacific	$ 5.2 bil.	1983
8.	Elf Aquitaine/Texas Gulf	$ 4.3 bil.	1981
9.	INA/Connecticut General	$ 4.2 bil.	1981
10.	Occidental/Cities Service	$ 4.0 bil.	1982

*Pending in March, 1984.

SOURCE: "The 10 Largest Mergers," *U.S. News & World Report,* March 26, 1984, p. 77. Basic data from W. T. Grimm & Company.

earnings. Diversification is one way to stabilize earnings. The theory of conglomerate diversification is drawn directly from the portfolio theory used for asset or security selection.[2]

Synergistic effects. The *synergistic effects* of business combinations are certain economies of scale resulting from the firms' lower overhead. Synergistic effects are said to be present when a whole is greater than the sum of the parts ("1 plus 1 equals 3"). The economies of scale that generally result from combination lowers combined overhead, thereby increasing earnings to a level greater than the sum of earnings as independent firms. Synergistic effects are most obvious when firms grow horizontally, since many redundant functions and employees can be eliminated. Staff functions such as purchasing and sales are probably most greatly affected by this type of combination.

Synergistic effects also result when firms are combined vertically, since certain administrative functions can be eliminated. For example, two presidents making $150,000 per year may not be required; the elimination of one of these salaries will

[2] A discussion of the key concepts underlying the portfolio approach to the diversification of risk was presented in Chapter 7. In the theoretical literature some questions exist relating to whether diversification by the firm is a proper motive consistent with shareholder wealth maximization. Many scholars argue that by buying shares in different firms investors can obtain the same benefits as they would from owning stock in the merged firms. It appears that other benefits need to be available to justify mergers.

provide a considerable savings. Conglomerate diversification also results in some synergistic effects, especially in the area of fund raising.

Fund raising. Often firms combine to enhance their fund-raising ability. A firm may be unable to obtain funds for internal expansion but able to obtain funds for external business combinations. Quite often, especially in the case of conglomerates, one firm may combine with another that has high liquid assets and low levels of liabilities. The acquisition of this type of "cash-rich" company immediately increases the firm's borrowing power and decreases its financial risk. This should enable it to raise funds externally at more favorable rates. Both mergers and holding company arrangements may enhance the firm's fund-raising ability when it combines with a high-liquidity, low-leverage firm.

Increased managerial skills. Occasionally a firm will become involved in a business combination to obtain certain key management personnel. A firm may have quite a bit of potential that it finds itself unable to develop fully due to deficiencies in certain areas of management. If the firm cannot hire the management it needs, it may find that combination with a compatible firm that has the needed managerial personnel is a solution. Of course, any combination, regardless of the specific motive for it, should contribute to the long-run maximization of owners' wealth. Combination with a firm that has a competent manager but a poor financial record is certainly not recommended.

Tax considerations. Quite often, especially in the case of conglomerate mergers, tax considerations are a key motive. The tax benefit generally stems from the fact that one of the firms has a tax loss carryforward, which can be applied against future income for up to 15 years.[3] Two situations could actually exist. A company with a tax loss carryforward could acquire a profitable company to utilize the tax loss. In this case, the acquiring firm would boost the combination's earnings by reducing the taxable income of the acquired firm. A tax loss carryforward may also be useful when a profitable firm acquires a firm that has such a carryforward. In either situation, however, the merger must be justified not only on the basis of the tax benefits but also on the basis of future operating benefits or on grounds consistent with the goal of long-run maximization of owners' wealth. Moreover, the tax benefits described are useful only in mergers—not in the formation of holding companies—since only in the case of mergers are operating results reported on a consolidated basis. An example will clarify the use of the tax loss carryforward.

EXAMPLE   The Perkins Company has a total of $450,000 in tax loss carryforwards resulting from operating tax losses of $150,000 a year in each of the past three years. To use these losses and to diversify its operations, the C. B. Company has acquired Perkins through a merger. C. B. expects to have *earnings before taxes* of $300,000 per year. Assuming that these earnings are realized, the Perkins portion of the merged firm just breaks even, and C. B. is in

---

[3] A 15-year carryforward is permitted on operating losses (includes losses on depreciable assets), while capital losses can be carried forward only five years. A discussion of tax loss carrybacks and carryforwards was presented in Chapter 2.

the 40 percent tax bracket; the total taxes paid by the two firms without and with the merger are calculated as follows:

Total taxes without merger

	Year		
	1	2	3
Profits before taxes	$300,000	$300,000	$300,000
Taxes (.40)	$120,000	$120,000	$120,000

Total taxes with merger

Profits before taxes	$300,000	$300,000	$300,000
Less: Tax loss carryforward	300,000	150,000	0
Taxable income	$ 0	$150,000	$300,000
Taxes (.40)	$ 0	$ 60,000	$120,000

With the merger, the total tax payments are less—$180,000 with the merger versus $360,000 without the merger. The combination is able to deduct the tax loss carryforward until 15 years have elapsed after the loss or the total tax losses have been exhausted, which happens, for this example, at the end of year 2. The tax advantages resulting from a merger involving a company with a tax loss carryforward should be clear from this example. ∎

Increased ownership liquidity. In the case of mergers, the combination of two small firms or a small and a larger firm into a larger corporation may provide the owners of the small firm(s) with greater liquidity. This is because of the higher marketability associated with the shares of larger firms. Instead of holding shares in a small firm that has a very "thin" market, the owners will receive shares that are traded in a broader market and can be liquidated more readily. Not only does the ability to convert shares into cash quickly have appeal, but owning shares for which market price quotations are readily available provides owners with a better sense of the value of their holdings. Especially in the case of small, closely held firms, the increase in the liquidity of shares obtainable through a merger with an acceptable firm may have considerable appeal.

RELEVANT VARIABLES

In evaluating possible combinations, the financial manager must consider not only the objectives mentioned in the preceding section but also the primary goal of the firm—to maximize the wealth of its owners over the long run. If achieving one or more of the objectives mentioned will contribute to the achievement of this primary goal, the combination should be made. To forecast the effects of a proposed combination on the firm's future performance, the financial manager must evaluate quantitatively certain key financial variables: earnings per share, dividends per share, market price of shares, book value of shares, and business and financial risk. As the discussion of valuation in Chapter 8 stressed, each of these variables is related to the valuation of corporate shares.

Earnings per share. Normally, the financial manager is looking for a reduction in the variability of earnings per share or some type of long-run increase in per-share earnings that will increase the market value of the firm's shares.

Dividends per share. The financial manager must also recognize and consider the importance of a suitable dividend policy. At the least, the precombination dividend will have to be maintained to stabilize the market price of the firm's shares.

Market price of shares. The market price per share of the merged firm is the key variable the financial manager attempts to maximize in selecting a suitable merger partner. Only if the market price of shares in the combined enterprise increases over the long run will the firm's overall objective be achieved. The value of the owners' holdings is most easily measured by the market price of their stock.

Book value of shares. In certain situations, firms are acquired for fund-raising purposes. In these combinations the amount paid for the stock of the acquired firm must be considered in light of the book value of the firm, since the firm is not being acquired for its earnings potential but for its favorable asset and financial structures. Since the book value of a firm does not directly reflect its valuation, this is not a key variable in the analysis of prospective acquisitions.

Business and financial risks. The effects of a proposed merger on the business and financial risks (see Chapter 13) of the resulting enterprise is of key importance in the valuation process. Investors in a firm's shares determine their value by discounting expected dividends at a rate highly dependent on the risk of the firm. If the firm becomes more risky as the result of a merger, its expected earnings and dividends will be discounted by investors at a higher rate. The net effect will be to lower the value of the owners' holdings if earnings are not expected to increase sufficiently to offset the increased risk. Risk and return were discussed in Chapter 7, and value was discussed in Chapter 8.

Although the variables just described are not equally easy to measure or predict, the financial manager must attempt to quantify and forecast them in order to get a better feel for the long-run effects of a proposed combination on the owners' wealth as measured in the marketplace. The financial manager's primary concern should be the effect on the earnings and the market price of the firm's shares.

Analyzing Prospective Mergers

This portion of the chapter is devoted to the various analytical decision-making techniques commonly used in evaluating and negotiating mergers.[4] As indicated

---

[4] A popular technique currently being used in mergers is the *leveraged buyout,* which involves the use of a large amount of debt — commonly secured by the acquired firm 's assets — to finance the purchase by the acquiring firm. The cash flows of the acquired firm are then used to repay the debt. This technique can be used as part of either a cash or a stock-exchange acquisition of a firm. Attention here is given only to straight cash and stock-exchange transactions; for a good review of the mechanics of leveraged buyouts, see Nicholas Wallner, "Leveraged Buyouts: A Review of the State of the Art," pts. 1 and 2, *Mergers & Acquisitions 14* (Fall 1979), pp. 4–13, and *14* (Winter 1980), pp. 16–26.

earlier, the term *merger* is used here to mean both consolidations and mergers. The two key variables of concern are earnings per share and market price per share. An important ratio in analyzing prospective mergers is the *price/earnings (P/E) ratio.*

Key topics in this section are cash purchases of companies, stock-exchange acquisitions, and the merger negotiation process.

CASH PURCHASES OF COMPANIES

When a firm is acquiring another firm for cash (debt is assumed to be the same as cash here), the use of simple capital budgeting procedures is required. Whether the firm is being acquired for its assets or as a going concern, the basic approach is similar.

Acquisitions of assets. In some instances a firm is acquired not for its income-earning potential but as a conglomeration of assets (generally fixed assets) that are needed by the acquiring firm. The cash price paid for this type of acquisition depends largely on what assets are being acquired. If the entire firm is acquired, the liquidation value of the firm is a reasonable price; if only certain key assets are purchased, no more than the market value of these assets should be paid. If the entire firm is purchased as a nongoing concern, consideration must also be given to the value of any tax losses.

To determine whether the purchase of assets is financially justifiable, the firm must estimate both the costs and the benefits of the assets. This is, in effect, the classic capital budgeting problem. A cash outlay is made to acquire assets and, as a result of their acquisition, certain future cash benefits are expected.

EXAMPLE   The VW Company is interested in acquiring certain fixed assets of the Bug Company. Bug, which has had some losses over the past five years, is interested in selling out, but it wishes to sell out entirely, not just get rid of certain fixed assets. A condensed balance sheet for the Bug Company is given.

Balance Sheet for Bug Company

Assets		Liabilities and stockholders' equity	
Cash	$ 2,000	Total liabilities	$ 80,000
Marketable securities	0	Stockholders' equity	120,000
Accounts receivable	8,000	Total liabilities and	
Inventories	10,000	stockholders'	
Machine A	10,000	equity	$200,000
Machine B	30,000		
Machine C	25,000		
Land and buildings	115,000		
Total assets	$200,000		

VW Company needs only machines B and C and the land and buildings. However, it has made some inquiries and has arranged to sell the accounts receivable, inventories, and machine A for $23,000. Since there is also $2,000 in cash, VW will get $25,000 for the excess assets. Bug wants $20,000 for the entire company, which means that VW will have to

Table 23.1   An Analysis of the Bug Company
Acquisition by the VW Company

Year(s)	Cash flow (1)	PV factor at 11% (2)	Present value [(1) × (2)] (3)
0	($75,000)	1.000[a]	$(75,000)
1–5	14,000	3.696[b]	51,744
6	12,000	0.535[a]	6,420
7	12,000	0.482[a]	5,784
8	12,000	0.434[a]	5,208
9	12,000	0.391[a]	4,692
10	12,000	0.352[a]	4,224
		Net present value	$3,072

[a] The present-value interest factor, PVIF, for $1 discounted at 11 percent for the corresponding year obtained from Table A-3.
[b] The present-value interest factor for an annuity, PVIFA, with a five-year life discounted at 11 percent obtained from Table A-4.

pay the firm's creditors $80,000 and its owners $20,000. The actual outlay required by VW after liquidating the unneeded assets will be $75,000 [($80,000 + $20,000) − $25,000]. In other words, to obtain the use of the desired assets (machines B and C and the land and buildings) and the benefits of Bug's tax losses, VW must pay $75,000. The *after-tax cash inflows* expected to result from the new equipment and tax losses are $14,000 per year for the next five years and $12,000 per year for the following five years. The desirability of this acquisition can be determined by calculating the net present value of this outlay using the VW Company's 11 percent cost of capital, as shown in Table 23.1.

Since the net present value of $3072 is greater than zero, VW should find acquisition of the Bug Company an acceptable investment. Of course, if VW has alternate ways of obtaining similar assets or must ration its capital, the acquisition may not be made. The importance of capital budgeting techniques in evaluating cash acquisitions of assets should be clear from this example. As long as the firm makes acquisitions that have positive net present values, the market value of the firm should be enhanced. ■

Acquisitions of going concerns. Cash acquisitions of going concerns are best analyzed using capital budgeting techniques like those described for asset acquisitions. The basic difficulty in applying the capital budgeting approach to the cash acquisition of a going concern is in the *estimation of cash flows* and certain *risk considerations that may result from the changed operating and financial structures.* The methods of estimating the cash flows expected from an acquisition are no different from the methods used in estimating cash flows in any capital budgeting decision. Prudent forecasting, along with the use of probability techniques, may be required.

If a firm acquires a company that has a considerably different operating or financial structure from its own, the effects of the new structures on the firm's overall cost of capital must be estimated. As the discussions of operating and capital structure in Chapter 13 showed, a shift in either of these structures may affect the firm's overall business and financial risk, thereby causing a change in its overall cost of capital. Only when a firm acquires another firm that has the same operating and financial structures is its cost of capital expected to remain fixed.

Therefore, whenever a firm considers acquiring for cash another firm that has a different operating or capital structure, it should adjust the cost of capital appropriately prior to applying capital budgeting techniques. An example will clarify the procedure.

EXAMPLE   The Stockade Company is contemplating the acquisition of the Wall Company, which can be purchased for $60,000 in cash. Both firms have similar operating structures and business risk; Stockade currently has a high degree of financial leverage, which is reflected in its 13 percent cost of capital. Because of the low financial leverage of the Wall Company, Stockade estimates that its overall cost of capital will drop to 10 percent after the acquisition. Since the effect of the less risky capital structure resulting from the acquisition of Wall Company cannot be reflected in the expected cash benefits, the postacquisition cost of capital (10 percent) must be used to evaluate the cash flows expected from the acquisition. The incremental cash inflows forecast from the proposed acquisition are expected over a 30-year time horizon. These estimated inflows are $5,000 for years 1 through 10, $13,000 for years 11 through 18, and $4,000 for years 19 through 30. The net present value of the acquisition is calculated in Table 23.2.

Since the net present value of the acquisition is greater than zero ($2357), the acquisition is acceptable. It is interesting to note that had the effect of the changed capital structure on the cost of capital not been considered, the acquisition would have been found unacceptable since the net present value at a 13 percent cost of capital is −$11,864, which is less than zero. ■

STOCK-EXCHANGE ACQUISITIONS

Quite often a firm is acquired through the exchange of common stock. The acquiring firm exchanges its shares for shares of the firm being acquired according to a predetermined ratio. The ratio of exchange of shares is determined in the

Table 23.2   An Analysis of the Wall Company Acquisition by the Stockade Company

Year(s)	Cash flow (1)	PV factor at 10%[a] (2)	Present value [(1) × (2)] (3)
0	($60,000)	1.000	($60,000)
1–10	5,000	6.145	30,725
11–18	13,000	$(8.201 − 6.145)^b$	26,728
19–30	4,000	$(9.427 − 8.201)^b$	4,904
		Net present value	$ 2,357

[a] Present-value interest factors for annuities, *PVIFA*, obtained from Table A-4.

[b] These factors are found using a shortcut technique that can be applied to annuities for periods of years beginning at some point in the future. By finding the appropriate factor for the present value of an annuity given for the last year of the annuity and subtracting the present value factor of an annuity for the year immediately preceding the beginning of the annuity, the appropriate interest factor for the present value of an annuity beginning sometime in the future can be obtained. You can check this shortcut by using the long approach and comparing the results.

merger negotiations. This ratio affects the various financial yardsticks that are used by existing and prospective shareholders in valuing the merged firm's shares.

Ratio of exchange. When a firm trades its stock for the shares of another firm, the number of shares of the acquiring firm to be exchanged for each share of the acquired firm must be determined. The first requirement, of course, is that the acquiring company have sufficient authorized and unissued and (or) treasury stock available to complete the transaction. Often the repurchase of shares, which was discussed in Chapter 14, is necessary to obtain sufficient shares for the transaction. Since the acquiring firm is *usually* larger and has a market for its shares and the smaller acquired firm may have closely held shares, the acquiring firm offers a certain amount for each share of the acquired firm. This amount is generally more than the current market price of publicly traded shares. Because of the difficulty of placing a value on and explaining the results of acquisitions of closely held firms, the discussion here assumes that the acquired firm's shares are publicly traded. The actual *ratio of exchange* is merely the ratio of the amount paid per share of the acquired firm to the market price of the acquiring firm's shares. It is calculated in this manner since the acquiring firm pays the acquired firm in stock, which has a value equal to its market price. An example will clarify the calculation.

EXAMPLE   The Huge Company, whose stock is currently selling for $80 per share, is interested in acquiring the Tiny Company in order to integrate its operation vertically. To prepare for the acquisition, Huge has been repurchasing its shares over the past three years. Tiny's stock is currently selling for $50 per share, but in the merger negotiations, Huge has found it necessary to offer $56 per share. Since Huge does not have sufficient financial resources to purchase the firm for cash, nor does it wish to raise these funds, Tiny has agreed to accept Huge's stock in exchange for its shares. Since Huge's stock currently sells for $80 per share and it must pay $56 per share for Tiny's stock, the ratio of exchange is .7 ($56 ÷ $80). This means that the Huge Company must exchange .7 shares of its stock for each share of Tiny's stock. ■

Owners of both the acquiring firm and acquired firm are concerned with the effect of the acquisition on certain financial variables. The focus is on the resulting earnings and market price per share, but attention is sometimes given to dividends per share, book value per share, and the business and financial risks of the merged company.

Effect on earnings per share. Ordinarily, the resulting earnings per share differ from the premerger earnings per share for both the acquiring firm and the acquired firm. They depend largely on the ratio of exchange and the premerger earnings per share of each firm. It is best to view the initial and long-run effects of the ratio of exchange on earnings per share *(eps)* separately.

Initial effect. When the ratio of exchange is equal to 1 and both the acquiring firm and the acquired firm have the same premerger earnings per share, the merged firm's earnings per share will initially remain constant. In this rare instance, both the acquiring firm and the acquired firm would have equal price/earnings ratios. In actuality, the earnings per share of the merged firm are generally above the

Table 23.3 Huge Company and Tiny Company Financial Data

Item	Huge Company	Tiny Company
(1) Earnings available for common stock	$500,000	$100,000
(2) Number of shares of common stock outstanding	125,000	20,000
(3) Earnings per share [(1) ÷ (2)]	$4	$5
(4) Market price per share	$80	$50
(5) Price/earnings ratio [(4) ÷ (3)]	20	10

premerger earnings per share of one firm and below the premerger earnings per share of the other, after making the necessary adjustment for the ratio of exchange. These differences can be illustrated by a simple example.

EXAMPLE   The Huge Company is contemplating acquiring the Tiny Company by exchanging .7 shares of its stock for each share of Tiny's stock. The current financial data related to the earnings and market price for each of these companies are given in Table 23.3. Although Tiny's stock currently has a market price of $50 per share, Huge has offered it $56 per share. As seen in the preceding example, this results in a ratio of exchange of .7.

To complete the merger and retire the 20,000 shares of Tiny Company stock outstanding, Huge will have to issue and (or) use treasury stock totaling 14,000 shares (.70 × 20,000 shares). Once the merger is completed, Huge will have 139,000 shares of common stock (125,000 + 14,000) outstanding. If the earnings of each of the firms remain constant, the merged company will be expected to have earnings available for the common stockholders of $600,000 ($500,000 + $100,000). The earnings per share of the merged company should therefore equal approximately $4.32 per share ($600,000 ÷ 139,000 shares). At first, it would appear that the Tiny Company's shareholders have sustained a decrease in per-share earnings from $5 to $4.32, but since each share of the Tiny Company's original stock is equivalent to .7 shares of the merged company, the equivalent earnings per share are $3.02 ($4.32 × .70). In other words, as a result of the merger, the Huge Company's original shareholders experience an increase in earnings per share from $4 to $4.32 at the expense of the Tiny Company's shareholders, whose earnings per share drop from $5 to $3.02. These results are summarized in Table 23.4.

The easiest way to explain the increased *eps* for the original Huge Company shareholders and the decreased *eps* for the original Tiny Company shareholders is to compare

Table 23.4 Summary of the Effects on Earnings per Share of a Merger Between the Huge Company and the Tiny Company at $56 per Share

Stockholders	Earnings per share	
	Before merger	After merger
Huge Company	$4.00	$4.32
Tiny Company	5.00	3.02[a]

[a] Based on .7 of the Huge Company's earnings per share.

Table 23.5 Effect of P/E Ratios on Earnings per Share

Relationship between P/E paid and P/E of acquiring company	Effect on *eps*	
	Acquiring company	Acquired company
P/E paid $>$ P/E of acquiring company	Decrease	Increase
P/E paid $=$ P/E of acquiring company	Constant	Constant
P/E paid $<$ P/E of acquiring company	Increase	Decrease

the price/earnings ratio of the original company to that based on the price paid for the acquired company. The possible outcomes are presented in Table 23.5. The usefulness of the relationships in Table 23.5 can be illustrated by comparing the P/E ratios associated with the Huge-Tiny merger. The Huge Company's P/E ratio is 20, while the P/E ratio based on the share price paid the Tiny Company was 11.2 ($56 ÷ $5). Since the P/E based on the share price paid for the Tiny Company was less than the P/E of the Huge Company (11.2 versus 20), the effect was to increase the *eps* for original holders of shares in the Huge Company (from $4.00 to $4.32) and to decrease the effective *eps* of original holders of shares in the Tiny Company (from $5.00 to $3.02).

Had Huge paid the Tiny Company $110 per share, which would result in a ratio of exchange of 1.375 ($110 ÷ $80), the effects on *eps* would be as shown in Table 23.6. The original holders of Huge Company stock would experience a drop in *eps* (from $4.00 to $3.93), while the original holders of Tiny Company's stock would experience an increase in *eps* (from $5.00 to $5.40). This is because the P/E ratio based on the share price paid for Tiny's stock was 22 ($110 ÷ $5), while the P/E of Huge Company stock was 20. As indicated in Table 23.5, whenever the P/E ratio based on the share price paid is greater than the P/E of the acquiring company, the earnings per share of the original owners of the acquiring company will decrease while the effective *eps* of the original owners of the acquired company increases. ■

Long-run effect. The long-run effect of a merger on the earnings per share of the merged company depends largely on whether the earnings of the merged firm grow. Especially when mergers to achieve horizontal or vertical integration are made, increases in earnings are likely. Combining the two firms may make it

Table 23.6 Summary of the Effects on Earnings per Share of a Merger Between the Huge Company and the Tiny Company at $110 per Share

Stockholders	Earnings per share	
	Before merger	After merger
Huge Company	$4.00	$3.93[a]
Tiny Company	5.00	5.40[b]

[a] $\dfrac{\$500,000 + \$100,000}{(1.375 \times 20,000) + 125,000} = \$3.93$

[b] $\$3.93 \times 1.375 = \$5.40$

SEVEN UNLUCKY MERGERS: SUPPOSE THEY HADN'T HAPPENED

To check out the mergers Wall Streeters call the decade's worst, *Fortune* estimated what each acquiring company would have earned in 1983 had the deals . . . not occurred. The exercise assumes that the dollar value of each acquisition had instead been used by the acquirer at the time to buy its own stock at the market

Acquiring company (Date of acquisition) Acquired company	Price	Business
Mobil (1974, 1976) Marcor	$1.86 billion in cash, notes, and common stock	Oil and gas Retail stores, paper packaging
Sohio (1981) Kennecott	$1.77 billion in cash	Oil and gas Copper and metal products
Exxon (1979) Reliance Electric	$1.24 billion in cash	Oil and gas Electric equipment
Baldwin-United (1982) MGIC	$1.16 billion in cash	Financial services Insurance and real estate
Atlantic Richfield (1977) Anaconda	$700 million in cash and common stock	Oil and gas Copper and minerals
Pan Am (1980) National	$400 million in cash	International airline Domestic airline
Wickes (1980) Gamble-Skogmo	$193 million in cash and common stock	Retailing and manufacturing Department and specialty stores

[a] Earnings through third quarter.

SOURCE: "Seven Unlucky Mergers: Suppose They Hadn't Happened," *Fortune*, April 30, 1984, p. 266.

possible for the sum of their earnings to exceed the total earnings of the firms when viewed separately. Often, although a decrease in the per-share earnings of the stock held by the original owners of the acquiring firm is expected initially, the long-run effects of the merger on earnings per share are quite favorable.

Since growth in earnings is generally expected by a business firm, the key factor enabling the acquiring company, which initially experiences a decrease in *eps,* to experience higher future *eps* than it would have without the merger is the fact that the earnings attributable to the acquired company's assets grow at a faster rate than those resulting from the acquiring company's premerger assets. An example will clarify this point.

EXAMPLE In 1984, the Huge Company acquired the Tiny Company by exchanging 1.375 shares of its common stock for each share of the Tiny Company. Other key financial data

price. This would have reduced the company's outstanding shares, increasing per-share earnings. The calculation also eliminates from the acquirer's books profits or losses of the acquired company. In every case calculated, the acquiring company's earnings would have been higher if the deal hadn't taken place.

Acquirer's 1983 after-tax profits Acquired company's contribution (Est.)	Acquirer's '83 earnings per share	
	Actual	If acquisition hadn't occurred (Est.)
$1.5 billion $41 million	$3.70	$6.12
$1.51 billion ($136 million)	$6.14	$8.01
$4.98 billion ($58 million)	$5.78	$6.17
($673 million)[a] ($148 million)[a]	($32.28)[a]	Not calculable
$1.55 billion ($155 million)	$6.03	$7.51
($51 million) Not calculable	($0.58)	Not calculable
$25 million $5 million	$1.72	$10.86

and the effects of this exchange ratio were discussed in the preceding example. The total earnings of the Huge Company are expected to grow at an annual rate of 3 percent without the merger, while the Tiny Company's earnings are expected to grow at a 7 percent annual rate without the merger. No synergistic effects are expected from the merger, and the same growth rates are expected to apply to the component earnings streams with the merger. Table 23.7 shows the future effects on *eps* for the Huge Company without and with the proposed Tiny Company merger, based on these growth rates.

Table 23.7 indicates that the earnings per share without the merger will be greater than the *eps* with the merger for the years 1984 through 1986; after 1986, the *eps* will increase above what they would have been without the merger as a result of the faster earnings growth rate of the Tiny Company (7 percent versus 3 percent). Although a few years are required for this difference in the growth rate of earnings to pay off, it can be seen that in the future the Huge Company will receive an earnings benefit from merging with the Tiny Company at a 1.375 ratio of exchange. The relationships in Table 23.7 are graphed in

Table 23.7   Effects of Earnings Growth on *eps* for the
              Huge Company without and with the
              Tiny Company Merger

Year	Without merger		With merger	
	Total earnings[a]	Earnings per share[b]	Total earnings[c]	Earnings per share[d]
1984	$500,000	$4.00	$600,000	$3.93
1985	515,000	4.12	622,000	4.08
1986	530,450	4.24	644,940	4.23
1987	546,364	4.37	668,868	4.39
1988	562,755	4.50	693,835	4.55
1989	579,638	4.64	719,893	4.72

[a] Based on a 3 percent annual growth rate.
[b] Based on 125,000 shares outstanding.
[c] Based on 3 percent annual growth in the Huge Company's earnings and 7 percent annual growth in the Tiny Company's earnings.
[d] Based on 152,500 shares outstanding [(1.375 × 20,000 shares) + 125,000 shares].

Figure 23.1. The long-run earnings advantage of the merger is clearly depicted by this graph[5]. ∎

This type of analysis should provide the financial manager with useful information for making the merger decision. The presence of synergistic effects or

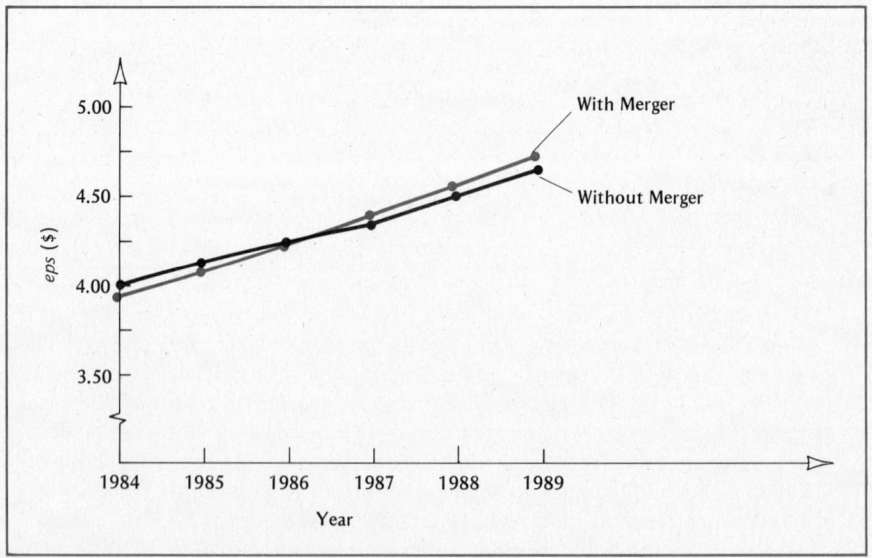

Figure 23.1   Future *eps* without and with the Huge-Tiny merger

[5] To properly discover whether the merger is beneficial, the earnings estimates under each alternative would have to be made over a long period of time, say 50 years, and then discounted at the appropriate rate. The alternative with the highest present value would be preferred. In the interest of simplicity, only the basic intuitive view of the long-run effect is presented here.

differential growth rates of earnings may suggest that even though the initial effect of the merger will be to lower *eps*, the long-run effect may be an increase in *eps*. The use of various assumptions to test the sensitivity of the long-run effects of a proposed merger should reduce the uncertainty associated with the merger decision.

Effect on market price per share. The market price per share does not necessarily remain constant after an acquisition; rather, adjustments take place in the marketplace in response to changes in expected earnings, the dilution of ownership, changes in business and financial risk, and certain other managerial and financial changes. Using the ratio of exchange, a *ratio of exchange in market price* can be calculated. This ratio, the *MPR,* is defined by Equation 23.1:

$$MPR = \frac{MP_{acquiring} \times RE}{MP_{acquired}} \qquad (23.1)$$

where

$$MPR = \text{market price ratio of exchange}$$
$$MP_{acquiring} = \text{market price for the acquiring firm}$$
$$MP_{acquired} = \text{market price for the acquired firm}$$
$$RE = \text{ratio of exchange}$$

A simple example can be used to illustrate the calculation of this ratio.

EXAMPLE In the Huge-Tiny example, the market price of the Huge Company's stock was $80 and that of the Tiny Company's stock was $50. The ratio of exchange was 1.375. Substituting these values into Equation 23.1 yields a ratio of exchange in market price of 2.2 [($80 × 1.375) ÷ $50]. This means that $2.20 of the market price of the Huge Company is given for every $1.00 of the market price of the Tiny Company. ■

The ratio of exchange in market price is normally greater than 1, which indicates that to acquire a firm, a premium over its market price must be paid. It would be unusual for a firm to acquire another firm by paying less than the firm's market price per share. Even so, however, the original owners of the acquiring firm may still gain because of differences in the two firms' price/earnings ratios. If a firm with a high P/E ratio acquires a firm with a low P/E ratio and the merged company maintains the higher P/E ratio, a rise in the market price of its shares may result. This can be illustrated by a simple example.

EXAMPLE The financial data in Table 23.3 for the Huge Company and Tiny Company can be used to explain the market price effects of a merger. If we assume that the ratio of exchange between the two stocks was .7, which means that $56 of the Huge Company's stock was given for each share of the Tiny Company's stock, substituting into Equation 23.1 gives us a ratio of exchange in market price of 1.12 [($80 × .70) ÷ $50]. If the earnings of the merged companies remain at the premerger levels, and if the stock of the merged companies sells at the Huge Company's premerger multiple of 20 times earnings, the values in Table 23.8 can

Table 23.8   Postmerger Market Price of the Huge Company Using a
.7 Ratio of Exchange and a P/E Ratio of 20

Item	Merged company
(1) Earnings available for common stock	$600,000
(2) Number of shares of common stock outstanding	139,000
(3) Earnings per share [(1) ÷ (2)]	$4.32
(4) Price/earnings ratio	20
(5) Expected market price per share [(3) × (4)]	$86.40

be expected.[6] Not only will the acquiring company have higher earnings per share, but the market price of its shares will also increase. ∎

Although the kind of behavior exhibited in this example is not unusual, the financial manager must recognize that only with proper management of the merged enterprise can its market value be sustained. Part of the boost in market price can justifiably be attributed to the fact that the acquired firm's stock may have been selling at a low P/E due to the thin market in which it was traded.[7] If the merged firm cannot achieve sufficiently high earnings while maintaining its current risk configuration, there is no guarantee that its market price will reach or maintain the forecast value. Nevertheless, a policy of acquiring firms with low P/Es can produce favorable results for the owners of the acquiring firm.[8] Acquisitions are especially attractive when the acquiring firm's stock price is high, since fewer shares must be exchanged to acquire a given firm.

Dividends per share. The dividend per share does not normally enter into the merger decision since the payment of dividends is a discretionary action based on firm and market factors. The primary concern of the acquiring firm is earnings per share, since earnings are believed to be a prerequisite to the payment of dividends. The dividend decision must be made once an acquisition has been consummated, but this decision is not a prerequisite to acquisitions.

Book value per share. The book value per share, like the dividend per share, is irrelevant when a firm is acquiring a going concern. If the firm being acquired is being obtained only for its assets, the book value per share may be helpful in determining the purchase price per share. When this type of acquisition is made, attention must

[6] In the absence of synergy, in a rational securities market, the P/E ratio of the combined firm should be the weighted average of the initial P/E ratios for the separate firms. For simplicity, this theoretical point is ignored.

[7] A *thin market* exists when a firm's stock is not actively traded due to the small number of owners or the small size of the enterprise. The stocks of such firms are usually traded over the counter, and as a result of their relative inactivity, the price at which they are traded may not reflect their true value or potential.

[8] It is interesting to note that most empirical studies have shown that the shareholders of the acquired firm benefit from the premium paid to them. However, the studies have also shown that the shareholders of the acquiring firm do not experience any significant gain from the merger.

also be given to the liquidity in the form of net working capital provided by the acquired firm. Both book value per share and *net working capital per share* are relevant in this situation. The postmerger book value depends to some extent on the accounting procedures used in consolidating the firm's statements. Description of the accounting techniques used in mergers can be found in most intermediate accounting texts.

Business and financial risk. Business risk, which concerns the firm's operating structure, is usually considered in making the initial merger inquiry. Analysis of business risk typically centers on an assessment of postmerger operating leverage and the stability of revenues and costs. Financial risk, which depends on the firm's financial (capital) structure, must normally be evaluated through a study of postmerger financial leverage. Occasionally, a desire to change the firm's business or financial risk is the primary motive for a merger. An accurate estimation of the changes in risk is important because of its effect on the postmerger market valuation of the firm's shares. If the total risk (business and financial) increases as a result of a merger, investors will discount the firm's earnings at a higher rate, thereby lowering its market price. The decreased market price will be reflected in a lower P/E ratio. If the total risk decreases, an increase in the market price of the firm's shares and its P/E ratio can be expected.

THE MERGER NEGOTIATION PROCESS

A merger can normally be initiated in either of two ways. When the management of an acquiring firm has found a suitable merger candidate, it can negotiate with the firm's management or directly with its stockholders. Negotiation with the management is generally preferred, though if such negotiations break down, the acquiring firm may make a direct appeal to the shareholders through tender offers.

Management negotiations. To initiate the negotiation process, the acquiring firm must make an offer based on a certain ratio of exchange. The merger candidate must then review the offer and, in light of alternative offers, agree or disagree with the terms offered. A desirable merger candidate usually receives more than a single offer. Normally, certain nonfinancial questions must be answered in the negotiations. These usually relate to the disposition and compensation of the existing management, product-line policies, financing policies, and the autonomy of the acquired firm.

The key factor will be the price per share offered, which is reflected by the ratio of exchange. If the acquired firm is offered a good premium over its market price along with certain other guarantees, the merger may be consummated. Occasionally there are lengthy negotiations in which the merger candidate plays one offer against another to obtain the best possible terms. Although the negotiations are generally based on the expectation of a merger, sometimes the negotiations will break down.

Occasionally, to satisfy the management of the acquired firm, certain *contingent payments* are built into the merger contract. In a cash transaction, *stock-purchase warrants* may be given to the management of a closely held company that is to be operated by its management as a subsidiary.[9] The warrants may be exercisable once the market price of the acquiring firm reaches a certain level; more often, however, they are tied in some way to the earnings of the subsidiary. The terms of this type of warrant generally state that if the subsidiary's accumulated earnings exceed a specified amount within a certain period of time, the management will receive or be able to purchase a certain number of shares of the firm's stock at a prespecified price. Sometimes achievement of the specified performance will provide for a *cash payment* equal to a certain percentage of earnings. The level of performance necessary to receive the contingent payment may be geared to average annual earnings or some other financial value. The contingent payments in a stock-exchange transaction are quite similar except that there is a greater likelihood that the payment will be made in stock instead of cash.

The use of contingent payments as a *sweetener* to stimulate the existing management of the acquired company to operate the firm, once it has been acquired, in a manner that will benefit the merged company is an attractive feature from both the acquiring firm's and the acquired firm's viewpoint. Sometimes a contingent payment is included as an undefined portion of the initial purchase price; in other cases it is used merely as an incentive for the subsidiary's management, which has been paid in full for the acquisition, to operate the firm efficiently and in the best interests of all. Here the contingent payment represents a type of profit sharing for the subsidiary management. When these types of payments are included, the acquiring firm is in effect providing a financial incentive to the management of the subsidiary to operate the subsidiary successfully.

Tender offers. When management negotiations for an acquisition break down, tender offers may be used in an attempt to negotiate a merger directly with the firm's stockholders. As explained in Chapter 14, a *tender offer* is made at a premium above the market price and is offered to all the stockholders of the firm. The stockholders are advised of the offer through announcements in financial newspapers or through direct communications from the offering firm. Sometimes a tender offer is made to add pressure to existing merger negotiations; in other cases the tender offer may be made without warning to catch the management off guard.

If the management does not favor a merger or believes that the premium in a projected tender offer is too low, it is likely to take certain defensive actions to ward off the tender offer. Common strategies include declaring an attractive dividend, informing stockholders of alleged damaging effects of being taken over, or attempting to sue the acquiring firm. These actions may deter or delay a tender offer. Deterring the tender offer by filing suit gives the management that is fearful of a takeover time to find and negotiate a merger with a firm it would prefer to be acquired by.

Holding Companies

A *holding company* is a company that has voting control of one or more other companies. The holding company may need to own only a small percentage of the

---

[9] Stock-purchase warrants were described in detail in Chapter 22.

outstanding shares to have this voting control. The number of shares required depends on the dispersion of ownership of the company. In the case of companies with a relatively small number of shareholders, as much as 30 to 40 percent of the stock may be required; in the case of firms with a widely dispersed ownership, 10 to 20 percent of the shares may be sufficient to gain voting control. A holding company desirous of obtaining voting control of a firm may use direct market purchases or tender offers to obtain needed shares.

ADVANTAGES OF HOLDING COMPANIES

The key advantages of the holding company arrangement are the leverage effect, protection from risk, legal benefits, and the fact that control can be obtained without negotiations.

Leverage effect. A holding company arrangement permits a firm to control a large amount of assets with a relatively small dollar investment. In other words, the owners of a holding company can *control* significantly larger amounts of assets than they could acquire through mergers. A simple example may help illustrate the leverage effect.

EXAMPLE   The Moses Company currently holds voting control of two subsidiaries — Company X and Company Y. The balance sheets for the Moses Company and its two subsidiaries are presented in Table 23.9. It owns approximately 17 percent ($10 ÷ $60) of Company X and 20 percent ($14 ÷ $70) of Company Y. It is assumed that these holdings are sufficient for voting control.

Table 23.9   Balance Sheets for the Moses Company and Its Subsidiaries

Assets		Liabilities and stockholders' equity	
Moses Company			
Common stock holdings		Long-term debt	$ 6
Company X	$ 10	Preferred stock	6
Company Y	14	Common stock equity	12
Total	$ 24	Total	$ 24
Company X			
Current assets	$ 30	Current liabilities	$ 15
Fixed assets	70	Long-term debt	25
Total	$100	Common stock equity	60
		Total	$100
Company Y			
Current assets	$ 20	Current liabilities	$ 10
Fixed assets	140	Long-term debt	60
Total	$160	Preferred stock	20
		Common stock equity	70
		Total	$160

The owners of the Moses Company's $12 worth of equity have control over $260 worth of assets (Company X's $100 worth and Company Y's $160 worth). This means that the owners' equity represents only about 4.6 percent ($12 ÷ $260) of the total assets controlled. From the discussions of ratio analysis, leverage, and capital structure in Chapters 4 and 13, you should recognize that this is quite a high degree of leverage. If an individual stockholder or even another holding company owns $3 of Moses Company's stock, which is sufficient for its control, it will in actuality control the whole $260 of assets. The investment in this case would represent only 1.15 percent ($3 ÷ $260) of the assets controlled. ■

The high leverage obtained through a holding company arrangement greatly magnifies earnings and losses for the holding company. Quite often a *pyramiding* of holding companies occurs when one holding company controls other holding companies. This type of arrangement causes an even greater magnification of earnings and losses. The greater the leverage, the greater the risk involved. The risk-return trade-off is a key consideration in the holding company decision.

Risk protection. Another advantage commonly cited for the holding company arrangement is that the failure of one of the companies held does not result in the failure of the entire holding company. Since each subsidiary is a separate corporation, the failure of one company should cost the holding company, at a maximum, no more than its investment in that subsidiary. Often, lenders to subsidiaries of holding companies will require the holding company to guarantee the subsidiaries' loans to protect themselves in the event that the subsidiary becomes bankrupt.

Legal benefits. Many states provide certain tax breaks to corporations chartered within the state. If a company were to merge with several other companies located in different states, the surviving company would receive these special tax benefits only in its state of incorporation. If, instead of merging, a holding company arrangement were used, whereby the subsidiaries still maintained their corporate identities, each of the subsidiaries would benefit from more favorable tax treatment, since they would be operating in their respective states of incorporation. Another legal benefit of the holding company is the fact that since each subsidiary is a separate corporation, any lawsuits or legal actions filed against the subsidiary will not threaten the remaining companies.

Lack of negotiations. Another major advantage of the holding company arrangement is the relative ease with which control of a subsidiary can be acquired. The holding company can gain control of a company simply by purchasing enough shares of its stock in the marketplace. If the holding company makes these purchases over a period of time, its seizure of control may go unnoticed up to a point; legal requirements for disclosure exist under certain circumstances. Stockholder or management approval is not generally required for a holding company to acquire control of a firm, whereas it usually is required for a merger.

DISADVANTAGES OF HOLDING COMPANIES

The key disadvantages commonly cited with respect to the holding company arrangement include multiple taxation, the magnification of losses, and high administrative expenses.

MERGERSPEAK: GREENMAIL, GOLDEN PARACHUTES, LADY MACBETH STRATEGIES . . .

Greenmail, golden parachutes, scorched-earth defenses, shark repellents, poison pills, Lady Macbeth strategies, white knights, and Pac-Man defenses sound more like video-game tactics than serious moves by adult masters of business administration in the world of corporate takeovers.

But serious they are. Despite their joy-stick titles, these are not the product of 20-year-old software moguls but of pin-striped strategists in the hostile takeover wars. And the effect of some of the tactics has become a poison pill for 42 million average stockholders.

In the long run, it is upon the support of those stockholders — as voters who influence members of congress who write regulatory law — that the relatively unhampered continuance of a free stock market system may depend.

Many corporate mergers are logical. As more industries enter a world market, mergers can add to efficiency and productive capacity in the competition for that vast market.

What does not make sense, in terms of the long-term health of the capitalist system, is the unfair practice called greenmail and its associated gambits.

Shark repellents and poison pills are schemes that protect corporate management against raiders, sometimes to the detriment of stockholders. Golden parachutes guarantee big payoffs to executives in case repellents don't work. A Lady Macbeth strategy is (pardon the gender change) a white knight who gallops up to save a company, then joins with the raider to do in the king and take control. Lady Macbeth, in this case, wants all the perfumes of Arabia not for spot cleaning but to rival Saudi assets.

Greenmail, in case you have missed some recent takeover battles, occurs when a corporate raider or group of raiders buys a minority position in the stock of a target company. This threat to win control then provokes a buy-back offer from the worried executives of the threatened corporation. The buy-back typically gives the greenmailers a sharply higher price per share than the other, more common holders of common stock can get for theirs. To add insult to injury, this extra expenditure of company (i.e., stockholders') money dilutes the value of the other shares. No Mafia protection seller could fail to admire the quick and unfair results of this system.

SOURCE: Earl W. Foell, "Takeover May Not Be Fair Game," Dayton *Journal Herald,* May 21, 1984, p. 11.

Multiple taxation. Since the income to the holding company from its subsidiaries is in the form of cash dividends, a portion of it is doubly taxed. The subsidiary, prior to paying dividends, must pay federal and state taxes on its earnings; when the holding company receives these earnings as dividends, it must claim 15 percent of them for taxes. In other words, although an 85 percent tax exemption on intercorporate dividends is permitted, the remaining 15 percent received by the holding company is considered taxable income. When a large proportion — currently 80 percent or more — of the subsidiaries' stock is held, the IRS effectively gives the holding company a 100 percent dividend exemption. If a subsidiary were part of a merged company, there would be *no* multiple taxation.

Magnification of losses. As the discussion of the leverage resulting from the holding company arrangement indicated, both earnings and losses are magnified. The magnification of losses when general economic conditions are unfavorable may result in the collapse of the holding company. The degree of risk is to some extent a function of the degree of pyramiding and the general stability of the subsidiaries' revenues and costs. However, since in general most businesspersons are risk averters, increased risk must be recognized as a very real disadvantage of holding companies.

High administrative expenses. A holding company is generally a more expensive form of business organization to administer than a single company created by a merger. The increased cost is generally attributable to the cost of maintaining each company as a separate entity and therefore not achieving all the economies available through a merger. Also, coordination between the holding company and its subsidiaries normally requires additional staff to maintain channels of communication. These diseconomies of administration can be viewed as a type of negative synergistic effect.

 MULTINATIONAL FINANCE

International Combinations

The motives for domestic business combinations stated in this chapter — growth or diversification, synergistic effects, fund raising, increased managerial skills, tax considerations, and increased ownership liquidity — as well as the factors emphasized in Chapters 1 and 2 — including the existence of tariff and nontariff barriers — are all quite applicable to MNCs' international combinations. Several additional points, though, need attention.

First, international joint ventures and acquisitions, especially those involving U.S. firms, have increased significantly in recent years. MNCs based in North America, Western Europe, and Japan have made substantial contributions to this increase. Moreover, a fast-growing group of MNCs has emerged in the past two decades, operating from such home bases as India, Pakistan, Mexico, Argentina, Brazil, Singapore, and Hong Kong, and this has added to the number and value of international acquisitions.

Foreign direct investments in the United States have gained popularity in the past few years, though the amount is still less than half the value of investment by American companies abroad. Most of the foreign (direct) investors in the United States come from one of seven countries: Britain, Canada, France, the Netherlands, Japan, Switzerland, and West Germany, with heavy investments concentrated in manufacturing, followed by the petroleum and trade sectors. Another interesting trend is the current rise in the number of joint ventures between companies based in Japan and firms domiciled elsewhere in the industrialized world, especially U.S.-based MNCs. While Japanese authorities continue their discussions (and debates) with other governments regarding Japan's international trade surpluses as well as perceived trade barriers, joint ventures and other forms of business combinations, acquisitions, and agreements continue to take place. In the eyes of some U.S. corporate executives, such business ventures are viewed as a "ticket into the Japanese market" as well as a way to curb a potentially tough competitor.

Developing countries, too, have been attracting foreign direct investments in both horizontal and vertical industries. Meanwhile, during the last two decades a number of these nations have adopted specific policies and regulations aimed at controlling the inflows of foreign investments, with a major provision being the 49 percent ownership limitation applied to MNCs. Of course, international competition among differently based MNCs has been of benefit to some developing countries in their attempts at extracting concessions from the multinationals. However, an increasing number of such nations have shown greater flexibility in their recent dealings with MNCs as the latter group has become more reluctant to form joint ventures under the stated conditions. Furthermore, given the present, as well as the expected, international economic and trade status, it is likely that as more Third World countries recognize the need for foreign capital and technology, they will show even further flexibility in their business agreements with MNCs.

A final point to note relates to the existence of international holding companies. Places such as Liechtenstein and Panama have long been considered favorable spots for forming holding companies due to their conducive legal, corporate, and tax environments. International holding companies control many business entities in the form of subsidiaries, branches, joint ventures, and other agreements. For international legal (especially tax-related) reasons, as well as anonymity, such holding companies have become increasingly popular in recent years. ●●

CHAPTER SUMMARY

● The common types of business combinations are consolidations, mergers, and holding companies.

● A consolidation involves the combination of two firms of similar size to form a completely new corporation.

● A merger involves combining two firms of unequal size in such a way that the larger of the firms maintains its corporate identity.

● A holding company is a corporation that has a controlling interest in one or more other corporations.

● Motives for business combinations include growth or diversification, synergistic effects, fund raising, increased managerial skills, tax considerations, and increased ownership liquidity.

● A firm can grow horizontally or vertically, or through conglomerate diversification.

● Motives for merging are not mutually exclusive; generally, a mixture provides justification for a business combination.

● Mergers can be transacted by paying cash or through the exchange of stock. In either case, the firm being acquired may be acquired for its assets or as a going concern.

● In cash purchases, traditional capital budgeting procedures using net present value can be employed to evaluate the economic feasibility of the transaction.

● If an exchange of stock is used to acquire a firm, a ratio of exchange of stock must be established. This ratio depends not only on the forecasted earnings per share and market price per share of the merged firm but also on dividends per share, book value per share, and the business and financial risk of the merged firm.

● A key relationship affecting the merged firm's earnings per share and market price per share is the relationship between the price/earnings ratio paid for the acquired firm and the price/earnings ratio of the acquiring firm.

● A merger can be negotiated with the firm's management or directly with the firm's stockholders. Not only do negotiations with management require a favorable cash price or exchange ratio, but certain nonfinancial factors must also be agreed upon. Often the management is given certain sweeteners as part of the payment price or to stimulate positive future performance. If a merger cannot be negotiated, tender offers can be used to purchase stock directly from the owners.

● A holding company can be created by gaining control of other companies, often with as little as 10 to 20 percent of the stock. The chief advantages of holding companies are the leverage effect, risk protection, legal benefits, and the fact that negotiations are not required to gain control of a subsidiary. The disadvantages commonly cited include multiple taxation, the magnification of losses, and high administrative expenses.

 ● International combinations — joint ventures and acquisitions, along with international holding companies — have come to exist for reasons similar to those leading to the creation of their domestic counterparts. Special factors affecting these combinations relate to international taxation, tariff and nontariff barriers, and various regulations imposed on MNCs by host countries.

KEY TERMS

conglomerate growth	ratio of exchange
consolidation	ratio of exchange in market price
holding company	subsidiary
horizontal growth	synergistic effects
horizontal integration	tender offer
merger	total integration
net working capital per share	vertical growth
pyramiding	vertical integration

QUESTIONS

23-1 What are *consolidations* and *mergers*? How are they different? How is the acquisition transacted in each case?

23-2 What is a *holding company*? What are the companies held by a holding company called? How does the holding company arrangement differ from both consolidations and mergers?

23-3 What are the differences among horizontal growth, vertical growth, and conglomerate diversification? In which case could "total integration" result? Why?

23-4 Often in mergers — especially in conglomerate mergers — tax considerations are a key motive for a combination. Why and in what situations may the acquisition of a firm with a *tax loss carryforward* be attractive?

23-5 What should be the financial manager's overriding concern in evaluating possible business combinations? What should this manager's viewpoint be with respect to (1) the earnings per share, (2) the dividends per share, (3) the market price per share, (4) the book value of shares, and (5) the business and financial risk of the firm?

23-6   How should the acquisition of a going concern be evaluated? What difficulties are often encountered?

23-7   What is a *ratio of exchange*? Is it based on the current market prices of the shares of the acquiring and acquired firm? Why or why not?

23-8   What are the important considerations in evaluating the long-run impact of a merger on the combined firm's earnings per share? Why may a long-run view change a merger decision?

23-9   What is a *tender offer*? How might it be used to arrange a merger? Are tender offers the primary tool used to arrange mergers?

23-10   What are the key advantages cited for the holding company arrangement? What leverage effect is involved?

23-11   What disadvantages are commonly cited for the holding company arrangement? What is *pyramiding*?

 **23-12**   In view of the multinational finance discussion in Chapters 1 and 2, along with the issues discussed in this chapter, discuss some of the reasons for the rapid expansion in international combinations of firms.

PROBLEMS

23-1   (**Tax Effects of Acquisition**)   The Whitower Watch Company is contemplating the acquisition of the Sport Watch Company, a firm that has shown large operating tax losses over the past few years. As a result of the acquisition, Whitower believes the total pretax profits of the consolidation will not change from their present level for 15 years. The total tax loss of Sport Watch is $800,000, while Whitower projects annual earnings before taxes to be $280,000 per year for each of the next 15 years. The firm is in the 40 percent tax bracket.

    a   If Whitower does not make the acquisition, what is the company's tax liability each year over the next 15 years?

    b   If the acquisition were made, how much would the company owe in taxes each year over the next 15 years?

    c   If Sport Watch can be acquired for $350,000 in cash, should Whitower make the acquisition based on tax considerations? (Ignore timing.)

23-2   (**Tax Effects of Acquistion**)   The General Restaurant Corporation is evaluating the acquisition of Student Prince Hot Dog Stands. Student Prince has a tax loss carryforward of $1.8 million. The tax loss resulted from earlier operations and can be broken down into the following schedule:

Years remaining	Loss amount
1	$ 400,000
2	200,000
3	600,000
4	100,000
5	500,000
Total	$1,800,000

General Restaurant can purchase Student Prince for $2.1 million. It can sell the assets for $1.6 million—their book value. General Restaurant expects earnings before taxes in the five years following the acquisition to be as follows:

Year	Earnings before taxes
1	$150,000
2	400,000
3	450,000
4	600,000
5	600,000

General Restaurant is in the 40 percent tax bracket.

a Calculate the firm's tax payments for each of the next five years *without* the acquisition.

b Calculate the firm's tax payments for each of the next five years *with* the acquisition.

c What are the total benefits associated with the tax losses from the acquisition? (Ignore timing.)

d Discuss whether you would recommend the proposed acquisition. Support your decision with figures.

23-3 **(Tax Benefits and Price)** Peterson's Pants has experienced losses in the past two years of $400,000 per year. Two firms are interested in acquiring Peterson's for the tax loss advantage. Studs Duds has expected income before taxes of $200,000 per year and a cost of capital of 15 percent. Glitter Threads has expected income before taxes for the next seven years as indicated:

Year	Glitter Threads earnings before taxes
1	$ 80,000
2	120,000
3	200,000
4	300,000
5	400,000
6	400,000
7	500,000

Glitter Threads has a cost of capital of 15 percent. Both firms are subject to 40 percent tax rates on ordinary income.

a What is the tax advantage of the acquisition each year for Studs Duds?

b What is the tax advantage of the acquisition each year for Glitter Threads?

c What is the maximum cash price each interested firm would be willing to pay for Peterson's Pants?

d Use your answers in a through c to explain why an acquisition candidate can have different values to different potential acquiring firms.

23-4 **(Asset Acquisition Decision)** The Gray Printing Company is considering the acquisition of Multicolor Press at a cash price of $60,000. Multicolor Press has liabilities of $90,000. Multicolor has a large press that Gray needs; the remaining assets would be sold to net $65,000. As a result of acquiring the press, Gray would experience an increase in cash inflow of $20,000 per year over the next ten years. The firm has a 14 percent cost of capital.

a What is the effective or net cost of the large press?

b If this is the only way Gray can obtain the large press, should the firm go ahead with the acquisition? Explain your answer.

c If the firm could purchase a press that would provide slightly better quality and

$26,000 annual cash inflow for ten years for a price of $120,000, which alternative would you recommend? Explain your answer.

23-5   **(Cash Acquisition Decision)**   The Toma Fish Company is contemplating acquisition of the Seaside Packing Company for a cash price of $180,000. Both firms have similar business risk. Toma currently has high financial leverage and therefore has a cost of capital of 14 percent. As a result of acquiring Seaside Packing, which is financed entirely with equity, the firm expects its capital structure to be improved and its cost of capital therefore to drop to 11 percent. The acquisition of Seaside Packing is expected to increase Toma's cash inflows by $20,000 per year for the first three years and by $30,000 per year for the following 12 years.

   a   Determine whether the proposed cash acquisition is desirable. Explain your answer.

   b   If the firm's capital structure would actually remain unchanged as a result of the proposed acquisition, would this alter your recommendation? Support your answer with numerical data.

23-6   **(Cash Acquisition Decision)**   Elkheart Oil is being considered for acquisition by Onagonda Oil. The combination, Onagonda believes, would increase its cash inflows by $25,000 for each of the next five years and $50,000 for each of the following five years. Both firms have similar business risk. Elkheart has high financial leverage, and Onagonda can expect its cost of capital to increase from 12 to 15 percent if the acquisition is made. The cash price of Elkheart is $125,000.

   a   Would you recommend the acquisition?

   b   Would you recommend the acquisition if the Onagonda firm could use the $125,000 to purchase equipment returning cash inflows of $40,000 per year for each of the next ten years?

   c   If the cost of capital does not change with the acquisition, would your decision in **b** be different? Explain.

23-7   **(Ratio of Exchange and *eps*)**   Flannagan's Public House is attempting to acquire the Moon Bar and Private Club. Certain financial data on these corporations are summarized as follows:

Item	Flannagan's Public House	Moon Bar and Private Club
Earnings available for common stock	$20,000	$8,000
Number of shares of common stock outstanding	20,000	4,000
Market price per share	$12	$24

Flannagan's has sufficient authorized but unissued shares to carry out the proposed acquisition.

   a   If the ratio of exchange is 1.8, what will be the earnings per share based on the original shares of each firm?

   b   If the ratio of exchanges is 2.0, what will be the earnings per share based on the original shares of each firm?

   c   If the ratio of exchange is 2.2, what will be the earnings per share based on the original shares of each firm?

   d   Discuss the principle illustrated by your answers to **a** through **c**.

23-8 (*eps* **and Merger Terms**)   United Manufacturing Company is interested in acquiring the Boren Machine Company by exchanging four-tenths shares of its stock for each share of Boren's stock. Certain financial data on these companies are given.

Item	United Manufacturing	Boren Machine
Earnings available for common stock	$200,000	$50,000
Number of shares of common stock outstanding	50,000	20,000
Earnings per share	$4.00	$2.50
Market price per share	$50.00	$15.00
Price/earnings ratio	12.5	6

United has sufficient authorized but unissued shares to carry out the proposed acquisition.
a   How many new shares of stock will United have to issue in order to make the proposed acquisition?
b   If the earnings for each firm remain unchanged, what will the postmerger earnings per share be?
c   How much, effectively, has been earned on behalf of each of the original shares of Boren's stock?
d   How much, effectively, has been earned on behalf of each of the original shares of United's stock?

23-9 (**Ratio of Exchange**)   Calculate the ratio of exchange (1) of shares and (2) in market price for each of the following cases.

	Current market price per share		
Case	Acquiring firm	Acquired firm	Price per share offered
A	$50	$25	$ 30.00
B	80	80	100.00
C	40	60	70.00
D	50	10	12.50
E	25	20	25.00

What does each ratio signify? Explain.

23-10 (**Expected** *eps* — **Merger Decision**)   At the end of 1984, Gordo Enterprises had 80,000 shares of common stock outstanding and had earnings available for common of $160,000. The Potut Company, at the end of 1984, had 10,000 shares of common stock outstanding and had earned $20,000 for common shareholders. Gordo's earnings are expected to grow at an annual rate of 5 percent, while Potut's growth rate in earnings should be 10 percent per year.
a   Calculate earnings per share for Gordo Enterprises for each of the next five years, assuming there is no merger.
b   Calculate the next five years' earnings per share for Gordo if it acquires Potut at a ratio of exchange of 1.3.

   c Calculate the next five years' earnings per share for Gordo if it acquires Potut at a ratio of exchange of 1.1.

   d Graph the earnings-per-share figures from **a, b,** and **c.** Explain the differences.

   e Which plan—**b** or **c**—is preferable from the viewpoint of each of the firms? Why?

23-11 (**Expected** *eps*—**Merger Decision**) B. S. Books wishes to evaluate a proposed merger into Plain Cover Publications. B. S. had 1984 earnings of $200,000, has 100,000 shares of common stock outstanding, and expects earnings to grow at an annual rate of 7 percent. Plain Cover had 1984 earnings of $800,000, has 200,000 shares of common stock outstanding, and expects its earnings to grow at 3 percent per year.

   a Calculate the expected earnings per share for B. S. Books for each of the next five years without the merger.

   b What would B. S. Books' stockholders earn in each of the next five years on each of their B. S. Books shares converted into Plain Cover shares at a ratio of (1) .6 and (2) .8 shares of Plain Cover for one share of B. S. Books?

   c Graph the pre- and postmerger earnings-per-share figures developed in **a** and **b.**

   d If you were the financial manager for B. S. Books, what would you recommend from **b,** (1) or (2)? Explain your answer.

23-12 (*eps* **and Postmerger Price**) Data for the Merwin Company and the Lyle Company are given. The Merwin Company is considering the acquisition of the Lyle Company by exchanging 1.25 shares of its stock for each share of Lyle Company stock. The Merwin Company expects to sell at the same price/earnings multiple after the merger as before merging.

Item	Merwin Company	Lyle Company
Earnings available for common stock	$225,000	$50,000
Number of shares of common stock outstanding	90,000	15,000
Market price per share	$45	$50

   a Calculate the ratio of exchange of market prices.

   b Calculate the earnings per share and price/earnings ratio for each company.

   c Calculate the price/earnings ratio used to purchase the Lyle Company.

   d Calculate the postmerger earnings per share for the Merwin Company.

   e Calculate the expected market price per share of the merged firm. Discuss this result in light of your findings in **a.**

23-13 (**Holding Company**) The Magna Company holds stock in company A and company B. A simplified balance sheet is presented for the companies. Magna has voting control over both company A and company B.   *(continued)*

Assets		Liabilities and stockholders' equity	
Magna Company			
Common stock holdings		Long-term debt	$ 40,000
Company A	$ 40,000	Preferred stock	25,000
Company B	60,000	Common stock equity	35,000
Total	$100,000	Total	$100,000
Company A			
Current assets	$100,000	Current liabilities	$100,000
Fixed assets	400,000	Long-term debt	200,000
Total	$500,000	Common stock equity	200,000
		Total	$500,000
Company B			
Current assets	$180,000	Current liabilities	$100,000
Fixed assets	720,000	Long-term debt	500,000
Total	$900,000	Common stock equity	300,000
		Total	$900,000

a   What percentage of the total assets controlled by the Magna Company does its common stock equity represent?

b   If another company owns 15 percent of the common stock of the Magna Company and by virtue of this fact has voting control, what percentage of the total assets controlled does the outside company's equity represent?

c   How does a holding company effectively provide a great deal of control for a small dollar investment?

d   Answer questions a and b in light of the following additional facts.

   (1)   Company A's fixed assets consist of $20,000 of common stock in company C. This provides voting control.

   (2)   Company C, which has total assets of $400,000, has voting control of company D, which has $50,000 of total assets.

   (3)   Company B's fixed assets consist of $60,000 of stock in both company E and company F. In both cases, this gives it voting control. Companies E and F have total assets of $300,000 and $400,000, respectively.

Chapter 24

Failure, Reorganization, and Liquidation

After studying this chapter, you should be able to:

1. Understand the types of business failures and their major causes.

2. Discuss procedures for initiating voluntary settlement for a failed firm and plans to sustain the firm under this arrangement.

3. Describe the objective and basic procedures for private liquidation of a failed firm under a voluntary settlement.

4. Explain bankruptcy legislation, petitions, and the procedures involved in reorganizing the firm under current bankruptcy laws.

5. Review the responsibilities of the trustee in the legal reorganization of the bankrupt firm.

6. Discuss the legal aspects, priority of claims, and discharge procedures for liquidating a bankrupt firm.

The preceding 23 chapters of this text have presented various theories, concepts, tools, and techniques for managing the finances of a business. Unfortunately, not all firms, even if they use these methods, are able to sustain themselves indefinitely; many firms fail each year. In some instances, the failure of the firm may be due to temporary phenomena that can be overcome with the cooperation of outsiders. In others, certain legal procedures can be employed to reorganize the failed firm and eliminate recognized weaknesses. If the weaknesses that caused the firm to fail cannot be eliminated, there are legal procedures for its liquidation.

Although financial managers do not like to think of the reorganization or liquidation of the firm, it is important that they be aware of the consequences of failure and the remedies available to the failed firm. This knowledge is important not only if the firm itself fails but also if the firm should become a creditor of a failed firm. The procedures for collecting at least a portion of the outstanding account when a customer that owes money fails should be understood.

The Nature and Causes of Business Failure

A business failure is an unfortunate circumstance. To provide a sense of the frequency and magnitude of business failure, some statistics are given in Table 24.1. The significant rise in business failures in 1980 and 1981 is clearly reflected by these data; the increase is attributable to the recession and extremely high interest rates experienced between 1978 and 1982. Similar high numbers of failures occurred in 1975 as a result of the severe recession experienced in the 1974–1975 period. Although the majority of firms that fail do so within the first year or two of life, other firms grow, mature, and fail much later. The failure of a business can be viewed in a number of ways and may be the result of one or more causes.

Table 24.1 Business Failure Statistics, 1970–1981

Year	Number of failures	Failures per 10,000 businesses	Average liability per failure[a]
1970	10,748	44	$176,000
1971	10,326	42	186,000
1972	9,566	38	209,000
1973	9,345	36	246,000
1974	9,915	38	308,000
1975	11,432	43	383,000
1976	9,628	35	313,000
1977	7,919	28	391,000
1978	6,619	24	401,000
1979	7,564	28	353,000
1980	11,742	42	395,000
1981	16,794	61	414,000

[a] Values rounded to the nearest $1000.

SOURCE: U.S. Bureau of the Census, *Statistical Abstract of the United States: 1984,* 104th edition (Washington, D.C.: U.S. Government Printing Office, 1983), Table 896, p. 535.

TYPES OF BUSINESS FAILURE

Firms may fail if returns are too low, if they become technically insolvent, or if they become bankrupt.

Low returns. A firm may fail because its returns are low or negative. A firm that consistently reports operating losses has failed to earn at a level that permits it to cover all its costs. From the point of view of existing and prospective shareholders, this performance is not desirable, and it will probably result in the deterioration of the value of the firm in the marketplace. If the firm has negative before-tax earnings, the owners' return is technically less than zero. If the firm cannot earn a return on its assets greater than its cost of capital, it may be viewed as having failed. Thus a firm that just breaks even each period may be considered a failure by its owners, for whose gain it is being operated. The consequences in the marketplace of failure due to low returns can be great, although outsiders cannot pressure the firm to liquidate. When returns are low, corrective action must be initiated and carried out by the owners and directors. Low returns, unless remedied, are likely to result eventually in a more serious type of failure.

Technical insolvency. *Technical insolvency* occurs when a firm is unable to pay its liabilities as they come due. When a firm is technically insolvent, its assets are still greater than its liabilities, but it is confronted with a *liquidity crisis.* If some of its assets can be converted into cash within a reasonable period, the firm may be able to escape complete failure. Though it cannot pay its bills, the firm's assets have not deteriorated and its liabilities have not increased to a point where they exceed the fair market value of the assets. Nevertheless, a technically insolvent firm is illiquid and cannot continue to conduct business without certain changes.

Bankruptcy. *Bankruptcy* occurs when a firm's liabilities exceed the fair market value of its assets. A bankrupt firm has a negative stockholders' equity.[1] This means that the claims of creditors cannot be satisfied unless the firm's assets can be liquidated for more than their book value. Although bankruptcy is an obvious form of failure, *the courts treat technical insolvency and bankruptcy in the same way.* They are both considered to indicate the financial failure of the firm.

Although poor returns to the owners may not be in line with the financial manager's goal of long-run owners' wealth maximization, they are not considered legal evidence of business failure. As long as a firm pays its obligations as they come due and does not allow its liabilities to exceed the fair market value of its assets, it is legally considered healthy. The laws relating to business failures are aimed primarily at protecting creditors. If creditors' claims against a firm are jeopardized, the law allows creditors certain recourse to the firm. Our concern in this chapter is with what the law — not the owners or management of a firm —considers to be business failure.

MAJOR CAUSES OF BUSINESS FAILURE

The major causes of business failure are a lack of managerial skill, economic activity, and corporate maturity.

Lack of managerial skill. The primary cause of business failure is mismanagement, which accounts for more than 50 percent of all business failures. Numerous specific managerial faults can cause the firm to fail. Overexpansion, poor financial actions, a poor sales force, and high production costs may result in the ultimate failure of the firm. Since a firm is generally organized in a hierarchical form, the top manager, president, and board of directors must share the responsibility for the failure of a firm as a result of mismanagement. It is the responsibility of the board of directors to monitor the president's activities, and, of course, the top managers normally report to the president. Each of these parties therefore contributes to the overall success or failure. Since all major corporate decisions are eventually measured in terms of dollars, the financial manager may play a key role in avoiding or causing a business failure. It is his or her duty to monitor the firm's financial pulse.

Economic activity. Economic activity — especially economic downturns — can contribute to the failure of a firm. If the economy goes into a recession, sales may decrease abruptly, leaving the firm with high fixed costs and insufficient revenues to cover these fixed outlays. In addition, rapid rises in interest rates during recession can further contribute to cash flow problems and make it more difficult for the firm to obtain and maintain needed financing. If the recession is prolonged, the likeli-

---

[1] Since on a balance sheet the firm's assets equal the sum of its liabilities and stockholders' equity, the only way a firm that has more liabilities than assets can balance its balance sheet is to have a *negative* stockholders' equity.

hood of survival decreases. The impact of the 1978–1982 recession on the number of business failures in 1980 and 1981 is clearly demonstrated by the data in Table 24.1.

Not all firms are equally affected by macroeconomic activity.[2] In fact, each industry can be viewed as operating in its own microeconomy. Although the national economy may be doing well, the industry in which the firm operates may be in a slump, and firms in the industry may fail. When the macro- or microeconomy is in a slump, competition within an industry is generally heightened. Increased competition is often a cause of business failures during a recession. The failure of a firm during an economic boom, on the other hand, is more often attributable to mismanagement.

Corporate maturity. Firms, like individuals, do not have infinite lives. A firm goes through the stages of birth, growth, maturity, and eventual decline. The idea that a firm, such as IBM, may mature and then decline is hard for many people to comprehend. Yet look what happened to the Penn-Central and many other railroads. Since our country can be considered industrially young, little more than 100 years having passed since Americans began mastering capitalism, the opportunity to observe the failure of businesses due to old age has not been that great. The life cycle of the firm, which is quite similar to a product's life cycle, is shown in Figure 24.1. Each stage of the firm's life is labeled in the figure. The firm's

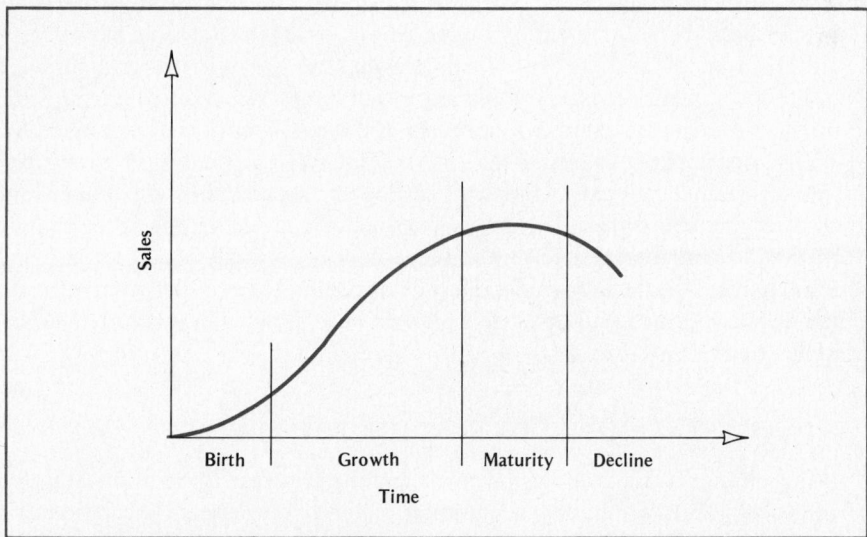

Figure 24.1 The life cycle of a firm

[2] The success of some firms runs countercyclical to economic activity, and other firms are unaffected by economic activity. For example, the sale of sewing machines is likely to increase during a recession since people are more willing to make their own clothes and less willing to pay for the labor of others. The sale of boats and other luxury items may decline during a recession, while sales of staple items such as electricity are likely to be unaffected. In terms of beta—the measure of nondiversifiable risk developed in Chapter 7—a negative-beta stock would be associated with a firm whose behavior generally is countercyclical to economic activity.

management should attempt to prolong the growth stage through acquisitions, research, and the development of new products. Once the firm has matured and begun to decline, it should seek to be acquired by another firm or liquidate before it fails. Good management planning should help the firm to postpone decline and ultimate failure. Single-product firms that fail to diversify are the most likely candidates for eventual failure.

Voluntary Settlements

When a firm becomes technically insolvent or bankrupt, it may arrange with its creditors an "out-of-court" settlement that leaves it in a position to continue operations. If the firm is technically insolvent, the *voluntary settlement* will probably permit the firm to continue operations. But if the firm is bankrupt, the settlement may result in liquidation. Regardless of whether the firm survives or is liquidated, a voluntary settlement enables it to bypass many of the costs involved in bankruptcy proceedings.

INITIATING A VOLUNTARY SETTLEMENT

A voluntary settlement is normally initiated by the debtor firm, since such a settlement may enable it to continue to exist or to be liquidated in a manner that gives the owners the greatest chance of recovering some of their investment. The debtor, possibly with the aid of a key creditor, arranges a meeting between itself and all its creditors. Quite often the meeting is arranged by the adjustment bureau of the local credit managers' association or a trade association. The adjustment bureau or trade association will then act as the mediator of the settlement.

The first item of business at the meeting is to select a committee of creditors to investigate and analyze the debtor's situation and recommend a plan of action. If an adjustment bureau is involved, its investigators may gather the necessary information, leaving the creditor committee with only the analysis and recommendation chores. The recommendations of the committee are discussed with both the debtor and the creditors, and a plan for sustaining or liquidating the firm is drawn up.

VOLUNTARY SETTLEMENT TO SUSTAIN THE FIRM

If the creditor committee recommends and the creditors agree to sustaining the firm's existence, a number of common plans may be used. The rationale for sustaining the firm is normally that it is reasonable to believe the firm's recovery is feasible. By sustaining the firm the creditors can continue to receive business from it. Common strategies for sustaining the firm include extension, composition, creditor control, and a combination of these approaches.

Extension. An *extension* is an arrangement whereby the creditors receive payment in full, although, as one might imagine, not immediately. Extensions are arranged when the creditors feel it is quite likely that the firm can overcome its problems and

THE CHARTER COMPANY BANKRUPTCY: FROM RICHES TO RAGS

Just last month [April 1984] the Charter Company, a $5.6 billion oil and insurance conglomerate that was once Wall Street's favorite, touted itself as a hard-charging, vibrant growth company. Its annual report, dated March 26, displayed a color photograph of smiling Charter chairman Raymond K. Mason, assuring shareholders that the company's "financial condition continues to be strong." In truth, however, Charter was weak — very weak. Twenty-five days later, the company declared bankruptcy and, in so doing, ended a four-year high-wire act during which it had struggled to shore up its shrinking cash supply through financial gyrations while its basic business was slowly bleeding to death.

The end of this corporate saga also closes a chapter in the colorful and volatile life of Mr. Mason, 57, a swashbuckling Florida legend whose penchant for deal-making transformed a small family lumber yard that he took over in 1963 into one of the nation's largest oil companies in the boom of the 70's. Mr. Mason was a king in his own world, shuttling between his castle in Ireland and a 60-acre former Du Pont estate here [Jacksonville, Florida]. He hobnobbed with the rich and powerful: Egyptian President Anwar el-Sadat came calling as did former President Gerald Ford.

But those days are over. His estate here — Epping Forest — has been sold to another oil company executive. His 2.7 million Charter shares, once worth up to $50 apiece, have sunk in value to $3.125 a share. His beloved Charter Company is about to be carved up by creditors who are trying to understand the complex financial empire that came tumbling down two weeks ago. And Mr. Mason has disappeared from public view. "He's no longer the wonder of Wall Street," said one Jacksonville businessman who, like many in this tight community, asked that his name not be used. "He is no longer the host of kings and princes. Charter Company was a major ego trip of a genius and that's out the window now. Mr. Mason is just another fellow that got overextended."

Charter's is more than the tale of a single company gone sour. Its dramatic history caps an era when the oil industry, spurred by OPEC price increases and soaring profits, was dominated by big-money dealmakers and breathtaking acquisitions. The good times generated nonstop earnings that pumped up corporate egos and lifted oil stocks. Yet, a worldwide oil glut ended life in this fast lane for some, and nowhere did it come more to a crashing halt than at Charter's executive suite in a gleaming office tower in downtown Jacksonville. Mr. Mason, ever the optimist, apparently tried for years to keep up a good face on his business through artful accounting that masked the sadder truth that the company was running out of cash — until events overtook him and he could do so no longer.

SOURCE: Leslie Wayne, "Charter's March into Bankruptcy," *The New York Times,* May 6, 1984, p. F-1.

resume successful operations. Normally, when creditors give an extension, they will agree *not* to grant additional credit to the debtor until their claims have been satisfied; they require cash payments for purchases until the past debts have been paid. Occasionally a creditor may agree to subordinate its claims to those of new creditors. This is done to permit the firm to get back on its feet so that repayment is more likely. Quite often the creditor committee will insist on certain controls. It may take legal control of the firm's assets or common stock, take a security interest in certain assets, or reserve for itself the right to approve all disbursements.

When the creditor committee makes its recommendations to the creditors, some creditors may dissent. To keep the firm from bankruptcy, a plan providing for the immediate repayment of the dissenting creditors may be arranged. If a large enough number of creditors dissent and no acceptable solution can be reached, liquidation may be the only alternative. To prevent this situation, the creditor committee is normally made up of representatives of both small and large creditors.

Composition. A *composition* is a pro rata cash settlement of creditor claims. Instead of receiving full payment of their claims, as in the case of an extension, creditors receive only a partial payment. A uniform percentage of each dollar owed is paid in satisfaction of each creditor's claim. The willingness of creditors to accept a composition arrangement depends on their general evaluation of the effects of liquidation. The creditors must weigh their estimate of the amount they would recover in the event of liquidation against the composition and the prospect of future profits from the firm's continued existence. A composition arrangement is quite similar to a reorganization in the event of bankruptcy except that many of the legal and administrative procedures and expenses are bypassed. As in the case of an extension, there may be dissenting creditors, in which case the alternatives are to pay them the full amount they are owed, let them recover a higher percentage of their claims, or liquidate the firm.

Creditor control. Occasionally the creditor committee's investigation results in the general finding that the current management cannot operate the firm so that it will have a reasonable chance for survival. In this case the committee may decide that the only circumstance in which maintaining the firm is feasible is if the operating management is replaced. The committee may then take control of the firm and operate it until all claims have been settled. Once the claims have been settled, it may recommend that a new management be installed prior to the extension of additional credit. The real danger of attempting to sustain a failing corporation through *creditor control* is the opportunity it provides for mismanagement suits by stockholders.[3] For this reason, creditors hesitate to take over the management of a failed corporation.

A combination of approaches. If the creditor committee recommends one of the preceding plans to the creditors and the creditors do not find the plan acceptable, it is likely that, through negotiations, a plan involving some combination of extension, composition, and creditor control will result. An example would be a settlement

---

[3] The existing ownership can sue creditors who are running the company and are unable to sustain the firm. In other words, if the creditor committee is in control when the firm fails, it can be held responsible instead of the original management that placed the firm in technical insolvency or bankruptcy. Even if the creditor committee is assured of winning a mismanagement suit, the time and cost of the litigation are serious drawbacks.

whereby the debtor agrees to pay 75 cents on the dollar in three equal annual installments of 25 cents on the dollar while the creditors agree to sell additional merchandise to the firm on 30-day terms if the existing management is replaced by a new management acceptable to them. Numerous variations and combinations of the plans are possible; the key concerns of creditors center on the likelihood and amount of long-run returns expected from sustaining the firm. If a greater return is expected from liquidation, attempts to sustain the firm are unnecessary.

VOLUNTARY SETTLEMENT RESULTING IN PRIVATE LIQUIDATION

After the situation of the firm has been investigated by the creditor committee, recommendations have been made, and talks among the creditors, the adjustment bureau or trade association, and the debtor have been held, the only acceptable course of action may be liquidation of the firm. Liquidation can be carried out in two ways — privately or through the legal procedures provided by bankruptcy law. If the debtor is willing to accept liquidation, legal procedures may not be required. Generally, the avoidance of litigation enables the creditors to obtain *quicker* and *higher* settlements. However, all the creditors must agree to a private liquidation for it to be feasible. Two aspects of private liquidation that should be highlighted are its objective and its organization.

Objective of liquidation. The objective of the voluntary liquidation process is to recover as much per dollar owed as possible. From management's standpoint, the objective is to recover as much of the shareholders' original investment as possible. The common stockholders, who are the true owners, cannot of course receive any funds until the claims of all other parties have been satisfied. It is the financial manager's responsibility to make sure that the liquidation process is carried out in a manner that is in the best interest not only of creditors but also of the owners.

Organization for liquidation. Liquidation procedures are generally carried out through the adjustment bureau or trade association initially used to organize a voluntary settlement. A common procedure is to have a meeting of the creditors at which they sign a legal contract *assigning* the power to liquidate the firm's assets to the adjustment bureau, the trade association, or a third party, which becomes the *assignee.* The assignee's job is to liquidate the assets, obtaining the best price possible. It may sell the assets at auction, piece by piece, or in bulk. This process of passing title to the firm's assets to a third party, which then liquidates them, is known as *assignment.* Certain legal procedures must be followed when assets are assigned. The *assignee* is sometimes referred to as the *trustee,* since it is entrusted with the title to the assets and the responsibility to liquidate them efficiently. Once the trustee has liquidated the assets, it distributes the recovered funds to the creditors and owners (if any funds remain for the owners). The final action in a private liquidation is for the creditors to sign a release attesting to the satisfactory settlement of their claims. If the creditors do not sign the release, the case may go into bankruptcy court.

Reorganization in Bankruptcy

If a voluntary settlement of a failed firm cannot be agreed upon, the firm can be forced into bankruptcy by its creditors.[4] As a result of bankruptcy proceedings, the firm may be reorganized or liquidated. This section of the chapter is concerned primarily with reorganization in the event of bankruptcy; the following section is devoted to liquidation procedures when bankruptcy is filed.

BANKRUPTCY

Bankruptcy in the legal sense occurs when the firm cannot pay its bills or when its liabilities exceed the fair market value of its assets. In either of these situations, a firm may be declared legally bankrupt. Generally, creditors attempt (if at all possible) to avoid forcing a firm into bankruptcy if it appears to have opportunities for future success. Although bankruptcy proceedings do not necessarily result in liquidation, there is a certain stigma associated with firms that have been reorganized through these proceedings. Voluntary settlements permitting the firm to continue to exist are generally preferable. Firms normally file for reorganization in order to develop a plan for continued existence.

Bankruptcy legislation. The first bankruptcy legislation in the United States was the American Bankruptcy Act of 1800. After a number of repeals and reenactments of this initial act, the Bankruptcy Act of 1898 was passed. The Bankruptcy Act of 1898 was the backbone of bankruptcy law for many years. It was reinforced by the *Chandler Act of 1938.* The *Bankruptcy Reform Act of 1978* (effective October 1, 1979) provided for sweeping changes in the law to allow bankruptcy cases to be resolved more quickly and efficiently. This law contains eight odd-numbered chapters (1 through 15). A number of these chapters would apply in the instance of failure; the two key sections are Chapters 7 and 11.

Chapter 7. Chapter 7 of the Bankruptcy Reform Act of 1978 covers liquidations. It details the procedures to be followed when liquidating a firm. This chapter typically comes into play once it has been determined that a fair, equitable, and feasible basis for reorganization does not exist, although a firm may choose not to reorganize and may instead go directly into liquidation.

Chapter 11. Chapter 11 resulted from the combination of Chapters X and XI of the Chandler Act. Chapter 11 outlines the procedures for reorganizing a failed firm whether its petition is filed voluntarily or involuntarily. If a workable plan for reorganization cannot be developed, the firm will be liquidated under Chapter 7.

Types of petitions. There are two basic types of reorganization petitions — voluntary and involutunary.

---

[4] For a more detailed discussion of the materials presented in this and the following section, see any basic business law text published after 1979.

Voluntary petitions. Any firm that is not a municipal or financial institution or a railroad can file a petition for reorganization on its own behalf. Insolvency is not required to file for *voluntary reorganization.*[5]

Involuntary petitions. Involuntary reorganization is initiated by an outside party, usually a creditor. An involuntary petition against a firm can be filed if one of the following three conditions is met:

1. The firm has past-due debts of $5000 or more.
2. Three or more creditors can prove they have aggregate unpaid claims of $5000 against the firm. If the firm has fewer than 12 creditors, any creditor owed more than $5000 can file the petition.
3. The firm is *insolvent,* which means (a) that it is not paying its debts as they come due, (b) that within the immediately preceding 120 days a custodian (a third party) was appointed or took possession of the debtor's property, or (c) that the fair market value of the firm's assets is less than the stated value of its liabilities.

REORGANIZATION PROCEDURES

The procedures for the voluntary or involuntary reorganization of a corporation (or any entity) are easily implemented. In the reorganization process, certain standard procedures must be employed to provide an acceptable solution. The procedures for the initiation and execution of corporate reorganizations under the Bankruptcy Reform Act of 1978 entail five separate steps: filing, appointment of a trustee, development of a reorganization plan, approval of the plan, and payment of expenses.

Filing. A reorganization petition under Chapter 11 must be filed in a federal district court. In the case of an involuntary petition, if it is challenged by the debtor, a hearing must be held to determine whether the firm is insolvent. If so, the involuntary petition is accepted.

Appointment of a trustee. The judge before whom the reorganization petition is submitted will evaluate it and, upon finding it acceptable, will enter an order approving it. If it is approved, the judge will appoint a trustee for the assets or, depending on the magnitude of the debtor's liability, permit the debtor to remain in possession of them.

Reorganization plan. After investigating the firm's situation, the trustee submits a plan of reorganization to the court. The plan is filed, and a hearing is held to determine whether it should be approved. The main requirement is that the plan be *fair,*

[5] Firms sometimes file a voluntary petition to obtain temporary legal protection from creditors or from prolonged litigation. Once they have straightened out their financial or legal affairs — prior to further reorganization or liquidation actions — they will have the petition dismissed. Although such actions are not the intent of the bankruptcy law, difficulty in enforcing the law has allowed this abuse to occur.

equitable, and *feasible.* The court's approval or disapproval is based on its evaluation of the plan in light of these standards.

Fair and equitable. A plan is considered fair and equitable if it *maintains the priorities* of the contractual claims of the creditors, preferred stockholders, and common stockholders. For example, holders of first-mortgage bonds must be given priority over common stockholders. It would also be unfair to eliminate the original common stockholders as owners if the valuation of the firm indicates that some equity still exists.

Feasible. The court must find the reorganization plan not only fair and equitable, but *feasible,* meaning it must be *workable.* The reorganized corporation must have sufficient working capital, sufficient funds to cover fixed charges, sufficient credit prospects, and sufficient ability to retire or refund debts as proposed by the plan. This requirement is intended to ensure that the reorganized firm can operate efficiently, compete with other companies in the industry, and avoid future reorganization or liquidation.

Approval of the reorganization plan. Once the court has determined that the reorganization plan is fair, equitable, and feasible, the plan, along with a summary, is given to the firm's creditors and shareholders for their acceptance. If the firm's indebtedness exceeds $3 million, the plan must first be submitted to the Securities and Exchange Commission, which makes an advisory report that is attached to the plan before it is reviewed by the creditors and shareholders. The SEC may either recommend or suggest rejection of the plan, but it is the creditors and shareholders who make the decision. Under the Bankruptcy Reform Act, creditors and owners are separated into groups with similar types of claims. In the case of creditor groups, approval by holders of at least two-thirds of the claims as well as a numerical majority of creditors in the group is required. In the case of ownership groups, two-thirds of the shares in each group must approve the reorganization plan for it to be accepted. Once approved, the plan is put into effect as soon as possible.

Payment of expenses. After the reorganization plan has been approved or disapproved, the trustee and all parties to the proceedings whose services were beneficial or contributed to the approval or disapproval of the plan file a statement of expenses. If the court finds these claims acceptable, the debtor must pay these expenses within a reasonable period of time.

THE TRUSTEE'S RESPONSIBILITIES

Since reorganization activities are largely in the hands of the court-appointed trustee, it is useful to understand the trustee's responsibilities. The key responsibilities are the valuation and recapitalization of the firm and the exchange of outstanding obligations for new securities.

Valuation of the firm. The trustee's first responsibility is the valuation of the firm to determine whether reorganization is appropriate. To do this, the trustee must estimate both the *liquidation value* of the enterprise and its value as a *going concern.* If the trustee finds that its value as a going concern is less than its liquidation value, he or she will recommend liquidation; if the trustee finds the opposite to be true, he or she will recommend reorganization. The procedure used to determine the liquidation value of the firm is similar to that described in the discussion of valuation in Chapter 8. Estimating the value of the reorganized firm as a going concern involves forecasting its sales and the earnings from those sales. By applying an appropriate *capitalization rate,* the present value of forecast earnings can be transformed into the value of the firm as a going concern. An example will clarify this approach.

EXAMPLE   Creditors of the Weak Company recently filed and had accepted a petition for the reorganization of the firm under Chapter 11 of the Bankruptcy Reform Act of 1978. The court assigned a trustee, who upon investigation found the firm's liquidation value (after expenses) to be $5 million. The trustee further investigated the firm's past operations and expected industry trends to estimate its future sales. On the basis of his estimate of future sales, the trustee felt safe in expecting the reorganized firm to generate after-tax earnings of $900,000 annually. In view of the firm's changed capital structure and prevailing capital market conditions, a capitalization rate of 15 percent was used to evaluate the estimated earnings. Assuming that the $900,000 annual earnings would continue indefinitely and using the procedure for capitalizing an infinite-lived stream of earnings (Equation 6.28), a value was found for the Weak Company as a going concern: $6 million [$900,000 × (1 ÷ .15)]. Since the firm's value as a going concern was estimated to be greater than its liquidation value ($6 million versus $5 million), the trustee recommended reorganization. If this situation had not resulted, the trustee would have recommended liquidation of the firm. ■

Recapitalization. If reorganization of the firm is recommended by the trustee, he or she must draw up a plan of reorganization. The key portion of the reorganization plan generally concerns the firm's capital structure. Since most firms' financial difficulties result from high fixed charges, the capital structure is generally *recapitalized,* or altered, in order to reduce these charges. Generally, debts are exchanged for equity, or the maturities of debts are extended. Sometimes *income bonds* are exchanged for debentures and mortgage bonds. An income bond requires the payment of interest only when earnings are available from which to make the payment.[6] The trustee, in recapitalizing the firm, places a great deal of emphasis on building a mix of debt and equity that allows the firm to service its debts and provide a reasonable level of earnings for its owners. The valuation of owners' returns after the recapitalization is one of the bases for the reorganization decision. An example will clarify the point.

EXAMPLE   The Weak Company's current (before recapitalization) capital structure, according to its books, is as follows:

---

[6] Although income bonds are generally considered undesirable investments because of the high degree of uncertainty associated with the interest payment, they are commonly used in corporate reorganizations. Since income bonds are a form of debt, their holders have preference over equity holders with respect to the receipt of interest and the recovery of principal.

Debentures	$ 2,000,000
Mortgage bonds	4,000,000
Preferred stock	1,000,000
Common stock	3,000,000
Total capital	$10,000,000

The high financial leverage of this plan is obvious from the debt-equity ratio of 1.5 ($6,000,000 ÷ $4,000,000). Since the firm was found to be worth only $6 million as a going concern, the trustee created a less highly levered capital structure with total capital of $6 million.

Debentures	$1,000,000
Mortgage bonds	1,000,000
Income bonds	2,000,000
Preferred stock	500,000
Common stock	1,500,000
Total capital	$6,000,000

Since interest on an income bond does not have to be paid unless earnings are available to pay it, it can be treated like equity in evaluating the firm's financial leverage. The new debt-equity ratio is .5 ($2,000,000 ÷ $4,000,000), which indicates a considerably safer capital structure for the recapitalized Weak Company. ■

Exchange of obligations. Once the best capital structure has been established in accordance with the firm's value as a going concern, the trustee must establish a plan for exchanging outstanding obligations for new securities. The guiding principle is to *observe priorities.* Senior claims must be satisfied prior to junior claims. To comply with this principle, senior suppliers of capital must receive a claim on new capital equal to their previous claims. The common stockholders are the last to receive any new securities. It is not unusual for them to receive nothing.[7] Security holders do not necessarily have to receive the same type of security they held before; often they receive a combination of securities. An example will clarify this process.

EXAMPLE   The exchange of securities involved in the reorganization of the Weak Company was as follows:

1. The $2 million in debentures were exchanged for $1 million in new debentures and $1 million in mortgage bonds.
2. The $4 million in mortgage bonds were exchanged for $2 million in income bonds, $500,000 of preferred stock, and $1.5 million of common stock.
3. The preferred stockholders received nothing.
4. The common stockholders received nothing.

Since the valuation of the firm allowed a total capitalization of $6 million, only the claims of the original debenture and mortgage bondholders were satisfied through the exchange

---

[7] This procedure is known as *absolute priority.* Although this procedure is most often applied in reorganization, the Bankruptcy Reform Act of 1978 does provide for *relative absolute priority,* which might under certain conditions permit recapitalization along lines more favorable to the lower-priority funds suppliers.

SUGGESTIONS FOR AVOIDING BANKRUPTCY

How can a company in trouble avoid bankruptcy proceedings? Here are some suggestions from Edmond P. Freiermuth, a Santa Monica, Calif., consultant who was a banker for 10 years, making many loans to small and medium-size businesses.

The first thing to do, he says, is analyze the extent of the company's financial difficulties and their causes. Then an estimate should be made of cash receipts and disbursements for the next three to six months.

The projection of cash in and out will probably show disbursements exceeding receipts. "Typically," Mr. Freiermuth says, "management hasn't been as aggressive as it could be in collecting accounts receivable and has let accounts payable go."

The remedy is to cut expenses as quickly as possible. "You have to take a hard look at all expenditures," he says, especially payroll. Usually, he finds more employees than are necessary because small-business owners tend to be reluctant to fire people.

One client hadn't cut its work force even though sales had plunged 50%. "It was incredible," Mr. Freiermuth says. And the concern had been threatened with legal action by creditors who, he says, "were furious."

He convinced the owners that they had to let go half the employees—50 people—for the company to avoid bankruptcy. The owners were able to placate the creditors by honestly stating the condition of the company and explaining what was being done to turn it around. It's a mistake to mislead creditors, Mr. Freiermuth says. They know something is wrong because they haven't been paid, and their cooperation is needed to keep the business out of bankruptcy proceedings.

Chapter 11 of the Bankruptcy Code offers a business protection from creditors while it tries to work out a settlement with them, but it is an expensive process, Mr. Freiermuth says. It involves legal fees that the business can ill afford, and it consumes time that the owners should spend turning the business around. Says the banker-turned-consultant, "I'm a strong believer in avoiding Chapter 11."

SOURCE: Sanford L. Jacobs, "Suggestions for Ailing Firms on How to Avoid Bankruptcy," *The Wall Street Journal,* January 23, 1984, p. 21.

process. The original preferred and common stockholders were virtually eliminated, and the original mortgage bondholders became the firm's new owners. ∎

The Weak Company example should make clear the priorities in reorganization and the close relationship between the value of the firm as a going concern, the recapitalization process, and the ultimate exchange process. In many cases, the original common stockholders will retain some ownership in the firm, although there is no guarantee. Once the trustee has determined the new capital structure and distribution of capital, he or she will submit recommendations to the court as described.

Liquidation in Bankruptcy

A bankrupt company may be liquidated under Chapter 7 of the Bankruptcy Reform Act of 1978. The liquidation of a bankrupt firm usually occurs once the courts have determined that reorganization is not feasible. A petition for reorganization must normally be filed by the managers or creditors of the bankrupt firm. If no petition is filed, if a petition is filed and denied, or if the reorganization plan is denied, the firm must be liquidated. Three important aspects of liquidation in bankruptcy are the legal aspects, the priority of claims, and the discharge of the firm.

LEGAL ASPECTS

When a firm is adjudged bankrupt, the judge may appoint a *referee* to perform the many routine duties required in administering the bankruptcy. The judge (in involuntary bankruptcies) or the referee (in voluntary bankruptcies) may appoint a *receiver* to take charge of the property of the bankrupt firm and protect the interest of creditors during the period between the filing of the bankruptcy petition and the appointment of a trustee or the dismissal of the petition. A receiver is sometimes used to protect the creditors' interests until a trustee is appointed.

Once the firm has been adjudged bankrupt, a meeting of creditors must be held between 10 and 30 days thereafter. At this meeting, creditors make their claims. The meeting is presided over by the judge or referee. The creditors appoint a trustee, who not only takes over the receiver's function but is also responsible for liquidating the firm, keeping records, examining creditors' claims, disbursing money, furnishing information as required, and making final reports on the liquidation. In essence, the trustee is responsible for the liquidation of the firm. Sometimes an advisory committee of three or more creditors is formed either to assist the trustee, or to manage the liquidation process in lieu of a trustee. Occasionally the court will call subsequent creditor meetings, but only a final meeting for closing the bankruptcy is required.

PRIORITY OF CLAIMS

It is the trustee's responsibility to liquidate all the firm's assets and to distribute the proceeds to the holders of *provable claims.* The courts have established certain procedures for determining the provability of claims.[8] The priority of claims, which is specified in Chapter 7 of the Bankruptcy Reform Act, must be maintained by the trustee in distributing the funds from liquidation. The order of priority is as follows:

1. The expenses of administering the bankruptcy proceedings.
2. Any unpaid interim expenses incurred in the ordinary course of business between filing the bankruptcy petition and the appointment of a trustee.
3. Wages of not more than $2000 per worker that have been earned by

---

[8] For a claim to be considered provable, the creditor must file in bankruptcy court within six months of the first creditor's meeting a signed statement specifying (1) the nature of the claim, (2) the amount of the claim, (3) whether any security is held against the claim, (4) whether and in what amount any payments have been made against the claim, and (5) that the claim is justly owed by the bankrupt party to the creditor. Written evidence of the claim must be filed with the creditor's statement.

workers in the three-month period immediately preceding the commencement of bankruptcy proceedings.

4. Unpaid employee benefit plan contributions that were to be paid in the six-month period preceding the filing of bankruptcy or the termination of business, whichever occurred first. For any employee, the sum of this claim plus eligible unpaid wages (item 3) cannot exceed $2000.

5. Unsecured customer deposits, not to exceed $900 each, resulting from purchasing or leasing a good or service from the failed firm.

6. Taxes legally due and owed by the bankrupt firm to the federal government, state government, or any other governmental subdivision.

7. Claims of secured creditors, who receive the proceeds from the sale of the collateral held. If the proceeds from the liquidation of the collateral are insufficient to satisfy the secured creditors' claims, the secured creditors become unsecured creditors for the unpaid amount.

8. Claims of unsecured and subordinated creditors. The claims of unsecured, or general, creditors, unsatisfied portions of secured creditors' claims, and the claims of subordinated creditors are all treated equally. Subordinated creditors must pay the amount required (if any) to senior creditors.

9. Preferred stockholders, who receive an amount up to the par or stated value of the preferred stock.

10. Common stockholders, who receive any remaining funds, which are distributed on an equal per-share basis. If the common stock has been classed, priorities may exist.

It can be seen from this list that the claims of certain nondebtholders have a higher priority than the claims of the secured creditors. The expenses of administering the bankruptcy proceedings, certain unpaid interim expenses, wages, unpaid employee benefits, certain unsecured customer deposits, and taxes are paid first. The secured creditors then receive the liquidated value of their collateral. The claims of unsecured and subordinated creditors, including the unpaid claims of secured creditors, are satisfied next and, finally, the claims of preferred and common stockholders. The application of these priorities by the trustee in bankruptcy liquidation proceedings can be illustrated by a simple example.

EXAMPLE The Failed Company has the balance sheet presented in Table 24.2. The trustee, as was her obligation, has liquidated the firm's assets, obtaining the highest amounts she could get. She managed to obtain $2.3 million for the firm's current assets and $2 million for the firm's fixed assets. The total proceeds from the liquidation were therefore $4.3 million. It should be clear that the firm is legally bankrupt, since its liabilities of $5.6 million dollars exceeds the $4.3 million fair market value of its assets.

The next step is to distribute the proceeds to the various creditors. The only liability not shown on the balance sheet is $800,000 in expenses for administering the bankruptcy proceedings and satisfying unpaid bills incurred between the time of filing the bankruptcy petition and the appointment of the trustee. The distribution of the $4.3 million among the firm's creditors is shown in Table 24.3. It can be seen from the table that once all prior claims on the proceeds from liquidation have been satisfied, the unsecured creditors get to divide the remaining funds on a pro rata basis. The distribution of the $700,000 among the unsecured creditors is given in Table 24.4. The disposition of funds in the Failed Company

Table 24.2   Balance Sheet for the Failed Company

Assets		Liabilities and stockholders' equity	
Cash	$ 10,000	Accounts payable	$ 200,000
Marketable securities	5,000	Notes payable — bank	1,000,000
Accounts receivable	1,090,000	Accrued wages[a]	320,000
Inventories	3,100,000	Unpaid employee benefits[b]	80,000
Prepaid expenses	5,000	Unsecured customer deposits[c]	100,000
Total current assets	$4,210,000	Taxes payable	300,000
Land	$2,000,000	Total current liabilities	$2,000,000
Net plant	1,810,000	First mortgage[d]	$1,800,000
Net equipment	80,000	Second mortgage[d]	1,000,000
Total fixed assets	$3,890,000	Subordinated debentures[e]	800,000
Total	$8,100,000	Total long-term debt	$3,600,000
		Preferred stock (5,000 shares)	$ 400,000
		Common stock (10,000 shares)	500,000
		Paid-in capital in excess of par	1,500,000
		Retained earnings	100,000
		Total stockholders' equity	$2,500,000
		Total	$8,100,000

[a] Represents wages of $800 per employee earned within three months of filing bankruptcy for 400 of the firm's employees.
[b] These unpaid employee benefits were due in the six-month period preceding the firm's bankruptcy filing, which occurred simultaneously with the termination of its business.
[c] Unsecured customer deposits not exceeding $900 each.
[d] The first and second mortgages are on the firm's total fixed assets.
[e] Subordinated to the notes payable to the bank.

liquidation should be clear from Tables 24.3 and 24.4. Since the claims of the unsecured creditors have not been fully satisfied, the preferred and common stockholders receive nothing.

Of the unsecured creditors, the bank holding the notes payable fares the best, thanks to the debentures subordinated to these notes. As a result of the subordination, the bank receives 45 percent of its claims ($450,000 ÷ $1,000,000), whereas the other unsecured creditors receive only 25 percent. The subordinated debenture holders receive nothing as a

Table 24.3   Distribution of the Liquidation Proceeds of the Failed Company

Proceeds from liquidation	$4,300,000
−Expenses of administering bankruptcy and paying interim bills	$ 800,000
−Wages owed workers	320,000
−Unpaid employee benefits	80,000
−Unsecured customer deposits	100,000
−Taxes owed governments	300,000
Funds available for creditors	$2,700,000
−First mortgage, paid from the $2 million proceeds from the sale of fixed assets	$1,800,000
−Second mortgage, partially paid from the remaining $200,000 of fixed asset proceeds	200,000
Funds available for unsecured creditors	$ 700,000

Table 24.4 Distribution of Funds Among Unsecured
Creditors of the Failed Company

Unsecured creditors' claims	Amount	Settlement at 25%[a]	After subordination adjustment[b]
Unpaid balance of second mortgage	$ 800,000[c]	$200,000	$200,000
Accounts payable	200,000	50,000	50,000
Notes payable — bank	1,000,000	250,000	450,000
Subordinated debentures	800,000	200,000	0
Totals	$2,800,000	$700,000	$700,000

[a] The 25 percent rate is calculated by dividing the $700,000 available for unsecured creditors by the $2.8 million owed unsecured creditors. Each is entitled to a pro rata share.
[b] The subordination adjustment concerns the notes payable to which certain debentures are subordinated. The debenture holders must pay what they can from their proceeds *up to* an amount sufficient to satisfy fully the claims of the holder of the notes payable (the bank).
[c] This figure represents the difference between the $1 million second mortgage and the $200,000 payment on the second mortgage from the proceeds from the sale of the collateral remaining after satisfying the first mortgage.

result of their obligation to the bank. The consequences in liquidation of subordinated debt for both the subordinated debtholders and the holders of debts to which other debts have been subordinated should be clear from this example. It is understandable that the firm must normally pay a higher interest rate to raise funds through sale of subordinated debts. They are simply more risky. ■

DISCHARGE OF THE FIRM

After the trustee has liquidated all the assets, distributed the proceeds to satisfy all provable claims in the appropriate order of priority, and made a final accounting of these proceedings, he or she may apply for the discharge of the bankrupt corporation. A *discharge* means that the court releases the bankrupt firm from all provable debts in bankruptcy except for certain debts that are immune to a discharge. If no objections to the discharge are filed, the court will discharge the firm. If objections are filed, the court will hear these objections and make the necessary decisions. If the debtor has not been discharged within the previous six years and did not become bankrupt because of fraudulent actions, he or she is free to enter into business again.

CHAPTER SUMMARY

● A firm's owners and managers may consider low or negative earnings a form of business failure, although these outcomes do not necessarily result in the reorganization or liquidation of the firm.

● Technical insolvency or bankruptcy is more commonly considered an indicator of failure. The technically insolvent firm cannot pay its bills; the bankrupt firm's liabilities exceed the fair market value of its assets. Both technical insolvency and bankruptcy are considered legal forms of bankruptcy.

● The major causes of business failure are lack of managerial skill, changes in general economic activity, and corporate maturity.

● One alternative for the financially failed firm is to arrange a voluntary settlement with its creditors.

● Voluntary settlements are initiated by the debtor and can take one of a number of forms. To sustain the firm, an extension, a composition, creditor control of the firm, or a combination of these strategies can be arranged.

● An extension is an arrangement in which creditors eventually receive full payment.

● Composition involves paying off debts on a pro rata basis.

● Creditor control involves the management of the firm by the creditors until their claims have been satisfied.

● The creditors must agree to any of these plans. If they do not, they may recommend voluntary liquidation, which bypasses many of the legal requirements of bankruptcy. If the firm is liquidated, its assets are assigned to a trustee.

● A failed firm that cannot or does not want to arrange a voluntary settlement can voluntarily or involuntarily file for reorganization or liquidation under the prevailing bankruptcy laws.

● Until 1979, the dominant bankruptcy statute for many years was the Chandler Act of 1938. The Bankruptcy Reform Act of 1978 (effective October 1, 1979) resulted in sweeping changes in the bankruptcy law, providing for quicker and more efficient resolution of bankruptcy cases. Its two key chapters from a corporate standpoint are Chapters 7 and 11.

● Chapter 7 details the procedures to be followed when liquidating.

● Chapter 11 outlines the procedures for reorganizing the failed firm whether it files voluntarily or involuntarily.

● Under Chapter 11, the judge will appoint a trustee. The trustee must determine the feasibility of reorganization by estimating the liquidation value of the firm and its value as a going concern.

● A firm that cannot be reorganized or does not petition for reorganization is liquidated under Chapter 7 of the Bankruptcy Reform Act of 1978. The responsibility for liquidation is placed in the hands of a creditor-appointed trustee, whose responsibilities include the liquidation of assets, the distribution of the proceeds, and an accounting of all his or her actions.

● If all claims are properly handled by the trustee and no objections are filed, the firm is discharged from all unpaid debts. If it has not been discharged within the previous six years, the firm is free to enter into business again.

KEY TERMS

assignment
bankruptcy
Bankruptcy Reform Act of 1978
Chandler Act of 1938
Chapter 7 (Bankruptcy Reform Act)
Chapter 11 (Bankruptcy Reform Act)
composition
creditor control
discharge (in bankruptcy)
extension
fair and equitable (reorganization plan)

feasible (reorganization plan)
involuntary reorganization
priorities (of creditors)
provable claim (in bankruptcy)
recapitalization
receiver (in bankruptcy)
referee (in bankruptcy)
technical insolvency
trustee
voluntary reorganization
voluntary settlement

QUESTIONS

24-1 How can a business that meets all its debt obligations technically be considered to have failed? Are firms that just break even each period considered failures? Why or why not?

24-2 What is the difference between *technical insolvency* and *bankruptcy?* How do the courts view these two situations?

24-3 What are the primary causes of business failure? What types of actions commonly cause business failure?

24-4 What is a *voluntary settlement?* What probable actions will result from a voluntary settlement of a technically insolvent or bankrupt firm? What is the advantage of a voluntary settlement as opposed to a legal settlement?

24-5 Define an *extension* and *composition* and explain how they might be combined to form a settlement plan that permits the continued existence of the firm.

24-6 What is the objective of voluntary liquidation? How is the voluntary liquidation process organized? What are (1) an assignment, (2) an assignee, and (3) a trustee?

24-7 Describe the two key chapters of the Bankruptcy Reform Act of 1978.

24-8 How are *voluntary* and *involuntary* reorganization petitions different? To file an involuntary petition, what are the three key conditions?

24-9 How is the trustee involved in (1) the valuation of the firm, (2) the recapitalization of the firm, and (3) the exchange of obligations using the priority rule in the reorganization of a bankrupt firm?

24-10 Under what conditions is a firm liquidated in bankruptcy? What legal procedures are associated with liquidating the bankrupt firm? What roles do the *referee,* the *receiver,* and the *trustee* play in the process?

24-11 In what order would the following claims be settled in distributing the proceeds from liquidating a bankrupt firm?
  a Claims of preferred shareholders
  b Claims of secured creditors
  c Expenses of administering the bankruptcy
  d Claims of common stockholders
  e Claims of general and subordinated creditors
  f Taxes legally due
  g Unsecured deposits of customers
  h Certain eligible wages
  i Unpaid employee benefit plan contributions
  j Unpaid interim expenses incurred between the time of filing and the appointment of a trustee

PROBLEMS

24-1 **(Voluntary Settlements)** Classify each of the following voluntary settlements as an extension, a composition, or a combination of the two.
  a Paying all creditors 30 cents on the dollar in exchange for complete discharge of the debt.
  b Paying all creditors in full in three periodic installments.
  c Paying a group of creditors with claims of $10,000 in full over two years and immediately paying the remaining creditors 75 cents on the dollar.

24-2 **(Voluntary Settlements)** For a firm with outstanding debt of $125,000, classify each of the following voluntary settlements as an extension, a composition, or a combination of the two.

     a Paying a group of creditors in full in four periodic installments and paying the remaining creditors in full immediately.

     b Paying a group of creditors 90 cents on the dollar immediately and paying the remaining creditors 80 cents on the dollar in two periodic installments.

     c Paying all creditors 15 cents on the dollar.

     d Paying all creditors in full in 180 days.

24-3 **(Voluntary Settlements — Payments)** The Peachtree Business Forms Company recently ran into certain financial difficulties that have resulted in the initiation of voluntary settlement procedures. The firm currently has $150,000 in outstanding debts and approximately $75,000 in liquidable short-term assets. Indicate, for each plan below, whether the plan is an extension, a composition, or a combination of the two. Also indicate the cash payments and timing of the payments required of the firm under each plan.

     a Each creditor will be paid 50 cents on the dollar immediately, and the debts will be considered fully satisfied.

     b Each creditor will be paid 80 cents on the dollar in two quarterly installments of 50 cents and 30 cents. The first installment is to be paid in 90 days.

     c Each creditor will be paid the full amount of its claims in three installments of 50 cents, 25 cents, and 25 cents on the dollar. The installments will be made in 60-day intervals, beginning in 60 days.

     d A group of creditors having claims of $50,000 will be immediately paid in full; the remainder will be paid 85 cents on the dollar, payable in 90 days.

24-4 **(Going Concern and Liquidation Value)** The following table summarizes the earnings after taxes, capitalization rate, and liquidation value of the six firms indicated. Earnings are expected to remain constant over an infinite time horizon.

Firm	Earnings after taxes	Capitalization rate	Liquidation value
A	$ 40,000	15%	$ 250,000
B	140,000	12	1,200,000
C	200,000	12	1,500,000
D	45,000	10	500,000
E	60,000	14	400,000
F	260,000	13	2,000,000

     a Calculate the value of each firm as a going concern.

     b If you were a trustee attempting to maximize shareholders' wealth, would you recommend reorganization or liquidation of each firm?

24-5 **(Reorganization)** Wrightsman Supply is in financial difficulty. The firm has a liquidation value of $1 million and has estimated after-tax earnings of $210,000 per year indefinitely. The firm has a capitalization rate of 12 percent. The trustee in reorganization has recommended the following proposed capital structure based on his valuation of the firm's worth.

Source of capital	Current structure	Proposed structure
Debentures	$ 500,000	$ 250,000
Mortgage bonds	1,250,000	250,000
Income bonds	0	500,000
Preferred stock	250,000	0
Common stock	500,000	750,000
Total	$2,500,000	$1,750,000

a Calculate the value of Wrightsman as a going concern. Would you recommend liquidation or reorganization? Why?

b Calculate and discuss the financial leverage in the current and proposed capital structures using the debt-equity ratio.

c Discuss the exchanges that would result from the proposed recapitalization. Indicate what amount, if any, and what type of capital each of the original suppliers of funds would receive.

d Briefly discuss the requirements of a reorganization plan and indicate the role of priorities in the exchange process.

24-6 **(Reorganization)** The Cannon Paper Company has an estimated liquidation value of $800,000. The firm's earnings are expected to remain at approximately $150,000 indefinitely, and the appropriate capitalization rate is estimated to be 15 percent. The firm's current and proposed capital structures are as follows:

Source of capital	Current structure	Proposed structure
Debentures	$ 500,000	$ 100,000
Mortgage bonds	450,000	200,000
Income bonds	0	400,000
Preferred stock	25,000	0
Common stock	925,000	300,000
Total	$1,900,000	$1,000,000

a Calculate the value of the firm as a going concern. Would you recommend liquidation or reorganization? Why?

b Calculate and discuss the financial leverage in the current and proposed capital structures using the debt-equity ratio.

c Discuss the exchanges that would result from the proposed recapitalization. Be sure to indicate what amount, if any, and type of capital each of the original fund suppliers would receive.

d Discuss the requirements of a reorganization plan and the role of priorities in the exchange process.

24-7 **(Comparison of Recapitalization Plans)** The current capital structure and five proposed capital structures for the Ralston Company are presented.

Source of capital	Current structure	Plan A	Plan B
Debentures	$2,000,000	$ 500,000	$ 0
Mortgage bonds	3,000,000	2,000,000	0
Income bonds	0	1,000,000	3,000,000
Preferred stock	1,000,000	0	0
Common stock	2,000,000	1,500,000	2,000,000
Total	$8,000,000	$5,000,000	$5,000,000

Source of capital	Plan C	Plan D	Plan E
Debentures	$1,000,000	$1,500,000	$1,000,000
Mortgage bonds	0	0	1,000,000
Income bonds	2,000,000	0	1,000,000
Preferred stock	500,000	0	1,000,000
Common stock	1,500,000	3,500,000	1,000,000
Total	$5,000,000	$5,000,000	$5,000,000

a Calculate the financial leverage in the current structure and each of the proposed plans using the debt-equity ratio. Compare the plans' leverage.

b For each of the proposed plans, indicate the exchanges that would result from recapitalization. Indicate what amount, if any, and type of capital each of the original funds suppliers would receive.

c Viewing the proposals from both creditors' and current owners' viewpoints, indicate which reorganization plan you believe to be the most fair, equitable, and feasible. Explain your answer.

24-8 **(Unsecured Creditors)** A firm has $450,000 in funds to distribute to its unsecured creditors. Three possible sets of unsecured creditor claims are presented.

Unsecured creditors' claims	Case I	Case II	Case III
Unpaid balance of 2d mortgage	$300,000	$200,000	$ 500,000
Accounts payable	200,000	100,000	300,000
Notes payable	300,000	100,000	500,000
Subordinated debentures[a]	100,000	200,000	500,000
Total	$900,000	$600,000	$1,800,000

[a] Subordinated to notes payable.

a Calculate the settlement, if any, to be received by each creditor in each case, *ignoring* the subordination.

b Determine the settlement, if any, to be received by each creditor in each case after adjusting for subordination.

c Discuss the effect of subordination on the settlement to be received by the senior issue, or notes payable, in each case.

24-9 **(Liquidation and Priority of Claims)** The Langston Company recently failed and was left with the following balance sheet.

Assets		Liabilities and stockholders' equity	
Cash	$ 80,000	Accounts payable	$ 400,000
Marketable securities	10,000	Notes payable — bank	800,000
Accounts receivable	1,090,000	Accrued wages[a]	500,000
Inventories	2,300,000	Unpaid employee benefits[b]	100,000
Prepaid expenses	20,000	Unsecured customer deposits[c]	50,000
Total current assets	$3,500,000	Taxes payable	250,000
Land	$1,000,000	Total current liabilities	$2,100,000
Net plant	2,000,000	First mortgage[d]	$2,000,000
Net equipment	1,500,000	Second mortgage[d]	800,000
Total fixed assets	$4,500,000	Subordinated debentures[e]	500,000
Total	$8,000,000	Total long-term debt	$3,300,000
		Preferred stock (10,000 shares)	$ 300,000
		Common stock (5,000 shares)	300,000
		Paid-in capital in excess of par	1,500,000
		Retained earnings	500,000
		Total stockholders' equity	$2,600,000
		Total	$8,000,000

[a] Represents wages of $250 per employee earned within three months of filing bankruptcy for 2000 of the firm's employees.
[b] These unpaid employee benefits were due in the six-month period preceding the firm's bankruptcy filing, which occurred simultaneously with the termination of its business.
[c] Unsecured customer deposits not exceeding $900 each.
[d] The first and second mortgages are on the firm's total fixed assets.
[e] Subordinated to the notes payable to the bank.

a The trustee liquidated the firm's assets, obtaining net proceeds of $2.2 million from the current assets and $2.5 million from the fixed assets. In the process of liquidating the assets, the trustee incurred expenses totaling $400,000. Because of the speed with which the trustee was appointed, no interim expenses were incurred.

(1) Prepare a table indicating the amount, if any, to be distributed to each claimant except unsecured creditors. Indicate the amount to be paid, if any, to the group of unsecured creditors.

(2) After all claims other than those of unsecured creditors have been satisfied, how much, if any, is still owed the second-mortgage holders? Why?

(3) Prepare a table showing how the remaining funds, if any, would be distributed to the firm's unsecured creditors.

(4) Discuss what effect, if any, the presence of subordinated debentures has on the payment to the bank holding the notes.

b Rework **a**, assuming that the trustee liquidated the firm's assets for $4.2 million — $2.2 million from the current assets and $2 million from the fixed assets.

c Compare, contrast, and discuss your findings in **a** and **b**.

24-10 **(Liquidation and Priority of Claims)**   The Mindy Corporation recently failed and was liquidated by a court-appointed trustee who charged $200,000 for her services. Between the time of filing of the bankruptcy petition and the appointment of the trustee, a total of $100,000 in unpaid bills was incurred and remain unpaid. The preliquidation balance sheet is as follows:

Assets		Liabilities and stockholders' equity	
Cash	$ 40,000	Accounts payable	$ 200,000
Marketable securities	30,000	Notes payable—bank	300,000
Accounts receivable	620,000	Accrued wages[a]	50,000
Inventories	1,200,000	Unsecured customer deposits[b]	30,000
Prepaid expenses	10,000	Taxes payable	20,000
Total current assets	$1,900,000	Total current liabilities	$ 600,000
Land	$ 300,000	First mortgage[c]	$ 700,000
Net plant	400,000	Second mortgage[c]	400,000
Net equipment	400,000	Subordinated debentures[d]	300,000
Total fixed assets	$1,100,000	Total long-term debt	$1,400,000
Total	$3,000,000	Preferred stock (15,000 shares)	$ 200,000
		Common stock (10,000 shares)	200,000
		Paid-in capital in excess of par	500,000
		Retained earnings	100,000
		Total stockholders' equity	$1,000,000
		Total	$3,000,000

[a] Represents wages of $500 per employee earned within three months of filing bankruptcy for 100 of the firm's employees.
[b] Unsecured customer deposits not exceeding $900 each.
[c] The first and second mortgages are on the firm's total fixed assets.
[d] Subordinated to the notes payable to the bank.   *(continued)*

a If the trustee liquidated the assets for $2.5 million — $1.3 million from current assets and $1.2 million from fixed assets,

    (1) Prepare a table indicating the amount to be distributed to each claimant. Indicate if the claimant is an unsecured creditor.

    (2) Prior to satisfying unsecured creditor claims, how much is owed to first-mortgage holders and second-mortgage holders?

    (3) Do the firm's owners receive any funds? If so, in what amounts?

    (4) What effect, if any, does the presence of the subordinated debentures have on the payments to the bank holding the notes?

b If the trustee liquidated the assets for $1.8 million — $1.2 million from current assets and $600,000 from fixed assets — rework your answers in **a**.

c Compare, contrast, and discuss your findings in **a** and **b**.

Appendix A

Financial Tables

Table A-1 Future-Value Interest Factors for One Dollar Compounded at k Percent for n Periods: $FVIF_{k,n} = (1 + k)^n$

Period	1%	2%	3%	4%	5%	6%	7%	8%	9%	10%
1	1.010	1.020	1.030	1.040	1.050	1.060	1.070	1.080	1.090	1.100
2	1.020	1.040	1.061	1.082	1.102	1.124	1.145	1.166	1.188	1.210
3	1.030	1.061	1.093	1.125	1.158	1.191	1.225	1.260	1.295	1.331
4	1.041	1.082	1.126	1.170	1.216	1.262	1.311	1.360	1.412	1.464
5	1.051	1.104	1.159	1.217	1.276	1.338	1.403	1.469	1.539	1.611
6	1.062	1.126	1.194	1.265	1.340	1.419	1.501	1.587	1.677	1.772
7	1.072	1.149	1.230	1.316	1.407	1.504	1.606	1.714	1.828	1.949
8	1.083	1.172	1.267	1.369	1.477	1.594	1.718	1.851	1.993	2.144
9	1.094	1.195	1.305	1.423	1.551	1.689	1.838	1.999	2.172	2.358
10	1.105	1.219	1.344	1.480	1.629	1.791	1.967	2.159	2.367	2.594
11	1.116	1.243	1.384	1.539	1.710	1.898	2.105	2.332	2.580	2.853
12	1.127	1.268	1.426	1.601	1.796	2.012	2.252	2.518	2.813	3.138
13	1.138	1.294	1.469	1.665	1.886	2.133	2.410	2.720	3.066	3.452
14	1.149	1.319	1.513	1.732	1.980	2.261	2.579	2.937	3.342	3.797
15	1.161	1.346	1.558	1.801	2.079	2.397	2.759	3.172	3.642	4.177
16	1.173	1.373	1.605	1.873	2.183	2.540	2.952	3.426	3.970	4.595
17	1.184	1.400	1.653	1.948	2.292	2.693	3.159	3.700	4.328	5.054
18	1.196	1.428	1.702	2.026	2.407	2.854	3.380	3.996	4.717	5.560
19	1.208	1.457	1.753	2.107	2.527	3.026	3.616	4.316	5.142	6.116
20	1.220	1.486	1.806	2.191	2.653	3.207	3.870	4.661	5.604	6.727
21	1.232	1.516	1.860	2.279	2.786	3.399	4.140	5.034	6.109	7.400
22	1.245	1.546	1.916	2.370	2.925	3.603	4.430	5.436	6.658	8.140
23	1.257	1.577	1.974	2.465	3.071	3.820	4.740	5.871	7.258	8.954
24	1.270	1.608	2.033	2.563	3.225	4.049	5.072	6.341	7.911	9.850
25	1.282	1.641	2.094	2.666	3.386	4.292	5.427	6.848	8.623	10.834
30	1.348	1.811	2.427	3.243	4.322	5.743	7.612	10.062	13.267	17.449
35	1.417	2.000	2.814	3.946	5.516	7.686	10.676	14.785	20.413	28.102
40	1.489	2.208	3.262	4.801	7.040	10.285	14.974	21.724	31.408	45.258
45	1.565	2.438	3.781	5.841	8.985	13.764	21.002	31.920	48.325	72.888
50	1.645	2.691	4.384	7.106	11.467	18.419	29.456	46.900	74.354	117.386

Table A-1 Future-Value Interest Factors for One Dollar Compounded at k Percent for n Periods: $FVIF_{k,n} = (1 + k)^n$ (continued)

Period	11%	12%	13%	14%	15%	16%	17%	18%	19%	20%
1	1.110	1.120	1.130	1.140	1.150	1.160	1.170	1.180	1.190	1.200
2	1.232	1.254	1.277	1.300	1.322	1.346	1.369	1.392	1.416	1.440
3	1.368	1.405	1.443	1.482	1.521	1.561	1.602	1.643	1.685	1.728
4	1.518	1.574	1.630	1.689	1.749	1.811	1.874	1.939	2.005	2.074
5	1.685	1.762	1.842	1.925	2.011	2.100	2.192	2.288	2.386	2.488
6	1.870	1.974	2.082	2.195	2.313	2.436	2.565	2.700	2.840	2.986
7	2.076	2.211	2.353	2.502	2.660	2.826	3.001	3.185	3.379	3.583
8	2.305	2.476	2.658	2.853	3.059	3.278	3.511	3.759	4.021	4.300
9	2.558	2.773	3.004	3.252	3.518	3.803	4.108	4.435	4.785	5.160
10	2.839	3.106	3.395	3.707	4.046	4.411	4.807	5.234	5.695	6.192
11	3.152	3.479	3.836	4.226	4.652	5.117	5.624	6.176	6.777	7.430
12	3.498	3.896	4.334	4.818	5.350	5.936	6.580	7.288	8.064	8.916
13	3.883	4.363	4.898	5.492	6.153	6.886	7.699	8.599	9.596	10.699
14	4.310	4.887	5.535	6.261	7.076	7.987	9.007	10.147	11.420	12.839
15	4.785	5.474	6.254	7.138	8.137	9.265	10.539	11.974	13.589	15.407
16	5.311	6.130	7.067	8.137	9.358	10.748	12.330	14.129	16.171	18.488
17	5.895	6.866	7.986	9.276	10.761	12.468	14.426	16.672	19.244	22.186
18	6.543	7.690	9.024	10.575	12.375	14.462	16.879	19.673	22.900	26.623
19	7.263	8.613	10.197	12.055	14.232	16.776	19.748	23.214	27.251	31.948
20	8.062	9.646	11.523	13.743	16.366	19.461	23.105	27.393	32.429	38.337
21	8.949	10.804	13.021	15.667	18.821	22.574	27.033	32.323	38.591	46.005
22	9.933	12.100	14.713	17.861	21.644	26.186	31.629	38.141	45.923	55.205
23	11.026	13.552	16.626	20.361	24.891	30.376	37.005	45.007	54.648	66.247
24	12.239	15.178	18.788	23.212	28.625	35.236	43.296	53.108	65.031	79.496
25	13.585	17.000	21.230	26.461	32.918	40.874	50.656	62.667	77.387	95.395
30	22.892	29.960	39.115	50.949	66.210	85.849	111.061	143.367	184.672	237.373
35	38.574	52.799	72.066	98.097	133.172	180.311	243.495	327.988	440.691	590.657
40	64.999	93.049	132.776	188.876	267.856	378.715	533.846	750.353	1051.642	1469.740
45	109.527	163.985	244.629	363.662	538.752	795.429	1170.425	1716.619	2509.583	3657.176
50	184.559	288.996	450.711	700.197	1083.619	1670.669	2566.080	3927.189	5988.730	9100.191

Table A-1 Future-Value Interest Factors for One Dollar Compounded at k Percent for n Periods: $FVIF_{k,n} = (1 + k)^n$ (continued)

Period	21%	22%	23%	24%	25%	26%	27%	28%	29%	30%
1	1.210	1.220	1.230	1.240	1.250	1.260	1.270	1.280	1.290	1.300
2	1.464	1.488	1.513	1.538	1.562	1.588	1.613	1.638	1.664	1.690
3	1.772	1.816	1.861	1.907	1.953	2.000	2.048	2.097	2.147	2.197
4	2.144	2.215	2.289	2.364	2.441	2.520	2.601	2.684	2.769	2.856
5	2.594	2.703	2.815	2.932	3.052	3.176	3.304	3.436	3.572	3.713
6	3.138	3.297	3.463	3.635	3.815	4.001	4.196	4.398	4.608	4.827
7	3.797	4.023	4.259	4.508	4.768	5.042	5.329	5.629	5.945	6.275
8	4.595	4.908	5.239	5.589	5.960	6.353	6.767	7.206	7.669	8.157
9	5.560	5.987	6.444	6.931	7.451	8.004	8.595	9.223	9.893	10.604
10	6.727	7.305	7.926	8.594	9.313	10.086	10.915	11.806	12.761	13.786
11	8.140	8.912	9.749	10.657	11.642	12.708	13.862	15.112	16.462	17.921
12	9.850	10.872	11.991	13.215	14.552	16.012	17.605	19.343	21.236	23.298
13	11.918	13.264	14.749	16.386	18.190	20.175	22.359	24.759	27.395	30.287
14	14.421	16.182	18.141	20.319	22.737	25.420	28.395	31.691	35.339	39.373
15	17.449	19.742	22.314	25.195	28.422	32.030	36.062	40.565	45.587	51.185
16	21.113	24.085	27.446	31.242	35.527	40.357	45.799	51.923	58.808	66.541
17	25.547	29.384	33.758	38.740	44.409	50.850	58.165	66.461	75.862	86.503
18	30.912	35.848	41.523	48.038	55.511	64.071	73.869	85.070	97.862	112.454
19	37.404	43.735	51.073	59.567	69.389	80.730	93.813	108.890	126.242	146.190
20	45.258	53.357	62.820	73.863	86.736	101.720	119.143	139.379	162.852	190.047
21	54.762	65.095	77.268	91.591	108.420	128.167	151.312	178.405	210.079	247.061
22	66.262	79.416	95.040	113.572	135.525	161.490	192.165	228.358	271.002	321.178
23	80.178	96.887	116.899	140.829	169.407	203.477	244.050	292.298	349.592	417.531
24	97.015	118.203	143.786	174.628	211.758	256.381	309.943	374.141	450.974	542.791
25	117.388	144.207	176.857	216.539	264.698	323.040	393.628	478.901	581.756	705.627
30	304.471	389.748	497.904	634.810	807.793	1025.904	1300.477	1645.488	2078.208	2619.936
35	789.716	1053.370	1401.749	1861.020	2465.189	3258.053	4296.547	5653.840	7423.988	9727.598
40	2048.309	2846.941	3946.340	5455.797	7523.156	10346.879	14195.051	19426.418	26520.723	36117.754
45	5312.758	7694.418	11110.121	15994.316	22958.844	32859.457	46897.973	66748.500	94739.937	134102.187
50	13779.844	20795.680	31278.301	46889.207	70064.812	104354.562	154942.687	229345.875	338440.000	497910.125

Table A-1 Future-Value Interest Factors for One Dollar Compounded at k Percent for n Periods: $FVIF_{k,n} = (1 + k)^n$ (continued)

Period	31%	32%	33%	34%	35%	36%	37%	38%	39%	40%
1	1.310	1.320	1.330	1.340	1.350	1.360	1.370	1.380	1.390	1.400
2	1.716	1.742	1.769	1.796	1.822	1.850	1.877	1.904	1.932	1.960
3	2.248	2.300	2.353	2.406	2.460	2.515	2.571	2.628	2.686	2.744
4	2.945	3.036	3.129	3.224	3.321	3.421	3.523	3.627	3.733	3.842
5	3.858	4.007	4.162	4.320	4.484	4.653	4.826	5.005	5.189	5.378
6	5.054	5.290	5.535	5.789	6.053	6.328	6.612	6.907	7.213	7.530
7	6.621	6.983	7.361	7.758	8.172	8.605	9.058	9.531	10.025	10.541
8	8.673	9.217	9.791	10.395	11.032	11.703	12.410	13.153	13.935	14.758
9	11.362	12.166	13.022	13.930	14.894	15.917	17.001	18.151	19.370	20.661
10	14.884	16.060	17.319	18.666	20.106	21.646	23.292	25.049	26.924	28.925
11	19.498	21.199	23.034	25.012	27.144	29.439	31.910	34.567	37.425	40.495
12	25.542	27.982	30.635	33.516	36.644	40.037	43.716	47.703	52.020	56.694
13	33.460	36.937	40.745	44.912	49.469	54.451	59.892	65.830	72.308	79.371
14	43.832	48.756	54.190	60.181	66.784	74.053	82.051	90.845	100.509	111.119
15	57.420	64.358	72.073	80.643	90.158	100.712	112.410	125.366	139.707	155.567
16	75.220	84.953	95.857	108.061	121.713	136.968	154.002	173.005	194.192	217.793
17	98.539	112.138	127.490	144.802	164.312	186.277	210.983	238.747	269.927	304.911
18	129.086	148.022	169.561	194.035	221.822	253.337	289.046	329.471	375.198	426.875
19	169.102	195.389	225.517	260.006	299.459	344.537	395.993	454.669	521.525	597.625
20	221.523	257.913	299.937	348.408	404.270	468.571	542.511	627.443	724.919	836.674
21	290.196	340.446	398.916	466.867	545.764	637.256	743.240	865.871	1007.637	1171.343
22	380.156	449.388	530.558	625.601	736.781	866.668	1018.238	1194.900	1400.615	1639.878
23	498.004	593.192	705.642	838.305	994.653	1178.668	1394.986	1648.961	1946.854	2295.829
24	652.385	783.013	938.504	1123.328	1342.781	1602.988	1911.129	2275.564	2706.125	3214.158
25	854.623	1033.577	1248.210	1505.258	1812.754	2180.063	2618.245	3140.275	3761.511	4499.816
30	3297.081	4142.008	5194.516	6503.285	8128.426	10142.914	12636.086	15716.703	19517.969	24201.043
35	12719.918	16598.906	21617.363	28096.695	36448.051	47190.727	60983.836	78660.188	101276.125	130158.687
40	49072.621	66519.313	89962.188	121388.437	163433.875	219558.625	294317.937	393684.687	525508.312	700022.688

Table A-1 Future-Value Interest Factors for One Dollar Compounded at k Percent for n Periods: $FVIF_{k,n} = (1 + k)^n$ (continued)

Period	41%	42%	43%	44%	45%	46%	47%	48%	49%	50%
1	1.410	1.420	1.430	1.440	1.450	1.460	1.470	1.480	1.490	1.500
2	1.988	2.016	2.045	2.074	2.102	2.132	2.161	2.190	2.220	2.250
3	2.803	2.863	2.924	2.986	3.049	3.112	3.177	3.242	3.308	3.375
4	3.953	4.066	4.182	4.300	4.421	4.544	4.669	4.798	4.929	5.063
5	5.573	5.774	5.980	6.192	6.410	6.634	6.864	7.101	7.344	7.594
6	7.858	8.198	8.551	8.916	9.294	9.685	10.090	10.509	10.943	11.391
7	11.080	11.642	12.228	12.839	13.476	14.141	14.833	15.554	16.304	17.086
8	15.623	16.531	17.486	18.488	19.541	20.645	21.804	23.019	24.293	25.629
9	22.028	23.474	25.005	26.623	28.334	30.142	32.052	34.069	36.197	38.443
10	31.059	33.333	35.757	38.337	41.085	44.007	47.116	50.421	53.934	57.665
11	43.793	47.333	51.132	55.206	59.573	64.251	69.261	74.624	80.361	86.498
12	61.749	67.213	73.119	79.496	86.380	93.806	101.813	110.443	119.738	129.746
13	87.066	95.443	104.560	114.475	125.251	136.956	149.665	163.456	178.410	194.620
14	122.763	135.529	149.521	164.843	181.614	199.956	220.008	241.914	265.831	291.929
15	173.095	192.451	213.814	237.374	263.341	291.936	323.411	358.033	396.088	437.894
16	244.064	273.280	305.754	341.819	381.844	426.226	475.414	529.888	590.170	656.841
17	344.130	388.057	437.228	492.219	553.674	622.289	698.859	784.234	879.354	985.261
18	485.224	551.041	625.235	708.794	802.826	908.541	1027.321	1160.666	1310.236	1477.892
19	684.165	782.478	894.086	1020.663	1164.098	1326.469	1510.161	1717.785	1952.252	2216.838
20	964.673	1111.118	1278.543	1469.754	1687.942	1936.642	2219.936	2542.321	2908.854	3325.257
21	1360.188	1577.786	1828.315	2116.445	2447.515	2827.496	3263.304	3762.633	4334.188	4987.883
22	1917.865	2240.455	2614.489	3047.679	3548.896	4128.137	4797.051	5568.691	6457.941	7481.824
23	2704.188	3181.443	3738.717	4388.656	5145.898	6027.078	7051.660	8241.664	9622.324	11222.738
24	3812.905	4517.641	5346.355	6319.656	7461.547	8799.523	10365.934	12197.656	14337.258	16834.109
25	5376.191	6415.047	7645.289	9100.305	10819.242	12847.297	15237.914	18052.516	21362.508	25251.164
30	29961.941	37037.383	45716.496	56346.535	69348.375	85226.375	104594.938	128187.438	156885.438	191751.000

Table A-2 Future-Value Interest Factors for a One-Dollar Annuity Compounded at k Percent for n Periods: $FVIFA_{k,n} = \sum_{t=1}^{n} (1 + k)^{t-1}$

Period	1%	2%	3%	4%	5%	6%	7%	8%	9%	10%
1	1.000	1.000	1.000	1.000	1.000	1.000	1.000	1.000	1.000	1.000
2	2.010	2.020	2.030	2.040	2.050	2.060	2.070	2.080	2.090	2.100
3	3.030	3.060	3.091	3.122	3.152	3.184	3.215	3.246	3.278	3.310
4	4.060	4.122	4.184	4.246	4.310	4.375	4.440	4.506	4.573	4.641
5	5.101	5.204	5.309	5.416	5.526	5.637	5.751	5.867	5.985	6.105
6	6.152	6.308	6.468	6.633	6.802	6.975	7.153	7.336	7.523	7.716
7	7.214	7.434	7.662	7.898	8.142	8.394	8.654	8.923	9.200	9.487
8	8.286	8.583	8.892	9.214	9.549	9.897	10.260	10.637	11.028	11.436
9	9.368	9.755	10.159	10.583	11.027	11.491	11.978	12.488	13.021	13.579
10	10.462	10.950	11.464	12.006	12.578	13.181	13.816	14.487	15.193	15.937
11	11.567	12.169	12.808	13.486	14.207	14.972	15.784	16.645	17.560	18.531
12	12.682	13.412	14.192	15.026	15.917	16.870	17.888	18.977	20.141	21.384
13	13.809	14.680	15.618	16.627	17.713	18.882	20.141	21.495	22.953	24.523
14	14.947	15.974	17.086	18.292	19.598	21.015	22.550	24.215	26.019	27.975
15	16.097	17.293	18.599	20.023	21.578	23.276	25.129	27.152	29.361	31.772
16	17.258	18.639	20.157	21.824	23.657	25.672	27.888	30.324	33.003	35.949
17	18.430	20.012	21.761	23.697	25.840	28.213	30.840	33.750	36.973	40.544
18	19.614	21.412	23.414	25.645	28.132	30.905	33.999	37.450	41.301	45.599
19	20.811	22.840	25.117	27.671	30.539	33.760	37.379	41.446	46.018	51.158
20	22.019	24.297	26.870	29.778	33.066	36.785	40.995	45.762	51.159	57.274
21	23.239	25.783	28.676	31.969	35.719	39.992	44.865	50.422	56.764	64.002
22	24.471	27.299	30.536	34.248	38.505	43.392	49.005	55.456	62.872	71.402
23	25.716	28.845	32.452	36.618	41.430	46.995	53.435	60.893	69.531	79.542
24	26.973	30.421	34.426	39.082	44.501	50.815	58.176	66.764	76.789	88.496
25	28.243	32.030	36.459	41.645	47.726	54.864	63.248	73.105	84.699	98.346
30	34.784	40.567	47.575	56.084	66.438	79.057	94.459	113.282	136.305	164.491
35	41.659	49.994	60.461	73.651	90.318	111.432	138.234	172.314	215.705	271.018
40	48.885	60.401	75.400	95.024	120.797	154.758	199.630	259.052	337.872	442.580
45	56.479	71.891	92.718	121.027	159.695	212.737	285.741	386.497	525.840	718.881
50	64.461	84.577	112.794	152.664	209.341	290.325	406.516	573.756	815.051	1163.865

Table A-2   Future-Value Interest Factors for a One-Dollar Annuity Compounded at k Percent for n Periods: $FVIFA_{k,n} = \sum_{t=1}^{n} (1 + k)^{t-1}$ (continued)

Period	11%	12%	13%	14%	15%	16%	17%	18%	19%	20%
1	1.000	1.000	1.000	1.000	1.000	1.000	1.000	1.000	1.000	1.000
2	2.110	2.120	2.130	2.140	2.150	2.160	2.170	2.180	2.190	2.200
3	3.342	3.374	3.407	3.440	3.472	3.506	3.539	3.572	3.606	3.640
4	4.710	4.779	4.850	4.921	4.993	5.066	5.141	5.215	5.291	5.368
5	6.228	6.353	6.480	6.610	6.742	6.877	7.014	7.154	7.297	7.442
6	7.913	8.115	8.323	8.535	8.754	8.977	9.207	9.442	9.683	9.930
7	9.783	10.089	10.405	10.730	11.067	11.414	11.772	12.141	12.523	12.916
8	11.859	12.300	12.757	13.233	13.727	14.240	14.773	15.327	15.902	16.499
9	14.164	14.776	15.416	16.085	16.786	17.518	18.285	19.086	19.923	20.799
10	16.722	17.549	18.420	19.337	20.304	21.321	22.393	23.521	24.709	25.959
11	19.561	20.655	21.814	23.044	24.349	25.733	27.200	28.755	30.403	32.150
12	22.713	24.133	25.650	27.271	29.001	30.850	32.824	34.931	37.180	39.580
13	26.211	28.029	29.984	32.088	34.352	36.786	39.404	42.218	45.244	48.496
14	30.095	32.392	34.882	37.581	40.504	43.672	47.102	50.818	54.841	59.196
15	34.405	37.280	40.417	43.842	47.580	51.659	56.109	60.965	66.260	72.035
16	39.190	42.753	46.671	50.980	55.717	60.925	66.648	72.938	79.850	87.442
17	44.500	48.883	53.738	59.117	65.075	71.673	78.978	87.067	96.021	105.930
18	50.396	55.749	61.724	68.393	75.836	84.140	93.404	103.739	115.265	128.116
19	56.939	63.439	70.748	78.968	88.211	98.603	110.283	123.412	138.165	154.739
20	64.202	72.052	80.946	91.024	102.443	115.379	130.031	146.626	165.417	186.687
21	72.264	81.698	92.468	104.767	118.809	134.840	153.136	174.019	197.846	225.024
22	81.213	92.502	105.489	120.434	137.630	157.414	180.169	206.342	236.436	271.028
23	91.147	104.602	120.203	138.295	159.274	183.600	211.798	244.483	282.359	326.234
24	102.173	118.154	136.829	158.656	184.166	213.976	248.803	289.490	337.007	392.480
25	114.412	133.333	155.616	181.867	212.790	249.212	292.099	342.598	402.038	471.976
30	199.018	241.330	293.192	356.778	434.738	530.306	647.423	790.932	966.698	1181.865
35	341.583	431.658	546.663	693.552	881.152	1120.699	1426.448	1816.607	2314.173	2948.294
40	581.812	767.080	1013.667	1341.979	1779.048	2360.724	3134.412	4163.094	5529.711	7343.715
45	986.613	1358.208	1874.086	2590.464	3585.031	4965.191	6879.008	9531.258	13203.105	18280.914
50	1668.723	2399.975	3459.344	4994.301	7217.488	10435.449	15088.805	21812.273	31514.492	45496.094

Table A-2 Future-Value Interest Factors for a One-Dollar Annuity Compounded at k Percent for n Periods: $FVIFA_{k,n} = \sum_{t=1}^{n} (1 + k)^{t-1}$ (continued)

Period	21%	22%	23%	24%	25%	26%	27%	28%	29%	30%
1	1.000	1.000	1.000	1.000	1.000	1.000	1.000	1.000	1.000	1.000
2	2.210	2.220	2.230	2.240	2.250	2.260	2.270	2.280	2.290	2.300
3	3.674	3.708	3.743	3.778	3.813	3.848	3.883	3.918	3.954	3.990
4	5.446	5.524	5.604	5.684	5.766	5.848	5.931	6.016	6.101	6.187
5	7.589	7.740	7.893	8.048	8.207	8.368	8.533	8.700	8.870	9.043
6	10.183	10.442	10.708	10.980	11.259	11.544	11.837	12.136	12.442	12.756
7	13.321	13.740	14.171	14.615	15.073	15.546	16.032	16.534	17.051	17.583
8	17.119	17.762	18.430	19.123	19.842	20.588	21.361	22.163	22.995	23.858
9	21.714	22.670	23.669	24.712	25.802	26.940	28.129	29.369	30.664	32.015
10	27.274	28.657	30.113	31.643	33.253	34.945	36.723	38.592	40.556	42.619
11	34.001	35.962	38.039	40.238	42.566	45.030	47.639	50.398	53.318	56.405
12	42.141	44.873	47.787	50.895	54.208	57.738	61.501	65.510	69.780	74.326
13	51.991	55.745	59.778	64.109	68.760	73.750	79.106	84.853	91.016	97.624
14	63.909	69.009	74.528	80.496	86.949	93.925	101.465	109.611	118.411	127.912
15	78.330	85.191	92.669	100.815	109.687	119.346	129.860	141.302	153.750	167.285
16	95.779	104.933	114.983	126.010	138.109	151.375	165.922	181.867	199.337	218.470
17	116.892	129.019	142.428	157.252	173.636	191.733	211.721	233.790	258.145	285.011
18	142.439	158.403	176.187	195.993	218.045	242.583	269.885	300.250	334.006	371.514
19	173.351	194.251	217.710	244.031	273.556	306.654	343.754	385.321	431.868	483.968
20	210.755	237.986	268.783	303.598	342.945	387.384	437.568	494.210	558.110	630.157
21	256.013	291.343	331.603	377.461	429.681	489.104	556.710	633.589	720.962	820.204
22	310.775	356.438	408.871	469.052	538.101	617.270	708.022	811.993	931.040	1067.265
23	377.038	435.854	503.911	582.624	673.626	778.760	900.187	1040.351	1202.042	1388.443
24	457.215	532.741	620.810	723.453	843.032	982.237	1144.237	1332.649	1551.634	1805.975
25	554.230	650.944	764.596	898.082	1054.791	1238.617	1454.180	1706.790	2002.608	2348.765
30	1445.111	1767.044	2160.459	2640.881	3227.172	3941.953	4812.891	5873.172	7162.785	8729.805
35	3755.814	4783.520	6090.227	7750.094	9856.746	12527.160	15909.480	20188.742	25596.512	32422.090
40	9749.141	12936.141	17153.691	22728.367	30088.621	39791.957	52570.707	69376.562	91447.375	120389.375
45	25294.223	34970.230	48300.660	66638.937	91831.312	126378.937	173692.875	238384.312	326686.375	447005.062

Table A-2 Future-Value Interest Factors for a One-Dollar Annuity Compounded at k Percent for n Periods: $FVIFA_{k,n} = \sum_{t=1}^{n} (1 + k)^{t-1}$ (continued)

Period	31%	32%	33%	34%	35%	36%	37%	38%	39%	40%
1	1.000	1.000	1.000	1.000	1.000	1.000	1.000	1.000	1.000	1.000
2	2.310	2.320	2.330	2.340	2.350	2.360	2.370	2.380	2.390	2.400
3	4.026	4.062	4.099	4.136	4.172	4.210	4.247	4.284	4.322	4.360
4	6.274	6.362	6.452	6.542	6.633	6.725	6.818	6.912	7.008	7.104
5	9.219	9.398	9.581	9.766	9.954	10.146	10.341	10.539	10.741	10.946
6	13.077	13.406	13.742	14.086	14.438	14.799	15.167	15.544	15.930	16.324
7	18.131	18.696	19.277	19.876	20.492	21.126	21.779	22.451	23.142	23.853
8	24.752	25.678	26.638	27.633	28.664	29.732	30.837	31.982	33.167	34.395
9	33.425	34.895	36.429	38.028	39.696	41.435	43.247	45.135	47.103	49.152
10	44.786	47.062	49.451	51.958	54.590	57.351	60.248	63.287	66.473	69.813
11	59.670	63.121	66.769	70.624	74.696	78.998	83.540	88.335	93.397	98.739
12	79.167	84.320	89.803	95.636	101.840	108.437	115.450	122.903	130.822	139.234
13	104.709	112.302	120.438	129.152	138.484	148.474	159.166	170.606	182.842	195.928
14	138.169	149.239	161.183	174.063	187.953	202.925	219.058	236.435	255.151	275.299
15	182.001	197.996	215.373	234.245	254.737	276.978	301.109	327.281	355.659	386.418
16	239.421	262.354	287.446	314.888	344.895	377.690	413.520	452.647	495.366	541.985
17	314.642	347.307	383.303	422.949	466.608	514.658	567.521	625.652	689.558	759.778
18	413.180	459.445	510.792	567.751	630.920	700.935	778.504	864.399	959.485	1064.689
19	542.266	607.467	680.354	761.786	852.741	954.271	1067.551	1193.870	1334.683	1491.563
20	711.368	802.856	905.870	1021.792	1152.200	1298.809	1463.544	1648.539	1856.208	2089.188
21	932.891	1060.769	1205.807	1370.201	1556.470	1767.380	2006.055	2275.982	2581.128	2925.862
22	1223.087	1401.215	1604.724	1837.068	2102.234	2404.636	2749.294	3141.852	3588.765	4097.203
23	1603.243	1850.603	2135.282	2462.669	2839.014	3271.304	3767.532	4336.750	4989.379	5737.078
24	2101.247	2443.795	2840.924	3300.974	3833.667	4449.969	5162.516	5985.711	6936.230	8032.906
25	2753.631	3226.808	3779.428	4424.301	5176.445	6052.957	7073.645	8261.273	9642.352	11247.062
30	10632.543	12940.672	15737.945	19124.434	23221.258	28172.016	34148.906	41357.227	50043.625	60500.207
35	41028.887	51868.563	65504.199	82634.625	104134.500	131082.625	164818.438	206998.375	259680.313	325394.688

Table A-2 Future-Value Interest Factors for a One-Dollar Annuity Compounded at k Percent for n Periods: $FVIFA_{k,n} = \sum_{t=1}^{n} (1 + k)^{t-1}$ (continued)

Period	41%	42%	43%	44%	45%	46%	47%	48%	49%	50%
1	1.000	1.000	1.000	1.000	1.000	1.000	1.000	1.000	1.000	1.000
2	2.410	2.420	2.430	2.440	2.450	2.460	2.470	2.480	2.490	2.500
3	4.398	4.436	4.475	4.514	4.552	4.592	4.631	4.670	4.710	4.750
4	7.201	7.300	7.399	7.500	7.601	7.704	7.807	7.912	8.018	8.125
5	11.154	11.366	11.581	11.799	12.022	12.247	12.477	12.710	12.947	13.188
6	16.727	17.139	17.560	17.991	18.431	18.881	19.341	19.811	20.291	20.781
7	24.585	25.337	26.111	26.907	27.725	28.567	29.431	30.320	31.233	32.172
8	35.665	36.979	38.339	39.746	41.202	42.707	44.264	45.874	47.538	49.258
9	51.287	53.510	55.825	58.235	60.743	63.352	66.068	68.893	71.831	74.887
10	73.315	76.985	80.830	84.858	89.077	93.494	98.120	102.961	108.028	113.330
11	104.374	110.318	116.586	123.195	130.161	137.502	145.236	153.383	161.962	170.995
12	148.168	157.651	167.719	178.401	189.734	201.752	214.497	228.007	242.323	257.493
13	209.916	224.865	240.837	257.897	276.114	295.558	316.310	338.449	362.062	387.239
14	296.982	320.308	345.397	372.372	401.365	432.514	465.975	501.905	540.471	581.858
15	419.744	455.837	494.918	537.215	582.980	632.470	685.983	743.819	806.302	873.788
16	592.839	648.288	708.732	774.589	846.321	924.406	1009.394	1101.852	1202.390	1311.681
17	836.903	921.568	1014.486	1116.408	1228.165	1350.631	1484.809	1631.740	1792.560	1968.522
18	1181.034	1309.625	1451.714	1608.626	1781.838	1972.920	2183.667	2415.974	2671.914	2953.783
19	1666.257	1860.666	2076.949	2317.421	2584.665	2881.461	3210.989	3576.640	3982.150	4431.672
20	2350.422	2643.144	2971.035	3338.084	3748.763	4207.926	4721.148	5294.422	5934.402	6648.508
21	3315.095	3754.262	4249.574	4807.836	5436.703	6144.566	6941.082	7836.742	8843.254	9973.762
22	4675.281	5332.047	6077.887	6924.281	7884.215	8972.059	10204.383	11599.375	13177.441	14961.645
23	6593.145	7572.500	8692.375	9971.957	11433.109	13100.195	15001.434	17168.066	19635.383	22443.469
24	9297.332	10753.941	12431.090	14360.613	16579.008	19127.273	22053.094	25409.730	29257.707	33666.207
25	13110.234	15271.582	17777.445	20680.270	24040.555	27926.797	32419.027	37607.387	43594.965	50500.316
30	73075.500	88181.938	106315.250	128058.125	154105.313	185273.000	222540.625	267055.375	320172.750	383500.000

Table A-3 Present-Value Interest Factors for One Dollar Discounted at k Percent for n Periods: $PVIF_{k,n} = \dfrac{1}{(1+k)^n}$

Period	1%	2%	3%	4%	5%	6%	7%	8%	9%	10%
1	.990	.980	.971	.962	.952	.943	.935	.926	.917	.909
2	.980	.961	.943	.925	.907	.890	.873	.857	.842	.826
3	.971	.942	.915	.889	.864	.840	.816	.794	.772	.751
4	.961	.924	.888	.855	.823	.792	.763	.735	.708	.683
5	.951	.906	.863	.822	.784	.747	.713	.681	.650	.621
6	.942	.888	.837	.790	.746	.705	.666	.630	.596	.564
7	.933	.871	.813	.760	.711	.665	.623	.583	.547	.513
8	.923	.853	.789	.731	.677	.627	.582	.540	.502	.467
9	.914	.837	.766	.703	.645	.592	.544	.500	.460	.424
10	.905	.820	.744	.676	.614	.558	.508	.463	.422	.386
11	.896	.804	.722	.650	.585	.527	.475	.429	.388	.350
12	.887	.789	.701	.625	.557	.497	.444	.397	.356	.319
13	.879	.773	.681	.601	.530	.469	.415	.368	.326	.290
14	.870	.758	.661	.577	.505	.442	.388	.340	.299	.263
15	.861	.743	.642	.555	.481	.417	.362	.315	.275	.239
16	.853	.728	.623	.534	.458	.394	.339	.292	.252	.218
17	.844	.714	.605	.513	.436	.371	.317	.270	.231	.198
18	.836	.700	.587	.494	.416	.350	.296	.250	.212	.180
19	.828	.686	.570	.475	.396	.331	.277	.232	.194	.164
20	.820	.673	.554	.456	.377	.312	.258	.215	.178	.149
21	.811	.660	.538	.439	.359	.294	.242	.199	.164	.135
22	.803	.647	.522	.422	.342	.278	.226	.184	.150	.123
23	.795	.634	.507	.406	.326	.262	.211	.170	.138	.112
24	.788	.622	.492	.390	.310	.247	.197	.158	.126	.102
25	.780	.610	.478	.375	.295	.233	.184	.146	.116	.092
30	.742	.552	.412	.308	.231	.174	.131	.099	.075	.057
35	.706	.500	.355	.253	.181	.130	.094	.068	.049	.036
40	.672	.453	.307	.208	.142	.097	.067	.046	.032	.022
45	.639	.410	.264	.171	.111	.073	.048	.031	.021	.014
50	.608	.372	.228	.141	.087	.054	.034	.021	.013	.009

Table A-3 Present-Value Interest Factors for One Dollar Discounted at k Percent for n Periods: $PVIF_{k,n} = \dfrac{1}{(1+k)^n}$ (continued)

Period	11%	12%	13%	14%	15%	16%	17%	18%	19%	20%
1	.901	.893	.885	.877	.870	.862	.855	.847	.840	.833
2	.812	.797	.783	.769	.756	.743	.731	.718	.706	.694
3	.731	.712	.693	.675	.658	.641	.624	.609	.593	.579
4	.659	.636	.613	.592	.572	.552	.534	.516	.499	.482
5	.593	.567	.543	.519	.497	.476	.456	.437	.419	.402
6	.535	.507	.480	.456	.432	.410	.390	.370	.352	.335
7	.482	.452	.425	.400	.376	.354	.333	.314	.296	.279
8	.434	.404	.376	.351	.327	.305	.285	.266	.249	.233
9	.391	.361	.333	.308	.284	.263	.243	.225	.209	.194
10	.352	.322	.295	.270	.247	.227	.208	.191	.176	.162
11	.317	.287	.261	.237	.215	.195	.178	.162	.148	.135
12	.286	.257	.231	.208	.187	.168	.152	.137	.124	.112
13	.258	.229	.204	.182	.163	.145	.130	.116	.104	.093
14	.232	.205	.181	.160	.141	.125	.111	.099	.088	.078
15	.209	.183	.160	.140	.123	.108	.095	.084	.074	.065
16	.188	.163	.141	.123	.107	.093	.081	.071	.062	.054
17	.170	.146	.125	.108	.093	.080	.069	.060	.052	.045
18	.153	.130	.111	.095	.081	.069	.059	.051	.044	.038
19	.138	.116	.098	.083	.070	.060	.051	.043	.037	.031
20	.124	.104	.087	.073	.061	.051	.043	.037	.031	.026
21	.112	.093	.077	.064	.053	.044	.037	.031	.026	.022
22	.101	.083	.068	.056	.046	.038	.032	.026	.022	.018
23	.091	.074	.060	.049	.040	.033	.027	.022	.018	.015
24	.082	.066	.053	.043	.035	.028	.023	.019	.015	.013
25	.074	.059	.047	.038	.030	.024	.020	.016	.013	.010
30	.044	.033	.026	.020	.015	.012	.009	.007	.005	.004
35	.026	.019	.014	.010	.008	.006	.004	.003	.002	.002
40	.015	.011	.008	.005	.004	.003	.002	.001	.001	.001
45	.009	.006	.004	.003	.002	.001	.001	.001	*	*
50	.005	.003	.002	.001	.001	.001	*	*	*	*

*$PVIF$ is zero to three decimal places.

Table A-3   Present-Value Interest Factors for One Dollar Discounted at k Percent for n Periods: $PVIF_{k,n} = \dfrac{1}{(1 + k)^n}$ (continued)

Period	21%	22%	23%	24%	25%	26%	27%	28%	29%	30%
1	.826	.820	.813	.806	.800	.794	.787	.781	.775	.769
2	.683	.672	.661	.650	.640	.630	.620	.610	.601	.592
3	.564	.551	.537	.524	.512	.500	.488	.477	.466	.455
4	.467	.451	.437	.423	.410	.397	.384	.373	.361	.350
5	.386	.370	.355	.341	.328	.315	.303	.291	.280	.269
6	.319	.303	.289	.275	.262	.250	.238	.227	.217	.207
7	.263	.249	.235	.222	.210	.198	.188	.178	.168	.159
8	.218	.204	.191	.179	.168	.157	.148	.139	.130	.123
9	.180	.167	.155	.144	.134	.125	.116	.108	.101	.094
10	.149	.137	.126	.116	.107	.099	.092	.085	.078	.073
11	.123	.112	.103	.094	.086	.079	.072	.066	.061	.056
12	.102	.092	.083	.076	.069	.062	.057	.052	.047	.043
13	.084	.075	.068	.061	.055	.050	.045	.040	.037	.033
14	.069	.062	.055	.049	.044	.039	.035	.032	.028	.025
15	.057	.051	.045	.040	.035	.031	.028	.025	.022	.020
16	.047	.042	.036	.032	.028	.025	.022	.019	.017	.015
17	.039	.034	.030	.026	.023	.020	.017	.015	.013	.012
18	.032	.028	.024	.021	.018	.016	.014	.012	.010	.009
19	.027	.023	.020	.017	.014	.012	.011	.009	.008	.007
20	.022	.019	.016	.014	.012	.010	.008	.007	.006	.005
21	.018	.015	.013	.011	.009	.008	.007	.006	.005	.004
22	.015	.013	.011	.009	.007	.006	.005	.004	.004	.003
23	.012	.010	.009	.007	.006	.005	.004	.003	.003	.002
24	.010	.008	.007	.006	.005	.004	.003	.003	.002	.002
25	.009	.007	.006	.005	.004	.003	.003	.002	.002	.001
30	.003	.003	.002	.002	.001	.001	.001	.001	*	*
35	.001	.001	.001	.001	*	*	*	*	*	*
40	*	*	*	*	*	*	*	*	*	*
45	*	*	*	*	*	*	*	*	*	*
50	*	*	*	*	*	*	*	*	*	*

PVIF is zero to three decimal places.

Table A-3 Present-Value Interest Factors for One Dollar Discounted at k Percent for n Periods: $PVIF_{k,n} = \dfrac{1}{(1+k)^n}$ (continued)

Period	31%	32%	33%	34%	35%	36%	37%	38%	39%	40%
1	.763	.758	.752	.746	.741	.735	.730	.725	.719	.714
2	.583	.574	.565	.557	.549	.541	.533	.525	.518	.510
3	.445	.435	.425	.416	.406	.398	.389	.381	.372	.364
4	.340	.329	.320	.310	.301	.292	.284	.276	.268	.260
5	.259	.250	.240	.231	.223	.215	.207	.200	.193	.186
6	.198	.189	.181	.173	.165	.158	.151	.145	.139	.133
7	.151	.143	.136	.129	.122	.116	.110	.105	.100	.095
8	.115	.108	.102	.096	.091	.085	.081	.076	.072	.068
9	.088	.082	.077	.072	.067	.063	.059	.055	.052	.048
10	.067	.062	.058	.054	.050	.046	.043	.040	.037	.035
11	.051	.047	.043	.040	.037	.034	.031	.029	.027	.025
12	.039	.036	.033	.030	.027	.025	.023	.021	.019	.018
13	.030	.027	.025	.022	.020	.018	.017	.015	.014	.013
14	.023	.021	.018	.017	.015	.014	.012	.011	.010	.009
15	.017	.016	.014	.012	.011	.010	.009	.008	.007	.006
16	.013	.012	.010	.009	.008	.007	.006	.006	.005	.005
17	.010	.009	.008	.007	.006	.005	.005	.004	.004	.003
18	.008	.007	.006	.005	.005	.004	.003	.003	.003	.002
19	.006	.005	.004	.004	.003	.003	.003	.002	.002	.002
20	.005	.004	.003	.003	.002	.002	.002	.002	.001	.001
21	.003	.003	.003	.002	.002	.002	.001	.001	.001	.001
22	.003	.002	.002	.002	.001	.001	.001	.001	.001	.001
23	.002	.002	.001	.001	.001	.001	.001	.001	.001	*
24	.002	.001	.001	.001	.001	.001	.001	.001	*	*
25	.001	.001	.001	.001	.001	*	*	*	*	*
30	*	*	*	*	*	*	*	*	*	*
35	*	*	*	*	*	*	*	*	*	*
40	*	*	*	*	*	*	*	*	*	*
45	*	*	*	*	*	*	*	*	*	*
50	*	*	*	*	*	*	*	*	*	*

*$PVIF$ is zero to three decimal places.

Table A-3 Present-Value Interest Factors for One Dollar Discounted at k Percent for n Periods: $PVIF_{k,n} = \dfrac{1}{(1+k)^n}$ (continued)

Period	41%	42%	43%	44%	45%	46%	47%	48%	49%	50%
1	.709	.704	.699	.694	.690	.685	.680	.676	.671	.667
2	.503	.496	.489	.482	.476	.469	.463	.457	.450	.444
3	.357	.349	.342	.335	.328	.321	.315	.308	.302	.296
4	.253	.246	.239	.233	.226	.220	.214	.208	.203	.198
5	.179	.173	.167	.162	.156	.151	.146	.141	.136	.132
6	.127	.122	.117	.112	.108	.103	.099	.095	.091	.088
7	.090	.086	.082	.078	.074	.071	.067	.064	.061	.059
8	.064	.060	.057	.054	.051	.048	.046	.043	.041	.039
9	.045	.043	.040	.038	.035	.033	.031	.029	.028	.026
10	.032	.030	.028	.026	.024	.023	.021	.020	.019	.017
11	.023	.021	.020	.018	.017	.016	.014	.013	.012	.012
12	.016	.015	.014	.013	.012	.011	.010	.009	.008	.008
13	.011	.010	.010	.009	.008	.007	.007	.006	.006	.005
14	.008	.007	.007	.006	.006	.005	.005	.004	.004	.003
15	.006	.005	.005	.004	.004	.003	.003	.003	.003	.002
16	.004	.004	.003	.003	.003	.002	.002	.002	.002	.002
17	.003	.003	.002	.002	.002	.002	.001	.001	.001	.001
18	.002	.002	.002	.001	.001	.001	.001	.001	.001	.001
19	.001	.001	.001	.001	.001	.001	.001	.001	.001	*
20	.001	.001	.001	.001	.001	.001	*	*	*	*
21	.001	.001	.001	*	*	*	*	*	*	*
22	.001	*	*	*	*	*	*	*	*	*
23	*	*	*	*	*	*	*	*	*	*
24	*	*	*	*	*	*	*	*	*	*
25	*	*	*	*	*	*	*	*	*	*
30	*	*	*	*	*	*	*	*	*	*
35	*	*	*	*	*	*	*	*	*	*
40	*	*	*	*	*	*	*	*	*	*
45	*	*	*	*	*	*	*	*	*	*
50	*	*	*	*	*	*	*	*	*	*

*PVIF is zero to three decimal places.

Table A-4 Present-Value Interest Factors for a One-Dollar Annuity Discounted at k Percent for n Periods: $PVIFA_{k,n} = \sum_{t=1}^{n} \dfrac{1}{(1+k)^t}$

Period	1%	2%	3%	4%	5%	6%	7%	8%	9%	10%
1	.990	.980	.971	.962	.952	.943	.935	.926	.917	.909
2	1.970	1.942	1.913	1.886	1.859	1.833	1.808	1.783	1.759	1.736
3	2.941	2.884	2.829	2.775	2.723	2.673	2.624	2.577	2.531	2.487
4	3.902	3.808	3.717	3.630	3.546	3.465	3.387	3.312	3.240	3.170
5	4.853	4.713	4.580	4.452	4.329	4.212	4.100	3.993	3.890	3.791
6	5.795	5.601	5.417	5.242	5.076	4.917	4.767	4.623	4.486	4.355
7	6.728	6.472	6.230	6.002	5.786	5.582	5.389	5.206	5.033	4.868
8	7.652	7.326	7.020	6.733	6.463	6.210	5.971	5.747	5.535	5.335
9	8.566	8.162	7.786	7.435	7.108	6.802	6.515	6.247	5.995	5.759
10	9.471	8.983	8.530	8.111	7.722	7.360	7.024	6.710	6.418	6.145
11	10.368	9.787	9.253	8.760	8.306	7.887	7.499	7.139	6.805	6.495
12	11.255	10.575	9.954	9.385	8.863	8.384	7.943	7.536	7.161	6.814
13	12.134	11.348	10.635	9.986	9.394	8.853	8.358	7.904	7.487	7.013
14	13.004	12.106	11.296	10.563	9.899	9.295	8.745	8.244	7.786	7.367
15	13.865	12.849	11.938	11.118	10.380	9.712	9.108	8.560	8.061	7.606
16	14.718	13.578	12.561	11.652	10.838	10.106	9.447	8.851	8.313	7.824
17	15.562	14.292	13.166	12.166	11.274	10.477	9.763	9.122	8.544	8.022
18	16.398	14.992	13.754	12.659	11.690	10.828	10.059	9.372	8.756	8.201
19	17.226	15.679	14.324	13.134	12.085	11.158	10.336	9.604	8.950	8.365
20	18.046	16.352	14.878	13.590	12.462	11.470	10.594	9.818	9.129	8.514
21	18.857	17.011	15.415	14.029	12.821	11.764	10.836	10.017	9.292	8.649
22	19.661	17.658	15.937	14.451	13.163	12.042	11.061	10.201	9.442	8.772
23	20.456	18.292	16.444	14.857	13.489	12.303	11.272	10.371	9.580	8.883
24	21.244	18.914	16.936	15.247	13.799	12.550	11.469	10.529	9.707	8.985
25	22.023	19.524	17.413	15.622	14.094	12.783	11.654	10.675	9.823	9.077
30	25.808	22.396	19.601	17.292	15.373	13.765	12.409	11.258	10.274	9.427
35	29.409	24.999	21.487	18.665	16.374	14.498	12.948	11.655	10.567	9.644
40	32.835	27.356	23.115	19.793	17.159	15.046	13.332	11.925	10.757	9.779
45	36.095	29.490	24.519	20.720	17.774	15.456	13.606	12.108	10.881	9.863
50	39.196	31.424	25.730	21.482	18.256	15.762	13.801	12.233	10.962	9.915

Table A-4   Present-Value Interest Factors for a One-Dollar Annuity Discounted at k Percent for n Periods: $PVIFA_{k,n} = \sum_{t=1}^{n} \dfrac{1}{(1+k)^t}$ (continued)

Period	11%	12%	13%	14%	15%	16%	17%	18%	19%	20%
1	.901	.893	.885	.877	.870	.862	.855	.847	.840	.833
2	1.713	1.690	1.668	1.647	1.626	1.605	1.585	1.566	1.547	1.528
3	2.444	2.402	2.361	2.322	2.283	2.246	2.210	2.174	2.140	2.106
4	3.102	3.037	2.974	2.914	2.855	2.798	2.743	2.690	2.639	2.589
5	3.696	3.605	3.517	3.433	3.352	3.274	3.199	3.127	3.058	2.991
6	4.231	4.111	3.998	3.889	3.784	3.685	3.589	3.498	3.410	3.326
7	4.712	4.564	4.423	4.288	4.160	4.039	3.922	3.812	3.706	3.605
8	5.146	4.968	4.799	4.639	4.487	4.344	4.207	4.078	3.954	3.837
9	5.537	5.328	5.132	4.946	4.772	4.607	4.451	4.303	4.163	4.031
10	5.889	5.650	5.426	5.216	5.019	4.833	4.659	4.494	4.339	4.192
11	6.207	5.938	5.687	5.453	5.234	5.029	4.836	4.656	4.486	4.327
12	6.492	6.194	5.918	5.660	5.421	5.197	4.988	4.793	4.611	4.439
13	6.750	6.424	6.122	5.842	5.583	5.342	5.118	4.910	4.715	4.533
14	6.982	6.628	6.302	6.002	5.724	5.468	5.229	5.008	4.802	4.611
15	7.191	6.811	6.462	6.142	5.847	5.575	5.324	5.092	4.876	4.675
16	7.379	6.974	6.604	6.265	5.954	5.668	5.405	5.162	4.938	4.730
17	7.549	7.120	6.729	6.373	6.047	5.749	5.475	5.222	4.990	4.775
18	7.702	7.250	6.840	6.467	6.128	5.818	5.534	5.273	5.033	4.812
19	7.839	7.366	6.938	6.550	6.198	5.877	5.584	5.316	5.070	4.843
20	7.963	7.469	7.025	6.623	6.259	5.929	5.628	5.353	5.101	4.870
21	8.075	7.562	7.102	6.687	6.312	5.973	5.665	5.384	5.127	4.891
22	8.176	7.645	7.170	6.743	6.359	6.011	5.696	5.410	5.149	4.909
23	8.266	7.718	7.230	6.792	6.399	6.044	5.723	5.432	5.167	4.925
24	8.348	7.784	7.283	6.835	6.434	6.073	5.746	5.451	5.182	4.937
25	8.422	7.843	7.330	6.873	6.464	6.097	5.766	5.467	5.195	4.948
30	8.694	8.055	7.496	7.003	6.566	6.177	5.829	5.517	5.235	4.979
35	8.855	8.176	7.586	7.070	6.617	6.215	5.858	5.539	5.251	4.992
40	8.951	8.244	7.634	7.105	6.642	6.233	5.871	5.548	5.258	4.997
45	9.008	8.283	7.661	7.123	6.654	6.242	5.877	5.552	5.261	4.999
50	9.042	8.304	7.675	7.133	6.661	6.246	5.880	5.554	5.262	4.999

Table A-4 Present-Value Interest Factors for a One-Dollar Annuity Discounted at k Percent for n Periods: $PVIFA_{k,n} = \sum_{t=1}^{n} \dfrac{1}{(1+k)^t}$ (continued)

Period	21%	22%	23%	24%	25%	26%	27%	28%	29%	30%
1	.826	.820	.813	.806	.800	.794	.787	.781	.775	.769
2	1.509	1.492	1.474	1.457	1.440	1.424	1.407	1.392	1.376	1.361
3	2.074	2.042	2.011	1.981	1.952	1.923	1.896	1.868	1.842	1.816
4	2.540	2.494	2.448	2.404	2.362	2.320	2.280	2.241	2.203	2.166
5	2.926	2.864	2.803	2.745	2.689	2.635	2.583	2.532	2.483	2.436
6	3.245	3.167	3.092	3.020	2.951	2.885	2.821	2.759	2.700	2.643
7	3.508	3.416	3.327	3.242	3.161	3.083	3.009	2.937	2.868	2.802
8	3.726	3.619	3.518	3.421	3.329	3.241	3.156	3.076	2.999	2.925
9	3.905	3.786	3.673	3.566	3.463	3.366	3.273	3.184	3.100	3.019
10	4.054	3.923	3.799	3.682	3.570	3.465	3.364	3.269	3.178	3.092
11	4.177	4.035	3.902	3.776	3.656	3.544	3.437	3.335	3.239	3.147
12	4.278	4.127	3.985	3.851	3.725	3.606	3.493	3.387	3.286	3.190
13	4.362	4.203	4.053	3.912	3.780	3.656	3.538	3.427	3.322	3.223
14	4.432	4.265	4.108	3.962	3.824	3.695	3.573	3.459	3.351	3.249
15	4.489	4.315	4.153	4.001	3.859	3.726	3.601	3.483	3.373	3.268
16	4.536	4.357	4.189	4.033	3.887	3.751	3.623	3.503	3.390	3.283
17	4.576	4.391	4.219	4.059	3.910	3.771	3.640	3.518	3.403	3.295
18	4.608	4.419	4.243	4.080	3.928	3.786	3.654	3.529	3.413	3.304
19	4.635	4.442	4.263	4.097	3.942	3.799	3.664	3.539	3.421	3.311
20	4.657	4.460	4.279	4.110	3.954	3.808	3.673	3.546	3.427	3.316
21	4.675	4.476	4.292	4.121	3.963	3.816	3.679	3.551	3.432	3.320
22	4.690	4.488	4.302	4.130	3.970	3.822	3.684	3.556	3.436	3.323
23	4.703	4.499	4.311	4.137	3.976	3.827	3.689	3.559	3.438	3.325
24	4.713	4.507	4.318	4.143	3.981	3.831	3.692	3.562	3.441	3.327
25	4.721	4.514	4.323	4.147	3.985	3.834	3.694	3.564	3.442	3.329
30	4.746	4.534	4.339	4.160	3.995	3.842	3.701	3.569	3.447	3.332
35	4.756	4.541	4.345	4.164	3.998	3.845	3.703	3.571	3.448	3.333
40	4.760	4.544	4.347	4.166	3.999	3.846	3.703	3.571	3.448	3.333
45	4.761	4.545	4.347	4.166	4.000	3.846	3.704	3.571	3.448	3.333
50	4.762	4.545	4.348	4.167	4.000	3.846	3.704	3.571	3.448	3.333

Table A-4 Present-Value Interest Factors for a One-Dollar Annuity Discounted at k Percent for n Periods: $PVIFA_{k,n} = \sum\limits_{t=1}^{n} \dfrac{1}{(1 + k)^t}$ (continued)

Period	31%	32%	33%	34%	35%	36%	37%	38%	39%	40%
1	.763	.758	.752	.746	.741	.735	.730	.725	.719	.714
2	1.346	1.331	1.317	1.303	1.289	1.276	1.263	1.250	1.237	1.224
3	1.791	1.766	1.742	1.719	1.696	1.673	1.652	1.630	1.609	1.589
4	2.130	2.096	2.062	2.029	1.997	1.966	1.935	1.906	1.877	1.849
5	2.390	2.345	2.302	2.260	2.220	2.181	2.143	2.106	2.070	2.035
6	2.588	2.534	2.483	2.433	2.385	2.339	2.294	2.251	2.209	2.168
7	2.739	2.677	2.619	2.562	2.508	2.455	2.404	2.355	2.308	2.263
8	2.854	2.786	2.721	2.658	2.598	2.540	2.485	2.432	2.380	2.331
9	2.942	2.868	2.798	2.730	2.665	2.603	2.544	2.487	2.432	2.379
10	3.009	2.930	2.855	2.784	2.715	2.649	2.587	2.527	2.469	2.414
11	3.060	2.978	2.899	2.824	2.752	2.683	2.618	2.555	2.496	2.438
12	3.100	3.013	2.931	2.853	2.779	2.708	2.641	2.576	2.515	2.456
13	3.129	3.040	2.956	2.876	2.799	2.727	2.658	2.592	2.529	2.469
14	3.152	3.061	2.974	2.892	2.814	2.740	2.670	2.603	2.539	2.478
15	3.170	3.076	2.988	2.905	2.825	2.750	2.679	2.611	2.546	2.484
16	3.183	3.088	2.999	2.914	2.834	2.757	2.685	2.616	2.551	2.489
17	3.193	3.097	3.007	2.921	2.840	2.763	2.690	2.621	2.555	2.492
18	3.201	3.104	3.012	2.926	2.844	2.767	2.693	2.624	2.557	2.494
19	3.207	3.109	3.017	2.930	2.848	2.770	2.696	2.626	2.559	2.496
20	3.211	3.113	3.020	2.933	2.850	2.772	2.698	2.627	2.561	2.497
21	3.215	3.116	3.023	2.935	2.852	2.773	2.699	2.629	2.562	2.498
22	3.217	3.118	3.025	2.936	2.853	2.775	2.700	2.629	2.562	2.498
23	3.219	3.120	3.026	2.938	2.854	2.775	2.701	2.630	2.563	2.499
24	3.221	3.121	3.027	2.939	2.855	2.776	2.701	2.630	2.563	2.499
25	3.222	3.122	3.028	2.939	2.856	2.776	2.702	2.631	2.563	2.499
30	3.225	3.124	3.030	2.941	2.857	2.777	2.702	2.631	2.564	2.500
35	3.226	3.125	3.030	2.941	2.857	2.778	2.703	2.632	2.564	2.500
40	3.226	3.125	3.030	2.941	2.857	2.778	2.703	2.632	2.564	2.500
45	3.226	3.125	3.030	2.941	2.857	2.778	2.703	2.632	2.564	2.500
50	3.226	3.125	3.030	2.941	2.857	2.778	2.703	2.632	2.564	2.500

Table A-4 Present-Value Interest Factors for a One-Dollar Annuity Discounted at k Percent for n Periods: $PVIFA_{k,n} = \sum_{t=1}^{n} \dfrac{1}{(1+k)^t}$ (continued)

Period	41%	42%	43%	44%	45%	46%	47%	48%	49%	50%
1	.709	.704	.699	.694	.690	.685	.680	.676	.671	.667
2	1.212	1.200	1.188	1.177	1.165	1.154	1.143	1.132	1.122	1.111
3	1.569	1.549	1.530	1.512	1.493	1.475	1.458	1.441	1.424	1.407
4	1.822	1.795	1.769	1.744	1.720	1.695	1.672	1.649	1.627	1.605
5	2.001	1.969	1.937	1.906	1.876	1.846	1.818	1.790	1.763	1.737
6	2.129	2.091	2.054	2.018	1.983	1.949	1.917	1.885	1.854	1.824
7	2.219	2.176	2.135	2.096	2.057	2.020	1.984	1.949	1.916	1.883
8	2.283	2.237	2.193	2.150	2.109	2.069	2.030	1.993	1.957	1.922
9	2.328	2.280	2.233	2.187	2.144	2.102	2.061	2.022	1.984	1.948
10	2.360	2.310	2.261	2.213	2.168	2.125	2.083	2.042	2.003	1.965
11	2.383	2.331	2.280	2.232	2.185	2.140	2.097	2.055	2.015	1.977
12	2.400	2.346	2.294	2.244	2.196	2.151	2.107	2.064	2.024	1.985
13	2.411	2.356	2.303	2.253	2.204	2.158	2.113	2.071	2.029	1.990
14	2.419	2.363	2.310	2.259	2.210	2.163	2.118	2.075	2.033	1.993
15	2.425	2.369	2.315	2.263	2.214	2.166	2.121	2.078	2.036	1.995
16	2.429	2.372	2.318	2.266	2.216	2.169	2.123	2.079	2.037	1.997
17	2.432	2.375	2.320	2.268	2.218	2.170	2.125	2.081	2.038	1.998
18	2.434	2.377	2.322	2.270	2.219	2.172	2.126	2.082	2.039	1.999
19	2.435	2.378	2.323	2.270	2.220	2.172	2.126	2.082	2.040	1.999
20	2.436	2.379	2.324	2.271	2.221	2.173	2.127	2.083	2.040	1.999
21	2.437	2.379	2.324	2.272	2.221	2.173	2.127	2.083	2.040	2.000
22	2.438	2.380	2.325	2.272	2.222	2.173	2.127	2.083	2.040	2.000
23	2.438	2.380	2.325	2.272	2.222	2.174	2.127	2.083	2.041	2.000
24	2.438	2.380	2.325	2.272	2.222	2.174	2.127	2.083	2.041	2.000
25	2.439	2.381	2.325	2.272	2.222	2.174	2.128	2.083	2.041	2.000
30	2.439	2.381	2.326	2.273	2.222	2.174	2.128	2.083	2.041	2.000
35	2.439	2.381	2.326	2.273	2.222	2.174	2.128	2.083	2.041	2.000
40	2.439	2.381	2.326	2.273	2.222	2.174	2.128	2.083	2.041	2.000
45	2.439	2.381	2.326	2.273	2.222	2.174	2.128	2.083	2.041	2.000
50	2.439	2.381	2.326	2.273	2.222	2.174	2.128	2.083	2.041	2.000

Appendix B

Answers to Selected End-of-Chapter Problems

The following list of answers to selected problems (and portions of problems) is included to provide "check figures" for use in preparing detailed solutions to end-of-chapter problems requiring calculations. For problems that are relatively straightforward, the key answer is given; for more complex problems, answers to a number of parts of the problem are included. Detailed calculations are not shown—only the final and, in some cases, intermediate answers, which should help to confirm whether or not the correct solution is being developed. For problems containing a variety of cases for which similar calculations are required, the answers for only one or two cases have been included. The only verbal answers included are simple yes-or-no or "choice of best alternative" responses; answers to problems requiring detailed explanations or discussions are not given.

The problems (and portions of problems) for which answers have been included were selected randomly; therefore, there is no discernible pattern to the choice of problem answers given. The answers given are based on what are believed to be the most obvious and reasonable assumptions related to the given problem; in a number of cases, other reasonable assumptions could result in equally correct answers.

2-1	a	$60,000
	c	$0.00
2-2		$80,000
2-3		Asset A; depreciation yr. 1 $4,250; yr. 2 $6,460; yr. 3 $6,290
2-5	a	Cash flow $74,980
2-6	a	EAC $18,000
	b	EAC $14,000
2-7	a	Juan $3,205; Maria $1,419
2-8	a	Long $1,000; Short $1,400

        b $25,650

        c $24,810

2-9   **a** Taxable income $15,170

        b $2,040.10

        c $2,015.10

2-11 **a** $33,600 book value

        b $24,560, $8,960, $0.00, −$3,440

2-12 **a** $167,000

        b $132,000

        c $52,000

2-14 **a** $72,624

        c $2,596

        d $86,028 total cash flow

           $47,972 total tax liability

2-15 **a** (2) $400,000 ordinary tax relief

        c (2) $800,000 ordinary tax relief

               $30,000 capital gains tax relief

2-17 A (1) $24,000

          (2) $24,000

       C (1) $120,000

          (2) $88,750

2-18 Incorporation

3-2   A $1,258.13

       C $47,520

       F $4,720

3-4   **a** $9,145

        b $594.43

        c $1,293.07

        d 42.42%

        e $1,887.50

        f 24.77%

3-6   **a** (1) 160 shares

          (2) 320 shares

          (3) 1,600 shares

3-7   A −$500 gross profit

          −$525 net profit

       B $7,000 gross profit

          $6,720 net profit

3-8   **a** $1,200

        b −$1,200

3-10 **b** 11%

        d 16%

3-12 **a** B 3.00%

           E 3.1%

3-14 **a** C 11%

        c C 13%

3-16 B 8%

       D 5.2%

4-1   Cash: Use

       Notes payable: Source

       Depreciation: Source

4-3	**a**	Current '81 1.88; '82 1.74; '83 1.79; '84 1.55
		Quick '81 1.22; '82 1.19; '83 1.24; '84 1.14
4-4	**a**	Average quarterly inventory $650,000
		Inventory turnover 3.69x
		Average age of inventory 97.6 days
4-7		ROE Raimer 1984 21.22%
		ROE Industry 1984 14.46%
4-9	**a**	Average collection period 20 days
		Debt ratio .55
		ROI 10.5%
4-10	**a**	Inventory turnover 2.33x
		TIE 2.8
		ROE 11.3%
5-1		Cash receipts Jun $86,250; Jul $82,500; Aug $92,500
5-2	**b**	Maximum financing $109
	c	Cash $25; notes payable $67
5-3		Minimum credit line $31,000
5-4	**a**	Nov $33,000; Dec $14,000; Jan ($7,000); Feb $37,000; Mar $67,000; Apr ($22,000)
	c	$37,000
5-7	**a**	Net profit after tax $216,857
	b	Net profit after tax $227,400
5-8	**a**	Total assets $9,080,000
5-9	**a**	Net profit after tax $67,500
	b	Total assets (% of sales) $729,000
		Total assets (judgmental) $697,500
6-1		C 1.188
6-2	**a**	A 10 yrs. $< n <$ 11 yrs.
	b	A 20 yrs. $< n <$ 21 yrs.
6-3		C $23,670
		F $110,920
6-5	**b**	annual $12,180
		semi $12,590
		qrtly $12,815
6-7		A $36,217.50
6-11		A $4,452
6-14		A $109,890
		B $91,290
6-15		A $11,805
		B $26,039
		C $52,410
6-17		C $2,821.70
6-18		A Invest
		B Forego
6-20		$1,336.68
6-22		A $4,656.57
6-24	**a**	A 12% $< k <$ 13%
6-28	**b**	A $250,000
6-29	**a**	$60,000
	b	$3,764.82
6-30		$15,575.10

7-1   **a**   X 12.5%
            Y 12.36%
7-2   A 25%
7-4   **a**   A 8
            B 20
7-5   **a**   R 10
            S 20
          b   R 25%
            S 25.5%
7-7   **a**   (4) Project 257 CV .366
                  Project 432 CV .354
7-8   **a**   F 4%
          b   F 13.38%
          c   F 3.345
7-13 **a**   .18 inc
          b   .096 dec
          c   .00 no change
7-16 A 8.9%
          D 15%
7-17 **b**   10%
8-2   A $10,870; B $2,000
8-5   **a** $1,156.88
8-6   A $1,149.66
          D $450.80
8-10 **a**   12.68%
          b   12.58%
8-12 $841.15
8-15 **a** $68.82
          b $7.87
8-17 **a** $72/share
          b $42.40/share
8-18 A $18.60
8-21 **a** $37.75
          b $60.40
8-22 $81.19
8-23 **a** $40.94
          b $23.06
          c   The equation is undefined.
8-26 2.67
8-27 **a**   14.8%
          b $29.55
9-1   **a**   Current expenditure
          b   Capital expenditure
9-3   **a** $13,340
          b $5,840
          c $0
          d   −$6,160
9-4   **a**   Asset A $2,920
                  Asset B $34,400
9-5   **a** $25,000
9-7   Initial investment $37,940

9-9   **a** yr. 1 $10,200; yr. 2 $14,960; yrs. 3–5 $14,280
9-11 yr. 1 $7,680; yr. 2 $9,024; yrs. 3–5 $8,832
9-13 **a** (1) $65,400
9-14 $80,320
9-17 **a** Initial investment $55,080

b	Year	CF
	1	$ 5,760
	2	10,040
	3	10,800
	4	17,040
	5	18,240

          c $29,400

9-19 **a** Alt. 1 $97,800; Alt. 2 $111,200

b Alt. 1	Year	CF	Alt. 2	Year	CF
	1	$24,500		1	$47,900
	2	32,400		2	60,800
	3	36,700		3	40,300
	4	46,700		4	20,300
	5	36,700		5	19,900

          c Alt. 1 $18,600
             Alt. 2 $34,800

10-1 **a** 20%
          b 10%
          c 60%
10-2 **a** 6 years
10-5 **a** (1) $2,675
             (2) accept
          b (1) $840
             (2) accept
          c (1) −$805
             (2) reject
10-6 A −$5,136
          C −$83,662
10-8 **a** $3,246 *NPV*
             1.32 PI; accept
10-11 A 17.43%
          B 8% < *IRR* < 9%
10-12 X 16%; accept
          Y 17%; accept
10-14 **a** $1,222
          b 1.067
          c 12%
10-18 **a** A 62.50%
          b A 3.67 years
          c A $3,655
          d 1.046
          e 14.61%
10-19 **a** $1,874,000
          c 6.10 years
          d *NPV* = $293,002; *IRR* = 13.79%
10-20 **b** *NPV* = $50,531

	c	15.95%
10-21	**a**	(1) Truck A Initial investment $54,992
		(3) Truck A Terminal cash flow $14,000
	c	(2) Truck A *NPV* $13,738
		(4) Truck A *IRR* 27.23%
11-1	**a**	A *NPV* $1,656
		B *NPV* $2,186
	c	A *NPV* $4,039
		B *NPV* $3,739
11-2		A *ANPV* $23,747.33
11-4	**b**	X $4,319 Y −$5,088; Y,X,Z
	c	X $920.04 Y $1,079.54; Y,X,Z
11-5	**a**	A PI 1.28
	b	F, C, and G
11-6	**a**	F, E, and G
	b	B, F, and G
11-8	**b**	*NPV* −$7,110
	d	*NPV* −$3,078
11-9	**b**	X Breakeven cash flow $8,949.88
		Y Breakeven cash flow $11,933.17
11-12	**a**	*NPV* Line S $8,500
		NPV Line T $8,200
	b	Range Line S $29,000
		Range Line T $16,000
	c	σ Line S $5,805.17
		σ Line T $3,355.59
	d	CV Line S .683
		CV Line T .409
11-16	**a**	*NPV* $22,320
	b	CE *NPV* −$5,596
11-18	**a**	Project E *NPV* $2,130
		Project F *NPV* $1,678
	b	$RADR_E$ 19%
		$RADR_F$ 15%
	c	NPV_E $834
		NPV_F $1,678
11-20	**a**	Project A *NPV* $5,391.10
		Project B *NPV* $730.00
	b	NPV_A $7,951
		NPV_B $4,330
12-2	**b**	12.4%
12-3	**a**	$980
	c	12.31%
	d	12.26%
12-4		A 5.66%
		E 7.10%
12-5	**a**	12.63%
	b	11.11%
12-7	**c**	16.54%
	d	15.91%
12-10	**a**	$k_a = 10.48\%$

12-11 **a** $k_a = 8.34\%$
        b $k_a = 10.85\%$
12-12 **a** $k_a = 13.55\%$
        b $k_a = 12.985\%$
12-13 **a** $k_i = 5.1\%$; $k_p = 8.4\%$; $k_n = 13.6\%$; $k_r = 13\%$
        b (1) $200,000
            (2) 9.71%
            (3) 10.01%
12-15 **b** Ranges of Total New Financing   **c** k_a for Each Range

Ranges of Total New Financing	k_a for Each Range
$ 0–$ 200,000	13.8%
$200,000–$ 500,000	14.6
$500,000–$ 750,000	15.4
$750,000–$1,000,000	17.0
Greater than $1,000,000	17.8

        e E, C, G, A, and H
13-1 **a** I 4,000 units; J 4,000 units; K 5,000 units
13-2 **a** 20,000 books
13-3 **a** $20,000
      b $12,000; $28,000
      c -20%; -40%; $+20\%$; $+40\%$
13-4 **a** 8,000 units; $508,000
      d *DOL* 5
13-6 **a** *eps* $.375
      b *eps* $1.275
      c *eps* $1.935
13-7 **a** *DFL* 1.5
      c *DFL* 1.93
13-8 **a** (1) 175,000 units
        (2) $9,333
        (3) 233,333 units
      b *DOL* 1.78
      c *DFL* 1.35
      d *DTL* 2.40
13-10 **a** $416,667
       b (1) $1.60
          (2) $4.30
       c 2.25
       d 3.76
       e 423% increase
13-12 **a** *eps* $-$$1.62; $0.18; $1.98
       c E(*eps*) $0.60; c(*eps*) $0.759; CV(*eps*) $1.27
13-14 **a** *eps* $12.00; $24.00
       b $40,000
13-16 **a** A $15,000
          B $12,000
       d *EBIT* $<$ $27,000, Choose B
          EBIT $>$ $27,000, Choose A
13-17 **a** Debt ratio 0% — Share price $24
       b (1) 40% debt ratio
          (2) 30% debt ratio
13-19 **a** *EBIT* $60,000, $240,000, $420,000

    d at 15% debt ratio, *eps* = $0.85, $4.02, $7.20

    e (1) at 15% debt ratio, E(*eps*) = $4.02

       (2) at 15% debt ratio, $\sigma(eps)$ = 2.45

    g $0 < EBIT < $80,000; choose 0%

      $80,001 < EBIT < $114,000; choose 15%

      $114,001 < EBIT < $163,000; choose 30%

      $116,001 < EBIT < $218,000; choose 45%

      $218,001 < EBIT < \infty$; choose 60%

    h at 15% debt ratio, share price = $38.29

    i Maximize *eps* at 60% debt ratio

      Maximize share value at 30% debt ratio

14-3 **a** $4.75/share

     b $0.40/share

14-4 **a** $1.60

14-5 **a** 1984 $1.60

     b 1984 $1.50

     c 1984 $1.30

14-6 **a** 1984 $0.70

     b 1984 $0.60

     c 1984 $0.74

     d 1984 $0.78

14-8 **a** Stockholder's equity $1,016,000, $1,000,000, $980,000, $940,000

     b Retained earnings $304,000, $240,000, $160,000, $0

14-9 **a** $2/share

     b 1%

     c 1%

     d $20/share

14-12 **a** Dec par from $3 to $2; no. of shares inc to 150,000

     b $80/share

     c Before stock split $100/share

      After stock split $66.67/share

14-13 **a** 19,047 shares

     b $2.10/share

     c $21.00/share

14-14 **a** *eps* = $4/share; P/E = 15

     b 16,129 shares

     c $4.13/share

     d $61.95/share

15-2 **a** (1) ROI 1.5%

       (2) ROI 3.0%

15-3 Avg. borrowing = $8,000; Annual loan cost = $1,200

15-4 **a** (1) Aggressive $820,000

         Conservative $2,380,000

       (2) Aggressive $680,000

         Conservative $1,680,000

15-5

	Aggressive	Conservative
a	$580,833	$1,184,000
b	$638,916	$1,036,000
c	$697,000	$ 888,000

15-7 **a** $10,000

     b $2,046.67

15-8   **a** Aggressive $30,000, Conservative $35,000
16-1   **a** 120 days
         b 3
         c $10,000,000
16-4   A +45 days
         B −5 days
16-5 $120,000 savings
16-6   **a** $583,658
         b $23,379
16-8   **a** 7 days
16-9   **a** $3,000,000
         b $420,000
16-12 **a** $27,000
         b −$4,950
16-14 Opportunity cost $5,967
16-15 Net benefit $80,000
16-16 $22,500 annual savings
16-19 **a** −$550, do not purchase
         c $700, purchase
16-20 **a** 19.25%
         f 2.95%
17-1   **a** A 66.0
             B 81.5
             C 76
17-2   **a** $125,000
         b $75,000
         c $9,000
17-3   **a** $180,000,000
         b $54,000,000
         c $30,200,000
         d $4,228,000
17-5   **a** $5,000
         b Net loss $1,800
17-6   Net loss $5,242
17-7   Cost of discount $26,460
         Additional profit $18,000
         Reduced investment in accounts receivable $31,833
17-9   **a** $14,000
         b Marginal bad debt expense $3,150
             Marginal investment in accounts receivable $8,034
17-11 Item
         $\overline{1 - C}$
         2 − B
         3 − B
17-12 **a** $1,875,000
         b $33,333
17-14 $20,000 additional profit
17-17 Reorder point − 150 tons
17-19 **a** EOQ 200 units
         b 122.22 units
         c Reorder point 33.33 units

18-1 **a** Dec. 25
18-2 **a** 36.73%
      f 55.67%
18-4 **a** X 8.08%
      b Forego
18-5 **a** Q 18.18%
      b Q borrow
      c Supplier S
      d Supplier S
18-6 $1,300,000
18-7 $375
18-8 14.29%
18-9 **a** 14.125%
      b 14.125%
18-10 **a** 9%
      b 13.06%
18-11 **a** $200,000
      b $152,000
18-14 **a** $1,173.33
      b $86,826.67
      c 16.22%
18-15 **a** $329,035
      b $2,765
      c 10.08%
      d 24.49%
18-17 **a** Center City $1,000
      First Local $1,083.33
      North Mall $1,050

19-2

	a	b
General creditors	$ 500,000	$ 500,000
A	1,000,000	2,000,000
B	1,500,000	2,500,000
C	1,000,000	0
D	1,000,000	0

19-4 Bond A $384,000
          B $360,000
19-5 **a** Bond A $16,667
      b Bond A $160,003.20
19-6 **a** Bond A $40,000
      b Bond A $16,000
19-7 **a** $80,000
      b $8,000
      c $1,680,000
      d Incremental initial outlay $2,840,000
      e Annual cash flow savings from new bond $364,000
      f Net savings $1,016,216; bond refunding should be initiated.
19-8 **a** Incremental initial outlay $1,294,000
      b Annual cash flow savings from new bond $178,933
      c Net savings $237,666; bond refunding should be initiated.
19-10 $3.60 per share spread
20-1 **a** $8.80, qrtly $2.20

b $8.80

c $35.20

20-2   A $15.00

20-3   **a** Preferred dividends $14.875/share

Common dividends $15.875/share

20-4   **a** 12.5%

b EAC $198,000, ROE 16.5%

c EAC $264,000, ROE 14.67%

d EAC $228,000, ROE 19%

20-6   **a** Common stock $10,000

Paid in capital $120,000

20-8   Case A: (1) 0 (2) 0 directors

(1) 0 (2) 3 directors

20-9   (1) Case A 0.033 shares

(2) Case A 20 shares

20-10 (1) Case A $0.50

(2) Case A R_e = $0.50

20-12 **a** 40,000 shares

b 0.08 shares

c 0.20 shares

d R_o = $0.148

R_e = $0.148

20-13 **a** 24,000 shares

b 12.5 rights

c 3,840 shares

d (1) $0.296

(2) R_e = $0.296

e $0.30 per right

21-1

Year	After-tax cash outflow
0	$40,000
1–11	24,000
12	(16,000)

21-3   A $96,875

21-4   A $47,807

21-5 $6,098

21-7   **a** Lessor R $115,776

b Lessor R $17,711

d Lessor S

21-8   **a** Net profit after tax/borrowing $6,000; Net profit after tax/leasing $8,280

c

	Borrowing	Leasing
(1) Debt ratio	.619	.617
(2) Total asset turnover	1.347	1.354
(3) ROI	2.85%	3.96%

21-10 A $299,800

21-11 Payment $30,085; yr. 1 interest $16,380, yr. 1 principal $13,705

21-12 Loan A; Interest rate = 16%

Loan D; Interest rate = 10%

21-13 Loan X_1; Interest year 2 = $1,098.36, Principal year 2 = $3,318.04

21-14 **a** (2) PV of lease = $13,420

b (1) Payment = $5,966.59

(4) PV of purchasing = $13,835.95

21-16   **a** $19,810.43
       c *PV* of lease = $53,171.20
          PV of purchasing = $54,064.20

22-1   **a** $50
      b $8

22-2   **a** 5.75 shares
      b 40 shares

22-3   **a** $1,250
      b $525

22-5   **a** $7
      b $87.50
      c 9.59%
      d $1,000, $1,062.50, $1,250.00

22-7   **a** *eps* $3.39
      b *eps* $4.00
      c *eps* $3.49

22-9   Bond A $735.30
      Preferred R $67.69

22-10   **b** $812.08

22-13   **a** 160 shares, 400 warrants
      b 20%
      c 125%

22-14   **a** 6.67%
      b 14.29%
      c Stock   (1) 0%
                    (2) −6.67%
        Warrants (1) −42.85%
                    (2) −100%

22-15   Option A $350
      Option B −$50

22-16   **a** $800
      b $200
      c $6 share

23-2

Year	a	b
1	$ 60,000	$ 0
2	160,000	0
3	180,000	0
4	240,000	0
5	240,000	160,000

      c $720,000

23-4   **a** $85,000
      b $19,320
      c $15,616

23-7

eps	a	b	c
merged firm	$1.029	$1.00	0.972
Flannagan's	1.029	1.00	0.972
Moon Bar	1.852	2.00	2.139

23-8   **a** 8,000 shares
      b $4.31/share
      c $1.72/share

credit standards   The minimum criteria for the extension of credit to a customer. Credit ratings, credit references, and the like are used in setting credit standards. [17]

credit terms   The repayment terms extended by a firm to its credit customers. They include the cash discount and cash discount period, if any, the net period, and the beginning of the credit period. [17, 18]

credit union   A financial intermediary that deals primarily in transfers of funds between consumers; membership is generally based on some common bond, such as working for the same employer or belonging to the same church. [3]

cross-sectional analysis   The comparison of different firms' financial ratios at the same point in time. Also the comparison of a firm's ratios to an industry average. [4]

cum dividends   See *dividends on.*

cum rights   See *rights on.*

cumulative preferred stock   Most preferred stock is cumulative, which means that all dividends in arrears must be paid prior to distributing any dividends to common stockholders. *Noncumulative preferred stock* does not entitle the holder to the eventual receipt of "passed" dividends but requires the issuer to pay only the current dividend prior to paying common stockholders. [20]

cumulative probability distribution   Distribution developed by determining the probability associated with obtaining at least each given value and plotting the cumulative probability of all occurrences less than or equal to the given value against the associated outcome. [7]

cumulative voting   A voting system in which each share of stock entitles the holder to as many votes as there are directors to be elected. This system gives minority shareholders an opportunity to elect some directors. [20]

current expenditure   Outlay made by the firm that results in benefits received within the year. [9]

current-rate method   Method of calculating balance sheet and income statement amounts for multinational companies under FASB No. 52. [4]

current ratio   A measure of liquidity calculated by dividing a firm's current assets by its current liabilities. The higher this ratio is, the more liquid the firm is considered. [4]

date of the invoice   See *credit period.*

date of record   The date on which holders of record in a firm's stock ledger are designated as the recipients of either dividends or stock rights. Stock usually sells *ex dividend* or *ex rights* beginning the fourth business day before the date of record; it generally sells *cum dividends* (with *dividends on*) or *cum rights* (with *rights on*) prior to the fourth business day preceding the date of record. [14, 20]

dealers   Traders on the over-the-counter exchange that make markets in certain securities by offering to buy or sell them at a stated price. The *bid* and *ask* prices represent, respectively, the highest price offered by the dealer to purchase a given security and the lowest price at which the dealer will sell the security. [3]

debenture   An unsecured bond whose holders have a claim on a firm's assets after the claims of all secured creditors have been satisfied. Unsecured bonds subordinated to other debts are called *subordinated debentures.* [19]

debt capital   Any type of *long-term* debt. Debt capital can be obtained by negotiated borrowing or through the sale of bonds. [13]

debt ratio   A measure of the degree of indebtedness calculated by dividing total liabilities by total assets. The higher this ratio, the greater is the amount of other people's money being used to generate profits and the more financial leverage the firm has. [4]

debt-equity ratio   A measure of the degree of indebtedness calculated by dividing the firm's long-term debt by its stockholders' equity. The higher this ratio, the greater the firm's financial leverage and risk. [4]

decision tree An expected-value-based approach commonly used when making capital budgeting decisions. This technique permits the various decision alternatives and payoffs as well as their probabilities of occurrence to be mapped out in a clear and easy-to-analyze fashion. The approach is not especially sophisticated since it uses subjective estimates of probabilities as a substitute for the statistical evaluation of risk. [11]

deductions from gross income In the calculation of personal taxes, this item includes a variety of trade and business expenses that may have been incurred by the individual, sole proprietorship, or partnership during the tax year. [2]

deep discount bond Bond issued with a very low coupon and sold at a price far below par value. [19]

default risk For a security, the possibility that the issuer will not pay the contractual interest or principal as scheduled. [3]

degree of financial leverage (DFL) A measure of a firm's *financial leverage;* the higher the DFL, the greater the financial leverage and therefore the greater the *financial risk.* [13]

degree of indebtedness The firm's debt position; measured by the debt ratio and the debt-equity ratio. [4]

degree of operating leverage (DOL) A measure of a firm's *operating leverage;* the higher the DOL, the greater the operating leverage and therefore the greater the *business risk.* [13]

degree of total leverage (DTL) A measure of a firm's *total leverage;* the higher the DTL, the greater the total leverage and therefore the greater the *total risk.* [13]

Depository Institutions Deregulation and Monetary Control Act of 1980 (DIDMCA) Legislation that signaled the beginning of the financial services revolution by eliminating interest-rate ceilings on most accounts and permitting certain institutions to offer new types of accounts and services such as NOWs, money market accounts, and discount brokerage. [3]

depository transfer check (DTC) An unsigned check drawn on one of the firm's bank accounts and deposited into its account at another bank. [16]

deposits to accumulate a future sum Amount that must be deposited annually in order to accumulate a certain amount of money at a certain point in the future. [6]

depreciable life The life over which an asset is depreciated. For tax purposes, an asset will fall into one of four property classes—each having specified *normal recovery periods* and *optional extended recovery periods*—under the *accelerated cost recovery system (ACRS).* See also *recovery period.* [2]

depreciation A charge against current income for a portion of the historical cost incurred with the acquisition of fixed assets. For tax purposes, depreciable lives and the rates of depreciation for each year are given under the *accelerated cost recovery system (ACRS)* guidelines established by the *Economic Recovery Tax Act of 1981.* [2]

depth of a market The ability of a market to absorb the purchase or sale of a large dollar amount of securities. [16]

direct lease Lease that results when a lessor owns or acquires the assets that are leased to a given lessee. See also *leveraged lease; sale-leaseback arrangements.* [21]

direct placement See *private placement.*

direct send Presenting checks for payment directly to the bank on which they are drawn. [16]

disbursement float Lapse between the time when a firm deducts a payment from its checking account ledger and the time when funds are actually withdrawn from its account. [16]

discharge Court release of the bankrupt firm from all provable debts in bankruptcy except for certain debts that are immune to a discharge. [24]

discount (bond) Amount by which a bond sells at a value less than par. [8]

discount loan Loan on which interest is paid in advance. [18]

discount rate In capital budgeting, the rate at which future cash flows are discounted in order to determine their present value; also called the *required return, opportunity cost,* or *cost of capital.* [6, 10]

discounting cash flows The inverse of *compounding;* determining the present value of a future amount. [6]

discrete probability distribution The simplest type of probability distribution showing only a limited number of outcome-probability coordinates; also called a *bar chart.* [7]

dispersion The distribution pattern of returns for a given asset. [7]

diversifiable risk The portion of an asset's risk that results from the occurrence of uncontrollable or random events such as labor strikes, lawsuits, regulatory actions, and loss of a key account. An investor tries to create a portfolio in which this risk, sometimes called *unsystematic risk,* is eliminated through diversification. Compare *nondiversifiable risk.* [7]

dividend Payment made by a firm to its owners, either in *cash* or in *stock.* The firm's directors periodically meet to decide whether to pay dividends and to determine the amount and form of the dividend payment. [2]

dividend reinvestment plans Plans offered by firms that allow stockholders to acquire additional shares, and even fractional shares, at little or no transaction cost. [14]

dividend yield The annual dividend on a share of stock divided by its prevailing per-share market price. The first term of the *Gordon model* represents dividend yield. [12]

dividends on Sale of stock prior to the ex dividend date, and with dividends; also called *cum dividends.* See also *ex dividend.* [14]

Dun and Bradstreet, Inc. The nation's largest mercantile credit-reporting agency. It provides a variety of types of credit information on any of millions of firms to its subscribers. It also publishes a variety of industry statistics, including industry-average financial ratios. [17]

DuPont formula A formula relating a firm's net profit margin and total asset turnover to its *return on investment (ROI).* The return on investment is equal to the product of the net profit margin and total asset turnover. [4]

earning assets A term commonly used to describe *fixed assets* since they generally provide the basis for a firm's earning power. Without plant and equipment, a firm could not produce a product. [17]

earnings per share (*eps*) Calculated by dividing the earnings available for common stockholders (EAC) by the number of shares of common stock outstanding. [4]

EBIT Earnings before interest and taxes. [4]

***EBIT-eps* analysis** A technique used to evaluate various capital structures in order to select the one that best maximizes a firm's *earnings per share (eps),* which is assumed to be consistent with the maximization of the owner's wealth. The financing plans are often shown graphically on a set of *EBIT* (x-axis) – *eps* (y-axis) axes. [13]

 economic exposure The risk, for a multinational firm, that since all future revenues and thus net profits can be subject to exchange-rate changes, part of its total diversifiable risk includes an element reflecting appreciation or depreciation of various currencies with respect to the U.S. dollar. [7]

economic order quantity (EOQ) model A technique for determining the optimum quantity of items to order or produce based on the trade-off between inventory ordering and carrying costs. The optimum quantity is that which *minimizes* the total cost of inventory or the sum of the ordering and carrying cost. [17]

Economic Recovery Tax Act of 1981 Legislation that established new rules and guidelines for the depreciation of assets for tax purposes. See also *accelerated cost recovery system.* [2]

efficient market A marketplace in which all investors are assumed to have the same accurate information with respect to securities. All investors view securities in light of a common holding period; there are no restrictions on investment, no taxes, and no transaction costs. None of the investors is large enough to affect the market significantly. The existence of efficient markets underlies the *capital asset pricing model (CAPM).* [3, 11]

efficient portfolio A portfolio that provides a maximum return for a given level of risk or a minimum risk for a given level of return. [7]

end of month (EOM) See *credit period*.

eps See *earnings per share*.

equipment trust certificates Certificates used by railroads, airlines, truck lines, and barge lines to finance the purchase of "rolling stock." A type of installment purchase arrangement that allows the firm to obtain the secured long-term financing necessary to finance fixed assets. [19]

equity capital Long-term funds provided by a firm's owners that do not mature at a future date, but have an infinite life. The basic sources of equity capital are preferred stock, common stock, and retained earnings. [13]

equity multiplier The ratio of total assets to stockholders' equity. See also *DuPont formula; modified DuPont formula*. [4]

estimated tax payments Quarterly payments made by self-employed persons, employed persons with outside income from which taxes are not withheld, and corporations as estimates of the tax due. [2]

Eurobond An *international bond* sold primarily in countries other than the country of the currency in which the issue is denominated. Compare *foreign bond*. [19]

Eurocurrency markets International markets for short-term borrowing. [18]

Eurodollar deposits Deposits denominated in U.S. dollars and deposited in banks located outside the United States. [16]

Euromarket A market (used largely by multinational companies) that provides for borrowing and lending of currencies outside their countries of origin. [3]

excess cash balance See *required total financing*.

excess earnings accumulation tax A tax levied by the IRS on any retained earnings above $250,000 (the amount currently exempt for all firms except personal corporations) that are believed to have been retained not for internal investments but rather to avoid the payment of taxes on dividends. [14]

excess itemized deductions For persons itemizing their nonbusiness expenses when calculating taxable personal income, the amount (if any) by which these itemized expenses exceed the *zero-bracket amount*. An adjustment for any excess itemized deductions is required to determine *taxable income*. [2]

ex dividend or ex right Phrases used to indicate that a stock is selling without a recently declared dividend or right. The ex dividend or ex right date is generally four business days prior to the *date of record*. If a stock is not selling ex dividend or ex right, then it is selling *cum dividend* or *cum right*. [14, 20]

exemptions (personal) In the calculation of federal income taxes, a $1,000 deduction is allowed for the taxpayer and each of his or her dependents. [2]

exercise price The price at which holders of *warrants* can purchase the number of shares on which they have an option. This price, which is set above the market price when issued, is sometimes called the *option price*. [22]

expected net present value One of the factors in the statistical measure of project risk in the capital budgeting decision. [11]

expected return For an investment, the expected change in value plus expected cash distribution over a given period, expressed as a percentage of the initial value. [3]

expected value A measure of central tendency, found by calculating the average value of the expected outcomes. If probabilities are attached to expected outcomes, the expected value can be calculated as the weighted average return, in which the weights used are the probabilities of the various outcomes. [7]

extension   An arrangement whereby, in order to sustain a failed firm, its creditors agree to let the firm repay its obligations over a specified period of time. [24]

external forecast   Sales forecast based on the relationships that can be observed between the firm's sales and certain economic indicators. [5]

external funds required   The amount of additional financing needed to allow the firm to meet its financing needs in the coming year. [5]

extra dividend   A dividend additional to the regular dividend, paid by the company when earnings warrant it. [14]

face value   See *par value*.

factor   A financial institution that purchases accounts receivable from business firms. The purchase is made at a discount from the accounts' value. Most *factoring* is on a *notification* basis. Normally, the factor accepts all the credit risks associated with the accounts by purchasing them on a *nonrecourse basis,* which means it must absorb any losses from uncollectible accounts. Some banks and commercial finance companies factor accounts receivable. [18]

FASB No. 52   Statement issued by the FASB regulating the financial statements of American multinational corporations. [4]

federal agency issue   An issue of an agency of the U.S. government, such as the Federal Home Loan Bank or the Federal National Mortgage Association. It is generally a short-term security with a slightly higher yield than Treasury issues. [16]

federal funds   Loan transactions from one commercial bank to another in which Federal Reserve banks are involved are transactions in federal funds. [3]

field warehouse   A storage area set up for a lender on the premises of the borrower so as to isolate inventory used as collateral for a warehouse receipt loan. [18]

financial and legal flows   Cash flows that include the payment and receipt of interest, the payment and refund of taxes, the incurrence and repayment of debt, the payment of dividends and stock repurchases, and the cash inflow from the sale of stock. [4]

financial asset   An asset such as a stock or bond. [8]

financial breakeven point   The level of *EBIT* necessary for a firm to be just able to meet its fixed financial obligations. In other words, the level of *EBIT* at which the *eps* just equals zero. The higher the financial breakeven point, the more financially risky the firm is considered. [13]

financial institution   See *financial intermediary*.

financial intermediary   An institution that channels the savings of various parties into loans or investments. Some financial institutions primarily lend money, while others primarily invest money in such earning assets as real estate, stocks, or bonds. The key financial institutions are commercial banks, mutual savings banks, savings and loan associations, credit unions, life insurance companies, pension funds, and mutual funds. [3]

financial lease   A long-term, noncancelable lease generally requiring the lessee to pay all maintenance costs. Compare *operating lease*. [21]

financial leverage   The ability of fixed financial charges such as interest and preferred stock dividends to magnify the effect of changes in earnings before interest and taxes *(EBIT)* on the firm's earnings per share *(eps)*. The more fixed financial charges a firm must meet, the higher is its financial leverage. [4, 13]

financial markets   The markets for short-term and long-term loans and investments. The two key financial markets are the *money market* and the *capital market*. [3]

financial planning process   Process of providing road maps for achieving a firm's long- and short-range objectives through guidelines and budgets; a structure for coordinating the activities of the firm and a control mechanism for evaluating actual outcomes. [5]

financial risk   The risk of being unable to cover financial costs. The greater a firm's *financial leverage* is, the higher its financial risk is. [12, 13]

financial supermarket   An institution at which a customer can obtain a full array of financial services such as checking, deposits, brokerage, insurance, and estate planning. [3]

finished goods inventory   Items that have been produced but not yet sold. [17]

first-mortgage bond   See *mortgage bond.*

fixed assets   See *earning assets.*

fixed asset turnover   Ratio used to measure the efficiency with which the firm has been using its fixed or earning assets to generate sales; calculated by dividing the firm's sales by its net fixed assets. [4]

fixed currency   Currency whose value with respect to another currency is fixed rather than floating. [7]

fixed operating costs   Costs (like rent) that are a function of time, not the volume of production or sales. [13]

fixed-payment coverage ratio   Ratio that measures the firm's ability to meet all fixed-payment financial obligations. [4]

fixed-rate note   A note on which the rate of interest is determined initially as a set increment above the *prime rate* and remains fixed at that rate until maturity. [18]

float   Funds that have been dispatched by a payer but are not in a form that can be spent by the payee. Float exists because of environmental as well as institutional imperfections in the collection-payment system. Many firms "play the float," writing checks against nonexistent deposits and depositing the money to "cover" the checks sometime prior to their presentation for payment. [16]

floater   See *variable-rate bond.*

floating currency   Currency whose value with respect to another currency is allowed to fluctuate on a daily basis. [7]

floating lien   A method of using accounts receivable or inventory as short-term loan collateral. A firm that has many accounts or items of inventory that, on the average, have a small dollar value will use this technique. The lender places a *lien* (claim) on all of the firm's accounts receivable or inventory, advancing a percentage against that lien which is usually less than half of the book value of the collateral. [18]

floating-rate note   A note on which the rate of interest is allowed to "float" at a predetermined increment above the *prime rate* over the term of the note. [18]

floor planning   A *trust receipt loan* under which the inventory of a seller of large, relatively expensive items finances these items. Floor planning is most common among retailers of autos, trucks, and boats. The borrower is required to remit the payment from a sale on its receipt to the lender. [18]

flotation costs   Sometimes called *issuance costs.* The total costs of issuing and selling a security. These costs are amortized over a specified period of time. [12]

foreign bond   An *international bond* sold mainly in the country of the currency in which the issue is denominated. Compare *Eurobond.* [19]

foreign exchange rate   The value of two currencies with respect to each other. Since the mid-1970s, the major currencies have had a *floating*—rather than *fixed*—relationship with each other. [7]

foreign exchange risks   Risks associated with doing business in foreign markets, where revenues and costs are based on foreign currencies whose exchange rates may fluctuate. [7]

forward exchange rate   A future day's exchange rate between any two of the major currencies. [7]

freely callable bond   A bond that can be retired at any time at the issuer's option. [3]

functional currency   The currency of the economic environment in which an entity primarily generates and expends cash; used in connection with the financial statements of multinational companies. [4]

future value   The value of a current sum or stream—annuity or mixed—at some future date assuming interest is earned at a specified rate over the period. Often called *compound value.* The process of finding future value is actually the inverse of finding *present value.* [6]

future-value interest factor   Multiplier used to calculate an estimate of how much a given sum will earn as of a given time in the future; found in a future-value interest table or a compound interest table. [6]

future-value interest factor for an annuity   Multiplier used to calculate an estimate of the future value of an annuity; found in a future-value interest factor for an annuity table. [6]

general partnership   A type of partnership in which all the partners have unlimited liability. See also *limited partnership, partnership, unlimited liability.* [2]

Gordon model   A commonly cited *valuation model* in which the value of the firm is equal to the present value of all future dividends expected over the firm's infinite life. The dividends are discounted at the firm's cost of equity capital. [8, 12]

government security dealer   A type of intermediary that purchases for resale various government securities and other money market instruments. [3]

gross income   In the calculation of personal taxes, all income that is subject to federal taxes. [2]

gross profit margin   The percentage of each sales dollar remaining after a firm has paid for its goods, calculated by dividing gross profits by sales. [4]

growth rate   The compound annual rate (stated as a percentage) at which a stream of cash inflows such as earnings or dividends grows over a period of years. [8]

historic weights   Capital structure proportions based upon the firm's historic capital structure and used in calculating the firm's *weighted average cost of capital (WACC).* They can be measured using either book or market values. [12]

holders of record   Owners of a firm's shares on the *date of record* indicated on the firm's stock ledger. Holders of record receive dividends or stock rights when they are announced. [14, 20]

holding company   A corporation having a controlling interest in (voting control of) one or more other corporations. To hold a controlling interest in a corporation often requires ownership of only 10 to 20 percent of the outstanding stock. [23]

horizontal growth   The combination of firms in the same line of business. Also called *horizontal integration.* [23]

horizontal integration   See *horizontal growth.*

income bond   A bond on which the payment of interest is required only when earnings are available from which to make the payment. Commonly used during the reorganization of a failing or failed business firm. [19]

income statement   A financial summary of the firm's operating results during the period specified. [4]

incremental after-tax cash flows   See *operating cash inflows; relevant cash flows.*

independent projects   Capital expenditure alternatives that compete with each other, but in such a way that the acceptance of one project does not eliminate the other projects from further consideration. [9]

inflation   A rise in price levels. [3, 11]

inflationary expectations   The average rate of inflation expected over the life of a loan or investment; the forecasted rate of inflation [3]

informational content of dividends   The fact that dividend increases cause owners to bid up the price of the stock based on future expectations. [14]

initial investment   The *relevant* cash outflow that should be considered in evaluating a prospective capital expenditure. It is found by netting all inflows and outflows occurring at time zero for a proposed expenditure. [9]

installation cost The cost of installing a new asset. The IRS requires that such costs be included as part of the capital expenditure for new equipment when calculating its depreciable value and any applicable investment tax credit. [9]

interest Payments made on money borrowed or received on money lent. [2, 6]

interest rate The cost of borrowing funds. [3]

interest rate risk The chance that a change in interest rates will result in a change in the value of a security. [3]

intermediate cash inflows Cash inflows received prior to termination of a project. [10]

intermediation The process by which savings are accumulated in financial institutions and then lent out or invested. [3]

internal forecast Sales forecasts based on a buildup of forecasts through the firm's sales channels. [5]

internal rate of return (*IRR*) A sophisticated way of evaluating capital expenditure proposals. The discount rate that causes the net present value of a project to just equal zero. If a project's *IRR* is greater than the cost of capital, the project is acceptable; otherwise, it should be rejected. Also called the *yield criterion*. [10, 11]

international bond A bond initially sold outside the country of the borrower and often distributed in several countries. See also *Eurobond* and *foreign bond*. [19]

intrayear compounding Compounding of interest more often than once a year. See also *semiannual, quarterly,* and *continuous compounding*. [6]

inventory turnover A ratio calculated by dividing the cost of goods sold by the inventory; hence, the number of times per year an item of inventory is sold. In general, a high inventory turnover is preferred. [4]

investment banker A financial institution that acts as a middleperson between the issuer and buyer of new security issues. It purchases securities from the government and business and sells them to the public. Its functions include bearing the risk of *underwriting* and *advising clients*. [3, 19]

investment company A financial organization that pools the funds of a large number of investors and invests them in a portfolio of securities. By purchasing a share in an investment company, a shareholder gets an interest in a diversified portfolio. A *mutual fund* is a type of investment company. [3]

investment opportunities schedule (IOS) A schedule (or graph) that lists the best (i.e., highest *internal rate of return* [*IRR*]) to the worst (i.e., lowest *IRR*) investment opportunities available to the firm at a given time. Used in combination with the firm's *weighted marginal cost of capital (WMCC)*, the optimal level of total new financing/investment can be determined. [12]

investment tax credit (ITC) To stimulate capital expenditures by businesses, the IRS offers an investment tax credit, which allows purchasers of both new and used capital equipment to deduct a certain amount from their *tax liability*. [2]

involuntary reorganization See *reorganization*.

itemized deduction The subtraction of a variety of nonbusiness expenses from adjusted gross income in calculating personal taxes due. [2]

joint and several liability The legal provision that in an equal partnership, any losses incurred by the firm must be satisfied by the partners, so that if partners A and B lack the resources to satisfy their share of a debt, partner C must bear the entire loss. [2]

key employee life insurance An insurance policy on the life of a key executive of a firm. Since the executive is of key importance, the firm must view his or her life as an asset, the removal of which would result in damages. Many lenders require a firm to maintain "key employee" insurance on the lives of certain executives as part of the loan agreement. [19]

labor-intensive firm A business requiring high labor inputs and relatively few fixed assets to produce finished goods. [9]

leasing Obtaining the use of specific fixed assets without actually taking title to them. The *lessee* receives the services of the assets *leased* to it by the *lessor,* which owns the assets. A periodic tax-deductible lease payment is required. An *operating lease* is generally a short-term cancelable arrangement, while a *financial,* or *capital, lease* is a long-term noncancelable agreement. [21]

least common life An approach to comparing unequal-lived projects: the shortest period of time over which projects can be repeated so as to cause them to terminate in the same year. [11]

legal entity The status of a corporation in law: A corporation can sue and be sued, make and be party to contracts, and acquire property in its own name. [2]

lessee Receiver of the services of the assets leased to him or her by the lessor who owns the assets. [21]

lessor Owner of assets leased to a lessee. [21]

leverage A term commonly used in finance to describe the ability of fixed costs to magnify returns to a firm's owners resulting from changes in the firm's revenues. [13]

leveraged lease Leasing arrangements that involve one or more third-party lenders. [21]

life insurance company The largest financial intermediary handling individual savings; transfers the savings of individuals received as premium payments into loans and investments. [3]

limited open-end-mortgage See *open-end mortgage.*

limited partner A partner in an enterprise (e.g., real estate or oil speculation) who invests therein but assumes no liability beyond the amount of that investment and is normally prohibited from being active in management of the firm. [2]

limited partnership A common type of partnership; an arrangement in which one or more partners can be designated as having limited liability as long as at least one partner has unlimited liability. [2]

line of credit The maximum amount of money or merchandise a lender or supplier, respectively, will extend to a firm without performing a further credit analysis. The firm can borrow or purchase on credit against the line as long as the amount owed is current and does not exceed the stated maximum. [17, 18]

liquidation value The value of a firm if all its assets are valued at their liquidation price and the resulting proceeds are reduced by the firm's debts and obligations to preferred stockholders. Also, the proceeds from the sale of a replaced asset. [8, 9]

liquidity The ability to pay bills as they come due. The liquidity of a firm is directly related to the level of cash, marketable securities, and other current assets it holds. [4]

liquidity crisis A situation in which a firm is unable to meet due bills, a period of "technical insolvency." [24]

liquidity preference General preference for shorter-term securities. [3]

liquidity risk The possibility that a potential loss in value will result from the need to quickly sell a security with low liquidity. [3]

load funds Mutual funds that charge transaction fees ranging as high as 8.5 percent. [3]

loan amortization The determination of the equal annual loan payments necessary to provide a lender with a specified interest return and repay the loan principal over a specified term. [6]

loan amortization schedule The annual schedule of payments to amortize a loan, showing annual reduction in principal and the portion of each payment representing interest and that representing principal repayment. [6]

lockbox system An arrangement whereby a firm has its customers mail their payments to geographically dispersed post office boxes, which are opened by its bank. The receipts are deposited in the firm's account, and any other enclosures are forwarded to the firm. This system speeds the collection process by reducing the time needed to mail, deposit, and clear checks. [16]

long term In finance, a period greater than one year. Fixed assets, noncurrent liabilities, and equity are the long-term assets, liabilities, and equities of the firm, respectively. Assets and liabilities with maturities of one to seven years are sometimes referred to as intermediate-term items. [4]

long-term capital gain Gain that results on assets held for more than six months; taxed at 40 percent of the ordinary income tax rate for individuals and at a flat 28 percent for corporations. [2]

long-term debt Debt having a maturity of more than one year; long-term debts of a business typically have maturities of between 5 and 20 years. [19]

long-term funds Financing needed by the firm over the long term; usually obtained through long-term debt and equity. [15]

loss on depreciable assets Results when a business firm sells a depreciable asset for less than its book value. The loss is the difference between the book value and the sale price of such an asset; such a loss may be deducted from operating income for tax purposes. [2]

M and M approach Theorists who believe an optimal capital structure does not exist; see also *traditional approach.* [13]

macroeconomics The area of economics concerned with the overall institutional and international environment in which the firm must operate. [1]

mail float The amount of time that elapses between the time a payment is placed in the mail and the time when it is received by the payee. [16]

majority voting A voting system in which each stockholder may cast one vote for each director for each share of stock held. This system is to the advantage of the majority shareholders. [20]

margin requirements Requirements set by the Federal Reserve Board that specify the proportion of the dollar price of a security purchase the buyer must provide; the buyer is permitted to borrow the balance. [3]

marginal analysis A type of analysis that is the heart of microeconomics and is frequently used in the financial decision-making process. It involves comparing the relative costs and benefits of various financial strategies in order to take actions consistent with the goal of maximizing the firm's overall profitability. [1]

margin purchases Purchases of securities made by borrowing a portion of the purchase price. See also *margin requirements.* [3]

marginal tax rate The rate at which additional income is taxed. [2]

market indifference curve Often called the *risk-return function.* A schedule of the discount rates associated with each level of project or firm risk. Estimation of this function is useful in adjusting discount rates for risk when analyzing capital expenditures. [11]

market portfolio A diversified portfolio of assets. [7]

market premium The amount by which the market price of a convertible security exceeds its *straight or conversion value.* The market premium is larger the closer the straight value is to the conversion value. [22]

market price The value of outstanding issues of stocks or bonds in the securities markets. [8]

market risk premium Represents the amount of return the investor must receive for taking the average amount of risk that would be associated with holding the market portfolio of assets. In terms of the *capital asset pricing model (CAPM),* it is the difference between the required return on the market portfolio and the risk-free rate. [7]

market value weights Capital structure proportions based on market values and used in calculating the firm's *weighted average cost of capital (WACC).* They can be based on either a historic or a target capital structure. [12]

marketable securities Short-term debt securities that can be readily converted into cash without sustaining a loss of principal. They include Treasury bills, Treasury notes, federal agency issues, negotiable certificates of deposit, commercial paper, banker's acceptances, Eurodollar deposits, money market mutual funds, and repurchase agreements. [16]

maturity   The number of years until a bond will be repaid in full. [8]

maturity date   The specific year in which an outstanding bond matures. [8]

maturity structure of debt   The proportions of long- and short-term debt held by the firm. [15]

maximization of wealth   See *wealth maximization.*

mercantile credit   Business firms extending credit to other business firms. [17]

merger   A combination of two or more firms in which one of the firms retains its initial identity and merely absorbs the others. Mergers are generally confined to the combination of two unequally-sized firms. The term "merger" is often used to describe what technically is a *consolidation.* [23]

microeconomics   The areas of economics concerned with the optimal operating strategies for firms or individuals. [1]

middle of month (MOM)   See *Credit period.*

minimum operating cash (MOC)   The minimum amount of liquidity a firm is estimated to need during the year, calculated by dividing total annual outlays by cash turnover. This estimate is based on a number of limiting assumptions. [16]

mixed stream of cash inflows   A stream of cash inflows that does not reflect any particular pattern. Any pattern of cash inflows other than an *annuity* is considered a mixed stream. [6]

MNC   See *multinational company.*

modified DuPont formula   A formula relating the firm's *return on investment (ROI)* to the *return on equity (ROE)*. The return on equity is calculated by multiplying the return on investment, which can be found using the DuPont formula, by the *equity multiplier,* which is equal to total assets divided by stockholders' equity. [4]

money market   An intangible market created by the suppliers and demanders of short-term funds. Not an organized exchange, but a communications network through which marketable securities transactions are made. Key money market instruments include *marketable securities,* which are short-term debt instruments such as Treasury bills, commercial paper, and negotiable certificates of deposit issued by government, business, and financial institutions, respectively. [3]

money market account   Account offered by commercial banks and other financial institutions that, subject to certain restrictions, pays interest at rates competitive with those for other short-term investment vehicles. [3]

money market mutual fund   Often called *money funds.* A fund holding a portfolio of marketable securities such as *commercial paper* and *banker's acceptances.* Yields are usually competitive with those of most other financial media. Shares in such funds can often be acquired without brokerage fees, and they provide instant liquidity. [3, 16]

mortgage bond   A bond secured with a lien on real property or buildings. Under a *blanket mortgage,* all assets are held as collateral. A *first-mortgage bond* gives the holder the first claim on secured assets; a *second-mortgage bond* gives the holder a secondary claim on the assets already secured by the first mortgage. [19]

 multinational company (MNC)   A firm that has assets and operations in markets other than its "home" country and draws part of its revenues and profits therefrom. [1]

multiple rates of return   More than one IRR for a project with *nonconventional patterns of cash flows.* [10]

mutual fund   An open-end *investment company* that sells its shares to the public and redeems them at a value representing their claim on the firm's total portfolio. [3]

mutual savings banks   Financial institutions similar to commercial banks except that they may not hold demand (checking) deposits. [3]

mutually exclusive projects A group of capital budgeting projects that compete with one another in such a way that the acceptance of one eliminates all the others in the group from further consideration. [9]

negative correlation The correlation that occurs when two series move in opposite directions. See also *correlation.* [7]

negotiable certificates of deposit (CDs) Negotiable instruments representing the deposit of a certain number of dollars in a commercial bank. Negotiable CDs have a good secondary market and a high yield. The amounts and maturities of a negotiable CD is usually tailored to the investors' needs. [16]

negotiable order of withdrawal (NOW) accounts Interest-earning savings accounts against which checks can be written. [3]

net cash flow Figure in the *cash budget* found by subtracting the cash disbursements from cash receipts in each month. [5]

net present value (*NPV*) The most common of the sophisticated tools for evaluating capital expenditure proposals. *NPV* is calculated by subtracting the initial investment required by a project from the present value of the projected cash inflows. If a project's *NPV* is greater than zero, the project is acceptable; otherwise, it should be rejected. [10, 11]

net present value profile A graph or schedule that depicts the net present value of a project (*y*-axis) for various discount rates (*x*-axis). This graph clearly depicts the project's *internal rate of return* as the *x*-axis intercept. [10]

net proceeds Funds actually received from the sale of a bond or stock after all underwriting and brokerage fees have been paid. [12]

net profit margin A ratio, calculated by dividing net profits after taxes by sales, that measures the percentage of each sales dollar remaining when all expenses including taxes have been deducted. [4]

net working capital A measure of a firm's liquidity that is useful in time-series comparisons. It is calculated by taking the difference between the firm's *current assets* and *current liabilities.* It is sometimes defined as the portion of a firm's current assets financed with long-term funds. [4, 9, 15]

new issue Bonds just being introduced to the market for sale. [8]

no-load funds Mutual funds that do not charge any transaction fees. [3]

nominal rate of interest The actual rate charged by the funds supplier and being paid by the funds demander. [3]

noncash charges Items that are deducted for tax purposes on a firm's income statement, but which require no actual cash outlay. Depreciation, amortization, and depletion charges are the most comon noncash charges. [2]

nonconventional cash-flow pattern Any pattern in which an initial outlay is not followed by a series of inflows. See also *conventional cash-flow pattern.* [9]

noncumulative preferred stock See *cumulative preferred stock.*

nondiversifiable risk A risk, often called *systematic* or *relevant risk,* attributed to forces that affect all firms and therefore is not unique to the given firm. Factors such as war, inflation, international incidents, and political events account for an asset's nondiversifiable risk. This risk can be measured by *beta.* Compare *diversifiable risk.* [7, 11]

nonnotification basis Arrangement for pledging or factoring of accounts receivable whereby the borrower collects payments of pledged or factored accounts and the lender trusts that the borrower will remit these payments as received; hence, the standard arrangement for *trust receipt loans.* Compare *notification basis.* [18]

nonparticipating preferred stock See *participating preferred stock.*

nonrecourse basis Basis on which most sales of accounts receivable are made to a *factor:* the factor agrees to accept all credit risks; if purchased accounts prove to be uncollectible, the factor must absorb the loss. [18]

nonvoting common stock   Issued when the firm's owners do not want to give up any voting power: usually class A common is designated as nonvoting, while class B would have voting rights. See also *common stock; cumulative voting system; majority voting system.* [20]

normal probability distribution   A symmetrical distribution that always resembles a bell-shaped curve, with each extension of the curve a mirror image of the other. [7]

normal recovery period   See *recovery period.*

note   An instrument stating the terms of a loan which include the maturity date and the interest rate charged. See also *single-payment note.* [18]

notification basis   Arrangement for financing—pledging or factoring—accounts receivable, whereby the customer whose account has been pledged or factored is notified to remit payment directly to the lender or factor. Notification is the standard arrangement for *factoring. Nonnotification* arrangements are generally preferred by borrowers but are less safe from the lender's viewpoint. [18]

objective probability distribution   Probability estimates of future outcomes occurring based on historical data. See also *subjective probability distribution.* [7]

open-end mortgage   A mortgage that permits the issuance of additional bonds under the same mortgage contract; may be a limited open-end mortgage that limits the firm to a specified maximum, typically stated as a percentage of the original cost of the pledged property. [19]

operating breakeven point   The level of sales at which all fixed and variable operating costs are covered, i.e., the point where earnings before interest and taxes *(EBIT)* equals zero. [13]

operating cash inflows   The incremental after-tax cash inflows resulting from use of the project during its life. [9]

operating flows   Cash flows that relate to the firm's production cycle. See also *cash flows.* [4]

operating lease   A short-term, cancelable lease that generally includes a clause requiring the lessor to maintain the leased assets, including repairs, insurance, and tax payments. Compare *financial lease.* [21]

operating leverage   The power of fixed operating costs to magnify the effects of changes in a firm's sales revenue on its earnings before interest and taxes *(EBIT).* The greater are a firm's fixed operating costs, the higher is its operating leverage. [13]

operating loss   Occurs when a firm has negative before-tax profits. The firm is permitted to apply this loss against past or future operating income, or both. Losses on the sale of depreciable assets used in the business or trade are treated as operating losses which can be deducted from current, past, or future operating income, or all of them. [2]

operating profit margin   The ratio, calculated by dividing operating profits by sales, that measures the *pure profits* earned on each sales dollar, ignoring interest and taxes. [4]

opportunity cost   See *cost of capital; discount rate; required return.* [6, 10]

optimal capital structure   The structure at which the overall cost of capital is minimized and the value of the firm is therefore maximized. [13]

option   An instrument that provides its holder with an opportunity to purchase an asset at a specified price on or before its expiration date. [22]

option buyer   Investor who purchases and sells options initially written by the writer. [22]

option writer   The maker of the contractual obligation in an option, responsible for meeting the terms. [22]

order costs (inventory)   The fixed clerical costs of placing and receiving an inventory order; normally stated as dollars per order. [17]

organized securities exchanges   Tangible organizations that provide facilities for transactions between suppliers and demanders of various types of securities. The exchanges are auction houses where listed securities are traded. The New York Stock Exchange is the largest of these exchanges. [3]

outstanding (seasoned) bonds   Bonds that have been on the market for some time. [8]

overall cost of capital   See *weighted average cost of capital.*

overdraft system   A banking provision whereby if the firm's checking account balance is insufficient to cover all checks presented, the bank will automatically lend the firm enough money to cover the overdraft. [16]

overhanging issues   Convertible securities that are not converted because the market price of the associated securities does not reach a level sufficient to force conversion. [22]

oversubscription privilege   Provision in a rights offering that allows distribution of shares for which the rights were not exercised to interested shareholders on a pro rata basis at the stated subscription price. [20]

over-the-counter (OTC) exchange   An intangible market for purchasers and sellers of unlisted stocks and bonds, linked by a sophisticated telecommunications network, NASDAQ. [3]

par value   The stated or face value of bonds or stocks. For stock, a relatively useless value except for bookkeeping purposes. Often, *no par* stock is issued. [8, 19, 20]

participating preferred stock   Preferred stock whose holders may receive more than the stated dividends by participating with common stockholders in dividend distributions beyond a certain level. Most preferred stock is *nonparticipating.* [20]

partnership   A business organization owned by two or more individuals. The partners' income is taxed as personal income, and the partners generally have *unlimited liability,* although certain partners in a *limited partnership* may have limited liability. [2]

payable-through draft   A draft drawn on the payer's checking account and payable to a given payee, but not on demand; approval of the draft by the payer is required before the bank pays the draft. [16]

payback period   The number of years required for a firm to recover the initial investment required by a project from the cash inflows it generates. Short payback periods are preferred. [10]

payment date   The actual date on which the company will mail the dividend payment to the holders of record. [14]

payout ratio   A firm's cash dividend per share divided by earnings per share. This ratio indicates the percentage of each dollar earned that is distributed to the owners in the form of cash. [14]

percent income statement   See *common-size income statement.*

percent-of-sales method   Forecast of sales and values for costs, expenses, assets, and liabilities expressed as a percentage of projected sales; method of developing a pro forma income statement or balance sheet. [5]

percentage advance   The amount which a lender is willing to lend against the book value of collateral, normally between 30 and 90 percent of that value. [18]

perfectly negatively correlated   In statistical analysis, two series that move exactly together; they would have a correlation coefficient of -1. [7]

perfectly positively correlated   In statistical analysis, two series that move exactly in opposite directions; they would have a correlation coefficient of $+1$. [7]

permanent (funds) need   Fixed assets plus the permanent portion of the firm's current assets. [15]

perpetual bond   A bond that pays a stated amount of interest periodically (annually or semiannually) over an infinite time horizon; in other words, its par value is never repaid. [8]

perpetuity   An annuity with an infinite life; in other words, an annuity that never stops providing the holder with x dollars at the end of each year. [6]

playing the float   Consciously anticipating the resulting float associated with the payment process; technique for maximizing disbursement float. [16]

pledge of accounts receivable   The securing of a short-term loan with certain of the firm's accounts receivable, generally on a "trust receipt" basis. Sometimes called an *assignment of accounts receivable.* [18]

political risk The implementation by a host government of specific rules and regulations that can result in the discontinuity or seizure of the operations of a foreign company in that nation. [1, 7]

portfolio A collection of assets that may consist of securities or physical fixed assets, or a mixture of both. [7]

positive correlation The correlation that occurs when two series move together. See also *correlation.* [7]

postimplementation audit Audit of a project several years after implementation in order to evaluate performance and take any appropriate action. [9]

preauthorized check (PAC) Check written for an agreed-upon amount by the firm and drawn on the given customer's checking account at a scheduled future date. [16]

preemptive rights Stock rights extended to most common stockholders that allow them to purchase new issues in order to maintain their proportionate ownership in the firm. This allows the existing owners to prevent the dilution of their interest in the firm. These stock rights are often sold rather than exercised or let expire. [20]

preferred stock A type of equity whose holders are given certain privileges, chiefly the right to receive a fixed periodic dividend. The claims of preferred stockholders are senior to those of the common stockholders with respect to the distribution of both earnings and assets. Preferred stockholders normally do not receive voting rights. [8, 20]

premium (bond) Amount by which a bond sells at a value greater than par. [8]

present value The value of a future sum or stream — annuity or mixed — of dollars discounted at a specified rate. The process of finding present value is actually the inverse of finding *future value.* [6]

present-value interest factor Multiplier used to calculate an estimate of the present value of an amount to be received in a future period; found in a present-value interest table. [6]

present-value interest factor for an annuity Multiplier used to calculate an estimate of the present value of an annuity; found in a present-value interest factor for an annuity table. [6]

president Also called *chief operating officer (CEO).* Corporate official responsible for managing day-to-day operations and carrying out policies established by the *board of directors.* [2]

price/earnings multiples approach to value A popular valuation technique whereby the expected per-share earnings of the firm are multiplied by the average *price/earnings (P/E) ratio* for the industry in order to estimate the firm's share value. [8]

price/earnings (P/E) ratio The ratio of the market price of a share of stock to the annual per share earnings. The higher this ratio the more optimistic investors are, and vice versa. [4]

price pegging Keeping the demand for an issue and therefore the price at the desired level by placing orders to buy the security; technique used by the investment banker to reduce the syndicate's risk and the issuance charges to the issuer. [19]

primary market Financial market in which securities are initially issued; the only market in which the corporate or government issuer is directly involved in the transaction. [3]

prime rate of interest The lowest rate of interest charged by the nation's leading banks on business loans to the best business borrowers. The prime rate is used as a reference point for lending rates and is known to fluctuate widely with changes in the supply of and demand for short-term unsecured loans. [3, 18]

principal The amount of money on which interest is earned by a depositor or an investor or the amount of money on which interest is paid by a borrower. [6]

private placement The sale of a bond or other security directly to one or a group of purchasers, normally large financial institutions such as life insurance companies and pension funds. Also called *direct placement.* [3, 18, 19]

probability The percentage chance of an event occurring, e.g., if an outcome is expected to occur seven out of ten times, the probability associated with that outcome is .7, or 70 percent. See also *objective probability distribution; subjective probability distribution; risk; uncertainty.* [7]

processing float   The time that elapses between the receipt of a check by the payee and the actual deposit of it in the firm's account. [16]

profitability   Revenues less costs, in the context of the profitability-risk tradeoff. [15]

profitability index (PI)   Sometimes called a *benefit-cost ratio.* Used to evaluate capital expenditure proposals, PI is calculated by dividing the present value of cash inflows from a project by the initial investment in it. If PI is greater than or equal to 1, a project is acceptable; otherwise, it should be rejected. [10]

profitability-risk trade-off   A trade-off common to many financial decisions, most commonly in the management of working capital. The lower the firm's liquidity, the greater the risk of *technical insolvency* and the higher the expected profits. This relationship between profitability and risk works both ways. [15]

pro forma balance sheet   See *pro forma statements.*

pro forma income statement   See *pro forma statements.*

pro forma statements   *Projected* income statements and balance sheets for future years. The cash budget and pro forma income statement act as inputs to the pro forma balance sheet. The sales forecast is the key input to all these statements. [5]

progressive tax rates   Tax rates that increase with increasing levels of taxable income, and vice versa. The federal income tax structure applicable to individuals as well as sole proprietorships and partnerships is subject to a progressive tax-rate schedule. [2]

prospectus   A portion of a security registration statement that may be issued to potential buyers of a security. A "red herring," or stamp indicating the tentative nature of the offer, is placed on the prospectus during the period in which it is being reviewed by the *Securities and Exchange Commission (SEC).* [19]

proxy   A statement in which the holder of stock transfers his voting rights to another party. Sometimes *proxy battles* erupt when outside groups attempt to gain control of a firm's management. [20]

proxy battle   Attempt to gain control of a firm by soliciting a sufficient number of stockholder votes to unseat the existing management. [20]

public offering   Sale of securities to the public through an investment banker. [3]

put option   An option to sell a given number of shares of stock on or before a specified future date for a stated *striking price.* [22]

pyramiding   The control by one holding company of other holding companies. [23]

quarterly compounding   Four compounding periods within one year, with one-fourth of the stated interest rate being paid four times a year. [6]

quick ratio   A measure of liquidity used when a firm is believed to have illiquid inventories; calculated by dividing the firm's current assets minus its inventory by its current liabilities. The higher the ratio is, the more liquid the firm is considered. Also called *acid-test ratio.* [4]

range   The most basic statistical measure of risk or variability. It is calculated by subtracting the lowest (i.e., worst or pessimistic) outcome from the highest (i.e., best or optimistic) outcome. The larger the range of a project, the more variability, or risk, it is said to have. [7]

ranking approach   Evaluating the relative attractiveness of capital projects on the basis of some predetermined criterion. [9]

ratio analysis   The use of various financial ratios for measuring a firm's performance. Commonly grouped into liquidity ratios, activity ratios, debt ratios, and profitability ratios. The key inputs to ratio analysis are the firm's income statement and balance sheet. [4]

ratio comparisons   The most common types of ratio comparisons are *cross-sectional* and *time-*

series comparisons. Cross-sectional comparisons compare the performance of similar firms at the same point in time; sometimes industry averages are used in cross-sectional comparisons. Time-series comparisons evaluate the firm's performance over time. [4]

ratio of exchange   In a merger or an acquisition, the ratio of the number of shares of the acquiring firm given for each share of the acquired firm. This ratio depends on the price paid for each share of the acquired firm and the market price of the stock in the acquiring firm. [23]

raw materials inventory   Items purchased by the firm for use in producing its products. [17]

real asset   An asset such as a machine or a building. [8]

real rate of interest   That rate which creates an equilibrium between the supply of savings and the demand for investment funds. [3]

realized values   The actual beginning-of-period purchase price and end-of-period sale price realized on an asset investment and used in the calculation of its rate of return. [7]

recapitalization   The process of changing a firm's capital structure by altering the mix of debt and equity capital without increasing the total amount of capital. This often occurs as part of a reorganization under the bankruptcy laws. [24]

recaptured depreciation   When a firm sells a depreciable asset used in business or trade for an amount greater than its book value, the premium over the book value and less than the initial purchase price is viewed as recaptured depreciation, which is taxable at the firm's ordinary tax rates. [2]

receipt of goods (ROG)   See *credit period*.

receiver   A party appointed by the judge or referee in bankruptcy to take charge of the property of a bankrupt firm and protect the interests of the creditors during the period between the filing for bankruptcy and the appointment of a *trustee* or the dismissal of the petition. [24]

recourse basis   A factoring agreement in which the factor does not agree to accept all credit risks; if purchased accounts prove uncollectible, the firm must repay the factor. Most factoring is done on a nonrecourse basis. [18]

recovery period   The period over which an asset is depreciated under the *accelerated cost recovery system (ACRS). Normal recovery periods* of 3 years, 5 years, 10 years, and 15 years as well as *optional extended recovery periods* are available for each of the four property classes, respectively. Under the normal recovery periods, specified depreciation percentages are given under ACRS; straight line depreciation incorporating the *half-year convention* is used over the optional extended recovery periods. [2]

red herring   A statement indicating the tentative nature of a securities offering, stamped in red on the *prospectus*. [19]

referee   Person appointed by the court to perform routine duties required in administering a bankruptcy. [24]

refunding   See *bond refunding*.

regional development company   An association generally attached to a local government that attempts to promote business development in the region by making attractive long-term loans to new and expanding firms. [19]

regular dividend policy   The payment of a fixed-dollar dividend in each period. [14]

relevant cash flows   The incremental after-tax cash flows associated with a proposed capital expenditure. These cash flows are referred to as the *relevant cash flows* since they are the only cash flows relevant to the capital expenditure decision. They consist of three cash flow components — *initial investment, operating cash inflows,* and *terminal cash flow.* [9]

removal cost   The cost of removing old assets. The IRS requires that such costs be deducted from the proceeds received from the sale of such assets. [9]

reorder point   The level of inventory at which the firm places an order. It may be stated as a specific number of items or as a certain level of items in a bin. [17]

reorganization   When a failed firm is reorganized, both its asset structure and its financial structure are changed to reflect their true value and an equitable settlement of claims is made. The reorganized firm then continues in existence, possibly with new owners who were previously creditors. [24]

repurchase agreement   An agreement whereby a bank or security dealer sells specific marketable securities to a firm and agrees to repurchase the securities at a specified price and time. [16]

required return   The level of return one must earn as compensation for taking a given level of *nondiversifiable risk*. The level of this return is specified by the *capital asset pricing model (CAPM)*. See also *cost of capital, discount rate,* and *opportunity cost*. [7]

required total financing   Figure obtained by subtracting the minimum cash balance from ending cash; also called *excess cash balance*. [5]

 reserve account   Device used prior to January 1976 by multinational companies to "smooth" international profits. Excess international profits due to favorable exchange fluctuations were deposited in this account, which was then used to make up for losses during periods of unfavorable exchange movements. [4]

residual theory of dividends   A theory that suggests that a firm pay cash dividends if and only if acceptable investment opportunities for these funds are currently unavailable. [14]

restrictive loan provisions   Provisions that place constraints on the operations of term borrowers, such as restrictions on working capital, fixed assets, future borrowing, combinations, salaries, security investments, the use of loan proceeds, and the payment of dividends. Sometimes called *restrictive covenants*. [19]

return   On an investment, the total gain or loss experienced on behalf of the owner over a given period of time. See also *cost of capital; discount rate; opportunity cost; required return; return on equity; return on investment*. [7]

return on equity (*ROE*)   A ratio measuring the return earned on the owners' (both preferred and common stockholders') investment, calculated by dividing net profit after taxes by stockholders' equity. It represents the end result of the *modified DuPont formula*. [4]

return on investment (*ROI*)   Sometimes called the *return on total assets,* calculated by dividing the firm's net profits after taxes by its total assets or by multiplying its net profit margin by the total asset turnover. The relationship between the net profit margin, total asset turnover, and return on investment is often referred to as the *DuPont formula*. [4]

return on total assets   See *return on investment*.

revenue stability   The relative variability of a firm's sales revenues. [13]

reverse stock split   Split in which a certain number of outstanding shares are exchanged for one new share. [14]

revolving credit agreement   A guaranteed line of credit arrangement in which the bank guarantees that, regardless of economic conditions, it will make available the amount of the line at any time during the term of the agreement. Often these agreements are written for two-year terms; they are more expensive than a simple line of credit. [18]

rights offering   An offering of a new issue of common stock to the firm's shareholders on a pro rata basis in accordance with their *preemptive rights*. [19]

rights on   Stock sold with rights; i.e., purchasers receive the rights. Also called *cum rights*. [20]

risk   Commonly used interchangeably with the term *uncertainty* to refer to the variability of returns associated with a project or forecast values of the firm. In a statistical sense, risk exists when a decision maker can use historical data to estimate the probabilities associated with various outcomes. Compare *uncertainty*. [7, 11, 13, 15]

risk-adjusted discount rate   A discount rate used in capital budgeting decisions that has been adjusted for the firm or the project's risk. The risk-adjusted discount rate is determined by adding an appropriate *risk premium* to the *risk-free rate of return*. [11]

risk-averse   One of three possible preference behaviors in regard to risk; most managers are risk-averse, since for a given increase in risk they require a greater than proportional increase in return. [7]

risk class   A term used to describe groupings of similar-risk projects. [11]

risk-free rate (R_F) The rate of return commonly required on a risk-free security. It is usually measured by the yield on a U.S. government security such as a Treasury bill. The *beta* for a risk-free security is equal to zero. [3, 7]

risk-indifferent One of the three possible preference behaviors in regard to risk; for the risk-indifferent manager, the increase in return corresponds directly to the increase in risk. [7]

risk premium The amount by which the required return on an asset or security j, k_j, exceeds the risk-free rate, R_F. In terms of the *capital asset pricing model (CAPM)*, it can be expressed as $b_j \times (k_m - R_F)$, where b_j is the asset's beta coefficient and k_m is the required return on the market portfolio. The higher this premium, the more risky the asset and vice versa. [3, 7, 11]

risk-return function See *market indifference curve.*

risk-return trade-off The relationship between the return expected from a given class of securities and its exposure to risk; the combined effect of risk and return on share price. [3]

risk-taker One of three possible preference behaviors in regard to risk; for the risk-taker, the required return exhibits a less than proportional increase as the risk increases. [7]

S corporation Certain corporations with thirty-five or fewer stockholders that are permitted by the IRS to be taxed like partnerships instead of corporations. It is a tax-reporting entity rather than a tax-paying entity. [2]

safety of principal The risk that the market value of a security will drop below the amount paid to purchase it. Concern over the safety of principal is especially important when making *marketable securities* investments. [16]

sale-leaseback arrangement An arrangement whereby a firm sells its existing assets to a leasing company, which then leases them back to the firm. This is often done to generate cash. This arrangement differs from a *direct lease* of assets originally owned by the lessor. [21]

sales forecast A key input to the firm's financial planning process: *external sales forecasts* are based on regression analysis and consideration of various macroeconomic factors; *internal sales forecasts* are obtained from the sales force. [5]

savings and loan associations Financial institutions that hold savings deposits, NOW accounts, and money market accounts but not demand (checking) accounts; lend primarily to individuals for real estate mortgage loans. [3]

seasonal dating A technique used by suppliers in seasonal businesses to escape inventory carrying costs. Goods are shipped to customers in advance of the selling season, but the credit period does not begin until the selling season arrives. Seasonal dating is a type of credit term. [18]

seasonal (funds) need Certain temporary assets; varies over the year. [15]

seasoned bonds See *outstanding bonds.*

secondary market A market for used securities (i.e., those that are not new issues). If a security has a secondary market, the holder should be able to sell it prior to its maturity. [3]

second-mortgage bond See *mortgage bond.*

secured short-term financing Financing that has specific assets pledged as collateral. [18]

securities exchanges Key institutions in the *capital markets* that provide a forum for trading stocks, bonds, options, and a variety of other investment vehicles. The two key types of exchanges are the *organized securities exchanges* and the *over-the-counter exchange.* [3]

security See *collateral.*

security agreement Agreement that specifies the collateral held against a loan, plus the terms of the loan against which the security is held. [18]

security market line (SML) The name given to the graphical depiction of the *capital asset pricing model (CAPM).* It is a straight line that reflects for each *beta* (x-axis) the associated required rate of return (y-axis). As traditionally shown, the SML presents the required or expected returns associated with all positive betas. [7]

selling group A group of investment bankers and stock brokerage firms formed to sell securities underwritten by an underwriter or underwriting syndricate. Members of the selling group are paid a certain amount for each security sold. [19]

semiannual compounding   Two compounding periods within one year, with one-half of the stated interest rate being paid twice a year. [6]

semivariable operating costs   Costs (e.g., commissions) that are fixed over a certain range of volume and change to a different level beyond that volume; also *semifixed costs.* [13]

senior debt   Existing debt that must be paid prior to subsequent debt. See also *subordinated debt.* [19]

sensitivity analysis   The analysis of the effect of changes in certain variables on an outcome in order to get a feel for the variability of outcomes, or risk, associated with a cash budget, a capital expenditure, or other risky situations. [7, 11]

serial bonds   Bonds issued in such a fashion that a certain portion of them come due each year. Serial bonds allow the issuer to refund debt on a scheduled basis. [19]

service (of debts)   How readily a firm can meet the fixed contractual payments typically required on a scheduled basis over the life of a debt. [4]

shelf registration   An SEC procedure that allows firms to file a master registration statement summarizing planned financing for a two-year period, and then file short statements when it wishes to sell any of the approved master statement securities during the period. [19]

short sale   A stock transaction made in anticipation of a drop in a security's price. The short seller sells stock belonging to another person or firm, promising to buy it back in order to replace it in the future. The idea is to sell high and buy low, so that the initial sale proceeds exceed the outlay required to repurchase the securities. Stockbrokers arrange short-sale transactions. [3]

short term   A period of time less than a year. Current assets are short-term assets, and current liabilities are short-term liabilities. [4]

short-term capital gain   Gain that results on assets held for less than six months; taxed as ordinary income. [2]

simulation   The process of generating outcomes of specific events using predefined probability distributions and random numbers. *Computer simulation* is commonly used to develop probability distributions associated with various financial decision outcomes. [5, 11]

single-payment note   Note obtained from a commercial bank when a borrower needs additional funds for a short period but does not believe this need will continue. [18]

sinking fund   A deposit or investment account into which borrowers are required to make periodic payments to provide funds for the retirement of their debt. A sinking fund is normally established in such a way that the deposits accumulate to the par value of the debt. *Fixed sinking-fund payments* represent prespecified annual dollar deposits or repurchases; *variable sinking-fund payments* require the firm to make deposits or repurchases based upon a set percentage of earnings. [19]

small business investment company (SBIC)   An institution licensed by the government that makes debt and equity investments in small firms, primarily those with high growth potential. [19]

sole proprietorship   A business owned by one person, who operates it for his or her own profit. The earnings are taxed as ordinary income, and the proprietor's liability is unlimited. [2]

specific cost of financing   The after-tax cost of obtaining the financing today, rather than the historically based cost of existing financing on the firm's books. [11]

spot exchange rate   That day's exchange rate between any two of the major currencies. [7]

spread   The difference between the price paid for a security by an investment banker and the sale price; also, the difference in interest rates between various debt instruments. [19]

standard deviation   A statistical measure of the variability of the historical or expected outcomes associated with a specified event; the square root of the average squared deviations from the mean. It is used as a measure of risk. [7]

standard deviation of *NPV* One of the factors in the statistical measure of project risk in the capital budgeting decision. [11]

standard loan provisions Provisions normally included in a term-loan agreement. Generally, they require the firm to operate in a respectable and businesslike manner. They deal with the accurate disclosure of financial data, the payment of bills, the protection of assets used for collateral, and the adequate repair and maintenance of assets. [19]

standby arrangement An arrangement whereby an underwriter agrees to purchase shares not subscribed to as a result of a rights offering. An issue of shares that is not fully subscribed is said to be *undersubscribed.* [20]

statement of changes in financial position A summary of the firm's "funds flow" over the period of concern — typically the year just ended. [4]

statement of retained earnings Statement that reconciles the net income earned during the year, and any cash dividends paid, with the change in retained earnings between the start and end of the given year. [4]

stock dividend A payment of stock to a firm's existing owners. It actually represents the distribution of something the owners already have. The effect of this action is merely to capitalize a portion of the firm's retained earnings. [14]

stockholders The true owners of a corporation; the holders of shares of stock in the corporation. [2]

stockholders' report Report provided annually to stockholders by publicly held corporations containing information on the firm's financial condition and plans for the coming year. [4]

stock options Options generally extended to members of a firm's management that permit them to purchase a certain number of shares of common stock at a stated price over a specified period. They are intended to motivate the management to perform well. [19]

stock-purchase plans Fringe benefits occasionally offered to employees that allow them to purchase their firm's stock at a discount or on a matching basis with the firm absorbing part of the cost. These plans provide the firm with an "internal source" of new equity capital. [19]

stock-purchase warrant See *warrant.*

stock repurchases The act of buying back the firm's own shares of common stock. The repurchased shares are called *treasury stock,* which represent the difference between the number of shares *issued* and the number of shares *outstanding.* Stock repurchases are sometimes used in lieu of paying cash dividends. The repurchase can be made by purchase in the open market, through a *tender offer,* or on a negotiated basis from a group of large shareholders. [14]

stock rights Certain purchase privileges provided to existing shareholders so that they do not run the risk of losing their proportionate control of the corporation. [20]

stock split A method of either increasing or decreasing (by a reverse stock split) the number of shares of stock outstanding while lowering or raising the market price per share. Stocks are split in order to stimulate trading activity. [14]

straight line depreciation A depreciation method in which the annual depreciation is calculated by dividing the cost of an asset by its normal or optional extended recovery period. [2]

straight security Nonconvertible bond or preferred stock; see also *convertible security.* [22]

stretching accounts payable A strategy of paying bills as late as possible as long as the firm's credit rating is not damaged, taking into consideration any cash discounts offered. By stretching its accounts payable, a firm "leans on the trade" and thereby reduces the amount of operating cash it requires. [16]

striking price Price at which the holder of the option can buy the stock at any time prior to the option's expiration date. [22]

subjective probability distribution Estimates of the probability of future outcomes occurring based on educated guesses, in the absence of historical data. See also *objective probability distribution.* [7]

subordinated debt   Debt whose holders have a claim on the firm's assets only after the claims of holders of *senior debt* have been satisfied. The subordinated debtholder is in a much riskier position than the senior debtholders. [19]

subscription price   The price at which the holder of stock rights can purchase a share of common stock. To make the rights attractive the subscription price is generally set below the prevailing market price at the time of the rights offering. [20]

subsidiary   Company controlled by a holding company. [23]

Super NOW account   Account offered by a commercial bank that, subject to certain restrictions, generally pays interest at rates competitive with those for other short-term investment vehicles. [3]

syndication   The process whereby an investment banker or a commercial bank diversifies the risk associated with a security issue or a loan by forming a group to share both the profits and the risk of the transaction. [19]

synergistic effects   The results of certain economies of scale that cause the total value of an organization to be greater than the value of the components summed. Synergistic effects often act as an impetus for business combination. [23]

systematic risk   See *nondiversifiable risk.*

target capital structure   The capital structure the firm wishes to retain over the long run. [12]

target dividend-payout ratio policy   Policy that the firm will attempt to pay out a certain percentage of earnings, but pays a stated dollar dividend and adjusts it toward the target as proved increases in earnings occur. [14]

target weights   Capital structure proportions often used in calculating a firm's *weighted average cost of capital (WACC).* The target weights are usually based upon certain desired capital structure proportions that in turn are typically based upon what is believed to be an "optimal capital structure." They can be measured using either book or market value. [12]

tax credit   A deduction allowed for any of a variety of reasons from one's tax liability. For personal income taxation, tax credits are given for child care, political contributions, and so forth. For corporate tax purposes, the most common tax credit is the *investment tax credit.* [2]

Tax Equity and Fiscal Responsibility Act of 1982   Legislation that amended and modified provisions for the depreciation of assets set forth in the Economic Recovery Tax Act of 1981. See also *accelerated cost recovery system.* [2]

tax liability   The amount actually owed in taxes to the government, after any tax credits have been deducted. [2]

tax loss carryback/carryforward   See *carryback/carryforward.*

taxable income   The amont of income that is subject to tax, after all deductions and exemptions have been subtracted. [2]

T-bill   See *Treasury bill.*

technical insolvency   A firm is technically insolvent if it is unable to pay its bills as they come due. Technical insolvency normally precedes *bankruptcy.* A firm can overcome technical insolvency through borrowing in many cases. [15, 24]

tender offer   A formal offer by a firm to purchase a given number of its own shares or the shares of another company at a specified price. The price at which a tender offer is made is usually set above the prevailing market price in order to attract sellers. Tender offers are used to repurchase the firm's own stock or in takeover attempts in which management negotiations have failed. [14, 23]

term loan   A loan having an initial maturity greater than one year; a *long-term loan.* [19]

term structure of interest rates   The relationship between the interest rate or rate of return and the time to maturity for a security. [3]

terminal cash flow The after-tax nonoperating cash flow occurring in the final year of the project, generally attributable to liquidation of the project. [9]

terminal warehouse A central warehouse used by a lender to store inventory held as collateral for a warehouse receipt loan. They are usually located in the borrower's vicinity. [18]

theoretical value of a warrant The amount one would expect the warrant to sell for in the marketplace. [22]

time draft An order to pay a specified amount at a specified time drawn on a bank. [16]

time-series analysis Evaluation of a firm's performance over time by means of ratio analysis. [4]

times interest earned A ratio, also called the *total interest coverage ratio,* that measures a firm's ability to pay contractual interest charges; calculated by dividing earnings before interest and taxes *(EBIT)* by annual interest expense. The higher this ratio, the better is the firm's ability to cover its interest charges. [4]

total asset turnover A ratio indicating the efficiency with which a firm uses its assets. It is calculated by dividing annual sales by total assets. The higher this ratio, the more efficient the firm's use of assets. [4]

total cost (inventory) The sum of the order and carrying costs. [17]

total interest coverage ratio See *times interest earned.*

total leverage The power of fixed costs — both operating and financial — to magnify the effects of changes in a firm's sales revenue on its earnings per share *(eps).* The greater the firm's fixed costs, the higher its total leverage. It reflects the combined effect of *operating leverage* and *financial leverage* on the firm's risk. [13]

total operating cost The sum of a firm's *fixed* and *variable* operating costs. [13]

total risk The risk that a firm will be unable to meet its operating and financial costs. The higher a firm's operating and financial *leverage,* the greater its total risk. In terms of securities, total risk is the sum of *nondiversifiable risk* and *diversifiable risk.* [7, 11, 13]

traditional approach to capital structure Theorists who assert the existence of an *optimal capital structure.* [13]

transit float The time that elapses between the deposit of a check by the payee and the actual availability of the funds. [16]

treasurer Member of a business firm commonly responsible for handling financial activities such as financial planning and fund raising, managing cash, making capital expenditure plans and decisions, managing credit activities, and managing the investment portfolio. [1]

Treasury bill (T-bill) A short-term obligation of the U.S. Treasury. Treasury bills are issued weekly. They have virtually no risk and have a strong secondary market. [3, 7, 16]

Treasury note A long-term obligation of the U.S. Treasury. Such notes have maturities of one to seven years, are virtually risk free, and have a strong secondary market. [16]

treasury stock Shares of stock that have been *issued* and then *repurchased* by a firm. Often stock is repurchased because all *authorized* shares are *outstanding* and the firm needs shares for stock options or stock-purchase plans. Occasionally, shares are repurchased as a way of paying dividends. [14, 20]

trustee (bond) The third party to a bond indenture — typically a trust department of a commercial bank, whose responsibility it is to make sure the issuer lives up to the numerous conditions in the bond indenture. The trustee is paid a fee and acts to protect the interests of the bondholders. [19]

trustee in bankruptcy A third party to a bankruptcy proceeding whose function it is to value and recapitalize the firm if it is to be reorganized or take charge of all aspects of its liquidation if the firm is to be liquidated. [24]

trust receipt loan A loan made against specific collateral that remains in the hands of the borrower but which can usually be identified by name or serial number. Trust receipt loans involving inventory are referred to as *floor-planning* arrangements. [18]

uncertainty   Commonly used interchangeably with the term risk to refer to the variability of outcomes associated with a specific project or event. In a statistical sense, uncertainty exists when a decision maker has no historical data from which to develop a probability distribution. [7]

uncorrelated   Assets that are completely unrelated in the sense that there is no interaction between their returns. [7]

underpricing   The act of selling a new security issue at a price below the prevailing market price, thereby reducing the proceeds below the current market price. Underpricing is usually necessary in order to create additional demand for shares when the market is in equilibrium (at the current price). [12]

underwriting   The investment banker's function of guaranteeing the issuer of a security that it will receive at least a specified minimum amount for the issue. The underwriter of an issue bears the risk that it will not sell. Alternatively, an investment banker may aid in the *private placement* of an issue or agree only to a *best efforts* offering whereby the risk of selling the issue is avoided. [19]

underwriting syndicate   See *syndication.*

unlimited funds   Situation in which a firm has sufficient funds available for capital expenditures to accept all independent projects that provide returns greater than some predetermined level. [9]

unlimited liability   A disadvantage of the *sole proprietorship* and *general partnership;* the owners' total wealth, not merely their amount originally invested in the firm, can be taken to satisfy creditors. [2]

unsecured short-term financing   Financing that does not have specific assets pledged as collateral. [18]

unsystematic risk   See *diversifiable risk.*

valuation   The process of measuring the value of an asset or liability. The term is used to describe the overall process of estimating the worth of a firm using its *book value, liquidation value, market value, price/earning multiples,* or a present value model such as the *Gordon model.* [8]

variable growth model   Model of expected growth in common stock value that allows for a change in the rate of growth. [8]

variable operating costs   Costs that vary directly with a firm's sales (for example, production costs). These costs are a function of volume, not time. [13]

variable-rate bonds   Bonds that have a floating coupon adjusted periodically in response to market conditions. Also called *floater.* [19]

vertical growth   The combination of a firm with suppliers of its raw materials or purchasers of its finished product. Vertical growth involves expansion either backward or forward through a channel of distribution or production. A firm controlling the entire production process is considered *totally integrated* vertically. [23]

vertical integration   See *vertical growth.*

voluntary reorganization   See *reorganization.*

voluntary settlement   An out-of-court settlement between a failed firm and its creditors with the purpose of avoiding the cost and inconvenience of bankruptcy proceedings. [24]

warehouse receipt loan   A loan secured with inventory that is controlled by the lender and can be removed for sale only with the lender's approval. Both *terminal* and *field* warehousing arrangements are used. A *warehouse receipt* is issued by the *warehouse official* to the lender; it describes the various items of collateral under his control. [18]

warrant   A certificate giving its holder the right to purchase a certain number of shares of common stock at a specified per-share price. A warrant is usually detachable, which means that the recipient can sell it without selling the security to which it was attached. Quite often, warrants are used to "sweeten" a debt or preferred stock issue or are used in the merger process. Warrants are traded on the security exchanges and may or may not have limited lives. [19, 22]

warrant premium The difference between the market value and the theoretical value of a *stock-purchase warrant.* The amount of the warrant premium typically depends upon the investors' expectations as well as their ability to get more leverage from the warrants than the underlying stock. This premium is largest when the market price of the stock and the warrant *exercise price* are close together. [22]

wealth maximization A long-run strategy of maximizing the value of the owners' investment in a firm, which is generally measured by the market price of the firm's stock. This strategy is for a variety of reasons not necessarily consistent with a strategy of profit maximization. [1]

weighted average cost of capital (WACC) A measure of the cost of capital calculated by weighting the cost of each type of capital (debt, preferred stock, and common stock equity) by the proportion of that type of capital in the firm's capital structure, using *book* or *market, historic* or *target* weights and aggregating the results. [12]

weighted marginal cost of capital (WMCC) A schedule or graph relating the firm's *weighted average cost of capital (WACC)* to the level of total new financing. The WMCC is an increasing function of the level of total new financing. In combination with the *investment opportunities schedule (IOS),* the WMCC provides a mechanism for finding the optimal level of total new financing or investment. The WMCC reflects the fact that the firm's raising more than a certain amount of a given type of financing also raises the specific cost of that financing, thereby raising the weighted average cost of capital for all amounts of financing. [12]

wire transfers Telegraphic communications that, via bookkeeping entries, remove funds from the payer bank and deposit them in an account of the payee bank. [16]

working capital management An area of finance concerned with the management of a firm's current accounts, which include its *current assets* and *current liabilities.* [15]

work-in-process inventory All items currently in the production process. [17]

yield The actual return received by an investor in a security. It depends on the price paid for the security and the annual interest or dividend payment expected. It is sometimes viewed as the internal rate of return on an investment. The phrase *yield to maturity* is used to refer to bond yields. [3]

yield criterion See *internal rate of return.*

yield curve A function or graph that shows the yields (*y*-axis) relative to the maturities (*x*-axis) for similar-risk securities. [3]

yield to maturity (YTM) The rate investors earn if they buy a bond at a specific price and hold it until maturity. [8]

zero-balance account A checking account in which a zero balance is maintained through daily transfers of funds from a master account sufficient only to cover checks presented against the zero-balance account that day. [16]

zero-bracket amount A type of blanket deduction from adjusted gross income available to taxpayers not wishing to itemize their nonbusiness expenses in the process of calculating taxable personal income. [2]

zero coupon bonds Bonds with a zero coupon rate, causing an investor's yield to result solely from gain in the bonds' value; sold at the deepest discount. See also *deep discount bond.* [19]

zero growth model Dividend valuation model that assumes a constant, nongrowing dividend stream. [8]

Index

D

Money Mkt Instruments
    90d Treasuries

    Fed Agencies

    CD
    Commercial Paper < 270d
    Bankers Acceptances
    Mutual Funds

Risk
    Default Risk
    Maturity Risk
    Marketability Risk
    contract Risk
    Tax Treatment Risk

This calculation is simple. Expanding the problem, we can compute the future value of the three flows at the end of the third period. The first flow of $150 is received today; the next flow of $200 is received one period from today; and the third flow of $300 is received two periods from today. The keystrokes using the standard method are:

[C] 150 [X] 1.1 [X] 1.1 [X] 1.1 [=] 199.65   (write down this number; it compounds three periods)

[C] 200 [X] 1.1 [X] 1.1 [=] 242.00   (write down this number; it compounds two periods)

[C] 300 [X] 1.1 [=] 330.00 [+] 199.65 [+] 242.00 [=] 771.65   (answer)(note — last flow compounds one period)

Instead, we could also have done the following:

[C] 150 [X] 1.1 [+] 200 [X] 1.1 [+] 300 [X] 1.1 [=] 771.65   (answer)

Again, it was not necessary to write down any intermediate results.

In the above example the future value was calculated under the assumption that all of the cash flows occurred at the beginning of the period. If, instead, the cash flows were to occur at the end of the period, it would be necessary to make a slight adjustment in the calculations. Assume that the cash flows from the above example occur at the *end of periods* one, two, and three. What is the future value of these flows at the end of the third period? The keystrokes for the standard method are:

[C] 150 [X] 1.1 [X] 1.1 [=] 181.50   (write down this number; flow compounds for only two periods)

[C] 200 [X] 1.1 [=] 220   (write down this number; flow compounds for only one period)

[C] 181.50 [+] 220 [+] 300 [=] 701.50   (answer) (the last flow does not earn any interest — it was just deposited)

The difference of $70.15 is caused by the fact that each flow earns interest for one period less. If these had been annuities, the first case would have been called an *annuity due* and the latter case an *ordinary annuity* (the *FVIFA* table in this book is for ordinary annuities). The alternative method would use the following keystrokes to get the same answer:

[C] 150 [X] 1.1 [+] 200 [X] 1.1 [+] 300 [=] 701.50   (answer)

Example 4: Present Value of Cash Flow Streams

For present values, a methodology that is the inverse of compound value is applied. The present value of $1,000 due in two periods discounted at 10 percent is equal to:

[C] 1000 [÷] 1.1 [÷] 1.1 [=] 826.44   (answer)

Again, it is easy to expand this technique to find the present value of a stream of cash flows. Assume you want to find the present value of the following cash flow stream using a 9 percent discount rate:

End of period	1	2	3
Cash flow	$200	$300	$400

Assume in this case you are going to use the present-value interest factors given in the PVIF table in this book. The following keystrokes would solve the problem: